Electronic Government:
Concepts, Methodologies, Tools, and Applications

Ari-Veikko Anttiroiko
University of Tampere, Finland

Volume IV

Information Science REFERENCE

INFORMATION SCIENCE REFERENCE
Hershey · New York

Acquisitions Editor:	Kristin Klinger
Development Editor:	Kristin Roth
Senior Managing Editor:	Jennifer Neidig
Managing Editor:	Jamie Snavely
Typesetter:	Michael Brehm, Jeff Ash, Carole Coulson, Elizabeth Duke, Sara Reed, Sean Woznicki
Cover Design:	Lisa Tosheff
Printed at:	Yurchak Printing Inc.

Published in the United States of America by
Information Science Reference (an imprint of IGI Global)
701 E. Chocolate Avenue, Suite 200
Hershey PA 17033
Tel: 717-533-8845
Fax: 717-533-8661
E-mail: cust@igi-global.com
Web site: http://www.igi-global.com/reference

and in the United Kingdom by
Information Science Reference (an imprint of IGI Global)
3 Henrietta Street
Covent Garden
London WC2E 8LU
Tel: 44 20 7240 0856
Fax: 44 20 7379 0609
Web site: http://www.eurospanbookstore.com

Library of Congress Cataloging-in-Publication Data

Electronic government : concepts, methodologies, tools and applications / Ari-Veikko Anttiroiko, editor.
p. cm.
Summary: "This collection meets the need for quality, authoritative research in this domain with an authoritative collection. Studies from the electronic government researchers worldwide enable libraries in academic, government, and other settings to provide a collection on topics like digital government, electronic justice, government-to-government, information policy, and cyber-infrastructure research and methodologies"--Provided by publisher.
ISBN 978-1-59904-947-2 (hardcopy) -- ISBN 978-1-59904-948-9 (e-book)
1. Internet in public administration. I. Anttiroiko, Ari-Veikko.
JF1525.A8E585 2008
352.3'802854678--dc22

2007045877

British Cataloguing in Publication Data
A Cataloguing in Publication record for this book is available from the British Library.

If a library purchased a print copy of this publication, please go to http://www.igi-global.com/reference/assets/IGR-eAccess-agreement.pdf for information on activating the library's complimentary electronic access to this publication.

List of Contributors

Contents
by Volume

Volume I

Section 1. Fundamental Concepts and Theories

This section serves as a foundation for this exhaustive reference tool by addressing crucial theories essential to the understanding of electronic government. Chapters found within these pages provide an excellent framework in which to position electronic government within the field of information science and technology. Insight regarding the critical incorporation of global measures into electronic government is addressed, while crucial stumbling blocks of this field are explored. With over 38 chapters comprising this foundational section, the reader can learn and chose from a compendium of expert research on the elemental theories underscoring the electronic government discipline.

Section 2. Development and Design Methodologies

This section provides in-depth coverage of conceptual architecture frameworks to provide the reader with a comprehensive understanding of the emerging technological developments within the field of electronic government. Research fundamentals imperative to the understanding of developmental processes within information management are offered. From broad examinations to specific discussions on electronic tools, the research found within this section spans the discipline while offering detailed, specific discussions. From basic designs to abstract development, these chapters serve to expand the reaches of development and design technologies within the electronic government community. This section includes more than 40 contributions from researchers throughout the world on the topic of electronic government.

Volume II

Section 3. Tools and Technologies

This section presents an extensive coverage of various tools and technologies available in the field of electronic government that practitioners and academicians alike can utilize to develop different techniques. These chapters enlighten readers about fundamental research on the many methods used to facilitate and enhance the integration of this worldwide phenomenon by exploring the use of RFID in various governments—an increasingly pertinent research arena. It is through these rigorously researched chapters that the reader is provided with countless examples of the up-and-coming tools and technologies emerging from the field of electronic government. With more than 40 chapters, this section offers a broad treatment of some of the many tools and technologies within the electronic government and IT community.

Volume III

Section 4. Utilization and Application

This section discusses a variety of applications and opportunities available that can be considered by practitioners in developing viable and effective electronic government programs and processes. This section includes over 50 chapters which review how the growing distribution and the increasing maturity of electronic government applications pose new issues. Further chapters provide a foundation towards the development of a theoretical framework for the implementation of electronic government systems via an extensive literature review. Also explored in this section is the repeated use of government Web sites and the users' satisfaction with these sites. Contributions included in this section provide excellent coverage of today's IT community and how research into electronic government is impacting the social fabric of our present-day global village.

Volume IV

Section 5. Organizational and Social Implications

This section includes a wide range of research pertaining to the social and organizational impact of electronic government around the world. Chapters introducing this section illustrate what types of social respon ibility issues need to be addressed in electronic government, who must address them, and how they might be addressed. Additional chapters included in this section provide important information on the role that the Internet is now playing in the delivery and take-up of government services by European citizens. Also investigating a concern within the field of electronic government is research on the public sector and innovative e-policies. With more than 38 chapters the discussions presented in this section offer research into the integration of global electronic government as well as implementation of ethical considerations for all organizations.

Volume V

Section 6. Managerial Impact

This section presents contemporary coverage of the social implications of electronic government, more specifically related to the corporate and managerial utilization of information sharing technologies and applications, and how these technologies can be facilitated within organizations. Core ideas such as training and continuing education of human resources in modern organizations are discussed throughout these chapters. Issues, such as utilizing segmentation techniques to identify significant differences in managerial beliefs and then associate these belief segments with e-CRM performance, are discussed. Equally as crucial, chapters within this section analyze the results of a survey conducted in 2005, in which IT executives were asked to describe the skills they felt were critical to keep in house now and in 2008. Also in this section is a case which examines the strategic positioning of BizE (disguised), an e-commerce start-up that serves small online businesses via an Internet portal.

Section 7. Critical Issues

This section contains over 20 chapters addressing issues, such as the digital public sphere, electronic government in business adoption, information security, e-democracy, deliberative democracy, and the digital rights managements process, to name a few. Within the chapters, the reader is presented with an in-depth analysis of the most current and relevant issues within this growing field of study. Issues, such as the growing threats to intellectual freedom through the loss of the information commons in the U.S., are discussed. Crucial questions are addressed and alternatives offered, such as the main conceptual dimensions of electronic government, while critically assess both the current responses and future prospects of Canada's public sector. Rounding out this section is an analysis of the extent to which local authorities in England and Wales have responded to the e-democracy agenda by examining their Web sites and assessing their potential to deliver democracy.

Volume VI

Section 8. Emerging Trends

This section highlights research potential within the field of electronic government while exploring uncharted areas of study for the advancement of the discipline. Introducing this section are chapters that set the stage for future research directions and topical suggestions for continued debate. Discussions exploring issues in Internet governance and personal privacy, which dominate legal theory's engagement with electronic government, are offered. Another debate which currently finds itself at the forefront of research is the notion of the e-mancipated citizen against the background of current trends in social and political participation of citizens. Found in these chapters, concluding this exhaustive multi-volume set are areas of emerging trends and suggestions for future research within this rapidly expanding discipline.

Preface

Paralleling the dynamic maturation of far-reaching distributed information and computing technologies has been an accelerated demand by citizens for electronic access to government services. Conversely, government administrators and officials have driven themselves to harness the cost, quality, and efficiency benefits that electronic service delivery offers. Profoundly traversing all facets of compound societies, electronic government implicates and impacts information science, political science, civic relations, electronic justice, security and privacy ethics, government-to-government interactions, and information policy.

During this period of time numerous researchers, academicians, and government officials have developed a variety of techniques, methodologies, and measurement tools that have allowed them to develop, deliver and at the same time evaluate the effectiveness of several areas of electronic government. The explosion of these technologies and methodologies have created an abundance of new, state-of-art literature related to all aspects of this expanding discipline, allowing researchers, citizens, and government officials to learn about the latest discoveries in the field of electronic government.

Due to rapid technological changes that are continually taking place, it is a constant challenge for researchers and experts in this discipline to stay abreast of the far-reaching effects of this worldwide expansion, and to be able to develop and deliver more innovative methodologies and techniques utilizing new technological innovation. In order to provide the most comprehensive, in-depth, and recent coverage of all issues related to this global phenomenon, as well as to offer a single reference source on all conceptual, methodological, technical and managerial issues, as well as the opportunities, future challenges and emerging trends related to electronic government, Information Science Reference is pleased to offer a six-volume reference collection on this rapidly growing discipline, in order to empower students, researchers, academicians, and practitioners with a comprehensive understanding of the most critical areas within this field of study.

Entitled "Electronic Government: Concepts, Methodologies, Tools, and Applications," this collection is organized in eight distinct sections, providing the most wide-ranging coverage of topics such as: (1) Fundamental Concepts and Theories; (2) Development and Design Methodologies; (3) Tools and Technologies; (4) Utilization and Application; (5) Organizational and Social Implications; (6) Managerial Impact; (7) Critical Issues; and (8) Emerging Trends. The following provides a summary of what is covered in each section of this multi volume reference collection:

Section 1, Fundamental Concepts and Theories, serves as a foundation for this extensive reference tool by addressing crucial theories essential to the understanding of electronic government. Chapters such as, "E-Government in the Information Society," by Lech W. Zacher, as well as, "Electronic Signature: The Core Legislation Category in Digital Economy," by Fjodor Ruzic, provide an excellent framework in which to position electronic government within the field of information science and technology. "Teledemocracy," by Ted Becker, offers excellent insight into the critical incorporation of electronic, interactive communications into government, while chapters, such as, "Introducing Mobile Government," by M. Halid Kuscu, Ibrahim Kushchu, and Betty Yu, address some of the basic, yet principle stumbling blocks of issues within electronic government. With over 38 chapters comprising this foundational section, the reader can learn and chose from a compendium of expert research on the elemental theories underscoring the electronic government discipline.

Section 2, Development and Design Methodologies, provides in-depth coverage of conceptual architecture frameworks to provide the reader with a comprehensive understanding of the emerging technological developments within the field of electronic government. "E-Government Development and Implementation," by Wayne Huang, Yining Chen, and K. L. Wang, offers research fundamentals imperative to the understanding of research and developmental processes within electronic government. From broad examinations to specific discussions on electronic government such as, Mohamed Ally's "Design of Government Information for Access by Wireless Mobile Technology," the research found within this section spans the discipline while offering detailed, specific discussions. From basic designs to abstract development, chapters, such as "If You Build a Political Web Site, Will They Come?," by Pippa Norris and John Curtice, serve to expand the reaches of development and design technologies within the electronic government community. This section includes over 40 contributions from researchers throughout the world on the topic of electronic government within the information science and technology field.

Section 3, Tools and Technologies, presents an extensive coverage of various tools and technologies available in the field of electronic government that practitioners and academicians alike can utilize to develop different techniques. Chapters, such as Paulo Roberto Santhias and Regis Cabral's, "Electronic Voting Machine," enlighten readers about fundamental research on one of the many methods in which citizens impact the electronic government community, whereas chapters, like "Radio Frequency Identification Technology in Digital Government," by Les Pang, explore the use of RFID in various governments—an increasingly pertinent research arena. It is through these rigorously researched chapters that the reader is provided with countless examples of the up-and-coming tools and technologies emerging from governmental information technology. With more than 40 chapters, this section offers a broad treatment of some of the many tools and technologies within the electronic government community.

Section 4, Utilization and Application, discusses a variety of applications and opportunities available that can be considered by practitioners in developing viable and effective government programs and processes. This section includes more than 50 chapters, such as "Application for Comprehensive E-Government," by Thomas Müllner and Dominik Grimm, which review how the growing distribution and the increasing maturity of electronic government applications pose new issues. Additional chapters, such as Ryad Titah and Henri Barki's, "E-Government Adoption and Acceptance: A Literature Review," provide a foundation towards the development of a theoretical framework for the implementation of electronic government systems via extensive literature review. Also considered in this section is the development of an integrated framework of intentions towards repeated use with a level of confidential information shared by a user as one factor and electronic government satisfaction derived from service performance as another factor as outlined by Sangmi Chai, T. C. Herath, I. Park, and H. R. Rao, in "Repeated Use of E-Gov Web Sites: A Satisfaction and Confidentiality Perspective." Contributions included in this section provide excellent coverage of today's electronic government community and how research into information technology is impacting the social fabric of our present-day global village.

Section 5, Organizational and Social Implications, includes a wide range of research pertaining to the social and organizational impact of electronic government in information technologies around the world. Introducing this section is Simon Rogerson's chapter entitled, "Aspects of Social Responsibility in the Information Society." This chapter illustrates what types of social responsibility issues need to be addressed, who must address them, and how they might be addressed, while discussing some of the basic aspects of social responsibility and the implications for the Information Society, drawing, in particular, from Corporate Social Responsibility. Additional chapters included in this section, such as, "User Attitudes to E-Government Citizen Services in Europe," by Jeremy Millard, provide important information on the role that the Internet is now playing in the delivery and take-up of government services by European citizens. Also investigating a concern within the field of electronic government and citizen concern is Ioannis P. Chochliouros and Anastasia S. Spiliopoulou-Chochliourou's, "Exploiting Public Sector Information through Innovative E-Government Policies." With over 38 chapters, the discussions presented in this section offer research on the integration of electronic government and computational access for all.

Section 6, Managerial Impact, presents contemporary coverage of the social implications of electronic government, more specifically related to the corporate and managerial utilization of information technologies and applications, and how these technologies can be facilitated within organizations. Core ideas such as training and continuing education of human resources in modern organizations are discussed through these chapters. "E-CRM and Managerial Discretion," by Tim Coltman and Sara Dolnicar, utilize segmentation techniques to identify significant differences in managerial beliefs and then associate these belief segments with e-CRM performance. Equally as crucial, chapters, such as "Changing IT skills: The Impact of Sourcing Strategies on In-House Capability Requirements," by Christine V. Bullen, Thomas Abraham, Kevin Gallagher, Kate M. Kaiser, and Judith Simon, analyze the results of a survey conducted in 2005, in which IT executives were asked to describe the skills they felt were critical to keep in house now and in 2008. Concluding this section is a chapter by Janis L. Gogan and Arnold Kamis, "A Not Quite Bountiful Thanksgiving at BizE." This case examines the strategic positioning of BizE (disguised) an e-commerce start-up that serves small online businesses via an Internet portal. During an economic downturn, BizE encounters difficulties with its new private-label strategy. With cash running dangerously low, executives reassess the new strategy and consider what they can do to ensure the company's survival.

Section 7, Critical Issues, contains over 20 chapters addressing issues such as the digital public sphere, electronic government in business adoption, information security, e-democracy, deliberative democracy, and the digital rights managements process to name a few. Within the chapters, the reader is presented with an in-depth analysis of the most current and relevant issues within this growing field of study. Elizabeth Buchanan and James Campbell's, "New Threats to Intellectual Freedom: The Loss of the Information Commons through Law and Technology in the US" explores the growing threats to intellectual freedom through the loss of the information commons in the U.S. as a direct result of advances and changes in technology and laws, while "The Critical Role of Digital Rights Management Process," by Margherita Pagani, analyzes the impact generated by the adoption of Digital Rights Management (DRM) processes on the typical Digital Media Management Value Chain activitie, while also analyzing the processes in the context of the business model. Crucial questions are addressed, such as that presented in Jeffrey Roy's chapter, "Service, Security, Transparency & Trust: Government Online or Governance Renewal in Canada?," which examines the main conceptual dimensions of electronic government and critically assess both the current responses and future prospects of Canada's public sector. "Local Democracy Online: An Analysis of Local Government Web Sites in England and Wales," by Lawrence Pratchett, Melvin Wingfield, and Rabia Karakaya Polat, closes this section by analyzing the extent to which local authorities in England and Wales have responded to the e-democracy agenda by examining their Web sites and assessing their potential to deliver democracy.

The concluding section of this authoritative reference tool, Emerging Trends, highlights research potential within the field of electronic government, while exploring uncharted areas of study for the advancement of the discipline. Introducing this section is a chapter entitled, "A Brave New E-World? An Exploratory Analysis of Worldwide E-Government Readiness, Level of Democracy, Corruption and Globalization," by Zlatko J. Kovačić which sets the stage for future research directions and topical suggestions for continued debate. Providing an alternative view of electronic government is the chapter, "E-Government as a New Frontier for Legal Theory," by Keith Culver. This chapter explores issues in Internet governance and personal privacy, which dominate legal theory's engagement with electronic government, while e-engagement of citizens plays an increasingly important yet still limited role in governments' interaction with citizens. Another debate which currently finds itself at the forefront of research within this field is presented by Valerie A.J. Frissen's research. "The E-mancipation of the Citizen and the Future of E-Government: Reflections on ICT and Citizens' Partnership" considers the notion of the e-mancipated citizen against the background of current trends in social and political participation of citizens. Found, in these chapters concluding this exhaustive multi-volume set, are areas of emerging trends and suggestions for future research within this rapidly expanding discipline.

Although the primary organization of the contents in this multi-volume is based on its eight sections, offering a progression of coverage of the important concepts, methodologies, technologies, applications, social issues, and emerging trends, the reader can also identify specific contents by utilizing the extensive indexing system listed at the end of each volume. Furthermore to ensure that the scholar, researcher and educator have access to the entire contents of this multi-volume set as well as additional coverage that could not be included in the print version of this publication, the publisher will provide unlimited multi-user electronic access to the online aggregated database of this collection for the life of edition, free of charge when a library purchases a print copy. This aggregated database provides far more contents than what can be included in the print version in addition to continual updates. This unlimited access, coupled with the continuous updates to the database ensures that the most current research is accessible to knowledge seekers.

Electronic government as a discipline has witnessed fundamental changes during the past two decades, allowing information seekers around the globe to have access to information which two decades ago, was inaccessible. In addition to this transformation, many traditional organizations and business enterprises have taken advantage of the technologies offered by the development of electronic government technologies in order to expand and augment their existing programs and practices. This has allowed practitioners and researchers to serve their customers, employees and stakeholders more effectively and efficiently in the modern virtual world. With continued technological innovations in information and communication technology and with on-going discovery and research into newer and more innovative techniques and applications, the electronic government discipline will continue to witness an explosion of information within this rapidly growing field.

The diverse and comprehensive coverage of electronic government in this six-volume authoritative publication will contribute to a better understanding of all topics, research, and discoveries in this developing, significant field of study. Furthermore, the contributions included in this multi-volume collection series will be instrumental in the expansion of the body of knowledge in this enormous field, resulting in a greater understanding of the fundamentals while fueling the research initiatives in emerging fields. We at Information Science Reference, along with the editor of this collection, and the publisher hope that this multi-volume collection will become instrumental in the expansion of the discipline and will promote the continued growth of electronic government.

Chapter 4.26
Challenges in Implementation of E-Procurement in the Indian Government

Ramanathan Somasundaram
National Institute for Smart Government, India

ABSTRACT

In this chapter, the concept of e-government procurement (e-GP), as it is being implemented in India, is explained. Furthermore, a set of six challenges encountered during implementation of e-procurement is discussed in depth. The six challenges discussed in the chapter are: lack of skilled personnel; multi-departmental implementation; inadequate IT and networking infrastructure; challenges in implementation of state-wide system; the need to regulate e-procurement market; and replicating best practices in federal-state setup. A practitioner's perspective is adopted to write this chapter. While this chapter deals specifically with e-GP in India, certain aspects of it can be generalized to e-GP implementations elsewhere in the world. Such generalization is possible since government procurement is driven by the same set of principles such as efficiency and transparency.

INTRODUCTION

The uptake of e-procurement in the government sector is on the rise. Developed nations such as Australia, Denmark, Singapore, the USA, Korea, and a few South American nations such as Chile and Brazil were the forerunners in implementing e-procurement. The forerunners got into e-procurement during the late 1990s. In India, the State of Andhra Pradesh pioneered with the implementation of e-procurement during early 2000. Elsewhere in Asia, Philippines and Indonesia have embarked on implementing e-procurement recently. Multi-lateral bodies such as the World Bank, Asian Development Bank, and Inter-American Development Bank have joined hands together to constitute a body for implementing e-procurement all across the developing and less-developed nations. This body, named Multilateral Development Bank e-Government Procurement (MDB-e-GP), is actively promoting implementation of e-procurement.

Government procurement is a voluminous activity, and in developing countries such as India, it is fast-growing. As per a country assessment report prepared by the World Bank, the Indian government is estimated to buy for US$100 billion each year. Similarly, across the globe, governments spend significant sums of money in public procurement. It is estimated that public procurement accounts for about 10-15% of a nation's GDP. In a country, the government is typically the largest buying entity. Despite the significance, there have not been many analytical write-ups on implementation of e-government procurement (e-GP). The implementation of e-procurement in the government setup is quite a challenging activity; in order to effectively deal with the challenges, it is vital that the nature of challenges are well-understood, and that the means to address the challenges are analyzed and discussed.

In this chapter, challenges encountered in implementation of e-procurement in India are explained. The explanation is preceded by the following sections:

1. Functional Overview of E-Procurement
2. Benefits of E-Procurement
3. Public Procurement in India
4. State of E-Procurement Internationally
5. State of E-Procurement in India
6. Geographical Scope Discussed in the Chapter

This chapter is written from a practitioner's perspective, one who is attempting to tackle the challenges being explained. While this chapter deals specifically with e-GP in India, certain aspects of it can be generalized to e-GP implementations elsewhere in the world. Such generalization is possible since government procurement is driven by the same set of principles, that is, efficiency, transparency, and accountability.

This chapter is written based on practical exposure, which the author has gained while implementing e-procurement in two state governments in India. The author was involved in preparation of a request for proposal (RFP), based on which a private partner will be selected for implementing an end-to-end e-procurement system in both the states. As part of the effort, the author has had the opportunity to interact with end users in government departments who undertake procurement, application service providers (ASP) community and nodal officers initiating the implementation effort. Moreover, he has been an integral part of the decision-making process within the government. The rich experience gained during the implementation effort is relied upon to write this chapter.

FUNCTIONAL OVERVIEW OF E-PROCUREMENT

E-procurement, as it is referred to in this chapter, is an integrated end-to-end application with the following modules:

1. Indent management (workflow system administering administrative and technical approval processes)
2. E-tendering (PKI-enabled electronic bid submission)
3. E-auctions (forward and reverse)
4. Contract management (preparation and verification of bills with respect of works and services contract)
5. Order management (for utilization of goods and services rate contracts)
6. Supplier enrollment
7. E-payments
8. MIS
9. Accounting

It is to be noted that in India, e-tendering is customarily referred to as e-procurement. It needs to be clarified that e-procurement is much more comprehensive than e-tendering. E-procurement

Figure 1. Functional overview of e-procurement

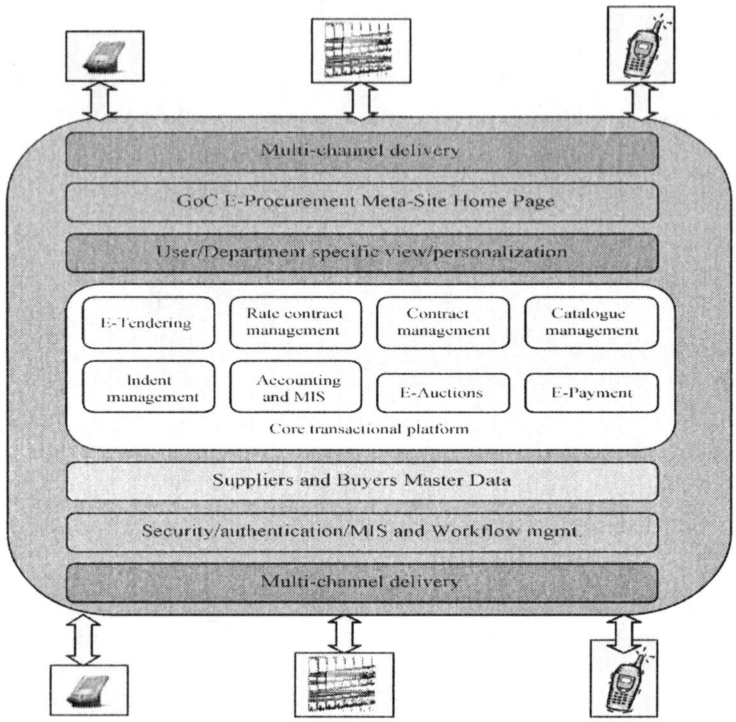

includes many other modules such as contract management and order management, which are equally if not more significant than the e-tendering. For seamless procurement operations, the e-procurement system has to be integrated with inventory management, budgeting, treasury, and payment gateways.

BENEFITS OF E-PROCUREMENT

The implementation of e-procurement in private enterprises, as it is claimed, has resulted in savings in the range of 10-15% of procurement value. It is logical to assume that government would likewise be able to save on a similar scale. Since government is typically the largest procurement agency in a country, the amount of savings in value terms is quite significant. If the Indian government can save 10% of its $100 billion a year procurement expenditure, then the resultant savings will be in the range of US$100 billion, or 4,500 billion Rupees (World Bank, 2003) (converting at US$1 = 45 Indian Rupees), an amount that will contribute significantly towards managing the fiscal deficit (Kaul, 2005).

Apart from efficiency, enhanced transparency is another important benefit resulting from e-procurement. Especially since the "*Right to Information*" Act (RTI Act), 2005, has come into force in India, the government is obligated to be transparent about its operations. Since procurement of works, goods, and services accounts for a major part of the operations, government agencies are flooded with queries about the procedure adopted for the award of contracts and the status of contracts (especially related to public works).[1] The amount of queries will increase in coming years when the RTI Act will come into full force, and as the number of works (e.g., roads, metro rail, and bridges) undertaken by the government will increase. Since e-procurement is implemented in the Internet environment, government agencies can voluntarily share with the public some information on tendering and contract management activities. Such information sharing will show the government in a good light and simultaneously minimize its workload.

In addition to efficiency and transparency, implementation of e-procurement results in many more benefits, a summary of which is provided below:

- Elimination of delays arising out of processing tenders manually and on paper
- Publication of tender notice/IFB in newspapers can be avoided, resulting in saving of time and money
- Cartel formation can be arrested, as any bidder interested will be able to participate with anonymity
- Fair, free, and fearless participation of tenderers becomes possible
- Improvement in work culture in the departments
- Database on goods, services, works, and contractors gets build up
- Economy of scale is achieved by aggregation of requirements
- Better access to procurement spend information and analytical reports

PUBLIC PROCUREMENT IN INDIA

Government procurement in India is a highly-dispersed activity. The estimated US$100 billion is spent by multiple offices across the country. Since procurement is essentially an expenditure activity, the locations and manner of expenditure depends on the allocation of funds and responsibility within the government. The procurement process is performed at multiple levels in government, and it is centralized as well as decentralized. Various methods employed in government procurement are explained in this section to give the reader an idea of the complexity involved in a move to e-procurement. The shift to e-procurement cannot be achieved if procurement, as explained below, is not handled electronically.

Rate Contract Negotiation

For rate contracts, a central agency empanels one (single rate contract) or more (parallel rate contract) suppliers to deliver a good/service for a price to all agencies within a given jurisdiction, which could be nation,[2] state,[3] department,[4] or office,[5] for a period of time.[6] The empanelment of suppliers is done based on a tendering process. An estimate of utilization, that is, the number of items which the government is expected to purchase, is provided based on the volume of procurement done in the previous years. In general, users on whose behalf the negotiation is done are not obligated to use the rate contracts. For example a government agency may choose to purchase an item such as furniture by using Directorate General of Supplies & Disposals (DGS&D's) rate contract or a contract negotiated by a state agency or by its own.

Rate Contract Ordering

There are two variations in rate contract ordering, which are: centrally-negotiated and decentrally-ordered; and centrally-negotiated and centrally-ordered:

- **Centrally-negotiated and decentrally-ordered:** The agencies negotiating rate contracts on behalf of the nation and a state hardly utilize the rate contracts which they have negotiated. Instead, ordering of items is done by agencies dispersed across the nation. The ordering is done in such a decentralized manner that the negotiating agencies are unaware of the extent to which the rate contracts are utilized. Likewise, rate contracts are centrally negotiated at the department level, for example, procurement of medicines and equipment by the Health Department. In case of departmental rate contracts, end users[7] in departments are typically obligated to order using the centrally-negotiated rate contracts.

- **Centrally-negotiated and centrally-ordered:** In some departments and offices, rate contract negotiation and rate contract ordering are done from a central location.[8] A bulk order is placed on suppliers using rate contracts, which is then distributed to various offices in the hierarchy as and when the need arises. The needed information is transmitted to the central location using requisitions.

ECV-Based Procurement

ECV is an abbreviation of estimated cost value. ECV is typically prepared for works procurement and for some types of services procurement. The basis for preparation of ECV is the schedule of rates (SOR), a price list maintained by departments. To do ECV-based procurement, Government agencies need to get two types of approvals: administrative and technical. While the administrative and technical approvals are given from the higher-ups in the hierarchy, the groundwork required for the preparation of the cost estimates is done by those lower in the hierarchy.[9] Typically, a project file moves back-and-forth in the hierarchy several times before the notice inviting tender (NIT) is issued. In line departments, such as the Public Works Department (PWD) and the Water Resources Department (WRD), the hierarchy is extensive, and it branches out from the secretariat at the top to subdivisional offices at the bottom. On the other hand, in boards and corporations, hierarchy tends to be short and, more importantly, the offices are co-located within a small geographical area and typically in the networked capital city.

Procurement in Line Departments, Boards and Institutions, and Urban Local Bodies

Procurement done by all the three agencies fall under rate contract-based procurement[10] and ECV-based procurement. However, the three agencies handle their procurement differently. Firstly, much of the procurement done by line departments falls under "*capital expenditure*," which results in the creation of assets (e.g., construction of highways and roads). The remaining part is spent on maintenance work, which in macroeconomics falls under "*revenue expenditure*." Since the value of capital expenditure tends to be high, multiples levels of authority have been created to develop and monitor the projects. Unless line departments have a "*Pay and Accounts*" office, payment for the work done by contractors is paid through the state's treasury department.

Boards and institutions are created specifically for a purpose, and they exist and operate with a high level of autonomy. Since government is engaged in many different activities, the purposes for which the boards and institutions are created vary significantly. For example, a board or an institution could be created specifically for the development of highways using World Bank loans,[11] for manufacturing of soaps and detergents,[12] for improving schooling infrastructure,[13] and for the development of metro rail.[14] Some of the organizations continue to exist perpetually, whereas others close down when the purpose is accomplished. Decision-making in these organizations is not as bureaucratic as that of the line departments; they operate in a focused manner and are therefore much more efficient. For reporting purposes, boards and institutions fall under one of the line departments.

Urban local bodies (ULB) comprises of zilla parishads (district-level committee), city and town corporations and taluk and gram panchayats (village-level committee). The administrative head of a ULB is Zilla Parishad (ZP), to which a sum of money is allocated each year as part of the budget. The ZP in turn allocates the money to "people-oriented" line departments reporting to it and panchayat organizations. The city and town corporations are typically autonomous bodies. They plough back the revenue earned and grants received to develop and maintain cities and towns. For implementation of development-oriented schemes, money is allocated to ZPs, in some cases, directly from the central government and alternatively through state government. In India, a move to decentralization is underway, and procurement handled by gram panchayats is expected to increase in future. So far, much of the procurement done at ULB falls under revenue expenditure. However, efforts are underway to increase the implementation of development-oriented projects through schemes funded by the central government.

Institutional Setup

In most of the Indian states, an institutional setup is not available to evolve procurement practices. In the country assessment report prepared by the World Bank, the lack of a policy-making department at the states and in the center is identified as a weakness of the regime. Some efforts are being taken by governments, either internally or using external agencies such as the World Bank and DFID, to study procurement practices. However, an organized approach is not adopted to internalize the best practices resulting from the study at the state level and promulgate the use of such practices across the nation. As of now, the reports generated by the committees and external agencies are not easily accessible, and best practices recommended in those reports often go unnoticed. Moreover, only two states in the country have institutionalized transparency in a Public Procurement act, which are Karnataka and Tamil Nadu. The legislation, as it is in the two states, needs to be amended to facilitate e-procurement. At the national level, there is a definite need to develop legislation on public procurement.

STATE OF E-PROCUREMENT INTERNATIONALLY

E-procurement is being actively implemented in many countries in the World. A few countries such as Singapore and Korea have had good success in implementing an end-to-end solution as a national initiative. E-procurement is implemented at the state level in federal nations such as Australia, the United States, and Canada. Efforts are now underway in the European Union to cohesively advance implementation of e-procurement in the entire community. In December, 2004, the European Commission has published an action plan for implementation of the legal framework for electronic public procurement (European Union [EU], 2004). Moreover, the EU has prepared a model functional requirements specification (FRS) document, which is used as the scale for certifying e-procurement systems. The Union members could then call for an EU certified e-procurement system and not self-engage in preparation of FRS and in evaluation of a technical specifications document. International standards on e-procurement are emerging, such as UNCTAD have taken efforts to develop an e-tendering standard.

In most countries that are in the forefront of implementing e-procurement, e-catalogue-based procurement is typically associated with e-procurement. In those countries, a lot of emphasis is laid on enhancing efficiency in goods procurement. There, e-procurement is implemented to increase operational efficiency and to introduce strategic sourcing.

Elsewhere in Denmark (www.gatetrade.com) and in the state of North Carolina in the United States (http://www.ncgov.com/eprocurement/asp/section/ep_index.asp), private-public-partnership (PPP) models have been used for implementing e-procurement. The state of Philippines is implementing e-procurement using the build-operate-transfer (BOT) model. In Singapore, the state government has developed an e-procurement solution on its own.

The Korean e-procurement system (http://www.korean.go.kr) is widely regarded as the state-of-the-art. Some of the noticeable features in the Korean system are: auto-bid evaluation where both technical and commercial bids are evaluated in minutes;[15] linkages with 30 procurement-related agencies such as Ministry of Finance, supplier certification agencies, e-guarantee and e-payment systems; and payment automation[16] (World Bank, 2004).

Multilateral development banks (MDB), such as the World Bank, Asian Development Bank, and Inter-American Development Bank have joined hands together to develop an organization specifically to foster implementation of e-procurement across the world. The organization named MDB e-Government Procurement (e-GP) group is now providing consulting services and the funds required for implementing e-procurement to many developing and less-developed countries. Thus, e-procurement is being implemented all across the world and not just in economically well-developed nations.

STATE OF E-PROCUREMENT IN INDIA

The concept of e-tendering is well publicized among government agencies in India. Except for a pioneering few, e-tendering is done in parallel with manual tendering, that is, bidders responding back to a tender could submit their bids online, or else submit the bids manually, or do both. The state of Andhra Pradesh is a pioneer in implementing a PKI-enabled e-tendering system that is used by government agencies all across the state. The government of Rajasthan has recently taken efforts to implement e-procurement at the state level. The efforts have fructified with the selection of an implementation agency, which is in the process of implementing the system across the state. Two other state governments, those of Karnataka and Chhattisgarh, are in the process of preparing a request for proposal (RFP) for implementation of a state-wide e-procurement system. While it is clear that the two state governments intend to adopt a private-public-partnership approach, the exact business model has not been decided as yet.

Typically, elsewhere in India, e-tendering systems are implemented at the departmental level. Departments individually take efforts to identify an e-procurement vendor, whose services they use. The business model adopted for funding these projects varies. For example, the payment could be made on a "fixed fee per tender" or "fixed fee per year" or "percentage of an ECV with cap" basis. In some of the states, departments place orders directly[17] to another government agency,[18] which in turn has a back-to-back agreement or a memorandum of understanding (MoU) with an e-procurement application service provider. In one of the states, having had the opportunity to study the contracts between government departments and another government agency to whom the order is placed, the author has learned that the payments are calculated in an arbitrary manner, not just in terms of the price quoted but in terms of the business model itself.

Apart from e-tendering, a system for administering the contract management aspects of e-procurement has been implemented in some of the public works departments. The system[19] is typically static in nature and implemented for the purposes of documentation and report generation. Such systems are prevalent in agencies that administer loans given by multi-lateral development banks. The business model typically adopted for procurement of the system is build-own-transfer (BOT). Many agencies have sunk in millions of rupees in deploying the systems and furthermore spending hundreds of thousand of rupees to upgrade and Web-enable the system. In this regard, it should be noted that implementation of the contract management module does not fully benefit government until it is integrated with the e-tendering module and supplier database. Only when the integration is done is it possible to automate technical-bid evaluation, a functionality that denotes an advanced state of e-procurement implementation.

The project management system implemented by the Karnataka State Police Housing Corporation (www.khspc.org) is a pioneering effort. As of now, more than 1,000 projects are managed using this system. Since the system is Web-based, information about the projects handled by the corporation is available on the net for the citizens to see. The drawback of the system, however, is that the project management module is a stand-alone system, and it is not integrated with the e-tendering module and supplier database.

Driven by business interests, e-procurement vendors have taken tremendous efforts to bring awareness about e-tendering in government agencies. Similarly, the success that the government of Andhra Pradesh has had in routing Rs. 36,000 crores[20] worth of procurement has publicized e-procurement across the country and elsewhere in the world too. The Central Vigilance Commission (CVC), on its part, has directed government agencies "*to eventually switch over to the process of e-procurement/e-sale wherever it is found to be feasible and practical*" (Central Vigilance Commission, p. 2).

In India, there are about 10 vendors operating in the e-procurement market. Most of them have a well-developed e-tendering product, which they have successfully implemented in several locations. A few of the vendors claim to have developed end-to-end e-procurement, as it is explained in the third section. The e-procurement market in India has good players, who have the capacity to implement large scale e-procurement projects.

There is a good amount of interest among Indian government agencies to implement e-procurement. So far, driven by self-propelled individuals, vendor marketing, and peer pressure, the e-procurement scene in India has emerged in an unorganized manner. In terms of capacity, e-procurement product vendors and the required workforce are available. Taking into account the state of development, interest, and capacity, the timing is just about right to initiate e-procurement implementation across the country in an organized manner and develop a technically sound, fully interoperable, end-to-end e-procurement system.

GEOGRAPHICAL SCOPE DISCUSSED IN THE CHAPTER

Two terms are used in this chapter to denote geographical scope, which are: state-wide e-procurement system; and national e-procurement system. In a state-wide e-procurement system, all procurement-related information flows,[21] handled by line departments, boards and institutions, and urban local bodies, (located within the geographical boundaries of a state) will be routed through a single, fully-integrated, end-to-end e-procurement application in a legally valid manner. In this chapter, an end-to-end system developed for central government agencies is termed as a state-wide system. The state-wide system will be regarded as fully implemented only when the e-procurement application is integrated with payment gateways, budgeting, and treasury systems. An integral part of implementing the state-wide system will be the development of an ecosystem, a policy-making organization, that will incorporate the best procurement practices in the state.

Under the national e-procurement system, implementation of e-procurement in all 29 Indian states, 6 union territories, and central government agencies is planned. To implement the national e-procurement system, certain aspects of the many state-wide systems are to be centrally developed/integrated. For example, there is a need for a contractor database at the national level; MIS data generated by many state-wide systems could be integrated to generate real-time data on government procurement at the national level. As part of the system, a national policy-making organization and e-Government Procurement-specific legislation has to be developed.

It is important to realize that the challenges in implementing nationwide e-procurement systems are different from those in implementation of state-wide e-procurement systems. One or more departments in a state may choose to take the initiative in implementing an e-procurement system for needs specific to them. However, such a decentralized approach is not considered as good practice, reasons for which are explained in the following section. From a researcher's point of view, nation, state, and department are three different units of analyses. Furthermore, federal-state nations such as India, the USA, Australia, and the European Union have a complex administrative structure, whereas small-sized countries such as Singapore, Denmark, and South Korea follow simpler structure. Given the categorization, it is proper to compare the implementation of e-procurement in India with other federal-state nations such as the USA, Australia, and the European Union, and likewise the effort taken by the state of North Carolina in the USA with that of the state of Andhra Pradesh in India.

CHALLENGES IN IMPLEMENTATION OF E-PROCUREMENT IN INDIA

One may get the initial impression that unavailability of financial resources is a barrier for implementing e-procurement in developing countries. From experience, the author has learned that India, despite being a developing country, has adequate financial resources for implementing e-procurement. For that matter, developing countries are able to get loans from donor agencies for implementing e-procurement. If a government chooses to adopt a PPP model and seek e-procurement as a service, then resource requirements are minimal. The private partner will need to implement the application and charge a service fee for transactions routed through the system. Since procurement is a commerce activity, the government can pay the private partner as per the usage and gradually purchase the application. For example, the government of Andhra Pradesh has implemented e-procurement quite successfully all across the state without making any upfront investment for setting up the e-procurement application.

The challenges in implementing e-procurement, as they are explained below, are mainly socio-political in nature. The deployment of e-procurement emerges as a key challenge since the system has to be deployed and accessed from a very large number of offices. Furthermore, the lack of skilled personnel is a critical challenge in the implementation of e-procurement. A set of six challenges is explained in detail below:

Challenge 1: Lack of Skilled Personnel

In a developing country such as India, the lack of an adequate number of skilled personnel in the government is probably the most significant challenge in implementing e-procurement. To implement e-procurement, government agencies will first need to specify things such as functional, technical, security, and service requirements, service level agreement (SLA) criteria, roll-out plan, and so forth. Furthermore, if e-procurement is implemented on a private-public-partnership (PPP) basis, then they have to decide on a business model and more importantly, customize the model to fit the e-procurement activity. The e-procurement project development is a comprehensive activity, and it requires skilled personnel to be on the job for a considerable period of time, usually between three and six months. Once the private partner is identified, then a team has to be deployed for a longer period of time to manage and monitor the implementation effort.

The implementation of state-wide e-procurement system is typically initiated by the department of IT/e-governance in tandem with public works departments. Employees in these departments typically lack the required skill sets to engage in the project development effort. Their understanding of e-procurement is obtained from vendors' marketing efforts and through hearsay. Such an understanding is inadequate to envision a state-wide end-to-end e-procurement system. Due to this inadequacy, government agencies implement e-tendering and often term it wrongly as end-to-end e-procurement.

As a remedy, government agencies look to hire external consultants to engage in the project development effort. Even for selecting the consultants, government agencies will need to prepare a terms of reference (ToR), for which they tend to lack the knowledge. If the government does prepare a ToR, then selecting an external consultant as per the laid-out procedural requirements is tedious. Except for the top management in the department of IT/e-governance and a few more employees, the rest in the department lack the capability to meaningfully engage in the project development effort. For the top management, e-procurement is only one of the many projects they have to handle, and hence efforts get diverted.

As it is often said in conferences and workshops, e-procurement, just like e-government, is not about "e" but about "procurement." Hence, one initiating the implementation of e-procurement needs to understand public procurement. In reality, however, only an exceptional few are aware of both the "e" and "procurement" attributes. If a project is implemented without proper understanding of both the attributes, then it is unlikely that the project will meet the desired objectives.

If the status quo has to change, then the government has to amend its human resource policies. Hiring of skilled personnel for a shorter duration of time has to be made simpler. Since salary structure is well-defined, government employees lack the incentive to initiate new projects. On the contrary, if an initiative taken by an employee does not fructify, then the employee becomes an easy target for criticism; thus the organization's own policies discourage personnel from taking initiatives. Furthermore, government personnel have to be trained at regular intervals. Unfortunately, government as it is lacks the institutional setup required for training its own employees. Unless skill sets of government employees are developed, implementation of e-procurement and, in a larger scale, e-government in a country as large as India will be difficult.

Challenge 2: Multi-Departmental Implementation

It is frequently mentioned that e-government cuts across departmental boundaries and mergers silos of operations within government. In a state-wide e-procurement system, procurement handled by multiple departments is routed through a single end-to-end application. Since a state-wide system is meant to be used by all departments in the state, the implementation authority has to consult with a wide range of stakeholders during project development and project implementation. Such a consultation process is fraught with difficulties because the department of IT, which typically is the implementation agency, lacks authority over other departments in the state. The lack of authority is typically overcome with several rounds of consultations, training, and negotiations. Unless one or more powerful authorities is fully involved in the implementation effort for a considerable period of time (ranging from three to six months), the project is unlikely to have the desired effect. The IT department may go ahead with project development on its own which, however, will have an adverse effect on uptake of the system. It definitely helps if a top ranking political or administrative authority in a state stamps his interest in the project.

Government agencies in India do not have information on procurement activities (procedures, spend break-up, etc.) in an easily retrievable manner. In order to prepare functional requirements and plan the system rollout, the implementation agency will need to gather procurement information from about 40 departments and around 100 government agencies. To undertake such a task, a high level of persistence is required.

Challenge 3: Inadequacy of IT and Networking Infrastructure

To implement an end-to-end e-procurement, IT and networking infrastructure across government offices is a basic requirement. In India, government agencies have inadequate IT infrastructure and connectivity problems in district and taluka (town and village) levels.

So far in India, there has not been a coordinated effort to improve the IT infrastructure. Instead, government agencies have taken efforts independently to computerize their offices. Often, computers are purchased just to utilize the funds allocated to an agency before the budget period lapses. The computers which are purchased in such a manner are typically shelved and hardly put to use. Additionally, government agencies purchase computers as part of externally-aided programs funded by donor agencies such as the World Bank. Since an asset management system is not in use in Indian government agencies, we lack information on IT readiness at the departmental level. Before initiating e-procurement implementation, one will need to collate the availability of IT infrastructure in the government.

Thanks to the deregulation of the telecom industry in India, broadband connectivity is becoming pervasive. As of now, broadband is readily available in all major cities, and its coverage is spreading towards smaller cities and towns. The government, as part of its Rs. 12,500 crores National e-Government Plan (NeGP), is in the process of implementing State-Wide Area Network (SWAN), which will bring Internet connectivity all across the country.

IT and network connectivity requirements are different for many e-procurement modules. For example, an e-tendering module is typically used at the district level (cities) offices and above, whereas a contract management module is used at the subdivisional offices (in remote areas) where a work gets implemented. Given the state of IT and network readiness in government, it is easier to implement the e-tendering aspect of e-procurement, since offices which handle the tendering work have better IT and network infrastructure when compared with offices that engage in contract management. Such distinction has to be taken into consideration while planning the rollout of the application function-wise and geography-wise.

Challenge 4: Implementation of State-Wide E-Procurement System

Given the awareness, peer pressure, and vendor marketing, many entities, departments and corporations, have independently taken the initiative to engage in e-procurement. Typically, the entities have implemented an e-tendering system, where tender information is uploaded/downloaded, and bid submissions are handled both manually and electronically in parallel. In a few exceptional cases, e-auctions are implemented, and 100% PKI-enabled e-bidding is put in place.

The independent efforts, while they have to be appreciated, typically have the following drawbacks:

1. A plan for scaling-up the initiative both function-wise and geography-wise is not envisaged.
2. Proper measures are not taken to secure data from e-procurement ASP in a restorable format, that is, if an ASP becomes dysfunctional, then the government may lose the past transactional data or, at the most, have it in a readable format.
3. Exit management strategy is not conceived.

4. Service level agreement (SLA) is not established with ASP.
5. Implementation of e-procurement is not looked at as an opportunity to reform processes, standardize formats, and make the necessary legislative amendments; hence, the manual system is at best handled in an electronic manner; the entities typically lack the mandate and the authority to implement reforms.
6. The business model adopted to remunerate ASPs for the service provided varies a lot; in some cases, ASPs are offered a fixed fee per tender and, in other cases, on an annuity basis; the rates quoted are quite varying and in the end, the government pays much more to ASPs than if they would have negotiated centrally as a single agency.
7. Often, a government agency is selected to implement e-procurement, which in turn has a back-to-back agreement with an ASP; the government agency charges a percentage of the fee, in the range of 10-15%, charged by an ASP for the services rendered; the process adopted by the government agency to select the ASP is often unclear, and contractual obligations between the two are not known to the entities using the system.
8. If there are any security loopholes in the e-procurement application, government agencies may be unaware of them since a security audit of the application is not typically done.
9. A set of suppliers will need to be trained to use multiple systems, to which they would resist.
10. To achieve a fully-integrated end-to-end system, an e-procurement application has to be integrated with external systems such as treasury systems, supplier database, and e-payment gateways; if multiple systems are operating in a state, such integration has to be done many times; since integration is an expensive activity, it is advisable to keep it to the minimum; moreover, opening sensitive applications such as the treasury to multiple e-procurement applications is not advisable.

A few of the drawbacks explained above get addressed inherently when a state-wide system is implemented. For example, with a state-wide system, the supplier community will have access to government procurement opportunities in a single location, and consequently they will need to be trained in using a single application. Some of the drawbacks such as exit management, rollout plan, SLA criteria, process reforms, and business model are addressed during the project development effort. Furthermore, in an effort to think of procurement at the state-level, an ecosystem in the form of a procurement cell could be created as part of the project development effort. The cell would address project monitoring, system audit, system maintenance, and process reform requirements.

To implement e-tendering and especially contract management/project management module, agencies have to invest significant sums of money, in some cases ranging in tens of millions of rupees. Such investments are asset-specific in nature and hence could be considered as sunk-costs. In addition to paying for the system, the agencies would have to invest in complementary activities such as project development, training, and publicity. Government agencies, which have already made such investments, may tend to get attached with their own efforts and consequently resist adopting the state-wide system. With further delay in planning state-wide e-procurement systems, many more islands of overlapping systems will emerge. The emergence of such islands will make it increasingly harder to implement state-wide systems. Fortunately in India, there are not so many legacy systems. In other words, the slate is clean. Unless urgency is shown in the implementation of state-wide systems, the government may lose the opportunity to develop end-to-end e-procurement systems consistently across the nation.

Challenge 5: The Need to Regulate E-Procurement Market

Procurement as an activity is done in a small or big way in almost all government offices in India. Government administration in India is the second largest in the world, and procurement done by the government is estimated at $100 billion each year. Moreover, if growth[22] in the Indian economy is taken into consideration along with investments made for infrastructure development,[23] the volume of government procurement will increase significantly in the years to come. If the government is to handle its geographically-widespread, voluminous, and fast-growing procurement electronically in an end-to-end manner, it will need to invest significantly in the implementation effort. The investment will be needed for planning, application deployment, training, hardware procurement, network installation, and purchase of security infrastructure. Apart from investing in implementation of e-procurement, the government will need to pay for maintenance, training, licenses, hardware, and software upgrades recurrently. Given the size of the market, its current state, and the effort required, business potential in the e-procurement market in the government sector is significant. The government has to outsource the implementation of e-procurement to external agencies in one form or the other. Thus it is no surprise that the market has more than 10 players showing active interest, including a few internationally-renowned firms.

Since the government represents the demand side of the supply-demand equation in the e-procurement market, it is not in a position to play the role of a regulator as it has done, for example, in the telecom industry. Despite the paradoxical situation, the need for regulation in the e-procurement market still remains. First and foremost, the process to be adopted for the selection of an ASP is not clear. In many cases, government agencies are selecting an e-procurement ASP without a tendering process. Such "back-door entry" creates distaste among the ASP community since equal opportunities were not given.

Second, a plan is not in place for e-procurement implementation in an organized manner all across the country. The implementation of such a plan should allow for experience sharing, and thus avoid reinvention of the wheel. Moreover, when a plan is in place, the ASPs will have clarity on the business that is available, which will cultivate healthy competition. For successful e-procurement implementation in the Indian government, it is vital that the ASPs work in harmony. Specifically for such, the government needs to regulate the e-procurement market.

Third, in the e-procurement market, a few of the ASPs are in dispute with one another, and consequently a couple of legal battles are ongoing. Especially in recent times, the disputes are getting spilled over and ASPs are resorting to trading accusations on the implementation efforts taken by the government and that too publicly. Citing the sensitive nature of procurement, government agencies are even threatened with public interest litigation (PIL) for the efforts they have taken in implementing e-procurement. Such behavior by the ASPs is destructive in nature, and it does not augur well to any of the stakeholders. Government agencies and, consequently, individuals in government are being accused by ASPs for the initiative they have taken to implement e-procurement. Such accusations will have a dampening effect in the uptake of e-procurement in the country. For the e-procurement scene to develop in an expeditious and harmonious manner, it is vital that ASPs are constructive and forthcoming. Disputes that ASPs have should be kept to themselves and not spilled over to the implementation locations. The need of the hour is a regulatory body that will monitor the market for destructive behavior and reprimand those who are found guilty.

Fourth, there is need to advocate the use of certain technology standards so that interoperability among the many e-procurement systems and with external systems will be possible. In this regard, the regulatory body will need to know the state of development of external systems such as treasury and budgeting systems across the nation. If the external systems are being developed in an unorganized manner, then integration with such systems will be difficult. When the regulatory body expresses its concern about the lack of standardization in a certain type of external system, then awareness will be created. Such awareness will catalyze the standardization of systems across many other national e-government initiatives.

Fifth, since government procurement is a sensitive activity, the use of certain security features is needed. In relation to this, there is need for an agency which will monitor advancement in technologies and advocate the use of the most advanced features.

Sixth, an e-procurement functional requirements specifications (FRS) standard needs to evolve to fit the procurement practices in the Indian government. The implementation of the FRS standard could be monitored through certification mechanisms. The European Union (EU) on its part has developed a FRS standard, which is accessible at the URL: http://europa.eu.int/idabc/en/document/4721/5874.

If the e-procurement market is not regulated at this juncture, then the e-procurement market would become fragmented, and islands of systems would emerge.

Challenge 6: Replicating Best Practices in Federal-State Setup

In India, the state of Andhra Pradesh (AP) pioneered the implementation of a state-wide e-procurement system in the year 2003. The system gained widespread usage within the state, and as of September 2005, Rs. 36,000 Crores worth of tenders are now handled through the e-tendering module. The AP system was developed on a PPP basis, where the private partner's name we shall call as "Company X" from here on. Even though AP's initiative was regarded as a best practice, many government agencies all across the country selected their own partner instead of opting to use the proven AP system implemented in government. In other words, the wheel was reinvented.

It is advocated that a best practice shall be replicated all across the nation so that the entire government setup receives benefits. So, why is this contradiction? Why did not other state governments use AP's proven e-procurement system? Could the federal government not have identified the AP's effort as a best practice and issued an order to all the state governments asking them to utilize the system? One may say that, had the federal government issued the order, and assuming that the order was adhered to by all the states, then the e-GP market in India would have been monopolized by Company X, which is not a desirable development. Alternatively, the federal government could have at least asked the states to replicate the procedure and frameworks adopted by AP and implement state-wide e-procurement on a PPP model. The federal government has not made such a policy, due to which e-procurement in India is emerging in a disorganized manner. Why has not the federal government made such a policy recommendation?

The key to answering the question lies in understanding the federal-state dynamics. As per the constitution, the states are autonomous bodies. The extent of autonomy given to states differs from one setup to another. In the USA, the states enjoy much higher autonomy than the states in India and Canada. Even if the federal government identifies a best practice and informs/recommends/suggests to replicate a best practice all across the nation, the state governments have the right to disagree with the advice and act as per their wish. In practice, some state governments look up to the federal government for direction whereas others prefer and even insist on acting independently. In the e-procurement context, the two alternatives get played out as follows: The ones who look up to the federal government for direction query as to why a national effort on e-procurement has not been taken. The others who insist on acting independently engage in the development of a state-wide system or, with further decentralization, a department-level system. We have studied why these alternative perceptions occur in the Danish context. From the study, it was found that those who perceive the nation as a single, independent entity seek the development of a centralized system at the national level. On the contrary, those who perceive state or a department as a single, independent entity argue for development of decentralized systems. In other words, the centralization versus decentralization "*debates originate due to differences in perception about the extent to which government is a single organization*" (Ramanathan, 2004, p. 3). Such an explanation holds true in the Indian context as well.

Regardless of the differences in perception, it is important that key stakeholders come together and agree on an approach for replicating best practices across the nation. Only when a plan is in place will e-procurement diffuse across the nation in a consistent manner.

CONCLUDING REMARKS

In this chapter, the concept of e-government procurement, as it is being implemented in India, is explained. Furthermore, a set of six challenges encountered during implementation of e-procurement are discussed in depth. The six challenges are intertwined and hence they shall not be treated independently. Instead, a concerted approach is required to address the challenges. To develop the approach, key stakeholders from all across the government have to set aside their differences and agree on a way forward. Unless urgency is shown in planning the state-wide systems, there is a risk that numerous islands of legacy systems will emerge. The emergence of the islands of systems will make it harder to implement the preferred state-wide end-to-end e-procurement system. Since public procurement is driven by the same set of principles everywhere, the rich descriptions and explanations in this chapter can be generalized to e-GP implementations in developing countries and in federal-state setup.

REFERENCES

Central Vigilance Commission. (2003, December 18). No. 98/ORD/1. Retrieved from http://cvc.nic.in/98ord12k312.pdf

European Union (EU). (2004, December 13). Action plan for the implementation of the legal framework for electronic public procurement. Commission of the European Communities. Retrieved from http://ec.europa.eu/internal_market/publicprocurement/e-procurement_en.htm

Kaul, V. (2005). *All you wanted to know about fiscal deficit.* Retrieved February 6, 2006, from http://www.rediff.com/money/2005/apr/12fiscal.htm

Ramanathan, S. (2004). *Diffusion of electronic public procurement in Denmark.* PhD thesis, Aalborg University, Denmark.

World Bank. (2003, December 10). *Procurement Services: South Asian Region* (India Country Procurement Assessment Rep. No. 27859-IN). Retrieved from http://www-wds.worldbank.org/servlet/WDSContentServer/WDSP/IB/2004/04/02/000012009_20040402111746/Rendered/PDF/278590IN.pdf

World Bank. (2004, July). Korea's move to e-procurement (No. 90). *Prem Notes: Public Sector.* Retrieved from http://www1.worldbank.org/prem/PREMNotes/premnote90.pdf

ENDNOTES

1 Recently, when roads in Mumbai went bad due to the incessant rains, many citizens groups had sought information about the efforts taken by the government to repair the roads. Such enquiries have become commonplace nowadays, and they get the media's attention too.

2 For example, Director General of Supplies and Disposals (DGS&D) is an agency that negotiates rate contracts on behalf of government agencies in India.

3 An example would be Chhattisgarh State Industrial Development Corporation (CSIDC), which is a state-specific rate contract negotiation agency.

4 Typically, the health department in a state negotiates rate contracts to meet its requirements.

5 City and town corporations, for instance, negotiate their own rate contracts for items such as street lights and phenyl.

6 Periods range from one to two years.

7 These end users are located in secretariat, district, and taluka levels.

8 The central location is typically the state capital.

9 Examples would include assistant engineer and assistant executive engineer, who are present at the district and taluka levels.

10 This can also be termed as non-ECV-based procurement.

11 Karnataka State Highways Improvement Project (K-SHIP)

12 Karnataka Soaps and Detergents Limited (KSDL), which manufactures the famous Mysore Sandal soap

13 Karnataka Residential Institutional Society (KRIS)

14 Delhi Metro Rail Corporation Limited (DMRCL)

15 The implementation of auto-bid evaluation functionality is one of the most challenging aspects of e-procurement. It can be done only when a supplier database is developed and linked with an evaluation engine. The logic underlying the evaluation engine has to be developed by the domain experts.

16 The Korean government makes payment to suppliers in less than 4 hours after the inventory inspection is done as against the regulatory requirements of 14 days. Due to such prompt payment, the number of suppliers bidding for government contracts has trebled.

17 This means without a tendering process.

18 Typically, it is an IT agency.

19 This system is also known as project finance management system (PFMS).

20 This was the exchange rate as of September 2005.

21 These include not just tendering, but also contract management, ordering, and workflow approvals, among others.

22 The Indian economy is growing at a rate of about 6-7% in the last few years. Given the steadfast buoyancy in the stock markets and the high expectations, it is likely that the current growth rate will at least be maintained in the next few years, if not enhanced.

23 The plan expenditure was estimated at 4.44% of the GDP in the year 2004-2005, and there is a strong lobby to increase the plan expenditure to 8% of the GDP so the economy would grow at the rate of 10-12% each year.

This work was previously published in E-Procurement in Emerging Economies: Theory and Cases, edited by A. K. Pani and A. Agrahari, pp. 76-100, copyright 2007 by IGI Publishing, formerly known as Idea Group Publishing (an imprint of IGI Global).

Chapter 4.27
The Dubai E-Government Project

James Piecowye
Zayed University Media Center, UAE

INTRODUCTION

Ranked 26th worldwide and second in the Middle East for its e-government initiative, the United Arab Emirates (UAE), and Dubai, in particular, is an excellent example of how e-government might be developed, implemented and advanced as a customer service-based concept (West, 2005).

The e-government project that continues to evolve in Dubai can be credited almost exclusively to the Emirate's leadership as embodied in Sheikh Mohammed Bin Rashid Al Maktoum, Crown Prince of Dubai, his vision and sheer tenacity to make grand ideas a reality.

It is not our intention in this article to suggest that the Dubai e-government project is without challenges and room for improvement. It is our intention, though, to present the Dubai case study as an evolving example of e-government from which to learn.

While the development and implementation of the e-government project is advancing in Dubai at a frenetic pace, the rollout of the concept to the public and the general acceptance and inclusion of the public in the larger governance process is still, to a large extent, a masterful work in progress.

The general global assessment of e-government delivery undertaken by Darrell West (2005) makes it very clear that progress is being witnessed worldwide when it comes to the implementation of e-government ideals. The greatest challenge to e-government, according to West (2005), is at times its very slow pace, its uneven nature and failure to adapt to changing conditions within which it exists. Dubai, in some instances to a lesser degree and others to a greater degree, is experiencing the same problems being experienced globally by those engaged in implementing e-government.

Fortunately, e-government performance in Dubai is improving rapidly, as budget, bureaucracy and institutional forces are pushed towards compliance. But what continues to be fundamentally lacking from Dubai's e-government project is a means of promoting and facilitating authentic e-governance where society as a whole has a means of engaging in meaningful interaction as a participant in the process of governance and not simply the service side of the state.

Dubai is one of seven Emirates that constitute the UAE federation. The country's constitution identifies it as an Arab state, with Islam as its religion and Arabic as its official language. The UAE is a member of the Arab League and the Gulf Cooperation Council (GCC), a regional group that joins the Gulf states of Kuwait, Saudi Arabia, Qatar, Bahrain, UAE and Oman. In general, GCC countries share many political, economic and social characteristics, including high reliance on an imported work force.

In the last decade, Dubai and the UAE have undergone phenomenal change. Fifty years ago, the country had little to no electricity, plumbing or simple infrastructure, such as surfaced roads and bridges. In 1950, there was no hospital and but a single school in Dubai. Dubai was a city comprised of barasti huts (housing made from palm fencing) and clay buildings lining sand streets. As late as the 1970s, according to Timothy Walters (unpublished), the literacy rate of the UAE hovered around 20%, with only a fraction of adults having any formal education.

Today, the landscape of Dubai has been radically transformed. Dubai is experiencing a level of prosperity never before seen. Physically, the city has been morphed from a sleepy regional trading post to the premier economic and tourist hub of the Middle East.

The transformation of Dubai is marked by its rapid installation of a modern infrastructure, the embracing of technology and both the vision and resources to rapidly roll out change to the general population. In 1999, Sheikh Mohammed Bin Rashid Al Maktoum championed the idea of launching a visionary e-government project to set the standard for such endeavours in the Middle East. More recently, in 2005, the idea of a government connecting to at least a large segment of its constituents is quickly becoming a reality.

This article will review why we believe Dubai might be considered an excellent e-government case study in the implementation of e-government as a customer-service concept. This article will also suggest that one of the greatest challenges of any e-government project is to include governance in the equation. This examination is primarily based on a synthesis of government publications available through the e-government portal www.dubai.ae, where examples of the e-government exercise are available, with other accounts of the Dubai e-government project.

BACKGROUND

According to the UAE Ministry of Economy and Planning, the UAE's population in 2003 was estimated to be 4.041 million (Dubai Development and Investment Authority, 2005). Dubai is the UAE's most populous city, with an estimated population of 1.071 million. Census results from 2000 shows that 80% of Dubai's population is comprised of expatriates. According to official government statistics, UAE nationals constitute 18% of the country's population, followed by other Arabs expatriates at 13%, Asians 63% and Europeans and others 4%. Dubai's population is similar in its diversity to the nation at large (Datadubai.com, 2005; Dubai Development and Investment Authority, 2005).

The diverse expatriate population of Dubai uses language as one tool of cultural expression and interaction. While English is the dominant language in the business and tourism industries, government agencies use both Arabic and English to cater for the Emirate's residents and visitors. In addition, Urdu, Hindi, Farsi, Tagalog, and Russian, along with other languages, are also widely used on a daily basis. Most schools in Dubai offer one or two languages as additional foreign languages for non-native speakers.

International schools in Dubai cater to the myriad of nationalities living in the Emirate. Expatriate children are not admitted to the UAE public schools in the country; therefore, they study in private institutions. Local authorities have licensed K-12 schools offering Lebanese, British,

American, French, International Baccalaureate and Indian curricula, to name just a few. American, Canadian and British-styled institutions of higher learning also provide higher studies to nationals and expatriates.

Dubai also plays a role as an international trading site. With an advanced infrastructure that includes world-class ports, airport, roads, free zones, a financial center, banks, insurance sector and retail outlets, to name just a few, Dubai attracts business as well as leisure visitors year round. To promote itself as a trade destination, the Dubai government organizes an annual shopping festival that attracts millions of visitors. In addition, it organizes a summer program of shopping and hotel promotions to revive the local economy during the months when temperatures soar and local residents take their annual leave abroad.

Dubai is one of the Middle East's most successful tourism destinations. According to the World Tourism Organization, Dubai has witnessed steady positive growth as a destination for the past decade, with only a marginal decline during periods of regional wars and instability. In 2002, Dubai achieved 31% growth in tourist arrivals—the world's highest for the year. In 2003, Dubai guests reached 4,980,228, with the majority coming from other Arab countries, Europe, Africa, Russia and the CIS republics and Asia. There is no question that Dubai is a city state in the throngs of rapid development.

THE IDEA OF E-GOVERNMENT

E-government can be defined as the electronic enablement of services provided or commissioned by the public sector specifically capitalizing upon applications of information and communication technology (ICT) tools to the wide range of service activities undertaken by the state.

The goal of any e-government project is to enhance the effectiveness and efficiency of a government's activities and, in many instances, alter the procedural relationship of the government with the public. This altered government/public relationship typically progresses through several distinct phases, according to Sami Atallah (2001): posting information; two-way communication; exchange of value; integrated service and exchange.

The move towards e-government by many first-world countries is fundamentally altering the government/public relationship on one hand and citizen/business relationship on the other. In the Middle East, change in the government/public and citizen/business relationship is no different.

What is different in the Middle East is the relationship of e-government to e-governance. In many democratic-styled countries, e-government and e-governance projects are being developed concurrently. E-governance might best be understood as the electronic enablement and management of democratic activities, ensuring a degree of fairness, transparency and ultimately participation in the public-policy process of the otherwise disenfranchised (Bovaird, 2005).

E-governence is less about access and more about the style and intent of leadership. E-governence, as Khosrow-Pour (2005) suggests, is about enabling new ways of debating and deciding public policy. E-governance is less an economic investment and more an investment in the populous itself, thereby facilitating a new means of listening and consulting the citizenship.

E-governance, thus, becomes about enabling democratic tendencies and efficient government. The ideals of e-governance are being talked about today across the Middle East in general, but have yet to be adopted in any meaningful way, including in the UAE.

Sami Atallah (2001) suggests that the most striking effect of e-government is seen in the enhancement of the communicative ability of governments. But e-government is not simply the reinvention of the communication structures of governments. E-government is the reinvention of the way the business of governance is conducted.

From information delivery, service procurement and delivery, the manner of conduct of the state is dramatically changing. What is coming about is the imposition of a customer service-centered mentality in the manner in which the state interacts with the population it serves.

The goal of e-government as it is being embraced today worldwide and, in particular, in Dubai, can be summarized as to provide unified quality services (UQS) under the common slogan "the customer first." Unified quality services are being promoted in the context of e-government embracing the use of technology to simplify customer/government transactions and create a better environment for efficient government operations (Dubai eGovernment, 2004).

The process of e-government is much more than simply facilitating UQS. What e-government is facilitating is the complete institutional, cultural change of government internally and as it is perceived by the public itself. What is being advanced is organizational change towards customer relationship management, with the goal being to meet and exceed customer expectations from the start to the end of the transaction (Bovaird, 2005).

THE DUBAI E-GOVERNMENT EXPERIMENT

The driving force behind e-government in Dubai is Sheikh Mohammed Bin Rashid Al Maktoum. His idea for e-government is embodied in the government's portal, www.dubai.ae, where customers can access a plethora of services being made available to them, in many cases, only electronically.

Sheikh Mohammed has set out two broad objectives for e-government in Dubai:

1. The government of Dubai shall e-enable 90% of its public services by 2007
2. Customers should conduct 50% of e-enabled government transactions through innovative channels by 2007 (Geray, 2004).

The Dubai e-government project is ambitious and premised on the simple idea that anything is possible if the right people are involved. Thus, what is constantly suggested within the Dubai government is that you are either part of the team or not, and those who are not up to the challenge of e-government are free to move on.

By 2007, it is expected that there will be:

1. E-enablement of 90% of public services (including identification of all online and off-line public services in each department and also service prioritization for e-enablement)
2. Implementation of e-service quality guidelines in all departments
3. Implementation of virtual governance by joining administrative boundaries through electronic integration and data sharing
4. Implementation of targeted marketing campaigns
5. Implementation of synergistic e-services to achieve expedited implementation and cost savings to the Dubai government (Geray, 2004).

The key to the success of the Dubai e-government project so far has been the ability of Dubai to re-invent the attitude of public service itself. Nowhere is this re-invention more prevalent than in the Department of Tourism and Commerce Marketing (DTCM). DTCM is a natural success story in Dubai because of the persistence of the Dubai government to continually try to accomplish the impossible and the desire of the Dubai government to see the Emirate become a unique tourist, financial, manufacturing and service destination.

The DTCM activities with e-government focus on connectivity to those who may want to come to Dubai and the eventual ease of their integration into Dubai. From general information to the obtaining of visas to the finding of suitable accommodations, the DTCM e-project embraces the idea of aiding the user first. The department considers its eServices a strategic gateway to the world. DTCM, as of December 2003, had 10 eServices, of which four were transactional and six informational (Dubai eGovernment, June 2004f).

THE DUBAI DIFFERENCE

What makes Dubai and its e-government initiative different than most other places in the world, according to Sheikha Lubna, CEO of Tejari (the first e-commerce supply chain market in the region), is that contrary to the practices in most parts of the world, where the corporate community and business sectors take the lead and impose their e-initiatives on society. the government sector in Dubai is the real leader in the transition into e-commerce (Dubai eGovernment, August 2004g).

Under the leadership of Sheikh Mohammed Bin Rashid Al Maktoum, the e-government initiative of Dubai has seen amazing advances. According to Sheikh Mohammed, "the e-government concept depends on many factors, two of which are: making essential improvements to the government services provided to the public, and prompting the public sector to deal with its customers as dynamically and easily as the private sector" (Dubai eGovernment, May 2004d, p. 2).

The Dubai e-government initiative has two basic guiding objectives: simplification of government transactions in the emirate, and creation of initiatives to help Dubai assume a leadership position in the IT-driven global economy (Dubai eGovernment, October 2004h).

To operationalize these two objectives, the Dubai e-government project has relied very heavily, but not exclusively, on cultivating a reflexive relationship with the private sector and business community. The Dubai government is very cognizant of the fact that its constituents comprise both individual residents and private industry, and its initiatives serve to satisfy the needs of both. In the case of private industry, the challenge is to get them to buy into the e-government initiatives by making the industry a key component of the goods and services supply train of the state.

According to Sheikh Mohammed Bin Rashid Al Maktoum, the success of any e-government initiative is premised on the symbiotic relationship of economics and social services that can only be realized if state and business interests work as partners.

The rapid movement towards the implementation of e-government and the changed mentality that comes with it has brought its own share of challenges. Dr. Khalid Al Khazraji, Undersecretary at the UAE Ministry of Labor and Social Affairs, considers one of the most significant challenges to the implementation of e-government in Dubai the changing of the attitudes of the employees who must buy into the current government-centered system to a customer-first e-government system. Part of the process of change can take place through re-training. The other, more difficult, aspect of change comes from convincing employees of the benefits of moving towards e-enabled government services (Dubai eGovernment, May 2004d).

Dubai has always been a pioneering state. In April 2000, Sheikh Mohammed Bin Rashid Al Maktoum called for the transition of the Dubai government into the new knowledge age, demanding that the departments of the Dubai government provide their services electronically within no more than 18 months! Between April 2000 and the time of Dubai e-government launch in October 2001, all the infrastructure for the rollout of the e-government project was put into place. After 2 years, Dubai government, through its e-government project, provided more than 600 electronic services. Dubai turned the initiative into a project and the project into an organization (Dubai eGovernment, April 2004c).

What distinguishes Dubai's e-government project from any other world wide is the constant desire to continually innovate. A further example of this innovation was seen in September 2005, when the Dubai government launched the first Arab electronic mobile phone e-government portal. The mobile phone portal was launched with 26 services divided into 10 categories: traffic and roads; health; business; aviation and flights; information about Dubai; information on Islamic issues; Emirates Airline; Real estate; and the Dubai stock market. The project is specifically intended to help enable the prime objective—the greater e-government project of 90% of all government services being available electronically (Dubai eGovernment, October, 2005h).

DUBAI E-GOVERNMENT IN ACTION

As of August 2004, the Dubai e-government exercise had 1,444 total online services. Of those, 173 were informational, 49 interactive and 1,222 transactional. The completion rate for transactions was 47% (Dubai eGovernment August, 2004g).

As of August 2004, there also were 20 government departments actively participating in the e-government project; this number is larger today, although exact statistics are not available. The Dubai municipality is by far the leading department, with 304 e-government services in total, of which 54 are transactional and 250 are informational. The Dubai Airport Free Zone Authority has 124 e-government services, of which 118 are transactional and 6 are informational. Links to various projects in the Dubai e-government project can be found at www.dubai.ae (Dubai eGovernment, March 2004b).

While Dubai was the first government to move towards e-government in the Middle East in 2001, according to measures of the effectiveness of these services by West (2005), even with its innovative approach, it is not the leader of e-government in the Middle East.

E-government ratings done by West (2005) put the UAE on par with Qatar in 26th place world wide, with an effectiveness rating of 30.1. Bahrain leads the e-government exercise in the Middle East, in 23rd place world wide, with an effectiveness rating of 31.

FUTURE TRENDS

What is being changed through the Dubai e-government project is the very nature of the state's relationship to its citizens, visitors and businesses. What is being seen is the transformation of residents to customers through the e-government project.

Dubai's e-government project is not, and never has been, intended as a solution to failed government development. No one knows this better than Sheikh Mohammed Bin Rashid Al Maktoum. What makes Dubai's case so interesting is that, for the most part, the state is rebuilding its services as the e-government project itself is being implemented. E-government is being used as a means to push improvement and enhancement, and not as a stopgap to brace failed programs and ideas that have become entrenched as part of the system (Atallah, 2001).

But it also needs to be remembered that there is a politico-administrative process at work as e-government is implemented. This politico-administrative process only works when it is understood that residents are not simply customers, but participants in the governmental process (Van Duivenboden, 2005).

For e-government to work, it needs to have a clear strategy that recognizes the commerce aspect of the exercise and simultaneously the governance aspects that are evolving and inextricably linked to effective government.

So far, the UAE, and Dubai in general, is concentrating on the e-government project only. There are hints of more open electronic channels between the Dubai's residents and the decision makers as seen through the Dubai municipality suggestion and complaint service, called "Have your Say." While this service provides a means of tracking the progress of submissions and has a mechanism to reward creative comments, it is a long way from a means of input into the public in the public-policy process of the Emirate (Dubai eGovernment, September 2005a).

CONCLUSION

There is no question that through the visionary leadership of Dubai and the rapid implementation of ICTs into the communication process of the government e-government has realized success in Dubai.

According to Qassim Sultan Al Banna, the adoption of ICTs and, ultimately, e-government has led to the Dubai government becoming more customer- and quality-centered in its delivery of products and services in an extraordinarily short period of time.

Dubai's e-government project has increased and expanded access to government services by enabling interaction with the Dubai government through a variety of ICTs, from mobile phones to the Internet. In many cases, the adoption of ICTs has actually reduced costs of service delivery by the state by as much as 30%, according to the Dubai government.

But the learning and adoption curve to a completely integrated e-government across society is steep. While the young e-generation is an early adopter, and a significant portion of Dubai's population, there still is much to be done to bring those skeptical of technology on board with the e-government project.

The 21st century brings with it a new expectation from businesses and individuals who require an environment that is conducive and one in which they can prosper. The Internet revolution is reshaping the world, and in this New Economy, it is critical for governments to re-invent themselves as it is for business to transform into e-business (Sheikh Mohammed Bin Rashid Al Maktoum, 2004).

REFERENCES

Atallah, S. (2001). E-government: Considerations for Arab States, United Nations Development Program. New York: The United Nations.

Bovaird, T. (2005). E-government and E-governance. In M. Khosrow-Pour, Practicing e-government: A global perspective (pp. 43-62). Hershey, PA: Idea Group Publishing. Retrieved from http://site.ebrary.com/lib/zu/Doc?id=10080038&ppg=1

Columbus Guides. (n.d.). Dubai City overview. Retrieved September 17, 2004, from www.cityguide.travel-guides.com/cities/dub/cityoverview.asp

DataDubai.com. (2005). Population of Dubai. Retrieved December 17, 2005, from http://datadubai.com/population.htm

Design, J. (2003). E-government expands in the Middle East as administrations set sights on world-leading service delivery. Retrieved November 1, 2004, from http://newsroom cisco.com

Dubai Development and Investment Authority. (2005). Dubai in figures. Retrieved December 17, 2005, from http://ddia.ae

Dubai eGovernment. (2004a). Technology partners. Retrieved September 14, 2004, from http://egov.dubai.ae/en.portal?EGOVPartners,Article_000008,1,&_nfpb= true&_pageLabel=view)

Dubai eGovernment. (2004b, March). E-service monitor. E4All, March, 5, 6.

Dubai eGovernment. (2004c, April). 1st Middle East eGovernment summit. E4All, 6, 2-14.

Dubai eGovernment. (2004d, May). We defeated all resistance to eTransformation by saying "nothing to impossible." E4All, 7, 4-6.

Dubai eGovernment. (2004e, May). 90% of e-services to be online by 2007. E4All, 7, 2-3.

Dubai eGovernment. (2004f, June). Dubai's online window from DTCM. E4All, 8, 7.

Dubai eGovernment. (2004g, August). Ask Dubai about DDB services. E4All, 10, 2-14.

Dubai eGovernment. (2004h, October). Dubai eGovernment in the eyes of IT pioneers. E4All, 12, 2-5.

Dubai eGovernment. (2005a, September). Have your say. E4All, 23, 11.

Dubai eGovernment. (2005b, October). Announcing the first government portal for mobile phones in the Arab World. E4All, 24, 2-3.

DubaiInc. (2004). Facts and figures. Retrieved September 15, 2004, from www.dubaiinc.com/

Geray, O. (2004). Implementing H.H. Sheikh Mohammed Bin Rashid Al Maktoum's vision for Dubai eGovernment: 2004-2007. Dubai: Dubai eGovernment.

Holme, D. (2005). Drop the 'e': Marketing e-governmentto a sceptical public and Web weary decision makers. In M. Khosrow-Pour, Practicing e-government : A global perspective (pp. 199-232). Hershey, PA: Idea Group Publishing. Available from http://site.ebrary.com/lib/zu/Doc?id=10080038&ppg=1

TheJudiciary.org. (2002). National profiles, 2002. Retrieved September 16, 2004, from www.thejudiciary.org/library/profiles/print/tc.html

Khosrow-Pour, M. (2005). Practicing e-government: A global perspective. Hershey, PA: Idea Group Publishing. Retrieved from http://site.ebrary.com/lib/zu/Doc?id=10080038&ppg=1

Piecowye, J. & Badran, B. (2004). Culture, communication, media, and hybridism: The Dubai case. In C. Ess & F. Sudweeks (Eds), Cultural attitudes towards technology and communication 2004 (pp. 399-410). Australia: School of Information Technology Murdoch University.

Sheikh Mohammed Bin Rashid Al Maktoum. (2004). E-government @ Dubai to revolutionize public service. Retrieved November 1, 2004, from http://dubaiinternetcity.com/html/10a-news.htm

Subbaroa, P. (2004). Population of Dubai. Retrieved September 15, 2004, from www.datadubai.com/population.htm

Sheikh Mohammed Bin Rashid Al Maktoum. (2004). Sheikh Mohammed inaugurates the e-government portal. Retrieved November 1, 2004, from http://shiekhmohammed.co.ae

UAE Interact. (2005). UAE population growth highest in Middle East. Retrieved December 17, 2005, from http://82.125.132.90/news/default.asp?cntDisplay=20&id=134

Van Duivenboden, H. (2005). Citizen participation in public administration. In M. Khosrow-Pour, Practicing e-government: A global perspective (pp. 415-446). Hershey, PA: Idea Group Publishing. Available from http://site.ebrary.com/lib/zu/Doc?id=10080038&ppg=1

Walters, T., Quinn, S. & Walters, L. (2005). Media life among gen zeds. International Journal of Cultural Studies 8(1), 65-86.

West, D. (2005). Global e-government, 2005. Retrieved December 18, 2005, from www.insidepolitics.org/egovtdata.html

KEY TERMS

E-Culture: The ordinary societal rudiments of interaction and acquisition taken for granted and sometimes ignored in any society, because they are so common, which are now mediated through ICT. Examples include activities such as conversations with friends via instant messaging or the ability to order goods and services through Web portals like Amazon.com.

E-Generation: The demographic born between 1995 and 2005 that has only ever known an environment employing ICTs for everything from entertainment to political participation.

E-Governance: The enabling of a new means of listening and consulting the citizenship, thereby enabling democratic tendencies and efficient socio-political development.

E-Government: The electronic enablement of all services provided or commissioned by the public sector capitalizing upon specific applications of ICT tools to the wide range of societal activities undertaken by the state.

E-Services: The exchange of goods and/or activities that in the past involved face-to-face communication but are now facilitated through an electronic, people-free interface.

Information Communication Technology (ICT): Devices utilizing microchip technology that enable enhanced information exchange.

Unified Quality Services (UQS): The use of technology to simplify customer/government transactions and create a better environment for efficient government operations.

This work was previously published in Encyclopedia of Digital Government, edited by JA. Anttiroiko and M. Malkia, pp. 410-415, copyright 2007 by Information Science Reference, formerly known as Idea Group Reference (an imprint of IGI Global).

Chapter 4.28
e-ASEAN and Regional Integration in South East Asia

Xiudian Dai
University of Hull, UK

INTRODUCTION

As a relatively new feature of the digital revolution in the Association of Southeast Asian Nations (ASEAN), e-ASEAN was initiated by the ASEAN economic ministers in September 1999 and endorsed by ASEAN leaders at their summit in Manila in November the same year, when the e-ASEAN Task Force was also set up (ASEAN Secretariat, 2003). At the Fourth ASEAN Informal Summit in Singapore in November 2000, a Framework Agreement was signed to serve as the legal foundation for the e-ASEAN initiative. To ensure success, the Senior Economic Officials Meeting (SEOM) was tasked to supervise, coordinate, and review the implementation of the e-ASEAN Framework Agreement. As stipulated in the e-ASEAN Framework Agreement, the SEOM reports to the ASEAN Economic Ministers (AEM) and assists the AEM in all matters concerning this Agreement (ASEAN, 2000, Article 13).

While there is no lack of literature discussing trade liberalisation and transborder cooperation in the ASEAN region, the impact of new information and communications technologies (ICTs) on the development of regionalism, and vice versa, remains a rather neglected area of study (Dai, 2003). The purpose of this article is to investigate the implications of the e-ASEAN initiative for regional cooperation and integration in South East Asia in the information age. In particular, the key challenges to achieving the objectives of the e-ASEAN initiative will be analysed.

BACKGROUND

It is widely perceived that new ICTs can significantly advance transnational co-operation and regional integration in both economic and political terms (Bangemann et al. 1994; European Commission, 2000). Transnational flows of communication are synonymous to the decline in the importance of national, geographical, and institutional boundaries (Castells, 1996). The launch of the European Information Society in the early 1990s serves as an example of public policy based on the notion that new ICTs can be a positive factor to regional integration (Dai, 2000; Federal Europe, 1995).

Generally speaking, e-ASEAN is "to develop a broad-based and comprehensive action plan including physical, legal, logistical, social and economic infrastructure needed to promote an ASEAN e-space, as part of an ASEAN positioning and branding strategy" (ASEAN Secretariat, 2003). Internally, the e-ASEAN initiative is to use ICTs "to speed up economic integration of the group" and, externally, to "help them compete better in the global economy" (Ng & Nurbanum, 2002, p. 39).

The promotion of regional economic growth and acceleration of regional peace and stability have been the key objectives of ASEAN since its establishment in 1967. In today's globally competitive world, ASEAN officials argue, "regionalism has to take on a larger meaning and scope than market integration alone" (ASEAN Secretary-General, 2000). It is perceived vital that, in close cooperation, ASEAN members endeavour "to acquire the technological prowess without which the ASEAN nations cannot hope to move forward economically" (ASEAN Secretary-General, 2000). A key question to be asked is whether or not the global communications revolution can be advantageous to regional integration in South East Asia.

E-ASEAN AND REGIONAL COOPERATION: CRITICAL ISSUES

Intra-regional cooperation among member states is manifested in the aims of e-ASEAN Framework Agreement: (1) co-operation to develop, strengthen and enhance the competitiveness of the ICT sector in ASEAN; (2) co-operation to reduce the digital divide within individual ASEAN member states and amongst ASEAN member states; (3) co-operation between the public and private sectors in realising e-ASEAN; and (4) the liberalisation of trade in ICT products, ICT services and investments to support the e-ASEAN initiative (ASEAN, 2000, Article 1).

Table 1. Access to ICTs in ASEAN, 2000 (Source: Based on figures from World Bank [2002], CIA [2005b] and Dai [2003])

Country	Telephone mainlines per 1000 people*	Mobile phones per 1000 people*	PCs per 1000 people*	Internet users (% of population)*	GDP per capita, PPP in US$**
Brunei	245	289	70.1	8.82	18,600
Cambodia	2 1	0	1.1	0.05	1,900
Indonesia	31	17	9.9	0.95	3,200
Laos	8 2		2.6	0.11	1,700
Malaysia	199	213	103.1	15.88	9,000
Myanmar	6	0	1.1	0.01	1,800
Philippines	40 8	4	19.3	2.65	4,600
Singapore	484	684	483.1	30.00	23,700
Thailand	92	50	24.3	3.79	7,400
Vietnam	32 1	0	8.8	0.25	2,500

*Notes: * Adapted from World Bank (2002) and Dai (2003); **All GDP figures are Estimated Purchasing Power Parity (PPP) of 2003, except for Brunei, for which the PPP figure is for 2002*

In order to achieve their objectives, ASEAN countries are committed to undertaking the following measures through the e-ASEAN initiative (ASEAN, 2000, Article 2):

- Facilitating the establishment of the ASEAN Information Infrastructure
- Facilitating the growth of electronic commerce in ASEAN
- Promoting and facilitating the liberalisation of trade in ICT products, ICT services, and of investments in support of the e-ASEAN initiative
- Promoting and facilitating investments in the production of ICT products and the provision of ICT services
- Developing an e-society in ASEAN and capacity building to reduce the digital divide within individual ASEAN Member States and amongst ASEAN Member States
- Promoting the use of ICT applications in the delivery of government services (e-government)
- Enabling advanced member states to assist the lagging member states to undertake capacity building

The signing of the e-ASEAN Framework Agreement has generated much enthusiasm within the public and private sectors across the ASEAN region. This is in part manifested in the large number of transnational ICT projects established in response to the launch of e-ASEAN involving project partners from different member states. Of a total of 40 ICT projects, 22 are within the field of e-commerce and the rest address the new and specialised market areas such as e-society, Information Infrastructure and e-governance (Dai, 2003). The dominance of e-commerce projects, in terms of the number of projects, serves as an indication that commercial organisations in the private sector are convinced of the potential opportunities to be afforded by e-ASEAN for promoting transnational e-commerce activities.

To make e-ASEAN a success, ASEAN countries would have to address a number of important issues. Among others, the existence of an intra-regional digital divide, national differences in the provision and application of cyberlaws and the competitive relationship between some ASEAN member states are the focal points of public debate.

Digital Inequality in ASEAN

Access to ICTs in ASEAN remains significantly uneven. Data presented in Table 1 shows a general trend in ASEAN: the region is clearly divided into countries moving along the fast lanes of the information superhighway and those crawling along the slow lanes. Singapore, Malaysia, and Brunei are the three ASEAN countries that are far ahead of the other member states in terms of penetration rate of main telephone lines, mobile phones, PCs (personal computers), and, last but not least, the Internet.

In 2000, when main telephone line and mobile phone penetration rate reached 484 and 684 per 1000 people (or 48.4% and 68.4%) respectively in Singapore, the corresponding rates for Myanmar were 6 and 0 per 1000 people and 8 and 2 for Laos. Commenting on the present situation of the telecommunications industry in Myanmar, the CIA (Central Intelligence Agency) believes the sector "barely meets minimum requirements for local and intercity service for business and government" (CIA, 2005a).

Concerning the Internet sector, the contrast between the advanced and the lagging countries in ASEAN adds another dimension of the intra-regional digital divide: while 30% of Singaporeans and just under 16% of Malaysians were Internet users in 2000, the proportion of Internet users among the population in the CLMV (Cambodia, Laos, Myanmar, and Vietnam) and Indonesia was below the 1% level.

The intra-regional digital divide in ASEAN does not come as a surprise. Rather, the picture

Table 2. Cyberlaws in ASEAN

Member State	Cyberlaw
Malaysia	• The Communications and Multimedia Act (1998) • The Malaysian Communications and Multimedia Commission Act (1998) • The Digital Signature Act (1997) • The Computer Crimes Act (1997) • The Telemedicine Act (1997)
Singapore	• Electronic Transactions Act (1998)
Brunei	• Electronic Transactions Order (2000)
Thailand	• Electronic Transactions Bill (Draft)
Philippines	• Electronic Commerce Act (2000)

of digital divide between ASEAN countries is in line with the differentiation in GDP per capita. Figures in Table 1 indicate that the three leading countries (Singapore, Brunei, and Malaysia) with higher ICT deployment rates are actually the three countries with much higher GDP per capita. To address the challenges posed by the digital divide, therefore, it is important to bear in mind that uneven access to ICTs is more than often associated with the varying levels of economic development.

Regional Governance of Cyberspace

One of the key objectives of the e-ASEAN initiative is to promote the harmonisation of cyberlaws across ASEAN. The e-ASEAN Framework Agreement states that "Member States shall adopt electronic commerce regulation and legislative frameworks that create trust and confidence for consumers and facilitate the transformation of businesses towards the development of e-ASEAN" (ASEAN, 2000).

The harmonisation of cyberlaws in ASEAN is faced with fundamental challenges. First, in addition to the digital divide in the sense of uneven access to ICTs, there is a gap in the provision of cyberlaws between different ASEAN countries. While some countries, notably Malaysia, have already become regional as well as world pioneers in enacting cyberlaws, others have hardly made any progress in the same field (see Table 2 for a list of cyberlaws in ASEAN).

The second challenge comes from the fact that social and political systems vary from country to country within the ASEAN region. Judged by their attitude towards the Internet, states in East and South East Asia fall into three different categories including the following (Hachigian, 2002):

- States with severely restrictive policies and rules towards all public use of the Internet (e.g., Myanmar and North Korea)
- States with moderately restrictive rules towards Internet access and contents (e.g., Vietnam, Singapore and China)
- States that actively promote Internet access and allow for online political pluralism, (e.g., Malaysia)

The different socio-political systems currently prevailing in ASEAN constitute a big challenge to the region's plan for harmonising cyberlaws for the simple reason that online contents and behaviours acceptable in one country may not necessarily be acceptable in another.

National vs. Regional Interests

In ASEAN countries, there is no lack of high profile ICT initiatives. For example, the Singaporean government has embarked upon an information age vision and strategy to "develop Singapore into a vibrant and dynamic global Infocomm Capital with a thriving and prosperous infocomm-savvy e-Society" (Infocomm Development Authority of Singapore, 2000, p. 5). Following closely the development in Singapore, the Malaysian government has developed a comprehensive strategy to fundamentally transform Malaysia from primarily an agricultural economy now into a developed country by the year 2020 and one of the policy measures for achieving this vision is the Multimedia Super Corridor (MSC) initiative. These national initiatives in ASEAN, however, remain largely disconnected and piecemeal efforts at the national, rather than regional, level—there seems to be a lack of any regional coordination.

Together, Singapore and Malaysia are arguably the two most ICT-savvy member states in the ASEAN region. This is reflected in the fact that these two countries have already put in place well-developed information age policy and strategies as well as cyberlaws, ahead of the other ASEAN countries. Not surprisingly, both Singapore and Malaysia would like to become the ICT hub for the South East Asian region. In this respect, Singapore's Intelligent Island initiative and Malaysia's MSC initiative are in direct competition—they compete for attracting external attention and inward investment. It remains to be seen whether this kind of competitive scenario could be changed and turned into genuinely interconnected initiatives. If this happened, ASEAN countries' common endeavour, that is, the e-ASEAN initiative, would be of much more substance.

FUTURE TRENDS

Given the critical issues faced by e-ASEAN, the overall impact of the initiative is broadly viewed as a positive one. More specifically, this impact is manifested in two ways: internally the initiative works as a positive factor to the process of regional integration among ASEAN members and, externally, it serves as a new mode of governance of the digital revolution at levels beyond the nation state.

Firstly, under the auspices of e-ASEAN, the promotion of Internet usage by individuals, businesses, and government organisations throughout the region has already established an additional platform for cross-border (or borderless) communication and transactions. Although there is an intra-regional digital divide between the member states, the level of Internet access and usage is improving throughout ASEAN. It is not unreasonable to believe that the Internet, as a cost-effective way of social and business communication, will play an even bigger role in promoting regional integration - national borders are still there but cross-border communication and e-commerce is already a reality on the Internet.

Secondly, if the collective effort of ASEAN countries in promoting the harmonisation of national cyberlaws proves successful, it would serve as an interesting example for the governance of ICTs in general and the Internet in particular at a regional or transnational level. To be sure, the simple fact that cyberspace does not have due respect for national and geographical borders is a major challenge for not only ASEAN countries but also the rest of the world in terms of governance.

The growing consensus in the public debate over the need for working towards a transnational or regional level of ICT governance leads to an interesting dimension for future research. The ASEAN Secretariat highlighted two specific issues that governments in the region need to address in order to implement the e-ASEAN initiative:

jurisdiction and taxation (ASEAN Secretariat, 2001). Regarding jurisdiction, the harmonisation of cyberlaws through the e-ASEAN initiative cannot by-pass controversial questions such as, among others, which national law to be used in resolving transnational e-commerce disputes and whether court judgement reached in one country could be enforced in another. The issue of e-commerce taxation is equally challenging: whose taxation regime should be used and to which state should taxes be paid when an e-commerce transaction occurred in more than one country and conducted in an "e-space," where there are no clearly defined national borders?

Outside ASEAN, the only comparable model of ICT regulation at a regional level is provided by the European Union (EU), where a regulatory framework for electronic communications has been adopted by member states. It would be worthwhile to undertake further research to compare and contrast the eASEAN model of cyberlaw harmonisation with the European model of communications regulation. A comparative study of this kind could shed light on the issue of whether regional or transnational level governance for ICTs is a desirable and practical solution to the challenges posed by the information age to the nation state at the national level in terms of governance and regulation.

CONCLUSION

The launch of the e-ASEAN initiative represents one of the most significant attempts at the regional level by a group of nation states to collectively explore the potential benefits that the global communications revolution brings with it. The main objective of the e-ASEAN initiative is to promote regional economic development and regional cooperation by effectively fostering an "e-space" within the region.

While it is not inconceivable that new ICTs in general, and the Internet in particular, could help overcome many traditional barriers, such as national boundaries and geographical distance, that hinder transnational cooperation, the same technologies poses a number of challenges to ASEAN political leaders. Firstly, before the intra-regional digital divide is effectively closed, many individuals and some parts of the ASEAN region will remain excluded from the digital revolution. This begs the question of who and which countries are going to benefit most from the e-ASEAN initiative. Secondly, cyberlaw harmonisation, one of the stated missions of the e-ASEAN initiative, is faced with a reality in which not all member states have passed legislations regarding cyberspace and those states with cyberlaws in place have their distinctive national approaches. It will be a daunting task to achieve a consensus over the governance and regulation of cyberspace at the regional level in ASEAN. Finally, some member states in ASEAN are torn between pursuing their national ICT agenda and the common e-ASEAN agenda. The fact that both Singapore and Malaysia wish to become a regional ICT hub has added a competitive feature to the emerging "e-space" in ASEAN, which goes against the key word of the e-ASEAN Framework Agreement—'cooperation!'

REFERENCES

Association of South East Asian Nations (ASEAN). (2000). e-ASEAN Framework Agreement. The 4th ASEAN Informal Summit, November 22-25, Singapore.

Association of South East Asian Nations (ASEAN) Secretariat. (2000). ASEAN electronic commerce legislation comparison table. Retrieved February 22, 2005, from http://www.aseansec.org/cyber_matrix.pdf

Association of South East Asian Nations (ASEAN) Secretariat. (2001). e-ASEAN reference framework for electronic commerce legal infrastructure.

Retrieved February 26, 2005, from http://www.aseansec.org/EAWG_01.pdf

Association of South East Asian Nations (ASEAN) Secretariat. (2003). Towards an e-ASEAN. Retrieved February 20, 2005, from http://www.aseansec.org/6268.htm

Association of South East Asian Nations (ASEAN) Secretary-General. (2000). Challenges and opportunities in information and communications technologies. Report (excerpts) to the 33rd ASEAN Ministerial Meeting, July. Retrieved February 24, 2005, from http://www.aseansec.org/6264.htm

Bangemann, M. (1994, May 26). Europe and the global information society: recommendations to the European council. Brussels: European Commission.

Castells, M. (1996). The rise of the network society. Oxford: Blackwell.

Central Intelligence Agency (CIA). (2005a). The world factbook. Retrieved February 28, 2005, from http://www.cia.gov/cia/publications/factbook/geos/bm.html

Central Intelligence Agency (CIA). (2005b). The world factbook. Retrieved February 28, 2005, from http://www.cia.gov/cia/publications/factbook/fields/2004.html

Dai, X. (2000). The digital revolution and governance. Aldershot: Ashgate.

Dai, X. (2003). Regionalism online: A case study of e-ASEAN. In C. Dent (Ed.), Asia-Pacific economic and security co-operation: New regional agendas (pp. 220-238). Basingstoke: Palgrave.

Federal Trust. (1995). Network Europe and the information society. London: The Federal Trust.

European Commission. (2000, December 12). Proposal for a regulation of the European parliament and the council on the implementation of the Internet top level domain "EU," COM (2000) 827 final, Brussels: European Commission.

Hachigian, N. (2002). The Internet and power in one-party East Asian states. The Washington Quarterly, 25(3), 41-58.

Infocomm Development Authority of Singapore. (2000). Infocomm 21: Singapore where the digital future is. December, Singapore, Retrieved August 28, 2002, from http://www.ida.gov.sg

Ng, E., & Nurbanum, M. (2002, September 38-44). E-enabling the ASEAN nations: Malaysia. Asia Pacific Information & Communication Technology.

World Bank. (2002). Data and statistics: ICT at a glance tables. Retrieved August 28, 2002, from http://www.worldbank.org/data/countrydata/ict-glance.htm

KEY TERMS

ASEAN: The Association of Southeast Asian Nations (ASEAN), representing a key regional trading block in the world, was established following the signing of the ASEAN Declaration on August 8, 1967 in Bangkok with five founding member states, namely, Indonesia, Malaysia, Philippines, Singapore, and Thailand. Brunei became the sixth member in January 1984. This was followed by the CLMV (Cambodia, Laos, Myanmar, and Vietnam) to join ASEAN in the 1990s. The main objectives of ASEAN include: (i) accelerating regional economic growth, social progress, and cultural development and (ii) promoting regional peace and stability. The 10 member states have a total population of about 500 million, covering a total area of 4.5 million square kilometres.

Cyberspace: A virtual or notional environment of electronic communications. The online environment facilitated by the Internet is the most popular type of cyberspace.

Digital Divide: Digital divide refers to the disparity in opportunities and abilities for making use of information and communications technologies that exists between different social groups and between different countries in the digital age.

e-ASEAN: Originally initiated by the ASEAN economic ministers in September 1999 and endorsed by ASEAN leaders at their summit in Manila in November the same year, e-ASEAN aims to develop an ASEAN "e-space." The e-ASEAN Framework Agreement, signed by the ASEAN member states at the Fourth ASEAN Informal Summit in November 2000 in Singapore, serves as the legal foundation for the e-ASEAN initiative.

E-Commerce: E-commerce refers to online electronic transactions involving the sale and purchase of physical goods or digital goods (e.g., software, digital films, and music, value added information in electronic format).

Information and Communications Technology (ICT): Information and Communications Technology (ICT), as defined in the e-ASEAN Framework Agreement, refers to "infrastructure, hardware, and software systems, needed to capture, process, and disseminate information to generate information-based products and services" (ASEAN, 2000, Article 1a).

Multimedia Super Corridor (MSC): Launched by the former Prime Minister Dr Mahatir in 1997 and remained as his pet project until his retirement, the Multimedia Super Corridor initiative (MSC) includes the creation of an ICT business and technology centre (Cyberjaya) to attract foreign direct investment (FDI); an "intelligent city" as the new federal government administrative centre (Putrajaya); a new international airport (i.e., the Kuala Lumpur International Airport (KLIA) and the Kuala Lumpur City Centre (KLCC)). The four "hot spots" are digitally linked through a fiber optic cable infrastructure offering high speed communications and a new motor way network. The MSC stretches over a designated development area of 50 kilometers long and 15 kilometers wide.

This work was previously published in Encyclopedia of Digital Government, edited by A. Anttiroiko and M. Malkia, pp. 416-421, copyright 2007 by Information Science Reference, formerly known as Idea Group Reference (an imprint of IGI Global).

Chapter 4.29
Effectiveness of E-Government Online Services in Australia

Xuetao Guo
University of Technology Sydney, Australia

Jie Lu
University of Technology Sydney, Australia

ABSTRACT

Electronic government (e-government) breaks down the barrier of distance and time, and offers the potential for government to better deliver its contents and services, and interact with citizens and businesses. Australia has been recognized as one of e-government leaders internationally. All the three levels (federal, state and local) of Australian government organizations have increasingly embraced e-government. With few years of e-government practices in Australia, it is critical to evaluate the current applications and explore more effective strategies for the next phase of e-government. This study aims to identify what factors affect the effectiveness of Australian e-government online services. In the study, a research model is proposed and data collections are completed based on two questionnaire-based surveys from internal and external users of Australian e-government Web sites respectively. Furthermore, data analyses are conducted to test proposed hypotheses. The findings show that Web presence quality and information quality influence effectiveness of e-government online services more than system quality from user perspectives. Several recommendations and future trends are also presented in the chapter.

INTRODUCTION

The Internet offers a tremendous opportunity for government to better deliver its contents and services and interact with citizens, businesses, and other government partners (Chen, 2002). Electronic government (e-government) breaks down the barrier of distance and time, and therefore offers the potential to enhance government service quality. E-government online services may not only provide benefits to citizens and businesses, but also offer the potential to reshape the public sector and remake the relationships between the citizens, businesses, and government (West, 2000).

A number of definitions of e-government have been offered in the existing literature (Devadoss, Pan & Huang, 2003); however, no single definition has been widely accepted (Scholl, 2003). The applications of information technology to government services are commonly referred to as e-government (Gordon, 2002; Holmes, 2001; Marchionini, Samet & Brandt, 2003; Scholl, 2003). Tapscott (1996) defined e-government as an Internet worked government, while Sprecher (2000) considered e-government as any way technology is used to help simplify and automate transactions between governments and constituents, businesses, or other governments. Wimmer and Traunmuller (2000) considered e-government as a guiding vision towards modern administration and democracy. According to them, e-government is concerned with the transformation that government and public administration have to undergo in the next decades. World Bank Group (worldBank, 2002) defined e-government as the use by government agencies of information technology (such as wide area networks, the Internet, and mobile computing) that have the ability to transform relations with citizens, businesses, and other arms of government, while New Zealand government (Anonymous, 2002) defined e-government as government agencies working together to use technology so that they can better provide individuals and businesses with government services and information. Taking a more comprehensive view, Aicholzer and Schmutzer (2000) saw e-government covering changes of governance in a twofold manner: (1) transformation of the business of governance, that is, improving service quality delivery, reducing costs and renewing administrative processes; (2) transformation of governance itself, that is, re-examining the functioning of democratic practices and processes. These definitions may be slightly different for each organization based on the community's values, goals and culture. However, a complete definition of e-government has to identify with consideration of all its users. In this study, we consider e-government users in two categories, internal and external users. The external users are citizen and business, while the internal users mainly imply the administration staff of a government agency or other government agencies.

E-government is much more than getting information and services online. It is transforming government administration, information provision and service delivery by the application of new technologies. It is delivering government services in ways that are most convenient to the client and citizen, while at the same time realizing efficiency gains, and streamlining government processes (Rimmer, 2002). E-government applications are very comprehensive. The challenges to e-government are not only technological but also economic, legislative and political; for example, electronic business, electronic management, electronic democracy and electronic politics (Pilipovic et al., 2002). Based on the involved parties, the most important classes of e-government applications are: government- to-citizen (G2C), citizen-to-government (C2G), government-to-business (G2B), business-to-government (B2G) and government-to-government (G2G). G2C applications focus on online services where government is working for citizens. G2B applications refer to supplying, information gathering and services for business. C2G and B2G applications are meant by communication between citizens, business and government agencies. And G2G concerns with communication amongst e-government users. Three components are required to support the e-government operational models that deliver a government-wide response. The three components are effective governance, business system, and physical infrastructure, which are explained below. Effective governance - the mandate or authority to act in a given situation, a framework for reporting and accountability, a recognised budget process and reward system. Business system - the operating business and decision-making processes that support cross-government activities. These include models for how response teams operate internally and processes to secure cooperation from different areas of government. Physical infrastructure – the information communication technology (ICT) and other systems needed to combine agency services for presentation to the community in an integrated way (Victoria, 2002).

So much of technology and information policy debate and discussion fall broadly under the header of e-government (Aldrich, Bertot & McClure, 2002). With the nearly all-inclusive domain of e-government, it is hard to conduct evaluation of e-government success. Thus, our study addresses online services delivery of e-government, which is termed as e-government online services. The concept of e-government online service implies those not-for-profit services delivered in the Internet environment by government agencies. Not-for-profit services address how to attract and keep customers returning, and to improve the service quality. The main contents of e-government online services are the delivery of all appropriate government services electronically, including complement (not replacement) of exiting written, telephone, fax and counter services; government information accessing; electronic payment and government-wide intranet for secure online communication (OGO, 2001).

Australia is a pioneer in the practices of e-government. Since the early 1990s Australia already had a clear e-government vision and began to develop its own e-government strategies. In February 2002, the Prime Minister announced that the 1997 commitment for all appropriate Commonwealth Government services to be online by 2001 had been achieved (NOIE, 2002b). Recently, Rimmer (2002), CEO of National Office for the Information Economy (NOIE) Australia, announced that the phase of government information and service online has been successfully completed, with over 1,600 Commonwealth government services online.

Internationally, Australia has been recognized as one of leaders in e-government. In 2001, on the basis of the assessment criteria developed by World Markets Research Centre (http://www.wmrc.com) to evaluate the "functionality" of national government Web sites around the world, Australia was ranked 3rd with 50.7% of federal government Web sites assessed conforming to all the assessment criteria. The US was ranked 1st with 57.2% of federal government Web sites conforming to all criteria (NOIE, 2002a). Australia was ranked second only to the United States according to a report from the United Nations released in June 2002, which had several key criteria such as sophistication of online services, Internet penetration rates, and Web presence of government (NOIE, 2002b). The Australian government has an important leadership role in enhancing the extent to which businesses and the community takes full advantage of the opportunities provided by the new technologies.

With few years of practices on e-government, it is clear that evaluating the current applications and exploring more effective ways for the next phase of e-government are critical. However, what factors influence the effectiveness of e-government online services? This study aims to identify and empirically establish the dimensions that underlie e-government online service effectiveness. We believe that our outcome will contribute to management scholars' and practitioners' understanding and developing efforts of effective e-government with accomplishment of the following tasks:

- identifying the development model and current practices of Australian e-government online services;
- identifying the underlying dimensions of the construct;
- developing a measure to evaluate user satisfaction from both internal and external user perspectives;

- empirically validating the construct; and
- exploring the theoretical and managerial implications of the findings.

The remainder of this chapter is structured as follows. Following a development model of Australian e-government online services and literature review in background section, the main thrust of the chapter is described, including a proposed research model, research methodology, data analyses and results, summary of findings, and several recommendations. Next, future trends in the area are presented. Finally, the conclusions are drawn.

BACKGROUND

Development Model of Australian E-Government Online Services

The government is committed to maximize the opportunities provided by the Internet. The potential for government using Internet to enhance services are now more evident than ever before. The challenge for government is to continually embrace the opportunities that the Internet provides and ensure that citizens, business and community needs and expectations are met. In addition to providing information, communication and transformation services, exciting and innovative transformation could occur with the new technologies and practices (Chen, 2002). E-government is an evolutionary phenomenon (Layne & Lee, 2001). The use of new technology and the demand of new service features will be required for the transformation of e-government. Therefore, we believe that the development model of e-government initiatives should be accordingly derived and implemented. Based on the observation on Australian e-government applications and our previous research (Guo & Lu, 2003), a development model of Australian e-government online services (shown in Figure 1) is proposed on the basis of Layne and Lee's (Layne & Lee, 2001) fourth-stage growth model of e-government. Our model is developed according to different levels of interaction ordered by complexity (Chen, 2002; Elmagarmid & McIver Jr., 2001; Gordon, 2002) and it is in four phases: phase 1 - information and service online; phase 2 – transaction-based online services; phase 3 – integrated online services; and phase 4 – intelligent online services. The detailed explanations of each phase are presented next. It

Figure 1. Development model of e-government online services

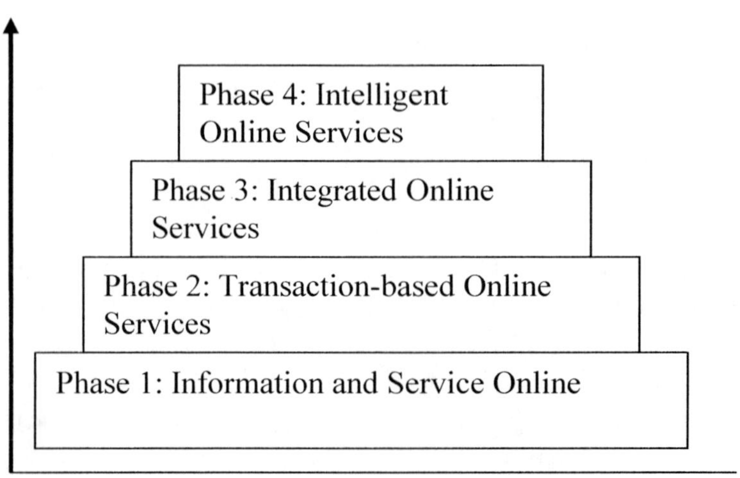

is expected that this model reflects the growth phases of Australian e-government online services and offers a strategic direction from technological perspective.

•Phase 1 - information and service online. One of the most common e-government applications is providing citizens with access to information and services. Governments produce vast volumes of information and an increasing amount of it is now available through the Internet and other electronic venues (Marchionini, Samet & Brandt, 2003). At this level, government information and services are delivered to its citizens and business through the Internet. Furthermore, by adding simple groupware functionalities such as Web forms, e-mail, bulletin and chat room, two-way communication is supported. Most early G2C and G2B services fall into this category (Chen, 2002). Most Australian governments' efforts on Web development belong to the first phase. Examples of functionalities at this phase are mostly limited to online presentations of government information. Our previous study (Guo, Lu & Raban, 2002) showed that the e-government Web sites deliver the static information in this phase. The Web site on this level provides catalogues of information, e-mail inquires and downloadable forms. "Provision of policy or service information (of 96.7% agencies offer the function)," "publication of organization information (of 90% agencies offer the function)," and "e-mail inquires (of 90% agencies offer the function)" are the three main functions that the majority of sample agencies provide on their Web sites.

•Phase 2 - Transaction-based online services. People also use government Web sites to complete transactions. Linked to direct deposit and other commercial transaction systems, increasing numbers of citizens are avoiding long lines, complicated phone menu systems, and postal delays by using government transaction processing systems. Around one quarter of Australian commonwealth e-government online services are in the second phase (Rimmer, 2002). The second phase of e-government focuses on service-oriented e-government activities, including linking database to online interfaces and paying bills online. For instance, citizens in New South Wales may renew their licenses via the Roads and Traffic Authority Web site (http://www.rta.nsw.gov.au/) with online payment. In Australian e-government context, many e-government applications fall into this phase. According to our previous research (Guo, Lu & Raban, 2002), the three functions fall into this level with reasonable complexity of functions, which are "site search engine," "directory" and "access to database," with percentage of 60%, 53.3% and 46.7% respectively. Four functions can provide two-way data interchange between clients and an agency, which are "online payment/online transaction (26.7%)," "registration (16.7%)," "sale of information, service or products (13.3%)," and "lodgement of return (6.7%)". In addition, in this phase agencies also move towards electronic procurement, by putting requests for proposal and bidding regulations online.

•Phase 3 - Integrated online services. Increasingly there are some whole-of-government requirements that cut across all agencies, some that bind a number of agencies together, and some that agencies can decide on an individual basis. The integrated online service delivery channels will be needed and it will link with existing delivery channels such as shop fronts and call centres. This phase would be able to provide clients with "one-stop shop," and make it unnecessary for clients to know the structure of government (Rimmer, 2002). This integration may happen in two ways: vertical and horizontal. Vertical integration refers to the different levels (local, state and federal) of government connected for different functions or services. Some Australian agencies' e-government activities are currently in this phase. As an example of vertical integration, a Tax File Number (TFN) registration system (http://www.

ato.gov.au) at a state might be linked to a national database for cross checking. Another example is Australian Business Number (ABN). ABN was introduced through A New Tax System (Australian Business Number) Act 1999, which also called for a system to share ABN information with all levels of government via the Australian Business Register (ABR). ABR allows clients to access or change their own details on the register. It allows businesses and their endorsed representatives to access and maintain their business information online. In contrast, horizontal integration deals with different functions and services in the same level of government. Customers are getting better services that are streamlined and integrated with other services offered by other governments or the private sector, and that make it easier to use the services and transact with government. Centrelink's Overseas Direct Deposit and the Department of Immigration, Multicultural and Indigenous Affairs' Citizenship e-lodgement services are prime examples of these services. With system integration of Australian Taxation Office, Medicare offices and Centrelink, Australian Family Assistance Office (http://www.familyassist.gov.au/) can process the claim of family assistance payments.

•Phase 4 - Intelligent online services. Providing high quality information and integrated communication services are no less challenging and may evolve into knowledge management services and become adaptive, personalized, proactive and accessible from a broader variety of devices (Gordon, 2002). In the previous three phases of E-government, although there have been a huge number of emails sent to government officials and agencies each year, there is not evidence to show their impact on government decision-making. This phase emphasizes on intelligent presentation of Web content, intelligent decision support, and direct citizen participation in government decision-making. In this phase, governments use information technology to provide more effective access to appropriate services by making more pathways available so that there is "no wrong door" to services. Governments can anticipate which service or information a citizen or business is likely to want in a given set of circumstances and then use information technology to fast track client access to these services or information. By using information technology in these ways governments have the opportunity to streamline business processes so that services are structured around clients rather than around government service providers.

Literature

Briggs et al. (2003) pointed out that the Internet is perhaps the most successful information system. As information systems ushered in flatter organizational structures, so the Internet ushers in globally distributed organizations and electronic commerce (e-commerce). Based on Briggs et al.'s (2003) point of view, e-government may be a new paradigm of information systems. In this study, like many research efforts (Gordon, 2002; Holmes, 2001; Marchionini, Samet & Brandt, 2003), e-government is considered as an application type of information technology, especially Internet. Although e-government can be seen as a sub-area of information systems, the evaluation of e-government can simply not adopt the measures of information system success. It should draw lessons from the measures of e-commerce success as well. Thus, literature from both areas may be appropriate for the research context.

Information System Success

There are many different definitions of information system success in the existing literature. Briggs et al. (2003) summarized them according to four perspectives. (1) From the end user's perspective, successful systems may be those that improve the user's job performance without inflicting undue annoyance. (2) From a management's

Figure 1. DeLone and McLean's (1992) model of information system success

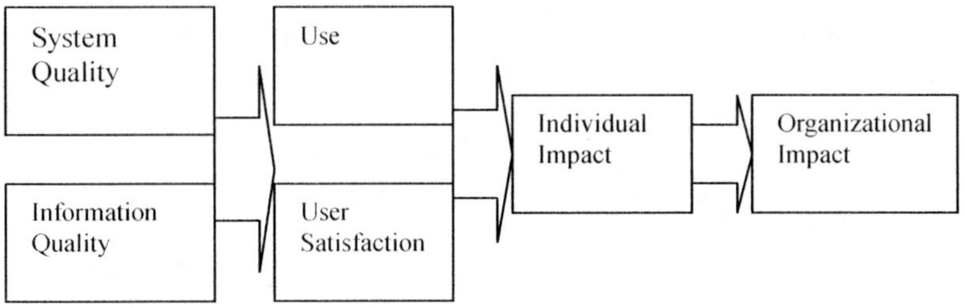

perspective, successful systems are those that reduce uncertainty of outcomes and have lower risks, and leverage scarce resources. (3) From a developer's perspective, successful information systems are those that are completed on time and under budget, with a completed set of features that are consistent with specifications and that function correctly. (4) From an innovator's perspective, successful information systems may be those that attract a large, loyal, and growing community of users.

A large number of research efforts on information system success evaluation can be found in the literature. Broadly, Garrity and Sanders (1998) viewed information system from two perspectives, an organizational viewpoint and a socio-technical viewpoint. The organizational perspective focuses on the quality of the interface and the information provided by an information system. The socio-technical viewpoint focuses on individual needs. According to Kim (1989), the surrogates developed for measuring information system success fall into three categories: user satisfaction (US) (Bailey & Pearson, 1983), level of system usage (Srinivasan, 1985), and information value regarding user decision performance (Gallagher, 1974). Seddon et al. (1999) reviewed 186 empirical papers in three major information system journals and proposed a two-dimensional matrix for classifying information system success measures. One dimension is the type of system studied, and another one is the stakeholder in whose interests the system is being evaluated. Communication theory is also used to understand the impact of information system at the individual level. For instance, Mason (1978) used the model of Shannon and Weaver (1949) to conduct a model. The basic elements of the Mason (Mason, 1978) model are receipt of the information, the evaluation of the information, and the application of the information leading to a change in recipient behavior and a change in the system performance.

More importantly, building on the work of Mason (1978) and comprehensive review of different information system success measures, DeLone and McLean (1992) proposed a model of information system success (shown in Figure 1) which depicted information system success measures in terms of six dimensions – system quality, information quality, use, US, individual impact and organization impact. The six interdependent and interrelated categories or components form DeLone and McLean (1992)'s information system success model. DeLone and McLean (1992) suggested that the effects of user participation on the subsequent success of different information systems may use satisfaction as their primary measure. System quality and information quality singularly and jointly affect both use and US. Use and user satisfaction are direct antecedents of individual impact. Additionally, the amount of use can affect the degree of US. The impact on individual performance should eventually have some organizational impact.

Since DeLone and McLean's (1992) model was proposed, a number of studies have undertaken empirical investigation of the multidimensional relationships amongst the measures of information system success (Rai, Lang & Welker, 2002; Seddon, 1997; Seddon & Kiew, 1996; Seddon et al., 1999; Wilkin & Castleman, 2003). However, it is difficult to measure information system success, because the general aim of information system development is to contribute to organizational effectiveness, to lead to higher productivity, better customer service, and better quality of working life. This has led to various measures of information systems to serve as surrogate for information system success (Iivari & Ervasi, 1994). US probably has been the most studied construct in information system research (Woodroof & Burg, 2003). Many researchers have investigated various dimensions of US (Bailey & Pearson, 1983; Davis, Bagozzi & Warshaw, 1989; Igbaria & Nachman, 1990), such as system accuracy, system timeliness, usefulness, ease-of-use, task importance, and quality of output. Other ways include content (such as accuracy and relevance), presentation (such as format and mode), and service quality (Woodroof & Burg, 2003). Much literature indicates that DeLone and McLean's (1992) model has been used as a basis of information system success measurement.

E-commerce Success

The quality of e-commerce Web sites may vary from high quality sites developed by professionals, to low quality sites constructed by inexperienced site developers. Many problems can arise when using Web sites, including page loading time which is often lengthy, out-of-date site content, privacy concerns, access to site contents, and lack of acceptance (Gehrke & Turban, 1999). Therefore, evaluation of e-commerce applications has been studied in many aspects and by different approaches, such as factors affecting customer relationship, consumer requirements, customer support, customer satisfaction, cost/benefits, and operational-qualitative and strategic-qualitative approaches. Based on the success stories from companies, Seybold (1998) provided eight success factors for e-commerce: targeting the right customers; owning the customer's total experience; providing a 360 view of the customer relationship; letting customers help themselves; helping customers do own jobs; delivering personalized service; and fostering community. Farquhar, Langmann and Balfour (1998) identified some generic consumer requirements, including ease of use, consistency in user interface, privacy, security, cost transparency, reliability, error tolerance, design for different type customers, order confirmation and system status information. Turban et al. (2002) proposed some Web-related metrics that a company can use to determine the appropriate level of customer support: response time; site availability; download time; up-to-date; security and privacy; fulfilment; return policy; and navigability.

Liu and Arnett (2000) identified four factors that were critical to e-commerce Web site success, including information and service quality, system use, playfulness, and system design quality. Elliot, Morup-peterson and Bjorn-andersen (2000) proposed a framework for evaluation of commercial Web sites to identify the key features and facilities of business-to-customer Web sites. The framework consists of six categories: company information and function; product/service information and promotion; transaction processing; customer services; ease of use; and innovation in services and technology. More research efforts can be found in the existing literature for e-commerce success measures (D'Ambra & Rice, 2001; Molla & Licker, 2001; Palmer, 2002; Teo & Choo, 2001).

E-Government Success

Some research efforts pay attention to the design of e-government. Heeks (2001) developed an IT-POSMO model and discussed the gap between current realities and design conceptions of e-government projects. ITPOSMO means Information, Technology, Processes, Objectives and values, Staffing and skills, Management systems and structures, and other resources (time and money). The research also suggested that mismatch of e-government initiatives can be assessed along those seven dimensions, and concluded that success or failure of an e-government initiative depends on the degree of mismatch between the design of that initiative and the realities.

Others focus on the measurement of e-government success. From a user's perspective, Lisle-Williams (2002) defined the successful e-government in three criteria: service quality, choice, and user experience. Service quality focuses on objective measures. Choice addresses not only personalization, but also privacy and anonymity. User experience refers to subjective and often influenced by small factors. Steyaert (in press) adopted e-commerce performance indicators – consumer awareness, popularity, contact efficiency, conversion, and retention, proposed by Watson et al. (2000) to analyze federal and state e-government service cases in USA. Consumer awareness deals with the number of visitors to a site. Popularity refers to the rank of the site. Contact efficiency indicates site usability and content. Conversion refers to customer satisfaction, transactions and time on the site. Retention deals with customer loyalty.

Two main categories of research results are government Web site evaluation and e-government success or failure criteria. Concerning the government Web site evaluation, DeConti (1998) proposed a methodology to evaluate and analyse the government Web sites in six areas: audience; purpose statement; objectives; Web specification; domain information; and Web presentation. Smith (2001) applied the evaluation criteria of Eschenfelder et al. (1997) to a sample of five Web sites of New Zealand government. The Eschenfelder et al. (1997) evaluation criteria are divided into two groups, information content criteria and ease-of-use criteria. Information content criteria are used to evaluate the nature of the information and services provided by the Web site, including orientation to the Web site, the content of site, currency, metadata, availability of services, accuracy and privacy. Ease-of-use criteria are used to evaluate the ease of use of the Web site, which includes links, feedback, accessibility, design and navigability. Huang, D'Ambra and Bhalla (2002) examined the adoption of e-government in Australian public citizens based on the technology acceptance model (TAM) (Davis, 1989). Huang, D'Ambra and Bhalla (2002)'s research effort focused on an actual system usage with two constructs, perceived usefulness and perceived ease of use. Their research indicated that the prediction of TAM theory was not supported by the findings. In addition, Burgess and Cooper (1999) proposed a Web site evaluation model called Model of Internet Commerce Adoption (MICA). The MICA model classified Web sites into three stages: inception, consideration and maturity. Sites in the inception stage provide basic information or have a basic Web presence. Sites classified in the consideration stage demonstrate an extension of basic information including e-mail, online inquiry and contact, information on extended services and general value-added information. Maturity stage sites include high-level value-added services, such as secure online transaction processing. Boon, Hewett and Parker (2000) tested the MICA model in the context of Australian local government Web sites and modified the model to make a clear distinction between the more progressive, sophisticated sites and those relatively simplistic sites.

MAIN THRUST OF THE CHAPTER

Research Model

This study focuses on the issue: what factors affect the effectiveness of e-government online services in Australia? DeLone and McLean's

Figure 2. Research model in this study

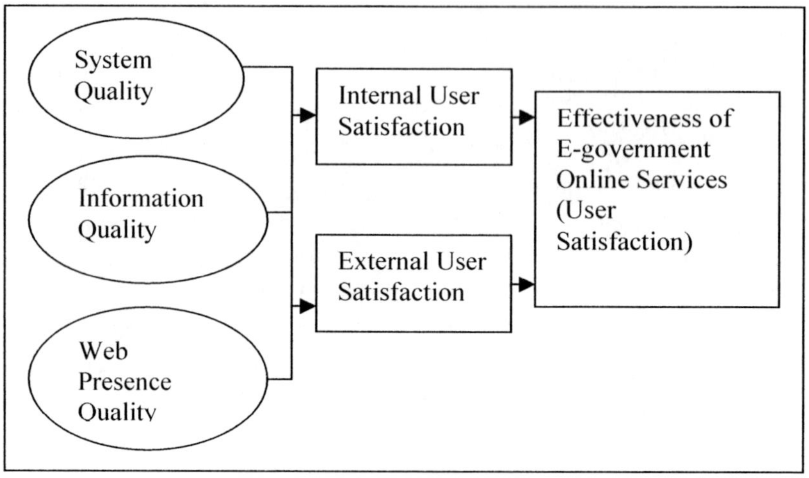

(1992) model explains the impact of information system at the individual and organizational level. A number of prior studies have used the DeLone and McLean (1992) model as basis of information system success (Rai, Lang & Welker, 2002; Seddon, 1997; Seddon & Kiew, 1996; Seddon et al., 1999; Wilkin & Castleman, 2003). In this study, our research model (shown in Figure 2) is partly adopted and extended from the DeLone and McLean (1992) model. Furthermore, another new construct, namely Web presence quality, is added to the DeLone and McLean (1992) model. We believe that Web presence quality is crucial in the online environment. The research model conceptualized information system success as effectiveness of e-government online services, which is measured by US. The research model shown in Figure 2 focuses on the investigation of the first two phases related to the development model of e-government online services (see Figure 1). This model presents the impact of three independent constructs (system quality, information quality and Web presence quality) on the dependent construct US, including both internal US and external US. The external US focuses on the public users, while the internal US emphasizes the inter-organizational users.

The effectiveness of e-government online services deals with both measures of information system success and that of e-commerce success. In the information systems arena, a search involved information system success measures and US. In the e-commerce arena, commercial Web site success measures were investigated. The measures in the research model are mostly derived from the measurement of information system success and e-commerce success. The relevant literature indicates that these measures are important for the three constructs, system quality, information quality and Web presence quality. However, there are no criteria to justify the weights of each measure (Liu & Arnett, 2000). Thus, the average scores of the variable, adopted in the prior study (Liu & Arnett, 2000), are used as a criterion for selection of the measures in this study.

User Satisfaction

Since the success of information systems is difficult to measure directly, many researches have turned to indirect measures such as US (Iivari & Ervasi, 1994). Cyert and March (1963) proposed the concept of US as a surrogate of information system success. Since then, many prior research

Table 1. List of constructs, measures and labels

Construct	Measure	Label
System Quality (SQ)	Accessibility	V1
	Feedback speed	V2
	Security	V3
Information Quality (IQ)	Information currency	V4
	Functionality	V5
	Content importance	V6
Web Presence Quality (WPQ)	User-friendly	V7
	Display format	V8
	Navigation efficiency	V9
User Satisfaction (US)	Internal user satisfaction	Internal US
	External user satisfaction	External US

efforts employed US to measure information success. US has been considered one of the most important determinants (Downing, 1999) and the most widely used measure of information system success (DeLone & McLean, 1992).

Moreover, in this study, US has been employed as a surrogate measure for e-government effectiveness. It is supposed that US can be affected by the three independent instructs - system quality, information quality and Web presence quality. Each independent construct includes a few measures. The constructs and the corresponding measures and labels are shown in Table 1.

System Quality

System quality refers to the technical details of the information system interface (DeLone & McLean, 1992). Many different measures of system quality have been adopted in the previous literatures, such as accuracy (Hamilton & Chervany, 1981), convenience of access, and reliability (Bailey & Pearson, 1983), rapid access, security, quick error recovery, precise operation and computation (Bhimani, 1996), and responsiveness and follow-up services.

In this study, the following three measures are adopted for system quality construct: accessibility, feedback speed, and security. In the Web-based e-government context, accessibility refers to access convenience of the system. Customers should be able to reach the company Web site at any time. This means that downtime should be as close to zero as possible. Feedback speed refers to availability and speed of responsiveness and contact management. Security concerns reliability of information systems. Security of online transaction is necessary to transmit financial information over the Web, because of increasing involvement of online transaction in e-government services.

Better system quality has been expected to lead in better effectiveness of e-government online services. Therefore, the following hypothesis is caused.

H1: system quality is positively associated with effectiveness of e-government online services.

Three measures, V1, V2 and V3, affect system quality. Therefore, this leads to sub-hypotheses H_{1-1}, H_{1-2}, H_{1-3}.

H_{1-1}: accessibility (V1) is importantly associated with system quality.

H_{1-2}: feedback speed (V2) is importantly associated with system quality.

H_{1-3}: security (V3) is importantly associated with system quality.

Information Quality

Information quality concerns the characteristics of information (DeLone & McLean, 1992). Many different information characteristics have been used as the measures of information quality, such as currency (Bailey & Pearson, 1983), accuracy, timeline, completeness, relevance (Ahituv, 1980; Bailey & Pearson, 1983), flexible and customized information presentation, service comparability, and service differentiation (Baty & Lee, 1995).

Based on the previous information quality construct, information quality is viewed as having three aspects, information currency, functionality, and content importance in this study. Information currency - it is relevant to timeline of information. Functionality – it concerns with website functions and information completeness to meet user needs. Content importance - this refers to relevance, completeness, and accuracy of information.

It is expected that increases of information quality will lead to the increase of effectiveness of e-government online services. This causes hypothesis 2.

H2: information quality is positively associated with effectiveness of e-government online services.

We have proposed that three measures, V4, V5 and V6, affect information quality. Thus, the following three sub-hypotheses are resulted in.

H_{2-1}: information currency (V4) is importantly associated with information quality.

H_{2-2}: functionality (V5) is importantly associated with information quality.

H_{2-3}: content importance (V6) is importantly associated with information quality.

Web Presence Quality

Web presence quality refers to the quality of e-government Web sites. There are a considerable number and variety of factors associated with Web site quality: for instance, high quality, text, graphics, image and animation (Ho & Wu, 1999), consistency in user interface, design for different customers, system status information (Farquhar, Langmann & Balfour, 1998), well defined hyperlink, help function, ease to use (Hamilton & Chervany, 1981), information availability and friendliness (Wan, 2000), present style, format and processing efficiency (Swanson, 1986). In this study, three measures are employed for Web presence quality, which are user-friendly, display format, and navigation efficiency. User-friendly concerns the availability of attracting users. Display format refers to presentation style of Web sites. Navigability efficiency means that a Web site must be easy to navigate in order to please customers.

In e-government online services, a Web site acts as an interface interacting with users. Thus, it is hypothesized that better Web presence quality will positively influence the effectiveness of e-government online services. This leads to hypothesis 3.

H3: Web presence quality is positively associated with effectiveness of e-government online services.

It is assumed that the measures V7, V8 and V9 affect Web presence quality. Therefore, the following three sub-hypotheses are led to.

H_{3-1}: user-friendly (V7) is importantly associated with Web presence quality.

H_{3-2}: format (V8) is importantly associated with Web presence quality.

H_{3-3}: navigation (V9) is importantly associated with Web presence quality.

Research Methodology

Sampling Method

In this study, non-probability sampling method (Dickman, 1998) was used to select sample Web sites from the federal or state entry point and their links. Non-probability sampling is usually based on someone's expertise about the population and can be used successfully even though the sample validity is unable to measure (Dickman, 1998). The samples were selected from those Web sites which the public can frequently use to find relevant information or do online transaction, other than those Web sites which offer only organizational information.

Questionnaire Design

Based on the Likert (1982) scale technique, a satisfaction score can range between one and five, where one represents the highest satisfaction and five is the highest dissatisfaction. For example, score 1 - extremely satisfied, score 2 - satisfied, score 3 - adequate, score 4 - dissatisfied, and score 5 - extremely dissatisfied. Our questionnaire was based on the four questions shown in Table 2. The content of each construct has been explained in Table 1. Target audiences need to highlight one number of the five scores. V1 – V3 are related to Question1, V4 – V6 refer to Question 2, V7 – V9 concern with Question 3, and "user satisfaction" offers the responses for Question 4.

Data Collection from Internal Users

In the study, the internal users imply the related government agency's staffs and they are familiar with the government online service activities. An e-mail-based survey was employed for data collection. The survey was operated through measures based on the previous literatures. Three pilot studies were conducted from selected agencies. Based on the responses from them, the format and readability of survey questions were modi-

Table 2. Questions in the questionnaire form of this study

Q.1. How do you assess the satisfaction of the following factors in system quality?	
V1: Accessibility	1 2 3 4 5
V2: Feedback speed	1 2 3 4 5
V3: Security	1 2 3 4 5
Q.2. How do you assess the satisfaction of the following factors in information quality?	
V4: Information currency	1 2 3 4 5
V5: Functionality	1 2 3 4 5
V6: Content importance	1 2 3 4 5
Q.3. How do you assess the satisfaction of the following factors in web presence quality?	
V7: User-friendly	1 2 3 4 5
V8: Display format	1 2 3 4 5
V9: Navigation efficiency	1 2 3 4 5
Q.4. Based on all the variables (V1 – V9), how do you assess the satisfaction of this E-government website?	
User satisfaction	1 2 3 4 5

fied. To test the organization level satisfaction, an Australian-wide government Web site search was completed to select the relevant government agencies. A hundred government agencies were selected from the Australian government entry point http://www.australia.gov.au and its links. Because some of these Web sites indicate to share one port with others and a few delivery failures occurred, only 80 valid questionnaires were sent out successfully. The data collection was undertaken during May and June 2002. In total 30 valid responses were received and a 37.5% response rate was obtained. Among the responses, it indicated that five (17%) were obtained from federal government, 19 (63%) were from state government, and six (20%) were received from local government. In addition, according to Dickman (1998), a small sample is one of less than 25 observations, while a sample of 25 or more will be deemed as large. The sample size is sufficiently large for valid data analysis.

Data Collection from External Users

The external users are those customers who regularly use the e-government Web sites. To test the external user satisfaction, eight questionnaires were e-mailed to research students and academic staff in Faculty of Information Technology at University of Technology Sydney, who were our colleagues and we were sure that they were regular users of e-government Web sites. Also it was assumed the participants should have certain knowledge of Web site design. Although the amount of questionnaires was not very large, the targeted audiences were, to a certain degree, experts on Web site design and Web site quality, so that more useful response than random audiences had been achieved. These expert audiences were required to visit all the 30 assigned Web sites and complete the survey questions. Six responses were received and a 75% valid response rate was obtained, which was considered a very high response rate.

Data Analysis and Results

Comparison of Internal and External User Satisfaction

The investigation results of US are shown in Table 3. From an internal user's viewpoint, the statistical data show that about 1/3 of agencies classify their feelings about the government Web sites as "satisfied," including 26.7% "satisfied" (ranking in 2) and 6.7% "extremely satisfied" (ranking in 4). Forty percent of agencies feel their site is "adequate" (ranking in 1). However, there are 23.3% that appeared "dissatisfied" (ranking in 3) and 3.3% "extremely dissatisfied" (ranking in 5). From an external user viewpoint, half of users consider their feeling about the government

Table 3: Comparison of internal and external user satisfaction (US)

Scale of US	Internal US			External US		
	No	*%*	*Ranking*	*No*	*%*	*Ranking*
1 - extremely satisfied	2	6.7	4	10	5.6	4
2 - satisfied	8	26.7	2	91	50.5	1
3 - adequate	12	40	1	63	35	2
4 - dissatisfied	7	23.3	3	14	7.8	3
5 - extremely dissatisfied	1	3.3	5	2	1.1	5
Total	30	100	Nil	180	100	Nil

Web sites as "satisfied" (ranking in1) and 35% feel "adequate" (ranking in 2).

More importantly, we have found that the average US from internal and external users are basically consistent, with 2.9 of the average US for internal users and 2.5 for external users. The responses show the score 1, score 4 and score 5 are in the same ranking, respectively ranking in 4, 3, and 5. The only difference is the ranking of score 2 and 3. Internal users ranked score 3 (adequate) on first, while external users ranked score 2 (satisfied) on first. The consistencey of two survey results have confirmed the validation of this survey. The little difference might be caused by the small population of external users. Furthermore, the total score of US may be obtained by averaging the whole responses, which is 2.7, beween satisfied (score 2) and adequate (score 3), and it is closer to score 3 (adequate). Thus, we conclude that the US of Australian Ee-government online services lies on an "adequate" level.

Reliability Analysis

The construct reliability is assessed in terms of Cronbach's a coefficient (Cronbach, 1951). Cronbach's a coefficient is regarded as a measure of internal consistency at the time of administration of the questionnaire. Cronbach's a coefficient of greater than 0.70 is an acceptable reliability (Nunnaly, 1978), but a lower threshold (e.g., 0.60 or above) has also been used in research literature (Huang, D'Ambra & Bhalla, 2002). In this study, model reliability of EUS are examined, which confirmed all Cronbach's a coefficients are above 0.7. Then total Cronbach's a coefficient of each construct is obtained by simply averaging the coefficients contained in each construct. Cronbach's a coefficient of both internal US and external US are listed in the Table 4. The results show that the constructs are reliable.

Hypotheses Testing

The three factors are examined in relation to their impacts on US. A one-way analysis of variables (ANOVA) is conducted with each factor as the independent variable, and internal US and external US as the dependent variables, separately. The ANOVA results with p-values of internal US are shown in Table 5. The ANOVA results with p-values of external US are shown in Table 6-1, Table 6-2, and Table 6-3, which show respectively the relationship between SQ, IQ, WPQ and external users.

It may be found from Table 5 that all nine measures have p-value<0.05. According to p-value, the measures fall into two groups: group 1 – two (V2 and V6) of the nine measures, which have p-value greater than 0.01 and less than 0.05. This means that V2 and V6 have important effects at 5% level; group 2 – the other seven measures (V1, V3, V4, V5, V7, V8, V9), which have p-value less than 0.01. This implies that the seven measures V1, V3, V4, V5, V7, V8, and V9 have significant effects at 1% level. Furthermore, the average p-

Table 4. Reliability analysis with Cronbach's a coefficient

Construct	No. of Indicator	Cronbach's α (Internal US)	Cronbach's α (External US)
System Quality	3	0.76 0	.73
Information Quality	3	0.71 0	.72
Web Presence Quality	3	0.80 0	.73

Table 5. ANOVA results to test relationship between constructs and internal US

Construct	Measure	Sum of Squares	df	Mean Square	F	*p*-value	Mean *p*-value
System Quality	V1	9.810	4	2.452	4.961	.004**	0.009 **
	V2	5.980	4	1.495	3.486	.021*	
	V3	10.843	4	2.711	5.203	.003**	
Information Quality	V4	3.760	4	.940	6.514	.001**	0.007 **
	V5	7.742	4	1.935	4.779	.005**	
	V6	8.621	4	2.155	3.756	.016*	
Web Presence Quality	V7	5.411	4	1.353	7.110	.001**	0.001 **
	V8	7.986	4	1.996	6.918	.001**	
	V9	9.821	4	2.455	7.356	.000**	

Table 6-1. ANOVA results to test relationship between SQ (V1, V2, V3) and external US

Measure	User no.	Sum of squares	df	ms	f	*p*-value	Mean *p*-value	
V1	1	1.750	2	.875	3.399	.048*	0.045*	0.042*
	2	2.567	2	1.283	3.726	.037*		
	3	3.819	3	1.273	1.753	.181		
	4	22.578	4	5.644	8.162	.000**		
	5	5.800	3	1.933	5.484	.005**		
	6	2.904	1	2.904	27.440	.000**		
V2	1	1.642	2	.821	3.026	.065	0.033*	
	2	2.042	2	1.021	2.434	.107		
	3	4.065	3	1.355	3.857	.021*		
	4	11.978	4	2.994	5.051	.004**		
	5	5.188	3	1.729	6.011	.003**		
	6	2.904	1	2.904	27.440	.000**		
V3	1	1.617	2	.808	8.559	.001**	0.047*	
	2	3.600	2	1.800	6.750	.004**		
	3	3.708	3	1.236	3.386	.033*		
	4	10.411	4	2.603	4.210	.010*		
	5	2.133	3	.711	3.467	.031*		
	6	.181	1	.181	2.018	.167		

$^{*}p<0.05$, $^{**}p<0.01$

values are 0.009 for SQ, 0.007 for IQ, and 0.001 for WPQ. Thus, the results from viewpoint of internal users support all three hypotheses, H1, H2 and H3. Meanwhile, all nine sub-hypotheses are also supported because of each p-value is less than 0.05.

In contrast, the Table 6-1, Table 6-2 and Table 6-3 indicate the viewpoint of external users. All measures (V1 – V6 and V8 – V9) have mean p-value less than 0.05, except V7 (user-friendly) with means p-value 0.074 (greater than 0.05). This result indicates that user-friendliness is not importantly associated with Web presence quality, and user-friendliness does not have significant effects on internal US. The hypothesis H_{3-1} should be rejected from the construct WPQ. The average p-values are 0.042 for SQ, 0.019 for IQ, and 0.024 for WPQ. The sub-hypotheses H_{1-1} H_{1-2}, H_{1-3}, H_{2-1}, H_{2-2}, H_{2-3}, H_{3-2}, and H_{3-3} are supported as well as p-values of V1 (0.045), V2 (0.033), V3 (0.047), V4 (0.014), V5 (0.031), V6 (0.011), V8 (0.033) and V9 (0.014) are less than 0.05. Therefore, we conclude that the results from the viewpoint of external users support all the three hypotheses. All sub-hypotheses are also supported by the results.

Table 6-2. ANOVA results to test relationship between IQ (V4, V5, V6) and external US

Measure	User no.	Sum of squares	df	ms	f	*p*-value	Mean *p*-value	
V4	1	5.267	2	2.633	6.971	.004**		
	2	2.417	2	1.208	6.591	.005**		
	3	3.919	3	1.306	3.122	.043*		
	4	11.711	4	2.928	3.724	.016*	0.014*	
	5	19.008	3	6.336	6.514	.002**		
	6	1.337	1	1.337	6.650	.015*		
V5	1	7.750	2	3.875	15.973	.000**		
	2	3.300	2	1.650	2.621	.091		
	3	1.708	3	.569	2.403	.090		
	4	18.411	4	4.603	5.363	.003**	0.031*	0.019*
	5	14.721	3	4.907	15.046	.000**		
	6	2.504	1	2.504	72.800	.000**		
V6	1	8.800	2	4.400	8.486	.001**		
	2	4.950	2	2.475	8.100	.002**		
	3	2.832	3	.944	5.295	.006**		
	4	18.478	4	4.619	2.970	.039*	0.011*	
	5	4.000	3	1.333	4.000	.018*		
	6	.300	1	.300	12.600	.001**		

$^{*}p<0.05$, $^{**}p<0.01$

Table 6-3. ANOVA results to test relationship between WPQ (V7, V8, V9) and external US

Measure	User no.	Sum of squares	df	ms	f	*p*-value	Mean *p*-value	
V7	1	4.692	2	2.346	12.239	.000**	0.074	
	2	3.442	2	1.721	2.918	.071		
	3	10.994	3	3.665	11.379	.000**		
	4	30.567	4	7.642	7.320	.000**		
	5	4.762	3	1.587	2.733	.064		
	6	.185	1	.185	1.089	.306		
V8	1	7.467	2	3.733	31.500	.000**	0.033*	0.024*
	2	4.950	2	2.475	4.243	.025*		
	3	5.094	3	1.698	11.398	.000**		
	4	19.678	4	4.919	5.777	.002**		
	5	5.221	3	1.740	3.942	.019*		
	6	.448	1	.448	2.144	.154		
V9	1	2.250	2	1.125	7.500	.003**	0.014*	
	2	4.492	2	2.246	3.593	.041*		
	3	12.375	3	4.125	14.315	.000**		
	4	23.578	4	5.894	7.447	.000**		
	5	3.008	3	1.003	3.576	.027*		
	6	2.700	1	2.700	7.088	.013*		

$^{*}p<0.05$, $^{**}p<0.01$

Summary of Findings

Apparently, the research outcomes indicate that the user satisfaction on Australian e-government online services lies only on an "adequate" level. Customers' expectations are only satisfied to a limited extent. The two surveys from both internal and external users have caused consistent results. All three main hypotheses, H1, H2 and H3, have been validated by the results of data analyses. According to the previous data analyses and results, we summarized the findings as follows.

System quality is positively associated with effectiveness of e-government online services

(H1); thus an increase in the quality of system leads to an increase in effectiveness of e-government online services. System quality includes accessibility, feedback speed, and security. A net positive effect from these factors will result in a positive effect on effectiveness of e-government online services. These factors should remain important considerations for the e-government developers and managers.

Information quality is positively associated with effectiveness of e-government online services (H2); thus an increase in the quality of information leads to an increase in effectiveness of e-government online services. Information currency, functionality and content importance constitute the construct of information quality. Thus, a net positive effect from these factors has resulted in a positive effect on effectiveness of e-government online services. Information currency, functionality and content importance should be considered as important factors when presenting information.

Web presence quality is positively associated with effectiveness of e-government online services (H3); thus an increase in the quality of Web presence leads to an increase in effectiveness of e-government online services. User-friendly, display format, and navigation efficiency are used to measure Web presence quality. Thus, a net positive effect from these factors will result in a positive effect on effectiveness of e-government online services. User-friendliness, display format, and navigation efficiency should be considered as important factors for Web designers. On the other hand, public users do not care about the user-friendliness factor. Easy to navigate and easy to find the relevant information are most important for them.

The results indicate that the viewpoints of evaluating the effectiveness of e-government online services are slightly different between the internal users and external users. Internal users address all nine factors to evaluate the satisfaction, which are accessibility, feedback speed, security, information currency, functionality, content usefulness, user-friendliness, display format and navigation efficiency. However, external users emphasize only the other eight factors except user-friendliness. We believe this is due to external users paying more attention to the service quality of e-government, and a small size of population from external users can also be another reason to cause the difference.

According to the internal users, all sub-hypotheses in the research model are fully supported. All the measures (accessibility, feedback speed, security; information currency, functionality, content importance; user-friendliness, display format, navigation efficiency) are positively associated to constructs separately. In contrast, from external users, the statistical conclusions partially support the sub-hypotheses in the research model. That is, user-friendliness is not positively associated with the Web presence quality. Others are positively associated with the constructs separately.

In addition, the results also demonstrate that the three constructs have different weight on affecting effectiveness of e-government online services. According to the internal users, the quality of Web presence has a highest weight among them, while system quality and information quality have almost equal weight on influencing effectiveness of e-government online services. Web presence quality is most important for promotion of effectiveness of e-government online services. That is, the quality of Web presence influences effectiveness of e-government online services most. On the other hand, from the external users, information quality and Web presence quality influence have approximately higher weight than system quality on influencing effectiveness of e-government online services. That is, information quality and Web presence quality influence effectiveness of e-government online services more than system quality.

Recommendations

In general, effectiveness of e-government online services may be achieved through making high user satisfaction. Based on the results, several recommendations are advanced to develop better e-government online services.

Firstly, government agencies and organizations should actively seek ways to promote quality of information and Web presence. This requires assisting users to find the information and services from the Web sites. It can be achieved by: improving navigation by adopting standard navigational devices and using them consistently throughout the site; facilitating browse through the provision of better site maps and/or indexes and the provision of navigational information on every page; providing more links to high demand content and ensuring that descriptive information is clear; providing search engines and stating clearly what and how they search.

Secondly, government agencies and organizations should focus on the way in which customers use the Web sites, so that Web developers can maintain user-oriented Web site design and content development. This includes: determining the purpose of the site and making this clear to the users and orienting them to the site; developing and organizing the site content around user groups. This requires identification and knowledge of the relevant user groups, their information and service needs and any access issues; improving the quality of instructions generally and providing for different level of skills and expertise from the novice to the sophisticated user where necessary.

Last but not the least, government agencies and organizations should also focus on assisting users to find the information that is not on the Web sites. This can be achieved by what follows. (1) Offering a comprehensive list of agency contacts and users should be able to send an e-mail enquiry directly to the relevant section/person. Users should expect appropriately detailed and relevant answers within a set period of time. (2) Facilitating links across government Web sites and other relevant Web sites.

FUTURE TRENDS

E-government is a dynamic concept of varying meaning and significance. Because e-government continues to evolve, the full measure of its success awaits assessment (Relyea, 2002). With the transformation of e-government and the changes of client needs, the applicable evaluation model would be developed to match the future practices of e-government. The limitation of this study should be addressed in further studies. First, a much larger sample should be required for greater precision. Second, more factors should be added to match more comprehensive applications. In order to attribute to maturity of e-government, we will need to continue to develop empirical-based theories of e-government evaluation.

A particular priority for Australian e-government is the integration or linking of related services that might be provided by the same agency, different agencies, agencies in other jurisdictions, and private sector partners, so that customers can carry out multiple transactions during a single instance of service (Rimmer, 2002). After completion of integrated e-government online service phase, higher level of e-government would implement intelligent services (Guo & Lu, 2003); for example, personalized relationship between citizen and government. All citizens can have an electronically maintained, personal profile of their financial interactions with the government to improve their personal efficiency. Thus, we identify personalization as one of our main direction in the future study. Personalization is a technique used to generate customized content for each client. Through personalization an organization can focus on customer intimacy and enhance its overall value. Although the full potential of personalization techniques have not broadly been realized, a few government agencies have launched to offer simple personalization function through provision of online personal profile.

CONCLUSIONS

This study has developed a research model to evaluate the effectiveness of Australian e-government online services. The specification of the research model is based on the theoretical and empirical sources. We have identified the underlying factors, system quality, information quality and Web presence quality, which influence significantly the effectiveness of e-government online services. The research results empirically demonstrate the relationships between the three conducts - system quality, information quality, Web presence quality, and user satisfaction. These relationships are useful in determining the development strategies of e-government online services. Government agencies need to understand these relationships in order to achieve better services.

E-government online services are still in an early stage. Demands of customers have not been understood completely and agencies are not so clear on how to present their information and services based on the needs of customers. Furthermore, the results obtained in this study have some important implications for development of e-government online services. Our results suggest that Web presence quality and information quality influence effectiveness of e-government online services more than system quality from user perspectives. This will help the relevant participants of e-government addressing management concerns of success strategy.

Although the study has been conducted in the context of Australian e-government online services, the research outcomes may assist practitioners and researchers, in the developed countries especially, who recognize the critical importance of e-government online services but remain unsure of how to implement the strategies effectively. On the other hand, the practitioners and researchers in the developing countries can draw lessons from the practices and experiences of e-government online services in Australia, and develop an effective strategy in combination with their own status.

REFERENCES

Ahituv, N. (1980). A systematic approach toward assessing the value of an information system. MIS Quarterly, 4(4), 61-75.

Aicholzer, G., & Schmutzer, R. (2000, September). Organizational challenges to the development of electronic government. Paper presented at the 11th International Workshop on Database and Expert Systems Applications, Greenwich, London.

Aldrich, D., Bertot, J.C., & McClure, C.R. (2002). E-government: initiatives, development and issues. Government Information Quarterly, 19, 349-355.

Anonymous. (2002). What is e-government? Retrieved March 18, 2003, from: http://www.e-government.govt.nz/programme/faqs.asp#a1.

Bailey, J.E., & Pearson, S.W. (1983). Development of a tool for measuring and analyzing computer user satisfaction. Management Science, 29(5), 530-545.

Baty, J.B., & Lee, R.M. (1995). Intershop: Enhancing the vendor/customer dialectic in electronic shopping. Journal of Management Information Systems, 11(4), 9-31.

Bhimani, A. (1996). Securing the commercial Internet. Communications of ACM, 39(6), 29-35.

Boon, O., Hewett, W.G., & Parker, C.M. (2000, June). Evaluating the adoption of the Internet: A study of an Australian experience in local government. Paper presented at the 13th International Bled Electronic Commerce Conference, Bled, Slovenia.

Briggs, R.O., Vreede, G.D., Nunamaker Jr, J.F., & Sprague Jr., R. H. (2003). Special issue: Information systems success. Journal of Management Information Systems, 19(4), 5-8.

Burgess, L., & Cooper, J. (1999, June). A model for classification of business adoption of Internet commerce solutions. Paper presented at the 12th International Bled Electronic Commerce Conference, Bled, Slovenia.

Chen, H. (2002). Digital government: Technologies and practices. Decision Support Systems, 34(3), 223 - 227.

Cronbach, L.J. (1951). Coefficient alpha and internal structure of tests. Psychometric, 16, 297-334.

Cyert, R., & March, J. (1963). A behavioral theory of the firm. Englewood Cliffs: Prentice-Hall.

D'Ambra, J., & Rice, R.E. (2001). Emerging factors in user evaluation of the World Wide Web. Information and Management, 38(6), 373-384.

Davis, F.D. (1989). Perceived usefulness, perceived ease of use, and user acceptance of information technology. MIS Quarterly, 13(3), 319-340.

Davis, F.D., Bagozzi, R.P., & Warshaw, P.R. (1989). User acceptance of computer technology: A comparison of two theoretical models. Management Science, 35(8), 982-1003.

DeConti, L. (1998). Planning and creating a government website: Learning for the experience of US states. Retrieved, June 16th, 2002, from: http://www.amn.ac.uk/idpm.

DeLone, W.H., & McLean, E.R. (1992). Information systems success: The quest for the dependent variable. Information Systems Research, 3(1), 60-95.

Devadoss, P.R., Pan, S.L., & Huang, J.C. (2003). Structural analysis of e-government initiatives: A case study of SCO. Decision Support Systems, 34(3), 253-269.

Dickman, G. (1998). Business statistics. Melbourne: Nelson.

Downing, C.E. (1999). System usage behavior as a proxy for user satisfaction: an empirical investigation. Information and Management, 35(4), 203-216.

Elliot, S.R., Morup-Peterson, A.S., & Bjorn-Andersen, N. (2000, June). Towards a framework for evaluation of commercial websites. Paper presented at the 13th International Bled Electronic Commerce Conference, Bled, Slovenia.

Elmagarmid, A.K., & McIver Jr., W.J. (2001). The ongoing march toward digital government. IEEE Computer, 34(2), 32-38.

Eschenfelder, K.R., Beachboard, J.C., McClure, C.R., & Wyman, S.K. (1997). Assessing US federal government Web sites. Government Information Quarterly, 14(2), 173-189.

Farquhar, B., Langmann, G., & Balfour, A. (1998). Consumer needs in global electronic commerce. Electronic Markets, 8(2), 9-12.

Gallagher, C.A. (1974). Perceptions of the value of a management information system. Academy of Management Journal, 1(1), 46-55.

Garrity, E.J., & Sanders, G.L. (1998). Dimensions of information systems success. In E.J. Garrity & G.L. Sanders (Eds.), Information systems success measurement. Hershey, PA: Idea Group Publishing.

Gehrke, D., & Turban, E. (1999, January). Determinants of successful Web design: Relative importance and recommendation for effectiveness. Paper presented at the 32nd Hawaii International Conference on System Science (HICSS'99), Hawaii, USA.

Gordon, T.F. (2002). Introduction to e-government. European Research Consortium for Information and Mathematics, 48, 12-13.

Guo, X.T., & Lu, J. (2003, September). Building intelligent e-government: A strategic development model in context of Australia. Paper presented at the CollECTeR (LatAm) Conference on Electronic Commerce, Santiago, Chile.

Guo, X.T., Lu, J., & Raban, R. (2002, October). An assessment of the characteristics of Australian government e-services. Paper presented at the 7th annual CollECTeR Conference on Electronic Commerce, Melbourne, Australia.

Hamilton, S., & Chervany, N.L. (1981). Evaluating information system effectiveness: comparing evaluation approaches. MIS Quarterly, 5(3), 55-69.

Heeks, R. (2001, September). Explaining success and failure of e-government. Paper presented at the European conference on E-government, Dublin.

Ho, C.F., & Wu, W.H. (1999, January). Antecedents of customer satisfaction on the Internet: An empirical study of on-line shopping. Paper presented at the 32nd Hawaii International Conference on System Science (HICSS'99), Hawaii, USA.

Holmes, D. (2001). eGov: eBusiness strategies for government. London: Nicholas Brealey Publishing.

Huang, W., D'Ambra, J., & Bhalla, V. (2002). An empirical investigation of the adoption of eGovernment in Australian citizens: Some unexpected research findings. Journal of Computer Information Systems, 43(1), 15-22.

Igbaria, M., & Nachman, S.A. (1990). Correlates of user satisfaction with end user computing. Information and Management, 19, 73-82.

Iivari, J., & Ervasi, I. (1994). User information satisfaction: IS implementability and effectiveness. Information and Management, 27(4), 205-220.

Kim, K.K. (1989). User satisfaction: A synthesis of three different perspectives. Journal of Information Systems, 4(1), 1-12.

Layne, K., & Lee, J. (2001). Developing fully functional e-government: A four stage model. Government Information Quarterly, 18, 122-136.

Likert, R.A. (1982). A technique for the measurement of attitudes. Archives of Psychology, 142, 44-53.

Lisle-Williams, M. (2002). Successful eGovernment. Retrieved November 6, 2002, from: http://www.egov.vic.au/Documents/webchannelsinfutureegov.pps.

Liu, C., & Arnett, K.P. (2000). Exploring the factors associated with Website success in the context of electronic commerce. Information and Management, 38, 23-33.

Marchionini, G., Samet, H., & Brandt, L. (2003). Digital government. Communications of the ACM, 46(1), 25-27.

Mason, R.O. (1978). Measuring information output: A communication systems approach. Information and Management, 1(5), 219-234.

Molla, A., & Licker, P.S. (2001). E-commerce systems success: An attempt to extend and respecify the DeLone and McLean model of IS success. Journal of Electronic Commerce Success, 2(4), 1-11.

NOIE. (2002a). The current state of play. Retrieved June 16th, 2003, from: http://www.noie.gov.au.

NOIE. (2002b). Advancing Australia: The information economy progress report 2002. Retrieved December 16, 2002, from: http://www.noie.gov.au/publications/NOIE/progress_report/NOIE_AA_S.pdf.

Nunnaly, J. (1978). Psychometric theory. New York: McGraw-Hill.

OGO. (2001). Government online: The commonwealth government's strategy. Retrieved June 16, 2002, from: http://www.govonline.gov.au/projects/strategy/GovOnlineStrategy.htm.

Palmer, J.W. (2002). Web site usability, design, and performance metrics. Information Systems Research, 13(2), 151-167.

Pilipovic, J., Ivkovic, M., Domazet, D., & Milutinovic, V. (2002). E-government. In V. Milutinovic & F. Patricelli (Eds.), E-business and e-challenges. Amsterdam: IOS Press.

Rai, A., Lang, S.S., & Welker, R.B. (2002). Assessing the validity of IS success models: An empirical test and theoretical analysis. Information Systems Research, 13(1), 50-69.

Relyea, H.C. (2002). E-gov: Introduction and overview. Government Information Quarterly, 19, 9-35.

Rimmer, J. (2002). E-government - better government. Retrieved March 26, 2003, from: http://www.noie.gov.au/publications/speeches/Rimmer/Breakfast/egov_sep18. htm.

Scholl, H.J. (2003, January). E-government: A special case of ICT-enabled business process change. Paper presented at the 36th Hawaii International Conference on System Science (HICSS'03), Hawaii, USA.

Seddon, P. (1997). A respecification and extension of the DeLone and McLean model of IS success. Information Systems Research, 8(3), 240-253.

Seddon, P.B., & Kiew, M.Y. (1996). A partial test and development of the DeLone and McLean model of IS success. Australian Journal of Information Systems, 2, 1-61.

Seddon, P.B., Staples, S., Patnayakuni, R., & Bowtell, M. (1999). Dimensions of information systems success. Communications of the AIS, 1(20), 1-39.

Seybold, P.B. (1998). Customer.com: How to create a profitable business strategy for the Internet and beyond. London: Random House.

Shannon, C.E., & Weaver, W. (1949). The mathematical theory of communication. Urbana, IL: University of Illinois Press.

Smith, A.G. (2001). Applying evaluation criteria to New Zealand government Website. International Journal of Information Management, 21, 137-149.

Sprecher, M.H. (2000). Racing to e-government: Using the Internet for citizen service delivery. Government Finance Review, 16(5), 21-22.

Srinivasan, A. (1985). Alternative measures of system effectiveness: Associations and implications. MIS Quarterly, 9(3), 243-253.

Steyaert, J.C. (in press). Measuring the performance of electronic government services. Information and Management.

Swanson, E.B. (1986). A note of informatics. Journal of Management Information Systems, 2(3), 86-91.

Tapscott, D. (1996). Digital economy. New York: McGraw-Hill.

Teo, T.S.H., & Choo, W.Y. (2001). Assessing the impact of using the Internet for competitive intelligence. Information and Management, 39(1), 67-83.

Turban, E., King, D., Lee, J., Warkentin, M., & Chung, H.M. (2002). Electronic commerce 2002: A managerial perspective. New Jersey: Pearson Education.

Victoria, M. (2002). Putting people at the centre: Government innovation working for Victorians. Retrieved March 18, 2003, from: http://www.mmv.vic.gov.au/egov.

Wan, H.A. (2000). Opportunities to enhance a commercial Website. Information and Management, 38(1), 15-21.

Watson, R.T., Berthon, P., Pitt, L., & Zinkhan, G. (2000). Electronic commerce - the strategic perspective. Texas: Dryden Press.

West, D.M. (2000). Assessing e-government: The Internet, democracy, and service delivery by state and federal government. Retrieved June 16, 2002, from: http://www.insidepolitics.org/egovtreport00.html.

Wilkin, C., & Castleman, T. (2003, January). Development of an instrument to evaluate the quality of delivered information systems. Paper presented at the 36th Hawaii International Conference on System Science (HICSS'03), Hawaii, USA.

Wimmer, M., & Traunmuller, R. (2000, September). Trends in electronic government: managing distributed knowledge. Paper presented at the 11th International Workshop on Database and Expert Systems Applications, Greenwich, London.

Woodroof, J., & Burg, W. (2003). Satisfaction/dissatisfaction: Are users predisposed? Information and Management, 40(4), 317-324.

WorldBank. (2002). A definition of e-government. Retrieved March 16, 2003, from: http://www1.worldbank.org/publicsector/egov/definition.htm

This work was previously published in Electronic Government Strategies and Implementations, edited by W. Huang, K. Siau and K.K. Wei, pp. 214-241, copyright 2005 by IGI Publishing, formerly known as Idea Group Publishing (an imprint of IGI Global).

Chapter 4.30
E-Governance in Australian Local Government: Spinning a Web around Community?

Kevin O'Toole
Deakin University, Australia

ABSTRACT

Local government in Australia is under pressure to modernize its structures in the new public management environment, as well as respond to increasing demands from its local electorates for better delivery of services and greater levels of participation in the democratic process. This article analyzes local government's response to these pressures through its use of information communication technologies (ICT) to execute its broad range of tasks. I begin by discussing e-governance in the light of Chadwick and May's (2003) three basic models of interaction between the state and its citizens: managerial, consultative, and participatory. Using data collected from an analysis of 658 local government Web sites in Australia together with existing survey research, I analyze the extent to which local government sites fit into the three models. The article then concludes with a discussion of the issues and problems faced by local government in its attempt to develop e-governance, as both an extension of its administrative as well as democratic functions.

INTRODUCTION

Australia's local governments, like many other institutions of governance around the world, are facing a raft of new challenges in the 21st century. The governance environment, within which local governments function, has undergone substantial change over recent years. The pressure for reform has seen major structural changes as state and federal governments seek to impose a new economic and political agenda upon the local institutions of governance (Baker, 2003). The focus of local government reform has revolved mainly around issues of statutory service obligations, financial accountability, local economic development and, to a lesser degree, democratic representation (Dollery, Marshall & Worthington, 2003). To some extent this has meant a more inward-looking local government framework, where compliance with competition policy guidelines and more efficient service delivery has dominated the agenda (Aulich, 1997).

More recently local governments have adopted Information Communication Technologies (ICT) in the form of Web sites in the hope of expanding their role in the new world of e-government. With large cash injections from the federal government's "Networking the Nation" program and local state programs to improve the reach of ICT, local governments have set about the task of relocating much of their activity online (Macdonald, 2001). The first wave of Web sites has been established on the Internet and local governments are now in the process of learning how to work in the world of e-government.

As this article demonstrates, the first rush of e-government, and for that matter e-governance, has brought mixed results for local government across Australia. Web sites exist for most local governments, but the types of e-government vary from place to place both within and between the state systems. The first section of this article discusses an analytical framework for understanding e-government. The second section outlines the background of local government across Australia. This is followed by a discussion of local government approaches to e-governance using data from a review of local government sites. The final section discusses the major issues that face any future development of e-governance for local government in Australia.

E-GOVERNMENT

In the Australian Local Government Association's report entitled *A Directional Roadmap for the Use of Electronic Technology by Councils*, e-government is defined as "the structured use of electronic technology to pursue the traditional goals of government in areas such as:

- the interface with government
- service relationships with people and businesses
- commercial relationships with business partners
- implementing sectoral and community based policy
- enhancing the role of citizens in democratic processes (i.e., e-democracy)
- interacting with other public institutions, and
- the conduct of government's own 'back-office' operations" (Australian Local Government Association, 2004, p. 10).

Such a list is instructive in the way it reaffirms the fundamental role of "government" in interfacing, implementing, conducting, and servicing. For all intents and purposes, it is business as usual for "government" without a lot of thought about increasing the reach of local democracy (Crabtree, 2001).

Others, however, consider that the shift to e-government involves a changing interaction between the government and its citizens. Chadwick and May (2003) argue that there are three basic models of interaction between the state and its citizens that underpin the notion of e-government: managerial, consultative, and participatory. The dominant approach is managerialism, which boasts a number of features:

> *... a concern for the "efficient delivery of services" of government information to citizens and other groups of users; the use of ICTs to improve flows of information within and around government; a recognition of the importance of "service delivery" to "customers"; the view that speeding up information provision is, by itself, "opening up" government; a general absence of user resources issues, such as the ability to receive and interpret information; and "control" and presentational professionalism (often termed spin) as defining logics.* (Chadwick & May, 2003, p. 272)

This approach to e-government is summed up by the Chief Information Officer for the Government of Canada, who states,

The ultimate goal is to use technology to strengthen Canada's economy and society; reduce the cost and burden of government processes and transactions; encourage innovation with government as a strategic procurer and model user of new technologies; and, optimize the effective and efficient delivery of government programs and services. (d'Auray, 2003, p. 36)

In this sense governments have sought to emulate the commercial world in the first instance by developing a form of e-government that includes four types of interaction:

1. Simple information
2. Allow access by citizens and businesses (even update particulars) —weak form of interactivity
3. Allow online transactions and purchases, or electronic sending of tender information
4. Integrated portal of all government services and information (Symonds, 2000)

These four stages are no different from many commercial sites in that they offer information and services online. The main difference is that the types of information and activity of e-government relate to services that are located in the public sector. People go online to government sites mainly "to download forms, find out about processes and rules, and generally to run their private affairs" (Rennie & Hartley, 2004, p. 10). E-government in this sense is a top-down governing process using online information and services that are often thought to be apolitical or more uninvolved (Griffiths, 2002).

A second model of e-government is consultative and thereby it facilitates the communication of citizen opinion to government (Chadwick & May, 2003, p. 278). This model embraces a "continuum of consultation, stretching from low-level information gathering towards (but not finally reaching) a fuller, quasideliberative level of interaction and consultation" (Chadwick & May, 2003, p. 279). Citizens are still the passive recipients of information, but at least they are encouraged to engage with government. Some consider this engagement a shift to e-governance that "is a technology-mediated relationship between citizens and their governments from the perspective of potential electronic deliberation over civic communication, over policy evolution, and in democratic expression of citizen will" (Marche & McNiven, 2003, p. 75). There is more emphasis on democratic governance where citizens are engaged in an active process of governing apart from their place as clients and consumers of state services. This is an extension of e-government, where all forms of ICT are used by governments and their agents to broaden the reach of public information and services, and engage citizens in some form of public engagement (Curtain, Sommer & Vis-Sommer, 2003, p. 2).

A third model is participatory and "conceives of a more complex horizontal and multidirectional interactivity" (Chadwick & May, 2003, p. 280). Here there is a demand from citizens to play a more active role in governing at all levels of government though greater ICT interactivity (Coe, Paquet & Roy, 2001). One simple definition of this type of e-governance refers to "two-way and horizontal power-using technologies to enhance democratic practice" (Griffiths, 2002, p. 185). In this sense the use of ICT becomes not merely a means of communication, but a way of facilitating interactivity between multiple sites in the political process (Geiselhart, Griffiths & Fitzgerald, 2003, p. 216). The main emphasis is upon "voluntary association and the development of new communities of interest" (Chadwick & May, 2003, p. 281). Through the use of bulletin boards, chat rooms, file sharing, and peer to peer networking, citizens can be involved in forms of deliberative democracy around opinion formation and political action in a new "cyber civil society" (Chadwick & May, 2003, p. 281).

There is partly a utopian vision in this participatory model that "paints a techno-dream of the Internet as a newly emerging public sphere in which people gather without the need for propinquity to politically organize, discuss and collectively resolve issues of the day" (Lim, 2002, p. 383). There is a sense here that new forms of e-democracy can enable citizens to propose, discuss, and vote upon new policy decisions directly. However, there are those who doubt that electronic direct democracy will be anything other than "politics as usual" (Barney, 2000; Crabtree, 2001; Moore, 1999; Norris, 2001). In the next sections we will explore the ways that local governments have developed their Web sites across Australia and evaluate them against these managerial, consultative and/or participatory models.

LOCAL GOVERNMENT: BACKGROUND

There are 721 local government bodies in Australia, including 97 indigenous community councils in Queensland, the NT, and WA and all come under the constitutional authority of the States and Territories. Virtually all of Victoria, Queensland, WA, and Tasmania come under the jurisdiction of some local government authority unlike NSW, SA, and the NT where there are large unincorporated areas. Uniquely in Australia, the Government of the Australian Capital Territory combines both state and local government functions, but it will not be treated as local government in this instance.

The population and size vary enormously as the federal government report on cost shifting indicates:

- the average population of local governing bodies is 26,400, however, 50% of councils have fewer than 6490 residents. Brisbane City Council has 899,604 residents, while Murchison in WA has 160 people;
- the Shire of East Pilbara covers the largest area of 378,533 sqare kms, while one of the smallest in area is the urban Shire of Peppermint Grove which covers 2 sqare kms. Some councils, including indigenous community councils, are recorded as having no area because their boundaries are not defined;
- the population of the metropolitan council of East Fremantle is 6,660, similar to the rural agricultural council of Buloke which has a population of 7,268. However, their areas are 3 sqare kms and 8002 sqare kms respectively. (House of Representatives Standing Committee on Economics Finance and Public Administration, 2003, pp. 6-7)

The legal framework for local government also differs from state to state but generally the functions and services of local government can include engineering, recreation, health, welfare, security, building, planning and development, administration, culture, and education. However, as the Cost Shifting enquiry found, local government has been taking on responsibility for a wide range of social functions that include management of health, alcohol and drug problems, community safety and improved planning, and accessible transport. Furthermore, the regulatory functions of local government have increased in areas like development and planning, public health, and environmental management (House of Representatives Standing Committee on Economics Finance and Public Administration, 2003).

Nevertheless, the expansion of these services is far from uniform across Australia, even within State and Territory Boundaries. For example, local government in Queensland, New South Wales, and Tasmania have local responsibility for water, while in other states water management falls under the jurisdiction of State government agencies. Local government in the Northern Territory does not have responsibility for planning, whereas in other states local governments have a significant yet differential role to play in the area (May, 2003).

Overall, local governments across Australia exhibit a wide variety of characteristics. Besides differences in population and geographic area, the range of functions they perform and in their legislative frameworks local governments also vary markedly in income and expenditure, the skills of employees, and physical, economic, cultural, and social environments. One significant differential is the ratios of elected members to their populations and the way the electorates are organized (Burdess & O'Toole, 2004; Kiss, 2003). The average population per councillor ranges from 258 in the Northern Territory to 8,122 in the State of Victoria (May, 2003). Electorates can be divided into wards or un-subdivided and voting in local government elections is compulsory in three states (New South Wales, Victoria, and Queensland), while the rest are voluntary (Kiss, 2003). There are also differences in voting procedures with many local governments opting for postal voting where it is either allowed or mandated, as in Tasmania (Kiss, 2003).

With such differences in the way that local government organizes itself in the different jurisdictions, any shift to new forms of communication such as ICT will most probably reflect those variations. The next section illustrates that process by outlining the results from research into ICT in Australian local government.

AUSTRALIAN LOCAL GOVERNMENTS AND ICT

To ascertain the extent of e-government at local government level two stages of data collection were conducted. The first stage entailed Web-search together with telephone and e-mail contact with local government associations to ascertain if they could assist by supplying any information and/or research they may have collected on e-governance. The second stage of the research entailed an analysis of all available local government Web sites in Australia together with existing survey research and also included a small number of case studies associated with different models of e-government.

Local Government Associations

At the national level and in each state the peak bodies represent and advocate the interests of local government and provide policy advice and strategic direction for councils throughout Australia. The Australian Local Government Association (ALGA) claims to represent 673 councils on a range of issues and has as one of its strategic priorities "connecting local governments through information technology" (http://www.alga.asn.au/about/). A significant boost to ALGA and other state local government associations was the Federal Government's "Networking the Nation" funding of $51 million that began in 2001, money that became available as a result of the part sale of Telstra (Macdonald, 2001).

The ALGA is a member of the Online and Communication Council (OCC) formally known as Online Council, whose membership includes ministers from the Australian state and territory governments. The OCC is a forum for commonwealth, state, and territory government ministers and local government to consider and reach agreement on national strategic approaches to the use of information and communications services. One of the key strategic priorities for the OCC is e-government and ALGA is involved in a Better Rural Services project that aims to increase the capacity of local government in rural areas to improve its ICT standard. The aims of the project are more focused on a managerial approach to e-government than any extension of community participation models, since it views ICT as "an enabler of innovation and productivity improvements" and an important tool "in the sustainability of local government" (http://www.alga.asn.au/policy/infotech/).

In the states and territories, the local government associations have developed a range of specific e-government projects, although it is not always a high priority policy area in some places. Generally state associations have promoted the use of ICT more in managerial terms, as a means of creating more efficient delivery of services and imparting information to ratepayers. As e-voting is not allowed by legislation in all jurisdictions, any campaign for changes to the voting procedures would require amendments to the legislation. However, all the associations have been supportive of their local governments in the development of local Web sites and there have been some attempts to use ICT to expand the reach of consultative and participative processes.

In New South Wales there is an online action initiative hosted by the Local Government Association of NSW and the Shires Association of NSW and funded by the Commonwealth Networking the Nation fund. It commenced in July 2001 with the aim of improving the availability of online services to enable rural councils to provide services more effectively to their communities using ICT. The second stage of the project entitled Local-e "Next Steps" mainly focused on service delivery functions such as e-services, e-mapping, e-procurement, standards and security, and portals (http://www.local-e.nsw.gov.au/). At present there is no specific policy on ICT in the NSW association.

In Victoria the two local government associations—The Municipal Association of Victoria (MAV) and the Victorian Local Governance Association (VLGA)—are both involved in e-government projects for local government. The MAV developed a Local Government Online Service (LGOS) delivery project that primarily focused on online payment, planning, and e-procurement systems as well as systems for connecting up local governments with state and federal governments. The project also included what the MAV entitled an e-democracy project where two councils—Melbourne and Cardinia—were involved in Web-casting their council meetings. The Web-casting only lasted for the trial period and both councils no longer Web-cast their meetings. The VLGA with its focus on governance issues has been actively involved in promoting e-democracy issues by distributing information on its own Web site. While there are no specific policy statements, a number of publications on the VLGA site that discuss the issues of e-governance are available.

In a bid to launch councils into the e-government era, the Local Government Association Queensland was successful in winning $7.5 million in federal government "Networking the Nation" funding to help establish Internet services in local councils. The aim was to use e-government to help councils to disseminate information to ratepayers and assist electronic payment of rates and charges. It was also expected that councils would use the online services to support residents and community groups by enabling e-mail services, community portals for groups to create Web sites, information and data collection services, and the ease of B-Pay for rate payments (Bell, 2003).

The Western Australian Local Government Association has minimal reference to e-government, although there is an indication that around 30 percent of councils have bill paying facilities. As part of their 5-year strategic plan they do indicate that one of their development goals is to "enhance Local Government's access to and use of technology" (http://www.walga.asn.au/policy/development). However, beyond this, the association does not have any fully articulated policies or projects that promote e-government.

The South Australian Local Government Association (SALGA) has been quite proactive in assisting local government to go online. A major initiative was the Electronic Services Program, a two-year $5.4 million program funded by "Networking the Nation" aimed at ensuring that regional local governments participate in the delivery of Web-based online services. SALGA has developed a tailor-made software package, entitled Unity DCW, that is used across the local government sector in South Australia and also in Tasmania and parts of New South Wales. While the package strongly emphasizes the managerial aspects of government, it does purport to "provide mechanisms for customers to provide feedback and take note of constructive criticism!" (SALGA, 2004).

In Tasmania there has been a concerted effort by the Local Government Association to experiment and expand ICT for more consultative and participative uses. The major project in Tasmania entitled LOGONS is aimed at online service delivery for local government and has the specific goal of providing the general public (mainly council customers) with online local government services (Local Government Association of Tasmania, 2002). One specific aspect of LOGONS has been the Interactions and Transactions project that aimed "to identify the tools and requirements that will allow councils to provide secure and customer friendly online transaction capability and participation in online forums" (Koerbin & Standish, 2004). There were two trials researching online communication using council Web sites, both of which will be discussed later in this section.

The Local Government Association of the Northern Territory (LGANT) has ICT projects including "NT Connect" and "I've Got Email", both designed to increase the exposure of local governments to ICT, especially in the remote areas. There are presently 46 community council Web sites designed to act as information pages for the local communities in remote areas. On the LGANT Web site, ICT development is placed first among its services to members (http://www.lgant.nt.gov.au/).

Local Government ICT Capacity

Local government's capacity for e-government is related to two issues: (1) local government's connection to communication networks; and (2) its ability to take advantage of the available technology. This is especially the case for rural and remote municipalities where fast communication networks are either nonexistent or reasonably expensive.

In many instances the physical capacity for the adoption of e-government across all municipalities in Australia is still problematic. A survey of 200 councils across Australia found that all councils had Internet access (Rural Industries Research and Development Corporation, 2004). However, 89% of urban councils were on broadband compared to 59% of those in rural areas. Across the country as a whole, 68% of councils were on broadband and 32% on dial up. Nearly 40% of councils not on broadband (equivalent to 10% of all councils) said they had no plans to upgrade nor did they indicate when they would do so. There were three main reasons given for remaining on dial-up: broadband was not available (62%); dial up was perceived to be cheaper (15%); and "dial up was best for their needs" (11%) (Rural Industries Research and Development Corporation, 2004, p. 31).

Beyond access to broadband is the construction of Web sites themselves and in this regard across Australia there are no common benchmarks. A report entitled *Services and Metadata on Local Government Web Sites* found that the Web sites are not very consistent in what constitutes a service, what service information is important to convey, how services are grouped on Web sites, and how to name these groupings (Farkus, 2004). The report also found that the information provided on local government Web sites fell into three categories:

- Council promotion—all sites provide detailed information about the Council, its role, structure, councillors, departments, sometimes meeting minutes, and history and other information about the Council and its functions

- Regional promotion—most sites provide some information about the region, its major center(s), tourist attractions, and sometimes economic development potential. Some sites include details of commercial tourist accommodation and venues; some provide or support local business directories
- Services information—everything else on most of the sites could loosely be described as "service-oriented" information, in the sense that it is not commercial, not advertising, not local news items. (Farkus, 2004).

Many local governments do have interactive online services, especially the payment of rates and it appears that where online capabilities are available ratepayers are using the Internet to make payments to councils (Rural Industries Research and Development Corporation, 2004). In states like Victoria this is almost uniform, whereas in Western Australia there are only 28% of councils that have online facilities for the payment of rates.

When it comes to the application of more extended models of e-government to include consultation and participation, there is even less capacity on local government sites. A review of local government Web sites was conducted in October 2005 to better understand the way that local governments had positioned themselves with regard to consultation and participation. All available Web sites (658 in total) were scanned in each state and territory to discover the interactivity of sites, especially with regard to citizen consultation and participation (see Tables 1 and 2). The overall percentage of local governments that had some form of online feedback mechanism on their sites was 40%. The types of feedback were usually contained in an online form that allowed people to post complaints, compliments, suggestions, comments, or "customer requests". Sometimes the forms were available on the home page under such headings as "have your say" or "feedback". At other times the forms were found in the contacts area or attached to the council activities part of the site. Most local government sites also included e-mail addresses, but for the purposes of this research it was the capacity to reach the council online that was used as the criterion for electronic feedback. Furthermore, those Web sites that offer feedback mechanisms asking for comments about the site itself were also excluded.

The types and placement of feedback forms varied from state to state and across the four categories of municipality (Department of Transport and Regional Services, 2005):

- Metropolitan developed or part of an urban center of more than 1,000,000 or population density more than 600/sqare km

Table 1. Number and percentage of state category for online feedback mechanism

	Metro	Regional	Fringe	Rural	Total
New South Wales	18 (53%)	19 (53%)	9 (82%)	29 (41%)	75 (50%)
Victoria	19 (86%)	20 (77%)	8 (80%)	14 (70%)	61 (78%)
Queensland	3 (100%)	12 (33%0	7 (64%)	18 (21%)	40 (29%)
Western Australia	11 (58%)	7 (64%)	7 (70%)	14 (31%)	39 (31%)
South Australia	15 (100%0	4 (57%)	3 (75%)	14 (49%)	36 (49%)
Tasmania	0	3 (38%)	0	7 (34%)	10 (34%)
Northern Territory	1 (100%)	3 (75%)	0	0	4 (6%)
Total	67 (71%)	68 (53%)	34 (71%)	96 (25%)	265 (40%)

Table 2. Number and percentage of state category for online consultation

	Metro	Regional	Fringe	Rural	Total
New South Wales	7 (21%)	4 (11%)	3 (27%)	0	14 (9%)
Victoria	3 (14%	3 (13%)	0	0	6 (8%)
Queensland	2 (67%)	4 (11%)	2 (18%)	0	8 (6%)
Western Australia	3 16%)	0	0	0	3 (2%)
South Australia	1 (7%)	0	1 (25%)	2 (4%)	4 (5%)
Tasmania	0	0	0	0	0
Northern Territory	0	0	0	0	0
Total	16 (17%)	11 (9%)	6 (13%)	2 (1%)	35 (5%)

- Regional Towns/City or part of an urban center with population less than 1,000,000 and predominantly urban in nature
- Fringe or a developing LGA on the margin of a developed or regional urban center
- Rural incorporating the agricultural and remote LGAs

The metropolitan and fringe municipalities accounted for the highest proportion of municipalities that have feedback mechanisms online (see Table 1). The size of metropolitan and fringe local governments and their proximity to better e-resources makes it easier for them to produce more sophisticated sites. However, even though the proportion was only 25%, the actual number of rural municipalities that had some form of online feedback mechanism was much higher than that of the metropolitan and fringe councils. Victoria's rural category had a high proportion at 70%, although with fewer and larger rural councils this is to be expected (Barlow, Chen, Chimonyo, Lyon & O'Loughlin, 2004). While the proportions in New South Wales and Western Australia were relatively low, the actual number was reasonably high, considering the size and technical difficulties of electronic delivery in those states.

Beyond the feedback mechanisms, there were few examples of councils (5%) supplying specific online facilities for comments on policy or planning proposals (see Table 2). While proposals for policy and planning changes were often posted on Web sites, the method of relaying comments was either by post or e-mail. Directions on these types of Web sites never included the use of the online feedback forms, even if they existed. To that extent any feedback loop took place outside of the Internet.

However, there were some quite advanced examples of online consultation and participation. The Perth Council's *City Interactive* site offers a range of functions that include online consultation and participation. The Melbourne City Council Web site contains a "have your say" section on its home page that includes three parts: consultation, feedback, and ideas. The consultation section gives residents the chance to read the documentation online, as well as supply online comments via Web communication. It also helps to target responses to specific policy issues rather than being lost in the more general feedback mechanisms.

Some municipalities attempt to involve people in dialogue about policy issues. The Bayside Municipality in Victoria includes an online form that gives residents the opportunity to request "to be heard" at committee meetings of the Council. While the actual presentation is not online, the fact that the council has an easy to complete online form gives residents a chance to have their opinions heard. There is also evidence that some Councils use Web sites to gather support for submissions to other levels of government. The Sutherland Shire in New South Wales has a permanent section on its site entitled "online surveys and petitions". When the site was accessed in October 2005, there was a petition seeking support against a desalinization plant in its region. These types of petitions are rare on local council sites at present, but they do extend the reach of local council engagement with their residents.

There were very few councils that took the further step of supplying a more participative model of e-governance where discussion forums could be both horizontal and well as vertical in nature. Besides large urban municipalities like Leichhardt Municipal Council in New South Wales and Brisbane City Council, there were also smaller municipalities like the Chapman Valley Shire located north of Geraldton in Western Australia. The Brisbane and Leichhardt examples are instructive in that the dialogue is monitored with feedback from the council about the issues raised. Brisbane also has a community reference panel made up of Brisbane residents who receive information on local issues and have a say about important decisions affecting the city. Currently there are more than 7,000 members in the "*Your City, Your Say*" community reference panel.

LOCAL GOVERNMENT IN THE DIGITAL AGE

Local government has followed the general trend of e-government by establishing Internet sites that offer a means of doing more of its business online through services such as paying rates, licenses, and charges or offering tender specifications, as well as communicating to the world at large the benefits of business investment in the municipality. Most local governments in Australia now have at minimum an Internet presence, but the extent to which local government has developed its capacity for moving to more consultative and participatory models of e-governance is not as certain. The tension between what some term the "local democracy model" and the "structural efficiency model" (May, 2003) will spill over into the direction that local governments will take in the development as well as, most importantly, the use of their Web sites.

To begin with, local governments in rural and remote areas face a "digital divide". While access to broadband is becoming more widespread across Australia, there are large areas that are still limited to dial up facilities (Rural Industries Research and Development Corporation, 2004). However, the digital divide is not restricted to access to the technical infrastructure but also to the social infrastructure that supports ICT (Rooksby, Weckert & Lucas, 2002). This includes sociodemographic factors such as income, gender, race, ethnicity, education, age, and location, as well as the availability of ICT support services. Furthermore, there are other local issues that are significant barriers to the expansion of e-democracy in local government. First, language and literacy are two interdependent issues in terms of the present communication channels to local government. Learning to participate in chat rooms, file sharing, and peer to peer networking not only involve language proficiency, but also the confidence to want to be included (Barry, 2002). At present some local government Web sites include languages other than English, but none provide the capacity for nonEnglish participatory mechanisms (Geiselhart et al., 2003). Second, education and training for engaging with local issues on the Web are fundamental for participation. In framing the way policy and planning issues appear on the Web, local officials will need to be aware to make the content readily accessible but also to motivate "underserved groups" to want to participate (Kretchmer & Carveth, 2001). Third, there is the issue of access for other disadvantaged groups, whether that is through disability or location.

Federal and state governments have provided a good deal of the infrastructure costs over recent years for ICT development, especially through the "Networking the Nation" program. However, like other government infrastructure programs, there is an initial outlay for the costs of development but then the ongoing maintenance is left to local government. Accordingly, ICT is not a high priority in many local governments, especially when there is significant "cost shifting" from other levels of government which the ALGA estimated could be between $500 million and $1.1 billion per annum (House of Representatives Standing Committee on Economics Finance and Public Administration, 2003, p. 29). Whether the cost shifting is purely in dollar terms, through the imposition of new service, or through costly compliance activity, local governments have become more cash strapped and thus looking to fund their basic requirements.

The ability of local governments to generate more local income is also thwarted by state government compliance requirements. For example, in NSW rate-capping severely limits the capacity of local government to raise local revenues (House of Representatives Standing Committee on Economics Finance and Public Administration, 2003). In this environment, the marked differences in the uses of ICT in the local government system across Australia are not unexpected. The size of local governments that range from approximately 900,000 to around 160 indicates the differences in the economies of scale and thus the ability to supply and maintain an appropriate ICT system. As it stands, local Government investment in electronic technology falls within a range of 1 to 3% of its own revenues (Australian Local Government Association, 2004).

There are also issues of on-going ICT support in some areas such as access to qualified professionals. As the Mayor of Barraba Shire Council in rural NSW stated:

In the rural areas ... you have great difficulty in attracting quality people to apply for positions, whether they are in police, health, education or any professional service, such as banking. It is not just in government areas, it is also in private enterprise. It is the professional services. ... So the responsibility of meeting the community expectation to attract those people there falls back on local government. ... Local government are then forced to spend their rate dollars on providing housing, incentives, rent subsidies or some other form of attraction. (House of Representatives Standing Committee on Economics Finance and Public Administration, 2003, p. 8)

This poses a major problem for rural and remote areas in supporting and maintaining ICT services, especially if there are significant demands upon local revenues to supply basic infrastructure services like roads. In such a climate a "local democracy model" that is more akin to a collaborative and a participatory approach to e-governance is likely to be subordinate to a "structural efficiency model" that focuses on a more managerial approach. The structure of the majority of local council Web sites indicates the dominance of a managerial mentality. The flow of communication is more often than not in one direction: from the council to their residents. Furthermore, in most sites the major interactivity between a council and its constituents is through the available rates and charges mechanisms. Consultative models are available through feedback mechanisms on a small minority of sites, but participation in the form of some online dialogue is very rare. Overall, it is fair to say that e-government at local level is dominated by a managerial model.

CONCLUSION

While it is apparent that local government in Australia has made some significant advances in its use of ICT in recent years, the results are far from uniform. Nearly all local governments have a Web site with basic information about the local area, minutes of council meetings, some access to public documents, and minimum contact details. A few others have developed interactive capacities that give citizens access to online payment of rates and charges or the ability to download forms. The "managerial model" is consistent with local government's role as a service provider. There are also a sizeable number of municipalities that give citizens some form of feedback mechanism, thus relaying their concerns directly to the local council. This is a weak form of the "consultative model", where citizens engage directly with local government through expression of their complaints, compliments, suggestions, comments, or "customer requests". Finally, there are a few local governments that allow their citizens to engage in conversations across and between other citizens, as well as with the local council itself. Such engagement emulates a participative model of horizontal and multidirectional interactivity.

The next phase in the development of e-government at local level will be a test of whether local governments continue to develop their Web sites towards more participatory models of e-governance. To retain Web sites merely as places where local governments can develop their commercial and in-house functions would be to miss an opportunity to increase the participation of their residents in a broader and more inclusive fashion. If local government claims to be the government nearest to the community it would be appropriate that it be the leader in the development of more participatory models of e-governance.

ACKNOWLEDGMENT

The author would like to thank Jenny Dennis for her tireless research assistance in the production of this article.

REFERENCES

Aulich, C. (1997). Competition in local government. In B. Dollery & N. Marshall (Eds.), *Australian local government*. Melbourne, Australia: McMillan.

Australian Local Government Association. (2004). *A directional roadmap for the use of electronic technology by councils*. Deakin, ACT: Australian Local Government Association.

Baker, G. (2003). Management reform in local government. In B. Dollery, N. Marshall & A. Worthington (Eds.), *Reshaping Australian local government: Finance, governance and reform*. Sydney, Australia: UNSW Press.

Barlow, S., Chen, P., Chimonyo, J., Lyon, A., & O'Loughlin, B. (2004). *E-Governance practice and potential in the local government sector*. Paper presented at the Australian Electronic Governance Conference, Center for Public Policy, Melbourne University. Retrieved May 28, 2007, from http://www.public-policy.unimelb.edu.au/egovernance/ConferenceContent.html#nancyotis

Barney, D. (2000). *Prometheus wired: The hope for democracy in the age of network technology*. Chicago: University of Chicago Press.

Barry, B. (2002). Social exclusion, social isolation, and the distribution of income. In J. Hills, J. Le Grand & D. Piachaud (Eds.), *Understanding social exclusion*. Oxford: Oxford University Press.

Bell, P. (2003). *Online transformation for council's business* [News Release]. Retrieved May 28, 2007, from http://www.lgaq.asn.au/portal/dt

Burdess, N., & O'Toole, K. (2004). Elections and representation in local government: A Victorian case study. *Australian Journal of Public Administration, 63*(2), 66-78.

Chadwick, A., & May, C. (2003). Interaction between states and citizens in the age of the Internet:

E-government in the United States, Britain, and the European Union. *Governance: An International Journal of Policy Administration and Institutions, 16*(2), 271-300.

Coe, A., Paquet, G., & Roy, J. (2001). E-governance and smart communities. *Social Science Computer Review, 19*(1), 80-93.

Crabtree, J. (2001). Whatever happened to the e-lection: A survey of voter attitudes towards new technology during the 2001 election. *iSociety*. Retrieved May 28, 2007, from http://www.egov.vic.gov.au/pdfs/electiondesigned1.pdf.

Curtain, G., Sommer, M., & Vis-Sommer, V. (Eds). (2003). *The world of e-government.* New York: The Haworth Press.

d'Auray, M. (2003). The dual challenge of integration and inclusion: Canada's experience with government online. In G. Curtain, M. Sommer & V. Vis-Sommer (Eds.), *The world of e-government.* New York: The Haworth Press.

Department of Transport and Regional Services. (2005). *Local government national report.* Canberra, Australia: Department of Transport and Regional Services.

Dollery, B., Marshall, N., & Worthington, A. (2003). Introduction. In B. Dollery, N. Marshall & A. Worthington (Eds.), *Reshaping Australian local government: Finance, governance and reform.* Sydney, Australia: UNSW Press.

Farkus, L. (2004). *Services and metadata on local government Web sites.* Canberra, Australia: Australian Local Government Association.

Geiselhart, K., Griffiths, M., & Fitzgerald, B. (2003). What lies beyond service delivery - An Australian perspective. In G. Curtain, M. Sommer & V. Vis-Sommer (Eds.), *The world of e-government.* New York: The Haworth Press.

Griffiths, M. (2002). *Forming audiences for e-democracy: Government policies, portals and pilots - And citizen literacies.* Paper presented at the 2nd European Conference on e-Government, St. Catherine's College, Oxford.

House of Representatives Standing Committee on Economics Finance and Public Administration. (2003). *Rates and taxes: A fair share for responsible local government.* Canberra, Australia: Commonwealth Government.

Kiss, R. (2003). Reasserting local democracy. In B. Dollery, N. Marshall & A. Worthington (Eds.), *Reshaping Australian local government: Finance, governance and reform.* Sydney, Australia: UNSW Press.

Koerbin, A., & Standish, C. (2004). E-*participation: TAS2000/141 interactions and transactions project.* Hobart: Local Government Association of Tasmania.

Kretchmer, S., & Carveth, R. (2001, September). The color of the net: African Americans, race and cyberspace. *Computers and Society, 9,* 14.

Lim, M. (2002). Cyber-civic space in Indonesia: From panopticon to pandemonium? *International Development Planning Review, 24*(4), 383-400.

Local Government Association of Tasmania. (2002). *LOGONS: Interactions and transactions.* Hobart: Local Government Association of Tasmania.

Macdonald, I. (2001). *Local government receives massive networking the nation funding* [Media Release]. Department for Regional Services, Territories and Local Government. Retrieved May 28, 2007, from http://www.ministers.dotars.gov.au/im/ releases/2001/july/m197_2001.htm

Marche, S., & McNiven, J.D. (2003). E-government and e-governance: The future isn't what it used to be. *Canadian Journal of Administrative Sciences, 20*(1), 74-86.

May, P. (2003). Amalgamation and virtual local government. In B. Dollery, N. Marshall & A.

Worthington (Eds.), *Reshaping Australian local government: Finance, governance and reform*. Sydney, Australia: UNSW Press.

Moore, R. (1999). Democracy and cyberspace. In B. Hague & B. Loader (Eds.), *Digital democracy: Discourse and decision making in the information age*. London: Routledge.

Norris, P. (2001). *Digital divide: Civic engagement, information poverty and the Internet worldwide*. Cambridge: Cambridge University Press.

Rennie, G., & Hartley, J. (2004). *Show-business for ugly people? Media politics and e-democracy.* Paper presented at the Australian Electronic Governance Conference Center for Public Policy, Melbourne University. Retrieved May 28, 2007, from http://www.public-policy.unimelb.edu.au/egovernance/ ConferenceContent. html#nancyotis.

Rooksby, E., Weckert, J., & Lucas, R. (2002). The rural digital divide. *Rural Society, 12*(3), 197-209.

Rural Industries Research and Development Corporation. (2004). *Broadband adoption by agriculture and local government councils: Australia and the USA*. Barton, ACT: Rural Industries Research and Development Corporation.

South Australian Local Government Association [SALGA]. (2004). *Building your Web site*. Retrieved May 28, 2007, from http://www.lga.sa.gov.au/webdata/resources/Files/ Build_A_Building_Your_Website_pdf1.pdf

Symonds, M. (2000, June 24). Government and the Internet - The next revolution. *The Economist, 355*(8176), 3-9.

This work was previously published in International Journal of Electronic Government Research, Vol. 3, Issue 4, edited by Mehdi Khosrow-Pour, pp. 58-83, copyright 2007 by IGI Publishing, formerly known as Idea Group Publishing (an imprint of IGI Global).

Chapter 4.31
Horizontal Process Integration in E-Government: The Perspective of a UK Local Authority

Jyoti Choudrie
University of Hertfordshire, UK

Vishanth Weerrakody
Brunel University, UK

ABSTRACT

This article examines how horizontal integration between the various departments of a local authority in the United Kingdom (UK) occurs. Following that the aim of this article is to extract the "success factors" in government intervention that support horizontal and vertical integration based on the strategies pursued in the UK in order to render favourable results if applied elsewhere. The research methodology consisted of an in-depth case study that used the research tools of interviews and referring to archival documents. This research is timely as the maturity of e-government increases the issues of integrating processes and systems across various government departments becomes pertinent. The conclusion and lessons that can be learnt from this research is that e-government integration on a horizontal level obtains significant efficiency and effectiveness as more and more public services are being centralized.

INTRODUCTION

Due to the advent of the Internet, business opportunities involving information and communication technologies (ICTs) have multiplied, persuading not only commercial enterprises, but also governments around the globe to invest profoundly into e-services. However, now the potential of a clear link between the use of ICTs and economic growth has become apparent, thereby urging numerous organisations and governments to invest profoundly into it (OECD, 2002). The e-services offered by governments are aimed at relaying information and public services to citizens over the Internet and is referred to in general as "e-government." E-government encompasses a broad spectrum of activities that are offered using ICTs and allows an improved service of the government to citizens (Northrup & Thorson, 2003). There are many varying definitions of e-government, but for the purposes of this paper, the following definition is offered. *E-government is an electronic technology that has the ability to transform relations within general government and between government bodies, citizens and businesses to better deliver its services and ultimately improve efficiency (World Bank, 2005).*

According to Lee, Tan, and Trimi (2005), various countries adopting the e-government initiative are at different levels of development, and to date very few governments have initiated the collaboration of government agencies across horizontal and vertical levels. With reference to the United Kingdom (UK), which is the backdrop of this research, in 1997 the Prime Minister announced that a quarter of all government services in the UK will be electronically delivered within five years (Phythian & Taylor, 2001). However, by the end of 2005 the deadline for providing 100% of the government services online had to be extended as most local authorities failed to meet the cut-off date; thereby causing the deadline to be extended to 2008 (www.computing.co.uk). It has been recognized as pertinent to offer services according to users' needs, as this enhances cooperation among agencies, which is categorically required in order to provide central services and present an enhanced user experience for citizens using the services (Traunmuller, 2004). Furthermore, Jaeger (2002) argues that e-government will need to promote horizontal and vertical integration of the various governmental branches in order to satisfy the citizens' need for a 24 hours and 7 days service.

Bearing in mind the importance of providing online public sector services, generally governments across the globe are considering ways of amalgamating back office systems, horizontally integrating Web applications across government agencies, and vertically combining levels in order to provide portals, seamless services, and information delivery to citizens more efficiently and effectively (Varshney, 2005). It has also been found that there is no local UK government Web site that can offer users the sophisticated functionalities and interactions associated with online private sector equivalents, such as banks and supermarket Web sites (www.computing.co.uk). Furthermore, many governmental agencies are affording only basic online services such as downloadable forms and transactions; whereas horizontal integration grants real-time systems offering a one-stop-shop for all e-services (Layne & Lee, 2001). Consequently, according to Norris and Moon (2005), very few governments offer much in the way of two- way transactional e-government or provide horizontal e-government integration.

In this article we undertake an examination of the horizontal integration among the various departments of a local authority that occurs in order to deliver e-services to the citizens in a particular vicinity. Therefore, the research question guiding this paper is: What can be learnt about the achievement of horizontal integration among local authorities in the e-government context in order to better deliver e-services to citizens? In line with that, the aim of this paper is to extract the "success factors" in government intervention that support horizontal and vertical integration based on the strategies pursued in the UK in order to render favourable results if applied elsewhere.

This research is timely since currently governments around the globe are becoming technically savvy and the issues of integrating various and diverse departments are becoming important. Subsequently, we intend to examine the possibilities of generalizing our findings to other geographical and/or cultural settings. We believe that our analysis will be useful to policy makers seeking to promote the use of online products and services to communities in a country in an equitable manner. Researchers in the area of process changes can also benefit by obtaining insights into the application of ICT policies at local levels.

Having offered an overview of the main issues regarding this paper the next section offers a literature review of the theory surrounding the framework and e-government and e-governance. Thereafter, a description and explanation of the research methodology is provided. Thereafter, the findings and analysis followed by a conclusion to the paper are provided.

STAGES OF GROWTH AND E-GOVERNMENT

When considering the e-government growth models there are several within the information systems (IS) literature, but in this section a brief description of some of them is provided and a reasoning for utilizing the main model of Layne and Lee is offered.

The development of information technology (IT) within organizations has been studied extensively in organizational research and IS literature, where it has been found that it can occur in a number of phases or stages (Janssen & Veenstra, 2005). Some of the more prominent growth models include Grover and Segars (2005), Layne and Lee (2001), Chandler and Emanuels (2002), UN (2002), Deloitte Research (2000), and Nolan (1979). Nolan (1979) was amongst the foremost to emphasize and publicise the stages of growth model by accentuating the intuitive appeal of the model. The stage model aims to deconstruct IS development into a series of stages, and development occurs from one stage to another. However, a drawback of the stage model is that it does not focus upon change management and organizational development strategies. This disadvantage implies that stage models should not be employed on their own but with a carefully selected change management strategy. This is because change management strategies require the addressing of various types of business management issues, such as the creation of a shared vision, dealing with resistance to change, obtaining political support, intervention strategies, or team building skills (Bruijn, ten Heuvelhof, & int Veld, 2002). However, in the e-government area many academics and researchers have proposed stages of e-government development. According to Siau and Long (2005) research conducted on existing e-government stage models, comparisons between models helped to develop a new e-government stage model with five stages: Web presence, interaction, transaction, transformation, and e-democracy. Therefore, the growth stage models of Gibson and Nolan (1974), the revised model of Nolan (1979) and Layne and Lee (2001) have been identified to be most appropriate for studying the changes. Gibson and Nolan (1974) and Nolan

Figure 1. Dimensions and stages of e-government development (Adapted from Layne & Lee, 2001)

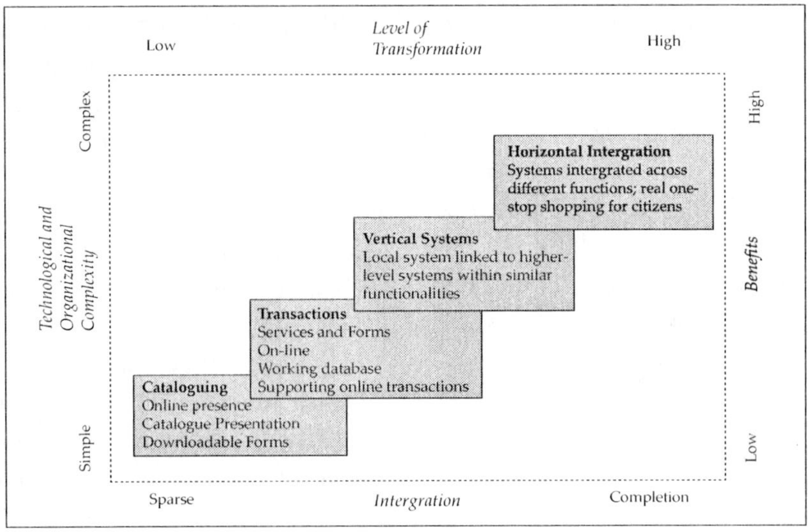

(1979) also describe stages of growth but offer much more detail, for instance, an investigation into initiation, formalization, and control, which is further broken into dimensions: (a) computer applications, (b) IT expert specialization, and (c) formal management and organization (Gibson & Nolan, 1974). The e-government area is still in the growth stages and is much more generic and does not follow a temporal continuum, thereby limiting the application of Gibson and Nolan (1974) and Nolan (1979) frameworks. Layne and Lee's model (2001) offers some similarities and synergies to Gibson and Nolan's (1974) models and Gibson's (1979) model by distinguishing the degree of development; however, the difference lies in the model not representing a temporal continuum, where one stage follows the other (Scholl, 2005). For the purpose of this paper and for the cited reasons the researchers selected the four-stage (cataloguing, transactions-based, vertical integration and horizontal integration) growth model by Layne and Lee (2001).

The four stage model above offers a way to map the evolution, maturity, and sophistication of e-government services both in terms of the organization and technical aspects. Furthermore, as illustrated in Figure 1 it outlines the multi-perspective transformation needed within government structures and functions for the exploitation of a one stop e-government Web portal.

The aforementioned discussion has offered the justifications for employing the four-stage growth model, which is the main framework of this research. However, the implementation of e-government impinges upon the information and communication technologies (ICTs) sector. Therefore, the next section describes the problems existent within the public sector and why and how ICTs could and may afford a solution.

Addressing Information and Communication Problems in the Public Sector

There are also many instances where information is clearly not available locally (within the organisation) to execute processes and service specific customer demands (Saxena & Wadhwa, 2003). This further complicates the process, as the required information may now need to be obtained from an external source outside the organisational boundaries of local government/councils (ibid). As in e-business, access to this information is also needed at a rapid speed in e-government, and thus demands instant communication and integration between processes and information systems in different agencies (ibid). This information communication and access process is illustrated in Figure 2 (which is a modification of the work by Saxena & Wadhwa, 2003).

As indicated in Figure 2, when a citizen requests information from a central government or local authority (council) Web portal, this information may always not be available within their respective internal systems. In this case, the internal systems of the respective government agency will need to request and interact with other organizations' (i.e., local government agencies, central government, local businesses, etc.) information systems to extract the required information to service the citizen's need. As mentioned before this demands the interaction between processes and IS/IT systems at both internal and external levels and thus needs an environment where integration and interoperability between disparate ICT systems is seamless. It is fair to suggest that realising this type of environment using traditional modes of enterprise application integration (EAI) is inconceivable given the nature of the diverse hardware and software systems that span government IT infrastructures (as in Figure 2). Given this context, the emerging concept of Web services cannot be ignored.

Figure 2. Information and communication infrastructure in e-government source (Adapted from Saxena & Wadhwa, 2003, p. 130)

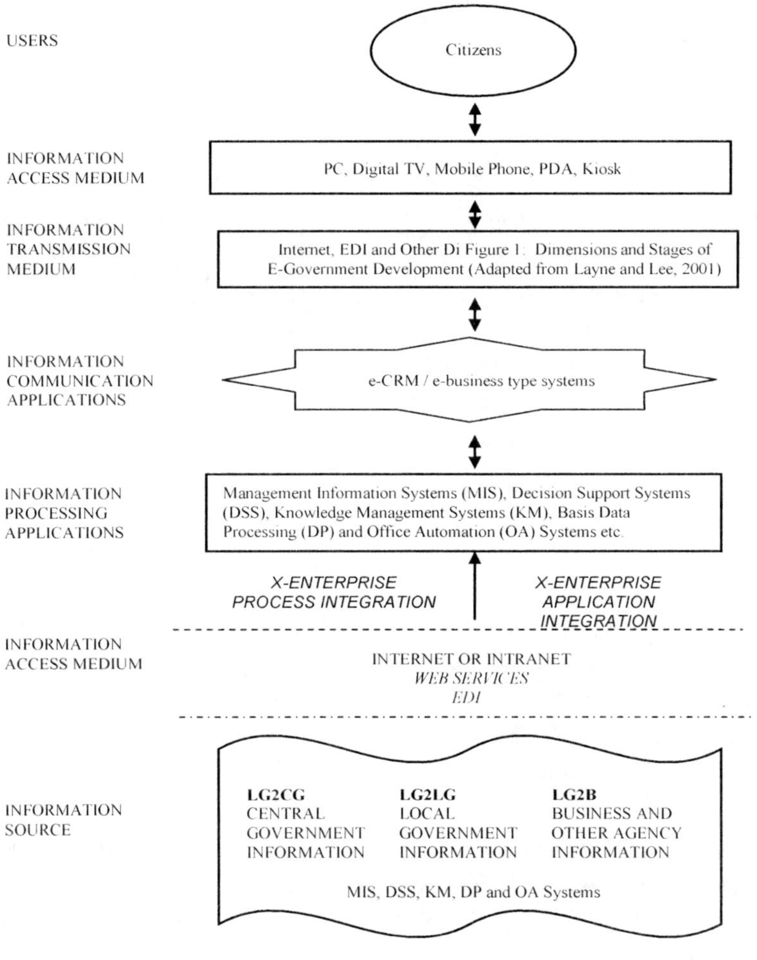

Web services breakdown applications into reusable components or services and enable the linking of these services within and across the enterprise using standards based on extensible mark up language (XML) (Fustes, 2003). It uses three XML-based standards: SOAP (simple object access protocol) for transmitting XML-encoded data and remotely accessing services in a platform independent way; UDDI (universal description and discovery language) for registering and discovering services; and WSDL (Web services description language) to provide an XML grammar for describing available Web services (Monson-Haefel, 2004). In comparison to the most common traditional EAI method, electronic data interchange (EDI), XML is specifically designed to use the Internet as the data transfer mechanism whereby business documents and services can be freely exchanged electronically, whereas the latter needs point-to-point connection between each participating system (Thompson, 2002).

Web services help EAI by providing the tools needed to manage end-to-end extended processes independently of the execution platform (Masood, 2002; Monson-Haefel, 2004). This is enabled through the use of SOAs, where, when the business needs to automate a business function or process, it merely plugs into a service like logging onto a Web site irrespective of whether this may be an internal application, or an external application that may be accessed over the Internet (Lawrence, 2004). Already organisations in the US such as DaimlerChrysler (Information Age, 2004b) and Jersey Post (Information Age, 2004b) and UK supermarket chains Sainsbury's (Information Age, 2004a) and Tesco's (Mclever, 2002) have used the Web services-SOA model to integrate their supply chains. Given this context, it is fair to suggest that government can draw from these successful cases of supply chain integration in their efforts to implement e-government.

In the context of e-government, as shown in Figure 2, an SOA/Web services environment could potentially replace EDI, Intranets, e-mails, and other forms of communication used to exchange information among government agencies. Also, XML can provide the common bridge between the various backend MIS, DSS, KM, DP, OA, as well as front-end CRM, ERP, and e-business type systems. In relation to Figure 1 (Layne and Lee's 2001 e-government development model), Figure 2 then illustrates some of the essential ICT concepts that need to work in synchrony to move from basic information delivery to vertical and horizontally integrated e-government services.

Having offered a theoretical overview of the main issues impinging upon this research, the next section describes and details the research methodology that was utilized for this research.

RESEARCH METHODOLOGY

Before stating the data collection a brief description of the local authority, the main context of this research, is offered. This will allow readers to obtain an understanding of the setting of this research.

Describing Council X

Case studies are viewed to fulfill three roles in research, exploratory, explanatory, or descriptive, depending upon the purpose (Yin, 1984). In the case of this research, a case study was considered to offer all three aspects as the case allowed us to explore the impacts of a process change. Then it allowed us to explain the changes that were obtained as a result of online products and services and finally, the findings following this section describe the undertaken changes. For the purposes of this research and to ensure that our pledge to the research organization was kept, anonymity of the case study had to be ensured and for this purpose we refer to our case study as Council X. Council X is an outer-London borough that is the second largest borough in the London region. The Council is currently home to 248,000 residents, which are vastly ranging in cultures and nationalities (Council Report, 2005). From the archival documentation and references from the Internet the following information regarding Council X was obtained. Council X was formed in 1965 and is London's second largest unitary borough covering 42 square miles. It covers the north-west corner of the former county of Middlesex and is the westernmost London borough. The borough also includes Heathrow airport and Northolt aerodrome. From the Census 2001 statistics it was found that of the resident population, 48% were male and 52% female. The average age of the population was 36.9 years in comparison to 38.6 years in England and Wales (Census, 2001).

Data Collection

As this research examined process changes, it was necessary to determine the reaction and opinions of various individuals. For this it was pertinent to collect data that focused upon words, and thus the data collection was a qualitative research approach (Miles & Huberman, 1994). The data was collected using face-to-face interviews with the main stakeholders involved in the process of the abandonment of motor vehicles at Council X during the period November 2005 to February 2006. According to Hellingsworth et al. (2001) it is necessary to conduct interviews with

Table 1. Snapshot of questions used for the data collection

	Questions for the Operations Development Manager
1.	What role does the customer contact centre provide to citizens?
2.	What is the procedure for a citizen to report an abandoned vehicle?
3.	What information do you require from the citizen to make a report of an abandoned vehicle?
	Questions for the Parking Services Support Manager
1.	What role does the abandonment of vehicles section provide to the overall service of removing abandoned vehicles?
2.	What is the procedure when the abandonment of vehicles section receives a report from the contact centre?
3.	What information is required for an Inspector to arrange the removal of an abandoned vehicle?

several members of the organisation as a comprehensive picture of requirements is gathered. The interviews (total of 10 were open-ended and contained semi-structured questions, as this allowed flexibility with the responses and allowed the researchers to probe further into matters related to e-government. As seen in Table 1 the questions do not require responses that are short and detailed. Rather they can allow the researcher to probe into the questions and yet not establish too stringent a boundary.

Before interviewing began, the participants were e-mailed with the interview questions so that the participants could familiarize themselves with the questions, and also to arrange a suitable date and time convenient for the participants (Smith, 2004). Furthermore, the participants were given a consent form regarding ethical considerations and their rights to withdraw from the study anytime without any prior notice or explanation. The interviews lasted approximately 30 to 45 minutes, and were undertaken in a meeting room of the council buildings. This allowed the researchers and respondents to build the necessary rapport and privacy for the required questions. The interviews were audio recorded with the consent of participants as this allowed an easier analysis of the information and allowed the participants to be quoted when writing the results of the research (Crane, 2005). Further, to validate and verify that the results were true and accurate, transcripts of the interviews were sent back to the respondents. This was done using the postal service and e-mail. The information was then transcribed onto a document and later analysed using coding and mainly, themes. That is, a thematic analysis process was utilized. This involved a process that involved encoding the qualitative information in order to identify a particular theme with the information; that is, if some sort of pattern is identified within the information that may have some relevance to the area of research (Boyatzis, 1998).

These explanations of the data collection and analysis are crucial, not only for this research, but for any research. The key findings obtained from the data collection phase are discussed in the next section.

THE NEED FOR PROCESS IMPROVEMENT AND INTEGRATION IN LOCAL GOVERNMENT: A CASE STUDY AT COUNCIL X

In section two a literature review identified numerous challenges that governments may face when e-enabling public sector processes. In this section we explore the impact of these issues in real life. Consequently, we examine the execution of a key public service process and related process management and integration issues in one of the largest local councils in the UK (identified as X).

Figure 3. Data flow diagram for abandonment of vehicles

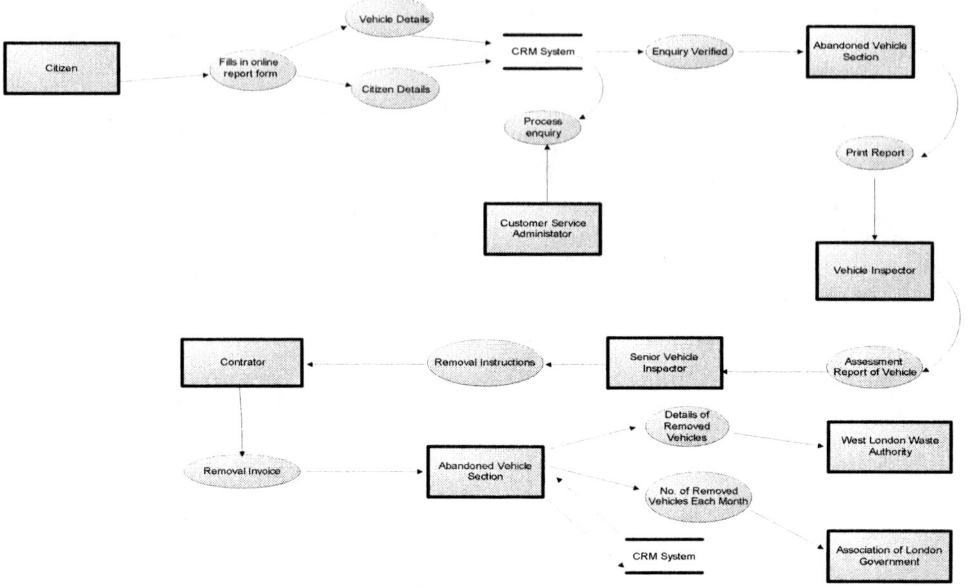

Since the aim of this research was to explore process management and integration aspects in local government, as said above, the researchers chose to focus on a key service provided by the council, the abandonment of motor vehicles. Given this context, interviews were conducted primarily at Council X's abandoned vehicles division (AMD). These interviews identified a scenario where lack of harmonisation and integration between business processes and underlying IS/IT systems has resulted in inefficient and ineffective process execution and service delivery in local government (LG). Based upon the information gathered from interviewing the service area participants from the abandoned vehicles division, the data flow diagram below illustrates the overall procedures of the entire service of reporting and removing abandoned vehicles.

The AMV process operates in the following manner: The citizen needs to report to the local authority the abandoned vehicle using telephone, fax, e-mail, or an online report form. The enquiry is sent to the central CRM (customer relationship management) system at the contact centre. The citizen's enquiry is automatically logged onto the system and a CSA (customer service administrator) is alerted about the enquiry via an e-mail system. Thereafter, the CSA determines whether the provided information by the citizen is accurate and correct by checking the system to see if the vehicle has been reported prior to the enquiry. If the vehicle is established as taxed, then the process must end. However, if the vehicle is untaxed then the enquiry is processed and marked onto the CRM system. The information is then sent to the abandoned vehicle section that has the responsibility to print out details of the enquiry and give it to an inspector. The inspector then must make a visit to the location and assess the condition of the vehicle and document the assessment. If the vehicle is taxed and does not look abandoned then the council cannot remove the vehicle and the process ends. However, if the vehicle is determined abandoned then the inspector will affix a message onto the vehicle stating that the council is aware of the vehicle. If the vehicle still remains after two days then the inspector revisits the vehicle and once again affixes a notice stating that the vehicle will be removed in 24 hours. Once the assessment report has been completed it is given to the senior vehicle inspector, who has the final decision to remove the vehicle. If the senior inspector decides to remove the vehicle then a legal document to remove the vehicle is sent through to the contractor. The contractor is responsible for the actual removal and disposal of the vehicle. The removal instructions are physically delivered to the contractor. Once the vehicle has been removed all the details are logged onto the CRM system and also statistical information is distributed to the West London Waste Authority and the Association of London Government.

The scenario above clearly contradicts Council X's vision for improved services in the context of e-government and highlights a number of process management problems in a key public service process. The key problems lie in delays caused when retrieving and exchanging information between different internal departments as well as external entities. This is further compounded by delays that occur when physically delivering or handing over documentation from one employee (vehicle inspector) to another (senior inspector) as well as when information and documents are passed to the external contractors.

Levels of Process and Systems Integration Required at Council X for Improved Service Delivery

Given the above context, moving from cataloguing to the horizontal integration stage in the e-government service delivery structure as outlined in the second section (see Figure 1: Layne & Lee, 2001) will require cross-functional as well as cross-organisational redesign of business processes and supporting software applications (Champy, 2002) in government institutions, at both local and national levels. Given the communication and information exchange problems at Council X, the primary focus therefore needs to be the integration and improved communication between internal as well as external processes and IT systems. Figure 4 maps the various problems encountered at Council X against Layne and Lee's (2001) framework for e-government development (see Figure 1) and the information processing and communication infrastructure model of (Saxena & Wadhwa, 2003) (see Figure 2). It is fair to suggest that this diagram outlines the kind of challenges that not only Council X, but many other local government

Figure 4. The levels of systems integration necessary to facilitate better LG services

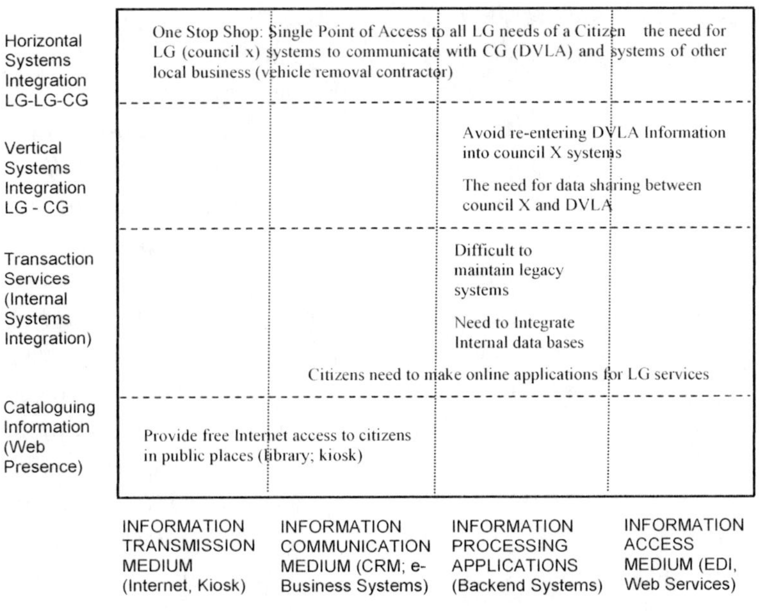

agencies will face when implementing e-government services. Figure 4 also illustrates the link between the various information systems and the level of integration required among these systems to overcome the challenges faced by local councils in general in the context of delivering efficient and effective local government services to citizens. As revealed before in the previous section and outlined in Figure 4 below, the main challenges that Council X faces revolve around integration and communication problems between various systems (such as internal data bases, ERP/CRM systems, Web-based systems, etc.) at both vertical and horizontal levels.

As outlined in Figure 4 the higher levels of e-service delivery required the harmonisation and integration of business processes and supporting ICT systems between the main stakeholders. In this case, the main stakeholders are the citizens, government agencies (Department of Vehicle License Applications-DVLA), employees (vehicle inspectors, administrators, and CSA in this instance), and business partners (contractors). Champy (2002) supported the view that harmonisation and integration of the processes and supporting ICT systems between the main stakeholders is imperative. While the integration between two or more of these entities may allow governments to deliver e-services at the cataloguing stage, in order to offer fully integrated e-services, the overall integration and harmonisation of all the above elements is imperative. However, this requires a high level of enterprise application integration (EAI) and this is where emerging technologies such as Web services can offer a fast and effective solution to councils (such as X) by helping to retain many existing (functional) applications in the council. However, instead of sojourning in relative isolation from each other, they can be integrated to create new services that are more attuned to the needs of the citizens.

At this point, it can be noted that the above description outlines the problems that are inherent within the existing process and systems. However, as mentioned before we propose a Web-based system portal (at a conceptual level) to overcome these issues and the following section details this.

A Proposal for Process Change and Integration Using a Web Portal

Currently, the business processes and supporting systems that make up the abandonment of motor vehicles (AMV) service were operating in isolation from each other resulting in several problems, more specifically in terms of communication. For example, a citizen was not aware of the outcome of his/her enquiry and the CSA in turn was not aware of the whole cycle. However, following the interviews and observations of the current system, a description of the newly designed integrated process for abandonment of vehicles in terms of a use case is offered. The use case below (Figure 5) describes the associations between actors and what is happening in the proposed redesigned web based system for processing abandoned vehicles at Council X.

The collaboration diagram in Figure 6 demonstrates the tasks carried out by a citizen in the new redesigned AMV process and the collaboration of each object in the system in order to perform tasks. The new process begins with the citizen logging into the main security user interface. From the new system a prompt is sent to the user for the provision of a username and password so that the services can be accessed. Once the username and password are verified by the system the main menu control appears. The main menu control allows the citizen to fill out an abandoned vehicle report form and the information captured in the form will be stored in a class named AV reports. The main menu control automatically assigns the AV report with a unique ID number so that the report is classified as an individual enquiry. Once the citizen has completed the report form, then the system obtains the AV details from the AV reports class and allows the user to view the

Figure 5. Associations between actors and the redesigned Web system

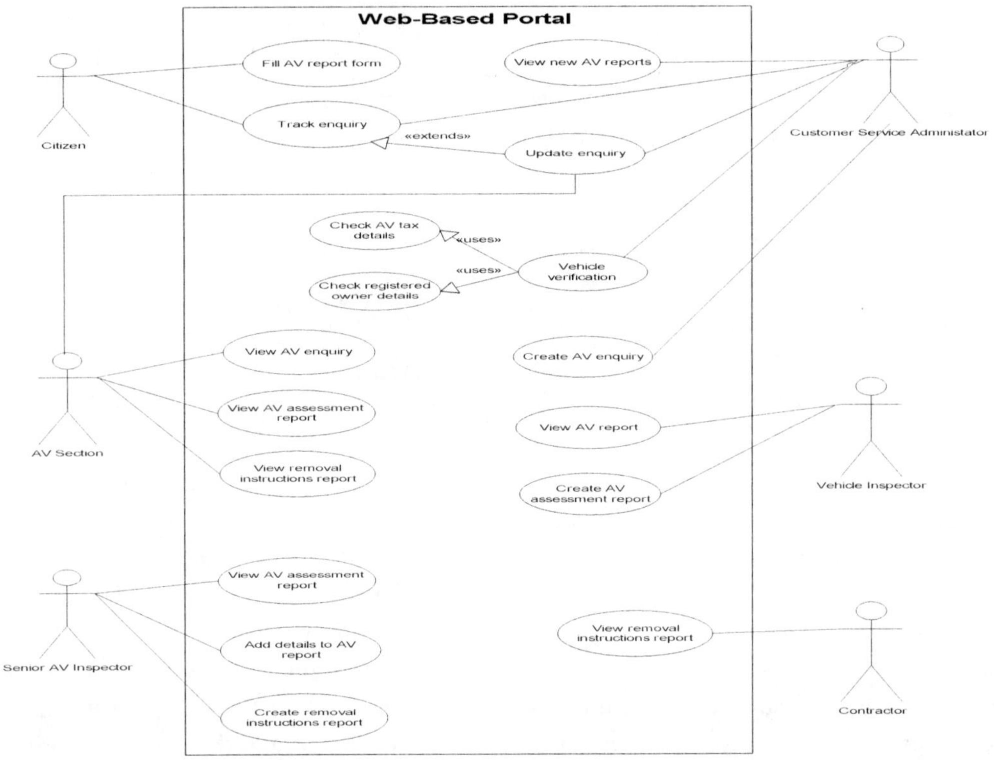

Figure 6. Collaboration diagram for citizen interaction with new Web-based portal

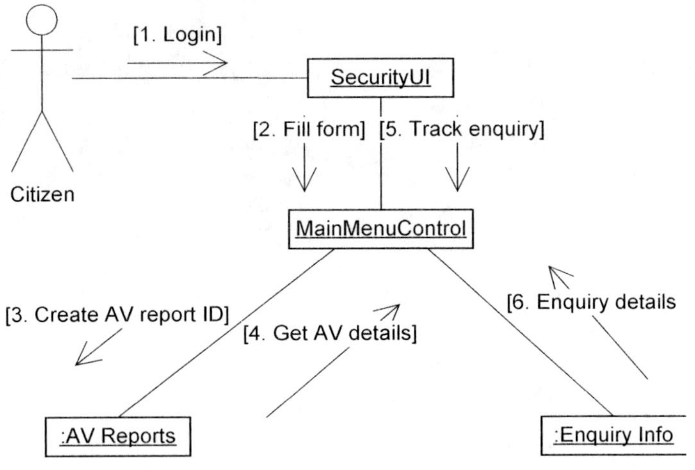

Figure 7. Collaboration diagrams for CSA interaction with the new Web-based portal

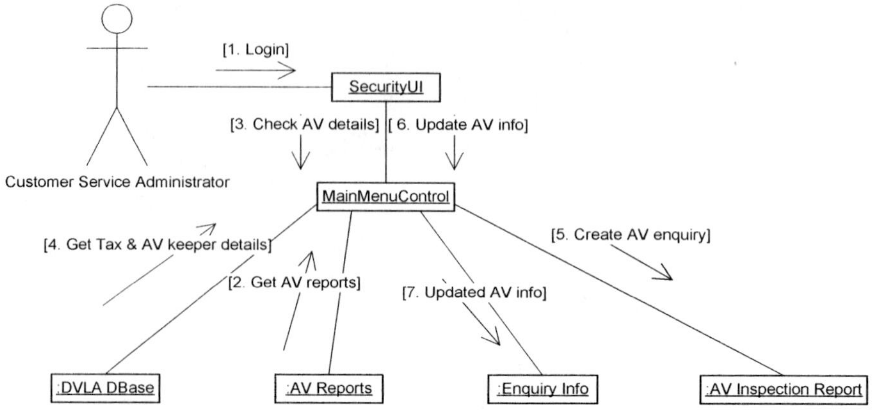

submitted report via the track enquiry facility. When the user selects the track enquiry facility from the main menu control the AV details are taken from the AV reports class and also the enquiry details are taken from the enquiry info class. The enquiry info class is updated by the customer service administrator with information regarding the progress of the investigation of the suspected abandoned vehicle.

The collaboration diagram in Figure 7 demonstrates how a customer service administrator will interact with the new system when attempting to perform tasks, in which objects in the system will need to collaborate together in order to perform those tasks. The process begins when the customer service administrator logs into a new system using a secure user interface. The secure user interface prompts the user to provide a username and password. The system then verifies the details and if the details are correct then access is granted. Once the CSA has successfully logged onto the system, the main menu control appears. At this point, the system alerts the CSA of recently received reports. Further, details of the reports are displayed to the user via the interaction of the class named AV reports. In order to verify the information from the AV report such as the vehicle tax and keeper details, the user needs to search the DVLA Database. Once the user selects the option to search the DVLA Database, the main menu control interacts with the class named DVLA DBase in order to get the TAX and AV keeper details to the CSA. Once the CSA has verified and checked the information the CSA needs to create an AV enquiry, which is stored in the class named AV inspection report. Once the CSA has sent the AV enquiry then the user is required to update the AV info, whereby details of the progress of the abandoned vehicle are presented for the viewing of the citizens.

Whilst this section has offered a practical outlook to this research, there is little known about whether this is a suitable system and also whether the issues identified in practice will be overcome by our proposed Web portal. In the next section we evaluate this further.

DISCUSSION AND ANALYSIS

As a result of the inefficiencies identified with the AMV service a new Web portal-based solution was proposed to provide a more integrated service to the citizen in the previous section. The new working model proposes to integrate the IS/IT systems of the contact centre, AV Section, DVLA and contractor horizontally with the aid of XML technology and a Web services model as proposed conceptually in Figure 2. This allows the sharing of information through one single Web-based portal.

In the new redesigned solution a number of new features have been incorporated into the design of the Web-based system for Council X. In particular, a citizen can report and also track the progress of an abandoned vehicle through one single Web-based portal. In the previous working model no such feature was available for citizens to track the progress of an enquiry electronically. Further, the Web-based portal also allows the administrators involved in the service of abandonment of vehicles to update the progress of an abandoned vehicle through the portal, which was also not possible in the previous working model. Equally, the Web-based portal provides a new feature, in which the CSAs can carry out a check on a suspected abandoned vehicle, in which tax and keeper details of the vehicle are directly viewable through the portal. However, in the existing working model Council X relied on the vehicle inspectors and citizens to physically check if the vehicle is taxed or not.

With the new portal the Abandoned Vehicle Section administrators have been offered a new horizontal process that can provide feedback to citizens regarding the abandoned vehicle at each stage of the investigation. In the current working model this feature is not available to the AV Section administrators or citizens. Vehicle inspectors are directly alerted through the portal and can also fill out an electronic assessment report form of an abandoned vehicle, which will be directly sent through to the senior vehicle inspector via the portal. The current working model offers the AV Section administrators a facility of printing out a copy of the initial report and giving it to an inspector. The inspector in turn would then physically visit the location, manually fill out an assessment report form and bring the report back for the viewing of the senior inspector. In the new system the senior inspector can view the assessment report directly through the portal and also create a removal instructions report electronically and send it through directly to the vehicle removal contractor. In contrast these features are not possible in the current process as the entire process relied on extended communication among the stakeholders involved in the process of abandonment of vehicles. With the new portal the vehicle removal contractor can also access the portal to view the instructions electronically and also print out the report. However, in the current process the AV Section administrators would physically visit the removal contractor's office to deliver the report for removal by hand. Overall, with the new system information and communication dissemination among entities involved in the service of removing abandoned vehicles at Council X was improved as the new working model demonstrates greater efficiency in delivering the service to citizens. Furthermore, duplication of information disseminated among entities is reduced in the new process model. Equally, the cycle time for removing a vehicle from the street is reduced as information is centralised and can be passed to various stakeholders a lot faster, thus the abandoned vehicle can be removed faster than the previously identified 10 working days for the current process.

Whilst the above discussion illustrates that the newly designed Web-based portal can work in theory, it was difficult to determine whether the new system does indeed satisfy the citizens' requirements. Although it was not possible to implement and test the proposed solution in practice, the system prototype was valuated using citizens. From the evaluation (summative evaluation method) it was learnt that there is greater efficiency of information flow and communication amongst the various stakeholders involved in the service of removing and reporting abandoned vehicles at Council X. As a rejoinder to this section. The observation and think-aloud protocol methods were used. Alongside the think-aloud approach a set of evaluation heuristics devised by Jakob Neilson were utilised in order to target usability problems with the interfaces (Mack & Neilson, 1993). There were eight respondents used for this purpose. This included a local authority

Table 2. Evaluation results

Result No.	Usability Problem Description
1	Two participants pointed out that the main menu tabs need to be highlighted in a different colour as they found it difficult to distinguish what Web page they were viewing. Therefore, the usability problem distinguished was related to the heuristic named visibility of system status, which will be improved in order to allow users to navigate the system more efficiently and effectively. "However, we like the way that the information is all in one place. We do not have to go to different pages or go to different desk (if we go to the offices of the council)."
2	One participant suggested that in the interface named abandoned vehicle report form (Figure 5.14) the citizen details such as name, address, and so on should automatically appear without inputting them.
3	One participant noticed that the track enquiry interface (Figure 5.15) has a button named 'E-mail Us,' which confused the participant as the user thought that there is a need to e-mail the council for some reason or another, therefore the system needs to be adjusted so that users are clearly notified with a message underneath explaining the intention of each control.
4	One participant pointed out that on the main login menu (Figure 5.13) the button named 'Logon' needs to be changed to 'Login', which relates to the heuristic named visibility of system status. Overall, both citizens found the system to be consistent and very informative for information that they required.

system's administrator, citizens (working)-3 and 4 citizens (mature students).

As an example of the problems that were inherent in the new system and some of the citizens' views of the new system, Table 2 is provided.

In terms of horizontal integration and efficiency it became evident that it is significantly a vision of efficiency and effectiveness as public services will be centralized and public agencies and businesses can share information in a seamless fashion. Stoltzfus (2004) identified that increased participation with citizens can make them feel that they have more of a voice in the policies and functions of government, are able to access information that may have once seemed inaccessible and are able to conduct business with government in a more understandable and effective manner. However, very few countries have excelled in the context of horizontal and vertical levels of integration in e-government (Weerakkody et al., 2007). Therefore, many academics and researchers have highlighted the need to collaborate and integrate IS/IT systems, processes across horizontal and vertical levels of government. According to Bekkers and Homburg, (2005) transaction level e-government services require a degree of integration and this can be achieved through vertical and horizontal integration of information systems. Furthermore, literature has distinguished that governments must utilize business process redesign initiatives in order to streamline processes and also integrate IS/IT systems using available standards such as XML and EAI techniques.

However, horizontal integration of IS/IT systems pose a number of barriers for governments and businesses trying to collaborate, such as participating organisations requiring compatible IS/IT infrastructures and standardised data definitions. Governmental agencies are surrounding by bureaucracy and red tape policies that discourage the change in governmental procedures (Weerakkody et al., 2006). Equally, organisations and people resist sharing information due to structural conflicts, managerial practices that discourage the sharing and integration of IS/IT systems. Conversely, according to Government Computing (2005) the UK public sector is looking upon making public services more efficient; many governmental agencies are considering shared services as a probable solution. However, the same article distinguished that issues regarding trust among governmental agencies and businesses are seen as a potential barrier and also smaller district councils have less funding to spend on such plans for sharing (Government Computing, 2005).

Having discussed and analyzed the results of this research in terms of theory and practice, the next section provides some conclusions and future directions to this research.

CONCLUSION

The main question driving this research was: What can be learnt about the achievement of horizontal integration among local authorities in the e-government context in order to better deliver e-services to citizens? The e-government context in this instance is the local authority; Council X. This research has demonstrated that horizontal integration between local authorities when implemented removes the perceived inefficiencies of an e-service (removal and reporting of abandoned vehicles) to the citizen. In this instance, the inefficiency existed in the entire process of removing and reporting abandoned vehicles. However, it was also learnt that the key service providers, for example the operations development manager, within the local authority did not think that there were any inefficiencies. In fact they thought the processes were efficient.

It was also learnt that due to the success of horizontal integration initiatives such as the removal and reporting of abandoned vehicles there were future plans to eventually integrate all the processes with the IS/IT systems. However, whilst integration of processes and IS/IT is important, another issue that is vital for any process change, which includes the horizontal integration of processes and systems is that the people aspect needs to be carefully considered and that is something that the e-government programme manager at Council X commented upon: "In terms of achieving a one-stop-shop service with integrated IS/IT systems, there are no problems from a technological viewpoint; however, it will require a change in people's attitude to accept technological changes."

Another aspect of horizontal integration within the e-government context that needs to be emphasized is the awareness of government policies. Although the DVLA database was integrated with the council Web-portal for this research, from a practical sense such an action cannot be undertaken as there are limitations-the DVLA discourages and prevents the sharing of information due to the Data Protection Act. However, as demonstrated in this research governmental agencies, central government and organisations need to be linked together in order to provide a one-stop-shop environment. For the success of a one-stop-shop environment each one of the parties must give up some power in order to truly reap the benefits of sharing across horizontal and vertical levels (Gupta & Jana, 2003).

In the above context, however, we can not ignore the progress made towards integrated service delivery by the UK government, where links to all 388 English local councils have now been implemented through the "direct.gov" Web portal (Government Computing, 2006). Using the address http://local.direct.gov.uk/mycouncil/ citizens can now link to access their respective local council services. However, we argue that this is merely a Web link and therefore only provides access to the same cataloguing and basic transaction level services that are already available through the local council Web sites. On the contrary, the evidence in Council X suggests that there are still a number of deeper process and systems integration issues that need to be addressed at both local and central government levels before fully integrated services are offered to citizens through a single point of access.

This research also proposed a Web-based solution incorporating process changes and better information exchange for the AMV process. Although theoretical in nature, there is no reason why such a solution cannot be implemented. In our proposed solution, due to the centralized Web site that is available for the AMV process, the local authority (Council X) can offer information to the central government departments about abandoned vehicles. This will prevent double counting or avoid cars being collected from sites. For the citizen this will ensure that residents are satisfied in the knowledge that their vicinities are being looked after and that their tax money is being utilized in an efficient and effective manner. Further, Stoltzfus (2004) identified that increased participation with citizens can make them feel that they have more of a voice in the policies and functions of government, are able to access information that may have once seemed inaccessible, and are able to conduct business with government in a more understandable and effective manner. However, a limitation that organizations, whether public or private should be aware of is that education, training, pre-preparation, and awareness is necessary when any substantial change such as this is being undertaken.

As with every research, there is always a future direction. This research focused upon only one local authority and one public sector service. Therefore, in future this research could be focused upon horizontal integration and ultimately a one-stop-shop environment on a national and even global aspect. Although some technological issues such as the application of XML were examined in this research, there are pertinent issues such as security and the impacts of the Data Protection Act that could be examined in the future. Further issues that can be explored upon such a topic are vertical levels of integration, the impacts of integration upon organizational change and the usability of the new services and portals for citizens.

ACKNOWLEDGMENT

The empirical study used in this paper was conducted by Mr. Gurjit Dhillon as part of his final year project/dissertation for the award of BSc (Honors) in computer science at the School of Information Systems, Computing and Mathematics at Brunel University. The authors wish to thank Gurjit for his contribution.

REFERENCES

Bekkers, V., & Homburg, V. (2005). *The information ecology of e-government.* Amsterdam: IOS Press.

Bruijn, H. de, Heuvelhof, E. ten, & Veld, R., int (2002). *Process management: Why project management fails in complex decision making processes.* Boston: Kluwer.

Boyatzis, R. (1998). *Transforming qualitative information.* Sage Publications.

Champy, J. (2002). *X-engineering the corporation: Reinventing your business in the digital age.* Warner Books.

Chandler, S., & Emanuels, S. (2002). Transformation not automation. In *Proceedings on the 2nd European Conference on E-Government*, Oxford, UK, (pp. 99-102).

Crane, J. (2005). *Qualitative research methods.* Retrieved December 6, 2005, from http://web.isp.cz

Deloitte Research (2000). *At the dawn of e-government: The citizen as customer.* Deloitte Consulting and Deloitte and Touche, New York.

Fustes, M. (2003). The unconstrained business. *Insight,* 3, 15-17.

Gibson, C. F., & Nolan, R. L. (1974). Managing the four stages of EDP growth. *Harvard Business Review, 52*(1), 76-88.

Government Computing Publication: March (2005)

Government Computing Publication: November (2005)

Government Computing (2006), A New Era Dawns: Local Directgov Programme, May 2006

Grover, V., & Segars, A. H. (2005). An empirical evaluation of stages of strategic information systems planning: Patterns of process design and effectiveness. *Information & Management,* 42, 461-479.

Gupta, M., & Jana, D. (2003). E-government evaluation: A framework and case study. *Government Information Quarterly,* 365-387.

Hazlett, S. A., & Hill, F. (2003). E-government: The realities of using IT to transform the public sector. *Managing Service Quality, 13*(6), 445-452.

Information Age (2004a). SeeBeyond empowers Sainsbury's transfomation. *Information Age,* B10-B11.

Information Age (2004b). Understanding, implementing and managing core technologies, Information Age advisory series. *Information Age, 1*(3), 26.

Janssen, M., & van Veenstra, A. F. (2005). Stages of growth in e-government: An architectural approach. *The Electronic Journal of E-Government, 3*(4), 193-200. Retreived from www.ejeg.com

Lawrence, A. (2004). From EAI to SOA. *Information Age, Infoconomy,* B8-B9.

Miles, M. B., & Huberman, A. M. (1994). *Qualitative data analysis: An expanded sourcebook.* Thousand Oaks, CA: Sage.

Jaeger, P. (2002). Constitutional principles and e-government: An opinion about possible effects of federalism and the separation of powers on e-government policies. *Government Information Quarterly,* 357-368.

Layne, K., & Lee, J. (2001). Developing fully functional e-government: A four-stage model. *Government Information Quarterly,* 18, 122-136.

Lee, S. M., Tan, X., Trimi, S., (2005). Current practices of leading e-government countries. *Communications of the ACM, 48*(10), 99-104.

Mack, R., & Neilson, J. (1993). Usability inspection methods. *SIGCHI, 25*(1), 28-33.

Masood, S. (2002). The missing link. November 2002, 31-32.

Monson-Haefel, R. (2004). *J2EE Web services.* Boston: Addison Wesley.

Nolan, R. L. (1979). Managing the crisis in data processing. *Harvard Business Review, 57*(2), 115-126.

Norris, D., & Moon, M. (2005). Advancing e-government at the grassroots: Tortoise or hare? *Public Administration Review, 65*(1), 64-72.

Phythian, M., & Taylor, W. (2001). Progress in electronic service delivery by English District Councils. *The International Journal of Public Sector Management, 14*(7), 569-584.

Saxena, A., & Wadhawa, S. (2004). E-business perspective of e-governance. In M. D. Gupta (Ed.), *Promise of e-governance: Operational challenges* (pp. 128-135). New Delhi: Tata-McGraw-Hill.

Scholl, H. J., Klischewski, R., & Moon, J. M. (2005). Minitrack: E-government infrastructure and interoperability. Proceedings of the 38th Hawaii International Conference on System Science, IEEE.

UN (2002). *Benchmarking e-government: A global perspective, assessing the progress of the UN member states.* Division of Public Economics and Public Administration (DPEPA). Nettelafrica.org/doc/NetTel%20Safari@the%20Equator%20(Uganda%202003)/Benchmarkingegovt.pdf

Varshney, A. (2005). New frontiers of social policy. Proceedings of Arusha Conference. December 12-15, 2005. Retrieved December 1, 2006, from http://siteresources.worldbank.org/INTRANET-SOCIALDEVELOPMENT/Resources/Varshney_Formatted.pdf

Weerakkody, V., Baire, S., & Choudrie, J. (2006). *E-government: A case for process improvement in the public sector.* Proceedings of the Hawaii International Conference on Systems Sciences (Hicss-39), January 2006.

Weerakkody, V., Janssen, M., & Hjort-Madsen, K. (2006). Realising integrated e-government services: A European perspective. *Journal of Cases in Electronic Commerce, 3*(2), 14-38.

World Bank (2005). *Definition of e-government.* www1.worldbank.org/publicsector/egov/definition.htm

Yin, R. K. (1984). *Case study research: Design and methods.* Beverley Hills, CA: Sage Publications.

This work was previously published in International Journal of Electronic Government Research, Vol. 3, Issue 3, edited by M. Khosrow-Pour, pp. 22-39, copyright 2007 by IGI Publishing, formerly known as Idea Group Publishing (an imprint of IGI Global).

Chapter 4.32
Integration and Enterprise Architecture Challenges in E-Government:
A European Perspective

Vishanth Weerakkody
Brunel University, UK

Marijn Janssen
Delft University of Technology, The Netherlands

Kristian Hjort-Madsen
Ministry of Science, Technology, and Innovation
The University of Copenhagen, Denmark

EXECUTIVE SUMMARY

Traditionally, government agencies are organized vertically around functional structures and there are almost no processes spanning departments and agencies. In such an environment, the co-ordination of business processes and integration of underlying information systems presents a significant challenge. Using case studies in three European countries, this research explores process and systems integration challenges in the European public sector and highlight opportunities for service improvement in the context of e-government implementation. While cross-organizational process and information systems integration barriers are seen in the literature as presenting the main technical challenge for realizing fully integrated e-government services, this research found that a legacy of rigid bureaucracy, established illogical routine tasks and lack of coordination of different information systems in the public sector were preventing the respective governments from expediting their e-government initiatives in Europe.

SETTING THE STAGE

As more and more citizens become internet savvy they demand faster delivery of public services and better insight into the status of their requests. While integrated service delivery requires the sharing of information among information systems of public agencies and harmonization of cross-organizational business processes, a debate that is facing many European governments' on-line agenda, at least in the short term, is how to precede best with this integration. Existing systems are typically build-using architectures that do not readily support enterprise-wide integration, thus requiring the development of new architectures to link on-line government (Allen, Juillet, Paquet, & Roy, 2001). The challenge is that many e-government initiatives require information exchange in networks across different governmental organizations. Most public institutions today manage technology in what is popularly described as "stove pipes" or "isolated islands of technology", with individual institutions implementing their own channels, Web page applications and supporting infrastructure. Traditionally, government agencies are organized vertically around departments. Cross-organizational processes can only be created by integrated information systems delivering timely and right information, and supporting cross-departmental processes. Current systems are often developed within the boundaries of departments without having in mind the "big picture" capturing the enterprise architecture of the whole organization. The existence of isolated, overlapping in function and content, highly fragmented, and unrelated computerized applications within the same public organization has resulted in a major interoperability problem and has led to "isolated islands of technology" (e.g. Peristera & Tarabanis, 2000).

E-government has evolved from the domain of e-business and as such needs business processes that can be continuously optimized and expanded outside the enterprise and outside internal enterprise systems (Fustes, 2003a; Champy, 2002). While the linking of these processes and IS require enterprise application integration (EAI) technologies, EAI has been an expensive and often problematic solution for many organizations engaged in e-business (Linthicum, 1999; Sutherland & Willem, 2002). These problems are multiplied in the public sector, where inefficient and bureaucratic business processes and disparate legacy IS/IT systems need to be integrated in an e-government environment (Weerakkody & Choudrie, 2005). In a resource limited environment such as government agencies, enterprise architectures should therefore not be merely about service delivery, but also about integrating and sharing resources and using common systems (Hanafin, 2004). Opportunities for joint-development, pooling of resources and coordination of efforts are often neglected due to the lack of overview. Although there a number of enterprise architectures available (e.g. Zachman, 1987; Bernard, 2004; Nora, 2006; Schekkerman, 2003; Office of the e-envoy, 2002; Danish Ministry of Science, White Paper on Enterprise Architecture, 2003) public managers find it difficult to translate the architecture to their specific situation, use these architectures to guide their decision-making and use these architectures as guidance for development from the existing situation. One of the reasons is that concepts are only vaguely defined, too abstract, or too technical defined (Kunda & Brook, 2000; Peristera & Tarabanis, 2000)

Given this context, the research question driving this article is *what are the process integration and enterprise architecture challenges faced by government when implementing integrated e-government services?*

To explore further the arguments set out above, this article is divided as follows. The next section describes the e-government development stages and examines the characteristics of Web services technology and enterprise architecture modeling, and how they could facilitate process and IS integration in e-government. This is followed by a summary of the methods used to carry out the research discussed in the article. The section afterwards then presents the results of an exploratory study in three different government agencies in the UK, Netherlands, and Denmark by examining key public service processes and related process and IS integration issues. The article concludes by summarizing the main research findings and discussing the enterprise architecture as well as process and IS redesign-requirements for delivering fully integrated e-government services.

To explore the arguments set out above in a deep and meaningful manner, a case study approach was considered to be suitable (Yin, 1994; Walsham, 1993). Case studies were conducted in a large local authority/council in the UK (Weerakkody, Baire, & Choudrie, 2006), Delft Municipality in the Netherlands (Janssen & Cresswell, 2005) and the Copenhagen hospital in Denmark (Hjort-Madsen, 2006). The detailed research approach of each case study is presented in the three referenced articles. As the main research instrument interviews were used, complemented with reports and minutes. In this article we aggregate the results of the case studies. The case studies were selected due to their variety in approaches and presenting typical issues. Moreover, the three countries are well comparable and are considered as innovative and frontrunners in different aspect. Consequently the case studies are complimentary and provide additional insights into various application and process integration challenges that the European public sector may face in the perspective of e-government.

RESEARCH CONTEXT: APPROACHES TO PROCESS IMPROVEMENT AND SYSTEMS INTEGRATION

The implementation of e-government implies different objectives and levels of transformation in public services in different countries. For instance, in the USA, the main objective is to automate and integrate different islands of information to simplify and maximize the benefits of technology (Navarra & Cornford, 2003), whereas in Europe the emphasis is to modernize public services and offer better services to citizens (Cuddy, 2003). For instance, the current program of e-government in the UK focuses on e-enabling local authorities in different regions in the UK with plans to implement a fully integrated service by 2008. In the national context of the UK, the direct.gov.uk Web portal provides a single point of contact for e-government, but is yet to function as a proper Web portal (that offers a gateway to local and national government Websites and provides a single point of contact for online service delivery) (Gant & Gant, 2001; Gant & Chen, 2001) .

Given the above context, examining Layne and Lee's (2001) representation of the different stages and dimensions of e-government development is appropriate (see Figure 1). Figure 1 captures the process transformation and integration aspects and the scope needed for a one-stop e-government Web portal.

In the cataloging stage in Figure 1, governments focus on establishing an online presence by publishing index pages or a localized site where electronic documents offer the public information relating to government services (Layne & Lee, 2001). This is the simplest and least expensive form of Web presence and from the government's perspective it helps to save staff time spent on answering basic questions (Bonham, Seifert, & Thorson, 2003). In the transaction stage the focus is on connecting the internal government systems to online interfaces thus allowing citizens to electronically transact with government institutions. While the speed of which this sector has progressed is disappointing, the process of developing and maintaining services in this stage are more complex than the first stage (Vasilaki, Laskaridis, Lepouras, Rouvas, & Georgiadis, 2003). In the third stage, vertical integration, federal, state, and local governments are expected to connect to each other to offer a higher level of integrated service. The main challenge is to ensure compatibility and interoperability between various government databases (Layne & Lee, 2001). The most complex stage is horizontal integration where different services and functions within the same level of government are integrated to provide a one-stop-shop for all major services

Figure 1. Dimensions and stages of e-government development (Adapted from Layne & Lee, 2001)

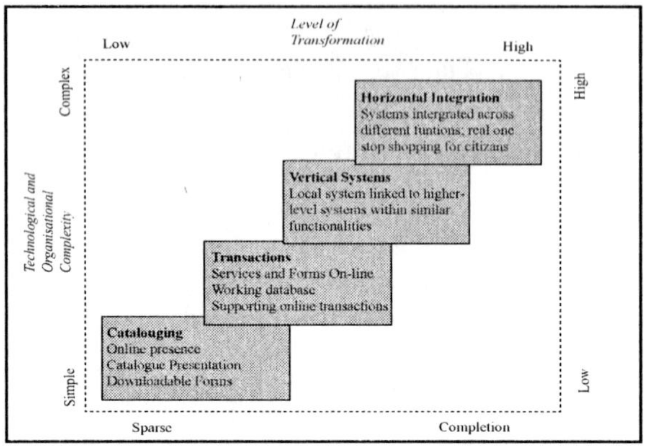

(Reffat, 2003). This according to Bonham et al., (2003) requires a transformation of how government functions are conceived, organized, and executed and is more difficult to realize than the first three stages.

Many stage models are focused on service provision to citizens and business, and not on helping to structure the architecture's maturity process, in other words, how the integration of front and back office systems should be arranged and evolve over time. Janssen and van Veenstra (2005) derived a five-stage growth model for the development of information architectures for local governmental agencies. The stage model consists of 1) no integration, 2) one-to-one messaging, 3) warehouse, 4) broker, and 5) orchestrated broker architecture. Starting with simple information architectures to more advanced process-based architectures able to deal with "spaghetti" of links and managing cross-organizational business processes. In the orchestrated broker architecture phase, an agency coordinates the provisioning of services and ensures process-based integration.

The above framework is not only hypothetical but has been researched in real life. Gant and Chen (2001) state that different countries around the world have strived at different speeds to move from the cataloging to transaction stage. The three countries studied in this article have approached this challenge in different ways:

- The UK is no exception where the country has managed to realize transaction level services in key public service processes such e-billing, e-payments, e-voting, and e-forms. Some local council have transformed customer facing processes and improved back office systems integration through SOA-Web services driven EA programs (Weerakkody, Choudrie, & Currie, 2004).
- In the Netherlands almost all government agencies are online and most of them provide basic transaction services. The foundation of the government is a service-oriented architecture to enable reuse and easy integration. Some of the public agencies started with transformation of their back offices and a small number has realized integrated service provisioning and adopt an orchestrated broker architecture.
- Denmark has been a "trend setter" in e-government with its early emphasis on Enterprise Architecture and the establishment of an Interoperability Framework with specific OIO-XML integration standards and more than 600 status assessments, standards, specifications and technologies used in e-government solutions. Many agencies have established EA programs with SOA as an important ingredient. Like the other two countries, there are, however, also severe collaboration difficulties in Denmark.

Although the above mentioned cases are encouraging, it can be argued that the transfer of public administrative processes from a an organization around functional silos to an e-enabled real-time automated, process-based state would involve rethinking and redesign of processes at both local and national government levels. There are also many instances where information is clearly not available locally (within the organization) to execute processes and service specific customer demands. This adds a further complexity to the process, as information now may need to be obtained from sources outside the organizational boundaries of local government/councils. Organizations part of different hierarchies need to collaborate for ensuring integrated service provisioning. Given this context, it is fair to state that progressing from the cataloging stage to the horizontal integration stage (in Figure 1) will require significant process and systems harmonization, change and integration. The next two sections review two developments that influence this progression—from an organizational and technical perspective.

Enterprise Architecture

In order to manage process changes and ensure systems integration, many public agencies are introducing new IS management programs to help align their strategies with business processes and IS and facilitate the coordination of resources. Some of the most prominent trends are associated with enterprise architecture (EA) (Pulkkinen & Hirvonen, 2005; Schekkerman, 2004), Information Management (McNurlin & Sprague, 2002), and Information Technology Governance (Weill & Ross, 2004). While the two later approaches take the viewpoint of the Chief Information Officer (CIO), the EA approach stresses the planning and management of all IS assets and their architecture together with organizational structures and processes. The purpose of an EA program is to guide an enterprise's business processes and the associated IS towards a common goal and to integrate business, data, information, and technology (Bernard, 2004; Boar, 1999; Zachman, 1987). The strength of an EA is that it embraces both the front and back-office focus along with a governance model that guides the use of IS from a business perspective. Thus, many public practitioners believe that EA is the solution to the vertical and horizontal integration and interoperability challenges that the public sector is facing today.

The challenge is that the concept of EA and IT architecture does not have a universally accepted definition in either the research or industry context (Ross, 2003). In a recently published textbook (Bernard, 2004) defines EA as "the analysis and documentation of an enterprise in its current and future state from an integrated strategy, business and technology perspective". And according to Richardson, Jackson, and Dickson (1990), an enterprise architecture defines interrelated data, hardware, software, and communications resources, as well as the supporting organization required to maintain the overall physical structure requires by the architecture. Some top-down architecture initiatives have been founded for the public sector such as the Federal Enterprise Architecture Program Management Office in the USA (FEAPMO, 2003) and the e-Envoy Office Framework including the Government Common Information Model (GCIM) (Office of the e-envoy, 2003), the Electronic Architecture in The Netherlands (NORA, 2006), and the national enterprise architecture in Denmark. Peristera and Tarabanis (2000) provides an overview of enterprise architecture methods for the public sector based on what they tried to model on one axis (process and data aspects) and the scope of the models on another axis (meta frameworks/methodology, generic models, specific industry applications). Schekkerman (2004) provides an overview of and describes the differences and commonalties of enterprise architecture frameworks.

The enterprise framework formula, in general terms, specifies how information technology is related to the overall business processes and outcomes of organizations, describing relationships among technical, organizational, and institutional components of the enterprise (CIOC, 2001; Fayad, Hamu, & Brugali, 2000; Gable, 2002; NASCIO, 2003; Richardson et al., 1990). Little is known about how EA frameworks can best be implemented and used in government agencies. Enterprise frameworks and overall information architecture concepts are quite general in order to be relevant for a wide range of organizations. However, organizations must adapt EA frameworks to their specific circumstances and needs. How this adaptation can best occur has not been extensively studied, nor have results of such adaptations been widely investigated. Yet, it is clear that EA should be understandable by all stakeholders in order to make it work. The creation of a shared vision, communication among stakeholders, and evaluation of the impact seem to be crucial aspects. One way of managing the complexities involved is to start a process to create a shared understanding

The primary strength of the EA approach is that it has greatly defined its concepts and instruments to predict and control complex technological systems. While many of the current models and concepts for the planning and management in government are one-dimensional and e-contextual in scope, there seems to be no other approach that can match EA in this regard and it is therefore not surprising that it is being used in most large IS projects in the private and public sector. The emphasis on preplanned and well-defined procedures in EA has the clear advantage that it offers high understandability and provides a good basis for teaching and knowledge transfer. EA encompasses a holistic approach to IS planning that provides an overview of the entire enterprise—from business to technology (Bernard, 2004; Schekkerman, 2004). In this way, it is an easy approach to communicate for consultants and practitioners (as well as academics) and it gives users of IS the perception of control. Furthermore, EA is oriented towards efficiency and effectiveness in the management and implementation of IS which seeks to conserve valuable resources in government.

However, so far, little empirical evidence exists on the actual implementation and management of EA in government agencies. The current approach to EA in many public agencies is that EA is defined as the planning and management of IS in a single organization (Hjort-Madsen & Gotze, 2004). In reality, however, the management of e-government initiatives is only sparsely structured based on ad-hoc cooperation in many inter-organizational settings. The principal obstacle in government is the high fragmentation where many actors get involved when offering e-services, and this article therefore draws on institutional theory from political science to capture the dynamic interaction between individual agencies in government. However, before we turn to the three empirical cases one of the technological enablers of e-government interoperability is first introduced.

The Use of Web Services Technologies

As stated before, internal systems of government agencies will often need to request and interact with other organizations' information systems to extract the required information (Saxena & Wadhawa, 2004). In an e-business or e-government context this process needs to be done at electronic speed and therefore ideally needs an environment where integration and interoperability between disparate IS/IT systems is exemplary. However, it is fair to suggest that realizing this type of environment using traditional modes of EAI can be costly and inefficient given the nature of the diverse hardware and software systems that span government IT infrastructures. In this regard, the emerging concept of Web services cannot be ignored. Web services promises to offer a solution to the EAI problem through the use of business process management (BPM) and service oriented architectures (SOA) where large service providers such as IBM, Microsoft, Sun and SAP are working together to develop a common platform and standards for modern EAI (Fustes, 2003a).

Web services break down applications into reusable components or services and enable the linking of these services within and across the enterprise using standards based on extensible mark up language (XML) (Fustes, 2003a). It uses three XML based standards: SOAP (simple object access protocol) for transmitting XML-encoded data and remotely accessing services in a platform independent way; UDDI (universal description and discovery language) for registering and discovering services; and WSDL (Web services description language) to provide an XML grammar for describing available Web services (Monson-Haefel, 2004). Web services helps EAI by providing the tools needed to manage end-to-end extended processes independently of the execution platform (Masood, 2002; Monson-Haefel, 2004). This is enabled through the use of SOA's, where, when the business needs to automate a business function or process, it merely plugs into a service like logging onto a Website irrespective of whether this may be an internal application, or an external application that may be accessed over the Internet (Lawrence, 2004; Zhang,, 2004). In comparison to the most common traditional EAI method, EDI, XML is specifically designed to use the Internet as the data transfer mechanism whereby business documents and services can be freely exchanged electronically, whereas the latter needs point-to-point connection between each participating system (Thompson, 2002). These protocols are not sufficient to support complex business processes. Web service orchestration, often using defacto standard Business Process Execution Language for Web Services (BPEL4WS or BPEL), is an XML-based technology to enable the process-based aggregation of different Web services (e.g. Janssen et al., 2006).

When using Web service, the existing application in the enterprise remains, but instead of staying in relative isolation from each other, they are seamlessly joined to create new services that are more attuned to the needs of the business (Fustes, 2003a). Currently the two main application servers for distributed computing, Microsoft's .Net and SUN's J2EE both support Web services (Monson-Haefel, 2004; Information Age, 2004a). Although Web services are not a fully mature technology yet, increasing numbers of private sector organizations and some public sector agencies both in Europe and North America have successfully adopted the Web services-SOA model to integrate their supply chains (Information Age, 2004b; Maclver, 2002; Information Age, 2004b). Given this context, it is fair to suggest that Web services may prove to be a cost effective EAI concept for e-government both in the long and short term. Moreover, these successful cases of Web services adoption offer the opportunity for the e-government context to understand the strengths and weaknesses of the concept before adoption.

CASE DESCRIPTIONS: A EUROPEAN PERSPECTIVE OF PROCESS AND SYSTEMS INTEGRATION IN E-GOVERNMENT

While a review of literature in the previous section identified numerous challenges that governments may face when e-enabling public sector processes from a theoretical stance, in this section we explore the impact of these issues in real life using three cases of e-government implementation and integration in Europe.

Case Study 1: Council Y in the UK

The first case that was studied is in the UK. Here we investigate the execution of a key public service process and related process and systems integration issues in one of the largest local councils in the UK (identified as Y). Located in northwest London, Council Y employs over 7,800 staff and owns 79 buildings that are available to the public. The services provided by council Y include central service departments (finance, law, administration and benefits services), housing services, library and community services, environment services and education. Council Y's electronic government statement states that "for council Y, e-government is about using ICT's to support the delivery of community strategy targets by making services more accessible, improving efficiency and supporting strong commitment to social inclusion".

Since the aim of this research was to explore process and systems integration aspects in local government, the researchers chose to focus on a key service provided by the council, the student loan application process. This process relates to the loan applications made by prospective university students to pay their tuition fees and subsistence during the course of their university studies. Given this context, interviews were conducted primarily at council Y's Local Education Authority (LEA). These interviews identified a scenario where lack of harmonization and integration between business processes and underlying IS/IT systems has resulted in inefficient and ineffective process execution and service delivery in local government (LG). Interviews with council Y staff that were responsible for the student loan application process identified two key activities relating to the process, which primarily revolved around the handling of different documents. These include processing the different applications received from students for loans and tuition fees (identified as PN1 forms) and confirmation of benefits (identified as CB2 forms). The first form (PN1) contains general information on the student such as personal details, income, parent's income, and so forth, while the second form (CB2) contains information about any benefits the student or their parents claim.

Once the student has filled out the two forms (PN1 and CB2), an administrator manually enters the details onto the LEA Computer system. At the same time information provided on the CB2 form is checked against the benefits agency records. Using this information the systems generates a financial assessment on the student, which is sent manually (by post) to an organization known as the Students Loans Company (SLC). To complement the investigation conducted at the LEA, as mentioned in a previous section, interviews were conducted with staff at the SLC, council Y's Benefits Agency and a student applying for the loan. The respective roles of these different entities and the sequence of activities that are executed to administer the student loan are outlined below.

Council Y's Benefits Agency: Council Y's benefits agency is just one of the local functions at Y. Their role is to provide benefits to citizens who are unemployed and are unable to work (such as income support and job seekers allowance). The LEA regularly needs information from the benefits agency to aid them in the process of making financial assessments for students. This is done using the confirmation of benefits-CB2 form. However, interviews with the benefits agency staff indicated that the LEA does not directly contact the benefits agency to obtain this information. Instead, the student is responsible to get part of the CB2 form completed by the benefits agency, which is then sent to the LEA by the student.

The Students Loan Company (SLC): The SLC is an organization set up to pay the tuition fees to the student's university. The SLC also pays the student an installment of loans throughout the academic year. The SLC does this by using the assessment information from the LEA. As noted earlier, interviews with staff at the SLC showed that there is no harmonization of processes and integration of systems between the LEA and SLC with the assessment information for every student being sent by mail on a regular basis.

The Student: Interviews with a university student in possession of a student loan confirmed the ineffectiveness of the lengthy process involved in the loan application process. It was revealed that the student applying for a loan and tuition fee payments, has to go through the same process every academic year. The student needs to fill out the first form (PN1) and the first section of the CB2 form. The student is then in direct contact with all the entities in the process including the LEA, SLC and the benefits agency. The student interviewed reported, "this is a very time consuming and lengthy process".

Current Working Model at the LEA in Council Y

By collating and analyzing the information gathered from all the interviewees, the authors present in Figure 2 a composition of the current working model of the student loan application process at the LEA in council Y.

Figure 2 shows that the process begins with the student filling out two forms, which include the PN1, and CB2 form. The PN1 form goes to the college or university the student is currently attending. The CB2 form goes to the benefits agency, where one section of the form is filled out and given back to the student. Once the two forms are complete, these are handed over to the LEA. The LEA then uses this information to make an assessment on the student's eligibility for the loan using an IT system at council Y's office. Once the assessment is made, the LEA passes this information manually to the SLC.

With the financial assessment received from the LEA, the SLC then enters this information into their computer system and sends the student a loan request form and the assessment information made by LEA. The loan request form is used by the student to indicate how much money they want to borrow. Once the SLC has received the completed loan request form, they are then able to start with installment payments to the student along with the tuition fee payments made to the student's university.

THE STUDENT LOAN APPLICATION PROCESS: IDENTIFYING THE KEY PROBLEMS

The scenario above clearly contradicts council Y's vision for e-government and highlights a number of process and IS integration problems in a key public service process. The first problem lies in the student handing the CB2 form to the benefits agency for them to complete one section of the form. If the student delays this process, this also delays the financial assessment process at the LEA in council Y. This is further compounded by delays that occur when the benefits agency is slow to give back the CB2 form to the student.

A second problem occurs with the exchanging of information between the LEA and SLC. The LEA receives a large number of requests from students, in particular during the period leading up to a new academic year, where each student loan

Figure 2. Student loan application process—use case model

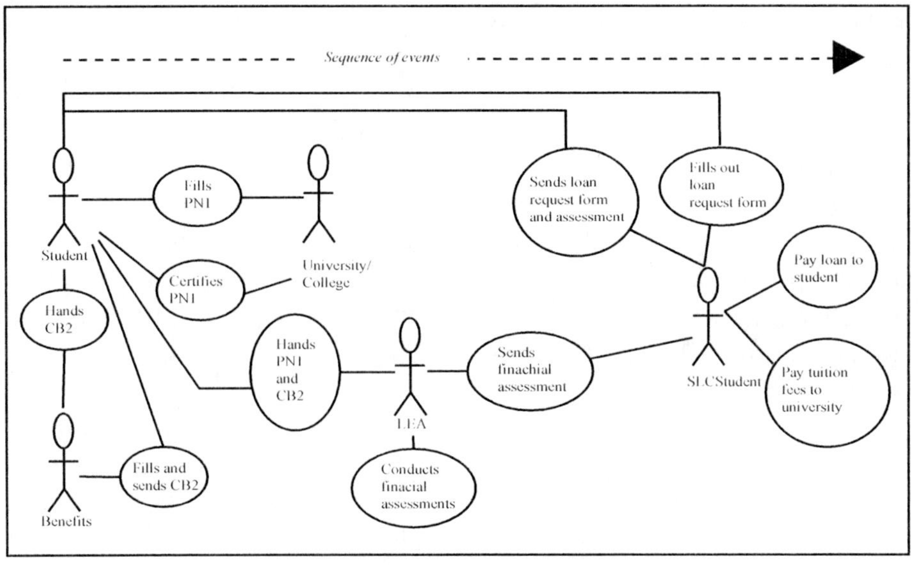

application can take between 2-3 weeks to assess. Once these assessments are made they are then sent to the SLC by post. One LEA worker stated during the interviews that, "using this method of communication can be sometimes troublesome when there are postal problems or delays". This can cause delays and financial difficulties to the students receiving the loan as well as the university enlisting the student. Furthermore, delays in obtaining the financial assessment information can result in delays in the student's enrollment process at the university/collage.

The last problem occurs with the "student loan request forms", which are sent to the students by the SLC. Delay can arise here again due to postal problems and lost or misplaced forms. This could mean that the student would need to contact the SLC and request a new form, which could take up to 1-2 weeks to arrive by post.

The Process Improvement Approach: A Web Services Based Solution

Given the above context, in order to reap the benefits of e-services and e-government, the student loan application process needs to be significantly improved. It was clear from our investigation that the lengthy cycle time and resulting process inefficiencies were caused mainly due to lack of harmonization and integration of process and supporting IS/IT systems (Champy, 2002) between various internal and external entities in the context of council Y. Hence, it can be argued that radical improvements (as in BPR: (Hammer & Champy, 1993) to the process can be made that would not only transform the student loan application process from manual to electronic, but reduce the cycle time by well over 50%. This would however require the integration and harmonization of processes and IS/IT systems between the LEA, SLC and Benefits Agency. With a new integrated system the following requirements need to be realized: a) the student should be able to hand both forms (PN1 and CB2) directly to the LEA; b) when the financial assessment has been made by LEA, the SLC should be able to access the information electronically through a direct link; c) the student should be able to access their financial assessment online, eliminating postal problems that can occur with hard copies; and d) the student should also be able to fill out the loan request form online.

In the context of e-government, the transfer of the student loan application process from a largely manual to an automated, e-enabled state would mean significant progress for council Y. Besides, empirical research in the UK strongly suggests that succeeding at the local (council) level is key for national level e-government success (Hackney & Jones, 2002; www.kable.com) whereby local best practices can be mirrored at national level. From an organizational perspective, the paradigm shift and change of culture that e-government would introduce to government institutions would certainly face resistance as seen in other forms of organizational change such as business process reengineering (Avgerou, 1993; Sahay & Walsham, 1997; Weerakkody & Hinton, 1999).

While this research has identified significant process inefficiencies in the student loan application process, yet we can argue that this is only one example of how a public sector process may be executed. However, previous research by the authors has also identified similar inefficiencies with various processes in other local government /councils (Weerakkody et al., 2004). As stated before, these process inefficiencies are caused largely due to the lack of integration and synergy between various internal departments and external government agencies. Although in the past rectifying these problems would have meant radical reengineering of business processes and changes to underlying legacy systems that may have also resulted in the implementation of expensive EAI solutions, we argue that in the present context Web services offer a realistic solution to this problem. The SOA—Web services concept offers the platform for processes and systems to communicate in well understood universally accepted protocols such as XML and HTTP thus rendering them completely independent to different technologies and software that may be used by various government agencies. In Figure 3 we outline a model based on Web services and SOA, which offers an integrated view of government processes and underlying systems in the context of e-government.

As outlined in Figure 3, the various applications used by government agencies expose themselves as services based on XML-SOAP protocols irrespective of hardware-platform or software. The model in Figure 3 is made up of three roles: service providers; user interface providers; and end-users (citizens in this case). Firstly, the government here has to assume the role of the service provider and needs to develop the infrastructure that enables them to expose their processes as Web services. Secondly, the user interface providers have to provide user-friendly interfaces or application software to access these Web services. Typical examples of interface providers may include google, msn, and yahoo. Their role here is to provide the channel for information to be passed between the user and the service provider. Finally, the users (citizens) can request for e-government information and services using various access mediums such as computers, PDA's, mobile phones and Kiosk. In an environment where there are disparate applications and hardware technologies (such as in the case of the public sector), the above model eliminates the need for major changes to software applications (legacy systems), which is both time consuming as well as costly. With tight budgets and project deadlines this is a luxury that many governments cannot afford.

Figure 3. A model for intergrating government processes and IT systems using Web

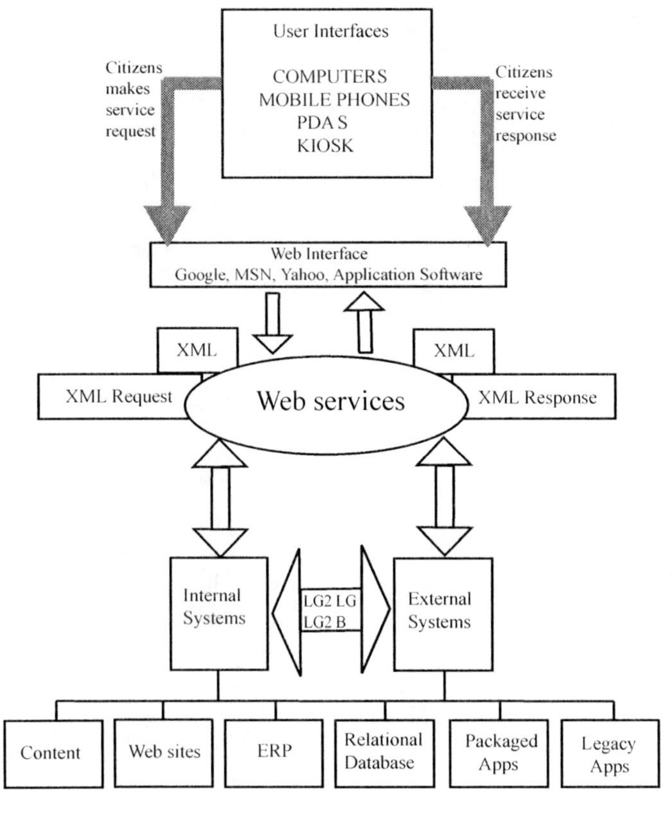

CASE STUDY 2: MUNICIPALITY OF DELFT

The integration aim of the Dutch government is that constituents should provide data only once and all government agencies should reuse this data by 2007 (www.elektronischeoverheid.nl). This can only be accomplished when governmental agencies share data and reuse the data in their processes. The Dutch municipalities are free to design their enterprise architectures and to choose appropriate software vendors. Often there is no central management with a municipality and departments can buy their own applications for each process. As a result, municipalities have a highly fragmented ICT-architecture, consisting of legacy systems for each product they offer. Municipality of Delft is a medium-sized municipality with 3000 employees consisting of various departments. The municipality consists of a large number of departments, which have developed their own, often heterogeneous, information systems. There is no overview of all systems and there is a need to reduce development and maintenance costs as budgets are decreasing. Managers were complaining about the lack of insight into the application architecture and that they are not able to make decisions to prioritize development. They merely assign budgets to development projects, but do hardly know what kind of results can be expected. As such they want to improve their understanding by developing an enterprise architecture. We investigated this case study by conducting a number of interviews and reading reports, which would result in the identification of the key challenges to process and systems integration (Janssen & Cresswell, 2005).

Figure 4. Architecture levels and horizontal and vertical dependencies

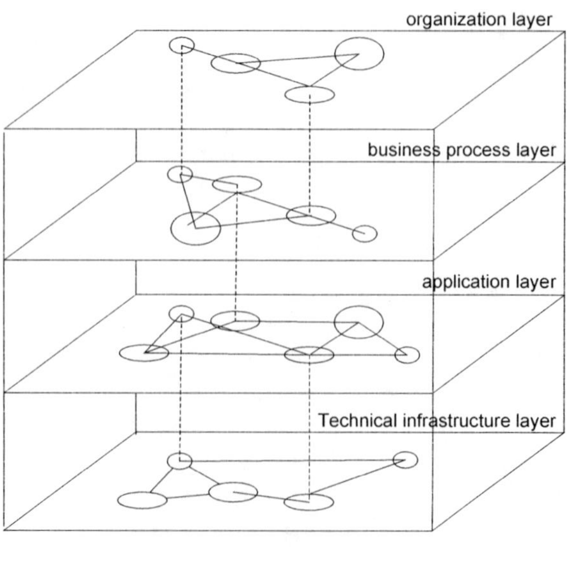

In general, architecture is perceived as having an inherently technical nature. Architects are only found within the ICT departments. This prevents the use of architecture as a strategic planning instruments and building of relationship between business and ICT. Architecture can be described using the organization, process, application, and infrastructure layers, and the complex horizontal and vertical relationships and connections between the various elements in the layers as shown schematically in Figure 4. In the following subsections we discuss the various architecture levels.

Organization Architecture

The municipality provides about 300 products to citizens and another 50 products to business. All customers interact with a one-stop service center. The service center aims at fulfilling service request, answering exceptional request and routing request to the right department. As such it manages the dependencies among the back-office departments.

From our interviews it appeared that service provisioning is in reality centered around departments. If citizens and business are familiar with the situation, they go often directly to the departments when requesting a certain service, although some managers mistakenly consider the service-center as a one-stop shop. The business processes of these products and services were analyzed and described, including the supporting information systems.

A critical factor for customer-oriented service provisioning is the sharing of information across departments, but also with outside agencies. As such external stakeholders should also be included in the enterprise architecture. The municipal departments communicate with external organizations to collect information, such as the chamber of commerce who owns and controls a registry of businesses, the police, fire, and justice departments.

Another challenge is the allocation of responsibility for the quality of service provisioning. When the terms of a permit changes and the permit request involves multiple departments; who is responsible for updating the permit terms on the Internet? If a business process changes, which organization unit is responsible for implementing the change?

Process Architecture

1. There are more than 350 services. Most of then are structured and standardize and a small number is unstructured and not-described. Most of the services are permit request consisting of the following process phase. Information phase: In this step information is collected by the citizens and business to gain an understanding of the services needed.
2. Intake phase: In this phase the customers request information and the data is filled out.
3. Execution phase: In this phase the service request is processed, often by various back offices. A service request is often split up in multiple sub processes that are executed by different departments using all kinds of systems.
4. Services provisioning phase: the results of the process are presented to the customers. This can result in granting or rejecting a permit
5. Complaint handling phase: A customer can file a complaint if he or she does not agree with the outcome.
6. Enforcement phase: Governmental agencies cooperate to ensure that people live to the terms and conditions of the permits. The information systems supporting enforcement are not connected to the system used in the preceding phases.

The current focus of the architecture was on the intake, execution, and service delivery processes. This is a too narrow focus can be concluded when viewing the process phases.

Application Architecture

Delft municipality application architecture is based on a plethora of different software standards, exchange formats, computing languages, platform, and operating systems. They have packages as well as custom-made software and open source and proprietary software in the front and back-office. Available applications include financial, human resource, and various workflow and document management systems. Many of the systems have fixed and rigid structures and some of them are not well or not documented.

The most advanced system is the Web-based applications based on a modular design available in the front office. A number of components have been developed that can be reused using scripting languages. Product information can be found on the Internet and some of the products can be ordered online. There is not systematic approach or strategy for making products online. Managers are very afraid that their Web-development department might turn gradually into a maintenance department. The updating of existing products might become more time-consuming that developing new components and scripts.

A small number of the applications have been integrated using a permutation of application integration technology. Delft has initially pursued a point-to-point approach in integrating new systems into its existing IS architecture. Based on request of public managers an ad-hoc connection between front and back office application was made without considering maintenance efforts. This results in a spaghetti-kind of integration as all systems will be connected with all other systems in the end.

The current services provision over the Internet can be positioned in the cataloging and transaction phase of Layne and Lee's (2001) e-government development framework outlined in Figure 1. Delft has a Web presence containing product information, there are downloadable forms for a limited number of products and for some products it is possible to conduct online transactions. In the latter case, most transactions are performed without any direct integration of front- and back-office applications. The stages of horizontal and vertical integration (Layne & Lee, 2001), characterized by integration of information systems across different functions and departments (Gable, 2002) therefore, are still far away.

THE PROCESS IMPROVEMENT APPROACH: ARCHITECTURE MODELING AND VISUALIZING

The aims of the enterprise architecture development process is to create a shared understanding of the environment where the municipality is currently in and to create a vision that is shared by and agreed on managers, technical experts and administrative staff. The involvement of staff of various departments to ensure that their view was included and commitment was created, was found to be of crucial importance for the initiating of this project. The vision in this context therefore was to develop a usable enterprise reference model for managing the development of information technology projects.

The architecture efforts resulted in a shared vision on the architectures that need to be developed. A architecture started with high-level standardization as interfaces, business rules, and protocols used need to be standardized for re-use. The vision on the architecture was based on a service-oriented architecture and the processes are managed using Web service orchestration technology, in other words, BPEL. Web service orchestration contains the business logic for managing the sequence of service invocations and requests. Service-oriented architectures enable the on-demand composition of new business processes using already existing Web services. Web services can be provided both internally or externally provided. Internal services might be used to request information, such as citizens' information, criminal records, and so on, or access functionality from these systems, like generating documents, storing documents, or processing payments. The orchestrator also guides the business process or workflow of users, in other words, which screen will appear in the Web browser of a user and which functional components and information sources need to be accessed. This provides benefits, such as the re-use of systems and components, the easy construction of new business processes out of existing building blocks, and even the re-use of complete processes by other public organizations.

Apart from the problems discussed in the preceding section the main challenges can be summarized as:

- **Overlap systems:** All kind of information systems having overlapping functionality exist;
- **Avoid creation of a spaghetti of integration:** Making products online available and the one-to-one integration of applications might lead to a spaghetti;
- **Multi-channel coordination:** There is a lack of coordination of customer channels such as Internet, call center and physical office;
- **Integral customer views:** Customer data and interactions are not stored at some

central place. Instead they are in the head of the people. When on employee does not grant a permit, the customer might try to get the permit from another employee;
- **Creation of shared vision:** it is important the persons have the same understanding of the problems and a shared vision on the future. Therefore a shared vision was developed and a reference architecture was used to guide this shared vision.

As can be seen from this list of problems, few of them have a purely technological nature and most of them can only be solved by a complex interaction on various architecture levels. In the opinion of the people who were involved in the action research, a reference architecture was appropriate to address these problems.

CASE STUDY 3: COPENHAGEN UNIVERSITY HOSPITAL

Copenhagen University Hospital (CUH) is Denmark's largest and leading hospital for patients needing highly specialized treatment and care. The IT department currently employs 110 IT professionals, supporting more than 300 applications besides the central Electronic Patient Record (EPR) system. The IS spans laboratory analysis applications, X-ray systems, and content management systems. These systems have been developed in almost every programming language in use over the last 20 years and the same level of heterogeneity applies for Application Programming Interfaces (API´s) and databases (Hjort-Madsen, 2006).

Since 1995, CUH has been part of the Copenhagen Hospital Corporation (CHC) where six hospitals in the Copenhagen area are working together in a loosely coupled structure. As the largest hospital in CHC, the hospital not only plays a prominent role when it comes to patient treatment but also as the primary hub for many shared IT-services within CHC. This development is likely to continue because the CHC is expected to grow within 2-3 years as part of a large structural reform in Denmark.

Since 2002, CHC had been working on an Enterprise Architecture and early in 2004 they delivered a descriptive EA blueprint for EPR-systems—called "The reference architecture for EPR"—based on the national EPR process model (G-EPR) for clinical data. This architecture describes the semantic and technical requirements for the six hospitals in the Copenhagen region. The CHC architecture does not focus on other relating applications besides the core modules of the EPR-system and CUH therefore decided that they needed their own EA.

The process of implementing an EA program at CUH started in the summer of 2004. The CUH CIO and his chief architect initiated the work, while other parts of the IT-organization and an external IT architect acted as reviewers. The first version of the reference architecture was completed in the first quarter of 2005.

PROCESS IMPROVEMENT APPROACH: THE CASE FOR AN ENTERPRISE ARCHITECTURE PROGRAM

Identifying the benefits and effects of having an EA program at CUH was difficult to envision at the outset of the program. While the IT-management wanted a set of descriptive EA blueprints describing CUH's technical and organizational requirements for every employee to use in their daily work, the system owners interviewed at the initiation of the EA program did not believe that the program would have any impact on their work. As one system owner interviewee said, "To me the enterprise architecture will probably not mean much for my choice of application, or how the application will fit into the overall architecture".

At first, the most obvious reason for implementing the EA program at CUH seemed to be the technical interoperability challenges inferred by the new EPR systems. But when analyzing the empirical data it becomes clear that economic, political, and institutional arguments for implementing the program were just as important.

The most obvious argument for implementing the EA program was an increased demand for interoperability and integration. Over time, several layers of historically separate IT-artifacts have accumulated internally. With the EA program CUH hopes to tie the existing applications, data, and infrastructure technologies together to increase the technical interoperability internally. Externally, the need for interoperability has grown due to increased environmental complexity and instability surrounding CUH. The structural reforms in Denmark will influence the Copenhagen hospital region, resulting in reorganizations and an increasing need for data to be exchanged in a network of private and public hospitals, medical practitioners, and specialists all over Denmark. This increases the demands for external interoperability and requires a high level of agility in the way that IS in the health sector are organized. Thus, the EA program is aimed at improving both the internal integration and the horizontal interoperability that enables an agile external collaboration.

The analysis showed that trends from the NPM tradition like strategic planning, incentive pay, performance appraisal and contracting out were high on the CUH CIOs agenda. The EA program was seen as a tool that could consolidate the IS infrastructure. The long-term goal of this consolidation is to limit both the heterogeneity of technological platforms and the diversity in products to reduce IT-costs. As the CIO said in one of the interviews:

this project is not only about technology and further integration. We want to save money by making our IT simpler with fewer vendors, less diverse applications and reduced maintenance costs in general; we must think about the future and this [EA] is a good tool for doing that.

With regards to the coming expansion of the Copenhagen health region, and the on-going process of pulling the hospitals in the existing region closer together, it was important that specific systems were assimilated along with their knowledge into the new hospital region and/or allowed to co-exist alongside until they can be replaced without destroying valuable knowledge. The current heterogeneity amongst the systems makes it impossible to migrate or rebuild systems at once, therefore leaving CUH no choice but to create interoperable services that are available to the healthcare region hospitals. The EA defines such common services needed and guides the acquiring, outsourcing, integrating, operating, and retiring of the IT-infrastructure.

Also, interviews with the IT-management revealed that the national EA work and CHC's EA blueprint for EPR-systems played a role for implementing an independent EA program at CUH. As the largest hospital in Denmark, CUH has always been very independent. And with the structural reforms underway in the Danish health sector, CUH again needs to position itself in a new organizational setting. The overall analysis clearly illustrates that there is little coordination between the different levels and functions of the Danish health sector. The implementation and management of IS has been decentralized as part of the NPM reforms, and while CUH is a part of CHC and the national health sector at large, in reality the individual hospitals work as independent actors that can manage IS the way they want — across the different levels and types of interoperability.

Defining how interoperability was to be governed across the organizational levels in CUH's EA programs was a difficult and time-consuming task. Both the CIO and the chief architect at CUH were aware of the EA work conducted by CHC and the national health sector with regard to EPR. In executing the EA work, the chief architect therefore found it challenging to define where the two EA program domains supplemented each other and where CUH needed its own architecture. CUH is part of CHC and the national health sector, but it makes many independent IS-decisions.

In the practical implementation of the EA program at CUH, many of the principles from the Copenhagen Hospital Corporation reference architecture could be reused. But to secure the local long-term consolidation of the 300 in-house applications, the CUH EA needed to be broad enough to engulf the functional heterogeneity of the systems. Because of this need and the institutional structure, CUH decided to focus its EA program primarily on technical aspects in its EA, namely applications and data.

Figure 5 illustrates how government has decentralized technical interoperability issues in the health sector and how the institutional setting determines the focus of EA programs in government. Based on the framework provided by Hjort-Madsen & Gøtze (2004), the figure makes a theoretical distinction between organizational interoperability (alignment of business processes that span intra- and inter-organizational boundaries), semantic interoperability (ensuring the precise meaning of exchanged information), and technical interoperability (technical issues of connecting information systems). The data analysis showed that the interviewees at CUH and CHC also perceived interoperability more broadly than as common standards for data sharing.

As outlined in Figure 5 at the government level, the processes that enable specific health care "life-events" (Leben & Bohanec, 2003) (e.g., cancer treatment) to span organizational boundaries are key, while technical aspects of actually implementing these "events" are left to the hospital corporations and/or the individual hospitals. The high-level semantic interoperability requirements are outlined in the national EPR process model (G-EPR) for clinical data, but the practical implementation of the semantic guidelines is left to the hospital corporations and individual hospitals.

For CUH, creating interoperability internally and externally was important. But the economic and political arguments for implementing the program proved to be just as important in a situation with large structural changes around the corner creates an uncertain environment where it is difficult for the hospital to justify investments that are not directly related to the day to day business. Because there is no overall coordination of the different e-government initiatives in the health sector there are no direct economic and/or immediate political incentives for CUH to share data and business functionality with other health care organizations. Hence, the EA program at CUH can be viewed as an attempt to keeping up with the national recommendations and the EA work at CHC and other hospitals as much as "rational"

Figure 5. Overview of interoperability across the health sector

motives such as increasing interoperability, consolidation, and value preservation.

One could ask why there is no overall coordination of this kind of e-government initiatives in the Danish health sector. One answer could be that EA is not the right tool for creating interoperability in government at large. The EA frameworks and models that we use in the public sector (e.g. Zachman, 1987) were built for private companies and have a limited organizational focus, while e-government is about seeing the "big picture". The interviews revealed that some of the system owners at CUH did not believe that EA would have any impact on their daily business, and we must therefore question the value of EA programs at this point because of this ambiguous governance setup in the Danish health sector.

CURRENT CHALLENGES: A CROSS-EUROPEAN E-GOVERNMENT PERSPECTIVE

From the background literature and the case studies presented in previous sections it is clear that the effective delivery of on-line public services will require the harmonization and integration of business processes and supporting IS/IT systems between various stakeholders such as government agencies, business partners, employees, and citizens. In this context, this research has identified significant process inefficiencies and IS integration issues in three different government agencies in three European countries. In the first case of council Y in London, it was clear that lack of coordination and integration between processes and IS systems in disparate organizations that needed to work in synergy was effecting the cycle time of the student loan application process. Although in the past rectifying these problems would have meant radical reengineering of business processes and underlying systems as well as implementation of expensive EAI solutions, in the present context we argued that Web services offers a realistic solution to this problem. The SOA-Web Services concept offers a platform for business processes and systems to communicate in well understood, universally accepted protocols such as XML and HTTP thus rendering them completely independent to different technologies and software that may be used by various government agencies. In Figure 3 we proposed a model based on Web services and SOA which offers an integrated view of government processes and underlying systems in the context of e-government.

In the second case, a reference enterprise architecture was developed for the Municipality of Delft using action research. This architecture is developed in collaboration with all stakeholders and represents a shared vision on the future. The aims in this case were to create a shared understanding of the situation where the municipality is right now and to create a vision that is shared and agreed on by managers, technical experts and administrative staff. The development of a reference architecture can be viewed as a kind of negotiation process between departments. At the beginning of the development process all departments had various ideas at different levels of details. During this process they shared their ideas, and the ideas became understood and diverged into shared ideas. The capturing of interdependencies among and within architecture layers, the visualization, and the development process of creating a shared model are probably the crucial elements contributing to an accepted and understandable architecture.

The reference architecture developed for the Municipality of Delft took into account overlap of functionality of applications within departments and is based on SOA and Web service orchestration. A similar architecture study can be performed across municipalities (councils in the case of UK), or even across more heterogeneous public agencies. Not only application functionality, but also complete services might be shared and bundled in some kind of centralized agency. Therefore, further research can focus on drafting an overall public administration architecture.

Table 1. The need for process and IS integration and improvement in e-government

	Student loan	Municipality	Hospital
Drivers	Process efficiency, reduced costs	Reuse, efficiency	Political motives, efficiency, reuse
Key characteristics	Fragmented departments Heterogeneous IS	Fragmented departments Heterogeneous IS	Fragmented departments Heterogeneous IS
Type of approach	Process Design	Bottom-up, technology driven	Enterprise architecture
Change management	Combination of radical and incremental change	Growth stages	Rigorous planning
Key challenges	Coordination between internal departments and across organizational boundaries	Shared vision	Coordination across organizational boundaries vertically and horizontally

In the third case (Copenhagen Hospital) an Enterprise Architecture was implemented. The primary strength of the EA approach is that it has greatly defined its concepts and instruments to predict and control complex technical systems. But, EA programs might demand so much rigor and organizational coherence that it impairs organizational agility. The question is whether EA is the right medicine for public organizations. Rigorous EA frameworks, vague definitions and organizational adoption are some of the largest challenges. Tomorrow's EA programs in government must therefore encompass public sector dynamics (and limitations) as well as being agile in the application of interoperable e-government services. The reality in most e-government settings is that there is a complex goal structure and strict legal norms, while interoperable services must still be delivered in a secure and transparent way. Narrowly defined, EA is about implementing IS architectures and interfaces, and this might not be sufficient to capture the complex dynamics in e-government systems development and management. Governments cannot be seen as one enterprise and the three case studies presented here therefore calls for a broader definition of interoperability in networks of cooperation where information and business processes are governed more rigorously across different levels (vertical) and functions (horizontal) of government. These arguments are further highlighted in Table 1 where we summarize the key drivers for change, characteristics of the current process and IS environment, and type of approach that was suggested for improved integration in the three cases examined in this article.

The three case studies also revealed different interoperability concerns at different levels of government and we therefore need to expand the traditional understanding of interoperability in public sector EA programs to embrace wider organizational, semantic, and technical issues. Many of the interoperability challenges arise because the management of IS has been decentralized in the public sector. The question is whether our traditional EA frameworks or EAI solutions can overcome this challenge when we strive to develop interoperability in networks of cooperation where information and business processes are governed across autonomous organizational levels and functions in government.

In conclusion, this research has attempted to offer a better understanding of some of the technological and organizational challenges that influence the realization of a fully integrated e-government service using literature and empirical research. It has also examined the capacity of two approaches, Web services technology and enterprise architecture, for understanding and improving process and systems integration in e-government. Although the empirical research relates to only three different pubic agencies in the UK, the Netherlands and Denmark, the diverse nature, size, location, and importance of the three agencies in the public agenda for e-government in the respective countries make our findings valid and relevant to the wider European context. The challenges can be used as starting points for further research.

REFERENCES

Allen, B.A., Juillet, L. Paquet, P., & Roy, J. (2001). E-Governance & government on-line in Canada: Partnerships, people & prospects, *Government Information Quarterly, 18*, 93–104.

Avgerou, C. (1993). Information systems for development planning. *International Journal of Information Management, 13*, 260-273.

Bernard, S. A. (2004). *An Introduction to Enterprise Architecture*. Author House: Indiana

Boar, B. H. (1999). *Constructing Blueprints for Enterprise IT Architectures*. John Wiley & Sons.

Bonham, M.G., Seifert, J. W., & Thorson, S.J. (2003). *The Transformational Potential of e-Government: The Role of Political Leadership.* 4th Pan European International Relations Conference: UK.

Champy, J. (2002). *X-Engineering the Corporation: Reinventing Your Business in The Digital Age*. Warner Books.

Cuddy, I. (2003, July 14). New moves for European eGovernment, http://www.egovmonitor.com/newsletter/yzdqasd86/talrln02.html, date accessed: June 02, 2003.

CIOC (2001). *A practical guide to federal enterprise architecture*. Washington DC, Chief Information Officer Council.

Danish White Paper on Enterprise Architecture (2003). Danish Ministry of Science, Technology and Innovation. http://www.oio.dk/arkitektur/eng.

Fayad, M.E. Hamu, D.S., & Brugali, D. (2000). Enterprise frameworks characteristics, criteria, and challenges. *Communications of the ACM, 43*(10), pp.39-46.

FEAPMO (2003). The Business Reference Model, Federal Enterprise Architecture Program Management Office, Version 2.0.

Fustes, M. (2003a), The unconstrained business. *Insight*, 3, pp.15-17.

Gable, J. (2002). Enterprise application integration. *Information Management Journal, 36*(2), 48-52.

Gant, J.P., & Gant, D.B. (2001). Web portal functionality and state government e-services, In *Proceedings of the 35th Hawaii International Conference on Systems Sciences*, Hawaii.

Gant, J., & Chen, Y. (2001). Transforming local e-government services: The use of application service providers. *Government Information Quarterly, 18*, pp.343-355.

Hackney, R. and Jones, S. (2002). Towards E-government in the Welsh (UK) Assembly: An information systems evaluation, ISOneWorld Conference and Convention, April 2002, Las Vegas, Nevada, USA.

Hanafin, M. (2004). Welcomes Speech Minister of State, European E-Government Conference ECEG2004: Dublin, Ireland.

Hammer, M & Champy, J (1993), Reengineering the corporation : A manifesto for business revolution. NY: Harper Collins Publishers Inc.

Hjort-Madsen, K., & Gøtze, J. (2004). Enterprise architecture in government - Towards a multi-level framework for managing IT in government. *Proceedings of ECEG04*, 365-374, Dublin, Ireland.

Hjort-Madsen, K. (2006). Enterprise architecture implementation and management: A case study on interoperability. *Hawaii International Conference on System Sciences (HICSS-39)*, January 5-7, Kauai, Hawaii

Information Age (2004a). J2EE v .NET, understanding, implementing and managing core technologies, information age advisory series. *Information Age, 1*(3), 34.

Information Age (2004b). Understanding, implementing and managing core technologies, information age advisory series. *Information Age, 1*(3), 26.

Janssen, M., & Cresswell, A. (2005). The development of a reference architecture for local government. *Hawaii International Conference on System Sciences (HICSS-38)* January 3-6. Hilton Waikoloa Village, Big Island.

Janssen M., & van Veenstra, A.F. (2005). Stages of growth in e-government: An architectural approach. *Electronic Journal of eGovernment, 3*(4), 193-200. http://www.ejeg.com/volume-3/vol3-iss4/v3-i4-art5.htm.

Kunda, D., & Brook, L. (2000). Identifying and classifying processes (traditional and soft factors) that support COTS component selection: a case study. *European Journal of Information Systems, 9*(4), 226-234.

Layne, K.J.L., & Lee, J. (2001). Developing fully functional e-government: A four stage model, *Government Information Quarterly, 18*(2), 122-136.

Lawrence, A. (2004), From EAI to SOA, information age. *Infoconomy, April 2004*, B8-B9.

Leben, A. and Bohanec, M. (2003), Evaluation of life-event portals: Multi-attribute model and case study. *KMGov 2003:* 25-36.

Linthicum, D. (1999). *Enterprise Application Integration*. USA: Addison Wesley.

Maclver, K. (2002). Sold. *Information Age, July 2002*, 20-22.

McNurlin, B.C., & Sprague, R.H. (2002). *Information Systems Management, 5th ed.* Prentice Hall: Pearson Education.

Monson-Haefel, R. (2004). *J2EE Web Services.* Boston: Adison Wesley.

Masood, S. (2002). The missing link. *Information Age, November 2002*, 31-32.

NASCIO (2003). Enterprise Architecture Maturity Model. Lexington, KY: National Association of State Chief Information Officers.

Navarra, D.D., & Cornford, T. (2003). A policy making view of e-government inovations in public governance. In *Proceedings of the Ninth Americas Conference on Information Systems*, Tampa, Florida.

Nora (2006). *Nederlands overheidsreferentiearchitectuur.* Samenhang en samenwerken binnen de elektronische overhead. ICT Programma Architectuur Elektronische overheid http://elo.asp4all.nl/atlas/referentiearchitectuur/ Last accessed April, 2006.

Office of e-Envoy UK (2002). e-Services Development Framework Primer v1.0b.

Peristera V., & Tarabanis, K. (2000). Towards an enterprise architecture for public administration using a top-down approach. *European Journal of Information Systems, 9*, 252-260.

Pulkkinen, M., & Hirvonen, A. (2005). EA planning, development and management process for agile enterprise development. In *Proceedings of the 38th Annual Hawaii International Conference on System Sciences.*

Reffat, R. (2003). *Developing a successful e-government.* Working Paper, School of Architecture, Design Science and Planning, University of Sydney, Australia.

Richardson, G.L., Jackson, B.M., & Dickson, G. (1990). A principle-based enterprise architecture: Lessons from Texaco and star enterprise. *MIS Quarterly, 14*(4), 385-403.

Ross, J. (2003). Creating a strategic IT architecture competency: Learning in stages. *MISQ Executive, 2*(1), 31-41.

Sahay, S. & Walsham, G. (1997). Social structures & management agency in India. *Organisation Studies, 18*, 415-444.

Saxena, A., & Wadhawa, S. (2004). E-business perspective of e-governence. In Gupta, M.D. (Eds.), *Promice of e-governance: Operational challenges*, pp.128-135. Tata-McGraw-Hill, New Delhi.

Schekkerman, J. (2004). *How to Survive in the Jungle of Enterprise Architecture Frameworks*. Trafford Publishing: Victoria.

Sutherland, J., & Willem, J. (2002). Enterprise application integration and complex adaptive systems. *Communications of the ACM, 45*(10), 59-64.

Thompson, J. (2002). Out with the old. *Information Age, July 2002*, 32-33.

Vasilaki, C., Laskaridis, G., Lepouras, S., Rouvas, S., & Georgiadis, P. (2003). A framework for managing the life cycle of transactional e-government services. *Telematics and Informatics, 20*, 315-329.

Walsham, G. (1993). *Interpreting Information Systems in Organisations*. Wiley: Chicester.

Weerakkody, V. and Choudrie, J. (2005), Exploring e-government in the UK: Challenges, issues and complexities, *Journal of Information Science and Technology, 2 (2)*.

Weerakkody, V., Choudrie, J., & Currie, W. (2004). Realising e-government in the UK: Local and national challenges. In *Proceedings of the 10th Americas Conference on Information Systems*, New York, August 2004.

Weerakkody, V.J.P., & Hinton, C.M. (1999). Exploiting information systems and technology through business process improvement, knowledge and process management. *The Journal of Corporate Transformation, Vol 6*, 1, March 1999, John Wiley & Sons, Ltd.: UK.

Weerakkody, V., Baire, S., & Choudrie, J. (2006). E-Government: The need for effective process management in the public sector. *Hawaii International Conference on System Sciences (HICSS-39)*, January 5-7, Kauai, Hawaii

Weill, P., & Ross, J.W. (2004). *IT governance - How top performers manage IT decision rights for superior results*. Harvard Business School Press: Boston.

Yin, R.K. (1994) Case Study Research, Design and Methods, Sage Publications, Newbury Park, CA.

Zachman, J.A. (1987). A framework for information systems architecture. *IBM Systems Journal, 26*(3), 276-292.

Zhang, J. (2004). An approach to facilitate reliability testing of Web services components, In *Proceedings of IEEE 15th International Symposium on Software Reliability Engineering (ISSRE 2004)*, Nov. 2-5, 2004, Saint-Malo, Bretagne, France, 210-218.

This work was previously published in International Journal of Cases on Electronic Commerce, Vol. 3, Issue 2, edited by J.N.D. Gupta, S.K. Sharma, and J. Hsu, pp. 13-35, copyright 2007 by IGI Publishing, formerly known as Idea Group Publishing (an imprint of IGI Global).

Chapter 4.33
Local E-Governments in Japan: IT Utilization Status and Directions

Sadaya Kubo
Setsunan University, Japan

Tatsumi Shimada
Setsunan University, Japan

ABSTRACT

This chapter explains the actual state of digital readiness of the local governments in Japan, and describes the stages of achievement in digitalization and the direction of digitalization. The items being analyzed are the digitalization of governmental administration, services to residents, and information security. Further, in order to clarify the direction of digitalization, we propose stages of progress of the digitalization of the local governments.

INTRODUCTION

In November 2000, the Basic Law on the Formation of an Advanced Information and Telecommunications Network Society was passed in accordance with the "Basic IT Strategy." Since then, there has been an increase in the emphasis placed on digitalization, under the guidance of the government, with the aim of establishing Japan as an IT nation. An IT nation comprises the construction of an e-government (Ministry of Public Management, Home Affairs, Posts and Telecommunication, 2005).

After self-evaluation, Japan came to the realization that it had not kept pace with the other developed nations with respect to its development into an IT nation. Therefore, the formulation of the concept of an e-government merits praise, considering that it was formulated as a national strategy and overcame the lack of a comprehensive IT approach by the government until that time. However, there are still several issues concerning e-government. In Japan, the government formulated a strategy to set up local e-governments, as well as to develop IT and communication infrastructure. The regional administrative bodies are making progress in the establishment of local e-governments through their own refinements within the IT strategy and communication infrastructure framework, while collaborating with the national government.

This chapter explains the actual state of digital readiness of the local governments in Japan, and describes the stages of achievement in digitalization and the direction of digitalization. The items being analyzed are the digitalization of governmental administration, services to residents, and information security.

In this chapter, we address the following three issues. First, digitalization can be classified into digitalization of organizations in order to improve their internal efficiency, and digitalization to improve services to residents. What is the current state of progress on each? Second, what is the current state of progress on information disclosure for the purpose of improving resident democracy and facilitating resident participation? Third, what is the current state of progress on information security for the purpose of satisfying residents' requirements?

Further, in order to clarify the direction of digitalization, we propose stages of progress of the digitalization of the local governments.

FRAMEWORK OF THE ANALYSIS AND RECOGNITION OF ISSUES

Several studies have examined the digitalization of local governments. They analyzed the effects of the digitalization of local governments on information and cost, the changing nature of public-private partnership, and the improvement of efficiency (Chen & Perry, 2003; Stamoulis, Gouscos, Georgiadis, & Martakos, 2001). Further, these studies also analyzed the increase in the provision of information services to the residents (Siau & Long, 2005), the increase in the autonomy of the residents as well as the improvement in the service provided to them (Marchionini, Samet, & Brandt, 2003). In many cases, the effects were studied only after the digitalization of local governments. However, since information technology (IT) is constantly developing, the effects and the process of digitalization should be studied simultaneously.

The digitalization of the local governments does not only imply the purchase of a personal computer, server, and network facility (Shimada & Ushida, 2003). Some examples of additional requirements are organized activity to increase the efficiency of the business process, development of the service model through information communication technology, and improvement of information security for the safety and relief of residents.

We consider that the digitalization of local e-government is carried out in three stages: computerization in offices, services to residents, and information security. Computerization in offices refers to the infrastructure of the e-government. Services to residents are put out by the e-government. Information security is important for the operation of the e-government.

Previous studies have measured digitalization through the types of technology used, the level of the information system, and the services provided by the system (Chen & Perry, 2003; Thompson & Rust, 2005). However, as far as other measurements, such as the measurement of the equipment, its practical use, and so on, that are essential for the efficient introduction of new technology are concerned, they are related to the improvement of services and cost reduction (Thompson & Rust, 2005). The improvement of services relate to the purpose of the organization and its information system (Brown & Brudney, 2004). These activities are related to the organization's approach toward its residents. In addition to these activities, the safety of the system and information security are also important. With regard to the Internet society, personal information and privacy are important considerations. Therefore, the digitalization of local governments must emphasize developing strong protocols and procedures to ensure information security. In this study, we analyze the digitalization from an integrated viewpoint that comprises the computerization of offices, services to residents, and information security.

As shown in Figure 1, these elements are interrelated and we believe they are associated with the realization of a local e-government. Moreover, the development of each element is thought to exist at several stages. They are considered to form a fundamental part of and play an important role in application and interaction.

Figure 1. Elements of e-government

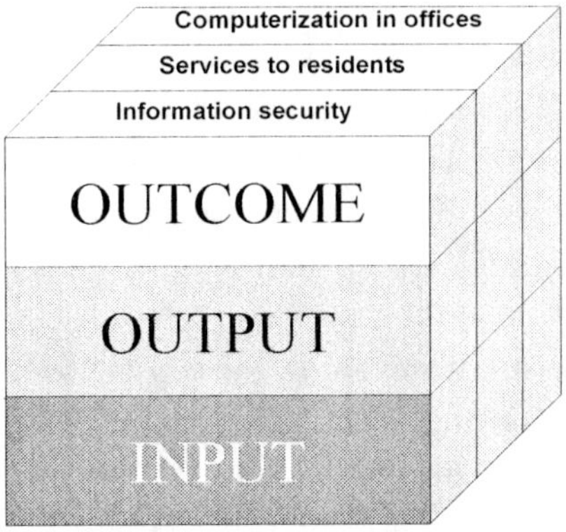

These elements are often undertaken and estimated separately. However, the contribution of digitalization cannot be measured merely by considering the amount of investment. We must focus on answering certain fundamental questions, such as "Is a system applied efficiently?" or "Does a system yield the desired results?" (Marchionini et al., 2003; Stamoulis et al., 2001). Therefore, we analyze the contribution of digitalization by considering the activities right from the investments in digitalization to its impacts. Our views on the progress of computerization are as follows. When measuring whether digitalization is "progressing" or "lagging behind," let us assume the following three levels:

- **Level 1:** The input (budget) level, as measured by the extent of the development of or investment in information and telecommunications infrastructure, for example, the number of people per PC, the speed of connection of a PC to the LANs (local area networks) and Internet connection speed, the extent of implementation of security policies and counter measures, and the extent of IT utilization in front and back office work.
- **Level 2:** The output (work) level, as measured by the number of employees who are capable of using a PC, e-mail, and so forth for work and the speed at which they work, the extent of the promotion of computerization or operating regimes, the extent of freedom of information and publicity activities for residents, the amount of support for services to residents, the extent of the framework for the participation of residents in administrative services.
- **Level 3:** The outcome (results) level, as measured by the extent of an increase in residents' satisfaction toward services rendered to them, the extent of investment outcomes such as greater energy efficiency through increased productivity, and so forth, the extent of any increase in workforce morale as a result of the workforce being freed from simplistic tasks, the extent to which infiltration by viruses or leakage of personal information is prevented or reduced through security countermeasures.

In general, from the above three levels described, a significant number of people are of the opinion that digitalization progresses due to level 1. However, level 1 only reflects the investment resources. To put this in the extreme, we can state that in order to achieve an increase in level 1, all that is required is to increase the capital directed toward this level. Moreover, level 2 being high does not necessarily mean that results have been achieved. This is because a high output does not necessarily correlate with a high outcome.

What is important is level 3. The question of whether digitalization is "progressing" or "lagging behind" should be evaluated at this level. However, in order to measure level 3, local governments should have the necessary skills and knowledge in system appraisals and administrative appraisal methods; if not, they will be unable to conduct effective appraisals. In the long run, even if one is able to understand this through a cost-benefit analysis, it may still be difficult for local governments that do not use digitalization on a daily basis and where it is yet to become second nature. There has recently been rapid progress in the introduction of public sector evaluation approaches in local governments. If this becomes common, there is no doubt that the ability to measure computerization at level 3 will improve.

In addition, it is necessary to achieve levels 1 and 2, since it is a fact that these levels are prerequisites to the realization of level 3. In short, the municipalities that do not give due consideration to level 3 and only aim at level 1 are likely to face difficulties. Moreover, it is difficult to increase outcomes solely with technology. Rather, this should be accomplished with technology coupled with work reforms and agile and flexible decision making and implementation. It is also vitally important to review any laws and ordinances, regulations, regimes, and procedures that restrict such decision making and implementation.

If the development of information and telecommunications infrastructure and the investment in computerization are carried out without the realization that IT should be utilized in order to raise outcomes, it will not contribute to administrative and financial reforms. Such investments in computerization cannot be said to be financially insignificant in comparison with empty box public works. It is important to remember that such investments will lead to financial pressure in the same manner that public works do.

The stages of progress are proposed for each category—computerization in offices, services to residents, and information security—along the same lines of thinking as earlier in this chapter.

RESEARCH DESIGN

We conducted a questionnaire survey on approximately 765 local governments; of these, approximately 500 responded to the questionnaire. Even in the past, the local governments in Japan have undergone several public investigations, and they have always actively cooperated with such research. Moreover, based on the response rate obtained in our study, it is clear that a high response rate is a feature of the local governments in Japan. The methods of the survey are:

- **Period of survey:** May-June 2004
- **Targets:** 765 local governments in Japan (prefectures, government-designated cities, special wards, and cities)
- **Total number of respondents:** 496 local governments (percentage of respondents: 64.8%)

The questions in the survey could be categorized as computerization in offices, services to residents, and information security.

Computerization in offices refers to the infrastructure of the e-government. The questions in this part of the survey were related to client and server machines, training provided to government employees, the use of integrated applications, and the appointment of a chief information officer (CIO).

Services to residents are put out by the e-government. The questions in this part of the survey included information services provided by the government's Web site, information interchange with the residents, the development of original services, and service estimation.

Information security is important for the operation of an e-government. The questions in this section focus on the framing of the security policy, management of client machines and the server room, checking of access logs, and education regarding information ethics.

We calculate the deviations in each part as well as in the total, which comprises all the deviations.

In this chapter, we propose five stages of progress for the three categories. The conceptualization of the stages of progress was based on the following perspectives (Kubo, Higashigawa, & Shimada, 2005): invested resources as the input, produced result as the output, and the effect of the input on the output as the outcome. These stages are based on our previous work. However, other studies have described several other stages and models. Kim's model (Kim & Kim, 2003) focused on organizational learning, digital democracy, information security, and cost efficiency. Reddick, on the other hand, used a two-stage model. Stage I involves the cataloguing of information online, while Stage II involves the completion of transactions online (Reddick, 2004). Another study developed a three-stage process of e-government. The first implies actually going online, that is, digitizing the government; the second refers to delivering interactive services to the citizens; and the third stage is increasingly interactive as it allows governments to use IT tools to engage citizens in the development of policies, programs, and services. These stages are similar to those that we consider for our analysis. Siau and Long (2005) proposed a five-stage model that entails Web presence, interaction, transaction, transformation, and e-democracy.

Although the direction of this model is appropriate, the range of its stages is far too broad. These activities are different during each stage. However, since the development of IT continues in relation to these activities, we believe that each stage of these activities should be examined in detail.

In order to analyze the development of an e-government, we focus on the stages of progress with regard to the services that are provided to the citizens. These stages will contribute to our understanding of the status and nature of digitalization. Thus, we propose our stages of progress for e-government.

OUTLINE OF THE RESULTS OF THE SURVEY

The results of our survey are listed in Table 1. In comparison with cities, prefectures, government-designated cities, and special wards had high scores in the total. Prefectures had a high score in the category of computerization in offices. Government-designated cities had a high score in the category of services to residents, and special wards had a high score in the category of information security.

A typical result is now provided for each category.

Computerization in Government Offices

Table 2 summarizes the results of the survey in the category of computerization in government offices. The introduction rate for LANs (99.6%) is high. The PC diffusion rate (the number of PCs per employee) is 71.5%. High tendencies are shown in these questions. The rate of establishment of a CIO is 61.6%. In the establishment of a CIO, cities and special wards had higher scores than prefectures and government-designated cities.

More than half the number of prefectures, government-designated cities, special wards, and cities (63.8%) had introduced geographic information systems (GIS). In the introduction of GIS, prefectures and government-designated cities have higher scores than cities and special wards. The rate of the introduction of electronics is 20.2 %. Here, prefectures and special wards accounted for more than 50 %, and the difference is large, while that of cities is low (15.6 %). The rate of introduction of electronic bidding is low (4.8 %). However, there was a large difference among prefectures. The rate of introduction of electronic document management is 34.1 %.

Table 1. The deviation of average

	Prefecture	Government-designated cities	Special wards	Cities
Computerization in offices	58.3%	55.7%	57.2%	48.9%
Services to residents	57.9%	59.8%	55.7%	48.9%
Information security	51.7%	50.6%	58.7%	49.5%
Total	56.0%	55.4%	57.2%	49.1%

Note: $*p<0.05$; $**p<0.01$

Excluding cities (30.8 %), this rate exceeds 50 %. As for the applications, cities are delayed as mentioned above.

The rate of execution of BPR (business process re-engineering) is 37.0 %. Government-designated cities and special wards had high scores, and the difference was large. The execution of BPR is all the more necessary in order that it can contribute to an increase in efficiency through information technology.

The rate of execution of reorganization is 34.6 %. However, prefectures, government-designated cities, and special wards accounted for more than 50 %. From these results, it can be considered that a reorganization of the organization should be more important for governments whose scale is large.

The rate of improvement of front office efficiency through investments in information technology is 73.3 %. However prefectures accounted for approximately 50 %, displaying an overall high tendency. The rate of improvement of back office efficiency through by investments in information technology is 90.2 %.

The rate of improvement of staff morale by release of routine work is 41.7 %. The rate of execution of system evaluation prior to digitalization is 53.6 %. Prefectures, government-designated cities, and special wards had high scores. The rate of execution of system evaluation after digitalization is 29.8 %. A low tendency can be seen pertaining to improvement of staff morale. However, system evaluation after digitalization is necessary to decide the aim of future digitalization.

Table 2. Computerization in government offices

	Prefectures	Government-designated cities	Special wards	Cities	Average
Installation of LAN in offices	100.0%	100.0%	100.0%	99.5%	99.6%
PC diffusion	86.5%	50.0%	77.8%	70.4%	71.5%
Appointment and job role of the CIO*	43.2%	40.0%	61.1%	63.7%	61.6%
Introduction and type of GIS*	83.8%	90.0%	66.7%	61.4%	63.8%
Introduction of electronic decision**	56.8%	30.0%	50.0%	15.6%	20.2%
Introduction of electronic bidding**	27.0%	10.0%	5.6%	2.8%	4.8%
Introduction of electronic document management**	61.1%	50.0%	50.0%	30.8%	34.1%
Execution of BPR**	67.6%	87.5%	94.4%	31.2%	37.0%
Reorganization*	55.9%	50.0%	50.0%	32.0%	34.6%
Increase in front office efficiency	52.9%	100.0%	77.8%	74.2%	73.3%
Increase in back office efficiency	88.2%	100.0%	88.2%	90.2%	90.2%
Improvement in staff morale by the release of routine work	46.9%	62.5%	55.6%	40.3%	41.7%
System evaluation prior to digitalization**	78.8%	100.0%	94.4%	48.9%	53.6%
System evaluation after digitalization	41.2%	44.4%	38.9%	28.1%	29.8%

Note: $*p<0.05$; $**p<0.01$

Services to Residents

Table 3 summarizes the survey results in the category of services to residents. The rate of enactment of the information disclosure ordinance is 98.8 %. A high tendency can be seen in this question. The rate of execution of Web accessibility is 35.6 %. In Web accessibility, prefectures had a high score and the difference among prefectures was large. Prefectures which have few direct relations with residents had high scores and the difference was large.

The rate of disclosure of regulations on a Web site is 83.6 %. The rate of publication of the governments' main policies, such as the city master plan, is 67.8 %. Excluding the cities, this is high.

Publications and the type of mail magazines for residents is 20.6 %. Prefectures scored the highest (94.6 %), followed by government-designated cities (40.0 %).

Special wards (27.8 %) and cities (13.5 %) had low scores. The rate of enabling a public comments facility on the Web site was 42.8 %. Excluding the cities, this is high, and the difference is large.

The rate of improvement of services to residents through digitalization is 90.7%. A high tendency is displayed in this question. However, there is a difference among cities. There are issues regarding the accuracy of the method of measuring this difference, because the answers are self-evaluated.

Information Security

Table 4 summarizes the survey results in the category of information security. In general, the scores for the rate of control (94.2%) of the server room, the use limitation (79.0%), and the security policy (86.2%) are high. The various fundamental components of information security are established.

Table 3. Services to residents

	Prefectures	Government-designated cities	Special wards	Cities	Average
Enactment of the information disclosure ordinance	100.0%	100.0%	100.0%	98.6%	98.8%
Provision of Web accessibility, taking into consideration the physical condition of the user and the environment of use**	81.1%	55.6%	44.4%	30.8%	35.6%
Disclosure of regulations on the Web site	89.2%	100.0%	88.9%	82.6%	83.6%
Disclosure of serial set on the Web site**	100.0%	100.0%	88.9%	63.5%	67.8%
Publication of the government's main policies such as the city master plan**	100.0%	100.0%	100.0%	78.3%	81.2%
Publication and type of mail magazines for residents**	94.6%	40.0%	27.8%	13.5%	20.6%
Enabling a public comments facility on the Web site**	94.4%	90.0%	88.9%	35.4%	42.8%
Improvement of services to residents through digitalization**	94.1%	100.0%	100.0%	89.8%	90.7%

The rate of the correspondence of each level exceeds 50%, except for government-designated cities. The rate of the special wards was 83.3%, and correspondence proceeds through it.

With regard to security education, while the average score was 35.3%, special wards also excelled with 61.1%. Since there was relative enforcement of the law, individual information protection displayed a high score (92.9%). Information ethics (41.4%) exceeded 50%, except in the case of cities. The cities have many contacts to residents. Therefore cities are required to the information ethics. An access log was acquired by 68.0%.

STAGES OF PROGRESS OF LOCAL E-GOVERNMENT

We propose the stages of progress for each category on the basis of the following assumptions. We assume that the fundamental stage—input—is represented by the infrastructure and the configuration of the rules for an information system. The next stage—output—is represented by activities that enable the effective use and planning for the expansion of and compliance to the new situation. The final stage—outcome—involves the estimation and verification of the effects through information technology and information systems. Although the Japanese administrative system aims at decentralization, the system still remains centralized. In Japan, the central government manages 40% of the all the work, while the remaining work is managed by the local governments. However, with regard to budget allocation, the central government enjoys 60% of the budget, while the local governments are only entitled to 40%. Thus, there is a 20% gap between the work and budget allocation. Therefore, most local governments seek financial assistance from the central government. Moreover, most local governments improve the input of digitalization through a block grant.

However, in order to improve the outcome of digitalization, it is necessary that these governments seek the participation and assistance of local residents. The estimation and verification of digitalization are important stages, and therefore, these are placed at a higher stage.

Table 4. Information security

	Prefecture	Government-designated cities	Special wards	Cities	Average
Access control in server rooms	100.0%	100.0%	100.0%	93.4%	94.2%
Implementation of restriction of and management method for client PCs	71.4%	80.0%	100.0%	78.7%	79.0%
Enactment of security policy	97.3%	90.0%	88.9%	85.0%	86.2%
Establishment of security as a countermeasure at every level*	57.1%	33.3%	83.3%	53.4%	54.4%
Information security training for the entire staff	27.8%	22.2%	61.1%	35.1%	35.3%
Enactment of ordinance or rules for the protection of personal information	100.0%	100.0%	100.0%	91.9%	92.9%
Enactment of information ethics rules such as netiquette and prevention of abuse**	61.1%	60.0%	72.2%	38.0%	41.4%
Checking access logs and notification	82.4%	87.5%	72.2%	66.4%	68.0%

Note: $*p < 0.05$; $**p < 0.01$

The Stages of Progress

Table 5, 6, and 7 list the stages of progress in the categories of computerization in offices, services to residents, and information security, respectively. These stages correspond to those conceptualized in the previous section. Progress in the category of computerization in offices comprises five stages: Stage 1: preparation of IT infrastructure; Stage 2: support of effective use; Stage 3: improvement of staff efficiency; Stage 4: expansion of applications with IT; and Stage 5: verification of the effects of computerization.

Progress in the category of services to residents comprises the following five stages: stage 1: disclosure of basic information; stage 2: improvement of basic services; stage 3: Internet use; stage 4: expansion of IT effectiveness; and stage 5: verification of services.

Progress in the category of information security comprises five stages: stage 1: enactment of the rules and clarification of the purpose; stage 2: technical correspondence; stage 3: independent correspondence; stage 4: integrated correspondence; and stage 5: improvement of staff consciousness.

We now verify the relationship between these stages of progress and the results of our survey. First, we consider the relationship between the increase in stage and degree of achievement. The degree of achievement is calculated by dividing the mean point by the full point in each stage.

We now describe the relationship among the stages and the changes in the degree of achievement for each category. All the governments that responded were categorized into 10 groups, each of which comprised approximately 50 governments in order of ranking. We then proceed to draw the graphs showing the change in the degree of achievement for the 10 groups. Based on the scores, we segment the local governments into 10 groups. Then, we compare the groups that scored

Table 5. The stage of progress for computerization in offices

Stage	Title	Content of question
5	Verification of the effects of computerization	Appointment and job role of the CIO Execution of BPR (business process reengineering) Reorganization System evaluation after digitalization
4	Expansion of applications with IT	Introduction and type of GIS Introduction of electronic decision Introduction of electronic bidding Introduction of electronic document management
3	Improvement of staff efficiency	Increase in back office efficiency Realization of a labor-saving method Periodical training of staff for effective IT use Improvement of staff morale by release of routine work Use of a lesser amount of paper
2	Support of effective use	Establishment of an IT help desk for staff use Systematic use of the mailing list Appointment of an IT leader and promotion of EUC Emphasis on labor saving as an objective and aim System evaluation prior to digitalization
1	Preparation of IT infrastructure	Installation of LAN in office PC diffusion Internet connection rate Distribution range of e-mail addresses

Table 6. The stages of progress for services to residents

Stage	Title	Content of question
5	Verification of services	Improvement of services to residents through digitalization Increase in front office efficiency Promotion of the relationship between local governments and residents or local enterprises
4	Expansion of IT effectiveness	Provision of Web accessibility, taking into consideration the physical condition of the user and the environment of use Setting up of an IT school for residents using the Web site Provision of individual services by residents IC card Methods of opinion collection Rebroadcast of the assembly by CATV
3	Internet use	Publication and type of mail magazine for residents Provision of system services such as reservation of facilities Enabling a public comments facility on the Web site Setting up a teleconference room and electronic bulletin board Emphasis on improved services for residents as the objective and aim of digitalization
2	Improvement of basic services	Delivery of certificates for extra time Placement of information terminal outside offices, such as for the reservation of various facilities
1	Disclosure of basic information	Enactment of the information disclosure ordinance Disclosure of regulations on Web site Disclosure of serial set on Web site Publication of the governments' main policies such as city master plan

Table 7. The stages of progress for information security

Stage	Title	Content of question
5	Improvement of staff consciousness	Checking access logs and notification Enactment of information ethics rules such as netiquette and prevention of abuse
4	Integrated correspondence	Establishment of security as a countermeasure for every level Penal regulations for outside trust dealers Checking access logs for e-mail and the Internet
3	Independent correspondence	Setup of access limitation to files and applications by job role and job grade Information security training for the entire staff (training to be held more than once every year) The rules pertaining to the information erasure process in the event of scrapping of machines Prohibition against sending e-mails to the private outside and Internet access
2	Technical correspondence	Implementation of restriction of and management method for client PC Access control in server rooms
1	Enactment of the rules and clarification of the purpose	Enactment of security policy Enactment of ordinance or rules for the protection of personal information

higher with those that scored low. Moreover, we analyze the relationship between the increase in the score and the increase in the degree of achievement at each stage.

The Degree of Achievement

Table 8 shows the degree of achievement at each stage. In all the cases, it is evident that the first stage shows the highest degree of achievement. Therefore, if the degree of achievement at a higher stage is greater than that at a lower stage, then, based on the proposed stages, digitalization will be difficult. However, for the categories of computerization in offices and services to residents, the degrees of achievement at stage 5 are higher than those at stage 2.

The degrees of achievement in the proposed stages follow an appropriate pattern. Accordingly, the attainment of a high degree of achievement at a higher stage is difficult. For example, integrated activities in each category are located in the fourth stage and their score was low. On the other hand, the lower stages contained independent correspondences, such as the enactment of rules. However, there were some cases wherein the numerical value of the evaluation and the verification deviated from the pattern (stages 2 and 5). However, it is likely that this was due to the manner in which the question was posed. Therefore, the proposed stages are fairly reflective of the actual situation.

Figures 2 to 4 show the degrees of achievement in each category. The line at the center of each of the figures indicates a 50% degree of achievement.

Computerization in Offices

Table 9 shows the relationship of the stages for computerization in offices. Figure 2 depicts the change in the degree of achievement in this category.

The existence of a relationship in this category could imply the preliminary stages and the applied stages of digitalization. If this is not the case, it appears that the contents of these questions can be simultaneously used for all the stages. Block grants are useful in the contingent progress because this content is treated in a parallel manner.

There are low correlations in stages 2, 3, and 4 in this category. Stages 1 and 5 appear to be independent of the other stages. Since the degree of achievement in stage 1 is extremely high, it is important to carry out stages 2 to 4 in an integrative manner.

The change in the degree of achievement displays the following characteristics:

- Stage 1 represents the fundamental stage, and there is a high degree of achievement.
- Stages 2 and 4 display the same trend in score for the order. It appears that these stages are carried out in an integrative manner.
- In stage 4, which has a type of GIS, electronic bidding has a low score and yields the difference in computerization.

Services to Residents

Table 10 shows the relationship among the stages for services to residents. Figure 3 shows the change in the degree of achievement in this category.

Table 8. The degree of achievement at each stage

	Stages				
Category	1	2	3	4	5
Computerization in offices	0.78	0.46	0.44	0.31	0.50
Services to residents	0.82	0.51	0.48	0.27	0.67
Information security	0.89	0.77	0.58	0.53	0.40

Figure 2. Computerization in the offices

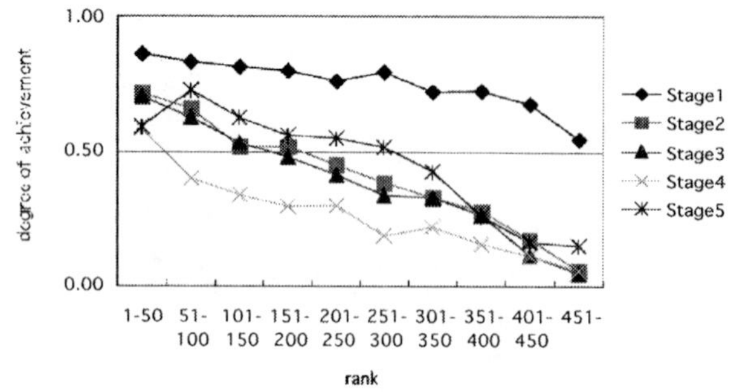

Figure 3. Services to residents

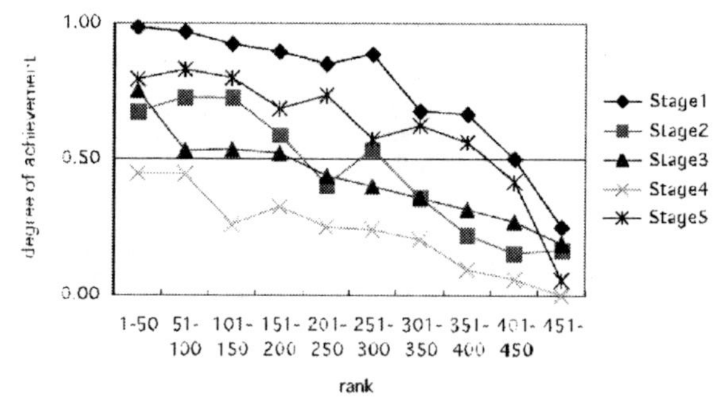

Figure 4. Information security

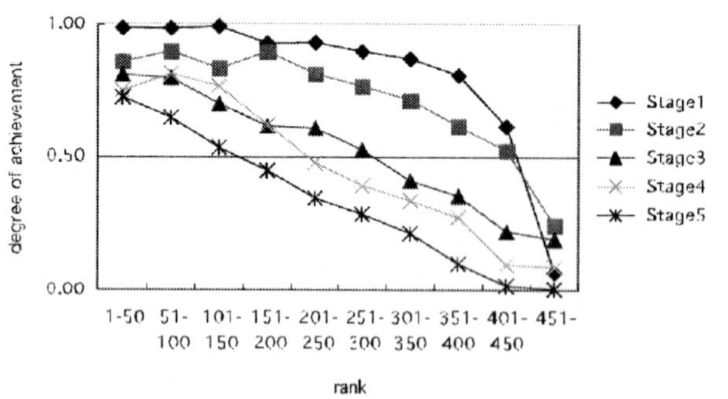

Table 9. Correlation of computerization in the offices

Stage	1	2	3	4	5
1	1				
2	0.14	1			
3	0.07	0.33	1		
4	0.17	0.34	0.28	1	
5	0.00	0.25	0.21	0.10	1

Table 10. Correlation of services to residents

Stage	1	2	3	4	5
1	1				
2	0.25	1			
3	0.27	0.42	1		
4	0.21	0.17	0.22	1	
5	0.18	0.12	0.14	0.11	1

There is a comparatively high correlation between improvement of basic services (stage 2) and Internet use (stage 3). It appears that local governments dealing with Internet facilities have already worked towards an improvement in these services. The effective use of IT relates not only to the technical characteristics of IT but also to the local government's vision or attitude toward this issue to date.

In this category, a relationship exists a tendency between degree of the stages and achievement as difficulties. However, the top 50 ranked local governments are strongly influenced by Internet use (stage 3). Further, the degree of achievement at stage 4 (expansion of IT effectiveness) has an influence on the top 100 ranked local governments.

Information Security

Table 11 shows the relationship among to the stages for information security. Figure 4 shows the change in the degree of achievement in this category.

The correlation of information security is stronger than that of the other two categories. Stages 1 to 4, 2 to 3, 3 to 4 and 5, and 4 to 5 display correlations above 0.3. These correlations become stronger with an increase in the stage. Therefore, it seems that activities in stage 2 are acceleration for higher stages.

Despite the low rank, the degree of achievement of enactment of the rule and clarification of the purpose (stage 1) and technical correspondence (stage 2) are over 0.5. On the other hand, the

Table 11. Correlation of information security

Stage	1	2	3	4	5
1	1				
2	0.14	1			
3	0.28	0.35	1		
4	0.35	0.25	0.45	1	
5	0.22	0.19	0.35	0.49	1

degree of achievement of improvement of staff consciousness (stage 5) increases linearly from the lower to higher ranks. Therefore, the development of information security can be gauged from the behavior and posture of the staff.

CONCLUSION

Digitalization of local governments progresses under the e-Japan strategy. This strategy attempts to increase the efficiency of administrative and financial services through the propagation of computerization and the improving of services to residents. Further, residents also demand the establishment of information security.

Regarding the actual situation of local governments, the computerization of the fundamental parts, such as the introduction of PCs and LANs, continues. However, use of the application for issues such as electronic decision making and electronic bidding, BPR, and the reorganization are not in progress. As a result, system evaluation becomes an issue.

Regarding the services to residents, static services by IT are satisfactory in such cases as the regulations and disclosure of serial set on the Web site. However, dynamic services such as mail magazines and public comments are all issues for the future. With regard to information security, the part of the systematic correspondence proceeds through the access control of the server room, the security policy, and so on.

From now, personal activities such as information ethics and security education will be a necessity. The proposed stages of progress have displayed the above characteristics. The examination of the roadmap of digitalization corresponding to each local government is necessary to output it from the input and then to proceed with the digitalization of local government to outcome.

When the proposed stages are applied to other countries, it is important to consider the following.

The State of IT Infrastructure

Japan has a strong background for the maintenance of IT infrastructure that is also supported by a national policy. Therefore, the computerization of local governments in other countries may be an extremely different process as compared with Japan.

The Range of the Official Services

In some countries, the private sector is the primary service provider for the citizens. However, since Japan delayed the use of the private sector in terms of being a service provider, it is possible that some of the proposed stages may not be applicable in these cases. Nevertheless, the stages that refer to the rules, correspondence, and evaluation will be valid and applicable. Therefore, we can use the stages proposed by us albeit with some adjustments according to the specific situations of different countries.

The Management of Personal Information

In Japan, the enactment of a law that protects personal information is a recent phenomenon. In the past, there was limited focus on the development of laws to protect personal information; moreover, the national consciousness toward such laws was not extremely high. However, other countries could have stricter regulations regarding information security, and their corresponding indexes may be higher.

Therefore, the analysis of the progress stages based on the actual condition of other countries is a subject for future study.

REFERENCES

Brown, M. M., & Brudney, J. L. (2004). Achieving advanced electronic government services: Opposing environmental constraints. *Public Performance & Management Review, 28*(1), 96-113.

Chen, Y. C., & Perry, J. (2003). Outsourcing for e-government: Managing for success. *Public Performance & Management Review, 26*(4), 404-421.

Kim, S., & Kim, D. (2003). South Korean public officials' perceptions of values, failure and consequences of failure in e-government leadership. *Public Performance & Management Review, 26*(4), 360-375.

Kubo, S., Higashigawa, T., & Shimada, T. (2005, May 15). The consideration of progress stages for computerization in local government. In *Proceedings of the 34th Conference on Japan Association for Management System* (In Japanese), Reitaku University, Chiba, Japan (pp. 138-141).

Marchionini, G., Samet, H., & Brandt, L. (2003). Digital government. *Communications of the ACM, 46*(1), 25-27.

Ministry of Public Management, Home Affairs, Posts and Telecommunication, Japan. (2005). *Information and communication in Japan.* Retrieved May 11, 2006, from http://www.johotsusintokei.soumu.go.jp/ whitepaper/eng/WP2004/2004-index.html

Reddick, C. G. (2004). Empirical models of e-government growth in local governments. *e-Service Journal, 3*(2), 59-84.

Shimada, T., & Ushida, K. (2003). Electronic government in Japan: IT utilization status of local governments. In G. Gingrich (Ed.), *Managing IT in government, business & communities* (pp. 111-126). Hershey, PA: IRM Press.

Siau, K., & Long, Y. (2005). Synthesizing e-government stage models: A meta-synthesis based on meta-ethnography approach. *Industrial Management & Data Systems, 105*(4), 443-458.

Stamoulis, D., Gouscos, D., Georgiadis, P., & Martakos, D. (2001). Revisiting public information management for effective e-government services. *Information Management & Computer Security, 9*(4), 146-153.

Thompson, D. V., Rust, R. T., & Rhoda, J. (2005). The business value of e-government for small firms. *International Journal of Service Industry Management, 16*(4), 385-407.

This work was previously published in Global E-Government: Theory, Applications and Benchmarking, edited by L. Al-Hakim, pp. 300-319, copyright 2007 by IGI Publishing, formerly known as Idea Group Publishing (an imprint of IGI Global).

Chapter 4.34
Organisational Challenges of Implementing E-Business in the Public Services:
The Case of Britain's National Mapping Agency

Francesca Andreescu
University of Greenwich, UK

ABSTRACT

Underpinning £136 billion of economic activity in the United Kingdom, Britain's National Mapping Agency is a commercialising public sector organisation having trading fund status and existing in the intersection of two different spheres—the public and the private. Recognised as a leading participant in the geographic information industry, within which it is forging partnerships with key private sector companies, the organisation has enthusiastically grasped e-business as an all-embracing phenomenon and implemented a new strategy that transformed the way it did business. Drawing on longitudinal data gathered over a period of four years, this article explores the processes of strategic and organisational transformation engendered by e-business implementation in this organisation and discusses the successful elements, as well as some of the challenges to its change efforts.

INTRODUCTION

A common theme within the management literature in recent years has been the take up of private sector management strategies and practices by public sector organisations, designed to increase efficiency, performance, and cost economy in the activities they performed. In the United Kingdom, more specifically, in the context of significant changes in their operating environments and pressures to increase efficiency and accountability, public sector organisations have been urged to experiment with new organising ideas, structures, and processes and transform the way they do business, by taking the opportunities and meeting the challenges that e-technologies and e-ways of working presented. As a result, public sector organisations have embraced e-business and have made innovative uses of Internet technologies to invent new business models or to enhance existing practices. E-business has been seen as a way of transforming these bureaucratic, centralised, and reactive organisations and their capabilities. Whilst the Internet created new commercial opportunities for public sector organisations, e-business was thus about exploiting those opportunities.

This article draws on findings from a study conducted over a period of four years in a commercialised public sector organisation to reveal the processes of strategic and organisational transformation engendered by e-business during the implementation of a complex structural and cultural change programme aimed at reshaping this organisation and rethinking how it provided value to its customers. The discussion will examine the dilemmas and constraints identified by managers in the interpretation of the e-business strategy concept and why its implementation in practice can be challenging. Whilst the Internet offers a technological solution, the findings of this case study suggest that the successful implementation of a wider e-business strategy depends on managing simultaneously a number of projects which cross organisational boundaries and link organisational and technological factors.

The article is divided into five main sections. The first section reviews recent e-business research and highlights that studies treating the concept of e-business as an all-embracing phenomenon and analysing in depth its implications are relatively rare. The second section of the article describes the methodology used in the study. Information on the contextual developments within the case study organisation is followed by a discussion of the research findings. The case study is used as a background for discussing some of the challenges and constraints that this commercialising organisation faces in implementing a wider e-business strategy. Finally, the concluding discussion highlights key lessons learnt and implications for practitioners.

E-BUSINESS AND ORGANISATIONAL CHANGE: REVOLUTION OR E-VOLUTION?

Increasing environmental pressures, global economic uncertainties, changes in public and community expectations, and pressures to increase public accountability have provided the momentum for British public sector organisations to examine the effectiveness of their management structures, systems, and processes. The emphasis is on achieving efficiency, effectiveness, and economy in the activities performed by public organisations and on developing their ability to compete with private sector organisations. As a result, many public sector organisations are now existing in the intersection of two different spheres—the public and the private (Kickert, 2001). They fit neither in the strictly public realm of state action nor in the strictly private realm of commercial relationships. They are expected to function like businesses—to be efficient, customer-driven, and client-oriented—yet they perform tasks that are inherently public. How to strengthen organisational capabilities in order to confront successfully the competitive pressures becomes, consequently, one of the biggest challenges for these organisations.

Research into appropriate e-business models has grown significantly over the past few years, with authors taking both theoretically and empirically based approaches to the development of taxonomies of business models suitable for the new economy. A number of business models focused upon individual business transactions that use the Internet as a medium of exchange, including both business-to-business and business-to-consumer (e.g., Becker & Berkemeyer, 2005; Carlton, 2001; Clay, 2001; Clegg, Chu, Smithson, Henney, et al., 2005; Gao, 2005; Garicano, 2001; Scott Morton, 2001; Smith, 2001). Interest has also tended to focus on new startups (Chaston, 2001; Clarke & Flaherty, 2004; Colombo, 2001) and on traditional organisations moving towards integrating electronic marketing and sales, purchasing, or customer service with their current businesses (e.g., Barnes, Hinton, & Mieczkowska, 2005; Bhaskar, 2005; Chen & Leteney, 2000; Hansen, 2000; Kotha, Rajgopal, & Rindova, 2001; Lee & Wang, 2001), or on the technology itself (Day & Schoemaker, 2000; Smith, 2001). Much research into the use of e-commerce, furthermore, has tended to focus on larger firms (Dutta & Segev, 1999), new business models for digital content (Barnes & Hunt, 2001; Boddy & Macbeth, 2000; Daniel, Wilson, & Myers, 2002; Mahadevan, 2000; Van der Wiele, Williams, Van Iwaarder, Wilson, & Dale, 2002), and the growth and development of dot-coms (Benoy, Cook, & Javalgi, 2001; Clay, 2001). Further studies revealed how the Internet has made possible types of business models previously very hard, or impossible, to implement (Mahadevan, 2000; Rayport, 1999; Timmers, 2000).

A key concern is how strategy can be developed in hypercompetitive markets where the speed of change makes traditional forms of analysis impractical (Hoffman & Novak, 2000; Ordanini & Pol, 2001; Venkatraman, 2000). Eisenhardt (1998, 1999) and Yoffie and Cusumano (1999a, 1999b) address this issue with concepts derived from complex systems theory and emergent strategy making. E-business has also confirmed the significance of the resource-based view of the firm. Competencies, such as knowledge management and the ability to integrate complex sets of technological and business skills, are identified as success factors in a number of case studies (e.g., Feeny, 2001; Harris, Coles, Dickson, & McLoughlin, 1999; Kotha, 1998; Sauer, 1993). Various studies also addressed the risks of Internet ventures, barriers to implementation, success factors, and steps needed to manage technology-driven change (e.g., Barua, Konona, Whinston, & Yin, 2001; Eisenhardt, 1999; Kotha et al., 2001; Porter, 2001).

In general, existing research has focused on issues related to the digital content provision (particularly online provision) and technologies or technology-based change generically, rather than focusing specifically on the organisational transformation required for successfully making the change to e-business. This topic is critically important because the majority of organisations are not startups, and many are not solely concerned with e-commerce and electronic markets. Rather, most organisations are traditional businesses which must grapple with finding a new architecture to meet the imperative of remaining competitive in an increasingly Internet-enhanced economy. Their concern is the adoption of e-business as an all embracing phenomenon, in other words, transforming key business processes with Internet related technologies (Deise, Nowikow, King, & Wright, 2000; Symonds, 1999). In particular, within the literature drawn on public sector organisations, the issue of how public sector organisations undergoing commercialisation can successfully make the transition from traditional approaches to e-business by taking advantage of e-technologies has received little attention.

Building upon these arguments, this article explores the processes of strategic and organisational transformation engendered by e-business implementation through an in-depth case study of a commercialising British public sector organisation within the geographic information industry. On doing so, the study aims to provide fresh insights into the internal transformation processes which occurred in an organisation evolving from the classical, bureaucratic, and centralised "public sector model" towards a new organisational form through embracing e-business as a corporate philosophy. We also aim to see whether practice had overtaken theory and, if so, what enhancements to existing theory could be learned from the practitioners in the field.

The definition of *e-business* adopted in this research takes the view that e-business represents:

the way in which organisations can gain value from the Internet technologies and encompasses not only e-commerce—selling and buying over a network, but also the way people within an organisation work together, the sharing of information and effective communication, the transactions and connections across a supply chain, between suppliers and distributors and consumers, as well as the relationships between individuals and institutions. (Symon, 2000, p. 6)

Thus, unlike other authors (e.g., Clegg et al, 2002; Poon & Swatman, 1999) who use the terms more or less interchangeably, this study seeks to distinguish between e-commerce and e-business. E-business is not just the sharing of business information, maintaining business relationships, and conducting business transactions by means of Internet-based technology; it is also about the organisation's social environment and the relationships between people and technologies. Such a perspective highlights the complex nature of the notion and shows that e-business goes beyond e-commerce, in that when implemented successfully, it transforms an organisation and its capabilities entirely.

RESEARCH APPROACH

The research reported here is drawn from findings from a four-year study of organisational change in Britain's National Mapping Agency, carried out between 2001 and 2004. The study adopted a longitudinal perspective on change concerned with the holistic and processual character of organisational transformations over time (Pettigrew, 1985, 1990).

An inductive research strategy was employed, which was both iterative and developmental. The research aim was not to confirm hypotheses, but to understand the *process* of e-strategy implementation and the perceptions of those involved and affected. What was important was the process by which the changes were introduced, the reaction by organisational members to those changes, and their perception of them.

Data Collection and Data Types

The time period for data collection was between 2001 and 2004. This research involved three main types of data: in-depth interviews, documentary data, and nonparticipant observation.

Data were collected from the organisation at two time points during the research period to track the internal changes over time:

- Time 1 (2001/2002), corresponded to the official adoption of the new "business model")
- Time 2 (2003/2004) corresponded to the incorporation and consolidation of strategic changes, allowing for change to become

Table 1. Number of respondents participating in interviews in Phase 1 and Phase 2

Position of Interviewee	Number in Time 1	Number in Time 2
CEO	1	1
Strategy Directors and Strategy Managers	6	5
Senior Managers		8
Senior Consultants	14	2
Project Managers	3	10
Line Managers	21	6
Individual Organisational Members	8	2
(Sales and Finance)	2	
Total Interviews = 89	55	34

partially "anchored" in new social structures and practices

A total of 89 interviews were conducted with the main actors involved in the strategic initiative programmes and in the implementation of change, such as deputy chief executive, corporate strategists, members of the top and middle management, other individual organisational members, and management consultants (Table 1). Most respondents had been with the organisation for a considerable period of time. This was supplemented with analysis of documentary evidence, including board minutes, strategy documents, reports of the steering committee, project teams, minutes of follow-up meetings, business plans, as well as nonparticipant observation.

During the field study, the researcher had access to the main participants, formal and informal meetings, existing minutes, and documentation highlighting some of the historical, processual, and contextual issues relevant to the e-business strategy implementation. In addition, the interviews emphasised both individual and shared interpretations of key participants concerning actions, events, views, beliefs, aspirations, and motives. All interviews were tape-recorded.

The following section will introduce the case study organisation and present the results.

Research Site

Britain's National Mapping Agency (NMA) is a quasiautonomous agency within the geographic information industry with trading fund status. It employs approximately 1,850 staff, 1,350 of whom are based at the head office, whilst the rest—cartographic surveyors and territorial sales representatives—are dispersed among a network of 80 local offices around the country.

NMA is recognised as a leading participant in the geographic information industry, within which it is forging partnerships with key private sector companies. Its principal activities are twofold: the maintenance of the National Topographic Database by recording and storing measurements of new roads, houses, and so forth, and the creation of products from it, such as paper map series and digital datasets used in geographic information systems (GIS).

The organisation offered an excellent opportunity to study the organisational change required in transforming a former government agency into an e-business, culturally, commercially, and technically. Confronted by powerful pressures to improve organisational performance under the government modernisation agenda, NMA implemented a complex e-business strategy, combined with a huge investment in technology new product development, which were designed to radically change the organisation's structure, management, and knowledge processes. To take advantage of the opportunities that e-technologies and e-ways of working presented, NMA charted an ambitious organisational transformation in which e-business was seen as a catalyst for change and e-strategy as a route map.

This knowledge-intensive organisation is a particularly interesting example of how a public organisation managed to overcome the constraints of its business context to fashion its own destiny. Unlike other public sector organisations with stable, incremental environments, NMA is operating in conditions of low environmental stability, with frequent, rapid changes in geographic information systems technology. Due to the emergence of new digital technology, the geographic information industry is on the verge of rapid growth, particularly in the market for location-based services. The overlay of layers of data to create new views creates good commercial opportunities for NMA, such as in the correlation of geographic, commercial catchment area and sociodemographic data for use in supermarket home delivery services.

All of these trends make the geographic information industry very different from the more traditional consumer and industrial markets in which many other public organisations operate. With an increasingly challenging environment, pressures to develop e-business under the government e-strategy in the public sector and emergence of new technologies, NMA is closer to the "relentlessly changing organisations" model of Brown and Eisenhardt (1998) in the high-velocity computer industry. There are these particular "high-tech" and "e-business" features of NMA that make this public sector organisation such an interesting case for management research in general, and for e-business change implementation in particular.

Key Facts About NMA

- Modern data collection using the geographic positioning system (GPS) and location information.
- Turnover from operating activities: £110 millions in 2004; most of the income comes from computerised geographic data, which is used extensively in both the private and public sector, with around £136 billion of Britain's GDP underpinned by it.
- Core markets by 2004: Public sector and utilities (32%); land and property (5%); consumer (12%); commercial markets (mobile communications and wireless; large retailers; banking, finance and insurance; transport and distribution) (51%).
- Has operated as a trading fund since April 1999, providing a greater degree of commercial flexibility and increased responsibility for its business planning and finances. As a trading fund the business has to make a profit but does not receive a subsidy from the taxpayer.
- A potential change in status towards a government-owned plc. was proposed in 2002 and rejected because it did not deliver the necessary benefits to the organisation. It was decided that it was in the public interest for NMA to remain a trading fund. However, enhanced financial freedoms and flexibilities have been granted by the government through a revised framework document in 2003.

Results

External Context

The *E-government Strategic Framework* (April 2001) set out a series of guiding principles for public sector organisations centred upon building services around citizens choices, making government and its services more accessible electronically and managing information and knowledge in more efficient ways to ensure easier online access and more effective use of all services. It set a series of e-government policies and targets for quasiautonomous agencies, stating as main objectives that 90% of low-value procurement transactions and 100% of document management should take place electronically by 2004 and that 100% of services should be available electronically by 2005. In order to meet these aims, public sector organisations must innovate within a common framework and manage their services as a business, focusing on cost effectiveness and funding mechanisms.

In line with these targets, Britain's national mapping agency was granted trading fund powers by Parliament in 1999 to give it direct responsibility for its own finances and freedom to develop new initiatives. In effect, this meant that NMA would remain obliged to serve the government by providing information across Britain whilst earning revenues in a commercial and increasingly competitive marketplace, reducing dependence on the taxpayer. Such a status provided the organisation with the opportunity to operate and compete commercially by earning commercial revenues for its geographical information in order to be self-funding, as well as be more accountable for the efficiency and effectiveness of its operations.

Internal Context

The organisation had a long history of unsuccessful reorganisations and frequent changes of Chief Executives. Since 1993, NMA has launched three different reorganisation initiatives under different governments, all of them recognised by managers and staff as "spectacularly unsuccessful."

Similar to other public sector entities undergoing public sector reform in the form of commercialisation, the efficiency and effectiveness of management processes were major challenges. NMA was a vertically integrated organisation, with an excessive degree of specialisation, rigid hierarchical divisions, and divided areas of activity with niches and boundaries that served no useful purpose. Underlying many of the problems of inefficiency and high costs was the monopoly situation that all costs could eventually be passed on to the market. The organisation was also a classic example of public service culture and organisational systems and processes. NMA's administrative structure based on departments and well-defined job categories had effectively prevented the organisation from operating in accordance with its own objectives and values. It was realised that, especially in the relationship between NMA's employees and its customers, too much importance was being given to resolving bureaucratic issues, to the detriment of customer service. In short, the internal structure worked against the integration of main business processes.

Drivers for Change

NMA has expanded considerably in recent years into commercial and leisure markets, both in the U.K. and internationally. The environment in which the organisation operated was characterised by emerging opportunities for the rapid expansion of the digital market and, in particular, location-based services offered via the Internet. That sat alongside its activities in the mature market for traditional paper-based mapping.

The severe market competition and threat of product substitution through the mass expansion of digital information and the new status of trading fund acted as drivers for revenue maximisation and for placing greater emphasis on increasing the utilisation of geographical data. A key aspect of becoming a trading fund was to move towards performance targets and a culture of measuring, and rewarding achievement linked to the business vision. This new "business model" meant that NMA had to strike the right balance between maintaining consistent and accurate geographical information for the whole of Great Britain whilst ensuring its operations are funded by earning income and generating profits from the licensing of data to both the public and private sectors. The organisation was also required to make an average return on the capital it employs—on average around £40 million—of at least 5.5% a year and to pay an annual dividend to the government based on each year's trading results. In response to this challenge, a series of organisation change initiatives began.

The Change Agenda: From Bureaucracy to E-Business

With the advent of a new Chief Executive Officer recruited from the commercial sector in September 2000, considerable impetus for change was being evidenced. A reevaluation of the business from the customers' perspective was completed and the need for the organisation to develop innovative products and services that could be delivered electronically was identified. The review undertaken by the executive team identified that the greatest hindrance to achieving NMA's corporate goals were its structures and work practices. Another major change that had to occur was a shift from the old culture of public monopoly to the culture of a market-oriented, customer-focused, and self-financing organisation. The nature and direction of the required cultural shift was a radical change for many employees, who had spent virtually all their careers in the relative security, comfort, and complacency of the old "public sector ethos" culture. The "cultural inertia" among the majority of employees, at all levels, was one of the major challenges to management in trying to achieve the transformation to the new system of efficient business operations.

Table 2. Projects under the e-strategy

Strategic Initiative	Corresponding Projects
Putting the customer first	*Customer Web sites* *New Web site for the organisation* *Customer Relationship Management* *On-line Service* *Digital Mapping*
Strategic alliances	*Establishment* *Joined-up government* *Alliance Extranet*
The new mapping agency	*New ways of working and Project Platinum* *Knowledge management* *"Help yourself" (personalised online support for all employees)* *Raising the return (a new financial model)*
Developing the market	*Developing the Digital National Geographic Database* *E-Brands* *Location-based standards* *E-Business channels* *Market Development team* *Pricing and licensing*
Enabling infrastructure	*Enhancing the IT infrastructure* *Off-site 24/7 availability* *Enterprise Wide Software Suite (ESS)*

Following the review, a new vision formed the foundation on which the organisation could be transformed into an e-business: *NMA and its partners will be the content provider of choice for location based information in the new information economy.* In October 2000, a cross-functional team from across NMA was established to develop the vision into a new strategy for the organisation. The team used the mission statement as a starting point for designing the structure and process of the change programme and translating it into a new e-strategy.

Fundamentally, the e-strategy was about transforming the business commercially, technologically, and culturally, by implementing a new business model, combined with a multimillion pound investment in technology and new product development. The main strategic priorities were:

- Commercial revenue—increase commercial revenue from existing assets
- Reduce costs and waste
- Invest in new brands, infrastructure, and capability
- Grow data products and help partners to develop their products
- Aggressive marketing for products
- Grow partners and enable them to add value to products
- Build the best data to enable "joined-up geography"

The key emphasis was on better knowledge management, focusing on the needs of businesses and individuals, and helping partners to create radically new products underpinned by data maintained by NMA. At the heart of the new strategy was the idea of NMA working together with partners to become the content provider of choice for location-based information. This meant establishing commercial agreements with various partners in which NMA was providing the geographical data and the partners were developing the software required for customising this data in different ways and translating it into innovative products and services under NMA's brand.

A series of *objectives* were established:

- Delivering excellence in all aspects of the business, employing e-business principles to exceed customer expectations
- Identifying, developing, and maintaining effective strategic partnerships
- Ensuring that the business strategy is clearly understood by staff, customers, partners, and the wider community
- Establishing NMA as the centre of excellence for innovation in location-based information
- Developing a business of progressive people with skills appropriate to an e-business
- Changing the internal culture

A range of projects were identified that would exploit e-business technology and approaches to improve performance. An initial assessment of costs, benefits, and timescales were prepared. At the end of the four-week period, NMA Executive and Nonexecutive Directors approved the strategy. More detailed planning and evaluation of implementation costs and benefits followed as development work began.

A major feature of the e-strategy implementation was the intention to place the organisation at the forefront of the new information economy by embracing cutting-edge technology for supplying geographical data and enhancing the versatility of NMA data. This involved the implementation of a groundbreaking new concept of mapping and the development of new products, by transforming the map-making process so that electronic data could be available to customers within 24 hours of being surveyed. The key aim was to replace the traditional paper map products with large-scale electronic mapping, so that most of the products and services offered by the organisation could be delivered electronically; digital mapping now accounts for some 80% of the organisation's turnover.

Amongst the most pioneering products were a digital database and online service named Master Map, featuring definitive digital data for the whole of Great Britain and an online integrated product called Pre-Build TM. The Master Map database provides intelligent and accessible data with the flexibility to link information across and between organisations, whilst Pre-Build TM offered highly-detailed digital mapping pinpointing buildings and roads tailored to the needs of utilities and telecommunication companies.

The successful implementation of the new strategy pivoted on the adoption of *e-business as a corporate philosophy*. As the Chief Executive remarked:

e-business is key to our future success, opening huge new opportunities for us and our partners. It requires new ways of working and both individual and team efforts right across the business. We have the best data to underpin the Master Map of Britain. Our e-initiatives will ensure we can create and supply that data when, where and how our customers want it—and at the same times e-enable ourselves. (Chief Executive, 2001)

Collecting, maintaining, and delivering geographical data was at the forefront of NMA's activity and the implementation of the new e-business strategy acted as a driver for the transformation of its core business processes—data collection and management. The e-strategy was thus seen as the necessary framework for driving forward business change. As some senior managers argued:

The "E" strategy allows us to reassess how we manage the collection and delivery of our data to remain at the forefront of the industry, offering agility and flexibility to our customers. (Director—Data Collection and Management, 2001)

The Digital Maps business cannot grow enough without the e-strategy. This work is critical because it will allow us to create and deliver more innovative products much faster to our customers. It will allow us to become far more efficient and cost effective across a wide range of activities. (Director—Digital Brands, 2001)

As the main supplier of geographical information in Britain, NMA needed not only to implement tangible customer benefits and to advance online services, but also to change the organisation's internal culture to a customer-led one. The prevailing view amongst over 90% of senior executives interviewed was that e-business was not only about electronic service delivery, but also that "e" should become embedded in the employees' ways of working, in terms of approach and attitude:

For the future NMA, there is no business but e-business! We must become a more agile organisation able to respond to our customers and partners needs at "internet-speed." ... The IT technology is the engine room of this change providing the infrastructure, information systems and user support in transforming the organisation. However, if we are to succeed in achieving our strategic aims and becoming an e-business, it is essential that we develop new ways of working. We must improve our day-to-day business practices and ensure that we get the best out of people, knowledge, systems and facilities. (Chief Technology Officer, 2001)

The process of strategy formulation resulted in a series of 21 investment projects that were grouped into 5 strategic initiatives reflecting their interconnected nature (Table 2).

Putting the customer first initiative involved the adoption of e-business principles and technology to ensure that each customer and partner is managed at segment and individual levels. In the words of the Initiative Manager:

This initiative is critical because it will allow us to create and deliver more innovative products much faster to our customers. It will allow us to become far more efficient and cost effective across a wide range of activities. (Initiative Manager, 2001)

Customers were offered online access to a wide range of mapping data, product demonstrations to show the versatility of NMA data and tailor-made Web gateways into the mapping agency, each fostering improved, more focused customer service. These gateways included facilities for the online ordering and delivery of existing data products at any time of the day or night or requests for special mapping surveys. Each customer Web site held information specific to that customer or partner as well as access to generic information and functionality available to wider groups.

By December 2002, the implementation of a portal Web infrastructure environment increased the efficiency of personalisation and customisation provided to customers. In parallel, the NMA Web site was redeveloped to become a gateway for location-based services and information and an enterprisewide software was implemented to allow better customer relationship management. Users of the new Web site were able to access location-based information and services either directly provided by NMA or indirectly by partners and account holders (customers and partners) could order digital and graphic mapping online.

The *strategic alliance initiative* involved the establishment of a strategic alliance to help drive the location-based information industry forward in a cohesive manner and develop collaborative working between NMA and other parts of the government with the help of e-business technology. It involved joined-up geography by using NMA data and referencing framework to combine other location-based information from other government bodies, for example, land ownership, local authorities, addresses, field parcels, and land use. It also marked a change in the way NMA was making available its datasets to users, by enabling partners to commercialise this data, on behalf of NMA, in a more flexible way. The initiative manager talks of the overall project as follows:

This initiative ensures that our NMA has the right strategic relationships to help grow the geographic information industry. Our organisation holds an important position in the location based informa-

tion industry but must work with key players in government and the private sector to realise the vision. (Initiative Manager, 2001)

The new mapping agency initiative focused on the people implications of the transformation of NMA into an e-business. The Project Manager states:

Whilst each of the other four strategic initiatives delivers in its own way significant change to the business, this initiative is the one that touches every single person in NMA. These projects are all closely related to our people and the way we do things. The focus is on simple and more effective ways of working whilst focusing on the needs of the customer. (Initiative Manager, 2001)

A programme called "New Ways of Working" addressed issues associated with the current organisational structure, people, culture, communication, and the way employees worked. The clear target was to make these elements more streamlined, adaptive, responsive, and customer-driven. This included changing the existing working practices, the implementation of new performance management, and reward systems focused on rewarding performance, changing the way information and knowledge are captured, coordinated, and made readily available within the organisation (knowledge management), and the implementation of a new software which allowed employees to manage their personnel records online whilst also eliminating unnecessary paperwork, procedures, administration, and costly support functions.

The organisation needed new competencies and skills among existing managers, so that they could drive forward the change programme. Current management capabilities were characterised by excellent technical abilities but poor people management skills, especially in terms of managing change and risk. It was considered that, in order to change the culture of the organisation, leaders and management teams had to develop themselves in readiness to embrace the new challenges and opportunities facing NMA. Therefore, a new programme entitled "Project Platinum" was designed to help leaders understand how they could influence the culture of the organisation, identify the competencies and skills required in leaders, and set in place a programme which could develop the behaviours supporting those competencies. As part of this initiative, a set-piece event—*NMA Experience*—was organised in December 2001. The event was attended by all the employees and was designed to explain to everyone the new vision and values of the organisation as an attempt to change the strong supportive civil service culture, rich in custom and practice, develop a new culture in line with the new direction of the organisation, and encourage creative and innovative behaviours. The core new values were identified as customer focused, quick, working together, able to take some risks, interested and excited by challenge, personally accountable, commercially oriented, and rewarded for results.

Developing the market initiative involved developing new partnerships and using new channels to reach new customers. In the past, NMA focused on an established core of customers in a relatively mature market with sectors such as central government, local government, and utilities. These customers increasingly expected better quality products and services in a market that was becoming more competitive. The organisation needed thus not only to develop the existing markets but also to find new markets and work with partners to develop new applications that will provide benefits to end customers. This involved adopting a proactive brand strategy, with a focus on digital location-based information and the launch of a new idea of geographic database—Master Map. Innovative in concept, Master Map was not a map in the traditional sense but a digital map framework through which customers could access the precise mapping data they needed. It offered a high level of flexibility and a complete reference system for Britain's geographical data. As the programme manager comments: "The initiative supports customers evolving needs, develops existing markets and opens new opportunities to ensure that NMA is the content provider of choice" (Initiative Manager, 2001).

Enabling infrastructure initiative involved building a robust new infrastructure of systems to underpin the e-business. A considerable amount of infrastructure has been put in place to support the whole of the e-strategy but particularly the Master Map idea. The Internet, extranet, and intranet applications were all upgraded and, in order to enhance customer benefit and operational efficiencies, the old systems were replaced with a single, integrated, enterprisewide software application platform. This integrated software package, called *Enterprise-Wide Software Suite* (ESS), offered a single repository for all NMA's data and was implemented in association with technology partners. One of the programme managers expressed a commonly held view:

The Enabling Infrastructure provides the foundation for the success of the e—Strategy. The application and technical environment that we build must provide the efficiencies that allow us to operate in an increasingly dynamic and delivery focused organisation. Information Technology (IT) provides the infrastructure, information systems and user support in transforming the organisation. Without a robust IT infrastructure none of the e-business activities will be sustainable. To a lesser or greater extent, we have all been frustrated when a system let us down, whether it be our own personal Internet Service Provider or a corporate system. As our business becomes increasingly dependent on IT systems, we have to avoid those frustrating (and potentially damaging) failures, as it is through the Enabling infrastructure initiative that we aim to do this. (Programme Manager, Enabling Infrastructure, 2002)

IMPLEMENTATION ISSUES

Organisational Restructuring

In order to successfully implement the e-business strategy, the structure of the organisation was reviewed and reorganised in November 2001. As the CEO summed up the rationale for this strategic initiative:

The need for accurate, reliable locational information underpins so many of the new services coming on stream and in Britain, no one has better locational information than us. ... But to stay at the forefront of the geographical industry we must keep pace with the market. That's why we're not only investing in e-business initiatives but have already put in place a whole new organisational structure to make it a reality. (Chief Executive, 2001)

The realignment of internal group structures and board responsibilities resulted in:

- The establishment of two brands businesses, based around distinct customer groups—Digital and Graphic Brands. The two brands' businesses were focused on introducing new and innovative ways of working with commercial and government partners to meet different customer group needs. Amongst such innovative approaches were the establishment of a joint-venture company with a commercial partner, with the aim of providing consistent and maintained points of interest data for the industry and an estimated £35 million content deal with a mobile phone operator that would allow mobile users to access coloured maps featuring real-time displays of various locations.
- The creation of a Business Change group that was charged with championing the transformation of the way the organisation did business and in particular managing the implementation of the e-business strategy.

Ownership of the Strategy

Ownership, accountability, and leadership were essential elements of the successful implementation of the NMA e-business strategy. As change was intended to be transformational and to affect all the aspects of the organisation and the levels within it, the entire programme has been top-down driven, with the provision of a clear, sustained direction that was well resourced and coordinated. The instigators of the transformation were the leaders of the organisation and the Strategy and Operating Board—including Executive and Nonexecutive Directors—had been heavily involved in the e-business strategy and monitor its implementation. In addition, each strategic initiative had a director-level owner who was accountable to the board for delivering the benefits of that initiative. Full-time initiative managers who focused on coordinating activity within their initiative have been appointed.

At project level, business owners have been identified, who were champions for their projects within the implementation. Project owners were responsible for ensuring that their projects delivered the benefits anticipated in the strategy. Where IT projects were involved in the delivery, the business owners worked in close conjunction with IT Programme and Project Managers.

Risk Management, Change Control, and Financial Monitoring at Appropriate Levels

Mechanisms have been implemented to ensure the adequate management of risks, costs, and change control during the implementation. The Operating Board received updates on implementation progress, including costs, on a fortnightly basis with a more detailed review undertaken six-weekly through a business health check exercise. In addition, a weekly implementation steering group (chaired by the Director of Business Change and including the Initiative Owner Directors) monitored strategic level risks, costs, and implementation progress. Significant changes to project contracts and business cases were approved by initiative owners and reported to the steering group. Furthermore, programme and project boards have been established within each initiative and these dealt with the day-to-day detail of implementation monitoring, cost control, and minor change control.

Internal Communication

In order to engage all employees in the business transformation associated with the implementation of the e-business strategy, considerable effort has been put into a coordinated programme of internal communication, which included:

- Face-to-face briefings with all staff in December 2000 and June 2001, including interactive and multimedia demonstrations of live and prototype systems
- Face-to-face briefings on quarterly basis with all field staff from December 2000 onwards
- Fortnightly update briefings at Operating Board—cascade briefed by managers to all staff and reported on Intranet
- A dynamic intranet site—regularly updated with project aims and progress
- Internal branding of the implementation activity to help focus all staff on the business transformation

Further Restructuring

In May 2002, a new Human Resources Director, recruited from the commercial sector, was appointed to drive forward the people side of the change programme. At her initiative, in August 2002, a team of senior managers undertook an eight-week review exercise (entitled "Emerald City") which involved looking forward to the future and identifying the challenges and opportunities that the organisation was likely to face in three to five years' time and how the business could be driven forward.

Following this review, in September 2002, the board announced a further restructuring of the organisation to help develop stronger teams and networks around the core processes (Figure 1) and to create a more flexible structure, with more flexible processes and communication patterns. This was accompanied by a review of staffing levels in different functional and subfunctional areas and 300 people were, consequently, released. A consequence of this restructuring was that a number of old divisions and functions were either eliminated or merged, in order to obtain a leaner, flatter structure and increase overall efficiency of the business.

The proposed new structure involved merging the Digital and Graphic Brands businesses into a single Sales and Market Development Group and creating a separate Programmes and Products Group, each headed by a Director. The Business Change Group activities were absorbed within other parts of the organisation. To give greater integration to corporate communications, the Corporate Communications Department has been integrated into the Human Resources and Corporate Services Group led by the HR Director. Minimal changes were introduced in the other groups.

As a result of these changes, the new structure due to be implemented starting with November 2002 incorporates seven major groups (Figure 2): strategy; human resources and corporate services; finance; information systems, Web, research and innovation; data collection and management; programmes and products; and sales and market development.

The previous structure created in November 2001 in relation to the e-strategy implementation served its purpose of focusing the organisation of work on developing new products and markets and gave an impetus to particular projects. It allowed NMA to strengthen its digital offering and also gave the graphic side of the business the confidence and space to develop, and between them both business groups could identify notable successes.

Figure 1. Core business processes in NMA

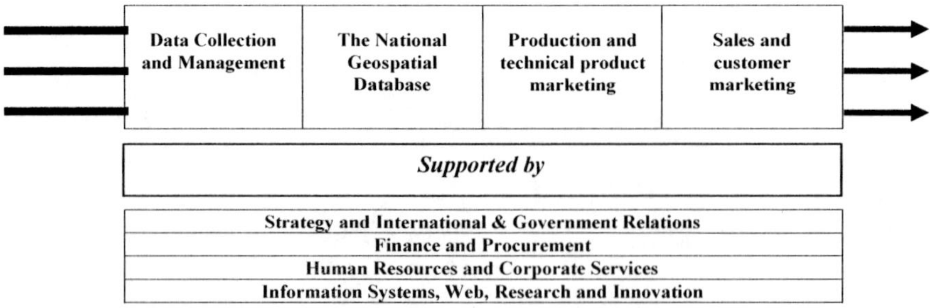

Figure 2. The new organisational structure

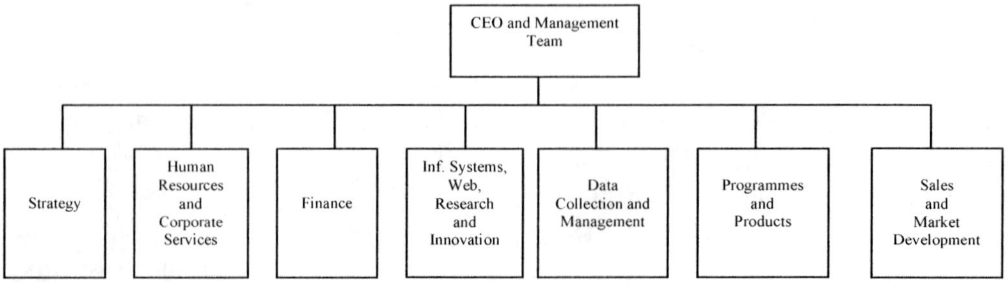

The new structure implemented in September 2002 offered a much higher level of functional flexibility. It gave clarity to the end-to-end processes of the business—from collecting data, through the production processes, and on the supply of data to partners and customers, whilst allowing the development of stronger cross-functional teams and networks around core processes. The number of hierarchical levels between top management and business groups teams has been substantially reduced and the seven groups have been organised along business processes, giving a lot of operational freedom to Group Managers. This freedom was balanced by a stronger planning process in the organisation, with group teams working with the strategy people on the overall planning.

The different cross-functional teams created meant increased horizontal communication between groups as well as vertical between the top management team and group teams, facilitated by the use of modern information technology. The new organisation of work was trying to combine the strengths of a functionally arranged organisational structure, offering a better coordination of the core business process with the flexibilities in terms of vertical communication offered by a process-based structure.

The transition from the old structure to the new one was a lengthy process. The old structure was effectively being moved to the new structure on a level by level basis. As employees in the positions made redundant under the voluntary redundancy scheme were leaving the organisation, the remaining positions were being rearranged in the new structure and staff were notified about the new positions. Transition structures were being used to prop up the old structure and keep the day-to-day operations going. The implementation of the new structure was finalised in August 2003.

In parallel with these structural changes, in order to track and predict customer, market, and brand profitability, a Corporate Balanced Scorecard with six performance dimensions (financial performance; quality of service; flexibility; competitiveness; resource utilisation; and innovation) has been introduced as a way of consolidating corporate performance measures and focus them upon core strategy components. The aim of introducing the balanced scorecard, in addition to other measurement tools such as customer satisfaction surveys, employee opinions, and monthly business health checks, was to provide the management board with the means to monitor the progress of the business on an ongoing basis. In addition, the strategy team could liaise better with individual business planners (Business Groups' Directors) for coordinating business processes across teams and establish integrated performance measures.

By December 2004, all the 21 projects comprising the e-strategy were fully completed and their success benchmarked against their key deliverables. A new business strategy 2005-2008, focused on how NMA will be meeting customer needs in the next four years, was created, building on some of the success aspects of the previous e-strategy: the creation of better data collection, maintenance and management systems as well as the development of new products and geographic solutions through partnerships with other public and private organisations. An event chart of the NMA "journey" is presented in Figure 3.

An overall assessment of the change efforts driven by the e-business implementation between 2000 and 2004 suggests the e-strategy implementation was a success. The progress made towards transforming the way the organisation worked was acknowledged by customers, partners, suppliers, and e-business experts, and employees noticed a marked improvement in their working environment. In addition to this feedback, the e-strategy was awarded five stars by the Government Office of the E-Envoy in 2004 and this rating indicated that the NMA's strategy was seen as a successful plan of action that has largely been met with key deliverables offering customers and staff new benefits. An operating profit of £9.4 million was forecasted by April 2005 thanks to careful management of costs, growth in revenue, and rigorous prioritisation of investments.

LESSONS LEARNED

The digital revolution offered huge opportunities for the organisation to improve the services that it provided to its customers, enhance its interaction with partners, and revolutionised the way people worked: first, by redrawing the way in which those services are provided to capture the full benefits of technology and, second, by tailoring the services to the needs of individual citizens, customers, and businesses. Electronic service delivery enabled NMA to become far more responsive and flexible, as well as creating the opportunity to harvest significant efficiency benefits.

The steps taken to meet the organisational challenges of implementing the e-business strategy across the organisation therefore provide a list of best practices for this particular situation (see Table 3). Several success factors relevant to e-business implementation emerged from this account:

First, one major lesson from this experience was that a successful organisational transformation involving e-business implementation requires clear leadership from the top management team. The NMA e-strategy has been created as the strategic blueprint to develop the business and firmly position it in the new information economy. The strategy was transforming the business at all levels, culturally, technically, and commercially. Fundamental to all of this activity was the requirement to create the environment in which NMA could successfully deliver its strategy for the business. This has required the Senior Management Team to clearly articulate the vision, purpose, goals, and values for the organisation and to communicate them clearly businesswide. It also required pulling together the leadership, communication, and engagement activity, whilst ensuring that all existing projects, initiatives, and everyday activities were aligned and integrated with this. This high level strategic activity was also about leveraging what was already in place and, most importantly, maintain consistency across cultural, behavioural, and leadership approaches.

Second, the case of Britain's National Mapping Agency shows that, in practice, the transition from government monopoly to commercial organisation whilst embracing e-business as a

Figure 3. Event chart, e-strategy implementation and follow-up (2000-2004)

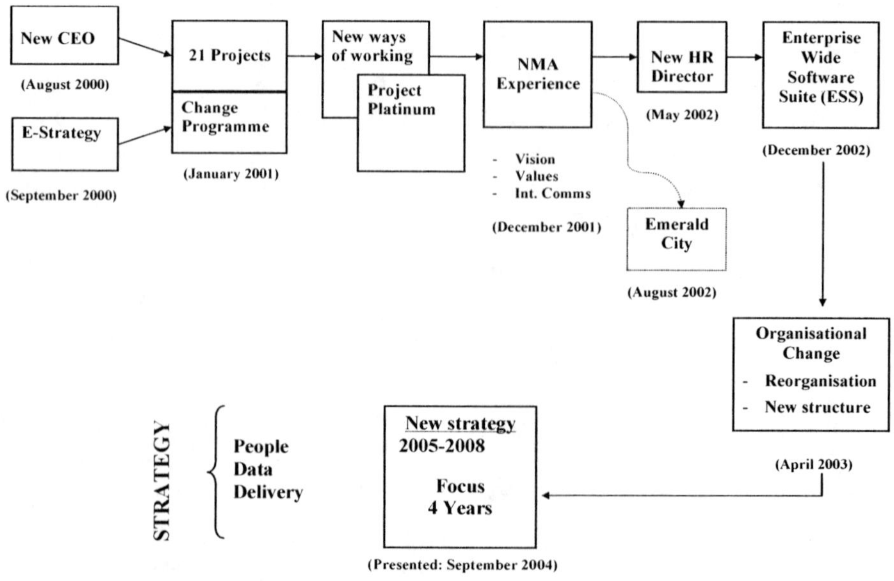

Table 3. Best practices for the implementation of the e-business strategy

No.	*Organisational Challenges*	*Steps Taken to Meet Organisational Challenges*	*Data from NMA*
1	Being "halfway" towards the private sector as a public sector executive agency moving towards a competitive commercial model	- Design a strategy that would capitalise on the unique position of the NMA on the market, as the biggest geographical information provider in U.K. with market-ready cutting-edge technology and high levels of internal capability - Establish strategic alliances to help drive the location-based information industry forward in a cohesive manner - Develop collaborative working between NMA and other parts of the government	"What we needed was a strategy that recognised our unique position. Something that enabled the organisation to have learning and, at the end of the experience, the learning would be resident in the organisation" (Corporate Strategist, 2001) "Who are our competitors? There is no single competitor for us. Because we are responsible for the national infrastructure of geographical information, there is no single other organisation who could and would want to replicate that, because it is hugely expensive to replicate that" (Senior manager, 2002)
2	Need to develop and communicate a clear e-business vision and the concept behind the change to the organisation as a whole and to all stakeholders, especially end users (customers and partners)	Communicate the why, where, and how of the change to the people involved in the 21 projects and to all employees by using mobilising events such as "NMA Experience." This builds confidence in the projects, lets the team know where they stand and where they are headed, and encourages commitment to the cause through the use of various internal communication mechanisms	"The top team and the board decided 'Right, this is our new strategy, this is were we are going, and this is our vision. We need to communicate that to everybody'" (Project Platinum Manager, 2002) "The essentials are around being absolutely clear about what it is you are trying to achieve and why — and I don't just mean the reorganisation. I mean: where do you want to be as a business?" (Senior manager, 2003) "What this event [NMA Experience] really did was to move the senior management up in the eyes of the workforce. It helped them understand that there was skill and ability in our senior team, and they were all committing to doing things in a different way and start leading the business more effectively" (Project Manager, 2002)
3	Create a feeling of ownership for the e-strategy at project level and a commitment at all levels of the organisation	- Get the project leaders and initiative owners involved early in the e-strategy projects - Communication events important in creating belief and feeling of ownership	"We put this plan together, represented by a railway journey. It's a single-track railway, a one-way journey, because we wouldn't be going back. It didn't have a starting-point because change has been going on forever, and we couldn't say if or when we would finish" (Chief Executive, 2001)
4	Need new effective communication channels between the project teams and between the Sales and Marketing teams and customers	- The project management teams were put in place to develop channels for and manage the communication between the different parties. Weekly, fortnightly, and quarterly status meetings help to keep all parties updated on each other's progress and on the progress of the e-strategy implementation as a whole	"After about three months we had improved the relationship between the project teams and the steering group. The steering group felt more comfortable and more confident in the ability of the teams to deliver" (Director of Business Change, 2002) "Communication forms the grounding for all the organisational work I have done. The communication, consultation and involvement strategy is what will make it happen" (Programme Manager, 2003)

Continued on following page

Table 3. Continued

No.	*Organisational Challenges*	*Steps Taken to Meet Organisational Challenges*	*Data from NMA*
5	Manage different customer segments: retain traditional loyal customers (public sector and utilities) whilst developing emerging markets (telecomm, retail, and insurance) and commercial partnerships	- From products to relationships: shift from a customer relationship management (CRM) focused on products or processes to a CRM philosophy focused on customer segments and the solutions they require - Identify the most profitable customer groups - Focus NMA's activity entirely on improving core business processes (data collection and management) and involve commercial partners in translating this digital data into business solutions that meet end users' needs through partnership agreements	"We need partners who would come and help us find/exploit certain niches in the market place. They are very well financed — e.g. Microsoft, big mobile operators and by enlarge our strategy is and will be in the future to partner with some of these companies rather than compete with them. So partnership development is an important part of our strategy, previously we worked with small partners, now we are trying to work with bigger ones, to get them develop solutions for us" (Senior Manager, 2002) "We place the customer rather than the product or process at the centre of the organisation to develop a stronger link between our different groups of customers and our data collection and management side of the business" (Business Improvement Manager, 2002)
6	Establish the right model of organisational design for the organisation	- Design and implement the right structure for an e-business starting from NMA's core business processes - Focus on core organisational competences: data collection, data management, exploitation of new technologies, and partner/customer management	"The normal practice would be: you take the external consultancy methodology cookbook and you apply things from it and other projects that you worked for, and you get a sense of the right way to do things … but this organisation is different and we wanted the structure to reflect what we do, not what consultants want us to do" (Board Member responsible for the structural change, 2003) "We did not want an off-the-shelf structure. Consultants came with a whole series of structural models, they came with the toolkit but didn't know how to fit it" (Strategist, 2003) "Don't expect everything to work without some adjustment and don't be afraid to review changes at an early stage to keep the reorganisation on track" (Business Group Director, 2003)
7	Top management commitment and the business case	- CEO with experience and personally identified with the e-strategy project - Have a multifunctional leadership team that is from sales, marketing, and IT -Involve senior management from sales and marketing in the strategy implementation	"The fundamentals are you need to have a really clear leader of the structure, somebody who has a very clear vision about what the endgame looks like" (Senior Manager, 2002) "Sales and Marketing senior management buy-in was absolutely fundamental for the process to work. … There must be a vision, there must be a strategy and there must be support behind it" (Senior Change Manager, 2003)
8	Political resistance to change of various stakeholders and managing simultaneously their diverse expectations	- Consistent communication allied to the use of facilitated workshops	"Consistency of message and purpose is one of the most important success factors in making change happen. Crystal-clear purpose, understood by all, including 'what it means for me,' should be made explicit" (NMA Employee, 2002)

Continued on following page

Table 3. Continued

No.	*Organisational Challenges*	*Steps Taken to Meet Organisational Challenges*	*Data from NMA*
9	External "customer acceptance" barriers and problems	- Communicate consistently with end users, at the beginning to build confidence, and throughout to communicate progress and to get feedback - Use customer relationship management to rebuild the confidence of customers who are confused about who they are actually buying products and services from	"The changes in our business processes — for example, procurement, reporting and customer relationship management, were so massive that the smallest error could have potentially serious consequences during business processes switching, damaging customer relationships and delivery channels for a lengthy period of time. Communicating proposed changes to our customers, users and clients was essential. They demanded honest, consistent and up-to-date information whether the news were good or bad. (Business Improvement Manager, 2002) "It was important to ensure all the time our customers, users and clients that we had a back-up or disaster recovery plan should something go wrong during the transition" (Sales and Marketing Manager, 2002)
10	Aligning the objectives of the 21 projects with the overall objectives of the e-business strategy and establishing timelines	- People involved in the projects have clear understanding of their roles and responsibilities - Good project management to avoid duplications and conflicting business objectives	"this great big machine called project planning comes in and it takes up vast amounts of time and systems space, because of all these critical paths which chunter away. Actually this is too big right now, and frightening people. (Senior Manager, 2002)
11	Blending major change with major continuity	- Integrate the e-commerce strategy with the business strategy and with the core operations from the start	"We needed to be able to adapt to shifting circumstances in market conditions and identify potential changes in course sooner rather than later" (Senior Marketing Manager, 2003)

corporate philosophy can be extremely challenging to achieve. Although e-business has enabled NMA to tap new customers and new revenues and opened up a space for importation of private sector practices into NMA, the strong public interest for its activities was still present. Yet the organisation was expected to operate commercially, cover its costs, and build up reserves through its own commercial style operations. That situated the organisation in the intersection of two different spheres—the public and the private. Becoming an e-business, in this context, required collaborative working not only with commercial partners but also with different parts of the government. The "in-between" situation thus tested to the full extent the capability of the organisation to lead and manage change, especially in terms of finding the perfect balance between fulfilling its still strategic role as national agency and providing high-quality services to its customers in a dynamic marketplace.

One of the senior managers interviewed described this situation with the following words: "We [as an organisation] want to behave as if we were situated in the commercial business sector, but we cannot escape our origins" (Senior Manager, 2004).

Third, the case findings demonstrate that successful organisational transformation involving e-business implementation relies on changing some fundamental business processes and attitudes. Close cooperation between many different sets of people—from middle managers to programmers, and from technical architects to system users within the organisation—is needed. This convergence of business process, creative, and technical skills created in NMA a new dimension for teamwork, which in turn shifted the culture of the organisation from "knowledge is power" to "sharing knowledge is power." Technology can be an important enabler but not a driver of knowledge sharing.

Finally, one key challenge in NMA was how to blend major change with major continuity. In this respect, a major lesson learnt from this organisation's experience was that it is essential to integrate the e-commerce strategy with the business strategy and with the core operations from the start. This echoes the findings of Dutta and Segev (1999) that successes result from close partnerships between commercial and IT managers, and that companies making e-commerce central to their organisation do better than those that make it an afterthought.

CONCLUSIONS

This article aimed to reveal the processes of strategic and organisational transformation engendered by e-business during the implementation of a complex structural and cultural change programme aimed at reshaping a commercialised public sector organisation and rethinking how it provided value to its customers. The discussion examined the dilemmas and constraints identified by managers in the interpretation of the e-business strategy concept and why its implementation in practice could be challenging. Whilst the Internet offers a technological solution, the findings of this case study suggest that the successful implementation of a wider e-business strategy depends on managing simultaneously a number of projects which cross organisational boundaries and linking together organisational and technological factors.

Whilst this reflective account may be unique, it does, however, provide pointers to other large organisations undertaking a similar e-transformation and reflects on the degree of organisational transformation required by traditional organisations in meeting this imperative and successfully making the change to e-business. In particular, the findings illustrate that an e-business strategy is not just about technology. It also embraces the business challenges that result from managing change in a fast moving environment, as well as the important issues of people, organisation, culture, communication, and how an organisation must create a process for delivering innovation.

Further empirical field studies in other settings would enrich the concepts developed in this study and would produce a definitive list of best practices. The case highlights, however, the complex nature of the notion of e-business in a public sector context and shows that when implemented successfully, it can transform entirely these organisations and their capabilities.

REFERENCES

Barnes, D., Hinton, M., & Mieczkowska, S. (2005). Enhancing customer service operations in e-business: The emotional dimension. *Journal of Electronic Commerce in Organizations, 3*(2), 17-33.

Barnes, S., & Hunt, B. (2001). *E-commerce and e-business: Business models for global success.* Oxford: Butterworth-Heinemann.

Barua, A., Konona, P., Whinston, A., & Yin, F. (2001). Driving e-business excellence. *Sloan Management Review, 43*(1), 36-45.

Becker, S. A., & Berkemeyer, A. (2004). A case study on a security maturity assessment of a business-to-business electronic commerce organization. *Journal of Electronic Commerce in Organizations, 2*(4), 1-19.

Benoy, J., Cook, R., & Javalgi, R. (2001). Marketing on the Web: How executives feel, what businesses do. *Business Horizons, 44*(4), 32-40.

Bhaskar, R. (2004). A customer relationship management system to target customers at Cisco.

Journal of Electronic Commerce in Organizations, 2(4), 1-19.

Boddy, D., & Macbeth, D. (2000). Prescriptions for managing change: A survey of their effects in projects to implement collaborative working between organisations. *International Journal of Project Management, 18*, 297-306.

Brown, S. L., & Eisenhardt, K. M. (1998). The art of continuous change: Linking complexity theory and time-paced evolution in relentlessly shifting organisation. *Administrative Science Quarterly, 42*, 1-34.

Carlton, D. W. (2001). Free riding and sales strategies for the Internet. *The Journal of Industrial Economics, 49*(4), 521-540.

Chen, S., & Leteney, F. (2000). Get real! Managing the next stage of Internet retail. *European Management Journal, 18*(5), 519-528.

Chaston, I. (2001). The Internet and e-commerce: An opportunity to examine organisational learning in progress in small manufacturing firms? *International Small Business Journal, 19*(2), 13-30.

Clarke, I., & Flaherty, T. B. (2004). Challenges of transforming a traditional brick-and-mortar store into a bricks-and-clicks model: A small business case study. *Journal of Electronic Commerce in Organizations, 2*(4), 74-87.

Clay, K. (2001). Prices and price dispersion on the Web: Evidence from the online book industry. *The Journal of Industrial Economics, 49*(4), 441-462.

Clegg, C. W., Chu, C., Smithson, S., Henney, A., et al. (2002). *E-business prospects: Findings from an expert panel.* London: Department of Trade and Industry.

Colombo, M. G. (2001). Technology-based entrepreneurs: Does Internet make a difference? *Small Business Economics, 16*(3), 177-190.

Daniel, E., Wilson, H., & Myers, A. (2002). Adoption of e-commerce by SMEs in the UK: Towards a stage model. *International Small Business Journal, 20*(3), 253-270.

Day, G., & Schoemaker, P. (2000). Avoiding the pitfalls of emerging technologies. *California Management Review, 42*(2), 8-33.

Deise, M. V., Nowikow, C., King P., & Wright, A. (2000). *Executive's guide to e-business, from tactics to strategy.* New York: John Wiley & Sons.

Dutta, S., & Segev, A. (1999). Business transformation on the Internet. *European Management Journal, 17*(5), 466-476.

Eisenhardt, K. M. (1998). Time pacing: Competing in markets that won't stand still. *Harvard Business Review, 76*(2), 59-70.

Eisenhardt, K. M. (1999). Patching: Restitching business portfolios in dynamic markets. *Harvard Business Review, 77*(3), 72-83.

Feeny, D. (2001). Making business sense of the e-opportunity. *Sloan Management Review, 42*(2), 41-52.

Gao, J. (2005). E-commerce issues in Australian manufacturing: A newspaper medium perspective. *Journal of Electronic Commerce in Organizations, 3*(4), 20-41.

Garicano, L. (2001). The effects of business-to-business e-commerce on transaction costs. *The Journal of Industrial Economics, 49*(4), 463-486.

Hansen, M. (2000). Networked incubators: Hothouses of the new economy. *Harvard Business Review, 78*(5), 74-84.

Harris, L., Coles, A. M., Dickson, K., & McLoughlin, I. (1999). Building collaborative networks. In P. Jackson (Ed.), *Virtual working: Social and organisational dynamics* (pp. 33-46). London: Routledge.

Hoffman, D., & Novak, T. (2000). How to acquire customers on the Web. *Harvard Business Review, 78*(3), 179-183.

Kickert, W. (2001). Public management of hybrid organisations: Governance of

quasi-autonomous executive agencies. *International Public Management Journal, 4*, 135-150.

Kotha, S. (1998). Cometing on the Internet: The case of Amazon.com. *European Management Journal, 16*(2), 212-222.

Kotha, S., Rajgopal, S., & Rindova, V. (2001). Reputation building and performance: An empirical analysis of the top-50 pure Internet firms. *European Management Journal, 19*(6), 571-586.

Lee, H. L., & Wang, S. (2001). Winning the last mile of e-commerce. *Sloan Management Review, 42*(4), 54-62.

Mahadevan, B. (2000). Business models for Internet-based e-commerce: An anatomy. *California Management Review, 42*(4), 55-69.

Ordanini, A., & Pol, A. (2001). Infomediation and competitive advantage in B2B digital marketplaces. *European Management Journal, 19*(3), 276-285.

Pettigrew, A. M. (1985). *The awakening giant: Continuity and change in ICI.* Oxford: Basil Blackwell.

Pettigrew, A. M. (1990). Longitudinal field research on change. Theory and practice.

Organization Science, 1, 267-292.

Poon, S., & Swatman, P. (1999). An exploratory study of small business Internet commerce issues. *Information and Management, 35*, 9-18.

Porter, M. (2001). Strategy and the Internet. *Harvard Business Review, 79*(2), 63-78.

Rayport, J. (1999). The truth about Internet business models. *Strategy and Business, Third Quarter*(16), 1-3.

Sauer, C. (1993). *Why information systems fail: A case study approach.* Henley-on-Thames: Alfred Waller.

Scott Morton, F. (2001). Internet car retailing. *The Journal of Industrial Economics, 49*(4), 501-520.

Smith, M. D. (2001). Consumer decision-making at an Internet shopbot: Brand still matters. *The Journal of Industrial Economics, 49*(4), 541-559.

Symon, C. (2000). The future at your fingertips. In S. Rock & J. Reeves (Eds.), *Building a successful e-business* (pp. 6-11). London: IBM Business Guide, Caspian Publishing.

Symonds, M. (1999, June 26). Business and the Internet: Survey. *The Economist*, pp. 1-44.

Timmers, P. (2000). *Electronic commerce.* Chichester, UK: John Wiley & Sons.

Van der Wiele, T., Williams, R., Van Iwaarder, J., Wilson, M., & Dale, B. (2002, September). *The e-business research network: Summary of the results of the Dutch pilot survey.* Paper presented at the British Academy of Management Conference.

Venkatraman, N. (2000). Five steps to a Dot.com strategy: How to find your footing on the Web. *Sloan Management Review, 15*(3), 15-29.

Yoffie, D., & Cusumano, M. (1999a). Judo strategy: The competitive dynamics of Internet time. *Harvard Business Review, 77*(1), 70-81.

Yoffie, D., & Cusumano, M. (1999b). Building a company on Internet time: Lessons from Netscape. *California Management Review, 41*(3), 8-28.

This work was previously published in International Journal of E-Business Research, Vol. 2, Issue 4, edited by I. Lee, pp. 39-60, copyright 2006 by IGI Publishing, formerly known as Idea Group Publishing (an imprint of IGI Global).

Chapter 4.35
Web Services in Government Policy
Case Study from UK National Health Service

Matthew W. Guah
University of Warwick, UK

ABSTRACT

The public sector accounts for a greater proportion of United Kingdom's information technology (IT) spending, but cutting edge success stories in government IT have suddenly been reported in the popular press. As a result of the electronic delivery of government services (i.e., the National Health Service, Defence and Criminal Justice systems) becomes more commonplace, the public sector is becoming increasingly dependent on technology. This chapter reports on three years of research, which looks at the application of Web services into United Kingdom healthcare as a fulfilment of numerous semi and unsuccessful IT projects, that fell short of delivering any tangible benefits. The author looks at the National Health Service's current IS strategy—fully dependent on Web services application – with the criteria of successful implementation, return on investment, increased productivity, innovation, and user benefits.

INTRODUCTION

Information technology (IT) strategies play an increasingly pivotal role in the overall strategies of a national healthcare organization, which has moved them in the focus of recent healthcare management research (Wilson & Lankton, 2004). Web services introduce a different business environment with respect to the institutional framework and the resource endowment of healthcare organizations. The institutions supporting the traditional mechanism for healthcare provision are less sophisticated or effective, and the health services are less well endowed with resources, especially in terms of maintaining valuable resources such as skilled labour in management—particularly IT staff.

Consequently, an understanding of emerging technology strategies in the health sector requires adoption and development of the theories currently applied in the management field, including transaction costs/agents theory and resource based theory and institutional theory. Such theories must account for how contextual influences moderate the strategic decisions taken by healthcare organizations. Recent empirical studies on healthcare organizations have begun to incorporate the specificity of the emerging technology context in their theoretical reasoning. In this chapter, the author takes this line of research further by applying the resource-based view (RBV) (Barney, 1991; Wernerfeld, 1984) to healthcare organizations to explain how Web services technologies are being implemented. The RBV has been found particularly suitable for analyzing organizations in high volatility environments (Eisenhardt & Martin, 2003), and has recently been applied to strategies in the health sector (Scott, Ruef, Mendel, & Caronna, 2004).

In recent years, e-government has received much attention by academics and practitioners as a wide-ranging initiative to use the latest IT to automate government services. One important area that has received large financial investment is healthcare services (Devaraj & Kohli, 2000; Majeed, 2003; Wilson & Lankton, 2004). Traditionally, government run healthcare services have not received large funding for IT, and this has led to a situation where disparate IT systems have produced pockets of efficiency alongside serious shortcomings in organizational processes and services.

Using Web-enabled IT systems as a way of empowering e-government within healthcare, the UK government has embarked upon the largest civil IT programme in the world to re-engineer organizational processes and services to enhance patient care. The current wave of Web-enabled IT systems is expected to play a large role in how the UK government fulfils its agenda for public reform in healthcare. Other examples of public sector reform include, e-democracy (voting and referenda by means of the Internet); Web-enabled delivery of products and services to citizens (healthcare, social services, tax payment, etc.); inter and intragovernmental communication and decision making (immigration and homeland security) enhanced by network applications and the digital integration of front and back office operations (Vriens & Achterbergh, 2004). These examples demonstrate that national governments are keen to adopt Web-enabled IT systems to improve public services.

The chapter is based upon a three-year research project that examined the UK's National Health Service (NHS) information systems strategy, where the National Programme for IT (NPfIT) is being implemented at a cost of $10 billion over 10 ten years. This research involved interviewing over 200 stakeholders in the NpfIT, including healthcare professionals (doctors, consultants, nurses, etc.), healthcare administrators (managers, administrators, secretaries and support staff), IT professionals (managers and technicians, IT vendor firms), government agencies (civil servants), and some patients. The cross-section of respondents enabled the researchers to derive a rich picture of how the NPfIT was perceived at all levels and spectrums within and outside the NHS. About 80% of the interviews were tape recorded and transcribed, with the results sent to the respondents for clarification. A qualitative approach to data collection and analysis using semistructured and open-ended questions was essential as a single, survey-based questionnaire was unsuitable given the variety and diversity of the stakeholders interviewed.

This chapter is divided into four parts. First we give an overview of the UK healthcare service and outline some of the political, economic, and social factors that influence IT expenditure. Second, we discuss the IT platform, which will enable large-scale change within the UK health sector. The technology we examine is Web services. Third, we present the case study, which discusses the current progress of the NPfIT. Next, we include a section that examines the key challenges of the NPfIT in the broader sociopolitical and economic context. Finally, we discuss the findings from our research and offer some guidelines to stakeholders in managing a large-scale, IT-enabled change programme.

WHAT IS WEB SERVICE?

Web services can be defined as "self-contained modular applications that provide a computation upon request" (Guah & Currie, 2005a, p. 14). These services can be published, located, or invoked over a network, usually the Internet, intranets, or LAN. The popularity of the World Wide Web over the last decade has generated more demand for the request of these services, partly because Web services are independent of the underlying systems providing the computation (Guah & Currie, 2005a). Considering that Web services architecture can provide universal interoperability of software applications, nearly any application in the world could interact with another software application regardless of geographical location, system hardware, operating systems, or programming languages. Thus, permitting a de facto standard for any particular type of computation permitting an organization the capacity to develop an information system for its use based entirely on the computational services is provided by the Web service paradigm.

On the other hand, the service provider is responsible for the process of service provision and therefore required to maintain of the system quality. The characteristics ensure the method of development also impacts the cost of maintaining the information.

In the simplest form, the foundation of Web services is the request/response paradigm. This paradigm involves a client in the Web services environment who requests a service via a specific protocol from a service provider. In response, the service provider, using a specific protocol, sends the service to the client—or a notification of why it cannot provide that service. Such a concept is used to implement the service-oriented architecture (SOA) which implements Web services, containing three entities and three operations.

However, benefiting from the advantages of Web services require an organization to place complete trust in the security of the service. The total relinquishing of an organizational information asset exposes that organization to malicious hackers, industrial espionage, and fraud. Therefore the service provider must equivocally assure the security of confidential data within Web services to win willingness of organizations to adopt this new technology as core parts of their IS strategies (Guah & Currie, 2005a).

THE UK NATIONAL HEALTH SERVICE

The UK National Health Service (NHS) is responsible for healthcare and services, serving around 60 million citizens and free at the point of delivery. The institution was created in 1948 by a parliamentary act initiated by the Labour government following a national healthcare review after World War II. Within the past six decades, the NHS has experienced both stability and change. Successive governments have introduced numerous policy documents designed to regulate, reengineer, and monitor all aspects of NHS care and service provision. In contrast, the NHS has, over the years, evolved many institutionalized mechanisms that make change difficult and often highly controversial.

One significant change from the late 1980s to early 1990s was the advent of compulsory competitive tendering (CCT), which fuelled an increase in the number of managers and administrators across the NHS (Scott et al., 2000). The rationale for creating an internal market through a new procurement strategy stemmed from political pressure to reduce costs by introducing the methods and practices more commonly found in the private sector. By the mid-1990s, decisions about organizationwide IT projects remained centralized at the level of government and the NHS Executive, although the NHS governance structure for IT was highly decentralized or division-based. IT divisions were spread across several regional authorities, with medical functions centrally controlled. This precluded many small IT service firms from gaining a foothold in the NHS, as their larger counterparts had the political, organizational, and technical capacity to deliver large-scale IT work.

In the late 1990s, the government increasingly recognized the opportunity to use IT to improve the delivery of service within the NHS. After a series of reviews of NHS IT service delivery, a more integrated and seamless IT method was recommended (DoH, 2000; Wanless, 2002). The NHS Information Authority (NHSIA) embarked on the Integrated Care Report Service (ICRS) project to provide, among other services, a nationwide electronic patient database. The result was a document called "Information for Health" that specified the need for the complete automation and integration of various patient information databases in the country (DoH, 2000). Such a system would be commissioned to selected IT service providers at a combined price of £6.3 billion (US $10 billion).

A DoH document published in 2002 stressed:

It is widely accepted that the NHS Plan to improve care and services in the NHS depends on a number of transformations in quality, speed and capacity of the organization. Information technology and the electronically stored information it handles are key enablers of some of this transformation. With modern IT, information can be captured once and used many times, working practices can be modernized and communications speeded up. (DoH, 2002, p. 3)

In spite of this vision for IT transformation in the NHS, the history of introducing large-scale IT development projects in the government sector have not been successful overall, with some suggesting a failure rate of 80% and others around 60% (Brown, 2001). The UK public sector spends around £2.3 billion per annum on IT, yet the government recognizes that "there is a history of failure of major IT-enabled projects, characterized by delay, overspend, poor performance and abandonment" (NAO, 2004, p. 3). The repercussions from these failures can reflect unfavourably upon government in general (Currie, 1997).

Yet against this backdrop of disappointing results from historical IT investments, the UK NHS is now embarking upon the largest civil IT programme in the world. This initiative has been enabled by the development of the Web services architecture, which will provide an IT platform to facilitate inter and intraorganizational data networks.

WEB SERVICE ARCHITECTURE

Since around 2000, Web services have emerged as a new "silver bullet" technology to transform organizational processes (Guah & Currie, 2005b). This form of emerging technology is expected to transfer IT from an internal to an external (outsourced) activity. Web services are defined as "self-contained modular applications that provide a computation upon request" (Boncella, 2004). These services can be published, located, or invoked over a network, usually the Internet, intranets, local area network, or wide area network. The growth in popularity of the World Wide Web within the last decade has generated more demand for the request of these services, partly because Web services are independent of the underlying systems providing the computation. Considering that Web services architecture can provide universal interoperability of software applications, nearly any application in the world could interact with another software application regardless of geographical location, system hardware, operating systems, or programming languages, thus resulting in a de facto standard that allows an organization to develop an information system based entirely on computational services provided by the Web service paradigm.

Figure 1. Evolution of Web services

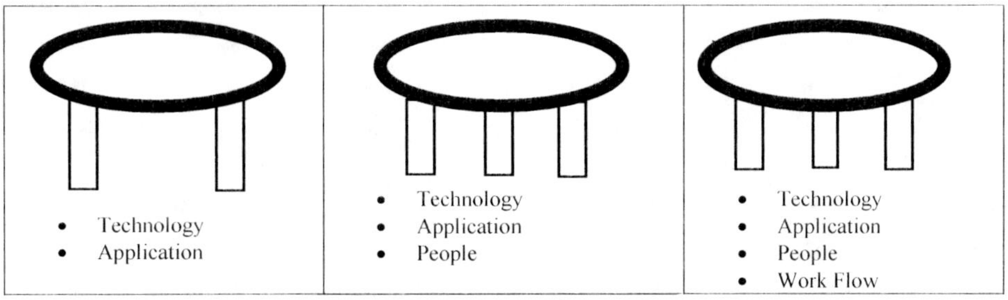

The service provider is responsible for the continuous availability of service as well as maintaining the system quality. These characteristics ensure that the method of development also impacts the cost of maintaining the information. In the simplest form, the foundation of Web services is the request / response paradigm: a client in the Web services environment requests a service via a specific protocol from a service provider. In response the service provider, using a specific protocol, sends the service to the client—or a notification of why it cannot provide that service.

Figure 1 shows that a more holistic approach to technology typically works better than a piece-meal approach to information systems solutions. Web services, as it is currently being implemented in most organizations, looks like a two-legged table. The three-legged table represents a version of Web services being sold by some vendors after the dotcom crash; this depiction incorporates people, where cultural changes are imperative if Web services are to be successful. The four-legged table depicts a mature model of Web services where workflow is further added; this model suggests that synergies exist between technology, people, and processes. The analogy here is that a two-legged table is less stable than a three-legged table, while a four-legged table is even firmer. At the present time, Web services remain an immature technology.

Further, benefiting from the advantages of Web services requires organizations to trust the security of the service. The service provider must therefore ensure the security of confidential data if Web services are to become a trusted technology. Boncella (2004) has outlined some requirements for Web services security measures:

- **Confidentiality:** a requirement that demands the assurances from a service provider the privacy of users and the prevention of information theft both in transit and data storage. Most Web services environments use symmetric and asymmetric encryptions to create cipher text for transmitting data between the client PC and server as well as data held in storage.
- **Integrity:** a requirement that demands the assurances that information would not be modified (intentionally or unintentionally) either during transit or in storage. An encrypted message digest—or digital signatures—can deal with integrity issues satisfactorily.
- **Nonrepudiation:** a requirement that demands the sender of a message to legitimately claim they intentionally sent a particular message. Digital certificates and public key infrastructure are frequently used for this assurance.
- **Authentication:** a requirement that demands the certifications of both sender and receiver of a particular message. Public key infrastructure and smart cards in combination with user name/password authentication methods are usually used to guarantee this authentication.

- **Authorization:** a requirement that demands the authentication entity can access only those information resources they must have either to request or provide a service. Once authenticated an entity authorization will be determined. Generally an authenticated entity has an associated access control list.
- **Availability:** a requirement that demands the provision of uninterrupted service to authenticated and authorized users. This is in addition to avoidance of the interruptions of services due to denial-of-service attacks.

Boncella (2004) demonstrates how Secure Sockets Layer and Public Key Infrastructure are being used in combination with firewalls to satisfy these requirements for conventional Web traffic using Internet protocol. Yet fears persist that these protections are not adequate to assure these requirements within a Web services environment (Guah & Currie, 2004). For e-government services to be successful, security will increasingly be a major issue. The key question about the use of Web-enabled technologies for the transfer of confidential data is: How can IT service providers ensure that inter and intraorganizational data flows across the Internet are safe and secure? This is especially important within the healthcare sector, where the use of Web services architecture will expose patient data to external networks on an unprecedented scale.

NATIONAL PROGRAMME: INFORMATION TECHNOLOGY

The National Programme for IT is an essential element in delivering the NHS Plan for reform over a period of 10 years. It is creating a multibillion pound information infrastructure, which should improve patient care by increasing the efficiency and effectiveness of clinicians and other NHS staff. The NPfIT is procuring, developing, and implementing a modern, integrated IT infrastructure and systems for all organizations in England up through 2010. These are being done by:

- Creating an NHS Care Records Service to improve the sharing of consenting patients' records across the NHS
- Making it easier and faster for GPs and other primary care staff to book hospital appointments for patients
- Providing a system for electronic transmission of prescriptions
- Creating a new National Network for the NHS (N3), ensuring that the IT infrastructure can meet NHS needs now and in the future
- Establishing reliable Picture Archiving and Communications Systems (PACSs) to capture, store, and distribute static and moving digital medical images
- Establishing a reliable Quality Management and Analysis System (QMAS) giving GP practices and primary care trusts objective evidence and feedback on the care delivered to patients
- Establishing a reliable contact systems including a central e-mail and directory service for the NHS

The competitive advantage of a service provider operating in the health sector is determined by its *ability to adapt its competencies* to the needs and capabilities of the specific technology and to utilize available local resources in the best possible combination with its own core competencies. Therefore, the service provider's choice of a service provision model is crucial for developing a resource mix that enables it to compete in the healthcare organizational context. Zhang, Chen, and Zhou (2005) refer to this as "information personalization," which continues to be the most difficult task in dealing with public sector information overload resulting from e-government initiatives.

Given the wide number of potential service providers (see Table 1), the NPfIT team had to

Table 1. Short-list of companies chosen to be service providers from a reduced long-list

SOUTHERN	EASTERN	NORTH WEST/WEST MIDLANDS	LONDON	NORTH EAST/ EAST MIDLANDS	NATIONAL PROVIDER
		SHORT-LIST			
Fujitsu	Accenture	CSC	BT Syntegra	Accenture	BT Syntegra
Southern Alliance	CaP Gemini Ernst & Young	BT Syntegra	IBM	Cerner	Lockheed Martin
PlexusCare	Cerner	Fujitsu			IBM
	PlexusCare	IBM			
		LONG-LIST			
Fujitsu	Accenture	CSC	BT Syntegra	Accenture	BT Syntegra
Southern Alliance	CaP Gemini Ernst & Young	BT Syntegra	IBM	Cerner	Lockheed Martin
PlexusCare	Cerner	Fujitsu	SAIC	Patient First Alliance	IBM
CTG Inc	PlexusCare	IBM	Xansa	Serco	Fujitsu
Lockheed Martin	Torex	McKesson/ Capita	Patni Computer Systems	Logica	Northrup Grumman
Wipro Techn.		Siemens	Compuware		McKesson/ Capita
					SAIC

take the preferences of the NHS service customers into consideration, which is an essential process of dynamic service composition planning (Zhang et al., 2005). Getting this stage of the project right significantly contributes to GP satisfaction with the service quality.

The national programme is being implemented via two means (see Table 2):

- National application service providers (NASP) are responsible for purchasing and integrating IT systems common to all NHS users at the national level.
- Local service providers (LSP) are responsible for delivering IT systems and services at the local level.

To facilitate this model, the nation has been divided into five regional clusters of strategic health authorities (London, North West, and West Midlands, North East, Southern, and Eastern). These regional clusters were created after consultation with Strategic Health Authorities (SHAs) on how best to deliver local IT solutions as part of the NPfIT. After much discussion, it was decided to split England into the five geographic regions in Figure 2—with each cluster comprising five, six, or seven SHAs who agreed to work together on the procurement and implementation of NPfIT services at local levels. Applications delivered at the local level are the responsibility of five selected Local Service Providers (LSPs) (see Table 2). The LSPs work closely with local NHS IT professionals and are overseen by a regional implementation director (RID) from the NPfIT. The LSPs will ensure that existing local systems are compliant with national standards and that data are able to flow between local and national systems. To do this, the NPfIT will deliver upgrades or replacements to hardware and software as appropriate and implement core local training for NHS staff.

The regional implementation directors (RIDs) led the LSP negotiations and are leading the implementation process across their individual areas. An RID manages a NPfIT support team and the relationship with the LSP, as well as coordinates deployment. An RID is part of the NPfIT management team and reports to the National Programme implementation director, but is also responsible to the regional cluster's board for delivery.

Table 2. Contracts with service providers for national or regional services

Primary Service Provision Model •NASP purchasing & integrating nationally •LSP delivering IT systems & services locally			
CONTRACTS (DEC-2004)	**SERVICE PROVISION**	**PROVIDER**	**LENGTH**
Care Records Service – NASP	National B	ritish Telecom 1	0 years
Care Records Service – LSP N	orth East A	ccenture	10 years
Care Re cords Service – LSP	Eastern	Accenture	10 years
Care Records Service – LSP L	ondon	Capital Care Alliance (BT)	10 years
Care Records Service – LSP N	orth West & West Midlands	CSC	10 years
Care Records Service – LSP S	outhern	Fujitsu Alliance	10 years
National Network for the NHS (N3)	National B	ritish Telecom 7	years
Choose and Book	National A	tos Origin 5	years
Contact (email) N	ational	Cable & Wireless	10 years

Figure 2. Five English regional clusters with approximate population

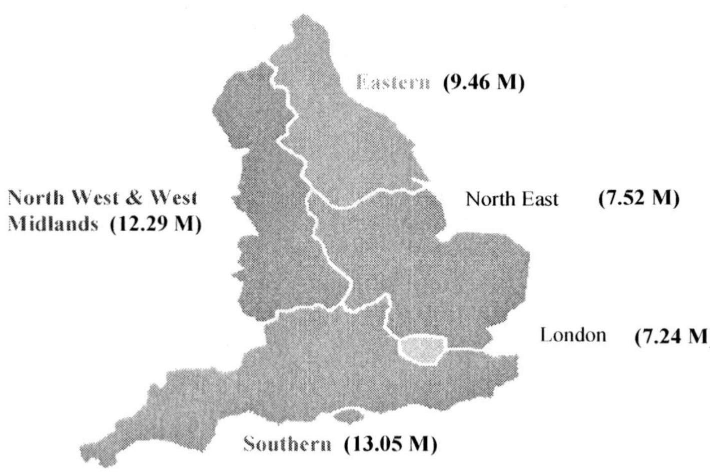

Current Achievements

Certain parts of the national programme have been achieved to date:

- **Autumn 2004:** Choose and Book was distributed at several hospitals implementing the first electronic booking of hospital appointments from GPs. The GP will make the appointment in negotiation with the patient.
- **Spring 2004:** The 1st phase of Care Record Service has been developed with basic health record including patient demographic information, birth and death notification, recording of allergies.
- **Winter 2005:** 1st phase roll-out of electronic transfer prescription service.
- **Summer 2004:** 1st phase roll-out of PACS (picture archiving communication system).
- **Autumn 2004:** Launch of Contact—a new service including E-mail and Directory Services (now available to all staff)
- **Autumn 2005:** Roll-out of QMAS—a system to provide timely feedback for GPs on the quality of care delivered to their patients
- **Summer 2004:** Establishment of National Service Desk (running from Leeds offices) for interim help desk purposes—temporarily operated in-house (since NPfIT did not initially contract for the provision of cohesive front line services)

FUTURE PROJECT PHASES

Other services planned for future phases of the national programme include:

- The 2nd phase of Care Record Service—planed for Summer 2005 to Summer 2006—will see health record grow to cover orders and results for diagnostic images and pathology, to support care pathways and notify GPs of emergencies and other out of hours encounters.
- The 3rd phase of Care Record Service—planned for 2006 to 2008—will provide support for all doctors and nurses to help with decisions. It will also include systems to support care at home using remote links to healthcare professionals anywhere in the community. This would provide better healthcare planning and enable access to facts and figures held on the NHS Care Record Service.
- The final phases of Electronic Transmission of Prescription and Picture Archiving and Communications Systems will be implementation by 2008.
- The final features incorporated to complete full integration between health and social care systems in England should be achieved by 2010.

The future phases demonstrate the difficulty of evaluating the two most important project variables—cost and value—as pointed out in Wanless' (2002) evaluation of management and operation in the NHS. However, the DoH has initiated a strong campaign to inform and engage the GPs and public about patient choice through the final months in 2005. In response to these delays, The Health Minister claimed:

This is the biggest civil IT project under way anywhere in the world today. Not everything is going to go smoothly all of the time, and we're not going to pretend to the public that it is. But one of the biggest challenges facing the NHS is the quality of its technology. If we don't get the technology we need, we won't get the service we want to see. (NHS Modernisation Agency, 2004)

While these delays are explained as technology problems, our research found that much of the delay could loosely be described as cultural issues. These included differences in political objectives between politicians, healthcare professionals, and workers; poor communication between the centre, regions, and individual hospitals; the problem of implementing new IT in conjunction with doing the day-to-day work within hospitals and GP surgeries; issues of security and confidentiality; the time lag between technology implementation and user training and uptake of the new system; and many other factors. These issues are discussed in the next section.

Criticisms of the NPfIT

There have been further objections to the NPfIT plans related to the protection of personal information, with opponents even suggesting that NHS patients' records would be connected to a more controversial e-government initiative—the national identity register requiring all citizens to carry ID cards on their person. However, the NHS has insisted that access to the system would be limited according to the requirements of the individual member of staff.

Many medical practitioners and hospital administrators also challenge the one-size-fits-all approach. NPfIT is intended largely to deliver healthcare data locally on a nationwide basis, but some IT directors in the NHS local trusts resent being pressured to run and manage a technology bought by London-based officials.

NPfIT receives its funding from the DoH, not from the businesses it is serving—which are run by GPs and NHS trusts. A common complaint about NPfIT in the NHS is that some medical practitioners and local trust IT directors believe they are being dictated to by the centre rather than receiving a service. Several regional trust boards have expressed concern about the local costs of introducing national systems. Some may be unable or unwilling to drop other work to spend large sums on a national scheme for which they feel no ownership. Some critics have argued that the NPfIT is led by a centralist approach, unlike the norm in the NHS of adopting systems of GPs' choice, built to standard specifications that followed a "data-centric" approach.

These concerns also show systemic cracks that have appeared in the structures of accountability within NPfIT. Different organizations are in partial control of delivery, including the DoH, Connecting for Health, clusters, suppliers, PCTs, hospital trusts, and GP organizations.

Further, the director of NHS IT, commenting on the delivery of a system to enable patients and doctors to book hospital appointments electronically, stated:

It is unfortunate we delivered it to schedule because if we had delivered it a year or two late, I think the user input would have caught up with the system being delivered. It is going to be interesting to see, over the next few months, whether the potential of that working technology platform with very high levels of availability is taken up locally in the NHS. (NHS Modernisation Agency, 2004)

The UK government's chief information officer, has rightly argued that governments cannot abandon schemes that should improve how citizens and the public sector interact simply because previous government IT projects have failed, and he recognizes that investment alone is not enough. Having seen the need for experienced professionals and best-of-breed solutions, Mr. Watmore has undertaken to increase levels of professionalism in government IT. However, there is also a need to recognize that IT problems are usually the result of bigger business challenges, and these business challenges of the IT-related government project should be the focus, not only IT itself.

THE CHALLENGES OF IMPLEMENTING IT-ENABLED HEALTHCARE SERVICE

The complexities of maintaining accurate and up-to-date information are well known to major corporations with large numbers of customers (Baskerville, 1993; Davies, 1989). The task being taken on by the UK government in regard to the NPfIT is massive in comparison with many large-scale private sector IT projects. This complexity is commensurate with increased risk as the NPfIT is both politically contentious and culturally and technologically diverse in scale and scope.

At the heart of many e-government initiatives is the focus on technology at the cost of what the citizen requires by way of improved services. This has led to widespread criticism that public money is being wasted on IT-enabled projects, which achieve little in terms of improving the quality of life of those it is intended to serve. Failure to identify and delineate between the perceived and actual benefits from e-government initiatives is often at the heart of many failures. In addition, the application of stringent performance targets may mean that "all the targets are being met" without considering whether "we are measuring the right targets." According to the UK government's chief information officer:

Not many private sector projects have to deal with the numbers of requests and people that government schemes do, and those that do often suffer the same problems when it comes to whether the system works and end users can actually use it. (NHS Modernisation Agency, 2004)

While it is understandable that government agencies focus upon a narrow range of performance targets to measure success and failure factors of IT projects, this is unlikely to pacify the critics of the NPfIT, many of whom resent any change to their working practices. In meeting the challenge of implementing the NPfIT, government will therefore need to work hard in convincing potential users of the various IT systems that their working lives will be improved and that patients will ultimately receive a better service. The failure to implement a large-scale management change programme in conjunction with the technical changes imposed upon the workforce will only exacerbate the problems of implementation.

Indeed, lessons from past IS research have shown that there is no such thing as an "IT failure," as all technology failures are more appropriately described as "management failures" (Currie, 1995). Using the label *IT failure* to describe an unsuccessful programme or project creates a perception that if only the technology had worked, then the result would have been successful. Such a perception tends to absolve management from any responsibility that the so-called IT failure was a result of their decision making and lack of proper project management.

The need to dispel some of the current perceptions in the media that the NPfIT is the next major "IT disaster-in-waiting" is therefore a critical task for senior politicians, healthcare executives, and IT service providers. Part of this task will involve "managing perceptions," not only to those who will use the various IT systems, but also to the media. One observation from our research is that the media recognize the public interest in stories about healthcare, particularly those that aim to "expose" poor practice. The vast amount of financial investment in the NPfIT offers a soft target for those wishing to publish an *expose* on the mismatch between the objectives and achievements of the programme to date. As a nationwide programme with several thousand users, all of whom will require different levels of access and need to share different databases and receive different levels of training, it is likely that media attention to any shortcomings of the programme will continue for several years to come. Further complications will arise with legislation such as the Freedom of Information Act or Data Protection Act.

Our research suggests that e-government projects should embrace these wider challenges rather than focus solely upon technology imperatives. If this is not done before technologies are identified and installed, the people affected by them are likely to develop attitudes and behavioural patterns that will circumvent their implementation. This scenario suggests the government needs to clearly identify strategies, methods, and techniques for winning the approval of those affected, rather than simply pursuing centrist (top-down) policies by imposing IT-enabled change upon people. This would require public sector officials to closely monitor the various IT projects from end-to-end and not just the IT implementation. Every large programme, like NPfIT, notably has problems and things that will go wrong. Identifying issues and risks early and reacting positively to problems within IT and across other project areas where any changes will have an impact is therefore critical.

While there is a need for highly skilled professional IT suppliers and consultants, the technology should not be the primary focus of such a massive project—a higher chance of ending up with another failed e-government initiative. Government IT strategists need to address the wider culture imperatives in the extent to which the organizational climate and people are predisposed to adopting new IT-enabled working practices. While this may seem self evident, our research shows that the top-down approach for IT adoption and diffusion is likely to engender feelings of resentment and frustration among healthcare workers, rather than a willingness to adopt and adapt to these changes. External service providers also have a role to play in this which extends beyond one of merely implementing new IT systems.

THE CRITICAL ROLE OF EXTERNAL SERVICE PROVIDERS

As part of the government agent for reforming public services, external IT providers are guaranteed a large role in the NPfIT with many large, long-term contracts being negotiated. The NPfIT seeks to develop applications in the NHS for the design of health service delivery processes across a range of clinical and nonclinical activities. Part of this agenda is to improve the internal and external supply chain of information flows across the NHS to enable healthcare professionals, managers and administrators, and patients to take more informed and better decisions on various aspects of health-related matters, from being able to electronically transfer patient information to allowing patients to choose and book convenient hospital appointments.

By attempting to emulate the methods and practices of private sector firms, in areas such as supply chain, procurement, cost effectiveness, workflow, and so forth, government and healthcare executives hope to transform the UK NHS from a less efficient and effective institution to a lean and agile one. However, the institutional structure, processes, and practices make this an enormous, if not impossible, task particularly in the short to medium term.

In selecting external service providers, our research suggests that one of the key challenges for government and healthcare executives is assessing the capabilities and skills of these firms. Many IT service providers do not have an extensive knowledge of healthcare products and services and, more importantly, the cultural values, attitudes, and beliefs that govern the behaviour of healthcare workers. For example, the cost imperatives that have been introduced by government force many NHS hospitals to evaluate whether or not they can offer a particular medical treatment (i.e., operations and drugs). This has resulted in concerns that patients are likely to receive specific treatments depending upon where they live or which hospital they use, rather than receiving a blanket service which is offered to all, irrespective of geographical region, postal code, or hospital.

As a result of the NPfIT, large IT service providers recognize that lucrative public sector contracts will be offered over a long period of time. Such contracts come at a time when many IT service providers have been damaged by the fall-out of the dotcom crash, where IT contracts were often delayed or even cancelled. But while the NPfIT offers IT service providers new business development opportunities, the healthcare sector is extremely complex and multifaceted, where rudimentary business decisions about cost-cutting and rationalization must be taken in the context of other, more immediate considerations (i.e., which may involve matters of life or death). IT service providers must therefore be sensitive to these issues as healthcare continues to be seen in the UK as a matter of right, and not merely one which is reducible to cost-cutting measures.

The DoH agenda for the NPfIT involves a number of different stages, starting with static applications used solely for providing information and ending with fully interactive databases over a complex WAN that are capable of handling a multitude of transactions that occur in the lifelong relationship between the NHS and its patients and partners. The NPfIT can take lessons from smaller e-government projects, the online tax return system, which demonstrates that transferring money online plays an important role in an e-government initiative to include financial transactions such as paying taxes, fees, or fines.

Trust, both in a functional use of the system and in e-healthcare security, can be seen as an important antecedent for the adoption of the NPfIT on the part of medical practitioners and patients alike. From the government's point of view, the potential for exerting influence seems to be somewhat limited. While national institutions in most Western countries are usually perceived as trustworthy, users' attitudes about having their medical records available online may be more skeptical. *IT service providers will therefore have to ensure that security of their systems are a top priority*, particularly when the media is eager to publish stories about lack of patient confidentiality and other negative aspects about IT-enabled change in the NHS.

POTENTIAL IMPACTS ON HEALTHCARE PROCESSES

A recent report of what works in terms of service improvement methodology within the NHS (NHS Modernisation Agency, 2004) points out 10 high impact changes. It illustrates what is possible when clinical teams equipped with the right tools and support networks are given the authority to review and streamline years of accredited processes.

Major changes in healthcare process are required for organizations in UK health and social care to adopt and to make significant and measurable improvements as a result of e-government initiatives. Though evidence based, these changes draw on the lessons learned from earlier work, build on the success already achieved (Atkinson & Peel, 1998), and illustrate the day-to-day experience and achievements of thousands of frontline clinical teams across the NHS.

If these changes were adopted systematically throughout the entire health sector:

- The experience of patients would be greatly enhanced by more appropriate and timely care
- Clinician hours, hospital bed days, and appointments in primary and secondary care would be saved by several hundred thousands
- Clinical quality and clinical outcomes would be tangibly improved
- It would be easier to attract and retain more good quality staff

The following quote, from a senior member of the NHS Modernisation Team, encapsulates this thinking:

We frequently see radiology and endoscopy departments where there are more than 100 separate patient queues within a single schedule. Many sites (hospitals) have been able to reduce the number of queues by between 50% and 80% and with no extra resources to reduce average waiting times by at least 50%. They have also been able to reduce Did Not Attends (DNAs) and cancellations as a by-product of shorter waits for patients. ... One by-product of the MA's work has been the definition of the data that is really required to successfully manage capacity, demand and utilisation. (anonymous interview)

The NPfIT is beginning to show signs of enhancing patient care in the few hospitals that have gone live with certain aspects of the phase implementation. At one NHS hospital, the new way of storing and sharing information is allowing patients to access information more easily when making decisions about their health and care. Patients have faster access to their medical records by using a secure Internet connection than is possible by requesting a paper copy. Once this is implemented across the NHS, this will allow diagnosis and treatment to be safer and speedier, as carers will have the right information available to them at the right time, including X-rays and other medical images. All these images will be stored electronically allowing them to be easily made available at different locations and forwarded to specialists for their advice. The emerging technologies are therefore bringing advantages over paper records and X-ray films that are still used in many parts of the NHS. Nondigital images, however, are frequently lost and sometimes difficult to read, and may lose their quality, as they are stored in a filing cabinet for long periods. One advantage of the new system is the facility to record details of everyone who has accessed an individual's NHS care record, which is not possible with paper records.

The stakeholders who are likely to benefit from the NPfIT programme are as follows:

Patients:

- Will eventually have access to their health record through a secure NHS gateway on the Internet, making patients more informed and involved in decisions about their own care and treatment.

- Provision of safer care with the availability of vital information for diagnosis and treatment (i.e., current medication, details of previous operations, test results, or allergies) regardless of geographical location and time of the day.
- Faster, easier, and a more convenient means of booking hospital appointments (at GP surgery or via telephone call, or over the Internet) allowing patients the luxury of discussing it with family, carers, or colleagues first.

Clinicians:

- Will have ready access to more comprehensive, up-to-date information to support diagnosis.
- Will be able to make more efficient referrals, gain alerts to contraindicated therapies, and significantly achieve early detection of disease outbreaks
- Will significantly reduce administrative burden dealing with chasing up referrals or missing notes.

The NHS management:

- Will provide better intelligence on how the NHS works and health of citizens by collecting anonymous information nationally.
- Will make it easier to observe and control the spreading of infectious diseases.
- Provide real number, in real time, not just a sample from spotter practices
- Will benefit from negotiating power. The first two years of NPfIT has saved the NHS over £430 million through the process of direct negotiation with suppliers and subcontractors.

KNOWLEDGE MANAGEMENT AND HEALTHCARE DELIVERY

Significant cost savings for better NHS intelligence for negotiating with suppliers and subcontractors have already been realized. In addition, however, better NHS intelligence can yield other benefits to the healthcare community, including the ability to more effectively respond to potential infectious disease crises.

To classify the KM elements of healthcare delivery, we consider a simple model in which we take the Modernisation Agency's integrated care pathways (NHS Modernisation Agency, 2004) as a descriptor of a generic process in care delivery. Clearly care pathways are no single process, but they reflect the emerging patient centred paradigm in healthcare (see Figure 3). Haines (2002) shows that KM must be targeted at providing the best support for each care pathway. Such a paradigm is followed by an analysis that asks where healthcare knowledge is stored. For the purposes of this analysis, we assume there are four types of knowledge repositories in a healthcare system:

1. **People:** This is perhaps the most obvious place to seek knowledge, particularly in medicine. One key element that distinguishes a medical consultation, for instance, from a counselling session, a tutorial, or a friendly conversation, is the knowledge possessed by the consultant. However, a great deal of healthcare knowledge is possessed and managed by people other than doctors—nurses and other professionals, as well, increasingly, as patients themselves. Finally, well people (those looking to remain well, and those operating as carers) are increasingly knowledgeable.
2. **Information sources:** This category includes paper-based and Web sites and other electronic information. Typical formats include journals, reference material, bulletins, and updates. With an increasing emphasis on process, this will also address strategic specifications for care delivery processes, details of local procedures, or to redesign those procedures (Guah & Currie, 2004).
3. **Data sources:** Here there is clearly scope for overlap with the previous category and,

Figure 3. Connecting sources of healthcare knowledge for data transfer

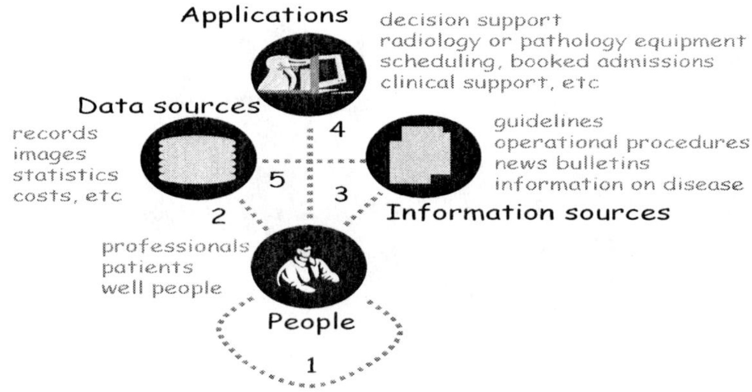

in some cases, with the next. However, data are meant to signify information that has not been processed. In this, we might typically place patient records, images, test results, perhaps even some statistics. The boundary with the previous category is not clean, but between them they define a spectrum of information, from raw digits to content.

4. **Applications:** Increasingly information about the system is contained in software applications and other equipment. For instance, while an MR machine might generate an image, the workflow system by which it picks up information about the patient, together with the PACS infrastructure may embody a great deal of information about the healthcare delivery system in which it operates. The same can be said about direct booking systems or decision support systems, particularly if they contain an element of drill-down description based on operational procedures.

Figure 3 shows the need for Web services to maintain continuously live repositories of knowledge as opposed to large repositories. For instance, many processes cannot be considered, even theoretically, because the referring clinician (GP) is unable to communicate with an appropriate specialist in real time. Thus, the patient (often using postal and telephone contacts) becomes part of knowledge transfer pathway that can take many weeks to return to the GP.

FUTURE IT CHALLENGES FOR THE NPFIT

With new emphasis now on e-government driving efficiency in the 21st century, IT has become more important than ever. Healthcare is a critical service to citizens where government needs to identify opportunities for increasing efficiency and cost control.

Public sector IT projects in UK—some may argue continental Europe—have not always led to successful outcomes (NAO, 2004). In an attempt to avoid these failures, the government has now introduced Gateway Reviews to evaluate IT projects at various points in their life cycles. There are six key goals for this review process. While this approach is formulaic and procedural, it is a step closer to recognizing the consequences of IT-enabled projects becoming overscoped and out of control (Currie, 1997).

Yet political imperatives of e-government are critical factors that affect public sector procurement for IT. Our research identified competing views about the IT procurement process with some defending the process and others highly critical of it.

According to the MD of a telecommunications and contact centre services company that sells heavily into the public sector:

One of the reasons public sectors IT projects fail is because public sector culture leads to the abdication of responsibility, especially with large projects. With these mega-projects, no one wants to get too close to them in case something bad sticks to them, so they create a structure where decision making responsibility is difficult to locate ... everyone and no-one is responsible! The larger the project, the more likely this will happen. The private sector usually has more stringent roles identified for managers, so this is what we need to do in the public sector.

An interviewee who heads project management software stated:

Government IT project failure isn't all down to individual cowardice or unwillingness to make a decision. The procurement cycles for many public sector projects are simply too long, leading to projects that can often fail to meet changing conditions. What this tends to do is shift focus away from what the organisation is trying to achieve and the outcome it wants to get. All of the brave creative thought that may have been there is stripped out. If the procurement phase of a project takes up too much time, the benefits can be eroded.

According to a member of the NPfIT team:

One reason IT procurement can take so long is that public sector bodies are bound to follow certain rules if the project meets selected criteria. For example, if the project value falls above a certain level, it must be put out to tender through the Official Journal of the European Commission (OJEC). The NHS had to advertize to the whole European Community, going through various rounds of responses. After a lengthy period of consulting with potential suppliers through this process, the service providers finally get to negotiate contracts. Many companies will bid low to get the business but will then define the project requirements so strictly that any minor change requires more investment by the public sector customer. Because projects almost always change, this can introduce extra costs and complexity into the project as it develops.

A CEO for an IT consultancy contributed his verdict:

Even when the contract negotiation phases reached, mistakes are made. Government negotiators were always forced to take the cheapest price in the past, and although this has changed slightly (the emphasis is now on "best value"), a culture of cheapness still exists within the public sector.

And according to a former member of the NPfIT team:

None of this is helped by the fact that many public sector IT projects are driven by politics. Public sector projects are driven by political cycles and so artificial deadlines are often set. They are driven by politicians, which creates a framework that isn't helpful. If politicians are driving the project, sometimes for overtly political reasons, it becomes difficult to set the projected benefits and deadlines of the project to benefit the real-world users at the sharp end.

These quotes demonstrate that one of the important differences between the public and private sector is that the political agenda can be a major driver of IT projects. Politicians played a key role in identifying and determining what needed to be changed in the NHS. Yet the follow-through of politicians was generally short-term, and this created a situation where it was difficult to impose a long-term agenda when the individuals taking these decisions were unlikely to be around, or indeed, accountable, for the results in the future. This scenario was highly criticized by many healthcare workers, who had become cynical about government policy making for the NHS.

Another key criticism about the IT procurement process was the highly bureaucratic procedures involved in selecting IT service providers. In the European Union, all Requests for Proposals (RFPs) had to be advertized across the EU. This meant that any IT service provider who was part of the EU could apply. Such a system was highly cumbersome and did not always lead to the best outcome. Thus:

The cultural and procedural elements of IT procurement within the EU are not conducive to getting the best deal. The *OJEC* (*Official Journal of the European Community*) system is the biggest single inefficiency that I can think of. It seems to rely on benchmarking of specific performance indicators rather than generating competitive tension among those who are interested in the tender. Once a contract is signed, then a lot of inertia creeps into it, and the project scope often loses its way. In terms of IT projects, it is better to take on bite-sized chunks, rather than trying to build the whole thing at once. This also makes your project more flexible because you can adapt future requirements as political conditions change. Using pilot projects can also help you to fly at least part of the project under the OJEC radar, keeping you within spending limits that do not require a huge European Commission-wide tender. Our experience is that many people run service lines as ad hoc items. You don't just want to know whether the application is alive and running or not. Identifying things like service levels and response times for your deployed IT service is also important. This will require a structured budget in advance.

Delineating IT projects into their component parts is a lesson that is often put forward as a key driver for success, yet one that is usually ignored. Scale and scope creep of IT projects is often depicted as a critical failure factor. Yet the IT projects that are part of the whole of the NPfIT are large scale and involve numerous stages. IT service providers will therefore need to work closely with all stakeholders if they are to avoid the common pitfalls of many large-scale IT projects.

CONCLUSION

While there is a great deal of academic literature on e-payment and e-government issues, this chapter combines both topics and proposes a framework and a measurement model that depicts important factors influencing patients' and medical practitioners' online behaviour. A structural equation modelling approach has been used to assess the relative importance and the strength of the relationships among different constructs, including users' previous experience, their trust in the availability of health information electronically, and their perceived convenience of the data access process.

The research results indicate that regional NHS trust (both in a frictionless use of the system and in e-healthcare security) can be seen as an important antecedent for the adoption of NPfIT on the part of the medical practitioners and patients alike. From the government's point of view, the potential for exerting influence seems to be somewhat limited. While national institutions in most Western countries are usually perceived as trustworthy, users' attitudes toward the medical data online may be more skeptical. This widely depends on users' previous experience with the automated systems, sadly through the interaction with businesses in the private sector.

This chapter has presented preliminary research findings about the NPfIT, which is the largest civil IT-enabled change programme in the world with the aim of automating various elements of healthcare service delivery. As a politically controversial, financially large, and technologically complex initiative, the NPfIT continues to attract positive and negative stories within the media. Our research findings confirm many of these negative reports. Yet, we also suggest that all large-scale IT-enabled programmes face similar challenges, and those relating to healthcare carry the addition burden of complex issues about how hospitals can control health costs while at the same time addressing other issues, such as meeting patient demands, ensuring the ability of service providers to deliver IT systems in line with national requirements, and the extent to which health workers are willing to change their working practices.

At the NPfIT, initiatives to control IT-enabled projects offer a potential solution to some of these issues, yet an increasingly bureaucratic approach is no substitute for winning the hearts and minds of the people who are affected by changes to working practices. While the NPfIT offers a unique and timely approach to standardizing the delivery of healthcare across the nation, we suggest that better communication channels are required to convince healthcare stakeholders that such changes are necessary and worthwhile. Finally, we suggest that, in meeting the challenges of a 21st century healthcare system, the NPfIT needs to be understood more as a large-scale programme to transform the culture of healthcare service delivery, rather than narrowly defined as an IT-enabled project evaluated on a narrow set of quantitative key performance indicators.

Analysis of data on the NPfIT to date indicated that there has to be an increase in the connection between service providers and medical practitioners to raise the efficiency of resulting applications. The implementation team also needs to increase the momentum actively in developing collaboration with users and strengthening user education to raise the utilization of the resulting information systems.

Handled properly, the public sector could work toward a more efficient, cost effective way of providing services with the aid of Web services applications. At this stage, any broader conclusion cannot be considered, given that the NPfIT is a 10-year project, part of a long-term modernization process for the future health service of the British people, still in its third year.

REFERENCES

Atkinson, C. J., & Peel, V. J. (1998). Transforming a hospital through growing, not building, an electronic patient record system. *Methods of Information in Medicine, 37*, 285-293.

Barney, J. (1991). Firm resources and sustained competitive advantages. *Journal of Management, 17*, 99-120.

Baskerville, R. (1993). Information system security design methods: Implications for information systems development. *ACM Computing Surveys, 25*(4).

Boncella, R. J. (2004). Web services and Web services security. *Communications of the Association for Information Systems, 14*, 344-363.

Brown, T. (2001). Modernization or failure? IT development projects in the UK public sector. *Financial Accountability & Management, 17*(4), 363-381.

Currie, W. L. (1995). *Management strategy for IT.* London: Pitman.

Currie, W. L. (1997). Computerising the stock exchange: A comparison of two information systems. *New Technology, Work and Employment, 12*(2), 75-83.

Davis, F. D. (1989). Perceived usefulness, perceived ease of use and of user acceptance of information technology. *MIS Quarterly, 13*(4), 982-1003.

Department of Health (UK). (2000). *NHS plan: An information strategy for the modern NHS.* London: Author.

Department of Health (UK). (2002). *Learning from Bristol.* Oxford: Capstone.

Devaraj, S., & Kohli, R. (2000). Information technology payoff in the health-care industry: A longitudinal study. *Journal of Management Information Systems, 16*(4), 41-68.

Eisenhardt, K. M., & Martin, J. A. (2003). Dynamic capabilities: What are they? *Strategic Management Journal, 21*, 1105-1121.

Guah, M. W., & Currie, W. L. (2004). NHS information quality and integrity: Issues arising from primary service provision. *International Journal of Healthcare Technology and Management, 6*(2), 173-188.

Guah, M. W., & Currie, W. L. (Eds.). (2005a). *Internet strategy: The road to Web services solution*. Hershey, PA: Idea Group.

Guah, M. W., & Currie, W. L. (2005b). Web services in national healthcare: The impact of public and private collaboration. *International Journal of Technology and Human Interaction, 1*(2), 48-61.

Haines, M. (2002). Knowledge management in the NHS: Platform for change. Retrieved May 9, 2006, from http://www.healthknowledge.org.uk

Majeed, A. (2003). Ten ways to improve information technology in the NHS. *British Medical Journal, 326*, 202-206.

National Audit Office. (2004). *Improving IT procurement*. London: The Stationary Office.

NHS Modernisation Agency. (2004). Review of waiting and booking information (ROWBI). Retrieved May 9, 2006, from http://www.content.modern.nhs.uk/NR/

Scott, W. R., Ruef, M., Mendel, P. J., & Caronna, C. A. (2000). *Institutional change and healthcare organizations: From professional dominance to managed care*. Chicago: University of Chicago Press.

Vriens, D., & Achterbergh, J. (2004). Planning local e-government. *Information Systems Management, 21*(1), 45-58.

Wanless, D. (2002). *Securing our future health: Taking a long-term view* (Final Report of an Independent Review of the Long-Term Resource Requirement for the NHS). London.

Wernerfeld, B. (1984, April-June). A resource-based view of the firm. *Strategic Management Journal,* 5, 171-180.

Wilson, E. V., & Lankton, N. K. (2004). Interdisciplinary research and publication opportunities in information systems and healthcare. *Communications of the Association for Information Systems, 14*, 332-343.

Zhang, D., Chen, M., & Zhou, L. (2005). Dynamic and personalized Web services composition in e-business. *Information Systems Management, 22*(3), 50-66.

This work was previously published in Global E-Government: Theory, Applications and Benchmarking, edited by L. Al-Hakim, pp. 238-260, copyright 2007 by IGI Publishing, formerly known as Idea Group Publishing (an imprint of IGI Global).

Chapter 4.36
Mechanism of E-Government Undertaking in Japan

Yuko Kaneko
University of Yamagata, Japan

INTRODUCTION

According to the report submitted by the Evaluation Committee of Experts, Government ICT Strategy Headquarters in December 2005 (ECE, 2005), Japan has already established the globally advanced e-government infrastructures for such services as online application and filing. The report also acknowledged that the quantity and quality of information, guidance and search engine at the government portal, "e-Gov", and individual government Web sites have reached almost the same level as those of the government Web sites of the other world-famous ICT nations.

These achievements have resulted from the continuous undertaking of introducing information and communication technologies (ICTs) in the government operations from 1960s (ECHMCA, 2001).

In this article, the successful accomplishments of e-government initiative are described followed by the analysis of institutional arrangements and mechanisms concerning e-government initiatives. Lastly, the future challenges will be suggested.

BACKGROUND

The Japanese government started its government-wide efforts for the management reform of administrative affairs in the late 1950s. Coincidently, the first computer in the national government was introduced by the Meteorological Agency in 1958. Since then, the government has been aggressively introducing computer and communication equipments and systems for improving efficiency and efficacy of public administration. This undertaking was not carried out independently by individual ministries. In 1968, the Cabinet decided on the future measures for the use of computers and at the same time an interministerial committee of computer use was established to promote the use of computers in more coordinated way. The committee was organized by a central management office, the former Administrative Management Agency of the Prime Minister's Office, consisted of the representatives from all the ministries and agencies who were the heads of the data processing divisions. The committee decided the computer utilization plan every fiscal year and all the ministries and agencies carried out necessary measures for promoting computer use in their organizations based on the plan (ECHMCA, 2001).

From 1960s to 1980s, the number of mainframe computers in the government kept on growing rapidly (Kaneko, 2004a). Batch processing of mass data by huge mainframes was the way of the day. Computers were utilized initially in the areas of research and statistics and then, by late 1970s, in such areas needing process of massive data as drivers' licenses, social insurances, and so forth (Kaneko, 2001). Databases for supporting policy formulation emerged later in the 1980s.

In the late 1980s, such remarkable development as downsizing, open-system, networking and user-friendly software was achieved in the ICT field. The government's undertakings to introduce personal computers (PCs) into policy planning/development and implementation lagged behind those of the private sector. With a view to promoting aggressive introduction and exploitation of ICT, a government-wide action program was needed. In 1994, the Cabinet decided upon a Master Plan for Promoting Government-Wide Use of ICT for realizing efficient and effective public administration by aggressively making use of ICT in all the government affairs.

Based on the master plan, the introduction of PCs and construction of LANs (local area networks) in the government offices progressed reasonably. Moreover, a WAN (wide area network) system (so-called Kasumigaseki WAN), connecting all ministries to facilitate the safe exchange of information between them, was constructed and it was put into operation in 1997 (Kaneko, 2004a).

Thus, it can be said that these continuous undertakings from 1960s have paved the way to the e-government initiatives.

ANALYTICAL VIEWPOINTS

All OECD countries have some sort of e-government program such as PAGSI in France, BundOnline in Germany and UK Online(OECD, 2003a, 2003b). Some are based on laws and top-level political commitment on the other hand other countries have a less ambitious e-government program, in which e-government is more a method to improve government outcomes within existing structures. As all countries have an e-government program, all countries have some sort of organizations with overarching responsibility for carrying out the program. The authority of these organizations differs widely from imposing mandatory obligation to offering solutions (OECD, 2005).

In this article, mechanism of e-government undertaking includes a national e-government program and institutional arrangements for implementing the e-government program. In describing the Japanese case, two viewpoints are adopted. One is the degree of political commitment concerning an e-government program and the other is the degree of the authority of the organization that is responsible for implementing an e-government program.

MAJOR ACHIEVEMENTS TOWARD E-GOVERNMENT

The Japanese e-government program envisages two main goals, one is to provide "user-oriented administrative services" and the other is to realize "streamlined public administration with high budget efficiency" (GOJ, 2003b). And the various initiatives have been executed based on these two goals. The major achievements of the government's actions toward e-government as of December 2005 (Kaneko, 2005)are described according to the goals of the e-government program.

Figure 1. Achievements in online processing

Achievements	Date
96% of all administrative procedures of the national government by on-line	Mar-05
GPKI (Government Public Key Infrastructure)	Apr-01
LGCA (Local Government Certification Authorities) services	Jan-04
E-payment system for fees and other revenues	Jan-04
E-bidding for procurement and purchasing	Mar-04

To Provide "User-oriented Administrative Services"

Online Processing

There has been real progress enabling citizens and businesses conduct online application and filing for almost all the national administrative procedures (GOJ, 2005). As of March, 2005, 96% of the targeted national administrative procedures are available online such as filing tax and applying for the social insurance system. As basic underpinning of online application, various initiatives have been completed such as GPKI enabling to confirm authenticity mutually, LGCA , enabling to confirm identification and the online payment systems allowing citizens to pay charges online. According to the survey conducted by the Ministry of Internal Affairs and Communications in 2004 (MIC, 2004), more than 80% of applications and filings were conducted online.

Improvement of the Government Portal "e-Gov"

A government portal site, "e-Gov" (http://www.e-gov.go.jp) has been in operation since April 2001 to make the people access the government information more easily and comprehensively (GOJ, 2005). Not only guidance for administrative procedures but also a powerful search engine to look for all the government Web sites, a law data retrieval system and extensive links to databases provided by the ministries are on "e-Gov." From January 2004, the public comment information has been integrated and the policy proposals from the citizens can be accepted at "e-Gov."

One-Stop Service

A single window service was started for the export/import procedures and the port control procedures in July 2003 (GOJ, 2005). Likewise, a new one-stop service for registration and other procedures related to owning automobiles was started in December 2005.

To Realize "Streamlined Public Administration with High Budget Efficiency"

ICT Infrastructure

Each official is provided with one PC and all ministries have completed deploying the ministry LAN environment, which is connected to the government-wide network, Kasumigaseki WAN enabling mutual access among ministry LANs (MIC, 2002). The network infrastructure in the government sector has been extended to involve LGWAN (local government-wide area network) linking the entire local governments and the judicial network (court network) linking the court branches (MIC, 2004).

Renovating Administrative Systems and Operations by the Use of ICT

While setting up various information systems including the network infrastructure, the budget allocation for building such systems and its cost efficiency are coming to be under public scrutiny. With a view to renovating administrative systems and operations by the use of ICT, the existing information systems together with the entire government business operations were sorted out and the operations needing renovation were specified for which optimization plans were to be decided (GOJ, 2004). In each optimization plan, concrete measures including integration or shared usage of systems, outsourcing as well as the estimated savings in time and costs are to be described. It was decided in January 2004 that the optimization plans for 79 operations were to be formulated by the end of March 2006. As of December 2005, 9 optimization plans targeting the common operation of the ministries and 12 targeting the specific operations of the individual ministries have been adopted.

Figure 2. Achievements in optimization

Achievements	Date
Adoption of Optimization Plans for 9 commonly applicable operations: Payroll, Procurement, Inventory Management, Benefits & Allowances, Travel Expenses, etc.	Dec-05
Adoption of Optimization Plans for 12 specific operations: Patent, Radio Wave Control, State Pension, National Forestry, Food Administration, Meteorological Services, etc.	Dec-05

NATIONAL E-GOVERNMENT PROGRAM

Introduction

Japan has a well-coordinated e-government program as "Program for Building E-Government" (GOJ, 2003b). This program is an action plan to implement the policies for realization of e-government included in "E-Japan Strategy," a national strategy for promoting the use of ICT in the whole society (GOJ, 2001, 2003a). The E-Japan Strategy was adopted based on the ICT Basic Law. In the following, the brief outline of the legal arrangement, the national ICT strategy and the e-government program (Kaneko, 2005) are described.

ICT Basic Law

In January 2001, the Basic Law on the Formation of an Advanced Information and Telecommunications Network Society (The ICT Basic Law) came into force. The objective of this law is to promote measures for the formation of an advanced ICT network society expeditiously and intensively. For this purpose, the law stipulates the basic ideas, principles and policies as well as organization for promoting measures strategically.

The law establishes the Strategy Headquarters for the Promotion of an Advanced Information and Telecommunications Network Society (ICT Strategy Headquarters).

Under the law, the Headquarters are to develop a priority policy program for the formation of an advanced IT network society, in light of the urgency to adapt the Japanese society to the world's rapid and drastic changes in the socioeconomic structure caused by the utilization of ICT.

E-Japan Strategy and Priority Policy Program

In January 2001, "E-Japan Strategy" was adopted by the ICT Strategy Headquarters (GOJ, 2001). It is a medium term national strategy aiming at making Japan the world's most advanced ICT nation within 5 years by such means as building the world's most sophisticated information and telecommunication network, which would make the citizens possible to access the Internet easily at low rates. The strategy shows the leading principles for preparing a priority policy program, a concrete work plan. The realization of e-government is identified as one of the high-priority policy areas in the Strategy.

In March 2001, the ICT Strategy Headquarters decided an E-Japan Priority Policy Program that included specific and detailed measures of the individual ministries. In the Priority Policy

Figure 3. Basic framework of policies for e-government in Japan

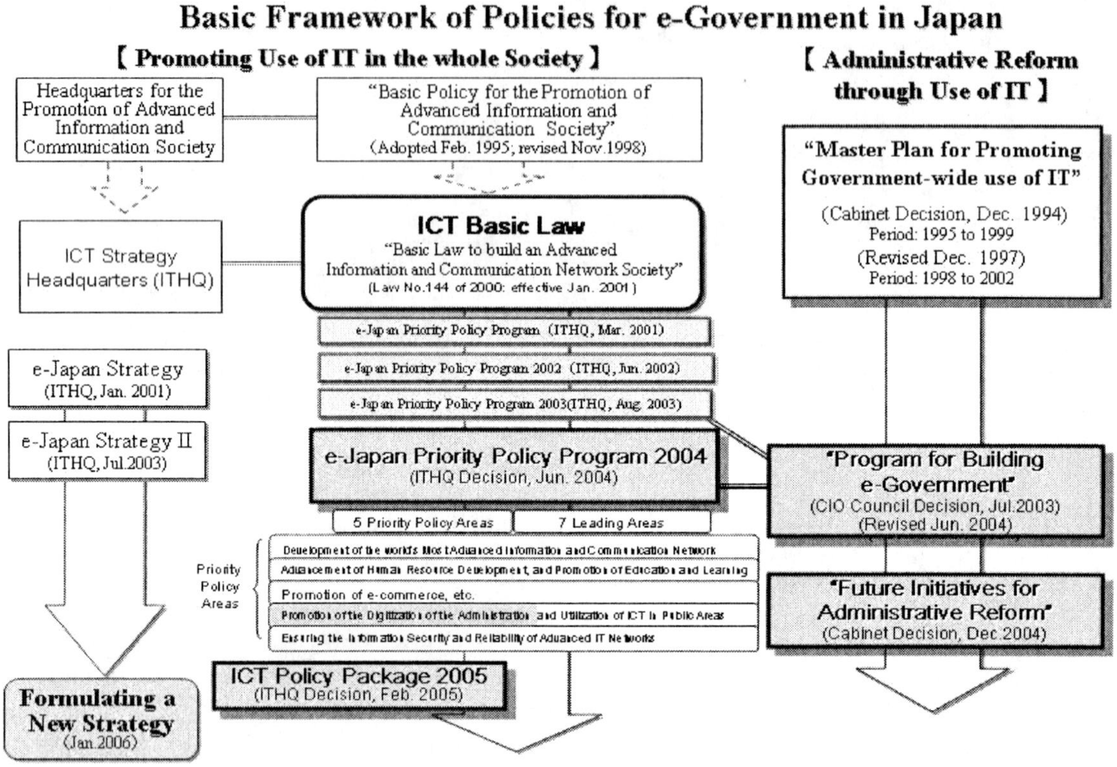

Program, government actions needed for the realization of e-government were described under the item of "Promotion of Digitization of the Administration and Utilization of ICT in the Public Sectors." The Priority Policy Program is an action plan for each fiscal year and it has been reviewed and amended once every fiscal year since then. The latest version, the ICT Policy Package 2005, was decided by the ICT Strategy Headquarters in February 2005.

Program for Building E-Government

As mentioned above, the Japanese government has been undertaking the management reform of administrative affairs by the use of ICT from the1960s. With the development of ICT, the government came to face the challenges to reinvent and reconstruct not only its computer systems but also its business processes *per se*.

In December 1994, the Cabinet decided upon "Master Plan for Promoting Government-Wide Use of ICT" covering from 1994 to 1998. This was virtually the first cabinet decision that stated the overall policy and enumerated concrete measures of utilizing ICT inside the government. With rapid installation of PCs and network infrastructures in the government offices as well as the explosive diffusion of PCs and use of the Internet in the society, the master plan was revised in 1997 to become a new 5-year plan covering from 1998 to 2002 (GOJ, 1997).

While the E-Japan Strategy and Priority Policy Programs consolidate all the ICT policies and programs, the revised master plan stood as it was as a blueprint for creating e-government and at the same time its main policies and measures were included in the E-Japan Strategy and Priority Policy Programs.

After the completion of the target period of the master plan, July 2003, a program for building e-government was decided as the successive plan to the master plan under the ICT Strategy Headquarters (GOJ, 2003b). The program is a

3-year plan from fiscal 2003 to fiscal 2005. Over the past 2 1/2 years, various policy initiatives have been undertaken based on the program

APPARATUS FOR PROMOTING E-GOVERNMENT

Introduction

In any OECD country, when a country has an e-government program, it has some sort of organizations with overarching responsibility for carrying out the program. Japan has such organizations, namely the ICT Strategy Headquarters, CIO Council, Inter-Ministerial Committee of Assistant CIOs as counsel bodies and the Administrative Management Bureau of the Ministry of Internal Affairs and Communications as a substantial driving body.

ICT Strategy Headquarters

The ICT Strategy Headquarters was established in January 2001 based on the ICT Basic Law. Headed by the Prime Minister, the Headquarters is composed of all ministers of state and ten acknowledged experts from the private sector. The main mission of the Headquarters is to hammer out ICT strategies including e-government policies. The Headquarters meets when fundamental policies or programs are to be decided. Since its establishment, the Headquarters met 34 times by December 2005. It is the place where the political leaders can take strong leadership to promote ICT policies for both the private sector and public sector. Based on the decisions by the Headquarters, ministries execute their own ICT policies such as constructing the advanced ICT networks and establishing necessary legal institutions enabling e-commerce rather independently.

CIO Council

As mentioned above, an interministerial body (Inter-Ministerial Committee of Computer Use) was established in the late 1960s with a central management office, the Administrative Management Bureau, playing an overarching role. The status of this committee was upgraded into "Inter-Ministerial Committee of Directors General on Computer Systems" in 1983 with a view to strengthening its coordination functions for accelerating the use of ICT for administrative reform. Under the Committee, some inter-ministerial meetings and taskforces were organized to improve ICT knowledge and skills, to exchange experiences

Figure 4. Apparatus for promoting e-government

and professional know-how among the officials and to foster common grounds for government-wide concerted undertaking of ICT use.

After the establishment of the ICT Strategy Headquarters, the Inter-Ministerial Committee of Directors General on Computer Systems was transformed into a Ministerial Chief Information Officers Council (CIO Council) under the ICT Strategy Headquarters in September 2002.

The Council, headed by the Assistant Chief Cabinet Secretary, is comprised of all ministry CIOs, who are usually the Directors General of the Minister's Secretariat or their equivalents. Ministry CIOs are in charge of overall systematic coordination and management of budgets, personnel, organizational structure, policies concerning the use of ICTs inside the respective ministries so that the CIO Council can effectively coordinate ICT matters across the whole government including budgets, personnel, and organizational structures and so on.

The Council is also a decision making body. All the important policies of e-government initiatives in principle have to go through the Council. Thus, the CIO Council is pushing forward various measures concerning e-government in an integrated and collective manner among ministries.

Under the CIO Council, like before, the Management Committee of CIO Council and some taskforces are organized to promote the coordinated works among ministries toward e-government.

Interministerial Committee of Assistant CIOs

Technical advisors to CIOs (Assistant CIOs) were appointed from among outside experts by December 2003 in respective ministries. Their mission is to support their ministry CIOs in business analysis and formulating optimization plans. At the same time, an interministerial committee of Assistant CIOs was organized under the CIO Council with a view to sharing experiences of respective ministries and exchanging views on technical matters; 21 meetings were held by December 2005.

Administrative Management Bureau, Ministry of Internal Affairs and Communications

In the centre of "e-government" initiatives is located the Administrative Management Bureau, Ministry of Internal Affairs and Communications. Together with the Cabinet Secretariat, the Bureau plays a secretariat role for the CIO Council and Inter-Ministerial Committee of Assistant CIOs and acts as a substantive promoter for e-government initiatives in Japan.

The bureau can be called a central management office. The establishment of the bureau dates back to the early 1950s when Japan regained its independence after its defeat in the World War II. The bureau has been in charge of promoting administrative reform, controlling the staff number of civil service, examining the establishment of public organizations and coordinating government information systems. In addition, the bureau has an authority to examine the annual budget requests for computer and communication systems and equipments from the individual ministries and to submit its comments to the Budget Bureau of Ministry of Finance. The comments of the bureau are seriously taken account of by the Budget Bureau during the budget preparation process. With its authorities for staff number control, organizational examination and ICT-related budget request, the bureau can effectively coordinate the government-wide undertakings for realization of e-government. Its coordination power is strong because the power is based on the laws. On the other hand, the bureau often convenes informal working sessions to exchange information, views and opinions between individual ministries. Fostering cooperative working relationship among ministries is one of the crucial conditions to smoothly and effectively implement government-wide reform measures including ICT exploitation (ECHMCA, 2001).

After the establishment of the ICT Strategy headquarters, the bureau came to carry out more innovative e-government initiatives with strong political support. It is often the case that every ministry resists to reform the current organizations and operations when the problems of current practices have not be identified. Without political commitment, the bureau can only implement reform measures after negotiation and compromise with the other ministries. The initiatives of the Headquarters are strong because the Prime Minister, Chairman, takes a strong leadership. The bureau can work out advanced reform measures with the support from the Headquarters.

Organizational Changes in the Government

As the use of ICT for management reform has been a government-wide undertaking from 1960s, each ministry has its own unit in charge of comprehensive control of own computer and communication systems and equipments inside the ministry. The unit, often called "Data Processing Division" or "Information Management Division" plays a role of a focal point of the ministry when ICT related interministerial cooperation and coordination are to be required. The head of such division became a member of the Inter-Ministerial Committee of Computer Use. And later a supervising official of the head of the division became the member of the Inter-Ministerial Committee of Directors General on Computer Systems and currently the CIO Council.

While an interministerial coordination institution was being established, each ministry created its own ICT promotion committee to promote the use of ICT in its operation of government affairs.

After the E-Japan Strategy was adopted, an executive office was newly established in the Cabinet Secretariat and additional officials were allocated to the Administrative Management Bureau of Ministry of Internal Affairs and Communications. In the respective ministries, to deal with new jobs such as making optimization plans and strict management of ICT procurement, ICT experts from the private sector were newly appointed as officials with limited term. In addition, various business affairs such as examining the current systems and making proposals for optimization are often contracted out to a third party firm, not to the vendors of the current systems.

On the other hand, the government has been cutting down the number of civil service based on a series of staff number reduction plan. The use of ICT in government operation improves the efficiency and is regarded as one of the effective means for a smaller government. From January 2001 to March 2005, 2.2 % of the national civil service was cut down due to the efficiency gain (GOJ, 2005).

FUTURE TRENDS

The current e-government program, "Program for Building e-Government" includes concrete measures that will have been carried out by the end of March 2006. Over the past 2 1/2 years since the program was formulated, various policy measures have been undertaken based on the program. Now, the government is in the process of evaluating the current progress and planning a new national ICT strategy to be decided in January 2006. A draft of the new strategy was released to the public on 8 December 2005. In the draft, the goal of e-government is set to realize citizen-oriented e-government in which citizen can find more convenient and high-quality services as well as to create more efficient e-government with program management offices (PMO) both for the individual ministries and for the government as a whole.

By now, some policy initiatives in the current e-government program have been accomplished, on the other hand some of them are in the process of implementation. The latter may be included in the new strategy. Major challenges to be included in the new strategy are mentioned in the following.

To Accelerate the Use of Online Applications

While progress has been seen that 96% of the national administrative procedures are now available online, its utilization rate as a whole is rather high (more than 80%) but that of general purpose online application systems remains low so far (MIC, 2004). The current challenge is to encourage and enhance the use of general purpose online application systems by citizens and businesses. To address this issue, the following initiatives are being executed.

- An action plan for encouraging online usage is expected to be prepared for those procedures with 100,000 or more applications a year or those frequently applied for by businesses by the end of March 2006.
- "E-Government Facilitators" have been appointed from among attorneys acting as a proxy for citizens and ICT expert since April 2005 so as to improve the public awareness toward online procedures.

To Develop and Enhance Government Portal "e-Gov"

Further works are conducted to ensure consistency in items common to "e-Gov" and ministry Web sites, including display positions on homepages. In addition, the government is working to improve "e-Gov" by extending links to the local governments, integrating reception systems developed by respective ministries.

To Promote "One-Stop Services" through "e-Gov"

Works are under way to integrate functions of accepting on-line applications to "e-Gov" as much as possible so that One-Stop Services will be realized to accept multiple applications all at once at "e-Gov." Moreover, it is expected that an e-government customer support center will open by the end of March 2006, where citizens can get necessary instruction how to operate e-government related procedures.

To Implement Optimization Plans

The government is now working hard on formulating all the optimization plans no later than the end of March 2006. The estimated savings in time and costs will be included in the optimization plans. From April 2006, the implementation phase of the optimization plans will be started. It is expected that this undertaking will realize streamlined public administration as well as better and more efficient public services.

CONCLUSION

In the Japanese undertaking toward e-government, political commitment for the e-government program is not so strong but the e-government program rather serves the administrative reform to streamline the government organization and operation. After the national ICT strategy was established, the central management office could promote more aggressive reform measures by the use of ICT due to the political commitment to the strategy. The overarching organization of the e-government program is formally the ICT Strategy Headquarters but the real promoter and facilitator of e-government program is the Administrative Management Bureau. Its coordinating power is relatively strong because its has authorities of controlling staff number, examining government organizations and budget requests for computer and communication systems and equipments stipulated by the laws.

The target date of the E-Japan Strategy has passed and now a new national ICT strategy is being prepared. From 2001 to 2005, various undertakings have been carried out in the public sector as well as the private sector to better exploit ICT in the Japanese society. Inside the government, based on the e-government program, the introduction of ICT into every day operation of government affairs is aggressively carried out. Still, the civil servants tend to behave themselves unconsciously assuming that paper-based communication, coordination and management of affairs are still right. Such paper-based organizational culture may hinder the progress of e-government (Kaneko, 2001, 2004b).

To transform such organizational culture into a new culture appropriate for e-governance, fostering of ICT-based thinking and improvement of ICT literacy among the civil servants should be promoted further by making use of the expertise and knowledge of the private sector. The strong leadership of the top management is indispensable. The top management should reflect on their assumption of the existing organizational culture and take the initiative in changing the culture in the government.

Successful transfer from the present government to e-government depends primarily on human factors. E-government will be managed and administered by real flesh and blood officials. An acceptance of the changes brought about by the use of ICT in procedures and techniques concerning government works and a positive attitude on the part of officials to the routine use of ICT will be necessary if e-government is to be successfully realized.

REFERENCES

Editorial Committee on the History of Management and Coordination Agency (ECHMCA). (2001). *Soumuchou shi* [History of management and coordination agency, prime minister's office]. Tokyo: Gyosei

Evaluation Committee of Experts (ECE). (2005). Hyuoka senmon chousakai houkokusho. [Report of the Evaluation Committee of Experts]. Retrieved January 5, 2006, from http://www.kantei.go.jp/jp/singi/it2/hyouka/051208honbun.pdf/

Government of Japan (GOJ). (1997). *Kaitei gyousei jouhouka suisin kihon keikaku* [Revised master plan for promoting government-wide use of information and communication technologies, cabinet decision]. Retrieved December 15, 2004, from http://www.soumu.go.jp/gyoukan/kanri/a_01_f.htm

Government of Japan (GOJ). (2001). *E-Japan strategy* [Decision by the IT strategic headquarters]. Retrieved December 15, 2004, from http://www.kantei.go.jp/foreign/it/network/0122full_e.html

Government of Japan (GOJ). (2003a). *E-Japan strategy II* [Decision by the IT strategic headquarters]. Retrieved December 15, 2004, from http://www.kantei.go.jp/foreign/policy/it/0702senryaku_e.pdf

Government of Japan (GOJ). (2003b). *Program for building e-government* [Decision by the CIO council]. Retrieved December 15, 2004, from http://www.kantei.go.jp/jp/singi/it2/cio/dai4/4siryou2.pdf

Government of Japan (GOJ). (2004). *Revised program for building e-government* [Decision by the CIO council]. Retrieved December 15, 2004, from http://www.kantei.go.jp/jp/singi/it2/cio/dai9/9siryou2.pdf

Government of Japan (GOJ). (2005). *Gyosei-kaikaku no jisshi joukyou* [Follow-up report of administrative reform initiatives in fiscal 2004]. Retrieved January 5, 2006, from http://www.guoukaku.go/jp/siryou/index_kouhyou.html

Institute of Administrative Management. (2004). *Japan's government and administration at a glance 2004.* Tokyo: Institute of Administrative Management.

Kaneko, Y. (2001, July 9-13). Promoting "electronic government"—With a focus on statistical activities. In *Proceedings of the 25th International Congress of Administrative Sciences,* Athens, Greece (pp. 833-849).

Kaneko, Y. (2004a, July 14-18). ICTs and a rejuvenated Japan post-ensuring diverse services for local communities. *In Proceedings of the 26th International Congress of Administrative Sciences,* Seoul, Korea (pp. 195-215).

Kaneko, Y. (2004b, July 14-15). Realization of the e-government: Japan's strength and challenges. In *Proceedings of the OECD E-Government Symposium-Making Change Happen,* Seoul, Korea (pp. 1-17).

Kaneko, Y. (2005, December 9). E-government framework in Japan. In *Proceedings of the 2005 International Symposium of the Korean Association for Public Administration,* Seoul, Korea (pp. 1-8).

Masujima, T. (2003). *Gyousei kaikaku no shiten to tenkai* [Perspectives on administrative reform and its evolution]. Tokyo: Gyosei.

Masujima, T., & O'uchi, M. (Eds.). (1995). The management and reform of the Japanese government (2nd ed.). Tokyo: The Institute of Administrative Management.

Ministry of Internal Affairs and Communications (MIC). (2002). *Gyousei jouhouka kihon chousa kekka houkokusho* [Report of the basic survey on the use of ICTs in the government]. Retrieved January 5, 2006, from http://www.soumu.go.jp/gyoukan/kanri/a_01_f.htm

Ministry of Internal Affairs and Communications (MIC). (2003). *Denshiseihu denshijichitai no shinten niyoru gyouseikari heno eikyou nikansuru chousakenkyuu houkokusho* [Research report on effects of e-government and e-local governments to administrative management]. Tokyo: Author.

Ministry of Internal Affairs and Communications (MIC). (2004). *Denshiseihu no suishin ni kansuru chousa kekka houkokusho* [Report of the survey on e-government initiatives]. Retrieved January 5, 2006, from http://www.soumu.go.jp/hyouka/seisaku_gyousei_f.htm

OECD. (2003a). *The e-government imperative.* Retrieved January 5, 2006, from http://webdomino1.oecd.org/COMNET/PUM/egovproweb.nsf/viewHtml/index/$FILE/E-Government%20Imperative%20Final().pdf

OECD. (2003b). *OECD e-government studies Finland.* Retrieved January 5, 2006, from http://webdomino1.oecd.org/COMNET/PUM/egovproweb.nsf/viewHtml/index/$FILE/E-GOV%20FINLAND.pdf

OECD. (2005, March 30). *E-government for better government.* Submitted to the Meeting of OECD E-Government Network, Paris.

KEY TERMS

Basic Law on the Formation of an Advanced Information and Telecommunications Network Society (ICT Basic Law): The law for promoting measures for the formation of an advanced ICT network society expeditiously and intensively, stipulating the basic ideas, principles and policies as well as organization for promoting measures strategically.

E-Japan Strategy: A medium term national strategy adopted by the ICT Strategy Headquarters in January 2001 aiming at making Japan the world's most advanced ICT nation within 5 years.

The strategy shows the leading principles for preparing a priority policy program, a concrete work plan.

E-Japan Priority Policy Program: An action plan materializing E-Japan Strategy for each fiscal year. It includes specific and detailed measures of the individual ministries. The first program was decided by the ICT Strategy Headquarters in March 2001. It was reviewed and amended once every fiscal year since then. The latest version, the ICT Policy Package 2005, was decided in February 2005.

Kasumigaseki WAN: A Wide Area Network system connecting all the ministries to facilitate the safe exchange of information between them. Kasumigaseki is the name of the area in Tokyo where most of the central government offices are located. It has been operational since January 1997.

Master Plan for Promoting Government-Wide Use of ICT: A cabinet decision of 1994. The first 5-year plan stipulating the overall policies and enumerated concrete measures of utilizing information technologies within the Government. Revised in 1997.

Ministerial Chief Information Officers Council (CIO Council): An interministerial organization established in September 2002 under the ICT Strategy Headquarters. Headed by the Assistant Chief Cabinet Secretary, and comprised of all ministry CIOs (usually the Directors General of the Minister's Secretariat), it is in charge of coordinating ICT matters across the whole government as well as deciding all the important policies of e-government initiatives.

Program for Building E-Government: A 3-year plan decided by the CIO Council in 2003 and incorporated into the Priority Policy Program 2003. It aims at realizing user-oriented public services and streamlined public administration with high budget efficiency.

Strategic Headquarters for the Promotion of an Advanced Information and Telecommunications Network Society (ICT Strategy Headquarters): The Headquarters established in January 2001 based on the ICT Basic Law, headed by the Prime Minister, and composed of all the ministers of state and ten acknowledged experts from the private sector. Its main mission is to hammer out IT strategies and polices of E-Japan initiatives.

This work was previously published in Encyclopedia of Digital Government, edited by A. Anttiroiko and M. Malkia, pp. 1203-1211, copyright 2007 by Information Science Reference, formerly known as Idea Group Reference (an imprint of IGI Global).

Chapter 4.37
Parliament and E-Governance in Finland

Paula Tiihonen
Parliament of Finland, Finland

INTRODUCTION

The Standing Committee for the Future in the Finnish Parliament has a motto: *It is the duty of parliament to observe the changing world, analyse it, and take a view in good time on how Finnish society and its political actors should respond to the challenges of the future. Democracy cannot be realised simply by accepting changes that have already taken place.* Indeed, parliaments have a role in e-governance all over the world, and this role will be discussed briefly in this article with a reference to the case of the Parliament of Finland.

BACKGROUND

Why are parliaments important? The information society and e-governance are on agendas all over the world. Every nation tries to jump into the knowledge-based society as quickly and as deeply as possible.

In November 2004, the World Bank organised a seminar on "e-Governance: From Successful Pilot to Sustainable Implementation" in India (Bangalore). One hot topic, especially in the debate in the press, was the effectiveness of this new and promising development aid called e-governance. Evaluation of development aid is not easy, but it seems that e-government initiatives in developing and transitional countries have not been particularly successful. It has even been calculated that 35% are total failures, 50% are partial failures, and only 15% are successes. There is no actual evidence that e-government failure rates in developing countries should be any lower than those in industrialised countries. But there are plenty of practical reasons to support the idea that e-government failure rates in those countries might be much higher.

One basic mistake has been that politicians, as decision makers and opinion leaders, have not been really committed to e-governance. For them, it has been just one issue of technology among others in line, not really their business at all. Still, e-governance, as with any other part of governance (Tiihonen, 2004), is not a task for experts—it is a matter of common interest, together building a better future for people.

What kinds of models concerning building e-government or e-governance, are in the world for the active use of politicians? Not many, but Finland—and, in this case especially, the Committee for the Future in the Finnish Parliament—offers one of these. The role of parliaments is the same all over the world: to reactively handle proposals for legislation and annual budgets given by governments. But, can a parliament be a forerunner and an active player for a new society? Yes. This can happen in Finland, where, in 1906, women were the first in the world to get full voting and candidature rights, which can be an explanation for why, after 100 years of this kind of great social innovation, the same Finnish Parliament was the first country in the world to decide that our common future is so important that politicians also have to take real responsibility for it.

The Committee for the Future was established at the beginning of the 1990s and functioned on a temporary basis from 1993 until 2000. Then, on December 17, 1999, in conjunction with adoption of the new constitution, Parliament decided to grant the Committee for the Future permanent status (http://www.parliament.fi/FutureCommittee).

The Committee for the Future in the Finnish Parliament has the same status as the other standing committees. Each of the standing committees has its corresponding ministry, and in the case of the Committee for the Future this is the Prime Minister's Office. From the very beginning, all 17 members of the Committee have been parliamentarians. Its current tasks are defined to be I) to prepare material to be submitted to the Finnish parliament, such as government reports on the future, II) to make submissions on future-related long-term issues to other standing committees, III) to debate issues relating to future development factors and development models, IV) to undertake analyses pertaining to future-related research and IT methodology, and V) to function as a parliamentary body for assessing technological development and its consequences for society (Arter, 2000).

POLITICS: FOR OR AGAINST NEW TECHNOLOGY, NEW THINGS?

Politics in this context is about values, attitudes, atmosphere and opinion building, and, not forgetting the most important, opinion leading. Normally, politics is against new technology and generally against change. It is said that voters do not always want all these new things. But in the Finnish case, the case is just the opposite, which is why politics is needed—to support new ideas, and, among them, new innovations and new technology (Tiitinen, 2004).

For the past fifteen years, we experts have told that in the New World—at least in the New Economy based on Information and ICT, on Knowledge and Wisdom—the role of the state and parliament no longer holds importance. Governmental tasks will be minimised, if not diminished all together. But again, the Finnish case has proven something else. On the contrary, the role of the governments in the new e-world or u-world is changing, but it is certainly not getting smaller. Without active participation by governments and parliaments, really useful, effective and economically valuable e-services—public and private—will never succeed. The state's role is to provide an enabling environment for the new development and support new initiatives for efficient economy and competitiveness. The state—in practice parliaments—have to take care of "fare play" among different players in the information society. In Finland, Parliament has to make sure that citizens have equal possibilities also in the e-governance.

In Finland, Parliament has taken an active role. Some examples: the state has for 50 years been responsible for equal school and education possibilities for all citizens which means free of charge education system from bottom up. The level of education, the strong input in polytechnics and engineering, have later supported the telecommunications R&D development. In the period of the last depression (at the beginning of the 1990s) the public policy incentive was to strongly increase R&D funding from public resources, which was just the opposite policy than in most countries. Today, the private sector is the major financier of R&D. The technology policy and the national strategy to build Finland as one of the leading information societies have enhanced the use of ICT, both in public administration, private business and every walk of life in society (Klus & Kalscheuer, 1997).

In general, and also in the knowledge economy, good governance without corruption plays an invaluable role. Institutions, both administrative and political, really do matter, even if we think that we are moving from governing to governance (Tiihonen, 2004). It is a fundamental task of parliaments to make sure that there are reliable, well-functioning and innovative governments, ministries, and other basic public institutions.

Here is one more example from Parliament. In 1997 the Committee for the Future was given a second official principal task, that of assessing the effects of technology on society. The following reasons were named as evidence that a need for assessment work existed:

The argument that there is a need for technology assessment in the Parliament can be justified in two ways. The accelerating development of science and technology is having substantial effects on society, economic development and the life of the individual. Technology assessment helps parliamentarians understand these influences better and take them into account in political decision making. The other justifying factor relates to Parliament's tasks and democracy. When legislative and budgetary proposals of significant importance for society are submitted for its consideration, Parliament must, if it is to be able to exercise oversight of the Government's actions, already have a good enough foundation of knowledge on which to assess these proposals.

Technology assessment linked in one way or another to parliamentary work has proved itself to be a successful solution in several European countries. What is meant by technology assessment in a parliamentary context is appraisal of the effects on society of using the results of scientific research and technology. The questions and needs stipulated by the parliament provide the point of departure. Technology assessment generally encompasses broader sectors of science and technology, such as biotechnology, mass communications, transport, energy, and so forth. From the very beginning, the Committee for the Future has examined technology and such phenomena of change in the structure of our society as globalisation, innovation, and governance as a development feature permeating the whole of Finnish society.

However, in Finland, one centrally important deviation from other parliaments was made right at the beginning. No unit independent of Parliament has assumed responsibility for technology assessment, as has been done in Germany, for instance; instead, the task is performed by the committee itself so the 17 Members of the Parliament sitting twice a week 2-3 hours in meetings. To support its work, the committee can commission studies from various research institutes or think tanks.

Some examples. It was 5 years ago that Parliament of Finland, while analysing Finland's future prospects, highlighted innovation, with special emphasis on its human aspects. With this respect to these challenges and opportunities the Committee decided to write a report on knowledge management at the level of politics and policy making (Suurla, Markkula, & Mustajärvi, 2002).

The subject of one of the most recent technology assessments was the Finnish knowledge society model—more specifically, its sustainability in its second phase (Himanen, 2004) The person invited to do the background research was Dr. Pekka Himanen of the University of California at Berkeley where Manuel Castells is a professor. Castells visited Finland and took part in discussions of the Committee. The Committee as a whole acted as the steering group for the work and deliberated the researcher's results in its meetings, and visited a common seminar in Berkeley, California, and so forth. The committee also used the results as an aid to prepare the presentation it gave as the basis for discussion at a plenary session. This report and its deliberation in Parliament attracted an exceptional amount of public attention. Altogether, the system of working together for the better information society—the dialogue between Parliament and the Government—was successful.

FUTURE TRENDS

The Finnish case is an example how important it is that power centres of politics are involved and really committed to build the information society. There are a lot of signs and weak signals that e-governance, in order to make a difference, needs more and more support from decision makers. The review of the Committee for the Future called Challenges of the Global Information Society (Himanen, 2004) came to the conclusion that the most critical aspect in the development of the information society is the development of the deep-set structure of society. These elements must explain why so many countries try to copy the Finnish model.

CONCLUSION

The Finnish model is unique. Perhaps it is too early to say anything about real success. One thing, however, is certain: the committee has taken its place in the Finnish parliamentary system as an innovative political body. First, it is an adage of political life at any level that the first step to power is to take the initiative and put yourself in a position where you can set the agenda. In the Finnish Parliament, the Committee for the Future has taken this adage seriously. It has created a new forum that works at the inner circles of the parliamentary system and—even more important—it has demonstrated that parliamentary measures can still be used to take the initiative within democracy.

Second, it is an excellent vantage point when the main task is dialogue with the Prime Minister's Office and government on future-related issues. The Committee for the Future is a good forum where parliamentarians can broaden their views beyond everyday politics and their own country's problems. The committee's work has become quite international in character. Quite a large proportion of the ministers in the present cabinet are former members of the Committee. They include the prime minister and the ministers of finance, labour, and the environment. Two important party leaders are members of the Committee. The present chairman of the committee, MP Jyrki Katainen, was chosen as the leader of the biggest opposition party (The National Coalition Party) in the summer of 2004, one year after the elections. He appreciates and enjoys his work on the Committee for the Future so much that he has continued to chair it.

REFERENCES

Arter, D. (2000). The model for parliaments in the future? The case of the Finnish committee for the future. *Politiikka*, *42*(3), 149-163.

Himanen, P. (2004). *Challenges of the global Information Society.* Helsinki: Parliament of Finland.

Klus, J. P., & Kalscheuer, B. C. (1997). *Finland-Wisconsin: A comparative study focusing on the job opportunities for Finland.* Helsinki: Parliament of Finland.

Suurla, R., Markkula, M., & Mustajärvi, O. (2002). *Developing and implementing knowledge management in the Parliament of Finland.* Helsinki: Edita.

Tiihonen, S. (2004). *From governing to governance.* Tampere: Tampere University Press.

Tiitinen, S. (2004, September). Communication on the Eduskunta's Committee for the Future in Inter-parliamentary Union, Geneva Session.

KEY TERMS

Commitment: Interaction dominated by obligations.

Democracy: Rule by the people.

E-Governance: A broader and more future oriented governing system of information society than e-government, which is the use of information technology in the internal processes of government and the delivery of government products and services to citizens and industry.

Parliament: A legislature.

Policy Making: A course of action adopted and pursued by a government, party, ruler or statesman.

Power: Possession of control or command over others.

State: An organized political community occupying a definite territory, having an organized government, and possessing internal and external sovereignty.

This work was previously published in Encyclopedia of Digital Government, edited by A. Anttiroiko and M. Malkia, pp. 1311-1313, copyright 2007 by Information Science Reference, formerly known as Idea Group Reference (an imprint of IGI Global).

Chapter 4.38
Development and Use of the World Wide Web by U.S. Local Governments

Carmine Scavo
East Carolina University, USA

INTRODUCTION

San Carlos, California (www.cityofsancarlos.org) claims to have developed one of the earliest local government Web sites in the world, posted on May 10, 1994 (San Carlos, 2006). From this early effort, United States (U.S.) cities moved rapidly onto the Web. Norris and Moon (2002), for example, report that some 4.4% of U.S. cities in a 2000 survey by the International City Management Association (ICMA) reported developing Web sites before 1995; 27.1% reported developing their Web sites in the 1995-'96 time period, and 68.5% reported their Web site developed after 1997. San Carlos' original Web site comprised one page; its current Web site now contains some 8,000 pages and uses some of the Web's most modern technology available, such as really simple syndication (RSS) and Flash Paper.[1] This article uses the example of San Carlos' Web site, along with two surveys of local government Web sites in the U.S., to illustrate the experience that U.S. local governments have had in developing and using Web sites in the pursuit of bettering governance. The article examines four local government Web applications—bulletin boards, promotions, service delivery and citizen input—and assesses their use by U.S. local governments. The article then addresses current issues of outsourcing Web site design and maintenance, and future issues of privacy, security, the digital divide and the possible effects of increased local government Web sites on U.S. civil society.

BACKGROUND

Some idea of the expanse and number of city Web sites can be obtained by consulting one of several search engines to locate local government Web sites. One such engine, containing links to some 10,235 Web sites, is State and Local Government (www.statelocalgov.net). This site provides not only links to local government Web sites in the U.S. but also to national organizations that represent state and local governments (e.g., U.S. Council of Mayors) and a functional area listing of service Web sites for state and local government (economic development, tourism, etc.). Another such engine is Official City Sites (www.officialcitysites.org), which not only lists local governments (towns, cities, counties, etc.) in the U.S. but also in Australia, Canada, France,

Germany, Japan, The Netherlands, New Zealand and the United Kingdom. The Official City Sites Web page is particularly attractive, with clickable stylized maps of the individual countries leading to individual maps or lists of sub-units within that country (states, provinces, etc.) and then to the local Web sites within those sub-units.[2]

LOCAL GOVERNMENT WEB APPLICATIONS

In previous work (Scavo & Shi, 1999; Scavo, 2003), we identified four types of Web applications that local governments tended to use: bulletin board applications; promotion application; service delivery applications; and citizen input applications. Bulletin board applications involve the use of a Web site to provide information about the services, personnel, programs and so forth provided by a government agency. Promotion applications have to do with the provision of information about the area—population characteristics; climate data; tourist attractions; and so forth. Service delivery applications are much more interactive than the previous two; involving the use of the Web to do such things as apply for licenses, pay taxes and make appointments. Last, citizen input applications allow citizens to communicate directly with government officials and personnel and also with each other (Scavo, 2005).

The four applications demonstrate an increasing level of Web application sophistication—the base is bulletin board usage. Posting basic information on government was the original function of local government Web sites—at first, some of this information was simply posted; later, much of the information became clickable, meaning that clicking on the name of the mayor, for example, would open a dialog box that would allow the user to send an e-mail to or chat with the mayor. Promotion applications are only somewhat more sophisticated than bulletin board applications. With these latter applications, information is posted, as with bulletin boards, but the information has a somewhat different focus and audience. Service delivery and feedback applications are more sophisticated than the previous two, with feedback being even more specialized than service delivery. Both of these applications require more technically sophisticated Web sites which, in turn, require more highly trained Web site designers and maintenance people, faster servers and, most likely, a greater financial investment by the local government in Web site design and operation. Scavo and Shi (1999) found empirical support for this hierarchy of applications and concluded that it seemed likely that local governments would introduce themselves to the Web by developing bulletin boards and promotion applications and then move into service delivery and feedback applications.

Scavo (2003) found that while U.S. local governments had generally improved their Web sites across the four utilizations from 1998 through 2002, there was a great deal of random movement within this increase. The mean score for all local governments on the overall Web feature scale increased dramatically between 1998 and 2002, as did the scores (some much less dramatically) for the sub-scales for the four utilizations, indicating improvement. However, the across-time correlations for the four sub-scales were low, varying between 0.00 and +.25, indicating a great deal of random variation among the Web sites. And, five local governments that had Web sites (one county and four municipalities) in 1998 did not have them in 2002, indicating some retrenchment.

The four applications are of varying interest to constituencies inside the city or those outside the city; promotion utilizations being the most interesting to external constituents (who may be considering relocating to the given area and want to investigate weather, schools, transportation facilities, etc.), and service delivery applications are of the greatest interest to internal constituents, who have the largest stake in the services local government provides (see Table 1).

San Carlos' Web site demonstrates good use of the four utilizations described above. Sections of the city's main Web page address the bulletin

Table 1. City Web utilizations by type of constituency

Constituency	Type of Utilization			
	Bulletin Board	Promotion	Service Delivery	Citizen Input
Internal	Primarily		Almost Wholly	Almost Wholly
External		Primarily		

board utilization (headlines, agendas and minutes, city newsletters, municipal code, news releases, job announcements, etc.), promotion (business guide, restaurant guide, schools, transportation, etc.), service delivery (garbage and recycling, guide to utility services, service requests and compliments, parcel and zoning information, permits by fax, etc.) and citizen input (forms on the Web, report traffic complaints, comment on development proposals, etc.). Users can click on any of the items and are directed to relevant Web pages for further information or contact.

In 2004, Brown University's Center for Public Policy surveyed federal, state and local government Web sites around the U.S. to examine the features that the Web sites provided. Some 1,873 Web sites in the 70 largest cities[3] in the U.S. were assessed for the types of features they offered to the user. The Brown study found that the most common types of services provided by these city Web sites were the renewal of library books and the payment of utility bills and parking tickets. Barriers to the increased use of Web sites to provide services were shown to be the inability to use credit cards and digital signatures on Web financial transactions. Only 14% of the Web sites allowed credit card use, while 6% allowed the use of digital signatures (West, 2004). These numbers, however, were a marked increase from those in the 2003 version of this survey.

CURRENT ISSUES IN LOCAL GOVERNMENT WEB SITE DESIGN AND MANAGEMENT

The evolution in Web site design by local government across the four applications described above was a phenomenon of the 1990s that may not have survived the transition to the new century. In the early 1990s, Web site design was often something that local government IT professionals learned on the job; few if any academic programs existed that taught such skills. Even as late as 1998, some city Web sites were designed as university class projects. By the early 2000s, much of this tentative introduction to the Web had been abandoned and even cities' initial forays into Web site use were quite sophisticated. Part of the reason for this is the changing nature of local government Web site administration and management. In 1998, national or regional Web-hosting companies did not administer a single one of the Web sites surveyed; by 2002, those same-type companies administered some 8% of the Web sites. As city Web sites became more sophisticated (and more expensive to design and maintain) and it became increasingly more difficult to recruit and retain IT professionals, an increased number of cities began contracting out the design and maintenance of their Web sites to national or regional companies who specialize in such activities. A 2001 ICMA survey found that 80% of U.S. city managers queried reported outsourcing Web site hosting, while 64% reported outsourcing Web site design and/or Web site operations and management (Norris, Fletcher & Holden, 2001). Web hosting companies, such as ProjectA (www.projecta.com), NIC (www.nicusa.com), the Alpha Group (http://alphais.com) and egovt.net—now part of cboss (www.cboss government.com), have all aggressively moved into local government Web management and design. Scavo (2003) found, however, that outsourcing of Web design and maintenance was much more popular for small cities in the U.S. than it was for larger ones. As of 2002, local governments that maintained their own Web sites showed a mean population somewhat more than 300,000; those that used local organizations showed a mean population of slightly less than 150,000; and those that contracted out Web design and maintenance showed a mean population of just more than 40,000.

Early criticisms of outsourcing of Web site design and management stressed the need to retain the expertise in Web-related matters that might be lost if the services passed out of the hands of local government into those of contractors. In partial response to this, professional associations like ICMA have developed low-cost or free Web design software (e.g., GovOffice) that can be easily adapted to a variety of city Web design uses (www.govoffice.com). Additionally, various organizations that support local governments in the U.S. have sought to reduce the costs of building internal Web expertise by publishing online manuals and offering other free or low-cost resources on Web site design and management. Some of these relevant organizations and their Web sites are The Center for Technology in Government (www.ctg.albany.edu), Government Technology (www.govtech.net) and Public Technology Inc. (http://pti.nw.dc.us).

FUTURE ISSUES IN LOCAL GOVERNMENT WEB SITE DESIGN AND MANAGEMENT

In recent years, one of the major issues surrounding Web usage has been the so-called digital divide—the difference in Internet and Web usage between relatively advantaged and disadvantaged groups in the population. While early differences in Internet and Web access usage between men and women, minorities and the majority, wealthy and poor, and even urban and rural dwellers have either narrowed greatly or largely disappeared, newer gaps persist. Several of the more pernicious problems that U.S. local government Web sites have yet to address are meeting the needs of users who are disabled, those who speak languages other than English and those with lowered literacy. The Brown study, for example, found that the cities they surveyed were not particularly successful in addressing these needs. Only some 21% of the Web sites surveyed passed the "Bobby" test (http://bobby.watchfire.com)[4], a widely used test of the accessibility of Web sites to the disabled, while only 17% of the Web sites provided some accommodation for non-English speakers.[5] And the mean grade level at which the Web sites were aimed was approximately 11.1, with some 71% of the Web sites aimed at the 12th-grade level at a time when the typical American is reading at the 8th-grade level (West, 2004). For all of these, however, there was a large degree of inter-city variation. Cities with the most accessible sites for the disabled were Cincinnati (95% of sites meeting the Bobby test) and San Diego (94%); those with the most accessible sites for non-English speakers were Houston (93%) and Kansas City (92%); while those with the most accessible sites for those with lowered literacy rates were Salt Lake City (mean grade level of 8.5) and Grand Rapids, Michigan (8.6).

Security and privacy are also issues that U.S. local government Web sites have shown varying degrees of success in addressing. For users to develop similar levels of trust in using the advanced features of service provision and feedback in local government Web sites as they have in the analogous features of business Web sites, local governments need to provide similar levels of security. Many users who would not give a second thought to ordering books online from Amazon.com hesitate when it comes to paying their local taxes online. Perhaps some of the reason for this has to do with the earlier evolution of e-business to e-government, but some of it may have to do with the lowered level of trust in U.S. government in general as opposed to business (Holzer, Meltiski, Rho, & Schwester, 2004). It is still odd, however, that users would, for example, input their credit card information into an e-business Web site with far more trust than they would input their voter information into an e-government Web site, when it would be far more troublesome to the user for the credit card information to be misused than it would be for the voter information to be misused.

Web site security has two different meanings—the first, discussed above, is the confidentiality of the information provided by the user to the Web site. The second, however, is the potential dangers in the information actually posted on the Web site. In the wake of the September 11, 2001 (9/11) terrorist attacks in the U.S., this second aspect of Web site security became a much greater issue in the U.S. than it had before. One immediate consequence of these attacks was a re-evaluation by many local governments about the openness of their Web sites, especially the provision of large amounts of information to potential terrorists. Earlier efforts—commonly known as community right-to-know laws—required U.S. local governments to publicly list potentially harmful chemicals (these lists moved from paper listings to Web-based listings over time). These requirements were relaxed since, in some places, such information was thought to be too useful to potential terrorists. For many years, government Web sites were touted as ways to inexpensively increase the amount of information the public could access; in response to 9/11, even such openness advocates as Steve Aftergood, the director of the Federation of American Scientists' Project on Government Secrecy, rethought the organization's stand on how much information should be made available to the public. In late 2001, Aftergood said in an interview, "I have had to come to terms with the fact that government secrecy is not the worst thing in the world ... There are worse things" (Toner, 2001, p. B4).

The managers of U.S. local government Web sites have also become much more cognizant of the sensitivities of user privacy. As more Web sites are being used to gather information on users, many U.S. cities have responded with elaborate privacy statements addressing the use of their Web sites. Several are indicative—Austin, Texas, for example, contains a 650-word policy statement that describes the types of information the site gathers on users (time of day of contact, day of week of contact, URL of site consulted before the city Web site, etc.), how that information is used (it will not be sold for commercial purposes but may be surrendered to law enforcement agencies requesting the information), the nature of the site's security routines, and that the site uses cookies. Austin's nearby neighbor, San Antonio, Texas, states in its privacy policy that it does not gather any personal information about users, except in the most general fashion—number of hits, for example. Other U.S. city sites take positions between these two, for example, certifying that they do not use cookies but that Web sites linked to the city Web site may indeed use cookies. Thus, there does not appear to be one standard for cities in terms of the types of information the sites gather about users, but there does appear to be an evolving standard that the user should be informed about what types of information is being gathered, how that information will be used and so on.

One additional future issue needs to be addressed—that of the type of local culture that increased use of Web-provided services may be creating. As more local government services are moved online, physical interactions between citizens and employees become less frequent. A result of this may be a lowered sense of empathy by citizens with local government employees. This tendency brings with it a larger question—can an Internet-based community replace a physical one? Will future citizens, whose predominant interactions with local government are on the Web, understand and appreciate physical problems and issues occurring in the communities in which they live? While there has been much speculation about the effect of Web-based interactions on civil society (Cain, 2001; Levine, 2002), there has been little empirical research on this issue; thus, this is a subject crying out for future research.

CONCLUSION

This article has examined the development and use of Web sites by U.S. local governments. The article demonstrates that local governments in the U.S. have been and remain very active in the development and use of Web sites to deliver services, promote local government activities, communicate with citizens and so forth. However, while there is a great deal of activity, there could be more—local government use of Web sites has not yet attained the level that U.S. business, for example, makes of the Internet.

Beyond the question of resource availability, a good part of the reason for this lowered level of development in government Web sites in the U.S. has to do with low levels of trust in U.S. government in general. Internet users who trust e-business to maintain the confidentiality of electronic financial information might not trust local e-government to do the same with other forms of electronic information. But the causality may run both ways—U.S. local governments that inspire trust from their citizens may also have an easier time implementing advanced Web functionalities that those citizens will use, while local governments that inspire lower levels of trust would have a more difficult time. Local government Web usage does not arise nor does it function in a vacuum; it is part of local government culture. Where that culture features mutual trust, local government Web sites can develop into very sophisticated instruments of e-government. When the culture features mistrust, that development will be stilted.

REFERENCES

Cain, B. (2001). The Internet in the (dis)service of democracy? *Loyola of Los Angeles Law Review, 34*, 1005-1021.

Holzer, M., Melitski, J., Rho, S., & Schwester, R. (2004). *Restoring trust in government: The potential of digital citizen participation.* Washington, DC: IBM Center for the Business of Government.

Levine, P. (2002). *The Internet and civil society.* The International Media and Democracy Project. Retrieved June 28, 2005, from www.imdp.org/artman/publish/article_29.shtml

Moon, M. (2002). The evolution of e-government among municipalities: Rhetoric or reality? *Public Administration Review, 62*(4), 424-443.

Norris, D., Fletcher, P., & Holden, S. (2001). *Is your local government plugged in? Highlights of the 2000 electronic government survey.* Washington, DC: International City Management Association.

Norris, D., & Moon, M. (2002). *Electronic government at the American grassroots—2002.* Retrieved October 25, 2004, from www.digitalgovernment.org/dgrc/dgo2003/cdrom/PAPERS/citsgovt/norris.pdf

San Carlos. (2006). City of San Carlos: The city of good living. Retrieved May 5, 2006, from www.cityofsancarlos.org/is/citywebsite.asp/

Scavo, C. (2003). World wide Web site design and use in public management. In G. David Garson (Ed.), *Public information technology: Policy and management issues* (pp. 299-310). Hershey, PA: Idea Group Publishing.

Scavo, C. (2005). Citizen participation and direct democracy through computer networking: Possibilities and experience. In G. David Garson (Ed.), *The handbook of public information systems* (2nd ed., pp. 255-280). New York: Marcel Dekker.

Scavo, C., & Shi, Y. (1999). World wide Web site design and use in public management. In G. David Garson (Ed.), *Information technology and computer applications in public administration: Issues and trends* (pp. 246-266). Hershey, PA: Idea Group Publishing.

Toner, R. (2001, October 27). Reconsidering security, U.S. clamps down on agency Web sites. *New York Times,* B4.

West, D. (2004). *Urban e-government: 2004*. Retrieved December 3, 2004, from www.insidepolitics.org/egovt01city.html

KEY TERMS

Blog: A Web log; basically, a diary posted on the Web available for users to access. Blogs can provide first-hand observations of events, reflections on current events and so forth.

Bobby Test: An online test of a Web site's accessibility to the disabled. The test reports the site's conformance with either the World Wide Web Consortium's (W3C) Web Content Accessibility Guidelines 1.0 or the U.S. Americans with Disabilities Act Section 508 Guidelines.

Branding: A marketing concept in which all pages on a Web site have a consistent, unique visual appearance, thus associating all of them with the agency or institution that sponsors the Web site.

Cookies: Short text files generated by a Web server and automatically stored in the user's computer for future access. Cookies store information about how the user has used the Web site in the past so that future use can be more customized. They can also store other personal information about the user; this information is transmitted to a relevant Web site when the user accesses that site.

Digital Divide: Differential Internet and Web access and usage by different groups—originally men and women or minorities and the majority; now rural and urban, non-native speakers and native speakers; disabled and non-disabled; and so forth.

Flash Paper: A program developed by Macromedia that allows documents to be formatted in a way that they can be easily transmitted to users over the Web.

Really Simple Syndication (RSS): A way of retrieving information on the Web where the user subscribes to a Web site or blog and information is delivered automatically to the user's e-mail address in conformance with the information supplied by the user in his or her subscription.

ENDNOTES

1. A history of the evolution of San Carlos' Web site can be found at http://web.archive.org/web/*/http://www.ci.san-carlos.ca.us/.
2. Official City Sites has recently changed its Web site since it has come under the management of bigdaddydata.com. The new version of the Web site does not function in the same way as the old one, and the information stated in this paragraph may not be able to be retrieved.
3. The Web sites represented executive offices, legislative offices and major service delivery agencies, such as health, human services, police, fire, taxation, and so forth.
4. Oddly, the San Carlos Web site also does not pass the Bobby test. The site showed two Priority One Accessibility errors and six Priority One User Checks. A variety of Priority Two and Three errors also were reported for the Web site.
5. These accommodations ranged from providing text translations into commonly used second languages to routing a user to one of several Web translation services.

This work was previously published in Encyclopedia of Digital Government, edited by A. Anttiroiko and M. Malkia, pp. 296-300, copyright 2007 by Information Science Reference, formerly known as Idea Group Reference (an imprint of IGI Global).

Chapter 4.39
A Multiagent Service-Oriented Modeling of E-Government Initiatives

Tagelsir Mohamed Gasmelseid
King Faisal University, Saudi Arabia

ABSTRACT

The recent technological developments have led to the emergence of a wide range of operational scenarios and significantly affected the formulation and implementation of e-government initiatives. While the failure of many e-government initiatives is attributed to many factors (organizational, institutional, technological and structural), the lack of consistent e-government modeling frameworks and universal architectures threatens the capacity of such initiatives to meet their objectives. Because of the complexities experienced in addressing e-government implementation issues, the use of multiple techniques can improve the likelihood of developing and implementing successful e-government initiatives. This article builds on previous work to advocate a "coupled" multiagent service oriented model for the implementation of the e-government initiative in Sudan. The use of service oriented measures and concepts of agency are considered to be necessary for improving overall consistency, integration, promptness and information sharing. Despite its potential benefits, the capacity of the proposed "coupled model" is contingent, among others, upon technological maturity and institutional flexibility.

INTRODUCTION

The use of the Internet and other related communication technologies has led to the emergence of multiple business models and dictated new axioms for information acquisition, sharing, and utilization. The increasing use of technological platforms is directly related to the emerging organizational transformations, and the growing importance of deploying universally enacted applications to improve the efficiency, effectiveness, and data quality in public and private organizations. Such applications range from electronic document interchange, through e-learning, e-business, e-commerce, e-banking to corporate models of e-government.

The last couple of years have witnessed an expanding deployment of e-government initiatives and applications at different scales. The emphasis, at the abstract level of analysis, continued to be on the use of information and communication technologies in public administrations (following customer-centered perspectives) to strategically enhance accessibility and delivery of government information, public services, and democratic processes to citizens, businesses, government employees, and other agencies (Hernon, Reylea, Dugan, & Cheverie, 2002; Andersen, 2004; Seifert, 2002; European Community, 2003; Hangen & Kubicek, 2002). The use of such a pool of technologies also reflects the existence of a wide range of institutional, structural, technological, and personnel-related factors.

The majority of e-government initiatives are aimed at improving government processes by cutting process costs, managing process performance, making strategic connections in government, and creating empowerment within the government architecture. Accordingly, connection between governments and citizens (and other stakeholders) can be improved (Hussein, 2006; Richard, 2001). In addition, the interactions associated with the use of such a rich pool of organizational and technological platforms in e-governance, creates a "task-oriented" forum of engagement between governments and other stakeholders (Davies, 2002; Paul & Thompson, 2004; Kim & Henriksen, 2006; Traunmüller & Lenk, 2002).

However, the increasing deployment of e-government applications neither means that governments and citizens will gain the "promised" benefits, nor that the level and magnitude of "downside" risks can be assessed. Estimates about the performance of existing applications in different countries show that almost 85% of the e-government systems are been regarded as totally or partially operational failures irrespective of their technological buildup. Such failure has been attributed to the lack of leadership and strategic thinking, technological infrastructures that facilitate accessibility, connectivity and network readiness, institutional infrastructures that secure an e-business climate, population e-aware, human capital, and legal infrastructure that maintains trust, information security, and privacy.

Successful implementation of e-government initiatives depends not only on the availability of resources, but most importantly on the adoption of appropriate implementation-oriented paradigms that describe the growth and evolution of e-governments. To avoid failures, such modeling paradigms must be practical enough to guide the implementation, monitoring, and maintenance of the entire e-government initiative. In addition to the growing percentage of failure of many e-government applications, the importance of focusing on the development of practical models and architectures originates also from the importance of managing the complexity associated with electronic interactions.

The main objective of this article is to address the context of e-government modeling by investigating architectural issues, taking the e-government initiative in Sudan as a case study. The chapter emphasizes the need for an integrated architectural approach for the management of distributed e-government services by coupling service-oriented architectures with multiagent technologies. While the second section of this article presents relevant literature in e-government development architectures, the third section discusses service-oriented concepts. The fourth section reflects on the e-government initiative in Sudan, with more focus in the fifth section on the process of coupling multiagent technologies with service-oriented architecture to be used for the development of the "coupled model" described in the sixth section. The seventh section addresses the advantages of the coupled model for the case study, potential limitations, and modifications with some conclusions provided in the eighth section.

E-GOVERNMENT DEVELOPMENT ARCHITECTURES: RELATED WORK

The importance of developing appropriate architectures is dictated by their importance for process identification, stakeholders and partners, attitudes and preferential matrix, connection management, resource utilization and monitoring. However, easy access to the Web has created the possibility for new business models and resulted in growth and evolution of multiple computing architectures, programming languages, and development approaches (Crawford, Bate, Cherbakov, Holley, & Tsocanos, 2005). Generally speaking, architecture can be defined as "the fundamental organization of a system embodied in its components, their relationships to each other and to the environment and the principles guiding its design and evolution" (Hillard, 2000). Within this context, the classification of processes and representation of stakeholders may improve data processing and information communication (Cook, 1996) because it supports improved coordination through the implementation of the principles of discontinuity and the definition of the boundaries to be articulated among components.

E-Government Modeling Context

The process of modeling e-government applications significantly affects information acquisition and representation. Existing e-government modeling themes address the process of implementation by allowing service providing agencies to be organized around departments that follow the vertical lines of command and structures in which each agency develops its own information system to publish metadata about the services it provides and enable users to interact electronically to request services. Because this feature leads to the lack of coordination and a unified theme, there has been a growing concern for the development of architectures that take into account the multiplicity of organizational and structural dimensions "such as line structures, rigidity of standard operating procedures and division of labor," technological factors, and legal frameworks. It is only this invented architecture that integrates all subsystems, subschema, and service groupings into service repositories. The information architectures used for the implementation of e-government initiatives need to be in pace with the growing call of citizens for quality, cost effective services, and responsiveness in such a dynamic and continuously changing environment (Janssen & Van Veenstra, 2005).

However, despite the contribution of powerful new technologies such as Web services, autonomic and utility computing and grid services (World Wide Web Consortium, 2002; Ganek & Corbi, 2003; Ross & Westerman, 2004; Foster & Kesselman, 2003), the lack of a consistent e-government architecture within which applications can be rapidly developed, integrated, and reused continues to exist. Because of the challenge that e-government solutions face with regards to the integration and interoperability of their applications with other multiple existing systems, emphasis continued to be made on the development of "open architectures."

According to Bernhard, van den Hoven, and Igl (2006), e-government architectures show some similar experiences as the domain of enterprise architectures:

1. The level of integration increased with time from rather low integration in early architectures to higher levels in current versions, in pursuit of independence and extensive coverage. Current architectures (like the German SAGA) are focusing on the adoption of technical standards (e.g., interfaces and communication protocols) to ensure interoperability between administrations.
2. The shift of emphasis from technical issues to business-driven approaches so as to broaden the scope to incorporate organizational and policy issues. This has led to the development of "layered architectures" that derive technical requirements and organizational processes from basic principles and a predefined policy.
3. A growing emphasis on addressing the dynamic elements of system evolution in e-government architectures because the e-government initiative is viewed as being

centered around continued modernization of governments and administrations.

Main E-Government Architectures

Over the years, various architectures for e-government are being proposed including, among others, the OSCI platform (Steimke & Hagen, 2003), the SeCo container (Greunz, Schopp, & Haes, 2001), the AIPA reference architecture (Arcieri et al., 2002), the eGOV project (Wimmer, 2002), the eMayor project (Kaliontzoglou et al., 2005) and the WebDG architecture (Medjahed et al., 2003). The aim of the eGOV project is to provide an open, extensible, and scalable platform for realizing one-stop e-government (Wimmer & Krenner, 2001; Tambouris, 2001; Wimmer & Traunmueller, 2002; Mühl & Krabina, 2003). It includes national and local service repositories and a service creation environment that allows the public sector to provide citizens and other public authorities with information and public services structured around life events, business situations, and portals in a customer-oriented form. Contrary to the eGOV framework, the e-service development framework (eSDF) is using a service-oriented pattern to develop interoperability specifications and standards for e-service to be used in the public sector (Benson, 2002; UK GovTalk, 2004). The Federal Enterprise Architecture aims at facilitating the federal government's transformations toward more citizen-centricity through five interrelated reference models designed to identify collaboration possibilities across organizational boundaries (Federal Enterprise Architecture, 2005). With the aim of increasing use by stakeholders and reducing cost of ownership, the enterprise information portals (EIPs) use amalgamation of software applications to enable companies to consolidate, manage, analyze, and distribute information across and outside the enterprise (Shilakes & Tylman, 1998). The extended enterprise application integration (EAI) aims at integrating and interconnecting the various databases, platforms, and applications using incompatible technologies to support flexibility, evolutionarity, and adaptability (Data Exchanger, 2002; Mediadev, 2002).

The majority of these architectures structurally view e-government applications in terms of "entities," transferable objects, service repositories, services, requests, reports, service providers, and requesters. They constitute a multiplicity of platforms for exchanging electronic requests (for service provision) among multiple entities including citizens, businesses enterprises, and government agencies, among others. Entities that provide services (i.e., service providers) act as facilitators that use their own resources or the resources of relevant partners to provide the requested service directly or in collaboration with other entities. They can also direct service requestors to the concerned service providing entities if they are different from the one initially approached for service provision.

The interaction between the service providing entities and the concerned partner service providing entities is usually viewed within the context of "front line" and "back line" offices. If this is the case then all requesting entities must request services through the front line office, which provides (on behalf of the back line office) the service requesting entity with all relevant information, undertakes all types of clearance (both documentary and financial) with the service requesting entity, and tracks service status (on behalf of the service requesting entity) with the back office. The process continues until the service is provided or the request terminated.

However, the use of the front and back line offices is regarded as a way to reduce the burden on the part of service requestors but in real practice it brings a wide range of internal organizational and institutional complexities. Viewing coordination and interaction within the context of e-government as back and front offices is based on the concepts of architectural classification and discontinuity, directed toward the maintenance of a matrix of customers' and interagency interactions. To accommodate the variability that may result from the use of front line and back line offices, the nature of the entity (mainly service providing entities) has resulted in some controversy. The main issue is whether it should be left abstract at the model level (as is the case in centralized e-government deployments) or should be materialized as a (fully or partially) automated portal in which human intervention is evident (as is the case in distributed e-government deployments) (Wimmer, 2002; Kaliontzoglou et al., 2005). However, centralized e-government deployment is best suited for cases where the major focus is on content distribution and searching. It is worth mentioning that it is difficult to implement in a portal services with complex workflow or services with security features such as digital signatures. On the other hand, e-government platforms with distributed components (such as specific applications, portals, application servers, and databases) can handle complex procedures by addressing the general e-government requirements (i.e., interoperability, security, and user friendliness) (Kaliontzoglou et al., 2005).

Although the "abstract form" may allow different degrees of technological maturity at the front and back line offices, it may also create some degree of institutional complexity and service instability. Whatever nature is assigned to the entity, there will be some difficulty in identifying how requesting entities will benefit from service repositories in practical terms. Generally speaking, it is only the specification attached to the nature of the service which determines the degree of dynamism and interactivity associated with crossorganizational and crossservice networking domains.

When considered individually, they fail to address at least some of the following requirements: The full support of a client-centered approach; the integration of both traditional and online delivery channels; the support for concurrent access points; versatility; and security (Goncalo & Rafael, 2006). Systems supporting electronic government should expose a high degree of adaptability to change in terms of transparency ease of accommodation and tailorability (Stamoulis et al., 2003; Eardley et al., 2003). According to Vassilakis et al. (2005), traditional approaches to service composition, service discovery, and service execution exhibit a number of drawbacks related to the following areas: a) a service's availability or lack of it, b) the concurrent execution of services, c) multiple and concurrent invocation of service, and d) the a priori knowledge of one or more discrete number of possible compositions that can take place in order to provide a composite service.

SERVICE-ORIENTED ARCHITECTURES REVISITED

The migration toward service-oriented architectures (SOA) has been advocated by the growing importance of ensuring more flexibility, efficiency, and timeliness of reusable government services based on open data standards, procedures, and nonproprietary technologies. The aim of SOA is to provide common access points for e-government services using common interface standards, procedures, and supporting services, together with the necessary information to make e-government services accessible, affordable and secure. As a result, stakeholders can submit service requests on their own behalf through the standardized mechanisms and procedures of the architecture to allow service providers to interact and provide the service requested.

A service-oriented architecture includes services created in a service layer with published interfaces that support the use of the service in distinct business domains. Because it is made up of interactive components together with their entire interconnections, it emphasizes interoperability and location transparency in a way that shapes both a structural and a behavioral view of the entire system (Michael, 2002). As a result it is possible to leverage application behavior among applications (reusing the same application functionality) without a significant amount of recoding or integration. In order to accommodate situational changes, the agility of the architecture provides the capability to change processes using existing services (single or composite) and information flows. Based on the extended reach features, such processes can be exposed to external entities" or legacy systems (such as Web services, ERP, and CRM), to improve collaboration. The concept of modularity in service-oriented architectures increases the range of manageable complexity, allows different parts of a large system to be worked on concurrently, and accommodates uncertainty (Baldwin & Clark, 2000). To improve monitoring and reduce complexity, software components are treated as "black boxes" that hide their implementation by providing controlled access to their behavior and data through an interface.

A service is a software component that is described by the meta-data, which can be understood by a program (Schmidt, Hutchison, Lambros, & Phippen, 2005). The distinguishing feature of a service is that the metadata descriptions are published to enable reuse of the service in loosely coupled systems, frequently interconnected across networks using shared development tools. Service functionalities can be deployed as a part of the entire application (composite service) or as a separate component. By putting the logic and methods necessary for the access and implementation of a particular service into a separate layer, the layer can exist well beyond the lifetime of any system it is composed into. In addition, since location transparency is a property of a service-oriented architecture, the resulting code mobility enables more flexibility in the movement of the service across different machines or providers in a way that makes it available irrespective of its location. Because services have published interfaces, they can be easily tested by creating and using test suites that can be run to validate the service independently from any application that uses the service. During the automated building process, services can also be tested independently and accordingly minimizes defects and improves quality.

E-GOVERNMENT INITIATIVE IN SUDAN: FROM VISION TO ACTION

The e-government initiative in Sudan is driven by the need to provide as many government services as possible through an accessible electronic network in pursuit of increasing the ease of transactions and rationalizing procedures. Within the context of the five-year National Information Strategy, the initiative aims at achieving this objective through the maintenance of transparency in governmental transactions and relationships, improving information dissemination and impartiality, and promoting participation in decision making. However, Sudan is still at the beginning of the road in the field of the computerization of various systems.

E-Government Modeling Perspective

The growth of e-government applications follows a waterfall-like conventional modeling perspective closely related to the Layne and Lee model, which includes four phases of e-government growth: cataloguing of information on a Web site, transactions on a Web site, vertical, and horizontal integration (Layne & Lee, 2001). While the cataloging of information phase establishes an online presence for governments, the transaction phase aims at building interfaces to enable users to gain universal access to databases and electronically perform transactions. Because the e-government project is viewed in a multilevel context, the vertical integration phase aims at linking local, state, and federal government systems and facilitating information accessibility among them as a prerequisite for the performance of functions and the provision of services. The horizontal integration phase, on the other hand, enables systems to be integrated across a landscape of different functions and services.

The e-government strategy in Sudan is divided into four phases (Abdorabo, 2004):

1. **Obtaining information about the service:** This is the first step toward the e-government, where the provider of the service provides information about the services that can be provided by a particular agency, such as documentary requirements, fees, and steps to be followed by service requestors such as obtaining forms and applying for service provision. Because considerable effort is put toward G2C applications, emphasis continues to be on viewing citizens as the main service requestors.
2. **Federal interaction:** Despite the fact that the name of this stage gives the impression of cross-system interaction, service requestors can only download forms from the Web site of the entire service providing agency, print, fill, and submit them.
3. **Bilateral interaction:** The aim of this phase is to enable service requestors to electronically submit their requests for the provision to service providers, fill and submit forms, get a response, and (it is hoped) make payment.
4. **Complete interaction:** In this phase, the service providing agency follows up the cases (i.e., applications for service provision placed by service requestors) and obtains additional information from other governmental agencies to enable service requestors to know the status of the request submitted. The process continues until a decision is taken with regards to service provision.

To move from vision to action, the following e-government executive steps are stated for implementation: (a) supporting information centers in federal ministries and in the states with computer systems and completion of building of local networks inside these units; (b) establishment of specialized databases as an infrastructure to provide electronic services; (c) linking local networks into a broad national network; (d) training employees in ministries and states; (e) establishment of the governmental services Web site on the network and (f) establishment of communication centers, in cooperation with the private sector in the urban towns and the rural areas.

The potential types of electronic services to be provided by the e-government project include (a) registration services (certificates of birth & death, marriage and divorce statements, real

Figure 1. E-government centralized implementation architecture

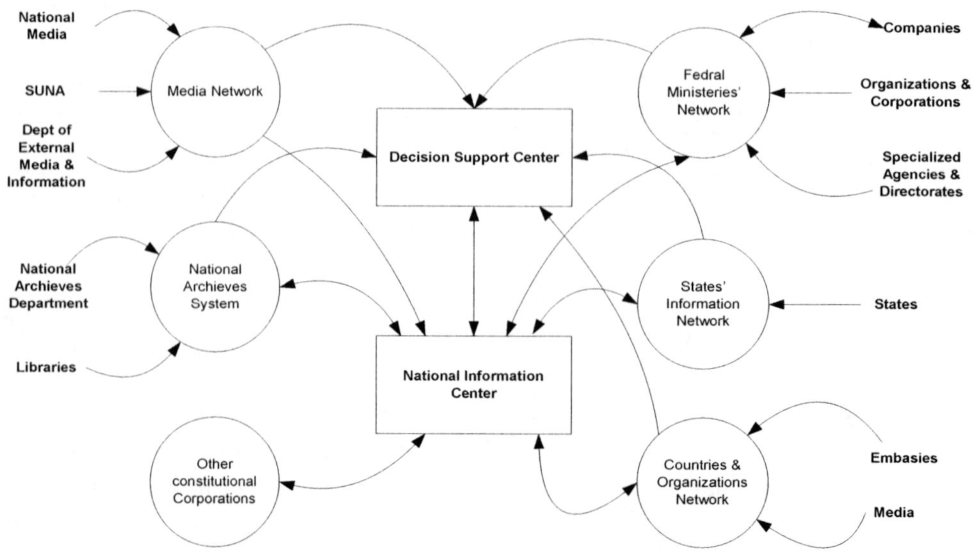

Figure 2. Fixed lines

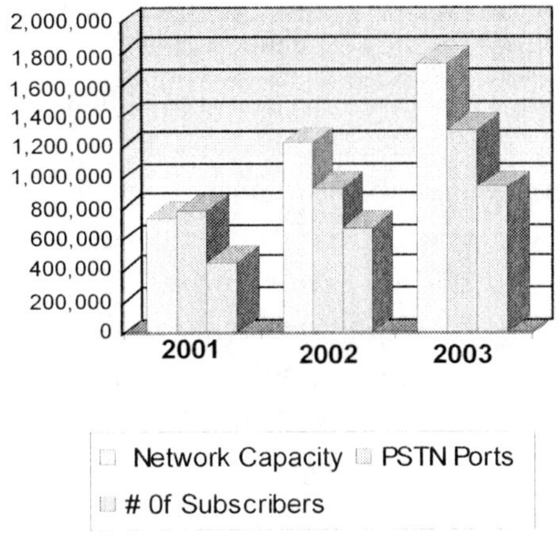

Figure 3. Data networks

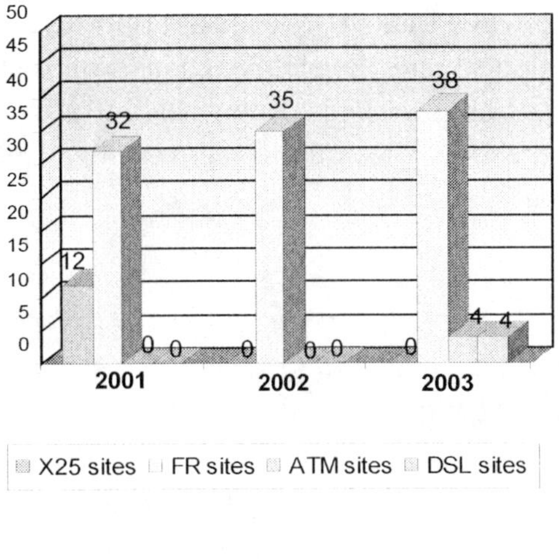

Figure 4. Data communication customers

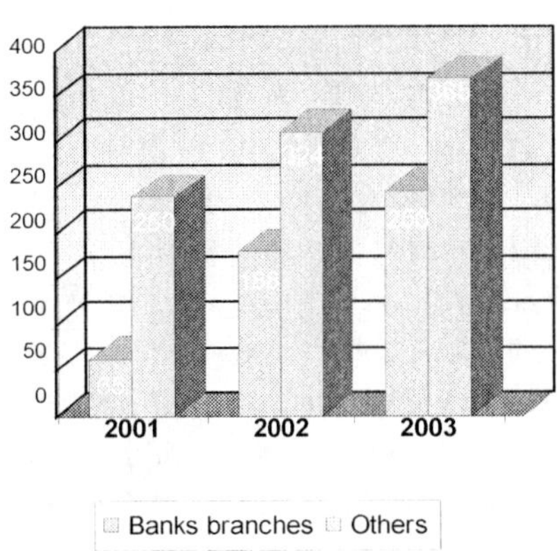

estate, ownership of vehicles, business names, national ID cards, and passports); (b) licensing services (local business licenses and registration procedures for educational institutions); and (c) payment-based services (taxes, fines, profits, and dividends).

As shown in Figure 1, in addition to the linear modeling approach used, the implementation of the initiative is guided by the centralized e-government deployment approach. In addition to the limitations associated with the modeling approach and architectural orientations adopted, the overall implementation theme of the entire e-government initiative reflects a provider rather than being a client-centric orientation.

Technological Preparedness and Infrastructure

In addition to the Internet and other related Web-based platforms, the implementation of e-government applications demands the incorporation of a wide range of hardware, software, and telecommunication technologies. This section provides some description of the telecommunication infrastructure used for the implementation of the e-government in Sudan. Figure 2 below shows the infrastructure with emphasis on fixed telephone lines till the year 2003, which includes a telephone network capacity of 1,738,600 lines, switches capacity 1,306,436 port, number of subscriber 936,756, and Tele-density 3.33 %. Figure 3 shows data networks where the first data switch was introduced in 1997. The technologies in use included X.25, Frame Relay, ISDN, ATM, and IP backbone. Figure 4 shows the main customers of data communication services, which include about 27 governmental and commercial banks consisting of about 256 branches with the potential to increase to 500 branches expected to enact electronically. Together with universities and other institutions, ministries have the potential to be connected to their branches through wide area networks. Figure 5 shows the Internet band-

Figure 5. Internet band width

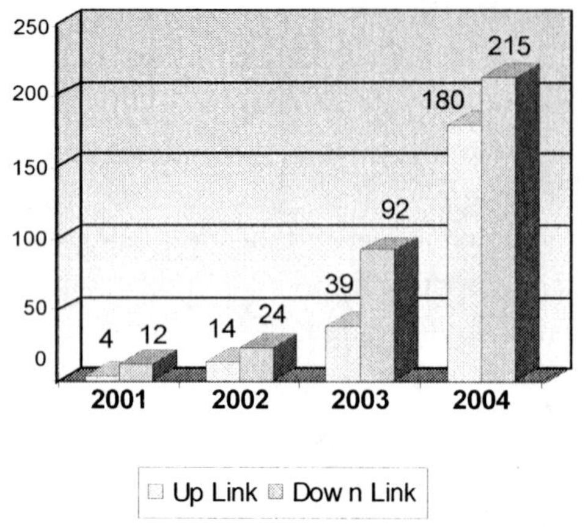

Figure 6. Number of ISPs

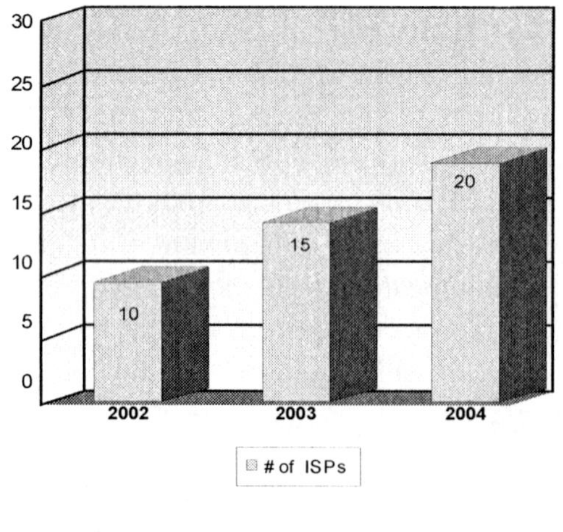

Figure 7. Internet dial-up users

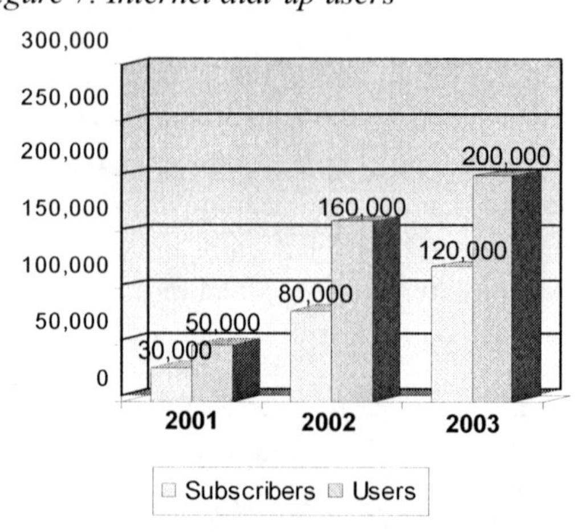

width where the first Internet presence in Sudan was witnessed in 1996. Internet Earth Station maximum capacity is STM-1 up & down link, the STM-1 via submarine cable Port Sudan-Jeddah, and STM-1 via Fiber cable Sudan-Egypt. Figure 6 shows the number of Internet service providers (ISP) whose number increased to 20 (till 2004) providing dial-up service covering about 75% of cities. Other ISPs are using national calls or VSAT stations to access the Internet and provide service to a network of about 1,000 Internet cafés. Figure 7 shows Internet dial-up users using a free Internet subscription.

The telecommunication network includes a fiber connection expanding over more than 6500 Km to facilitate the use of the advanced STM-16 & STM-64 rings SDH Technology and Digital Microwave Links connecting rural areas to the O.F. Backbone. Recently, the use of ATM is expanding to constitute the basic infrastructure for the development of e-government-related enabling systems.

COUPLING SERVICE-ORIENTED ARCHITECTURES AND MULTIAGENT CONCEPTS

The process of coupling alternative computing paradigms is widely used. Different projects have adopted service orientation concepts to address different perspectives by coupling service-oriented architectures with other technologies and paradigms. The Terregov Project (2005) adopted the principles of an SOA based on interoperable components with dynamic support for finding services because information, services, and administrations are regarded as being spread over several information systems. The architecture contains a set of collaborative tools for e-government Web services that are semantically enriched. The Ontogov—ontology-enabled e-government service configuration project (ONTOGOV, 2006) incorporated service orientation concepts with ontological perspective by developing, testing, and validating a semantically enriched (ontology-enabled) platform that will facilitate the consistent composition, reconfiguration, and evolution of e-government services. Janssen and Van Veenstra (2005) coupled the concepts of information brokerage with service-oriented architectures for the composition of new business processes using Web services in the context of e-government. Sean and O'Reilly (2004) used service-oriented architectures (SOA) and XML representations of data as the basis for service delivery and modernization of e-government in Ireland.

Because this article adopts a distributed e-government deployment approach, service-oriented architectures are coupled with multiagent systems' technologies. An intelligent agent is an autonomous, computational software entity that has access to one or more heterogeneous and geographically distributed information sources, and that pro-actively acquires, mediates, and maintains relevant information on behalf of users or other agents. The autonomous behavior of these agents is determined by their pro-activeness, reactive and deliberative actions, and social interactions. In a multiagent system, agents jointly use knowledge and resources to solve problems in a context-dependent way (Gasmelseid, 2007a).

Within the context of a distributed work environment software agents can assist in facilitating coordination, cooperation, and interaction among government agencies. Accordingly, these agencies can develop effective communication capabilities by benefiting from the resulting horizontally integrated services. Their use would also enhance user interaction and mobility by benefiting from the embedded user, service, and physical mobility that support service accessibility and uniformity of service points.

Software agents can also assist with the management of channel conflicts when multiple service-providing agencies find themselves operating on a network of front line and back line offices. Channel conflict exists because e-government services are provided online and accessed by all citizens through multiple channels including computers, kiosks, face-to-face, mail, fax, and new electronic channels like the Web, electronic mail, and videoconference—irrespective of their communication-use attitudes and literacy. Unless properly managed, channel conflict significantly challenges service interoperability. Software agents could also assist users in avoiding a conjugation of different delivery channels that appears when several contacts between the user and the provider of service are necessary with regards to the provision of a single service.

The use of multiagent systems will also reduce the side effects associated with cultural difference that exist among the various government levels and stakeholders. Such differences have their ramifications on the attitudes, preferences, and "style" of the user's electronic interactions. The use of multiagent systems can assist in coordinating service provision and limiting the effects of power struggles by creating and implementing service congruence mechanisms.

The use of multiagent systems can also assist in addressing security issues by enabling the entire system to prevent, avoid, detect, or prepare for breaches of security that threaten the confidentiality, integrity, or availability of information processed and used electronically (Gasmelseid, 2007a, 2007b). Especially for distributed e-government deployment approaches the importance of security and the use of alternative methods originates from the critical need of improving user confidence and interaction through improved privacy, confidentiality, and authentication (Wimmer & von Bredow, 2002; Lambrinoudakis et al., 2003). Because information will be fed to software agents to act upon, there is a chance to build effective security layers to be adhered to by all agents interacting in the architecture.

However, although security requirements vary with the concrete application, emphasis continued to be on authentication (the ability to properly and securely identify system users); authorization (the ability to grant access privileges to the resources based on the available users' identities); confidentiality (the capacity to prevent information from being accessed or understood by unauthorized users or systems); integrity (the ability to prevent information from being intentionally or unintentionally corrupted or tampered with); availability (the ability to grant access to resources within a reasonable period of time); and non-repudiation (the ability to prevent any user from later denying his intervention in a given process or transaction) (Lambrinoudakis et al., 2003; Arcieri et al., 2004; Boudriga, 2002; Caloyannides et al., 2003; Joshi et al., 2001).

The relevance of the software agents' paradigm stems from the possibility to use a wide range of object-oriented features to conceptualize both the domain and context of e-government applications by articulating roles, players, and relationships on the one hand, and drawing road maps for system-wide critical success technical factors including security and authentication on the other hand. The context of modeling e-government as back line and front line offices brings to attention the concept of viewing agents as a network of superior and subordinate agents possessing multiple and heterogeneous, yet related, tasks within the prevailing chain of relationships and a set of verification and authentication processes.

A MULTIAGENT SERVICE-ORIENTED MODEL FOR E-GOVERNMENT IN SUDAN

The architecture described in this article follows a distributed e-government deployment. While many authors have classified agents in accordance with their potential capabilities as information, Internet, search, and task agents, using the concept of agent sets as building blocks of a multiagent service-oriented organization provides additional insights as shown in Figure 8 below. The rationale of using agent sets stems from the fact that users have no standardized mode of activity-handling as they can use their agents to search information about a service, implement procedures, browse necessary documentation and locations (service procedures), and request the service through the e-government infrastructure. So, architecturally, users may either have different agents to perform different functions or multifunction agents to enable the management of preferences, task prioritization and the balancing of the entire utility matrix.

The agent sets attached to service requesters and "providers" reflect the priorities and preferences of service requestors and the dynamics of service declaration, assignment, or provision. The interaction among different agent sets is governed by standardized service level agreements (SLA), business level agreements (BLA), and agent level agreements (ALA).

As shown in Figure 9, the entire framework is based on the creation, updating, and management of the following modules:

a. Service requesting module denoting the framework of interaction between service requestors and the entire e-government infrastructure.
b. Service declaration, publishing, management, and provision module in which all entities operating and interacting in the service provision grid state and implement an agreed upon route of cooperation.
c. Service tracking module concerned with maintaining service logs, service requesting, and provision status reports, and update of the qualities of publishable services. Requests are instances of services that request entities to create and upload to providing entities when they need to request a service. To be able to integrate the process of service provision, these entities must keep a record of the successive events and results of the requests they receive, and whenever needed, they create reports to describe their state.

Figure 8. Architectural agent sets' perspectives

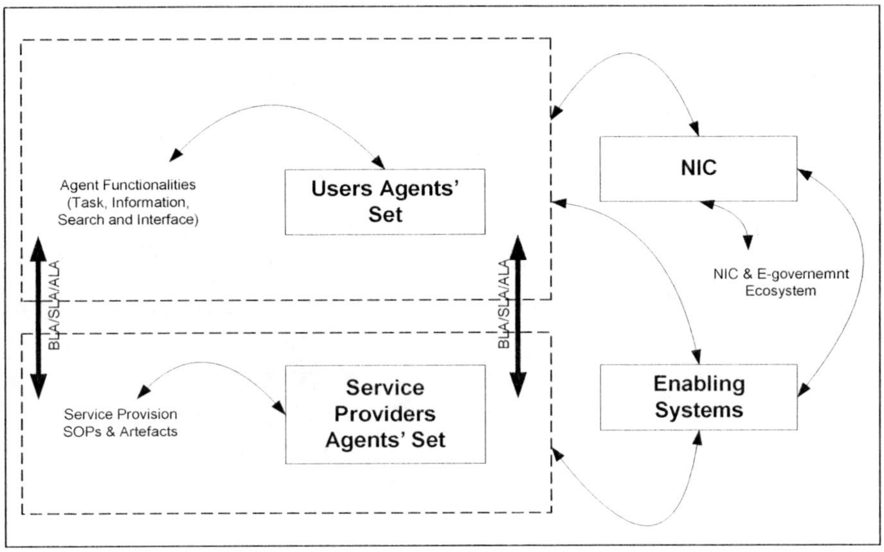

Figure 9. Coupled distributed e-government architecture

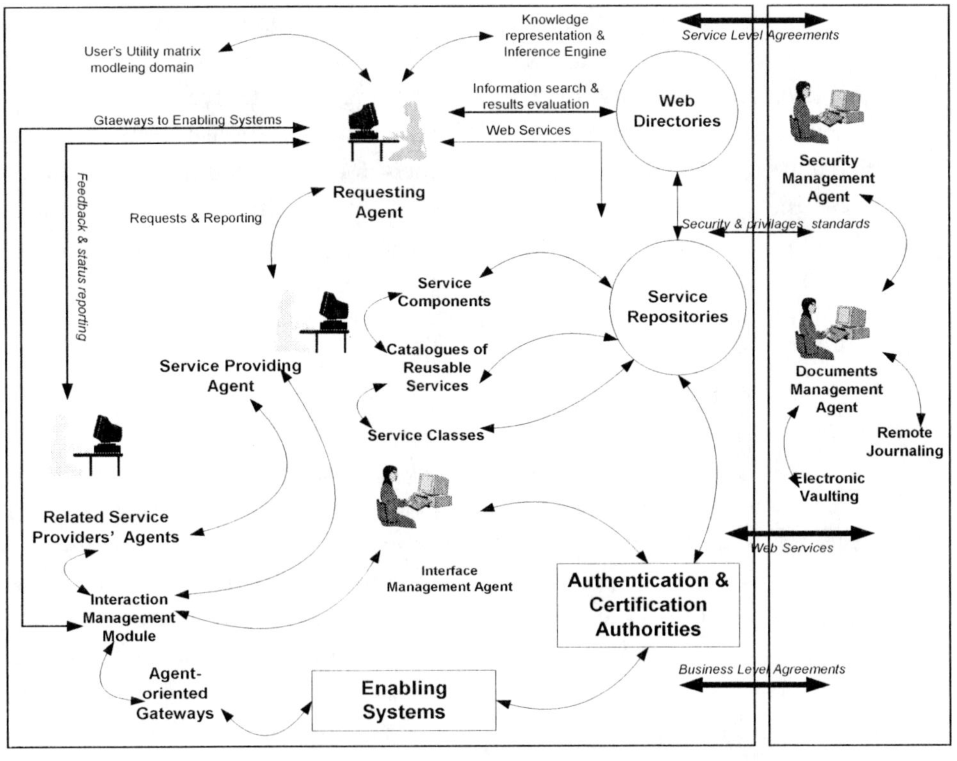

> The importance of such a module stems from the fact that when front line and back line structure is adopted, the availability of service requesting and provision reports is essential for service tracking and user notification.

The basic aim of incorporating such modeling modules is to assist in the articulation of the functionalities of agent sets and associating them with the services to be offered by the entire multiagent SOA organization. Within the context of the proposed architecture, the concepts of front line and back line offices are left loose and incorporated as modules to facilitate information sharing, code reusability and interagent communication because the entire architecture follows a distributed e-government deployment approach.

The optimization of these modules across the landscapes of the entire e-government project is also affected by agent-specific integrated components (interface engines, knowledge representation algorithm and functionalities) and system-wide ecosystem procedures (security procedures and measures, authorization, authentication, and data back-up). However, when using software agents such repositories can be shared as they can be a part of the corporate sharable resources.

However, services are interacted and transacted using the front line and back line office paradigm by adopting the concept of agent sets. The user requests the service from the service providing entity by authorizing his entire agent to do that on his behalf. If the service is entity-specific then interaction will be limited among the entity, the agent, and his owner. If not, then the front line office authorizes its agent set to communicate, on behalf of the user's agent, with the back line office agents set to request the service. The service-providing agent takes the responsibility of collecting necessary documentation from the user's agent and, if necessary, authorizes and manages (in collaboration with other agents) electronic payment through enabling systems. Its roles expand to include user's agent authentication, authorization, and notification. It also tracks the status of the service requested and sends feedback to service requestors.

Coupling SOA with agent sets provides the possibility to address the potential difficulties associated with the use of the front and back line offices paradigm when integrated large-scale e-government applications are being deployed. The implementation of such paradigm is associated with some difficulties that, if not properly managed, will move the whole context into disarray. Generally speaking, the front-back-office paradigm suits situations where services are provided by different organizational units that coordinate and collectively orchestrate their activities and processes within the same chain of command, that is, superior-subordinate relationship. In this case, there is room to challenge and address the difficulties associated with the paradigm within the domain of information sharing, work coordination, and conviviality. However, if the relationship between the front line and back line office exists outside the unified chain of command, the process of service management will be affected by the lack of organizational flexibility necessary for offering some degree of transparency, openness, and prompt response. In their process to follow their localized chain of command, the failure of different offices to alter or adapt to existing structure-based standard operating procedures to accommodate the need for frequent communication across multiple lines of command is another implementation challenge.

The process of communication among organizational units may also be challenged by a wide range of institutional, organizational, and personnel issues. If the service is provided by different entities operating within different chains of command, then each of them must have full knowledge about the services it can provide and accordingly publish metadata to describe it (in a schema-subschema fashion) as a part of relevant service repositories. Within this context, with the lack of standardized universally accessible communication measures and data formats (together with the failure and/or unwillingness of any entity to adhere to such measures), communication problems will challenge the interactive service requesting –and provision process and the ability of entities to share, load and upload, and access service objects using normalized formats. In addition, even for entities operating within the same chain of command, there is a potential of conflict because they are usually organized as profit, cost, or responsibility centers. Because the process of service provision demands some entities to undertake some functions on behalf of others, the potential suboptimization and power struggles significantly affect the quality of service and user satisfaction. Especially when the entities engaged in the process of service provision are enacted in a value chain, both front line and back line offices must possess reasonable degrees of technological maturity and the capacity to manage technology intensive acquisitions. The variety of status on the technology adoption curve, technological infusion, and institutional preparedness are all, among others, significant change factors.

Using the distributed loose defined entities, connections among service providing entities are viewed as a value chain rather than a chain of commands. The functionality of the entire value chain is governed by multiple service and business level agreements. The failure or lack of adherence to these agreements will result, under practical situations, into different communication and reporting difficulties. Such agreements are backed by a trust chain managed by the security agent in collaboration with the document management agent using different security layers.

If the service requesting entity provided its agent sets with advanced context awareness and mobility capabilities, those agents can sense and act upon contextual information and move across different servers to carry out different functions. Due to the huge amounts of forms, documents, and data to be uploaded, downloaded, and exchanged during the service requesting –and provision process, the question of data backup emerges as an important issue for agents and their migration to search for services, service providers, service provision terms, consult with its owner, submit a request for a service and track it through. The architecture proposes the use of remote transaction journaling and electronic vaulting systems to facilitate data and system mirroring. Electronic vaulting allows effective control of data protection, outsourcing the data backup, offsite storage, archiving, and management of recovery tasks. Although electronic vaulting services use a delta backup scheme that transmits only data that has changed, electronic vaulting still requires a good bandwidth in order to do simulations either on specific data presentation applications (such as spreadsheets) or by running its software to find out how long it will take to back up with the user's bandwidth. Remote transaction and server journaling accelerates the recovery time after an unexpected shutdown and significantly improves the availability of data, the capacity of the server, and storage systems to maintain a continuous record of these transactions in a separate file (i.e., a journal). Moreover, remote journaling also provides an extremely fast and reliable mechanism for backup by moving critical data-change information to a remote location as it offloads the processor's load required for applying a replication activity to the backup machine, and puts the remaining processing load on the production machine beneath the operating system (IBM). It also reduces the latency of replication data and processes, which also increases the transaction integrity of databases.

Implementation of this work will be done using XML and Concordia to gain the functionalities of mobility, accessibility, and interoperability.

COUPLING FEATURES AND DEPLOYMENT CONSIDERATIONS

When taken individually, the concepts of agency and service orientations may provide different advantages and limitations with regards to task accomplishment, user engagement, and the rationalization of institutional procedures. The process of coupling has the potential to pool the merits of both concepts, and at the same time presents some challenges that deserve paramount attention.

Situational Relevance and Advantages

The coupled architecture is relevant for the implementation of distributed e-government initiatives under the following situations:

a. When the service cycle is completely automated and computer-based on a network of interconnected legacy systems for service requesting and provision. The process of tax authorization, negotiation, adjustment, and settlement, for example, can be significantly enhanced by such coupling. Using their entire agent sets, requesting entities (business enterprises) can authorize their tax agent sets to cross reference the internal accounting system and financial statements to get the value of tax due, interface (foreword) through the coupled architecture with the entire service provider (tax administration) to negotiate the amount of tax and interface (backward) with the tax-paying entity to get the final authorization from functional decision makers or their respective agent sets to settle tax through bank transfers or any other electronic method.
b. When there is an environment of orchestrated regulatory domains governing the different levels or scales of service provision. Especially for government service provision, there tend to be different regulations (both procedural and documentational) adopted by different government levels (federal vs. state) that significantly reduce the capacity of the requesting entity to request the service or complete its processing cycle. For the entire coupled model to be of more operational benefit it is preferred that there should exist an integrated, yet orchestrated, regulatory context to enable free mobility of service requesting agent sets, otherwise additional effort is needed to modify the overall interface capacity and knowledge engine of service requesting agent sets in pursuit of improving their learning and adaptation skills.

The coupled architecture has the following advantages for the e-government initiative in Sudan:

a. It reduces entry requirements for service requestors and increases the span of implementation by expanding the context and definition of "service requesting entities" from citizens to include business enterprises.
b. Because it is using the concept of "agent sets" it supports the rationalization of procedures and reducing complexities, redundant processes, and inefficiencies.
c. It reduces implementation failures associated with the centralized implementation model currently in use.
d. Because the process of coupling is based on the concepts of system integration and multi-dimensionality, it has the potential to provide additional support due to the recent developments witnessed with regards to the deployment of the integrated banking network (the national transactions' exchange facility managed by the Central Bank).

Potential Limitations

Although the majority of e-government initiatives are devoted to the provision of government services to citizens, little has been done to investigate the potential of these initiatives in reengineering government agencies and improving their operational efficiency. The proposed model can be used in the future at a larger scale for the provision of sophisticated services (such as electronic medicine and computer supported collaborative work systems). While this may provide government units with the opportunity to assess their operational capacity to manage electronic processes it also improves operational efficiency through training and enhanced information sharing among different and remote trajectories using different types of data and interfaces. However, the following limitations are expected from the process of coupling agent and service-oriented concepts.

In addition to other limitations, the deployment of a coupled framework can be challenged by the difficulty or the lack of willingness to create "learning organizational sets" to support the dimensions of agents' sets. The functionality of the entire coupled framework or model depends exclusively not only on the ability of service providing agencies to provide services but also on the ability of these agencies to operate as learning organizational sets each with its own learning capacity that contributes to the overall learning curve. Although the adoption of agency concepts supports this dimension, in real term service providing agencies must be dynamic enough in preparing and fine-tuning their data sets in a way that allows for mobile agents' navigation and data access.

Foreseen Modifications

However, the following modifications and changes, among others, are expected to improve the potential and capacity of the model to support the implementation of the e-government initiative in Sudan as well as in similar situations:

1. Incorporating additional learning and autonomy dimensions to accommodate multichannel considerations and shift of customer orientations and preferences. This may not only demand a significant change in the agent sets to be used, but also shifts the context of knowledge acquisition, representation, and sharing.
2. To support mobility (user, service, and equipment) associated with Internet connections and user transactions, the use of the model to a large extent demands the integration of additional powerful mobility, context awareness, and ubiquity to support service requestors and enhance the operational efficiency of government units with regards to the provision of sophisticated services. This demands building long-term trusted preservation services through the use of service interaction protocols and evidence records to support other sophisticated service.

Therefore, future research might systematically test the interconnections between the effectiveness of e-government initiatives and the dynamics of the social, political, and economic environment. Special emphasis can be put on the effect of resource availability on e-government growth and implementation at different levels of governance. The extent to which the migration to democracy and institutional or political reforms affects the effectiveness of e-government applications is another variable to consider.

Critical research is also important to further address the concerns for interoperability in an open distributed environment, semantic and ontological management issues, standardization of agent-specific and collective processes to maintain an integrated value chain that crosses the boundaries of command chains, and ensuring security and effectiveness of enabling systems such as electronic payment and user authentication and authorization. In addition to the growing number of implementation platforms, taking special care to theses issues, among others, gives an insight about the transformational capacity of the entire e-government project to benefit from the unprecedented developments to be exhibited in computing paradigms and user activities and attitudes.

CONCLUSION

The article is advocating the use of multiagent systems technology and the concepts of service orientation as a form of coupling multiple e-government implementation paradigms. The proposed agent-oriented and service-based modeling approach adopted takes basic concepts addressed by previous research and attempts to reduce their merits to the case of the e-government initiative in Sudan. While the use of such a research method enriches our understanding about the reasons that lead to the failure of many e-government projects, it also provides a testable platform that guides the movement from vision to action, especially in developing countries. The architecture proposed in this article supports the development and implementation of e-government initiatives by establishing a coupled atmosphere that includes the basic conditions necessary for allowing the entities involved in the provision of governmental services to share resources and cooperate with each other. The architecture supports the implementation of flexibly enacted agent sets either as single life entities or composite ones by providing the possibility of concurrent service provision and access through integrated delivery channels. The proposed architecture is oriented toward relaxing e-government implementation variables by coupling service-oriented concepts and the widely spreading and consolidated agents' technologies. The basic aim is to incorporate an effective enabling environment that offers more capabilities to support authentication, authorization, confidentiality, integrity, and nonrepudiation. Moreover, the architecture follows a distributed pattern where all resources (including knowledge) are accessible to all service providing entities and all channels are open for service requestors. Because of their operational capabilities, the use of agent sets supports such distribution.

The article raises the importance of viewing the implementation of e-government initiatives by not only considering technological build–ups, but also by understanding the variety of institutional, organizational, and managerial dimensions. While the benefits and merits of the proposed coupled model are based on the use of an integrated approach, its linkage to the case study of the e-government of Sudan has facilitated the articulation of modifications and future work. Addressing the limitations mentioned in this article goes hand in hand with the overall effort to strategically manage and implement the entire e-government project in the case studied as well as in similar ones.

REFERENCES

Abdorabo, A. (2004). E-Government and IP Symposium for the Arab Region, UAE – Dubai.

Alexandros, K., Panagiotis, S., Thanos, K., & Despina, P. (2005). A secure e-government platform architecture for small to medium-sized public organizations. *Electronic Commerce Research and Applications, 4(2),* 174-186.

Arcieri, F. et al. (2002). Experiences and issues in the realization of e-government services. *Proceedings of the 12th International Workshop on Research Issues in Data Engineering: Engineering E-Commerce/E-Business Systems* (pp. 143-148). New York: IEEE.

Arcieri, F. et al. (2004). A layered IT infrastructure for secure interoperability in personal data registry digital government services. In *Proceedings of the 14th International Workshop on Research Issues on Data Engineering: Web Services for E-commerce and E-government Applications* (pp. 95-102). New York: .

Baldwin, C. Y., & Clark. K. B., (2000). *Design rules: The power of modularity.* Cambridge, MA: The MIT Press.

Benson, T. (2002). E-service development framework primer. eGIF4 Project, 1.0b version. Office of the e-Envoy, Cabinet Office., UK.

Bernhard, K., Jeroen, H., & Guenther, I. (2005). In principle: Towards an open architecture for e-government identity management, Working Paper No. 2504, ISSN: 1667-738X, Center for Technology and Innovation Management. Retrieved November 25, 2006, from http://www.cetim.org/wps

Boudriga, N. (2002). Technical issues in securing e-government. *Proceedings of the IEEE International Conference on Systems, Man and Cybernetics, (2)* (pp. 392-397).

Caloyannides, M. et al. (2003). US e-government authentication framework and programs. *IT Professional,* 5(3), 16-21.

Cook, M. A. (1996). *Building enterprise information architectures: Reengineering information systems.* New Jersey: Prentice Hall.

Crawford, C. H., Bate, G., Cherbakov, L., Holley, K., & Tsocanos, C. (2005). Toward an on-demand service-oriented architecture. *IBM Systems Journal, 44*(1), 81-108.

DataExchanger (2002). Pierre Audoin Conseil, "Guide comparatif EAI".

Eardley A. et al. (2003). Methods for developing flexible strategic information systems: Is the answer already out there? In N. Patel (Ed.), *Adaptive evolutionary information systems.* Hershey, PA: Idea Group Publishing.

European Community. (2003). The role of e-government for Europe's future. Communication of the European Commission. Retrieved December 15, 2005, from http://europa.eu.int/information_society/eeurope/2005/doc/all_about/egov_communication_en.pdf

Foster, I., & Kesselman, C. (Eds.). (2003). *The Grid 2: Blueprint for a new computing infrastructure.* San Francisco: Morgan Kaufmann Publishing.

Ganek, A. G., & Corbi, T. A. (2003). The dawning of the autonomic computing era. *IBM Systems Journal, 42*(1), 5-18.

Gasmelseid, T. (in press). From Operational Dash Boards to E-Business: Multiagent Formulation of Electronic Contracts, accepted, the International Journal of E-Business Research, (in print), Idea Group Publishing, USA.

Gasmelseid, T. (2007b). Engineering Multiagent Systems accepted Encyclopedia of Information Ethics and Security, (in print), Idea Group Publishing, USA.

Gonçalo, P. D., & José, A. R. (2006). A simple model and a distributed architecture for realizing one-stop e-government. *Electronic Commerce Research and Applications,* doi:10.1016/j.elerap.2006.02.001.

Greunz, M., Schopp, B., & Haes, J. (2004). Integrating e-government infrastructures through secure XML document containers. *Proceedings of the 34th Annual Hawaii International Conference on System Sciences (HICSS-34), (2)* (p. 5004).

Hillard, R. (2000). IEEE-std-1471-2000: Recommended practice for architectural description of software-intensive systems. Retrieved February 15, 2007, from http://standards.ieee.org

IBM. iTera Echo² High Availability for IBM iSeries, http://www.ibm.com

Janssen, M., & Van Veenstra, A. (2005). Stages of growth in e-government: An architectural approach. *The Electronic Journal of e-Government, 3*(4), 193-200.

Joshi, J. et al. (2001). Digital government security infrastructure design challenges. *Computer Security, 34*(2), 66-72.

Kaliontzoglou, A., et al. (2005). A secure e-government platform architecture for small to medium-sized public organizations. *Electronic Commerce Research and Applications, 4*(2), 174-186.

Lambrinoudakis, C. et al. (2003). Security requirements for e-government services: A methodological approach for developing a common PKI-based security policy. *Computer Communications, 26*(16), 1873-1883.

Layne, K., & Lee, W. (2001). Developing fully functional e-government: A four-stage model. *Government Information Quarterly, 18*(2), 122-136.

McGrath, S., & O'Reilly, C. (2004). A service-oriented approach to e-government architecture. Proceedings of the XML-Europe 2004, Amsterdam, The Netherlands. Retrieved November 22, 2006.

Medjahed, B. et al. (2003). Infrastructure for e-government Web services. *IEEE Internet Computing, 7*(1), 58-65.

Mediadev (2002). Pourquoi et comment faire communiquer les applications. Livre blanc.

Stevens, M. (2002). Service-oriented architecture introduction, part 1. Retrieved April 26, 2005, from www.developer.com/design/article.php/1010451.

Mühl, F., & Krabina, B. (2003). Online one-stop government - Eine Integrierte Plattform: Ergebnisse des EU-Projekts eGOV. In Maria Wimmer (Ed.), *Quo vadis e-Government? State-of-the-art 2003, Proceedings of eGOV Days OCG series, 165* (pp. 156-165).

ONTOGOV project (2006). Retrieved December 30, 2006, from http://www.sciencedirect.com/science?_ob=RedirectURL&_method=externObjLink&_locator=url&_cdi=6902&_plusSign=%2B&_targetURL=http%253A%252F%252Fwww.ontogov.com%252F

Ross, J. W., & Westerman, G. (2004). Preparing for utility computing: The role of IT architecture and relationship management. *IBM Systems Journal, 43*(1), 5-19.

Schmidt, M., Hutchison, B., Lambros, P., & Phippen, R. (2005). The enterprise service bus: Making service-oriented architecture real. *IBM Systems Journal, 44*(4), 781-797.

Shilakes, C., & Tylman, J. (1988). Enterprise Information Portal. Merrill Lynch.

Stamoulis, D. et al. (2003). A teleological development of "design-decisions-independent" information systems. In N. Patel (Ed.), *Adaptive evolutionary information systems*. Hershey, PA: Idea Group Publishing.

Steimke, F., & Hagen, M. (2003). OSCI: A common communication standard for e-government. Lecture Notes in Computer Science, 2739, 250-255.

Tambouris, E. (2001). An integrated platform for realizing online one-stop government: The eGOV Project. In *Proceedings of the DEXA International Workshop "On the Way to Electronic Government."* Los Alamitos, CA: IEEE Computer Society Press.

Terregov Project (2005). Retrieved October 20, 2005, from http://www.sciencedirect.com/science?_ob=RedirectURL&_method=externObjLink&_locator=url&_cdi=6902&_plusSign=%2B&_targetURL=http%253A%252F%252Fwww.terregov.eupm.net

The Federal Enterprise Architecture, Program Management Office Web site (2005). Retrieved October 29, 2005, from http://www.feapmo.gov

UK GovTalkTM (2004). Retrieved September 2006, from www.govtalk.gov.uk

UN (2003). World public sector report: E-government at the crossroads, United Nations, New York.

UNPAN, Benchmarking e-government (2002). A global perspective, United Nations Online Network in Public Administration and Finance, New York.

Vassilakis, C., Anya, S., Dimitrios, T., & Dimitris, G. (2005). A blackboard-oriented architecture for e-government service composition. Managing modern organizations with information technology. 309-312.

Web Services, World Wide Web Consortium (2002). Retrieved July 25, 2006, from http://www.w3.org/2002/ws/

Wimmer, M., & Traunmueller, R. (2002). Towards an integrated platform for online one-stop government. *ERCIM News, Special Theme: e-Government, 48*.

Wimmer, M. (2002). A European perspective towards online one-stop government: The eGOV project. *Electronic Commerce Research and Applications, 1*(1), 92-103.

Wimmer, M., & Bredow, B. (2002). A holistic approach to security aspects in e-government. *Proceedings of the 35th Hawaii International Conference on System Sciences (HICSS-35) (5)* (p. 128b).

Wimmer, M., & Krenner, J. (2001). An integrated online one-stop government platform: The eOGV Project, 9th Interdisciplinary Information Management Talks. Proceedings of the Schriftenreihe Informatik, Universitätsverlag Trauner, Linz, (pp. 329-337).World Bank. A definition of e-government. Retrieved 25 November 25, 2006, from www.worldbank.org/publicsector/egov

This work was previously published in International Journal of Electronic Government Research, Vol. 3, Issue 3, edited by M. Khosrow-Pour, pp. 87-106, copyright 2007 by IGI Publishing, formerly known as Idea Group Publishing (an imprint of IGI Global).

Chapter 4.40
A Roadmap for Ambient E-Service:
Applications and Embracing Model

Yuan-Chu Hwang
National Chengchi University, Taiwan

Soe-Tsyr Yuan
National Chengchi University, Taiwan

ABSTRACT

Most of the existing mobile services were designed based on the client/server architecture. Those mobile services neither paid much attention to mobile users' interactions with their environments nor considered the collective efforts between the mobile users in a dynamic peer group. In this article, the notion of ambient e-service is so defined as to identify a new scope of mobile e-service, which address dynamic collective efforts between mobile users (enabled by mobile peer-to-peer technology), dynamic interactions with ambient environments (envisioned by location-based service), the moment of value (empowered by wireless technologies), and low cost service provision. The notable features of ambient e-services are the exhilarated linkage based on social context and significantly rapid growth of connections. We also present an ambient e-service framework that characterizes ambient e-services with three dimensions (value stack, environment stack, and technology stack), followed by several exemplars of ambient e-service applications. Moreover, we present the ambient e-service embracing model (ASEM) that addresses the integrated consideration of trust, reputation, and privacy required for fostering the growth of ambient e-services and steers the directions of future fruitful relevant research.

INTRODUCTION TO AMBIENT E-SERVICE

The notion of ambient e-service is defined to identify a new scope of mobile e-services. Until now, there have been two different design paradigms in mobile commerce. Most of the current mobile commerce applications are grounded in the client/server architecture, where the only interactions involved are between a service provider and a mobile user. Mobile users are standalone. Users under such service environments cannot interact with each other easily. Although the issues of human-computer interaction with mobile devices has been brought to public attention for the last several years (Paternò, 2003). In current mobile service scenarios, interactions, or cooperation between mobile users are not considered as important issues. Therefore, collective efforts from mobile user groups cannot be produced.

Fortunately, the Peer-to-Peer (P2P) technology with mobile devices makes it possible for mobile users to communicate with each other easily. Mobile users can exchange information wirelessly under a sensors-enabled environment. Ambient e-service is designed based on the P2P architecture that highlights the collaborative interactions of mobile users.

The notion of ambient e-services addresses dynamic collective efforts between mobile users (enabled by mobile-P2P), dynamic interactions with ambient environments (envisioned by location-based services), moment of value, and low cost service provision. The collective effort is based on the collaborative interactions of mobile users, which facilitate the low cost service provision. In a sensor-enabled environment, information presentations are embedded in everyday objects such as pens, walls, or doors. It makes the environment become an interface of the context information. Using the Mobile P2P Technology, users can exchange their information wirelessly and proceed highly extensive interactions. Grounded on location-based service, location information of mobile users can be retrieved. Hence, ambient e-service can provide personal, timely, and relevant services to mobile users.

Comparing with the client/server design, an ambient e-service has two major distinguished features. First, under the client/server architecture, it is not possible to effectively attain the collective efforts that are tailored to the contexts of the user. Second, with the P2P design, the number of connections grows by a significantly rapid pace especially in an open space. For a better understanding of ambient e-services, we will use an ambient e-service framework (as shown as Figure 1) to identify some possible deliverables (values) of ambient e-services and address the technologies required to support the applications of ambient e-services.

This framework is composed of three dimensions, the value stack, the environment stack, and the technology stack. The descriptions of the stacks will be detailed as follows.

Value Stack

The ambient value stack comprises five layers indicating the supporting value layers for ambient e-services (deliverables of higher levels requiring the provision of deliverables of lower levels). The basic layer is the "context information," which is attained from the ambient sensor environments. A mobile user can interact with the environments (e.g., entering a room) and the context sensors, then retrieve context information with the device

Figure 1. Ambient e-service framework

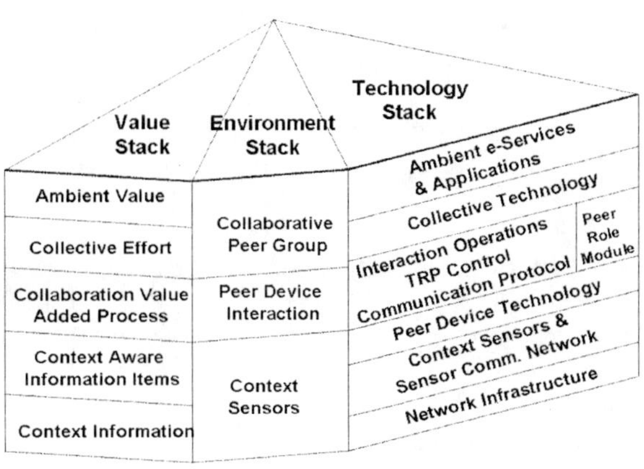

carried by the user (e.g., informing the user of his or her location). Comparing the user's profile, the second layer "Context Aware Information Items" sends information items to the user that matches his or her preferences. The information items received from the environments may be useful to the user, but sometimes some of the information items may be irrelevant. With the communication ability, a mobile peer can collaborate with another mobile peer and exchange carried information items stored in their mobile devices. Through these collaboration interactions, it may be the case that there is someone whose information items are valuable to me and thus I can exchange or trade with them with a micro payment or a barter process. This is called "Collaboration Value Added Process."

Not only communicating with only one peer, a peer can also interact with a peer group of multiple peers. Aiming at the same goal or interests, a peer group can collect their abilities to accomplish the goal that is impossible for a single peer to reach. Therefore, "Collective Effort" represents the power of a peer group (or multiple peer groups). The ambient value subsequently refers to the collective efforts, which include the peers' interactions and peer groups' interactions.

Environment Stack

The environment stack consists of three layers indicating the supporting environment layers for ambient e-services (environments of higher levels comprising those of the lower levels). The sketched stack diagram is shown in Figure 2.

The "Ambient Context Sensors" is the bottom layer, which include three categories of environments. Schilit, Adams and Want (1994) claim that the important aspects of context are: where the user is, who the user is with, and what resources are nearby.

The user environment includes the user context, the activity context, and the social context. The user environment represents the profile of a user, such as peer identification, where the user is, who the user is, the user's preference, their privacy concern, their social situation, and relations with others, etc. The physical environment includes the physical context and the device context. The physical environment refers to things like temperature, noise, lighting level, and device context. The computing environment includes the network context and the services context. The computing environment represents the network connectivity, available processors, cost of computing, bandwidth, and available nearby services, etc.

Figure 2. Ambient environment stack

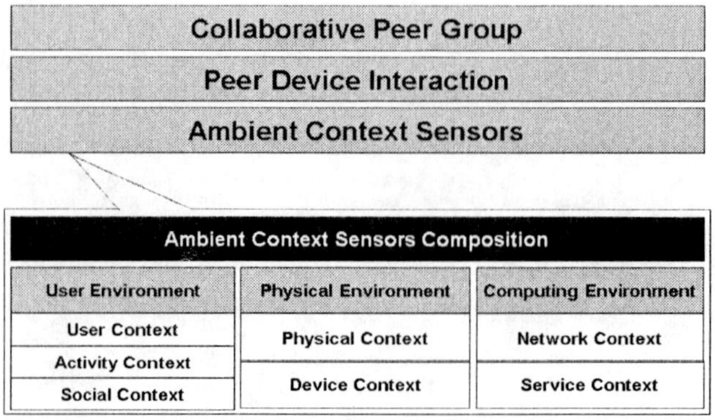

The layer "Peer Device Interaction" represents environments (featuring peer-to-peer interactions) in which mobile users may exchange their experience and trade attained information items with nearby peers. The "Peer Device Interaction" layer rests on the "Ambient Context Sensors" layer; that is, all peers' information items originally come from the interaction with the dynamic environments of the bottom layer.

The top layer of the environment stack represents environments featuring peer groups' interactions and collaboration. Peer groups can collect all peers' power for certain objectives (e.g., collective buy, forming a task-oriented workforce group, etc.).

Technology Stack

The technology stack is shown in Figure 1. Network infrastructure is the fundamental of all ambient technology stacks. The wired and wireless hybrid network infrastructure provides the basic communication infrastructure for context sensors and peer devices. Above the network infrastructure layer, context sensors and sensor communication can interact with the surrounding peers. Peer devices function on top of the sensor communication network and the mobile device's hardware, operation systems, and software platforms.

The layer above the peer device technology layer has two folds: (1) For peers to interact with each other, a peer communication protocol is required (similar to that in Web services). (2) In ambient environments, peers may just know nearby peers for quite a short period of time. How can a peer trust the nearby peers? Is it possible to build a reputation system for the aforementioned situation so that it is feasible to trust unfamiliar peers? Similarly, privacy control should be addressed in ambient e-services. Resting on trust, reputation, and privacy control as the dependable basics, mobile users can engage ambient interactions to handle some operations between peers. These operations are the likes of "discovery," "request," "respond," "bargain," "transact." and "delivery."

Since a mobile user plays different roles in different interactions, the peer role module can be applied to the peer in response to the dynamic roles rendered. Mobile users, who have the information items required by other users, play the seller role by applying the seller module. The surrounding peers (who have attained various kinds of information) then can play as the broker role by applying the broker module. Mobile users, who need the information from others, apply the buyer module and play the buyer role (who can trade or barter with other mobile users).

Beyond the peer-to-peer interactions, peer group collective effort is the communal power of peers. Collaborative technologies that support peer and peer groups to work together underlie the key character of ambient power. Based on the collective technology, ambient e-services can be unfolded in various applications, which we will discuss in the next section.

The remaining sections of this chapter are organized as follows: Next section exemplifies several ambient e-service application scenarios, followed by the challenges and the state of the art for embracing ambient e-services. In the ASEM section, we present an embracing model of ambient e-services in terms of its framework design. In addition, we illustrate the roadmap and impact of the embracing model in the roadmap section. Finally, a conclusion and the directions of our future work are provided in final section.

AMBIENT E-SERVICE APPLICATIONS

It will be useful, to begin with, making a distinction between two kinds of ambient e-services. One is for the distributed trading; another is for the distributed collaboration. Please note that the social context and the rapid growth of connections are the major incentives of applying the ambient e-service design. The two characteristics are not mutually exclusive; of course, one scenario may apply both of the ambient characteristics.

This section aims to identify several important ambient e-service application scenarios presuming ambient environments of mobile commerce are provided. Without loss of generosity, the physical context of location is referenced and considered in the ambient environments addressed in the following scenarios, naturally relating to the LBS (Location-Based Service) research. As mentioned in the introduction section, ambient e-services aim to identify a new scope of mobile e-services mainly addressing dynamic collected efforts between mobile users (enabled by M-P2P) and dynamic interactions with ambient environments (envisioned by LBS).

Since LBS was categorized into four major types (transaction services, information services, navigation and tracking services, and safety services), we accordingly exemplify some scenarios reflecting the LBS types as well as exhibiting dynamic collected efforts based on M-P2P.

We introduce an ambient shopping mall scenario to be a representative of ambient transaction services. The shopping mall scenario can easily be modified to act as ambient safety services. The information items distribution cooperation scenario then is considered as an exemplar of ambient information services. The cooperative peer group scenario then can be instantiated into ambient navigation and tracking services. As to the ambient location information acquisition scenario, it can be considered as an instance of ambient transaction services, ambient information services or ambient navigation and tracking services. We'll take the ambient shopping mall scenario for detail description in the next subsection.

These applications differ from the past mobile e-services in addressing dynamic collected efforts between mobile users and dynamic interactions with ambient environments. The collective efforts of mobile users are not possible in the primal mobile services framework that deploys the services with the client/server architecture. Moreover, mobile devices in ambient e-services applications are very personal to the users, and thus the social contexts retained in the personal devices (e.g., the social relationships in the vicinity) can unfold the e-services of high complexity and security than that of no social contexts in sensor networks. E-services with the social context environment render ambient e-services capable of providing the most appropriate collaborative power for mobile users anywhere whenever needed.

Ambient Shopping Mall Scenario

In Figure 3, a picturesque view of the ambient shopping mall scenario is presented. In a shopping mall (fully equipped with wireless network infrastructures), information items (e.g., advertisement or sales promotion information) can be broadcast to passing-by peers with Info_BC_Station. This means the attained information items of a peer vary based on the peer's interactions with the shopping mall ambient environments.

The ambient e-service addressed in this scenario will be delineated for the case of new customers of high buyer perishability (entering the shopping mall and being in a rush to buy certain items without the knowledge of where to buy and how to buy cheap given relevant sales promotion). Those new customer peers carrying mobile devices can communicate with nearby peers when they just enter the shopping mall.

In such scenarios, the goal of ambient shopping mall e-service is to provide a new channel for customers to get needed information. The

Figure 3. Ambient shopping mail scenario

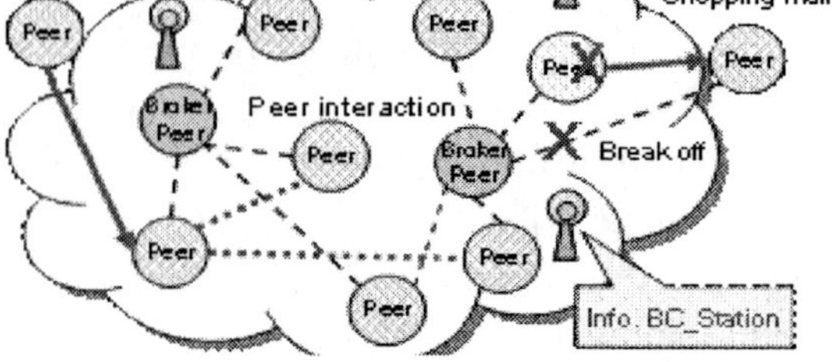

assumption of this scenario is that the contents of information items kept in peers are different from one another based on their membership status (i.e., preference, location). Mobile users will receive the information items based on their user context such as their preferences or membership data. Those members with higher loyalty points will get a higher discount e-coupon. This would encourage customers to join the membership program.

All mobile peers have their temporary peer ID number, preference, context data, transaction history, and the information attained information items. Peers can do basic operations such as bargain and payment. Mobile peers can apply different role modules to do specific operations. There are the buyer modules, the seller modules, and the broker modules for mobile peers.

When a peer applies the seller module, it can respond a buyer's product discovery operation. If a seller peer has the information items that the buyer required, the seller then responds the buyer's request and starts a bargain operation with the buyer peer. After the payment process, the seller delivers the information items to the buyer. The operations performed by the buyer module are complementary to those performed by the seller module. But the buyer module has been designed not only to handle the transactions with seller module, but also to request the package service from the broker module.

The broker module is applied to those peers who will stay in the mall for a long time and own more complete information items. The broker module is designed for peers serving as service providers. The broker module has the "generate" package, which can generate services of producing information items of the buyer's interests and preference. (Similar to service bundles in Baida, Gordijn, Akkermans, Saele, & Morch, 2005). Package templates are used for the broker module to produce a service package in an easy way. Also, the broker module has the same ability as the seller module that can deliver the products.

Although the effective reach is one of the shopping mall's goals. If the contents of information items are the same for everyone, both client/server and P2P designs can pass the items to the public but in different ways. However, mass broadcasts like spam mails will annoy customers and they will be reluctant to join this shopping program, attaining the contrary results. When considering user differentiation, content differentiation will be in relation to user profiles and to ambient context sensors in the environment stack (that subsequently will involve social context and correlate to the privacy concerns of the customers). Those concerns make the P2P design more applicable than the client/server architecture.

A UML class diagram is depicted (as shown in Figure 4) and represents the relationships between the different modules, as well as the peer module basic functions.

Information Items Distribution Cooperation Scenario

The information items distribution cooperation is an ambient e-service based on a mobile advertising infrastructure. Distributor companies can broadcast shop's advertisement items (e.g., e-coupons) through an ambient advertising infrastructure,

Figure 4. Class diagram of the ambient shopping mall scenario

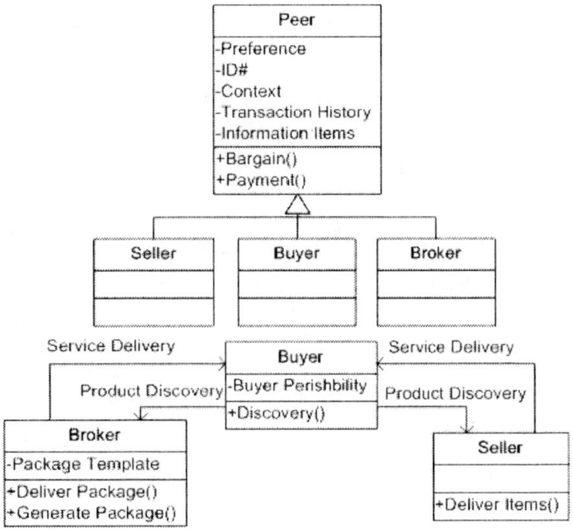

which dispatches advertisement items relevance to their preferences to proximate users. Shops may be geographically distant from the broadcast stations of the distributor companies. In this scenario, e-coupons are considered as valuable information items. When a mobile user passes through a shop and wants to buy certain products but is short of the relevant e-coupons, the mobile peer can probe the surrounding environment to see if there are some nearby peers that own the desired e-coupons.

The P2P design combined with social awareness will make the connections not only in a rapid growth, but also with persuasiveness, being more powerful than the client/server design. Moreover, e-coupons become a valuable information item if the contents of information items are different. In this business model, mobile users can get some financial benefit by exchanging their e-coupons, and thus be attracted to join the program so as to create a large scale of the participants. That is a win-win situation for both customers and the shops.

Figure 5 depicts a UML class diagram of the scenario, representing the relationships, attributes, and operations between all participators. When a mobile user (the barter initiator) passes through a shop and is lacking certain e-coupons, the peer can discover the e-coupons from the ambient peer groups. Whenever the requested e-coupons are found and owned by another peer (the barter responder), the barter initiator requests a bartering process with the barter responder. E-coupons can be distributed not only to the mobile users falling into the broadcast range of the distributor companies, but also to the primary target peers (who really need the certain e-coupons in the right time and right place).

Ambient Location Information Acquisition Scenario

There are mobile services providing location-based services for mobile users with devices of handheld positioning technologies. For instance, Pocket Map delivers nearby restaurants or theater

Figure 5. Class diagram of the information items distribution cooperation scenario

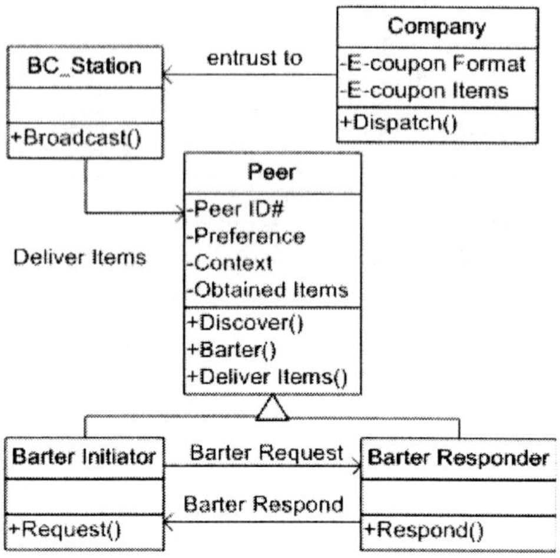

information to mobile users who have the current location information. Those services require location information of the mobile user as a basis to provide various services. Some mobile services simply furnish a mobile user his or her current position with their positioning technologies.

However, it is often the case that not every mobile device is empowered with the handset positioning technology or subscribes certain positioning mobile services. Consequently, mobile users of no positioning-empowered devices and no subscribed positioning services cannot attain desired location-based services. Fortunately, these peers can attain the location information from the nearby peers (possessing the location information) and then engage their desired location-based services (as long as those location-based services do not require precise location information). Figure 6 shows a picturesque view of this scenario.

In this scenario, only when the peer is in a certain distance will the location information be useful. The question now arises: What specific information do I pass to the nearby peers? Do I provide my location information to everyone nearby or just some peers with different characteristics (e.g. in the same virtual community)? Considering the privacy sensitive data, the ambient e-service's social context with privacy concern is the better choice for this scenario. Figure 7 represents the interactions between participators. With the location information, the mobile user then is able to undertake some location-based services.

Cooperative Peer Group Scenario

The cooperative peer group scenario is classified into the application category of distributed collaboration (as depicted in Figure 8). Not only the one to one interaction, mobile users can form peer groups (who have the same interests or same goal) to work together. For example, when the workforce is dynamically deployed in the exhibition center and the environment has customers coming and going, workforces can receive and update the exhibition center task ontology from the BC_Station (similar to as mentioned in the shopping mall scenario but with different information). To support real-time collaboration of distributed group work between mobile workforces, peers may exchange their current working content information to find the best fit candidate peers for dynamic tasks encountered based on their social context (profile, relationship, or experience) so as to maintain workforce task assignments of optimal allocations. In such scenario, peer groups become powerful because of the collective efforts. Various workforces can be dynamically allocated appropriately to resolve the subtasks involved in a goal, enhancing the total performance.

Figure 6. Ambient location information acquisition scenario

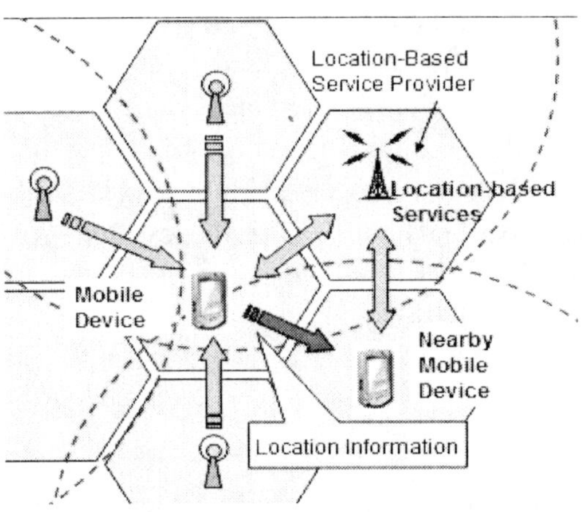

Ambient E-Services Infrastructure

The ambient e-services infrastructure is depicted as a diagram shown in Figure 9, which represents the participators' attributes, operations, and the relationships between them. This diagram captures the major concepts of the scenarios mentioned earlier. This diagram also highlights the peer interactive efforts with others. That is the major concept of the ambient e-services. These interactions and collaboration makes the mobile users to form certain peer groups and gain more power than a standalone mobile.

Figure 7. Class diagram of the ambient location information acquisition scenario

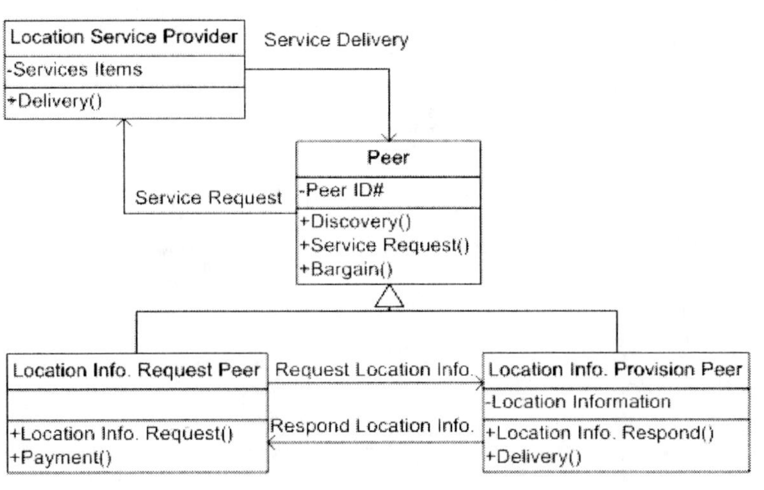

Figure 8. Cooperative peer group scenario

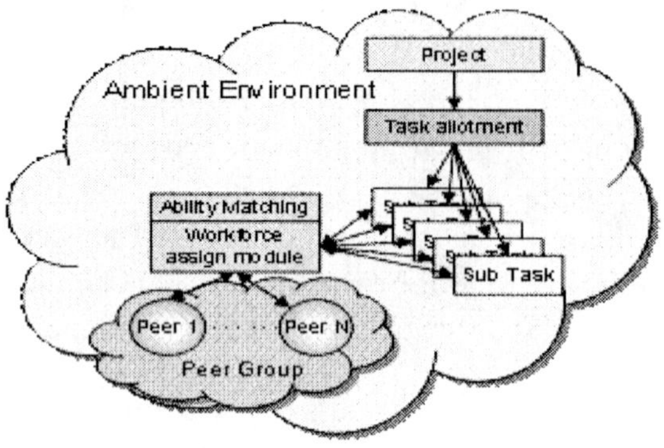

CHALLENGES FOR EMBRACING AMBIENT E-SERVICE

Different from the past mobile e-services, ambient e-services address dynamic collective efforts of mobile users and dynamic interactions within ambient environments. It makes mobile commerce become a new paradigm and will develop certain revolutionary business models. Therefore, we definitely need to put emphasis on how this new ambient era progresses.

In general, ambient e-services bring two important issues, the social and economic issues. The social issues include the user interaction behaviors, intellectual property rights problems, and security issues, etc. For ambient e-service implementation, user behavior and their interactions are very complex. Not only have the security issues that influence the user's willingness to join in an e-service, the legal issue is also troublesome. How do we protect intellectual property in ambient e-services? Since the user interface and the usability of ambient e-services are quite different from the primal mobile commerce. Those issues should also be concerned as a vital social issue awaiting future studies.

The economic issues include the pricing issues of e-services, the bargain and payment issues, and the collaboration and utility issues. Regarding the economics issues, one of the most important issues is the pricing utility issue. Ambient e-services require several kinds of supporting infrastructures, such as sensor networks, wired/wireless network infrastructures, broadcast stations, and service providers. The ambient value is delivered with the combined efforts of the supporting infrastructures. Accordingly, how to price ambient e-services and how to divide the revenue between the infrastructure providers will also become an important issue.

Figure 9. Class diagram of the ambient e-service infrastructure

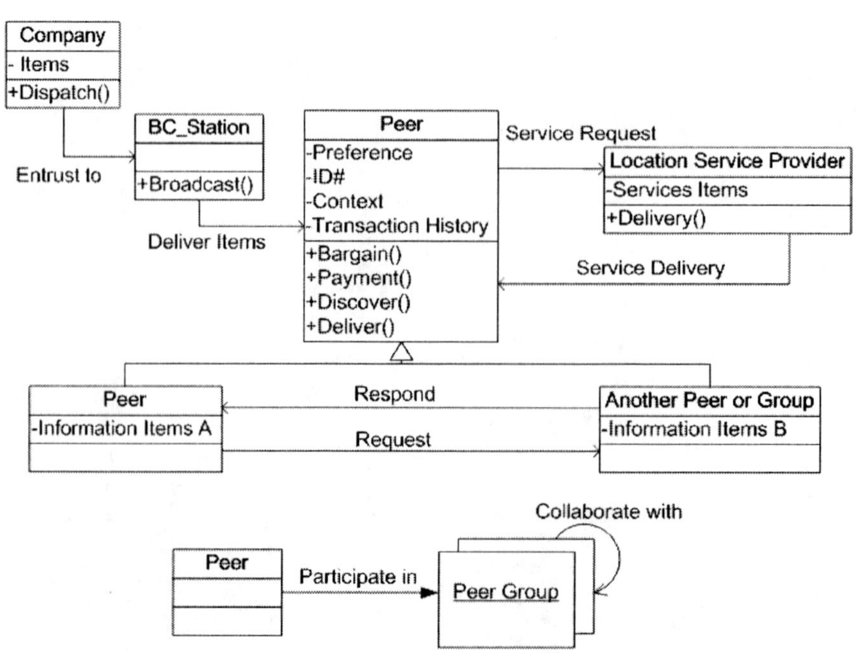

Figure 10. Issues of ambient e-services

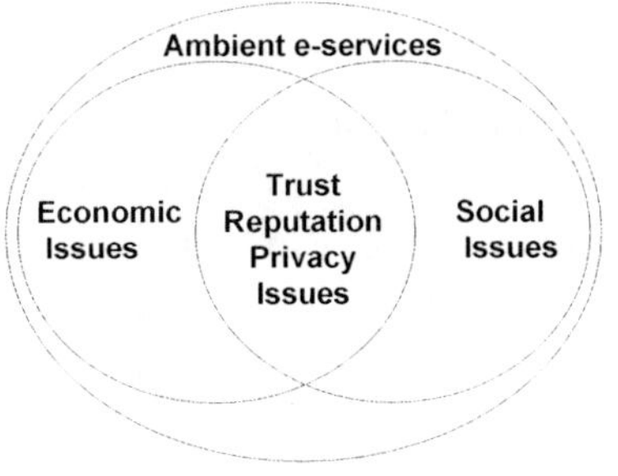

However, a core issue is involved in both the social issues and the economics issues (as shown in Figure 10). That core is the issue of trust, reputation, and privacy. In a dynamic environment of ambient e-services, who can be trusted? Is the mobile user trustworthy? What do they know about me? These questions underlie the interactions and collaborations between mobile users. Accordingly, trust, reputation, and privacy issues act as the groundwork of ambient e-service.

The Relationship Between Trust, Reputation, and Privacy

Ambient e-services rest on the interactions and collective efforts of the surrounding environments and nearby participating peers. However, in the ambient environments of ad-hoc networks, peers are not familiar with others. Unlike the fixed Internet environment, there are no permanent databases of historical data that can be analyzed in the ambient environments. Consequently, it is rarely to see trust mechanisms with which peers interact with each other in the ad-hoc network domain. However, before cooperating with other peers, peers need to guard themselves and seek who can be trusted based on the peers' reputations.

Over the past few decades, a considerable number of studies have been made on trustworthiness in different circumstances. The trust problem was recently brought to light by electronic commerce scenario. Numerous attempts have been made by scholars to show trust is the essence of e-commerce success. There is sufficient evidence to prove that reputation is usually considered as a core manner of how trust is manipulated and demonstrated in e-commerce scenarios. One may notice that privacy and security are the foundation for users to participate in such e-commerce programs. Surprisingly, little attention has been given to explore the relations between trust, reputation, and privacy and their impact to the e-commerce. However, the trust, reputation, and privacy issues are the core for users to embrace the e-service business model.

On the other hand, privacy may have different meanings and significance to different mobile users. Privacy must be considered together with all other requirements: functionality, usability, performance, costs, security, and so on (Shand, Dimmonck, & Bacon, 2003). However, the privacy concern is a primitive barrier for mobile users to embrace ambient e-services. When users do not feel safe about their sensitive data, they may not participate in the e-services. In other words, the more participants an e-service has, the more power the ambient e-service would embody. The collective power comes into view only when the number of the connections reaches above a certain threshold. Accordingly, transcending this threshold is a crucial problem for developing ambient e-services. Privacy-aware ambient e-services are believed to encourage users to participate in the services for attaining collective power. Figure 11 then summarizes the semantic interactions of trust, reputation, and privacy (that underlie the embracing of ambient e-services).

Embracing Challenges

Various features of ambient e-service applications make our lives convenient and safe. Ambient e-services facilitate people to communicate and collaborate with others. Although there might exist some technical problems for ambient e-services, those problems will be solved through the continuous new techniques and innovations.

However, user participation will become the major barrier when we boost ambient e-service applications into public. From the past experi-

Figure 11. Semantic interactions of trust, reputation, and privacy

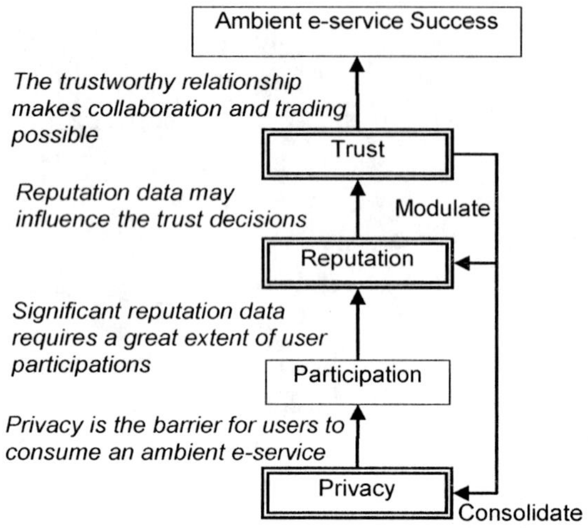

ences, no matter how good a system could be, or how high the value of the system function can achieve, a system will never be popular if users can not trust the system or truly understand how it works. In other words, the problem of user acceptance toward ambient e-service applications is worthy of further discussion.

Many existing systems that might be useful to customers, users may be still reluctant to participate owing to the fear of invasions of privacy (even though the system functions provisioned are powerful and of potential benefits). See Hoy, Grubbs, & Phelps (2003) and Odlyzko (2003). In other words, the privacy concern goes deeply into the heart of the trust problem. Users will participate in those services only when they believe their private data is well protected and they feel safe to join in. With participants' trust and interactions, ambient e-service applications are then able to become popular.

Trust and reputation studies have been proposed for large open environments, such as e-commerce and recommendation systems. Although trust and reputation are different in how they are developed, they are closely related. There are many researches focusing on how to translate trust from reputation data, and reputation has been the major criterion to measure the trustworthiness.

However, existing studies have been focused on reputation computation, and translation from reputation to trust. What seems to be lacking are a consideration of the relationship between trust, reputation, and privacy and integrating those abstract ideas into a whole framework.

In other words, it is required to devise a framework that integrates and analyzes the relationship between trust, reputation, and privacy (so as to embrace ambient e-service applications). Moreover, this framework needs to take into account the nature of ambient e-service environments (distributed interactive network environments of trust and reputation data stored in every user's handheld devices).

For driving the values of collective actions, there are four features required for the environment of ambient e-services. They are as follows:

- **Convenient:** Mobile users can conveniently interact with others in the environment.
- **Safe:** Mobile users may exchange experience for safety protection cooperation but only when the environment provides a certain level of protection that satisfies their privacy requirement.
- **Fair:** In the environment, communications are free from fears and with fair interactions.
- **Collaborative:** The environment supports collaborative actions between mobile users, realizing the collective power of mobile users.

To embrace ambient e-services, the aforementioned challenges and features mainly rest on two directions:

- **Dynamic identity management:** The dynamic identity management problem refers to the dynamic organization of ambient e-service user groups and each user's identity in the ambient environment. Owing to the nature of ambient e-services, every mobile device carries a temporary identity. The identity may be alive only for a certain short period of time under a limited communication range. Mobile users may leave or enter the e-service environment, update the user identity and refresh the environment composition. Accordingly, the problem of dynamic identity management in light of the trust, reputation, and privacy issues has to be carefully resolved.

- **Ambient data management:** In an ambient environment, data spreading across the devices of mobile users, which complicates the handling of the trust, reputation and privacy issues. The problem of ambient data management therefore rest on the assurance of the following objectives: (1) seamless unlinkability (2) convenient data access, (3) ambient data access, and (4) carefree heterogeneous data source (that will be addressed afterward).

State of the Art

Existing relevant researches exhibit certain deficiencies. Ambient e-services are similar to the applications on mobile ad-hoc networks, which is a collection of autonomous peers or terminals that communicate with each other over relatively bandwidth-constrained wireless links. Since the peer nodes are mobile devices, the network topology may change rapidly and unpredictably over time, the network structures underlying ambient e-services are mainly decentralized. Accordingly, all network activities including discovery of the topology and delivery of messages must be executed by the peers themselves.

To embrace ambient e-services, it is inevitable to take into account the characteristics of the ambient e-service environments (short-lived identity, distributed environments, peer-to-peer communication network structures, lightweight computation, limited storage, and connection-constrained wireless networks).

The problems involved in embracing ambient e-services are two folds: dynamic identity management and ambient data management. Existing relevant research activities (together with their deficiencies from the embracing consideration) are to be briefed as follows.

The Dynamic Identity Management for Ambient E-Services

The ambient data management problems from the embracing consideration include (1) dynamic identity management and (2) the deficiencies of existing researches:

Dynamic Identity Management

Due to the nature of the ambient e-service environments, the identity is temporarily assigned to each peer. Once a peer enters an ambient e-service environment, a temporary peer ID is issued with the technology of mobile identity management (Roussos, Peterson, & Patel, 2003). In current researches, in order to collect user's reputation data or compute their trustworthiness, the historical transaction data is open for reference. One may trace back to the identity owner to find who the user is. For privacy concern, we should protect the identity, and keep sensitive data from others. In studies (Enzmann & Schneider, 2004, 2005), identity is issued as one to one relationship, but the connections between identity and transaction data are restrained by using the blind signature technique.

The Deficiencies of Existing Researches

In an ambient e-service environment, the mobile peers' composition is dynamic. Users may not stay in the environment for a long time. Mobile peers in such environment form a dynamic-organized structure. Unlike in the fixed Internet environment, peers do not have permanent ID. Lack of sustained identification, the trust and reputation data for mobile peers cannot be tracked. Accordingly, the trust and reputation information cannot be retained. Therefore, the ambient e-service environment should consider the refreshing of participants composition and the checking of the updated identities. Because of the ambient e-service application focus on the nearby peers' interactions, the overhead of checking the updated identities is only for a finite range and thus the communication cost is manageable. However, the issues of environment identity refreshing and identity updating for ambient e-services still await acceptable mechanisms in the future.

The Ambient Data Management for Ambient E-Services

The ambient data management problems from the embracing consideration include (1) seamless unlinkability management, (2) convenient data access control, (3) ambient data access control, and (4) carefree heterogeneous data source (An in-depth discussion of these four issues will be detailed in the ASEM section).

Seamless Unlinkability Management

Unlinkability means that users are unable to determine whether the same user caused certain specific operations in the services. In providing the seamless unlinkability management, some studies make the transactions becomes public data for normal requesters but keep the details of transaction information from the public (Enzmann et al., 2004, 2005). The others then make the recommendations or the reputation data unlinkable to their original identities (Gupta, Judge, & Ammar, 2003). Since these mechanisms were designed for the fixed-Internet environments, they are not appropriate for ambient s-services owing to their nature (temporary identity, dynamic network composition, etc.). The seamless unlinkability management problem subsequently becomes complex in the ambient e-service environment.

Figure 12. The construct of ASEM framework

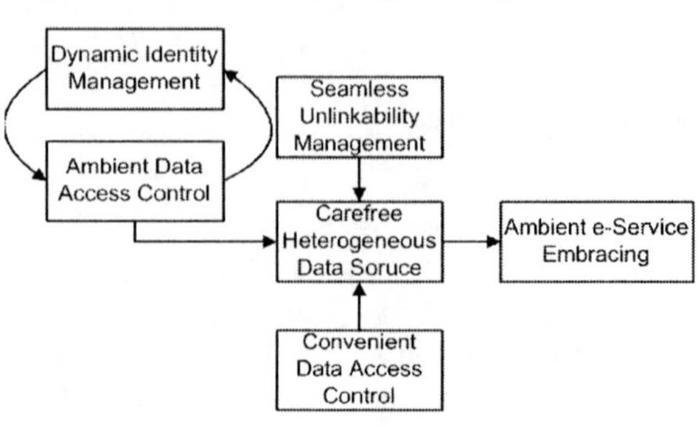

Convenient Data Access Control

This refers to making information requester access the data as easy as possible while keeping the real identity from each other. Some studies address easy authentication of data access (Wilhelm, Staamann, & Buttyan, 2000) and easy data authorization (Lin, Lu, & Yu, 2004; Wilhelm et al., 2000). A pessimistic approach to trust is also proposed to guard the agent from malicious execution environments (Wilhelm et al., 2000). Many studies work on the provision of secure data access control and authorization/authentication procedures for secure transaction. In contrast to the complex data access control procedures proposed in existing researches, what ambient e-services require is a convenient solution.

Ambient Data Access Control

The issue of ambient data access control involves the distributed data storage problem. Most of current studies related to the trust, reputation and privacy issues are focused on the fixed Internet environment (Ashrafi & Kuilboe, 2005, Enzmann et al., 2004, 2005; Golbeck, Parsia, & Hendler, 2003; Kinateder & Rothermel, 2003; Lin et al., 2004; Sabater & Sierra, 2002). Little is known about the wireless peer-to-peer environment (Wilhelm et al., 2000).

Few studies mention to update the trust data in the wireless distributed network environments (Lin et al., 2004; Shand et al., 2003).

Due to the storage and communicational limitation of mobile devices, not all the trust data could be retrieved wherever needed or stored in the mobile devices. Naturally comes to a question--"How the trustworthiness is computed?" There are two approaches about how to acquire available trust data. The local computation design calculates the trust data only from the locally obtained data (Aberer & Despotovic, 2001; Gupta et al., 2003; Shand et al., 2003; Twigg, 2003), while the global trust computation calculates from the entire trust data stored in disparate sources (Aberer & Despotovic, 2001; Castelfranchi, Falcone, & Pezzulo, 2003; Lin et al., 2004; Mui, Halberstadt, & Mohtashemi, 2003; Sabater et al., 2002). The methods to obtain trust data then involve the problem of convenient data access control.

Heterogeneous Data Source

The trust or reputation computation can be originated from two directions of heterogeneous sources. One is calculating from the experience; the other is to calculate without experience.

Over the past few decades, a considerable number of studies have been conducted on using good experience as the source of reputation computation (Golbeck et al., 2003; Mui et al., 2003; Sabater et al., 2002; Shand et al., 2003). Some studies involve recommendations based on good experience (Shand et al., 2003; Twigg, 2003). Besides good experience, bad experience is also important. Studies on trust management based on bad experience are also proposed (Aberer et al., 2001; Mui et al., 2003). The bad experiences are represented as optional information to confirm the positive experience information.

It has been recognized that trust can be generated without direct experience in three ways. The first way is grounded on prediction that is based on indirect data sources. For instance, one may get the trust or reputation data from the user groups the targeted users belongs in or have the general trust ideas about those groups (Mui et al., 2003; Sabater et al., 2002) based on the trustworthy group or communities' certificates. The second way is to compute one's trustworthiness from the other persons that you trust, like the FOAF project (Golbeck et al., 2003). Using collaborative content-based filtering is then the third way to compute trust without direct experience.

When dealing without direct experience, the importance of malicious prevention is addressed in(Castelfranchi et al., 2003). Uncertainty management and risk reasoning are also considered in (Twigg, 2003). Very few attempts have been made at the fraud and deception for the mobile environment, especially under the privacy concern.

The Deficiencies of Existing Researches

The concern with heterogeneous information source has been growing in recent years (Hertzum, Andersen, Andersen, & Hansen, 2002). Some trust and reputation systems have been proposed and various methods are provided for collecting participants' trustworthy information. Unfortunately, it is not suitable for the ambient e-service environments due to the difference in the environment architecture and design ideas. For instance, a distributed trust and reputation management framework for e-services was proposed to solve the trust issues in a distributed environment (Lin et al., 2004). In this framework, a distributed broker-based architecture was employed to gather enough information so as to make a confident judgment of the trustworthiness. Nevertheless, this solution was so designed with the client/server architecture that the brokers and the users had to live within the fixed Internet. This system has some similarities to the ambient framework, exerting the collective efforts of the broker peers to build up the trust and reputation management system. However, this system works only in the fixed Internet and is not suitable for the ambient e-service wireless peer-to-peer environments. These challenges are still awaiting future research to counteract.

AMBIENT E-SERVICE EMBRACING MODEL (ASEM)

In this section, we present a framework called Ambient e-Service Embracing Model (ASEM) that addresses the core elements (of relevance to the integrated concern of trust, reputation, and privacy) required in dynamic identity management and ambient data management so as to assure such desired features as convenience, safety, fairness and collaboration for mobile users when they engage ambient e-services.

The ASEM framework considers the conceptual ideas of trust, privacy, and reputation as an integrated construct as shown in Figure 12. The construct of Figure 12 manifests the core elements of the model together with their dependency relationships. In other words, the embracing of ambient e-services is harvested from carefree heterogeneous data source that subsequently relies on convenient data access control, seamless unlinkability and ambient data access control (that is mutually correlated with dynamic identity management). As follows are the itemized descriptions of the core elements and their dependency relationships:

- **Dynamic identity management:** Since a user identity exists only when the user is within an ambient environment, the identity would expire when the ambient e-service is unreachable. Accordingly, dynamic identity management aims to enable the identities dynamically issued being different when a mobile peer leaves the environment and re-enters the environment again (even though the mobile device used is the same).
- **Ambient data access control:** Owing to the dynamic structures of participants' composition, the updating of the environment of the distributed data storage becomes indispensable (for subsequent accounting of the integrated concern of privacy, reputation, and trust). Ambient data access aims at facilitating the manipulation of this updating and accessing in the ambient environments.
- **Correlation of dynamic identity management and ambient data access control:** Ambient data access control relies on dynamic identity management for that the updating of the environment of the distributed data storage requires the knowledge of the dynamic composition structures of participants of their dynamically issued identifiers. Conversely, dynamic identity management depends on ambient data access control because a dynamically issued identity would be recorded in the device storage of a mobile user.
- **Seamless unlinkability management:** Owing to the privacy concern, the e-service providers are allowed to attain only the needed information from the mobile users. In other words, the e-service providers acquire information from untraceable identities. A blind or unlinkable identity from user's trust, reputation records should be furnished when a mobile user poses a query to the e-service providers. Seamless unlinkability identity aims at designing unlinkability so as to encourage the carefree access of the heterogeneous data sources when embracing ambient e-services.
- **Convenient data access control:** Due to physical limitations of mobile devices of users, ambient e-services require an easy authorization and authentication process. This process has to take into account such questions as what kinds of authentication are required for different ambient e-services. How many steps or parameters can be involved in authentication execution for

being considered as an easy authentication process. Convenient data access control aims to assure the required convenience in the carefree access of the heterogeneous data sources when embracing ambient e-services.

- **Carefree heterogeneous data sources:** Since the trust or reputation data is treated as a particularly major factor that influences the risk assessment of ambient e-services, the heterogeneous data sources from which trust or reputation is obtained become substantial. Heterogeneous data sources, in general, include the data based on experience, the information gathered without experience, the information based on the social relationships among mobile users. Accordingly, these heterogeneous data sources are of different weights to influence safety and fairness of ambient e-services. In other words, carefree heterogeneous data sources intend to ensure such a carefree perception (i.e., safety and fairness) in ambient e-services. This perception significantly affects the success of ambient e-service embracing.

The conceptual idea of trust, reputation, and privacy concerns for ambient e-services are now consolidated as an integrated model of ASEM. However, it is required to further determine what level of trust (and its attributes) for different ambient e-services should be provided so as to yield the success of ambient e-services and their implementation. We need a structured methodology to solve the short-lived identity's problems under the nature of ambient e-service environment. A set of metrics should be designed in order to enable the benchmark processes of ambient e-service systems implementation in the future.

In our work of Hwang and Yuan (2006), a multiple layered anonymous pseudonym system was proposed which combines interaction trust and creditability investigation enabling users to collaborate with nearby peers to establish a rapid reputation under a short-lived identity environment. In addition, an ASEM measurement design was proposed in Hwang and Yuan (2005), which identifies possible measurements for each core element of ASEM. However, different ways of rendering the infrastructure into implementations (and the evaluation of the implementations) are beyond the focus of this chapter. In the following sections, we are trying to provide a vision about how to explore the collective effort in the ambient e-service environments.

ROADMAP FOR AMBIENT E-SERVICES

We have proposed an ambient e-service framework, followed by an ASEM model for embracing and adopting ambient e-service applications. This model is believed to bestow ambient e-services fundamental guidelines for their future development in research, platforms, or applications. In other words, the roadmap for ambient e-services is two-fold: One is for the application service domain, which represents the remarkable diversity of ambient e-service applications grounding on ASEM. The other is for the platform design domain, which manifests possible solutions in shaping the ambient e-service platform design.

Application Service Domain

Ambient e-service scenario applications presuming ambient environments of mobile commerce are provisioned. As mentioned in the introduction section, ambient e-services mainly address dynamic collective efforts between mobile users and dynamic interactions with ambient environments. The ambient e-service applications are categorized reflecting the LBS types (transaction service, information service, navigation, and tracking service and safety service) as well as exhibiting dynamic collected efforts based on the peer-to-peer design.

We'll take the "Ambient shopping mall scenario" for example. The Ambient shopping mall scenario is classified as a distributed transaction service. In a shopping mall (fully equipped with wireless network infrastructures), information items (e.g., advertisement or sales promotion information) can be broadcast to passing-by peers with information broadcast station. Peers in different locations receive different information items depending on their preference. This means the experience and attained information items of peers are different to their locations and user context (e.g., user preference or interest). That is, the attained information items of a peer vary based on the peer's interactions with the shopping mall ambient environments. The customers are not required to go all over the shopping mall to receive the broadcast information items, but just pay little money to acquire a suitable information items service package based on their preferences. Alternatively, a mobile agent peer for customer can inquire with nearby peers for what they want and proceed a bartering process. This will help the new entering customers in hurry to efficiently acquire the shopping mall information.

This scenario delineates not only the case of new customers with high buyer perishability (entering the shopping mall and being in a rush to buy certain items without the knowledge of where to buy and how to buy cheap given relevant sales promotion), but also carry out the collective efforts of mobile users (e.g., collective bargaining, collective buy, or some collective agreement). Through a transaction e-service, information items (e.g., e-coupons) can be distributed not only to the mobile users falling into the broadcast range of the distributor companies, but also to the primary target peers (who really need the certain e-coupons in the right time and right place).

However, in such an ad-hoc structured environment, peers might not recognize each other. Should we trust the entire information sources? There are no evidences that all the peers are trustable. What if there is someone trying to acquire my sensitive information? There is a possibility of act of swindling; hence, users should protect themselves from any possible forms of harm. Considering a mobile user's willingness of participation, the safety and privacy issue remain the major concern. If the number of participants of an e-service diminishes, the e-service application would collapse. Accordingly, a convenient and safe environment would encourage users to participate and interact with each other.

Since different e-service applications should cope with different circumstances and bear different restrictions, the framework of ASEM outlines the guidelines for the implementation of ambient e-service. For example, if the trading process employs a bartering mechanism (that does not involve real money), the required level of trust is comparatively lower than those using official currency. In other words, various ambient e-service applications are of particularly different concerns of the factors outlined in ASEM and lead to different ambient e-service implementation.

ASEM also enables diminishing the chance of fraud and deceit. Mobile users can obtain necessary decision information of certain assured quality from nearby sources (e.g. mobile users, service providers). Different information sources are exerted to facilitate great utilities derived in behalf of users. Once the risk level of transactions can be curtailed, the convenience interactions of ambient e-services would be more prevalent and aggrandizing the chances of realizing the power of the collective efforts between mobile users.

Platform Design Domain

In this section, we bring up some ideas for the future design of ambient e-service platforms (that constitute dynamic identity management, ambient data access control, seamless unlinkability management, and convenience data access control).

Dynamic identity management and ambient data access control particularly concern the nature of an ambient e-service's environment (e.g., wireless communication distance, handheld device storage capacity, and temporary identity). For the example of the shopping mall scenario application, the communication ranges of the ad-hoc wireless networks centered on a mobile user vary from place to place. The mobile user is required to update the surrounding nearby peer list at their current location, and check if there are other peers' offerings fitting their needs. That is, the information update of the surrounding peers is necessary. However, the desired update type (update frequency) varies between applications. In the shopping mall application, it is not necessary to engage a constant update of the list of the surrounding peers because the movement of a user often is not so fast. Accordingly, a periodical update type is a right choice of the update-type design for the ambient shopping mall scenario.

This short-term lifetime identity is a unique property in ambient environments. As mentioned in the ASEM section, Dynamic Identity Management aims to issue different identities for a mobile peer when the peer leaves the environment and re-enters the environment again (even though the mobile device used is the same). However, existing P2P systems/solutions are still with long-lived identities. For instance, as addressed in Resnick, Zeckhauser, Friedman, and Kuwabara (2000), reputation systems generally take on three properties: (1) entities are long-lived; (2) feedback about current interactions is captured and distributed; (3) past feedback guides buyer decisions. In other words, the identities in ambient e-service environments are short-lived and localized, and thus existing methods/solutions requiring long-lived identities can not be applied to our environments.

On the other hand, the nature of ambient environment (localized/short period lifetime's identities) could result in the material change of the reputation's basics as well as other issues (trust/traceability/privacy). How to derive a reputation system coping with the nature of ambient environments accordingly becomes new a challenge to straighten out.

Regarding seamless unlinkability management, the requirements for different ambient e-service scenarios are also different. In the ambient shopping mall scenario, if a transaction involves just information items, the amount of necessary information required would be less than those transactions that involve real money. Required security level for privacy concern (e.g., identity tracing back concern, transaction records) can be handled by associating weights with respect to a user's unique needs and circumstances. A blind signature method provides higher untraceable level than the pseudo identity. Alternatively, a user may have various role identities for different transactions, and this then involves both dynamic identity management and seamless unlinkability management.

Convenience data access control facilitates the ambient e-service realization. A single sign-on authorization is more acceptable than those complex authorization processes. While the identity authentication can be achieved by various techniques (e.g., Strong authentication, password, etc.), the proper method is based on a users' unique needs and preference.

Respecting the heterogeneity of data sources, since all data sources have their own risk levels (e.g., risk probabilities), carefree heterogeneous data sources should draw upon the entire data sources so as to enable the computation required for decision making. This computation takes into account the risk level, heterogeneity, and the quantity of available data. However, an economic evaluation method is indispensable due to the computational limitation of ambient handheld devices.

Benefits of ASEM

ASEM aims to provide the design guidelines of the platforms/infrastructures for supporting ambient e-services with a safety and trustworthy environment as well as congregating the collective effort of mobile users within the environment. In this section, the benefits of ASEM from the socio-economic perspective are briefly discussed (in addition to the justification of ASEM rendered being technologically possible as addressed in previous sections).

From the economic view for privacy invasion, anecdotal evidence shows that people are willing to disclose personal information for potential monetary savings (Russell, 1989), and people do join Web sites for free gifts and catalogs. Those evidence supports that individuals respond to economic incentives in deciding whether to disclose information. On the other hand, in various organizational and marketing contexts, concern of privacy invasion have been shown to depend on information control, outcomes arising from disclosures, information type and sensitivity, perceived relevancy of information use, and target of disclosures. Hoffman, Novak, and Peralta (1999) claimed that nearly 63% of consumers would not provide information to Web sites owing to lack of trust.

From the socio-economic view, our method is to be evaluated in terms of a cost-benefit analysis and expect the majority benefit would eliminate privacy invasion. In other words, with our method privacy of a person's persona would be appropriately protected because all the real personal identities are hidden. Seamless Unlinkability Management enables users to control their owned information in accord with the information type and sensitivity; users are able to decide whether to disclosure the information or not, as well as the target of their information disclosed to.

Furthermore, users within the ambient environment may provide various data sources (i.e., experience or subjective opinions) for others to make a strategic decision. These collective efforts encourage the building of the sense of ambient trust by engaging the reliability of fraud detection in ambient e-service environments.

However, some systematical costs are required. Making decisions with heterogeneous data source provide a comparative reliability rather than depending on their own information, especially in the dynamic environment. When the number of peers exceeds the limit of computation capability, the complexity of data management and computation will become a major problem especially in a Peer-to-Peer environment. For preliminary estimates, establishing a trustworthy ambient environment with privacy protection might have to trade with some efficiency loss. Therefore, the trade-off between the cost and benefit is a major issue for further research. At the moment, this chapter mainly focuses on the framework prospect, but we intend to provide a vision of collective wisdom within ambient e-service environment. However, the implementation or systematical evaluations are not the focus of this chapter.

In summary, with the supporting infrastructures (delimited by ASEM), ambient e-service applications are believed to bring us a new carefree information/service era. Let's take the shopping mall scenario for example. Mobile users can acquire desired information items very conveniently. That is, even a user communicating with other unknown mobile users, there is still measurable data for the user to consider, such as numerous nearby unknown users' experience or opinions gathered to serve as a reference material for advanced transaction decisions. Users can determine their actions based on various information sources, and decide which one is suitable for their current needs. Fraud and untruthful activities can also be diminished with the collective effort from those participants.

CONCLUSION

Ambient e-services address dynamic collective efforts of mobile users dynamically engaging interactions in the ambient environments, rendering a new paradigm of mobile commerce promising revolutionary business models. This chapter presents an ambient e-services framework characterizing three supporting stacks. The ambient value stack describes the value process in ambient environments. The ambient technology stack identifies the technology process to ensure connectivity and security in ambient interactions and cooperation between peers and then realize powerful collective efforts. The environment stack then represents the ambient basics for the collaborations.

Ambient e-services applications can be divided into two types. One is for the distributed trading; another is for the distributed collaboration. However, social context and significant rapid growth of connections enabled by P2P are the two major incentives for applying ambient e-service to such revolutionary business models. We exemplify several ambient e-service applications. Those applications differ from existing mobile e-services (grounded on client/server design) in terms of the focus of the dynamic interactions between peers in dynamic ambient e-service environments.

In this chapter, we also present another framework called Ambient e-Service Embracing Model (ASEM) that addresses the core elements (of relevance to the integrated concern of trust, reputation and privacy) required for assuring such desired features as convenience, safety, fairness and collaboration for mobile users when they engage ambient e-services. This framework manifests the relationship between the issues of dynamic identity management and ambient data management. The framework abstracts the trust, reputation, and privacy concerns into an integrated consideration. Since different e-service applications are of different circumstances and bear different restrictions, the framework of ASEM also outlines the guidelines for the implementation of ambient e-service applications and the platforms.

The fruitful future research includes a further in-depth evaluation of ASEM, a complete design of the ASEM core elements, and a fielded implementation of certain ambient e-services deriving economic models of ambient e-services.

REFERENCES

Aberer, K., & Despotovic, Z. (2001). Managing trust in a peer-2-peer information system. In *Proceedings of the Conference on Information and Knowledge Management* (pp. 310-317). CIKM01. November 5-10, 2001, Atlanta, Georgia.

Ashrafi, N., & Kuilboer, J. P. (2005). Privacy protection via technology: Platform for privacy preferences (P3P). *International Journal of E-Business Research, 1*(2), 56-69.

Baida, Z., Gordijn, J., Akkermans, H., Saele, H., & Morch, A. Z. (2005). Finding e-service offerings by computer-supported customer need reasoning, *International Journal of E-Business Research, 1*(3), 91-112.

Castelfranchi, C., Falcone, R., & Pezzulo, G. (2003). Integrating trustfulness and decision using fuzzy cognitive maps. *Trust Management 2003, LNCS 2692* (pp. 195-210).

Enzmann, M., & Schneider, M. (2004). A privacy-friendly loyalty system for electronic marketplaces. In *Proceedings of the 2004 IEEE International Conference on e-Technology, e-Commerce, and e-Service* (EEE04), Taiwan.

Enzmann, M., & Schneider, M. (2005). Improving customer retention in e-commerce through a secure and privacy-enhanced loyalty system. *Information Systems Frontiers, 7*(4-5), 359-370, December 2005.

Golbeck, J., Parsia, B., & Hendler, J. (2003). Trust networks on the semantic Web. *Proceedings of Cooperative Intelligent Agents 2003.*

Gupta, M., Judge, P., & Ammar, M. (2003). A reputation system for peer-to-peer networks. *NOSSDAV'03.* (Jun. 1-3, 2003) 144-152.

Hertzum, M., Andersen, H., Andersen, V., & Hansen, C. (2002). Trust in information sources: Seeking information from people, documents, and virtual agents. *Interacting with Computers, 14*(5), 575-599.

Hoffman, D. L., Novak, T. P., & Peralta, M. A. (1999). Building consumer trust online. *Communications of the ACM, 42*(4), 80-85.

Hoy, Grubbs, M., & Phelps, J. (2003). Consumer privacy and security protection on church Web sites: Reasons for concern. *Journal of Public Policy and Marketing, 22*(1), 58-70.

Hwang, Y. C., & Yuan, S. T. (2005). Ambient e-service embracing model. In *Proceedings of the 7th IEEE International Conference on E-Commerce Technology* (pp. 535-538). (CEC2005) Germany.

Hwang Y. C., & Yuan S. T. (2006). Technical report: Exploring collective wisdom in ambient e-service environment: implementation method and evaluations. Taiwan: National Cheng-Chi University.

Kinateder, M., & Rothermel, K. (2003). Architecture and algorithms for a distributed reputation system. *Trust Management 2003, LNCS 2692* (pp. 1-16).

Lim, E., & Saiu, K. (2003). *Advances in mobile commerce technologies.* Hershey, PA: Idea Group Publishing.

Lin, K., Lu, H., & Yu, T. (2004). A distributed trust and reputation management framework for e-services. *IEEE International Conference on Services Computing*, Shanghai, China.

Mui, L., Halberstadt, A., & Mohtashemi, M. (2003). Evaluating reputation in multi-agents systems. In R. Falcone, S. Barber, L. Korba, & M. Singh (Eds), *Trust, reputation, and security: theories and practice* (pp. 123-137). Berlin: Springer-Verlag.

Odlyzko, A. (2003). Privacy, economics, and price discrimination on the Internet. *The 5th International Conference on Electronic Commerce* (ICEC 2003). ACM Press.

Paternò, F. (2003). Understanding interaction with mobile devices. *Interacting with Computers, 15*(4), 473-478.

Resnick, P., Zeckhauser, R., Friedman, E., & Kuwabara, K. (2000). Reputation systems: Facilitating trust in Internet interactions. *Communications of the ACM, 43*(12), 45-48.

Roussos, G., Peterson, D., & Patel, U. (2003). Mobile identity management: An enacted view. *International Journal of E-Commerce, 8*(1), 81-100.

Russell, C. (1989). Kiss and tell *American Demographics, 11*(12), 2.

Sabater, J., & Sierra, C. (2002). Reputation and social network analysis in multi-agent systems. *The 1st International Joint Conference on Autonomous Agents & Multiagent Systems* (pp. 475-482). AAMAS'02, July 15-19, 2002, Bologna, Italy.

Schilit, B., Adams, N., & Want, R. (1994). Context-aware computing applications.In *Proceedings of the 1st International Workshop on Mobile Computing Systems and Applications* (pp. 85-90).

Shand, B., Dimmonck, N., & Bacon, J. (2003). Trust for ubiquitous, transparent collaboration. In *Proceedings of the 1st IEEE International Conference on Pervasive Computing and Communications* (PerCom'03).

Twigg, A. (2003). A subjective approach to routing in P2P and ad hoc networks. *Trust Management 2003* (pp. 225-238), LNCS 2692.

Wilhelm, U. G., Staamann, S. M., & Buttyan, L. (2000). A pessimistic approach to trust in mobile agent platforms. *IEEE Internet Computing* (pp. 40-48), September-October.

This work was previously published in International Journal of E-Business Research, Vol. 3, Issue 1, edited by I. Lee, pp. 51-73, copyright 2007 by IGI Publishing, formerly known as Idea Group Publishing (an imprint of IGI Global).

Chapter 4.41
Automating Governmental Cross-Agency Processes Using Web Service Orchestration:
A Gap Analysis

Jeffrey Gortmaker
Delft University of Technology, The Netherlands

Marijn Janssen
Delft University of Technology, The Netherlands

ABSTRACT

In response to the demand for better service provisioning, governments from all over the world are looking for technologies to automate their cross-agency processes. This chapter investigates the applicability of Web service orchestration for the automation of governmental cross-agency service delivery processes by investigating a case study of a business counter. Our case study shows that Web service orchestration using BPEL4WS is a feasible technology for automating governmental cross-agency service-delivery processes, but also shows a gap between the capabilities of Web service orchestration technology and the organizational arrangements needed for automating the processes. We identified three organizational issues that at least need to be addressed before governments can profit fully from the advantages of Web service orchestration technology: (1) ensuring correct and in-time execution of business processes; (2) information sharing; and (3) responsibility and accountability.

INTRODUCTION

As an increasing number of governmental service-delivery processes involve multiple (semi-) autonomous agencies, a huge challenge for governments from all over the world is designing their cross-agency processes. This is caused by the inherent structure of public administration and by the need to become more customer-centric. First, the fragmented nature of governments (e.g., Wimmer, 2002) causes the activities that make up a single, atomic governmental service, for example, a liquor license, often involve several governmental agencies. Under the influence of governmental reforms, such as New Public Management (NPM) (e.g., Hood, 1991), governments became more decentralized, leading to more departments, agencies, or even external parties involved in service-delivery processes. An example is a liquor license, which includes tasks to be performed by several municipal departments, the fire department, the justice department, and the police.

The second main reason for cross-agency processes is the aim to reduce the administrative burdens, or "red tape," for citizens and businesses and to become more citizen centric (e.g., Cabinet Office, 2000; Dutch Government, 2003, 2004; Ongaro, 2004). The clients of the government, citizens, and businesses expect the public sector to increase their attention on customer service, just as businesses have done in response to the rise of Internet technologies (Donnelly, Wisniewski, Dalrymple, & Curry, 1995; McIvor, McHugh, & Cadden, 2002). This requires governments to rethink their service offerings, for example, start the joint offering of a permit to build a house and a permit to tear down the old building in place. Several (semi-) autonomous agencies working together to reach a common goal, here to deliver a service, is often called "joined-up government" (Ling, 2002; Pollitt, 2003).

Crucial to the improvement of governmental service delivery and the reduction of administrative burdens is the automation of cross-agency service-delivery processes. To offer seamlessly integrated services, the service-delivery processes of the different subservices should be coordinated. The cross-governmental collaboration in the delivery of services to its citizens is getting more and more attention and is one of the main issues in national e-government strategies (Accenture, 2005).

A promising technology that offers many advantages to the problem of automating cross-agency processes is Web service orchestration (Gortmaker, Janssen & Wagenaar, 2004). Web service technology is based upon the notion of a service-oriented architecture (SOA), an architectural paradigm according to which application functionality is not provided by large monolithic information systems, but is instead created by using relatively small-grained components which can be invoked as Web services. SOA provides the ability to register, discover, and use services, where the architecture is dynamic by nature. Web service orchestration coordinates Web services by means of a process flow in which the Web services are invoked according to a predefined sequence. Automating cross-agency business processes using Web service orchestration offers flexibility in business processes, so changes in law can be supported quickly. Moreover functionality encapsulated in components can be reused in various business processes and investments in legacy systems can be leveraged (Gortmaker et al., 2004).

The objective of this chapter is to investigate the feasibility of Web service orchestration technology for the automation of cross-agency processes, based on a case study of cross-governmental service-delivery processes at a business counter. First, we present an overview of Web service orchestration technology and introduce the business counter and its processes. Thereafter, we present a prototype to demonstrate the feasibility of Web service orchestration for the automation of cross-agency processes, and conclude that several important organizational-related issues need to be addressed when employing Web service orchestration for supporting cross-agency business processes.

RESEARCH APPROACH

In order to investigate the feasibility of Web service orchestration, both a literature review into Web services and Web service orchestration, and a case study were conducted.

The case study was conducted at the business counter for the hotel and catering industry at a medium-sized municipality in the Netherlands. This case was chosen because it is regarded as a best practice in the Netherlands as an account-manager-operated one-stop-shop. At the business counter, we analyzed five representative cross-agency service-delivery processes in detail: two processes that are needed for pouring liquor, a license to place gambling machines, an environmental permit, and a license for organizing special events. The processes were analyzed and a gap analysis was made by conducing semistructured interviews with policy makers, operational managers, back office employees, IT staff, customer representatives, and account managers from the business counter. Due to the explorative nature of this case study, interviews were conducted in a semistructured fashion, without a strict interview protocol, but with the use of some open questions to start and guide the interviews. A total of 12 people were interviewed between one and three times. Also, relevant memos, strategy statements, Web sites, and internal reports were studied.

WEB SERVICE ORCHESTRATION TECHNOLOGY

In this section we present a brief overview of Web service orchestration technology and related protocols. A more in-depth presentation of SOA, the Web service technology stack and Web service orchestration can be found in Gortmaker, Janssen, and Wagenaar (2005) and Janssen, Gortmaker, and Wagenaar (2006). Web service orchestration technology is based upon the notion of a *service-oriented architecture* (SOA). Due to its loosely-coupled nature, the SOA-paradigm is very suitable for orchestrating service-delivery processes that run across relatively autonomous agencies. Agencies can provide services to other agencies that can invoke them as subservices in their business processes. A SOA makes it possible to quickly assemble new compound services out of existing services.

Web services are an important technology for realizing SOA. Web services are a technology that enables the provisioning of functionality, on an application level, or on a business level, by means of a standardized interface in a way that they are easily invoked via Internet protocols. Web services are said to be modular, accessible, well-described, implementation-independent, and interoperable (Fremantle, Weerawarana, & Khalaf, 2002).

Web service technology consists of a collection of protocols needed to implement a SOA. This "Web service stack" first defines basic technologies, such as HTTP, XML, and XML schema for the creating of documents and communication between the different Web services. The basic functionality of a SOA is provided by the message and description layers. The interface of a Web service is defined by means of Web Service Definition Language (WSDL), and the messages by which the services can be invoked are defined using SOAP (simple object access protocol). To make it easier to discover existing Web services, a service provider can register its Web services in a Web service directory through UDDI (Universal Description, Discovery and Integration).

Higher on the Web services stack are the standards for service composition, combining two or more services together to obtain a new composite service. These are different ways to create composite services. One form of constrained aggregation is coordinating them by means of a process flow that invokes the different subservices. Service composition using process flows comes in two flavors: Web service orchestration and Web service choreography. The difference between these two forms is subtle, and they are therefore sometimes erroneously considered as synonyms. There is, however, a major distinction between the two. Web service choreography specifies only the possible sequences between the public message exchanges between different agencies. Web service orchestration requires that the whole process needed for offering the service is defined at one place. This is an executable process, defined from the perspective of one participant, and offers an overview of all internal and external Web services that need to be invoked in the process.

As choreography does not require the responsibility for the whole process to be located at one place, it is less suitable for the coordination of cross-agency service delivery processes. It can, however, be used for coordinating interactions between different agencies within the service-delivery process.

Wohed, Van der Aalst, Dumas, and Hofstede (2003) define an executable business process as specifying "the execution order between a number of constituent activities, the partners involved, the messages exchanged between these partners, and the fault and exception handling mechanisms." In Web service orchestration, these activities are typically performed by Web services that are invoked from a process by means of their standardized Web service interface.

Many competing proposals for process specification languages, including ebXML BPSS, WSCI, WSFL, XLANG, BPML, have been made, but the standard language for Web service orchestration is BPEL4WS, Business Process Execution Language for Web Services (Andrews et al., 2003), BPEL for short, a specification developed by IBM and Microsoft, based on their respective standards WSFL and XLANG. BPEL can be viewed as a layer on top of WSDL, as it uses the properties of Web services that are specified by means of WSDL.

A process that is specified in BPEL consists of two types of activities: basic activities that specify the tasks that are to be performed, such as *receive* an invocation, *reply* to the service requester, *wait* for a specified amount of time, and structured activities as *switch* for conditional branching, *while* for repeating parts of the business process, and *sequence* for performing tasks in parallel. The structured activities determine the structure, or the sequencing of the process, and the basic activities determine what happens in the process, for example, the invocation of a WS, receiving a message from a Web service, and so forth.

BUSINESS COUNTER

Although the business counter for the hotel and catering industry is viewed as a best practice as it consists of account managers functioning as one-stop shops and passing permit applications through to the back office, in the current situation, there is hardly any ICT support. A model describing the high-level interactions between the actors involved is depicted in Figure 1. For almost all permit applications, the applicant has to schedule an appointment with the business counter, after which the account manager coordinates the interactions with the back office and the other agencies. Many of the permit requests exceed the desired lead times.

The entrepreneurs, the customers of the business counter, are often bound to the opening hours of their own business and face difficulties having to meet the openings hours of the business counters. Moreover, they would like to have a faster response time and insight into the status of their requests, as this enables the further development of their business. The city council recognizes the entrepreneurs' needs and wants to know if Web service orchestration technology is suitable for improving the cross-agency processes.

A liquor license[1] is one of the most important permits for the hotel and catering industry. Every restaurant or café that pours alcohol is obliged to apply for a license. For requesting a license, an entrepreneur can contact the business counter. After this first contact, an intake interview is planned, where civil servants of the business counter, the back office, and sometimes of other involved agencies are present. After this meeting, the entrepreneur has to fill in an application form and return it, together with the needed official documents, for example, a floor plan.

Hereafter, the name, address, and place of residence of the applicant are checked. If the applicant lives in the municipality, this activity is performed by the back office, otherwise a request has to be sent to another municipality. Next, the

Figure 1. Actors and interactions in liquor-licensing process

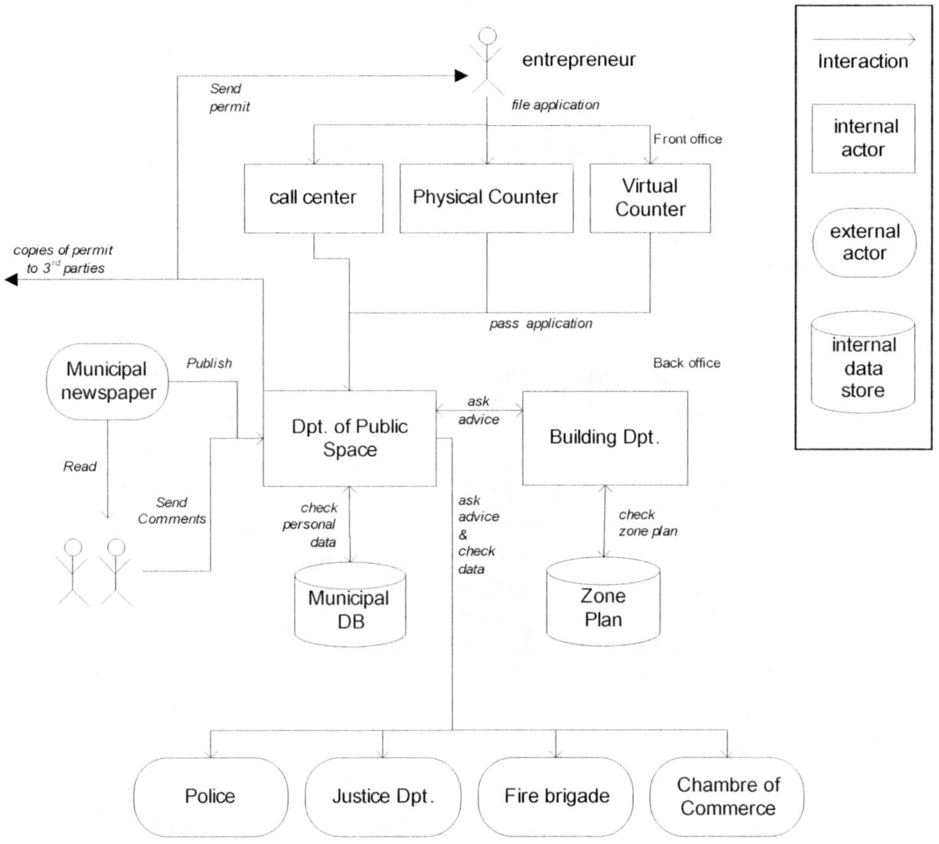

justice department is asked for advice; they check whether the applicant has a criminal record or not. The police are also asked for advice about the applicant, but look for "softer" evidence, for example, fines, crimes that were not proven, or for which someone has not been sentenced yet. Also the fire department is asked for advice concerning the construction and safety of the building. Finally, the building department has to check whether the building meets all legal requirements.

On the basis of these advices, the back office employee draws up a license, or a letter stating the reasons for refusing the license. Copies of the issues license are sent to third parties such as the police, the chamber of commerce, and the fire department.

WEB SERVICE ORCHESTRATION AT THE BUSINESS COUNTER

To determine the feasibility of Web service orchestration for supporting cross-agency processes, a prototype of automating the liquor-licensing process using BPEL4WS was built. Figure 2 shows a graphical representation of a part of the cross-agency process implemented in BPEL. As real-life BPEL processes are usually very complex and consist of many elements, only part of the process could be shown. Also several process steps, mostly concerning the assigning of variables, were omitted from the picture. The figure contains a screenshot from Oracle JDeveloper BPEL Designer, the process designer belonging to their orchestration server, Oracle BPEL Process Manager (Oracle, 2004).

On the left of Figure 2 the file menu is shown, the BPEL process constructs are shown on the middle and right part of the figure. The process is started (see call out 2 in Figure 2) after the applicant initiates the BPEL process (1) by filling in an online application form on the client. First, an internal Web service (4) to check whether the form is correctly filled in, the "InputCheckService," is invoked (3). When not all fields are filled in correctly (5), an error-message is prompted back to the applicant (6). When the application is complete, two simultaneous subprocesses are started (7): the application is published in the municipal newspaper (8) (which was not implemented in this prototype) and a Web service at the police (10), "Advice_Police," is invoked (9) to get information about the criminal record of the applicant. Only a Web service providing access to the business processes of the police is shown in this picture, but every agency or organization, the justice department, the fire department, or the chamber of commerce that can offer Web service access to its business processes can be linked into a cross-agency process in similar fashion. The complex decision-making process on the license request is also not shown in the figure.

GAP ANALYSIS

The prototype of the liquor-licensing process demonstrates that Web service orchestration using BPEL4WS is a feasible technology for automating the cross-agency processes at the business counter.

Although Web service orchestration is a suitable technology for automating governmental cross-agency processes, we found that several organizational-oriented issues need to be addressed when implementing Web services orchestration for automating cross-agency processes. We categorized the main issues into three categories: (1) ensuring the correct and in-time execution of subprocesses, (2) facilitating the sharing of information among the agencies, and (3) allocating responsibilities and ensuring accountability

Figure 2. Screenshot of BPEL-editor showing part of the liquor-licensing process

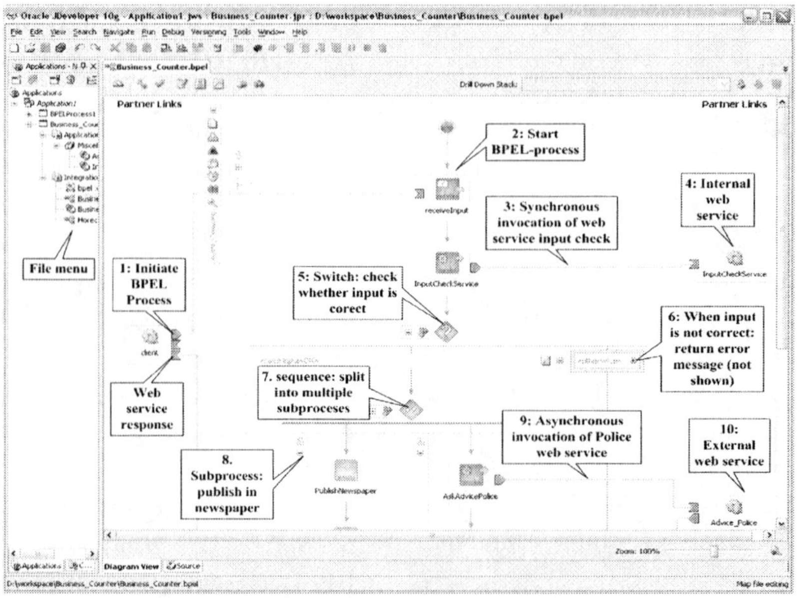

among agencies participating in the cross-agency processes. These three categories of issues will be discussed in more detail in the following subsections.

Correct and In-Time Execution of Business Processes

One of the main issues that should be dealt with when automating business processes is to ensure that every subservice in the cross-agency service-delivery process is fully completed in time. This aspect is further complicated by the fact that in cross-agency processes there is no hierarchical control of one agency over all the other agencies.

At the business counter, we found that guarding the lead times of the overall liquor-licensing process is a major problem, as some of the required subservices sometimes take a long time to complete, or are even not completed at all.

This problem was mentioned many times during the interviews, by employees of the business counter, employees of the governmental back offices, but also by the customers, who were frustrated that obtaining a permit could take so much time. One of the customers stated that it took so much time for a liquor license to be obtained. Although there were formal lead times that needed to be met by the municipality, there were no direct sanctions on those lead times, such as is the case with certain building permits, which are automatically granted if the lead times are exceeded. From the interviews with the employees at the municipality it turned out that it was relatively easy to extend a deadline. Deadline extension was possible by simply sending a letter to the requester. These employees indicated that other agencies involved in the licensing process not reacting in time were the major cause of these delays. One striking example is checking the address of applicants that live in another municipality, which has to be performed by the other municipality. This simple check can in practice take as long as three weeks or more, and can take as much as four requests before an answer can be expected. As there is no formal way of requesting the other municipalities to perform this task in time, controlling the lead times is difficult to accomplish.

A solution to this problem could be ensuring correct and in-time execution of every subservice by agreeing upon service levels between agencies, but simply agreeing beforehand upon service levels between the business counter and the different agencies is not sufficient. The service levels need to be constantly monitored, and mechanisms that respond when a service fails, when a service does not produce the required answer, or does not answer in time, should be put in place.

Information Sharing

Each actor has a registry storing different kinds of data. Data were sometimes found to be inconsistent between registries; that is, address data are updated by one agency but not by the others. Changes in data necessary for executing the activities of agencies should be immediately shared among these actors. The sharing of information between governmental agencies can also help to avoid opportunistic behavior of permit requesters. If one agency or department rejects a permit they might try to acquire the permit at another agency or department. Sharing of information should result in consistent decision making. Another advantage of information sharing is that entrepreneurs only have to fill in the personal data that has been changed in time or has to be added newly. When there are only two agencies involved, information sharing is still relatively straightforward. When multiple agencies that all use and update each others information, as is often the case with cross-agency service-delivery processes, are involved, this becomes more difficult.

In the case study at the business counter many issues related to inadequate information sharing were found. First, the customers complained about having to fill in the same information again every time applying for another license. Inconsistencies among different governmental databases were also found, as one customer stated that his business was registered under at least three different names in the databases of the tax office, the municipality, and the chamber of commerce. The employees at the business counter and the back office indicated that sometimes it was difficult to obtain a consistent view on the status of an application. When a customer was, for example, requested for additional information by the back office employee, the employee at the business counter would not always know this the next time he had a meeting with that customer. In other words, there was not something like an integral customer view. According to the employees at the municipality, that was also noticed by some "customers," as customers had the tendency to just ask another employee the same question when they got a negative answer from the first employee. Furthermore it was interesting to notice that the municipality did not have an overview of the licenses and permits granted in the past. If an overview was asked about, for example, the number of restaurants in the municipality, this was answered by asking the fire department, as they had their own database which apparently was more accurate. Even within the municipality, a different back office, such as the building department, had its own database. This database was also not linked to other databases within the municipality.

Currently, many of these problems were solved informally, by telephone, or by face-to-face communication. In case of the automation of these cross-agency processes, this ad-hoc way of solving problems is not possible anymore and a more robust information-sharing mechanism should be put in place. The issue of information sharing will become even more important when in 2007 a new law comes into effect. This law states that citizens cannot be asked to provide personal data already available somewhere else within the government (Dutch Government, 2003).

A major issue with information sharing is privacy (e.g., Ali Eldin & Wagenaar, 2004). Not all agencies need access to all collected personal data. A typical example is the data resulting from the check of the criminal record of the applicant. This data is privacy-sensitive and not relevant for other agencies. Therefore it should not be provided to other parties, such as the building department and the chamber of commerce.

Accountability and Responsibility

A major issue with orchestration is the allocation of responsibilities among the many actors. Who takes the overall responsibility for monitoring the progress and ensuring the quality of the individual performers and products/services provided? Who is accountable for failure when different services provided by external partners are orchestrated into the business processes? Clearly defined responsibilities and formal organizational procedures stating how to deal with these questions need to be agreed upon by all agencies involved in order to avoid surprises and ad-hoc actions when trying to deal with them.

Accountability is an important requirement for the whole public sector (Bovens, 1998). For governmental service-delivery processes, it is especially important that the processes are transparent, non-discriminating, and consistent, and that the decisions made in the process are well motivated, and made by the right person. Citizens and businesses no longer accept a black-box view of the service delivery process, but want to know what steps are taken in a decision-making process.

Ensuring accountability for governmental service-delivery processes running across different organizations is especially difficult, as it has to cope with different (semi-) autonomous agencies that are involved in the process.

Problems with accountability of the cross-agency processes at the business counter were the inability to provide status information or to account for lead times by employees in the front office, as they did not have enough information for this. But also back office employees that often had difficulties explaining why lead times were exceeded, or what the status of an application was. The division of responsibilities was not always clear between the business counter and the back office. This was partly because before the business counter was put in place, the employee at the business counter used to work at the back office. Also employees at the business counter and back office stated they were each others stand in, even though they both had direct colleagues who would be more logical candidates for this from an organizational point of view. This makes it difficult and not transparent to answer questions of customers about why a certain decision was taken, or whether the correct procedures were followed.

Ensuring accountability of cross-agency service-delivery processes requires specialized coordination mechanisms that ensure that the outcome of every process step is recorded, and that the overall process has run the way it was supposed to. No one should be able to change the stored information, as the information might be used as evidence.

FUTURE TRENDS IN WEB SERVICE ORCHESTRATION

Business process automation was traditionally the field of workflow management (WfM) and business processes consisted mostly of human performed activities without using functionality offered by information systems. Nowadays, a shift from WfM towards BPM (Business Process Management) is occurring, where on top of the design, configuration, and enactment of business processes, also a module to analyze these processes is present (Van der Aalst, Hofstede, & Weske, 2003). Although Web service orchestration is a very promising technology, the developments in the orchestration market go rapidly. Orchestration servers are incorporating more and more levels of functionality. It is expected that future BPM products will be more and more capable to deal with invoking Web services and that BPEL implementations will offer more and more advanced workflow capabilities, or in other words that the paradigms behind Web service technology and business process management (BPM) will merge slowly (Zhao & Cheng, 2005).

We also observe that the Enterprise Application Integration market is converging with the Workflow/BPM market with as a provisional climax the acquiring of leading BPM-vendor Staffware by Enterprise Application Integrator Tibco (Tibco, 2004). Considering the current momentum behind BPEL, other BPM vendors are expected to support BPEL in the near future, all resulting in large BPM or business process integration suites with BPEL support that are capable of coupling applications, processes, and businesses.

CONCLUSION

The objective of this chapter is to investigate the feasibility of Web service orchestration technology for the automation of cross-agency processes. Based on a case study of cross-governmental service-delivery processes at a business counter and using a prototype we conclude that Web services and Web service orchestration in particular have huge potential for the automation of governmental cross agency service-delivery processes. We also conclude that the following three categories of organizational-oriented issues need to be addressed when implementing Web services orchestration for automating cross-agency processes to leverage the full potential of Web service orchestration technology: (1) ensuring the correct and in-time execution of subprocesses, (2) facilitating the sharing of information among the agencies, and (3) allocating responsibilities and ensuring accountability among agencies participating in the cross-agency processes. Further research focuses on supporting public managers in dealing with these issues when designing their automated cross-agency processes.

REFERENCES

Accenture. (2005). *Leadership in customer service: New expectations, new experiences.* Retrieved June 23, 2006, from ftp://www.accenture.com/NR/rdonlyres/F4CE4C8-9330-4450-BB4A-AF4E265C88D4/0/leadership_cust.pdf

Ali Eldin, A., & Wagenaar, R. (2004). *Towards users driven privacy control.* Paper presented at the 2004 IEEE International Conference on Systems, Man and Cybernetics, The Hague.

Andrews, T., Curbera, F., Dholakia, H., Goland, Y., Klein, J., Leymann, F., et al. (2003). *Business process execution language for Web services version 1.1.* Retrieved June 23, 2006, from ftp://www6.software.ibm.com/software/developer/library/ws-bpel.pdf

Bovens, M. (1998). *The quest for responsibility: Accountability and citzenship in complex organisations.* Cambridge: Cambridge University Press.

Cabinet Office. (2000). *E.gov: Electronic government services for the 21st century.* Retrieved April 28, 2006, from http://www.number-10.gov.uk/su/delivery/foreward/frames.htm

Donnelly, M., Wisniewski, M., Dalrymple, J. F., & Curry, A. C. (1995). Measuring service quality in local government: The SERVQUAL approach. *International Journal of Public Sector Management, 8*(7), 15-20.

Dutch Government. (2003). *Actieprogramma Andere Overheid* (Action Program New Government). Retrieved December 10, 2005, from http://www.elo.nl/elo/Images/actieprog_elekt_overheid_12-98_tcm70-16092.pdf

Dutch Government. (2004). *Meer ruimte voor ondernemers door minder lasten—Van lastenproductie naar lastenreductie* (More room for entrepreneurs by decreasing the administrative burdens—from production to reduction of administrative burdens). Retrieved December 10, 2005, from http://www.minfin.nl/IPAL04-100.DOC

Fremantle, P., Weerawarana, S., & Khalaf, R. (2002). Enterprise services. *Communications of the ACM, 45*(10), 77-82.

Gortmaker, J., Janssen, M., & Wagenaar, R. W. (2004). *The advantages of Web service orchestration in perspective.* Paper presented at the 6th International Conference of Electronic Commerce, ICEC 2004, Delft, The Netherlands.

Gortmaker, J., Janssen, M., & Wagenaar, R. W. (2005). *Towards requirements for a reference model for process orchestration in e-government.* Paper presented at the TED Conference on E-Government, Bolzano-Bozen, Italy.

Hood, C. (1991). A public management for all seasons? *Public Administration, 69*, 3-19.

Janssen, M., Gortmaker, J., & Wagenaar, R. W. (2006). Web service orchestration in public administration: Challenges, roles, and growth stages. *Information Systems Management, 23*(2), 44-45.

Ling, T. (2002). Delivering joined-up government in the UK: Dimensions, issues and problems. *Public Administration, 80*(4), 615-642.

McIvor, R., McHugh, M., & Cadden, C. (2002). Internet technologies: Supporting transparency in the public sector. *International Journal of Public Sector Management, 15*(3), 170-187.

Ongaro, E. (2004). Process management in the public sector: The experience of one-stop shops in Italy. *International Journal of Public Sector Management, 17*(1), 81-107.

Oracle. (2004). *Oracle BPEL Process Manager.* Retrieved April 28, 2006, from http://otn.oracle.com/products/ias/bpel/index.html

Pollitt, C. (2003). Joined-up government: A survey. *Political Studies Review, 1*(1), 34-49.

Tibco. (2004). *TIBCO® Staffware Process Suite*. Retrieved April 28, 2006, from http://www.tibco.com/software/process_management/staffware_processsuite.jsp

Van der Aalst, W. M. P., Hofstede, A. H. M. t., & Weske, M. (2003). *Business process management: A survey*. Paper presented at the Business Process Management International Conference (BPM 2003), Eindhoven, The Netherlands.

Wimmer, M. A. (2002). A European perspective towards online one-stop government: The eGOV project. *Electronic Commerce Research and Applications, 1*(1), 92-103.

Wohed, P., Aalst, W. M. P. v. d., Dumas, M., & Hofstede, A. H. M. t. (2003). Analysis of Web services composition languages: The case of BPEL4WS. In *Proceedings of the Web Application Modeling and Development, Conceptual Modeling, ER 2003,* (LNCS 2813, pp. 200-215). Berlin-Heidelberg: Springer-Verlag.

Zhao, J. L., & Cheng, H. K. (2005). Web services and process management: A union of convenience or a new area of research? *Decision Support Systems, 40*(1), 1-8.

ENDNOTE

1 A café needs two licenses to be allowed to pour alcohol: (1) a license to pour alcohol, and (2) a license to open a café. For the purpose of this chapter, we consider the integrated "liquor-licensing-process" which combines the two licenses.

This work was previously published in Global E-Government: Theory, Applications and Benchmarking, edited by L. Al-Hakim, pp. 52-64, copyright 2007 by IGI Publishing, formerly known as Idea Group Publishing (an imprint of IGI Global).

Chapter 4.42 Certificate Management Interoperability for E-Government Applications

Andreas Mitrakas
European Network and Information Security Agency (ENISA), Greece

ABSTRACT

Secure e-government aims at supporting public administration in delivering enhanced public services. In e-government, electronic signatures and certification services are used to invoke trust and security in services and applications. Certification services, however, are often on offer in an apparent geographical or contextual isolation threatening to create new fault lines across e-government services that rely on them. As public administration often operates at multiple levels and in a compartmental manner, the risk is that limitations in the interoperability of certification services might hamper trust and security in the whole value chain of e-government. Drawing from the case of small public administrations, this chapter proposes a certification service architecture and approach to support interoperability in secure e-government services.

INTRODUCTION

The promise of e-government for a simplified and efficient Public Administration (PA) has been regarded by governments worldwide as a means to carry out public policy and enhance services to citizens and organisations. E-government aims at introducing to public administration, information, and communication technologies (ICT) at a mass scale in a way previously unknown and for tasks often impossible to carry out without ICT. Online citizens and organizations gain access to 24/7 services over an array of transactions with the PA and often in combination with private sector or other third party services. Cross-border interoperability is a critical aspect in delivering such services. Electronic signatures are an infrastructure technology upon which e-government applications rely to ensure authentication and non-repudiation of transactions. While electronic authentication is often associated with identity management, non-repudiation is essential for critical e-government applications that require the undisputed commitment of the signatory. Using electronic signatures in cross-border transactions across multiple application environments may become an awkward experience due to interoperability limitations that may lead to setbacks in trust. It is therefore becoming critical to allow for the seamless validation of electronic signatures in multiple application environments. This chapter addresses certain issues related to certification authority (CA) services across e-government infrastructures and it reviews prevailing models to assess their suitability for interoperability in e-government. Emphasis is placed on the suitability of these models for applications made available by e-government organizations, particularly small ones that typically rely on limited resources that cannot necessarily sustain demanding deployments in terms of technology used and organisational cost. In building trusted e-government services, grasping the trust requirements of each application is an essential prerequisite. Since trust is likely to be based on certificate-based services, ensuring interoperability across the board is a priority for administrations in the Member States but also for the European Union (EU) in an effort to enhance interoperability and encourage cross-border deployments. After providing a short overview of the state of art, the remainder of this chapter presents existing interoperability models. Furthermore, this chapter presents a proposed interoperability model that leverages on an overarching interoperability capability.

BACKGROUND: TRUST AND E-GOVERNMENT

While the EU E-Europe initiative has focused on government services online, seamless access to government information services and decision-making procedures have also been seen as a priority (Prins, Eifert, Girot, Groothuis, & Voermans, 2001). The envisaged application environment for e-government seeks to meet the expectations of citizens and businesses alike especially with regard to providing efficient and cost effective e-government services (UNCTAD, 2001). Applications of e-government aim at citizens and business with varying levels of involvement and service functionality. These applications may often rely on electronic signatures to safeguard the transmission of user and transaction data. Online e-government services that leverage upon electronic signatures for citizens include for example: taxation, social security, registration services, etc. Typical e-government applications that require the identification of organisations include social security contributions, corporate tax, VAT submissions, company registries, and electronic public procurement. More recently, the set up of official registries such as those required for accountants and companies, also rely on the use of electronic signatures. In certain areas a drive toward greater cooperation among PAs can be observed, that is often motivated by the need to service a larger population in the EU internal market or leverage upon a greater range of services. In some cases, cooperation may also be instantiated by interactions at a political level that have led to successful deployments, like for example, the European Digital Tachograph (see, Council regulation (EC) No 2135/98 of 24 September 1998 amending Regulation (EEC) No 3821/85 on recording equipment in road transport and Directive 88/599/EEC concerning the application of Regulations (EEC) No 3820/84 and (EEC) No 3821/85). As it can be expected in complex transaction areas such as electronic procurement, a combination of technologies and a multitude of interoperability options have to be taken into consideration to allow for the seamless cooperation among PAs and provide appropriate interactions with private sector services. In such environments, PA processes may require re-designing to ensure interoperability and accessibility.

Figure 1. Evolution of e-government transactions

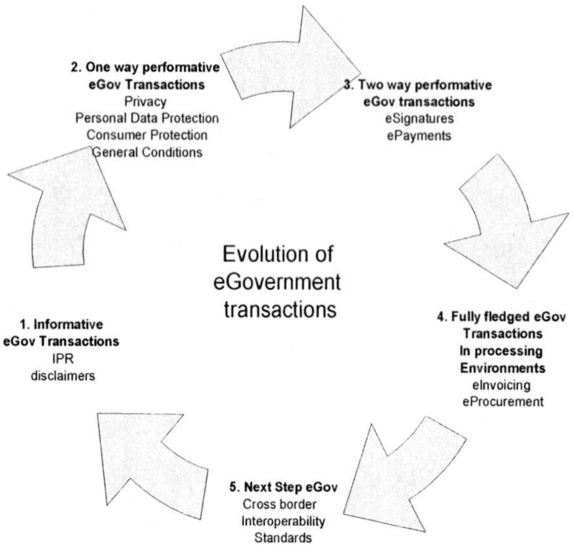

While cross-border PA services are desirable, their need cannot always be justified by the way PAs work and the sort of services they offer. PA cooperation typically occurs in selected and clearly defined areas where there has been a manifestation of the need to cooperate. Sometimes PA cooperation can be instantiated through dedicated applications. Identification services have been singled out as a centerpiece in e-government efforts to provide personalized and efficient services to citizens (Mitrakas, 2002). In the EU, cross-border e-government services have been deemed essential to support the mobility of the citizens and stimulate competition among public administrations that is likely to lead to greater efficiency and better services for citizens and organizations (Blivet, Mitrakas, & Moyal, 2001).

In spite of the obvious benefits that interoperability presents, PAs in Member States often maintain a silo approach that sometimes constrains them from leveraging upon or offering cross-sector and cross-border services (Eymeri, 2001). Operating in isolation and setting up silo constraints can be well justified in a nation-centric PA that only serves internal needs. For a PA, however, that seeks to cooperate with other organisations and participate in the EU internal market, there is scope in opening up services to parties that do not necessarily reside in its own jurisdiction. The shift toward e-government is the means to effect this change. Therefore, public interest can be interpreted as the need toward greater cooperation among PAs for the purpose of enhancing services rendered within the EU internal market by using electronic means.

Identity management is a critical application that evidences the shift toward e-government. By allowing the authentication of citizens and organizations across the board in a range of other e-government applications, identity management is a critical undisputed element in the e-government application lifecycle. Managing identities for e-government, a complex application area, requires a relatively high degree of interoperability to allow for the delivery of services across multiple PA platforms that can be accessible through e-government services. Opening up such functionality to other Member State PAs is an additional challenge to tackle.

Much like other application environments, e-government has also passed from a stage of one-sided communications to a performative level of transactions that involve multiple actors in both the private and public sector. The figure below illustrates the evolutionary stages of e-government stages that seek to add to cross-border functionalities.

To date the role of PA is twofold acting as issuer of identities, like for example electronic identity or more often as a relying party, that validates and accepts electronic signatures that citizens use. Relying parties require mechanisms that permit the validation of electronic signatures from resources that the issuing authority makes available. This approach, as it can be expected, has significant merits within the domain of a single PA irrespectively of the level in which it might be applied, being local, regional, federal etc. Interestingly enough in private sector applications this challenge has largely been addressed through market oriented solutions. A challenge for PAs is how to leverage on market solutions to allow for interoperable identity management and other e-government applications made available through PA.

PAs face significant shortcomings when identity management centric e-government services are made available at a cross-border level. Currently the open question for a PA is how to access a validation resource especially in the case where that PA relies on a certificate that has been issued by a foreign CA that belongs to a PA in another Member State. Accessing that resource is a necessary step before validating and accepting that certificate. To date there has been no real life evidence of large-scale cooperation among EU Member State PAs to ensure the validation of electronic identities issued by various authorities. Pursuant to the increase in e-government deployments, future e-government services are likely to depend on the rate of interoperability at the certificate validation level in a way that ensures seamless services.

A critical question is whether information society beneficiaries, that include citizens, businesses, and other PAs, have a right to interoperability of information society services. Article 2 of the EU Treaty stipulates sustainable information society that establishes a right to information society services. While at a Member State level this right might be interpreted as granting access to and affording e-government services at the EU level, interoperability becomes critical to give effect to the sustainability of information society service. Within the EU, internal market rules that sometimes depend on information society services rely on the requirement for interoperability to assume a meaningful form. The ubiquitous business and private use of public open networks has resulted in a surge of regulation concerning an array of issues, among which certification services promise to tackle the issue of identity management and identity assurance in a hard to secure environment. It has been argued that citizens have political and moral rights against the state that are prior to the welfare of the majority. In this regard, legal rights can extend beyond those explicitly laid down (Dworkin, 1977). In terms of information society services, beneficiaries require access to meaningful services in a way that enhances the internal market and ensures other basic rights such as the protection of personal data. While interoperability of certification services is a viable means to exercise and enjoy the right to accessing e-government applications it should be encouraged and afforded protection in a meaningful way.

An additional question relates to whether the EU level is the most appropriate to address interoperability of e-government services especially in the certificate management area. With regard to e-government interoperability, it is necessary to underline the importance of adhering to the principles of proportionality and subsidiarity (Mousis, 2002). Especially for e-government certification services for the purpose of identity management, it is expected that cross-border deployments will observe the principle that regulation that can be regulated at a national level within a Member State does not have to be addressed at an EU level. From the conception of policy to its implementation, the level at which action is taken, like for example from the EU to local levels, and the selection of the instruments used, must be in proportion to the objectives pursued. Consequently, before launching an initiative, it is essential to check if public action at the EU level is really needed. Additionally it has to be established whether action at EU level is the most appropriate to address the issue at hand (Hix, 1999).

To enhance certificate management services for e-government interoperability, it is necessary to seek the appropriate level of cooperation as well as an operation model that is suitable with respect to the technical and operational features of the applications involved. In e-government, various trust models can be considered and implemented to meet the requirements of diverse types of applications. To date these models can mostly be based on bilateral agreements, cultural or organizational preferences, and trust requirements. These models, however, often face limitations with regard to scalability and acceptance for mass deployments. To make e-government services evolve, a certain degree of national control might have to be substituted by a shared responsibility among e-government services. The released level of control can be entrusted to a mutually shared body that will be designate by the PAs involved. To enhance the EU internal market, by means of e-government services, it is critical to ensure that PAs share the vision and service the goal for e-government interoperability.

LEGAL CONSIDERATIONS

Electronic signatures and their subsequent regulation in the EU are a critical element in the question of certification services for identity management. With the EU Directive 99/93/EC, electronic signatures acquired a legal meaning next to the technical one that they already had. Directive 99/93/EC on a Common framework for electronic signatures has made a significant impact on e-government applications by laying the ground rules and pro-actively encouraging the standardisation of certificate based signature services (Mitrakas, 2003). One important objective that this Directive has accomplished is averting the fragmentation of the internal market of electronic signatures within the EU that has spared a critical part of the internal market with regard to information society (Aalberts & van der Hof, 1999). While further steps are required to enhance interoperability levels across the EU, state of the art implementations in several application areas including identity management manifest the value of electronic signature standards.

Directive 99/93/EC introduces three classes of electronic signatures, namely a general class of electronic signatures, advanced electronic signatures, and advanced electronic signatures based on qualified certificates and created by a secure signature creation device. A specific type of electronic signatures, known as qualified signatures, meets certain formal requirements and is afforded the same legal effect as hand-written signatures, according to article 5.1 of the Directive. The effect of advanced electronic signatures, which are based on a qualified certificate and are created by a secure signature-creation device is that they meet the legal requirements of a signature in relation to data in electronic form in the same manner as a hand-written signature satisfies those requirements in relation to paper-based data; and that they are admissible as evidence in legal proceedings. Furthermore, an advanced electronic signature is a generic type of electronic signature that meets the conditions of uniquely identifying the signatory while the signatory remains associated with the signed data (Mitrakas, 2006).

Article 5.2 of the Directive 99/93/EC addresses the legal effect of signatures that do not meet the requirements of qualified signatures. These types of signatures are afforded significant recognition provided that supportive evidence ensures their trustworthiness.

The signatures of article 5.2 can also be used for identification and authentication, like when using S/MIME, for example. These types of signatures are within the focal area of organisations seeking to make available e-government applications available where hand-written signatures are not necessary for the purpose of non-repudiation of a transaction. In the EU, electronic signatures have in some cases epitomised the security requirements mandated for certain e-government applications. Since electronic signatures ensure already the non-repudiation of the transaction, the authentication of the transacting parties, the confidentiality of the communication, and the integrity of the exchanged data, they are also supported by a stringent set of audit and compliance rules that ensures the quality and level of services offered by a certification service provider (Caelli, Longley, & Shain, 1991; Pfleeger, 1997). Applications such as national electronic identity schemes based on electronic signatures provide the functionality and control that governments need to manage large populations of users of their electronic systems (Deprest & Robben, 2003). Electronic signatures for the purpose of authentication provide e-government services with the ability to centralise and focus their security requirements as well as complement additional security requirements that it might actually have.

An increasing number of deployments and applications make use of qualified signatures for the purpose of non-repudiation. In a paper-based environment, law requires hand-written signatures in a relatively small number of formal transactions, a tendency that might be projected in electronic transactions also. It can be argued that the assertions on qualified signatures have thus far paid little service to the general use of electronic signatures. This tendency can be amended by improvements in the available technology and more importantly the drive toward raising the current rate of penetration of electronic transactions also for e-government.

Directive 99/93/EC permits Certification Service Providers (CSP) to make services available without seeking for ex ante authorisation by Member States' authorities prior to commencing operations. It remains at the Member States' discretion, however, to decide how they ensure supervision of CSPs according to the provisions of the Directive. The Directive does not preclude establishing private sector based supervision systems or oblige certification service providers to apply for supervision under any applicable accreditation scheme. The Directive therefore permits the split between the legally establishing a CSP in one Member State while the provision of services remains in another.

In deploying interoperable electronic signatures in the EU, standardisation has played a significant role especially in terms of the deliverables of the European Electronic Signatures Standardisation Initiative (EESSI) that hold a pivotal position. The EESSI standards have been promulgated by the European standardization organizations as the European Telecommunications Standards Institute (ETSI) and European Committee for Standardization/Information Society Standardization System (CEN/ISSS). The EESSI standards can be further extended to reflect the current and specific needs of industry and PAs. EESSI standards have also addressed the matter of electronic signature validation that is an essential requirement to establish trust in a chain of certificates that are used in e-government applications. To carry out cross-border public services it is necessary to have the ability to check the validity of the electronic signatures that are in use. Checking the validity of an electronic signature requires controlling a directory that contains status information of digital certificates. Such directory contains all certificates that have been revoked or suspended at the time a request is made. Information published on such directories must be kept up to date regularly or provided in real time.

TRUST MODELS FOR CERTIFICATE SERVICE MANAGEMENT

Several models are currently available to deploy validation authority services across multiple domains. While some of them are based on private sector experience from electronic commerce, others have evolved exclusively to serve e-government needs. A critical factor to the future deployment of these models is likely to be the applications they shall be called to support, the rate of technology use within the PA as well as the type and level of public e-government services on offer. Present day monolithic approaches of a single model per Member State are likely to be replaced by a tailor made model based on an application centric approach.

Documented and enforceable policy plays a significant role in determining the conditions in which certificate services are rendered. A certificate policy for example is used to ensure the policy objectives for the CSP with regard to security requirements of certificate management. A certification practice statement is also used to ensure how such objectives are met (ETSI TS 101 456). At the application level, relying parties may use signature policies to assess the validity of electronic signatures. A signature policy describes the scope and the usage of electronic signature with a view to address the operational conditions of a given transaction context (ETSI 102 041). A signature policy is a set of rules under which an electronic signature can be created and determined to be valid (ETSI TS 101 733). A signature policy determines the validation conditions of an electronic signature within a given context. A context may include a transaction type, a legal regime, a role assumed by the signing party, etc. Policies are the means to invoke trust and convey information in electronic commerce by defining appropriately indicated trust conditions (Mitrakas, 2004). Additionally certificate policies and certification practices statements remain entirely under the domain of the application service provider and are, typically audited for compliance.

As validation of identities is a critical issue that e-government services address to enhance interoperability, the remainder of this section presents prevailing models for e-government validation authority interoperability.

Cross-Certification

Cross-certification aims at establishing a trust relationship between two CAs. Cross certification is carried out by setting an interoperability path for one or more applications between two discreet certificate management domains or two CAs within the same certificate domain (Lloyd, 2001). According to the IETF PKIX Group, "A Cross-certificate is a certificate issued by one CA to another CA which contains a CA signature key used for issuing certificates." This definition is consistent with the X.509 standard in which it stated that a certification authority can be the subject of a certificate issued by another certification authority. In this case, the certificate is called a cross-certificate whereby the issuer of a certificate and the subject are different CAs. CAs issue certificates to other CAs in order to authorise the subject CA, as is the case of strict hierarchies. Alternatively, cross certificates are used in order to recognise the existence of the subject CA as is the case in a distributed trust model. Cross-certification is a unilateral action that typically applies within a strict hierarchy where a superior CA issues a certificate to a subordinate one. Advantages associated with cross-certification include that each domain remains autonomous from any external trust considerations and the internal trust relationship between the relying parties and the trust anchor (i.e., hierarchically superior CA) within the domain are not affected. Open issues in cross-certification render its administration uneconomical due to the large number of bilateral agreements that have to be executed as well as potentially time-consuming negotiations

Cross-Recognition

A Task Group within the Telecommunications and Information Working Group of APEC (APEC TEL, 2001) defines cross-recognition as "An interoperability arrangement in which a relying party in one PKI domain can use authority information in another PKI domain to authenticate a subject in the other PKI domain, and vice versa" (APEC TEL, 2001). The CA accreditation schemes of the UK (tScheme) and The Netherlands (TTP. NL) follow a similar approach whereby an authority appointed by Law to accredit CSPs, grants approval on the basis of successfully passing an audit based on specific criteria. Some steps have already been taken for the mutual recognition between accreditation schemes that operate in various Member States.

Cross-recognition differs from cross-certification because there is no mutual or unilateral recognition between CAs. Cross-recognition is based on the notion that independent CAs would somehow be licensed or audited by a mutually recognized trusted authority (e.g., an accreditation authority or an independent auditor). A foreign CA is regarded as trustworthy if it has been accredited by a formal accreditation body or has been successfully audited by a trusted independent auditor. Accreditation can be accomplished on the basis of successful assessment according to specific mutually recognized criteria. Cross recognition requires cooperation between PA and private entities that are entrusted with the approval of the CA services. Deterrents for Cross-recognition include:

- A relying party is expected to make the trust decisions rather than the CAs but it is not yet clear how the relying party will gather the information necessary to make an informed decision
- Cross-recognition may not be acceptable in cases where high levels of assurance or trust are required especially where the control of the chained CAs must remain at arms length due to application constraints

Bridge CA

Bridge CAs use cross-certification as the basis for inter-domain interoperability. A bridge CA is effective in the diminution of the number of bilateral agreements required by the cross-certificate entities. The bilateral cross-certification agreements that are required in a fully meshed approach is: n*n, where n represents the number of participating CAs, making it a complicated and laborious endeavour that has limited ability to scale. Acting as an intermediary, a bridge CA introduces one organization to another. It is, therefore, no longer necessary for each organization to enter into a bilateral cross-certification with any other organization. Each participating CA gets cross-certified with the bridge CA. The conditions of trust are described in a certificate policy that prevails for the entire domain of cross certification. Where certificate policies overlap, participating organizations can have a trusted path to each other's resources via the bridge CA. A bridge CA can significantly reduce the overhead required especially when the number of organizations that belong to the same policy is extended (ETSI TS 101 733, ETSI TS 102 042). Open issues for a bridge CA mostly associate with the policy (i.e., certificate policy or certification practice statement each CA applies and they include):

- Certificate Policy usage and assurance levels that might clash with application limitations and might require format and content mapping
- Certificate Profiles that might nurture conflicts related to key usage (i.e., authentication, non repudiation, or both)
- Client software configuration that might require building the trust path or that alternatively is required to rely on trust anchors included in one's own browser

Certificate Trust List and Bridge CA

A Certificate Trust List (CTL) is a signed PKCS#7 data structure that contains a list of trusted CAs. Within the CTL, a hash of the public key certificate of the subject CA identifies whether a CA is trusted. The CTL also contains policy identifiers and supports the use of extensions. From an inter-domain interoperability perspective, the CTL essentially replaces the cross-certificate pair. The relying party trusts the issuer of the CTL, who in return allows the relying party to trust the CAs conveyed within the CTL. The relying party can access a CTL by including one or more of the operational protocols defined within the IETF PKIX working group or via an out-of-band distribution mechanism. Like any of the other alternatives discussed in this chapter, acceptable practices and procedures are required in order for this mechanism to be a viable alternative to achieve inter-domain interoperability. Particularly important is to establish what constitutes a trusted CTL issuer and determine the criteria that the CAs must adhere to before they can be deemed "trusted."

A bridge CA enables organisations to communicate with one another on a secure and authenticated basis. Certificate management resources of discreet CAs are linked together by incorporating previously issued top root certificates into the Bridge-CA network. A CA that registers with a bridge CA can have its own certificates recognised by all other participating organizations without having to individually negotiate the reciprocal recognition of its root. The European Bridge-CA is an implemented model of the bridge CA concept carried out by the Teletrust association in Germany (www.teletrust.de).

The program Interoperable Delivery of European E-Government Services to public Administrations, Businesses, and Citizens (IDABC) of the European Commission has underlined the need for further interoperability in the area of certification services within the EU. The IDABC bridge CA has been deemed necessary to add trust to e-government applications. The IDABC CA model, however, does not necessarily seek to cross-certify participating CAs, by approving their policies (Certification Practice Statement—CPS) etc. The IDABC bridge CA distributes a signed list of the root certificates of the CAs approved for use by the Member States for their respective PAs (ETSI TS 102 231, ETSI TR 102 030). By making the CA's root certificates available either through signed lists or via a repository, IDABC expects to act as a gateway so that relying parties establish trust with a CA within the PA originating from another Member State (Callens, 2003).

Root CA

A Root CA model is based on the assumption that trust derives from one trusted source that is organized in a strict hierarchical order. A root CA is the trust anchor for all relying parties within a given domain. Subordinate CAs may be deployed, however relying parties will not rely on any certificates issued by a subordinate CA, unless a valid certificate path can be traced back to the root CAs. In a strict hierarchy, a subordinate CA features one superior CA. Further, subordinate CAs are not permitted to have their own self-signed certificates while only the root CA has a self-signed certificate. Strict hierarchies:

- Comprise of one root CA and zero or more subordinate CAs
- Are appropriate for business cases where policy controls are to be enforced in a "top-down" approach
- Have been established to support specific vertical applications within an industry (e.g., Identrus)

In strict hierarchies, the consequences of compromise of a root CA private key could be severe. In addition, there is no single root CA that applies to every PKI domain, so it is not possible to maintain a strict hierarchy across all conceivable domains. This means that one of the other methods previously discussed must be used to establish a trust relationship between these otherwise isolated domains. In specific implementations, an added benefit of the Root CA model permits the trusted root to undertake the operation of the directory of certificates if a CA fails to find a successor in case of ceasing operating, which is a clear benefit for the relying party. Open issues for cross-recognition include CA reluctance to accept subordination out of fear for the market or hierarchical position.

There are issues regarding the overlapping validity periods of the keys of the CAs.

Looking at the root CA model it is hard to avoid noticing the demanding security requirements, however justified they might be, that might limit scaling. Currently it is not conceivable to attain to the desired interoperability levels for multiple CAs operating across the EU under the root CA model. In this regard, the German regulator's view is that "Until such time, legally recognized digital signatures may only be used in international business transactions if the correspondent has been issued certificates by a German CA." The Digital Signature Act (see, Gesetz über Rahmenbedingungen für elektronische Signaturen (Signaturgesetz - SigG)1) of May 16, 2001 (BGBl. I S. 876) as such does not prohibit the establishing of offices abroad by German CAs for the acceptance of certificate requests and the provision of signature components. However, this has been considered to be a mere temporary solution until a more suitable model is adopted.

AN INTEROPERABILITY ARCHITECTURE FOR E-GOVERNMENT

The e-mayor project aims at setting up and operating a platform for secure e-government exchanges of data for multiple applications of small e-government organisations. While typical of these organisations is the need to be cost effective due to the budgetary constraints the benefits from interoperating with counterparty organisations in other Member States can have a significant impact on citizen perception for e-government. Often e-government solutions might have to be made available by small PAs that face specific shortcomings in terms of resources and expertise. In such cases certificate management infrastructure must be adapted to the needs of small PAs and meet specific requirements such as scalability, simplicity in the use, and low access to resources. While this section proposes an architecture that meets these objectives and fulfils the interoperability requirements among heterogeneous entities. Figure 2 presents an overview of the recommended architecture.

End entities such as citizens and small PAs that are entitled to request services within the proposed infrastructure must register locally within their certificate service of their own administration. To facilitate the interactions among various small PAs certificate services must become sufficiently interoperable in order to recognize each other's root and allow end entities carrying out end user transactions.

For the end-entity certificate validation, an overarching validation authority (oVA) makes

Figure 2. Certificate interoperability for small PAs

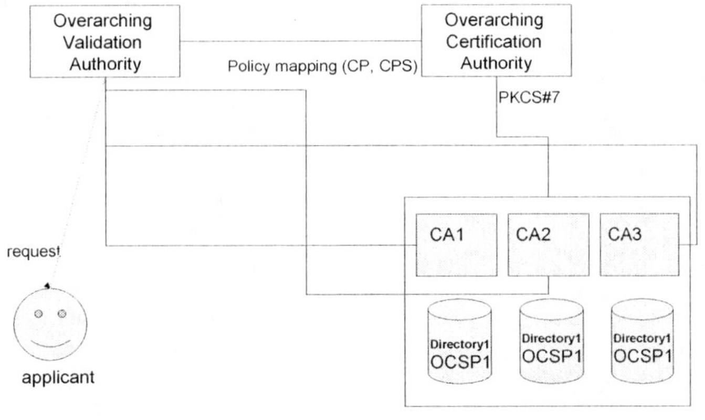

available validation services by redirecting certificate validation requests to the appropriate validation service of a local CA. An oVA provides the end entity with the technical capability to check the certificate status through an appropriate application. Using a certificate trust list that is composed by a list of predefined and trusted CAs is a desirable add on. Browsers and other applications have the ability to allow users to add other root certificates besides the ones included therein by default as needed. The end user can therefore update the default lists of CA roots to match their individual requirements.

The potential risk is the ease in which root certificate updates can take place within end entity applications, could potentially be exploited by malicious actors to add false root certificates that can be further used to carry out bogus and fraudulent transactions with PAs. To overcome this problem, a list of trusted CAs is digitally signed by a dedicated Overarching Validation Authority (oCA). An oCA is a technical facilitator and is entrusted with the competence to set up a policy and a technical framework to support the cross-border recognition of certificates issued by the various local CAs that service the small PAs. An oCA can address the critical issue of the recognition of local CAs in a large number of contexts, being geographic, organizational, etc.

The previous represents a basic interoperability model for PAs. The following section expands this basic concept by elaborating certain elements that are of interest to the PA with regard to the application environment that interoperability is sought.

FURTHER STEPS

The policies that each local CA makes available may additionally be mapped and reconciled against each other in order to ensure organisational and legal interoperability. Policy mapping is an additional albeit optional step to complement the basic model presented before. By taking a flexible approach toward policy interoperability, the proposed model allows for an enhanced level of transactions in heterogeneous PA services that require the validation of certificates and subsequently the management of identities of end users. Mapping and reconciling policy frameworks in overlapping transactions might however threaten transactions, which are based on the use and acceptance of varying terms. A typical hard case might involve for example overlapping policy conditions, which apply to certificates issued by different CAs. The situation is exacerbated when CAs that do not have the means to recognise one another issue certificates that can be used in the same transaction environments (ETSI TS 102 231). Although such certificates may well be complementary to a transaction framework the varying assurance levels they provide might threaten the reliability of the e-government application environment as a whole (Mitrakas, 2005a). Reconciling the methods used across various electronic signing environments is likely to contribute to creating trust in e-government services.

Besides policy mapping, setting up equivalence levels is a significant requirement that might also have to be introduced at a later stage in order to ensure compliance with prevailing rules and reconcile the differences among the approach toward voluntary accreditation conditions according to article 3.2 of 99/93/EC. To date the degree of equivalence among accreditation schemes across the EU Member States is unclear with the consequence of possibly inhibiting the use of certification services in cross-border transactions for PA purposes. Using intermediaries is recommended to ensure equivalence levels according to prescribed criteria. Intermediaries could collect applicable policies in a repository as well as specify audit conditions and provide advance notice concerning the legal status of the scheme or legal requirements under which a certificate has been issued or a root operates (Mitrakas & Bos, 1998). Policy mapping tools based on decision support systems could be developed in order to facilitate the management of disparate policies of participating CAs.

An additional issue associates with the way that operational requirements of an oCA are addressed. Based on present day experience whenever a new CA seeks recognition by the oCA its name and root certificate have to be added to the master trust list that is signed by the oCA and subsequently distributed to the implicated end entities. Distributing updated trust lists might face scalability shortcomings if there are more than a small number of CAs used by the various PAs across the EU. This problem could be addressed by setting up a single reference directory for CAs that seek the inclusion of the root in a given trust list. By accessing the directory of CA roots, an end entity that transacts with the PA enhances its ability to establish the trustworthiness of the CA issuing the certificate in question because it can directly validate the certificate path online. The role of the oCA can be limited to providing the secure publication of the directory as well as ensuring the inclusion of a pointer to the directory by all trusted local CAs. Including CAs in a directory however is likely to require a classification mechanism for the CAs included therein (ETSI TS 102 231).

Furthermore, an area of future attention could address policy frameworks related to the application layer in an e-government transaction. To respond to transparency requirements it is expected that online applications will increasingly become more demanding in explaining to the end user what they do and actually warranting the performance. Through a combination of dedicated legislation and policy (e.g., CPS) part of this requirement has been addressed. It remains to be seen how providing comprehensive description of the technical features and functionality of the online e-government application might be tackled. In e-government it is still required to enhance the features that invoke trust and safety to the benefit of end users. Policies for the application layer are likely to become more in demand in e-government applications where the requirement for transparency in the transaction and accountability of the parties involved is higher than in electronic business (Mitrakas, 2005a). Finally, specifying policies further to meet the needs of particular application areas, groups or organisations are additional expectations, like for example in the area of eProcurement. In e-government it is expected that interoperability will be enhanced through best practices and standards regarding policy in specific vertical areas. Typical content for an application layer policy may include aspects associated with the kinds of underlying services that are involved, the profile of the providers that make these services available, architectural premises, disclosures with regard to databases, personal data, validation services as well as liability or warranty that might be offered to the end user. The scope of application layer policy is to contribute to the transparency of the application platform that might ultimately lead to trust and legal safety (Mitrakas, 2005b).

Further standardisation is a way to effect the desired changes to enhance interoperability in e-government CA services. A set of overarching rules has yet to emerge and be accepted for this architecture to become fully operational. While political support at the EU level is necessary for the set up and operation of an overarching infrastructure that is trusted by CAs more initiatives are necessary to contribute toward establishing a framework of best practices in cross-border CA service recognition for the PA. Applications for e-government are likely to provide the additional drive like for example in the area of identity management especially for such areas as electronic invoicing and electronic public procurement (CWA 15236:2005).

While interoperability remains a constant requirement for information society, e-government applications need to also benefit in a way that allows applications from various PAs to work together. Identity management is a key e-government application that has the ability to render interoperability requirements applicable across multiple functional applications such as e-procurement and e-invoicing. A much needed improvement would be to strive for a policy framework that meets the requirements of law and associated applications.

CONCLUSION

To date Member States' e-government services have developed certification services across multiple platforms. The Directive 99/93/EC does not necessarily address the issue of the cross-border recognition of CA services for the purpose of validating identities in an identity management environment that is leveraged upon e-government applications. Furthermore, policy requirements of the e-government application layer remain fragmented. The EESSI standards and several PA and industry initiatives have strived to address this issue with some success. However, present date standards have but succeeded to provide entwined solutions that work well when a small number of strings of two or more strands are brought together. Lacing together however does not necessarily provide an answer to interoperability in a complex application area as e-government where multiple PAs originating from a vast number of contexts must trust each other to provide end-to-end services. As interoperability of services across EU Member States becomes ever more demanding additional efforts are necessary in order to set the guidelines required. New architecture elements including enhanced policy mapping tools, intermediaries to establish equivalence levels between CAs and one or more directories for trusted CA roots can provide the additional functionality needed in e-government. Failing to come up with a scalable interoperability solution is likely to put at risk sophisticated infrastructures and turn them yet again to modern day information silos for PAs that are able to merely operate in the local context alone. Failure to meet interoperability requirements risks impacting the beneficiaries of e-government services that typically seek to operate and contribute to the success of the EU internal market. The strong drive in support of applications, such as electronic identity for the movement of persons, as well as electronic public procurement, for public sector transactions are likely to provide the necessary impetus to achieve certificate service interoperability. Policy and Law must follow suit and facilitate the need of end users to rely on appropriate identity resources to carry out secure electronic transactions.

ACKNOWLEDGMENT

This chapter has been drafted within the framework of the e-mayor project (IST- 2003-507217) co-funded by the European Commission. While the views expressed herein are strictly personal and reflect the author's involvement in the e-mayor project on behalf of Ubizen NV (a Cybertrust company), in no way do they represent those of the author's employer past or present. The author wishes to thank Dr. Abdel Youssouf for his valuable insight.

REFERENCES

Aalberts, B. P., & van der Hof, S. (2000). *Digital signature blindness, Analysis of legislative approaches toward electronic authentication.* Deventer, The Netherlands: Kluwer.

APEC eSecurity Task Group. (2001). *Achieving PKI interoperability.* Canberra, Australia: APEC.

Blivet, L., Mitrakas, A., & Moyal, M. (2001). *Pre-inventory of smart card based PKI projects in the European Union.* Brussels: eEurope Smart Cards Report.

General Description of the Business Counter

We investigated a case study to research the need for support for implementing process orchestration and to identify some main areas in which a reference model should be able to provide support. We selected the business counter as it is regarded as a best practice in The Netherlands and it wanted to orchestrate their cross-agency processes and was willing to cooperate.

The business counter provides all municipal services that are provided to the hotel-and catering industry. Typical examples are services specific to the hotel-and catering industry, such as a liquor license, a license to operate gaming machines, and a pavement café license, but also more generic business-permits, such as a parking permit, and an environmental permit. As these permits and licenses require the input from many different municipal departments and governmental agencies, their service-delivery processes are cross-agency processes that need to be orchestrated. Figure 3 provides a high-level overview of the business counter.

Although the business counter is viewed as a best practice, there was hardly any ICT support at the time of investigation. For almost all services, the requester has to schedule an appointment with the business counter, after which the account manager coordinates the interactions with the back-office and the other agencies. Processing the permit-application, asking other departments for advice, and drafting the final permit are for most processes all done without the support of information systems other than traditional office applications.

Case-Study Approach

The case study at the business counter was conducted between July 2003 and May 2004, and in total we interviewed nine different persons at the municipality and also some representatives of the businesses in hotel and catering industry. At the municipality we interviewed persons at the business counter itself, employees at the different functional departments, and key ICT-staff to get an overview of the information systems in place.

Figure 3. High-level overview of the business counter

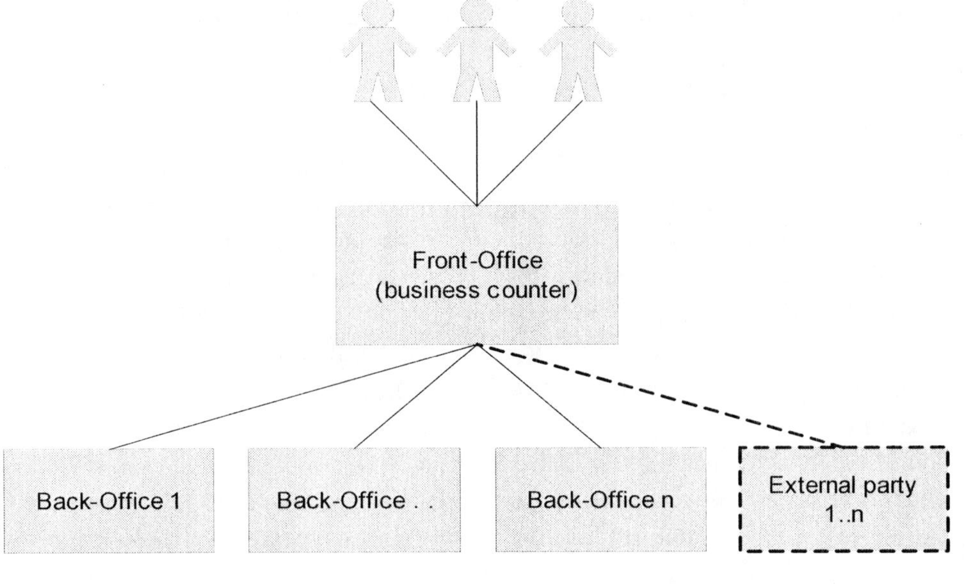

We studied five processes at the business counter in detail: a license to open a café, a liquor license, a permit to organize special events, a permit to operate gaming machines, and an environmental permit. These processes were chosen, as the permit to open a café, the liquor license, and the gaming license processes together represent most of the work for the business counter and is the most complex cross-agency process. During the case study we found that these processes all ran largely in parallel and the organization of the process over different departments and agencies was very similar. For this reason, the permit to organize special events, and the environmental permit were also analyzed, as the first is almost completely being taken care of by the licenses team, and the second is almost completely performed by the team environment supervision.

The issues that are defined in the next section are based on the analysis of all five processes that were analyzed at the business counter and the different departments involved in the service-delivery processes. This chapter uses the example of the liquor licensing process to illustrate the issues that are identified in the remainder of this chapter.

Liquor Licensing Process

A liquor license is one of the most important permits for the hotel and catering industry. Every restaurant or café that pours alcohol is obliged to apply for a license. For requesting a license, an entrepreneur contacts the business counter. After an initial intake meeting, the entrepreneur fills in an application form and returns it, together with the needed official documents, such as, for example, a floor plan. Hereafter, the name and address of the applicant are checked, the justice department and the police are asked for advice whether the applicant has a criminal record. Finally, the building department checks whether the building meets all legal requirements and the application for a liquor license is published in the municipal newspaper. Based on these advices, the back-office employee draws up a license or a letter stating the reasons for refusing the license.

Short lead-times on license-request are crucial to entrepreneurs. Also, the data provided to the government by the entrepreneurs often contains privacy-sensitive information. The cross-agency aspect and the nature of the liquor-licensing process put high requirements on security throughout the whole process. The sensitivity of the information involved (e.g., information on criminal record of applicant) requires secure communication and strict information-access-control. Moreover, the importance of giving thorough advice on granting a license or not requires strict control on who performs these process-steps. These issues are already difficult enough to deal with in a single-agency setting, but are even more difficult in a cross-agency setting, where responsibilities are scattered over different agencies, and are not always known beforehand. Too rigid access control on information may also lead to rigid inflexible processes, where agencies cannot anticipate customer needs.

Requirements on Cross-Agency Business Processes

This section discusses the main requirements on cross-agency processes. These requirements represent the areas in which a reference model should provide support. We derived the requirements from the case study and clustered the requirements into three main categories: (1) ensuring the correct and in time execution of business processes, (2) secure information-sharing, and (3) accountability.

Correct and In-Time Execution of Business Processes

As the process orchestrator is responsible for the overall service-delivery-process, one of the main tasks a process orchestrator must perform is to ensure that every sub-service in the cross-agency service-delivery process is completed in the right way, performed by the right person, and in time.

Service-levels can help in ensuring correct and in-time execution of every sub-service, but simply agreeing beforehand upon service-levels between the business counter and the different agencies alone is not enough. The service-levels need to be constantly monitored and mechanisms that respond when a service fails, when a service does not produce the required answer, or does not answer in-time, should be put in place.

At the business counter, the correct and in-time execution of cross-agency processes is very important, as the entrepreneurs requesting a liquor license, want information about whether the license will be granted or not as soon as possible. Often, entrepreneurs have to wait for the completion of the licensing process before they can open their café or restaurant. For the entrepreneur, each delay results in losing money. For the business counter, there are legal deadlines on the liquor-licensing process that must be met. As the business counter depends on other agencies or departments to perform certain tasks, it cannot completely control the lead-times of these sub-processes. For example, the sub-process of checking the identity of an entrepreneur that has its residence in another municipality can take a lot of time and repeated requests before it is finally completed. The business counter bases its decision to grant or deny a liquor license on the tasks performed by other agencies, for example the check for a criminal record at the business counter. It is therefore important that these tasks were executed correctly (i.e., by someone having the right responsibility, by not skipping certain checks, etc.) before an answer is sent back.

Secure Information Sharing

The secure sharing of information among different governmental agencies is crucial. When different agencies are all involved in one service-delivery process, they should all have access to the customer-data that is relevant to them. Authorization of users and especially the ability to present only the information that is relevant for them is a key issue. Within a single organization this may be solved relatively easy, for example by means of a large data warehouse, but in a governmental setting where many of the involved agencies have their own autonomy, this is much more complex. As the responsibilities are fragmented among many governmental agencies, so are its information-systems, making information sharing between multiple agencies far from straight forward.

Agencies that perform sub-services need the business counter to provide them with information about the customer, as they need this data in performing the process. At the business counter, the building-department, for example, needs information about the applicant of the liquor license; about the kind of restaurant it is requesting the liquor license for, and so forth. This "one-way" sharing of data is relatively straight forward, but when different agencies start updating data that is required by other agencies, there is a need for robust information-sharing mechanisms.

The issues of secure information-sharing will become even more important when the law comes into effect requiring that citizens cannot be asked to provide personal data that is already given to the government in general, which could be another agency (Dutch Government, 2003). Another major issue with information sharing is privacy. Not all agencies need all available customer information. For privacy reasons, every agency should only have access to the information they needs. An example is the information resulting from the check of the criminal record at the justice department. This data is not relevant and therefore should not be provided to other parties, such as the building department.

At the business counter, different departments and agencies that are involved in the liquor licensing and related processes all have different information-systems that are not able to communicate with each other. An entrepreneur mentioned that the tax office, the municipality, and the chamber of commerce identified his restaurant using three different names. Entrepreneurs had to fill in forms which requested the same information over and over again, for different, but also for the same departments and agencies. Not sharing information also makes enforcement more difficult. The lack of an integrated customer view makes it difficult to get an overview of all the permits a specific café or restaurant has been granted.

Accountability

Accountability is an important requirement for the whole public sector. For governmental service-delivery processes, it is especially important that the processes are transparent, non-discriminating, and consistent, and that the decisions made in the process are well motivated and made by the right person. Citizens and businesses no longer accept a black-box view of the service delivery process, but want to know what steps have to be taken in order to reach the final decision.

Ensuring accountability for governmental service-delivery processes that run across different organizations is especially difficult, as it has to cope with different (semi-) autonomous agencies that are involved in the process. For example, the decision not to grant a liquor license, because the police have strong suspicions against the applicant, should be very well motivated.

Ensuring accountability of cross-agency service-delivery processes requires specialized coordination mechanisms that ensure that the outcome of every process step is recorded, and that the overall process has run the way it was supposed to. No one should be able to change the stored information, as the information might be used as evidence.

At the business counter, for the process of granting a liquor license, accountability is an important requirement in different ways. Entrepreneurs want the business counter to account for their acceptance/rejection decisions. When a license is rejected based on "soft" evidence by the police that the person wanting to open a café may be a criminal, the business counter needs to be able to account for not granting the permit based on this information. Next to the entrepreneurs, the citizens also want the business counter to account for their decisions on the granting of liquor licenses. For example, when a license for a café in a residential area is granted, the business counter will have to account for their decision. In this case, it is important to show that all procedures have been followed rigidly.

APPLICABILITY OF EXISTING REFERENCE MODELS

The case study at the business counter provided the requirements for a reference model supporting governmental decision-makers in implementing process orchestration in e-government. The coordination issues that were identified in the previous section are the main issues that governmental decision-makers are facing in our case study, but might not be exhaustive as they are based on a single case study. This section will evaluate whether the two existing reference models meet the requirements that were identified in the previous section.

Workflow Reference Model

To evaluate applicability of the workflow reference model, it will have to be translated into orchestration-concepts. The obvious link is on the level of with Web service orchestration, instead of process orchestration. Analogous to workflow management, in Web service orchestration there also exists a central "orchestration server" to enact the process-flow. Examples are Oracle's BPEL Process Manager (Oracle, 2004),

Microsoft Biztalk 2004 (Microsoft, 2004), and IBM Websphere Business Integration Server Foundation (IBM, 2004). Analogous to workflow, process definition and monitoring tools are also needed. External applications can be invoked by means of their Web service interface and human tasks can be supported by invoking a Web service interface to someone's e-mail client. Web service orchestration also relies on invoking Web services for interfacing with other orchestration servers. A process that is defined in BPEL can be made available as a Web service itself, and thus be called by a process on another orchestration server.

From this translation of the workflow reference model into cross-agency Web service orchestration-terms, it can be concluded that there is quite a large resemblance between workflow and Web service orchestration. The requirements that need to be addressed in cross-agency processes, including accountability, secure information sharing, and correct and in-time execution of the process remain unaddressed by this model. The reference model provides no support for guarding lead-times, or how to facilitate information-sharing. Instead, the reference model focuses on technical components, and technical interfaces. This is, analogous with the initial goal of the workflow reference model, more relevant to vendors of orchestration technology, than to governmental decision-makers.

Extended-SOA Reference Model

The extended-SOA reference model is focused on providing roles and functionality for Web-services market (i.e., the selling and buying of Web-services). The model identifies a service-provider, service-requester, service-aggregator, service-operator, and even a market maker. Several of these roles can of course be performed by the same organization, but the model seems to be more tailored to situations where service requesters buy or rent services from service-providers on a services market.

Nevertheless, large parts of this reference model are still relevant to the situation of implementing process orchestration at the business counter. Especially the composite services layer is very relevant, as offering a service as a liquor license where sub-processes at different agencies are incorporated into the overall service-delivery process, is an example of composition. The managed-services-level appears to be less relevant in the case of the business counter, but may become so in the future, when Web service orchestration is adopted on a larger scale.

The business counter corresponds to the role of service aggregator in the reference model. It aggregates services that are provided by other agencies (service-providers), and provides these aggregated services to the customer. The reference model does address many of the issues that the decision-makers are facing by means of the tasks that the service-aggregator must perform.

The functionality in the composite services layer: coordination, monitoring and conformance checking, and agreeing on service levels of the incorporated services matches with the requirements that were identified at the business counter. Although it does address issues like the monitoring of component service, the calculation of QoS on aspects like security, cost, and performance, it does not provide any guidelines about how to fill them in. Decision-makers can use this reference model only to identify the roles and functionality that they need to consider, but will have find ways to implement these roles themselves.

CONCLUSION

The goal of this chapter is to investigate the applicability of two existing reference models to support governmental decision-makers for implementing process orchestration in e-government. We investigated the two models, derived requirements from practice and evaluated the models using these requirements.

The case study shows that cross-agency processes need to satisfy requirements that can be clustered in three categories: the correct and in-time execution of business processes, secure information sharing, and accountability.

We evaluated the two reference models using these requirements. Neither of the models can provide governmental decision-makers with enough support to design cross-agency processes satisfying the requirements. The workflow reference model is too much focused on technology implementations, and therefore fails to address the non-technical coordination issues, and although the e-SOA reference model does address many of the issues, the model remains rather abstract, only pinpointing the required functionality, but not indicating how this should be filled in. Moreover, this reference model aims at supporting Web services markets and not cross-agency processes.

To support governmental decision-makers in implementing process orchestration in e-government, a new reference model is needed meeting the above-mentioned requirements. Further research will focus on designing such a reference model.

REFERENCES

Andrews, T., Curbera, F., Dholakia, H., Goland, Y., Klein, J., Leymann, F., et al. (2003). *Business process execution language for Web services* (Version 1.1). Retrieved February 13, 2006, from http://www.ibm.com/developerworks/library/ws-bpel/

Castellano, M., Pastore, N., Arcieri, F., & Summo, V. (2004, June 17-18). *An e-government interoperability framework for cooperation among public administrations.* Paper presented at the 4th European Conference on e-government, Dublin Castle, Ireland.

Contenti, M., Termini, A., Mecella, M., & Baldoni, R. (2003). An eService-based framework for inter-administration cooperation. In M. A. Wimmer (Ed.), In *Proceedings of the 4th IFIP International Working Conference on Management in Electronic Government: KMGov 2003*, (Vol. 2645/2003, pp. 13-24). Rhodes, Greece: Springer-Verlag Heidelberg.

Dutch Government. (2003). Actieprogramma Andere Overheid (in Dutch).

Dutch Government. (2004). Meer ruimte voor ondernemers door minder lasten—Van lastenproductie naar lastenreductie (In Dutch).

Fremantle, P., Weerawarana, S., & Khalaf, R. (2002). Enterprise services. *Communications of the ACM, 45*(10), 77-82.

Gortmaker, J., & Janssen, M. (2004). *Business process orchestration in e-government: A gap analysis.* Paper presented at the 15th IRMA International Conference, New Orleans, LA.

Gortmaker, J., Janssen, M., & Wagenaar, R. W. (2004). *The advantages of Web service orchestration in perspective.* Paper presented at the 6th International Conference of Electronic Commerce, ICEC 2004, Delft, The Netherlands.

IBM. (2004). *Websphere business integration server foundation.* Retrieved July 13, 2004, from http://www-306.ibm.com/software/integration/wbisf/features/

Lawrence, P. (1997). *Workflow handbook 1997.* Chichester, UK: John Wiley & Sons LTD.

McIvor, R., McHugh, M., & Cadden, C. (2002). Internet technologies: Supporting transparency in the public sector. *International Journal of Public Sector Management, 15*(3), 170-187.

Microsoft. (2004). *Microsoft biztalk server home.* Retrieved July 13, 2004, from http://www.microsoft.com/biztalk/

Oracle. (2004). *Oracle BPEL process manager.* Retrieved July 13, 2004, from http://otn.oracle.com/products/ias/bpel/index.html

Papazoglou, M. P., & Georgakopoulos, D. (2003). Service-oriented computing. *Communications of the ACM, 46*(10), 24-28.

Pasley, J. (2005). How BPEL and SOA are changing Web service development. *IEEE Internet Computing, 9*(3), 60-67.

Piccinelli, G., & Williams, S. L. (2003). *Workflow: A language for composing Web services.* Paper presented at the Business Process Management: International Conference, BPM 2003, Proceedings, Eindhoven, The Netherlands.

Stojanovic, Z., & Dahanayake, A. (2005). *Service-oriented software system engineering: Challenges and practices.* Hershey, PA: Idea Group Publishing.

The Open Systems Joint Task Force. (1999). *Common lexicon and acronym dictionary.* Retrieved September 28, 2004, from http://www.acq.osd.mil/osjtf/html/terms.htm

Van der Aalst, W. M. P. (2003). Don't go with the flow: Web services composition standards exposed. *IEEE Intelligent Systems, 18*(1), 72-76.

WFMC. (2001). *Workflow management coalition workflow standard—interoperability Wf-XML Binding* (No. WFMC-TC-1023).

WFMC. (2002). *Workflow process definition interface—XML process definition language* (No. WFMC-TC-1025).

WFMC. (n/a). *About the WFMC—Introduction to the workflow management coalition.* Retrieved July 12, 2004, from http://www.wfmc.org/about.htm

Wimmer, M. A. (2002). A European perspective towards online one-stop government: The eGOV project. *Electronic Commerce Research and Applications, 1*(1), 92-103.

Wohed, P., Aalst, W. M. P. V. D., Dumas, M., & Hofstede, A. H. M. T. (2003). Analysis of Web services composition languages: The case of BPEL4WS. In *Web application modeling and development, conceptual modeling—ER 2003* (LNCS 2813, pp. 200-215), Berlin-Heidelberg: Springer-Verlag.

Zhao, J. L., & Cheng, H. K. (2005). Web services and process management: A union of convenience or a new area of research? *Decision Support Systems, 40*(1), 1-8.

This work was previously published in Secure E-Government Web Services, edited by A. Mitrakas, P. Hengeveld, D. Polemi, and J. Gamper, pp. 217-232, copyright 2007 by IGI Publishing, formerly known as Idea Group Publishing (an imprint of IGI Global).

Chapter 4.44
The Impact of the Role of the Government of Egypt on Electronic Commerce Development and Growth

Sherif Kamel
The American University in Cairo, Egypt

Ahmed Ghoneim
Cairo University, Egypt

Sherine Ghoneim
Cairo University, Egypt

ABSTRACT

Information and communication technology with a focus on the digital economy and the implications of the development of electronic commerce is increasingly playing an active role in the development and growth of the global economy. The implications are wide and diversified. This includes the facilitation of trade transactions and acceleration of movement of capital through the new rules of the digital economy with the removal of time and distance barriers. The impacts are varying in density and effectiveness between developed and developing nations. Electronic commerce could be beneficial to business and socioeconomic development in the north (developed world) as well as in the south (developing nations). Small and medium-sized enterprises stand a unique opportunity worldwide to optimally leverage their capacities and excel from the diversified communication channels the digital economy presents. However, one challenge remains critical and that is the growing digital divide emerging between developed and developing nations as well as within developing nations themselves, which could deepen income and wealth inequalities.

In that respect, the government role in developing nations in preventing the widening of the digital divide is becoming increasingly vital with implications that vary and affect business, culture and the society at large. During the past two decades, electronic commerce has had a diversified variety of impacts on organizations of all types and sizes. Such impacts differed from one country to another and from one environment to another, depending on the local conditions and the adaptation of the society. Implications related to the management and leadership of the organizations, their vision, mission and strategies, policies, governance, the organizational learning, ethics and culture among other elements.

This chapter demonstrates the role of the government of Egypt in introducing, diffusing and institutionalizing electronic commerce. Electronic commerce represents a tremendous challenge and at the same time a great opportunity for growth and development, and hence it needs an institutional role to regulate it. Electronic commerce promises great potentials for developing nations giving poor nations and their populations additional access to markets, information, and other resources that would have otherwise been inaccessible. However, there has been a great fear of a digital divide emerging between developed and developing nations. Hence, the governments' involvement of developing nations, such as Egypt, in preventing the appearance or the widening of the digital divide is of paramount importance. With respect to electronic commerce, the role of the government is highly different from its traditional role in other conventional areas that have been subject to extensive research, such as infrastructure and social services amongst others. It is different because electronic commerce is a newly ventured domain for government involvement that requires substantial thinking and structuring of the role it should play; it is more or less a comprehensive new role with aspects related to setting the rules for market operations as well as developing control measures to handle the risk factor associated with electronic commerce-related investments. Electronic commerce represents both a challenge and an opportunity for a developing nation such as Egypt with potentials for growth and development. This chapter introduces electronic commerce in Egypt with a focus on the prevailing status and the institutional role of the government to regulate electronic commerce and develop the electronic trading industry.

INTRODUCTION

The information and communication technology infrastructure and the development of electronic commerce are both playing an increasingly active role in changing and growing the global economy in a digital way. The implications are wide and diversified, including the facilitation of trade transactions and acceleration of movement of capital through innovative rules irrespective of time and distance differences. Electronic commerce could be beneficial to business and socioeconomic development in the north (developed world) as well as in the south (developing nations), but the impacts could vary in density and in effectiveness due to one critical challenge, and that is the growing digital divide emerging between developed and developing nations as well as within developing nations, which could deepen income and wealth inequalities.

Therefore, the government role in developing nations in preventing the widening of the digital divide is becoming increasingly vital with implications that vary and affect business, culture and the society at large. During the past two decades, electronic commerce had diversified impacts on organizations of all types and sizes. Such impacts differed from one country to another and from one environment to another depending on the local conditions and the adaptation of the society. The implications related to the management style and leadership of organizations, their vision, mission and strategies, policies, governance, the organizational learning, ethics and culture among other elements. This chapter demonstrates the role of the government of Egypt in introducing, diffusing and institutionalizing electronic commerce, which represents a challenge and an opportunity for development and hence needs an institutionalized role to regulate it. This chapter introduces electronic commerce in Egypt with a focus on the prevailing status and the institutional role of the government to regulate electronic commerce and develop the electronic trading industry.

A THEORETICAL FRAMEWORK

There are a number of issues that need to be highlighted when addressing the theoretical framework of the role of the government in electronic commerce development and growth, and that includes (a) the importance of institutions in developing healthy market economies; (b) the sequence of institutional building and reform; and (c) the NIE approach in explaining how institutions are formed.

a. **The importance of institutions in developing healthy market economies:** There is an overall consensus that institutions are needed to support market function properly. According to the World Bank Development Report, institutions support markets by helping to manage risks from market exchange, increasing efficiency and raising returns; hence reducing the transaction costs arising from inadequate information, incomplete definition and enforcement of property rights. Institutions that fit the developed economies are different from the ones that fit economic environments of developing countries (World Bank, 2001; World Bank & OECD, 1998). Hence, it can be safely argued that developing countries experiencing transition to market economies are in need of new forms of institutions that are not necessarily adopted by industrialized countries and that are needed to ensure the functioning of their infant market economies.

b. **Sequence of institutional building:** The ultimate goal of institutional building in developing countries is to create a market-friendly environment, with supportive government services that ensure its functioning. But agreement on this ultimate goal does not resolve the crucial issue of how to get there, which is ideally through a series of sequential steps that could be defined as follows: (a) to recognize inadequate institutions; (b) to focus on functions that need to be improved, mainly related to smoothing information asymmetries, defining and enforcing property rights and contracts, and regulating competition (Islam, 2002); and (c) to concentrate on relevant institutional design or structure that fits with the overall institutional environment prevailing in the economy. It is important to note that the heterogeneity of the three steps across different countries led NIE theorists to conclude that there is no blueprint for institutional development across all countries and there is no one specific sequence for it (Islam, 2002; Clague, 1997). Respectively, each country should follow a series of steps according to its own priorities, taking into consideration the differences in constitutional orders, cultural endowments, and inherited institutional arrangements. The NIE approach underlines the need for incentives to undertake reform. It emphasizes that what is required are reform strategies based on a careful understanding of the incentives facing actors in the current situation and on an examination of different alternatives to change the institutional equilibrium (Clague, 1997).

c. **An NIE model of building institutions:** With respect to reform, there is always a need to investigate demand and supply. Demand usually varies from one organization to the other. Demand for institutional change is normally made either by agents who expect that new arrangements will provide them with better opportunities of capturing gains that are lost under existing arrangements (greater efficiency), or by actors dissatisfied by the current distribution of income or wealth. Important factors motivating the demand for institutional change are relative product and factor prices, the law making process, level of technology, and the size of the market (Zaki, 1999). With respect to supply, institutions are created by principals (political rulers or the owners of resources) to govern their relationship with other principals and with their agents (citizens, bureaucrats and employees), and principals are motivated to create institutions that maximize their individual utility. However, an important element that needs to be put into consideration is the cost required for the physical and human infrastructure needed for the design and implementation of new institutional reforms. Moreover, some laws usually need to be changed and here there is an associated cost of alternative choices (of institutional arrangements) available in the social, political and economic domains (Zaki, 1999).

Integrating the demand and supply sides together implies that the pressure of a competitive market as suggested by North (1990) is the most viable mechanism for selecting the most efficient economic institutions. The market's competitive pressure will select socially beneficial forms of economic organization, regardless of the intentions of the actors. If, instead, the creation of institutions is left in the hands of any dominant actor—such as the state, or a cohesive self dominant class—the product will be institutional rules that will give that actor a strategic advantage with respect to other actors, regardless of how socially sub-optimal the outcome of these institutions may be.

BACKGROUND

Electronic commerce promises great potentials for developing nations providing additional access to markets, information, and other resources that would have otherwise been inaccessible. However, the growing challenge of the digital divide and the need to develop measures to prevent it is of paramount importance to governments in developing nations such as Egypt. With respect to electronic commerce, the role of the government is different as opposed to other conventional domains requiring extensive research and substantial restructuring of the role it should play, including setting new rules for market operations and developing control measures to handle the risk associated with electronic commerce-related investments.

The role of the government in the functioning of the economy has experienced continuous change with an objective to pave the way for increased private sector participation. With respect to electronic commerce, the role of the government is different; it is not conventional in the sense of retreating or reducing its engagement, but rather

Table 1. Internet users by region (Source: Computer Industry Almanac, 2003)

Region	Users (000)				Users/1,000 People			
	1995	1998	2000	2005	1995	1998	2000	2005
Worldwide	39,479	150,887	318,650	717,083	6.94	25.44	52.45	110.52
North America	26,217	82,989	148,730	229,780	89.4	275.7	479.1	715.4
Western Europe	8,528	34,741	86,577	202,201	21.67	87.54	217.5	501.4
Eastern Europe	369	2,983	9,487	43,767	1.26	10.2	32.7	151.8
Asia-Pacific	3,628	24,559	57,607	171,098	1.11	7.24	16.57	45.90
South/Central America	293	2,722	10,766	43,529	0.62	5.48	21.1	78.6
Middle East/Africa	444	2,893	7,482	26,708	0.48	2.89	7.22	23.6

Table 2. Forecast of total electronic commerce (B2B and B2C) in billions of U.S. dollars (Source: Forrester Research, 2001)

Region	2002	%	2006	%	CAGR % 2002-2006
Developing Asia and Pacific	87.6	3.8	660.3	5.1	65.7
Latin America	7.6	0.3	100.1	0.8	90.5
Transition Economies	9.2	0.4	90.2	0.7	77.0
Africa	0.5	0.0	6.9	0.1	91.1
Total Developing Nations	104.9	4.6	857.5	6.7	69.1
North America	1677.3	73.1	7 469.0	58.2	45.3
Developed Europe	246.3	10.7	2 458.6	19.2	77.7
Developed Asia and Pacific	264.8	11.5	2 052.1	16.0	66.8
Total Developed Nations	2188.4	95.4	11 979.7	93.3	53.0
World Total	2293.5		12 837.3		

it is a comprehensive new role that encompasses (a) setting the rules for market operations and (b) controlling the risks associated with investments. The role expected to be played by the government should focus on removing deterrents of electronic commerce such as lack of Internet connectivity. Despite rapid growth of the Internet, its access and penetration in developing nations is far below that in developed countries, as shown in Table 1, which demonstrates the growth rate of the Internet. It is important to note that in recent years many developing nations have experienced much more rapid diffusion of the Internet for the given availability of telephone lines than in some developed nations.

In developing nations, the collaborative role of the government and the private sector will be crucial in the diffusion of innovation and in the use of the Internet across the society at large, especially in remote and rural areas. This will be important to maintain the gaps created that lead to the digital divide and can also help reduce it. For example, the average OECD country has 70 times the number of telephone mainlines in developing nations than in sub-Saharan Africa, excluding South Africa. Wilson and Rodriguez (2000) found that an index of country inequality with respect to access to communications including personal computers, Internet hosts, facsimile, mobile phone and televisions deteriorated substantially during the 1990s.

Electronic commerce can generate productivity gains by reducing transaction costs, even if the effects so far have proven to be small and limited (Oliner & Sichel, 2000). However, it is projected that within the United States electronic commerce could reach around 6 trillion US dollars by 2004 (Bermudez et al., 2000; Economist, 1999). At the global level, electronic commerce may account for around 25% of world trade by 2005 (United Nations Conference on Trade and Development, 1999). But the distribution of Internet access among nations worldwide is extremely unequal and despite the rapid growth in Internet access in developing nations, developed nations still account for the majority of Internet subscribers (Suttle, 2000). However, recently, there is a growing share of Internet users in developing nations and in 2001, developing nations accounted for 33% of new Internet users worldwide (United Nations Conference on Trade and Development, 2002). Moreover, electronic commerce is also growing in developing nations but more slowly than the number of Internet users. In developing nations, the proportion of Internet users who are at the same time electronic commerce practitioners is lower than average owing to lower per capita income in addition to other factors such as low credit card usage, lack of relevant and needed products and services and poor logistics and fulfillment services (United Nations Conference on Trade and Development, 2002). In that respect, the gap between developed and developing nations in terms of access to and use of the Internet is smaller than the one in terms of electronic volumes (www.ecom.or.jp).

It is important to note that business-to-business predominates over business-to-consumer but remains small in developing nations. Table 2 shows that while the shares of developing nations in both business-to-business and business-to-consumer global electronic commerce are expected to remain small in the medium term, business-to-business could remain much weaker, with the proportion between business-to-business and business-to-consumer being 2.5 times smaller in developing nations than in North America (United Nations Conference on Trade and Development, 2002). It is important to note that as long as business-to-business does not take off in developing nations, electronic commerce volumes will remain negligible. Therefore, major efforts need to be put together to improve the infrastructure in developing nations, because business-to-business represents a unique developmental opportunity for developing nations since it can help enterprises and firms generate efficiency gains at all stages of their production and distribution processes. Such gains are vital for development since they effectively affect the competitiveness level, lead to increasing levels of productivity and respectively improve income levels for the economy at large.

IMPACT OF INTERNET GROWTH ON ELECTRONIC COMMERCE

The phenomenal growth of the Internet has certainly been one of the driving forces for the introduction and diffusion of electronic commerce worldwide. The Internet with its massive innovative capacities will no doubt boost efficiency and enhance market integration domestically and globally, especially in developing nations that are most disadvantaged by poor access to information. However, it is important to note that it can also have negative implications for nations that will not have access to information. The Internet, as an output of the information and communication technology evolution, is the largest network of computers in the world, providing a wealth of information and knowledge that reaches over 655 million users worldwide (www.nua.ie). Table 3 shows the current and projected global Internet population.

Electronic commerce is one of the most important topics in today's global business environment. Consequently, understanding the degree to which the Internet will change business and society is a vital research topic. The global society is currently witnessing a phase of transition from an Information Age that was physical to an Information Age that is digital (Lynch & Lundquist, 1996). This transition promises to cut costs, save time, increase revenue and provide a general digital

Table 3. Global online population Source: cyberatlas.internet.com (23 June 2003)

Worldwide Internet Population 2002	Projection for 2004
580 million (Nielsen//Net Ratings) 655 million (International Telecommunications Union)	709.1 million (www.eMarketer.com) 945 million (Computer Industry Almanac)

sense of the world as one global digital village where people can communicate anytime and anywhere, and where time and distance barriers are reduced and in many ways removed (Kamel, 1995). Today, it costs only a small amount to use the Internet and the cost is going down by the day. In the near future, it will cost virtually nothing (Tapscott, 1996). While the underlying costs of telecommunications are collapsing, the Internet usage is experiencing an unprecedented exponential growth (Kalakota & Whinston, 1996). At the policy level, national and regional plans are being formulated as part of a global consensus to deregulate national networks, to open up nations and territories to competition, to forge alliances between former competitors and to wire up the three-quarters of the world that is still unconnected, in order to minimize the growing digital divide between developed and developing nations that is being perceived as an integral part of the global information society (European Union, 1997).

ELECTRONIC COMMERCE IN EGYPT

The government of Egypt has been instrumental in establishing the nation's information and communications infrastructure to support its developmental plans. The decision made at the highest level of policy making in 1985 was to build a national information infrastructure to become the platform for development of all sectors and industries through better allocation of resources and rationalization of the decision making process by using timely, relevant and accurate information. Since 1985, a public-private sector partnership for development had a remarkable impact on the build-up of Egypt's information infrastructure (Kamel 1995b). It included a large number of projects with effective implications on the different building blocks of the infrastructure including hardware, software, information, interconnectivity and human resources. Today, the information and communication technology sector is one of the largest in the Arab region (International Telecommunications Union, 2001). The Internet was introduced to Egypt in 1993 (Kamel, 1998a). Its use developed from being used solely by the government and academic institutions to becoming more of a standardized search and communication tool used by everyone in the society. The Internet use is constantly being encouraged by the government and by private investors who establish their own Internet service providers.

The Internet was first introduced to Egypt by the Egyptian Universities Network of the Supreme Council of Egyptian Universities. In 1994, as an attempt to diffuse the Internet usage among the society, the Cabinet of Egypt Information and Decision Support Center (IDSC) and the Regional Information Technology and Software Engineering Center (RITSEC) provided free Internet access on a trail basis to the public, private, government and non-government organizations to entice the users to venture into the new technology. This was done with the financial support of the government to aid in the exposure of the local market and to pave the way for the commercialization of the Internet services. The free access formula was accredited for contributing to the boost in the rate of growth of Internet users, especially within small and medium sized enterprises and industry and sector professionals (Kamel, 1998b). In 1996, the government replaced its free Internet access policy with an open access policy and Internet services for the commercial domain were privatized, and 12 Internet service providers started their operation. Today, there are around 50 ISPs serving over 2.2 million Internet users (Fahmi, 2003). Most of the Internet usage in Egypt is for business information gathering (Loch, Straub & Kamel, 2003). Egypt tops the index of bandwidth in the region with a score of 2.11 (American Chamber of Commerce in Egypt Report, 2002). In January 2002, the government of Egypt launched an initiative through its ministry of communications and Information

Technology providing free nationwide access to the Internet to all citizens of the country, creating a larger demand for connectivity coupled with the establishment of over 3,000 Internet cyber-cafes in Metropolitan Cairo as well as other locations, and demonstrating the tangible intention of the government to diffuse the use of the Internet among the society.

The Internet evolution in Egypt demonstrates the active role played by the government. With the privatization of the Internet in 1996, the role of the government did not come to an end. The government still provides strong support for different Internet service providers in the form of upgrading the infrastructure to enable them to offer better connection speeds to their users as well as providing them with technical support. Additionally, the government is helping in training software developers in collaboration with local vendors and leading multinationals in the field. In terms of information as web content, the government is trying to magnify the outcome with an objective to make the Internet more relevant and appealing to the community (www.idsc.gov.eg). The efforts exerted by the government include the development of awareness and utilization of the Internet. There are also efforts done by non-government organizations such as the dissemination of economic information and applications developed by the private sector as information providers to encourage business transactions over the Internet. Some of these efforts are taking the form of portals, which are diversified between Arabic search engines, content sites for specific industries, online shopping sites, career services and special sites promoting trade and investment in Egypt (American Chamber of Commerce in Egypt, 2002). The development of portals and web sites in Arabic is one of the major challenges that hinder the growth of the Internet use in Egypt. A booster took place in 2001 with the launch of MSN Arabia; the portal is a product of a partnership between Microsoft Corporation and LinkdotNet, the largest private Internet service provider in Egypt. Other successful examples of Arabic content portals include gn4me.com, arabia.com, masrawy.com and moheet.com.

Moreover, the government has invested time and effort in making national economic information available on the Internet. For example, Egypt's State Information Service (SIS) (www.sis.gov.eg) includes information on investing in Egypt, its economic growth, foreign trade, agriculture and irrigation, industry, energy, transportation and tourism, among others. Additionally, the Information and Decision Support Center (IDSC) publishes its monthly economic bulletin online (www.economic.idsc.gov.eg). The bulletin includes key economic indicators reflecting the performance of the economy. The Egyptian Center for Economic Studies (ECES), an independent organization, publishes online series of articles to contribute to the discussion of ideas and policy options for enhancing economic development in Egypt. The Economic Research Forum (ERF) (www.erf.org.og) is a non-governmental organization whose mission is to provide an institutional mechanism to initiate and fund policy-relevant research, to disseminate research results, and to function as a resource base for researchers. The forum's web site has searchable databases with working papers, conference proceedings, and other publications. Moreover, the Egyptian International Trade Point (EITP) (www.tpegypt.gov.eg) was established in 1993 under the ministry of foreign trade to create international trade efficiency using the Internet, and it represents Egypt's electronic link to UNCTAD's Global Trade Point Network (GTPN). The web site targets listing of trade opportunities for Egyptian businesses, providing information on international customs, banks and packaging requirements, and establishing a database for Egyptian exporters and importers. Relating this to the theoretical model mentioned above, it is observed that the supply side was highly active.

Egypt is viewing electronic commerce as a venue to support business and socioeconomic development plans, where it provides opportunities for increasing trade, promoting investment, facilitating business transactions, providing a larger and more varied market and supplying an unparalleled marketing tool. Electronic commerce as a medium for foreign trade is a catalyst for export, implying a potential increase in Egypt's exports and a better formula for its balance of trade that will eventually have positive impacts on its economy. It can also enable the country to experience a more open economy and increase its comparative advantage worldwide. Many sectors could benefit from electronic commerce besides trading; this includes financial services (insurance, banking, trading); tourism; entertainment; music; advertising and marketing; information services, education and training; the media (electronic books, newspapers, journals, news services) as well as other services such as medicine and real estate. Moreover, it can create job opportunities where Egyptians will have the opportunity to venture and establish small and medium enterprises with global market access. For examples, software developers will be baled to work for international customers. The government of Egypt has formulated a national plan demonstrating its vision to prepare itself for a more competitive and global market environment that is enabled by the Information Age. The plan attempts to capitalize on the cutting-edge information and communication technology that could help rationalize the decision-making process and optimize the allocation of resources within the context of developing nations with all local conditions that relate to culture, norms and values (Kamel, 2000). The objective of formulating and implementing electronic commerce technologies has a strategic objective in leveraging the nation's business development and socioeconomic status. However, it is believed that in order to realize such a long-term objective, the following needs to be realized: (a) to formulate a framework for electronic commerce coherent with the national political, social and legislative environment and compatible with the global environment; (b) to develop the national information infrastructure required for electronic commerce; (c) to promote the use of electronic commerce through pilot projects; (d) to improve awareness and stimulate cooperation among all concerned parties including the government, the industry, the private sector and the general public and (e) to develop the human resources required for successfully enabling electronic commerce. Estimates for electronic commerce in Egypt are only available with respect to business-to-consumer commerce, indicating that only 6% of Internet users make purchases online based on a sample survey of 452 Internet users (American Chamber of Commerce in Egypt, 2002).

INSTITUTIONAL ROLE OF THE GOVERNMENT OF EGYPT

Egypt is in the early stages of adopting electronic commerce; the regulatory framework that defines the environment in which firms conduct business has evolved over decades and centuries. However, it has been adjusted to the needs of the old economy. No wonder then that the Internet economy, characterized by no frontiers, intangibility and to a certain degree, anonymity, requires adaptation of existing laws, rules and regulations. Because of the speed of electronic commerce development, the adaptation process in many cases lags behind, resulting in legal uncertainty (ECATT Report). As electronic commerce stretches over the borders the need for regulation at a national and international level prevails as a requirement. In principle, the institutional role of the government is based on the classical definition of Douglas North, where he identified institutions, or at least the formal institutions which we are concerned with, as the rules and regulations and their enforcement (North, 1990). Since institutions, using such definition, are wide, we will concentrate on the main issues that are of vital importance for electronic commerce, namely security issues which incorporate issues related to encryption and authentication in specific as well as telecommunications, taxation and banking at large. Unsecured transmission on the Internet is often cited as the main deterrent for a rapid growth of electronic commerce. Although much progress is being made in terms of security, the Net is still considered to pose a risk for commercial transactions. Although such lack of security stems from the fundamental design of the basic protocol suite, security measures can be implemented at various levels of Internet communications which are heavily affected by the institutional framework that governs such transactions. Establishing the required institutional infrastructure for electronic commerce is a challenging task. The difficulties encountered in establishing such infrastructure are embedded in the interrelation between the rules and regulations governing the electronic commerce activity per se and the rules and regulations in other domains, and especially in the telecommunications and financial sectors which highly affect the functioning of any electronic commerce transaction.

Formulation of an Electronic Commerce Law for Egypt (The Institutional Infrastructure)

The government has undertaken a number of initiatives to enhance electronic commerce such as the establishment of the Internet Society in Egypt's electronic commerce committee in October 1997; the issuance of ministerial decree number 2 in 1999 by the ministry of trade and supply to formulate a committee to develop the electronic commerce legislation; and, the formulation of the national telecommunications and information technology plan in January 2000 (Brown, 2000). However, all these initiatives remain short of providing an efficient institutional infrastructure capable of handling the promotion, governance and diffusion of electronic commerce. The main deterrent affecting tailoring a law for electronic commerce is a number of critical issues affecting the economy in general and electronic commerce in specific that do not have a foundation in the legal system in Egypt. This includes the legal enforceability of electronic documents, the lack of verifiable means for identities and transactions, controlling anonymity and providing a balance between privacy of deals and national security (United Nations Conference on Trade and Development, 2000).

It is important to note that nations have two alternatives to deal with the legal and institutional requirements of electronic commerce; either having a comprehensive law that regulates all issues related to electronic commerce, an option which a large number of countries have chosen including India, Malaysia, Canada and Germany, or opting for passing specific legislation as electronic commerce develops, an option chosen by the United States. Based on available documentations, Egypt has chosen the first option with efforts being put together to formulate a comprehensive law dealing with electronic commerce with a separate law for electronic signature (www.un.or.at). The currently drafted Egyptian electronic commerce law is comprehensive, dealing with issues related to electronic documents, electronic signature, authentication, encryption, consumer protection, fraud, privacy, taxes and tariff treatment and dispute settlement. However, the law is not detailed and delegates a large number of issues to the executive decree. Moreover, it gives the responsible minister a large room of discretion. Such two aspects have an advantage of making the law flexible but, on the other hand, it increases the uncertainty aspect by making the rules subject to continuous change and vulnerable to pressures from different interest groups. Another separate law is devoted for the electronic signature issue, which is still a draft as well. Following is a presentation of a number of important aspects related to the institutionalization of the role of the government with respect to electronic commerce and covering privacy, security, banking and taxation.

a. **Privacy versus Anonymity:** Often the anonymity of the Internet makes it more attractive and increases the level of communications, but the anonymity suitable for political free speech often causes hindrance to commerce. Lack of identity can facilitate fraud and deception and can lead to numerous crimes that may not be possible in physical markets. Similarly, credit card frauds can occur even when merchants ask for proof that only the real owner can provide. A survey undertaken in the some Arab countries in 1998 revealed that only 33% of Internet service providers accept payments through their web sites, and only 20% provide a means for secure transactions (NUA Internet Surveys, 1998). Verification services based on digital signatures are being offered by commercial enterprises but still it is not pervasive and no explicit agreement across governments is enacted. Therefore, no matter what systems are supported in the market, continued international cooperation is imperative to achieve an interoperable encryption system capable to provide identity, confidentiality and non-repudiation. The current law in Egypt is tough on privacy violations. For example a firm cannot monitor employee electronic mails unless there is permission. In the banking sector, information cannot be given out even between banks without the consent of the customer (Brown, 2000). Thus the electronic commerce legislation addressing privacy must be carefully drafted to take into account principles in the local market yet recognizing how these principles may conflict with national security concerns and electronic commerce legislation laws in other countries. The current electronic law drafted preserves privacy.

b. **Authentication:** The biggest vacuum in the legal framework for electronic commerce is lack of verifiable means for identities and transactions (Whinston, Stahl & Choi, 1997). Authentication refers to the ability to verify the identity of persons involved in transactions, which is vital for electronic commerce and can be addressed through a certificate authority, which is a public or private entity that issues digital certificates to be used by sellers and buyers to authenticate identities and messages or to assert that a deal has occurred. Digital certificates operate to verify identity or right to access information or services online; they can also identify web sites and software that are being sent over the web. In the drafted law there is no mentioning of the authentication issue; however, it is dealt with in the electronic signature drafted law. No certificate authority was identified but it is expected that there will be a number of national certificate authorities.

c. **Encryption:** To secure confidential and authenticated messages, encryption and digital signature technologies that provide content-level security are already being adopted. Network level security secures the conduit, while encryption secures the content traveling through the conduit. At present the widespread use of encryption technologies is discouraged by the lack of technology to integrate encryption into applications, rather than by any impediments imposed by policy (Whinston, Stahl & Choi, 1997). The drafted law contains a provision on encryption; however it defers all of its details to the executive decree with the exception of identifying explicitly the governmental third party that will be responsible for archiving the encryption keys. Hence, the law preserves the secrecy issue but no assessment of the mechanism of ensuring the encryption process can be provided, as it is contained in the executive decree yet to be issued. The challenge that the government is likely to face arises from the relative lack of human and physical resources that are capable of handling such issues. The review of scrutiny and privacy issues in the law revealed that wording of the law emphasizes their importance; however, it delegates a large number of crucial details to the executive decree.

However, if it is assumed that the executive decree includes the necessary remaining provisions it is important to know whether this ensures the success of having an efficient institutional framework for the promotion of electronic commerce. The answer is contingent on the availability of two crucial determinants: (a) the enforceability of such law and other related laws should be guaranteed; and (b) the laws related to telecommunications, banking and taxes and customs administration should be restructured to include the electronic commerce patterns of conducting business in a market economy. With respect to the first issue, it is important to note that Egypt lacks the needed human resources to ensure the success of the law. Human capacities in the fields of law and Information Technology are inadequate and require extensive training to meet the challenge of implementing the law. Law enforcement officials must be aware of how to gather, preserve, and authenticate electronic evidence. This will not only require substantial training of law enforcement personnel, but also sufficient experience with such evidence by investigators, prosecutors, defense counsel, courts, and others until clear rules and standards are established. The volume of electronic evidence that requires analysis is also increasing substantially. The increasing use of computers and the Internet often means that information or records of communications that were previously never retained or routinely destroyed can be recovered, but such recovery may still require sophisticated computer techniques to handle them. With respect to the second issue, the existing laws related to telecommunications, banking, taxation and customs administration are either not ready to deal with electronic commerce or contain loopholes that can impede its success.

d. **Telecommunications:** Electronic commerce is dependant upon an infrastructure that delivers high quality and high-speed connections. The telecommunications law determines the deployment of advanced services, the extent of universal service, the awarding of licenses to telecommunications providers and the scheme for the awarding of federal government spectrum. The telecommunications law is therefore essential for the success of electronic commerce and should be given as much attention as any electronic commerce legislation (Brown, 2000). The liberalization of the telecommunications sector is currently taking place by limiting government participation in services provision and confining it to the role of a policymaker. Success has been attained in the liberalization of Internet services and the provision of mobile and payphone services. Law Number 19 and Presidential Decree Number 101, both of 1998, were issued to separate telecommunications services provision (operator and the service provider) from the regulatory functions. The newly created Telecommunications Regulatory Authority (TRA) was assigned the independent regulatory functions and Telecom Egypt (TE) took responsibility only as the sole operator and service provider. In 1999, a new telecommunications law was drafted to further liberalize the telecommunications sector (American Chamber of Commerce in Egypt, 2001). TRA is tasked by the law to establish a number of policies and regulations that will ultimately affect electronic commerce; however, the problem arises from the fact that TRA is not separate from the government, creating a conflict of interest, and does not shield it from political influence, which is most likely to affect the progress of electronic commerce. Therefore, it is crucial that TRA is granted more independence to ensure its efficiency and its separation from the political influence.

e. **Banking:** Egypt suffers from a divide between traditional local banking and international banking practices. For example, a paper system is still utilized to perform clearinghouse functions even though an electronic system would be more efficient. The current paper-based banking system deters electronic commerce. There is nothing that legally prevents banks from operating over the Internet, but because of security concerns they simply are not comfortable with Internet transactions. Thus, banks do not accept payments or transactions online even though they are not legally refrained from doing so. The general reluctance of banks to facilitate online credit card transactions is partially due to the lack of firm legislation to regulate the process. The Central Bank of Egypt perceives the importance of an electronic commerce law for the banking industry. Moreover, fraud legislation is needed to reduce risk and the criminal law needs to be modified to take into account bank practices. Liability should be clearly defined and privacy must be addressed because customer information cannot be exchanged, even among banks, without the prior permission of the customer (Brown, 2000; Business Monthly, 2001). Nevertheless, some private firms are moving forward and implementing IT services and devices, and hoping that the law will catch up. For example, some financial institutions are implementing a smart card system to encourage customers to engage in electronic transactions, with some of these cards having stored value in a chip and others operating as a debit card, such as Citibank, as well as Bank Misr, which started issuing pre-paid Internet cards, and most recently, the National Bank of Egypt started offering the Ahly Internet Card.

Another deterrent in the banking legislation is the inability to open a current account through an Egyptian bank for dealing directly with credit cards. This is due to the fact that the transaction is to be effected through an online server with the credit card service donor (Visa, MasterCard, etc.) which bankers call—the credit card center. In the case of Egypt, the number of credit card centers does not encourage expanding Internet transactions. Therefore, the web stores have to depend on a third party to deal with credit cards' collection of money, which is likely to increase the transaction costs and affect negatively the progress of electronic commerce in Egypt. Moreover, the credit card community in Egypt did not really boom until 1998, when banks started to include personal finance in the domain of their business activity. Prior to that date, banks followed a stiff regime in the process of credit cards issuance. As it was a must in order to issue a credit card to hold and block a time deposit collateralizing the limit with which the credit card is issued—not only this but also banks set relatively high limits as a minimal for issuance—this was around 3,000 U.S. dollars on average. However, since 1998, the banking system experinced major positive changes where banks started to enroll consumer finance in their business portfolios accompanied by an expansionary activity in issuance of credit cards. The rationale of holding time deposit collateral was evaded as the introduction of international banks to the banking industry pushed clean basis credit cards to existence.

Banks currently ask for a proof of residence, personal ID and an official letter from the employer for issuing the credit card. However, the limiting factor is that all banks set a minimal wage limit of at least 250 U.S. dollars—which is the wage level that bank officials see appropriate to lower payback risk.

f. **Taxation:** The distinction between sales and income tax becomes unclear when business is conducted via electronic commerce. However, most of all the fluidity of online taxable entities makes it difficult to establish at any one time what is being taxed, who should be taxed and who can impose taxes. If there is an attempt to apply tax laws to electronic commerce, the first task should be to determine which digital products are taxable under which tax mechanisms such as sales tax, income tax or royalty tax. In the case of tangible (physical) products sold over the Internet, existing tax laws will apply with less difficulty, but in the case of intangible (digital) products there need to be new definitions. For example, while shrink wrapped software is considered tangible property subject to sales tax, downloaded software from the Internet is considered intangible and may not be subject to sales tax. Even when digital products are defined as tangible properties the nature of the Internet may require tax code revisions or a new approach toward taxing transactions. According to existing worldwide regulations, businesses must collect and pay sales taxes if they maintain a substantial presence in the taxing jurisdiction and the same applies in the case of products that are intangible and related taxation (Whinston, Stahl & Choi, 1997).

The challenge is to design a taxation system that is capable of handling both tangible and intangible products and how to avoid circumvention from one mode of trade to the other to escape taxes and at the same time enhance electronic commerce. Moreover, the proposed regulation should be analyzed through a policy framework that ensures that online conduct is treated in a manner consistent with the offline conduct in a technology-neutral manner. The drafted law mentions explicitly the tax treatment of online vendors and advertisements on the Internet; however it deferred the tax treatment of electronic transactions to the executive decree and was silent about the treatment of products and services traded via the Internet. Moreover, the law mentions that Egypt will respect all the international agreements that are signed, implying the exemption from taxes and other duties on electronic transactions and digital products traded via Internet. The World Trade Organization (WTO) members agreed on temporary moratorium against the imposition of customs duties on electronic transactions per se since 1998 and have extended such moratorium (www.wto.org). Nevertheless, it should be mentioned that the existing estimates of lost tariff revenues related to the digital products are likely to be minimal, in the case of Egypt not exceeding 0.1% of total import duties and 0.01% of the total governmental revenue (Mattoo & Schuknecht, 2000; Schuknecht & Perez-Esteve, 1999). Hence, institutional concerns related to that matter should be left as the last step, as any advancement in that regard is likely to result in more costs than revenues.

ELECTRONIC COMMERCE READINESS

The extent of electronic commerce readiness is governed by the degree of information and communication technology diffusion and the institutionalization of the electronic commerce enabling environment. First, although computer penetration and access to the Internet has been growing steadily over the last years, it will take some time until a critical mass is realized. Second, a legal infrastructure governing business and financial transactions and protecting consumer rights cannot be taken for granted. Within this context, the extent of electronic commerce readiness in Egypt has been fairly limited, with the small number of Internet users (2.2 million) and the relatively prohibitive information and telecommunications costs, if compared in terms of per capita income to those in developed countries (Fahmi, 2003). However, it is readily apparent that the difficulties surrounding electronic commerce in Egypt have more to do with traditional ways of conducting business than with legal barriers. For example, one of the barriers is the fact that Egypt is a cash-based society and paper transactions are the dominant mode of conducting electronic commerce; whereas there are slightly over 600,000 credit card users but cards cannot be used online because most of the banks in Egypt do not authorize their use for transactions over the Internet. When linked to the theoretical framework and the model, the demand side is rather weak due to special concerns of weak institutions in other related fields. Table 4 demonstrates the barriers to electronic commerce in Egypt following the measures adopted by the benchmarking telework and electronic in Europe report (ECATT, 2000).

Table 4. Barriers to electronic commerce in Egypt

Lack of awareness of added value There is considerable skepticism with regard to the added value of electronic commerce applications due to lack of interest by firms and users for online presence and shopping, respectively, due to lack of access or for security reservations.
Suitability of products for distribution Not all products can be sold on the Internet. Statistics indicate that for many online shoppers in the Arab region (Egypt included), in 48% of the cases the main reason for buying online is the lack of product availability in the local market, followed by ease of purchase (45%), convenience of comparing products online (32%), comparing prices (24%) and ease of payment (21%). There is a lack of existence of well-established distribution networks to support remote products distribution. Currently, a hybrid model of traditional and online distribution networks is being deployed.
Costs and performance The limitations of narrow band access have hampered electronic commerce evolution. Moreover, online shopping is perceived by many as an expensive pastime for Internet users rather than an efficient alternative to traditional shopping. The free Internet model introduced in 2002 might improve the situation.
Data security Compared to private value added networks, the Internet causes considerable security concerns due to its open architecture, necessitating specific technological measures to make data exchange secured and reliable, such as encryption, which are costly. In the Middle East, users generally prefer sending credit card details by alternative methods such as the phone (27%), fax (31%) or email (15%) (DIT, 1998). There is a need to improve security and there is also an evident need for allowing for alternative payment methods to complement the use of the fairly limited credit card use in the society, such as cash on delivery, which suit the local consumer and allow for building trust and alleviating consumer concerns with regard to exchanging payment details over the Internet.
Consumer protection In business-to-consumer electronic commerce, building trust requires measures that protect consumers from fraud and entitle them to consumer protection rights when buying from shops and retail outlets. There is a need to enhance buyers' awareness and to engage trust in online shopping. A vital user's concern lies in the collection of personalized data about shoppers in databases that may be used for purposes beyond the consent of the shopper, which needs to be dealt with in an appropriate copyright statement and could take the form of a new law for intellectual property rights relevant to the issues of the software industry.
Lack of critical mass Online marketplaces work better with more consumers and suppliers involved. In Egypt, the market is still relatively small and in its early stages of development. Respectively, the problem is the lack of buyer demand to make online selling a viable and sustainable option but the situation is gradually improving though diversification in market segments that might have not been accessible through traditional retail outlets.

Table 5. Role of the government in setting up an electronic commerce environment

Role of the Government		
National strategy and institutional framework	*National ICT infrastructure*	*Community development*
• To ensure that the legal framework is favorable to electronic trading, defining the legal and regulatory measures that apply to governing business and inter-firm transactions and collaboration, including contract and commercial law, taxation and measures of arbitration and dispute settlement. • To develop the legislative framework addressing the cost and accessibility of telecommunications, intellectual property, privacy and the free flow of information. • To empower national agencies and encourage the creation of efficient and independent business associations, chambers of commerce and industry associations to coordinate electronic trading. • To foster the promotion and application of electronic trading through its use in public sector organizations. • To develop a strategic and shared vision for electronic commerce.	• To develop the national ICT infrastructure and competitively price to enable electronic trading. • To provide reliable low cost and widespread technological resources. • To improve continental interconnectivity and provide gateways to international telecommunication networks. • To establish national VANs dedicated to the provision of electronic commerce solutions to help set up the foundations of business-to-business environment. • To partner with international donor agencies to fund and develop the electronic trading infrastructure. • To encourage the private sector to support, help establish and use the information infrastructure. • To coordinate activities between industry practitioners and service providers. • To establish a framework ensuring the participation of all key players and beneficiaries in the industry.	• To maintain the flexibility to accommodate changing market and legal requirements. • To maintain state-of-the-art technology by establishing a monitoring mechanism to account for changes in the business requirements and technology developments. • To design, develop and implement national policies and plans adopting information and communication technologies within various sectors. • To promote the use of information and communication technology to improve the government and industry-based effectiveness. • To set an example through the adoption of electronic government applications and utilize electronic commerce trade facilitation applications in streamlining international trade processes with respect to import and export procedures. • To encourage the private sector to play an effective role in preparing the grounds for inter-firm partnerships through raising their awareness of potential electronic commerce trading benefits. • To encourage the private sector, NGOs and the media to play an active role in promoting electronic commerce.

Table 6. Role of the private sector, NGOs and the media in setting up an electronic commerce environment

Role of the Private Sector	Role of NGOs	Role of the Media
• To ensure that the role of the private sector could be reflected through stimulating growth and assuming market leadership in developing national ICT through investment and capitalizing on new business opportunities. • To support managers of small and medium size enterprises in information and communication fields. • To establish an organizational framework that eliminates constraints and supports business development. • To encourage the formulation of information services agencies.	• To identify the needs of rural communities and contribute in developing the capacity of its people to minimize the digital divide. • To assess the public concerns with respect to information and communication technology infrastructure needs. • To promote the concern of the workforce to different employers and the government.	• To spread awareness in rural areas of the importance and benefits of the information and communication technology evolution and its implications on business and societal development. • To promote electronic commerce in different newspapers, radio and television channels to provide an easy, accessible, and cheap means of diffusing information to end users. • To provide broad channels of communication to rural and remote communities.

ROLE OF SOCIETY'S BUILDING BLOCKS IN SETTING UP AN ENABLING ELECTRONIC COMMERCE ENVIRONMENT

In the case of developing a national electronic commerce industry, the role of the government is a prerequisite, particularly in the early stages, and the government is expected to play a regulatory role, establish the ICT infrastructure and coordinate efforts at the top policymaking level as well as set an example to the best practice (Ghoneim, 2000).

However, other building blocks in the society have an integral role in enabling an electronic commerce environment. This includes the roles that could be played by the private sector and non-governmental organizations. Table 5 demonstrates the roles that could be played by the government of Egypt and that relate to (a) national strategy and institutional framework, (b) national information and communication technology infrastructure and (c) community development.

With respect to the private sector, non-governmental organizations and the media, there is also a vital role that can be played and that can help seize the numerous business opportunities made available and arising from adopting electronic commerce, as shown in Table 6.

CONCLUSION

Egypt's social and economic development is to a large extent determined by its most precious resource, "human resources", through its size and quality. The intellectual capital of a developing nation like Egypt represents a critical factor for its development and growth in the 21st century. It is important to note that the success of the economy will be determined by the quality of its human resources as the importance of natural resources steadily diminishes worldwide. Therefore, preparing the society for the Information Age necessitates appropriate investments in developing its human resources. In that respect, there is a growing need to formulate a new comprehensive policy to entice the use of information and communication technology in decision-making through accessing a wide scope of national and international information sources covering different sectors coupled with the development and improvement of knowledge capacities to be able to optimize the use of information to serve the different developmental efforts. Electronic commerce represents a dynamic model for the information society but neither the people nor the firms in many developed and developing nations are prepared for the new technology. Therefore, there is an invaluable need for more awareness creation and readiness to be provided by governments as well as public and private authorities. From a socioeconomic perspective there is a need for public and widespread participation in the evolving information society and for avoiding the risk of creating classes of information haves and have-nots. Electronic commerce will have a profound impact on businesses, institutions and individuals but there is a need to set up a favorable electronic commerce environment to face the challenge of strong internationalization of markets, globalization of corporate strategies, and the increasing mobility of capital and know-how that characterize the economic process worldwide. Finally, to relate the policy recommendations to the institutional framework, it seems that the institutions on the demand side need to be strengthened as well as institutions related to the indirect supply of electronic commerce, which is needed to reach a conducive environment for electronic commerce to function.

REFERENCES

American Chamber of Commerce in Egypt. (2001, April). *Business monthly.*

American Chamber of Commerce in Egypt. (2001, July). *Telecommunications in Egypt.* Business Studies Series.

American Chamber of Commerce in Egypt. (2002, April). *Information Technology in Egypt.* Business Studies Series.

Brown, M. (2000). *Advancing e-commerce in Egypt: Legal and regulatory recommendations.* Report submitted to the Ministers of Economy and Foreign Trade and Communication and Information Technology.

Chase, L. (1998). *Internet world: Essential business tactics for the Net.* New York: John Wiley and Sons, Inc.

Clague, C. (1997). The new institutional economics and institutional reform. In C. Clague (Ed.), *Institutions and economic development: Growth and governance in less developed and post socialist countries.* The John Hopkins University Press.

Electronic Marketing Bulletin. Available: *www.emarekter.com* (last visited December 10, 2001).

European Commission, Information Society Directorate General. (2000, August). *Benchmarking telework and e-commerce in Europe (ECATT) final report.*

Fahmi, H. (2003). The world of telecommunications. *Al Ahram Newspaper,* 8 June.

Ghoneim, S. (2000). *Developing a national EDI strategy: Opportunities & challenges.* Unpublished Ph.D. Dissertation, The Management School, Imperial College of Science, Technology & Medicine, University of London, UK.

Hammond, R. (1996). *Digital business.* London: Coronet Books.

Hashem, S., & Ismail, M. (1998, November). The evolution of Internet services in Egypt: Towards empowering electronic commerce. *Proceedings of the Global Marketplace for SMEs Conference,* Manchester, UK.

Information and Decision Support Center. Available: www.idsc.gov.eg (last visited: January 10, 2002).

Institute of Development Studies (IDS). (2001). *Policy brief,* Issue 14. University of Sussex.

Internet Society of Egypt. Available: *www.ise.org.eg* (last visited: January 09, 2002).

Internet Surveys. Available: *www.nua.ie* (last visited: October 20, 2001).

Islam, R. (2002). Institutions to support markets. *Finance and Development, 39*(1), March.

Kalakota, R., & Whinston, A. (1996). *Frontiers of electronic commerce.* Addison Wesley.

Kamel, S. (1995, May 21-24). Information superhighways, a potential for socioeconomic and cultural development. *Proceedings of the 6th International IRMA Conference on Managing Information and Communications in a Changing Global Environment,* Atlanta, Georgia, USA.

Kamel, S. (2000). Electronic commerce in Egypt. In M. Khosrow-Pour (Ed.), *Managing web-enabled technologies in organizations: A global perspective.* Hershey, PA: Idea Group Publishing.

Kosiur, D. (1997). *Understanding electronic commerce.* Redmond: Microsoft Press.

Lynch, D.C., & Lundquist, L. (1996). *Digital money: The new era of Internet commerce.* New York: John Wiley and Sons, Inc.Matto, A., & Schuknecht, L. (2000). *Trade policies for electronic commerce* (World Bank Paper, No. 2380).

Merriam-Webster's Collegiate Dictionary. (2000). *10th Edition.*

Ministry of Communication and Information Technology. Available: *www.mcit.gov.eg* (last visited: February 5, 2002)

Mintz, S. (1998). *The Internet as a tool for Egypt's economic growth* (an International Development Professionals Inc. Report).

Noll, R.G. (1997). *The international dimension of regulatory reform: With applications to Egypt* (Series of Distinguished Lectures, No. 8). Cairo: The Egyptian Center for Economic Studies (ECES).

North, D.C. (1990). *Institutions, institutional change and economic performance (political economy of institutions and decision).* Cambridge: Cambridge University Press.

NUA Internet Surveys (1998, April 23). *Electronic commerce in the Arab world - An overview*. Available: (*www.nua.com*).

Rodrik, D. (1997). Trade and the demand for social insurance. *Has globalization gone too far.* Washington, D.C.: Institute for International Economics.

Schuknecht, L., & Perez-Esteve, R. (1999). *A quantitative assessment of electronic commerce* (WTO Staff Working Paper ERAD-99-01).

Silverstein, B. (1999). *Business-to-business Internet marketing.* USA: Gulf Breeze Maximum Press.

Tapscott, D. (1996). *The digital economy promise and peril in the age of networked intelligence.* USA: MacGraw Hill.

Whinston, A.B., Stahl, D.O., & Choi, S. (1997). *The economics of electronic commerce.* IN: Macmillan Technical Publishing.

World Bank. (2001). *Building institutions for markets* (World Bank Development Report). Oxford: Oxford University Press.

World Bank and OECD. (1998). *A framework for the design and implementation of competition law and policy.* Washington, D.C. and Paris.

UNCTAD. (2000). *Building confidence: Electronic commerce and development.* United Nations.

Zaki, M. (1999). *Egyptian business elites: Their visions and investment behavior.* Cairo: Konrad Adenaur Stiftung and the Arab Center for Development and Future Research.

This work was previously published in The Social and Cognitive Impacts of e-Commerce on Modern Organizations, edited by M. Khosrow-Pour, pp. 253-276, copyright 2004 by IGI Publishing, formerly known as Idea Group Publishing (an imprint of IGI Global).

Chapter 4.45
The Impact of M-Government on Organisations: A Mobility Response Model

Ibrahim Kushchu
Mobile Government Consortium International, UK

Seda Arat
Mobile Government Consortium International, UK

Chet Borucki
Temple University, Japan

ABSTRACT

Adoption of mobile technologies by government organizations not only benefits the parties who use these services, but also has positive impact on the internal workings of the public sector. Those government entities which initiated mobile applications have visible gains in productivity and cost and operational savings. This new way of performing tasks also undoubtedly has some repercussions on the organizational structure, civil worker, and the business processes. This chapter tries to underline some of the issues that might arise in these areas by examining some ongoing mobile government projects.

INTRODUCTION

Wireless technologies are leading the trend toward a ubiquitous and pervasive living environment enabling individuals and organizations to communicate and perform specific tasks anytime and anywhere. Tablet PCs, mobile phones, PDAs, and smart-phones are becoming an indispensable part of the personal and professional lives of an increasing number of people in an increasing number of countries, with time-saving applications both on and off the job. Location, and to some extent, context-based mobile applications are allowing users to benefit from not only the mobility, but also the information and guidance that these devices provide.

Advancements in information and communication technologies (ICT) and especially the rapid adoption of mobile phones around the world contributed to the introduction of new mobile technology applications and services in recent years. Hence, mobile technologies offer solutions to a wide range of audiences ranging from individuals to businesses and government institutions in a world where speed and efficiency matter the most. The benefits and consequent improvements in efficiency and service that earlier generation technologies have provided are evident in activities that are now often taken for granted, for example, banking or paying bills online, or what is commonly referred to as e-commerce. Applications of information technologies in the governmental sector are sufficiently different from those in the private sector such that they are commonly referred to as e-government. However, special consideration is warranted for those government applications and services made available to the citizens specifically via the use of mobile technologies, hence the emergence of the field of mobile government or m-government (Kushchu & Kuscu, 2003).

At first glance, applying wireless solutions to the bureaucratic, slow-paced, and rigid public sector entities may seem a little out of place, but the increasing number of mobile government applications around the world show that there are indeed many opportunities for governments to improve and enhance their services, cut down on operational costs and create a better functioning organization. Traffic updates, navigation assistance, emergency assistance, weather updates, notification for tax and bill payments, field inspections, and tracking systems for stolen vehicles, all of which are possible with mobile technologies, are some of the more common applications used by governmental agencies (Yu & Kushchu, 2004). Though these applications have much promise, their widespread acceptance by governmental agencies is still in question.

Kushchu and Borucki (2004) further argue that while mobile government applications can have immediate and significant benefits for end users, many of the governmental units offering mobile solutions have yet to achieve major gains, especially in terms of workplace productivity. Given the bureaucratic nature of governmental agencies, critical changes in decision-making processes and shared values under guiding organizational culture and organizational structure tend to occur much slower than they do in private sector companies. The authors contend, however, that as the demands of its citizens continue unabated, governments would be eventually forced to accelerate the diffusion of mobile technologies. Once accustomed to convenient services received from private sector organizations such as airlines, banks, and utility companies that allow timely sharing of information and seamless transactions without face-to-face interactions, it is not unreasonable for the public to expect the same from governmental agencies.

In our opinion, it is important to understand the impact of mobile technologies on government administration as there are implications for the success of well-planned, integrated, and widely-adopted m-government applications. A technology-influenced state of administrative efforts, whether broad e-government initiatives or mobile-specific m-government initiatives, can potentially lead to the re-definition of job descriptions and duties, improved relationships between citizens and other governmental agencies, and promote new policies for enhancing services. However, where government agencies tend to lag private sector organizations in the diffusion of technology is in essential internal changes in organizational structure, hierarchical decision-making processes and politically-oriented shared values or culture. The inherent characteristics of governmental administrations understandably are difficult to change but in the short run, various efficiency gains in terms of speed, improved services, and cost savings may be possible.

Having introduced mobile technologies and their utilization in the governmental sector, the remainder of this chapter is organized as follows. In the next section, we provide an overview of mobile government and its differentiating characteristics followed by an assessment of the impact that mobile technology has on governments. We then review and evaluate the typical responses that governmental organizations have exhibited in response to the pressures exerted by mobile technologies. Five case studies will be discussed (four from the United Kingdom and one from Hong Kong) in part to illustrate the challenges and opportunities presented by the applications of mobile technologies in governmental agencies and to show that there are examples where considerable efficiency gains have been possible. Furthermore, the chapter will highlight some potential changes that might occur in governmental organizations in terms of structure, the attitudes and skills of the civil worker and business processes as a result of utilizing mobile technologies. We close the chapter with a summary of our findings and implications for future research.

M-GOVERNMENT AND ITS DIFFERENTIATING CHARACTERISTICS

M-government pertains to the strategy and implementation of governmental services through a mobile platform to provide end users, both citizens and civil servants, the benefit of obtaining services and information from anywhere at anytime (Arazyan, 2002; Kushchu & Kuscu, 2003). As indicated earlier, the specific use of mobile technologies and applications is what differentiates m-government from any other developments in the public sector using new technologies, including e-government. Based on a study of mobile technologies (Yu & Kushchu, 2004), and their practical applications in governmental agencies (Cilingir & Kushchu, 2004), the following differentiating factors are apparent:

- Convenient accessibility and availability:
  - M-government facilitates the adoption of online governmental services by end users through the improved convenience it offers. Citizens can use the online governmental services not only "anytime" but also "anywhere".
  - In contrast to laptop computers, for example, mobile devices are always "switched on". Usually, these devices remain in an inactive state, but applications can "wake up" the device. This is also serves to differentiate m-government from e-government applications.
  - Mobile devices are designed to be mobile—or carried around by the user. Thus, applications can be designed to provide instant information to the users. An example is to send out warnings about forthcoming bad weather conditions or emergencies.
- Precision and personalisation in targeting users and delivering content:
  - A computer can be shared among different users, but mobile devices are intended and designed for personal use by one individual—a person generally does not "share" use of a cell phone with others, for example. This means that personalized information can reach the same user at any time through that one specific device.
  - M-government increases the acceptance, adoption and the usage of online governmental services by reaching end users through a more personal, familiar and friendly device.
- Larger and wider user base:
  - M-government reaches a larger number of people through mobile devices, which often far exceeds the wired Internet user community.

- o M-government reaches a variety of audiences, including people who have no training or experience with computers and the internet, but are active users of mobile communication.

MOBILE TECHNOLOGY'S PRESSURES ON GOVERNMENTS

The impact of these differentiating characteristics of mobile technology places considerable pressure on governments, to a varying degree. Some are technology related and others are related to public expectations and the governments' position to improve its services and business, and can be summarized as follows.

- **The pressure to meet increased expectations:** Trends in a high rate of adoption of mobile Internet applications and services in the private sector lead to higher expectations for timely service from governmental agencies. This requires more efficient government units with employees who need more accurate and timely information readily available regardless of where they are working (Yu & Kushchu, 2004).
- **Pressure towards adoption of new technologies:** The emergence of the mobile Internet and the high level of mobile penetration world-wide exerts pressure on governmental agencies to catch up with the developments in the technology. The development of 3G mobile network services makes the provision of mobile government applications possible and more accessible than using the wired Internet. The evolution of mobile Internet technologies, standards and protocols allows faster and more sophisticated (voice and multimedia) application developments (Yu & Kushchu, 2004).
- **Pressure towards further improving e-government efforts:** M-government is best viewed as complementing, rather than replacing e-government. End users can access the applications from a new platform from "anywhere" through mobile devices. However, there are certain applications that are only possible with mobile technologies such as location dependent information delivery (Cilingir & Kushchu, 2004; Yu & Kushchu, 2004).
- **Pressure for increased governmental efficiency and effectiveness:** The essential value of mobility is often observed in faster responses and reach to a wider user base, resulting in economies of scale in performing various governmental tasks.
- **Pressure for supporting economic development, especially for rural areas of developing countries:** Mobile applications in many developing countries are being used to "leapfrog" wired e-government efforts where there is not enough infrastructure of wired Internet in terms availability of networked computer and skilful users of computers (Ghyasi & Kushchu, 2004).

To appropriately respond to these pressures, there is a call for significant improvements in the internal structures, decision-making processes, and culture of many governmental agencies. Although provision of these new mobile technology developments is mostly related to improving government services for external users, such improvements would be incomplete without bringing significant changes to government organizations themselves. Kushchu and Borucki (2004) suggested that governments are giving more priority to satisfying the requirements of external stakeholders such citizens and businesses rather than intra-governmental agencies, units, departments, and so forth at local, state, and national levels. However, recent case studies, which will be summarized next, indicate that some governmental agencies are trying to attend to both external customer needs and internal organizational transformations in traditional policies procedures, and practices, with varying degrees of success.

TYPICAL RESPONSES

According to Kushchu and Borucki (2004), governments implement mobile technologies either as a response to complement their existing e-government initiatives or as a response to take advantage of the benefits of mobility. Their observations were summarized in the form of a "response model" which appears in Figure 1. The model highlights three interrelated issues: First, it identifies what is special about mobile technologies as a set of unique characteristics of mobile government developments. Second, the various pressures bureaucratic governments face in adopting mobile technologies and transforming themselves into effective and efficient administrative organizations are highlighted. Finally, based on examination of various mobile government applications (Cilingir & Kushchu, 2004; Ghyasi, Farshid, & Kushchu, 2004; Yu & Kushchu, 2004), the model enumerates the "response" of governments to address those pressures. In brief, the response model suggests that much remains to be done for current m-government applications to be able to serve governments with effective tools of administration.

Various m-government applications and business models have been developed and implemented to address the pressures identified earlier. In general, there are two categories of responses: those complementing e-government efforts and those exploiting the unique essence of mobility.

- **Upgrading efforts:** Here, governments endeavor to upgrade their applications and services to confront technological and user expectation pressures, and these include m-government applications that are complementary to e-government applications. Such "add on" mobile applications are intended to increase the value provided by e-government applications and enhance end user convenience. Thus, the value of electronic government applications is enhanced by adding the "anywhere" component to the "anytime" value proposition.

Figure 1. The response model (Source: Kushchu and Borucki (2004), A Mobility Response Model for Government)

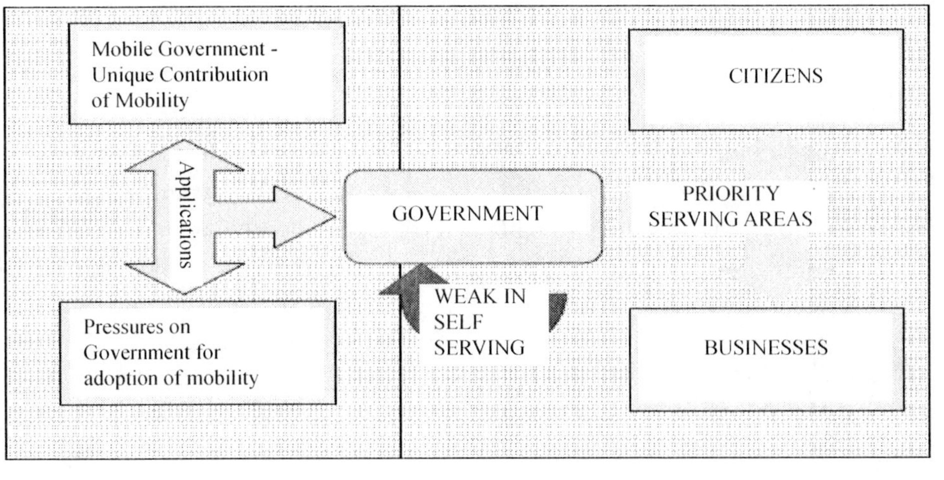

- **Innovative efforts:** These efforts are intended to build m-government applications that create a novel and unique set of benefits stemming from unique characteristics of mobile technologies and the nature of m-government applications. A new definition of value is created with the implementation of mobile applications, and this category of services is not dependent on e-government applications and the real value stems from the mobility itself.

CASE STUDIES ON MOBILE TECHNOLOGY DIFFUSION AND M-GOVERNMENT

There are many ongoing mobile government projects in different parts of the world where attention seems to be paid to the goals of both external user satisfaction and internal organizational efficiency and effectiveness. It is still very early to be able to clearly identify the impact of mobile government on the organization since most of the mobile government projects are smaller-scale, local in origin, and involve a small number of civil servants in few departments.

One such project initiated by the Office of the Deputy Prime Minister in United Kingdom is "Project Nomad". Project Nomad aims to facilitate the use of mobile technologies in interested local government organizations by offering a wide range of assistance varying from research and business case design to technical issues such as planning, technology selection, data integration, and management and organizational issues. Some local organizations that participate in this project are Cambridgeshire County Council, Sheffield City Council, North Somerset Council, Norwich City Council, London Borough of Sutton, London Borough of Greenwich, London Borough of Lewisham, Barnsley Metropolitan Borough Council, Kirklees Metropolitan Council, and Cumbria County Council.[1]

North London Strategic Alliance Street Wardens Pilot Project Overview (UK)

North London Strategic Alliance (NLSA) Street Wardens Pilot Project, a collective effort of four London Boroughs (Enfield, Haringey, Barnet, and Waltham Forest) is a mobile government application aimed at streamlining the operations of street wardens. The scope of this pilot project is currently limited to environmental crime and abandoned vehicles.

This application allows the street wardens to fill in information regarding the incident at the scene using a mobile device like a XDA2 smart phone or Pocket PC. These mobile devices have GPRS and Bluetooth connectivity. Thus, all information provided by the warden is instantly transferred to a password secured database accessible via the Internet. These mobile devices also have mapping capabilities.

With this new application, the wardens do not have to go back to the office to enter the information into the database and therefore can be responsive to more incidents. Furthermore, the accuracy of the information is improved. For instance, the wardens can take pictures of environmental crimes by their mobile devices to support their formal letter to the citizens.

Regarding the impact on internal organizational efficiencies and overall effectiveness, the following have been observed:

- 20% time savings in report writing for wardens;
- Increase in the response rate of wardens to incidents (they can be on the road longer since they do not have to return to the office);
- Elimination of duplicate work (before wardens who filled in the report by handwriting had to go back to the office to re-enter the information into the database making reporting inefficient);

- Increase in the accuracy of reporting and reduction in citizen claims and legal costs due to visual evidence; and
- Cost savings for each council for abandoned vehicles.[2]

Barnsley Metropolitan Borough Council, Berneslai Home Impact Team Officers Mobile Data Project Overview (UK)

Impact Team Officers Mobile Data Project is owned by Berneslai Homes which is an "Arms Length Management Organization" of Barnsley Metropolitan Borough Council. Bereslai Homes is a new organization within the borough specifically created to establish better relations with the tenants living in the council housing by listening to their concerns. One key tenant concern raised has been anti-social activities. In order to find a solution, Bereslai Homes introduced the Impact Team Officers to replace the existing Council Estate Officers. These new officers will spend their time in the estates to be closer to the tenants. This requires the officers to be highly mobile. Thus, the project permits 42 Impact Team Officers to use Bluetooth enabled mobile phones and iPAQ handheld devices to instantly transfer their reports on anti-social behavior taking place in council housing estates while still at the site.

Previously, the Council Estate Officers were to write their reports once they return to the office and then upload it to the council's IT system. Their interactions with the tenants were limited since they were generally present at the estates whenever there was a complaint. However, with the new project, the Impact Team Officers will spend their entire time on the premises completing and transferring their reports wirelessly without the need to go back to the office.

Since Berneslai Homes is an organization established by Barnsley Metropolitan Borough Council to oversee the council housing issues, the information systems of both entities have been integrated for smoother operations and knowledge sharing.

Reported efficiencies gained include the following:

- Operational efficiency in the form of elimination of duplicate work, minimization of traveling time, attending more tenant complaints, and so forth;
- Cost savings since less office space and workstations are needed; and
- Better service offering to tenants.[3]

Mobile Working at Barking and Dagenham Project Overview (UK)

Mobile Working at London Borough of Barking and Dagenham Project enables six void inspection surveyors, who deal with 2,000 void inspections every year to use Pocket PCs to transfer their findings electronically back to the office. Prior to this project, the surveyors were relying on Dictaphones to keep a record of the inspection results and then taking the tapes to the office for two typists to type. A paper-based questionnaire was also filled out by the surveyor in each site visit. The old process was burdensome necessitating the surveyors to return to the office to hand in the tapes and the questionnaires.

Under this project, these surveyors not only can transfer data like inspection results and questionnaires seamlessly, but can also access additional information such as timescales, tenancy agreements, and so forth, in the field. The organization is planning to extend this project to include the remaining 12 surveyors who are annually in charge of 80,000 responsive repairs.

Mobile Working at Barking and Dagenham Project increased productivity in the following ways:

- Surveying time has been improved and increased by 2 hours per day compared to before.

- Void turnaround has been cut down by at least 2 days.
- Some savings achieved in HR since there was no need for the two typists anymore.
- Less office space is required since the surveyors don't have to go back to the office.
- The quality of the surveyors reports and the gathered data has improved.
- Surveyors are able to access more information outside of the office which contributes to the quality and accuracy of their reports.[4]

Norwich City Council Street Scene Project: Parking Services Overview (UK)

Norwich City Council Street Scene Project enables 34 parking attendants to report illegal parking and environment related issues using their handheld devices to the central parking system called Langdale. In the past, these parking attendants had to go back to office to upload the information. Since monitoring litter, graffiti, abandoned vehicles, fly posting, and fly tipping is also among their secondary duties, the parking attendants in addition prepared reports concerning these environmental issues to be passed on to the relevant authorities for further action via e-mail. Moreover, at the beginning of each working day, the attendants had to be present at the office to be briefed by the Parking Team Leader.

With this project, the attendants will be able to upload their reports on illegal parking to Langdale system wirelessly without going back to the office. They will also be able to submit their environment-related reports to parties concerned like City Care or Environmental Health (Comino system) electronically. In other words, this project will allow the parking system and environmental health system to be loosely integrated to work more effectively together. The project will also eliminate the need for attendants to be present in the office every morning for the daily briefing since a messaging system will be developed to inform them of new developments each time they connect to the system.

Thanks to the mobile technology deployment, Norwich City Council Street Scene Parking Services expects to observe:

- Increase in productivity by around 15% (from 60 to 75%);
- One man hour saving per parking attendant every day (if the attendants were to be out in the streets rather than staying in the office in this "non-patrolled" time period, it is estimated that 6,000 additional tickets would be issued annually and the organization would make additional £112,000 revenue);
- Less paper work since the environmental reports will be sent to parties concerned electronically; and
- Less office space since the parking attendants do not need an office to perform their tasks anymore. Instead they will be using a new depot at the city center.[5]

Environment Protection Department of Hong Kong Mobile Field Inspection System Overview (Hong Kong)

Environment Protection Department (EPD) of Hong Kong is the authority in charge of environmental issues and, to this end, conducts regular inspections on chemical waste collectors and compiles the compliance results. Before the realization of the Mobile Field Inspection System, the inspectors were writing their reports on paper and then re-entering the same data to the database at the office. This business process was not very efficient. Therefore, EDP introduced a mobile field inspection system which uses touch-screen PDAs to enter the inspection information at the scene. The inspectors are also able to review the results of past inspections through their PDAs to have a better knowledge about the inspected waste collector. Once the data is stored in the PDA, it is transferred directly to EDP's back-end system through synchronization.

As for EDP Mobile Inspection System, some of the savings are:

- Increase in productivity by around 10%;
- 1.5 man hour saving per inspection team on a daily basis; and
- Elimination of duplicate work.[6]

THE IMPACT OF MOBILE GOVERNMENT ON THE INTERNAL ORGANIZATION

Though the five projects described previously are quite small in scale with limited involvement of civil servants and in only a few departments, they do suggest that some progress is being made in accomplishing the dual goals of end-user satisfaction and internal governmental agency efficiency and effectiveness. In this section, we summarize some of the potential impacts of mobile technologies on organizational structure, civil workers, and business processes.

The Impact on Structure

One expected outcome of utilizing mobile government applications is increase in productivity in line with the increasing demands of the citizens for faster and better service. Increase in efficiency and productivity due to mobile government applications is inevitable as exemplified earlier and may reflect itself in the structure of the organization in following possible ways:

1. **Reduction in the number of people performing the job.** A small though appropriate example is the laying off of the two typists who are no longer needed in case of the "Mobile Working at Barking and Dagenham" Project.
2. **Establishment of new virtual departments.** The London Borough of Barking and Dagenham is considering whether to ask the six void inspection surveyors to be home based since they do not require office space anymore to perform their tasks. The borough is also thinking about expanding the project to include other surveyors. In due course, this department could turn into a virtual one. We can expect to see a similar approach in other projects we have explained previously. Another example for a virtual department is the National Department of Seniors in Canada which offers local, regional, and national services to Canadians in English and French. Although this department is not part of the existing organizational structure, its online services are guaranteed by a group of civil workers working in the local, regional, and national government entities (Robillard, 2003).
3. **Consolidation of divisions/departments so that complementary or parallel departments are replaced with fewer functional departments and reduction in hierarchical levels due to these consolidations.** In all these projects, since it's only the wardens, inspectors, surveyors, attendants, and officers who are affected by new mobile applications and it is simply using a new tool to do the same task, a major potential effect on the organizational structure in this form will be very unlikely at least for the time being. But as more interrelated departments start using mobile applications, department consolidations are to be expected. In the transition phase, it is very likely that these interrelated departments will first integrate their databases or information sharing processes and then gradually move into a full-scale consolidation.

The Impact on Civil Workers

In the case of some mobile government applications, the civil workers may be required to acquire some new skills like learning how to use a new wireless device or how to enter information via wireless networks. Although these devices and applications may be user friendly, depending on the age and background of the users, adaptation may take longer than anticipated hindering the success of the project or causing delays in outcomes. Furthermore, some adjustments in the civil workers' job descriptions may be required or the new application may call for hiring new people with different skills into the organization.

Before the introduction of the NLSA Street Wardens Project, 12 wardens who are part of the pilot were handwriting the information at the scene and then going back to the office to enter that information into a database to be accessed and shared by other departments. This meant a waste of time because of the duplication of work. Furthermore, the wardens were not quick enough in attending new incidents since some of their working time was allocated to staying at the office to prepare the report. Once this project was introduced, the street wardens were required to use mobile devices to perform their task of entering information on the incident at the spot. These mobile devices freed the wardens from spending unnecessary time at the office. However, since this was a new tool with many features, all wardens using these devices were trained for half an hour to an hour. The training sessions, which also involved senior management, were relatively short because the software was developed with simplicity and user friendliness in mind. However, extra training was required for those who were not used to information technologies.

Likewise, the inspectors at EDP were entering information by hand and then transferring it to the database manually. With the new system, the work process is streamlined and the inspectors have more time at inspection sites. Although they still need to go back to the office to synchronize the data with their back-end system, with the introduction of new devices like Blackberry, it is very likely that in the near future, the inspectors would be able to send their reports through their device without going to the office. The PDAs were designed for easy use, so the training time was short.

As part of the Barnsley Metropolitan Borough Council, Berneslai Home Impact Team Officers Mobile Data Project, all Impact Team Officers were given a two-day training session in which they learned how to use the device and connect to the database and how to use the forms available to them. Additionally, to assist officers further, eight people were trained to act as "super users" to be the main contact point when officers faced problems. In the initial stages, management also monitored the officers to see how often they use the mobile solution and tried to understand the reasons behind infrequent use by some officers. Although these training sessions were successful, during the implementation phase, some technical problems were encountered that affected the motivation of the officers making them wary of the benefits of deploying mobile technologies. Therefore, it is of utmost importance that the civil workers who will be part of the mobile solution are encouraged to take part during the planning and implementation phase so as to convince them that they can perform better and save time by using these applications.

It would not be wrong to conclude that using wireless technologies to perform certain tasks may reduce the amount of personal communication between people. For instance, rather than going to the office and asking for additional information from a colleague, the civil worker may simply use his/her device to retrieve that information, never directly communicating with anyone from his/her office. In other words, face-to-face communication may be replaced with human-to-machine communication and any interdependencies between individuals or departments can be dealt with through the wireless system.

Although the mobile government application is aiming to make the working process of civil workers more efficient, due to the location-based nature of the application, it is possible to track them. On one hand, this helps to identify where each civil worker is located and may improve efficiency when it comes to calling the person on duty located closest to the incident. On the other hand, the civil workers may feel that they are being monitored and tracked. This may also have some legal repercussions as these projects become full scale.

The Impact on Business Processes

Introduction of mobile technologies may suggest that the organizational structure will become flattened with fewer hierarchical levels and looser connections between employees. Moreover, being able to access recent information "anytime and anywhere" may require a more integrated approach to mobile government solutions. The cases we have analyzed support this contention. For instance, an inspection report prepared by one warden in one borough using mobile technologies may need to be shared by other boroughs in London or even across the UK and accordingly may require a unified business process. Since currently the information within different government organizations and different departments within the same government organization is scattered, mobile government can help to combine all organizational knowledge on a real-time basis so that process time and costs are reduced. For instance, Norwich City Council Street Scene, Parking Services Project allows efficient information flow and sharing between parking services and environmental health. Similarly, Berneslai Homes and Barnsley Borough Council have integrated information systems which allow the civil workers who have different roles/tasks in the same process to perform faster and more efficiently.

Figure 2.

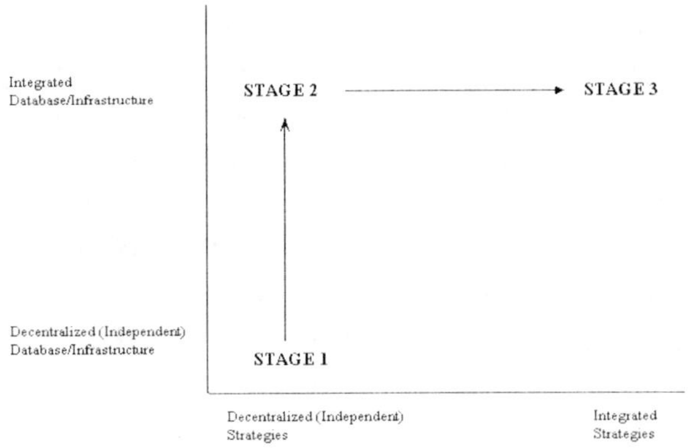

There is no doubt that with the introduction of mobile government, the civil workers involved are more mobile than before. They no longer have to go to the office to do their job. In other words, they do not require any office space. As a result, these civil workers could be viewed as virtual workers. They can be informed about the incident, prepare and send their report via their mobile devices, hence, never needing to go to the office to fulfill their duties. This encourages a more flexible environment and promotes looser connections when it comes to peer-subordinate relationships. However, having virtual workers raises some important issues that require attention such as performance evaluation and working efficiently and effectively, both individually and collectively, as part of a team without direct supervision.

The biggest impact of mobile government is likely to be on streamlining business processes on a single, shared platform by gathering, updating, and processing data from all departments anytime and anywhere. Figure 2 shows the evolution of mobile government. Although it's too early to predict the progress of mobile government strategies, it is possible to expect that initially the mobile government strategies will be decentralized since they will be first tried out locally rather than on a city or country basis. Accordingly, the database and infrastructure supporting these strategies will be independent of a unified database or infrastructure. In the second stage, as mobile government applications become more common and successful, more local authorities will adopt it. This will pave the way for a common, unified database and infrastructure within and among various government units. In the later stage, a more integrated mobile government strategy will be favored within the government as a whole and an integrated database and infrastructure will allow the information to be shared across all government entities.

CONCLUSION

Recently, governments around the world are setting very aggressive targets to move towards e-government and mobile government. This bureaucratic or top-down approach, which to a great extent is a result of external pressures from citizens and businesses, may fall short of visibly identifying strategies as to the content (what) and process (how) of this shift to e- and m-government. In other words, governments should have a roadmap that clearly identifies when it is necessary to make the change, what needs to be changed and how to make it happen.

We have tried to identify the impact of utilizing mobile government applications on the organizational structure in light of some real-life examples presented in the previous sections. Although these case studies are insufficient in allowing us to reach more than general conclusions, they do suggest that some governmental agencies are embracing mobile technologies and are following through with some internal changes in structures, policies, and practices in an attempt to reap benefits more often seen in private sector companies. However, at least for the near future, it is not likely that we will see wide-scale major structural changes in public institutions due to mobile government. This is mainly because most of the mobile government initiatives are at the local level with the involvement of very few departments and civil workers.

Furthermore, these applications seem to have insufficient impact on the workings of the organization to necessitate a major structural change. The case studies, as few and as limited as they are, indicate that change occurred not in the formal structure of the organization, but rather in the way the tasks were accomplished. In other words, there were some changes in the business process and workflow of the departments involved. We should also note that structural changes require more time and energy, and structure in whatever form should support strategy and fit with other internal organizational components such as organizational culture, though clearly, in governmental agencies, there are many cases where both structure and culture need to be changed. As more and more departments embrace mobile government applications, a more unified mobile government strategy as well as more integrated infrastructure and databases within the government is likely to be observed. Once this level of adoption is achieved, it would be possible to witness some major changes in the structure of the government organization due to bottom-up pressures coming from those local or regional departments that have benefited from m-government applications. These changes might be in the form of virtual departments, consolidation of some departments into one or reductions in headcounts.

Additionally, we can argue that the role of the civil worker, who is part of the mobile government service, is likely to be re-defined making him/her a more independent, mobile agent accountable to not only one but many different departments by fulfilling his/her tasks under the mobile government project. It is quite possible that the shift to e- and m-government applications will make governments more functional organizations since the tasks would be completed by different people with different skills and job descriptions working at different departments at different parts of the country, though a process-oriented structure may be more desirable. This would also facilitate a working environment where the relationships are loosely defined giving more flexibility to the civil worker while performing his/her tasks.

Although the examples used in this chapter are small-scale and there are no issues of rejection of the concept on the part of the civil workers, it may be of importance to dwell a little on the resistance to change on the part of the employees as a result of mobile government initiatives. Habits, fear of the unknown, security, and economic factors are some reasons why people can be resistant in accepting new approaches. We have already mentioned some effects of mobile applications on the civil worker. As a consequence of these changes, employees might think of these applications as a threat that will lead to redundancies or the loss of jobs, or may have a feeling that they are losing control to machines. The fear of not being able to acquire the skills or concerns over future competencies may make the employees suspicious to these applications. Interpersonal communication should be at the center of this process in order to persuade the parties involved to willingly be part of the change rather than forcing them to agree to the set goals. Forcing employees to accept something that they do not believe in or something they see as a threat will bring resistance and hindrance during the transition phase and may lead to total rejection later on. In other words, employees should be motivated and supported all throughout this process through proper education and training.

The culture of an organization is of utmost importance when it comes to embracing change without much difficulty. At times, organizational culture needs adjustment to fit the change. Lucienne Robillard, President of the Canadian Treasury Board, and member of Parliament for Westmount-Ville-Marie gives an example from the Seniors Department in Canada in a speech delivered on May 8, 2003:

...What is also changing, quite significantly, is the role of the individual public sector employee and his or her relationship to information, clients, organization and colleagues. Drawing from our "Government on Line" experience, we are beginning to understand that cultural rather than structural change may be more important at this time. And that our approach to information, information systems and understanding the concept of "communities of practice" may be more radical and necessary than 'machinery' change... (Robillard, 2003)

There is no doubt that mobile government applications not only make the lives of the citizens easier, but also increase the productivity within the government organizations. However, while adopting it, a careful consideration should be made as to its effects on the work processes, the civil workers, the span of control, and the formal structure of the government entity. Longitudinal research with case studies of larger governmental agencies in different contexts would provide data on when diffusion of mobile technologies is successful and under what conditions, and would further shed light on the impact of these technologies on internal organizational functioning.

REFERENCES

Arazyan, H. (2002). *m-Government: Definition and perspectives*. Retrieved January 17, 2005, from http://www.developmentgateway.org/download/143909/mGovernment_Interview_2.doc

Cilingir, D., & Kushchu, I. (2004). E-government and m-government: Concurrent leaps by Turkey. In D. Remenyi (Ed.), *European Conference on E-Government (ECEG 2004)*, Trinity College, Dublin, June 17-18 (pp. 813-821). Department of the Taoiseach, Dublin, Ireland; Reading, UK: Academic Conferences International.

Ghyasi, A. F., & Kushchu, I. (2004). m-Government: Cases of developing countries. In D. Remenyi (Ed.), *European Conference on E-Government (ECEG 2004)*, Trinity College, Dublin, June 17-18 (pp. 822-829). Department of the Taoiseach, Dublin, Ireland; Reading, UK: Academic Conferences International.

Kushchu, I., & Borucki, C. (2004). *A mobility response model for government*. Retrieved January 15, 2005, from http://www.mgovlab.org/library/mgovlab/mgovlab_ikcb.pdf

Kushchu, I., & Kuscu, H. (2003). From e-government to m-government: Facing the inevitable. In the *Proceedings of the European Conference on E-Government (ECEG 2003)*, Trinity College, Dublin, July 3-4 (pp. 253-260). Reading, UK: Academic Conferences International.

Robillard, L. (2003). *When e-government becomes simply government: Making the case for radical incrementalism in public sector governance.* Speech. Crossing Boundaries Conference. Retrieved April 30, 2005, from http://www.tbs-sct.gc.ca/media/ps-dp/2003/0508_e.asp

Yu, B., & Kushchu, I. (2004). The value of mobility for e-government. In D. Remenyi (Ed.), *European Conference on E-Government (ECEG 2004)*, Trinity College, Dublin, June 17-18 (pp. 887-899). Department of the Taoiseach, Dublin, Ireland; Reading, UK: Academic Conferences International.

ONLINE

A Mobile Working Solution for London Borough of Barking & Dagenham Project. Retrieved April 30, 2005, from http://www.projectnomad.org.uk/docstore/15/pdf/357_MobileWorkingSolutionForLondonBoroughoBarkingandDagenham.pdf

Barnsley Metropolitan Borough Council, Berneslai Home Impact Team Officers Mobile Data Project. Retrieved April 30, 2005, from http://www.projectnomad.org.uk/docstore/12/doc/193_BarnsleyApprovedCaseStudy26January2005.doc

Norwich City Council Street Scene Project—Parking Services. Retrieved April 30, 2005, from http://www.projectnomad.org.uk/docstore/12/pdf/367_NorwichCityCouncilStreetScene.pdf

NLSA Street Wardens Project Case Study. Retrieved January 17, 2005, from http://www.projectnomad.org.uk/7xJ5321CSn17443NQj5vOnxf4Si3SI66/docstore/12/doc/34_North%20London%20Strategic%20Alliance%20-%20Final%20Report%20Version%201%20-%201st%20December%202004.doc

Project Nomad—http://www.projectnomad.org.uk/

http://www.asiawireless.net/cust-002.php

http://www.palmone.com/au/solutions/enterprise/studies/hk_edp.html

ENDNOTES

1 http://www.projectnomad.org.uk/ and http://www.localegovnp.org.uk/default.asp?sID=1095853022025

2 http://www.projectnomad.org.uk/7xJ5321CSn17443NQj5vOnxf4Si3SI66/docstore/12/doc/34_North%20London%20Strategic%20Alliance%20-%20Final%20Report%20Version%201%20-%201st%20December%202004.doc

3 http://www.projectnomad.org.uk/docstore/12/doc/193_BarnsleyApprovedCaseStudy26January2005.doc

4 http://www.projectnomad.org.uk/docstore/15/pdf/357_MobileWorkingSolutionForLondonBoroughoBarkingandDagenham.pdf

5 http://www.projectnomad.org.uk/docstore/12/pdf/367_NorwichCityCouncilStreetScene.pdf

6 http://www.asiawireless.net/cust-002.php and http://www.palmone.com/au/solutions/enterprise/studies/hk_edp.html

This work was previously published in Mobile Government: An Emerging Direction in E-Government, edited by I. Kushchu, pp. 134-153, copyright 2007 by IGI Publishing, formerly known as Idea Group Publishing (an imprint of IGI Global).

Chapter 4.46
Skills for Electronic Service Delivery in Public Agencies

Salvador Parrado
Spanish Distance Learning University, Spain

ABSTRACT

The text analyses the strategy of OECD countries in order to introduce the needed skills for launching e-government services at the national level. The chapter further establishes the four sets of e-government related skills that are needed within the three relevant communities of public servants: information technology community, information management community and service community. It additionally discusses the framework to identify skill gaps through the revision of different assessment toolkits. Finally, it offers an overview of how ICT-related skills can be outsourced. This chapter draws on documents, policy papers and interviews with experts and managers of national e-government strategies from OECD countries.

INTRODUCTION

This chapter deals with the needed skills to implement an e-government strategy. It was commissioned by the Public Management Service [PUMA] of the OECD as part of its e-Government Task Force initiative. The present text, as an updated version, benefits from numerous comments and questions gathered from seminar participants and interviewees.[1] It highlights the most important strategies of OECD countries in relation to e-skills.

Although competencies and skills are used in the text interchangeably, competencies have a broader meaning. They are characteristics of an individual which underline performance or behavior at work. Competency is an observable, measurable pattern of skills, knowledge, abilities, behaviors and other characteristics that an individual needs in order to perform successfully work roles or occupational functions (Barker, 2001). According to this definition, general competencies could be oral communication, problem solving, customer service, while technical competencies are, for instance, infrastructure design, network management, and systems integration. In this chapter, the emphasis is placed on ICT- (Information and Communication Technology) related skills for top managers of public bureaucracies that deliver services electronically.

Two different dimensions have been assigned to electronic service delivery (ESD) or e-government (see Bovaird & Lenihan). One dimension refers to the electronic provision of services and the new capacity to collect, integrate and manage information for the use of the public or for tracking broad societal changes and evaluating governmental actions. Another dimension has a wider meaning. It implies the use of ICT to expand public space enabling the direct participation of stakeholders—citizens, businesses, mass media, NGOs (non-governmental organizations), and other levels of government — in government activities. For the sake of simplicity the concept of "e-government services" encompasses both dimensions in the text.

ESD needs that the right skills are in place. The search for generic skills for the Information Age Society is mostly the concern of Anglo-Saxon countries like Australia, Hong Kong, the United States, Canada and the United Kingdom. In other OECD countries, the work on skills is not emerging, or the search for the right skills is narrowed down to ICT-specific skills for the IT community. While there is recognition that government strategists and business managers are not always fully aware of the implications (software, hardware, relationships with other stakeholders and citizens) of the ICT, the content of training of these professionals lack IT-related contents. Different reasons can be offered for this. Some interviewees have underlined the strong division among IT specialists and generalists and the relatively high control of the formers not only on the technical aspects of e-government strategies but also on the non-technical dimension, i.e., on the overall service strategy. In many non Anglo Saxon countries, the launch of e-government service has been seen as an opportunity for IT specialists to control service delivery.

In order to tackle the issue on skills, four questions will be addressed in the chapter. How can different groups or communities of public servants be identified in relation to e-government services? What ICT skills are linked to different communities? Which instruments could assess the existence of e-skills in those groups or communities? How could the gap of needed skills be filled?

COMMUNITIES OF PUBLIC SERVANTS AND E-GOVERNMENT

The introduction of ICT in the public sector to achieve e-government has facilitated the further specialization of different communities of professionals and has fostered the need of increasing communication needs among communities.

The Canadian government (Treasury Board of Canada Secretariat) has identified three communities [information technology (IT) community, information management (IM) and community and service community (SC)]. Other governments, however, tend to merge the IT and the IM community and accordingly, their skills, under the same label of IT specialists. The differentiation of these two communities proves to be useful for rightly approaching the topic on e-skills.

The information technology (IT) community is relatively easy to recognize. It is basically formed by technical staff that work primarily in fields such as information technology supplies and services, telecommunications, IT consultancy, multi-media and Internet-based products and services. The limits of the information management (IM) community are more blurred. Specialists and managers responsible for the provision of information management services constitute this community. The work of IM professionals encompasses professions like librarians, archivists, and access to information and privacy specialists, communication managers and records managers among others. The members of this community hypothetically have the role of shaping the content management to be produced for different output media.

The service community (SC), formed by general managers and front line staff, provides services to citizens and other stakeholders by traditional or electronic means. The SC is made up of generalists. They develop the whole life cycle of a service. All legal, financial, managerial and other professional experts typically belong to the service community.

The first two communities share the "supply side." They have to meet the business requirements of the demand-side or "end-user" organizations, i.e., the service community.

The boundaries among communities are less clear than suggested by the definitions. For instance, an IT specialist may be appointed (or promoted) to a generalist position. In this post, he ought to master both business- and ICT-related skills. Likewise, it is, for instance, quite difficult to determine whether the design of a portal should be led by an IT specialist, an IM specialist or a generalist. While the IT specialist can claim the connection of the hardware and software to the existing hardware and software of the organization, the IM specialist may focus on the content that should be published in the different output media and the service community member may claim that the portal is another, different interface for service delivery. In many instances, the technological and the content sides of a portal are defined by an IT specialist if the organization lacks IM specialists or IT knowledgeable general managers to face the e-challenge.

These overlaps entail at least one consequence on skills. There are some skills that all three communities should share because they are pursuing the common enterprise of delivering better services through electronic means. Therefore, the more technical communities should be aware of business skills, while general managers should have acquaintance with technical skills.

Figure 1. Communities and skills

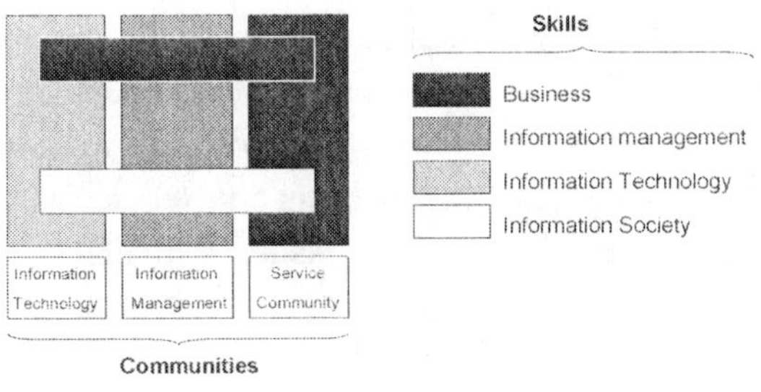

CLUSTERS OF E-SKILLS

Three sets of skills relate directly to e-government: information technology (IT) skills, information management (IM) skills and information society (IS) skills. Although boundaries among IT, IM and IS skills are blurred, a common-sense distinction has been used to link IT and IM skills with "hard" (technical) skills and IS skills with the "soft" ones. IS skills refer exclusively to the ability of recognizing how to make better use of technology for information systems and service provision of the organization.

E-government service requires a combination of skills in each community (see Figure 1), and business and IS skills are cross-cutting for the three communities. The service community should at least have some IS skills, while business skills should be added to the repertoire of the IT and IM communities

The focus of the section will be on IT, IM and IS skills. The skills will be clustered around four sets: (a) strategy and planning, (b) system development, (c) system implementation and (d) service and user support. These clusters are an adaptation of materials from the British Cabinet Office and the Skills Framework for the Information Age (SFIA).

Information Technology (IT) Skills

Information Technology (IT) skills (see Box 1) must be accompanied by business skills for the success of an e-government service. IT skills cannot improve a poorly designed service, and can never replace business skills altogether. IT specialists should take into account the overall service strategy in drafting the IT system (strategy and planning), and establishing networks, databases,

Box 1. IT skills

a) Strategy and planning:
It implies understanding the principles…

- … of the service strategy, facilitating thus the implementation of the e-government service.
- … of the organisational information system
- … of change management for helping to design the transition from traditional service delivery to e-government services.

Also…

- Designing the technological strategy of the organisation by developing the ICT architecture in terms of components, interfaces, standards, data security and payment for services.
- Auditing existing technological instruments and their adequacy to the strategy of the organisation
- Exploring the existing IT software solutions in the market, in the partners, in other stakeholders and in the public sector in order to achieve the goals of interoperability and interchangeability of data and information with other departments and organisations.

b) System development:

- Establish the communications network of data, voice, text, image and the like.
- Design the database structures and foreseeing its maintenance
- Design or acquiring and adapting the adequate software in order to meet the service needs
- Define the terms for the adequate acquisition of external supply of hardware, software, operational and maintenance services when applied
- Test e-services using a variety of mechanisms like web sites, digital TV, electronic kiosks, and digital signatures.
- Design instruments in cooperation with partners and stakeholders for integrating processes and exchanging data
- Facilitate the communication exchange between IT managers, end-users of the service community and customers.
- Design the electronic system to redress customers.

c) System implementation:

- Install new hardware and software, changing components of hardware and software and integrate them with the existing hardware and software systems.
- Administer the network of the organisation and maintaining the database structures
- Implement the security measures of the system in terms of authorisation, provision of authentication of services, investigation of unauthorised access and the like.
- Implement the e-payment policy of the organisation.
- Help to implement or implementing the web sites and other output media.
- The continuous evaluation of the system through selected performance indicators.

d) Service and user support:

- The maintenance of hardware and software systems
- The reception of problems reported by the users and the provision of technical fixes
- The training of end-users to make an appropriate use of technology and by designing proper tools for continuous computer literacy policy

and acquiring appropriate software and hardware (system development). Furthermore, IT specialists have to integrate the technical infrastructure with the service requirements (system implementation) and the support of the customer organization, the end-users and the customers (citizens) in the use of ICT systems (service and user support).

IT specialists should have "hard" technical skills that help to design and implement the technical elements (hardware, communication and software) of the e-government service. Moreover, they should have "soft" skills (IS and business skills) for understanding and matching the business strategy to the new technologies.

Information Management (IM) Skills

IM skills allow the adequate deployment of knowledge resources between the different parts of the organization and between the organization and other partners, stakeholders, customers and the general public. In the road from dispersed to integrated electronic services, IM skills play an extraordinary role. Leadership in IM means understanding the business-related issues associated with the management of information and ensuring that IM functions and services are positioned to address those issues, especially in an e-government context.

Box 2. IM skills

a) Strategy and planning: IM specialists should take into account the overall service strategy in drafting the IM system strategy by:

- Understanding the business, the processes and the overall strategy of the organisation in order to better design the information system.
- Helping to identify relevant sources of information and relevant information to the business of the organisation and to the external stakeholders, partners and citizens
- Filtering and codifying information in line with the service strategy of the organisation
- Designing the strategy for information management in the organisation by developing the formats for exchanging, retrieving and sharing information within the organisation and with external partners, stakeholders and customers.
- Auditing existing information management systems and their adequacy to the strategy of the organisation
- Exploring the existing information management practices in the market, in the partners, other stakeholders and the public sector in order to achieve the goals of interoperability and interchangeability of data and information.

b) System development

- Designing the system of retrieving and keeping information electronically for future use.
- Helping to establish the contents to be provided for various output media and target groups.
- Designing the technical system to update and maintain information in different output media.

c) System implementation and maintenance

- Administering and maintaining the archive system composed of traditional and electronic means.
- Administering and maintaining the knowledge contents from external and internal sources of information and making sure that these contents are available to relevant groups.
- Implementing the content management system for various output media and target groups.

d) Service and user support: Finally, among the IM skills should be included the support of the customer organisation, the end-users and the customers (citizens) in the use of information. Thus, IT skills should imply:

- The continuous evaluation of the system through selected performance indicators
- The maintenance and the update of the information
- The reception of problems reported by the users
- The design of training programmes to facilitate an appropriate use of information through the new tools by helping the service community, and eventually the citizens, in navigating and interrogating information sources, assessing and evaluating information, creating, recording and storing information, i. e., designing proper tools for continuous information literacy policy.

IM skills complement business skills. The IM community should take into account business skills to deliver e-services effectively, while the service community needs some IM skills in order to plan and implement e-services adequately.

The Canadian government has undertaken promising work on IM skills and the contribution of IM leaders to e-government. An IM Competency Working Group was set up to oversee the project on Competency Profile. As a starting point, an online repository of actual work descriptions was established. The committee is identifying common traits in the work descriptions for positions that are aligned to the needs of e-government. According to an interviewee, the work seems to show that these positions will require more specialized skills, a higher use of technology, involve advisory functions and carry a higher level of accountability (see also TSCS, 2004).

Ed Fine (2003) suggests that IM leaders should be aware of a mix of traditional and emerging roles, including responsibility for: "strategies, policies, standards, good practices; enterprise-wide, integrated information architecture; managing information flows within core business processes; enabling innovation and risk management through information sharing and supporting service delivery with content rich extranets."

Corporate information flows are complex and there is an increasing need to understand and manage them. IM skills (see Box 2) are distributed among different professions, especially librarians and archivists. While librarians have focused largely on the acquisition and the distribution of external information; record managers (archivists) have developed their own particular discipline from an inner perspective in many public agencies, while in others they are involved in the design and implementation of portals. Advisory cabinets, internal advisers, consultants, strategic planners are also examples of information rich areas that often set up their own information systems away from the organizational systems. The concepts of information sharing, utilization and creation imply a level of information handling skills which has been taken for granted but not explored in depth.

Although Librarian and Information Specialists (LIS) and Record Management (RM) skills are of enormous importance in an e-service strategy, it seems that both professions have had little impact on the management of information and knowledge of public organizations. The service community seems to rely little on LIS and RM professionals, because of their perception as professions that seldom engage with "the business" (TFPL, 1999).

Information Society (IS) Skills

IS skills imply, especially for the service community, the ability of recognizing how to make better use of ICT resources in order to implement a responsive e-government strategy. IS skills complement the business skills and intersect at some points with the IT and IM skills (Figure 2).

An e-government strategy requires that the whole organization gain information and computer literacy. Four sets of IS skills are key for the service community (see Box 3):

a. Relationship management with suppliers, with end-users, with customers and with other stakeholders.

Figure 2. Skills for e-government initiatives

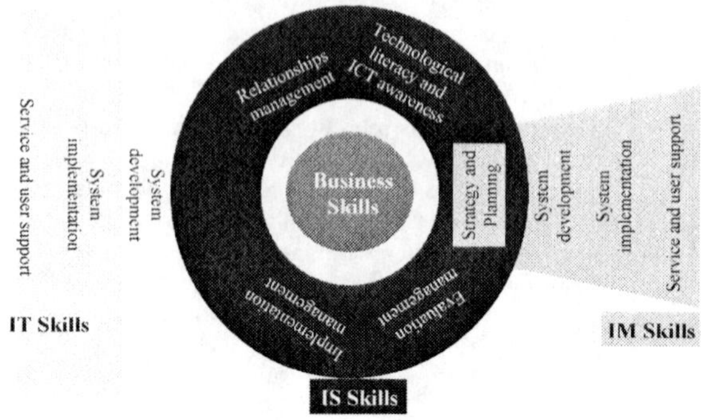

b. Technological literacy and ICT awareness to support the business strategy.
c. Implementation management.
d. Evaluation management.

These sets of IT, IM and IS skills, or similar ones, should enable the relevant managers to ensure that the information systems are beneficial to the activities of the organization, that the relevant technologies are contributing to the effective e-government service, that the information resources are managed in an effective and efficient way, that the agreements between the supply and the demand side are effectively negotiated and that the organization can successfully plan and implement an e-government service. While the three sets of skills are of great importance, it is taken for granted that IT/IM specialists are aware of the new technologies and the potential use for delivering e-services. However, top managers of the service community seem to be unaware of the potential of new technologies and the training and recruiting programs do not often include IS skills.

ASSESSMENT OF CURRENT LEVEL OF E-SKILLS

The development of an e-service strategy should entail an assessment of the current capability (skills availability) of the organization. Several

Box 3. IS skills

a) Relationships management: An e-government strategist should…:
(regarding citizens-customers)

- Decide the level of involvement of customers in decision-making and in consultation of e-services.
- Decide the level of responsiveness vis à vis customers in e-services.
- Consult citizens on how e-government services should be planned.
- Help to design the frameworks for redressing customers.

(regarding suppliers)

- Establish long-lasting relationships with ICT specialists from outside and from in-house. In case of external supply, this entails ensuring the efficient acquisition of ICT supplies and defining the basic and broad requirements of ICT-based services (based on Smart Cards, Call Centres, Cell Phones, Webs…) to be delivered.
- Define the level of ICT integration with suppliers of different services (not necessarily ICT services) and other stakeholders.

(regarding end-users or in-house staff)

- Ensure that the in-house end-users of information systems have the adequate support and training
- Involve all end-users in the use of the information system. End-users should not only be able to get information from the system but also give inputs to it.
- Consult end-users on how the e-government service should be planned

(regarding partners)

- Identify common sources of cooperation to achieve seamless government.
- Help to establish governance principles of transparency, responsiveness, responsibility and equity among different partners.

b) Technological literacy and ICT awareness to support business strategy and management: An awareness of ICT and the acquisition of the right technological literacy implies understanding:

- … the meaning of technology developments in terms of the information system of the organisation and also in regards to the e-government service strategy. This also includes a continuous scanning of technological tools that could support the business strategy.
- … the principles underlying the ICT architecture of the organisation and the possibility of innovation and expansion.
- … the broad technical aspects of ICT supply and provision in order to do an adequate monitoring of the activities of suppliers.
- … the principles of an information system strategy
- … and setting the limits of the use of information by staff, suppliers, customers, and partners.
- … the standards for security, privacy and authentication work, so that these standards can be met.
- … the principles of risk management that are ICT related

c) Implementation management: The e-government strategist should …

- Establish the relationships and responsibilities between the supply-side (technology) and the demand-side (e-services)
- Ensure that the end-users deliver e-services in an appropriate manner by meeting quality standards.
- Combine traditional channels and electronic channels of e-government service delivery.

d) Evaluation management: The e-service strategist should be able to…

- Identify and apply a library of indicators (with other stakeholders if necessary) in order to adequately evaluate the impact of a strategy of e-services.

national approaches assess the current level of skills: the British Cabinet Office focuses on available skills and skill gaps; the Canadian government concentrates on competencies and jobs skills profiles; and the KPMG proposal for the German BundOnline initiative analyses the readiness of an organization to deliver e-services with mention to e-skills.

The E-Business Skills Assessment Toolkit

This toolkit was developed as an instrument to help Departments identifying the skill gaps in their organization as part of developing an e-service strategy. Besides, the toolkit should deliver a cross-government view of skill-related issues and gaps to the British Cabinet Office. The toolkit provides a comprehensive checklist of all possible requirements, and it assesses separately two sets of skills: technical professional skills and business system management skills. The British Central IT Unit (CITU) of the Cabinet Office merges the IT and IM skills in the first set and the business and IS skills in the second one (Cabinet Office, 2000).

Each set of skills (technical and business) is broken down into seven clusters or areas of skills. For each cluster, a questionnaire of nine questions assesses the relevance of listed skills for the successful implementation of the organizational e-strategy, the critical skills for that success, the internal or external availability of these skills and the skill gaps among other aspects. The assessment of each question is marked in a three-point scale. Unavailability of a critical skill indicates that the organization should fill the gap as soon as possible. An aggregate result of unavailability of certain critical skills across different departments and agencies requires also further central action.

According to an interviewee from the Cabinet Office, many departments incorporated the results of their analysis using the toolkit into their early e-service strategies. This allowed them to consider skills issues as part of the risk analysis and for remedial action to be taken where necessary. Departments had to assess their skill needs in the context of whether the technological systems had been outsourced or were still provided by the in-house staff. In the event of outsourcing, some of the responsibility for identifying and addressing skill needs would rest with the provider. The current situation seems to suggest that things have moved on more generally. Besides monitoring the requirements for skills with the skills assessment toolkit, departments and central government are increasingly focusing on taking action to address a broader range of skill needs that are included in the category of business skills and information society skills. These skills include: leadership, project and program management, related commercial skills and IT literacy. In other words, the British agencies realize that more technical skills (hard skills) are important, but not enough to address an e-service strategy. The business strategy should have priority, while IT awareness is an important complement.

The toolkit provides a very useful and detailed checklist of almost every single skill that an e-government service would require. However, it is not very clear who should fill in the questionnaire, based on a self-assessment exercise. While it would make sense that the human resource unit co-ordinates the exercise, extensive consultation with specialists and business managers is required. Finally, the process of self-assessing the skill needs of the organization seem to represent a burden for some organizations, especially those that are unable or unwilling to undertake such an enterprise. Perhaps a more simplified version would help some agencies in identifying skill gaps.

The IT Job Competency Profiles

Canada's Treasury Board Secretariat (2000) explored the adoption of a community-led, competency-based approach to HR Management for the IT Community. IT Job Competency Profiles are one key element of the process. A competency-based approach has potential to allow the flexible, adaptable responses required in dynamic modern organizations. It also reflects an assumption that the knowledge and experience of individual public servants will be more critically important. Furthermore, the role of managers will increasingly involve encouraging and supporting individuals willing to take initiative to manage their own development and career progression. Competency profiles can help to identify optimal candidates in staffing processes; link development and training to sustained high performance and provide valid foundation for recruitment, selection and training (Barker, 2001).

The IT Job Competency Profiles provide a common basis for comparing requirements for similar positions within and across departments and jurisdictions. Improved awareness of the skills and competencies needed in various types of positions allows IT professionals and managers to make better informed decisions about learning and training plans to meet both individual and organizational goals. But competencies are only useful if the competency profiles are kept up-to-date, and if there is a consistent, effective and accepted way of assessing competencies of applicants for positions, and of employees for development and for effective performance management and work assignments.

Processes are being developed to assess and record individual competencies which, if successfully implemented across the community, could reduce the substantial time and other resources devoted to retesting job applicants and employees for competencies they have already proven. Moreover, Canada is implementing the first version of a Web-based self-assessment tool to allow individuals to compare their personal qualifications to the competencies required in IT positions for which they may wish to prepare themselves.

Adopting a community-wide competency taxonomy should help to reinforce the Canadian government's commitment to lifelong learning by providing an incentive to improve qualifications in anticipation of a range of career possibilities, rather than focusing on training individuals for specific positions. The organization benefits from having individuals with increased ability to perform in their current positions, and from the flexibility of being able to draw on pre-qualified individuals when positions come open. The IT Competency Profiles and the accompanying assessment tools being developed in Canada have the potential to provide the basis for an inventory of individual competencies and learning plans. Such an inventory would put both individual departments and the overall IT Community in a better position to predict skill gaps, allocate learning resources and do succession planning.

Canada's competency-based approach identifies skills for particular types of jobs, while the British Skills Assessment Toolkit is a generic tool that assesses whether the required skills exist in the organization. It does not matter whether these skills are in one particular job or not. Unlike the British toolkit, Canada's approach makes possible very detailed career and training plans customized for each individual in each hierarchical level and an overall assessment of specific capacities across the community. This richness of information entails a considerable amount of work, making it more suitable for agencies already used to the competency approach and more generic job descriptions, but probably less suited for public agencies that still use traditional job assessments.

The types of information that the competency-based approach can provide include whether a candidate for a position has the competencies and skills or has the potential to attain those competencies and skills required; the types of training and/or development an individual would need to qualify for a specific position; and whether there is a career path for the individual within the particular organization or whether they should expect to move outside that organization to achieve career goals. In contrast, the e-skills assessment toolkit has a broader focus and it provides information about whether the candidate's particular skills exist somewhere in the organization, in a team or in an individual position-holder. The Canadian approach allows not only the organizational-level HR planning possible with e-skills assessment, but also allows significant HR planning at the individual and group level in order to meet changing job requirements.

The Net-Readiness Analysis

The Net-Readiness Analysis has been devised by KPMG for the BundOnline 2005 strategy of the German Government and has been placed in the e-government manual of the German Federal Office for Information Security (*Bundesamt für Sicherheit in der Informationstechnik*). The Net-Readiness analysis is a self-assessment instrument that should help to evaluate the e-government capacity of an organization.

The analysis is undertaken through a questionnaire that could be answered either by single individuals or by teams within the organization. The analysis follows the four dimensions of a model (technology, learning skills, leadership and organization). Each part is structured around 10 questions and each one accounts for 50 points. With the overall addition of points, a Net Readiness Scorecard can be built up. For each position in the final scale, there is a label of the organization in terms of Net Readiness and a subsequent list of recommendations can follow after working out the position of the organization in this scale.

For instance, a "visionary organization" (more than 180 points) is, according to KPMG, an organization that is a pathfinder in e-government services and is very successful in its Internet activities. This organization may serve as a model for other agencies. A "savvy organization" (between 120 and 179 points) has awareness for the potential results that e-government can trigger and the organization is able to follow and understand what the competitors or similar organizations do in terms of e-government services. In this kind of organization, some resources have been allocated for e-government strategies and some processes are under study of being changed or have already been changed. The challenges would be to extend these partial initiatives to an overall picture.

This instrument offers a first approach to the e-capacity of a specific public organization. However, there are some problems linked to the ICT skills in this instrument. Firstly, skills represent a minor part of this assessment tool, and although there are recommendations to improve the skills of the organization after the exercise, this cannot be followed from the questions for each dimension. Secondly, this instrument is based on numeric overall points that give a general idea of how "agnostic" or "visionary" an organization is in terms of e-government. An overall numeric mark does not help very much in terms of searching for the specific gaps of the system. Therefore, this instrument could be used as a starting point, but—in terms of skills—more specific tools are needed.

Assessing ICT-Related Skills: Getting the Fittest Instrument for the Organization

It is difficult to establish the same and unique guidelines that could be followed by different countries. Some governments are designing central systems to identify and assess the level of ICT skills in public organizations while other governments are fully unaware of how to plan the improvement of ICT skills in public agencies. The research into OECD countries showed that most countries have not given much importance to the need of IS skills for the service community (especially for top managers). In some organizations, human resource managers are used to dealing with job profiles or with self-assessment tools, while many public agencies have never undertaken a self-assessment of any kind. In these conditions, there is not a best-for-all tool. Each organization should select and use an adequate instrument to fit the current HRM practices of the organization.

The assessment of e-skills gap for the three communities is an urgent job for many public agencies. In some cases, the specific needed skills are very obvious and any common sense self-assessment exercise can tell that without any specific methodology. In other cases, some instruments may help identify the skills gap. The British and the Canadian tools seem to be good instruments to tackle this question but at the same time they are complex (too many questions, too many sets of skills) and hard to use for inexperienced or busy managers. That was at least the reactions of managers in related ICT services in countries where self-assessments for required skills have not been implemented.

At OECD seminars, an easier-to-use tool was presented (Parrado, 2002). It can be summarized as follows. The more detailed lists of skills (from the Skills Assessment Tool, for instance) are useful for those organizations that are used to work with skills; other newcomer organizations should focus on the core skills.

Once the short list of skills has been decided upon, a decision should be made on the appropriate questions that could help identify the skills gap. The organization could use four parameters to assess the importance of particular skills for the e-strategy, the availability of these skills, the need to maintain them in-house and whether or not the organization should undertake further actions.

Further actions could be graphically represented by a traffic light system. Red meaning that urgent actions should be enacted; amber implying that further actions should be planned and/or implemented; green meaning that the organization has the proper capacity in these skills.

The self-assessment exercise should be undertaken by representatives from each community: IT, IM and SC.

The output cards should show that the different sets of skills cannot always be seen isolated, as there are strong connections among different sets of skills and different communities (see Figure 2). It is not necessary to ascertain exactly whether a skill is very important or not. Several outside observers may think differently about one particular skill, even though it is important in the perception of the leading staff of the organization (from the three communities). If a particular skill is important and not available, something must be done.

Nevertheless, in some public agencies, some questions still remain. Would the leadership be able to clearly link importance and availability of skills to their strategy? Would they be able to undertake such an exercise or would they need external help for this self-assessment? They could always seek for advice from consultancy firms from the private sector. There are other solutions from within the public sector through different means of recruiting and training (see Settles) or by means of competence centres (see next section).

OUTSOURCING E-SKILLS?

Once skills gap have been identified, can the organization fill the gap with in-house skills or does it need to buy those needed skills from an external contractor?

It was previously suggested that the skills assessment tool could contain a question on whether a specific skill (or set of skills) should be taken care of in-house or not. This requires further explanation. It is almost impossible to offer a list of those skills that should necessarily remain in-house for all kinds of organizations and services in all countries. This issue should be examined through an assessment exercise of the concerned organization.

The Finnish Ministry issued a policy decision of the Council of State on the Development of Information Management of State Administration in which concerns were developed around the idea of outsourcing information management tasks. The document explicitly mentioned that attention should be "paid to the maintenance of adequate leadership, planning, acquisition and information-security know-how in the office. In outsourcing, the risks and total costs thereof, the tasks of the office and the nature of the services subject to outsourcing as well as especially the possibilities of the office to steer and inspect the appropriate handling of the outsourced services and information security shall be taken into consideration." The Ministry of Finance announced that regulations and instructions relating to outsourcing would be issued.

According to interviewees from the Finnish Ministry of Finance in the Finnish government, the analysis of outsourcing of IT functions has been done for five agencies. At first, the Ministry of Finance analyzed the skills these departments currently have and which ones would be required in 2006. Apparently, the differences were not daunting. Basic skills that should remain in-house were: project management, data security, IT strategy and procurement skills, although these skills may change for different agencies.

Outsourcing is then an important strategy to buy skills that cannot be found in-house but it also entails risks if the outsourced skills are core to the e-government service and the external provider fails to provide them adequately. There are then two different questions: What questions do we pose to know if specific skills could be contracted out? Once a decision has been reached to contract out, what checklist of questions could be used to do a pre-outsourcing exercise?

Regarding the first question, some dimensions could be offered. These dimensions relate to risk management issues, to the privacy, confidentiality and security of data on customers and to the relationship between the business skills and ICT-related skills under scrutiny. By checking those dimensions against the list of skills, any organization should have a fair idea of what could be outsourced or not.

Regarding the second issue, the pre-outsourcing exercise, a checklist of different items grouped in four sets could help an organization to identify how the IT services could be outsourced (see Box 4). Two basic skills are involved in the exercise: Are the skills available in the organization to do the pre-outsourcing exercise? Are the skills available to monitor the contract? (Adapted from Gramatikov, 2002.)

The first issue of Box 4 is critical. If the team considering outsourcing lacks decision capability, external aid should be sought. Ideally, the drafting team should consist of people from the different identified communities (IT, IM and the Service Community). At least one member of the team should have a legal background, while another person at least should be a financial expert. While it is assumed that the managerial, legal and financial expertise can be traditionally found in any organization, the required ICT expertise may be absent. Moreover, the outsourcing team should check if the hard skills of the clusters "Strategy and planning" and "System development" are present in the IT community of the organization so that the outsourcing exercise can be safely made.

The second issue of Box 4 refers to the present relationship of the IT function and the service. In this regard, the outsourcing team should collect performance indicators of the current IT infrastructure and question whether the current level of IT is enough for the organization and can help

Box 4. Check-list for outsourcing ICT related skills

Pre-outsourcing question on skills
- What is the skill level of the organisation for deciding the pre-outsourcing conditions?

IT function and the e-government service
- Is the organizational IT function clearly defined or definable?
- How critical is the IT service level for the performance and the strategies of the organization?
- What are the strengths and weaknesses of the internal provision of IT?
- What are the middle and long-term perspectives of the internal and external provision of IT?

Cost of e-government services and market competition
- Does the market provide for cost optimisation?
- What is the total cost of operating the service?
- What is the total cost of ownership of the IT assets?
- What is the level of competition on the market?

Skills level to manage the contract
- What are the experience and the skill level of the organization in management of complex contractual relations?

to satisfy the services demand. A list of indicators can be helpful in this regard (Gramatikov, 2002) (see Box 5).

This kind of information will help to compare the bids and to decide whether the market can provide the service at a sufficient quality.

Regarding the third issue of Box 4: "Cost of e-government services and market competition," the outsourcing team should be able to ascertain the total cost of ownership for hardware, software and network components of the IT and to assess the different offers from the market. A vague perception of the cost of the services is of little help when the public manager has to conduct cost-benefit analysis. Thus, price and levels of service performance are the two components of the outsourcing decision. In order to ease this task, the outsourcing team can break down the IT services to be outsourced into functions and separate from the rest those generic functions for which there are more standardized parameters and the outsourcing decisions are easier to handle. The list of Box 6 offers some suggestions (Gramatikov, 2002).

The final set of questions (Box 5) refers to whether the outsourcing team has the required skills for managing the contract. This means to:

- Draft the specifications of the IT services which will be transferred outside and determine, for instance, the Service Level Agreements that provide the regulation of responsibilities of the parties according to the demand for and supply of the service within the contract.
- Determine the incentives for excelling performance and penalties against underperformance.
- Set up and maintain an effective system for controlling the IT-provided services.
- Finish the outsourcing contract in due time (for updating the system) or in case of risk of disruption of the e-government service.

The outsourcing exercise is a complex task and some help from other public agencies is welcomed. The German government has devised Competence Centres in order to coach and complement in-house e-skills of different agencies. These centres could also be of help in outsourcing exercises, although their primary functions are rather different.

The five competence centres designed by the German government have the following features:

Box 5. Indicators for assessing current IT infrastructure

- number of servers and desktops in use in the organization
- percentage of uptime
- request for desktop help per day
- lines of source code
- proprietary and off-the-shelf applications used in the organization
- transactions per second, hour, day or week
- mean bandwidth capacity
- mean delay time for processing, storing, publishing, printing etc. requests
- time for learning the system
- interoperability with existing internal or external systems
- level of compliance with planned IT systems
- level of standardization required for the organization IT system

1. **Processes and Organization.** The competence centre should help the agency to align the processes of the organization through analyzing the workflow and undertaking process reengineering when necessary with the designed e-government services.
2. **Job Processing and Document Management.** The competence centre should foster the cooperation between those involved in document-intensive processes in accordance with specific rules and methods. Its activities should cover those that establish the order in which individual steps of a job are to be processed and which staffing, material and organizational resources are needed for implementation.
3. **Data Security.** The competence centre on this issue will help agencies to ensure and get the citizens' trust on e-government services through the correct set up of the encryption and authentication instruments, the enhance of confidentiality by protecting data against unauthorized access, the establishment of integrity by protecting data against incorrect manipulation and the assurance of authenticity by ensuring that a message actually comes from the person or institution claiming to be the sender of the communication.

In the three previous competence centres, activities are centrally planned but locally provided. However, the next two competence centres offer basic components that are suited for central planning and central provision:

4. **Content Management System (CMS).** The CMS is to provide topical, relevant content for various output media and target groups, as well as implementing their creation, requirement for the provision and the ongoing updating of considerable information offerings of authorities on the Internet. Some public agencies may not have the CMS, therefore, a centrally provided solution might be of great help.
5. **e-Payment Platform.** The provision of a central platform for payment requires that different interfaces are integrated within the respective application.

The competence centres will be staffed with 25 to 30 experts from the German public administration and external industry experts/IT consultants. The centres will initialize, monitor and coach projects from different federal agencies. In doing so, these competence centers would be an optimal solution to help the organization in two ways: either fostering the in-house work for implementing the e-government services or assessing them in the outsourcing exercise. Thus, the skill gaps can be filled with external aid under public sector supervision.

CONCLUSION

This chapter has collected and analyzed leading experiences of OECD countries in identifying communities of public servants, in using instruments to assess e-skill gaps (at the individual- and agency-level) and offering some ideas about how to fill those skill gaps.

Box 6. Functions of IT services

- desktop maintenance, application development and implementation, data warehousing, transition from legacy systems to client-server environment, network access services, helpdesk services, LANs and WANs, virtual private networks, identification and authorization services, internet and intranet
- applications development and maintenance, EPR systems, payroll processing, accountancy applications,
- various data centre and databases applications, electronic fund transfers, B2Government applications, e-procurement etc

The identification of three different communities: information technology (IT), information management (IM) and service community (SC) should help to further identify their leaders, the sets of skills they need for e-service strategies, and the gaps in e-skills for individual-, organizational- and community-levels.

From the different international experiences it seems that four sets of skills are needed for e-service strategies: information technology (IT), information management (IM), information society (IS), and business skills. These sets of skills (except business skills) have been kept to the most meaningful ones and have been broken down into four clusters in this chapter. IS skills are important because they constitute the link between technology and business from the perspective of the service community. Business skills are relevant for members of the IT and IM community in order to adequately integrate the technology into the service. IT skills have been sufficiently developed in some countries while IM skills are rarely attracting the attention from governments. These skills seem to hold the key to the future of e-government services as they should be able to connect communities of public servants, stakeholders and the general public.

There are basically two approaches for identifying skill gaps. One is based upon job Competency Profiles, which is used for the individual-, the organizational- and the community-level (Canadian approach). The other approach is based upon skill needs of an entire agency (British approach). It has been suggested that both approaches are useful instruments, but they should match the current HRM practices of the organization. For agencies with less developed HRM, more easy-to-use tools are advised.

In order to fill the skill gaps, we have discussed just one option: outsourcing (while training and recruitment have been dealt with in the chapter from Settles in this book).

For the outsourcing exercise, it is recommended to build up a pre-outsourcing team with members from the three communities (IT, IM, Service community) from the organization that should go through a check-list. The team should check the dangers of outsourcing particular skills, the relationship between the IT and the service, the costs of different providers and the capabilities of the organization in order to monitor the contract. In the pre-outsourcing exercise, public competence centres, shaped after the German experience, could be of great help.

REFERENCES

Barker, S. M. (2001). Information technology competency-based job profile. Retrieved June 25, 2004, from *http://www.opm.gov/compconf/postconf01/it/sbarker.htm*

British Computer Society. (2004). Retrieved June 29, 2004, from *http://www1.bcs.org.uk*

BSI. (2002). Chefsache E-Government: Leitfaden für Behördenleiter. E-Government Handbuch. Bonn: Bundesamt für Sicherheit in der Informationstechnik. Retrieved June 26, 2004, from *www.e-government-handbuch.de*

Bundesregierung. (2001). Umsetzungsplan für die eGovernment-Initiative [Implementation plan for the "BundOnline 2005" eGovernment initiative.] Retrieved June 25, 2004. from *http://www.bmi.bund.de/downloadde/16396/Download.pdf*

Cabinet Office. (2000a). Successful IT: Modernising government in action. Retrieved June 29, 2004, from *http://www.ogc.gov.uk/index.asp?docid=2632*

Cabinet Office. (2000b). E-business skills assessment toolkit. Retrieved June 20, 2004, from *http://e-government.cabinetoffice.gov.uk/Resources/Guidelines/fs/en*

Cabinet Office. (2000c). Skills in the information age. Retrieved June 20, 2004, from *http://e-government.cabinetoffice.gov.uk/Resources/OtherPublications/fs/en*

Fine, E. (2003). The IM leadership initiative. Retrieved June 27, 2004, from *http://www.cio-dpi.gc.ca/oro-bgc/imli-ilgi/pres/initiative/page01_e.asp*

Gramatikov, M. (2002). Outsourcing of public information systems. UNPAN. Retrieved June 26, 2004, from *http://unpan1.un.org/intradoc/groups/public/documents/untc/unpan003861.pdf*

Melitski, J. (2002). The world of e-government and e-governance. Retrieved June 26, 2004, from *http://www.aspanet.org/solutions/egovworld.html*

Ministry of Defence. (2000a). Modernising defence training: Report of the dDefence training review (volume 1). Retrieved June 26, 2004, from *http://www.mod.uk/linked_files/dtr_vol1.pdf*

Ministry of Defence. (2000b). Modernising defence training: Report of the defence training review (volume 2). Retrieved June 26, 2004, from *http://www.mod.uk/linked_files/dtr_vol2.pdf*

Ministry of Defence. (2001). Armed forces e-skilling (chapter 4). Retrieved June 26, 2004, from *http://www.mod.uk/linked_files/deb2001_ch4-10.pdf*

Parrado, S. (2004). ICT related skills for e-government. Paper presented for the *OECD E-Government Project at the Seminar on Reform of Public Administrations OECD*, Paris, September 23-24.

Skills Framework for the Information Age. (2004). Retrieved June 20, 2004, from *http://www.e-skills.com/cgi-bin/wms.pl/335*

Treasury Board of Canada Secretariat. (1999). Strategic directions for information management and information technology: Enabling 21st century service to Canadians. Retrieved June 26, 2004, from *http://www.tbs-sct.gc.ca/Pubs_pol/ciopubs/TB_OIMP/sdimit_e.html*

Treasury Board of Canada Secretariat. (2000). IT job competency profiles. Retrieved June 26, 2004, from *http://www.cio-dpi.gc.ca/oro-bgc/learning/jswg-gtpc/it-comprofil-ti/it-comprofil-ti00_e.asp*

Treasury Board of Canadian Secretariat. (2004). Retrieved June 26, 2004, from *http://www.cio-dpi.gc.ca/oro-bgc/im/im_e.asp*

ENDNOTE

1 I would like to acknowledge the help from Santiago Segarra, Ernesto Abati, Luis Felipe Paradela, Tomás Muñoz, Tony Bovaird, David Hickman, Ed Fine, Helen McDonald, Sandra Bogdanovic, Ralf Kleindiek, Timo Hauschild, Olavi Köngäs, Olli-Pekka Rissanen, Masaaki Nakagawa and Brigid Feeny. I am also very thankful for the help of Elizabeth Muller from OECD. Errors of this document are entirely mine.

This work was previously published in Practicing E-Government: A Global Perspective, edited by M. Khosrow-Pour, pp. 310-328, copyright 2005 by IGI Publishing, formerly known as Idea Group Publishing (an imprint of IGI Global).

Chapter 4.47
Requirements Analysis and General Functional Model of Seamless, Citizen-Oriented Service Delivery

Elena Mugellini
University of Applied Sciences of Western Switzerland, Switzerland

Maria Chiara Pettenati
University of Florence, Italy

Omar Abou Khaled
University of Applied Sciences of Western Switzerland, Switzerland

ABSTRACT

Seamless services provide citizens with what they need to know in a particular topic without having to know which government level or agencies they must contact to get it. Seamless services meet efficiency targets, reduce costs, and respond to citizen demands for improved services; they help governments to be more citizen-centered, outcome-oriented, efficient, and accountable. This chapter outlines main requirements for the delivery of seamless services and presents a general functional model (e-government service marketplace) for the delivery of shared services to citizens at the transaction level (i.e., supporting a complete online handling of a service). The main functionalities of the e-government service marketplace are analyzed in detail. Advantages, disadvantages, and the impact of this concept on the three fundamental axes (social, economic, and technical) are discussed as well. The chapter ends with some insights on future trends and open issues about seamless services delivery and enabling systems.

INTRODUCTION

The rapid emergence and growth of information and communication technologies (ICTs) in everyday life of citizens has pushed government to transform itself into an electronic government (e-government) to serve citizens. The main limits in traditional public administration practices are mainly due to the bureaucracy complexity among the departments, excessive and time consuming duplication/multiplication of paperwork which lead to long waiting time both for citizens and for public administration officers.

Due to the complexity of administrative procedures (which is somehow necessary in order to protect and guarantee citizens' rights) the interaction with public administration can be perceived by citizens as a complex and time consuming experience. As a consequence, traditional services and service delivery processes would benefit from a redesign and reorganization according to a more *citizen-oriented approach*. Government needs to take advantage of information and communication technologies and new business models to improve efficiency and effectiveness of internal processes as well as change the nature and quality of government interaction with both citizens and businesses allowing *seamless service delivery*. Government could take advantage of ICTs not just putting existing paper-based processes into digital form but rather starting a profound transformation of the way it provides services as well as interacts with citizens. Thanks to seamless service e-government practices, government could become more efficient, transparent, and responsive by allowing citizens to have 24-hour, 7-day interactive access to all governmental services as well as perform online transactions with governmental agencies at a distance.

This chapter outlines the main requirements for the provision of such shared services and presents a general functional model (e-government service marketplace) for seamless service delivery. It discusses the advantages and disadvantages as well as the impact of e-government service marketplace concept according to the three fundamental e-government perspectives: social, economic, and technical. It provides a case study of e-government service marketplace concept application and eventually it provides some insights on future issues and emerging needs of seamless service delivery.

It is worth noting that privacy and security issues are beyond the scope of this chapter; as a consequence, they will not be analyzed in-depth.

BACKGROUND

E-government refers to the use by government agencies of ICT to improve the way public administration interacts with citizens and businesses, and to improve the efficiency of the administrative process. Enhanced quality of service has been a major component of public administration reform over the past two decades, and the use of ICT in order to generate improvements in services has been a primary driver for e-government activity. In particular the use of the Internet has given a major boost to citizen-oriented, seamless services, and online services are increasingly seen as part of a broader strategy which aims to improve citizen satisfaction and interest in e-government. Online service targets have also been effective in motivating public administrations to examine the potential of the Internet and related technologies by applying them to existing services. One-stop offices, advice bureaus, information kiosks, and call centers have attempted to bring together information and services from different governmental agencies.

In order to evaluate e-government progress in some countries several stage models describing the evolution of public services have been developed (AOEMA, 2004; Persson & Goldkuhl, 2005; Suh, 2003). These models divide the development of e-government into several stages from simple information provision to more complex services (Table 1). All these models divide the development of e-government into several stages from simple information provision to more complex services.

Table 1. E-government development stages

<table>
<tr><th></th><th colspan="5">E-Government Service Development Stage Models</th></tr>
<tr><th rowspan="7">Service Stages</th><th>ANAO (ANAO, 1999)</th><th>SAFAD (Statskontoret, 2000)</th><th>Layne &Lee (Layne & Lee, 2001)</th><th>UN/ASPA (Ronaghan, 2001)</th><th>Capgemini (Capgemini, 2005)</th></tr>
<tr><td rowspan="2">publishing information</td><td rowspan="2">information</td><td rowspan="3">catalogue</td><td>emerging</td><td rowspan="2">information</td></tr>
<tr><td>enhanced</td></tr>
<tr><td>interactive information</td><td>interaction</td><td>interactive</td><td>one-way interaction</td></tr>
<tr><td>transaction</td><td>transaction</td><td>transaction</td><td>transaction</td><td>two-way interaction</td></tr>
<tr><td rowspan="2">data sharing</td><td rowspan="2">integration</td><td>vertical integration</td><td rowspan="2">fully integrated or seamless</td><td rowspan="2">transaction</td></tr>
<tr><td>horizontal integration</td></tr>
</table>

All of them start off with a stage of providing information to the public. Only the United Nations/American Society for Public Administration (UN/ASPA) model splits this stage into two distinct/separate levels: emerging and enhanced. After this, the models begin to differ from each other in a more substantial way. The Australian National Audit Office (ANAO), Swedish Agency for Administrative Development (SAFAD), and UN/ASPA continue with an interaction stage where there is increasing interaction between the agency Web site and the client.

Layne and Lee (2001) continue in their second stage, transaction, where internal systems of public administrations are integrated with the Web sites. This stage corresponds to the third stage in the ANAO and SAFAD models or the fourth stage in the UN/ASPA model. On the contrary the Capgemini model presents some differences as its fourth stage (transaction) corresponds to the third (partially) and fourth stage of ANAO or SAFAD models.

It clearly appears how differences between different models are usually minor differences and that there is a common trend to classify as the last level (i.e., the level that requires the highest level of technological sophistication, transformational effort, and economical investment) the one that requires a complete integration between several administrations in order to provide seamless (or integrated) transactional services. In other words despite different names of equivalent stages in different models, essentially the direction of e-government development always begins with only a presence and basic information where the technology is treated as simply another site on which to post information. Sites then move to a stage where interaction and communication between citizens, businesses, and governmental officials are developed and are the main focus. The next step is provision of real e-service delivery where the focus is on transactional service and citizens are able to accomplish complete routine tasks online. This stage requires an extensive use of technology that is not only a new way ("e-way") of doing traditional government but has the possibility of creating new and different ways for government to serve the citizens. For the sake of clarity in the rest of the chapter (when speaking about a stage model for service provision), we will refer to the four-stage Capgemini model (Figure 1).

As Figure 1 shows, while stages 1 and 2 provide a low level of service provision which requires a low level of technological sophistication, stages 3 and 4 require a high level of technological sophistication which allows for the delivery of high level services.

To date, e-government has enjoyed a level of political support in different countries, which have seen it as a tool to modernize public administration, as a symbol of modernity, as a way of promoting the development of ICT industry, and the move to an information society. The initial impressive results of e-government activities—the rapid appearance of several government Web sites and the development of portals—made information easy to find without requiring additional substantial funding. However after this initial enthusiastic phase, fewer efforts have been made to reach the next stages of e-service provision (stages 3 and 4 in Figure 1).

According to the Capgemini report (Capgemini, 2005) on online availability of public services (the survey covered 17 countries and examined 20 basic public services), the online sophistication of public service delivery in Europe is situated between one-way interaction (stage 2) and two-way interaction (stage 3) (measurement October 2004). Moreover when results are broken down into the target groups, citizens and businesses, it appears that online sophistication for governmental services are significantly higher for businesses than for citizens. The results of the survey also sketch out e-government progress: e-service improvements in the period 2001-2004 register an increase of six percentage points (Capgemini, 2005). This means that over the last three years, online development of public service has improved but much work still remains to reach the highest level of complete transactional public services (Halligan & Moore, 2004). There is more and more need for providing the glue interconnecting separate initiatives and efforts into a single and global approach (an integration model enabling the collaboration between participating governmental agencies and citizens).

The next stages of e-government will involve the development of hidden infrastructure, joined-up back-office systems, possible reengineering of administrative processes and more considerable funding with benefits which are likely to emerge slowly and be less evident. However this new phase is essential for seamless service delivery becoming a reality. The logic of customer-focus, seamless, and integrated e-government and the

Figure 1. Capgemini four-stage model

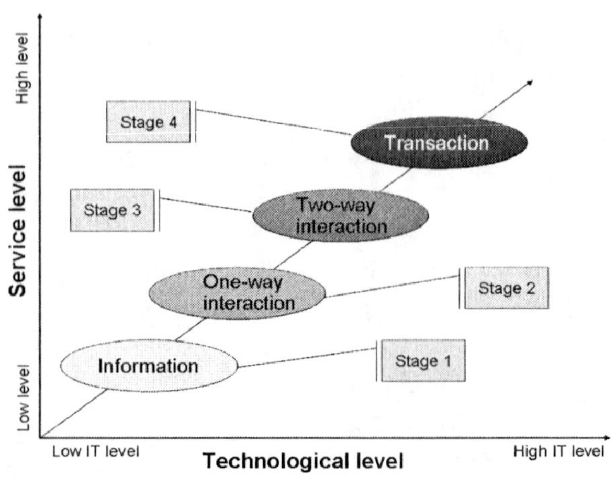

need to work in cooperation to ensure interoperability and reduce duplication applies as much as across jurisdictions as it does across agencies at the same level of government, and involves a number of issues, including:

- Ease-of-use and user-friendliness
- Personalized and accessible services
- Support of citizen migration across different countries
- Respect of public administration autonomy
- Integration of public administration legacy system
- Private and public service integration
- Continuous improvement and evolution of e-government solutions

In the following a detailed analysis of requirements for seamless service delivery from both citizen and public administration point of view is provided.

REQUIREMENTS FOR SEAMLESS SERVICE DELIVERY

As services become more complex, efficiency considerations require greater cooperation between agencies in areas such as shared processing, data exchange, and authentication. The need of collaboration between agencies thus has both "front-office" (service to the customer) and "back-office" (efficiency in e-government) components (Mugellini, Abou Khaled, Pettanati, & Franco, 2005). The front-office refers to how public administration organization and efficiency is perceived from citizens; in this case the main requirements for a seamless service delivery concern user satisfaction about government services (user-friendliness, information accessibility, ease-of-use, etc.). On the other hand back-office refers to the internal operations of an organization that are not accessible or visible to the general public; in this case the main requirements for a seamless service delivery are about integration of heterogeneous information systems, interoperability between agencies, and so forth. Hence, the main requirements for a quality service delivery change align with the two different points of view: the citizen point of view and the public administration point of view.

From the citizen point of view the main requirements for seamless service delivery are about citizen-centered, effective, and efficient services; in particular the following needs can be outlined:

- **Focus on users' needs:** So far, services offered by public administrations were mainly focused on the expectations of the administrations themselves rather than on the real needs of the citizens. Public services should not be designed around public administration needs. Instead, they should be centered according to citizen needs (for instance either increasing the number of online services or decreasing administrative response time).
- **User-friendly services:** Provide citizen-oriented services hiding to the citizen the complexity and fragmentation of public administration performing the necessary operations for collecting the information to deliver government services instead of the citizen. Citizen comfort depends on the ergonomics of the services offered: the simplicity of the tasks to be carried out and the terminology used, but also the uniformity of presentation of services provided by different agencies. Moreover the move from one administration to another should not be troubling for the citizen: similar data should have similar names and similar actions have to be presented in the same way.
- **Personalized services:** Personalization of services over time by tailoring what the government provides to the individual citizen (Accenture, 2004). The development

of e-government permits personalized processing, centered on the individual needs of each citizen; services can interpret available data within the context of a particular time, whereby services and information change as certain events occur.

- **Access and accessibility:** Provide 24/7 service availability (i.e., provide services to citizens every time they need them, wherever they are, increasing access possibilities while reducing delays). Services should be completely available to anyone with Internet access, or an opposite terminal should be provided, in order to save citizens from having to travel for simple matters (a better access to public services is important in peripheral or rural areas).
- **Transaction handling:** Allow service delivery at the transaction level (the highest interaction level between citizen and administration, supporting online handling of a complete service). Users can enter information and engage in electronic transaction with the administration. Seamless services at the transaction level require real-time responsiveness by government agencies to the service demand of citizens and the administration ability to share data with the other governmental agencies. This way, citizens can obtain high-level services without having to provide the same documentation or data time and time again and without having to move to several administrations.
- **Support migration across different countries:** Help citizens during their migration from one country to another. Since the integration of Europe into a single market, the citizens of the European Community member states should be able to migrate from one European country to another with as few problems as possible. Yet, mobile European citizens have to deal with time and money consuming administrative procedures. If the collecting of required documents costs a lot of time and money for citizens in their home country, for foreign citizens, the situation is even worse.
- **Quality of service:** Citizens should benefit from the information given, which must be up to date and offer relevant self-service options. Seamless services should improve citizen life providing simplified procedures and preventing them from wasting money and time. Moreover services should enable users to find out the status of their official papers or the progress of their requests and should reduce as much as possible the need for users to provide redundant information already held by the authorities.

From the administration point of view the main requirements of quality seamless service delivery include, among others, data reuse, services sharing as well as legacy system integration. Hence "interoperability" and "integration" are crucial issues for developing and implementing seamless services. It is worth noting that interoperability is not only a technical issue dealing with distributed computing, but it deals also with information sharing among different administrations and the redesign of administrative processes to support more effective delivery of e-government services. Three levels of interoperability are relevant to seamless service delivery: technical, semantic, and organizational (European Commission, 2003). The first one refers to technical issue of connecting computer systems, defining common communication protocols, and data formats. The second one concerns the exchange of information in an understandable way even between applications that were not initially developed for this purpose. The third one refers to enabling processes cooperation between agencies at the same level of government as well as across different jurisdictions. The main requirements for seamless service delivery according to the administration point of view are:

- **Flexibility:** Refers to efficient reuse of information while respecting technical and political capabilities of different administrations. *Reuse* refers to the possibility of reusing services and information instead of duplicated them at different agencies. *Efficiency* refers to the ability to quickly and easily create new services using a combination of new and already existing services. Finally "respect technical and political capabilities" means allowing each administration to provide services according to different interoperability levels that do not require the same level of technological sophistication.
- **Data storage:** Seamless services require the administrations to share information they hold. The qualitative and economic advantages of e-government are based on the possibility of sharing and exchanging data regarding the citizens. Therefore appropriate data storage and access mechanisms are required.
- **Integration of legacy systems:** Refers to promoting integration of legacy systems allowing a gradual transition from already existing information systems to the new ones. Different and heterogeneous applications should be able to exchange data and participate in a business process regardless of the implementation details (for instance, operating system or programming languages) underlying those applications, thus allowing technical interoperability.
- **Shared services:** Refer to the consolidation of administrative or support functions (human resources, information technologies, etc.) from several departments or agencies into a single organizational entity (Accenture, 2005); that is, services provided by different agencies are shared and composed in order to deliver more complex services to citizens, allowing organizational interoperability.
- **Interagency cooperation:** Public services are composed of several activities involving different agencies and frequently need to link and use data from multiple and diverse information resources. Therefore in order to deliver seamless services to citizens, it is necessary to enable a real interagency cooperation which allows services and information sharing, reducing the need for users to provide redundant information already held by the authorities. Interagency cooperation is about definition of sharing rules, cooperation policies as well as a common standard language thus allowing for organizational and semantic interoperability.
- **Horizontal and vertical integration:** Refers to promoting integration among agencies and departments within the same level of government (horizontal) and integration of central government services with state, local, or municipal services (vertical) (OECD, 2004). While horizontal integration has long been a goal of many countries and is still a challenge area, governments are now beginning to look beyond this to the next challenge: vertical integration. Vertical integration adds a layer of complexity to the e-government challenge but it is a fundamental challenge to integrate services for a seamless interaction for citizens.
- **Scalability and evolution over time:** Provide a flexible, scalable, and evolutionary solution in order to support changing and evolving needs of public administration. As public sector administrative organization, functional division, as well as legislative regulations evolve continuously, it is necessary to provide a technology-independent solution for seamless service delivery which facilitates system evolution over time. Finally, the use of standards and modeling techniques for formalizing system specification and conceptualization allow a better support of system evolution over time.

Table 2. Seamless service delivery requirements

Seamless service delivery requirements	
Citizen point of view	**Public administration point of view**
Focus on users' needs	Flexibility
User-friendly	Data storage
Personalized	Shared services
Access and accessibility	Integration of legacy system
Online handling of a complete service	Interagency cooperation
Practical value	Horizontal and vertical integration
Support migration	Scalability and evolution over time

Table 2 summarizes the requirements elicited throughout the previous paragraphs for quality seamless service delivery.

Many interesting solutions have been developed so far, the majority of them based on providing an Internet site where citizens can find information about governmental agencies and providing limited interaction functionalities (Belgium Web site, n.d.; Austrian Web site, n.d.). While some portal provides information concerning service delivered by multiple administrations together with contact information, another portal goes one step further providing downloadable forms to request services. Very often, no support for complete online handling of the whole service is provided.

More recently various middleware solutions are emerging as the dominant approach to technical integration in several countries, allowing a cooperative data exchange for the delivery of certain services (such as business services or taxation) or for providing increased quality services to citizens (services at stages 3 and 4) (Baldoni, Mecella, Contenti, & Termini, 2003; Pappa et al., 2003; Riedl, 2001). However a middleware oriented approach limits somehow the flexibility of the proposed solution in terms of both its integration with heterogeneous systems and its evolution over time. In order to design a flexible and interoperable system capable of easily evolving over the time a model-driven approach for system conceptualization and formalization is necessary. A model-driven system design, which is implementation and technology independent, allows overcoming limits of technology oriented systems in terms of reusability, interoperability, and transferability across different contexts. Moreover as front-office and back-office components are the two faces of the same coin, issues of both quality service provision and administration interoperability have to be fulfilled in order to provide seamless services. In order to address all these requirements it is necessary to provide an operating model of shared service, that is, a model of cooperative and open service sharing and information reuse between agencies. The concept of the e-government service marketplace aims at proposing a conceptual approach for defining an operating model of shared services which abstracts from implementation constraints and technological details hence easing flexibility, interoperability, and evolution over time.

THE CONCEPT OF E-GOVERNMENT SERVICE MARKETPLACE

The e-government service marketplace (eGovSM) concept (Mugellini, Abou Khaled, Pettanati, & Kuonen, 2005) proposes a general functional model for shared, interoperable, and evolutionary services for citizens enabling and promoting

Figure 2. E-government service marketplace

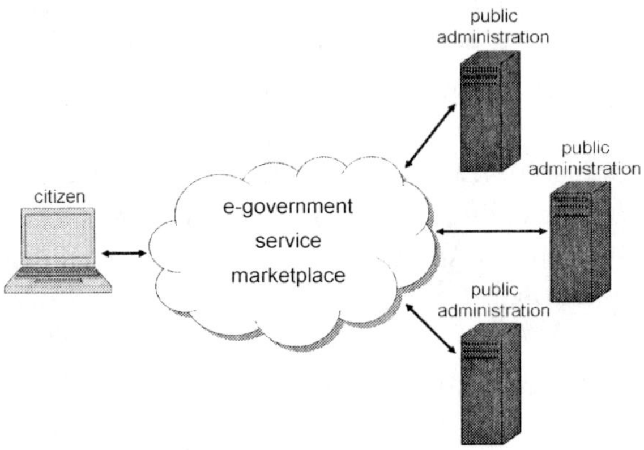

Figure 3. E-government service marketplace domain

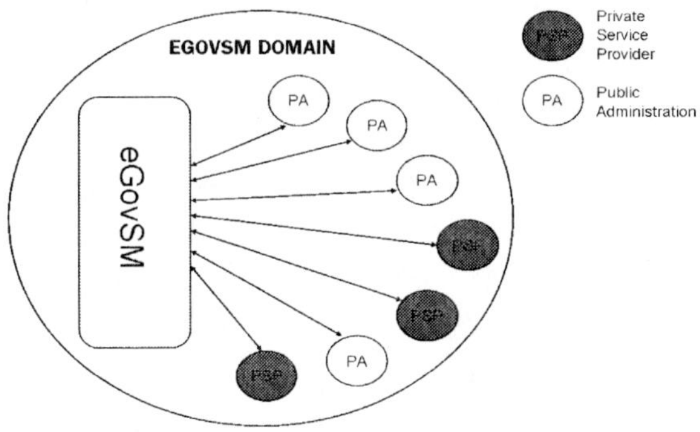

horizontal and vertical integration of agencies within the public sector. According to the e-government service marketplace concept, agencies are provided with organizational and technical flexibility because their back-office structures are independent of marketplace front-line structures. The concept of e-government service marketplace refers to an open and common virtual space for providing enhanced services to citizens which facilitates citizens' interaction with administrations hiding from citizens public administration complexity and fragmentation (Figure 2). Citizens gain value from increased access and reduced delays, improved service delivery, and less interaction with intermediaries, while administrations can flexibly share services and information as they are not required to meet the same level of technological sophistication.

The e-government service marketplace promotes the reuse of information as well as the sharing of services provided by different agencies. As it happens in a traditional marketplace (or "supermarket"), where a citizen can buy the products the citizen needs without caring about production and delivery process, the e-government marketplace aims at providing e-government services to citizens without requiring them to be aware of public administration complexity. For instance, for the delivery of a document, citizens will not be concerned with administration responsibility or geographical location of information. On the one hand, the e-government service marketplace can be considered an "interoperability intermediary" acting between agencies allowing the reuse and sharing of information at both horizontal and vertical levels (Figure 2). It allows interconnection and integration of multiple government agencies in order to deliver seamless services; services and information provided by multiple agencies are integrated and composed in order to support the online handling of a complete transaction (stages 3 and 4 of service provision). On the other hand, it can be considered a "communication intermediary" acting between the public administration and the citizen (Figure 2). It makes it easier for citizens to interact with public administrations, rebalancing relations between citizens and administrations and presenting e-government services in a citizen-oriented way. As stated before, the e-government service marketplace purpose is not only to use technologies to increase the efficiency of administrative process. It aims also to make it easier for citizens to interact with public administrations by presenting and structuring e-government services according to a citizen-oriented approach.

Moreover, as shown in Figure 3, the e-government service marketplace provides an open environment where commercial activities coexist with government services. While at its start-up eGovSM will start by integrating services of various public administrations (PA), then it will be open to, and it will promote as well, the participation of business company and private service providers (PSP). This way the marketplace will represent a common access point to "enriched governmental services." For instance if a citizen needs a driving license document the eGovSM will provide not only the "getting your driving license" service (public service) but also the service "driving school subscription" (private service). The e-government service marketplace domain is therefore defined as the ensemble of the e-government service marketplace and the administrations and private service providers connected to it (Figure 3). This domain represents somehow the "knowledge" of the e-government marketplace, that is, the service providers it knows about. All the administrations and private service providers that subscribe to the e-government service marketplace will be part of its domain.

As the e-government marketplace proposes an approach gradually integrating all the areas of public administration involved (state, regional agencies, administrations in the health and welfare sector), at the beginning not all the agencies will join the system sharing electronically their services and information. Moreover there will be agencies that will require a direct interaction with the citizen even if they participate in the marketplace—this is the case of a hospital where, for instance, an eyes check-up requires the citizen to physically move to the hospital.

Figure 4 shows the entities involved in the marketplace and possible interactions between them. The figure highlights three different types of public administrations (PAs). PAs of "type A" represent administrations subscribed to the eGovSM that automatically provide data to the marketplace without requiring the citizen to interact with them. PAs of "type B" represent administrations subscribed to the eGovSM that, even if they can automatically provide data to the marketplace, require a direct interaction with citizens (for example a hospital in case of a medical check-up). Finally PAs of "type C" represent administrations that are not subscribed to the eGovSM and hence require a direct interaction with citizens to provide data. As Figure 4 shows, citizens interact directly with the eGovSM and agencies of types B and C.

The e-government service marketplace has to hide the regulatory, administrative, and procedural complexity to citizens presenting simple

Figure 4. Gradual integration of public administrations

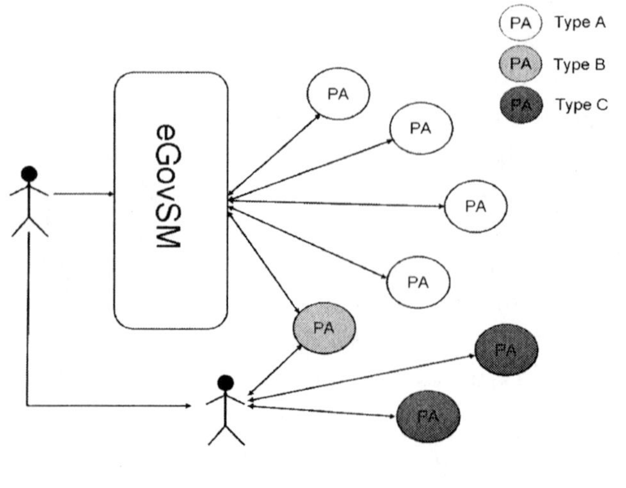

services which meet users' needs. The development of "global" services, defined on the basis of actions in the daily life of the citizen, regardless of how many administrations are involved (state, regional authorities, the health, the welfare sector, etc.), facilitates citizen interaction with the public sector. As the e-government service marketplace aims at facilitating citizen life not requiring users to provide information held by agencies time and time again, it has to provide a mechanism for identifying citizens which allows the automatic retrieving of this information. Often the delivery of a service is a complex process (consisting of multiple operations to perform) involving several agencies. The eGovSM has to guarantee an appropriate coordination as well as execution of all these operations. Finally it has to manage the interaction with administrations and private service providers. The main functions the e-government service marketplace ought to be able to perform are:

- Citizen interaction management
- Citizen identification
- Administrative process coordination
- Public administration interaction management

In the following paragraphs a more detailed description of these functions is provided.

Citizen Interaction Management

The eGovSM represents a common access point to public services presented and structured according to a citizen-oriented approach. By citizen-oriented service, we mean reorganizing the processes of services provision and delivery on the basis of citizens' needs rather than the internal needs of the government, as has been the practice so far. The problem lies in the fact that the existent organization of government is based on a division of work between several fields or competences (Vintar, Kunstelj, & Leben, 2002). Accordingly, administrative procedures and services are adapted and distributed over several public institutions. However, the problems of citizens do not usually apply merely to one single competence or one single public institution; instead they involve multiple institutions. Consequently these processes are complicated, time consuming, and expensive. The solution to these problems lies in the introduction of services designed around possible life events of the citizens. The life-event approach (Dipartimento per l'Innovazione e le Tecnologie, 2002; Life Event Portal, n.d.) considers government operations from the perspective of everyday life. Its main purpose is to overcome the existent structure and complexity of public institutions. One life event has to comprise all services as well as the corresponding processes needed to solve the customer's problem from the beginning to the end. In this way, all services needed to solve a particular problem or situation, are either linked or integrated into one single service. According to this model, citizens' life is described providing a list of events that (when occurring) result in a series of transactions between a citizen and different public sector organizations (Figure 5). Examples of life events could be "looking for a job," "moving home," "getting the driving license," "retiring," "having a baby," and so on.

The e-government service marketplace provides access to services aggregating them according to "life event metaphor" making the various public administrations involved in the delivery of such services transparent to citizens (Figure 5). The marketplace concept of service consists in either the transmission or the reception of a document between offices. In the context of this chapter a document can be an official document (well-structured information) or "raw" information (not structured information).

The citizen interaction manager is also responsible for updating life events and services according to changes to the law or to the administrative process associated to the service. Moreover the

Figure 5. Seamless and citizen-oriented services in the e-government service marketplace

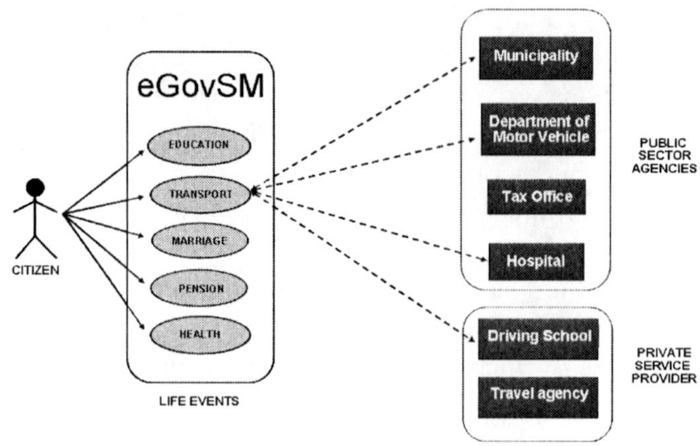

e-government service marketplace will enable users to find out about the status of their official papers or the progress of their service requests. To conclude, the citizen interaction management can be defined as the following:

- The citizen interaction manager component is responsible for managing all the interactions between the citizen and the marketplace. Its main role is to organize, structure, and present governmental services according to citizens' needs (the life event metaphor). Moreover it has to manage and supervise citizen service request, for instance, informing the citizen about service request progress or possible alternatives in case the target administration is not yet electronically connected to eGovSM.

Citizen Identification

The delivery of seamless services requires an exchange of information between the e-government marketplace and the agencies that hold citizen data. Hence, the eGovSM needs a mechanism to find, according to the requested service, which administrations to contact in order to retrieve the necessary information (as previously defined, the delivery of a service corresponds to the transmission or reception of a document). In other words to deliver a service to the citizen, it is necessary to identify such a citizen. Such an identifier will contain information about the citizen that allows verifying if the citizen who is requesting the service meets the requirements for obtaining such service as well as identifying the agencies that hold the information necessary for delivering the service. Several identification options are possible (Ministère de la Fonction Publique, 2003): single significant identifier, single nonsignificant identifier, several nonsignificant identifiers, and single significant federated identifier. The single significant identifier, which can be general or sector-based, suggests somehow the identity of the citizen; hence it is not the best solution for protecting the privacy of citizens. On the contrary the nonsignificant single identifier does not contain citizen personal information; that is, it is not related to the identity of the citizen, but it has to be associated to sector identifiers. Then the problem arises from the necessity of a look-up table to match the single nonsignificant identifier with the sector identifier and, above all, the storage of this table. However this solution provides a greater protection of citizen freedom as it allows users to decide and manage which identifier accesses the different services. The same, in case of several nonsignificant identifiers allowing the access to different services, the problem of the look-up table and its storage still exists. Finally the single significant federated identifier allows citizens to use a single identifier to access all the services. This identifier contains citizen personal information, but as it is "federated" neither the government nor the identity federator itself are able to make the connection between the different identifiers (i.e., there is not a look-up table stored somewhere). According to the needs of the e-government service marketplace, the most suitable solution for the citizen identifier is the federated one. Each federated identifier will uniquely identify a citizen. This identifier will federate all the information about the citizen (such as name, birth date, birthplace, or sector-specific identifier) necessary to the e-government marketplace for identifying, every time, a service requested, the administration that holds a particular set of citizen data. It is worth noting that this identifier is not for privacy protection or security issues. Therefore other security mechanisms, for guaranteeing respect of privacy as well as positively identifying the citizen requesting the service, are required. The e-government service marketplace will manage this federated identifier but neither the marketplace itself nor any of the administrations will store the identifier; that is, there is not a centralized database of all the federated identifiers.

The management of the identifier will include the generation of the identifier and successive use. As the identifier federates specific information and country-specific sector identifiers, federated identifiers belonging to different countries will have a different structure (country-specific identifier structure). Hence, each e-government service marketplace will be able only to create and interpret identifiers belonging to its origin country. The creation of the identifier is done online by the e-government marketplace; a citizen wishing to obtain an identifier provides an ensemble of information the e-government marketplace uses, after a verification phase where the system checks the correctness and truthfulness of information provided by the citizen with the public administration, to create the identifier. The identifier is stored on an electronic card; thus only the citizen possesses it (in those countries where an electronic identity card has already been activated, it can be envisaged to stock the identifier on the identity card).

To conclude, the citizen identification functionality can be defined as the following:

- The citizen identifier is a federated identifier, containing citizen personal data, which allow the e-government service marketplace to find out the governmental agencies that hold citizen data. This identifier has a general structure which can be adapted according to country-specific needs. This identifier is not for security issues.

Administrative Process Coordination

As Figure 6 shows, life events are used to facilitate citizen navigation and search of services. However citizens do not consume a life event since this general structuring concept only represents the access interface to public services. Public services are the concrete products and services citizen are applying for. At the same time each public service consists of several processes—elementary operations to perform in order to deliver such a service. These elementary operations include among others prerequirements verification, constraints check, and information retrieval (see Figure 6).

Usually laws and administrative provisions fragment all the aspect of the life of a citizen according to multiple sectors (i.e., taxation, municipality, health, etc.). This fragmentation causes difficulties in delivering services to citizens, such as services composed of several activities involving different agencies and frequently need to link and use data from multiple and diverse information resources. Therefore in order to deliver seamless services to citizens it is necessary to coordinate

Figure 6. Life events to processes mapping

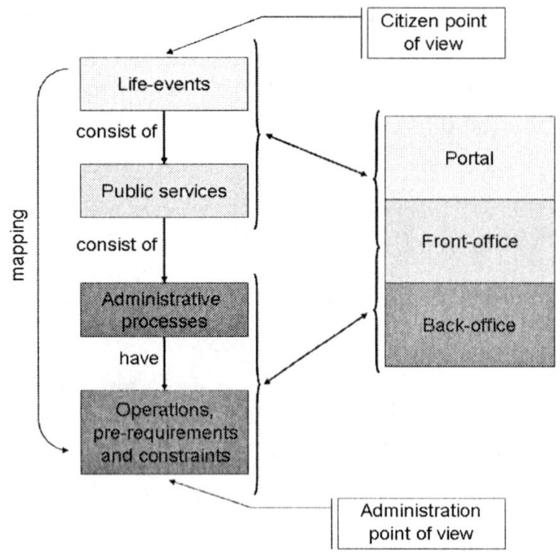

the execution of all these activities and monitor the correct course of the whole process instead of the citizen. Citizens will not have to supply different government agencies with the same information and documentation time and time again. Instead they will ask the government service marketplace for the service they need and the e-government marketplace will manage all the operations to obtain such a service (constraint verification, requirements check as well as information retrieve and exchange) on behalf of the citizen, thus reducing as much as possible the need for users to provide redundant information already held by the authorities. When a citizen requests a given service, as a service is usually composed by several activities involving different agencies, the marketplace has to perform all these activities in order to correctly deliver the final service to the citizen. The marketplace translates the requested service (expressed according to life-event metaphor) into the corresponding administrative process and executes this process to deliver the document to the citizen. For each service provided by the marketplace a description of the process associated with such service is given as well. As administrative procedures and services are distributed over several public institutions, the e-government service marketplace has to coordinate the execution of distributed tasks. Since service delivery is not only a mere retrieval of information but is subjected to the satisfaction of specific constraints, the e-government marketplace has also got to guarantee that all the constraints are satisfied before completing the delivery of a service.

The e-government service marketplace is responsible for verifying if the citizen requesting the service meets the requirements for obtaining the service and, if it is the case, coordinating the operations for collecting the necessary information and creating the final document to be delivered.

It is worth noting that in order to respect public administration authority in delivering official documents, the marketplace will create, by default, only the "logic document" (i.e., an electronic document containing all the information required in the final document without formatting style and without the "status" of official certificate). This logic document will be sent to the administration responsible for delivering it to the citizen and the administration itself will create the physical official document. On the contrary if the administration delegates this function to the e-government service marketplace, the system will create the final document and deliver it to the citizen instead of the agency.

As stated, in order to provide seamless services to citizens, the e-government service marketplace has to exchange and retrieve a certain number of data regarding the user. Therefore citizen personal data has to be stored somewhere; several options are possible (Ministère de la Fonction publique, 2003): centralization, generalized exchange, or decentralization. The first option (centralization) requires centralizing all the data and administrative files of each user of the administration. This solution is not implemented in any country for evident reasons of privacy and individual freedom. The second option (generalized exchange) allows an indiscriminate exchange of data between administrative departments, which enables users to benefit from really simplified services as data held by one agency are accessible to any other; but on the other hand it does not offer a sufficient protection of citizen personal data. Finally the third option (decentralization) implies a decentralized storage of data with a controlled exchange between agencies. Data storage remains decentralized within each agency in respect of privacy and individual freedom issues. The e-government service marketplace implements a decentralized approach; it does not store a local copy of citizen data; data remains stored only within each agency as it has been the practice so far.

To conclude, the administrative process coordination can be defined as:

- The administrative process coordination is about the translation of a public service (expressed according to life-event metaphor) into the corresponding administrative process and the execution of all the operation associated to such a process (constraints verification, requirements check, etc.).

Public Administration Interaction Management

As elicited in the previous requirement analysis allowing public administration interoperability while integrating legacy systems is a key factor towards improving the quality of service delivery. Public administration interoperability has to be made possible respecting public administration autonomy and integrating legacy systems. For this reason eGovSM reach for interoperability by proposing a service-oriented approach, that is, distributed and independent administrations participate to the marketplace activity by exchanging services that provide a complete abstraction of the legacy systems explained later. Moreover each administration wanting to join the marketplace has to subscribe to it, declaring its availability to provide services and share data. In order to respect technical and political capabilities of public administrations, as well as providing a certain flexibility, as not all the agencies are at the same level of technological sophistication, eGovSM provides different subscription profiles, corresponding to different levels of interoperability both for providing as well as receiving data from the marketplace. Concerning the transmission of data from an agency to the eGovSM, four different subscription profiles are provided. In this way eGovSM allows each administration to interact and cooperate with the marketplace according to its capability. The "Profile 0" refers to administrations that are not able to provide electronic data. The "Profile 1" refers to administrations that can provide elementary electronic functionalities (they are able to respond to yes/no questions). The "Profile 2" refers to administrations that are able to provide a richer set of functionalities (they can provide the marketplace with information or documents). The "Profile 3" refers to administrations that implement an instance of the eGovSM system. In the last case the administration information system is fully eGovSM compliant and it is able to provide the same functionalities of the eGovSM system. Concerning the communication of data from the eGovSM to the government agencies, each agency has two subscription possibilities: it can accept or not data from the marketplace. It is worth noting that considerations about public administration that have been done so far are valid for the private service provider as well.

Table 3 relates the four profiles with the three different types of public administrations previously introduced.

To conclude, public administration interaction management can be defined as the following:

- Public administration management is about providing different levels of interoperability and legacy system integration in order to allow a gradual involvement of agencies with different levels of technological sophistica-

Table 3. Public administration types and subscription profiles

Subscription profiles / Types of PA	Profile 0	Profile 1	Profile 2	Profile 3
Type A		X	X	X
Type B		X	X	X
Type C	X			

tion. The public administration manager is responsible for localizing and contacting agencies as well as integrating services and information of various administrations.

EGOVSM FORMALIZATION: THE MODEL-DRIVEN APPROACH

The concept of e-government service marketplace has been formalized using a model-driven approach which allows the development of a flexible, interoperable, and scalable environment. Using a system modeling approach makes it possible to define the system at business domain level and then translate it in a software system meeting the requirements of system generality, extensibility, and interoperability. In a continuously changing and evolving world as public sector (and also evolving technologies), it is very important to design a flexible system which is easy to maintain and reconfigure in order to meet changing and evolving needs of administrations. Moreover in a heterogeneous world as public sector, it becomes fundamental to provide different levels of abstractions in system representation and view in order to make possible and facilitate the communication between different actors involved (engineers, administrators, managers, etc.). A model-driven design allows specifying the concept without taking care of any implementation constraints or technological details. Model-driven approach refers to the use of models at different levels of abstraction in order to formally describe an information system. Separation and formalization, that is, modeling, are recognized as the best practices for system design and development. Modeling techniques allow the same model specifying system functionalities to be realized on multiple platforms. They allow different applications to be integrated by explicitly relating their models, enabling integration and interoperability and supporting system evolution as technologies change rapidly.

Arrangements and middleware solution for integrating back-office systems with customer-oriented interface may give the impression that collaboration and cooperation between agencies can be achieved primarily at the technical level. In practice this is unlikely to be the case. In effect collaboration for seamless service delivery is more than technical issues and it is likely to involve implementation of integration models, service delivery policies and standards, service quality, presentation of information and material, and a decision-making process. For these reasons a middleware-oriented approach, which concentrates and takes care only of technological constraints and implementation details, is not enough and a more conceptual (technology-independent) approach is required. This is why the concept of e-government service marketplace is first of all a conceptual model for a shared infrastructure enabling seamless service delivery, which can be afterwards converted into a physical and operational architecture (which will only correspond to one of the possible implementation solutions). Interoperability, integration, and evolution are crucial issues e-government has to deal with. As stated before, the main e-government objectives are to better deliver services to citizens, improve interactions with citizens, and provide more efficient government management. In order to achieve these goals a real collaboration between administrations and a fully integrated heterogeneous public administration information system is required (European Commission, 2003). Using modeling techniques to formalize an e-government system allows specifying system functionalities in a technology-independent way, thus enabling integration and interoperability and supporting system evolution. The e-government service marketplace has been formalized using a document based modeling approach (document engineering). Document engineering (Glushko, 2003) is evolving as a new scientific discipline for specifying, designing, and implementing systems belonging to very different business domains by using XML technology (World Wide Web Consortium, n.d.). The use of XML technology (Daum, 2003) allows the design and specification of a flexible, interoperable, and scalable system. It allows the description and formalization of the system in a technology-independent way, making it portable across different development environments, thus achieving maximum reusability and interoperability.

This allows us to provide a standard definition of the system which will be common for all implementation while guaranteeing a certain level of flexibility. According to the e-government service marketplace model, only basic functionalities and behaviors are defined, making possible to add and adapt this "basic" system specification to the specific needs of a particular context. This would eventually allow different administrations, even of different countries, to customize the system according to their needs while remaining fully compliant, thus interoperable, with other systems. The definition of the concept of e-government service marketplace transcends country-specific requirements and identifies elements that can be transferred across different contexts. Moreover the modeling of the eGovSM in a technology-independent way facilitates system evolution over time as public sector administrative organization, functional divisions as well as legislative regulations evolve continuously.

EGOVSM REPLICATION: THE CONCEPT OF E-GOVERMENT SERVICE MARKETPLACE NETWORK

The concept of "network of e-government service marketplace" refers to an ensemble of interconnected e-government service marketplace domains, within a country or distributed over several countries. These multiple domains are able to work in a cooperative manner thus providing seamless services to a wider range of citizens. Interconnecting different e-government service marketplace domains allows sharing and integrating the knowledge of each of them, while respecting their autonomy and operational independence. The concept of network of e-government service marketplace represents an interesting solution to respond to the need of providing seamless services at the European level (pan-European services) while at the same time allowing each country to decide about implementation details of the eGovSM concept (for instance, which information the federated identifier should contain, life-events classification, and implementation and possible subscription profiles).

As Figure 7 shows, the network of eGovSMs will include all the known eGovSM domains. Each eGovSM has not to know about all the other domains, it is sufficient that each domain is known for at least another one. When an eGovSM is set up, it has to subscribe to (at least) another one in order to become part of the network.

This way each e-government service domain can be considered as a virtual organization in the grid (Foster, Kesselman, & Tuecke, 2001) domain. A Virtual Organization is defined as a dynamic set of individuals or institutions defined around

Figure 7. The concept of e-government service marketplace network

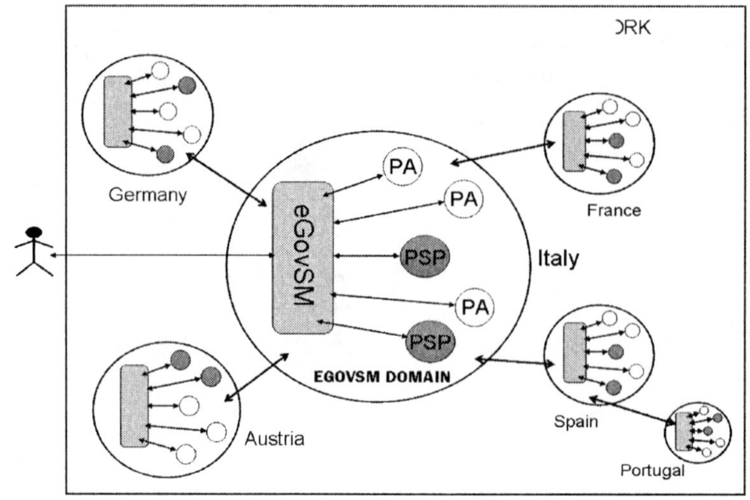

a set of resource-sharing rules and conditions which share resources in a coordinated, secure, and flexible manner (Joseph & Fellenstein, 2004). Entities of an eGovSM domain (public administrations and private service providers) share information and services with the e-government service marketplace of that domain according to the sharing rules defined in such a domain (which can be different from domain to domain). The other domains have neither direct knowledge nor access to these resources and information. They only know about and can refer to the eGovSM of that domain. The concept of network of eGovSM seems to suitable represent an interagency cooperation at European level (see Figure 7), where each country has its own eGovSM platform which with the other service providers (governmental agencies and private businesses) forms the eGovSM domain of such a country. EGovSMs of different countries are part of the whole network and thus collaborate in order to provide pan-European seamless services. Citizens, by interacting only with one of the eGovSM of the network (see Figure 7), can access all the services offered by the whole network. This concept scales at a national level as well. For instance, different regions of the same country can implement their own eGovSM system. In this case each eGovSM domain contains agencies at local and regional levels, has its own, specific sharing rules, and collaborates with the other regional-level eGovSM domains in order to provide seamless services at the national level.

THE CASE OF PROVISIONAL DRIVING LICENSE DELIVERY

To further illustrate the application of the developed framework, we used it to apply the concept of e-government service marketplace for the delivery of a Provisional Driving License in the Italian context. The case study is summarized to illustrate the main features of the framework and should not be considered a complete and exhaustive presentation of the e-government service marketplace functional model.

For any kind of government service there are a plethora of official forms that citizens are requested to fill in; moreover each form has its own prerequisites and routing cycle, each with its own fees. As a result, a simple service like the delivery of Provisional Driving License becomes a quite

Figure 8. Provisional driving licence delivery: Sequence diagram

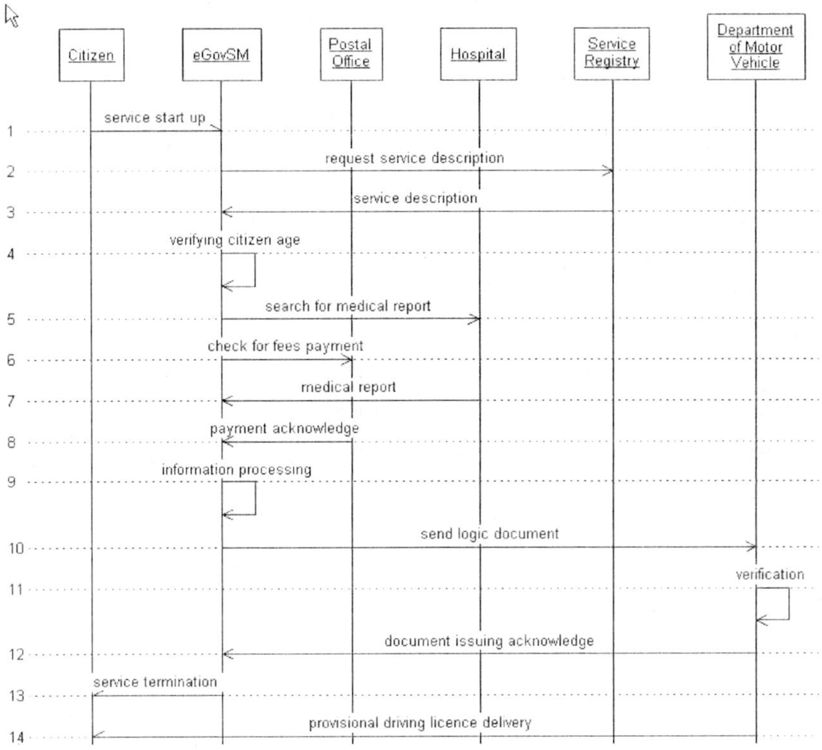

complicated and time-expensive task requiring citizens to move to several governmental agencies, providing the same information multiple times.

The Provisional Driving License (named "Foglio Rosa" in Italian) is a document issued by the Department of Motor Vehicle (responsible for delivering all services concerning driving licenses and vehicles) that allows a citizen to take driving lessons on the road for a six-month period. After the citizen has been issued the Provisional Driving License, the citizen has to pass the Final Driving Theory and Practical Driving Test to obtain the Full Driving License. The delivery of the Provisional Driving License has some conditions attached to it:

- The citizen must be 18 years old or over
- The citizen must exhibit an identity card or a passport
- The citizen must hold "moral requirements" (e.g., not to be a criminal, etc.)
- The citizen must provide a medical report (including an eyesight report)
- The citizen must pay the appropriate fees
- The citizen must provide two passport-type photographs

The traditional procedure for the delivery of such service requires the citizen to move to the postal office to pay the fees, to the hospital for medical check-up, the photos, and eventually to the Department of Motor Vehicle with all the previously collected documents and information and apply for obtaining a document ("Foglio Bianco") that allows the candidate to drive while waiting for the delivery of the Provisional Driving License. Once moral requirements are checked and confirmed the Provisional Driving License is issued and delivered to the citizen (which has to move to the Department of Motor Vehicle again). The eGovSM allows easing the whole procedure by reducing interaction between citizen and agencies and providing this service as a unique transaction to the citizen. Case handling, decision, and delivery of the requested service are completely treated by eGovSM via the Web by integrating participating agencies (hospital, postal office, department of motor vehicle, and so on). The citizen wishing to apply for a Provisional Driving License accesses the eGovSM via the portal and applies for the service (see Figure 8). The request is handled by the eGovSM that, as a first step, retrieves the document ("Process Descriptor") describing the entire process of Provisional Driving License from a dedicated registry. This document describes in a machine-readable way tasks and requirements that have to be executed and satisfied in order to deliver the service (for instance, verifying whether the applying citizen is 18 years old and over or holds moral requirements).

By following the instructions contained in the Process Descriptor, eGovSM checks whether the citizen is of age, whether the citizen has done the medical examination and payed the fees and, if this is not the case, eGovSM stops the process and informs the citizen about requirements that have not been satisfied or missing information.

Figure 9. Impact of the e-government service marketplace

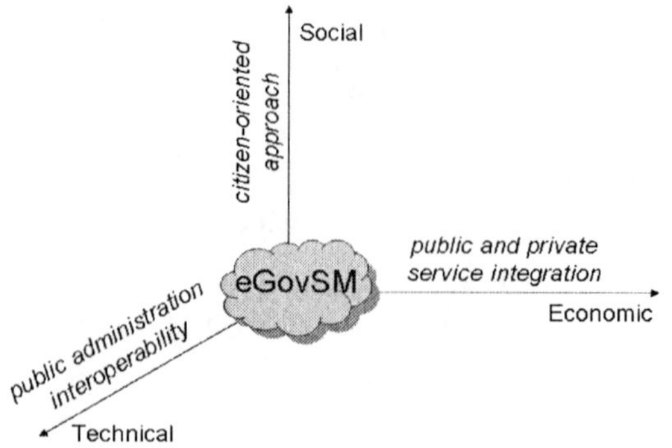

Public administrations involved in the process of service delivery are located by processing the information contained in the citizen identifier (for instance, the "birthplace" information contained in the identifier tells the system the origin region of the citizen and allows focusing information search on specific governmental agencies). Once all requirements are satisfied and required tasks performed the eGovSM system provides the Department of Motor Vehicle with the logic document, that is, an electronic version of the final document to be delivered (meanwhile the citizen is informed by the eGovSM about the progress of the request). The Department of Motor Vehicle has to check the validity of the document, inform the eGovSM about it, and issue the final document to the citizen.

ANALYSIS OF BENEFITS OF EGOVSM SEAMLESS SERVICE DELIVERY

A shared and seamless service delivery has a major impact on e-government evolution process and several types of interconnected benefits can be identified. More specifically the impact of the concept of e-government service marketplace can be analyzed and evaluated according to three different perspectives:

- The social perspective
- The economical perspective
- The technical perspective

In fact, the use of information and communication technologies in public administration in order to improve service delivery process has tangible and intangible benefits from the social, economic, and technical points of view (Figure 9).

The Social Perspective

The social perspective refers to benefits which are perceived from citizens (i.e., customers of the service) or civil servants (i.e., the persons who are involved in or responsible for guaranteeing a quality service delivery to the customers). According to this point of view, an increased user's satisfaction is the main objective to reach. The user's satisfaction can be expressed in terms of:

- **Improved quality of information:** The user-friendliness and citizen-oriented approach for service delivery allow improving the way citizens interact with government agencies, making it easier for them to obtain the services they need without being concerned with "administrative" details which are not relevant for them.
- **Reduced administrative burdens:** The use of ICT in the provision of public services makes it possible to significantly reduce the administrative burdens for citizens that use these services. Citizens will have neither to move from an administration to another one wasting time and money, nor to provide the same information time and time again.
- **Improved access and accessibility:** Access and accessibility are two key issues enabling citizens to obtain online information. *Access* refers to the real possibility of consulting or acquiring government information electronically. *Accessibility* is the ease with which one can actually make use of the possibility of consulting government information electronically. Therefore accessibility emphasizes the perspective of end users of government information and their capacity to find, digest, and use relevant information. Improving the accessibility of online information can be achieved in terms of specific life events, that is, classifying and presenting services to citizens according to events that make sense in their lives.
- **Improved service level:** A major benefit of seamless service delivery is the improved service level. More precisely in terms of increased time availability and flexibility (24/7 availability, multichannel delivery) and transparency (availability of more detailed and complete information about the service). Using a Web-based system for service delivery allows citizens to access the services wherever they are and according to their device (PDA, PC, mobile phone, etc.). Improving service delivery is a means for decreasing time in completing transaction and reducing cost associated with citizen to government interactions. Moreover it allows improving civil servants work; it allows improving efficiency of civil servants by automating tedious and repetitive tasks and reducing cost of transactions for government processes. The rise in the use of online services will shorten queues at the counters, thus easing the work of the reception staff and enabling them to provide a better service.
- **Personalized service:** Increased capabilities for custom-made services (i.e., the possibility to customize electronic service delivery). Personalized services will inform citizens about the progress of their request or they will allow citizens to adapt to their needs the home page of the e-government service marketplace portal.
- **Multichannel service delivery:** The need to preserve choice is fundamental to any customer-focused strategy. Providing alternative delivery channels (for instance, phone and kiosk) and indeed choice of online access points improve chances of ensuring access and effectiveness. The e-government service marketplace mainly provides service via a Web-based interface (i.e., it requires an access via personal PC or dedicated kiosk), but it can be easily configured to provide information on other alternative channels thanks to the use of a model-driven specification approach.
- **Improved support to citizen mobility:** Since the integration of Europe into a single

market, citizens of the European Community member states should be able to migrate from one European country to another with as few problems as possible. Yet, mobile European citizens have to deal with time and money consuming administrative procedures. If the collecting of required documents costs a lot of time and money for citizens in their home country, for foreign citizens, the situation is even worse. The concept of a network of e-government service marketplaces capable of cooperating across national borders can handle this problem and facilitate the migration of citizens.

The Economical Perspective

The economic perspective refers to economic benefits which can be obtained at the public administration. According to this point of view, the e-government service marketplace allows for:

- **Enriched public service:** The concept of e-government service marketplace provides an open environment where commercial activities can coexist with government services. This way the marketplace represents a common access point to "enriched governmental services." For instance if a citizen needs a driving license document, the eGovSM provides not only the "getting your driving license" service (public service) but also the service "driving school subscription" (private service).
- **Improved public-private partnership:** Public-private integration can improve e-government by direct provision to end users of government services. This integration can add value for both parties. Integration with nongovernment activity complements seamless government services. Public-private partnerships can help integrate and improve the delivery of government services both to benefit customers and to increase efficiency. So public-private partnerships can be, and have to be seen as, a means not only to share risk and investment, to bypass budgetary constraints, or to access specialized skills (for instance, for software development) but also to provide better services to citizens, thus maximizing benefits of e-government.
- **Reduced cost:** The automation of service delivery process and the use of electronic communication with citizens can lead to significant cost savings. The use of ICT enables the public sector to increase its services processing and delivery capabilities, while requiring less time and fewer personnel. This way a rebalancing from tedious and repetitive tasks towards more customer-oriented activities of civil servant work can be possible. Moreover according to the concept of e-government marketplace each agency is not obliged to implement an instance of the system with clear economic advantages and cost savings.
- **Decreased budgetary barriers:** Budgetary constraints can work against e-government seamless service delivery implementation especially for small agencies where the costs for a system development can be prohibitive. The concept of e-government service marketplace, as it does not require each administration to develop and implement an instance of the system architecture, represents a suitable solution for different-budget contexts.
- **Reduced process time:** The digitalization of public services can also significantly reduce the time it takes to process and deliver a service (process time), therefore saving precious time for public administration officials. Because data can be submitted electronically by customers and shared between different organizations, service information can be reviewed online in real

time, allowing a greater responsiveness on the part of the administration.

- **Improved quality of information and information supply:** The direct input of data in electronic format by public service users reduces the number of errors, thus decreasing the number of citizen enquires or complaints, and makes it possible to build quality management information systems. Furthermore, the shared use of information and databases, made possible by electronic networks can also improve the quality of information and data supply.
- **Increased efficiency:** Improved information supply and service delivery contribute to increase the efficiency (i.e., the capability to convert resources and inputs into effects and impacts) of public service delivery. Tasks and costs can be more efficiently distributed, both within and between public sector agencies.
- **Increased economic competitiveness:** Seamless service delivery can provide a major contribution to increasing economic competitiveness at local, regional, national, or international levels. By streamlining bureaucratic procedures and increasing public sector efficiency, it plays a significant role in raising the productivity levels in the economy as a whole (IDABC eGovernment Observatory, 2005).

The Technical Perspective

The technical perspective refers to benefits the information and communication technologies bring to the public administration. The main advantages the concept of e-government service marketplace carries can be expressed in terms of:

- **Improved cooperation:** The concept of e-government service marketplace facilitates the cooperation at the technical level between agencies allowing seamless service delivery based on a shared service operating model. The e-government marketplace concept has the potential to improve collaboration across agencies and organizations but there are a number of regulatory barriers to pass beyond (for instance, accountability rules, designed to ensure responsible use of public resources by clearly identifying who does what, can impede collaboration as it may be unclear who is accountable for shared service delivery).
- **Shareable infrastructure:** A lack of compatible infrastructure between agencies can impede interagency collaboration, but the expense of implementing modern infrastructure can be a major barrier to the implementation of e-government initiatives. A shared infrastructure among agencies is one way of overcoming this problem.
- **Improved interoperability:** The concept of e-government service marketplace facilitates the interoperability between agencies according to two different aspects: integration of legacy systems and flexibility and independence from a specific technology.
- **Reuse of information:** Information is not duplicated multiple times and collected at different locations but it is reused when needed, thus avoiding useless replication of data and promoting decentralization of information.
- **Integration of legacy system:** The use of a service oriented paradigm allows integrating heterogeneous legacy systems. Distributed and independent administrations participate to the marketplace activity by exchanging services that provide a complete abstraction of the legacy systems.
- **Reduced process time:** The availability of electronic data makes it possible to automate and "e-enable" key steps of the decision-making and service delivery process.
- **Increased efficiency and flexibility:** On the one hand according to the marketplace

concept each administration can participate and join the system according to different levels of integration and interoperability. This way allows creating a network of collaboration between different administrations while respecting their technical and political capabilities. Clearly the administration that evolves and improves its services has the ability to strengthen its participation to the e-government service marketplace by increasing its level of cooperation. On the other hand the concept of e-government service marketplace modeled in a technology independent way allows the development of different, yet interoperable, systems. Moreover its generality makes possible its development and utilization in different countries.

- **Evolution over time and scalability:** The concept of e-government marketplace allows a gradual participation and integration of each administration. The multiple subscription profiles it provides make possible for each administration to join the marketplace according to its technical and political capabilities.

FUTURE TRENDS AND OPEN ISSUES

As the field of seamless service delivery continues to grow and develop, much research should be done to fully take advantage of innovative approaches and technologies for e-service provision. Several pending or emerging issues that should be better investigated include the following:

- **Investigate emerging paradigm:** For distributed and shared collaboration. Given the high speed at which services are growing and changing continuously, shared and seamless service delivery is at the basis of grid service concept. According to the definition of grid, within a virtual organization it is possible to use in a flexible and shared manner distributed and heterogeneous resources all over the world in order to provide seamless, yet very complex, services. The concept of e-government service marketplace can be extended and enriched to make it more efficient in a distributed and heterogeneous world has the public sector is. The integration of grid concept can bring several advantages by making the discovery of services more dynamic, efficient, flexible, and distributed on a world-scale basis.
- **Measure performance:** Several performance measures should be used to evaluate efficacy and success of shared infrastructure for seamless e-service provision. For instance the amount of staff time to develop and set up such an infrastructure, the number of accesses on the site, the number of downloads, the number of problems resolved should be carefully measured and analyzed (Pavlichev & David Garson, 2004).
- **Provide legislative support for seamless service:** As previously stated collaboration between agencies for seamless service delivery is not only a technical issue; in order to promote and support interadministration data exchange, service sharing, and accountability, an adequate and accurate legislative support is required. For instance digital signature mechanism for the future development of seamless service delivery needs to be adopted and integrated in present systems. The evolution of the law, in order to remove regulatory barriers to the development of seamless and shared services, is a fundamental component of the e-government development process. The development of seamless service delivery should be supported by a special legislation on shared and integrated services.
- **Measures improvement in citizen life:** It is crucial to research the effects of seamless

e-service delivery and what differences it is making in the citizens' lives. It is fundamental to understand whether citizens find it too difficult to use or whether they do not experience lower costs or more effective government. Improvement in citizen life could be measured in terms of increased level of citizen satisfaction with government and government services, increased level of citizen trust in government, or costs saved by seamless service provision (in terms of money and time).

- **Account for privacy issues:** Further efforts to continue to develop policies and technical solutions around the key areas of security, authentication, and data storage in order to preserve and protect privacy of individual citizens' data are needed. In fact, if not handled correctly, this issue, more than any other, has the potential to undermine the support and development of e-government and seamless government initiatives.

CONCLUSION

Seamless delivery of public service is a fundamental challenge e-government has to deal with. As public services are very complex ones, in order to provide seamless service at the transaction level, different and multiple requirements, from both citizen and public administration point of view, have to be satisfied. The emerging concept of e-government service marketplace proposes a general functional model for shared and interoperable services enabling integration between agencies both at horizontal and vertical levels. This chapter has reviewed the requirements for seamless service delivery from both citizen and public administration points of view. It has presented a general functional model for seamless, citizen-oriented service delivery (eGovSM), and its main functionalities. The impact and advantages of this concept on the three main axes (social, economic, and technical) have been discussed as well. The chapter ends providing some insights on future trends and open issues about seamless services delivery and enabling systems.

REFERENCES

Accenture. (2004). *eGovernment leadership: High performance, maximum value* (Technical report). Retrieved April 28, 2006, from http://www.accenture.com/xdoc/en/industries/government/gove_egov_value.pdf

Accenture. (2005). *Driving high performance in government: Maximizing the value of public-sector shared services* (Technical report). Retrieved April 28, 2006, from http://www.accenture.com/xd/xd.asp?it=enweb&xd=industries%5Cgovernment%5Cinsights%5Cmaximizing_value.xml

ANAO. (1999). *Electronic service delivery, including Internet use, by commonwealth government agencies* (Technical report). Retrieved April 28, 2006, from http://www.egov.vic.gov.au/pdfs/rpt18-00.pdf

AOEMA. (2004). *E-government from a user's perspective* (Technical report). Retrieved April 28, 2006, from http://www.apectel29.gov.hk/download/bfsg_14.pdf

Austrian Web site. (n.d.). Retrieved April 28, 2006, from http://www.help.gv.at/

Baldoni, R., Mecella, M., Contenti, M., & Termini, A. (2003). Report on EU-PUBLI.com architecture prototype. Deliverable. Retrieved April 28, 2006, from http://research.unisoft.gr/Eupublicomsite/workspace1/deliverables.htm

Belgium Web site. (n.d.). Retrieved April 28, 2006, from http://www.belgium.be

Capgemini. (2005). *Online availability of public services: How is Europe progressing?* Web based survey on electronic public service. Retrieved

April 28, 2006, from http://europa.eu.int/information_society/eeurope/2005/doc/highlights/whats_new/capgemini4.pdf

Daum, B. (2003, March). *Modeling business objects with XML schema.* Morgan Kaufmann.

Dipartimento per l'Innovazione e le Tecnologie. (2002). *Front-office e servizi di e-government per cittadini ed imprese* (Technical report). Retrieved April 28, 2006, from http://www.innovazione.gov.it/ita/intervento/normativa/allegati/avviso_allegato1.pdf

European Commission. (2003). *Linking up Europe: The importance of interoperability for eGovernment services* (Technical report). Retrieved April 28, 2006, from http://www.csi.map.es/csi/pdf/interoperabilidad_1675.pdf

Foster, I., Kesselman, C., & Tuecke, S. (2001). The anatomy of the grid: Enabling scalable virtual organization. *International Journal of High Performance Computing Applications, 15*(3), 200-222.

Glushko, R. J. (2003, September 24-25). Document engineering. *Symposium on Coevolution of Technology Business Innovations*, San Jose, CA.

Halligan, J., & Moore, T. (2004). *E-government in Australia: The challenges of moving to integrated services* (Technical report). Retrieved April 28, 2006, from http://unpan1.un.org/intradoc/groups/public/documents/un/unpan019249.pdf

IDABC eGovernment Observatory. (2005). *The impact of e-government on competitiveness and jobs* (Technical report). Retrieved April 28, 2006, from http://europa.eu.int/idabc/en/document/3851/254

Joseph, J., & Fellenstein, C. (2004). *Grid computing.* IBM Press.

Layne, K., & Lee, J. (2001). Developing fully functional e-government: A four stage model. *Government Information Quarterly, 18*(2), 122-136.

Life Event Portal. (n.d.). Retrieved April 28, 2006, from http://www.oasis.gov.ie/siteindex/by_life_event.html

Ministère de la Fonction publique, de la Réforme de l'Etat et de l'Aménagement du territoire Secrétariat d'Etat à la Réforme de l'Etat. (2003). *Plan stratégique de l'administration électronique (PSAE) 2004-2007* (Technical report). Retrieved April 28, 2006, from http://www.adae.gouv.fr/article.php3?id_article=315

Mugellini, E., Abou Khaled, O., Pettenati, M. C., & Kuonen, P. (2005, March 29-April 1). eGovSM metadata model: Towards a flexible, interoperable and scalable eGovernment service marketplace. In *Proceedings of the IEEE Conference on E-Technology, E-Commerce and E-Service, EEE05*, Hong Kong, China (pp. 618-621).

Mugellini, E., Abou Khaled, O., Pettenati, M. C., & Franco, P. (2005, March 2-4). eGovernment service marketplace: Architecture and implementation. In *Proceedings of the TED Conference on eGovernment*, Bolzano, Italy (pp. 193-204).

OECD e-Government Studies. (2004). *The e-government imperative.* OECD Press.

Pappa, D., Kavadias, G., Spanos, E., Tambouris, E., Hoholis, D., Erkkilä, T., et al. (2003). Platform integration and deployment report, description of the trials. Deliverable. Retrieved April 28, 2006, from http://www.egov-project.org/gr/deliverables.htm

Pavlichev, A., & David Garson, G. (2004). *Digital government: Principles and best practices.* Hershey, PA: Idea Group Publishing.

Persson, A., & Goldkuhl, G. (2005, February 14-15). Stage-models of public e-services — Investigating conceptual foundations. In *Proceedings of the 2nd Scandinavian Workshop on e-Government*, Copenhagen, Denmark.

Riedl, R. (2001). The conceptual system architecture of the FASME Project. Deliverable.

Retrieved April 28, 2006, from http://www.ifi.unizh.ch/egov/Deliverable_6.1.pdf

Ronaghan, S. A. (2001). *Benchmarking e-government: A global perspective* (Technical report). Retrieved April 28, 2006, from http://www.nettelafrica.org/docs/NetTel%20Safari@the%20Equator%20(Uganda%202003)/Benchmarkingegovt.pdf

Statskontoret. (2000). *The 24/7 agency: Criteria for 24/7 agencies in the networked public administration* (Technical report). Retrieved April 28, 2006, from http://www.statskontoret.se/upload/Publikationer/2000/200041.pdf

Suh, S. Y. (2003). *Promoting citizen participation in e-government* (Technical report). Retrieved April 28, 2006, from http://unpan1.un.org/intradoc/groups/public/documents/UN/UNPAN020076.pdf

Vintar, M., Kunstelj, M., & Leben, A. (2002, April 25-27). Delivering better quality public services through life-event portals. In *Proceedings of the 10th NISPAcce Annual Conference*, Cracow, Poland.

World Wide Web Consortium. (n.d.). XML schema part 0: Primer. Retrieved April 28, 2006, from http://www.w3.org/TR/xmlschema-0/

This work was previously published in Global E-Government: Theory, Applications and Benchmarking, edited by L. Al-Hakim, pp. 21-51, copyright 2007 by IGI Publishing, formerly known as Idea Group Publishing (an imprint of IGI Global).

Chapter 4.48
ICTs, Empowerment, and Development: Articulating Grassroots Analysis Through Participatory Approaches

Hannah Beardon
ActionAid, UK

ABSTRACT

The digital divide has its roots in the political and power dynamics that underlie all inequality. It follows, therefore, that the response from the development sector should be rooted in learning from the long experience of tackling inequality and unequal power relations in many other fields. This chapter draws on the example of the Reflect ICTs Project to show how participatory theories, tools, and processes can be applied to ensure that ICT initiatives fundamentally address power and empowerment issues rather than ignoring or, worse, exacerbating them. The project methodology is described and some findings shown, in an attempt to show how attention to the human communication dimension of ICTs can make applied technology more sustainable and appropriate for poor communities in their struggle to access their rights.

INTRODUCTION

Information and communication technologies (ICTs) can be an empowering force, providing access to rapid communication and timely information. According to a recent study of ICT for Development (ICT4D) projects in Africa, access to communications technologies can improve people's livelihoods, access to services, agricultural practices, participation in government (and government's accountability and transparency), incomes, voice, security, social relationships, and health.

Where people are struggling to access even their most basic needs, such as clean water or school for their children, information and communication technologies may not appear to be a priority. However, within a rights- or empowerment-based approach to development, there are many types and levels of work: whether to enable people to access their rights; to influence policy makers; to enhance communication between actors; or to develop new methodologies, tools, and resources. Information and communication are at the heart of all these. As such ICT4D can be an important part of the empowerment process, if (and only if) explicitly placed within a wider movement to achieve equity and social change through access to and realisation of human rights.

Learning from the Past

The so-called *digital divide* is a term which, although of relatively recent coinage, deals with concepts and problems of long-standing in the development world. For the divide between those who can avail themselves of ICTs for rapid and efficient communication and those who suffer from lack of timely and reliable information has at its root the same dynamic as any other gap between rich and poor, have and have-not, exploiter and exploited. As such, the same theories and practices which have evolved in the development sector in the past 50 years also have great significance for the field of ICTs for development or empowerment.

This chapter draws on the example of the Reflect ICTs Project to show how participatory theories, tools, and processes can be applied to ensure that ICT initiatives fundamentally address such gaps rather than ignoring or, worse, exacerbating them.

The project, which has been running pilots in Burundi, India, and Uganda since 2003, highlights in its methods and findings the importance of recognising politics and power relations at all levels, and of forming transparent and effective partnerships between different actors in the field. Here, some of the methods are shared and their applicability to different contexts discussed, based on a review of some of the perspectives and theories underlying the work.

BACKGROUND

Participatory theories, such as Participatory Rural Appraisal (PRA) and Participatory Learning in Action (PLA), have evolved over the last two decades to enable and encourage a shift in relationships within the development sector. This means away from a traditional paternalistic donor/beneficiary paradigm towards a situation where the traditional *targets* of development — the poor, women, older people, refugees, and so forth — could become the drivers of change in their own environment. Values such as equality, empowerment, solidarity with the poor and marginalised, and gender-equity are explicitly held at the heart of such approaches.

Participation is the vital ingredient in the PLA process (Ruland, 2003). Participation is understood as a process, not an event, whereby local people undertake their own analysis, reflection, and action. Theories, tools, and methods have been developed to understand and deal with the dynamics of power, confidence, and culture that create elites, amplify some voices, and drown out others. It acknowledges the ways that built pedagogies constrain some learning practices and enable others, and the works to create dimensions that catalyse empowerment through participation (Monahan, 2000). The most famous include visual and oral methods for facilitating appraisal, analysis, and planning. Examples of such tools and reviews are available in a number of literatures (Wilcox, 1994; UNDP, 1997; Belgeonne & Brookes, 1999; Allen & Kilvington, 2001; Allen, Kilvington & Horn, 2002; Bates, Bruce, Doig, & Gitonga, 2002), including Communication and Power (CIRAC, 2003), on which this project is partly based.

The focus on group dynamics and power relations is not simply an objective one, but involves a transformation of our own roles as researchers and practitioners as well. This relationship is transformed from one of doing, directing, or transferring technology, to one of facilitating, sharing, enabling, catalysing, as well as learning and reflecting ourselves.

The early theories and methods have been used, adapted, rejected, and reinvented for innumerable contexts and thematic focuses so we now have what Robert Chambers describes as:

A growing family of approaches, methods, attitudes, and behaviours to enable and empower people to share, analyse, and enhance their knowledge of life and conditions, and to plan, act, monitor, evaluate, and reflect. (Chambers, 2004)

ICTs in Participatory Theory

In light of this shifting relationship and empowerment focus, information and communication technologies have an interesting (potential) significance, for information and communication are at the very heart of the appraisal, analysis, and action which make up this approach to development. Good choices are well-informed choices. People can make more appropriate decisions or plans if their local analysis is rooted in an understanding of the larger-scale processes which influence them. Technologies, including video, radio, and the Internet, can be put to use to ensure both that information flows adequately and that voices are heard more fairly. As the Rockefeller Foundation states on its Web site (www.rockfound.org):

Communication can enable poor people to move from being passive recipients of externally generated development interventions to being effective advocates for the enrichment of their own lives and, finally, generators of their own development.

The Reflect ICTs Project was designed as a participatory approach to ICTs for Development. In essence, the aim is to test the assumption that ICTs chosen by communities based on a thorough and participatory analysis of their communication and information needs (and practices) will be more useful, more empowering, more sustainable, and ultimately have more impact. The project builds on the existing work of Reflect practitioners in the pilot locations and around the world.

The Reflect Approach

Reflect is an approach to adult learning (see Figure 1) and social change, which is used by over 350 organisations in 60 countries (CIRAC, 2002). It began as a fusion of the pedagogical theories of Paulo Freire, who argued that education is not a neutral process and therefore must be deliberately designed to liberate (Freire 1968, 1994), with participatory methodologies such as PRA (Chambers, 1994). The result was an approach to adult learning which focuses on power relations and works through systematising and deepening people's existing knowledge to enable them to base their choices and actions on thorough analysis (Archer & Cottingham, 1994; Phnuyal, Archer, & Cottingham, 1998).

Although Reflect originated as an approach to adult literacy, it has in recent years evolved to link empowerment with communication practices more broadly, including access to information and influence over decision makers. People need to articulate their views through any available or appropriate means of communication — oral, written, visual, or audio — to strengthen their participation in decisions that affect their lives.

Some of the principles and methods behind this are collected in the recent Reflect publication *Communication and Power* (CIRAC, 2003). With this, local groups and community organisations are able to own and adapt the resources and techniques of PRA to strengthen their voices and sharpen their struggle for change. In different contexts this means different things, whether communication for peace and reconciliation in

Figure 1. Women from Bubel reflect circle, Orissa, India

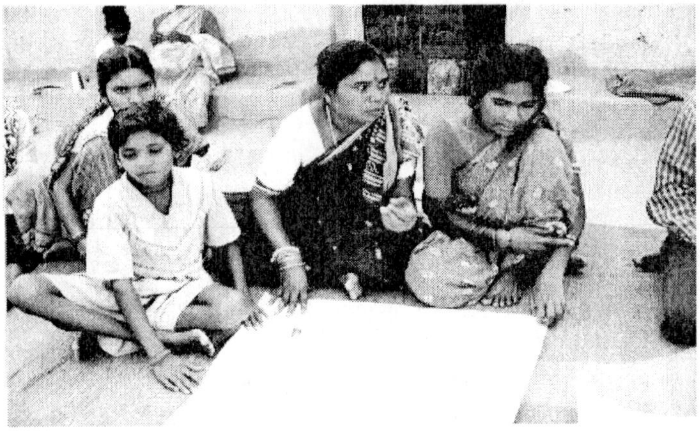

Burundi, holding local institutions accountable through budget tracking or school management in El Salvador and Mali, challenging racism in the UK, or accessing land rights in South Africa. More examples are available on the Reflect Web site (www.reflect-action.org).

With this changing focus of Reflect, and the emergence of the digital face of the resource gap, the Reflect ICTs Project was born. The project, funded for three years by the UK Department for International Development (DFID), aims to build on the emerging understanding of the relationship between communication and power, not only to provide a critical analysis of existing ICT for Development work, but also to provide resources and models for applying participatory principles and theories to future ICT projects.

ISSUES AND PERSPECTIVES

Though ICT for Development is a relatively new field, it has taken a well-trodden path. A technology which the market has made cheaply and easily available to the more advantaged and wealthy, then becomes considered important or necessary to those the market does not reach — the poor and marginalised. Various powerful individuals, international and local non-governmental organisations (NGOs), governments, and their departments and agencies develop policies and plans in order to make these technologies and their valuable impact more widely available. Meetings, conferences, and summits are convened; articles, papers, and books published, trying to understand why technology is not being taken up, reaching the poorest, or making a difference.

From a participatory or empowerment perspective, it is possible to see a link between the involvement of people in decisions made for and about their lives, and the sustainability and impact of development interventions. Too many failed or questionable development projects suffer from a surplus of good ideas and intentions from the top and a deficit of real involvement and understanding at the grassroots. So what looks good on paper does not translate directly into reality. Plenty of evidence, anecdotal or otherwise, exists of such failures: of fully equipped telecentres in Argentina remaining unused, or complex computer systems aimed at decentralising land registration in India ending up in the hands of the same corrupt elites who routinely use their power to deny poor people their constitutional rights (Sanjoy, 2003).

Participatory theory has emerged from an understanding that development must not be done on behalf of others, but must be based in locally generated processes. The field of ICT for development or empowerment also needs to follow such logic to avoid such failures and be fair to those in whose name the work is done. The value of a computer or a video lies not in its existence, but in its use. Empowerment is not an easy process, and requires taking sides and making waves. It is a political process, whereby the voices of poor and marginalised people are strengthened and broadcast to *challenge* the status quo that exploits them. Information and communication can transform, if the aim is to expand meaningful participation in decision making. But for this to be possible, attention needs to be paid not only to the technologies applied, but also (and more importantly) to the *relationships and processes* that underlie interventions and policies.

This places at the centre of project planning the question: How can the voices and knowledge of poor people be sufficiently represented in policies, technology design, and implementation? This is a question which the Reflect ICT project aims to highlight, but also to tackle through example and by developing transferable methodologies and tools.

A Critical View of ICTs

It is common to find evangelistic attitudes towards ICT for development, and this project and learning is based very much in a critical analysis of the tools and approaches in the field. ICTs may have a lot of potential for empowerment, but they also have potential to be tools for exploitation and cultural imperialism. In fact, there is probably a lot more evidence of the latter than the former in existence.

As is argued in the publication *ICTs for Development: Empowerment or Exploitation* (Beardon, 2004), modern ICTs are generally the product of powerful western and commercial cultures, and both are designed to meet the needs of that community first and also to fit in with their existing logic and communications culture. If such technologies are promoted blindly throughout the world, it could in effect consolidate existing power relations between cultures and communities in the world. It could also have the practical effect on the ground of relegating traditional forms of knowledge and its expression to second-best or lower value.

Other negative effects of the introduction of ICTs can be the *brain-drain* effect of equipping people with skills and education without the accompanying opportunities, meaning that they leave the local community to find opportunities elsewhere. Even where this may be a positive impact for the individual involved and their family, it should still be recognised that any change in their individual circumstances does not constitute empowerment as such. While these people cannot determine the terms of their employment, or appropriate the technology to meet the needs of their own communities, they remain vulnerable to exploitation.

This means that ICT projects and initiatives which are aimed to empower and strengthen local cultures and strategies need to be explicitly designed for this. If technology is merely introduced with no awareness of these issues, then the exact opposite may end up taking place, weakening local traditions and structures which are the basis for survival strategies. ICT projects that are not explicitly aimed at empowerment of the poorest and most vulnerable — that is, real structural change — are also likely to end up replicating and consolidating the status quo.

Whether at household or community level, those who already have the best opportunities and advantages will be the first to avail of the new technologies provided. In all three of the Reflect ICT pilots, the groups noted that women have little access to, or control over, existing information technologies such as radio and newspapers. A gender analysis, as part of a wider power analysis, should form the basis of any empowerment-focused ICT project.

LEARNING AND RECOMMENDATIONS

The Reflect ICTs Project was developed in order to combine the experience and techniques of participatory theory with the potential of ICTs for empowerment and development. This potential is great, and not to be ignored, since access to timely and reliable information is the heart of a rights or empowerment-based approach to development. Only with strong communication capacity can people really influence the decisions — or access the rights and benefits — that affect them. Reflect participants across the world have shown how they can use a collective analysis of their situation to bring about real and significant changes.

The basis for the Reflect ICT project is a set of resource sheets for facilitators to use in order to encourage analysis of the value of information, the strengths and weaknesses of existing and traditional communication practices, and potential means of improving access to information and communication capacity. Existing Reflect groups in the three pilot locations of Ruyigi (Burundi), Bukuuku (Uganda), and Balangir (India) used the sheets to build a comprehensive picture of the context into which any new technologies would be applied. This includes analysis of the appropriateness of different technology to different sections of the community including women, youth, social classes, and so on. From this analysis was developed a plan for a community communications system, which combined new technology resources with clearly defined and accountable roles and relationships.

In the case of these three pilots, limited funding for the new system was pre-assured. However, it is hoped that the resource sheets will go on to be used either for community groups to develop clear proposals for funding and resourcing from outside, and/or for donor groups and implementing agencies to strengthen the participatory needs assessment element in their own programmes.

The Facilitated Process

The process was structured around five Reflect ICT resource sheets (Beardon, 2004), which set out some key issues for communication and provide simple exercises to encourage discussion and contextual analysis. The first of these looks at the value of information, and how it can make a difference to people's lives and livelihoods. Participants are encouraged to think of examples from their own experience and develop them into analysis of general factors and trends.

The second sheet explores the different factors which make a piece of information useful or meaningful, which can include the source, format, media, relevance of the information, or capacity or confidence of the person receiving it. It is this analysis which feeds into the design process of a communication system that really fits the needs and culture of a community. In many cases people may not use information unless it comes from an already known and trusted source. So new technologies and media must be introduced carefully and only to strengthen existing networks and information sources.

Another sheet helps groups to think through the value and purpose of documenting their own knowledge, then how best this can be done. Exercises and facilitated discussions help them to think through who might wish to share their knowledge, what the implications might be, and what media could be used to store and transmit it. In the first place, it encourages people to recognise the knowledge they have, as often people take their own knowledge for granted. This is also an important step in building people's own confidence to communicate.

The other sheets help groups to identify specific information gaps and evaluate different strategies and resources for overcoming these. Visualisation techniques such as matrices can be used for groups to list and rank the different communications media and technologies in terms of their availability, appropriateness, or affordability. Finally there is a sheet to help with planning, highlighting areas to be considered in a funding proposal or work plan.

The Diverse Pilot Contexts

The three pilot locations emerged through a process of communication and consultation with active Reflect implementing organisations. When the project was in conceptualisation, Reflect practitioners and organisers were encouraged to get involved, share ideas, and participate through the Reflect network. Where there was clear convergence between the aims and ideas of the Reflect ICT project concept and the existing work and direction of Reflect implementing organisations or networks, strong links were made, and from there the three pilot locations were chosen. Although all three pilot locations are poor, rural areas, they each have marked differences in terms of size, terrain, infrastructure, social and economic realities, and as a result, in pertinent issues.

Burundi

In this society dealing with and emerging from conflict, Reflect is oriented towards promoting peace and strengthening the role of women in building peace and reconstruction. Communication is key to this, as mistrust and misinformation have been key factors in perpetuating the conflict at local and national levels.

There are currently 91 circles operating in Ruyigi province, offering a space for Hutu and Tutsi neighbours to meet and talk, share accurate information, and rebuild confidence and collaboration. Participation is around 60% male and 40% female, and in total approximately 1,000 people participate regularly in groups involved in the pilot. A newsletter called *Ejo* is compiled by ActionAid of contributions from Reflect participants, and is distributed in villages and in refugee camps to promote accurate and trusted information on conflict, development, gender, health, and other relevant issues. Cultural activities are also promoted and organised to bring communities together.

Table 1. Access to communications media: Burundi

	Women	Men	Youth	Aged	Leaders	Ex-combatants	Refugees	Students
Radio		X			X		X	
Radio magazines		X	X					X
Ejo newsletter	X	X	X		X	X	X	X
Mobile video	X	X	X		X			X
Letter		X	X		X	X	X	X
Telephone					X		X	X
Cinema			X					
TV					X			X
Markets	X			X	X	X	X	
Meetings	X	X	X	X	X	X	X	
Churches	X		X	X	X	X	X	X
Internet								X
Cultural events	X	X	X	X	X	X	X	X
Schools	X	X	X		X			X

As Table 1 shows, women and older people are specifically disadvantaged in access to communications media, relying mostly on face-to-face contact. This type of analysis, deepened through the Reflect ICT process, enabled the team and participants to devise a communications system which caters for these excluded groups. New equipment, including Internet-connected computers, are being used to strengthen the scope and quality of *Ejo*, while both content and receivers for video and radio are integrated into the Reflect process. The analysis shown in Table 1 also highlighted for Reflect facilitators the role of access to information as an indicator of vulnerability to conflict — a key for future programme work.

India

This pilot is located in Balangir in the state of Orissa, near the Bay of Bengal. The majority of the population live below the poverty level and literacy is under 40% (among women only 21%). Reflect is used by 19 local organisations in 344 villages to support popular planning and mobilisation processes. The organisations form a network known as Collective Action for Drought Mitigation in Balangir (CADMB) and supported by ActionAid India; 112 of these villages are involved directly in the Reflect ICT pilot, with the others indirectly involved through facilitators forums, public meetings, and collective planning.

In total, nearly 5,000 people participate directly in Reflect groups in Balangir, of whom 42% are women. Sixty-six percent are from scheduled castes and tribes, meaning the lowest social status, as opposed to only 37% of the general population.

The focus of the project in this area is transparent and accountable governance. A drought-prone area, many of the poorest people are forced to sell their land or migrate seasonally to nearby cities and industrial areas. Food security, land rights,

Figure 2. Matrix developed by Patharla Reflect circle shows information needs

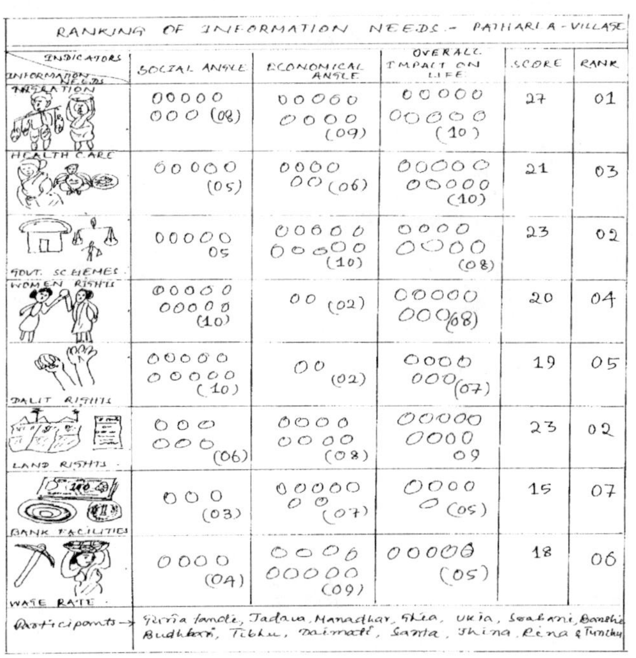

RANKING OF INFORMATION NEEDS - PATHARLA-VILLAGE

INDICATORS / INFORMATION NEEDS	SOCIAL ANGLE	ECONOMICAL ANGLE	OVERALL IMPACT ON LIFE	SCORE	RANK
MIGRATION	(08)	(09)	(10)	27	01
HEALTH CARE	(05)	(06)	(10)	21	03
GOVT. SCHEMES	05	(10)	(08)	23	02
WOMEN RIGHTS	(10)	(02)	(08)	20	04
DALIT RIGHTS	(10)	(02)	(07)	19	05
LAND RIGHTS	(06)	(08)	09	23	02
BANK FACILITIES	(03)	(07)	(05)	15	07
WAGE RATE	(04)	(09)	(05)	18	06
Participants →	Girija landi, Jadara, Manadhar, Shea, Ukia, Seabani, Banshi, Budhbari, Tibhu, Daimati, Santa, Jhina, Rena & Tunchy				

Figure 3. Map by Kundamal Reflect group showing available sources of information

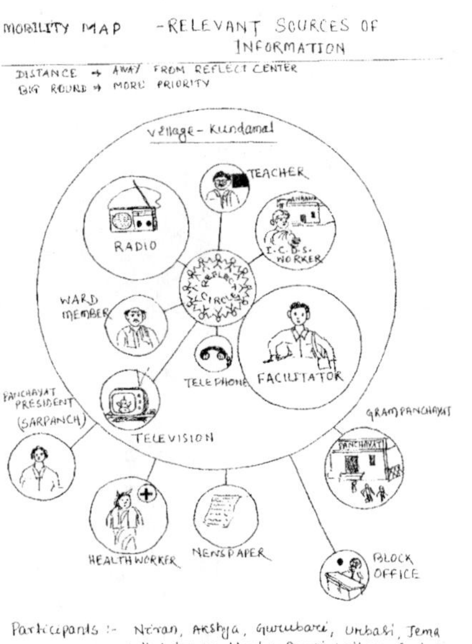

and labour protection are all key issues, and at the heart of them all is good information about rights and entitlements available in the constitution and state laws. In many cases in the pilot area, information is withheld by the local elites, and the poorest people are kept in the dark about funds or entitlements which are their rights. In this situation it is clear that information is not neutral, and access to it needs (see Figure 2) to be carefully targeted and monitored.

The initial analysis carried out in Reflect circles showed that poor people depend on other people, such as facilitators, health workers, or elected representatives, for information (see Figure 3). Televisions, telephones, and even radios are out of reach of the majority of people, and literacy levels are so low as to make printed information require interpretation.

As a result of such analysis, the emerging communication system relies heavily on oral communication and accountable, informative relationships. There is great emphasis on not only the articulation of information needs at the village level, but the communication of these needs to the appropriate authorities and advocacy at different administrative levels to ensure that the needs are both heard and met. Equipment, including video and radio, as well as cultural troupes, leaflets, and public meetings, have been funded in order to increase information flow among and between village communities.

Uganda

Bukuuku sub-county is in Eastern Uganda, bordering the Democratic Republic of Congo. The area has 25 villages and a total population of slightly more than 25,000 people. Most households live in absolute poverty (less than $4 per day) despite fertile soils and good agricultural conditions. In large part this poverty is due to poor market information, leaving local farmers vulnerable to exploitation. Another key development issue is health, in particular HIV/AIDS, and with family sizes averaging 8 to 10, access to education is also a major problem.

There are 12 Reflect groups in the area, each with an average of 30 members, most of whom are women (see Figure 4). In addition there are seven school knowledge groups, which are Reflect groups based in the local primary (5), secondary (1), and tertiary (1) educational institutions to address issues relating to local youth. Since the introduction of the Reflect ICTs project, new circles have been introduced and the demand is increasing. Literacy and Empowerment, a lo-

Figure 4. Reflect participant listening to a radio set provided by project

Table 2. Matrix by Bulera Reflect group ranking ICTs

	Accessible	Available	Affordable	Appropriate	Rank
Posters	3	1	0	10	**6**
Local council	10	5	4	10	**4**
Alarm	10	10	10	10	**1**
Radio	5	10	5	10	**3**
Phone	4	10	2	10	**5**
Drum	10	10	10	10	**1**
Newspapers	0	1	1	10	**7**
Video	0	0	0	10	**8**
Oral	10	10	10	10	**1**
Music/drama	10	6	7	10	**2**
Meetings	10	10	10	10	**1**
Letters	5	8	6	10	**4**

cal community-based organisation, implements Reflect, training and supporting facilitators and circles, and manages the ICT project with support from ActionAid Uganda.

The Uganda pilot has the best access to telecommunications infrastructure and conducive ICT government policy, and both mobile and fixed-line telephones are widespread. However, the Reflect circles' analysis showed that poor people still rely on trusted, well-informed individuals and organisations to access required social and economic information (see Table 2). Meetings, cultural events, and social gatherings were ranked as the most widely used and useful media of communication, while radio, video, and telephone were desirable but less accessible. Internet awareness was quite low, especially among adults.

Due to the smaller scale of the pilot, the groups were able to plan for a centralised resource centre with Internet access and training, bolstered by radio sets for each circle. Databases have been established to catalogue local knowledge of herbs which can be used to treat opportunistic diseases related to HIV, and another to list and monitor all orphans living in the area. Training is tailored to the needs of the groups, and additional funding and sponsorship is being sought to meet capacity needs. Women in particular are targeted for training on ICT use.

Some Interesting Insights

The actual findings of the pilot communities are part of the planning process and not to be taken as stand-alone facts and figures. However, they provide an interesting opportunity for researchers and policy makers to compare the outcomes of grassroots-level analysis with their own assumptions in applying new ICTs to poverty reduction.

In all three pilot areas, oral communication was the primary and most trusted source of information. This may be through local health or child care workers, leaders or facilitators, or through mutual exchange at meetings and gatherings such as church or market. Beyond this, media such as radio, cultural performances, posters, and leaflets or newspapers were considered useful and accessible. Due to high levels of illiteracy in all areas, textual information is only accessible to many through an interpreter and is therefore not directly effective.

Thus, literacy can be treated as one important factor in determining existing access to and control over ICTs. Other factors include social class, education, income, and gender. In Orissa, for example, the cost of a black-and-white television set is more than the value of the land of most villagers. In Uganda, where households do own radio sets, they are usually controlled and operated by the male head of household, who chooses what to listen to. In Burundi, Reflect facilitators noted that vulnerable groups, such as the very poor, widows, elderly, and displaced people, were less able to access reliable information about security threats which make them still more vulnerable to the effects of conflict.

The types of information that people wanted to access also differed between groups. For example, in Uganda, while everyone wanted market and credit information, men and boys were more interested in job opportunities while women and girls in health and women's rights. The youth were more interested in HIV prevention and reproductive health than their parents.

In each pilot the funds for ICTs were spent differently, but in all three places the resulting plan was a combination of technologies and people to transmit information and queries. In this way, the community communications systems continue to build on people's preference for face-to-face communication. The resulting systems were influenced heavily by the size and level of infrastructure in each area.

- Uganda, being a smaller-scale pilot, has been able to create a central information/ resource centre, backed up by training and advice sessions, equipment, and continued activities of Reflect circles.
- In India, where the scale is much larger (over 100 villages), the groups have developed a complex network of local organisations, committees, and individuals to support the flow of existing information to Reflect participants and their communities, as well as advocating to different levels of government for better information provision. At different levels this network is using the Internet, video and radio programmes, travelling cultural troupes, and printed information.
- In Burundi insecurity has created a problem of mobility, and the main technologies being adopted are radio and video, and the Internet will be used to support and strengthen an existing community newsletter as well as linking Diaspora communities.

FUTURE TRENDS FOR ACTION AND RESEARCH

The Reflect ICT Process aims to enable groups to develop and define their own knowledge — about their context, needs, and existing patterns and prejudices. Theirs is not the only knowledge needed to ensure a good, effective ICT project or programme. However, it is necessary to ensure that their perspective is heard and informs the decisions of other players in the process, including technology experts, policy makers, and donors. It appears that effective and equal working relationships between these different actors, built on mutual respect and transparency, is the key to a sustainable intervention. More research is needed to understand the nature of such relationships and how existing modes of working in development need to adapt in order to allow them to flourish.

As such, the Reflect ICTs model is useful for strengthening the grassroots analysis element of any ICT for Development project. The model can be made more effective in combination with other perspectives, expertise, and resources.

Policy advocacy is also important in order to strengthen the impact and reach of the Reflect ICT Project, and approach this in two areas. Firstly there is the question of directly influencing ICT policy. Grassroots analysis of information needs and the applicability of different ICTs should be heard and considered by those making policy decisions at local, national, and international levels. It is up to projects, organisations, and research institutions to help to establish this link.

There is also the question of what happens to the types of information and analysis that participants in projects such as this are creating and documenting. As documentation of analysis improves through participation in such projects, there is scope for forging greater linkages between the issues arising from such grassroots-level analysis and the development, advocacy, and aid agendas of NGOs and donors at national and international levels.

CONCLUSION

This chapter argues that in order to unlock the full potential of ICTs for empowerment and rights-based development, the knowledge and resources of the full range of stakeholders need to be combined. It is not only donors, technicians, and large implementing organisations who hold the key to successful project planning and implementation. A large and essential chunk of the knowledge and expertise needed rests with the people and communities who are the intended beneficiaries.

The Reflect ICT Project has been created to build on and complement existing participatory theories, approaches, and techniques, and make sense of ICTs and the digital divide in this context. The aim is to provide a model for developing this grassroots analysis of communication needs and appropriate technologies. However, finding ways to effectively bring this perspective together with all the other essential elements of good ICT for development policy and practice is a challenge still very much ahead of us.

REFERENCES

Allen, W., & Kilvington, M. (2001). *Building effective teams for resource use efficiency* (Landcare Research Contract Rep. LC0001/060). Lincoln, New Zealand.

Allen, W., Kilvington, M., & Horn, C. (2002). Using participatory and learning-based approaches for environmental management to help achieve constructive behaviour change. Retrieved March 31, 2005, from http://www.landcareresearch.co.nz/research/social/par_rep.asp

Archer, D., & Cottingham, S. (1996). *REFLECT mother manual*. London: ActionAid.

Bates, E., Bruce, N., Doig, A., & Gitonga, S. (2002). *Participatory approaches for alleviating indoor air pollution in rural Kenyan kitchen* (Boiling Point No. 48) (pp. 12-15).

Beardon, H. (2004). *ICT for development: Empowerment or exploitation*. London: ActionAid.

Belgeonne, C., & Brookes, H. (1999). *PSE and participatory learning*. London: WWF-UK.

Chambers, R. (1994). The origins and practice of participatory rural appraisal. *World Development, 22*(7), 953-969.

Chambers, R. (2004). Notes to accompany PRA/PLA familiarisation workshops. Retrieved from http://www.ids.ac.uk/ids/particip/research/pra/pranotes04.pdf

CIRAC. (2001). *Reflect global survey*. London: CIRAC.

CIRAC. (2003). *Communication and power*. London: CIRAC.

Freire, P. (1968). *Pedagogy of the oppressed*. New York: Seabury.

Freire, P. (1994). *Pedagogy of hope: Reliving pedagogy of the oppressed*. New York: Continuum Publishing Company.

Gerster, R., & Zimmerman, S. (2003). *Information and communication technologies and poverty reduction in Sub-Saharan Africa: A learning study*. Richterswil: Gerster Consulting.

Monahan, T. (2000). Built pedagogies and technology practices: Designing for participatory learning. In *Proceedings of the Participatory Design Conference*. Palo Alto, CA: CPRS.

Phnuyal, B., Archer, D., & Cottingham, S. (Eds.). (1998). *PLA notes 32: Participation, literacy and empowerment*. IIED.

Ruland, C. D. (2003, March). Participatory learning and action. *Youth Lens*.

Sanjoy, A. (2003). Critical analysis of the Gyandoot project. Retrieved from http://www.reflect-action.org

UNDP. (1997). *UNDP guidebook on participation: Empowering people: A guide to participation*. UNDP.

Wilcox, D. (1994). The guide to effective participation. Partnerships online. Retrieved March 31, 2005, from http://www.partnerships.org.uk/guide/index.htm

KEY TERMS

Digital divide: The condition of one group (the dominant group) having an advantage over another group (the marginalised group) concerning computer or technological skills. It can also refer to the general lack of access to computers and the Internet, which affects women, children, various ethnic groups, and older citizens.

Empowerment: Involves a process which pays attention to power relations and their impact on the opportunities individuals and communities have to create changes in their lives. Empowerment is about structural changes. More than simple service delivery, it is about building capacity of people to make demands and influence decision making.

Empowerment Processes: The processes of empowerment can be at individual, group, or community level, and include capacity building and participatory approaches.

ICT for Development (ICT4D): When ICTs assist to meet development objectives, in particular global development goals for poverty reduction, education, health, and environment as a tool for economic growth.

Participatory Approaches: Techniques to promote participation in development though a focus on Participatory Learning and Action (PLA) information exchange. In particular, participatory approaches allow a community to express and analyse the realities of their lives, plan themselves what action needs to be taken to change the situation, and monitor and evaluate the results by themselves. Participatory approaches have been used in many settings in development both in rural and urban aspects.

Participatory Learning in Action (PLA): An umbrella term of methodologies in participation of people in the processes of learning about their needs and opportunities, and in the action required to address them. PLA techniques are being used to encourage community members to express their ideas and needs.

Participatory Rural Appraisal (PRA): A label given to a growing family of participatory approaches and methods that emphasise local knowledge and enable local people to make their own appraisal, analysis, and plans. It evolved from rapid rural appraisal—a set of informal techniques used by development practitioners in rural areas to collect and analyse data.

This work was previously published in Empowering Marginal Communities with Information Networking, edited by H. Rahman, pp. 44-61, copyright 2006 by IGI Publishing, formerly known as Idea Group Publishing (an imprint of IGI Global).

Chapter 4.49
A Dynamic Two-Phase Commit Protocol for Adaptive Composite Services

Weihai Yu
University of Tromsø, Norway

Calton Pu
Georgia Institute of Technology, USA

ABSTRACT

Next-generation applications based on Web services impose additional requirements on the use of coordination protocols with various optimizations, such as the two-phase commit protocol (2PC). This article analyses the well-known 2PC optimizations "presumed commit" and "presumed abort," and presents an improved 2PC that is suitable for Web-service-based applications. More specifically, the protocol allows every individual service provider to choose dynamically the most appropriate presumption for any distributed transaction. This new capability is especially useful when a composite Web service is integrating component services that make different presumptions in their commit protocols. The protocol does not introduce extra overhead to the previous 2PC variants in terms of number of messages and log records, and it is easy to understand and realize. Our simulation shows that the choice of appropriate presumption has significant influence on system performance, and that in some heterogeneous settings, combining different presumptions in individual transactions outperforms adopting only one single presumption.

INTRODUCTION

One of the goals of Web services is to enable next-generation applications to be dynamically composed of invocations on different data services. The composition of services can be specified using Web services flow specification languages such as BPEL4WS (BPEL4WS, 2003). Consider, for instance, a virtual manufacturer consisting of a chain of distributed outsourced services such as marketing, R&D, procurement, manufacturing and distribution. Tasks within this supply chain typically consist of access to one or more data services. For example, approval of some engineering changes might involve updates in data services of a number of component manufacturers. Technically, these tasks can be modeled into a number of distributed transactions. For many of these transactions, it is crucial that global atomicity, among other properties, is guaranteed: Either the entire transaction gets succeeded or nothing takes effect. The global atomicity becomes a non-trivial property when composing heterogeneous component services, one of such technical challenges being addressed in this article.

In addition to guaranteeing correctly the global atomicity of composite Web services, the runtime overhead and delay of commit protocols may lead to increased data contention that in turn leads to poor scalability and performance of applications. Trade-offs of various kinds are therefore necessary. At a higher level, weaker properties than global atomicity are adopted in order to achieve better scalability and performance at the expense of more sophisticated application logic. A complex task, such as the approval of engineering changes mentioned previously, is usually not modeled into a single globally atomic distributed transaction. Instead, application semantics and alternative correctness criteria are explored for long-running activities (Elmagarmid, 1992). However, globally atomic distributed transactions are still necessary to simplify application development. In theoretical models such as process algebra (Fokkink, 2002), processes are composed of actions that are assumed to be atomic, so that no exploration of their inner structure is needed. In practice, the complex task is decomposed into smaller inter-dependent atomic transactions, using mechanisms like recoverable message queues and compensation (Leymann, 1998). The smaller atomic transactions are distributed, typically involving a data service and a recoverable queue at a different site (Bernstein & Newcomer, 1997). This article contributes to the support of the smaller atomic transactions, where we provide global atomicity but relax the overhead and delays associated with the presumption part.

Atomic commit protocols are a key element in supporting global atomicity of distributed transactions. *Two-phase commit protocol* (*2PC*) is the de facto standard atomic commit protocol (Bernstein et al., 1987; Gray & Reuter, 1993). It is widely agreed that 2PC is important to guarantee correctness properties in the complex distributed world, whilst at the same time it reduces parallelism due to high disk and message overhead and locking during windows of vulnerability. Liu et al., (1994) even showed that distributed *commit* processing can have more effect on system performance than distributed *data* processing. With an increasing number of potential atomic actions in an N-tier application architecture based on Web services, the performance penalty of commit processing may be aggravated as the system grows in scale and size.

There are a number of optimizations to the basic 2PC (Chrysanthis et al., 1998; Gray & Reuter, 1993; Lampson & Lomet, 1993; Mohan et al., 1986; Samaras et al., 1995). Some of them are so widely used that they are built into commercial systems and become part of transaction processing standards, including OMG transaction service (OMG, 1998) and its Java mapping Java transaction service (Sun Microsystems, 1999), XA (X/Open, 1991), and the newly proposed WS-AtomicTransaction (WS-AtomicTransaction, 2005) for Web services.

Standard efforts reflect this composition for transactional Web-service-based applications. WS-Coordination (WS-Coordination, 2005) provides a general framework for supporting coordination among different service providers. Under this framework, two particular coordination types are defined: WS-BusinessActivity (WS-BusinessActivity, 2005) is used for decomposing a complex task into a set of inter-dependent atomic transactions; WS-AtomicTransaction (WS-AtomicTransaction, 2005) is used for providing global atomicity of distributed transactions.

While these interfaces support the composition of different variants of commit protocols, a serious technical challenge arises when component services choose commit protocols with potentially incompatible presumptions that may jeopardize global atomicity of the composite service. Instead of forcing the components to make the same presumption, we believe a better solution is to develop an adaptive commit protocol that is capable of integrating component protocols with different presumptions and guarantee global atomicity.

Web-service-based applications may be dynamically composed of data services that are typically heterogeneous. The dynamic and heterogeneous nature of Web services compositions sets specific requirements on applying different optimizations as follows.

1. **Compatibility:** The optimizations used by different service providers might be incompatible with each other and therefore cannot be jointly applied.
2. **Dynamic choices:** No optimization is the best in all run-time situations. Often the choice of the most suitable optimization can only be made dynamically based on the run-time situation and application demand.
3. **Adaptation:** Data and Web services are usually autonomous management entities. The next-generation service providers, in addition to obeying global optimization rules, should be able to automatically tune themselves and apply local optimizations in order to maximize the utilization of its own local resource and the satisfaction of its own combined set of clients (see, for example, Weikum et al., 2002).

In this article, we narrow our focus on one particular set of well -known 2PC optimizations that are based on presumptions of the outcomes of distributed transactions when no information about the transactions is available at the coordinator. These optimizations are coined with the names *presumed nothing* (*PrN*), *presumed abort* (*PrA*) and *presumed commit* (*PrC*) (Gray & Reuter, 1993; Lampson & Lomet, 1993; Samaras et al., 1995).

The compatibility issue has been an active research topic in the multi-database area for many years. The incompatibility of presumptions was first identified in (Al-Houmaily & Chrysanthis, 1996,1999), where a new protocol called *presumed any* (*PrAny*) was proposed. PrAny allows participants with different presumptions to be part of a global multi-database transaction. PrAny, however, does not allow a participant to change presumption during its entire life time and therefore does not meet the dynamic-choices and adaptation requirements where a data service should be able to dynamically adapt to the current environment by choosing the most appropriate presumption.

Standardization efforts assure compatibility by allowing but one 2PC variant, namely PrA (OMG, 1998; Sun Microsystems, 1999; X/Open, 1991). WS-AtomicTransaction (WS-AtomicTransaction, 2005) allows different participants to choose different protocols for the termination of the same atomic transaction. The purpose is to enable special treatment for participants with different roles. For example, a caching server that does not support transaction durability should use Volatile2PC so that it can enter a special phase zero to send updates to the backend durable server before that backend server is informed to prepare. All participants supporting durable transactions must use the same Durable2PC, which is PrA. Therefore, dynamic choice and adaptation is not supported by the current WS-AtomicTransaction specification.

There have also been efforts on dynamically choosing the (likely) best presumptions for homogeneous database systems, though PrA is generally considered to "win" the game, due to its simplicity and its better combination with the particularly useful optimization for read-only transactions (Mohan et al., 1986; Samaras et al., 1995). In

System R* (Mohan et al., 1986), a coordinator can choose between PrA and PrC on a transaction-by-transaction basis, at the start of 2PC. Different presumptions, however, cannot be mixed in one transaction. This restriction is reasonable for homogeneous distributed databases such as System R*, but it prevents Web-service-based applications to satisfy the adaptation requirement. For example, a recoverable queue manager, which is typically dominated with short update operations, may favor PrC due to less forced disk writes in the commit case. A distributed transaction in favor of PrA as a whole (e.g., most of its sub-transactions are read-only in a particular period) should not force this queue manager to use PrA.

In this article, we construct an improved 2PC (called *DPr—dynamic presumption*) where different presumptions can be dynamically combined in one transaction. The choice of presumption can be made as late as a participant service provider returns from its normal execution, i.e., just before the 2PC starts. Furthermore, the protocol does not introduce extra overhead to the previous 2PC variants in terms of number of messages and log records. Finally, the protocol is easy to understand and realize. The protocol supports increased compatibility among the component commit protocols by allowing dynamic choice of presumptions, and can adapt to different presumptions automatically.

The rest of this article is organized as follows. We start with system model and correctness requirements. The readers unfamiliar with 2PC can then find an overview of 2PC and its optimizations based on presumptions. The section INQUIRIES AND PRESUMPTIONS addresses the important issues regarding presumptions and when it is safe to discard information about a transaction. This is followed by the presentation of the DPr 2PC protocol in its entirety and correctness proof of the protocol. Then, we present the results of our performance study and describe how the protocol can be implemented for Web services with legacy transaction management engines. After the discussion on previous related work, we conclude with a summary of the main contributions and directions of future work.

SYSTEM MODEL AND CORRECTNESS REQUIREMENTS

A distributed transaction is started at a *client* process (service consumer) and expanded when services at other processes (service providers) are invoked as sub-transactions. The only way for processes to share information is via message passing.

A transaction is terminated via 2PC. 2PC is started at the client (called *coordinator* of 2PC) when all service invocations are successfully returned (the return messages are named *WorkDone*). The processes at service providers are *participants* of 2PC.

Processes may fail by stopping, and may restart when failures are repaired. Messages can be duplicated or lost, but they cannot be corrupted. Timeout is used to detect remote process failures and message losses.

2PC must guarantee the *atomic commitment properties* (Bernstein et al., 1987) among processes that are not read-only:

- **AC1:** All processes that reach an outcome reach the same one.
- **AC2:** A process cannot reverse its outcome after it has reached one.
- **AC3:** The *Commit* outcome can only be reached if all participants voted *Yes*.
- **AC4:** If there are no failures and all participants voted *Yes*, then the outcome will be *Commit*.
- **AC5:** Consider any execution containing only failures that the protocol is designed to tolerate. At any point in this execution, if all existing failures are repaired and no new failures occur for sufficiently long, then all processes will eventually reach an outcome.

Furthermore, the log garbage collection property must also hold (Al-Houmaily & Chrysanthis, 1996,1999):

- **LGC**: all processes can eventually forget about transactions and garbage-collect their logs.

The latter is important because it has much to do with the presumptions, the purpose of which is to leave out some acknowledgement messages and the corresponding logging overhead and at the same time still allows the coordinator to draw correct conclusion about the outcome of transactions when *no information* is available about the transactions in question. Under certain presumption, some participants will never acknowledge the outcome message, rendering it impossible for the coordinator to distinguish between the participants that have successfully terminated and those that are still hanging. A naïve solution is that the coordinator never forgets a transaction without receiving acknowledgements from all participants. While this might allow us to guarantee the atomic commitment properties AC1-AC5, it is impractical, because the coordinator will never be able to discard information pertaining to some terminated transactions either from the main memory or from the stable log.

OVERVIEW OF 2PC AND PRESUMPTION-BASED OPTIMIZATIONS

2PC consists of two phases: A *voting phase* and a *decision phase*. In the voting phase, the coordinator asks the participants to get prepared to commit by sending a *Prepare* message and collects the votes from the participants. In the decision phase, the coordinator decides and notifies the participants of the outcome of the transaction. If it has collected *Yes* votes from all participants, the outcome is *Commit*; otherwise, the outcome is *Abort*, since either a participant has voted *No* or some vote has not been successfully delivered due to some system or communication failure. With a *No* vote, a participant either has aborted the transaction or decides to abort the transaction unilaterally. With a *Yes* vote, a participant declares that it is prepared to commit: It assures that it is able to either commit or abort, even in case of subsequent system failures. The decision, however, must be made by the coordinator. The participant cannot make any decision unilaterally after sending the *Yes* vote.

The resilience of 2PC to system or communication failures is achieved by logging the relevant events of the protocol. The coordinator force-writes a decision record (*Commit* or *Abort*) prior to notifying the outcome to the participants, so the decision, once made, will survive subsequent system failures. Each participant force-writes a *Prepare* record prior to sending the *Yes* vote. The force-write of the *Prepare* log record flushes enough information about the transaction to disk so that it is able to either commit or abort, even in case of subsequent system failures. Before sending an acknowledgement, the participant force-writes (possibly in a lazy fashion) an outcome record (*Commit* or *Abort*). This assures that the participant will never ask the coordinator about the outcome of the transaction. After receiving acknowledgements from all participants, the coordinator writes an end record (*CommitEnd* or *AborEnd*) and the protocol terminates.

The coordinator maintains a *protocol table* in the main memory. For every transaction, the protocol table records the status information of every participant (vote, acknowledgement, etc.). The coordinator uses this information to conduct the progress of the protocol. The information of a transaction is discarded from the protocol table when the protocol terminates. The entire protocol table is lost upon system crash at the coordinator. On recovery, the log is used to re-establish the protocol table for non-terminated transactions at the time of the crash. Note that if no information about a transaction is found in the protocol table, either has the protocol terminated, or the decision has not been made yet before the crash, thus the coordinator can safely decide to abort the transaction. This is the hidden presumption of the *presumed nothing* (PrN) 2PC.

The *presumed abort* (PrA) 2PC makes this presumption explicit to spare a few messages and log records. When the outcome is *Abort*, the coordinator simply notifies the participants of the outcome. No log record is needed at the coordinator and no acknowledgements from participants are expected. At a participant, the *Abort* record is not required to be force-written, since this is the end of the protocol at the participant: No acknowledgement will be sent to the coordinator.

The *presumed commit* (PrC) 2PC, on the other hand, is designed to reduce the cost when the outcome is *Commit*. Missing information about a transaction in the protocol table is interpreted by the coordinator as the *Commit* outcome of the transaction. To avoid making false interpretation, the coordinator must force-write an *Init* log record before sending the *Prepare* message. When the decision is *Commit*, the coordinator force-writes a *Commit* record and then notifies the participants of the outcome. No acknowledgements are expected from the participants. At the participants, the *Commit* log records are not required to be force-written. Therefore when the outcome is *Commit*, PrC spares the messages for acknowledgements and the *CommitEnd* log record at the coordinator, and the *Commit* records at participants become no-forced. All these savings are at the cost of the extra forced *Init* log record, no matter what the outcome would be.

The presumption-based optimizations can be combined with optimizations for read-only transactions. Basically, if only read operations are performed at a participant, upon receiving a *Prepare* message, the participant can reply with a *Readonly* vote and release all local resources. A coordinator need not notify the participants with *Readonly* votes of the outcome of the transaction. With PrA, if all participants have voted *Readonly*, the coordinator need not do anything in addition to releasing all local resources. With PrC, however, upon receiving *Readonly* votes from all participants, the coordinator must write a *Readonly* log record to logically undo the *Init* log record.

INQUIRIES AND PRESUMPTIONS

Traditionally all participants and the coordinator adopt a single presumption. In order to support dynamic choice of different presumptions, there are two key issues to be addressed for the coordinator to draw correct conclusion about the outcome of a transaction:

1. During what period of time *must* the coordinator keep the information pertaining to a transaction?
2. In the *no-information* case, how can the coordinator be aware of the presumption used by a participant?

Note that PrN also presumes abort. In other words, the extra messages and log records in PrN that PrA leaves out are in practice not necessary. The existence of PrN is mainly of historical reasons. In the discussions that follow, we focus ourselves on PrA and PrC only. Figure 1 illustrates the concepts presented below. Double lines indicate messages that will be re-sent if no acknowledgements are received in time. The read-only and voting *No* cases are not shown in the figure.

Participant In-Doubt Windows

Definition 1 (*Participant in-doubt window*): A participant is within the *in-doubt window* of a transaction if it cannot decide by itself the outcome of the transaction, i.e., without getting it from the coordinator. An in-doubt window is opened when

Figure 1. Forced-availability and in-doubt windows

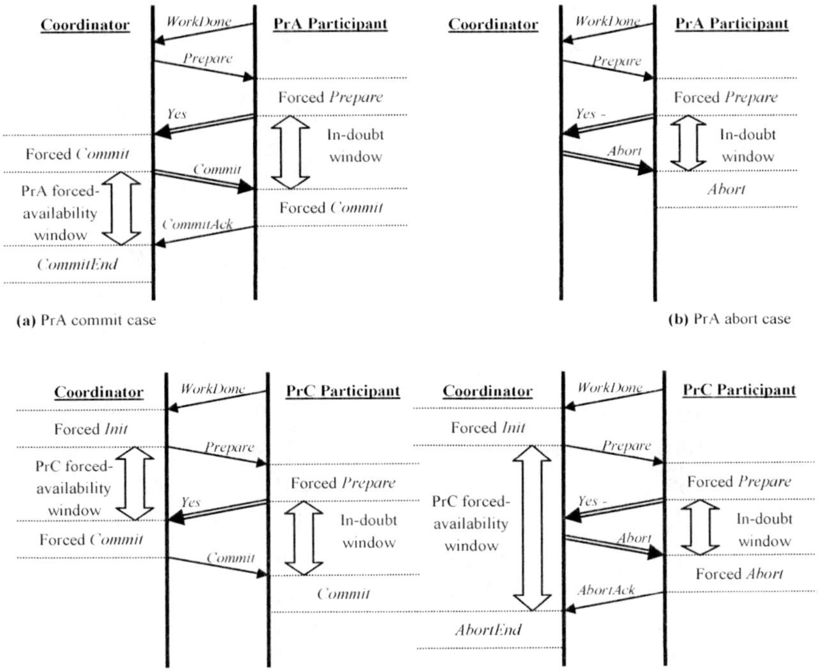

(a) PrA commit case

(b) PrA abort case

(c) PrC commit case

(d) PrC abort case

a participant sends out a *Yes* vote; it is closed when the protocol is terminated at the participant. An in-doubt window is *stable* if the events signifying its opening and closing are on stable storage. A 2PC is *in-doubt window complete* if all in-doubt windows will eventually be closed.

Comments:

- In the literature, participant in-doubt windows are sometimes also called *windows of vulnerability, uncertain periods,* or *prepared states* of participants. The concept is independent of the presumption adopted, though its implementations can bear slight differences in whether some log records are forced or no-forced (Figure 1).
- If a participant is not within an in-doubt window of a transaction, it will *never* ask the coordinator about the outcome of the transaction. Either does it appear to the participant that the 2PC has not started, so it can unilaterally abort the transaction, or has the 2PC already completed at the participant (e.g., it has voted *Readonly,* or has finished commit or abort).
- An in-doubt window must be stable. Once an in-doubt window is opened, it must remain so until explicitly closed despite of subsequent system failures. More specifically, before sending a *Yes* vote, a participant must force-write a log record to stably record the opening of an in-doubt window. The *Prepare* log record serves this purpose, among others. At the termination of 2PC, a participant must write an (forced or no-forced) outcome log record (*Commit* or *Abort*).
- All in-doubt windows must be closed eventually. There are two reasons for this. For one, 2PC must eventually terminate at all participants (AC5). By its definition, this means that in-doubt windows at all participants must eventually be closed. For the other,

the log records pertaining to an in-doubt window can only be discarded when the in-doubt window is closed. This is crucial for guaranteeing the LGC property.

Coordinator Forced-Availability Windows

Definition 2 (*Coordinator forced-availability window*): For a transaction, a coordinator is within the *forced-availability window* of a participant if it cannot use the presumed outcome of the participant in responding to the inquiries of the participant about the outcome of the transaction. A forced-availability window is *stable* if the events signifying its opening and closing are on stable storage. A 2PC is *forced-availability window complete* if all forced-availability windows will eventually be closed.

Comments:

- Coordinator forced-availability windows are closely related with the current state of the coordinator and the presumptions of the participants. Figure 1 illustrates forced-availability windows in different situations.
- In the case of PrA, a forced-availability window is opened when the coordinator decides that the outcome be *Commit*; it is closed when the coordinator is acknowledged that all participants have finished committing the transaction (Figure 1a). Before a forced-availability window is open, if no information about the transaction is available (due, for example, to a system crash), the coordinator can safely decide that the outcome of the transaction be *Abort*, which is the same as the presumed outcome. After a forced-availability window is closed, the coordinator knows for sure that it will never be asked about the outcome of the transaction (since all participants have closed their corresponding in-doubt windows). Notice that when the outcome is *Abort* or *Readonly*, no forced-availability window is ever opened (Figure 1b).
  The case of PrC is somewhat more sophisticated. A forced-availability window is opened as early as the coordinator sends out a *Prepare* message; it is closed either when it decides that the outcome be *Commit* or *Readonly* (Figure 1c) or when it knows for sure that all participants have finished aborting the transaction (Figure 1d). Before the coordinator sends out a *Prepare* message, no participant has ever opened an in-doubt window of the transaction and thus there will be no inquiry about the outcome of the transaction. After the decision of *Commit*, the coordinator can safely respond to any inquiry with the presumed outcome *Commit*. On the other hand, if the outcome is *Abort*, the coordinator has to keep the information about the transaction until it knows for sure that all participants have finished aborting the transaction and so no inquiry about its outcome will come.
- A forced-availability window must be stable. Once a forced-availability window is opened, it must remain so until explicitly closed despite of subsequent system failures.
  In the case of PrA, before sending the *Commit* message, the coordinator must force-write a log record to stably record the opening of the forced-availability window. The *Commit* log record serves this purpose. After receiving all acknowledgements from committed participants, it writes a no-forced *CommitEnd* record (Figure 1a).
- In the case of PrC, the coordinator must force-write an *Init* log record, in prior to the *Prepare* message, to stably record the opening of a forced-availability window. Before sending the *Commit* message, the coordinator force-writes a log record to stably record the closing of the forced-availability window

(Figure 1c). The *Commit* log record serves this purpose. (Notice the different roles of the *Commit* log record in PrA and PrC. In PrA, it stabilizes the *opening* of a forced-availability window, whereas in PrC, it stabilizes the *closing* of a forced-availability window.) If all participants voted *Readonly*, the coordinator writes a *Readonly* log record to close stably the forced-availability window. When the coordinator receives acknowledgements from all aborted participants, it writes a no-forced *AbortEnd* log record to record stably the closing of the forced-availability window (Figure 1d).

- All forced-availability windows must be closed eventually. This is crucial for guaranteeing the LGC property, because the log records pertaining to a forced-availability window can only be discarded when the forced-availability window is closed.

Knowing the Presumptions

When a participant has finished executing the request from the client, it chooses the presumption to be used and includes this one-bit information (*presumption-bit*) in the return message (*WorkDone*). Later, it also includes the presumption-bit in the *Prepare* log record. This stable information is now associated with the in-doubt window and will never be improperly discarded. When the coordinator writes the *Commit* log record, it also includes the presumptions of all participants in the record. This is necessary because the same *Commit* log record serves different purposes for PrA and PrC participants. The explicit knowledge of the presumptions of the participants is needed to properly garbage collect the log: the coordinator must be careful not to discard the *Commit* log record when it closes the forced-availability window for PrC participants while there still remain in-doubt PrA participants.

When a participant inquires about the outcome of the transaction, it includes the presumption-bit in the inquiry message. Usually, a re-sending of *Yes* vote message serves this purpose. The coordinator will then use this information to give the correct answer.

THE DPR 2PC

The basic structure of the DPr 2PC is very much the same as the earlier 2PC variants. Namely, it consists of a voting phase and a decision phase. The types of messages and log records are also the same. We highlight the new features below:

- A coordinator maintains in main memory a *protocol table* (*PTbl*) that contains an entry for every transaction that has entered 2PC. For every transaction, it maintains a list of participants, their presumptions and votes (if voted).
- The messages *WorkDone*, *Yes* and log record *Prepare* contain the presumption-bit of the participant. The messages *Prepare* (if the coordinator can override the presumptions), *Commit*, *Abort* and the coordinator log record *Commit* contain presumptions of all participants.
- Before the protocol starts, the coordinator has received *WorkDone* messages from all participants and therefore is aware of their preferred presumptions. The coordinator may choose to override the preferred presumptions of the participants and include this information in the *Prepare* message. We will not explore this feature further.
- The coordinator maintains a forced-availability window for all PrC participants (if any) and a forced-availability window for all PrA participants (if any). Care is taken to properly close all forced-availability windows so that the log can be correctly garbage collected.
- Each participant includes the presumption-bit in the *Prepare* log record which opens an in-doubt window. Care is taken to properly

close all in-doubt windows, so that the log can be correctly garbage collected.

- The participants only acknowledge the outcomes that are different from the presumed ones. The duplicated outcome messages are also acknowledged. (The messages include the presumptions of participants, so the participants know the presumptions even when the in-doubt windows are closed.)
- On recovery from a system crash or on timeout of an expected outcome message, a participant inquires the outcome by re-sending the *Yes* vote message. The message includes the presumption-bit.
- The coordinator responds to the participant with the presumption included in the *Yes* vote message when no information about the transaction is available.

Figure 2 shows the normal process of DPr for transaction *Tx*. Release of locks in the strict two-phase locking (S2PL) is also included in the protocol. The S2PL adopted here does not allow update operations to be triggered during 2PC. Note that the *Prepare* message is multicasted first to PrA participants and then, after the *Init* log, to PrC participants. This avoids unnecessary delay at PrA participants. Recovery is executed when a process is restarted after a crash (Figure 3). The log garbage collection program is run periodically (Figure 4). The logs of a transaction are garbage collected if the corresponding windows (forced-availability windows for coordinator and in-doubt windows for participants) are closed.

CORRECTNESS

Theorem 1 (LGC participant): A 2PC participant guarantees the LGC property if and only if it is in-doubt window complete.

Proof:

IF: That a participant is in-doubt window complete indicates that it will eventually close the in-doubt window of any transaction. After that, it will never ask about the transaction. Thus all information about the transaction can be discarded.

ONLY IF: We prove by contradiction. Consider an in-doubt window of a transaction that will never be closed. Suppose the logs pertaining to that transaction can be garbage collected. Now consider the case where the outcome is the same as the presumed outcome of the participant (*Commit* for PrC participant and *Abort* for PrA participant). After sending out an outcome message, the coordinator can forget about the transaction without the acknowledgement of the participant. Now, none of the coordinator and participant has any information about the transaction. If the outcome message is lost, the transaction can never be atomically terminated. □

Theorem 2 (LGC coordinator): A 2PC coordinator guarantees the LGC property if and only if it is forced-availability window complete.

Proof:

IF: That a 2PC is forced-availability window complete implies that for any transaction, the coordinator will eventually close all forced-availability windows of the transaction. When all forced-availability windows are closed, the coordinator can discard all information about the transaction. As long as the coordinator can obtain the presumptions used by the participants (using the presumption-bit in the inquiry) the coordinator can always use the presumed outcome in responding to the inquiries in the no-information case.

ONLY IF: We prove by contradiction. Consider the forced-availability window of a transaction that is never closed. Suppose now the logs pertaining to the transaction can be garbage collected. Now the coordinator has no information about the transaction after a system crash. If an inquiry comes, the coordinator will reply using the presumed outcome. This is incorrect, because the

Figure 2. DPr 2PC normal process

```
Coordinator voting phase:
C1. Insert Tx in PTbl;
    Send Prepare message to all PrA participants;
    If there are PrC participants,
        Force-writes Init log record;
        Send Prepare message to all PrC participants;
    Wait for replying vote messages.
Coordinator decision phase:
C2a. Upon receiving Yes vote message:
C2a-1. Tx does not exist in PTbl:
    If the message contains PrC,
        Reply with Commit message;
    Otherwise,
        Reply with Abort message.
C2a-2. The outcome is available in PTbl:
    Reply with that outcome.
C2a-3. Otherwise:
    Update PTbl;
    If all participants have voted Yes or Readonly,
        Force-write Commit log record;
        Send Commit message to all participants
         who voted Yes;
        If there is PrA participant,
            Wait till CommitAck messages from all PrA
             participants have arrived;
            Write CommitEnd log record;
        Remove Tx from PTbl.
C2b. Upon receiving No vote
        or timeout of a vote message:
    Send Abort message to all participants
     who did not vote No or Readonly.
    If there is PrC participant,
        Wait till AbortAck messages from all PrC
         participants have arrived;
        Write AbortEnd log record.
    Remove Tx from PTbl.
C2c. Upon receiving Readonly vote message:
C2c-1. Tx does not exist in PTbl
        or the outcome is available in PTbl:
    Skip.
C2c-2. Otherwise:
    Update PTbl;
    If all participants have voted,
        If all votes are Readonly,
            If there is any PrC participant,
                Write a Readonly log record;
            Remove Tx from PTbl.
        If some votes are Yes,
            Do the same as C2a-3.
C3a. Upon timeout of CommitAck from PrA
participant:
    Re-send Commit message to the participant.
C3b. Upon timeout of AbortAck from PrC
participant:
    Re-send Abort message to the participant.

Participant voting phase:
P1. Upon receiving Prepare message:
    If the vote is Yes,
        Release all read locks;
        Force-write Prepare log record;
        Reply with Yes vote message;
        Wait for outcome message.
    If the vote is No,
        Release all locks;
        Reply with No vote message.
    If the vote is Readonly,
        Release all locks;
        Reply with Readonly vote message.
Participant decision phase:
P2a. Upon receiving Commit message:
P2a-1. First Commit message:
    Release all write locks;
    For PrA participant,
        Force-write Commit log record;
        Reply with CommitAck message.
    For PrC participant,
        Write Commit log record.
P2a-2. Duplicated Commit message:
// there is already Commit log record
// or Tx is unknown
    If the presumption in the message is PrA,
        Reply with CommitAck message.
P2b. Upon receiving Abort message:
P2b-1. First Abort message:
    Release all write locks.
    For PrA participant,
        Write Abort log record.
    For PrC participant,
        Force-write Abort log record;
        Reply with AbortAck message.
P2b-2. Duplicated Abort message:
// there is already Abort log record
// or Tx is unknown
    If the presumption in the message is PrC,
        Reply with AbortAck message.
P3. Upon timeout of outcome message:
    Re-send Yes vote message.
```

forced-availability window is still open and the outcome is the opposite of the presumed one. □

Theorem 3 (Correctness of DPr 2PC): The DPr 2PC satisfies the properties AC1-5 and LGC.

Proof:

AC3 and AC4 are obvious from code (C2a-3 and C2c-2).

AC2 is also straightforward. When a participant reaches an outcome, it closes the in-doubt window and will never inquire about the trans-

Figure 3. DPr 2PC recovery process

Coordinator recovery process:
C4. Scan log backward:
For every *Commit* record, if there are associated PrA participants but no corresponding *CommitEnd* record,
Insert the transaction in *Ptbl*;
Send *Commit* to all participants;
Wait for *CommitAck* from all PrA participants;
For every *Init* record without corresponding *Commit* or *AbortEnd* record,
Insert the transaction in *Ptbl*;
Send *Abort* to all participants;
Wait for *AbortAck* from all PrC participants;
Enable normal processing of the protocol.

Participant recovery process:
P4. Scan log backward:
For every *Prepare* record without corresponding *Commit* or *Abort* record,
Send *Yes* vote message to coordinator;
Wait for outcome message;
Enable normal processing of the protocol.

Figure 4. DPr 2PC garbage collection of logs

Coordinator garbage collection of logs:
C5. Scan log backward:
For every *CimmitEnd* or *AbortEnd* record,
Discard all records of the transaction.
For every *Commit* record without corresponding *CommitEnd* record,
If there is no associated PrA participant,
Discard all record of the transaction.

Participant garbage collection of logs:
P5. Scan log backward:
For every *Commit* or *Abort* record,
Discard all records of the transaction.

action again (P2a-1 and P2b-1). The coordinator only makes a decision in two disjoint cases (C2a-3 and C2c-2, or C2b). Nowhere in the protocol will the coordinator make a new decision.

AC1:

In the protocol where the decision is made by the coordinator, AC1 can also be stated like this: If a decision has been made by the coordinator, all participants will reach the same outcome.

In the *Commit* case, the coordinator force-writes a *Commit* log record before notifying the participants of the decision (C2a-3). This opens a forced-availability window for PrA participants and closes a forced-availability window for PrC participants. If a participant does not receive the *Commit* message, it inquires the coordinator by re-sending a *Yes* vote message (P3, P4). In the case of a PrA participant, since the coordinator has not received *CommitAck* from this participant, the forced-availability window is still open. It can find the *Commit* decision in the protocol table and reply with a *Commit* message (C2a-2). In the case of a PrC participant, if the coordinator still has the transaction in the protocol table, it can find the *Commit* decision there (C2a-2); if the coordinator does not have any information about the transaction, it will use the presumed outcome of PrC and reply with a Commit message (C2a-1). In all these cases, the coordinator will respond with the same *Commit* message. Thus all participants will reach the same *Commit* outcome.

The *Abort* case is similar and is thus not repeated here.

AC5:

There are three possible failures: Coordinator failure, participant failure and communication failure.

The open forced-availability windows are stably logged and will survive system failures. The coordinator recovery procedure can re-establish all forced-availability windows that are open at the moment of coordinator failures (C4). Similarly, the open in-doubt windows are stably logged and will survive system failures. The participant recovery procedure can re-establish all in-doubt windows that are open at the moment of coordinator failures (P4).

A coordinator will detect possible participant and communication failures by timeout and re-sends an outcome message (C3a and C3b). A participant will detect possible coordinator and communication failure by timeout and re-send a *Yes* vote message (P3).

Thus, if all these possible failures are repaired and no new failures occur for sufficiently long, both the coordinator and the participants will eventually reach an outcome.

LGC:

The protocol is forced-availability window complete (C2a-3, C2b and C2c-2) and in-doubt window complete (P2a-1 and P2b-1). According to Theorem 1 and Theorem 2, both the coordinator and the participants satisfy LGC. □

PERFORMANCE EVALUATION

Simulation Model

To evaluate the performance of DPr 2PC, we developed a simulator using a closed queuing model, which is similar to the ones (Chrysanthis et al., 1998; Gupta et al., 1997; Liu et al., 1998) for studying commit protocols for homogeneous distributed database systems. Important pa-

Table 1. Simulation parameters

NumSP	Number of SPs	6
NumSC	Number of SCs	12
NumSPPages	Number of pages at a SP	3000
NumSPDataDisks	Number of data disks at a SP	1
NumSPLogDisks	Number of log disks at a SP	1
NumSCLogDisks	Number of log disks at a SC	1
MPL	Transaction multiprogramming level at a SP	8..56 (low lock contention) 4..28 (high lock contention)
ParticipantSize	Number of page accesses per participant at a SP	4 (low lock contention) 12 (high lock contention)
Participant-ReadonlyRate	Percentage of read-only participants at a SP	0.0, 0.1, 0.7, 0.9
Participant-ReadOpRate	Percentage of read operations per updating participant	0.3
BufferHitRate	Buffer hit rate at a SP	0.9
ExecMode	Transaction execution mode (parallel or sequential)	parallel
DistDegree	Number of participants per transaction	2
PageProcessing-Time	Processing time of a page in CPU and main memory	2ms
DiskSeekTime	Disk seek time	10ms
DiskTransferTime	Disk rotation and transfer time	10ms
IPCDelay	Inter-process message delay at same site	0.5ms
MsgDelay	Message delay between different sites	5ms

rameters of the model and their settings for the experiments are summarized in Table 1. In the description below, we refer to these parameters in parentheses.

The model consists of a number of clients or service consumers **SCs** (*NumSC*) and a number of data service providers **SPs** (*NumSP*). Each SC is associated with a transaction manager that functions as coordinators of distributed transactions started at this SC. Each SP consists of a database and a transaction manager that functions as participants of distributed transactions.

A database is modeled as a collection of data pages (*NumSPPages*). Concurrent read and write operations on the data pages are controlled by strict two-phase locking at page level. Deadlocks are avoided using timeouts. A transaction is aborted when a timeout for lock acquiring occurs.

Each database and transaction manager is associated with a number of disks with their own FCFS queues (*NumSPDataDisks*, *NumSPLogDisks* and *NumSCLogDisks*). The time used for a forced disk IO involves both disk seek time (*DiskSeekTime*) and disk rotation and transfer time (*DiskTransferTime*), whereas the time used for a no-forced disk IO is only disk rotation and transfer time.

The system workload is modeled using the multiprogramming level per SP (*MPL*, number of concurrent sub-transactions) as well as the characters of the SPs and the sub-transactions at the SPs. A distributed transaction starts at a SC and invokes its sub-transactions at the randomly chosen SPs, in parallel or sequentially one after the other (*DistDegree*, *ExecMode*). A sub-transaction consists of a sequence of read or write operations on data pages (*ParticipantSize*). A read-only sub-transaction consists only of read operations (*ParticipantReadonlyRate*). An updating sub-transaction consists of both read and write operations (*ParticipantReadOpRate*). Each read or write operation spends some time in CPU and main memory (*PageProcessingTime*), and may or may not involve disk IOs according to the buffer hit rate (*BufferHitRate*). The resources consumed by a sub-transaction are thus determined by the characters of both the SP (*PageProcessingTime*, *BufferHitRate*) and the sub-transaction (*ParticipantSize*, *ParticipantReadonlyRate* and *ParticipantReadOpRate*), which is SP specific. A transaction terminates by running 2PC. When a transaction terminates, a new one starts immediately at the same SC with sub-transaction at new randomly chosen SPs.

Experimental Results

Our primary performance concern is transaction throughput. In every experiment, transaction throughput (number of committed sub-transactions per second at the SPs) is measured at different multiprogramming levels. In the first two groups of settings, the SPs are characterized with low and high lock contentions respectively (*ParticipantSize* 4 and 12 respectively). In both groups of settings, several simulations are run for SPs characterized with different rates of read-only sub-transactions. In what follows, a SP is denoted **ro0*x*** when its *ParticipantReadonlyRate* is set to 0.*x*. For example, all sub-transactions at a ro00 SP (*ParticipantReadonlyRate* 0.0) are updating, whereas 90% of the sub-transactions at a ro09 SP (*ParticipantReadonlyRate* 0.9) are read-only. In simulations where SPs have homogeneous workload character (e.g., all SPs are ro09), only PrA and PrC are compared. When SPs have heterogeneous workload characters, DPr is compared with PrA and PrC. The last group of settings consists of SPs with both low and high lock contentions. We focus on short transactions, because our experiments (not shown here) indicate that with long transactions, the choice of particular commit protocols is only a second-order factor to the total system performance.

The performance results are shown in Figure 5.

Figure 5. Performance of 2PC optimizations

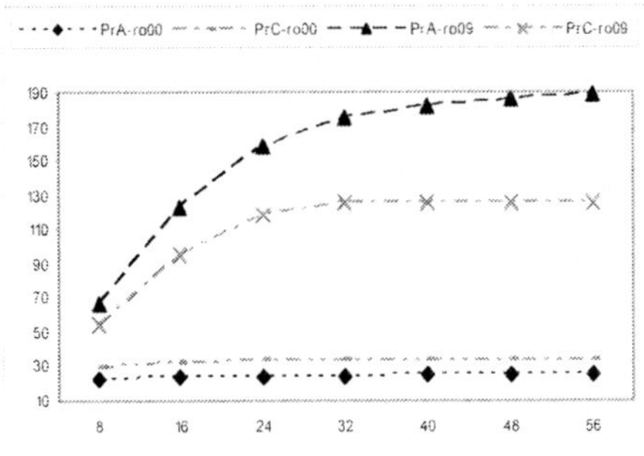

a. Low lock contention, homogeneous workload

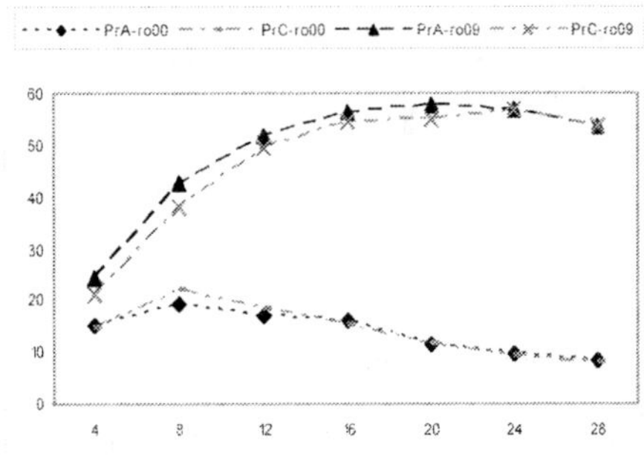

d. High lock contention, homogeneous workload

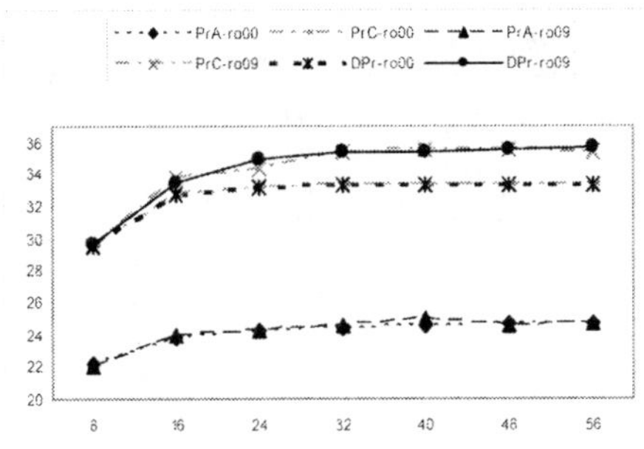

b. Low lock contention, most services updating

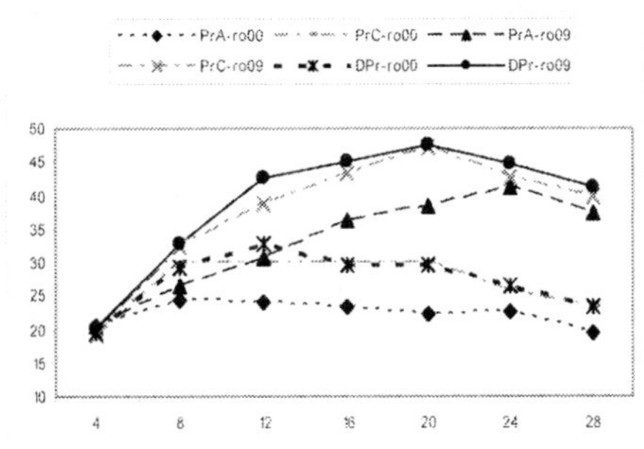

e. High lock contention, most services read-only

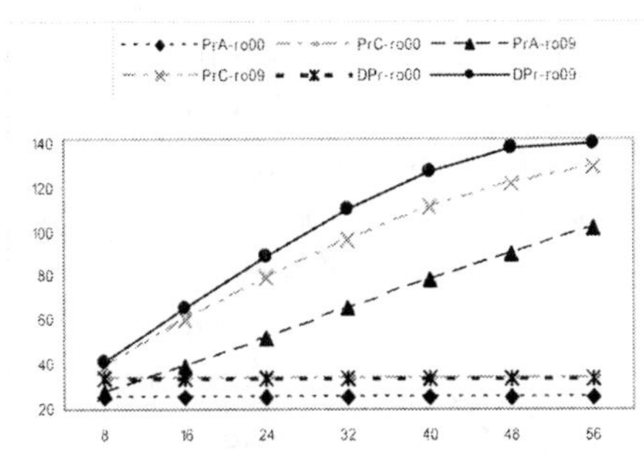

c. Low lock contention, most services read-only

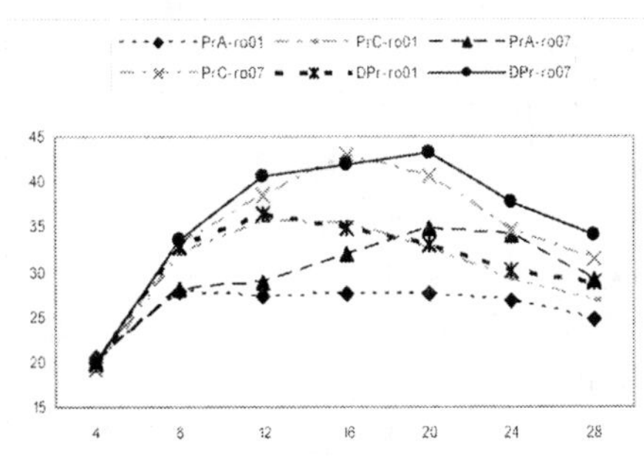

f. Low and high lock contention

x-axis: multiprogramming level (number of concurrent sub-transactions) at SPs
y-axis: transaction throughput (committed sub-transactions per second) at SPs

Performance At Low Lock Contention

When lock contention is low, the number of disk IOs is the primary performance factor in choosing a proper 2PC. Table 2 summarizes the number of disk writes in the commit case.

In the first two experiments, the SPs have homogeneous workload characters, either all are ro00, or all are ro09 (Figure 5a). These are followed by two experiments where the SPs have heterogeneous workload characters, either one of the SPs is ro00 and the others are ro09 (Figure 5b), or vice-versa (Figure 5c).

Table 2. Number of log writes in commit case (force, no-force)

	Coordinator log		PrA participant log		PrC participant log	
	updating	read-only	updating	read-only	updating	read-only
PrA	(1,1)	(0,0)	(2,0)	(0,0)	-	-
PrC	(2,0)	(1,1)	-	-	(1,1)	(0,0)
DPr	(2,0)	(1,1)	(2,0)	(0,0)	(1,1)	(0,0)

Table 3. Lock holding from start of 2PC

	Read locks		Write locks
	PrA participants	PrC participants	PrA or PrC participants
PrA	1 MsgDelay		3 MsgDelay + 1 DiskForce$_{coordinaror}$ + 1 DiskForce$_{participant_PrA}$
PrC		1 DiskForce$_{coordinator}$ + 1 MsgDelay	3 MsgDelay + 2 DiskForce$_{coordinaror}$ + 1 DiskForce$_{participant_PrC}$
DPr	1 MsgDelay	1 DiskForce$_{coordinator}$ + 1 MsgDelay	3 MsgDelay + 2 DiskForce$_{coordinaror}$ + 1 max(DiskForce$_{participant_PrA}$, DiskForce$_{participant_PrC}$)

In the homogeneous updating case (Figures 5a with ro00), PrC outperforms PrA by around 25%. The peak throughput is primarily bound by the log disks at the participants. In the homogeneous read-only case (Figure 5a with ro09), PrA outperforms PrC by up to 33%. In this case, the amount of log writes at the participants is largely reduced and the disk queuing time at both the participants and the coordinators becomes significant.

In the heterogeneous case, where most of the SPs are ro00 (Figure 5b), throughputs at all SPs, including the ro09 SP, are bounded by the log disks at the ro00 SPs. In the PrA case, all SPs even show nearly identical throughputs. This is due to the synchronous effect of 2PC: The fast participants have to wait for the slow ones to get committed globally. In the experiment, PrC outperforms PrA by up to 25% at the ro00 SPs and up to 30% at the ro09 SP. With DPr where PrC is used at ro00 SPs and PrA at the ro09 SP, the performance of DPr is almost identical to PrC. With DPr, the use of PrA at only one participant does not improve total performance compared to PrC, because the *Init* log is still needed for every transaction and therefore the queuing time at the log disks of the coordinators remains the same as PrC.

However in the heterogeneous case where most of the SPs are ro09 (Figure 5c), the different SPs show very different performance characters. The ro00 SP shows considerably poorer performance than the ro09 SPs. At the ro00 SP, PrC outperforms PrA by up to 25%, since the log disk at this SP is the resource with the most contention. Somewhat unexpected, PrC also outperforms PrA by up to 30% at the ro09 SPs. This again is due to the synchronous effect of 2PC such that the performance of the fast SPs is pulled down by the slow SP. The DPr uses PrC at the ro00 SP and PrA at the ro09 SPs. At the ro00 SP, DPr shows performance nearly identical to PrC; whilst at the ro09 SPs, DPr outperforms 2PC using only PrA or PrC (by up to 35% and 15% respectively).

Performance at High Lock Contention

When the level of lock contention is high, both the time transactions spend on acquiring locks and on disk queuing plays an important role. Table 3 summarizes the time locks must be held from the beginning of the protocols. The time in Table 3 can be obtained with the help of Figure 1. For example, in the PrC case, write locks at a SP can only be released after 3 messages (*Prepare*, *Yes* and *Commit*), 2 forced disk writes at the coordinator (*Init* and *Commit*) and 1 forced disk write at the participant (*Prepare*).

In all experiments, performance thresholds are reached and the performance begins to decline when transactions spend over 20% of their lifetimes waiting to acquire locks. This is in line with the well-known 2PC threshold results (e.g., Thomasian, 1996).

In the homogeneous updating case with ro00 SPs, PrC outperforms PrA by around 10% at the peak (Figure 5d with ro00). Although PrC participants must wait one more $DiskForce_{coordinator}$ to be able to release write locks, a larger $DiskForce_{participant\_PrA}$ reduces this difference. In the homogeneous read-only case with ro09 SPs, PrA outperforms PrC by around 5% (Figure 5d with ro09).

Interestingly, in the heterogeneous case where the majority of SPs are ro09 and one SP is ro00 (Figure 5e), PrC outperforms PrA by up to 20% at all sites. At the ro00 SP, PrC outperforms PrA to a larger degree than in the homogeneous ro00 case. At the ro00 SP, $DiskForce_{participant\_PrA}$ becomes larger than in the homogeneous ro00 case, due to faster ro09 SPs. At the ro09 SPs, PrC still outperforms PrA. Like in the case with low lock contentions, this is due to the synchronous effect of 2PC such that the performance of the fast SPs is pulled down by the slow SP. The DPr uses PrC at the ro00 SP and PrA at the ro09 SPs. Again in this setting, DPr outperforms both PrA (by around 25%) and PrC (by around 5%) at all SPs.

Performance at Mixed Low and High Lock Contentions

In our last experiment, we mix SPs with low and high lock contentions and low and high ratio of read-only sub-transactions (Figure 5f). Most of the SPs have high lock contention and 70% of sub-transactions are read-only (the ro07 SPs), whereas one SP has low lock contention and 10% of sub-transactions are read-only (the ro01 SP).

The experiment shows similar performance trend as in the previous settings. PrA works generally poor due to the ro01 SP. PrC outperforms PrA in general (by up to 25% at all SPs) due primarily to the much better performance at the worst performed ro01 SP. DPr outperforms both PrA (by up to 30%) and PrC (by up to 5%) at all SPs.

IMPLEMENTATION FOR WEB SERVICES

We now explain how DPr 2PC can be implemented for transactional Web services. A typical composite Web-service-based application consists of compositions of individual component Web services in terms of, for example, BPEL4WS flows (BPEL4WS, 2003). Each composition consists of a number of smaller atomic distributed transactions. A distributed transaction is coordinated by a transaction manager (TM), known as the coordinator, and TMs associated with the component Web services, known as the participants.

To fully utilize the functionality of DPr 2PC, all 2PC messages, as well as the *Commit* log record at the coordinator and the *Prepare* log records at the participants, should contain the presumption bits (section THE DPr 2PC). This additional information requires only minor extensions to current standards for distributed transaction processing, which allow for but PrA 2PC (OMG, 1998; Sun Microsystems, 1999; X/Open, 1991;WS-AtomicTransaction, 2005). Several commercial transactional Web service engines already exist, e.g., BEA Tuxedo (BEA Systems), Websphere App Server (IBM Corporation), .NET Enterprise Services (Microsoft), etc. They have evolved from the earlier transaction monitor and later distributed object/component middleware products. Basically, they implement PrA 2PC that comply with current standards with minor vendor-specific extensions. It is therefore reasonable to assume that legacy TMs and protocols without the presumption bits all use PrA. We will show below how an implementation of DPr 2PC can support backward compatibility with existing TM implementations.

In a transactional Web services environment enhanced with DPr 2PC, there are two types of TMs: DPr-aware and PrA-only TMs. Existing TMs conforming to current standards are PrA-only. We consider two cases. In the first case, the coordinator TM of a distributed transaction is DPr-aware. If the coordinator receives a message from a participant without a presumption bit, it assumes the participant to be legacy TM or component and that the participant adopts the PrA presumption. In the second case, the coordinator TM is PrA-only. The *Prepare* message from the coordinator thus does not contain presumption bits. A DPr-aware participant, upon receiving such a *Prepare* message, is forced to adopt the PrA presumption. Similarly, if a DPr-aware participant receives a *Commit* or *Abort* message of an unknown transaction without presumption bits, it assumes that the coordinator TM is PrA-only and acknowledges only the *Commit* message. In both cases, no modification to the existing TMs is needed for them to work correctly in an environment enhanced with DPr 2PC.

This implementation strategy shows an incremental and backward-compatible migration path from the current PrA-only transactional Web service engines to a richer DPr environment, while preserving global atomicity of the composite Web services.

RELATED WORK

Our work builds on significant previous contributions on selecting an appropriate presumption dynamically or combining different presumptions in one transaction. Previous research efforts have resulted in various solutions in specialized cases. The DPr 2PC can be viewed as generalizing the previous specialized solutions.

In system R* (Mohan et al., 1986), the coordinator can choose between PrA and PrC on a transaction-by-transaction basis, at the start of 2PC. The coordinator includes the chosen presumption in the *Prepare* message. Every participant includes the presumption in the *Prepare* log record, so this information is not lost before the protocol terminates. The presumption is also included in the inquiry messages by the recovery processes of participants, so the coordinator can use this information in responding to inquiries when no information is available in the protocol table. Garbage collection of logs is not discussed. Our protocol reduces to the 2PC in System R*, when all participants adopt the same presumption.

The presumed-either 2PC (Attaluri & Salem, 2002) is a further optimization of the System R* 2PC using the principle similar to group commit. Instead of force-writing an *Init* log record as in the PrC 2PC, the coordinator writes a no-forced *Participant* record when some participants of the transaction are known. The *Participant* records might be piggybacked by forced writes possibly on behalf of some other transactions. When 2PC starts, if all *Participant* records are already on disk, the coordinator may choose either PrA or PrC; otherwise PrA is the only choice left.

PrAny (Al-Houmaily & Chrysanthis, 1996,1999) allows a transaction to have participants with different presumptions. DPr shares some similarity with PrAny. Particularly, the concept of forced-availability window corresponds to "safe state" in (Al-Houmaily & Chrysanthis, 1999). The main difference lies in how the coordinator knows the presumption of a participant. In PrAny, a coordinator records on its local stable storage the presumption employed by each participant. As a result, a participant is restricted to one particular presumption during its entire lifetime. Moreover, PrAny is not strictly correct with regard to garbage collection of logs, though the information about presumptions that is not garbage collectable is very small in the static world. Our protocol reduces to PrAny (and satisfies completely the LGC property) when no participant will change its presumption in its entire lifetime.

(Al-Houmaily & Chrysanthis, 1996) shows a different approach to dynamically applying presumptions. A participant still cannot change its used presumption. Instead, an agent sits between the coordinator and a participant as an adapter. Additional disk writes are necessary by the agent when the presumption used by the participant is different from the one known to the coordinator. Although this approach may save a few acknowledgement messages in some cases, it in effect increases disk writes at the agent.

With regard to the requirements presented in the INTRODUCTION, our protocol supports all three whereas the previous work only partially supports some of them: PrAny supports compatibility; system R* and presumed-either support dynamic choices; none of these support adaptation of presumptions for service providers.

Relevant to composite services is the area of coordination of agents, which has been an active research topic, originated in the area of distributed artificial intelligence. The goal is to coordinate individual agents to achieve coherent composite behavior (see, for example, Destani 2005; Singh, 2000). Recently, it has been applied to e-commerce (Chen, 2000) and the composition of Web services (Singh, 2003). The multi-agent coordination typically includes both hierarchical agreements and peer-to-peer cooperation, thus becoming a rich environment for heterogeneous composition. Consequently, DPr 2PC can be used as an optimization method for multi-agent systems.

Our performance study differs from earlier work (Chrysanthis et al., 1998; Gupta et al., 1997; Liu et al., 1998) in two respects. First, we study 2PC in heterogeneous settings whereas all previous work assumed homogeneous workload across all sites. Homogeneous workload is unrealistic for applications based on Web services. Secondly, the number of coordinators (i.e. number of service consumers) is taken into account in our study. As our experimental results show, the ratio between the number of service providers and the number of service consumers has a significant impact on systems' performance. Particularly when PrC is used, the log disks at the coordinators can easily become a performance bottleneck.

CONCLUSION AND FUTURE WORK

We observed some new issues concerning supporting distributed transactions in the next-generation applications based on Web services, and developed a 2PC protocol call DPr 2PC that addresses these issues for a set of well-known 2PC optimizations. Particularly DPr 2PC allows participants with different presumptions to be dynamically combined in one distributed transaction. This extends the previous work where either all participants adopt the same presumption or participants cannot change presumptions in their entire lifetime. The protocol bears the same structure of the previous 2PC variants, is easy to understand and implement, and does not introduce extra overhead in terms of number of messages and log records.

We have also quantitatively investigated the performance of various 2PC optimizations under different workloads. In general, PrC 2PC outperforms PrA 2PC when most transactions are updating, due primarily to the queuing time at log disks at service providers. However, PrA 2PC outperforms PrC 2PC when most of transactions are read-only and the queuing time at log disks at service consumers becomes relevant. When lock contention is high, PrA 2PC may perform slightly better if the log disks at the service providers are not overly congested. In a heterogeneous setting, DPr 2PC gives the best performance. Particularly when most service providers are dominated with read-only sub-transactions and thus favors PrA, DPr 2PC show clearly better performance than traditional PrA and PrC 2PCs.

While DPr 2PC meets all the three requirements listed in the INTRODUCTION for Web-service-based applications, several interesting research challenges remain. For example, our performance study included a representative but relatively small number of variables; factors beyond those used in our study may influence the choice of the appropriated presumptions. Another interesting question, not addressed in this article, is how much intervention is needed from the application developers to make the best choice of the presumptions. DPr 2PC supports adaptation of service providers with respect to the presumptions they can choose. A third challenge for future work relates to adaptation of DPr 2PC itself and the support for automatic choice of presumptions based on runtime context of systems.

ACKNOWLEDGMENT

This research is supported in part by the Norwegian Research Council and University of Tromsø under the project Arctic Beans during the first author's sabbatical leave at Georgia Tech. The second author is partially supported by NSF, AFOSR, and Hewlett-Packard.

REFERENCES

Al-Houmaily, Y. J. & Chrysanthis, P. K. (1996). Dealing with incompatible presumptions of commit protocols in multidatabase systems., *Proceedings of the 11th ACM Annual Symposium on Applied Computing*, (pp. 186-195). Philadelphia, PA.

Al-Houmaily, Y. J. & Chrysanthis, P. K. (1999, May 31 - June 2). Atomicity with incompatible presumptions. *Proceedings of the 18th ACM SIGACT-SIGMOD-SIGART Symposium on Principles of Database Systems*, (pp. 306-315). Philadelphia, PA.

Attaluri, G. K.& Salem, K. (2002). The presumed-either two-phase commit protocol, *IEEE Transactions on Knowledge and Data Engineering, 14*(5), pp. 1190-1196.

BEA Systems, BEA Tuxedo, http://edocs.bea.com/tuxedo/tux81/index.htm

Bernstein, P. A., Hadzilacos, V., & Goodman, N. (1987). *Concurrency control and recovery in database systems*, Reading, MA: Addison-Wesley.

Bernstein, P. A.& Newcomer, E. (1997). *Principles of transaction processing*, Chapter 4, Queued Transaction Processing, Morgan Kaufmann Publishers, Inc.

BPEL4WS (2003). Business Process Execution Language for Web Services version 1.1. Retrieved from ftp://www6.software.ibm.com/software/developer/library/ws-bpel.pdf.

Chen, Q. & Dayal, U. (2000, September). Multi-agent cooperative transactions for e-commerce,. *Proceedings of the Fifth Conference on Cooperative Information Systems*, (pp. 311-322). Eilat, Israel.

Chrysanthis, P. K., Samaras, G., & Al-Houmaily, Y. J. (1998). *Recovery and performance of atomic commit processing in distributed database systems,* In V. Kumar and M. Hsu (eds.), Recovery Mechanisms in Database Systems, (pp. 370-416), Prentice Hall PTR.

Dastani, M., Arbab, F. & de Boer, F (2005, July 25 - 29). Coordination and composition in multi-agent systems,. *Proceedings of the fourth International Joint Conference on Autonomous Agents and Multiagent Systems*, (pp. 439-446), Utrecht, The Netherlands

Elmagarmid, A. E. (1992). *Database transaction models for advanced applications*, Morgan Kaufmann Publishers.

Fokkink, W. (2000). *Introduction to process algebra*, Springer-Verlag.

Gray, J. & Reuter, A. (1993). *Transaction processing: Concepts and techniques*.Morgan Kaufmann Publishers.

Gupta, R., Haritsa, J., & Ramamritham, K. (1997, May 13 - 15). Revisiting commit processing in distributed database systems,. *Proceedings of 1997 ACM SIGMOD International Conference on Management of Data*, (pp. 486-497).Tucson, AZ.

IBM Corporation, Websphere Software, http://www.ibm.com/websphere

Lampson, B. W.& Lomet, D. B. (1993, August 24 - 27). A new presumed commit optimization for two phase commit,. *Proceedings of 19th International Conference on Very Large Data Bases*, (pp. 630-640).Dublin, Ireland,

Leymann, F.& Roller, D. (1998, February 23 - 27). Building a robust workflow management system with persistent queues and stored procedures,. *Proceedings of the IEEE International Conference on Data Engineering*, (pp.254-258). Orlando, FL

Liu, M. L., Agrawal, D., & El Abbadi, A. (1998). The performance of two-phase commit protocols in the presence site failures. *Distributed and Parallel Databases*, *6*(2), 157-182.

Microsoft Inc., .NET Enterprise Services, http://msdn.microsoft.com/webservices/enterpriseservices/default.aspx

Mohan, C., Lindsay, B. G., & Obermarck, R. (1986). Transaction management in the r* distributed database management system. *ACM Transactions on Database Systems*, *11*(4), 378-396.

OMG (1998). Object Management Group, *CORBA Services Specification*, Chapter 10, Transaction Service Specification, December, 1998.

Samaras, G., Britton, K., Citron, A., & Mohan, C. (1995).Two-phase commit optimizations in a commercial distributed environment. *Distributed and Parallel Databases*, *3*(4), 325-360.

Singh, M. P. (2000). Synthesizing coordination requirements for heterogeneous autonomous agents. *Autonomous Agents and Multi-Agent Systems*, *3*(1),107-132.

Singh, M. P. (2003, July 14 - 18). Distributed enactment of multiagent workflows: temporal logic for web service composition, *Proceedings of the second International Joint Conference on Autonomous Agents and Multiagent Systems*, (pp. 907-914). Melbourne, Australia.

Sun Microsystems (1999). *Java Transaction Service 1.0*, December, 1999.

Thomasian, A. (1996). Two-phase locking performance and its thrashing behavior, In V. Kumar (eds.), *Performance of Concurrency Control Mechanisms in Centralized Database Systems*, (pp. 166-214), Prentice Hall PTR.

Weikum, G, Moenkeberg, A., Hasse, C., & Zaback, P. (2002, August 20 - 23). Self tuning database technology and information services: from wishful thinking to viable engineering,. *Proceedings of 28th International Conference on Very Large Data Bases*, (pp.20-31). Hong Kong, China.

WS-AtomicTransaction (2005). Web Services Atomic Transaction, Version 1.0. Retrieved from http://xml.coverpages.org/WS-AtomicTransaction200508.pdf, August, 2005.

WS-BusinessActivity (2005). *Web Services Atomic Transaction, Version 1.0*. Retrieved from http://xml.coverpages.org/WS-BusinessActivity200508.pdf, August, 2005.

WS-Coordination (2005). *Web Services Coordination, Version 1.0*. Retrieved from http://xml.coverpages.org/WS-Coordination200508.pdf, August, 2005.

X/Open (1991). X/Open Company Ltd., *Distributed Transaction Processing: The XA Specification*. Document number XO/CAE/91/300.

This work was previously published in the International Journal of Web Services Research, Vol. 4, Issue 1, edited by L. J. Zhang, pp. 80-100, copyright 2007 by IGI Publishing, formerly known as Idea Group Publishing (an imprint of IGI Global).

Chapter 4.50
A Metamorphic Testing Approach for Online Testing of Service-Oriented Software Applications

W. K. Chan
City University of Hong Kong, Hong Kong

S. C. Cheung
Hong Kong University of Science and Technology, Hong Kong

Karl R. P. H. Leung
Hong Kong Institute of Vocational Education, Hong Kong

ABSTRACT

Testing the correctness of services assures the functional quality of service-oriented applications. A service-oriented application may bind dynamically to its supportive services. For the same service interface, the supportive services may behave differently. A service may also need to realize a business strategy, like best pricing, relative to the behavior of its counterparts and the dynamic market situations. Many existing works ignore these issues to address the problem of identifying failures from test results. This article proposes a metamorphic approach for online services testing. The off-line testing determines a set of successful test cases to construct their corresponding follow-up test cases for the online testing. These test cases will be executed by metamorphic services that encapsulate the services under test as well as the implementations of metamorphic relations. Thus, any failure revealed by the metamorphic testing approach will be due to the failures in the online testing mode. An experiment is included.

INTRODUCTION

The service-oriented architecture (SOA) is an architectural reference model (Bass et al., 2003) for a kind of distributed computing such as the Web services (W3C, 2002). It promises to alleviate the problems related to the integration of heterogeneous applications (Kreger et al., 2003; Mukhi et al., 2004). In this reference model, a SOA application is denoted by a collection of self-contained communicating components, known as *services*. The model also emphasizes that each service should make little or no assumption about its collaborating services. This setting advocates the dynamic composition of a service by using different configurations of supportive services, creating behavioral differences amongst different invocations of a service. Typical end-users of a SOA application, such as bank customers using an online foreign exchange trading service, may expect consistent outcomes each time they use the service. The customers may further compare the online foreign exchange service of a bank to similar services of other banks to judge whether the service is of good quality. If a B2B service provider is driven by a predefined business strategy to, for example, maintain its market share, then the criteria to define functional correctness of the service may vary according to its environment. In other words, testers need to integrate the environment of a service to check test results.

Services may be subject to both the off-line testing and the online testing. Unlike the testing of conventional programs, services bind dynamically to other peer services when it is tested online. While the off-line testing of services is analogous to the testing of conventional programs, the online testing of services needs to address new issues and difficulties.

Testers may generally apply certain static analyses or testing techniques to assure the correctness of a software application. The evaluation criteria of the functional correctness, on the other hand, must be predefined. For a unit testing, testers also want to address the test case selection problem and the test oracle problem (Beizer, 1990). We restrict our attention to the latter problem in this article.

A test oracle is a mechanism that reliably decides whether a test succeeds. For services, as we will discuss, formal test oracle may be unavailable. The expected behavior of a service that represents business goods and services changes according to the environment. Such an expected behavior is relative to the behaviors of competing services or other services. Intuitively, it is hard to define the expected behavior explicitly in the first place. Tsai et al., (2004) for example, suggest using a progressive ranking of similar implementations of a service description to alleviate the test oracle problem. The behaviors of different implementations of the same service vary in general. Test results of a particular group of implementations cannot reliably be served as the expected behavior of a particular implementation of the same service on the same test case. Also, a typical SOA application may comprise collaborative services of multiple organizations, knowing all the implementations are impractical (Ye et al., 2006). For example, a travel package consultant may wrap up services of various hotels, airlines, and entertainment centers to personalize tour packages for a particular client. Without the implementation details, static analysis appears infeasible to assure the implementation quality. The black box approach for test results checking remains viable and popular to assure the correctness of a software application.

Metamorphic testing is a promising approach to the test oracle problem in the testing of conventional scientific programs (Chan et al., 1998; Chen et al., 1998, 2002). Instead of relating an output to its input, metamorphic testing relates multiple input-output pairs via well-defined relations, called metamorphic relations.

This article extends the preliminary version (Chan et al., 2005a) to propose an online testing approach for testing services. The main contributions of the preliminary version (Chan et al., 2005a) include:

1. It proposes to apply the notion of metamorphic testing to services computing to alleviate the test oracle problem. It constructs

more test cases to reveal faults than those ordinarily required when test oracles are known.

2. It proposes to realize the metamorphic testing mechanism as a metamorphic service in services computing that encapsulates a service under test, executes test cases and cross-validates their test results. Such realization seamlessly integrates the existing SOA framework. It automates the construction of follow-up test cases and their test results checking.

The main extended contributions of this article include:

3. It devises the use of the successful test cases for off-line testing as the original test cases for online testing. Since, in an off-line testing, the environment of services can be controlled by testers, test oracle could be defined. Thus, any failure revealed by our metamorphic testing approach will be due to the failures in the online testing mode.
4. It refines the testing approach presented in the preliminary version of this article to take the successful test cases from the off-line testing phase into account.
5. It evaluates the revised proposal against a control experiment having no prior confirmation of test results through an experiment. The experimental result indicates that our proposal is superior to the control experiment. The control approach suffers from an extra 16% effort to check test results and a 13% reduction of failure detection.

The rest of the article is organized as follows. The next section introduces the concepts of services, metamorphic testing and other preliminaries. After that, we describe our testing proposal. Our approach will be illustrated by a sample scenario, followed by an experiment on the feasibility of applying the proposal in a SOA application. Based on the experimental results, we compare our approach to related work, and discuss our experience. Finally, we conclude the article and outline the future work.

PRELIMINARIES

In this section, we briefly introduce the notion of service, metamorphic relation, and metamorphic testing. We also discuss how a metamorphic relation can be aligned with the notion of service and discuss our assumptions. Finally, we clarify our terminologies on online testing and off-line testing.

Service

A *service* in SOA is a self-contained application function, packaged as a reusable component, for the use in a business process (Colan, 2004). It can describe itself so that other services may discover and locate the service. Services also use simple and self-contained messages with well-defined interfaces for communications. Those interfaces are neutral to different hardware or software platforms to support the execution of a service. Metamodels, such as XML Schema (W3C, 2001), are often used to govern the syntactic validity of the messages.

For example, the Web services (Curbera et al., 2002; W3C, 2002) use the *Web service definition language* or WSDL (W3C, 2005) to let each service of an application define the syntactic and interoperability requirements. It also uses the *universal description, discovery and integration* or UDDI (OASIS, 2005) to offer applications a unified and systematic way to locate services from common registries. The *simple object access protocol* or SOAP (W3C, 2003) is then used to support XML[2]-based messaging between peer services.

In general, there are two types of services, namely *stateless* and *stateful*. They are analogues to conventional programs and object-oriented programs, respectively. Both types are popular in these days.[3] Intuitively, in terms of modeling, one may use a stateless service with self-addressing stateful messages to simulate a stateful service. We thus restrict ourselves to consider stateless services in this article.

Metamorphic Relation (MR)

As a service is a self-contained and function-oriented component, some functional properties of the service should be identifiable; otherwise, it would be difficult for collaborating services to identify the usefulness of the service. One way to display the functional properties of a service is to show the connection of multiple invocations of the service.

A metamorphic relation, or MR, is an existing or expected relation over a set of distinct inputs and their corresponding outputs for multiple executions of the target function (Chen et al., 1998, 2002, 2003). For example, consider a sorting program *Sort*( ) that sorts the input list of integers into a list of integers in ascending order. The expected result of *Sort*(⟨*1,4,3*⟩) is ⟨*1,3,4*⟩, which is same as that of *Sort*(⟨*1,3,4*⟩). Generalizing the scenario would lead to the formulation of the relation: *Sort*(*X*) = *Sort*(*Sort*(*Y*)) *if X* = *Y*.

Readers can easily observe that in the above example, the expected output of the input ⟨*1,4,3*⟩ is only induced implicitly. This relieves testers to predetermine the expected behavior of a test case in an absolute term. It is particularly important when a tester is conducting the online testing of a service, for the reason that the concrete expected behavior of a service may depend on other peer services, which may not be under the control of the software developers or testers of the service under test.

A metamorphic relation can be formally described as follows:

- Suppose that f is an implemented function under test. Given a relation r over n distinct inputs $x_1, x_2, \ldots, x_n$, the corresponding n computation outputs $f(x_1), f(x_2), \ldots, f(x_n)$ must induce a necessary property r_f

A metamorphic relation MR_f of f over n inputs and n outputs can be defined as follows:

$$MR_f = \{(x_1, x_2, \ldots, x_n, f(x_1), f(x_2), \ldots, f(x_n)) \mid r(x_1, x_2, \ldots, x_n) \Rightarrow r_f(x_1, x_2, \ldots, x_n, f(x_1), f(x_2), \ldots, f(x_n))\}$$

We observe that, when a service is seen to be a function, and all input and output messages are self-contained, the notion of metamorphic relation readily applies to services. We will give an example after the introduction of metamorphic testing in the following section.

Metamorphic Testing (MT)

Metamorphic testing or MT (Chen et al., 1998, 2002, 2004) is a program testing technique that employs the mathematical relations, namely metamorphic relations, to conduct testing. It has been applied to numerical applications (Chan et al., 1998) and context-aware applications (Chan et al., 2005c).

It uses *successful test cases* to alleviate the test oracle problem when a test oracle is unavailable or expensive. Given a program P of target function f with input domain D. A set of test cases T, $\{t_1, \ldots, t_k\}$ ($\subset D$), can be selected according to any test case selection strategy. Executing the program P on T produces outputs $P(t_1), \ldots, P(t_k)$. When they reveal any failure, testing stops and debugging begins. On the other hand, when no failure is revealed, these test cases will be termed as *successful*. A set of successful test cases is called a successful test set.

Testers may apply the metamorphic testing approach to continue to verify whenever some necessary property of the target function f is satisfied by the implementation P. The metamorphic testing approach constructs the *follow-up* test set T', $\{t'_1,\ldots,t'_m\}$ ($\subset D$), automatically from the initial successful test set T, with the reference to some given metamorphic relation.

Let us cast an example in the services computing setting. Suppose that S is an expected USD–HKD exchange service, accepting deal orders in USD and returning deal orders in HKD; x and y are two deal orders; $g(\ )$ is a function that accepts a deal order and returns its deal order amount. Further suppose that the following metamorphic relation sample is given, meaning that doubling the deal order in USD, doubling the resultant amount in HKD:

$MR_a(x, y, S(x), S(y))$:
$2g(S(y)) = g(S(x))$ if $g(x) = 2g(y)$

Consider a successful test case x_1 = "a deal order of US\$20,000." The metamorphic testing approach constructs automatically another test case y_1 = "a deal order of US\$10,000" based on the condition $g(x) = 2g(y)$ of MR_a. Suppose P is an implementation of S. If the comparison $2g(P(y_1)) = g(P(x_1))$ fails, the MT approach reveals a failure due to the pair of failure-causing inputs x_1 and y_1. As x_1 is successful in the first place, the identified failure should be due to the test case y_1

In the MT terminology, x_1 is termed as the *original test case*, and y_1 is termed as the *follow-up test case*. By checking the results amongst multiple input-output pairs, metamorphic testing bypasses the need to define the expected result explicitly to alleviate the test oracle problem. We refer readers to (Chan et al., 2005c; Chen et al, 2002, 2003, 2004; Tse et al., 2004) for more details about metamorphic testing.

In this article, we assume that MRs are provided by testers. Verification is generally undecidable, thus, we further assume that the provided MRs describe some necessary conditions of the expected behavior of the program under test. In practice, we recommend testers to define their MRs in a style so that they are directly coded in certain executable specification languages such as Prolog. As such, the implementation of MRs is a non-issue when testers use our methodology. In the next section, we further describe a few major assumptions of our proposal.

Assumptions and Terminologies

In this section, we list out a few major assumptions to establish our model for the online testing of services. These assumptions facilitate us to propose an infrastructure, namely metamorphic service, to be discussed in the metamorphic service section. We also clarify our terminologies on off-line testing and online testing.

We make the following assumptions: A service could be wrapped up by another (wrapper) service. It is based on the understanding that services are loosely coupled amongst themselves and they recognize one another through the common service registries. We assume that in the common service registries, the entries of the former service are replaced by those of the latter service for the testing purpose. This allows the latter service to query and catch messages for the former one. In our model, we use a message as a *test case* or *test result* of a service. This kind of treatment is also adapted by other researchers (Tsai et al., 2004; Offutt & Xu, 2004). It enables the wrapper service to construct test cases and evaluate their test results.

Furthermore, we agree with other researchers that a service is self-contained and independent to the contexts of other services. It also outputs results on every input.

We refer the term *online testing* to the testing of a service under the SOA environment, and the term *off-line testing* to the testing of a service without interaction with other services relevant to the service under test. We also term *off-line testing* and *testing in the off-line mode* interchangeably, and *online testing* and *testing in the online mode* interchangeably. Moreover, for the off-line testing, we refer a *stub service* as a service, since it is obvious in the context that the service under test does not interact with any other peer services of the SOA application when it is subject to an off-line testing. In the next section, we will present our testing proposal.

AN ONLINE TESTING APPROACH

In this section, an online testing methodology will be presented. We propose to test a service in two distinct modes, namely off-line mode and online mode. Informally, we propose to use the test oracle available to the off-line testing and make it also available to the online testing via metamorphic relations. In the overview section, we first introduce the two modes of testing. Next, in the metamorphic service section, we propose a core design artifact of our approach, the metamorphic service, which serves as a surrogate of the services under test to relay messages. At the same time, it constructs follow-up test cases and evaluates results accordingly. It then summarizes the methodology in the testing in the online mode section.

Overview

The off-line mode tests a service in the absence of interacting services. We view that it strongly resembles the convention techniques for the unit test of a conventional program. Many test data selection strategies (such as dataflow testing [Beizer, 1990; Zhu et al., 1997]) and test oracle construction for the unit test of conventional programs have been researched for years. As testers could control the off-line environment (such as providing test drivers and stub services, and messages), it is relatively easier to define test sets to test a service and validate the test results in such a mode. Thus, whether a test case reveals a failure or not, for off-line testing, can be determined through the checking of their test results against certain test oracle.

The above observation motivates us to apply the successful test cases of an off-line testing as the original test cases for the online testing mode. In the sequel, we restrict ourselves to discuss the online testing mode. We presume that a set of successful test cases for the off-line testing is available.

For online testing, as these original test cases are determined to be successful in advance, any violation of a corresponding metamorphic relation should be due to the failures of the follow-up test cases. Thus, when their corresponding follow-up test cases are for online testing, our approach pinpoints the online failure-causing inputs automatically even if the test oracle for online testing is not available. Figure 1 depicts the relation between off-line testing and our proposal for online testing.

Interested readers may compare the above strategy and the strategy that an original test case is unknown to be successful. In the latter strategy, when a violation of a metamorphic relation is detected, testers still need to further evaluate whether the violation is due to the original test case (no matter if it is in the off-line or online testing mode) or the follow-up (online) test case. Therefore, this alternative strategy may incur more overheads than our proposal. We will further study this issue in our empirical experiment in the experiment section.

We will introduce a fundamental building box of our approach in the metamporphic services section, and then elaborate our online testing approach in the rest of this section. To ease our discussion, in the sequel, we use a metamorphic relation with two input-output pairs. The extension of the approach to more than one input-output pair is not hard.

Figure 1. The Integration between off-line and online testing

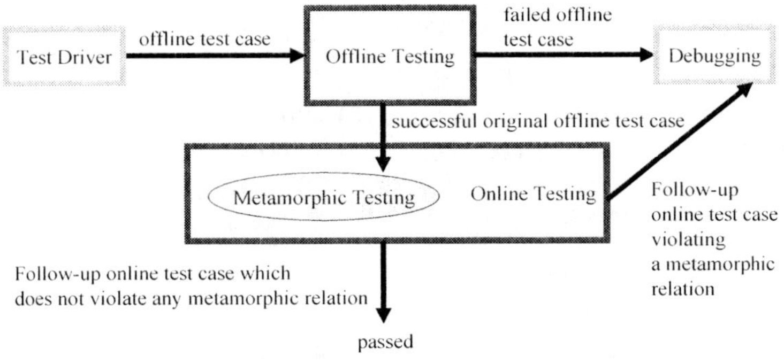

Metamorphic Service (MS)

We formulate a metamorphic service as a service that has the characteristics of being an access wrapper (Mecella & Pernici, 2001; Umar, 1997) and being an agent to conduct metamorphic testing. A metamorphic service imitates all the data and application access paths of the service being encapsulated. It also embodies the program logics, which is the implementation of metamorphic relations, to compute follow-up test cases based on an incoming (or outgoing) message, and evaluates test results according to the implemented metamorphic relations.[4]

Since a metamorphic service is a service, which dynamically discovers a service implementation to receive a follow-up test case. The result of the follow-up test case will be sent to the metamorphic service for the detection of failures. The metamorphic service checks the test results against other test cases by using its metamorphic relations. Any violation of an implemented metamorphic relation reveals a failure.

Testing in the Online Mode

The testing in the online mode validates whether a service can interact correctly with other services. The following shows the self-explanatory methodological steps for this mode.

(ON-1). For a service under test *S*, collect the set of service descriptions D_S that represents the services interacting with *S*.

(ON-2). Design a metamorphic relations MR_i applicable to test *S* in the online mode.

(ON-3). Implement MR_i in the metamorphic service *MS* of the service *S*.

(ON-4). Repeat Steps (ON-2) to (ON-3) until no additional metamorphic relation is required for online testing.

(ON-5). For each available successful off-line test case t_o, do

- i. *MS* uses applicable MR_i to construct the following-up test case t_f of t_o.
- ii. *MS* invokes *S* to execute t_f.
- iii. *MS* obtains the corresponding results t_f
- iv. If *MS* detect a failure by using MR_i, then report the failure and go to Step (ON-7).
- v. Repeat Steps (On-5-i) to (On-5-iv) until no more applicable MR_i.

(ON-6). Report that no failure is found.

(ON-7). Exit

Step (ON-1) collects the service description that the service under test intends to collaborate. They facilitate testers to define and implement relevant metamorphic relations[5] in Steps (ON-2) and (ON-3) respectively.

If a tester does not identify any further metamorphic relation, Step ON-4 naturally stops, because there is no additional metamorphic relation in the tester's context. On the other hand, if a tester knows a metamorphic relation, but is incompetent to implement such a relation, it is obvious that the tester cannot use such a metamorphic relation according to our methodology; unless the tester seeks helps to implement the metamorphic relation.

Step (ON-5) uses an original test case to construct a follow-up test case. It also invokes the service under test to execute the follow-up test case, and collects the test result of the follow-up test case. Next, it evaluates the results until no more implemented and applicable metamorphic relation is available. When it detects a violation of any metamorphic relation, in Step (On-5-iv), it reports the failure and stops the testing. Otherwise, the process iterates, using another original test case until no more original test case is available. If no failure could be detected by any test case, the process will report such a case in Step (ON-6) and stop at Step (ON-7).

After presenting our approach in this section, the next section will demonstrate a way to use metamorphic testing to reveal failures related to the relative correctness for the testing of a service. We will then present an empirical experiment of our proposal in the experiment section.

AN ILLUSTRATION SCENARIO

In this section, our proposal for online testing will be further illustrated by an example. We first describe an application and its faults. Then, we illustrate how these faults can be revealed.

Figure 2 shows a foreign exchange dealing service application with five services, namely FXDS1 to FXDS5. In particular, FXDS2 is embraced by a metamorphic service. We denote the metamorphic service as *MS*. It has three metamorphic relations, namely MR1, MR2 and MR3. To ease our discussion, we restrict ourselves to discuss the exchange of US dollars to Renminbi.

A bank normally offers cross-currency rates inquiry services. A sample USD–RMB exchange rate is a pair of values such as 8.2796/8.2797. The first value and the second value in the pair refer to the *bid rate* and the *ask rate*, respectively. The difference between the two values in such a pair is known as the spread. We will use this rate for the following illustration, and assume these rates to be provided by the service FXDS4.

Suppose the expected behaviors of FXDS2 include:

1. A uniform exchange rate for any deal order.
2. A better, or at least the same, exchange rate to its clients than its rivals (e.g., the service FXDS3).
3. Checks on the exchange rates from central banks dynamically (e.g., the service FXDS4 for Central Bank of China, or FXDS5 for European Central Bank).

Also suppose that the implementation FXDS2 contains the following two faults (see (Table 2):

a. It uses the bid rate or the ask rate to process a deal order non-deterministically.
b. The rate provider logic has faults to cause it to use the minimum (that is, the worst rate) instead of the maximum (that is, the best rate) for its rate calculations.

To test the service FXDS2, testers can apply our testing proposal, which is illustrated as follows.

Testers first formulate metamorphic relations. For the requirement (i), testers can check whether the output amount of service FXSD2 for a deal order is proportional to the deal order size. It forms the first metamorphic relation:

Figure 2. A foreign exchange services system.

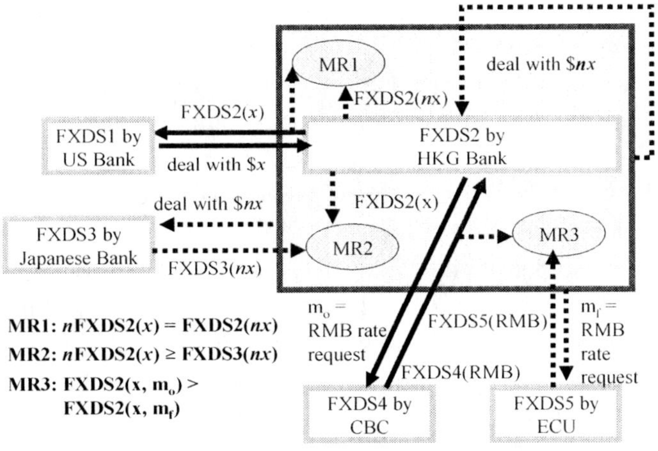

MR1: nFXDS2(x) = FXDS2(nx).

Consider an original test message t_o: a deal order of x (= US$100). FXDS2 correctly uses the above bid rate to output a message FXDS2(US$100) = 827.96 = 8.2796 × 100 in the off-line testing mode by using stubs. The metamorphic service *MS* constructs a follow-up test case t_f: a deal order of US$200 = 2 × x. It then passes this message to FXDS2 to execute in the online testing mode. (This is shown as the top-right dotted arrow in Figure 2).

Suppose, unfortunately, FXDS2 incorrectly uses the above ask rate and outputs FXDS2(US$200) = 1655.94 = 2× 827.97. Since both messages FXDS2(US$100) and FXDS2(US$200) can be checked by *MS* via MR1, we have, 2 × FXDS2(US$100) = 1655.92 ≠ 1655.94 = FXDS2(US$200). It violates the equation MR1. Hence, a failure related to the fault (*a*) is revealed and reported by the metamorphic service.

Readers may be interested to know the results of other combinations of using bid and ask rates for either the original or the follow-up test cases. When the original test case and the follow-up test cases use the bid rate or the ask rate, the equation MR1 will be ineffective to reveal the fault. However, when the original test case incorrectly uses the ask rate and the follow-up test case correctly uses the bid rate, MR1 would reveal the fault.

Let us continue to describe the scenarios to reveal the fault (*b*). We also begin with the formulations of two metamorphic relations. For the requirement (ii), testers may enlarge or shrink a deal order size by a multiplier. (In practice, a deal order size applicable to a global bank may not be applicable to a small foreign exchange shop at a street corner.) Such a follow-up deal order will be forwarded to a competing service (e.g., FXDS3). Next, one can determine whether the output of FXDS2 of the same order size is better than or equal to that provided by a rival service. This formulates the metamorphic relation:

MR2: nFXDS2(x) ≥ FXDS3(n x).

For the requirement (iii), testers may formulate the metamorphic relation:

MR3: value(FXDS2(x)) > value(FXDS2(y))
if centralbank(FXDS2(x)) = m_o and centralbank(FXDS2(y)) = m_f

Alternatively, in a shorthand notation:

MR3: FXDS2(x, m_o) > FXDS2(x, m_f)

MR3 means that if the target exchange is between USD and RMB, then the rate, provided by the Central Bank of China via the rate request m_o, should be strictly better than that due to any other rate request m_f from other central banks. We note that we choose to show the outgoing messages that interact with other services as parameters in the metamorphic relation in the shorthand notation to ease our discussion. We also deliberately use a different notation (that is, m_o and m_f, instead of t_o and t_f) for outgoing messages that serve as test cases for the metamorphic testing being illustrated.

According to MR2, a follow-up test case m_f can be formulated: Deal order of US$60 = 0.3 × 200. Suppose that an implementation of the service FXDS3 is discovered dynamically, and the latter correctly receives m_f and returns a message FXDS3(US$60) = 60 × 8.2796 = 496.776 to *MS*. Both messages FXDS2(US$200) and FXDS3(US$60) are verified by the metamorphic service via MR2. We have, 0.3 × FXDS2(US$200) = 496.782 > 496.776 = FXDS3(US$60). It satisfies MR2. Hence, no failure will be reported by *MS* for this particular follow-up test case.

On the other hand, for online testing, in the execution of a deal order as the input, FXDS2 needs to communicate with services of central banks to collect relevant exchange rates. Thus, the original test case t_o will trigger an outgoing message m_o, a USD–RMB rate request, for such a purpose. Suppose that FXDS2 discovers both FXDS4 and FXDS5 to provide the quotes of exchange rates for USD–RMB. For the illustration purpose, further suppose that the exchange rate provided by the European Central Bank via FXDS5 for USD–RMB is 8.2795/8.2798. This spread is wider than that provided by FXDS4, and thus is poorer.

MS uses the metamorphic relation MR3 to produce the follow-up test case m_f of m_o. Owing to the faults (*a*) and (*b*), FSDS2 incorrectly selects the ask rate of the service FXDS4 to process the deal order. FSDS2 will output a message FXDS2(US$100) = 827.98 = 8.2798 × 100. We have, in the shorthand notation, FXDS2(US$100, m_o) = 827.96 < 827.98 = FXDS2(US$100, m_f). It violates MR3, and *MS* reports a failure due to the combination of faults (*a*) and (*b*).

We have illustrated the usefulness of using a metamorphic service for the testing of services. In reality, there are domain-specific rounding practices compliant to the international accounting practice. Since rounding rules are a part of the application domain, it is natural for the designed metamorphic relations to take this type of rounding rules into account. This type of domain-specific rounding does not affect the metamorphic approach for services testing. It is worth mentioning that there could be implementation-specific rounding errors also. We refer readers to a previous work on metamorphic testing (Chen et al., 2003) for using a metamorphic approach to identify failures in the presence of the implementation-specific rounding errors. In the next section, we report an experiment that applies our proposal and discuss observations.

EXPERIMENT

In this section, we examine two issues in our proposal through an empirical experiment. We would like to study the testing overhead when some of the original test cases have failed. This is to validate our proposal to use successful test cases applicable to off-line testing as the original test cases for online testing. Our rationale is that if the overhead, on the contrary, is marginal; it is unnecessary to predetermine the successfulness of original test cases. This also helps reduce the testing effort for the online testing of services.

The Subject Program

The subject service implements a service-oriented calculator of arithmetic expressions. It is developed in C++ on Microsoft Visual Studio for

.NET 2003 as a Web services. It consists of 16 classes with 2,480 lines of code.

Functionally, the calculator accepts an arithmetic expression consisting of constants of designated data type and arithmetic operators. The set of supported operators are $\{+,-,\times,\div\}$ in which each operator is overloaded to enable every operand belonging to different data types. Five data types of operands are supported: integer, long integer, decimal, floating-point number, and floating-point number with double precision. Each operator is implemented as a supportive service of the subject service.

The subject service parses the inputted arithmetic expressions, locates other services, and composes the results from the results returned by its individual supportive services. In the case where different data types are associated with an operator in a sub-expression, the subject service is responsible to resolve the appropriate data types and to pass the sub-expression to an applicable supportive service. In the design of the application, we choose to allow at most three concurrent instances of the above logic in the subject service. They, together with an expression dispatcher instance, compose our subject service. The expression dispatcher discovers the above supportive services of the subject service, and sends outgoing and receives incoming messages for the latter services. The metamorphic service for the subject service is composed of the dispatcher and a program unit that implements a set of metamorphic relations, which will be explained in the next section.

All the above services are developed by a team of five developers. They have completed certain formal software engineering training. Before doing the experiment, they have gained at least one year of research-oriented and application software development to develop location-based systems, mobile positioning systems and common business applications.

Experimental Setup

In this section, we describe the setup configuration for the testing of the subject service. Specifically, we present the selection of the original test cases, the metamorphic relations, and our experience in finding and implementing the metamorphic relations for the experiment.

As described previously, every instance of services is executed on a designated machine. In total, 14 personal computers are used. All the machines to collect our data are located in the Compuware Software Testing Laboratory of the Hong Kong Institute of Vocational Education (Tsing Yi).

The selection of the set of the original test cases is a black-box combinatorial testing approach. This allows the test cases to serve as the original test cases for both the off-line testing mode and online mode. Consider an arithmetic expression of length 3, which we mean to have an expression having three values and two operators (e.g., $13 + 0.45 - 7$). In our experiment, there are five types of data type and four types of operator. In total, there are 2,000 (that is, $5^3 \times 4^2$) combinations, not counting the possible choices of value to initialize each variable. Since the length of an arithmetic expression could be ranged from zero to a huge figure, we choose to fix the length to three in this experiment. This minimizes the potential problem of using a very long expression to compare with a very short expression in our subsequent analysis. We also initialize test cases that do not cause integer value overflow, and the overflow of other data types alike. We are aware that we have implemented some design decisions in the test case selection process. We minimize these highlighted threats by designing our metamorphic relations *neutral* to these design decisions.

In ideal cases, a user would perceive every calculation as if it is derived analytically using mathematics. However, some expressions would incur rounding errors due to the limitation of programming or system configuration. Different orders of evaluations of an expression could thus produce inconsistent results. A good calculator would provide consistent results to its users. For example, the arithmetic expression "(1 ÷ 3) × 3" would be evaluated as "(1 × 3) ÷ 3" by a good calculator.

We follow the above general guideline to formulate our metamorphic relations. We first describe how we determine and implement metamorphic relations. Next, we will describe the chosen metamorphic relations.

The arithmetic operators for the calculator application domain naturally define associative and commutative properties amongst arithmetic operators. We use these properties as the basis to design our metamorphic relations. This aligns with our objective to design such relations neutral to the selection of the original test cases. Since these properties naturally occur in the domain application, we experience a marginal effort to design associative and commutative relations and convert them into their corresponding formats in the sense of metamorphic relation. Furthermore, since the .NET framework for C++ directly supports the chosen operators, the effort to implement the metamorphic relations in our experiment is also marginal.

The types of metamorphic relation used in the experiment are as follows. Suppose *A*, *B* and *C* are operands of some data type in the set {integer, long integer, floating point number, floating point number with double precision}, and θ_1 and θ_2 are overloaded operators in the set {+, –, ×, ÷}. Consider the expression "(A θ_1 B) θ_2 C." A commutative-property rule to generate the follow-up test cases is: "(A θ_1 B) θ_2 C" ⇒ "C θ_2 (A θ_1 B)". It derives the follow-up test case "C θ_2 (A θ_1 B)" based on the original test case "(A θ_1 B) θ_2 C."

Let us denote our subject service by *S*. The corresponding metamorphic relation of the above commutative rule would be: *S*("(A θ_1 B) θ_2 C") = *S*("C θ_2 (A θ_1 B)"). A metamorphic relation derived from an associative rule is *S* ("(A θ_1 B) θ_2 C") = *S*("A θ_1 (B θ_2 C)"). We also design variants of the follow-up test case derivation rules to deal with the division operator: "(A × B) ÷ C)" ⇒ "(1 ÷ C) × (A × B)," and other similar rules alike. The generation of test cases is implemented as logic in our program.

Let us continue the discussion on the execution of test cases. Even a program is ideal; messages could still be lost or corrupt in a distributed environment. Our subject application does not implement a sophisticated fail-and-retry strategy to handle these anticipated scenarios. To compensate the lacking of this kind of strategy, we choose to abort the execution of a test case when a service returns no output after a timing threshold. After some trials-and-errors in our laboratory environment, we choose the threshold to be 50 seconds per execution of a pair of (original and follow-up) test cases. A typical test case will yield the result with three seconds.

Based on the implementation of the subject application, we create additionally six consecutive faulty versions of the set of supportive services. Each version injects one additional mutation fault to its immediate ancestor. The six consecutive faults are created in the following order: changing a "+" operator to the operator "–"; changing a "–" operator to the "+" operator'; changing a "×" operator to a "–" operator; swapping the operand of a "÷" operator; changing a "–" operator to the "×" operator; and changing a "×" operator to a "+" operator. These faults support operands of the following data types respectively: floating-point number with double precision, integer, decimal, floating-point number with single precision, long integer, and floating-pointer number with single precision.

The following configurations were deployed for off-line testing and online testing.

- The subject application (the subject service with the original version of the supportive services) simulates an off-line testing environment. The original non-faulty versions of the supportive services serve as stub services for the off-line testing, in the sense of conventional testing. Inexperienced developers implement the subject service and, thus, it naturally contains real faults. Some random test cases do reveal failures from the subject service. We however have reviewed that a set of test cases for the subject service for off-line testing are successful. This set of test cases could be used as the original test cases for online testing according to our approach. We refer this set of test cases to as the set of original test cases in the experiment.

- A faulty application (the subject service with a faulty version of the supportive services) simulates an online testing environment. A faulty version of the supportive services is not identical in behavior to its original counterpart (the test stub used in the off-line testing). The six faulty versions therefore facilitate us to re-use the above set of original test cases yet provide failed test results for some of the elements. This allows us to compare the effect of failed original test cases. In order to avoid biases towards a particular faulty implementation, we put all original test cases and their results of the faulty versions in the same pool for analysis and treat them homogenously.

In total, we executed 22,503 follow-up test cases and also 22,503 original test cases. These two figures are the same because we use metamorphic relations with two input-output pairs in this experiment. For the original version, we execute 3,987 pairs of test cases, and for each faulty version, we execute 3,086 pairs of test cases. To facilitate us to evaluate the effectiveness of test cases, we also mark every test case to be successful or failed, according to the expected result of the arithmetic expression. The result is shown in the next section.

Empirical Results

In this section, we will present the empirical results of the experiment and discuss our observations from the results. In summary, our experimental result shows that our approach uses 16% less in terms of effort to detect 13% more in terms of failures, compared to the control experiment having no prior confirmation of test results of original test cases.

We first analyze the overhead, including failed original test cases for online testing. According to the previously mentioned experimental setup, we have collected a pool of 18,516 (= 3,086 × 6) pairs of test cases from the six faulty versions. Some of the pairs contain failed original test cases. We evenly partition the pool into 18 groups so that each group consists of around 1,000 test cases. For the i-th group (for i = 1 to 18), we use database queries to help us randomly draw around $5i$ percent of its elements having failed original test cases and all elements having successful original test cases to calculate the overhead in terms of test result checking. The total number of elements drawn from each group is shown in Table 1.

Table 1. No. of elements drawn from selected groups

Group	2	4	6	8	10	12	14	16	18	Total
Percentages of failed test cases drawn	10%	20%	30%	40%	50%	60%	70%	80%	90%	-
No. of elements drawn	767	791	809	839	885	904	945	973	997	7,910

The calculation of the *overhead* of a test pair is as follows.

- If no violation of the associated metamorphic relation is detected, then the overhead value is zero. It is because the test pair cannot reveal any failure.
- If a violation of the associated metamorphic relation is detected, then the overhead value is equal to the number of actual failure-causing test case(s) in the test pair. In other words, if both test cases are failure-causing inputs, the overhead value will be two; otherwise, it will be one.

We further define that the number of additional test result checking to confirm the failure-causing inputs for a set of test pairs, denoted by Ω, is the sum of the overhead of every test pair in the set.

Figure 3 shows the value of Ω for 10%, 20% and up to 90% of total number of the failed original test cases of a group for the calculation. The mean value is 141 and the standard derivation is 29.4. (We are aware that there are inadequate numbers of data to calculate a good standard derivation statistically. We show the value just to give readers an impression about the skewness of data set.)

As expected, the value of Ω increases when the percentage increases. When more failed original test cases are added to a set for the calculation of Ω, the chance to detect a failure increases.

However, as we increase the number of test cases from 762 (for group 2) to 997 (for group 18), the change in Ω is moderate and is equal to 77 (= 173 – 96). When around 10% of failed original test cases are included, the value of Ω is 96. This initial value, 96, is even larger than the cumulated change, 77, increasing the percentages from 10% to 90%.

It confirms our assertion that the inclusion of small percentages of failed original test cases for the online testing of a service accounts for a major source of overhead in terms of additional test result checking. This substantiates our recommendation of using successful original test cases only for online testing to alleviate the test oracle problem.

We also observe that the overall percentage is not high. The mean is 15.9%. It suggests that even testers had to include inevitably some failed

Figure 3. The overheads for different percentages of failed original test cases

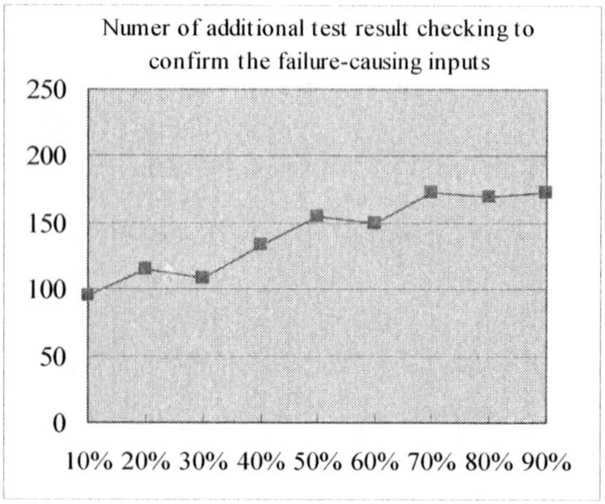

Figure 4. The number of missed detection of failure-causing inputs

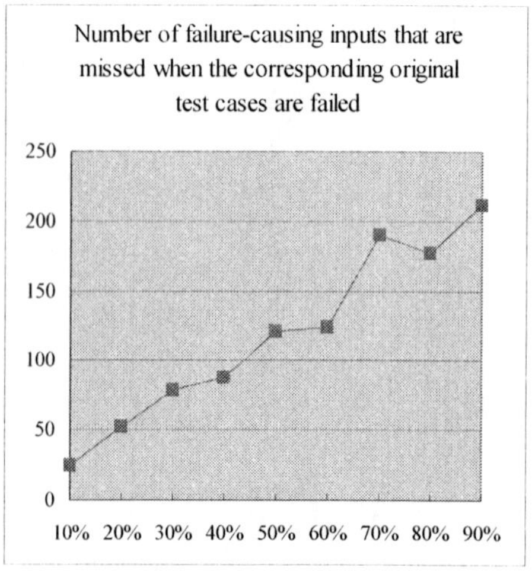

original test cases; measures should be taken to minimize such an inclusion.

We further examine the chance that we would miss to detect a failure if some failed original test cases are used for online testing. In our experiment, we use simple equations (instead of inequality) as metamorphic relations deliberately. We recall that, in our methodology, an original test case is known to be successful. It follows that any failure detected by the metamorphic testing approach would be due to the failure of the follow-up test case. On the other hand, when no violation of a metamorphic relation (in the form of equation) could be detected, the follow-up test case will be regarded as successful in the experiment.

For a set of test pairs, we define ω as the number of test pairs that each pair consists of one failed original test case and one follow-up test case, and at the same time, the associated metamorphic relation cannot detect the failure. The ω thus measures the missed opportunities to detect failures for online testing.

We also use the data sets reported in Table 1 to calculate ω for each group. The results are shown in Figure 4. The mean value is 118.7, that is, 13% of all failure-causing cases. The corresponding standard derivation is 64.2. The minimum is 25 for Group 2 (that is, the 10% group) and the maximum is 212 for Group 18 (that is, the 90% group).

The trend of missed detection of failures ω is increasing as the percentage of failed original test cases included in a group increases. Moreover, the number of missed detection appears proportional to the percentages of failed original test cases in the data set. This observation looks interesting and warrants further investigations.

RELATED WORK

Literatures on function testing research for SOA applications or Web services are not plenty. Bloomberg (2002) overviews a few major types of testing activity for testing Web services. We refer interested readers to the work of Bloomberg (Bloomberg, 2002) for the overview. In the rest of the section, we review selected related work on providing tools for testing, exception handling testing, generation of test cases and test result evaluation for service-oriented programs.

The use of the testing tool is an indispensable part to automate testing activities. Dustar and Haslinger (2004) propose to develop an experimental testing tool prototype to conduct batch mode and online mode testing. Their tool is reported to expect to handle several types of testing such as functional test and reliability test. Deng et al., (2004) extend AGENDA, a database application testing tool that populates database instances as a part of a test case, to test Web-based database applications. Rather than populating test database instances, SOATest (Parasoft, 2005) also reads data from different data sources to conduct testing. On the Internet, there are quite a few tools to conduct load and stress tests for Web services. Their discussions are not within the scope of this article.

To generate test cases, Offutt and Xu (2004) propose a set of mutation operators to perturb messages of Web services. They also suggest three types of rules to develop test cases based on the XML schema of messages. Their initial result on a sample application shows that 78% of seeded faults can be revealed. These faults include communication faults in SOAP, faults in statements for database query languages and conventional faults. The mutated messages could be considered as a method to construct follow-up test cases in the sense of metamorphic testing. Their empirical study of their approach is valuable. Rather than injecting faults to messages, Looker and Xu (2003) inject faults in SOAP-based programs to test the programs for robustness.

Chen et al., (2004a) also aim at testing for robustness. They focus on testing the exception handling of Java Web services through a data flow coverage approach. They propose to inject faults to system calls to trigger exception throws and require test cases to cover the exception-oriented def-use relations. Through their subject programs are Java-based Web service program; their techniques are not specialized to services testing.

Tsai et al., (2004, 2005) propose an approach to testing Web services that each service has multiple implementations with the same intended functionality. They apply test cases to a set of implementations of the same intended functionality progressively. Their test results are ranked by a majority voting strategy to assign a winner as the test oracle. A small set of winning implementations is selected for the integration testing purpose. At an integration testing level, they follow the same approach except using a weighted version of the majority voting strategy instead. To deal with the test case selection problem, their research group (Tsai et al., 2002a) proposes to generate test cases based on WSDL. Although WSDL-based testing has been proposed for a few years and implemented in testing tools such as SOATest (Parasoft, 2005), their version of WSDL (Tsai et al., 2002b) extends the standardized WSDL (W3C, 2001) to include features to express semantics. It is not difficult to use other voting strategies instead of the majority voting strategy in their approach.

The advantages of semantics checking are also observed by other researchers. An immediate example is our adaptation of metamorphic relation in this article. Keckel and Lohmann (2005), on the other hand, propose to apply the notion of design by contract to conduct testing for Web services. They suggest defining formal contracts to describe the behavior of functions and interactions of Web services. Based on the contracts, combinatorial testing is suggested to apply to conduct conformance testing against the contracts of intended services.

Our approach uses metamorphic relations to construct follow-up test cases. It is not a fault-based approach; whereas Looker and Xu (2003) suggest a fault-based approach to testing for program robustness. In addition, unlike the work of Offutt and Xu (2004), these follow-up test cases in our approach are intentional to allow automated test result evaluations. A follow-up test case triggers a service to produce an output. The output of a follow-up test case is allowed to be different from the output of the original test case. Hence, it can be applied to configurations when multiple implementations of the same functionality are too expensive to be used. This distinguishes our work from Tsai et al., (2005). Our approach checks test results amongst themselves; whereas the work of Keckel and Lohmann (2005) checks the test results against some formal contract specifications. Chen et al., (2004a) is a white-box-centric approach; whereas ours is a black-box-centric approach. The tools (Dustar & Haslinger, 2004; Parasoft, 2005) appear to be developed as an integrated testing tool that includes a number of different testing modules. Their architectures are unclear to us at this moment. Our metamorphic service is an access wrapper to facilitate off-line and online testing of a service. We aim at reducing the amount of non-core elements from our metamorphic service. In this way, when exposing the function to other services, we would like to develop the approach further so that it enjoys a good scalability.

DISCUSSION

We have presented an approach to online testing and an experiment on a simple application to study metamorphic testing for services testing in the previous sections. The approach is useful for the online testing of a service if testers have difficulties to obtain the expected results of a test case in a cost-effective manner. The test oracle problem has been identified for many years (see also Beizer, 1990). In practice, many testers validate their software without a formal test oracle. Metamorphic testing is an approach towards the problem when a metamorphic relation exists and could be identified. We believe that this trend will continue for services testing.

In the rest of this section, we discuss the threat to validity of the experiment. The evaluation of using the metamorphic testing approach for services testing in the online mode is conducted in a small application. The application domain of the subject application is generic that it uses the basic computing functionality, namely a fundamental set of arithmetic operations and basic (communicative and associative) properties to define metamorphic relations. It is unknown about the impact on the results when certain domain-specific knowledge is taken into account to both define metamorphic relations and selections of test cases. We merely use a small number of faulty versions to conduct the experiment to discuss our findings. The statistics may be different if other faulty versions are used. Our subject program does contain real faults and hence some metamorphic relation instances are violated even if the original version is used. We believe that it is common for a typical testing of a newly-coded software program. However, the assumption is not valid if other rigorous quality assurance techniques such as rigorous regressions, code inspections or formal methods have been applied to a software development project. We have evaluated our approach on the Microsoft .NET 2003 platform only. The present implementation of the subject program is not portable to other platforms. There is a threat to interpret the empirical results in other configurations. We have reviewed the set test cases and the set follow-up test cases, and use a commercial spreadsheet to help us to check whether the target relation is maintained in the reviewed samples.

CONCLUSIONS AND FUTURE WORK

Testing services in a services-computing environment needs to deal with a number of issues. They include: (i) The unknown communication partners until the service discovery; (ii) the imprecise blackbox information of software components; (iii) the potential existence of non-identical implementations of the same service; and (iv) the expected behavior of a service potentially depending on the behavior of competing services. In this article, we treat a service as a reusable software module with a well-defined function. A service can introduce itself so that other services can discover and use the service. Services communicate amongst themselves through well-defined messages and interfaces. A message is an input or an output of a service.

We have presented a testing approach to the online testing support of service-oriented applications. We formulate the notion of metamorphic service; the service that has the characteristics of being an access wrapper, the wrapper encapsulates the access for the service under test and implements the metamorphic testing approach. We also propose to use the successful test case for off-line testing as the original test case for online testing, as test oracle is much more likely to be available for off-line testing. Using our online testing methodology, testers builds a bridge between the test oracle available in the off-line testing mode and the test oracle problem encountered in the online testing mode. The services approach to conducting an online test alleviates the problem (i). It delays the binding of communication partners of the follow-up test cases after service discovery. Our realization of the metamorphic testing approach alleviates the problems (ii), (iii) and (iv).

We have also conducted an experiment to evaluate the feasibility of our proposal. The experimental results encouragingly indicate that, on average, when the set of original test cases are unknown to be successful, an extra 16% effort to check test results and a 13% reduction of failure detection are observed. This supports our proposal that original test cases should be (much) better to be successful, particularly when the checking is (much) less costly when it can be conducted in the off-line testing mode.

There are quite a number of future directions of research. We have not evaluated our proposal extensively. We plan to conduct more experiments. The way to control the chain reaction of the follow-up test cases generations due to interferences of multiple metamorphic services warrants more researches. We also plan to measure the degree of code coverage or fault coverage of our approach.

ACKNOWLEDGMENT

We would like to thank the program co-chairs of The First International Workshop on Services Engineering (SEIW 2005) for inviting us to extend the preliminary version (Chan et al., 2005a) to contribute to the special issue. We would also like to thank anonymous reviewer of the article. Special thanks should be given to Mr. Kwong–Tim Chan, Mr. Hoi-Shun Tam, Mr. Kwun-Ting Lee, Mr. Yuk-Ching Lam and Mr. King–Lun Yiu of the Hong Kong Institute of Vocational Education (Tsang Yi) who do the experiments presented in this article. Part of the research was done when Chan was with The University of Hong Kong. This research is supported by grants of the Research Grants Council of Hong Kong (Project Nos. HKUST 6170/04E and CITYU1195/03E).

REFERENCES

Bass, L., Clements, P., & Kazman, R. (2003). *Software architecture in practice*. Addison Wesley.

Beizer, B. (1990). *Software Testing Techniques*. New York:Van Nostrand Reinhold.

Bloomberg, J. (2002). Testing web services today and tomorrow. Retrieved from http://www-106.ibm.com/developerworks/rational/library/content/rationaledge/oct02/webtesting_therationaledge_oct02.pdf

Chan, F.T., Chen, T.Y., Cheung, S.C., Lau, M.F., & Yiu, S.M. (1998). Application of metamorphic testing in numerical analysis. In *Proceedings of IASTED International Conference on Software Engineering (SE 1998)*,(pp. 191–197). Calgary, Canada: ACTA Press.

Chan, W. K., Cheung, S. C., & Leung, K. R. P. H. (2005a). Towards a metamorphic testing methodology for service-oriented software applications, The First International Workshop on Services Engineering (SEIW 2005). In *Proceedings of the 5th Annual International Conference on Quality Software (QSIC 2005)*. Los Alamitos, CA:IEEE Computer Society.

Chan, W. K., Cheung, S. C., & Tse, T. H. (2005b). Fault-based testing of database application programs with conceptual data model. In *Proceedings of the 5th Annual International Conference on Quality Software (QSIC 2005)*. Los Alamitos, CA:IEEE Computer Society.

Chan, W. K., Chen, T. Y., Lu, Heng, Tse, T. H., & Yau, S. S. (2005c). A metamorphic approach to integration testing of context-sensitive middleware-based applications. In *Proceedings of the 5th Annual International Conference on Quality Software (QSIC 2005)*. Los Alamitos, CA: IEEE Computer Society.

Chen, F., Ryder, B., Milanova, A., & Wannacott, D. (2004a). Testing of java Web services for robustness. In *Proceedings of the International Symposium on Software Testing and Analysis (ISSTA 2004)*, (pp. 23–34).New York: ACM Press.

Chen, T. Y., Huang, D. H., Tse, T. H., & Zhou, Z. Q. (2004b). Case studies on the selection of useful relations in metamorphic testing. In *Proceedings of the 4th Ibero-American Symposium on Software Engineering and Knowledge Engineering (JIISIC 2004)*, (pp. 569–583). Madrid, Spain: Polytechnic University of Madrid.

Chen, T. Y., Tse, T. H., & Zhou, Z. Q. (2002). Semi-proving: An integrated method based on global symbolic evaluation and metamorphic testing. In *Proceedings of the ACM SIGSOFT*

International Symposium on Software Testing and Analysis (ISSTA 2002). (pp. 191–195). New York:ACM Press.

Chen, T. Y., Tse, T. H., & Zhou, Z. Q. (2003). Fault-based testing without the need of oracles. *Information and Software Technology, 45* (1), 1–9.

Chen, T.Y., Cheung, S.C., & Yiu, S.M. (1998). *Metamorphic testing: A new approach for generating next test cases* (Tech. Rep. HKUST-CS98-01). Hong Kong: Hong Kong University of Science and Technology, Department of Computer Science.

Chunyang Ye, S.C. Cheung & W.K. Chan (2006). Publishing and composition of atomicity-equivalent services for B2B collaboration. In *Proceedings of the 28th International Conference on Software Engineering (ICSE 2006).* Los Alamitos, CA:IEEE Computer Society.

Colan, M. (2004). Service-oriented architecture expands the vision of Web Services, part 1: Characteristics of service-oriented architecture. Retrieved from http://www-128.ibm.com/developerworks/webservices/library/ws-soaintro.html

Curbera, F., Duftler, M., Khalaf, R., Nagy, W., Mukhi, N. & Weerawarana, S. (2002). Unraveling the web services web: An introduction to SOAP, WSDL, and UDDI. *IEEE Internet Computing, 6* (2), 86–93.

Deng, Y., Frankl, P., & Wang, J. (2004). Testing web database applications, SECTION: Workshop on testing, analysis and verification of web services (TAV-WEB) papers. *SIGSOFT Software Engineering Notes, 29* (5).

Dustar, S., & Haslinger, S. (2004). Testing of service-oriented architectures: A practical approach. In *Proceedings of the 5th Annual International Conference on Object-Oriented and Internet-Based Technologies, Concepts, and Applications for a Networked World (NODe 2004),* (pp. 97–112). Berlin, Heideberg: Springer-Verlag.

Frankl, P. G. & Weyuker, E. J. (1988). An applicable family of data flow testing criteria. *IEEE Transactions on Software Engineering, 14* (10), 1483–1498.

Kapfhammer, G. M., & Soffa, M. L. (2003). A family of test adequacy criteria for database-driven applications. In *Proceedings of the 9th European software engineering conference held jointly with 11th ACM SIGSOFT international symposium on Foundations of software engineering (ESEC/FSE 2003)* (pp. 98–107). New York: ACM Press.

Keckel, R. & Lohmann, M. (2005). Towards contract-based testing of Web services. *Electronic Notes in Theoretical Computer Science, 116*, 145–156.

Kreger, H. (2003). Fulfilling the web services promise. *Communications of the ACM, 46* (6), 29–34.

Looker, N., & Xu, J. (2003, October). Assessing the dependability of SOAP RPC based Web services by fault injection. In *Proceeding of IEEE International Workshop on Object-Oriented, Real-Time and Dependable Systems*, Capri Island.

Mecella, M. & Pernici, B. (2003), Designing wrapper components for e-services in integrating heterogeneous systems. *The VLDB Journal, 10* (1), 2–15.

Mukhi, N. K., Konuru, R., & Curbera, F. (2004). Cooperative middleware specialization for service oriented architectures. In *Proceedings of the 13th international World Wide Web conference on Alternate track papers & posters (WWW 2004)*, (pp. 206–215) New York: ACM Press.

OASIS (2005). Universal Description, Discovery and Integration (UDDI) version 3.0.2. Retrieved from http://uddi.org/pubs/uddi_v3.htm

Offutt, J. & Xu, W. (2004). Generating test cases for web services using data perturbation, SECTION: Workshop on testing, analysis and verification of web services (TAV-WEB) papers, *SIGSOFT Software Engineering Notes*, *29* (5).

Parasoft Corporation (2005). SOATest, Retrieved from http://www.parasoft.com/jsp/products/home.jsp?product=SOAP&itemId=101

Rajasekaran, P., Miller, J. A., Verma, K., Sheth, A. P. (2004). Enhancing Web services description and discovery to facilitate composition. In *Proceeding of The First International Workshop on Semantic Web Services and Web Process Composition (SWSWPC 2004)*, LNCS 3387, (pp. 55-68). Berlin, Heideberg: Springer-Verlag.

Tsai, W. T., Chen, Y., Paul, R., Huang, H., Zhou, X., & Wei, X. (2005). Adaptive testing, oracle generation, and test case ranking for Web services. In *Proceedings of the 29th Annual International Computer Software and Applications conference (COMPSAC 2005)*, (pp. 101–106). Los Alamitos, CA :IEEE Computer Society.

Tsai, W. T., Chen, Y., Cao, Z. Bai, X., Hung, H., & Paul, R. (2004). Testing Web services using progressive group testing. In *Proceedings of Advanced Workshop on Content Computing (AWCC 2004)*, LNCS 3309, (pp. 314–322). Berlin, Heideberg:Springer-Verlag.

Tsai, W. T., Paul, R., Wang, Y., Fan, C., 7 Wang, D. (2002a). Extending WSDL to facilitate Web services testing. In *Proceedings of The 7th IEEE International Symposium on High-Assurance Systems Engineering (HASE 2002)*, (pp. 171–172) Los Alamitos, CA: IEEE Computer Society.

Tsai, W. T., Paul, R., Song, W., & Cao Z. (2002b). Coyote: An XML-based framework for Web services testing. In *Proceedings of The 7th IEEE International Symposium on High-Assurance Systems Engineering (HASE 2002)*, (pp. 173–176). Los Alamitos, CA: IEEE Computer Society.

Tse, T. H., Yau, S. S., Chan, W. K., Lu, H., & Chen T. Y. (2004). Testing context-sensitive middleware-based software applications. In *Proceedings of the 28th Annual International Computer Software and Applications Conference (COMPSAC 2004)*, (pp. 458–466). Los Alamitos, CA:IEEE Computer Society.

W3C (2003). SOAP Version 1.2 Part 1: Messaging Framework. Retrieved from http://www.w3.org/tr/soap12-part1/

W3C (2002). Web Services Activity, Retrieved from: http://www.w3.org/2002/ws

W3C (2005). Web Services Description Language (WSDL) Version 2.0 Part 1: Core Language. Retrieved from http://www.w3.org/tr/wsdl20/

W3C (2004). Extensible Markup Language (XML) 1.0 (Third Edition). Retrieved from http://www.w3.org/TR/2004/REC-xml-20040204/

W3C (2001). XML Schema. Retrieved from http://www.w3.org/xml/schema

Umar, A. (1997). *Application reengineering. Building web-based applications and dealing with legacy.* Cliffs, NJ: Prentice-Hall, Englewood

Zhu, H., Hall, P. A. V., & May, J. H. R. (1997). Software unit test coverage and adequacy. *ACM Computing Survey, 29* (4), 366–427.

ENDNOTES

1. All correspondence should be addressed to Dr. W. K. Chan at Department of Computer Science and Engineering, Hong Kong University of Science and Technology, Clear Water Bay, Kowloon, Hong Kong. Tel: (+852) 2358 7016. Fax: (+852) 2358 1477. Email: wkchan@cse.ust.hk .
2. XML stands for Extensible Markup Language (W3C, 2004).

[3] IBM also proposes to design stateless Web services when it introduces service-oriented architecture (see http://www-128.ibm.com/developerworks/Webservices/library/ws-soaintro.html)

[4] We refer readers to Section 0 for the role of a tester in the design and implementation of metamorphic relations, and refer readers to Section 0 for the illustration to construct test cases in the metamorphic approach.

[5] Although services are highly recommended to publish their functional properties for other services to judge its usefulness in their areas of concerns and to subscribe to use the service, yet the design of metamorphic relations, the implicit form of functional properties, is not within the scope of this paper. We refer interested readers to a case study (Chen et al., 2004) on the selection of effective metamorphic relations for more details.

This work was previously published in the International Journal of Web Services Research, Vol. 4, Issue 2, edited by L. J. Zhang, pp. 61-81, copyright 2007 by IGI Publishing, formerly known as Idea Group Publishing (an imprint of IGI Global).

Chapter 4.51
E-Auctioning by the U.S. Federal Communications Commission

Trevor R. Roycroft
Roycroft Consulting, USA

INTRODUCTION

Market economies rest on a foundation of the private ownership of resources. Certain resources, however, have been managed outside of the market mechanism, even in the United States' decidedly pro-free-market economy. The management of radio frequencies, or spectrum, is a prime example of government control of a valuable resource. Spectrum management is practiced by governments around the globe, and the experience of the U.S. Federal Communications Commission (FCC) provides a valuable illustration of how management of this resource may be improved through the use of electronic resources.

BACKGROUND

The portion of the electromagnetic spectrum consisting of the frequencies ranging from 3 kilohertz (KHz) to 300 gigahertz (GHz), commonly known as radio frequencies, represents a natural resource that may be exploited through technological means. When considered in the context of other naturally occurring resources, radio frequencies are unique. On a geographic basis, radio frequencies are limited but are uniformly distributed. As long as the strength of the radio signal is controlled, the same amount of radio frequency is available per square mile in the U.S., Uganda, or any other nation. Each nation must live with what is available within its borders; the import and export of radio frequencies is not possible. While the resource is limited, it is continuously renewable—each frequency becomes available again at each new moment in time.

In addition to the geographically limited nature of the resource, various portions of the radio-frequency spectrum have properties that affect their usefulness. As the frequency of a radio wave increases, the wavelength decreases. Smaller wavelengths have a higher likelihood of being deflected by physical objects such as buildings, foliage, or even water droplets in the atmosphere in the form of rain, snow, or fog. Longer wavelengths easily can penetrate objects. These differences in the physical properties of spectrum make certain frequency ranges more useful (and more valuable) than others. The differences in the quality of spectrum place further impetus for management of the resource. By matching the performance needs of a technology with a spectrum range, the resource can be used more effectively. For example, broadcast radio, which may encounter significant environmental barriers associated with mobile receiving units (in automobiles) or stationary receiving units (inside dwellings) benefits from the use of relatively longer wavelengths associated with the AM and FM frequency bands. On the other hand, satellite-to-earth transmission can rely on a fixed ground station antenna that can be oriented skyward to avoid physical barriers such as walls and trees and, thus, can perform well with relatively shorter wavelengths associated with higher frequencies.

Concerns regarding interference between competing users of spectrum have been the prime motivation for strict control of most of radio-frequency resources (Noam, 1998). Analog technologies, which were associated with early radio-frequency applications, suffered functional degradation if they were not guaranteed the exclusive use of a specific radio frequency. Thus, management of radio frequencies by the FCC and other governmental bodies around the globe traditionally are based on an approach that systematically organizes the spectrum resource into logical groupings and then assigns exclusive rights to use the spectrum to certain individuals or organizations.

U.S. POLICY AND SPECTRUM MANAGEMENT

In order ro facilitate the management of spectrum in the U.S., the entire range of radio frequencies is divided into bands or blocks that are associated with specific applications or technologies, such as broadcast television or cellular telephones. These divisions are known as allocations. Within the allocation of radio frequency, the bands face further subdivision, known as allotments. Allotments are associated with a specific geographic area; for example, a specific frequency to be used as a television channel in a specific metropolitan area or a frequency to be used by cellular telephone companies in a rural area. With these divisions, the spectrum then may be assigned, or licensed. The grant of a license gives the user the ability to provide the specified service in the geographic area and may impose additional conditions on the use of the radio frequencies, including the type of technology (analog vs. digital) and the strength of the signal.

Assigning Spectrum in the U.S.

While economists have advocated private property rights for spectrum for years (Coase, 1965), U.S. law prohibits private ownership of spectrum (Shelanski & Huber, 1998). Thus, administrative means were traditionally used to manage the resource (FCC, 1997b). Applications that had the most significant potential to suffer from interference degradation, such as broadcast radio and television, required significant capital investments, which led to relatively little competition for the required spectrum resource. In geographic areas where the economics of the market was substantial enough to lead to higher demand for the resource, comparative hearings were used to determine which of the competing entities would be eligible to receive an exclusive license. In a comparative hearing, the competing interests (typically a broadcast radio or television station) would present their cases before an administrative law judge, who ultimately decide whether the public interest would be better served by one or the other of the competing interests.

Impact of Cellular Technology

With technological change, significant difficulties emerged with the then-existing approach to spectrum management. While radiotelephones were commercialized in the 1950s, the development of analog cellular telephone technology during the 1970s offered the potential for a much broader dissemination of wireless telephony. By carefully limiting signal strength, a limited amount of spectrum could be reused in multiple adjacent cell sites. While the previous radiotelephone service might enable 40 to 50 simultaneous calls in a metropolitan area, the new cellular technology potentially enabled thousands of simultaneous calls, which generated the possibility of a much larger subscriber base (Rappaport, 2002). The new technology required that spectrum be licensed to companies that essentially would resell use of the radio frequency to the public, which the FCC deemed Commercial Mobile Radio Service (CMRS). Underlying the distribution of spectrum for the initial cellular telephone technology was a policy of duopoly. In each geographic area, only two licenses would be granted, with one offered first to the local telephone company serving the geographic area and the second available to other businesses. The limited availability of licenses combined with the commercial potential of the new service led to high levels of demand for available licenses. As a result, the FCC was confronted with a new problem with the allocation of spectrum resources. Multiple competing interests were interested in the limited number of licenses, with 200 applicants vying for the first 30 licenses made available (FCC, 1997b). Comparative hearings were the only means by which the FCC could settle the issue of which of the limited number of licenses should go to whom. Complicating the comparative hearing process was the similarity of the applicants. As a result, the administrative process was faced with numerous situations that, for all practical purposes, were ties between competing interests. The inefficiency of the comparative hearing process led to significant delays in the distribution of the initial cellular licenses.

Following the problems associated with the distribution of spectrum licenses through comparative hearing, the FCC sought authority for an alternative mechanism—lotteries. Given the prevalence of ties in the qualifications of those seeking licenses, the theory of the FCC lottery scheme was based on random selection from a qualified pool of interested parties. With the winner picked randomly, ties would be broken, and the speed of distribution would be promoted. However, the process of qualifying lottery participants also introduced delays, with the first prequalifications taking about two years. To remedy this situation, the FCC sought further authority from the U.S. Congress to eliminate the need for prequalification. With prequalification eliminated, lottery participants quickly obtained licenses, but now another set of problems emerged. As the public became aware of the value of the resource that was being given away through the lottery process, large numbers of individuals sought to participate in the lotteries. Given the pre-Internet period, the paperwork required by the FCC to participate in a lottery presented a hurdle for those uninitiated in the operations of U.S. federal government agencies. Thus, third-party businesses, which came to be known as license mills, emerged. The license mills would process and submit the necessary paperwork for participation in a lottery. This rent-seeking activity resulted in hundreds of millions of dollars of revenue for the license mills (Hazlett & Michaels, 1993).

While the rent-seeking activity associated with the license mills was socially wasteful, further problems emerged after the licenses were awarded. Licenses were awarded relatively quickly; however, the licenses were not put to immediate use. Rather, a secondary market for licenses emerged, resulting in windfall profits for license holders. Delays once again were introduced into the process of distributing licenses while lottery winners sought the highest bidder for their licenses.

The problems associated with the distribution of spectrum licenses led the FCC to approach Congress again to revise the method by which licenses could be granted for spectrum, resulting in the establishment of the FCC's electronic auctions.

AUCTIONS

Auction authority was granted to the FCC as part of the Omnibus Budget Reconciliation Act of 1993. The auction authority that was granted to the FCC was quite limited. The interests of broadcasters and other entities who already utilized spectrum resources without charge were protected by the law. The authority granted to the FCC limited the auction process to spectrum that was to be newly transferred from governmental use to non-governmental use and that also was to be used by the licensee to generate revenues from subscribers for transmitting and receiving signals over the licensed spectrum (47 USC, §309(j)(9) and §309(j)(2)(A)).

The newly available spectrum ultimately was used to enable a variety of new services, including digital cellular services (Personal Communications Services [PCS]), fixed high-speed data services (LMDS), direct broadcast satellite service (DBS), and paging services (FCC, 1997b). The legislation required that the FCC take a flexible approach to determine the best bidding method for the spectrum resource.

Designing an Efficient Auction

Every market transaction is based on information. The price at which an object is bought and sold depends on the information available to the buyer and to the seller. With regard to the newly available spectrum that the FCC was charged with selling, there was a distinct asymmetry of information between the seller (the FCC) and potential buyers (companies interested in providing wireless services). Obviously, the FCC wanted to generate the highest level of revenues possible from the sale of spectrum rights, while the buyers wanted to pay as little as possible. Thus, designing an auction structure that resulted in the highest level of revenues was a priority for the FCC.

Spectrum rights have an interesting economic characteristic. Unlike an object of art or a piece of sports memorabilia, which may have a unique personal value to the purchaser, spectrum rights are likely to provide a similar value to any purchaser. This situation is known in the economics of information as common values (Baye, 2000). For example, suppose that the FCC were to auction five new licenses to provide a new digital wireless service to the Boston, Massachusetts, market area. Because the service is new, *ex ante*, no firm knows the exact value of these licenses. To any firm winning a license, however, it is likely that the profits associated from providing the service will be similar. In formulating a bidding strategy for a license, each bidder estimates the costs and revenues expected if the license were to be won. Once this calculation is completed, the bidder has an estimate of the highest bid that they would possibly be willing to make. While it is likely that the various bidders would come up with similar valuations of the licenses, it is unlikely that the valuations would be identical. There would be some variation in the valuations.

This situation results in a potential risk to any prospective buyer. If common values are present, then the high bidder in any auction is likely to be the party that has experienced a random variation in calculating the expected value of the license on the high side (i.e., the winner likely will pay too much for the object). This outcome has been dubbed the winner's curse. Of course, potential bidders are aware of the winner's curse; thus, rational bidders will follow a bidding strategy that leads them to shave their bid (i.e., to not bid as much as they think the object is actually worth). From the seller's perspective, the winner's curse will lead to lower auction revenues, as buyers will not be willing to bid up to their true valuation of the object. Thus, the FCC was interested in developing an auction format that would mitigate the impact of the winner's curse.

Figure 1. How an FCC auction is initiated (FCC Wireless Bureau Web site)

How is an FCC Auction Initiated?

1. Comment Public Notice
(Approximately four to six months prior to auction)
A public notice is released seeking comment on auction procedures.

2. Procedures Public Notice
(Approximately three to five months prior to auction)
A public notice is released providing potential participants with the procedures, terms, and conditions for the auction event.

3. Seminar
(Approximately 45 days prior to auction)
A free pre-auction seminar is conducted for potential participants in order to introduce them to the auction rules and process. The bidding software is demonstrated.

4. Short-Form (FCC Form 175) Application Filing Deadline
(Approximately 30 days prior to auction)
Form 175 application, which must be filed electronically, collects basic information about the applicant.

5. Filing Status Public Notice
(Approximately one week after the filing deadline)
After the deadline for filing, the FCC reviews all timely filed short-form applications and deems them accepted, incomplete, or rejected. The status of the applications is communicated to the public through the release of this public notice.

6. Upfront Payment Deadline
(Approximately two weeks prior to auction)
Potential bidders must submit a refundable deposit, which is used to purchase the bidding units required to place bids in the auction.

7. Short-Form Application Resubmission Deadline
(Approximately two weeks prior to auction)
Form 175 applications that were deemed incomplete must be refiled by this deadline, which often coincides with the upfront payment deadline.

8. Qualified Bidders Public Notice
(Approximately 10 to 12 days prior to auction)
This public notice lists the bidders qualified to participate in the auction.

9. Qualified Bidders Registration
Immediately following the release of the Qualified Bidders Public Notice, the bidder registration process begins.

10. Mock Auction
(Approximately two to three days prior to auction)
To ensure that bidders understand the auction process, the FCC sponsors a mock auction as a service to the qualified bidders. The mock auction allows bidders to work with the bidding system, become comfortable with the rules and conduct of the auction, and familiarize themselves with the telephonic bidding process.

11. Auction Begins

Compounding the FCC's auction design problem was the complexity of the objects to be auctioned. Policy objectives of promoting competition in the provision of wireless services and also promoting small-business participation in the auction process resulted in the creation of numerous market areas. For the PCS auctions, a total of 493 market areas (known as basic trading areas) were used, and multiple licenses were available within each Basic Trading Area. This led to the availability of more than 2,500 licenses for 10-year terms (Bykowsky, Cull, & Ledyard, 2000). Thus, a potential bidder would be very concerned about the complementary and substitute relationships of licenses and would be faced with a complex and risky environment.

Electronic Simultaneous Multiple-Round Auctions

In order to solve these problems, the FCC developed electronic auctions, which allow users to participate over the Internet or by telephone. All licenses are made available for bidding during the entire auction period, which creates the simultaneous nature of the auctions. The auction is conducted in rounds, each having a set duration. At the end of each round, the bids are posted on a Web site for review by the bidders. This format allows bidders to evaluate the bids placed by other participants.

While the duration of rounds is established by the FCC, the number of rounds are not. Bidding is allowed to continue until all bidder activity ceases. When this occurs, the auction is closed.

The FCC's approach also allows bidders to place combinatorial (package bids) in which the bidder can place bids on groups of licenses. Package bidding is particularly important where complementary relationships between licenses exist. For example, a firm that is planning on offering service on a regional basis might want to purchase licenses in two or three basic trading areas. With the package bidding approach, a firm could place bids on the entire group of licenses in which it was interested. Package bidding will tend to increase auction revenues, since it encourages bidders to reveal their perceptions on the values of groups of licenses.

Look and Feel of the Auction Web Interface

The auction interface requires qualified bidders to log in, and then it presents menus of information, including public notices associated with the specific auction, pages where bidding histories can be reviewed, and pages where bids can be placed. Several screen shots from the FCC's auction Web interface have been provided in the appendix.

FCC Auction Structure and the Winner's Curse

Recall that the winner's curse is related to the bidder's lack of information. When formulating their bidding strategies in isolation, bidders will be reluctant to place bids up to their estimate of their true values. While prohibiting collusion, the FCC's auction structure offers an opportunity for bidders to exchange information by viewing all of the bids that are placed in each round. For example, if a potential bidder, when formulating its bidding strategy, calculates a value of $500,000 for a specific license, and after two or three rounds of the auction, the high bids observed are significantly lower than $500,000, then the bidder might want to reevaluate the analysis underlying its bid. Perhaps it made a mistake or overlooked something in the development of its valuation.

FCC AUCTION OUTCOMES

As of early 2005, the FCC had conducted 55 auctions, which generated about $44 billion in revenues, all of which have not been collected. The results of the auction process have overcome some of the difficulties associated with the granting of spectrum licenses through administrative hearings and through lotteries. Auctions generally have delivered the spectrum into the hands of those who can put it to use quickly (FCC, 1997b), and the auction process has a tiebreaker, as there can be only one winning bidder per license.

PROBLEMS WITH FCC AUCTIONS

As was discussed earlier, the auction approach utilized by the FCC encourages the sharing of information through the public availability of bidding information. Auction participants, however, are not allowed to exchange information privately, to stake out claims to certain licenses, or otherwise to collude (FCC, 2003). However, auction participants have been found to signal one another regarding their intentions by incorporating desired basic trading area numbers into their bid values (Cramton & Schwartz, 2000), a practice that the FCC now carefully monitors (FCC, 1997a). The biggest problems associated with the FCC's auction process have not been a result of the auction process itself but relate instead to separate policy mandates regarding small business participation in the auction process. Some have pointed to the general inefficiency of these set aside programs (Hazlett & Boliek, 1999), but the ultimate problem that emerged from the small business set-asides resulted in the authority to manage spectrum being partially wrestled from the FCC.

In order to accommodate the more limited financial capability of smaller-scale bidders, the FCC auction rules allowed winning bidders to pay off their winning bids on an installment plan. Following the completion of these so-called entrepreneur block auctions, several winning bidders encountered financial difficulties, and some filed for bankruptcy protection prior to paying off their installments. A pressing question that then needed to be answered was how the licenses of a bankrupt bidder would be disposed. The FCC thought that they should be returned so they could be auctioned off again. However, the jurisdiction of federal bankruptcy courts was now involved, and a process of judicial review that led to the U.S. Supreme Court was undertaken. Ironically, the Supreme Court ruled in favor of the license holders, which allowed the licenses to be treated as an asset of the bankrupt bidders. The result of these bankruptcies has been to reduce collections of auction revenues (CBO, 2002). It also removed the FCC from the process of controlling the distribution of these licenses.

FUTURE TRENDS

Despite the problems encountered to date, the FCC auction process generally is viewed as a success (Cramton, 1998, Hazlett, 1998), but there are dissenters (Morris, 2004). The structure of the FCC's auctions have been adopted by other nations following problematic outcomes with other formats (Anadalingam, 2001). Some non-U.S. auction formats have been viewed as successful (Crandall, 1998). Licenses for third-generation wireless services have been auctioned throughout Europe (Anderson, 2002). While there is no question that auctions are superior to other methods for generating revenues, whether they promote good spectrum management policy is an issue of concern. Spectrum licenses are founded on the assumption that the services utilizing the spectrum will suffer from interference. New technologies, such as digital spread spectrum, utilize intelligent devices, which are capable of coping better with interference. Some have suggested that the future of spectrum management will not require much management due to these new technologies (Noam, 1998). A major impediment to the advancement of these new technologies may be the existing licensing of spectrum, which leaves little room for the deployment of these new technologies (GAO, 2004). Of course, economists point to the superiority of property rights in spectrum (Hazlett, 2005); thus, it likely will be some time before the dust settles on the long-term need to license spectrum and to use auctions for that purpose.

CONCLUSION

Auctioning spectrum licenses is a major innovation in the governmental management of natural resources. The complexity of the economic process has been mitigated significantly due to the use of electronic resources. The ability to conduct simultaneous multiple-round auctions would have been limited significantly absent electronic means to process and distribute information in real time. Electronic spectrum auctions, as conducted by the FCC, have provided valuable lessons in the application of electronic technology to achieve policy objectives.

REFERENCES

47 U.S.C. §151 through §614. Communications Act of 1934. Retrieved May 4, 2006, from http://www.access.gpo.gov/uscode/title47/chapter5_html/

Anadalingam, G. (2001). On the use of Vickrey auctions for spectrum allocation in developing countries. *Proceedings of the 29th Research Conference on Communication, Information and Internet Policy, Telecommunications Policy Research Conference,* George Mason University School of Law, Arlington, VA. Retrieved May 4, 2006, from http://www.arxiv.org/pdf/cs.CY/0109065/

Anderson, C. (2002). Winner's curse: The 3G auctions were the last party of an old regime. *Wired, 10*(5). Retrieved May 4, 2006, from http://www.wired.com/wired/archive/10.05/change.html/

Baye, M.R. (2000). *Managerial economics and business strategy.* Boston: Irwin McGraw-Hill.

Bykowsky, M. M., Cull, R. J., & Ledyard, J. O. (2000). Mutually Destructive Bidding: The FCC Auction Design Problem. *Journal of Regulatory Economics, Vol. 17,* 205-228.

CBO. (2002). *The budget and economic outlook: Fiscal years 2003 to 2012, appendix B.* Washington, DC: U.S. Congressional Budget Office.

Coase, R. H. (1965). Evaluation of public policy relating to radio and television broadcasting: Social and economic issues. *Land Economics, 41,* 161-167.

Cramton, P. (1998, October). The efficiency of the FCC spectrum auctions. *Journal of Law and Economics, XLI,* 727-736.

Cramton, P., & Schwartz, J. A. (2000). Collusive bidding: Lessons from the FCC spectrum auctions. *Journal of Regulatory Economics, 17,* 229-252.

Crandall, R.W. (1998, October). New Zealand spectrum policy: A model for the United States. *Journal of Law and Economics, XLI,* 821-840.

FCC. (1997a). In *Re-applications of Mercury PCS II, LLC for facilities in the broadband personal communications systems in the D, E, and F blocks, notice of apparent liability for forfeiture,* FCC 97-388. Retrieved May 4, 2006, from http://wireless.fcc.gov/auctions/11/releases/fc970388.pdf/

FCC. (1997b). The FCC report to Congress on spectrum auctions. Federal Communications Commission, Wireless Telecommunications Bureau. *In the Matter of FCC Report to Congress on Spectrum Auctions,* WT Docket No. 97-150, FCC 97-353, October 9, 1997. Retrieved May 4, 2006, from http://wireless.fcc.gov/auctions/data/papersAndStudies/fc970353.pdf/

FCC. (2003). *In re-application of Northeast Communications of Wisconsin, Inc. For C Block facilities in the 710-716 and 740-746 Bands, notice of apparent liability for forfeiture.* DA 03-2723, August 27, 2003.

FCC Wireless Bureau Web site (n.d.). FCC auctions home. Retrieved May 4, 2006, from http://wireless.fcc.gov/auctions/default.htm?jon=about_auctions&page=3

GAO. (2004). *Spectrum management: Better knowledge needed to take advantage of technologies that may improve spectrum efficiency.* Washington, DC: U.S. General Accounting Office.

Hazlett, T. W. (1998, October). Assigning property rights to radio spectrum users: Why did FCC licenses auctions take 67 years? *Journal of Law and Economics,* XLI, 529-575.

Hazlett, T. W. (2005, Summer). Spectrum tragedies. *Yale Journal of Regulation, 22*, 242.

Hazlett, T. W., & Boliek, B. E. L. (1999). Use of designated entity preferences in assigning wireless licenses, *Federal Communications Law Journal, 51*(3), 639-662.

Hazlett, T. W., & Michaels, R. J. (1993). The cost of rent-seeking: Evidence from cellular telephone license lotteries. *Southern Economic Journal, 59*(3), 425-435.

Morris, A. C. (2004). Spectrum auctions: Distortionary input tax or efficient revenue instrument? *Proceedings of the 32nd Research Conference on Communication, Information and Internet Policy. Telecommunications Policy Research Conference,* George Mason University School of Law, Artlington, VA. Retrieved May 4, 2006, from http://web.si.umich.edu/tprc/papers/2004/381/Adele_Morris_ on_Spectrum_Auctions_updated_1.pdf/

Noam, E. (1998, October). Spectrum auctions: Yesterday's heresy, today's orthodoxy, tomorrow's anachronism. Taking the next step to open spectrum access. *Journal of Law and Economics, XLI*, 765-790.

Rappaport, T. S. (2002). *Wireless communications principles and practice* (2nd ed.). Upper Saddle River, NJ: Prentice Hall.

Shelanski, H. A., & Huber, P. W. (1998, October). Administrative creation of property rights to radio spectrum. *Journal of Law and Economics, XLI*, 581-607.

KEY TERMS

Allocations of Spectrum: The categorization and division of spectrum into blocks that are then associated with a specific technology; for example, broadcast television.

Allotments of Spectrum: Divisions of spectrum allocations on a geographic basis; for example, broadcast television station 5 in New York City.

Basic Trading Area: A geographic region used by the FCC determines service areas for PCS wireless licenses. The entire U.S. and some of its territories are divided into 493 non-overlapping BTAs.

Combinatorial Bidding: Allowing auction participants to place bids on groups of licenses.

Comparative Hearings: Method used in the U.S. to award spectrum prior to the advent of cellular telephones.

Hertz: The number of cycles per second.

License: The right to use a specific portion of the radio frequency in a specific area for a set term.

Radio Frequencies: The portion of the electromagnetic spectrum ranging from 3 kilohertz (kHz) to 300 gigahertz (300 GHz).

Simultaneous Multiple-Round Auction: An auction process in which all licenses are available for bid at the same time.

Spectrum: Radio frequencies.

Winner's Curse: Tendency in common value auctions for the high bidder that wins due to variation in the formulation of a bid on the high side.

Chapter 4.52
Using Digital Hotlines in an Anti-Corruption Campaign

Paula F. Saddler
Association of Certified Fraud Examiners, USA

INTRODUCTION

Throughout the world, people are just as concerned about corruption as they are about unemployment, poverty, and physical security. Governments can support citizens in their fight against corruption by using digital hotlines to investigate wrongdoing and to strengthen fraud-prevention efforts. Best practices in managing digital hotlines can be packaged into a module that is rolled out to all units of government from the national to the local level.

BACKGROUND

Every year, Transparency International (TI) prepares a barometer of global corruption, and in 2004, TI interviewed 50,000 people in 60 countries. TI reported that for 2004 and 2003, the public perceived political parties as the sector most affected by corruption, followed by parliament/legislature, the police, and the legal system/judiciary. Similarly, when asked to rate the impact of corruption on different spheres of life, people ranked 70% for politics, 60% for business, and 40% for family and personal life.

Petty administrative corruption also was mentioned by 78% of respondents as a concern. Worldwide, one in 10 persons interviewed said someone in their household had paid a bribe in the previous 12 months.

Corruption, especially in the public sector, is a worldwide epidemic that is growing rather than shrinking. TI reported that for 2004, 43% of respondents expected the level of corruption to increase in the next three years (Transparency International, 2005). With corruption on the rise, governments will need powerful and effective tools to combat fraud and abuse.

ESTABLISHING HOTLINES

One such powerful tool is a digital fraud hotline, which should be integrated into an anti-corruption campaign. Even though some countries have passed whistle blower protection laws, their application is riddled with problems, and the whistle blower often ends up frustrated, disappointed, and unemployed (Calland & Dehn, 2004). Furthermore, the original problem that was identified by the informant often is not corrected, which discourages public servants from blowing the whistle (Devine, 2004). A conventional hotline using telephone and mail allows citizens to remain anonymous when filing a complaint, thus reducing the fear of retaliation, which may motivate them to actively fight corruption (USGAO, 1988). A digital hotline multiplies the opportunity for safe reporting to a vastly larger audience.

How Hotlines Function

A hotline is a system that facilitates the reporting of wrongdoing or violations of the code of conduct directly to the sponsoring organization (SO). If the SO initiates an investigation, it may result in administrative sanctions according to the rules of the SO or in legal complaints filed with the national judicial system. Technology for hotlines has advanced from telephones or physical snail mail to Internet technology that now supports sophisticated features such as the following:

- Receiving and storing a large number of complaints from informants.
- Allowing informants to remain anonymous, if they so chose.
- Rapid notices to officials of an SO when a complaint is received.
- Supporting a real-time online dialogue between an informant and officials of the SO who are in different time zones.
- Classifying complaints by a variety of categories and characteristics.
- Ability to quickly adjust the classification scheme of complaints as needed.
- Ability for informant to log in (anonymously) and to track progress on his or her case.
- Maintaining a log of how a case is investigated.
- Recording the outcome of a case, such as actions taken against an employee and whether assets were recovered.
- Quickly customizing reports for detail and summary statistics.
- Preparing and distributing reports automatically on a schedule.

The sophistication of digital hotlines has been fueled by the fact that managing hotlines has become a growth business in the last 15 years. The number of vendors that provide digital hotline services has been growing because fraud and corruption are alive and thriving.

The Global Fight Against Corruption

Many public interest organizations are fighting corruption in both the public and private spheres. Notable international efforts include the drafting of a Convention Against Corruption that is sponsored by the United Nations Office of Drug Control (UNODC). This convention was ratified by 37 national governments, and it entered into force on December 14, 2005 (UNODC, n.d.(d)).

How Can the Digital HotLine Support Anti-Corruption Efforts?

The UN Convention Against Corruption recommends best practices for governments to foster honesty and integrity of citizens as they fulfill their obligations, whether in the public or private arena. With 71 articles organized into eight chapters, there are four main pillars of the anti-corruption model that are listed as follows (UNODC, n.d.(a)):

1. National anti-corruption policies and mechanisms
2. Strengthening judicial integrity and capacity
3. Promoting integrity in the public and private sectors
4. Denying the proceeds of corruption and recovering illicit assets

Creating a Hotline is a Best Practice

Article 8 of the convention recommends developing a code of conduct for public officials as well as a system to facilitate the reporting of acts of corruption to appropriate authorities

UNODC notes that critical components in enforcing a standard of conduct include ethics training, credible public complaint systems, public awareness about their rights, and appropriate disciplinary measures. (UNODC, n.d.(a), p. 6)

Who Owns the Hotline?

Developing national policies, strategies, and action plans is critical to effectively fighting corruption. Article 5, Paragraph 1 of the convention stipulates that states shall develop and implement coordinated anti-corruption policies that are based on laws and good management principles such as integrity, transparency, and accountability and that encourage the participation of society (UNODC, n.d.(a)).

This can be accomplished by creating a special anti-corruption body, which Article 6 recommends establishing, to oversee and implement the policies outlined in Article 5 as well as to increase and disseminate knowledge about preventing corruption (UNODC, n.d.(a)).

Therefore, Article 6 supports establishing a governing body over the hotline to oversee management, which mirrors the same concept that there should be high-level governance over information technology resources (IT Governance Institute, n.d.). A key responsibility of this governing body over the hotline would be to review all complaints filed to ensure that there is follow-up on all serious cases that are reported and that this oversight would extend to protect the whistle-blower, as well (USGAO, 1989). Hopefully, this governing body also would oversee the overall anti-corruption efforts of the government entity, and a hotline would be only one responsibility.

Article 6 also recommends that this governance body be independent and free from any undue influence. It should have the power to advocate for and/or resolve conflicts in laws and regulations so that there is a consistent policy that protects whistle blowers in all cases. Oversight is needed to ensure that public agencies do not bury complaints and punish the whistle blower for political reasons. One troubling trend is that national laws can negate whistle blower rights in favor of protecting national security, which denies the public's right to know about wrongdoing in this sector (Devine, 2004).

Members of this hotline governing body should not come exclusively from public service but also should include members of NGOs and community-based organizations that can bring independence to the exercise of oversight. Governments should reach out to find suitable NGOs to serve on such a body. Once again, Article 13 of the Convention confirms the importance of involving NGOs in efforts to prevent and fight against corruption and to raise public awareness about the threats that corruption poses (UNODC, n.d.(a)).

Content of the Web Site for the Hotline

A digital hotline can harness data processing power to provide a vast amount of information to anyone. Since a hotline sits on a Web server, the site where the informant first accesses the hotline, called the landing page, can be linked to many other Web sites that are devoted to fraud prevention and education.

A recommended best practice is that a landing page for a hotline should include the following:

- Purpose of the hotline and how it relates to the anti-corruption efforts of the sponsoring organization (SO).
- Instructions on how to file complaints.
- Reports on complaints received and their status (to the extent that it can be released

to the public) without jeopardizing the investigation.

- Educational materials. There should be links to other Web sites that have information on ethics. Citizen responsibility to report frauds and links to individual hotlines of the inspector generals of the various government departments.
- Links to NGOs and civil-based societies that support and counsel whistle blowers.
- Results of cases that were investigated and links to information services that track court cases.

A model Web site for anti-corruption that has these features is the Hong Kong Independent Commission Against Corruption (ICAC) (n.d.), which incorporates hotline features with fraud prevention advocacy. The ICAC has had spectacular success over the last 30 years in becoming a model for clean government (UNODC, n.d.(c)).

Web Site Content Promoting Transparency in Government

Strengthening the integrity and capacity of judges and prosecutors is another important goal of the UN Convention that is discussed in Article 11 (UNODC, n.d.(a)). A landing page should be linked to information about the fate of prosecutions adjudicated in courts of law and internal administrative actions taken by government. Publishing the outcomes of these cases tells everyone how well investigators, prosecutors, and judges perform their jobs.

Publishing the results of cases also reinforces the credibility of the hotline and the underlying fraud prevention effort. If a person is wavering about whether to report wrongdoing, throwing light on the entire process can reassure him or her that a personal sacrifice will make a difference.

Support for Whistle Blowers

Before an informant reports a wrongdoing, he or she should understand that such an act may adversely impact his or her personal and professional life. Support resources for informants should be included on the landing page. Some NGO advisors help to evaluate the appropriateness of the acts that whistle blowers plan to expose and whether there is a more suitable remedy for something that actually may be an administrative grievance. In planning the Web site, government units should explore whether there are local NGOs that can provide this support.

Whistle blowers should have a voice on the landing page. But when is it appropriate for the whistle blower to report about what happens as a result of filing a complaint? Citizens are naturally curious about what happens to a complaint, and reports of outcomes lend more credibility to the hotline. Thorny issues, however, revolve around how the status of the whistle blower gets reported (if they chose to identify themselves), who should report it and when, and how to verify information reported by the whistle blower.

Informants should be warned that even if they wish to conceal their identities, it may be discovered during an investigation. Dire things may happen to informants and whistle blowers who are identified—they may lose their jobs; they may suffer severe economic consequences; or, if they remain employed, they may be reassigned to meaningless tasks. They also may become burdened with expensive legal bills. In one developed country, public servants have had their security clearances revoked, which means that they not only lose their jobs but also become blacklisted from any work that requires a security clearance (Devine, 2004).

In a developing country, where one or two companies dominate a sector of the economy, being stigmatized as a whistle blower can mean never working in that particular sector again. Subsequent employment obtained in a different sector may require that the person start over on a junior level in a new profession, which results in long-term loss of income (Dimba, Stober, & Thomson, 2004).

Required Infrastructure for Telecommunications Within the Country

Digital hotlines require an effective telecommunications infrastructure in the country. One organization that brings information and communications technology to the poor is the United Nations Development Programme (UNDP). It has an extensive Web site of information and projects in this area, and governments should explore possible services that UNDP may be able to offer in the country.

Requirements for a Successful Digital Hotline

Adequate financial and IT resources alone will not guarantee success, especially if there is a high volume of complaints at startup. There has to be adequate capacity in order for both investigators and the internal justice system to handle an increased workload. Investigators, prosecutors, and judges or administrative tribunals have to complete cases promptly after they are initiated through the hotline. Long delays with inadequate and incomplete reports will quickly destroy the credibility of the hotline and the related anti-corruption effort (PcaW, n.d.).

FUTURE TRENDS

Any public entity that is establishing a digital hotline should consider the following topics:

- Is the national infrastructure for telecommunications adequate to support widespread access to the digital hotline?
- What are the objectives for the hotline, based on national, state, or local needs?
- Who owns the hotline; who is the governing body, and what is its power?
- Who manages it on a day-to-day basis?
- Structure of the hotline—What are the client agencies and how can their hotlines be coordinated?
- Telephone operators—How important is it to have telephone operators who talk with informants, and when and how should those operators be used?
- Who are the users—Are reporters restricted only to citizens, to employees, to vendors, or to any person living in the country?
- Marketing the hotline—What kind of advertising campaign will encourage citizens to use the hotline?
- Support to whistle blowers—What support and advice should be given to informants in order to warn them about the risks of filing a complaint?
- Funding—What is the budget, and how will costs be apportioned among public entities that share a hotline?
- Reports from the hotline:
- What are the annual operating reports, and who will receive them?
- When can a complaint and its investigation be disclosed to the public?
- What reports should be disclosed to the public and when?

- Feedback to the informant—When and how should the SO give feedback?
- Evaluating Effectiveness—What are the indicators of success for the hotline by quality and quantity?

CONCLUSION

A digital hotline is a vehicle for citizens to report fraud and abuse in the public sector and, with its related Web-based technology, serves as a platform to support a culture of zero tolerance toward corruption. A digital hotline can bolster the faith and confidence of the public that its government is committed to running clean operations without corruption. If citizens believe that they can make a difference and that they will be protected from acts of retaliation, they will blow the digital whistle that they are given, and they will blow it loudly.

REFERENCES

Calland, R., & Dehn, G. (2004). *Whistleblowing around the world, law, culture and practice*. London: Public Concern at Work.

Devine, T. (2004). WhistleBlowing in the United States: The gap between vision and lessons learned. In R. Calland, & G. Dehn (Eds.), *Whistleblowing around the world, law, culture and practice* (pp. 74-100). London: Public Concern at Work.

Dimba, M., Stober, L., & Thomson, B. (2004). The South African experience. In R. Calland, & G. Dehn (Eds.), *Whistleblowing around the world, law, culture and practice* (pp. 143-152). Cape Town: Open Democracy Advice Centre (ODAC).

Hong Kong Independent Commission Against Corruption (ICAC). (n.d.). About the ICAC—History. Retrieved October 26, 2004, from https://www.icac.org.hk/eng./main/index.html/

IT Governance Institute (ITGI). (n.d.). Retrieved October 30, 2004, from http://www.itgi.org/

(PCaW). (n.d.). Recognizing retaliation. The risks and costs of whistleblowing. Retrieved October 30, 2004, from http://www.whistleblower.org/article.php?did=34& scid=720008/

Transparency International. (2005). Global corruption report 2005. Retrieved December 3, 2005, from http://www.globalcorruptionreport.org/download.html/

United Nations Office on Drugs and Crime (UNODC). (n.d.(a)). United Nations convention against corruption enters into force on 14 December. Retrieved October 25, 2004, from http://www.unis.unvienna.org/unis/pressrels/2005/uniscp528.html/

(UNODC). (n.d.(b)). Priorities for the provision of technical assistance—Global programme against corruption. Retrieved October 26, 2004, from http://www.unodc.org/corruption_gpac_strategy_jul04.pfd

(UNODC). (n.d.(c)). Global programme against corruption conference: Prevention: An effective tool to reduce corruption. Vienna, December 1999. Retrieved October 26, 2004 from: http://www.unodc.org/Cicp2.pdf

(UNODC). (n.d.(d)). United Nations convention against corruption last update: Thursday, 17 November 2005. Retrieved December 3, 2005, from http://www.unodc/unodc/en/crime_signatures_corruption.html

US General Accounting Office (USGAO). (1998, April 19). Fraud hotline. GAO testimony. Doc. No. 135603. Statement of Charles A. Bowsher, Comptroller General of the United States before the Subcommittee on Government, Efficiency, Federalism, and the District of Columbia Committee on Governmental Affairs, United States Senate. Retrieved October 26, 2004, from http://www.gao.gov/reports.htm/135603.pdf

(USGAO). (1989, November 13). Briefing report to the Chairman, Subcommittee on General Services, Federalism, and the District of Columbia, Committee on Governmental Affairs, U.S. Senate, Inspectors General, fraud hotline operations. Retrieved October 26, 2004, from http://www.gao.gov/reports.htm/139970.pdf

KEY TERMS

Complaint: A statement by a person that there has been wrongdoing by one or more employees of an organization. It has to be investigated to determine if the information is true.

Confidential Informant (CI): Person who reports information about wrongdoing. This person does not want his or her identity revealed to the public.

Corruption: The misuse of entrusted power for private gain. (Downloaded from the TI Web site on December 4, 2005, from http://www.transparency.org/faqs/faq-corruption.html.)

Hotline: A system that facilitates the discovery of wrongdoing. It facilitates communications between an informant or a whistle blower and the sponsoring organization (SO), which investigates and prevents wrongdoing.

Informant: A person who discloses information about wrongdoing. This person may remain anonymous or can reveal his or her identity only to a select person within an entity, in which case this person becomes a confidential informant.

Information Technology Governance Institute (ITGI): Assists managers in fulfilling their responsibility to ensure that information technology is aligned with the business and delivers value efficiently and effectively (http://www.itgi.org).

Non-Governmental Organization (NGO): Serves the public interest. Its finances and management are independent of government.

Public Interest Disclosure Act (PIDA): A Part of employment law in the United Kingdom that defines what is a protected disclosure for wrongdoing. The law applies to all workers in the UK, whether they are employed in public, private, or voluntary sectors.

Sponsoring Organization (SO): Any entity involved in activities that has employees and volunteers and that hosts a hotline designed to receive complaints of abuse and corruption.

Support Groups for Whistle Blowers and Confidential Informants: Offer counseling and legal assistance to whistle blowers.

Transparency International (TI): An NGO that brings civil society, business, and governments together in a powerful global coalition in order to combat corruption (http://www.transparency.org/).

United Nations Development Programme (UNDP): The United Nations global development network. UNDP helps countries to attract and use development aid effectively (http://www.undp.org). UNDP is active in information and communication technologies for development and has a wealth of information from a network of 166 countries in which it works (http://sdnhq.undp.org/it4dev). UNDP also supports e-governance and citizen participation in government through access to information (http://www.undp.org/governance/sl-egov.htm)

United Nations Office on Drug and Crime Control (UNODC): A United Nations organization that supports the Global Programme against Corruption, Vienna International Centre, P.O. Box 500, Room E1272, A-1400 Vienna, Austria. Tel: +43(1) 26060-4406; Fax: +43(1) 26060-5898.

United States General Accounting Office (GAO): Supports the Congress of the United States to improve the performance and to ensure the accountability of the federal government for the benefit of the American people (www.gao.gov).

Whistle Blower: An employee who discloses an abuse of power that betrays the public trust.

Whistle Blowing: The act of an employee who voices concerns about wrongdoing in the workplace or through an independent entity associated with it. Whistle blowers do not conceal their identities and often communicate their concerns to supervisors, managers, executives, regulators, or the public (Calland & Dehn, 2004).

Wrongdoing: Any action by an employee that does not comply with the code of conduct, applicable laws, rules, regulations, or operational guidelines of the employing organization or that violates the laws of the country. Besides illegal acts, wrongdoing includes waste, mismanagement, abuse of authority, or posing a substantial and specific danger to public health and safety (Devine, 2004).

This work was previously published in the Encyclopedia of Digital Government, edited by A. Anttiroiko; M. Malkia, pp. 1595-1600, copyright 2007 by Information Science Reference, formerly known as Idea Group Reference (an imprint of IGI Global).

Chapter 4.53
Business Models for M-Government Services

Gertraud Peinel
Fraunhofer FIT, Germany

Thomas Rose
Fraunhofer FIT, Germany

ABSTRACT

This chapter reports on experiences gained in the sustainable implementation of mobile e-government services. Sustainable operations require appropriate business models and partnerships for the implementation and provision of services. The lessons learned are based on experiences gained in major European research projects for the implementation of information services for environmental information and for the provision of mobile services. This chapter will briefly present the mobile services provided in these projects and then turn to the specific dimensions of interest: added values materialized by the combination of m-government, business models, and, in particular, revenue models for financing the services. Specific attention will be devoted to public-private partnerships for implementing, maintaining, and operating the services. Each dimension will be discussed in terms of pros and cons. The section on business models will be completed by a summary of specified experiences gained with different stakeholders.

INTRODUCTION

This chapter revolves around the customer and business aspects of mobile government services. Rather than wallowing in pure e-government issues or IT science and technologies, we want to talk about *business*. This business stance compasses the exploration of business partnerships and models as well as the market investigation of service content, that is, the design of use-oriented and citizen-centred services.

Governmental information services and in particular online services towards the citizen still fell a step short of success. They are mainly created to meet the demands of legislations and regulations concerning information needs, but mostly do not entertain and attract the citizen, for example, by additional services taking into account individual situations, or by impelling people to a more active information exploration stance. A significant share of information services fell short concerning intuitive presentations and user interfaces for navigation, in particular taking into account normal citizens as customers. Instead, raw numbers and/or a large amount of reports dominate. One reason for this lack of customer orientation are diverging perceptions of the information strategy of authorities: merely offering *access* to information to the public versus pro-active information *dissemination* (Craglia & Masser, 2001). The latter requires processes taking into account also modern information technologies and customer-oriented thinking (even though we respect possible problems by transferring the concepts of e-commerce to e-government (Adams, Haston, Gillespie, & Macintosh, 2003; Stahl, 2005).

M-government services often require not only pull but also push functionalities such as sending of SMS notifications: In contrast to pure Web services, the sending of SMS has to be financed explicitly. Experiences from the Government of Malta mGov project (Government of Malta—Ministry for Information Technology and Investment, 2003) as well as project USE-ME.GOV (USE-ME.GOV Consortium, 2005b) showed that authorities tend to cover the expenses of mobile services, since other funding possibilities and business models with private organizations are eyed suspiciously.

The following sections will further elaborate on the range of business and revenue models for running m-government services in a sustainable way, and accompanied information strategies based on the results of EC-funded projects.

BACKGROUND

Projects APNEE and APNEE-TU

Project APNEE (Air Pollution Network for Early warning and on-line information Exchange in Europe—APNEE, 2006) evaluated the potential of raising money with m-government information services; or at least to create a win-win situation between public and private partners. It implemented ubiquitous information services available on mobile phones (WAP, SMS, MMS), PDA, street panels, voice servers, and Internet. These services are operated in public-private partnerships while each partnership creates dedicated value for the end user, that is, the citizen as customer.

APNEE has been launched during the hype of the content industry. Only a few years ago, content was considered king for the telecommunication industry. Environmental information was ranked third place in customer interviews about attractive content. Moreover, the Information Society Technologies programme for information technology development and deployment of the European Union begun to promote citizen-centered services, that is, services and in particular information services that generate added value for many citizen. Hence, the ingredients for a success story were in place.

APNEE materialized on these ingredients and delivered a multichannel dissemination platform for air quality information, which was successfully evaluated in field trials in several European regions. Based on the successful implementation of an online information service for the citizen, a major European field trial was launched with project APNEE-TU (Take-UP measure).

The vision of APNEE was to establish an information service which informs citizens about the current air quality taking into account the current location of the citizen (different values depending on region), the preferences of the citizen (i.e., sensitive to ozone, pulmonary diseases, limits, alert intervals), and the availability of different information access channels (mobile: mobile phones, smart phones, PDAs, street panels; at home: PC with Internet, voice server) (Peinel & Rose, 2004).

APNEE finally operates air pollution information service in Norway, Germany, Spain, France, and Greece on different channels according acceptance and business models. The success of the online information services stayed with APNEE from a citizen's point of view. However, the business partnerships changed significantly while getting closer to the commercialization of the services and the products built.

USE-ME.GOV

Project USE-ME.GOV developed an open platform for m-government services that is both cost-effective and efficient. These crucial attributes can be especially beneficial for smaller and financially weak local authorities. This open platform for m-government services fosters usability, sharing, openness, interoperability, and scalability, thus enabling service deployment and access. The project also elaborated business models for the sustainable operation of such services while at the same time considering the sharing of services by several authorities as well as public-private partnerships between authorities and commercial companies.

IST initiatives for improving services to the citizen and businesses are prevailingly promoted and implemented by individual authorities and organizations. Nowadays even smaller towns operate their own Web site with access to general public information, whereas larger cities and institutions use to offer a wider range of more sophisticated electronic (Web-based) services (Leenes & Svensson, 2002).

However, the richness and quality of these services vary significantly. In particular small authorities, for example, in rural areas, have limited financial, technical, and human resources in order to implement and deploy electronic services with the same quality as large organizations (ibid). This aspect becomes even more critical for the deployment of mobile services because of a higher complexity of service implementation, required organizational changes, as well as higher costs for commercial exploitation due to complexity of value chain.

Authorities are usually organized in departments each with own responsibilities, tasks, structure, and customers. Often hardware, and moreover software differ from door to door and are not shared (also named "patchwork" in a study from DB Research (2005), or "information silos" as described for example in Kane (2004) and Saxena (2005)). On the other hand, mobile operators or portals are searching for content to promote their new mobile technologies and approach public organizations to deliver services on Internet and wireless networks. Once contracted, one department connects to the mobile operator in charge and "somebody" implements a proprietary bridge to one specific operator interface. This bridge can normally not be reused for other applications or other mobile operators.

Authorities are now actively searching for mobile solutions to implement regulations and recommendations from state, national, and European bodies calling for e-government, e-governance, and of course m-government. But due to often missing technical background, monetary shortcuts, administrative regulations, and less experience about mobile market interdependencies, they are hesitating to invest time and money in solitaire solutions with a high degree of propriety and accordingly major investments.

The deployment of an open service platform that can be shared by networked authorities and institutions (e.g., on a regional scale) in terms of technical resources as well as commercial exploitation harmonizes the quality of public services and overcomes related *divide* phenomena. On the other hand, resource sharing explored on the basis of attractive business models will also provide the conditions for cost-efficient m-government services namely in geographical areas with low Internet penetration, since penetration of mobile technologies already got ahead of Internet penetration.

Hence, project USE-ME.GOV's key results was to support authorities entering the mobile market with an open source platform allowing:

- To share common modules with other departments or other authorities (for example subscription, alerting components)
- To secure development and operation by open source transparency
- To attract further mobile operator independent of respective interfaces
- To estimate efforts, outcome, and benefits in advance

The platform has been finalized and validated in four European regions and will be operated on the basis of different business models depending on the individual validation results. Sharing of the platform, sponsoring, and public-private partnerships prevail.

VALUE CHAINS FOR MULTICHANNEL SERVICES

Business partners are normally not considered in the supply chain of e-government or m-government services (Abramowicz, Bassara, Filipowska, Peinel, Rose, Wisniewski, & Zebrowski, 2005). But, telecommunication companies have the technological know how and infrastructure to deliver services on a large scale and on multiple channels. Moreover, portal operators and content syndicators are eager to get new content in order to provide new and better services. On the other hand, environmental authorities and research organizations have profound knowledge about and access to environmental data, but they are not experts on the use of modern information and telecommunication technology for reaching the citizen with their messages. Thus, the ingredients for a successful business partnership are available in principle. Rather than mimicking other partner's roles at low quality, organizations should team-up for business.

APNEE implemented a value chain with several stakeholders:

- **Authorities and non-governmental environmental organizations:** Provide the data and the knowledge about the data, its sources, measurement networks, quality measures and of course legislation background.
- **Research institutes and universities:** Supplement this information with forecasting models and impact analysis.
- **Private portal operators:** Are bringing in the contacts and knowledge about information markets and specific customer requirements. Therefore, they supplement the data with background information (like health impacts) and user-friendly visualization means.
- **Telecommunication operators:** Are delivering the information and service to the customers via multichannel platforms. They might also enhance the service with location based features.

This value chain proved to be successful because:

- High-quality data is available
- The impacts of air pollution elements are well researched.
- Internet and mobile end user devices are common and widespread; multichannel service provision will therefore better reach the citizen.
- Telecommunication providers host multichannel systems and are eager for content with demand.
- Authorities want and have to reach the public with modern communication means.
- Authorities and NGOs foster the capitalization of their data and services to create value.

Figure 1. Structure of the information value chain in APNEE(-TU)

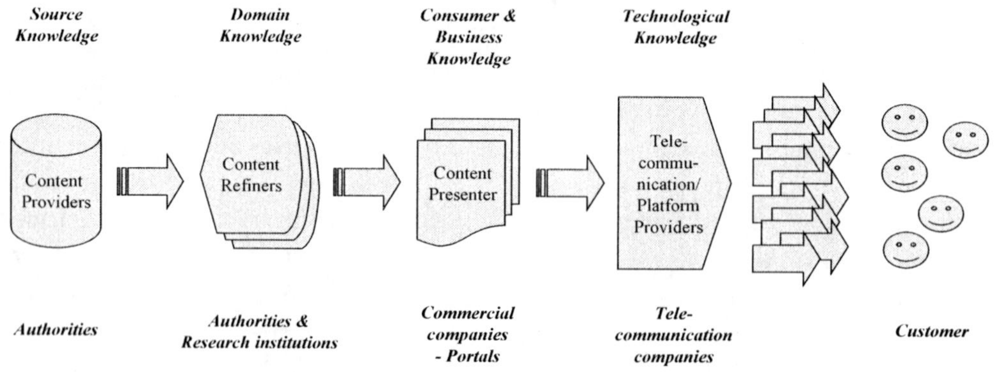

Telecommunication operators were first inclined to host valuable content themselves and blocked any integration attempts. Now they increasingly offer standardized interfaces to their infrastructure leaving the market to portal operators and information providers. This opening allows authorities an easier implementation of multichannel information services for reaching the public—provided they are able to master questions of usability, interaction mechanisms, and use of medium.

BUSINESS EXPERIENCES GAINED

APNEE has evaluated several business opportunities and models to establish e-government services as a sustainable business. One specific business perspective has been explored by telecommunications providers and operators in early phases: establish air quality information as premium content, such as traffic information, and charge the citizen on a use or subscription basis. This business idea has not proven profitable for a mass market. It will only generate revenues for niche markets, although there is again a significant difference among Northern and Southern European countries. Since the participating telecommunication companies focused their business on the big picture, this business concept has not been further elaborated in APNEE(-TU). The change of business interest might also be caused by a vanishing of content-related businesses in general or by missing content delivery frameworks for environmental information.

Although new directives for the publication of public sector information (PSI) have been published (European Commission, 2000b), they do not specify how to implement and regulate this publication. There are in particular no content delivery frameworks to offer online information to external entrepreneurs that might turn them into commercial and professional services. Formal content delivery contracts between public information providers and commercial syndicators have proven critical in the course of APNEE. Contracts have been negotiated at national levels, for example, in Germany where the federal states (*Länder*) and the federal environmental agency wanted to use APNEE services with online data managed by a federal environmental institute. Yet, there is no European framework. Content delivery management is further compounded by competition issues. Can we transfer a set of services operational in Germany to Spain and use publicly certified data online from Spanish sources? Our talks with authorities showed a clear reluctance to offer the data to foreign companies.

There has been a major shift from telecommunication companies as service syndicators towards public administrations as provider of APNEE-like services as for example in Norway. Public administrations might use APNEE services to elevate their service quality in the context of government-to-citizen and e-government initiatives. Hence, the pendulum moved backwards from high quality content for commercial information services on a charge basis towards information services to be offered by public authorities. Air quality information as a life style service commercially operated is somehow in between with the addition of a niche market for dedicated groups of citizens. APNEE services will likely be offered as additional modules to existing air quality management systems and be offered to public bodies in charge of air quality monitoring.

OPTIONS OF REVENUES

A joint provision of services by private and public bodies might be based on a rather classical thinking of costs, revenues, and financiers. This approach of finding one party who pays the bills has been aged out by many examples of Internet projects. Based on experiences gained in this business community, we present a number of potential financing sources for the integration and operation of mobile services, which have been elaborated in the USE-ME.GOV project. These business model recommendations include a checklist of options to evaluate when planning m-government services (USE-ME.GOV Consortium, 2005a). The following is the list of recommendations that should be considered for financing m-government initiatives:

- National and international funding
- Public-private partnerships (in low cost or win-win relationships)
- Advertising and sponsoring
- Payment by the citizens (at least for push services)
- Sharing of the service or the platform with other authorities
- Or some combination of these all options.

National and International Funding

At the start of project USE-ME-GOV, the participating authorities put their faith in national and international funding sources as financing option. Even though national or European funding seems to be the easiest way to support m-government activities, this solution neglects the advantages of partnerships with private organizations as stated in the next section (but of course also avoids any problems related to it). But, with public purses under strain, such financing is often limited in amount and time, and this might not allow a flexible answering to increased or extended customer demand, not to talk about required expenses for further adaptations to new technologies. Public funding should be used to support innovations, start-up, or implementation phases of projects, but not the permanent operation of such undertakings.

Public-Private Partnerships (in Low Cost or Win-Win Relationship)

Public-private partnerships (PPP) between stakeholders of governmental information service value chains combine partners from the public and the private sector. They are by nature differently structured, have a different policy and business aim, and underlie different legislations. But, partnerships between public organizations and private companies would allow a simple business model: Authorities deliver their data and service to a well-defined interface, and commercial organizations pick it up, polish, and perhaps revalue them for their respective business purposes, obeying the syndication rules agreed upon, that is, concerning the end-user price. This business model could fertilize the market of public sector information, gives each commercial partner a fair access, and avoids competition by public authorities operating such services themselves.

In APNEE-TU, the German Internet and WAP services operated by a commercial company did not cause any extra costs for the citizen (the implemented SMS information services, which have been tested in the project, did not survive the validation: accepted price and number of potential customers did not reach the threshold of the commercial partner). The company offered the Internet and WAP services for free to extend their information portal with this information in order to attract more customers which might in turn invoke services with costs. Unfortunately, this PPP by service level agreement did not survive more than three years, since: (1) the commercial company took over risks and costs (monthly amount for data provision by the authority) of the partnership; and (2) the authority did not support the partnership with a common objective, engagement, or investment. Finally, the commercial company changed their business interest and online presence, and the German APNEE services were abandoned tacitly.

Not every possible service has to be and should be operated by authorities, not only from a financial and effort point of view, but also because governmental activities should not interfere with the private market. In some states of Europe and in the U.S., the competition of the government with the private sector are forbidden by law to avoid precluding other entities from developing markets (Software and Information Industry Association, 2001; Weiss, 2002). "A further objective [*of the EC competition law*] is the avoidance of situations in which a government agency or organization might be perceived as abusing its monopoly supply position with regard to distribution, pricing, licensing and competition" (INSPIRE DPLI Working Group, 2002).

But, partnership must be carefully negotiated, since delegating the service provision to commercial partners might hinder governmental policies concerning reaching all citizens (for example, by having no influence on the provider policy regarding customer selection) or concerning free information to satisfy specific information needs of the public (commercial providers might want to charge for the information). It must also be assured that private companies do not control the information flow between citizen and government and thus influence and filter content and reach.

PPPs can also be used for the initial implementation: the private sector carries the cost of initial implementations in order to prove the effectiveness of the technology, and further costs are covered by the government, if the service is successful (Goldstuck, 2004). The government of Hong Kong already established specific PPPs for electronic services delivery named the *electronic service delivery (ESD) scheme*. Here, the private sector operator is responsible for developing, financing, operating, and maintaining the system, and the government starts to pay transaction fees to the operator after the transaction level has reached a pre-agreed volume. The commercial operator is allowed to make use of the information infrastructure for advertisements and e-commerce services for additional income. The business risk to the government is low; while the private sector operator has continuous incentive to promote the wider use of the e-government services and to introduce service enhancement. "This also drives the development of e-commerce in the business sector" (Government of the Hong Kong Special Administrative Region, 2004).

Another option for a PPP is that the commercial company builds and operates the mobile service, and charges the customer/citizen for using the service. Revenues can be shared between authority and private partner, or retained completely by the private company as reimbursement for efforts. This business model is successfully implemented in the U.S. with a company named NIC (National Information Consortium, Inc.) currently operating 18 U.S. state portals through the so-called "self-funded model" (NIC Homepage, 2005).

The negotiation and implementation phases in APNEE and USE-ME.GOV showed problems and advantages of these public-private partnerships, which will be described in the following sections.

Problems of Partnerships

We experienced in the projects the following conflicts (which either have been solved by individual agreements or are still under negotiation).

- **Law concerning exchange of data and ownership/copyright of data:** Even the EC provides with the new directives on access to public sector information and communication of environmental data (European Commission, 2000b, 2003) a first indication on how to deliver public data and services to external parties, other issues of such a deal are still open for negotiation: do authorities have to deliver to ALL external customers, including customers from other countries with different legislation? Are external parties allowed to process the data? Allowed to resell the data? We experienced that a reselling might be condoned by the authorities due to an unclear legal position about this in some states. In face-to-face discussions, most authorities showed a strong reluctance when asked to sell their data and services to other countries.
- **PPP contracts missing:** Still, generally accepted contracts for information services operated in PPPs are rare in most European countries. This means that for each binding agreement lawyers have to negotiate service level agreements between the accuracy-oriented authorities and the reliability-oriented commercial providers. Among other problems, the latter normally integrates in content provision contracts passages about penalties if the provision fails or is not available in time, and this demand is certainly not acceptable for public organizations. Nationwide and moreover European-wide standard contracts would ease this negotiation process and spare time and costs.
- **Documentation ownership:** Information services should inform the public sufficiently and extensively. This means that for example environmental services should not just send raw measurement values, but indices and additional information about health impacts and actions to undertake, in order to allow the citizen to assess the danger of air pollution. This background, general, and regulation information—be it text, pictures, videos, animations—should be backed by authorities and research competences. But, the ownerships of such documentation might be problematic to settle. What is legally allowed on a public or research site must be clarified in ownership before presented on a commercial site. This could result in a tiresome fight to detect who is the originator and such owner of which piece of information.
- **Niche product versus public policy:** It is public policy to reach most citizens in order to inform and protect. On the other hand, commercial organizations tend to concentrate on the biggest part of the picture and therefore do not want to invest in niche services, which might result in low revenues with high investment. A successful partnership must therefore try to balance the investment on the private and the public site for a win-win-situation of both parties.
- **Intermediator:** Authorities are rightly careful when external parties intermediate the channel to the citizens. One topic of caution is the potential misuse of individual data of the citizen. While authorities are judged as trustful, private companies have to overcome the suspicion of customers concerning the use of their sensitive data. Also, the USE-ME.GOV validation interviews showed a clear expression of mistrust by citizens with

regard to data privacy when commercial companies are involved in service provision. It should also be controlled that the data and information is not changed and tampered for specific business needs, say for advertisement of pharmacies. The contract between public and private organizations must be flexible enough to allow additional financing on the private site, but it ought to be strict with regard to misuse and incorrect interpretations on the other side.

Advantages of Partnerships

We also want to highlight the clear benefits both partners can capitalize on:

- **Provision of multichannel services:** Authorities should implement multichannel services to get a maximum reach towards the citizen, anyhow, anywhere, and anytime (European Commission, 2004). But the required investment confronts with the current problematic financial situation of most public organizations. Especially mobile services have to be tested on a large amount of devices to be useful for a larger audience due to a large variety of mobile standard implementations. In addition, the number of new devices appearing year for year on the market results in never-ending tests and adaptations. Following the APNEE approach, authorities do not have to waste taxes and efforts to join this rush of new technologies but can concentrate on data delivery to private operators. The latter are already operating implementation centres for the transfer and test of content to new devices and can such serve the most common and most up-to-date technology.
- **New information markets:** The PIRA study (European Commission, 2000a) estimated in the year 2000 that public sector information presents an economic value of between 28 billion and 134 billion Euro per annum in Europe and this market is still underdeveloped. The business chain of APNEE showed that PSI can be successfully exploited creating a win-win situation for all partners. Other services based on PSI like water quality, or for example statistical data can be implemented in the same way. From the citizen point of view, these kinds of information services with PSI is not yet offered, and hence new demand with emerging commercial value can be created.
- **Market driven approach of commercial partners:** Certainly commercial partners are market and customer oriented. We also suppose they are more creative in getting value out of data and services and are hence inventing new service types and new demand: "by assembling, arranging, and organizing it *[public sector information]* in useful ways; by combining it with information from other sources; by adding indexing, cross-referencing and annotations; and by updating and expanding databases to make sure that they are comprehensive, timely and accurate" (Software and Information Industry Association, 2001). One example idea from the APNEE partners was to invent a *Bio-feel-good-index* like the already established bio-weather. This index should approach the new generation of health-concerned citizens and give information about the daily environmental condition. We see this example as a new concept of extending pure environmental information to new promising "information products". Extending public information or services with other information or services to new "products" improves public services and such provides more value for citizens.
- **Bundling of information:** Combining several sources (different types, different regions) to an information bundle (like also presented in the item before) fosters

also the information awareness of citizen. New visualization means like maps with zooming and smart map facilities (Peinel & Rose, 2001) covering a larger region like the whole country seduces to information detection and exploration. Citizens tend to be curious not only about the situation in their neighborhood, but they also want to compare with other regions, check also water, weather, sun, UV, and the like.

- **Reselling of data:** The information provision from authorities can certainly not be bound to only one commercial partner. Other interested parties have the same right to access the data. But, it might be easier for them to "buy" now the data from the already-established private partner because it already knows the semantics and use. Provided reselling of data is allowed, this will spread the availability and use.

Advertising and Sponsoring

Citizens do not expect to receive "content" for free and are therefore not strictly against advertising integrated in information services; this was also demonstrated by a survey made by the mobile operator Amena, partner in USE-ME.GOV. Given the choice of (1) the payment of a service, (2) advertising for financing, or (3) no service at all, advertising was clearly the favorite. Even advertisements on e-government portals have been debated for quite some time among the actors (see, for example, Peterson, 2000), apparently reluctance still prevails. A survey of e-government services showed in 2005 that only around 4% of government Web sites world-wide relied on ads (the same as the year before) (West, 2005). They were presented as banners, pop-ups, and fly-by advertisements.

The author of Koppell (2001) compared governmental Web sites with a bus and a park. Either like a park, "a public space that shouldn't be marred by clever click-through ads..." or like city buses "literally wrapped in advertising". Citizen and authorities preferring the latter view will not care about advertising combined with public services. And as the author finalizes his opinion in favor of advertisements: "Talk is cheap. But someone has to pay for the servers and software that will make e-government work. If you're not willing to pay for them, maybe *Motel 6* will be."

We experienced in project APNEE-TU (Peinel & Rose, 2004) that the authorities involved did not object to commercial advertising on the same interface where the environmental information is presented (probably because it was not an authority operated interface but a commercial one). But they restricted the type of advertising. Naturally, they forbid commercials for unhealthy products like cigarettes and offending material like gambling and the like. We would expect the same opinion for all authorities, and this will require controlled advertising by special contracts or by special advertising companies.

We define sponsoring as financial support of an information service by an external non-public party, with the service in turn showing the sponsor's name on the Web or mobile interface, and/or mentioning them in other official publications. If advertising is not well accepted by citizens, sponsoring could be a more discreet possibility of financial support. Sponsoring requests should not be targeted only to pure commercial companies. Public organizations seeking for additional funding should also consider to approach NGOs, other public bodies, societies, chambers, unions, and the like. As an example, automobile clubs might sponsor a public infrastructure complaint service as additional support service for their members, since deteriorated streets and highways are of special concern for car drivers.

Payment by Citizen

Most authorities are reluctant to ask the citizen for payment of services, even push services that require an active transmission of data which in turn causes costs on the invoker side. Citizens would argue that the tax payer is stressed enough with payments to the state, so governmental services should be as free as possible. On the other hand, there is no argument that authorities have to provide their services with all the bells and whistles on every channel available for free; specific personalized services with a clear added-value could be supported by the citizen with an additional payment. A second argument has already been mentioned—the competition to the private market, and the possible exploitation of public sector information by new marketable services thus creating new value, and in turn new tax revenues.

If authorities decide to claim a reimbursement from the citizens, the revenue model can be based on subscriptions, pay-per-use, or transactions. Payment can be done by micro-payment systems such as FirstGate or Mobipay, via the phone bill and transfers to the authority by the mobile operator, or by direct cash in the office (for example, when a notification about the pickup of a passport should be sent by mobile phone to the citizen, the notification fee is included in the total issue fee and directly payable). Concerning professional micro-payment offers (like PayPal, Firstgate), it should be noted that such services "eat" a large percentage of the overall revenue, and such a reduction has to be taken into account when calculating the overall service revenues and of course also when calculating the price customers have to spend.

Also, citizens in different European countries show a different acceptance of technology and use. This results also in a difference of pricing acceptance. As project APNEE showed, North-European countries accept higher prices for mobile services than citizens from southern Europe (Peinel & Rose, 2004). In addition, younger and older customers differ in their acceptance of technology, especially with regard to mobile technology. It should be carefully evaluated who is the normal customer for the intended service in order to be not confronted with the digital divide phenomena.

Sharing of the Service or the Platform with Other Authorities

All costs and efforts can be naturally reduced if several authorities share the service and operation of the mobile offer. This sharing can be done with commercial organizations too, but sharing with other authorities might be easier to carry out considering trust, privacy, and regulations. On the other hand, this sharing can also pose some problems since other departments and moreover other authorities have very probably different leadership and work-sharing models, hierarchy, and structure. Consider the diverse organizational structures in countries with a federal constitution.

But the advantages are clear:

- Sharing of costs and efforts, exchange of experiences and results.
- Provision of a larger dissemination field for services, possibility to offer cross border services (also municipality borders), giving one anchor point for all services—one-stop shop.
- Stronger negotiation position against mobile operators by bundling and increasing customer base.
- Implementation of chained and combined services (i.e., move from one city to another; notifications of a move in one service instead of two notifications at two city portals).
- Bundling of services according to citizen needs, not the authority structure.

IT investments and operational costs are especially difficult for smaller authorities, municipalities, or rural civil services, which do not only have low IT resources and investment for establishing electronic service delivery, but also serve a great variety of service types to, for the most part only a limited number of customers (citizens). Well-known and often cited examples of e-government services are mostly operated by larger authorities with a large clientele and more focused business segments like tax offices (Leenes & Svensson, 2002). The authors Leenes and Svensson also strongly recommend the sharing of services between authorities to lower investment, and also to bundle services in central access points for citizens.

RECOMMENDATIONS

Public authorities need to have an open mind for PPPs, as they offer them the opportunity to expand their service portfolio by sharing the investment with private partners (and possibly reduce development and operational costs by reuse of infrastructure and value-added mobile network operator services [Dietz, 2005]). Private companies, on the other hand, can open new market opportunities with new services based on public sector information.

Due to the experiences in APNEE, we believe in the success of PPPs. Even we experienced a "cultural" habit of authorities to retain the custom of power control in their hands to avoid any intervention or meddling. Until now, there also seems to be a tendency of public authorities to hide behind the reliability shield. Authorities retain their behaviour to convey also those information to the public that has proven to be water tight. The hidden objective is to minimize risks of reliability claims by information processors and information receivers.

However, in light of current and emerging budget restrictions, public authorities have to start establishing mutual contracts with syndicators for the provision of information as well as to settle the range of services that might operate with the information provided.

Moreover, European legislations in terms of EU directives pave the way for new business services based on public sector information (European Commission, 2000b). Public sector information has been gathered and maintained in enormous quantities and typically come with premium quality. PPP will enable a collaborative exploitation of this information with commercial business. One major obstacle to this business bonanza so far has been the variety of technical interfaces that are not standardized among authorities and different national initiatives. Industry and commercial standardization bodies come as natural partners to these exploitation initiatives. Projects that build upon public information, for example, information public due to the act of free information in the United States, have already taken-off with success in the U.S. (European Commission, 2000a). However, in Europe many cross-border initiatives and hence businesses fail due to different implementations of frameworks that are actually striving for European uniformity. In addition, we experienced animosity when authorities were asked to provide information cross-border to "unknown" recipients.

CONCLUSION

We have been arguing that authorities need to reconsider their financing options. Rather than limiting their minds to governmental do-it-yourself, they ought to open their line of thinking to already established financial mechanisms and modes of operations in the commercial market. Advertising, payment by the citizen, and public-private partnerships for a sharing of business risks and operating costs are additional options to be considered to enable service provision while minimizing public investments. In addition, sharing of services between authorities and departments gives the advantages of establishing a one-stop-government, sharing of experiences and efforts, as well as stronger position when negotiating with commercial providers.

Project APNEE provides the evidence for the PPP approach presented. In the course of the project various business models have been applied. By the end of the project, the services are operated as different value chains resulting in a variety of partnerships that are contingent upon regional preferences as well as business interests. Hence, the entire spectrum of business options needs to be explored and suitable partners have to be identified. On the other hand, USE-ME.GOV has produced recommendations on when certain options are most favorable and which caveats have to be taken in account. Results serve as guidelines for sustainable m-government services.

ACKNOWLEDGMENT

APNEE has been supported by the European Commission DG XIII under contract IST-1999-11517, APNEE-TU under contract IST-2001-34154. Project USE-ME.GOV is supported by the EC under contract IST 6FP 002294.

REFERENCES

Abramowicz, W., Bassara, A., Filipowska, A., Peinel, G., Rose, T., Wisniewski, M., & Zebrowski, P. (2005). Technical implications and business recommendations for building open and interoperable platform for m-services provisioning. In I. Kushchu, & M. H. Kuscu (Eds.), *Proceedings of the First European Conference on Mobile Government*, Brighton, UK, July 10-12 (pp. 7-16). Brighton, UK: University Sussex.

Adams, N. J., Haston, S., Gillespie, N., & Macintosh, A. (2003). Conventional and electronic service delivery within public authorities: The issues and lessons from the private sector. In R. Traunmüller (Ed.), *Proceedings of the 2nd International Conference, EGOV 2003* (Vol. LNCS 2739, pp. 129-134), Prague, Czech Republic, September 1-5. Berlin, Heidelberg: Springer-Verlag.

APNEE. (2006). Air pollution network for early warning and on-line information exchange in Europe. Project Homepage. Retrieved November 18, 2006, from http://www.apnee.org

Craglia, M., & Masser, I. (2001). *Access to geographic information: A European perspective.* Paper presented at the ESF-NSF Workshop on Access to Geographic Information and Participatory Approaches Using GI, Spoleto, Italy, December 6-8. Retrieved April 2002, from http://www.shef.ac.uk/~scgisa/spoleto/craglia.pdf

DB Research. (2005). E-government in Germany: Much achieved – Still much to do! *E-conomics, Digital economy and structural change*. Retrieved April 2006, from http://www.dbresearch.com/PROD/DBR_INTERNET_EN-PROD/PROD0000000000188264.PDF

Dietz, U. (2005). Mobile government and mobile network operators – Is cooperation possible. In I. Kushchu, & M. H. Kuscu (Eds.), *Proceedings of the First European Conference on Mobile Government 2005*, Brighton, UK, July 10-12 (pp. 133-142). Brighton, UK: Sussex.

European Commission. (2000a). Commercial exploitation of Europe's public sector information (Final report). Retrieved June 2005, from ftp://ftp.cordis.lu/pub/econtent/docs/commercial_final_report.pdf

European Commission. (2000b). *Directive 2003/98/EC of the European Parliament and of the Council of 17 November 2003 on the re-use of public sector information.* 2003/4/EC, Official Journal L 345, p. 90-96.

European Commission. (2003). *Directive 2003/4/EC of the European Parliament and of the Council of 28 January 2003 on public access to environmental information and repealing Council Direc-*

tive 90/313/EEC. 2003/4/EC, Official Journal L 41, p. 26-32.

European Commission. (2004). *Final Report of the Multichannel delivery of e-government services - June 2004 (EN)* (Short report): EC, Enterprise DG, Interchange of Data between Administrations. Retrieved June 2005, from http://europa.eu.int/ida/servlets/Doc?id=16867

Goldstuck, A. (2004). *Government unplugged, Mobile and wireless technologies in the public service*. Centre for Public Service Innovation, South Africa. Retrieved April 2006, from http://topics.developmentgateway.org/egovernment/rc/filedownload.do~itemId=379174

Government of Malta—Ministry for Information Technology and Investment. (2003). Mobile government services of the government of Malta. Retrieved December 2005, from http://www.mobile.gov.mt/?mb:lang=en

Government of the Hong Kong Special Administrative Region. (2004). Public-private sector partnership. Retrieved November 2005, from http://www.info.gov.hk/digital21/e-gov/eng/init/index.htm

INSPIRE DPLI Working Group. (2002). Data policy & legal issues working group position paper. Retrieved August 2005, from http://www.ec-gis.org/inspire/reports/position_papers/inspire_dpli_pp_v12_2_en.pdf

Kane, B. (2004). *Connecting The dots – Why Danish IT architecture does not result in interoperability*. ITU - IT University of Copenhagen. Retrieved May 2006, from http://www.interop.dk/fileadmin/user_upload/Brian_Kane_Thesis_EAI_FINAL_public_version_v3.pdf

Koppell, J. (2001). Your ad here. *Industry Standard, Online Magazine*, February 5, 2001. Retrieved December 5, 2005, from http://www.newamerica.net/index.cfm?pg=article&DocID=100

Leenes, R. E., & Svensson, J. (2002). Size Matters – Electronic service delivery by municipalities? In R. Traunmüller, & K. Lenk (Eds.), *Proceedings of the Electronic Government – First International Conference, EGOV 2002* (Lecture Notes in Computer Science 2456), Aix-en-Provence, France, September 2-5 (pp. 150-156). Springer.

NIC Homepage. (2005). NIC Inc. Retrieved March 2006, from http://www.nicusa.com

Peinel, G., & Rose, T. (2001). Graphical information portals: The application of smart maps in GeoNet 4D. *Journal of GeoInformatica, 5*(4), 327-344.

Peinel, G., & Rose, T. (2004). Dissemination of air quality information: Lessons learnt in European field trials. In the *Proceedings of the EnviroInfo 2004*, Geneva, Switzerland, October 21-23. Retrieved from http://www.enviroinfo2004.org/cdrom/Datas/Fullpaper.htm

Peterson, S. (2000). This space for rent. *Government Technology, Online Magazine*, December 2000. Retrieved November 1, 2005, from http://www.govtech.net/magazine/story.php?id=3024&issue=12:2000

Saxena, K. B. C. (2005, October). Towards excellence in e-governance. *International Journal of Public Sector Management, 18*(6), 498-513.

Software and Information Industry Association. (2001). Promoting public-private cooperation in e-government – Not competition. In Congressional Internet Caucus and its Advisory Committee (Ed.), *Briefing book outline: E-government*. Internet Issue Compilation Books. Retrieved November 17, 2005, from http://www.netcaucus.org/books/egov2001/pdf/netcaucu.pdf

Stahl, B. C. (2005). The ethical problem of framing e-government in terms of e-commerce. *The Electronic Journal of e-Government, 3*(2), 77-86.

USE-ME.GOV Consortium. (2005a). Recommendations for the planning of mobile services in public administrations (Deliverable D3.1) (public deliverable). USE-ME.GOV Homepage. Retrieved March 1, 2006, from http://www.usemegov.org

USE-ME.GOV Consortium. (2005b). USE-ME.GOV Project Homepage. Retrieved March 1, 2006, from http://www.usemegov.org/

Weiss, P. (2002). *Borders in cyberspace: Conflicting public sector information policies and their economic impacts*. U.S. Department of Commerce, National Oceanic and Atmospheric Administration, National Weather Service.

West, D. M. (2005). *Global e-government*. Brown University's Taubman Center for Public Policy. Retrieved October 2005, from http://www.insidepolitics.org/egovt05int.pdf

This work was previously published in Mobile Government: An Emerging Direction in E-Government, edited by I. Kushchu, pp. 86-105, copyright 2007 by IGI Publishing, formerly known as Idea Group Publishing (an imprint of IGI Global).

Section 5
Organizational and Social Implications

This section includes a wide range of research pertaining to the social and organizational impact of electronic government around the world. Chapters introducing this section illustrate what types of social responsibility issues need to be addressed in electronic government, who must address them, and how they might be addressed. Additional chapters included in this section provide important information on the role that the Internet is now playing in the delivery and take-up of government services by European citizens. Also investigating a concern within the field of electronic government is research on the public sector and innovative e-policies. With more than 38 chapters the discussions presented in this section offer research into the integration of global electronic government as well as implementation of ethical considerations for all organizations.

Chapter 5.1
Aspects of Social Responsibility in the Information Society

Simon Rogerson
De Montfort University, United Kingdom

ABSTRACT

The Information Society must be based on fundamental assumptions about information and human information rights, access, privacy, self-determination and personal control rather than on privilege, power and special interest. Those involved in the planning, development and implementation of the information systems that turn the Information Society into a reality are the custodians of the greatest change agent yet devised. They must recognise their social responsibilities and act accordingly for the benefit of society and its citizens. This chapter serves as an illustration of what types of social responsibility issues need to be addressed, who must address them and how they might be addressed. It discusses some of the basic aspects of social responsibility and the implications for the Information Society, drawing in particular from Corporate Social Responsibility. Five disparate cases illustrate how concepts are turned into real organisational policy. Two example applications, electronic voting and electronic patient records are used to illustrate the types of social responsibility issues that need to be addressed in order to tackle the digital divide and satisfy the needs and aspirations of stakeholders.

INTRODUCTION

The social impact of computing technologies is growing at an increasing rate. Computers are changing where and how we work, learn, shop, eat, vote, receive medical care, spend free time, make war and establish social relationships. This revolution is not merely technological and financial, it is fundamentally social and ethical. It is a revolution that has spawned an Information Society with the potential to be either empowering or enslaving. In this dangerous world the stakes are much higher, and consequently considerations and applications of social responsibility must be broader, more profound, and above all effective. This will increase the chance of an Information Society that effectively utilizes information and the related technologies to promote human well-being.

There is much evidence to show that there exists a digital divide. DeHann (2000) argues that "in an age of globalization, an age where the gap between the rich and the poor nations continues to widen, business leaders more than ever need to embrace social responsibility as a successful business strategy." Considering the world as a village of 100 people, DeHann says we would find that: 80 would live in substandard housing; 66 would not have safe drinking water; 66 would never have made a phone call; 50 would suffer from malnutrition; six (all from the U.S.) would own one-half the wealth; one would have a college education; and one would own a computer.

There is an increasing awareness among people of such inequalities and the potential of the Information Society to redress the balance. The demand on organizations to act in a socially responsible manner may well increase. In 1999 Environics International undertook The Millennium Poll on Corporate Social Responsibility involving representative samples of 1,000 citizens in each of 23 countries on six continents. The report of the poll included the following four public expectations of organizations in the future:

- Demonstrate their commitment to society's values and their contribution to society's social, environmental, and economic goals through actions.
- Fully insulate society from the negative impacts of company operations, and its products and services.
- Share the benefits of company activities with key stakeholders, as well as with shareholders.
- Demonstrate that the company can make more money by doing the right thing, in some cases by reinventing its business strategy.

These expectations set a challenging agenda for those involved in the planning, development, and implementation of the Information Society. However, this public expectation is likely to be dulled because of people's tendency to be somewhat unquestioning about technological advancement and solutions. Indeed Hamelink (2000) claims people have complete trust in technological solutions to personal and social problems, have a tendency to seize any technological advance, and tend to equate technological progress with progress of civilization. There is thus a need to be proactive about social responsibility.

Against this backdrop, the purpose of this chapter is to explore some of the key aspects of social responsibility within the evolving Information Society with particular emphasis on the role of organizations. The objective is to highlight the types of problems and challenges faced by those planning, developing, and operating systems that turn the Information Society into a practical reality.

UNDERSTANDING SOCIAL RESPONSIBILITY

As mentioned earlier the Information Society can be a dangerous world. Johnson (1997) explains that the potential benefit of the Information Society is being devalued by antisocial behavior, including unauthorized access, theft of electronic property, launching of viruses, racism, and harassment. These have raised new ethical, cultural, economic, and legal questions that have led many to consider the feasibility and desirability of regulation in this area. Similarly, it is questionable whether technological countermeasures will be very effective either. The absence of effective formal legal or technological controls presents grave dangers to this virtual society.

The international aspect of the Information Society, the transient nature of the content, and the rapid evolution of the techniques and strategies raise specific difficulties for the application of penal and commercial law. It is extremely difficult to determine which laws apply, who is responsible, and what proof is required in the event of a transgression. It is probably unattainable to create international law that can provide legal guarantees for this global community. This would require agreement on universal rights and wrongs that may well be possible for obvious cases, such as the dissemination of child pornography, but is very difficult for debatable issues, such as individual privacy and intellectual property. For this reason society must turn to social responsibility to provide the necessary checks and balances in order for the enormous benefits of the Information Society to be realized.

But what is social responsibility? The term has been used differently in many contexts such as business, health care, libraries, and marketing. It has been used in terms of both organizational responsibility, usually termed corporate social responsibility, and individual responsibility. Corporate social responsibility is probably the most studied area. Potentially much can be applied from this area to the Information Society and as such is worthy of some further consideration.

Corporate Social Responsibility

There are many definitions of Corporate Social Responsibility (CSR). For example, Kilcullen and Kooistra (1999) suggest CSR is the degree of moral obligation that may be ascribed to corporations beyond complying with the laws of the state. Baker (2002) defines such moral obligation in a practical sense in that CSR is how companies manage the business processes to produce an overall positive impact on society. This agrees with DeHann's (2000) view that social responsibility is about achieving commercial success in ways that honor ethical values and respect people, communities, and the natural environment. The general concept of positive societal impact is elaborated upon in the definition by Holme and Watts (reported by Baker, 2002). This points to the improvement of the quality of life of the workforce and their families, as well as of the local community. The implication here is that there must be a positive relationship between an organization and its stakeholders. This relationship is explicitly stated in the CCBC (2002) definition, which is that CSR is "the overall relationship of the corporation with all of its stakeholders. These include customers, employees, communities, owners/investors, government, suppliers, and competitors. Elements of social responsibility include investment in community outreach, employee relations, creation and maintenance of employment, environmental stewardship, and financial performance."

CSR does not appear to be a universal concept. For example, Baker (2002) explains that, in Ghana, CSR is concerned with sustaining livelihoods and that it must respect cultural differences, while in the Philippines the focus seems philanthropic and is about business giving back to society. He suggests this is different from the European approach, which focuses on operating the business in a socially responsible way, complemented by investment in communities, but only for solid business case reasons. This view of Europe appears at odds with the definition used by Hines et al. (2000) in their research on European attitudes towards CSR. They suggest social responsibility activities go beyond profit making and focus on environmental protection, employee welfare, ethical trading, and involvement in the local community within which an organization operates.

CSR Policy

CSR must have practical worth. The UK Government in its "Business and Society: Corporate Social Responsibility Report 2002" suggests that the concepts and principles discussed above need to be translated into organizational policy and operational practice. It explains that responsible organizations do three things:

- Recognize that their activities have a wider impact on the society in which they operate.

- Take account of the economic, social, environmental, and human rights impact of their activities across the world.
- Strive to achieve benefits by working in partnership with other groups and organizations.

The five cases that follow illustrate typical practice and policy across a broad range of organizations. The italicized text in each case contains extracts from the organization's policy documents.

Policy Case 1. Lever Brothers Limited (see Zairi, 2000)

Lever Brothers is a long-established chemical manufacturer in the north of England. The emphasis of their social responsibility approach is on safety, the environment, and employee welfare. It appears quite local in its focus and does not move far beyond the company's core business. While the policy states the principles are for employees to follow, the five statements seem more appropriate to organizational action than individual action.

> *Lever lays down the following principles for employees to follow in order to effectively focus on societal value-added:*
>
> 1. *We recognize that our employment policy, not least the commitment to training and personal development and our emphasis on safety, health, and environment, has a positive impact on the world outside the working environment.*
> 2. *We improve the well-being of society at large both by the generation of employment in companies which service and supply us, and in our marketing activities.*
> 3. *We use a world-class expertise base in human safety to ensure the consumer safety of our products.*
> 4. *We take great care to minimize the environmental impact on all our operations from raw material procurement, product design, manufacture, and distribution to use and disposal.*
> 5. *Lever has a long and proud tradition of involvement with the community. This originated when William Hesketh Lever first established Port Sunlight village to improve the living conditions and well-being of his employees.*

Policy Case 2. British Columbia Ministry of Education (2001)

This is a pragmatic framework for an educational setting. It does not provide a comprehensive definition of social responsibility, but it does clearly set out expected norms of behavior for individuals. It is easily understood but challenging to realize. It might also be considered as a code of conduct.

> *The framework for the BC performance standards for social responsibility provides educators, students, and families with a common set of expectations for student development in four categories. Most of these have more than one component.*
>
> ***Contributing to the Classroom and School Community***
>
> - *sharing responsibility for their social and physical environment*
> - *participating and contributing to the class and to small groups*
>
> ***Solving Problems in Peaceful Ways***
>
> - *managing conflict appropriately, including presenting views and arguments respectfully, and considering others' views*
> - *using effective problem-solving steps and strategies*

Valuing Diversity and Defending Human Rights

- *treating others fairly and respectfully; showing a sense of ethics*
- *recognizing and defending human rights*

Exercising Democratic Rights and Responsibilities

- *knowing and acting on rights and responsibilities (local, national, global)*
- *articulating and working toward a preferred future for the community, nation, and planet—a sense of idealism*

Policy Case 3. Hudson's Bay Company (2002)

Hudson's Bay Company is Canada's oldest corporation and largest department store retailer. This is their statement of philosophy. It recognizes the potential tension between profit and societal needs. The emphasis is on establishing an acceptable organizational culture that promotes broad social responsibility.

> *Hudson's Bay Company believes that a company is obligated to be accountable to all of its stakeholders in all it operations and activities. Socially responsible companies consider the full scope of their impact on communities and the environment when making decisions, balancing the needs of stakeholders with their need to make a profit.*
>
> *Companies need to:*

- *demonstrate commitment to their espoused values by actively contributing to social and environmental goals, as well as economic ones;*
- *insulate society from negative impacts of the companies' operations, products, and services; and*
- *share the benefits of company activities with key stakeholders.*

Policy Case 4. Assistants.Com (2002)

Assistants.Com is an online software house that subscribes to open source principles. Again this is a statement of philosophy. There is an attempt to link social responsibility positively to self as well as others. This is different from the other cases, which all focus only on the relationship with others.

> ***Our principles***
>
> *Social Responsibility—We believe that there is no purpose in getting wealthy for the sake of wealth. As we have been lucky enough to be given quality education in high-demand skills, we have no real problem maintaining our financial commitments. Rather, we hope to create sites which provide value to others and we hope to use the proceeds in a rewarding manner. We are not a non-profit, but we recognize the importance of social responsibility, not to the world, but to our own happiness.*

Policy Case 5. AASL Information Literacy Standards (1996)

This policy again focuses on individual behavior, but this time in a library setting. It provides clear policy regarding the range of modern information resources. This policy covers the individual in the role of user of technology, creator of information, and member of the library community.

> ***Category III: Social Responsibility***
>
> *The student who contributes positively to the learning community and to society is information literate and:*
>
> ***Standard** 7: Recognizes the importance of information to a democratic society, as described by the following indicators:*

1. *seeks information from diverse sources, contexts, disciplines, and cultures;*

2. *respects the principle of equitable access to information.*

Standard 8: *Practices ethical behavior in regard to information and information technology, as described by the following indicators:*

1. *respects the principles of intellectual freedom;*
2. *respects intellectual property rights;*
3. *uses information technology responsibly.*

Standard 9: *Participates effectively in groups to pursue and generate information, as described by the following indicators:*

1. *shares knowledge and information with others;*
2. *respects others' ideas and backgrounds and acknowledges their contributions;*
3. *collaborates with others, both in person and through technologies, to identify information problems and to seek their solutions;*
4. *collaborates with others, both in person and through technologies, to design, develop, and evaluate information products and their solutions.*

The five cases illustrate a variety of approaches to turning social responsibility concepts and principles into practical policy. When combined they emphasize the importance of creating employment and supporting personal development, public welfare, environmental care, shared responsibility, reasoned problem resolution, respect for others, distributed benefits, and equality of opportunity and access. Such themes are particularly important, given that most modern organizations operate in the context of the Information Society.

Psychologists working online serve as a good illustration of how such themes are relevant for those working within a modern organization in the Information Society. King and Poulous (1999) explain, "Psychologists 'apply and make public their knowledge of psychology in order to contribute to human welfare' (APA, 1992). Online psychologists who maintain a website advertising their services often include a wealth of information about psychological disorders and their treatment. This psycho-educational service is available to the public 24 [hours] a day, can be accessed to the advantage of anyone, not necessarily a client, and is generally provided free of charge. In situations where a recipient of services is in a geographically remote location, online therapy may be the only psychological therapy available to them." In this situation the psychologist's traditional approach has been transcended with the advent of the Information Society. In this new situation, public welfare, distributed benefit, and equality of access are all promoted through exploiting the temporal and geographic independence of the online world.

This type of transformation is common across many types of work. The social responsibility principles discussed above and the practical adaptations in the five case illustrations can be used to derive a set of strategic pointers for applying social responsibility within the Information Society as follows:

- Develop a socially responsible culture within the organization which nurtures moral individual action.
- Consider and support the well-being of all stakeholders.
- Account for global common values and local cultural differences.
- Recognize social responsibility is beyond legal compliance and effective fiscal management.
- Ensure all business processes are considered from a social responsibility perspective.
- Be proactive rather than reactive.

From this discussion there appears to be three concepts to draw from CSR and its practical adaptation: adoption of a stakeholder approach, focus on welfare and quality of life, and account for cultural diversity. These can be related to specific issues in the Information Society. Dhillon (2002) identifies five broad issues of social responsibility that permeate the Information Society. These are privacy and confidentiality, accessibility, property rights, freedom of speech, and quality and reliability of systems. The three concepts underpin each of these five broad issues. For example, freedom of speech is directly constrained by Internet censorship. This could affect many stakeholders such as the community, employees, and competitors. Damage to freedom of speech will degrade quality of life. Internet censorship is accepted and even promoted in some countries, while in others it is seen as grossly unacceptable.

THE DIGITAL DIVIDE

As society's dependency on technology increases, so the risk increases of creating both dangerous systems and restrictive systems. Technological dependency has a tendency to limit choice implicitly or explicitly as resource availability reduces for maintaining non-technological facilities. There is an increasing need within society to be computer literate. However, it will be several generations before the digital solution is widely accepted as the traditional and obvious solution. Acceptance is affected by whether a sense of ownership of systems exists within the using community. Such challenges point to the need on the part of planners and developers of systems to accept their social responsibility and act in a way that addresses the digital divide. Lack of education, poverty, and technology aversion all play their part in sustaining the digital divide.

People's perception of IT is an important factor in realizing the huge societal benefit that IT offers. In an international survey by British Telecommunications (1998), people were asked whether they felt advances in information and communication technologies would have a positive or negative effect on aspects of their lives. More than 40% of people globally felt there would be a positive effect on the amount of leisure time available, but interestingly more than 40% of people globally felt it would have a negative effect on the amount of human contact. This feeling was particularly strong in the U.S. (67%) and South Africa (84%). More than 70% of people globally felt it would have positive effect on flexible working. Such perceptions of ICT, causing major changes in work, leisure, and the way people interact, need to be borne in mind by all involved in providing systems. As part of their social responsibility, providers need to be sensitive of such perceptions and work with those directly and indirectly affected to allay their fears concerning, for example, redundancy and becoming disenfranchised.

STAKEHOLDERS IN THE INFORMATION SOCIETY

As mentioned earlier social responsibility should be a proactive action rather than a reactive action. Those involved must consider and act upon the interests of all stakeholders. The identification of stakeholders is therefore an essential element of proactive social responsibility. Many would argue that shareholders or owners or investors are the primary stakeholders in a business and that their welfare should be maximized, but at what cost and to whom? The traditional view of stakeholders is not sufficient, as consideration tends to be restricted to primary users, developers, decision makers, financiers, and legal experts. It is essential to adopt a wider perspective that includes those directly and indirectly affected by the move to the Information Society. This broadening is essential as it includes not only traditional stakeholders viewed from the widely accepted business perspective, but also social actors who Schot (2001) defines as "those who experience the effects of evolving technologies but [traditionally] are not actively involved in the development of technologies. They can be consumers, citizens, employees, companies, social groups, etc." This broader stakeholder consideration encourages

IT professionals to be more sensitive about the systems they design and implement.

However, it is not just IT professionals who have a role to play in promoting social responsibility in the Information Society. It must include all those with some responsibility for IT systems. Johnson (2000) suggests responsibility for technology must start with those who created it, but that users of the technology have a shared responsibility for the consequences. This remains true for information technology. However, there is a wider group of people responsible for IT systems. These can be subdivided into people who commission the systems, people who develop the systems, people who operate the systems, people who use the systems, people who make overall policies under which the systems are developed and operated, and people who actively promote the systems. Each of these subgroups has a role to play in ensuring that systems are beneficial to society.

Participation of Senior Executives

The strategic vision of an organization is driven by its senior executives. This is true of all types and all sizes of organization. It is therefore imperative that senior executives are actively supportive of social responsibility within all areas of operation. There is concerning evidence that this might not be so for IT.

In April 2001, Synstar International, a leading pan-European provider of IT and business availability services, published a survey titled, "Information Technology: Does the Board Understand the Importance of IT Yet?" The survey investigated the changing role of the IT manager in the UK, Germany, and Benelux across the retail, banking, insurance, and automotive market sectors. Three questions in this survey of IT managers and directors are relevant to the issue of social responsibility.

- Question 4b: The board makes decisions without considering the IT implications—agree or disagree?
- Questions 5: What is the average IT literacy of your company's board of directors?
- Question 7: What are the reasons why IT managers/directors are rarely on the board?

Responses to these questions are shown in Table 1.

Overall, 37% of IT managers and directors reported that the board makes decisions without considering the IT implications. The UK (42%) and the automotive sector (40%) were the worst. This, coupled with the belief of about a quarter that their boards had poor or very poor IT literacy, is very concerning. Even more so when 22% responded that the reason why there is not an IT representative on the board is because either the board considers IT peripheral to its business, or the board does not value or understand IT.

These findings suggest that the private sector has some fundamental issues to address if social responsibility related to IT is going to be realized. DeHann (2000) points out, "When social responsibility is a strategic initiative, it is embedded in all aspects of the company's operations." It is therefore concerning that IT companies have little strategic focus on social responsibility. For example, Foley and Jayawardhena (2001) report, "Interviewees acknowledged the growing impact of the Internet on society, but for most (72%) this had little impact on their corporate social responsibility strategies. Indeed, only 15% of IT businesses are currently involved in Internet access projects with local community groups and only four are supporting projects to help households or individuals to have Internet access from home." Without due consideration and support at the board level, responsible computing within organizations is unlikely to become an accepted

Table 1. Percentage of IT managers and directors agreeing

	Q4b—Board does not consider IT	Q5—Board has poor or very poor IT literacy	Q7—Main reason: Board thinks IT peripheral to business	Q7—Main reason: Board does not value or understand IT
Overall	37%	23%	22%	22%
UK	42%	19%	12%	28%
Germany	36%	28%	28%	8%
Benelux	28%	18%	32%	38%
Retail	39%	25%	23%	29%
Banking	34%	17%	24%	20%
Insurance	36%	21%	23%	16%
Automotive	40%	28%	18%	20%

common value. It will mean that critical events will always dictate action based upon efficient and effective expediency rather than social benefit. This seems unacceptable.

ILLUSTRATIONS OF SOCIAL RESPONSIBILITY IN PRACTICE

The Information Society offers new ways of undertaking existing activities. The introduction of electronic voting and electronic patient records are two examples of this new order. These are discussed in detail as they serve to illustrate the sorts of societal issues that need to be addressed during the planning, development, and implementation of facilities within the Information Society. Such issues can only be effectively addressed if a social responsibility approach is adopted.

Electronic Voting

Electronic voting offers real advantages, including the possibility of voting from more convenient locations and the chance for disabled voters to vote on equal terms with others. However, voting is one activity where equal access is of vital importance. Robert Mugabe sought to influence the result of the Zimbabwe presidential election by making it easier to vote for those who he thought would vote for him, and more difficult for those he thought would vote against him. Unlike most public services, when it comes to voting, it is not good enough to make voting much easier for some people without making it easier for all. Voting systems cannot rely on a technology that some have easy access to, but a significant proportion is struggling to use. This alone seems to suggest that simply making it possible to vote using home computers will be unfair.

E-voting also raises tough issues of security and secrecy. Virtually no other transaction with government requires the same degree of secrecy, even from other family members. History has shown that if secrecy is not maintained, there will be attempts to buy votes, to coerce voters, and to use undue influence in other ways. It is no good, therefore, if problems are encountered, to go back to receipts as in other electronic transactions: receipts are just what would be needed to buy and sell votes, and make sure coercion has worked.

If voting is allowed away from supervised polling stations, how do we know that there is not someone else in the room coercing the voter? If we get to the stage where systems are routinely supplied with cameras, then it might be possible for there to be checks that the voter is not being coerced, but this in turn will cause worries about privacy, and could be very labor intensive.

There is a clear requirement for the election authorities to know that each person who is submitting a vote is genuinely entitled to submit a vote, and has not already done so. Yet at the same time, the requirement for secrecy means that how the voter has voted should not be revealed to those in authority. This problem does not seem to be logically insoluble: issuing every voter in an election an identity code for that election, but which cannot be improperly linked back to the identity of the individual, is part of the solution.

A fundamental problem for electronic voting, or electronic counting of votes, is: how do we know that we can trust the systems to give us a 'result' that accurately reflects how people have cast their votes? This is not just a case of how we avoid farces like Florida in the U.S. Presidential election. The question of knowing whether we can trust systems goes deeper. If you use ICT to cast a vote, how do you know that when you tell it 'vote for candidate X' it really does so? It might tell you that it has, but how do you know it is not telling lies? Part (but not all) of the problem here is with viruses. If you are using a multipurpose computer with a mainstream operating system, you are wide open to virus attacks. Sure you might have 'virus protection', but virtually all 'virus protection' systems only protect you against viruses that they already know about, and there is no guarantee that it will know about a virus that changes votes as you cast them.

Assuming that all votes that are sent do genuinely reflect the intentions of the voters, how do we know they have been counted accurately? We could ask the computer to count them again, and be amazed when it comes to exactly the same result as last time (unless we are using the punch cards they used in Florida …). But that does not tell us that it has counted them correctly either time. Part of the solution here is for the software that does the counting to be open to inspection by the political parties (or experts they nominate), but that does not tell us that it has been compiled in the way that we expect. So the compiler needs to be open to inspection, and the computer that the compiler runs on, and so on, and so forth. Transparency is therefore essential. Even if we are confident the votes in the database are correctly counted, we also need to know that they were recorded correctly in the first place, and the database has not been improperly modified. It is far from easy to ensure this in the face of people who might be determined to rig an election.

Electronic Patient Records

The Electronic Patient Record (EPR) allows providers, patients, and payers to interact more efficiently and in life-enhancing ways. It offers new methods of storing, manipulating, and communicating medical information of all kinds, including text, images, sound, video, and tactile senses, which are more powerful and flexible than paper-based systems. The policy of governments appears to favor a national healthcare infrastructure with a longitudinal patient record, covering a patient's complete medical history from the cradle to the grave. Such developments raise a number of issues.

EPRs can facilitate the doctor-patient relationship through use of computerized notes that the doctor and patient share and contribute to. However, EPRs can harm the relationship and undermine trust. For example, in the U.S. there are medical data clearinghouses that sell medical patient data to insurance companies, police departments, employers, drug companies, and so on. Consequently, patients are becoming reluctant to tell their doctors everything about their medical symptoms and the causes of them. This is damaging the doctor-patient relationship, which depends heavily upon confidentiality and most importantly threatens to damage quality of care. There is clearly a tension and trade-off between the need-to-know and the right to confidentiality that must be addressed. This is an issue that has been exacerbated by ICT. Violations of medical confidentiality may appear to be easier because of the efficiency of computerized systems. The damage to the patient whose confidentiality is violated may be proportionately greater because of the amount of data held within the EPR.

Electronic access to medical information requires careful scrutiny. A patient's right to informed consent should prevail. A patient should have control over her/his data, preventing casual distribution that might be harmful. A patient should also have the right not to be informed of medical facts, for example, genetic data that might affect self-esteem and the way in which one lives one's life. The ability to invoke only partial access is important. For example, a woman who had had an abortion might visit a surgeon for an unrelated ailment. She should have the right to decide whether or not to allow that physician access to data other than what could be termed as her general health status. Electronic access to patient data can be beneficial. For example, the administering of prescriptions via electronic transactions from doctor to pharmacist to patient with the aid of digital signatures for authorization could improve service significantly.

The movement of EPRs over the Internet, intranets, and extranets raises concern, for the further from the original source, the greater the risk of inaccuracy, falsification, duplication, manipulation, and unauthorized distribution. There is little effective control over data use over computer networks. Ethical practices are not well defined for the vast array of disclosures to secondary users, such as managed care evaluators, insurance companies, and so on. For example, categorizing and profiling patients may engender discriminatory and/or exclusionary effects. Data banks of health maintenance organizations, and drug companies are gathering information and storing it in computerized form. By linking their computers, these organizations can trade information across computer networks. Information has thus become a tradable commodity. The legitimacy of this medical information trading needs to be established and assurance sought that data is completely anonomized.

Practical Considerations

The discussions about electronic voting and electronic patient records illustrate the range of complex social responsibility issues surrounding the application of computer technologies in the Information Society. Democracy and healthcare are fundamental elements of free society. For the Information Society to flourish, key planks such as these need to be effectively and sensitively addressed. Clearly the two examples highlight a range of matters, such as privacy, intellectual property, trust, and access that need to be addressed during planning, development, and implementation. Table 2, based on the three concepts and five issues mentioned earlier, shows how social responsibility factors inculcate the computer-based systems of the Information Society.

Furthermore, a fundamental underlying issue is complexity. Bucy (2000) argues that the systems

Table 2. Social responsibility issues and concepts penetration

	stakeholder approach	*welfare and quality of life*	*cultural diversity*
privacy and confidentiality	E-vote EPR	E-vote EPR	EPR
accessibility	E-vote EPR	E-vote EPR	E-vote EPR
property rights	EPR	EPR	EPR
freedom of speech	E-vote	E-vote	E-vote
quality and reliability of systems	E-vote EPR	E-vote	E-vote

of the Information Society are, in their current form, too complicated for the many people to use and derive benefit. They require a certain level of cognitive ability to navigate successfully. For this reason he argues, "There is reason to believe that the digital divide will not be completely remedied through universal physical access to computer technology alone." The need to simplify systems radically should form a major design principle for the Information Society.

The attitude of those involved in the planning, development, and implementation of IT systems will greatly influence the nature of the Information Society. Recruitment of people committed to the social responsibly approach is vital. DeCremer and Van Lange (2001) suggest that people can be divided into two categories: those with pro-social orientation and those with pro-self orientation. They explain that, "relative to pro-selfs, pro-socials exhibit greater levels of cooperation in a variety of social dilemmas, seek out greater opportunities to enhance collective outcomes and equality of outcomes, and tend to give social dilemmas a stronger cooperative (rather than competitive) meaning." In other words pro-socials are much more likely to adopt a social responsibility approach. There is thus a compelling argument that profiling done during recruitment of IT personnel should be used to identify this trait in order to increase the chances of engaging staff committed to social responsibility. Ongoing staff development should also promote a pro-social culture and attitude. In this way it is more likely that the wide range of issues and concepts associated with applications such as electronic patient records and electronic voting will be tackled.

These types of practical consideration point to the need for a comprehensive IT management approach that promotes social responsibility. An effective approach is suggested by Erbschloe (2002). He puts forward 10 principles of socially responsible information technology management as follows:

- Appropriately staff IT departments
- Fairly compensate IT workers
- Adequately train computer users
- Provide ergonomic user environments
- Maintain secure and virus-free computer systems
- Safeguard the privacy of information
- Ethically manage intellectual property
- Utilize energy-efficient technology
- Properly recycle used computer equipment
- Support efforts to reduce the digital divide

These principles offer strategic guidance on many issues, including the ones discussed in this chapter, facing those providing systems for the Information Society.

CONCLUSION

Consider this interesting observation by Blanchette and Johnson (2002) concerning a characteristic of the Information Society:

The nature of public/institutional memory is dramatically changing due to the evolving character of information technologies. While preserving the opportunity for a second chance might have been easily achieved in the past, it has become increasingly difficult today. The ongoing balancing of 'discard and forget' and 'preserve and evaluate' has been skewed in favor of the latter. Unless data retention issues are addressed explicitly as part of a comprehensive policy approach to personal privacy, we will gradually move to a panoptic society in which there is little social forgetfulness and little, if any, opportunity to move on beyond one's past and start afresh.

IT systems have never been designed to forget; this has never been on the development agenda. But perhaps in the future it should be for the sake of individuals living in the Information Society. Overall, the Information Society must be based on fundamental assumptions about information and human information rights, access, privacy, self-determination, personal control, and not privilege, power, special interest. Those involved in the planning, development, and implementation of the systems that turn the Information Society into a reality are the custodians of the greatest change agent yet devised. They must recognize their social responsibilities and act accordingly for the benefit of society and its citizens.

This chapter has discussed some of the important aspects of social responsibility in the Information Society. It serves as an illustration of what types of issues need to be addressed, who must address them, and how they might be addressed.

REFERENCES

AASL/AECT National Guidelines Vision Committee. (1996). *AASL Information Literacy Standards*. Retrieved October 7, 2002, from: www.gananda.k12.ny.us/library/mshslibrary/infolit.htm.

American Psychological Association (APA). (1992). Ethical principles of psychologists and code of conduct. *American Psychologists, 47,* 1597-1611.

Assistants.Com. (2002). *Social responsibility*. Retrieved October 4, 2002, from: www.theassistants.com.

Baker, M. (2002). *Corporate social responsibility—what does it mean?* Retrieved October 4, 2002, from: www.mallenbaker.net/csr/CSRfiles/definition.html.

Blanchette, J., & Johnson, D.G. (2002). Data retention and the panoptic society: The social benefits of forgetfulness. *The Information Society, 18,* 33-45.

British Columbia Ministry of Education. (2001). *Performance standards social responsibility: A framework.* October.

British Telecommunications plc. (1998). BT world communications report 1998/99. Retrieved October 1, 2002, from: www.bt.com/global_reports/1998-99/implicat.htm.

Bucy, E.P. (2000). Social access to the Internet. *Press/Politics, 5*(1), 50-61.

CCBC (Canadian Center for Business in the Community). (2002). Corporate social responsibility: Better businesses, better world. Retrieved October 4, 2002, from: www.conferenceboard.ca/ccbc/csr_topic/.

DeCremer, D., & Van Lange, P.A.M. (2001). Why pro-socials exhibit greater cooperation than pro-selfs: The roles of social responsibility and reciprocity. *European Journal of Personality, 15,* S5-S18.

DeHann, C. (2000). Why corporate social responsibility? *Proceedings of the OTE Conference,* Spain (October 4).

Dhillon, G. (2002). *Social Responsibility in the Information Age: Issues and Controversies.* Hershey, PA: Idea Group Publishing.

Environics International Ltd. (1999). *The millennium poll on corporate social responsibility.* Toronto, Canada.

Erbschloe, M. (2002). *Socially Responsible IT Management.* Burlington, MA: Digital Press.

Foley, P., & Jayawardhena, C. (2001). *Corporate Social Responsibility in the IT Industry.* London: The Stationery Office.

Hamelink, C.J. (2000). *The Ethics of Cyberspace.* London: Sage Publications.

Hines, C., Cumming. R., Lewis, S., & McLoughlin, K. (2000). *European attitudes towards corporate social responsibility.* London: MORI. Retrieved October 4, 2002, from: www.businessandsociety.net/uusi/tutkimukset+raportit/europe_eng.html.

Hudson's Bay Company. (2002). Social responsibility: HBC's definition of social responsibility. Retrieved October 4, 2002, from: www.hbc.com/hbc/socialresponsibility/intro.asp?section=social.

Johnson, C.J. (2000). Taking responsibility for technology. *The Internet Encyclopedia of Technology and Culture.* Retrieved October 4, 2002, from: faculty.erau.edu/pratta/Archive/t/takingtech.html.

Johnson, D.G. (1997). Ethics online. *Communications of the ACM, 40*(1), 60-65.

Kilcullen, M., & Kooistra, J.O. (1999). At least do no harm: Sources on the changing role of business ethics and corporate social responsibility. *Reference Services Review, 27*(2), 158-178.

King, S.A., & Poulos, S.T. (1999). Ethical guidelines for online therapy. In J. Fink (Ed.), *How to Use Computers and Cyberspace in the Clinical Practice of Psychotherapy* (pp. 121-132). Northvale, NY: Jason Aronson Inc. Publishers.

Schot, J. (2001). Constructive technology assessment as reflexive technology politics. In P. Goujon & B.H. Dubreuil (Eds.), *Technology and Ethics: A European Quest for Responsible Engineering* (pp. 239-249). Leuven, Belgium: Peeters.

Synstar International. (2001). Information technology: Does the board understand the importance of IT yet? April. Retrieved October 7, 2002, from: www.synstar.com/publications.html.

UK Government. (2002). *Business and society: Corporate social responsibility report 2002*. London: Department of Trade and Industry. May.

United States Internet Council. (2000). State of the Internet report. Retrieved October 7, 2002 from: www.usic.org.

Zairi, M. (2000). Social responsibility and impact on society. *The TQM Magazine, 12*(3), 172-178.

This work was previously published in Social and Economic Transformation in the Digital Era, edited by G. Doukidis, N. Mylonopoulos, and N. Pouloudi, pp. 31-46, copyright 2004 by IGI Publishing, formerly known as Idea Group Publishing (an imprint of IGI Global).

Chapter 5.2
Balancing Individual Privacy Rights and Intelligence Needs:
Procedural-Based vs. Distributive-Based Justice Perspectives on the PATRIOT Act

Kathleen S. Hartzel
Duquesne University, USA

Patrick E. Deegan
Duquesne University, USA

ABSTRACT

This chapter explores how individuals using different justice perspectives to evaluate the appropriateness of the USA PATRIOT Act will logically arrive at different views on the fairness of the legislation. Some pundits believe the USA PATRIOT Act creates an increased risk for the privacy rights of US citizens. Excerpts from both Department of Justice and ACLU documents concerning the USA PATRIOT Act are presented. An analysis of these excerpts suggests that the Department of Justice applies a procedural justice perspective to demonstrate the fairness of the Act in terms of the way the law will be applied. The ACLU applies an outcome-based justice perspective that focuses on the potential for the Act to disproportionately penalize specific demographic groups. Different justice perspectives lead to different fairness judgments.

INTRODUCTION

This chapter presents a social justice perspective on people's attitudes about revealing personal data in exchange for increased government sanctioned-intelligence activity. The degree of personal and corporate data that law enforcement officials and intelligence agencies need in order to provide more comprehensive protection from terrorist attacks threatens to erode individual privacy rights granted by the Constitution and defined by the legal system. Are people willing to trade their personal privacy and autonomy to protect themselves and others or to trade privacy for convenience and profit? How does a society determine whether it is just to compromise privacy rights for increased security? Finally, if an individual's privacy has been compromised, how does that person judge the fairness of this sacrifice in relation to more effective government intelligence and increased physical safety of persons and property?

Comparing the merits of decreasing the threat of terrorist action to the personal costs of a decrease in individual privacy rights is important because of the technological capabilities available today. Technology can, and should, be used to help identify behavior leading to criminal acts. However, the processing capability of information technologies, the vast number of transaction databases with personal identifiers, and the ability to retrieve, integrate, and create virtual alter egos is cause for alarm. Public data of a personal nature, such as deaths, births, sales, and property transfers, have been a constant in our society. However, the difficulty, time, and expense involved in retrieving the data made it difficult to integrate the data and view it as a whole. Information technologies can remove physical barriers to accessing data and can facilitate the integration of data from multiple sources. This is especially true when this data is placed on the Web and in other publicly accessible databases. The aggregation of this public personal data can be too intrusive to be deemed appropriate for a public record (Perkins, 2002).

When electronic profiles of individuals are created, they typically are built with data collected for other, often innocent, purposes—yet they can serve as the basis for initiating more invasive intelligence activity against foreign nationals and US citizens alike. Furthermore, with today's technology, the time and cost necessary to assemble profiles are negligible after the data retrieval and integration algorithms are developed and legal clearances are available. Thus "the body of evidence" necessary to cost-justify an investigation of individuals is minuscule. As a consequence, targeting of intelligence activities could be somewhat arbitrary or capricious. Unfortunately, even the innocent subjects of this type of investigation may suffer irreparable harm once their privacy has been violated. Thus, information technologies can be used to threaten the privacy of individuals, as well as to protect them from other threats.

PRIVACY RIGHTS VS. INTELLIGENCE NEEDS

We value our privacy from a young age. As small children we decide that we can change our clothes by ourselves. As preteens, we lock our diaries because our thoughts are private. As teenagers, we lock the bedroom door so we can be alone—free from the intrusions of Mom and Dad. As adults, the details of our relationships with other people are considered private. Typically, people do not want their financial transactions, whereabouts, or medical histories publicized. Despite our intimate familiarity and desire for privacy, definitions of privacy are often nebulous or incomplete. This is because privacy is a multifaceted concept. The classic definition of privacy is the right to be left alone (Warren & Brandeis, 1890). Privacy is also considered the right to control the use of personal information about one's self (Westin, 1967). Roger Clarke (1999) defines privacy as "the interest that individuals have in sustaining a 'personal space', free from interference by other people and organizations." He further specifies four dimensions of privacy: (1) Privacy of the person, which deals with the physical body—compulsory medical tests and treatments are representative of this category; (2) Privacy of personal behavior, which deals with what we do—this includes our religious, political, and sexual activities; (3) Privacy of personal communications, which implies personal conversations are not to be recorded; (4) Privacy of personal data, which means data about ourselves should not be revealed to other parties without our consent.

Another reason for the lack of clarity in defining privacy—in addition to its being a multidimensional concept—is that privacy is not an absolute right. As members of society, certain personal information must be made available to others. For example, the privacy of an individual's health records can be and should be compromised when public health demands it. Another example is the need of potential creditors to know about an individual's credit history in order to assess the risk of nonpayment before approving a loan.

As a society, we rely on the government to protect us from foreign powers, organizations, and their agents who would chose to do us harm. But, in order to avert a threat, you must be aware of the danger. Thus we need "intelligence." The US Government's Intelligence Community (2003) defines intelligence as:

A body of evidence and the conclusions drawn therefrom that is acquired and furnished in response to the known or perceived requirements of consumers. It is often derived from information that is concealed or not intended to be available for use by the acquirer ... The Intelligence Community deals with both classified and unclassified information. Its analysts produce finished intelligence by analyzing, evaluating, interpreting, and integrating such information (raw intelligence) from various sources.

The USA PATRIOT Act (**U**niting and **S**trengthening **A**merica by **P**roviding **A**ppropriate **T**ools **R**equired to **I**ntercept and **O**bstruct **T**errorism) was drafted in response to the September 11, 2001 terrorist attacks on the US, and passed October 24, 2001. The Act extends many of the same tools that law enforcement uses in the war on crime and drugs to the war on terrorism. It applies to foreign nationals and US citizens alike. The USA PATRIOT Act is designed to protect America from clear and present dangers, but it does so at a cost to our previously acquired privacy rights. The Act has been both applauded for aggressively equipping law enforcement and intelligence agencies with the access to information that they need to fulfill their missions, and also widely protested and criticized for eroding individual privacy rights.

On September 1, 2002, in an address to the Eighth Circuit Judges Conference, John Ashcroft, US Attorney General, stated that the mission of the Department of Justice had changed in focus from the prosecution of illegal acts to the prevention of terrorist acts. In other words, intelligence activity will be the focus. Ashcroft (2002) acknowledged the conundrum that increasing intelligence activity creates. He said, "I am concerned about the expansion of preventative law enforcement. That is why we have undertaken this challenge, mindful that we seek to secure liberty, not trade liberty for security." Given this change in the stated mission of the Department of Justice, an analysis of the justifying perspectives is both timely and relevant to future policy decisions.

SOCIAL JUSTICE PERSPECTIVES

The social justice and organizational justice literatures are concerned with perceptions of fairness in the allocation of rewards and punishments within a given population. The literature reports that people essentially use two evaluation heuristics to judge the fairness of a given situation; these heuristics are called distributive justice and procedural justice. Distributive justice is focused on the outcome of the allocation; it is rooted in equity theory and posits that each party should be rewarded based upon his or her relative contribution. The greater one's contributions, the greater his or her reward should be. The tenets of this line of reasoning have expanded to include the needs of the constituents, particularly in the social and political realms. One prominent area where distributive heuristics have been applied to demonstrate the unjust allocation of outcomes is in gender and racial representations in society. For example, if a particular demographic group is 20% of the general population, do its members hold 20% of the higher paying, more desirable jobs? Conversely, do members of this group comprise more than 20% of the prison population or of those unemployed? If a specific group does not receive a proportionate share of society's rewards (i.e., a good job) or receives a disproportional share of negative outcomes (i.e., prison sentences), there might be distributive injustice.

On the other hand, procedural justice is concerned with the process or rules used to determine the allocation of rewards or punishments. This line of reasoning emanated from the legal setting, where studies have confirmed that defendants viewed both positive and negative outcomes more fairly if they believed the process by which the outcome was determined was fair (Walker, Lind, & Thibaut, 1979). Investigation into this phenomenon revealed that a major factor in the perception of a process as fair was whether or not a participant felt he or she was treated with respect and had a chance to be heard. Having a chance to present one's case is called having a "voice." When participants have a voice in the process, they tend to judge the process as more fair, irrespective of the outcome, because they feel that they have had some control over the process (Van den Bos, 1999).

Rasinski (1987) summarized the differences in people's social justice views in this way: "People who believed that proportionality should be the basis on which benefits are distributed in society emphasized procedures in their judgments of what is fair in society, whereas those who endorsed egalitarianism stressed the fairness of the outcome" (p. 209). He further noted that this tendency increased with higher levels of education. However, other research does not view the choice as ideological, but rather as a more base response. Greenberg (1987) suggested that when people's own outcomes are favorable, they tend to rate outcomes as fair regardless of the fairness of the procedures. But when they receive low-level outcomes, procedures become very important. Whether an individual will apply a procedural justice heuristic, distributive justice heuristic, or a combination of both heuristics to judge the fairness of any given situation is often situational.

It stands to reason that if a distributive justice paradigm is to be used to evaluate outcomes, the individual must not only have knowledge of his or her own outcomes and inputs, but must also know about the outcomes of others and their contributions to the system (Van den Bos, Lind, Vermunt, & Wilke, 1997; Van den Bos, Wilke, Lind, & Vermunt, 1998). Social comparison is a critical factor in evaluating the justness of one's own outcomes relative to the outcomes of those competing for the same or similar resources (Messick & Sentis, 1983). When the knowledge of the outcomes others receive is absent, the individual must look at the fairness of the procedures as a proxy (Van den Bos, Wilke, Lind, & Vermunt, 1998).

Judicial proceedings, employee compensation, employee hiring, immigrant entitlement, affirmative action, landlord-tenant relations, retail exchange, social welfare, and presidential policies are representative of the domains where the body of work in justice theories has been tested and applied.

PRIVACY AND JUSTICE

It is clear that if all electronically processed information were made available and then integrated, most people would feel vulnerable and some would be harmed through the misuse of personal information. However, the typical citizen is not in a position to directly impact information privacy policy and its laws and regulations. As individual citizens, we cannot decide for society as a whole what information about individuals should be private (medical history), what information should be public (phone numbers, marriage licenses), what information becomes corporate property (purchase history, customer profiles), what information must be available for government use (tax information, criminal history), and what information should be available for intelligence activity. Although private citizens do not individually determine public policy, collectively individuals do form public opinion, and public opinion drives the decisions of officials and other public servants. Thus, the citizens' perceptions of the fairness of data access policies are important, both pragmatically and ethically.

Generally, the literature on the privacy implications of data integration and secondary data use weighs individual privacy rights against corporate financial motives. However, when we discuss unfettered access of intelligence agencies to personal data, we are weighing our individual privacy rights against the government's ability to protect not only our property, but also our lives. Creating public policy and the corresponding laws and regulations that dictate intelligence agency power and its limitations would be easy if individuals all had the same political ideology, social standing, knowledge, health consideration, and backgrounds. However, what makes us individuals also makes us different in terms of what we value and what we fear. The strong and diverse reaction to the USA PATRIOT Act is a prime example of the lack of consensus in our society as far as what is a fair and just response to terrorist threats.

The procedural and distributive justice dichotomy can be used to partially explain the variation in the public's reaction to initiatives such as the USA PATRIOT Act. But using these theories to assess the fairness of this legislation is more difficult than applying them to more traditional problems, such as hiring and promotion decision, because of the timing and the availability of information. If you are interviewing candidates for a job opening, you know that there is a position available, you know the job requirements, and you have the candidate's resume. After the decision is made, the outcome is known. The procedural rules for candidate selection may or may not be known. However, if there was no diversity in the people chosen for positions or if candidates with better qualification were dismissed, the heuristics used to determine the "fairness" of the outcome may negatively affect perceptions of the distributive and procedural justice.

It is interesting to point out that the US Government and the American Civil Liberties Union (ACLU) use procedural and distributive heuristics to argue and convince others concerning the USA PATRIOT Act. As is shown in the example below, the ACLU uses a distributive tone in explaining its arguments against the PATRIOT Act and the U.S. Government relies on a procedural tone to argue for support of the PATRIOT Act. A brief example of this can be seen by comparing a part of President Bush's State of the Union Address dealing with the PATRIOT Act (The White House, 2004) to language found on the ACLU's PATRIOT Act Web site (ACLU, 2004). The relevant language is underlined and in italics.

State of the Union Address, January 20, 2004 (Procedural Defense)

Inside the United States, where the war began, we must continue to give our homeland security and law enforcement personnel every tool they need to defend us. And one of those essential tools is the PATRIOT Act, which allows federal law enforcement to better share information, to track terrorists, to disrupt their cells, and to seize their assets. For years, we have used similar provisions to catch embezzlers and drug traffickers. If these methods are good for hunting criminals, they are even more important for hunting terrorists.

President Bush is using a procedural heuristic to show that the PATRIOT Act is very similar to other accepted practices regarding the capture of common criminals. The message here is clear. The government only wishes to do that which it has been doing to "catch embezzlers and drug traffickers." The same procedures that are used and have been tested and approved for the capture of everyday criminals should be applied to the capture of terrorists.

From ACLU Web Page on the USA PATRIOT Act (Distributive Attack)

Just 45 days after the September 11 attacks, with virtually no debate, Congress passed the USA PATRIOT Act. Many parts of this sweeping legislation take away checks on law enforcement and threaten the very rights and freedoms that we are struggling to protect. For example, without a warrant and without probable cause, the FBI now has the power to access your most private medical records, your library records, and your student records... and can prevent anyone from telling you it was done.

The Department of Justice is expected to introduce a sequel, dubbed PATRIOT II, that would further erode key freedoms and liberties of every American.

The ACLU uses a distributive heuristic to show how arbitrary the use of the PATRIOT Act could possibly be. They seem to be conveying the message that the rules and procedures will not protect you, and the allocation of justice has no relation to whether an individual is a terrorist. This excerpt also uses the distributive heuristic to ask why should innocent Americans have their "key freedoms and liberties" further eroded? The use of the particular language plays on the fears of American citizens who are concerned that their privacy will be infringed upon despite little or no connection to a terrorist plot.

Department of Justice (DOJ) and ACLU Arguments on the PATRIOT Act

One of the more controversial parts of the PATRIOT Act is Section 215. Section 215 amends the Foreign Intelligence Surveillance Act of 1978 to allow for access to "business records" and sets up congressional oversight. The Department of Justice and the ACLU have very different views on what Section 215 allows the government to access. Soon after the passage of the PATRIOT Act, the Justice Department created a Web site (www.lifeandliberty.gov) to provide support for the Act. On August 20, 2003, the ACLU released a report refuting the claims made by the Justice Department's Web site. Both groups state that their own position is "Reality" and the other group's is a "Myth." These documents provide an excellent opportunity to look further at how organizations will use social justice perspectives to sell their ideas concerning privacy rights. In the following examples, the relevant language is underlined and in italics.

ACLU and Justice Department Language Dealing with Library Records

From Government Web site (http://www.lifeandliberty.gov/subs/u_myths.htm) *(Procedural Defense)*

- **Myth:** The ACLU has claimed that "Many [people] are unaware that their library habits could become the target of government surveillance. In a free society, such monitoring is odious and unnecessary... The secrecy that surrounds Section 215 leads us to a society where the 'thought police' can target us for what we choose to read or what Web sites we visit." (ACLU, July 22, 2003)
- **Reality:** The PATRIOT Act specifically protects Americans' First Amendment rights, and terrorism investigators have no interest in the library habits of ordinary Americans.

Historically, terrorists and spies have used libraries to plan and carry out activities that threaten our national security. If terrorists or spies use libraries, we should not allow them to become safe havens for their terrorist or clandestine activities. The PATRIOT Act ensures that business records—whether from a library or any other business—can be obtained in national security investigations with the permission of a federal judge.

The phrase "business records—whether from a library or any other business—can be obtained in national security investigations with the permission of a federal judge," shows a procedural justification as it appeals to our sense of fairness that before any step is taken, the proper legal procedures will be followed because a judge will properly scrutinize the government action.

From ACLU (2003) report (Distributive Attack)

- **Myth:** Congress states Section 215 "specifically protects Americans' First Amendment rights."
- **Reality:** Section 215 specifically authorizes the FBI to investigate Americans based in part on their First Amendment activity, and to investigate others based *solely* on their First Amendment activity.

The only thing that Section 215 says about First Amendment rights is that United States citizens and permanent residents can't be investigated under the provision based "solely" on their exercise of those rights. What this means in practice is that, if you're a United States citizen, the FBI can't obtain your library records or your medical records or your genetic information simply because you wrote a letter to the editor criticizing the war in Iraq. If the FBI wants to investigate you, they need to base the investigation on something else as well—something unrelated to the First Amendment. This doesn't mean that the FBI has to have probable cause, or that they need to have any evidence at all that you're engaged in criminal activity. The "something else" could be that you were born in the Middle East, or that you took a trip to Pakistan last year. In fact, the "something else" might even be what one or your friends or associates did, if the FBI thinks that records about you will shed light on that person's activities. As long as the "something else" isn't related to First Amendment activity, it can count as a basis for the investigation. Those who aren't United States citizens or permanent residents don't get even this minimal protection. For example, Canadians in the US on NAFTA visas can be investigated solely because of the books they borrowed from the library, the websites they visited, or the fact that they belong to the Federalist Society or ACLU.

This is an example of applying distributive rationale to judge the Act because it clearly states that privacy rights can be intruded upon due to factors outside of direct terrorism action. This places a heavy burden on those groups that have questionable reputations despite little evidence to label them terrorists.

ACLU and Justice Department Language Dealing with Business Records

From Government Web site (http://www.lifeandliberty.gov/subs/u_myths.htm) *(Procedural Defense)*

Examining business records often provides the key that investigators are looking for to solve a wide range of crimes. Investigators might seek select records from hardware stores or chemical plants, for example, to find out who bought materials to make a bomb, or bank records to see who's sending money to terrorists. Law enforcement authorities have always been able to obtain business records in criminal cases through grand jury subpoenas, and continue to do so in national security cases where appropriate. In a recent domestic terrorism case, for example, a grand jury served a subpoena on a bookseller to obtain records showing that a suspect had purchased a book giving instructions on how to build a particularly unusual detonator that had been used in several bombings. This was important evidence identifying the suspect as the bomber.

This example of language reviews a specific event that shows how the procedure works. The Justice Department again relies on a procedural tone to show how the law will not infringe on an individual's privacy. The argument used is that the system, including that of a grand jury, will keep the infringement on privacy to a minimum while yielding positive results.

From ACLU (2003) report (Distributive Defense)

- **Myth:** Congress states Section 215 of the Act can only be used to obtain "business records."
- **Reality:** Section 215 is not limited to business records.

The DOJ's Web site states that Section 215 of the PATRIOT Act "[a]llows federal agents to ask a court for an order to obtain business records in national security terrorism cases." The site suggests again and again that Section 215 concerns only "business records." In fact, Section 215 authorizes the FBI to order any organization to turn "any tangible thing" over to the government. The provision is much broader than the DOJ now admits. The FBI could use Section 215 to demand:

- *Personal belongings, such as books, letters, journals, or computers*
- *A list of people who have visited a particular Web site*
- *Medical records, including psychiatric records*
- *A list of people who have borrowed a particular book from a public library*
- *A membership list from an advocacy organization like Greenpeace, the Federalist Society, or the ACLU*
- *A list of people who worship at a particular church, mosque, temple, or synagogue*
- *A list of people who subscribe to a particular periodical*

In fact, at a June 2003 hearing before the House Judiciary Committee, the Attorney General himself boasted that the FBI could use the law even to obtain genetic information. The DOJ misleads the public by repeatedly referring to the law as a "business records" provision.

Language as used in this ACLU passage applies distributive heuristics to appeal to the reader's sense that—despite any procedural promises on the part of the government—the outcome of any particular case is not sure to be equitable or just. Instead, the ACLU argues against the PATRIOT Act by listing specific intrusions that may infringe upon our privacy. This passage also shows a disproportionate risk in relation to the reward. If you happen to be a member of a group that is suspect, your privacy may be violated even if your group has little connection to terrorism.

Applying a distributive justice heuristic to determine whether or not outcomes would be fair requires speculation and a tolerance for a high degree of ambiguity, given the outcomes are not known. Additionally, wealth, birth country, and political ideology are all among the factors that can make you more or less visible to the system, and thus more or less at risk.

Clearly, neither heuristic is sufficient to predict how the privacy-security exchange could be judged as fair across the population, a priori. It is more likely that the heuristics provide for speculative and post-hoc justification and criticism of policies. In other words, the justice paradigm applied, and its rationale and conclusions are more likely presented in support of one's ideological stance than as a product of the judgment process.

It is the government's responsibility to address the terrorist threat. Often in executing this duty, the government adopts another set of procedures and policies that are aimed at better protecting us. Of course, it is easier to implement procedures than to guarantee results. Therefore, parties responsible for outcomes have an incentive to adopt a procedural justice position. On the other hand, it is easy to select isolated cases where the outcomes were exceptionally favorable or exceptionally unfavorable and present these extreme cases as either representative or in the "this could happen to you" vein. This characterization is a speculative or post-hoc construction of a distributive justice perceptive.

CONCLUSION

It would be comforting to believe that people make judgments about the fairness of policies and their effects using some rationale heuristic. Unfortunately, that is not a universal truth. In fact, it may be the exception. Although we as humans want to see things as they are, our biases, ideological stances, and fears are self-sustaining. Psychologically, we tend to give those aspects of a situation that support our predisposition a lot of salience, and under weigh those aspects that are counter to our beliefs.

For those who value individual privacy rights highly and do not believe that they should be compromised at any cost, the potential cost of allowing unprecedented access to private information can not be justified. For those who believe increased security outweighs the rights of any individual to keep secrets, "fair procedures" must be put in play and followed. To influence those who can see both points, or who do not have an opinion, explaining procedures and posing hypothetical outcomes can be effective techniques to engender support. The privacy advocates present hypothetical outcomes effectively by using worst case scenarios to elicit fear. On the other hand, the government has to deal with the fear factor stemming from the events of 9/11. However, we believe those responsible for implementation of policies that change the status quo must present a realistic set of potential outcomes. They should emphasize the most likely outcomes and also acknowledge the extreme outcomes to be credible.

REFERENCES

American Civil Liberties Union (ACLU) (2003). Seeking truth from justice: PATRIOT propaganda: The Justice Department's campaign to mislead the public about the USA PATRIOT Act. Washington, DC: ACLU. Retrieved May 25, 2004 from: http://www.aclu.org/Files/getFile.cfm? id=13098

American Civil Liberties Union (ACLU) (2004). USA PATRIOT Act. Retrieved May 25, 2004 from: http://www.aclu.org/SafeandFree/SafeandFree.cfm?ID=12126&c=207

Ashcroft, J. (2000). National security: Justice department's new mission. *Vital Speeches of the Day.* September 1, LXVIII(22), 706-708.

Clarke, R. (1999). Introduction to dataveillance and information privacy, and definition of terms. Retrieved September 29, 2003 from: http://www.anu. edu.au/people/Roger.Clarke/DV/Intro.html

Greenberg, J. (1987) Reactions to procedural injustice in payment distributions: Do the means justify to ends? *Journal of Applied Psychology, 72*(1), 55-61.

Messick, D.M. & Sentis, K. (1983). Fairness, preference, and fairness biases. In D.M. Messick & K.S. Cook (Eds.), *Equity theory: Psychological and sociological perspectives* (pp. 61-94). New York: Praeger.

Perkins, R. (2002). Can public data be too public? *Target Marketing*, March, *25*(3), 51, 54.

Rasinski, K.A. (1987). What's fair is fair—Or is it? Value differences underlying public views about social justice. *Journal of Personality and Social Psychology, 52*(1), 201-211.

US Intelligence Community. (2003). Retrieved October 1, 2003 from: http://www.intelligence.gov/2-character.shtml

Van den Bos, K. (1999). What are we talking about when we talk about no-voice procedures? On the psychology of the fair outcome effect. *Journal of Experimental Social Psychology, 35*, 560-577.

Van den Bos, K. (2001). Uncertainty management: The influence of uncertainty salience on reactions to perceived procedural fairness. *Journal of Personality and Social Psychology, 80*(6), 931-941.

Van den Bos, K., Lind, E.A., Vermunt, R., & Wilke, H.A.M. (1997). How do I judge my outcome when I do not know the outcome of others? The psychology of the fair process effect. *Journal of Personality and Social Psychology, 72*(5), 1034-1046.

Van den Bos, K., Wilke, H.A.M., Lind, E.A., & Vermunt, R. (1998). Evaluating outcomes by means of the fair process effect: Evidence for different processes in fairness and satisfaction judgments. *Journal of Personality and Social Psychology, 74*(6), 1493-1503.

Walker, L., Lind, E.A., & Thibaut, J. (1979). The relationship between procedural and distributive justice. *Virginia Law Review, 65*(8), 1401-1420.

Warren, S., & Brandeis, L. (1890). The right to privacy. *Harvard Law Review, 4*(5), 193-220.

Westin, A. (1967). *Privacy and freedom*. London: Bodley Head.

The White House (2004). George W. Bush's State of the Union Address, January '02. News release. Retrieved May 25, 2004 from: http://www.whitehouse.gov/news/releases/2004/01/20040120-7.html

This work was previously published in Information Ethics: Privacy and Intellectual Property, edited by L. Freeman and A.G. Peace, pp. 180-196, copyright 2005 by Information Science Publishing (an imprint of IGI Global).

Chapter 5.3
Citizen Relationship Management

Alexander Schellong
Harvard University, USA,
and J.W. Goethe University, Germany

INTRODUCTION

Citizen relationship management (CiRM) refers to a cluster of management practices, channel, and IT solutions that seek to use private sector customer relationship management (CRM) in the public sector. Goals can be improving citizen orientation, better accountability, and changing the citizen government relationship. I begin with an overview of citizen orientation in government and the emergence of CiRM. The following section starts with a look at the underlying principles, goals, and components of customer relationship management. Accordingly, there is an in depth discussion and definition of citizen relationship management. Aspects such as the citizen government relationship, technology, public participation, and organizational changes are addressed. Finally, future trends and conclusions are drawn.

BACKGROUND

It is one of the central interests of government to improve the relationship with its constituents. Public administration (PA) is often ignored in the discussion of the citizen government relationship although it plays a vital role in how the government exerts its role within society. Administrative practices and capabilities are often subsumed within the general discussions of government and governmental obligations to citizens. In fact, with a few exceptions, philosophical foundations of the administrative component of government are seldom discussed at all (Rohr, 1986; Waldo, 1984). On average, citizens have more contacts with public servants than their elected representatives throughout their life. They experience policies and the structure of the state through their interactions with the public administration, the latter being for instance law enforcement or public service agencies. Local public administrations are a strong factor for trust building in the discussed relationship.

The intense competition in the private sector and parallel service sector growth has fostered research and focus on customer management related topics (Bretthauer, 2004; Laing, 2003). Furthermore, private sector customer service orientation had an influence on expectations towards public sector services.

Improving public services can be tracked back to the beginning of the 20th century. Throughout the late 1970s and since the emergence of neo-economic new public management (NPM) and its components like total quality management (TQM) (Berman & West, 1995), a customer-driven government has been on the agenda for public servants and researchers (OECD, 2003; Osborne & Gaebler, 1992). This is due to the fact that customer demands are perceived as an agent for organizational change (Lowenthal, 1994). Today, NPM has become a normative model, especially how we think about the role of public administrators, public services, and their goals (Denhart & Denhart, 2003). In fact, as shown by Schedler (2003) or Hood and Peters (2004), there is no common way or understanding of NPM. Despite components like TQM, which is a set of management and control activities based on statistics, leadership of top management and involvement of all departments and levels of employees aimed at quality assurance and citizen orientation, NPM tended to have a one-sided, internal focus on issues such as economic controlling (Traunmüller & Lenk, 2002). This might also relate to NPM's missing theoretical foundation (Frederickson & Smith, 2003; Lynn, 1998).

Customer approaches to government service increased in the 1990s (Albrecht, 1993; Gore, 1993; Kißler, Bogumil, Greifenstein, & Wiechmann, 1997; Swiss, 1992. Especially true with the managerial/consumerist notion of deconstructing citizens as a consumers raised concerns among researchers (Barnes & Prior, 1995; Hood, 1995). A major objection is that the citizen government relationship is redefined as a passive commercial transaction, rather than an interactive political engagement. It strengthens the idea of elitist politics and reduces a complex relationship to a simplistic voluntary one (Box, 1999). Furthermore, it supports short term politics undermining long term political goals (Swiss, 1992).

The emergence of electronic government (e-government) in the late 1990s added new momentum to the NPM oriented reforms and research on public services improvement through online applications (Abramson & Morin, 2003; Ashford, Rowley, & Slack, 2002; Caldow, 1999; Cook, 2000; Fountain, 2001a; Gisler & Spahni, 2001). I define e-government as the use of information technology to support government operations, engage citizens, and provide government services (Dawes, 2002). ICT neutralises time, spatial, and hierarchical limits of the public administration and public services.

Concurrent with these developments, first publications on public sector customer relationship management appeared (Accenture, 2003; Bleyer & Saliterer, 2004; Hewson Group, 2002; Freeland, 2002; Janssen & Wagenaar, 2002; Kavanagh, 2001; Richter, Cornford, & McLoughlin, 2005; Sharpe, 2000; Souder, 2001; Trostmann, 2002). At this point, it is neither possible to identify a clear research stream on CRM in the public sector, an adapted model or theoretical framework nor to identify the broad existence of public managers responsible for CRM. Other terms used are constituent relationship management or citizen relationship management. This article employs the term citizen relationship management.

CUSTOMER RELATIONSHIP MANAGEMENT

Customer relationship management can be defined as a holistic management approach, enabled by technology with a broad customer focus, to start, maintain and optimize relationships and to make customers more loyal/profitable. CRM requires a customer centric business philosophy and culture to support effective marketing, sales and service processes. This is an aggregation of existing perspectives on CRM (Payne & Frow, 2004). For a detailed overview of definitions and research streams see: (Zablah, Bellenger, & Johnston, 2004). Some authors emphasize a single technology solution, others a series of customer-oriented technology solutions and the final group stresses the holistic approach.

CRM's main goal is to optimize the customer lifetime value (CLV) within the customer lifecycle (Homburg & Bruhn, 2005). Customers are long term assets and thus major factors for competitive advantage (Peppers & Rogers, 2004). Further advantages are supposed to be a reduction of marketing costs, strengthening customer loyalty and satisfaction, reduced price sensitivity, new opportunities for up- and cross-selling and erect exit barriers (Janssen & Wagenaar, 2002).

CRM builds on principles of relationship marketing (Berry, 1983). Unlike transaction marketing which focused on a one time transaction (selling process), relationship marketing is about attracting, maintaining and enhancing customer relationships. Other influences come from TQM, business process reengineering (BPR) (McAdam & Donaghy, 1999), and knowledge management (KM) (Alavi & Leidner, 2001; Grover & Davenport, 2001; Nonaka, 1994. Note that TQM and BPR are already included in NPM. Several trends like ICT developments, rigid global competition, and growing knowledge in marketing research (i.e., one-to-one marketing (Peppers & Rogers, 1993), permission marketing (Godin, 1999)) had an impact on the evolution of CRM.

Besides its strategic/organisational component, customer relationship management can be divided into three parts: collaborative CRM, operative CRM, and analytical CRM. Collaborative CRM is focused on channel management. Channel options are:

- Shop/outlets/counter
- Internet
- Telephony (call center)
- Mobile
- Sales force

Collaborative CRM involves decisions about appropriate/ economic channel combinations, keeping single customer view and offering a consistent customer experience across channels. Particularly, electronic channels are very attractive as their self-service potential offers the chance to reduce costs (Kracklauer, 2003).

Processes in the back and front offices are integrated through operational CRM. Software applications can be enterprise resource planning (ERP), sales automation (SA), computer-aided selling (CAS) or knowledge management systems.

Organization and interpretation of customer data through data mining or OLAP and creation of a 360 degree view on customers are within the area of analytical CRM. Data warehousing, database management and data mining systems are an important part of the technological component of CRM.

Basic principles of CRM are personalization (products, information, services), integration (planning processes, business process reengineering, product development, collaboration), interaction (channels, long-term communication, surveys), and selection/ segmentation (identify the top 20% of customers who make 80% of the profit (pareto rule), termination of unprofitable customers). Moreover, quality/performance measurements, change management, and a strategy/ measures promoting customer oriented culture are vital to any CRM concept or project.

Figure 1 summarizes these principles and visualizes the importance of the holistic approach of a CRM/CiRM. Thus, CiRM is about:

- Organization (change)
    - Culture

  - Processes
  - Structure
  - Responsibilities
  - Networked governance
  - Cross-boundary collaboration
- Interactions
  - Channels
  - Participation
- Service range
  - Offering
- Insights
  - Analysis
  - Segmentation
  - Personalization
  - Performance measurement

CITIZEN RELATIONSHIP MANAGEMENT (CIRM)

While identifying and retaining the most profitable or most costly citizens in a commercial sense would contravene against basic principles of social justice, delivering high quality citizen oriented public services is a government policy.

Citizen relationship management (CiRM) can be defined as a strategy enabled by technology with a broad citizen focus, to maintain and optimize relationships and encourage participation. This represents a working definition because CiRM is an emerging research area. CiRM is not a theory but rather a management concept. However, it is possible to build a theory on its impact which has yet to be done.

The main goal of CiRM is to create and optimize the relationship with citizens by embedding their opinions throughout public administration instead within a certain processes/ agency, certain hierarchy level or elected officials. Citizens are a valuable asset in service planning and provision (i.e., cost reductions). A responsive, accessible and citizen focused public administration that creates opportunities for participation can build a close

Figure 1. The CiRM framework

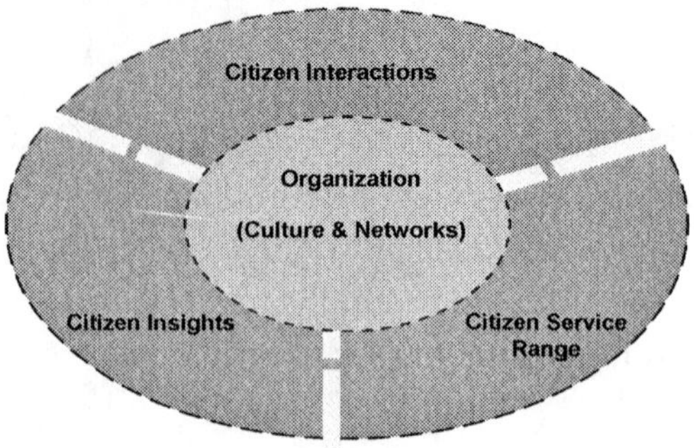

citizen relationship strengthening democracy and legitimating its role.

Though, understanding and application of CiRM by PA practitioners is currently different than the academic discussion or business claims. Reviewing projects in the U.S. and UK, CiRM is mostly applied in conjunction with call centers (311) or citizen service centers (citizen interactions, citizen service range) with a focus on it's technological component at the local level. Technological collaboration across agencies and jurisdictional boundaries occurs, however change and collaboration on the organizational level or other aspects of CiRM is in its early stages.

Miami/Dade County is one of the first cases of a multi-jurisdictional collaboration and a multi-channel, closed loop environment with access to information and services of over 30 municipalities and their agencies in its final level of development. To achieve this, the county takes a gradual approach by bringing in new partners one at a time to cope with any inherent challenges and risks.

Citizen Government Relationship

Before addressing CRM a deeper understanding of the citizen government relationship is needed. It can be reached through an analysis of the reciprocal factors and circumstances of both actors. In fact, psychology of the citizen as a customer/con-

Figure 2. CiRM technology framework

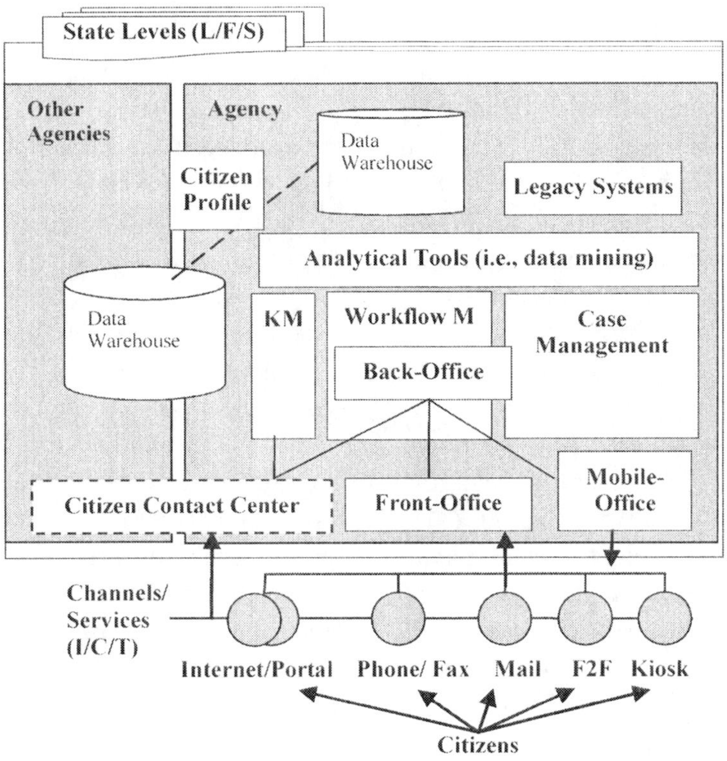

sumer of public services (demand side) as well as public service operations from citizen perspective is not very well researched (Reddick, 2005). To learn more about citizens, public administrations use surveys, focus groups and to a lesser extent citizen counsels. Unfortunately, most of (80%) of this kind of market research serves mainly to reinforce existing conclusions which is also the case for private businesses (Deshpande, 2001).

A major difference exists between customer business and citizen government relationships that offer interesting CiRM scenarios. Citizens in most countries are loyal to their government and public administration (Fountain, 2001b), something that would be a dream for any business. Citizens consider obligations to other, present and even future citizens. They have the moral and legal right (and obligation) to build or to participate in the institutions that provide public services. This is not the case for consumers.

Finally, some questions remain unanswered. Could CiRM help improving public participation? What do citizens think about their roles and segmentation? Are satisfied citizens more active or passive participants?

Contributions of a CiRM Technology Framework

A CiRM technology framework (Figure 2) enables public managers to respond in an accurate and appropriate manner to citizens' inquiries. Public servants have access to citizen profiles and knowledge base while they are in contact with constituents regardless of the channel or state level (local, county, federal state, federal). Currently most relevant channels for information (I), communication (C), and transaction (T) type services are counter/ one-stop service centers, inbound telephone, Web self-service, automated email response and kiosks.

Administrators can build new and real-time databases for future orientation. By cross-referencing citizen surveys with service usage and other related data from multiple organizations they can offer more personalized information, services and identify emerging problems (O'Looney, 2002), process or policy improvements. Since this would be an iterative process it fosters innovation.

Citizen Data

According to a study by Accenture, a consulting company, two thirds of government agencies are not using citizen data they are collecting (Accenture, 2001). Citizen data can be grouped into profile data (i.e., name, address, age, or education), service data (i.e., complaints, suggestions, or questions), contact data (i.e., contact person at agency, date of contact) and service data (i.e., type of service, usage time, costs). Research by Schellong and Mans (2004) revealed that citizens would even allow a personal profile to be saved and shared across public authorities. Those are: name, address, date of birth, education, and the current employment status. Personal history of utilized public services (25%) and personal income (12%) are barely accepted for citizen data profiles. Nevertheless, citizens have more trust in government than in private sector internet services. Information sharing is absolutely necessary to realize the desired benefits of such systems. However, local authority data silos, laws, regulations and culture pose difficult obstacles to overcome (Bannister, 2001).

Citizen Participation

CiRM attempts to integrate citizens into PA. Citizen participation is two-fold. First, it means self-service/ co-production. The more automated and standardized (by heavy use of ICT), services can be organized, the more money can be saved by PA and the more work is done by citizens. Organized well, it can raise satisfaction levels as experience from other sectors (i.e., banking) shows. However, design flaws will generate dissatisfied customers using other channels. Efficiency gains can be neutralized if the streamlining potential of ICT in conjunction with self-services is mainly used to reduce the work force in the PA. A case manager that has to work on comparative more cases can be equal or less citizen oriented (in terms of response time, case handling) than before.

The second form of participation is citizen feedback/complaints on service provision (main focus), policies and any form of political issue (sub focus). Citizens reactions are good indicators of policy outcomes (Vigoda, 2002). Analytical CiRM might be able to provide the technical tools to analyze them. Unfortunately, research on citizen participation draws pessimistic conclusions on the willingness of citizens for continuous engagement (Roberts, 2004; Vries, 2000. In addition, many public administrators believe that greater citizen participation increases inefficiency, delays, and red tape (King, Feltey, & Susel, 1998).

Organizational Changes

Beyond a change of the external relationships the internal relationships change. Agencies, departments, and public managers have to collaborate closely. Consolidations and changes of processes can be necessary measures. Individuals and organizational units need to treat each other like customers to be consistent with the intended cultural change of CRM and seamless service environment. Additionally, CiRM systems can give clerks low in the hierarchy more accountability as the rules they are to follow can be embedded within the software and not the decision maker (Fountain, 2001a). As claimed by Janowitz and Delany (1957) CiRM systems in combination with other applications might finally connect the substantive knowledge (i.e., clients, face-to-face contacts) of lower level employees with the functional knowledge (i.e., strategy, communication, management) of upper-level administrators or policy makers and avoid their isolation and at the same time give them clear information.

However, a knowledge-centric system and organization requires a front-line worker who has a broad understanding of goals, strategies, stakeholders, and how their work fits in this context. A term being used is system-level bureaucrat (Reddick, 2005). How these people capable of executing such a new role can be attracted to public administration and how upper-level administrator will react to sharing the power of "knowing" has yet to be determined. Furthermore, transparencies through reorganization and ICT will cause political battles over such issues like ownership of data (Fountain, 2001a).

Private sector CRM lessons

Technology facilitates improving citizen orientation or satisfaction, yet it is not required. The same conclusion is true for the private sector CRM (Rigby, Reichheld, & Schefter, 2002). Improving office hours, accelerating service processes through redesign, training employee friendliness are just some "offline" examples that have and had a positive impact on citizen satisfaction/citizen orientation (Bogumil, 1997). CRM does not mean that the PA starts offering new services demanded by the citizens and identified through data base analysis or market research. In the medium term, it rather supports tailoring existing services to citizens needs.

Recent empirical studies suggest that CRM technology only has a moderate to weak impact on overall success of companies' relationship building efforts (Reinartz, Krafft, & Hoyer, 2003). Reported failure rates of private sector CRM solutions can be up to 70% (Verhoef & Langerak, 2003). Interestingly similar success rates (20-30%) are reported from public sector TQM projects (Bennington & Cummane, 1997; Kelemen, 2000).

The organizational challenges inherent in any CRM initiative and the diversity of people involved pose another threat (Agarwal, Harding, & Schumacher, 2004). A large number of internal and external stakeholders creates accountability problems and makes behavioural/organizational change difficult. Many projects fail because of the lack of coordination between strategy and processes. Not establishing clear business goals before launching a CRM effort is one of the most common and important source of these problems (Ebner, Hu, Levitt, & McCrory, 2002). Public Administrations need a broad understanding of all processes and the demand side (here citizens). Continuous Leadership and communication by elected officials and executive administrators is a key to success even when there is strong opposition caused by the inherent changes over a longer period of time.

The 311/CiRM initiative in New York City is such a case. The 22 Mio USD project was planned and implemented during a budget crisis, fire stations were closed down and more than 20 administrative call centres were consolidated, but the success, especially from the citizen side, was so overwhelming that neither the media nor other political actors opposed.

Costs are as critical to companies as they are to cities, counties or federal states with tight budgets. It takes up to 36 months until a CRM strategy/system is implemented—a rather long time lag in the political sphere. Costs in the private sector usually run from 60 to 130 Mio. USD (Rigby, Reichheld, & Schefter, 2002), (Ebner, Hu, Levitt, & McCrory, 2002). Costs for a public 311 call-centres for cities like Miami, New York City or Chicago are around 15-25 Mio USD. Therefore, sunk costs have to be considered before a CRM solution chosen. Switching between systems and solutions is merely impossible and not economically justifiable towards taxpayers. Furthermore, a rise in quality of service and information transparency can lead to an increase in its use, raising costs by enlarging facilities or staff.

CRM systems rely heavily on databases and establishing connections to legacy systems (Foss, Stone, & Woodcock, 2003). To be efficient, information systems need to exchange data horizontally and vertically on all state and agency levels. Front and back-offices have to be integrated to offer a "closed loop" environment. A certain level of standardization is required. There needs to be more research on how far (state levels, standardization) and where (authorities, services, type of data) this is feasible. The idea runs contrary to the general understanding of federalism and call for subsidiarity particularly at the local level. Virtually, institutional boundaries would be removed. This conclusion is also true for e-government. However, the chances of creating more, rather than cutting red tape are high if we consider a paper by Peled (2000).

A government connected at all state levels (a term being used is joined up government (National Audit Office, 1999; Pollitt, 2003) and data bases with citizen profiles is on the one hand much more efficient and implies major improvements but raises a vast array of questions from a democratic viewpoint. These include questions on controlling data access and how to protect it and again on the effect of the role of the citizen within the state. At its very core, such a scenario also underpins the collectivist concept of citizenship, which places primary needs on the broader

Table 1. Major differences between private and the public sector CRM environment

Private Sector CRM	Public Sector CRM
Competition (some)	Monopoly
Market orientation	Jurisdiction
Million relationships	Billion relationships
Homogeneous product range / controllable quantity	Huge number of heterogeneous products (services) / uncontrollable due to political decision making
Personalization	"One size fits all"
Segmentation (Pareto rule 20-80)	Segmentation possible/no termination of unprofitable citizens
Processes flexible	Processes static
Budget/sunk costs	Budget/sunk costs
Legacy systems (IT)	Legacy systems (IT)
	Poor service image
Organization culture	Organization culture
	Human resources (lack of knowledge, salaries not competing with private sector)
Laws	Laws
	Federalism
	Political influence (planning cycle)
Profit orientation/maximising the shareholder value	Democratic understanding

needs of society and social justice rather than the narrow needs of individuals. Another are of concern is that if citizens and their demands are better understood politicians might misuses this as a source of power. Table 1 summarizes major differences between in the private and the public sector and the constraints on the use of CRM.

FUTURE TRENDS

Citizen Relationship Management offers new opportunities for local government (borough, city, county) in the next years. Cases like New York City or Miami/Dade County are first indications where developments are heading. In general, there is not enough data available. Besides various operative aspects like channels, data analysis or technologies research needs to focus on inter-organizational arrangements and the use of information in decision making. Does CiRM and e-government lead to a new form of government and governance or are they just enhancing the status quo?

CONCLUSION

I argued that former attempts of improving citizen orientation in the public sector have partly failed. E-government and CiRM share many objectives, tools, implications and to a certain extent the role of ICT. Indeed, CiRM adds a clear customer strategy to e-government. As demanded by Marshall (1990) CiRM and its bidirectional channel character can enhance citizenship in the administrative process. So far e-government falls short of providing researchers and professionals with a concept on creating a citizen oriented organization and public services. This is where CRM fills the gap. Implicitly or explicitly, ICT can not be the main driver of internal change processes. However, the use of ICT combined with external pressures (constituents) has change potential but may also fail due to the same reasons NPM did not meet its expectations: the logic of bureaucratic politics and multiple stakeholders within the government sphere. Instead of theoretic disquisitions on a brave new CiRM or e-government world we need more empirical evidence on many aspects of public administrations and public services to approach the obstacles in an appropriate way. The most pressing issue is the structural change of the state which is inevitable if we want to truly benefit from CiRM, ICT and other concepts. In this regard, many questions concerning understanding, ownership, control, use, responsibility, collaboration, laws, processes, and costs have to be answered by research.

REFERENCES

Abramson, M. A., & Morin, T. L. (2003). *E-government 2003*. Boulder: Rowman & Littlefield.

Accenture. (2001). *Customer relationship management: A blueprint for government.*

Accenture. (2003). *CRM in government: Bridging the gaps.*

Agarwal, A., Harding, D. P., & Schumacher, J. R. (2004). Organizing for CRM. *The McKinsey Quarterly*. Retrieved April, 9, 2004, from http://www.mckinseyquarterly.com

Alavi, M., & Leidner, D. E. (2001). Review: Knowledge management and knowledge management systems: Conceptual foundations and research issues. *MIS Quarterly, 25*(1), 107-136.

Albrecht, K. (1993). Total quality service. *Quality Digest, 13,* 26-28.

Ashford, R., Rowley, J., & Slack, F. (2002, September). Electronic public service delivery through online kiosks: The user's perspective. In R. L. Traunmüller, Klaus (Ed.), *Electronic government. Proceedings of the 1st International Conference, EGOV 2002,* Aix-en-Provence, France (2456 ed., pp. 169-172). Berlin: Springer.

Bannister, F. (2001). Dismantling the silos: Extracting new value from IT investments in public administration. *Info Systems Journal, 11*, 65-84.

Barnes, M., & Prior, D. (1995). Spoilt for choice? How consumerism can disempower public service users. *Public Money & Management, 15*, 53-58.

Bennington, L., & Cummane, J. (1997). The road to privatization: TQM and business planning. *International Journal of Public Sector Management, 10*(5), 364-376.

Berman, E. M., & West, J. P. W. (1995). TQM in American cities: Hypotheses regarding Commitment and Impact. *Journal of Public Administration Research and Theory, 5*(2), 213-230.

Berry, L. L. (1983). Relationship marketing. In L. L. Berry, G. L. Shostack, & G. D. Upah (Ed.), *Emerging perspectives on services marketing* (pp. 25-28). Chicago: American Marketing Association.

Bleyer, M., & Saliterer, I. (2004). Vom Customer Relationship Management (CRM) zum Public/Citizen Relationship Management. *Verwaltung und Management, 10*(6), 1-9.

Bogumil, J. (1997). *Vom Untertan zum Kunden?: Möglichkeiten und Grenzen von Kundenorientierung in der Kommunalverwaltung.* Berlin: Edition Sigma.

Box, R. (1999). Running government like a business: Implications for public administration theory. *American Review of Public Administration, 29*(1), 19-43.

Bretthauer, K. M. (2004). Service management. *Decision Sciences, 35*, 325-332.

Caldow, J. (1999). *The quest for electronic government: A defining vision.* Washington, DC: Institute for Electronic Government, IBM Corp.

Cook, M. E. (2000). *What citizens want from e-government.* Albany: Center for Technology in Government, SUNY at Albany.

Dawes, S. S. (2002). *The future of egovernment.* Albany: Center for Technology in Government, SUNY at Albany.

Denhart, J. V., & Denhart, R. B. (2003). *The new public service: Serving, not steering.* Armonk, NY: M.E. Sharpe.

Deshpande, R. (2001). *Using market knowledge.* Thousand Oaks, CA: Sage Publications.

Ebner, M., Hu, A., Levitt, D., & McCrory, J. (2002). How to rescue CRM. *The McKinsey Quarterly* (Special Edition: Technology).

Foss, B., Stone, M., & Woodcock, N. (2003). *Customer management scorecard.* London, Sterling: Kogan Page.

Fountain, J. E. (2001a). *Building the virtual state—information technology and institutional change.* Washington, DC: The Brookings Institution.

Fountain, J. E. (2001b). Paradoxes of public sector customer service. *Governance: An International Journal of Policy and Administration, 14*(1), 55-73.

Frederickson, H. G., & Smith, K. B. (2003). *The public administration theory primer.* Boulder, CO: Westview.

Freeland, J. (2002). *The ultimate CRM handbook: Strategies and concepts for building enduring customer loyalty and profitability.* New York: McGraw-Hill.

Gisler, M., & Spahni, D. (2001). *eGovernment—Eine Standortbestimmung.* Bern, Switzerland; Stuttgart, Germany; Wien, Austria: Paul Haupt.

Godin, S. (1999). *Permission marketing: Turning strangers into friends, and friends into customers.* New York: Simon & Schuster.

Gore, A. (1993). *Creating a government that works better and costs less: Report of the national performance review.* New York: Random House.

Grover, V., & Davenport, T. H. (2001). General perspectives on knowledge management: Fostering a research agenda. *Journal of Management Information Systems, 18*(1), 5-21.

Hewson Group. (2002). Customer relationship management in the public sector. Retrieved October 5, 2002, from http://:www.hewson.co.uk/public_sector/crm_public_ sector_more.htm

Homburg, C., & Bruhn, M. (2005). *Handbuch: Kundenbindungsmanagement*. Wiesbaden, Germany: Gabler.

Hood, C. (1995). Contemporary public management: A new global paradigm? *Public Policy and Administration, 10*(2), 104-117.

Hood, C., & Peters, G. (2004). The middle aging of new public management: Into the age of paradox? *Journal of Public Administration Research and Theory, 14*(3), 267-282.

Janowitz, M., & Delany, W. (1957). The Bureaucrat and the public: A study of informational perspective. *Administrative Science Quarterly, 2*(2), 141-162.

Janssen, M., & Wagenaar, R. (2002, October 1-2). *Customer relationship management in e-government: A Dutch survey.* Paper presented at the European Conference on E-Government, St Catherine's College Oxford, UK.

Kavanagh, S. (2001). Constitutent relationship management systems: A primer for public managers. *Government Finance Review, 17,* 1-5.

Kelemen, M. (2000). Too much or too little ambiguity: The language of total quality management. *Journal of Management Studies, 37*(4), 483-498.

King, C. S., Feltey, K. M., & Susel, B. O. (1998). The question of participation: Toward authentic public participation in public administration. *Public Administration Review, 58*(4), 317-326.

Kißler, L., Bogumil, J., Greifenstein, R., & Wiechmann, E. (1997). *Moderne Zeiten im Rathaus?* Berlin: Edition Sigma.

Kracklauer, A. H. (2003). *Collaborative customer relationship management: Taking CRM to the next level.* Berlin, New York: Springer.

Laing, A. (2003). Marketing in the public sector: Towards a typology of public services. *Marketing Theory, 3*(4), 427-445.

Lowenthal, J. N. (1994). *Reengineering the organization: A step-by-step approach to corporate revitalization.* Milwaukee: ASQC Quality Press.

Lynn, L. E. (1998). The new public management: How to transform a theme into a legacy. *Public Administration Review, 58*(3), 231-237.

Marshall, D. (1990). The restorative qualities of citizenship. *Public Administration Review, 50*(1), 21-25.

McAdam, R., & Donaghy, J. (1999). Business process re-engineering in the public sector. *Business Process Management Journal, 5*(1), 33-52.

National Audit Office. (1999). *Government on the Web.* London.

Nonaka, I. (1994). A dynamic theory of organizational knowledge creation. *Organization Science, 5*(1), 14-37.

O'Looney, J. (2002). *Wiring governments: Challenges and possibilities for public managers.* Westport: Quorum.

OECD. (2003). *The e-government imperative.* Paris: OECD Publication Service.

Osborne, D., & Gaebler, T. (1992). *Reinventing government: How the entrepreneurial spirit is transforming the public sector.* Reading, MA: Addison-Wesley.

Payne, A., & Frow, P. (2004). The role of multichannel integration in customer relationship management. *Industrial Marketing Management, 33*, 527-538.

Peled, A. (2000). Do computers cut red tape? *American Review of Public Administration, 31*(4), 414-435.

Peppers, D., & Rogers, M. (1993). *The one to one future: Building relationships one customer at a time*. New York: Currency/Doubleday.

Peppers, D., & Rogers, M. (2004). *Managing customer relationships*. Hoboken, NJ: John Wiley & Sons.

Pollitt, C. (2003). Joined up government: A survey. *Political Studies review, 1*, 34-49.

Reddick, C. G. (2005). Citizen interaction with e-government: From the streets to the servers? *Government Information Quartlerly, 22*, 38-47.

Reinartz, W. J., Krafft, M., & Hoyer, W. D. (2003). *Measuring the customer relationship management construct and linking it to performance outcomes*. Working Paper Series of the Teradata Center for Customer Relationship Management, Duke University.

Richter, P., Cornford, J., & McLoughlin, I. (2005). The e-Citizen as talk, as text and as technology: CRM and e-government. *Electronic Journal of E-Government, 2*(3). Retrieved July 13, 2005, from http://www.ejeg.com/.

Rigby, D. K., Reichheld, F. F., & Schefter, P. (2002). Avoid the four perils of CRM. *Harvard Business Review, 80*(4), 101-109.

Roberts, N. (2004). Public deliberation in an age of direct citizen participation. *American Review of Public Administration, 34*(4), 315-353.

Rohr, J. A. (1986). *To run a constitution: The legitimacy of the administrative state. Law*. Lawrence: University of Kansas Press.

Schedler, K. (2003). Local and regional public management reforms in Switzerland. *Public Administration, 81*(2), 325-344.

Schellong, A., & Mans, D. (2004, May 24-26). *Citizens preferences towards one-stop government*. Paper presented at the DG.O 2004—The National Conference on Digital Government Research, Seattle.

Sharpe, R. (2000). *Citizens' preferences—Measuring the acceptability of e-channels*. London: Kable Ltd.

Souder, D. (2001). CRM improves citizen service in Fairfax county. *Public Management, 83*(4), 14-17.

Swiss, J. E. (1992). Adapting total quality management (TQM) to government. *Public Administration Review, 52*(4), 356-362.

Traunmüller, R., & Lenk, K. (2002, September). *Electronic government. Proceedings of the 1st International Conference, EGOV 2002*, Aix-en-Provence, France (LNCS ed. Vol. 2456). Berlin: Springer.

Trostmann, T. (2002). CERM—Citizen Encounter and Relationship Management. *eGov Präsenz, 2*(2), 32-35.

Verhoef, P. C., & Langerak, F. (2003). Strategically embedding CRM. *Business Strategy Review, 14*(4), 75-80.

Vigoda, E. (2002). From responsiveness to collaboration: governance, citizens, and the next generation of public administration. *Public Administration Review, 62*(5), 527-540.

Vries, M. S. (2000). The bureaucratization of participation. *International Review of Administrative Sciences, 66*(2), 325-348.

Waldo, D. (1984). *The administrative state: A study of the political theory of American public administration* (2nd ed.). New York: Holmes & Meier.

Zablah, A. R., Bellenger, D. N., & Johnston, W. J. (2004). An evaluation of divergent perspectives on customer relationship management: Towards a common understanding of an emerging phenomenon. *Industrial Marketing Management, 33*, 475-489.

KEY TERMS

311: The number was approved by the U.S. Federal Communications Commission in 1997. It is a single point of contact call centre for all non-emergency public services.

Citizen Relationship Management (CiRM): A strategy or management approach enabled by technology with a broad citizen focus to maintain, optimize relationships and encourage citizen participation.

Customer Lifetime Value (CLV): Model to measure the customer value over time. Present net value and expected future value minus costs associated with a customer.

Customer Relationship Management (CRM): A holistic management approach enabled by technology with a broad customer focus to start, maintain, optimize relationships and make customers more loyal/profitable. CRM requires a customer centric business philosophy and culture to support effective marketing, sales. and service processes.

Enterprise Resource Planning (ERP): Software solution to assist organization with all aspects of operational planning

Online Analytical Processing (OLAP): Approach and tool to analyze complex queries of multidimensional databases. It belongs to the broader family of business information tools which include data mining or relational reporting.

Total Quality Management (TQM): A set of management and control activities based on statistics, leadership of top management and involvement of all departments and levels of employees aimed at quality assurance and citizen orientation.

This work was previously published in the Encyclopedia of Digital Government, edited by A. Anttiroiko and M. Malkia, pp. 174-182, copyright 2007 by Information Science Reference, formerly known as Idea Group Reference (an imprint of IGI Global).

Chapter 5.4
Civil Servants' Resistance Toward E-Government Development

Mila Gascó
International Institute on Governance of Catalonia, Spain

INTRODUCTION

As the new UNPAN E-Government Readiness Report (2004) stated, during the last years, governments worldwide have made rapid progress in embracing information and communication technologies for electronic government. All over, several projects have been carried out in order to offer more and better information to citizens and to improve public service delivery. Nevertheless, not all of them have been successful. Several factors have restrained governments at all levels from implementing thriving e-government initiatives.

Research has shown that workers' resistance to change is one of the major obstacles that organizations face when trying to implement innovation change processes. The public sector is not an exception. Due to its intrinsic characteristics, the introduction of information technology and, particularly, of electronic government programs requires paying special attention to the potential crisis situation to which these initiatives could lead. The intention of this article is to make clear how public servants experience and react to those changes that result from the adoption of information and communication technologies (ICTs) within the public administration; that is, to analyze the people dimension of change.

BACKGROUND

More and more, governments and public administrations are getting used to the new tools brought about by the new information era. The Internet and a growing array of information and communication technologies have modified widely the possibilities for organizing the government and the state. In particular, digital government projects have become a powerful way to contribute to public administration reform and modernization processes that have been taking place in many countries during the last two decades.

Indeed, electronic government has the potential to cut transaction costs all the way to zero in some cases (Fountain, 2001) and, therefore, to obtain efficiency gains, to become more transparent, to reduce corruption, and to enhance public service delivery. In short, it may lead to a more citizen-oriented government that offers an improved range of services and that, in return, increases the level of satisfaction among the population as well as the acceptance of the public sector (Bertelsmann Foundation, 2002).

It has been argued that, despite all its latent benefits, electronic government initiatives failure (total or partial) is far more prevalent than success. From analysis of both theoretical and real-world examples, Heeks and Bhatnagar (1999) concluded that the root causes of this situation are seen to lie in what they called conception-reality gaps; that is, those gaps that exist between the way in which digital government projects are conceived and the realities into which they are introduced.

In a sense, electronic government initiatives are not different from any other government actions, which means that they also are subject to unintended consequences that fundamentally are due to the adoption of imitation strategies on the one hand and to the introduction of change processes into a particular type of institution—the bureaucratic one—on the other hand. These two variables represent two conception-reality gaps. Thus, when the conceptual model does not take into consideration both the environment and the organization implementation context, electronic government programs tend to fail.

As Heeks and Bhatnagar (1999) put it, all information technology projects operate within a change context that has two main components. The first refers to the wider environment outside of the organization. It is characterized by the presence of other institutions, a specific level of development of new technologies, a particular state of the economy and the markets, several political pressures, or a variety of cultures and other social systems. That is why electronic government projects developed within the framework of a particular geographic context have to cope with the challenges of that specific country, region, or city. Imitation strategies that generally have been indifferent to economic, social, and political systems usually have been unsuccessful. For example, "a patient information system was developed in the US to support improved health resource management. When similar reforms based around IS were introduced in the UK, they ran into difficulties. British nurses found it hard to use the new information system because of the U.S.-inspired assumptions it made about the planning and costing of patient care" (Heeks & Bhatnagar, 1999, p. 69).

Even greater can be the problems of transfer from more advanced countries to developing ones, such as the failure of several public administration reform processes in Latin America or other regions of the world already have shown. The World Bank and other international institutions support has depended on the attention paid by the beneficiary countries to those IT policies considered as the correct ones by the lending organizations. This coercive isomorphism has been accompanied by a mimetic isomorphism, which implies that the political and economic elites who have been trained in the United States or in Great Britain have considered these countries' electronic government initiatives as examples to follow. As a consequence, important attributes, such as an inadequate technological infrastructure, an unstable political environment, a limited local skills base, an important restriction on money, or a wide acceptance of patronage practices, have not been taken into consideration when designing digital government solutions. This lack of knowledge frequently has led to partial or total project failure.

The second component that Heeks and Bhatnagar (1999) cited is the organization within which the technology is located. This has an organizational culture, a political dimension, a set of overt or covert management strategies related to change, and both formal and informal structures. Specifically, the public organization is a bureaucratic one. Therefore, electronic government initiatives are necessarily conditioned by the obstacles and problems to which this type of structure gives rise, such as referring all political decisions to the law, stressing a culture of legality, emphasizing senior public managers' control over extremely predictable and rational processes, impeding adaptation to new times as a result of its slow nature, and avoiding quality-oriented structures (Gascó, 2005).

This assertion explains why private sector information technology practices that have proved to be successful often fail when they are transferred to public administration. Failure is not only a consequence of the broadly studied and analyzed dissimilarities that exist between the private and the public sectors, such as pursuing different objectives, being accountable to different stakeholders, or having different types of customers (Allison, 1983), but is a consequence of the prevailing public administration culture. In sum, "government is not a business. Forcing governments into private sector thinking usually causes more problems than it solves" (Osborne & Gaebler, 1992, p. 20).

PUBLIC OFFICIALS' RESPONSES TO INNOVATION: RESILIENCE TO CHANGE

The difficulties that arise from the implementation of imitative electronic government strategies within the bureaucratic public organizations give rise to feelings of fear, anxiety, and uncertainty among their employees, which minimizes the likelihood of project accomplishment. Although, generally speaking, resistance to change has been widely accepted as a natural reaction, it is cited, however, as one of the major obstacles that the public sector faces when trying to implement any sort of change (Kearns, 2004). Just as any other government program, digital government initiatives can lead to failure due to the public servants' negative responses and attitudes about the changes being implemented.

Private companies also may be affected by resistance to innovation projects. Nevertheless, the two conception-reality gaps mentioned in the previous section in relation to the introduction of electronic government programs aggravate the public sector employees' resistances to change in comparison to the opposition experienced by the private arena staff. Although it is important to notice that imitation policies usually do not bring about the necessary commitment from the upper and middle public managers (they are often perceived as imposed strategies), reluctance to electronic government projects is mainly the result of the public sector bureaucracy's attributes. Thus, its job definition and tasks precision, its routines and procedures uniformity, its hierarchical structure, its isolated departments, its organization continuity, its risk aversion, and its reliability are some of the bureaucratic structure characteristics that give rise to a close system based on certainty and exact prevision, a system that is perceived by its members as a stable and secure one (Gascó, 2003, 2005).

Given this environment, the introduction of electronic government actions may result either in resistance to change due to a lack of clear evidence about its positive impact (Heeks & Davis, 1999) or technology enactment in ways that reproduce, preserve, or even strengthen the ongoing social relationships and performance programs (Fountain, 2001, 2002). Since the use of information technology generally leads to uncertain and unexpected organizational changes, the most common reaction to innovation projects is distrust. Kearns (2004) maintained that organizational change usually is related to information technology and can take many forms. According to her, technology may provoke changes in service delivery, business processes, people's roles and responsibilities, or structures and facilities.

Some of the more important resistance-to-change issues brought about by the implementation of digital government projects are as follows:

1. **Loss of Jobs:** Wirszycz (1997) noted that there is continuing evidence of a fear among employees that the introduction of computers will lead to a loss of jobs. Because technological change is implemented recurrently to automate internal processes, it often is regarded as a senior management pretext to downsize or to cut back on overtime hours. Along with the added stress from being asked to master the technology, this fear is a significant force hindering the move toward improved public service delivery. Many other authors have supported this statement; among them are the Working Group on E-Government in the Developing World (2002) and Fountain and Osorio-Urzua (2001). Public servants' unfamiliarity with technology accentuates this perception, because they may feel that their skills and expertise will become redundant and that they will not be capable of developing the new abilities and behaviors that the new electronic government initiatives may require. Particularly in Spanish or Latin American contexts, where stability has resulted in life jobs and, therefore, in aging workers not used to transformation processes, this view has become a remarkable obstacle that hinders change.
2. **Resistance to Cooperate:** Most of the electronic government initiatives that are being implemented require a stout collaboration among different departments within the public administration. This is so, because these kinds of programs are transverse and affect the functioning of several areas (Danish Technological Institute & Institut für Informationsmanagement Bremen, 2004). Nevertheless, in the bureaucratic public sector, departments operate as Taifas kingdoms,[1] which means that they are reluctant to share information and to work together, and that they view other units as competitors for resources and control. The existence of several subcultures within the public sector (scientists, politicians, and bureaucrats) reinforces this behavior. Each of them tends to "(a) require different data, information, and knowledge to do its work; (b) have different abilities and propensities to collect and acquire its own data; (c) gather data about the world in different categories, using different metrics that have specific and not always easily translated meanings; and (d) have different requirements for and uses of the outputs of its information. ... As a result, each subculture sees itself with different roles in, contributions to, and purposes for its value chain; these differences can lead to challenges in coordinated and productive information sharing" (Drake, Steckler, & Koch, 2004, p. 68).
3. **Lack of Clear Leadership:** The previous situation results in another effect. To keep everybody content, several people are assigned to a project group that actually leads to a situation in which there is certain confusion about who really is in control of the electronic government initiative. The need of a leader is important from an operational point of view. As stated by the UNPAN (2003), "the chief executive officer of the public sector must be committed to e-government, lead and build broad support for it, and be eager to learn. This generates the all-important positive signals that the civil service needs to receive from its top leadership" (p. 9). However, political and senior management's strong commitments may not always be easy to attain. Two facts lead to this conclusion. On one hand, electronic government strategies still are considered new within public

administration (education or health policies have been implemented for decades; it is obviously not the same with digital government programs). On the other hand, the vast majority of electronic government projects has not yet achieved their objectives and, therefore, has not clearly been evidence for all their proclaimed benefits.[2] As a consequence, skepticism has been a widespread attitude among public sector top managers who, in response, have chosen to be cautious when acclaiming ICT projects.

4. **Reform Fatigue:** The public sector has had more than its fair share of reform projects fail. This past experience also has shaped the perceived value of benefits and, therefore, has promoted a behavior against change (Gascó, 2005). In Bourn's (2002) words, "the history of government information technology has led to a poor IT culture for many government organizations, arising from a previous bad experiences with IT projects or procurement. ... Previous experience of ICT projects that ran over budget, brought few costs savings or even failed to work altogether can lead to reluctance to invest in web-based technologies. ... Alternatively, the organizational response to previous bad experience with IT can be a 'hands-off' approach by all staff outside the IT department, because they do not want their careers tainted through association with any more disasters" (pp. 3-4). Thus, past heritage conditions new projects of change.
5. **Deficient Telecommunications Infrastructure:** As explained in the preceding section, magnificent digital government projects that have succeeded somewhere else are undertaken in context with different premises. Too often, the available IT infrastructure is not taken into consideration when designing digital solutions. Under these circumstances, which usually give rise to important delays and unpredicted difficulties, even the most committed employee may develop a feeling of frustration and, therefore, of resistance to change. Other concerns can be found when reviewing electronic government literature, such as fear of extra work (i.e., during the earlier stages of a project, legacy technology may need to run in parallel with the new system) or inappropriate use of outside consultants and contractors (due to the public sector inexperience with IT, digital government projects too often are introduced and managed by third-party teams and contractors and consultants). Nevertheless, the intention of this section has been to highlight those matters that have been addressed more commonly.

FUTURE TRENDS

Electronic government projects are underway almost everywhere in the world. More and more, governments are exploring the possibilities that information and communication technologies offer in order to build a better-quality democracy and to deeply change public administrations. But in order for these to be successful, civil servants' engagements are needed unquestionably. That is why the future design of digital government plans must include specific actions in order to obtain public employees' commitments.

Much has been said about how to overcome those feelings and perceptions that result in reluctance to change when electronic government or other types of programs that involve the use of information and communication technologies within the public sector are implemented. Gascó (2005), for example, stated that, in fact, the classic organization theory recommendations about how to deal with change in private companies also are suitable in the public context. Thus, education and communication strategies, support, negotiation, and participation must accompany the technological innovation transformations, considering that long-time bureaucratic behaviors cannot be eradicated with isolated short-run courses of action. Yet, despite the validity of these general and broad proposals, change management in public organizations must take place in specific ways.

First, there is a need for proper and complete information about the project to be undertaken. Communication is an essential motivational exercise aimed at gaining support and understanding of the workforce. That is why the communication plan has to take into consideration the following elements:

1. Both written and verbal communications of the facts have to take place before the initiative actually starts.
2. The extent to which communication is successful depends on the communication skills of the participants and the degree of common grounding in the lexicon shared by them. The effective transaction of knowledge and ideas may be hampered by fundamental differences in professional subculture grammars (Drake et al., 2004; Vann, 2004).
3. The language of external consultants, often hired as agents of IT change, is fundamentally opposed to the language of public agencies and departments (Vann, 2004).
4. Electronic government leaders might find that their listening abilities are more important than their abilities to communicate their own perspectives on the change to employees (Piderit, 2000). Dialogue and conversation should take place more frequently than top-down information display. In addition, innovation should be marketed. However, overselling the benefits of IT projects may not be effective in securing employee support, if employees already accept that the new programs will have some positive outcomes but feel that a different perspective is required (Piderit, 2000).
5. Public servants' responses to change may evolve over time. Paying attention to this evolution implies constantly reviewing the message that is communicated.

Second, training ought to take place. But education strategies must focus on two aspects. On the one hand, instruction has to be concerned both with keeping skills up and with sending cultural messages throughout the organization. As a consequence, computer literacy cannot become the only goal to pursue. On the other hand, people who are going to be sent to training should get involved in real projects. Public administration managers too often have abused learning and have adopted it as the only solution to overcome resistance to change.

Finally, planning for change is an imperative, as it may allow one to gain control over the uncertainties inherent in the change process as well as to ensure backout strategies and rollback abilities in the event of serious unforeseen problems (Kearns, 2004). The certain and secure public sector context should allow for these types of arrangements.

CONCLUSION

The need for efficacy and efficiency has given rise to multiple attempts to reform and to modernize the public sector. During the last years, a new tool—information and communication technologies—has become available to do so. Its adoption within the public context often has resulted in the design of digital government initiatives. Nevertheless, many of these new programs have failed totally or partially. The existence of conception-reality gaps, which refers to the disparities that exist between the way the projects are conceived and the public sector realities in which they are introduced, has been said to explain these breakdowns. Particular emphasis has been placed on the bureaucratic attributes of public organizations and on the ensuing resistance of change to which they may lead.

This article has endeavored to claim that reluctance to change is a common and natural phenomenon when introducing information and communication technologies into the public sector. For that very reason, the biggest challenge to creating electronic government or even just installing a new IT system is not the technology but the cultural changes that must be made to accommodate it.

REFERENCES

Allison, G. (1983). Public and private management: Are they fundamentally alike in all unimportant respects? In J. Perry & K. Kraemer (Eds.), *Public management: Public and private perspectives* (pp. 72-91). Palo Alto, CA: Mayfield Publishing.

Bertelsmann Foundation. (2002). Balanced e-government. Retrieved November 3, 2004, from http://www.begix.de/en

Bourn, J. (2002). Better public services through e-government: Academic article in support of better public services through e-government. *National Audit Office*. Retrieved December 1, 2004, from http://www.nao.org.uk/publications/nao_reports/01-02/0102704-III.pdf

Danish Technological Institute & Institut für Informationsmanagement Bremen (2004). Reorganisation of government back-offices for better electronic public services—European good practices (back-office reorganization): Final report to the European Commission. Retrieved December 29, 2004, from http://europa.eu.int/information_society/activities/egovernment_research/doc/back_office_reorganisation_volume1_mainreport.pdf

Drake, D., Steckler, N., & Koch, M. (2004). Information sharing in and across government agencies. The role and influence of scientist, politician, and bureaucrat subcultures. *Social Science Computer Review, 22*(1), 67-84.

Fountain, J. A. (2001). *Building the virtual state. Information technology and institutional change*. Washington, DC: Brookings Institution Press.

Fountain, J. A., & Osorio-Urzua, C. A. (2001). Public sector: Early stage of a deep transformation. In R. Litan, & A. Rivlin (Eds.), *The economic payoff from the Internet revolution* (pp. 235–268). Washington, DC: Brookings Institution Press & Internet Policy Institute.

Fountain, J.E. (2002). A theory of federal bureaucracy. In J. Nye, & E. Kamarck (Eds.), *Governance.com. Democracy in the information age* (pp.117-140). Washington, DC: Brookings Institution Press.

Gascó, M. (2003). New technologies and institutional change in public administrations. *Social Science Computer Review, 21*(1), 6-14.

Gascó, M. (2005). Implementing e-government projects: Organizational impact and resilience to change. In D. Garson (Ed.), *Handbook of public information systems* (2nd ed.) (pp. 83-91). Boca Raton, FL: Dekker/CRC Press.

Heeks, R., & Bhatnagar, S. (1999). Understanding success and failure in information age reform. In R. Heeks (Ed.), *Reinventing government in the information age. International practice in IT-enabled public sector reform* (pp. 49-74). London: Routledge.

Heeks, R., & Davis, A. (1999). Different approaches to information age reform. In R. Heeks (Ed.), *Reinventing government in the information age. International practice in IT-enabled public sector reform* (pp.22-48). London: Routledge.

Kearns, B. (2004). *Technology and change management*. Dublin: Dublin Institute of Technology School of Computing. Retrieved December 15, 2004, from http://www.comp.dit.ie/rfitzpatrick/MSc_Publications/2004_Brenda_Kearns.pdf

Osborne, D., & Gaebler, T. (1992). *Reinventing government: How the entrepreneurial spirit is transforming the public sector.* Reading, MA: Addison-Wesley.

Piderit, S. K. (2000). Rethinking resistance and recognizing ambivalence: A multidimensional view of attitudes toward an organizational change. *Academy of Management Review, 25*(4), 783-794.

UNPAN. (2003). *World public sector report 2003. E-government at the crossroads.* New York: United Nations. Retrieved December 10, 2004, from http://unpan1.un.org/intradoc/groups/public/documents/un/unpan019207.pdf

UNPAN. (2004). *Global e-government readiness report 2004. Towards access for opportunity.* New York: United Nations.

Vann, J.L. (2004). Resistance to change and the language of public organizations: A look at "clashing grammars" in large-scale information technology projects. *Public Organization Review, 4*, 47-73.

Wirszycz, R. (1997). Smashing the glass hurdles of human fear. *Government Computing, 11*(10), 12.

Working Group on E-Government in the Developing World. (2002). *Roadmap for e-government in the developing world. 10 questions e-government leaders should ask themselves.* Los Angeles, CA: Pacific Council on International Policy & Western Partner of the Council on Foreign Relations. Retrieved December 23, 2004, from http://www.pacificcouncil.org/pdfs/e-gov.paper.f.pdf

KEY TERMS

Change Management: The process, tools, and techniques used to manage people effectively and the associated human resource issues that surface when implementing change.

Conception-Reality Gap: A gap that exists between the way in which reform is conceived and the public sector realities into which it is introduced.

Electronic Government Initiatives: Those actions based on information and communication technologies (particularly, the Internet) carried out in order to increase public sector efficiency, to improve citizen-oriented public services, and to provide a more transparent performance network.

Organizational Change: The design and implementation in a deliberate way of a structure innovation, policy, new goal, or operational transformation.

Partial Electronic Government Failure: Electronic government projects that are implemented but have something wrong with them (e.g., unattained goals or undesirable outcomes).

People Dimension of Change: How employees experience and react to change processes.

Resistance (or Resilience) to Change: A restraining force moving in the direction of maintaining the status quo.

Total Electronic Government Failure: Electronic government projects that are never implemented or that are implemented but soon abandoned.

ENDNOTES

1 The Taifas kingdoms were small Spanish realms that resulted from the disintegration of the Caliphate of Cordoba in 1031. This expression is generally used to illustrate the independent functioning of departments or areas that are close together geographically but do not have any relationships among them.

2 Because of the bureaucratic nature of public sector organizations, initiatives and goals undertaken within this context take a long period of time to achieve. One of the features that particularly boosts process slowness and results delay is overregulation, that is, the need to fulfill too many laws and procedures in order to implement a project of change.

This work was previously published in the Encyclopedia of Digital Government, edited by A. Anttiroiko and M. Malkia, pp. 190-195, copyright 2007 by Information Science Reference, formerly known as Idea Group Reference (an imprint of IGI Global).

Chapter 5.5
Social Critiques of Electronic Voting

Andrew Ó Baoill
University of Illinois, USA

INTRODUCTION

The use of computers in the electoral process—to count punch-card ballots, or to maintain a register of voters—has been in place in many countries for some time. We now see many countries move to more thoroughly integrate computers into the voting experience, by introducing what are commonly known as "electronic voting" systems. The use of such systems in public elections combined with the role of voting in creating and maintaining democratic institutions requires that we pay attention to the impact that changes to the electoral process have on the construction of the public nature of elections.

BACKGROUND

The essential characteristic of an electronic voting system, as discussed here, is that voting takes place through the use of a computer or specialized electronic interface—commonly called direct recording electronic (DRE) equipment. Such systems usually also collate votes and calculate results through electronic means, but this latter characteristic is shared with other systems not considered here (Cranor, 2001). In restricting ourselves to systems with an electronic interface, it is important to note essential differences between electronic voting in polling stations, voting in kiosks, and remote Internet-enabled voting where voters can vote from any Internet-enabled computer (Chen, Roberts, & Gibson, 2002). Although all three forms constitute electronic voting and introduce computing technologies to the voting process, they have quite different impacts.

Media attention to electronic voting often focuses on system failures, and expert-driven critiques of the technical shortcoming of the various systems, such as the need for a voter verified audit trail (VVAT). Social critiques, if considered at all, are often relegated to anecdotal accounts of the ease of use (or lack thereof) of the system. However, much of the rationale put forward for the transition to electronic voting presumes a social critique, such as arguing that "the practice of voting ... has not kept pace with social and economic change" (Pratchett, 2002, p. 4). It behooves us, then, to interrogate the social impacts of electronic voting, given particularly the centrality of voting to our social and political structures. In doing so we focus on three main aspects. First, we examine general social critiques of technological development and the implications of these for discourse around electronic voting. Second, we examine the impact of electronic voting on the public nature of elections. Third, we examine issues of usability and participation. There is, necessarily, overlap between these various areas–both questions of public space and usability can be understood to turn on the issue of accessibility and inclusivity–but these headings provide a convenient point of departure for a consideration of the questions to be addressed.

EXPERTIZATION AND TECHNOCENTRIC DEBATE

Much analysis of electronic voting stems from a neutral conception of technology, divorced from any consideration of the cultural context of technology's production or consumption. Linked to this is a belief that any problems with the implementation of a technology are technical in nature, and can be addressed by technical fixes. This frame can be used, for example, to explain debate over the need for—and means of implementing—a voter verified audit trail in electronic voting systems. Alternative approaches arise from those who view technology as existing primarily within a cultural framework. Kling, for instance, challenges the "tool" metaphor, arguing (1996, p. 20) that "part of what is required ... is a willingness to examine computer issues as part of a larger socio-technical system, not just as a component." For such theorists an exclusive concentration on, for example, cryptography, or questions in computer science has at least three troubling aspects. First, it ignores issues that cannot necessarily be considered within a technological frame, such as the nature of the public-private divide or the interplay of technology and culture. Such issues form the basis of the remaining sections of this article.

Second, a neutral conception of technology is tied to a view that newer, more "high-tech" solutions are somehow necessarily better, by virtue of their novelty and innovation. Such an approach doesn't accommodate a belief that a technology may be "sufficiently advanced" or that technological innovation is not synonymous with progress. One report, for instance, chides voting processes (Pratchett, 2002, p. 4) explicitly for having "changed very little in over 100 years." Illich has criticized the cycle of obsolescence that emerges in a society where:

> *Periodic innovations in goods or tools foster the belief that anything new will be proven better.... The "better" replaces the "good" as the fundamental normative concept.* (Illich, 1973, p. 74-75)

Illich is wary of a situation where "a few corporate centers of decision-making impose compulsory innovation on the entire society" (1973, p. 73) and concerned with the manner in which a certain form of technology gains what he calls a "radical monopoly" over the accepted range of approaches to social innovation. Efficiency and speed, modernization, an image as a technologically advanced society: all become aims in themselves, irrespective of whether they are needed to address identified problems. A more techno-skeptic approach would prompt greater scrutiny of, and skepticism about, the rationale for introducing electronic voting, asking, for instance, whether its introduction is focused on a necessary change, or whether it is the most effective solution to identified problems with the existing system. To what extent might electronic voting circumscribe or influence the possibility of future choices, such as–to take a topical issue in the U.S.—the introduction of instant run-off voting?

Third, full engagement with the issues raised within a technocratic framework frequently requires a level of expertise and knowledge that serves to exclude most people from discussion concerning matters of great public importance. In a similar vein, Mercuri notes in relation to electronic voting that:

Electronic balloting and tabulation makes the tasks performed by poll workers, challengers, and election officials purely procedural, and removes any opportunity to perform bipartisan checks. Any computerized election process is thus entrusted to the small group of individuals who program, construct, and maintain the machines. (Mercuri, 2001)

PUBLIC-PRIVATE DIVIDE

Apart from the purely functional matter of electing officials, elections are seen by some to act as a legitimating ritual (Hoffman, 2000; Oostveen & van den Besselaar, 2004), serving as a symbolic process that both acknowledges and, in doing so, creates the "public." One can usefully ask how adoption of electronic voting—particularly Internet voting—might affect the significance of voting as "a symbol which unite [sic] people in a common commitment toward democracy" (Monnoyer-Smith & Maigret, 2002, p. 283). There seem to be two related issues at play in such a critique. First, by removing the solemn, and sometimes arcane, aspects of the ritual of voting we risk obliterating the cultural markers that identify an election as an important social act. Some observers (Schaffer, 2002) go so far as to suggest that moves designed to "clean up" elections may, perversely, be linked to disenfranchisement and demobilization. Second, voting becomes increasingly refigured as an individual act. Barber already criticizes the existing system of secret voting in representative democracies:

Our primary electoral act, voting, is rather like using a public toilet: we wait in line with a crowd in order to close ourselves up in a small compartment where we can relieve ourselves in solitude and in privacy of our burden, pull a lever, and then, yielding to the next in line, go silently home. (Barber, 1984, p. 188)

With Internet voting we do not even need to attend a public place, thus reducing even further the social nature of the act of voting. However, this is also true with absentee or postal ballots, and so this criticism, as leveled at Internet voting, is perhaps best understood as one of remote voting generally. Barber's dislike of the secret ballot is, it should be noted, somewhat unusual, but it does raise the question: why secret? The secret ballot was introduced to protect individual voters from coercion and manipulation, and to prevent vote selling. Remote voting, in which oversight by election officials is absent, and where it cannot be assumed that voters will be free from intimidation or observation, removes these protections. Thus there are concerns (Oostveen & van den Besselaar, 2004, p. 6) that "with remote voting…family members, colleagues, or employers may try to influence the voter's decision…Internet voting is expected to substantially increase the scale of these problems."

For Jürgen Habermas elections and similar systems are the necessary but fallible "legal institutionalization of the general conditions of communication for a discursive formation of will" (1992, p. 450)—necessary because in practice we need some means to move from debate to action, fallible because of temporal and other constraints under which voting occurs. Systems put in place for holding elections should encourage the discursive, reflective formation of opinion by individuals, rather than an "unpolitical follower mentality" (Habermas, 1992, p. 450) where people act only for their own personal short-term preferences. In this context, processes that make voting more convenient for individuals, but which diminish the social, deliberative and discursive elements of the electoral process are doing both the voter and society a disservice. Given the limited amount of discourse occurring under contemporary systems, as described by Barber, it is legitimate to ask whether electronic voting will actually have a significant negative impact in this regard. Consider the limited communication undertaken by political activists outside polling stations in many jurisdictions. Does this qualify as discourse that is no longer possible with remote voting, or is it purely ritual? Would Internet voting encourage voters to be more reflective, searching out information on candidates as they vote, or encourage them to view voting as no different from buying an item online? A further question, that of public access to source code for software used in electronic voting systems has also been raised, entangling the electoral system in debates over open source software, free software, and the privatization of core public services (Commission on Electronic Voting, 2004; Ó Baoill, 2004).

USABILITY AND PARTICIPATION

The introduction of electronic voting has often been enthusiastically received by disability advocate groups, in part because such systems often include features that enable blind voters to cast their vote in private, without assistance from a third party—something that is not generally possible with older manual systems—and other features that improve the ability of voters with disabilities to participate in the electoral process. As a result of the newfound equality of access these systems provide, advocacy groups have also sometimes opposed the addition of VVAT functionality to DREs, as the paper record generally returns blind voters to requiring an intermediary to participate in the voting process. It should be noted that not all electronic voting systems include features that facilitate use by blind voters, something that can in turn lead disability advocacy groups to withhold support (Commission on Electronic Voting, 2004).

Others support electronic voting on the basis that it can reduce or eliminate the unintentional casting of invalid votes by individuals. In certain cases, however, public debate has highlighted dissatisfaction with systems that also disrupt the possibility of intentionally casting a blank or invalid vote (a "spoilt" vote). In Ireland, debate on the planned introduction of a DRE system led to public outcry at the seeming removal of the ability to cast a spoilt vote (Commission on Electronic Voting, 2004; Ó Baoill, 2004). It is accepted that most spoilt votes result from inadvertent error. However, the debate in Ireland resurrected attention (Ó Baoill, 2004) to a "case [in which] a puppet character is reputed to have "secured" more ballot papers in Tallaght (a large suburb of Dublin) than one of the three candidates during the national Presidential election in 1990" something viewed as indicative of social discontent in that area. Can an intentional "spoilt" vote be a valid social statement? Debates such as this show that voters and "pollsters"—those "in charge of collecting and elaborating the poll results, or...otherwise involved in voting systems and processes"—often "have different expectations of how a polling system should perform" (Oostveen & van den Besselaar, 2004, p. 7). This highlights the importance of research such as that of Oostveen and van den Besselaar, where voters are asked to articulate what they believe to be the important issues arising from electronic voting.

The issue of computer proficiency also arises, with some professing concern that "the voter population will include people with little or no computer experience" (Larsen, 1999, p. 57). Given the heterogeneous target user group—comprising all those eligible to vote–any existing "digital divide" across race, gender, or other, lines offers potential for a distortion of participation rates and subsequent results (Oostveen & van den Besselaar, 2004). Some proponents hope to mitigate any negative impact of this through the use of multi-channel delivery with remote voting possible through mobile phones, digital television, and other interfaces, while maintaining the option of voting in a polling station for "the foreseeable future" (Pratchett, 2002). The Indian DRE system is frequently cited (Commission on Electronic Voting, 2004, p. 316; Gill, 2001) as being successful despite large numbers of voters who are illiterate or have little or no computing experience, though some argue (Mercuri & Camp, 2004) that the system "made it easier for partisan operatives to commandeer and control entire polling booths." Mercuri addresses some specific issues that arise in the case of remote Internet voting:

Off-site Internet voting creates unresolvable problems with authentication, leading to possible loss of voter privacy, vote-selling, and coercion. Furthermore, this form of voting does not provide equal access for convenient balloting by all citizens, especially the poor, those in rural areas not well served by Internet service providers, the elderly, and certain disabled populations. For these reasons, off-site Internet voting systems should not be used for any government election. (Mercuri, 2001)

To approach the issue another way, and using the case of one vulnerable social group for whom electronic voting might have an impact—those with learning disabilities–careful design may, for example, reduce the risk of inadvertently spoilt ballots, a tangible benefit, though electronic voting cannot be expected to be a cure-all (Bell, McKay, & Phillips, 2001) since barriers to voting for this group go beyond what might be addressed by electronic voting. In addition, *remote* voting might facilitate voting by this group, but would also remove the protection from coercion that a polling station provides.

It is important also to ask whether it is possible to examine usability divorced from more general societal questions of equity and cultural diversity. To the extent that usability can be usefully addressed, we must also ask what the practical impact of improved usability might be. Some governments, for instance, have seen electronic voting and remote voting as means to address falling participation rates (DETR, 1998, Wilson, 1999). However there are conflicting reports regarding the impact of such approaches, from estimations of "relatively insignificant" impact (Mercuri, 2002) to "indications [of] higher voter participation" (Chen et al., 2002). Done (2002) examines a 2000 presidential preference election in Arizona in which remote Internet voting was available and finds a significantly higher rate of participation than the previous (1996) election. The increase in remote paper voting was, however, almost as much as the number who used remote Internet voting and Done acknowledges that the increase resulted from a "combination of outreach, legal argument, process, and technology" (2002, p. 8). Overall the research available indicates that "e-voting on its own is unlikely to stimulate greater levels of democratic engagement" (Pratchett, 2002, p. 8) with at least one study finding postal ballots to have a significantly greater impact than remote Internet voting (Norris, 2003). Also significant—particularly in light of our earlier discussion of the social ritual conception of elections—is the claim (Internet Policy Institute, 2001, p. 24) that "previous reforms designed to make voting more convenient ... have had very little if any impact on turnout levels and virtually none on the composition of the electorate."

While convenience and increased usability can benefit specific user groups such as the blind or those with learning difficulties as discussed above, they do not appear to have an impact on general issues of voter engagement and involvement. Hoffman asks whether the increased convenience of Internet voting would "outweigh the possible further erosion of the "civic ritual" of physically casting your vote at your local polling place" (2000, p. 221), bringing us back to our earlier discussion of the public nature of voting and forcing us to consider how to balance benefits for particular groups against losses for the overall population.

It has also been suggested that remote voting might have an impact on voter behavior other than merely on participation rates (Oostveen & van den Besselaar, 2003), and some work has been done on tools to measure this impact (Hammer & Traugott, 2004). Internet voting could have a significant impact; Hoffman (2000), for instance, draws attention to the "disintermediating" function of the Internet, which could effectively erase the current delay between receiving information and acting on it by voting. While some have seen benefits for, for instance, smaller political parties, in integrating an information portal or "lobby space" into a remote voting interface (Chen et al., 2002), Hoffman clearly worries that such developments might reduce reflection, inducing more knee-jerk reactions, and endangering both the deliberative and representative nature of current democratic systems. One's personal approach to these questions must inevitably be informed by one's own conception of the role and function of democracy (Barber, 1984). However, researchers such as Norris show (2003) that acceptance of the benefits of the Internet for the campaign process need not require that one support the use of computers or the Internet in the voting process.

FUTURE TRENDS

The theoretical questions that have been raised, and the evidence to date, suggest that there is plenty of room for fruitful debates in this area. More research is needed on the impact on turnout of various innovations—including changes in technology and changes in the location of voting (kiosk voting, remote voting). Such research should attempt to identify the relative contribution of different factors—distinguishing, for example, the impact of remote voting in general from that of Internet voting—and be awake to the various demographic components that may further influence (changes in) participation rates. Given the attention paid to the purported ease of use of DREs and Internet voting there is also space for comparative, systematic research on the relative usability of various systems (Caltech/MIT Voting Technology Project, 2001, p. 72), which will, of course, depend in turn on factors such as the electoral system in use and cultural and social settings.

Further, there have been calls (Hammer & Traugott, 2004) for researchers to identify impacts other than simply the "top line" one of participation. Does electronic voting have an impact on voter behavior—such as participation in "second tier" ballots? What impact might changed usability for vulnerable groups—either improved, for the blind, or declining, in the case of the computer illiterate—have not only on results, but also on the electoral process and the greater political environment? What impacts do DREs and remote Internet voting systems have on the potential for discourse in and around the voting process–what opportunities are gained, what lost? The unique role of elections also suggests that this area would provide particularly interesting material for examinations of free and open-source software—with issues of privatization, commercialization, intellectual property, security of a crucial application, and expertization all arising in this single case.

CONCLUSION

The political momentum behind the introduction of electronic voting has often been strong, often driven by a sense that existing systems are anachronistic and inappropriate for our current society, or by a belief that electronic voting will provide an improved usability that will combat apathy and declining participation rates. Social research in the area would indicate that, as Norris notes, "technological quick fixes, while superficially attractive, cannot solve long-term and deep-rooted civic ills" (2003, p. 10). Rather, we should ensure that changes to these important systems are made in light of a holistic consideration of social and cultural effects.

REFERENCES

Barber, B. R. (1984). *Strong democracy: Participatory politics for a new age*. Berkeley: University of California Press.

Bell, D. M., McKay, C., & Phillips, K. J. (2001). Overcoming the barriers to voting experienced by people with learning disabilities. *British Journal of Learning Disabilities, 29*(4), 122-127.

Caltech/MIT Voting Technology Project. (2001). *Voting: What is, what could be*. Pasadena; Cambridge: Caltech; MIT.

Chen, D. P., Roberts, D. W., & Gibson, D. R. (2002). *Submission to the inquiry into electronic democracy* (Submission). Melbourne: Scrutiny of Acts and Regulations Committee.

Commission on Electronic Voting. (2004). *Secrecy, accuracy, and testing of the chosen electronic voting system* (No. 1). Dublin: Commission on Electronic Voting.

Cranor, L. F. (2001). Voting after Florida: No easy answers. *The CPSR Newsletter, 19*(1), 2-6.

DETR. (1998). *Modern local government: In touch with the people* (White Paper). London: Department of the Environment, Transport, and the Regions.

Done, R. S. (2002). *Internet voting: Bringing elections to the desktop* (Grant Report). Arlington, VA: The PricewaterhouseCoopers Endowment for the Business of Government.

Gill, M. S. (2001). Insights from India. *Journal of Democracy, 12*(2), 138-140.

Habermas, J. (1992). Further reflections on the public sphere (T. Burger, Trans.). In C. Calhoun (Ed.), *Habermas and the public sphere* (pp. 421-461). Cambridge, MA; London: MIT Press.

Hammer, M. J., & Traugott, M. W. (2004). The impact of voting by mail on voter behavior. *American Politics research, 32*(4), 375-405.

Hoffman, L. J. (2000, 4-7 April). *Internet voting: Will it spur or corrupt democracy*. Paper presented at the Tenth conference on Computers, freedom and privacy: Challenging the assumptions, Toronto, Ontario, Canada.

Illich, I. (1973). *Tools for conviviality*. New York: Harper & Row.

Internet Policy Institute. (2001). *Report of the national workshop on internet voting: Issues and research agenda*. National Science Foundation.

Kling, R. (1996). Computers as tools and social systems: The car-computer analogy. In R. Kling (Ed.), *Computerization and controversy: Value conflicts and social choices* (2nd ed., pp. 16-21). San Diego, CA: Academic Press.

Larsen, K. R. T. (1999). Voting technology implementation. *Communications of the ACM, 42*(12), 55-57.

Mercuri, R. (2001). *Rebecca Mercuri's statement on electronic voting*. Retrieved 14 July, 2005, from http://www.notablesoftware.com/RMstatement.html

Mercuri, R. (2002). A better ballot box? *IEEE Spectrum, 39*(10), 46-50.

Mercuri, R. T., & Camp, L. J. (2004). The code of elections. *Communications of the ACM, 47*(10), 52-57.

Monnoyer-Smith, L., & Maigret, E. (2002). *Electronic vote and internet campaigning: State of the art in Europe and remaining questions*. Paper presented at the First International Conference on Electronic Government.

Norris, P. (2003). *Will new technology boost turnout? Evaluating experiments in e-voting v. all-postal voting facilities in UK local elections.* John F. Kennedy School of Government (Harvard University) Faculty Research Working Papers Series, RWP03(034).

Ó Baoill, A. (2004, 17-18 June). *The case against electronic voting in Ireland.* Paper presented at the 4th European Conference on e-Government, Dublin, Ireland.

Oostveen, A. M., & van den Besselaar, P. (2003, April). *E-voting and media effects, an exploratory study.* Paper presented at the EMTEL Conference, London.

Oostveen, A. M., & van den Besselaar, P. (2004). Internet voting technologies and civic participation: The users' perspective. *Javnost—The Public, 11*(1), 1-18.

Pratchett, D. L. (2002). *The implementation of electronic voting in the UK.* London: LGA Publications.

Schaffer, F. C. (2002). Might cleaning up elections keep people away from the polls? Historical and Comparative Perspectives. *International Political Science Review, 23*(1), 69-84.

Wilson, D. (1999). Exploring the limits of public participation in local government. *Parliamentary Affairs, 52*(3), 246-259.

KEY TERMS

Electronic Voting System: A voting system in which voters record their votes by means of an electronic interface, or DRE.

DRE (Direct Recording Electronic Voting) Device: A piece of equipment that allows voters to record their vote directly into electronic form. It can thus be differentiated from systems in which voters record their votes in, for example, paper form, with the votes later being collated and counted using an electronic system.

Kiosk Voting: The concept that voting might be possible in public places that would not have the trappings of a full traditional polling station. This is often thought of as being enabled by Internet voting, and might supplement, or be a transitional step to, remote Internet-enabled voting.

Remote Internet-Enabled Voting: Remote voting system in which the voter casts their vote on an Internet-enabled computer, which in turn transmits the vote over the Internet to a central server. Such a system might use a secure website or a specialized software application on the voter's computer.

Remote Voting: The situation where a voter need not attend a special venue, such as a polling station, in order to vote. Examples include postal ballots, remote Internet-enabled voting, and voting using alternative channels such as mobile phone messaging services.

Voter Verified Audit Trail (VVAT): A generally paper-based system run parallel to an electronic voting system that provides an independent record of the votes cast. One such system would involve a paper ballot being printed after the voter casts a ballot on the electronic system, allowing the voter to accept (verify) or reject that paper record.

This work was previously published in the Encyclopedia of Digital Government, edited by A. Anttiroiko and M. Malkia, pp. 1460-1465, copyright 2007 by Information Science Reference, formerly known as Idea Group Reference (an imprint of IGI Global).

Chapter 5.6
Electronic Surveillance for the Public Good

Liz Lee-Kelley
University of Surrey, UK

Ailsa Kolsaker
University of Surrey, UK

ABSTRACT

The central government in the UK is determined to employ new surveillance technology to combat the threat of terrorist activities. This chapter contributes to the important debate on the relationship between citizens and the government, by discussing not whether electronic surveillance should be used, but rather, when it is acceptable to the populace. From our analysis, we conclude that a reconciliation of state-interest and self-interest is critical for the success of e-governance; as such, electronic surveillance's mission has to be about serving the law-abiding majority and their needs, and its scope and benefits must be clearly understood by the visionaries, implementers, and the citizenry.

INTRODUCTION

Many contemporary social theorists argue that concerns that advances in electronic technologies would lead to panoptican societies have proved unfounded (see Bauman, 1998; Bogard, 1996; Boyne, 2000). The popular discourse of the Information Age embracing direct and indirect surveillance, supported by extensive systems of data capture and retention is overly technology-focused and insufficiently cognizant of cultural norms and impulses. The panoptican society implies a docile populace, an inactive community upon which Lyon's (2003) conception of profiling and surveillance of any number of individuals perceived as undesirable or dangerous are conducted. Yet, there is much to suggest that modern Western citizens are far from docile. According to Boyne (2000) and drawing on Mathieson's (1997) idea of the viewer society, Western reaction to the panoptical impulse renders it redundant by the propensity of normal, socialised subjects to engage actively in self-surveillance. This is illustrated by the ascendancy of the celebrity culture, the popularity of the "Big Brother," and similar reality television programmes, and the use of Web cams for "private" viewings. There is also a visible hunger for immediacy in knowledge and awareness of current events, and viewers' willingness to contribute to the dissemination process is redefining the role, content, and delivery of mass media. A recent example is the use of digital and mobile phone cameras in December 2005 to capture and provide evidence of the UK Buncefield oil depot fire (reputed to be the biggest industrial blaze in Europe), where the BBC news team actually used video images of the blaze relayed to them by nearby witnesses. The age of citizen journalism has arrived.

From a Foucauldian perspective the active engagement of citizens in these pursuits should come as no surprise. Foucault (1980) argues that participants in communities of practice not only internalise and accept behavioural norms, but also actively shape members' dispositions, and reinforce norms, controls, and exclusions. In the present context, far from being passive subjects of a regime, modern citizens must be viewed as active, willing contributors who not only accept, but sanction prevailing social practices. This is the synoptican society envisaged by Mathieson (1997) where surveillance has evolved from the few watching the many to the many watching the few. The individual as an active member of the media society has become habituated to being a watcher and is not overly concerned with being watched. Although Boyne (2000) has suggested ego investment in the continuation of this state of affairs, we would add that the thrill factor of being among the firsts to be at the scene of a dangerous or catastrophic event is also a strong motivator.

This is not to say, however, that the spectre of the panoptican society has disappeared completely. Current debates on the benefits and disbenefits of electronic technologies have begun to focus increasingly upon public surveillance. It might be argued that the voluntary participation of the citizenry actually increases the menace of the panoptican spectre, as those in power and with arguably a higher order agenda of monitoring and enforcing law and order could interpret the public's synoptic tendencies as evidence of tacit acceptance of all surveillance practices. The machinery of surveillance stands by and is ready to be employed—but by whom, for whom, in whose name, and in whose interest?

In this chapter we query whether a society that engages in apparently harmless (although some would argue, frivolous and mindless) voyeurism has now entered into what might be described as the panoptic-synoptican era where the watched are also watchers themselves. Rather than taking a populist view of the citizenry being reduced to what Lyon (2001, p. 41) has called a "digital person" quivering under an all-seeing, all-knowing Big Brother, this chapter examines the underlying logic for the growing tendency by the UK government towards electronic surveillance to instigate political and social changes for the public good. We consider public reaction not in isolation but as a general indicator of the power relationships between state and the citizenry, to provide an explanation of public distinction between acceptable and nonacceptable electronic governance.

MECHANISMS OF SURVEILLANCE

The UK has one of the most extensive and sophisticated surveillance systems in the world (FIPR, 2005). Indeed, the headlines and leading articles in the Independent newspaper (2004) claimed that around 20% of the world's closed-circuit television (CCTV) cameras could be found in the UK alone. Other recent press headlines also highlighted the extent to which new surveillance technology is being deployed—and welcomed—in a variety of contexts across the UK (Electronic Design, 2005; Liberty, 2005).

Border guards routinely employ thermal imaging devices in addition to the more mainstream CCTV cameras to monitor the citizenry and overseas visitors as they enter and exit UK airports, sea-ports, and the Channel Tunnel. Currently, a new generation of surveillance cameras are being trialled for UK airports. These Passive Millimetre Wave Radar cameras are supposed to be able to detect metallic objects concealed under our clothes. Although increasingly intrusive, citizen resistance to this kind of surveillance approach has been minimal, as it is widely recognised that technology can play a key role in locating explosive devices, illegal substances, contraband goods, illegal immigrants, and so on.

Surveillance technology is also used widely in other contexts. Military applications are finding their way into civilian crime detection and law enforcement. An example is the remote controlled airship which is rumoured to be under review by the London Metropolitan Police. In the central business district of London—the City—there are reported to be over 10,000 CCTV cameras (Electronic Design, 2005). A further 6,000 cameras are located throughout the London Underground (*The Guardian*, 2005). Station assistants are now trained to use the CCTV software to spot unattended baggage and to scan for untoward behaviour. These suspicious behaviour systems are new and untested in the judiciary system; significantly, the criteria for deciding suspicious behaviour are secret. Another little publicised example is the London Borough of Newham's supposed role as the beta-cite for the possible roll-out of Visionics' Mandrake facial recognition system across other London boroughs. This system has a database of faces and logs the times and dates of passersby at specified public areas. Amongst its many potential uses, it can be an effective tool for enforcing curfews and protecting private or "no-go" areas. Once again, the criteria for inclusion in the database and extent of public awareness or agreement are unknown.

The stated reasons for the increased use of surveillance technology vary. Before the London bombings on July 7, 2005, the emphasis was upon ensuring that those living in the UK have permission to be here, whilst post July 7 the main emphasis has been upon safeguarding the public against acts of terrorism. Since July 2005 government debate has moved on from whether as a society we ought to employ surveillance technology to where and how it ought to be deployed, despite protests from civil liberty groups such as Statewatch which have argued vociferously that there is no proven link between the presence of surveillance systems and crime prevention. Certainly, CCTVs do not seem to have a deterrent effect on brawls and drunkard behaviour common at weekends and after bars' closing hours in the larger cities, nor are they able to prevent more hideous crimes such as the recent alleged rape of a teenage girl in a pub toilet in Brighton, Sussex (*BBC News*, June 18, 2005).

In a densely populated but mobile world, one has to question whether any state can really hope to maintain a comprehensive overview of the activities of its population. For the UK with its mix of immigrant cultures, religions, and beliefs, it is unlikely that any surveillance short of that exercised in the old communist regimes would be sufficient to deter transgressors. Besides, new software techniques such as facial recognition, although promising, are costly and have yet to prove themselves. Despite these obvious hurdles, the UK government appears determined to invest in even greater deployment of surveillance technologies. For example, aside from an agenda to double the number of CCTV cameras on the London Underground by 2010, there is also a plan to introduce airline-style checks on the rail-link between Paddington station and Heathrow airport and at certain points on the London Underground.

Other imminent installations include the much criticised proposal to introduce biometric identity cards (ID) by 2007. The ID cards are intended to have two key benefits: first, to prevent terrorism and, second, to ensure that those entitled to use public services are able to do so. Total estimated cost ranges between £10.6 to £19.2 billion (LSE, 2005), with no figure given for ongoing updates as people are born, marry, change names, move house, and eventually die. The scheme has been much criticised for a number of naïve assumptions, such as that the cards will be impossible to forge; criminals and terrorists will be easily detected since they will not possess an ID card; ID cards will make crimes easier to solve, and it has been suggested by numerous groups that the ID card scheme is simply a smokescreen for establishing a national citizen database. The government's unwaivering belief in the scheme is taken as evidence (by protest groups and factions of the media) that amongst politicians the panoptican mentality is in the ascendancy once again. Yet, despite media interest and civil liberty groups' protestations, there has been little reaction from the public at large, either about ID cards or indeed concerning the increasing use of surveillance technology in general.

PUBLIC PERCEPTION OF E-GOVERNMENT: A PARADOX

Although authors such as Haggerty and Ericson (2001) may argue that the object of contemporary systems of surveillance is not punishment or control, we posit that e-governance in the Labour government context can be interpreted as the super-ability to observe, control, classify, and divide the population into categories of rich, poor, fraudster, bankrupt, crime risk, and so forth. That is, e-government or e-governance is a conduit with which our Labour government can deliver its Third Way ideology of state involvement and regulation. Public and private organisational policies of exclusion and inclusion may then be exercised based on the identified categorisations.

Possibilities for technology surveillance are numerous and extensive. Public intrusion into private lives is reinforced regularly by government broadcasts, such as a campaign by the DVLA advertising their ability to identify and fine late or overdue car-tax licences. Technology enabled eavesdropping or snooping of the unsuspecting populace includes police officers, M15 agents, and even private investigators working for government (and commercial) agencies. Indeed, the high penetration of mobile communication devices and mobile personal organisers (collectively known as MDs) in the UK makes phone-tapping easy, effective, and cost-efficient. As individuals carry their MDs with them, their location can be pinpointed and their conversation monitored—safely at a distance and without the need for excessive manpower. Defence electronic manufacturers such as TRW regularly sell specialised MDs to the security forces. Although most people are unaware of, or affected by, the surveillance on them, the discovery of being "spied on" can be a traumatic experience especially when there appears to be little recourse since the police are not obliged to confirm one's suspicion one way or the other. There is an independent watchdog—the Investigatory Powers Tribunal—but it would appear that neither it nor its predecessor have ever supported any complaint over phone tapping or electronic surveillance in the last 18 years (*BBC News*, November 12, 2003). In theory, any and every member of the population with a suitable mobile device is capable of being monitored; in practice, only a few are targeted—and even fewer will ever know that they are being watched. There is no way of confirming the extent of this kind of covert surveillance.

Despite the British public's tendency to have a fairly cynical view of politicians and their government agencies, individuals who have to endure any form of private surveillance are still surprised and hurt by the inability or unwillingness of public institutions and the legal system to protect them against this intrusion. If queried, it is likely that an individual will admit to some idea of the capability of technology for use in personal surveillance, but has somehow elected not to think about it or to continue in the belief that existing judicial and legal frameworks are sufficient to protect against such blatant violations of personal privacy. To do otherwise, would rock the very foundations of consensual democracy and accountability.

Whilst the Freedom of Information Act, which came into full force in January 2005, ameliorates the imbalance to some extent by allowing citizens to access categories of information previously held out with the public domain, unilateral exclusions and the need to pay for every request for disclosure diminishes its stated purpose of openness, transparency and ubiquitous access. The government's reply to the Science and Technology Select Committee's report on "the scientific responses to terrorism" (E-Envoy, 2003) provides a further hint of things to come and highlights the conflict between confidentiality and accountability. In the document the government reiterates its duty to ensure public safety and national security as well as its commitment to utilise "the best science and technology available" towards that goal. At the same time, the government considers it inappropriate and dangerous to release information that might be used by terrorists and the criminal fraternity. Resistance by those in public service to complete openness and free informational exchange highlights the difficult balance between respecting citizens' right to know and keeping secret information that they have deemed necessary to protect the law-abiding public from internal and external threats. Indeed, there are already some rumours of increased shredding of government documents.

Another case in point is a classified report by the National Criminal Intelligence Service (NCIS) agency proposing to require all communications service providers (CSPs) "to retain communications data originating or terminating in the UK, or routing through UK networks, including any such data that is stored offshore" for a period of seven years. The motive may be justified in terms of tackling cybercrime, but the wide-sweeping and indiscriminate retention methodology is open to question as it infringes the principles of the Data Protection Act (1998) and the Human Rights Act (1998).

Similarly, in the name of fighting money laundering and other financial crimes, the whole of the UK financial services industry is required to keep comprehensive records of their customers, which they, as effective owners of the data, could also use for their own marketing efforts. Blau's (1964) conception of human beings as value maximisers emerges here as those in official capacities or positions of trust are likely to desire some form of pay-off and as such, are inclined to selfish acts; the outcome of which could be the exploitation of the very public the surveillance mechanisms are allegedly designed to protect. Once again, it is unlikely that individuals would ever know how exactly and by whom the knowledge about their personal and financial data are being stored and used. It would seem that individuals are expected by the state and those in power to have faith and rely on the safety mechanisms of the larger "abstract systems" (Giddens, 1991). The question remains: who is watching the watchers? More to the point, what is the basis of our apparent lack of concern or apathy over the decisions and acts of others taken on our behalf? Of concern to the authors is the political reasoning that an apparently moral motive for public benefit is sufficient virtue in justifying such wide ranging power—to quote Martin Hollis (1998, p. 9), "it is not the sleep of reason which begets monsters."

Anxiety over being watched is very real as reflected in a U.S. Gallup Poll pre-September 11 which reported that people found the loss of privacy more disturbing than the prospect of nuclear war. Presumably the belief or paranoia—founded or otherwise—that the likelihood of government intrusion is much higher than nuclear conflict. Moreover, the tension between public access and protection of civil liberties in other areas of e-government is evident: public lethargy and marked reluctance to adopt government online services resulted in the discontinuation of the business section of the ukonline.gov.uk portal in April 2004. In the E-Envoy's fourth UK Online report, it had to acknowledge that although public awareness of online government services registered 96% of Britain's population, three quarters of them have never visited a government Web site. In a similar vein, public outcry against speed cameras has forced a review of the number and location of speed cameras across the UK.

The irony is that as society grows increasingly opaque, with individuals becoming more and more distant from their neighbours, more is known by the government about individuals. The long-term implications of a simultaneous erosion of societal closeness and increase in state knowledge about citizens are significant in terms of the tacit, consensual agreement between government and citizens. Once the state knows more about citizens than the citizens themselves, the ability of citizens to question and call to account the government for actions done in their name is diminished significantly. It could be argued that the populace is to be blamed for its own acquiescence and submission to increasing public profiling practices—perhaps the technology and media-led leisure pursuits in Western societies, as in the UK, have produced a generation that is largely ambivalent to the idea of being watched. That is, this apparent lack of public response is symptomatic of Foucault's constitution of participatory, self-regulating subjects and therefore a feature of Mathieson's synoptican society. But this explanation may be too superficial and the relatively subdued reaction to government surveillance practices, so far, may be attributable to good planning and communication (if one were generous) or simply, a fortuitous balance between peoples' expectations of their right to privacy and their right to personal safety. Alternatively, this may be the population's reaction to a perceived Orwellian approach to systematic governance and control manifested as a deliberate withdrawal and disengagement from the larger political and social domains.

Policy makers are reliant on their vision being implemented with competence, care, and good faith which, given the numerous failed citizens' charters and withdrawal of the recent UK Computer Within Reach programme (owing to poor distribution, faulty hardware, and exorbitant help-line costs) would suggest a disconnection between the visionaries and the administrators or implementers. The European Court of Human Rights' landmark judgement on the Geoff Peck case in 2003 highlights the problem of over-reliance on the "truth" of CCTV footage and the lack of a code of conduct or regulatory framework in the UK for government agencies and regulatory bodies such as the Broadcasting Standards Commission and Independent Television Commission, including the police. Mr. Peck, who was suffering from depression and attempting to commit suicide, was caught on camera with a knife. Without obtaining Mr. Peck's permission, the council had released the unpixelled video footage to first the local media, and even more inappropriately, to the BBC's special programme called "Crime Beat." Recent government's embarrassment and furore over a recent spate of whistle-blowing by civil servants (e.g., Katherine Gun from GCHQ) and accusations by a former cabinet minister of spying on Kofi Annan the UN Secretary General, are further indications of the rift between conflicting public policies and private beliefs. Other incidents include the PM Blair's office having to defend accusations of embellishing "evidence" to support the invasion of Iraq; Home Secretary Blunkett's resignation over the possible misuse of his position to fast-track a visa application; and the implied involvement of the PM himself in events leading to the death of senior government scientist David Kelly. How will the interest of each be reconciled with the interest of all? Who is to decide what public interest is and how can that be best protected without encroaching on individual rights?

Government decisions and actions may be explained as poor political judgement, inadequate systems, and procedures or mere error, but any indiscriminate or inappropriate use of power (whether perceived or real) is a regression away from the basic tenet of "government of the people by the people" envisioned by Abraham Lincoln in his Gettysburg address (1863). An ICM poll which revealed that people are three times more likely to trust the BBC than the government (Daily Telegraph, 2004) is a telling indictment of public disillusionment and growing cynicism of the benevolence of the government. On one level this relates to the growing unease about personal privacy, tracking, data storage, and sharing. On another such concerns reflect failing participation rates in civic society from a lack of respect for politicians, increasing suspicion of their motives, and growing distance between the government and its people; creating a situation of the more the government knows about the citizens, the less people would relate and trust the government to act in their interest.

We use a recent example to illustrate this point. Government concern for public safety resulted in a UK-wide ban on using a mobile phone while driving. However, a RAC study reported that 4 out of 10 drivers were still ignoring the mobile rules (*BBC News*, 2004); leading road safety campaigners to lobby for tougher penalties and for a total ban on *all* hands-free devices. This scenario offers an interesting insight into the kaleidoscope of modern UK society: in response to public opinion, health reports and in carrying out its role as state guardian, the government uses legislation to communicate the message that talking on the mobile phone while driving is dangerous to oneself and to others and must be stopped. Those affected are unconvinced and choose to show their distrust of this unwelcome interference through continuing use. Road safety campaigners (society's self-appointed watchers) react by calling for even greater sanctions and control measures.

The public may be forgiven if their perception is one of an increasingly integrated, comprehensive network of survey and control, in which those in power such as corporations, the government, and society's viewers or watchers appear to "co-operate" and "pool" their surveillance resources to produce a panoptic-synoptican form of totalitarianism beyond the hierarchical Orwellian Big Brother state. The difference between the muted response to growing and intrusive e-surveillance and the refusal to accept and participate in the more mundane services of online government and other e-government initiatives and legislatures is the basis of our thesis that the UK citizenry can and does distinguish between acceptable and unacceptable use of technology by the government, and that acceptability is anchored on a careful match between self interest and state interest. The government needs to understand this basic concept before assuming that in the panoptic-synoptican era, initiatives will automatically be accepted simply by claims that they provide for the greater good.

POWER VS. CONSENSUAL GOVERNANCE

Our discussion so far points to the rapid expansion of surveillance technology with only limited unease from the population to the increased monitoring of their daily lives. This lack of reaction may be desensitisation from the insidious synoptican society. Some authors have already surmised that this apparent citizen compliance is evidence of an increasingly authoritative state and an impotent public where rulers tend to put the pursuit and retention of power before all other scruples (e.g., Lyon, 2001)—and one which, in philosopher Plato's (427-347 BC) view, is a regrettable but natural outcome of democracy (see *The Republic,* Murphy, 1951; Kraut, 1997). He predicted that democracy would plunge into dissension and conflict with an indulgence of desire and permissiveness that erodes respect for political and moral authority, in which the young no longer fear and respect their teachers; they constantly challenge their elders and the latter ape the young. Plato opined that against this background would rise a "popular champion" who is tempted to "grasp the reins of the state." In Plato's analysis the "keeper" controls "the beast" by a study of its moods, wants, and habits. For the animal to be properly tamed it is important to know which of the creature's tastes and desires are admirable, or shameful, good or bad, right or wrong. It is possible that the UK Labour government views itself as that champion whose legitimacy and power is supported by its role as protector of the citizens, from external threats, and increasingly from their own actions, thus keeping in check democracy's tendency towards destructive chaos. Surveillance technology offers all this and more.

However, this perspective continues to propagate the idea of the top-down panoptic ability of a government with a reputation for limitless power and using the malevolent presence of widespread, 24/7 surveillance to intrude on society and individuals—for their own good, of course. We venture that, unlike the "old" panoptican era where there was no route by which those who were subjected to surveillance might redress the balance, new and more accessible technology has spearheaded a new synoptic movement in which the primary targets of surveillance (the citizens) are able to scrutinise their neighbours and critically, the keeper. This redresses the balance of power between groups in society and returns to the individual, the rights of control and self-determination, and the choice of the venue, manner, and extent of disclosure. We have entered the panoptic-synoptican era where technology has produced a media society of state and private watchers with complex motivations, and is legitimised through the generalised idiom of "public interest and right to know." In short, technology has created a new equality in terms of the ability to observe, record, and publish. This provides a powerful armoury against any perceived misuse of power by the government as evidenced by the recent spate of exposés on public and political figures.

We support John Mill's (1859) assertion that while individual liberty is paramount and "the only purpose for which power can rightfully be exercised over any member of a civilised community, against his will, is to prevent harm to others" (Mill, 1859-1869/1989, p. 68), growing infringements on individual liberty are to be expected as the state expands to cope with the pressures of the modern age. In 21st century society, governments such as the UK's have to grapple to control complex and interrelated international problems that have potentially devastating impact at the local level. If surveillance may be viewed as an attempt by the state to protect its citizenry from loss or harm, compliance could be interpreted as a pragmatic response to external threats. In pursuing this interpretation we also draw upon the work of Thomas Hobbes (1588-1679) which marks the emergence of the modern liberal and addresses the balance between the liberty of the individual and the power of the state. In *Leviathan* (1660), Hobbes investigated the circumstances under which inherently and profoundly self-interested human beings would put their rights of self-government to one side in the name of upholding peace, national security, and the long-term interests of the state. An external threat to national security creates precisely the conditions within which citizens are likely to acknowledge the need to balance individual liberty with state power in order to guarantee social and political order. We should not be surprised, therefore, by citizens' compliance with increased surveillance at border crossings and in other areas of possible harm from terrorist or criminal acts. Indeed we may even interpret their reaction as further evidence of the veracity of Hobbes' observation (which echoes Machiavelli's stance in *The Discourses*) that individuals act ultimately in their own self-interest. Despite privacy in the Western society being traditionally a valued human right, the basis of citizens' acceptance to intrusion is their recognition that the cost of personal safety is the sacrifice of a certain amount of privacy.

In Hobbes and Mills' analysis, when equality and security are in conflict, the former must give way to the latter. Although equality does not mean privacy, the conception of equality of power is underlined by the right to (of individuals) and the respect for privacy and confidentiality by the state. In our own analysis, the willingness to be subjected to any form of monitoring is context specific, and is given only when individuals perceive that the stated benefits of e-governance will satisfy their needs or protect them from external threats. In addition, individuals need to be confident that any information held on them by government authorities and agencies is within the legal bounds, that it is properly and securely stored with appropriate access authorisations and, when accessed, the information is treated with utmost sensitivity. While the government's vision of a "joined-up," fully integrated e-government has been communicated as desirable progress, the population appears less excited at the prospect of the crumpling of the "Chinese walls." Therein lies the basis of the acceptance paradox; whereas intrusion via e-surveillance is understood as protecting and preserving personal safety against some unwanted and unknown threats, information accumulated on individuals across government departments and agencies induces the Big Brother syndrome of unwarranted state interference. It also exposes the individual to threats of data loss, administrative errors, and, for some, the possibility of higher tax assessments and possible detection for any legal or moral transgressions. Besides, a single-platform e-government is vulnerable and subject to technical failure and deliberate or inadvertent malpractice, thus adding to the concern about the intentions of policy makers, the competency of those responsible for keeping citizens' data intact and safe. As a result, recent government's efforts to encourage citizens to interact with public sector agencies and to participate in policy-making "citizens councils" have produced minimal results. The dilemma between knowledge acquisition for benevolent governance and preservation of individual privacy grows increasingly more acute.

The government's ambition of using technology to access all the information about every citizen is legitimised through the emotive objective of public interest and safety. When supported by an equally ambitious legislative framework (e.g., the Regulation of Investigatory Powers Act) and backed by the EU's position on the retention of telecommunications data, it effectively drowns out individual cries against public snooping. It also ignores the public's ability to assess forms and reasons for intrusion. At stake here is not just a concern about individuals being reduced to electronic ciphers and losing their personal freedom, nor about an untrustworthy government; it is about the possibility of governance and protection being implemented under a flawed rationale, and one which is conducted with apparently little regard or awareness of the citizens' views and their evaluation of the impact on their lives. It is about the extent to which we can believe that our elected government and custodian of the nation truly have our interest at heart. In the UK, the use of cameras on London buses serves a dual purpose—they protect drivers from possible attack and dissuade rowdy behaviour by some passengers. Additionally, to keep bus lanes free from selfish and unthinking drivers, bus drivers are entrusted with the ability to photograph the culprits. In this example, there is convergence of state-interest and self-interest. The mutual advantage for those who have to police undesirable behaviour and those on the receiving end is clear, and when perceived as such, there is little negative reaction or protest. To be accepted, government surveillance policies and practices need to be appreciated as genuine efforts to provide and protect the citizenry.

GLOBALISATION EFFECTS OF TECHNOLOGY ON GOVERNANCE

An important development is the emergence of a friction-free boundless global economy where the largest corporations operate and coordinate supply chains and distribution networks with precision and efficiency, and smaller organisations have had to revise their strategies likewise in order to survive. As global trade becomes the norm rather than that enjoyed by multinational organisations, governments are forced to review their stance on border control, trade levy, taxation, merger and acquisition regulation, and other trade-related policies. Further, increasing access by citizens of different nations to various levels of the media society also makes it impossible for individual governments to ignore the globalisation effects of technology and to continue to govern and legislate in isolation. There is no longer a terrorist problem in any specific country; terrorism is a global feature faced by a growing number of countries regardless of religion, colour, or creed. As demonstrated by the September 11, 2001 and July 7, 2005 incidents, individuals or groups with terrorist or criminal intent, as part of the panoptic-synoptican society, have been able to use technology to hatch their plots, survey the targets, and coordinate actual attacks. To protect their peoples, there is a need for greater coordination across nations. Aside from cultural and sovereign issues, there is the challenge of managing international relationships and providing governance on a vast scale.

We envisage that governments will have little choice but to continue investing in the latest technology for surveillance and control. A possible application is radio frequency identification (RFID), which can improve the government's ability to conduct surveillance activities en mass. It is possible to track individuals or groups of individuals using passive RFID tags. Small and portable, these tags are armed with a tiny antenna that does not require an internal energy source. When a surveilled target passes a reader (say an individual attempting to enter or leave a designated secure area), it will send a pulse of electromagnetic energy or radio wave that briefly activates the tag, which can be set to raise either a silent or audible alarm while relaying data on the individual to the relevant authorities. Commercial applications began by embedding a RFID tag in a product or a pet's collar for location purposes, although more innovative uses of the technology are emerging. Recent examples of RFID use include tagging deceased victims post Hurricane Katrina. The bodies are tagged and their medical records loaded on a RFID chip. Sister nightclubs in Barcelona, Spain, and Rotterdam, Holland apparently use temporary RFID implants as automated passes to their VIP lounges. Customers with the implants can order food and drinks with a wave of their arm. As an effective surveillance system, RFID can be deployed in almost any public or high-security area such as prison establishments, government buildings, military bases, airports, railway stations, and border controls.

Other digital advances include emerging ubiquitous technologies such as Digital Multimedia Broadcasting (DMB) and High Speed Downlink Packet Access (HSDPA) which underpin the development of 21st century mobile televisions (TVs). DMB service is already available in Korea, and its hardware market is expected to grow quickly. Other developments include Internet protocol TVs which have recently been launched in Hong Kong, Japan, and Italy. Wibro technology is another form of mobile Internet offering merged communication, broadcasting, and data services. These developments are amongst the most recent moves towards ubiquitous computing (ubi-comp). Ubi-comp can overcome traditional problems of citizen access and computer efficacy since the central precept of ubi-comp is that computer chips can be embedded into the structural fabric of our lives—whether at home, at the office, on lampposts, park benches, doorways, shopping malls, bank counters, and in cars or other forms of public transport. That is, mass broadcasting is not only possible, it can provide the government with the ability to reach and keep its citizens "informed" anytime and anyplace. In turn, individuals can interrogate the system for further information on anything of particular interest or concern. If installed with the latest microcamera technology, these ubi-comp systems will allow the government to watch its citizens in numbers and from across locations, something that is not feasible currently.

In e-governance terms, therefore, new and emergent technologies such as RFID and ubi-comp possess significant panoptic capabilities. They have the potential to curtail and reverse current synoptic practices of private viewers and society watchers, thus reverting to the few watching the many. For any government keen to use technology to perform its role as protector or to impose its political ideology and retain power over the people, these new advances offer almost limitless possibilities. And when conducted in partnership with large, global corporations, it can easily be interpreted as the rebirth of Orwellian draconism—the difference is that 21st century e-surveillance has the potential to be even more intrusive and extensive, operating as a global network. Imagine a world where unseen eyes are watching our every activity (or inactivity), and where the term "ubiquitous" refers to the possibility of entire populations being watched by the omnipresent few. This rather pessimistic projection does ignore parallel technological developments which individuals can use to preserve their synoptic abilities. Besides, raised on a diet of liberty and fair play, and having enjoyed the freedom of citizen broadcasting, it is unlikely that the UK public will want or allow the return of a purely panoptic society.

CONCLUSION

The UK government has put in place electronic systems which have the potential both to serve citizens and inhibit their freedoms. The government in reacting to recent terrorist events, has seen it necessary to forego the freedom of the masses in the pursuit of a small number of transgressors. For their part, citizens have demonstrated a high level of tolerance of potentially panoptic surveillance as they go about their daily business. That tolerance is based upon the consensual notion of state and citizens working as partners in our present panoptic-synoptican society. Technology has enabled the watched to turn their lens on the watchers, and increasing cooperation between the media and members of the public has given rise to a new generation of viewers, many of whom have taken upon themselves to act as self-appointed guardians of "truth," putting pressure on the accountability and transparency of government policies. There is little room for secrecy in our modern media-hungry society—the latest news, gossip, exposés, and public debate are instantaneously uploaded onto various media platforms for public consumption, making it difficult to distinguish what is in "the public interest" or who is protecting it and why. We caution that in the light of recent tendencies by certain disaffected factions towards anarchy and violence, failure by the government to understand the reasons behind public acceptance of some but not all of its e-governance efforts, and make explicit their objectives and scope of any new initiative, will only fuel any discord.

Regardless of the surveillant power of new technologies, the possession of power does not automatically legitimise it. Not all surveillance is considered unequivocally intrusive and we have demonstrated by our examples, when inappropriate assumptions of compliance have evoked vocal and active resistance. For Western democracies such as the UK, what is required is the employment of technology to enhance the credibility of the government as a "steward of society." The government should be careful not to use technology as a disciplinary instrument against the masses or to suppress dissenting views. From our discussion, it is clear that people are not overly disturbed by the type or even extent of surveillance, but they will not accept a government that is not open and convincing about the reasons and nature of surveillance. When the object for surveillance is transparent and evaluated as truly beneficial, then acceptance is likely. The central London congestion charge system is an apt example where all number plates are scanned and matched against a vehicle record and payment database. The logic for its implementation was made clear from its conception and as people begin to reap the benefits of a less congested London, it soon becomes another routine of daily life. We conclude that citizen compliance to e-surveillance is achieved only when there is a match between state and private interest.

REFERENCES

Bauman, Z. (1998). *Globalization: The human consequences.* Cambridge: Polity.

BBC News. (2003, November 12). Should we carry ID cards? Retrieved April 29, 2006, from http://news.bbc.co.uk/1/hi/uk_politics/3264165.stm

BBC News. (2004, November 23). Drivers ignoring "mobile rules." Retrieved April 29, 2006, from http://news.bbc.co.uk/1/hi/uk/4034353.stm

BBC News. (2005, June 18). Rape "filmed on mobile phone." Retrieved April 29, 2006, from http://news.bbc.co.uk/1/hi/england/southern_counties/2998818.stm

Blau, P. (1964). *Exchange and power in social life.* New York: John Wiley & Sons.

Bogard, W. (1996). *The simulation of surveillance.* Cambridge: Cambridge University Press.

Boyne, R. (2000). Post-panopticism. *Economy and Society, 29*(2), 285-307.

Daily Telegraph. (2004, February 1). This house seems to be full of bullies and wimps. Retrieved April 29, 2006, from http://www.telegraph.co.uk/opinion/main.jhtml;sessionid=HCXHDWLT2DDBDQFIQMGCM5OAVCBQUJVC?xml=/opinion/2004/02/01/do0104.xml&secureRefresh=true&_requestid=89500

E-Envoy. (2003, June). www.ukonline.gov.uk and www.e-envoy.gov.uk Web site traffic figures. Retrieved April 29, 2006, from http://e-envoy.gov.uk/MediaCentre/CurrentPressReleaseArticle

Electronic Design. (2005, August 4). Electronics can protect subways against terrorism. Retrieved April 29, 2006, from http://www.elecdesign.com/Articles/ArticleID/10799/10799.html

European Court of Human Rights. (2003, January 28). Chamber judgement in the case of Peck v. the United Kingdom. Retrieved April 29, 2006, from http://www.echr.coe.int/Eng/Press/2003/jan/Peckjudeng.htm

Foucault, M. (1980). *Power/knowledge: Selected interviews and other writings 1972-1977.* Brighton: Harvester Press.

Foundation for Information Policy Research (FIPR). (2005, November). Surveillance and security. Retrieved April 29, 2006, from http://www.fipr.org/surveillance.html

Giddens, A. (1991). *Modernity and self identity.* Cambridge: Polity.

Guardian. (2005, August 11). Eyes have it. Retrieved April 29, 2006, from http://society.guardian.co.uk/e-public/story/0,,1546355.html

Haggerty, K., & Ericson, R. (2001). The surveillance assemblage. *British Journal of Sociology, 51*(4), 605-622.

Hobbes, T. (1660/1996). *Leviathan.* In J. C. A Gaskin (Ed.). Oxford: Oxford University Press.

Hollis, M. (1998). *Trust within reason.* Cambridge: Cambridge University Press.

Independent. (2004, January 12). Big brother Britain. Retrieved April 29, 2006, from http://news.independent.co.uk/uk/this_britain/article73167.ece

Independent. (2004, January 12). How average Briton is caught on camera 300 times a day. Retrieved April 29, 2006, from http://news.independent.co.uk/uk/this_britain/article73158.ece

Kraut, R. (Ed.). (1997). *Plato's republic: Critical essays*. Lanham, MD: Rowman & Littlefield.

Liberty. (2005). CCTV. Retrieved April 29, 2006, from http://www.liberty-human-rights.org.uk/privacy/cctv.shtml

Lincoln, A. (1863, November 19/1946). The Gettysburg Address. In R. P. Basler (Ed.), *The collected works of Abraham Lincoln*, Vol. II. Retrieved April 29, 2006, from http://showcase.netins.net/web/creative/lincoln/speeches/gettysburg.htm

London School of Economics. (2005, June 27). The identity project: An assessment of the UK Identity Cards Bill and its implications. Retrieved April 29, 2006, from http://www.lse.ac.uk/collections/pressAndInformationOffice/newsAndEvents/archives/2005/IDCard_FinalReport.htm

Lyon, D. (2001). *Surveillance society: Monitoring everyday life*. Buckingham, Open University Press.

Lyon, D. (2003). *Surveillance after September 11*. Cambridge: Polity.

Machiavelli, N. (c. 1517/1950). *The prince and the discourses*. New York: Modern Library.

Mathieson, T. (1997). The viewer society: Michel Foucault's "Panopticon" revisited. *Theoretical Criminology, 1*(2), 215-234.

Mill, J. S. (1859-1869/1989). On liberty. In S. Collini (Ed.), *'On liberty' and other writings*. Cambridge: Cambridge University Press.

Murphy, N. R. (1951). *The interpretation of Plato's Republic*. Oxford: Clarendon.

This work was previously published in Global E-Government: Theory, Applications, and Benchmarking, edited by L. Al-Hakim, pp. 100-113, copyright 2007 by IGI Publishing, formerly known as Idea Group Publishing (an imprint of IGI Global).

Chapter 5.7
E-Social Policy and E-Social Service Delivery

Rose Melville
The University of Queensland, Australia

INTRODUCTION

E-social policy is an important aspect of the information society development and e-governance agenda (Fitzpatrick, 2000, 2003; Loader, 1998). To date, it has not received the same amount of critical scholarship and research activity as traditional areas of social policy, but this is changing as policy scholars focus on the whole gamut of e-governance concerns. E-social policy is concerned with the social implications of information technology communication (ITC) technology in its broadest sense. E-service delivery is a narrower term, encompassing the range of ITC used by governments, churches, charities, other non-government organisations (NGOs), and community groups to deliver social and community services online. Initially, most services provided online by governments were of a commercial and business nature (Curtin, Sommer, & Vis-Sommer, 2003), but e-service delivery has evolved quite rapidly in the fields of health, education, social security, and one-stop community information systems. It is better developed in OECD countries and in specific social policy fields (social security, housing, health, education, and community care) whereas in other countries it is very poorly developed and resourced, if it exists at all (Polikanov & Abramova, 2003). Despite this uneven development, there are many innovative examples of ITC use in farming production and trade, e-health services and promotion, education, environmental pollution management, and enhancement of development strategies in poorer nations. However, there is still a long way to go in bridging the digital divide–the unequal access to ITC of richer and poorer nations. This is a global social policy concern.

BACKGROUND

E-social policy is a relatively new field of academic inquiry and research. Pioneer researchers in this field include Fitzpatrick (2000, 2003), Hudson (2002), and Loader (1998). In recent years, Henman [and colleagues] has made a substantial contribution to the critical analysis of e-social policy (1999, 2001a, 2001b, 2004a, 2004b, 2004c).

Fitzpatrick (2002) explains the low profile

among social policy analysts. Firstly, early figures on ITC use indicated that it was dominated by the U.S. and Europe, with only 1% of the world's population using the Internet. English is the dominant language of this new technology, and few people predicted the phenomenal growth of ITC around the world. It was, therefore, seen as a marginalised issue. Secondly, social policy analysts failed to see the connections between the global communication explosion; the rapid spread of neo-liberal and public choice ideologies (Melville, 1999) that accompanied economic globalisation (Bardouille, 2001); and the radical restructuring of government and public sector activities and roles with welfare reform, especially in advanced Western post-industrial societies. Thirdly, the primary focus of social and political scientists was on the potential of *e-governance* rather than e-social welfare delivery to enhance democratic, civil rights, and political relationships (Fitzpatrick, 2000, p. 376).

More social policy scholars are turning their focus on e-social policy. The work of the Community Informatics Research and Applications Unit at Teeside University in social care and delivering community services has attracted considerable attention (Thomas & Loader, 2000). John McNutt, a U.S. academic, has played a pioneering role in e-social policy activism. McNutt has hosted an e-social policy Web site on *Yahoo!* for many years, and recently published an exemplary text in this field (Hicks & McNutt, 2002). The *Journal of Critical Social Policy*; *European Journal of Social Policy*; and the *Journal of Information, Communication, and Society* regularly feature e-social policy initiatives.

From a government perspective, the justification for using online service delivery revolves around public sector management issues, such as efficiency and effectiveness and enhanced citizen or consumer satisfaction. Governments promote the view that e-service delivery reduces costs and provides savings through better use of staff time, increased choice and freedom, and improved time management for consumers and providers. The potential of ITC technology to overcome constraints of time, travel, physical ability, age, and geographic boundaries for disadvantaged individuals and groups is very appealing to policy makers and service users alike. However, many transactions in social service fields are more complex than simple online business transactions such as downloading a form or providing information. They require face-to-face interactions in the absence of appropriate technology to deal with multi-faceted transactions.

A key debate concerns *equity* and *access* to e-service delivery, especially among those who have traditionally been the focus of social service and development intervention; for example, the poor, the computer illiterate, the disabled, the aged, and women at both a national and global level. Perron (2004) is an excellent source on the state of ITC in developing nations. Debate about the "digital divide" (Selwyn, 2002, p. 2) and of the role of computer illiteracy in perpetuating poverty and inequality within countries and between countries are common in the literature (Perron, 2003; Norris, 2001). The available statistics on class, gender, age (International Telecommunications Union, 2004) and cross-national comparison of Internet usage (Perron, 2004) suggests that the primary beneficiaries of e-service delivery are the technologically and economically richer Western nations, especially post-industrial welfare-state societies. However, even within these societies, technology does not provide a quick fix for overcoming structural inequalities or social exclusion (Hudson, 2003). It may lead to new forms of inequality and social exclusion. What is important for social policy analysts to examine are the policies and strategies put in place by governments and transnational bodies, such as the United Nations, to reduce (and eliminate) these inequalities.

Many of the debates about the ITC (including e-social policy) are polarised. They are based on pre-existing assumptions about the social,

Table 1. Summary of key e-social policy and e-service delivery

Issues	Authors
Major government incentives to use e-service delivery (neo-liberal discourses that emphasise the role of individuals to manage risk, user pay [customer choice] for their social and economic needs, increased economic globalisation, restructuring of work, the welfare state, the reduced role of the state, and new public management emphasis on cost efficiency and effectiveness)	Melville (1999); Bardouille (2001); Clarke (2004); Fitzpatrick (2000); Hudson (2002); Hood (1995); Rhodes (1996); OECD (1998; 2003); Policity.com (2001); Commonwealth of Australia (2002); Cabinet Office-UK (2002); Perri 6 (2004); Snellen and van Donk (1998)
Potential of ITC to overcome social problems	Stonier (1983); Wellman, (1999; 2001); Davies (n.d.)
Social exclusion and digital divide—social inequality	Hudson (2002); Selwyn (2003); Kirschenbaum, & Kunamneni (2001); Perron (2004); Loader (1998a)
Social regulation and increased surveillance of social service beneficiaries	Henman and Dean (2004); Marston (2004); Henman (1999)
Technical capacity of ITC to develop complex interactive forms of service delivery and costs of infrastructure, staff time, and resources necessary for 24/7 operations	Hudson (2002); Liikanen (2003); Wittkemper and Kleindiek (2003)
Social nature of ITC	Fitzpatrick (2000, 2003); Loader (1998a, 1998b); Kitchen (1998); Ballamy and Taylor (1998)
New "virtual rights" instead of "social rights" required in an information society	Fitzpatrick (2000)
Inadequate skill levels, ITC infrastructure of non-government sector to deliver social services online	Wyatt and Aitken (2001)

economic, and political nature of technology in modern society. For example, there are those who argue that technology determines social behaviour and interaction, and others who argue that technology is socially shaped (Bellamy & Taylor, 1998, p. 18-19). Table 1 provides a summary of key debates.

Some writers (Bellamy & Taylor, 1998; Stonier, 1983; Wellman, 2001) hold a very utopian perspective of ITC—promoting it as possessing power to promote social change (Bellamy & Taylor, 1998; Stonier, 1983) for all, but especially those in poorer nations. The World Bank and the United Nations are strong advocates in the inherent capacity of ITC to solve their social problems. Barry Wellman is an exemplar of this position. Wellman (2001, p. 40-41) writes "the good news is that the cost of computing is becoming so low that in the developed world the digital-social class divide should get smaller just as the digital gender gap." Both Perron (2004, p. 180) and Sen (2000) argue that the falling costs of ITC (together with the scientific, political, and academic knowledge available about it) and e-democracy potential has the capacity to address basic social problems such as HIV/AIDS, unemployment, and human rights. E-social policy is concerned with addressing poverty and unequal access to healthcare, and securing basic human rights such as employment, freedom, and well-being.

Other writers hold a more dystopian view of the control aspects of ITC (Bellamy & Taylor, 1998). Marston (2004), using a Foucaldian "governmentality" framework, argues that e-service delivery is a mechanism that increases the surveillance and governing of the unemployed and social welfare consumers (Marston, 2004). Perron (2004) focuses on the way in which ITC maintains poverty and inequality globally, and questions whether it is a "panacea for deep-seated economic deprivation or for the existence of social divisions in a capitalist [neo-liberal market] economy" (p. 197).

Other concerns relate to the social nature of the technology used in e-service provisions. On one hand, it has the capacity to provide existing and innovative forms of social services online, yet at the same time it has the potential to increase the surveillance and governing of the poor, disabled, elderly, young, and other marginal groups. It is a two-edged sword both ambiguous and contradictory in nature.

E-SOCIAL POLICY AND E-SERVICE DELIVERY

Advents of new technology sometimes force us to develop new definitions and new typologies. As it is a relatively new field of policy analysis, defining e-social policy is not an easy task.

Fitzpatrick (2003, p. 131) writes "e-social policy is concerned with a critical examination of the social implications of these new technologies." He goes onto outline ten key areas requiring urgent attention by policy researchers:

- "The changing nature of work, employment, use of ITC in home and office—blurring of these boundaries
- Broader economic and social trends associated with ITC
- Increasing speed of communication that is changing our sense of presence and being, coupled with the dominance of English language
- The levels of e-commerce, e-business and e-shopping are still increasing–need to examine the implications of this on market and social relations
- New technologies have become the sites of both criminal activity and policing
- New forms of surveillance are emerging that involve the use of biometrics to classify and catalogue people in public and private data bases
- Rapid advances in e-health technology that is transforming the relationship between provider and consumer
- Educational pedagogies are changing through the use of ITC
- Major changes are occurring in public management that create increased tension between two conflicting needs–security and freedom
- The way in which new technologies maintain and create new forms of social exclusion" (Fitzpatrick, p.131-133)

Selwyn (2002, p. 1) claims e-social policy involves the critical examination of government rhetoric about the heroic potential of ITC to bring about "social inclusion by examining the problems that it sets out to address, the substance of these policies, and the perceived rationales and benefits for doing so." In doing so, we can assess whether ITC policies and programs promote social and economic change through social inclusion or maintains the digital divide and social exclusion. Loader (1998a) does not set out to define e-social policy, but the questions he raises about ITC fall within the traditional boundaries of social policy. Loader (1998a, p. 4) emphases "issues of social inequality, the manner in which computer-mediated communications can alter identities based around locality, gender, race, age, disability, or religious fundamentalism (Cable, 1994; Jones, 1995), and the capacity of government supranational policies to address issues of access, skills and universal carriage."

Attempts to define e-social policy raise similar issues to those in social policy. For example, we need to ask (as Titmuss (1974), a renowned social policy scholar, did) what kinds of political, moral, ethical, and ideological values are embedded in ITC. Who will benefit and who will lose out in the new cyber-landscape? Titmuss (1974, p. 4) wrote that "policy can be taken to refer to the principles that govern action directed towards given ends, and it, therefore, implies change: changing situations, systems, practices, and behaviours." Embedded in the notion of policy is the "belief that we can promote change of one sort of another" (Titmuss, 1974, p. 4-5). The goals (and outcomes) of social policy vary considerably and are highly contested. Policy goals are based on principles, such as "access, equity, egalitarianism, equality, social justice norms, needs, freedoms, rights and responsibilities" (Blakemore, 1998, p. 16-19); however, the interpretation and application of these principles are mediated by political, economic, social, cultural, religious, historical, and ideological contexts, producing different outcomes in societies over time.

E-social policy incorporates all forms and uses of ITC for economic, social, political, cultural, and recreational purposes. It involves what Fitzpatrick (2000, p. 375) calls "cybercriticalism"—a critical analysis of the social implications of ITC, the moral and political values associated with various policy initiatives, and an assessment of the social change that accompanies it.

E-SOCIAL SERVICE APPLICATIONS

E-social service delivery takes many forms. It is used in healthcare and telemedicine, education, organising volunteers, housing, social and community care, the provision of information on social services, and the processing and payment of social security benefits (income maintenance or social security payments). It is not possible in this brief overview to outline these in any detail. E-service delivery is defined broadly as:

...concerned with the delivery of public [social] services over digital networks and media—whether by government bodies or by private bodies under contracts or licence–to individual citizens and organisations. This includes [social] services provided by NGOs, churches, charities and community groups to consumer groups (Perri, 2003, p. 16; italics added).

It is important to note that e-service delivery (except in health and education) seldom involves the *physical delivery of services*. Table 2 provides several examples of e-service delivery provided by public sector agencies.

E-health is prominent in discussions about e-service delivery (see a recent issue of the *Journal of Information, Communication, and Society*, 2004.) Ravi (2000) provides an excellent overview of new telehealth initiatives in healthcare. He notes that healthcare professionals have been using ITC "[telegraphy—signalling by wires—telephony, radio and television] to exchange e-health related information since the mid-19th century, but recent advances in new shared media [Internet and virtual reality] [are changing the] way people relate, communicate and live" (Ravi, 2000, p. 989). Gaby and Henman (2004, p. 1-2) observe that new tensions are emerging in the traditional doctor-patient relationship as a result of better-informed health consumers (who can obtain a large volume of medical and traditional healthcare knowledge through the Internet). The increased access to health information, support groups, diagnosis, and treatments is accompanied by concern about the quality of information online. This is seen as increasing risk management for doctors and governments, who are keen to reign in the heightened power of consumers in the

Table 2. Summary of e-service delivery application (Burrows et al., 2000; Ravi, 2000; Gaby & Henman, 2004; Marston, 2004, Hagan & Kubicek, 2000; Liikanen, 2003; Loader, Hardey, & Keeble, 2004)

Policy field	ITC used to deliver services	ITC used by consumers of services
Health	Teleradiology, teledermatology, and telepsychiatry; shared virtual reality; Internet; new networked ITCs with digital cameras, videos and scanners; email; and videoconferencing.	Internet chat rooms, email discussion lists, self-help and support news groups, narratives on personal Web sites, and newsgroups. [Internet-based health care alternatives practitioner—providing diagnostics services and selling health products, herbs, pharmaceuticals, home care, and physical aid products].
Income maintenance (social security)	Web/internet sites for information and downloading claim forms; call centres; Web kiosks; processing claim forms and payments; electronic assessment techniques; job profiling software; short messaging service (SMS); interactive voice recognition.	Community-based job Web sites, e-mail, and chat rooms.
Education	Enrol online; pay fees online; study subjects delivered partly or completely online; And obtain post-secondary and tertiary certificates, diplomas, and degrees online.	Internet sites for sharing educational resources, chat rooms, e-mail discussion lists, Web logs, news groups, and bulletin boards.
Personal and community care	Electronic service delivery systems (e.g., case management) and data transfers between statutory and non-government authorities (e.g., elderly) (County Durham Project, 2004).	Wide range of self-help and support group using newsgroups, Multi-user domains (MUDs) for survivors of abuse, chat rooms, bulletin boards, and e-mail for online social and personal support
Sources: (Burrows et al., 2000; Ravi, 2000; Gaby & Henman, 2004; Marston, 2004, Hagan & Kubicek, 2000; Liikanen, 2003; Loader, Hardey, & Keeble, 2004)		

knowledge-diagnosis-treatment chain without relinquishing the potential benefits of e-health initiatives (Gaby & Henman, 2004).

FUTURE TRENDS

Governments operating in an increasingly competitive and neo-liberal globalised economy (Melville, 1999) concerned about cutting costs to deliver services in a more efficient and effective manner will continue to exploit ITC. On a global scale, the challenge is to use the technology to bring about social change and improve the social and material deprivation experienced by those in poorer nations. This is a big task, as the cost of ITC infrastructure is still unaffordable for many developing countries. The number of people with access to telephones, personal computers, internet cafes, and Web kiosks in those countries is much lower than in Western countries (Perron, 2004). Social inclusion, not exclusion, needs to be at the forefront of government e-service delivery polices (Hudson, 2003). This means funding public access to computers and self-service kiosks, training and skilling people in using ITC technologies, and overcoming the cultural ambivalence towards technology by the groups it is intended to assist (Hudson, 2002). This cultural bias towards ITC is expressed differently in countries around the world. For example, Canadians have embraced e-service delivery in large numbers, whereas it is still at a low level in Britain (d'Auray, 2003). The gender and age digital divide is slowly improving in most Western nations, but the class (economic) divide is still to be overcome.

Issues of social justice, access, and equity remain core social policy concerns. Ways of reformulating the basis of entitlement and social rights in an increasingly marketized and privatized welfare state pose many challenges to policy analysts. Fitzpatrick (2000, p. 393) calls for the recognition of "virtual rights: these being rights possessed by the massless citizens which overlap with, but are nevertheless distinct from their civil, political and social rights to cater for the changes occurring in a post-capitalistic socio-economic context." The potential for ITC and e-service delivery to advance social inclusion and increased equality exists. This includes using the Internet to provide job market information for young unemployed, email discussion groups for sexual assault survivors, or telemedicine in remote or rural regions. Paradoxically, there is also potential for it to be used politically as a tool for increased surveillance and control of recipients of state and privatised social services (Hudson, 2002; Marston, 2004). As governments continue to experiment with e-democracy and e-service delivery, the need for widespread public debate within nation states and transnational policymaking organisations increases.

There will be increasing concerns about maintaining the privacy and confidentiality of citizens' data accumulated in large networked public and private organisations. This is especially so within a policy that emphasises increasingly seamless and networked integration of service provision by one-stop agencies (COA, 2002; Hudson, 2002; Wittkemper & Kleindiek, 2003) and personalised electronic portals. According to Hudson (2000), private companies are now accumulating large amounts of personal data previously collected by government agencies under competitive tendering arrangements. These companies hold considerable power over governments who have depleted their ITC expertise by contracting it out or by abolishing these positions and now rely on private firms. These changes herald a set of complex dilemmas concerning privacy, security, and the changing relationships citizens have with the state. What may emerge is a quasi-state or "digital shadows" (Hudson, 2002, p. 524) consisting of private identities based on data from private/public firms combining credit histories with benefits records to assess the likehood of social security fraud.

There are still many technological problems to be resolved before physical services are delivered online. Most e-service delivery is limited to providing information and support. Technology is being developed that has the potential to revolutionise e-service delivery. The Canadian government is leading the world in experimenting with a securely coded digital signature (known as *epass*) to enable online forms to be completed (d'Auray, 2003). We will no doubt see more interactive, multi-dimensional, and multi-user technology in e-service delivery in the future.

CONCLUSION

The challenge for e-service delivery (and ITC generally) will be to alleviate deeply entrenched poverty and social problems in poor nations as well as rich ones. Serious global problems such as the scarcity of natural resources and environmental degradation may force nations to develop global institutions that ensure developing nations share in the world's wealth, including new forms of ITC such as e-social policy. The capacity of e-social policy to deliver social goods and services will depend ultimately on resolving deeply held ideological divisions about the distribution and redistribution of goods and services between and within nations. These are age-old debates within the field of social policy.

Finally, e-social policy should be seen somewhere along a continuum between potential and constraints rather than a either gloom and pessimism or outright unmitigated optimism. The technology itself does not function in a deterministic manner on social beings, but instead is open to resistance and change by those who use it.

REFERENCES

Alder, M., & Henman, P. (2001). e-Justice: A comparative study of computerization and procedural justice in social security. *International Review of Law Computers, 15*(2), 195-212.

Bardouille, N. (2000). The transformation of governance paradigms and modalities. *Round Table, 353*, 81-106, London.

Bellamy, C., & Taylor, J. A. (1998). *Governing in the information age.* Buckingham: Open University Press.

Blakemore, K. (1998). Ideas and key concepts in social policy. In *Social policy.* London: Open University Press.

Burrows, R., Nettleton, S., Pleace, N., Loader, B., & Muncer, S. (2000). Virtual community care? Social policy and the emergence of computer mediated social support. *Information, Communication, & Society, 3*(1), 95-121.

Cable, V. (1994). *The world's new fissures.* London: Demos.

Clarke, J. (2004). Standing of shaky ground: The problems of welfare states. In *Changing welfare, changing states: New directions in social policy.* London: Sage.

Commonwealth of Australia. (2002). *Better services, better government: The federal government's e-government strategy.* Canberra: National Office of Information Economy.

Curtin, G. G., Sommer, M. H., & Vis-Sommer, V. (2003). The world of e-government. *Journal of Political Marketing, 2*(3/4).

d'Auray, M. (2003). The dual challenge of integration and inclusion: Canada's experience with government online. In G. G. Curtin, M. H. Sommer, & V. Vis-Sommer (Eds.), *The world of e-government. Journal of Political Marketing, 2*(3/4).

Davies, W. (n.d.). *You don't know me, but ... social capital & social software.* London: The Work Foundation. Retrieved from www.theworkfoundation.com

Fitzpatrick, T. (2000). Critical cyberpolicy: Network technologies, massless citizens, virtual rights. *Critical Social Policy, 20*(3), 375-407.

Fitzpatrick, T. (2003). Introduction: New technologies and social policy. *Critical Social Policy, 23*(2), 131-137.

Gaby, S., & Henman, P. (2004, April 13-14). E-health: Transforming doctor-patient relationships with a dose of technology. *Refereed Conference Proceedings, Australian Electronic Governance Conference*, Centre for Public Policy, University of Melbourne, Melbourne. Retrieved March 3, 2005, from http://www.unimelb.edu.au/publicpolicy.egovernance/papers/

Hagen, M., & Kubicek, H. (2000). *One-stop-government in Europe: Results of 11 national surveys.* Germany: University of Bremen.

Henman, P. (1995). Computer technology—A political player in social policy processes. *Journal of Social Policy, 26*(3), 323-340.

Henman, P. (1999). The bane and benefits of computers in Australia's department of social security. *The International Journal of Sociology and Social Policy, 19*(1/2), 101-129.

Henman, P. (2004b). E-government and the electronic transformation of modes of rule: The case of partnerships. *Journal of systemics, cybernetics, and informatics, 2*(2).

Henman, P., & Adler, M. (2001). Information technology and transformations in social security policy and administration: A review. *International Social Security Review, 54*(4), 23-47.

Henman, P., & Dean, M. (2004a, April 13-14). The governmental powers of welfare e-administration. *Refereed Conference Proceedings, Australian Electronic Governance Conference*, Centre for Public Policy, University of Melbourne, Melbourne. Retrieved March 3, 2005, from http://www.unimelb.edu.au/public-policy.egovernance/papers/

Hick, S., & McNutt, J. G. (2002). *Advocacy and activism on the Internet: Perspectives from community organization and social policy*. Chicago: Lyceum Books.

Hood, C. (1995). Emerging issues in public administration. *Public Administration, 73*, 165-183.

Hudson, J. (2002). Digitising the structure of government: The UK's information age government agenda. *Policy & Politics, 30*(4), 515-531.

Hudson, J. (2003). E-egalitarianism? The information society and new labour's repositioning of welfare. *Critical Social Policy, 23*(2). 265-290.

International Telecommunications Union. (2004). Key global telecom indicators for the world telecommunciation services sector. Retrieved March 20, 2004, from http://www.itu/ITU-D/ict/statistics/at-glance/KeyTelecom99.html

Jones, S. (1995). *Cybersociety: Computer-mediated communication and community*. London. Sage.

Kirschenbaum, J., & Kunamneni, R. (2001). *Bridging the organizational divide: Towards a comprehensive approach to the digital divide*. Oakland, CA: PolicyLink National Office.

Kitchin, R. (1998). *Cyberspace*. New York: John Wiley & Sons.

Liikanen, E. (2003). eGovernment: An EU perspective. In G. G. Curtin, M. H. Sommer, & V. Vis-Sommer (Eds). *The world of e-government. Journal of Political Marketing, 2*(3/4).

Loader, B. (1998a). *Cyberspace divide: Equality, agency, and polity in the information society*. London: Routledge.

Loader, B. (1998b). Welfare direct: Informatics and the emergence of self-service welfare? In J. Carter (Ed.), *Postmodernity and the fragmentation of welfare*. London: Routledge.

Loader, B., Hardey, M., & Keeble, L. (2004). Wired for the third age: An evaluation of an electronic service delivery project for older persons. Retrieved April 6, 2005, from http://www.cira.org.uk/wiredindex.html

Margetts, H., & Dunleavey, P. (2002). Cultural barriers to e-government. In *Building public services through e-government*. Report by the Comptroller and Auditor General, HC, 704-111. London.

Marshall, T. H. (1964). *Class, citizenship, and social development*. Chicago: Chicago University Press.

Marston, G. (2004, April 13-14). Take a number: Employment services and e-government. *Refereed Conference Proceedings, Australian Electronic Governance Conference*. Centre for Public Policy, University of Melbourne, Melbourne. Retrieved from http://www.unimelb.edu.au/public-policy.egovernance/papers/

Melville, R. (1999). The state and community sector peak bodies: Theoretical and policy challenges. *Third Sector Review, 5*(2), 25-41.

Norris, P. (2001). *Digital divide: Civic engagement, information poverty and the Internet worldwide.* Cambridge, UK: Cambridge University Press.

Pavlichev, A., & Grason, D. A. (2004). *Digital government: Principles and best practices.* Hershey, PA: Idea Group Publishing.

Perri, 6. (2004). *E-governance: Styles of political judgement in the information age polity.* Basingstoke: Palgrave Macmillan.

Perrons, D. (2004). *Globalisation and social change: People and places in a divided world.* London. Routledge.

Pierson, C. (1991). *Beyond the welfare state.* Cambridge: Polity Press.

Policity.com. (2001). ESD clearinghouse. Retrieved April 3, 2005, from http://www.policity.com/esd/

Polikanov, D., & Abramova. I. (2003). Africa and ICT: A chance for breakthrough? *Information, Communication, & Society 6,* (1), 42-56.

Rhodes, R. (1996). From institutions to dogma: Tradition, eclecticism, and ideology in the study of British public administration. *Public Administration Review, 56,* 507-516.

Riva, G. (2000). From telehealth to e-health: Internet and distributed virtual reality in health care. *CyberPsychology & Behaviour, 3*(6), 989-998.

Selwyn, N. (2002). E-stablishing an inclusive society. Technology, social exclusion, and UK government policy making. *Journal of Social Policy, 31*(1), 1-20.

Sen, A. (2000). *Development as freedom.* New York: Anchor Books.

Snellen, I., Th, M., & van de Donk, W. B. H. J. (1998). *Public administration in an information age.* Amsterdam: IOC Press.

Stonier, T. (1983). *The wealth of information: A profile of the post-industrial economy.* London: Methuen.

Thomas, D., & Loader, B. (2000). *Cybercrime.* London: Routledge.

Titmuss, R. (1974). What is social policy. In *Social policy: An introduction.* London: George Allen & Unwin.

Wellman, B. (2001). Physical place and cyberplace: The rise of network individualism. In Keeble, L., & Loader, D. (Eds.), *Community informatics: Shaping computer-mediated social relations.* London: Routledge.

Whittkemper, G., & Kleindiek, R. (2003). BundOnline 2005—The E-Government Initiative of the German Federal Administration. In G. G. Curtin, M. H. Sommer, & V. Vis-Sommer (Eds.), *The world of e-government. Journal of Political Marketing, 2*(3/4).

Wyatt, J., & Aitken, H. (2001). *E-enabling the voluntary and community sectors–Final Report–November 2001.* Glasgow: Ashbrook Research and Partnerships Online.

KEY TERMS

Access: A term used to describe the ability of people, more commonly those associated with welfare state provision, to secure and/or use goods and services in society. There is an assumption that access is based on a notion of getting a share of resources (not necessarily an equitable or equal one) and needs that are hard to define or measure.

Digital Divide: A term that capture the inequalities in access to technology between countries and, in particular, the technological divergence between richer and poorer nations.

Egalitarianism: According to Blakemore (1998, p. 22), this is a utopian or "ideal" goal in the pursuit of equality in society. It is based on the notion that we can find ways to ensure that all people are treated equally in every area of life—the same income levels, health outcomes, lifespan, education levels, and so forth. This will ensure the same results and outcomes in life experiences and quality of life for everyone. Inequality will disappear because there will be no differences between people.

Equality: In Blakemore's (1998, p. 23) typology, this term refers to equality of opportunity. To overcome inequality, unfairness, and injustice in the ways individuals and groups are treated in society, mechanisms are established to remove barriers to employment, recruitment, promotion, education, and access to welfare services and benefits. The conservative approach argues that we can never fully remove differences between people in terms of abilities and attributes. A progressive view argues that positive action or, in some cases, positive discrimination is necessary to ensure equality of opportunity.

Equity: A term used to describe the difference the goals of egalitarianism and equality. Equity means treating people so that we can achieve a similar end-state or outcome. An equitable approach, according to Blakemore (1998, p. 24) involves treating people fairly but not differently, so that some form of equally is achieved at the end. Some will get more than others because their needs are greater. This approach will not ensure equal outcomes for all individuals and groups as espoused by the egalitarian utopians.

E-Social Policy: A new term used to describe research and critical policy analysis investigating the social implications of the use of technology in social life.

E-Service Delivery: A term used to describe the provision of a range of social services (primarily non-physical) uses a wide variety of ITCs.

Neo-Liberalism: The revival of the beliefs of classical market-based liberalism. Neo-liberalism has become entwined with public choice theory. Neo-liberalism advocates the power of the market to regulate all aspects of society. Three core tenets of neo-liberalism are that markets are superior, governments have been taken over by minority interest groups, and governments do too much. The solution is to curb the power of interest groups and roll back the state by using market mechanisms.

Social Exclusion: A contentious and ambiguous term used by British and European policymakers to describe the complex interplay of social, political, geographic, and spatial deprivation accompanying economic and material deprivation (i.e., poverty). Many see it as a broader and more comprehensive notion (see, Selwyn, 2002).

Social Inclusion: A term developed to describe the advantages of access to social, political, economic, geographic and spatial resources, and goods and services in society. This includes economic and social relationships that provide support, networking, information, and other less tangible goods and exchanges that privileges those "included" in mainstream society compared to those who are "excluded" (see Selwyn, 2002).

Social Policy: This term describes an academic discipline and a range of social services.

Virtual Rights: A term coined by Fitzpatrick (2000, p. 393) to describe the "cyber rights" of massless citizens in a post-industrial social and economic context. It draws on the tri-typology of rights (civic, social, and political) originally devised by Marshall (1964).

Welfare State: A term used to describe the institutional arrangements that have been set up to provide state services and goods to those who cannot fend for themselves in the market economy. According to Pierson (1991), it defines: (a) a particular form of state; (b) a distinctive form of polity; or (c) a specific type of society.

This work was previously published in the Encyclopedia of Digital Government, edited by A. Anttiroiko and M. Malkia, pp. 726-733, copyright 2007 by Information Science Reference, formerly known as Idea Group Reference (an imprint of IGI Global).

Chapter 5.8
Legislative Bases for Personal Privacy Policy Specification[1]

George Yee
National Research Council Canada, Canada

Larry Korba
National Research Council Canada, Canada

Ronggong Song
National Research Council Canada, Canada

ABSTRACT

The growth of the Internet has been accompanied by a proliferation of e-services, especially in the area of e-commerce (e.g., Amazon.com, eBay.com). However, consumers of these e-services are becoming more and more sensitive to the fact that they are giving up private information every time they use them. At the same time, legislative bodies in many jurisdictions have enacted legislation to protect the privacy of individuals when they need to interact with organizations. As a result, e-services can only be successful if there is adequate protection for user privacy. The use of personal privacy policies to express an individual's privacy preferences appears best-suited to manage privacy for e-commerce. We first motivate the reader with our e-service privacy policy model that explains how personal privacy policies can be used for e-services. We then derive the minimum content of a personal privacy policy by examining some key privacy legislation selected from Canada, the European Union, and the United States.

INTRODUCTION

The rapid growth of the Internet has been accompanied by a proliferation of e-services targeting consumers. E-services are available for banking, shopping, learning, healthcare, government services, and many other areas. However, each of these services requires a consumer's personal information in one form or another. This leads to consumer concerns over unwarranted leakage, storage, and/or exploitation of their private information. Indeed, consumer savvy regarding their rights to privacy is increasing. In Canada, recent federal privacy legislation known as the Personal Information Protection and Electronic Documents Act (PIPEDA) (Government of Canada) has forced businesses to seek consumer permission before collecting personal information. Similar legislation exists in the European Union (European Union, 1995) and in the United States for healthcare (U.S. Government). In this light, e-services must respect consumers' personal privacy if they are to be successful.

A promising solution for management of private information in e-services is to employ consumer personal privacy policies, that is, a consumer expresses his/her privacy preferences in a personal privacy policy. Once the e-service provider agrees with this privacy policy, it is then the provider's responsibility to comply with it. These are the basic tenets of our e-service privacy policy model (explained in the section *E-Service Privacy Policy Model [EPPM]*) to motivate the need for personal privacy policies). However, what should go into the personal privacy policy? In this work, we answer this question by examining privacy legislation from Canada, the European Union, and the United States. (Although we could have looked at privacy legislation in other countries as well, we settled on these three because our audience is expected to be mostly from these regions and thus be subject to privacy legislation from them). The result is the minimum personal privacy policy, that is, one that contains the necessary elements to satisfy privacy legislation, but one that can contain extra privacy provisions according to consumer wishes. We shall indicate what some of these "extra provisions" could be. Policy-based management approaches have been used effectively to manage and control large distributed systems. As in any distributed system, e-services may also use a policy-based framework to manage the security and privacy aspects of operations.

For privacy policies, there are related works such as P3P (W3C), APPEL (W3C, 2002), PSP (Carnegie Mellon University), and EPAL (IBM), which are languages for expressing privacy preferences in policies. Web sites use P3P to divulge their privacy policies to consumers. APPEL is a specification language used to describe a consumer's privacy preferences for comparison with the privacy policy of a Web site. PSP is a protocol in the research stage that provides a basis for policy negotiation. EPAL is a markup language for privacy preferences. These works are not necessary for the purposes of this chapter. They only serve as illustrations of what has been done in the related area of capturing privacy preferences in a form amenable to machine processing. Our work differs from P3P, APPEL, PSP, and EPAL in that we look at privacy legislation and other regulations in order to derive a core set of privacy attributes that are required by law in the content of a consumer personal privacy policy, rather than be concerned with expressing preferences in machine processable form. In fact, the example personal privacy policies we give in this chapter are expressed in English. Therefore, we are not proposing another policy language but rather looking at what content must be in personal privacy policies to satisfy privacy legislation. Our example privacy policies may well be expressed in P3P, APPEL, PSP, or EPAL. We are not aware of any other work that derives personal privacy policy content requirements from privacy legislation.

The rest of this chapter is organized as follows. The section *E-Service Privacy Policy Model (EPPM)* describes our model of using personal privacy policies to protect consumer privacy. This is followed by the section *Privacy Legislation*, which examines privacy legislation from Canada, the European Union, and the United States and derives privacy attributes for inclusion in personal privacy policies. The next section, *Personal Privacy Policy Specification*, integrates the privacy attribute findings from *Privacy Legislation* into the minimum personal privacy policy that satisfies privacy legislation. The last section gives our conclusions and ideas for future work.

E-SERVICE PRIVACY POLICY MODEL (EPPM)

Before explaining our e-service privacy policy model, it is useful to describe what we mean by an e-service. An e-service is a service that is offered by a provider to a consumer across a computer network. A stock quotation service is often used as an example of an e-service. Here a consumer would logon to the service from a computer, and after appropriate user authentication, would make use of the service to obtain stock quotes. Accessing one's bank account through online banking is another example of an e-service. Here the provider is the bank, and the service consists of allowing the consumer to check the balance, transfer funds, or make bill payments. The network is usually the Internet, but could also in principle be a private enterprise network. At any time, one provider may be serving many consumers, and many providers may be serving one consumer. For the purposes of this chapter, the business relationship between provider and consumer is always one-to-one, that is, the service is designed for one consumer and is provided by one provider (although this provider may make use of other providers to compose its e-service), and payment for the service is expected from one consumer. In addition, service providers may also be service consumers, and service consumers may also be service providers.

The e-service privacy policy model describes the origin and use of personal privacy policies to protect consumer privacy for e-services. This model consists of six phases as given in Table 1. These phases would occur in ascending numerical order. In this model, a provider of a particular e-service has a privacy policy for that e-service, stating what private information it requires from the consumer and how the information will be used. The consumer has a privacy policy stating his/her privacy preferences for using a particular e-service, for example, what private information the consumer is willing to give to the provider and with whom the information may be shared. An entity that is both a provider and a consumer has separate privacy policies for these two roles.

For Phases 3 and 4, a privacy policy is attached to a software agent that acts on behalf of a consumer or a provider as the case may be. Prior to the activation of a particular service, the agent for the consumer and the agent for the provider undergo a privacy policy exchange in which the policies are examined for compatibility. The service is only activated if the policies are compatible (Yee & Korba, May 2005), in which case we say that there is a "match" between the two policies. In addition, *we assume that in general, the provider always asks for more private information from the consumer than the consumer is willing to give up.* Figure 1 illustrates Phases 3 and 4. For the purposes of this work, it is not necessary to consider the details of service operation.

Further detailed descriptions of how to carry out individual phases of this model are beyond the scope of this work; however, we include in Table 1 some references to Yee and Korba, who have works describing how some of the phases may be carried out.

PRIVACY LEGISLATION

Canada

In Canada, federal privacy legislation is enacted in the *PIPEDA* (Government of Canada) and is based on the Canadian Standards Association's *Model Code for the Protection of Personal Information* (Department of Justice), recognized as a national standard in 1996. This Code consists of 10 Privacy Principles that for convenience, we label as CSAPP (Table 2). Since the privacy provisions of

Table 1. E-service privacy policy model phases

Phase	Description	Reference
1. Formulate	Privacy policy creation; every e-service consumer needs to have his/her own personal privacy policy that expresses his/her privacy preferences for using a particular e-service; every provider also needs one or more privacy policies expressing what private information it needs for it's e-services.	Yee and Korba (January 2005) describes methods for creating personal privacy policies
2. Search	E-service consumer knows the type of e-service he/she needs (e.g., book seller) and searches the Internet (e.g., using Google) for such an e-service.	-
3. Match	Before an e-service is engaged, the service consumer and service provider exchange and compare their individual privacy policies for the e-service to see if there is a match. If there is a match, Phase 5 is entered next. Otherwise, Phase 4 is entered next.	Yee and Korba (May 2005)
4. Negotiate	Consumer and provider negotiate with each other to try to arrive at a mutually agreed privacy policy. If this negotiation is successful, Phase 5 is entered next. Otherwise, Phase 2 is entered next (consumer searches for another provider).	Yee and Korba (January 2003, May 2003)
5. Engage	The consumer engages the e-service.	-
6. Comply	The provider must comply with the personal privacy policy of the consumer or comply with their mutually negotiated privacy policy.	Yee and Korba (July 2004, March 2005)

Figure 1. Exchange of privacy policies (PP) between consumer agent (CA) and provider agent (PA)

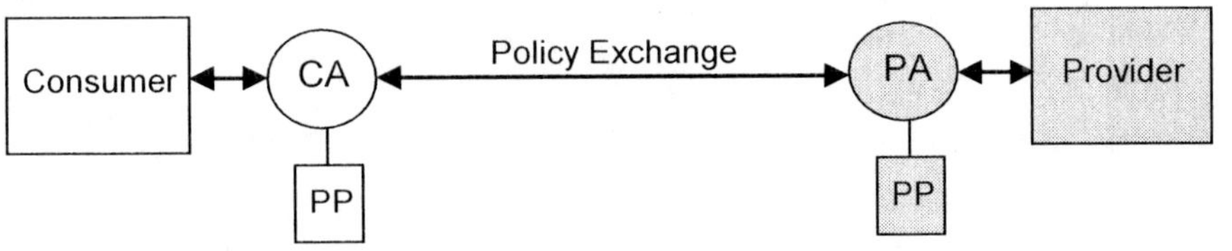

PIPEDA are represented by CSAPP, we examine CSAPP rather than the more complicated text of PIPEDA itself.

To identify some attributes of private information collection using the CSAPP, we interpret "organization" as "provider" and "individual" as "consumer." In the following, we use CSAPP.n to denote Principle n of CSAPP. Principle CSAPP.2 implies that there could be different providers requesting the information, thus implying a *collector* attribute. Principle CSAPP.4 implies that there is a *what* attribute, that is, what private information is being collected. Principles CSAPP.2, CSAPP.4, and CSAPP.5 state that there

Table 2. CSAPP — The 10 Privacy Principles (Canadian Standards Association)

Principle	Description
1. Accountability	An organization is responsible for personal information under its control and shall designate an individual or individuals accountable for the organization's compliance with the privacy principles.
2. Identifying purposes	The purposes for which personal information is collected shall be identified by the organization at or before the time the information is collected.
3. Consent	The knowledge and consent of the individual are required for the collection, use, or disclosure of personal information, except when inappropriate.
4. Limiting collection	The collection of personal information shall be limited to that which is necessary for the purposes identified by the organization. Information shall be collected by fair and lawful means.
5. Limiting use, disclosure, and retention	Personal information shall not be used or disclosed for purposes other than those for which it was collected, except with the consent of the individual or as required by the law. In addition, personal information shall be retained only as long as necessary for fulfillment of those purposes.
6. Accuracy	Personal information shall be as accurate, complete, and up-to-date as is necessary for the purposes for which it is to be used.
7. Safeguards	Security safeguards appropriate to the sensitivity of the information shall be used to protect personal information.
8. Openness	An organization shall make readily available to individuals specific information about its policies and practices relating to the management of personal information.
9. Individual access	Upon request, an individual shall be informed of the existence, use, and disclosure of his or her personal information and shall be given access to that information. An individual shall be able to challenge the accuracy and completeness of the information and have it amended as appropriate.
10. Challenging compliance	An individual shall be able to address a challenge concerning compliance with the above principles to the designated individual or individuals accountable for the organization's compliance.

are *purposes* for which the private information is being collected. Principle CSAPP.5 implies a *retention time* attribute for the retention of private information. Principles CSAPP.3, CSAPP.5, and CSAPP.9 imply that the private information can be disclosed to other parties, giving a *disclose-to* attribute. Thus, from the CSAPP we derive five attributes of private information collection, namely *collector*, *what*, *purposes*, *retention time*, and *disclose-to*.

The Privacy Principles also prescribe certain operational requirements that must be satisfied between provider and consumer, such as identifying purpose and acquiring consent. Our EPPM and the exchange of privacy policies automatically satisfy some of these requirements, namely Principles CSAPP.2, CSAPP.3, and CSAPP.8. The satisfaction of the remaining operational requirements depends on compliance mechanisms (Principles CSAPP.1, CSAPP.4, CSAPP.5, CSAPP.6, CSAPP.9, and CSAPP.10) and security mechanisms (Principle CSAPP.7).

European Union (EU)

Privacy in the EU is defined as a human right under Article 8 of the 1950 European Convention of Human Rights and Fundamental Freedoms (ECHR). The implementation of this Article can be traced to The Directive (European Union Directive). Similar legislation and enforcement structures as the European model exist in Canada, Australia, Norway, Switzerland, and Hong Kong.

The Directive applies to all sectors of EU public life, with some exceptions. It specifies the data protection rights afforded to "data subjects," plus the requirements and responsibilities obligated for "data controllers" and by association "data processors" (Deitz, 1998). This triad structure of entities balances data subject fundamental rights against the legitimate interests of data controllers (see Figure 2). The Directive places an obligation on member states to ratify national laws implementing its requirements.

The data subject is a person who can be identified by one or more pieces of data related to his physical, physiological, mental, economic, cultural, or social identities. Even data associated with an individual in ambiguous ways may be deemed reasonable personally identifiable information. Following Article 1 of the ECHR, the fundamental right to data protection falls not to the nationality of the data subject, but as an obligation to a party that relies on the data subject (Council of Europe Convention 108). The parties that rely on the data subject are the data controller and, by association, the data processor.

The data controller is an entity that determines the purpose and means of processing personal data and is defined as the holder of ultimate accountability as it relates to the correct processing and handling of the information from the data subject. The data processor is an entity that processes personal data on behalf of the data controller.

For e-services in this work, the data subject maps to the e-service consumer and the data controller and data processors together map to the e-service provider, as depicted using gray in Figure 2.

EU privacy principles (Table 3) abstracted from the complexities of legislation have been developed to simplify compliance with privacy regulations. Analyzing an approach using the principles as a guide offers a fruitful means for determining the effectiveness and pitfalls of the approach. We thus use these principles to derive privacy attributes based on EU privacy legislation. For convenience, we label these principles as EUPP, with EUPP.n meaning Principle n of EUPP.

Looking at Table 3, we note that the EUPP has much in common with the CSAPP. We see that EUPP.2 has "who is processing his personal data and for what purpose" implying the privacy attributes *collector* (for "who"), *what* (for "personal data"), and *purpose*. Purpose is also confirmed by EUPP.3. EUPP.7 talks about exchanging personal data implying the *disclosed-to* attribute. While retention time is not mentioned explicitly, EUPP.3

Figure 2. A schematic representation of the roles of the three entities defined in the directive

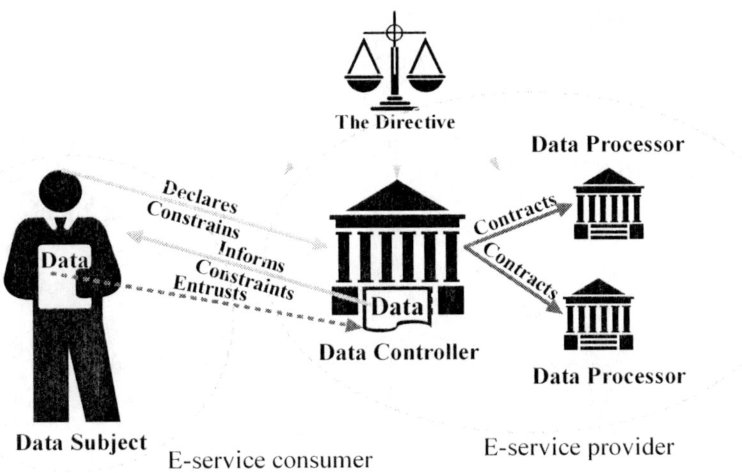

Table 3. European Union privacy principles

Principle	Description
1. Reporting the processing	All non-exempt processing must be reported in advance to the National Data Protection Authority.
2. Transparent processing	The data subject must be able to see who is processing his or her personal data and for what purpose. The data controller must keep track of all processing it performs and the data processors and must make it available to the user.
3. Finality & purpose limitation	Personal data may only be collected for specific, explicit, legitimate purposes and not further processed in a way that is incompatible with those purposes.
4. Lawful basis for data processing	Personal data processing must be based on what is legally specified for the type of data involved, which varies depending on the type of personal data.
5. Data quality	Personal data must be as correct and as accurate as possible. The data controller must allow the citizen to examine and modify all data attributable to that person.
6. Rights	The data subject has the right to improve his or her data as well as the right to raise certain objections regarding the execution of these principles by the data controller.
7. Data traffic outside EU	Exchange of personal data to a country outside the EU is permitted only if that country offers adequate protection. The data controller assures appropriate measures are taken in that locality if possible.
8. Data processor processing	If data processing is outsourced from data controller to processor, controllability must be arranged.
9. Security	Measures are taken to assure secure processing of personal data.

mentions, "not further processed in a way that is incompatible with those purposes," which can be partly enforced using retention time. In addition, EUPP.8 talks about arranging for controllability, which is supported by retention time. In any case, retention time as a privacy attribute can only help the cause of privacy protection. The remaining aspects of the EUPP refer to operational requirements (e.g., EUPP.1, EUPP.9). We thus conclude that the privacy attributes *collector*, *what*, *purposes*, *retention time,* and *disclose-to* are also supported by the EUPP, and moreover, that the EUPP does not introduce any additional attributes.

United States

In the United States, privacy protection is achieved through a patchwork of legislation at the federal and state levels. Privacy legislation is largely sector-based (Banisar, 1999). At the Federal level there are presently more than a dozen privacy laws. Some of these laws are: Privacy Act of 1974 as amended (5 USC 552a), Electronic Communications Privacy Act of 1986, and Right to Financial Privacy Act of 1986. Laws applicable to the private sector include: Family Educational Rights and Privacy Act of 1978, Privacy Protection Act of 1980, and Video Privacy Protection Act of 1988. As can be seen, the laws typically apply to specific technologies or privacy threats to, for example, bank records, government databases, or video rental history. The laws serve as operational boundaries rather than requirements, and there is no national all encompassing code for privacy protection. As such, the United States laws are less effective at protecting personal privacy than either the legislations of the European Union or Canada. The United States is not the leader in privacy protection (Banisar, 1999; Hurley, 1999;

Milberg, Burke, Smith, & Kallman, 1995). However, there is one very hot area where privacy is treated very seriously, and that is the area of personal health information privacy, as exemplified by the Health Insurance Portability and Accountability Act (HIPAA) (U.S. Government). We therefore examine the privacy provisions of HIPAA for privacy attributes.

The following three paragraphs are quoted from U.S. Government-1 and give a good background on HIPAA privacy provisions:

The following overview provides answers to general questions regarding the Standards for Privacy of Individually Identifiable Health Information (the Privacy Rule), promulgated by the Department of Health and Human Services (HHS).

To improve the efficiency and effectiveness of the health care system, the Health Insurance Portability and Accountability Act (HIPAA) of 1996, Public Law 104-191, included 'Administrative Simplification' provisions that required HHS to adopt national standards for electronic health care transactions. At the same time, Congress recognized that advances in electronic technology could erode the privacy of health information. Consequently, Congress incorporated into HIPAA provisions that mandated the adoption of Federal privacy protections for individually identifiable health information.

In response to the HIPAA mandate, HHS published a final regulation in the form of the Privacy Rule in December 2000, which became effective on April 14, 2001. This Rule set national standards for the protection of health information, as applied to the three types of covered entities: health plans, health care clearinghouses, and health care providers who conduct certain health care transactions electronically. By the compliance date of April 14, 2003 (April 14, 2004, for small health plans), covered entities must implement standards to protect and guard against the misuse of individually identifiable health information. Failure to timely implement these standards may, under certain circumstances, trigger the imposition of civil or criminal penalties.

The Privacy Rule is too long to use here (even the summary of the Privacy Rule takes 25 pages). We instead present a summary of HIPAA health information privacy rights from U.S. Government-2 (Table 4). For convenience, we label Table 4 as HIPR and use HIPR.n to mean the n-th right of the HIPR, which has eight rights.

Looking at the HIPR, we note that the HIPR has much in common with the CSAPP and the EUPP. We see that HIPR.3 states, "You can learn how your health information is used and shared by your provider or health insurer." This implies a *collector* ("by your provider") and a *what* ("your health information"). HIPR.4 contains "used or shared for many other purposes," implying a *purpose* attribute. HIPR.7 talks about sharing your health information with other entities, implying a *disclose-to*. The HIPR does not mention *retention time*, but the much more detailed Privacy Rule of the HIPAA (see above) mentions "retention of records." The remaining aspects of the HIPR refer to operational requirements (e.g., HIPR.1, HIPR.2) some of which are similar to the CSAPP and EUPP (e.g., HIPR.1 and HIPR.2 relate well with EUPP.6, CSAPP.6, and CSAPP.9). We thus conclude that the privacy attributes *collector, what, purposes, retention time,* and *disclose-to* are also supported by the HIPR and HIPAA. Moreover, the HIPR does not introduce any additional private information attributes.

PERSONAL PRIVACY POLICY SPECIFICATION

Based on Table 4, the contents of a personal privacy policy should, for each item of private information, identify (a) *collector*—who wishes to collect the information, (b) *what*—the nature of the information, (c) *purposes*—the purposes for which the information is being collected,

Table 4. HIPAA consumer privacy rights

	Your Health Information Privacy Rights: Providers and health insurers who are required to follow this law must comply with your rights to...
1	**Ask to see and get a copy of your health records** You can ask to see and get a copy of your medical record and other health information. You may not be able to get all of your information in a few special cases. For example, if your doctor decides something in your file might endanger you or someone else, the doctor may not have to give this information to you. • In most cases, your copies must be given to you within 30 days, but this can be extended for another 30 days if you are given a reason. • You may have to pay for the cost of copying and mailing if you request copies and mailing.
2	**Have corrections added to your health information** You can ask to change any wrong information in your file or add information to your file if it is incomplete. For example, if you and your hospital agree that your file has the wrong result for a test, the hospital must change it. Even if the hospital believes the test result is correct, you still have the right to have your disagreement noted in your file. • In most cases the file should be changed within 60 days, but the hospital can take an extra 30 days if you are given a reason.
3	**Receive a notice that tells you how your health information is used and shared** You can learn how your health information is used and shared by your provider or health insurer. They must give you a notice that tells you how they may use and share your health information and how you can exercise your rights. In most cases, you should get this notice on your first visit to a provider or in the mail from your health insurer, and you can ask for a copy at any time.
4	**Decide whether to give your permission before your information can be used or shared for certain purposes** In general, your health information cannot be given to your employer, used or shared for things like sales calls or advertising, or used or shared for many other purposes unless you give your permission by signing an authorization form. This authorization form must tell you who will get your information and what your information will be used for.
5	**Get a report on when and why your health information was shared** Under the law, your health information may be used and shared for particular reasons, like making sure doctors give good care, making sure nursing homes are clean and safe, reporting when the flu is in your area, or making required reports to the police, such as reporting gunshot wounds. In many cases, you can ask for and get a list of who your health information has been shared with for these reasons. • You can get this report for free once a year. • In most cases you should get the report within 60 days, but it can take an extra 30 days if you are given a reason.
6	**Ask to be reached somewhere other than home** You can make reasonable requests to be contacted at different places or in a different way. For example, you can have the nurse call you at your office instead of your home, or send mail to you in an envelope instead of on a postcard. If sending information to you at home might put you in danger, your health insurer must talk, call, or write to you where you ask and in the way you ask, if the request is reasonable.
7	**Ask that your information not be shared** You can ask your provider or health insurer not to share your health information with certain people, groups, or companies. For example, if you go to a clinic, you could ask the doctor not to share your medical record with other doctors or nurses in the clinic. However, they do not have to agree to do what you ask.
8	**File complaints** If you believe your information was used or shared in a way that is not allowed under the privacy law, or if you were not able to exercise your rights, you can file a complaint with your provider or health insurer. The privacy notice you receive from them will tell you who to talk to and how to file a complaint. You can also file a complaint with the U.S. Government.

(d) *retention time*—the amount of time for the provider to keep the information, and (e) *disclose-to*—the parties to whom the information will be disclosed. Privacy policies across different types of e-services (e.g., e-business, e-learning, e-health) are specified using these attributes (see Figure 3) and principally differ from one another according to the values of the attributes *what* and *purposes*. For example, an e-commerce privacy policy might specify credit card number as *what*

Figure 3. Example of consumer personal privacy policies

Policy Use: E-learning *Owner*: Alice Consumer *Proxy*: No *Valid*: unlimited	*Policy Use*: Bookseller *Owner*: Alice Consumer *Proxy*: No *Valid*: June 2005	*Policy Use*: Medical Help *Owner*: Alice Consumer *Proxy*: No *Valid*: July 2005
Collector: Any *What:* name, address, tel *Purposes:* identification *Retention Time:* unlimited *Disclose-To*: none *Collector:* Any *What:* Course Marks *Purposes:* Records *Retention Time:* 2 years *Disclose-To*: none	*Collector:* Any *What:* name, address, tel *Purposes:* identification *Retention Time:* unlimited *Disclose-To*: none	*Collector:* Any *What:* name, address, tel *Purposes:* contact *Retention Time:* unlimited *Disclose-To*: pharmacy *Collector:* Dr. A. Smith *What:* medical condition *Purposes:* treatment *Retention Time:* unlimited *Disclose-To*: pharmacy

and payment as *purposes*, whereas an e-learning privacy policy might specify marks as *what* and student assessment as *purposes*.

Figure 3 gives three examples of consumer personal privacy policies for use with an e-learning provider, an online bookseller, and an online medical help clinic. The first item in a policy indicates the type of online service for which the policy will be used. Since a privacy policy may change over time, we have a *valid* field to hold the time period during which the policy is valid. The proxy field holds the name of the proxy if a proxy is employed to provide the information. Otherwise, this field has the default value of "no." The address and telephone contact of the proxy may be specified as an informational item in the privacy policy itself. These policies need to be expressed in a machine-readable policy language such as APPEL (W3C, 2002) (XML implementation).

A personal privacy policy thus consists of "header" information (policy use, owner, proxy, valid) together with 5-tuples or privacy rules, where each 5-tuple or rule represents an item of private information and the conditions under which the information may be shared:

<collector, what, purposes, retention time, disclose-to>

A personal privacy policy therefore consists of a header plus one or more privacy rules.

As we mentioned in the Introduction, this is a minimum personal privacy policy that satisfies the privacy legislation of Canada, the European Union, and the United States (for personal health information), since it can contain additional privacy provisions. Additional provisions could include, for example, (a) elaborated retention time using conditions such as "6 months unless I call to have it deleted right away," (b) negative purposes such as "not for purposes A or B," (c) negative disclose-to such as "not to be disclosed to persons C or D," and d) operational items such as requesting a report as in HIPR.5 or requesting different means of contact as in HIPR.6.

CONCLUSIONS AND FUTURE RESEARCH

We began by introducing our E-Services Privacy Policy Model that describes how personal privacy policies can be used to protect personal privacy in an e-services environment. We then examined privacy principles and rights representative of privacy legislation from Canada, the European Union, and the United States and derived five attributes of private information collection for use in specifying personal privacy policies, namely *collector, what, purposes, retention time*, and *disclose-to*. We showed that these attributes are supported by the privacy legislation of all three geographic regions. Moreover, these attributes are complete in the sense that no other privacy attributes are required by the legislation, although one could add additional modifiers to the attributes and include operational items in the policy. In addition, we believe that the five attributes lead to a policy that is very understandable and manageable by the average e-service consumer, which is important if the EPPM is to succeed. In this sense, the possible additional privacy provisions mentioned would only complicate matters and may not be used by most consumers.

Ideas for future research include: (a) expressing our personal privacy policy using a policy language such as APPEL (W3C, 2002) to investigate ease and practicality of use, and (b) have consumer volunteers express their privacy preferences using our privacy policy to gauge how well consumers adapt to it and whether or not it meets the requirements for a variety of e-services in different domains. The latter work would explore how personal privacy policies may be used with Web services via their implementation protocols (e.g., UDDI, WSDL, and SOAP).

REFERENCES

Banisar, D. (1999, September 13). Privacy and data protection around the world. In *21st International Conference on Privacy and Personal Data Protection.*

Carnegie Mellon University. (n.d.). Privacy Server Protocol Project. School of Computer Science, Robotics Institute and eCommerce Institute, Internet Systems Laboratory. Retrieved August 13, 2002, from http://yuan.ecom.cmu.edu/psp/

Council of Europe Convention 108. (n.d.). *Convention for the Protection of Individuals with Regard to Automatic Processing of Personal Data.* Retrieved from http://conventions.coe.int/treaty/EN/Treaties/Html/108.htm

Deitz, L. (1998). Privacy and security — EC's privacy directive: protecting personal data and ensuring its free movement. *Computers and Security Journal, 17*(4), 25-46.

Department of Justice. (n.d.). *Privacy provisions highlights.* Retrieved July 3, 2002, from http://canada.justice.gc.ca/en/news/nr/1998/attback2.html

European Union Directive. (1995). Directive 95/46/EC of the European Parliament and of the Council of 24 October 1995 on the protection of individuals with regard to the processing of personal data and on the free movement of such data. Unofficial text retrieved Sept. 5, 2003, from http://aspe.hhs.gov/datacncl/eudirect.htm

Government of Canada. (n.d.). Personal Information Protection and Electronic Documents Act. Retrieved February 28, 2005, from http://www.privcom.gc.ca/legislation/index_e.asp

IBM. (n.d.). *Enterprise Privacy Architecture Language (EPAL).* Retrieved March 9, 2005, from http://www.zurich.ibm.com/security/enterprise-privacy/epal/

Milberg, S. J., Burke, S. J., Smith, H. J., & Kallman, E. A. (1995, December). Values, personal information, privacy, and regulatory approaches. *Communications of the ACM, 38*(12), 65-74.

U.S. Government. (n.d.). *Office for Civil Rights—HIPAA: Medical privacy—National standards to protect the privacy of personal health information.* Retrieved February 28, 2005, from http://www.hhs.gov/ocr/hipaa/

U.S. Government-1. (n.d.). *General overview of standards for privacy of individually identifiable health information*. Retrieved February 28, 2005, from http://www.hhs.gov/ocr/hipaa/guidelines/overview.pdf

U.S. Government-2. (n.d.). *Your health information privacy rights*. Retrieved February 28, 2005, from http://www.hhs.gov/ocr/hipaa/consumer_rights.pdf

W3C. (2002, April 15). *A P3P Preference Exchange Language 1.0 (APPEL1.0)* (W3C Working Draft). Retrieved August 12, 2002, from http://www.w3.org/TR/P3P-preferences/

W3C. (n.d.). *The Platform for Privacy Preferences*. Retrieved August 12, 2002, from http://www.w3.org/P3P/

Yee, G., & Korba, L. (2003, January). Bilateral e-services negotiation under uncertainty. In *Proceedings of the 2003 International Symposium on Applications and the Internet (SAINT2003)*, Orlando, Florida, USA.

Yee, G., & Korba, L. (2003, May). The negotiation of privacy policies in distance education. In *Proceedings of the Information Resources Management Association International Conference 2003 (IRMA 2003)*, Philadelphia, Pennsylvania, USA.

Yee, G., & Korba, L. (2004, July). Privacy policy compliance for Web services. In *Proceedings of the IEEE International Conference on Web Services (ICWS 2004)*, San Diego, California, USA.

Yee, G., & Korba, L. (2005, January). Semiautomatic derivation and use of personal privacy policies in e-business. *International Journal of E-Business Research, 1*(1), 54-69.

Yee, G., & Korba, L. (2005, March). An agent architecture for e-services privacy policy compliance. In *Proceedings of the IEEE 19th International Conference on Advanced Information Networking and Applications (AINA 2005)*, Tamkang University, Taiwan.

Yee, G., & Korba, L. (2005, May). Comparing and matching privacy policies using community consensus. In *Proceedings of the Information Resources Management Association International Conference 2005 (IRMA 2005)*, San Diego, California, USA.

ENDNOTE

[1] NRC Paper Number: NRC 48270

This work was previously published in Privacy Protection for E-Services, edited by G. Yee, pp. 281-294, copyright 2006 by IGI Publishing, formerly known as Idea Group Publishing (an imprint of IGI Global).

Chapter 5.9
User Attitudes to E-Government Citizen Services in Europe:
Report from the Field

Jeremy Millard
Danish Technological Institute, Denmark

ABSTRACT

In 2005, the eUSER project undertook a questionnaire survey covering about 10,000 households in 10 European Union member states, the purpose of which was to provide some of the first systematic evidence in Europe of citizen user behaviour and their attitudes to the use of public services, and particularly the role of e-services in this context. The survey focused on a number of themes—the public's use of government services, the different channels (or media) employed, the nature of potential future demand for e-government, the barriers and experiences in using e-government, and the socio-economic attributes of e-government users compared with non-users. The results provide important new information on the role that the Internet is now playing in the delivery and take-up of government services by European citizens. Face-to-face contact is still the most important channel for contacting government in Europe. In some countries (e.g., the UK), however, telephone and post have overtaken face-to-face. Results also show that potential demand for e-government services is about 50% of all government users and could be higher. One quarter of individual e-government users have acted as intermediaries for family members or friends, and one quarter have also done so on behalf of their employer. Most barriers that users anticipate they will meet when using e-government relate to difficulty in actually starting, with a feeling that face-to-face is better and the fear about data privacy important. However, once citizens have used e-government services, the barriers appear less, though still important, and relate mainly to the difficulty of feeling left alone with problems or questions.

INTRODUCTION

In 2005, the eUSER project[2] undertook a questionnaire survey covering approximately 10,000 households in 10 European Union member states,

Chart 1. Type of service used in contact with government

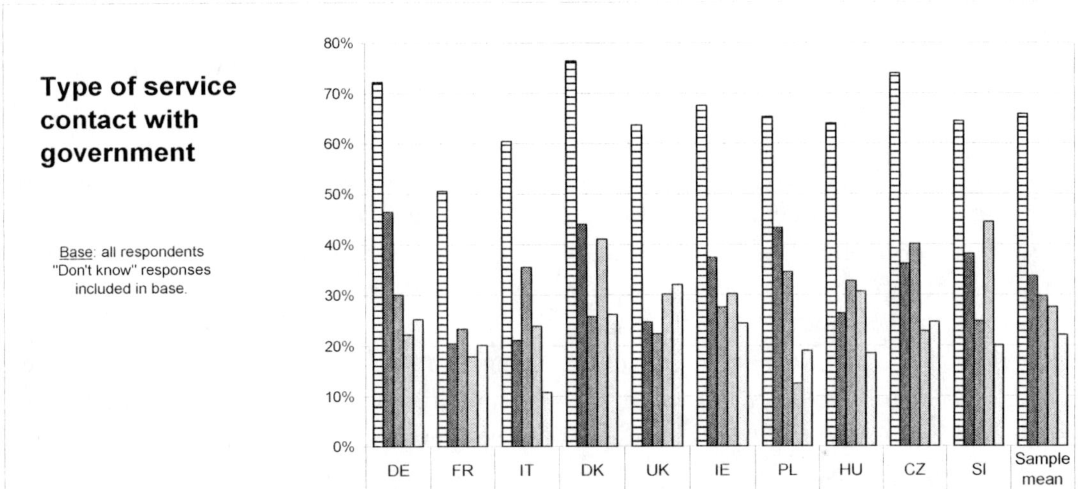

	DE	FR	IT	DK	UK	IE	PL	HU	CZ	SI	Sample mean
Had any contact with PAs in last 12 months	72%	51%	60%	76%	64%	68%	65%	64%	74%	64%	66%
Paying taxes (administration)	47%	20%	21%	44%	25%	37%	43%	26%	36%	38%	34%
Declaration or permits (administration)	30%	23%	36%	26%	22%	28%	35%	33%	40%	25%	30%
Use of public services and facilities (everyday life)	22%	18%	24%	41%	30%	30%	13%	31%	23%	44%	28%
Receiving financial benefits and grants (everyday life)	25%	20%	11%	26%	32%	24%	19%	19%	25%	20%	22%

both old and new.[3] In order to achieve as close to a random sample as possible, this was completed using either telephone or direct interview, with the responses being keyed into a database. The purpose of the survey was to provide some of the first systematic evidence in Europe of citizen user behaviour and attitudes to the use of public services, and particularly the role of e-services in this context.

The eUSER project surveyed the use by citizens of, and their attitudes toward, three sets of e-services, in e-government, e-health, and e-learning. The e-government part of the survey focused on a number of themes – the public's use of government services, the different channels (or media) employed, the nature of potential future demand for e-government, the barriers and experiences in using e-government, and the socio-economic attributes of e-government users compared with non-users. The results provide important new information on the role that the Internet is now playing in the delivery and take-up of government services by European citizens.

Some selected initial results of the eUSER survey are presented in this article. Fuller and final results became available at the end of 2005 from the author or the eUSER Web site.

USE OF GOVERNMENT SERVICES

As illustrated in Chart 1, across the 10 EU member states in the sample, almost 70% of all respondents had contact with the Public Administration (PA) in the last 12 months. There is, however, some variation between countries, with the more southern EU member states (France and Italy) having somewhat less contact, whilst there is not much difference between the central and northern member states and the new member states of Eastern Europe.

Although usage levels overall do not differ greatly between service types, the first two administrative services tend to be the most highly used. There are likely to be two reasons for this. First, these are the services that are most ubiquitous and available because the PAs have tended to roll these out first. Second, because they are legally enforced if the citizen is in a specific situation, the citizen is obliged to use the service.

More significantly, there are quite large differences between countries in the use of different service types. In several countries, some everyday life services are used more than some administrative services, for example, in Denmark and Slovenia the use of public services and facilities, and in the UK both the use of public services and facilities and receiving financial benefits and grants. In the southern European countries of France and Italy, the use of tax services is considerably lower than elsewhere, although the UK is also quite low. These differences probably reflect cultural contexts and legal regimes in different countries. The new member states tend to closely resemble the average usage patterns, with the exception mentioned earlier of Slovenians having higher levels of contact for public services and facilities.

Other data show how respondents felt about the ease or difficulty of using services. The differences between type of service and country are not large but do nevertheless show interesting variations. Although overall ease of use is quite high with a score of about 3.5 out of 5, the EU 10 average shows that the most difficult-to-use services are those involving the transfer of finances, either paying taxes or receiving benefits with the latter the most difficult of all.

Amongst the different member states, Denmark scores the highest in terms of ease of use, and this could be due to a combination of better-designed services and/or more skilled users. There do not appear to be any real differences between older and newer member states.

Chart 2 shows that the media channel used when contacting government is still overwhelming face-to-face. In some countries, such as the UK and Ireland, however, the use of the postal services and the telephone has overtaken face-to-face. Overall, new information and communication technology (ICT) media provide access for

Chart 2. Media channel used when contacting government

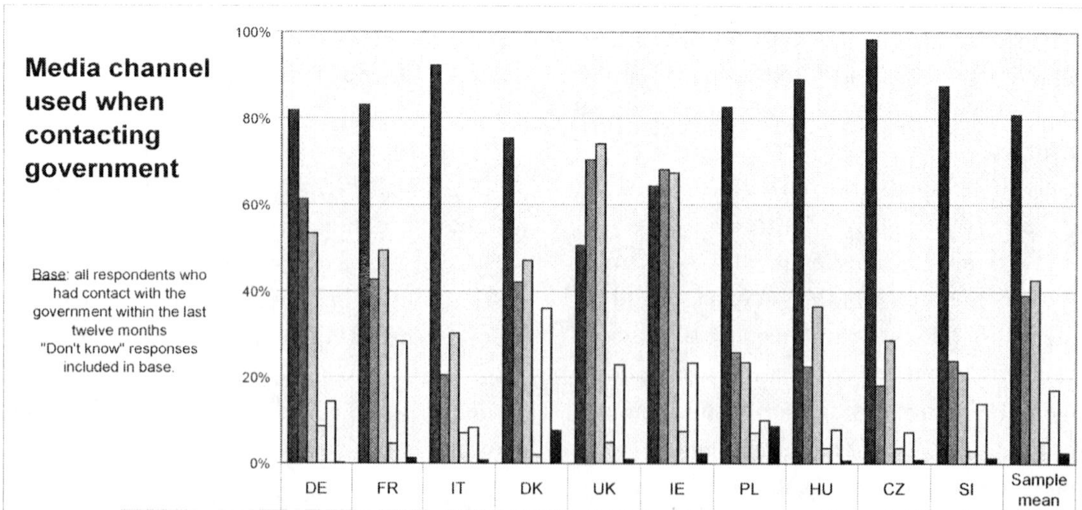

	DE	FR	IT	DK	UK	IE	PL	HU	CZ	SI	Sample mean
Face-to-face visits	82%	83%	92%	75%	51%	64%	83%	89%	98%	88%	81%
Post	61%	43%	21%	42%	70%	68%	26%	23%	18%	24%	39%
Telephone	53%	49%	30%	47%	74%	67%	23%	36%	29%	21%	43%
Fax	9%	5%	7%	2%	5%	7%	7%	4%	4%	3%	5%
Internet or e-mail	14%	28%	8%	36%	23%	23%	10%	8%	7%	14%	17%
SMS	0%	1%	1%	8%	1%	2%	9%	1%	1%	1%	3%

about 20% of all contacts with government, 17% of this via the Internet or e-mail and 3% via short message service. Denmark's use of ICT for contacting government is the highest, whilst the older member states generally, with the exceptions of Germany and Italy, show higher ICT usage than the new member states. Slovenia has the most use of ICT of the new member states in the sample, at about the same level as Germany.

POTENTIAL USE OF E-GOVERNMENT SERVICES

Another set of questions in the survey asks about the future intentions of all government users to use Internet or e-mail for contacting government. Comparing the responses to the existing use of Internet/e-mail by government users shows that the intention of these respondents to use e-government in the future has the potential to rise from the present 20% level of contacts to 47%. This is a substantial potential rise of well over 100%, although respondents were not asked to indicate when they are likely to use e-government, and it is known from previous surveys that not all future predictions of use translate into actual use. Nevertheless, strong potential interest is clearly present and shows that policies to encourage future use amongst users of government services are likely to fall on fertile ground.

There are few large differences between countries, though Denmark is clearly the member state with the highest intended future use at 63% and Hungary the lowest at 33%. The intentions of government users in the new member states to use e-government in the future appears also to be slightly less than those of older member states, with Slovenia again the leading new member state somewhat ahead of Germany the most lagging older member state.

In terms of intentions to use different levels of e-government services, the survey shows that potential demand is highest for information ser-

Chart 3. E-government users: Own purpose, for family or friends, or for employer

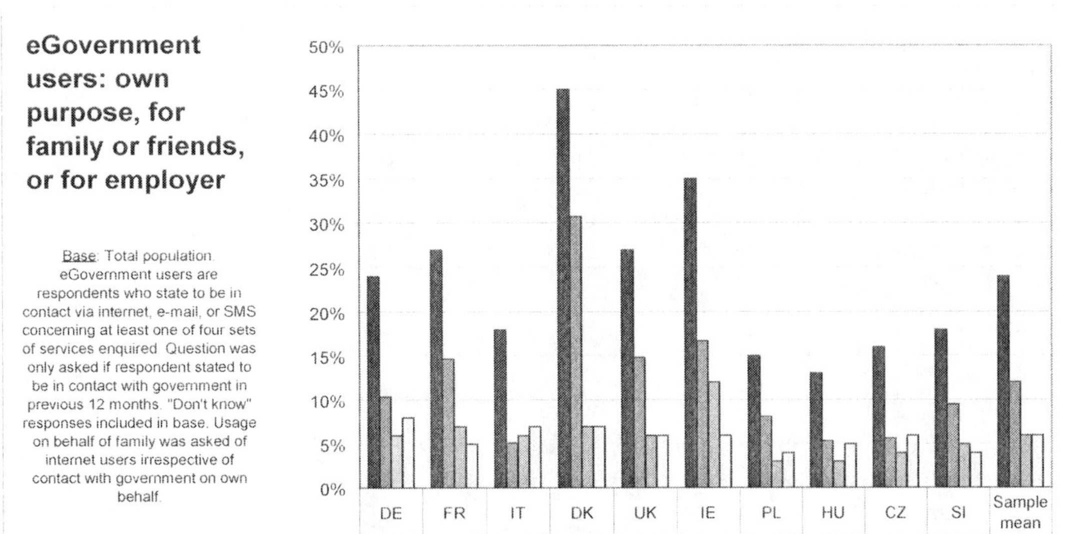

	DE	FR	IT	DK	UK	IE	PL	HU	CZ	SI	Sample mean
eGov total users	24%	27%	18%	45%	27%	35%	15%	13%	16%	18%	24%
eGov: own purpose	10%	15%	5%	31%	15%	17%	8%	5%	6%	9%	12%
eGov on behalf of family or friends (acting as intermediary)	6%	7%	6%	7%	6%	12%	3%	3%	4%	5%	6%
eGov as part of job (on behalf of employer)	8%	5%	7%	7%	6%	6%	4%	5%	6%	4%	6%

vices in all countries in the sample. Next comes communication services and finally transaction services, that is, the least sophisticated services are in most demand. Of the two transaction services, making payments is more likely to be used than using a digital signature, which indicates that the latter remains a significant barrier to e-government use. Differences between countries appear to be insignificant in terms of potential demand across the different levels of service.

USE OF E-GOVERNMENT ON BEHALF OF WHOM?

Using e-government services on behalf of others is an important factor in the overall use of such services. On average, one half of e-government users do so, and of these again one half do so on behalf of family and friends and one half on behalf of their employer as part of their job. There are also important differences between countries, with the older member states generally having higher percentages of the adult population acting as intermediaries for family or friends (lead by Ireland) and as part of their job on behalf of their employer (lead by Germany), whilst the new member states have a higher proportion of their use of e-government characterised by acting on behalf of others. This is likely to be because of the greater access problems and lower digital skills in these countries, and probably reflects the different stages of development of the information society. This is also shown in Chart 3.

The data on the number of persons helped by an intermediary who is family or friend shows a significant bias toward the new member states, as shown in Chart 4. As also reflected in the data presented in Chart 3, this is likely to be because of the greater access problems and lower digital skills in these countries where more people in the population need to share online access facilities and probably reflects the different stages of development of the information society. Part of the

Chart 4. Average number of persons assisted by family or friends acting as intermediary

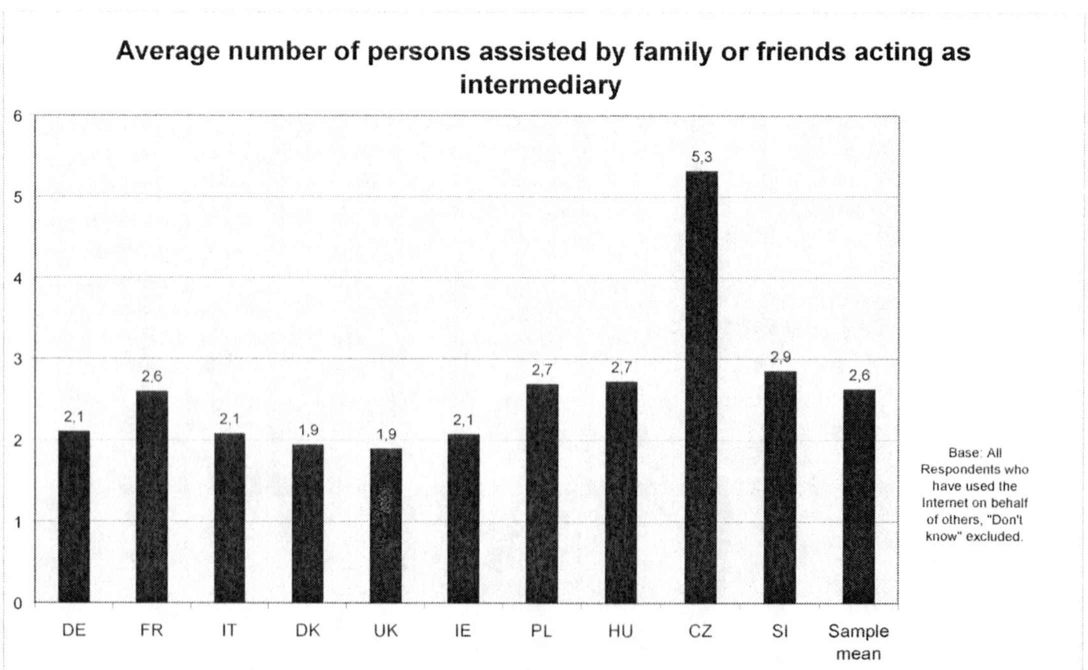

explanation for this could also be that it reflects different levels of development (particularly sophistication and user friendliness) of e-government services.

Seen from the perspective of persons receiving help from an intermediary when accessing e-government services, other data collected show that on average 17% of all e-government users did so partially and 7% did so completely. Support from an intermediary seems to be highest in the new member states (reflecting the data in Charts 3 and 4), where the relative number of "don't know" answers or the lack of an answer were also received, suggesting less familiarity with the idea of getting help from an intermediary in these countries.

ANTICIPATED AND EXPERIENCED BARRIERS TO E-GOVERNMENT SERVICES

Another part of the survey looks at barriers to the take-up of e-government by citizens, which are anticipated by many citizens as very important before the services are actually used. Most important is that well over half of potential users think they need face-to-face contact for a specific service. There are also fears about supplying personal information online expressed by 45% of users, but there is also lack of knowledge about whether the service they need is actually available online. Less widespread but still important barriers are potential users' impression that there is too much effort involved or that they have insufficient technical means. There are also important differences between countries but no distinction between older and newer member states. Danish and Slovenian users are generally less inclined to anticipate barriers to use, whereas the Czech Republic and Italy anticipate the biggest barriers. The latter two countries together with Poland emphasise particularly the need for face-to-face contact. In the UK, Ireland, and Hungary, fears about supplying personal information online are much higher than average.

These anticipated barriers before using e-government are generally much higher than the barriers actually experienced once e-government is used. After actual experience with e-government services, fewer users experience barriers or difficulties (between 17% and 32%) compared with the number of users who perceive barriers before use (between 25% and 58%). The most important difficulty experienced after use appears to be that the user feels that there are significant problems or questions the online service cannot deal with. There are also concerns that the online service cannot cater to the user's own individual needs, whereas the least problematic but still important factor is that the online service is felt to be too complex to use.

LEVELS OF SATISFACTION WITH E-GOVERNMENT SERVICES

As shown in Chart 5, overall satisfaction levels with e-government are very similar to overall satisfaction with government services generally with scores between 3.0 and 3.5, which indicates that adding online services to the government service portfolio does not change such perceptions. This can be interpreted both positively, that is, that the early days of online services with all the attendant difficulties has been very successful, or negatively, that is, that online services should be improving service quality and hence satisfaction. However, the relationship between service quality and user satisfaction is probably not a straightforward one.

Service fulfilment (able to completely do or get what's wanted from the electronic service) scores second highest after up-to-date and accurate information, but the least satisfactory is an aspect of transparency (easy to see whether an e-mail message has reached the right person).

Chart 5. Satisfaction with e-government by country

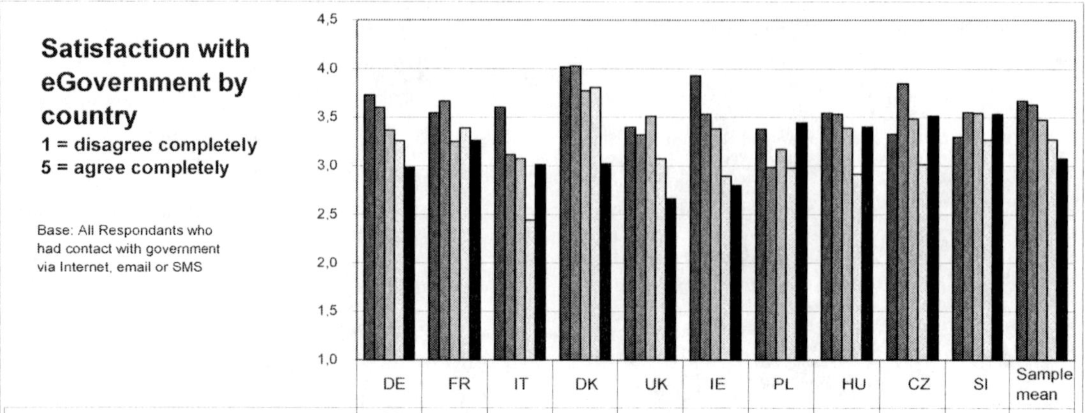

	DE	FR	IT	DK	UK	IE	PL	HU	CZ	SI	Sample mean
Information on public web sites was up-to-date and accurate	3,7	3,5	3,6	4,0	3,4	3,9	3,4	3,5	3,3	3,3	3,7
Able to completely do or get what wanted from the electronic service	3,6	3,7	3,1	4,0	3,3	3,5	3,0	3,5	3,9	3,6	3,6
Public websites provided enough information about what to do in specific situation	3,4	3,3	3,1	3,8	3,5	3,4	3,2	3,4	3,5	3,5	3,5
The online government services used can take account of personal circumstances	3,3	3,4	2,4	3,8	3,1	2,9	3,0	2,9	3,0	3,3	3,3
Easy to see whether an email message has reached the right contact person in the government agency	3,0	3,3	3,0	3,0	2,7	2,8	3,4	3,4	3,5	3,5	3,1

Chart 6. Identification methods for e-government: Use and ease of use

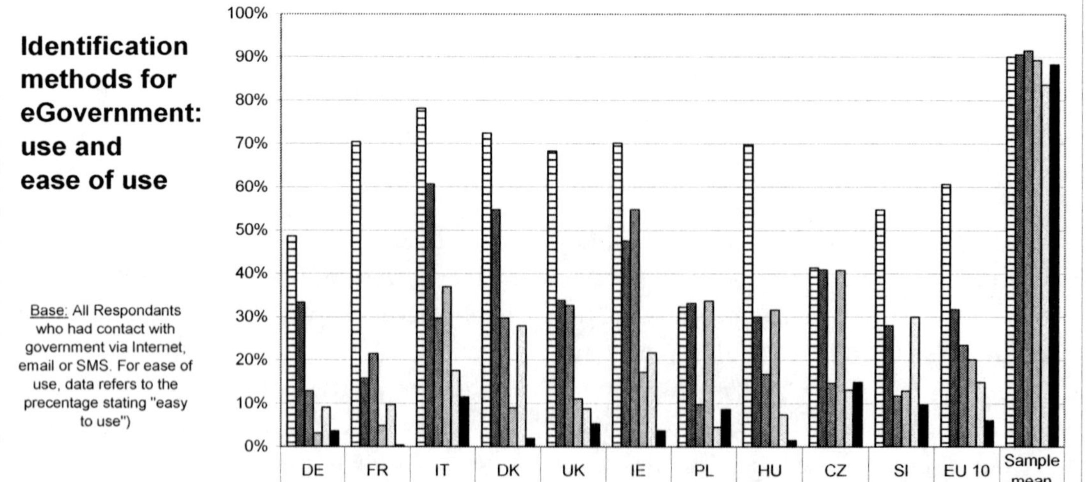

	DE	FR	IT	DK	UK	IE	PL	HU	CZ	SI	EU 10	Sample mean
User ID & password	49%	70%	78%	72%	68%	70%	32%	70%	41%	55%	61%	90%
PIN code	33%	16%	61%	55%	34%	48%	33%	30%	41%	28%	32%	91%
Credit card	13%	22%	30%	30%	33%	55%	10%	17%	15%	12%	23%	92%
SMS messaging	3%	5%	37%	9%	11%	17%	34%	32%	41%	13%	20%	89%
Digital Signature	9%	10%	18%	28%	9%	22%	5%	7%	13%	30%	15%	84%
Specialised smart cards	4%	0%	12%	2%	5%	4%	9%	2%	15%	10%	6%	88%

In terms of country differences, Denmark leads in terms of satisfaction and it also leads in terms of use of e-government services, which could be due both to a combination of better-designed services and/or more skilled users, and probably reflects the general level of development of the information society in that country. The UK shows the lowest satisfaction levels, and there appear to be no differences between the older and newer member states.

IDENTIFICATION METHODS FOR E-GOVERNMENT

As Chart 6 shows, there are marked differences in the use of the currently available user identification methods, with the most used tending to be the simplest, cheapest, and least secure, though, for the most commonly used e-government services, arguably secure enough. In terms of ease of use, differences are slight; only the use of digital signatures is a little lower than the others. However, it is probable that once citizens get used to a particular method, its ease of use from their perspective increases.

There are also important differences between countries, with Italy leading on the use of user ID/password and Personal Identification Number (PIN) codes compared to Poland, which has the lowest use of these. Indeed two of the four new member states (Poland and the Czech Republic) do not show the pattern typical of the eight other countries in which user ID/password and PIN codes are by far the most common methods. The data seem to indicate that in these two countries at least, some focus and investment has been made on more "advanced" methods, particularly the use of specialised smart cards, in comparison with the other methods. In terms of the most "advanced" methods, Slovenia and Denmark lead on the use of digital signatures and the Czech Republic on the use of specialised smart cards. The very high use of credit cards in Ireland is probably related to the fact that some revenue-raising transaction services (such as motor tax) are now fully available online.

MAIN CONCLUSION

Face-to-face contact is still the most important channel for contacting government in Europe—81% of all citizens who contacted government in the last year did so in person, although not necessarily exclusively by this channel. However, in some countries, telephone and post have overtaken face-to-face (for example, in the UK with 74% telephone and only 51% face-to-face).

In the countries surveyed, about 11% of the adult population have used the Internet to access government services, and of those who have contacted government in the last year, this figure rises to 20%.

However, potential demand for e-government services is about 50% of all government users and could be higher.

Potential demand for e-government is mainly for information services, then communication services, and lowest for transaction services.

In terms of government services generally, citizens rate their overall satisfaction at about 3.5 out of 5.0, a figure that is almost identical to that for e-government services.

One quarter of individual e-government users have acted as intermediaries for family members or friends, and one quarter have also done so on behalf of their employer. Greater proportions of the total adult population in the older member states have used e-government on behalf of others in this way, but the share of e-government users doing so on behalf of others is greater in the new member states. Twenty-four percent of individual e-government users have received help in using e-government services from a family member or a friend.

Most barriers that users anticipate they will meet when using e-government relate to difficulty in actually starting, with a feeling that face-to-face is better and the fear about data privacy important. However, once citizens have used e-government services, the barriers appear less though still important, and relate mainly to the difficulty of feeling left alone with problems or questions.

When citizens need to identify themselves when using e-government services, most use simple well-know methods (such as user ID and password and PIN codes), which are not always suitable for legal or financial transactions. User identification is still a barrier to communication and transaction services, although the evidence also shows that once more sophisticated methods are employed (such as digital signature or smart cards) they are often rated as just as easy to use as the more well-known methods.

ENDNOTES

1. An earlier version of this article was previously published as: Millard, J. (2005, October). User attitudes to eGovernment Citizen Services in Europe. *eGov Magazine*. Noida, India: CSDMS (Centre for Science, Development and Media Studies). Available at http://www.egovonline.net
2. http://euser-eu.org
3. The old member states in the sample were: Denmark, France, Germany, Ireland, Italy, and the UK. The new member states in the sample, which joined the European Union in May 2004, were: the Czech Republic, Hungary, Poland, and Slovenia.

This work was previously published in International Journal of Electronic Government Research, Vol. 2, Issue 2, edited by D. F. Norris, pp. 49-58, copyright 2006 by IGI Publishing, formerly known as Idea Group Publishing (an imprint of IGI Global).

Chapter 5.10
User Help and Service Navigation Features in Government Web Sites

Genie N. L. Stowers
San Francisco State University, USA

ABSTRACT

This article examines the user help and service navigation features in government Web sites and compares them across levels of government. These features are critical to ensuring that users unfamiliar with government are able to successfully and easily access e-government services and information. The research finds clear patterns in the use of similar help and navigation features across governments, leading to a conclusion that these features are diffusing in the public sector Web development field. The article concludes by stating that Web developers should work to overcome a second digital divide, one of a lack of knowledge of Web site organization and government structure. Users need to be actively assisted to find information by Web developers.

USER HELP AND SERVICE NAVIGATION FEATURES IN GOVERNMENT WEB SITES

This article reports on efforts to make American state, local, and federal e-government portals more user-friendly by providing user help, service navigation, and organizational structures to assist potentially novice users in finding e-government information and services.

Once users have access to the Internet and learn how to use computers, they still have to understand how to navigate Web sites and find the information or services they need. Then, they have to understand how to interact with the Web site so that they can access those services. Governments need to provide more proactive user help features, service navigation features, and organizational structures to actively assist users in finding information and services they desire; otherwise, they can create a second digital divide, one between those who understand Web site structure and organization structure, and those who do not. As Hargittai (2003, p. 3) puts it, many a Web developer "wrongly assumes that gaining access to the Internet obliterates any potential inequality that may result from lack of access to the new medium. There are factors beyond mere connectivity that need to be considered when discussing the potential implications of the Internet for inequality. In addition to relying on basic measures of access to a medium, one needs to consider more nuanced measures of use such as user 'skill'. " 'Skill' is defined as the ability to locate content online effectively and efficiently."

USABILITY IN PUBLIC SECTOR WEBSITES

Today, West (2005) suggests that there is a great degree of variation among the organization and structure of current public sector Web sites, and that not all sites are organized in a user-friendly fashion. Indeed, there is little formal focus on these elements, and their importance sometimes goes unheeded. Many government portals and Web sites are designed with government workers in mind, not the ordinary users without experience in government or with the use of Internet services.

Bridging the "digital divide" does not mean just making computers themselves accessible, but also involves making the Web sites themselves more user-friendly and easy to use—removing barriers due to lack of experience with the Internet (Nielsen, 2000; Rosenfeld & Morville, 1998). Designers and developers of public sector Web sites must assume that those using their sites have limited training and experience and will need sites that are easy to use and designed with usability and effective information architecture in mind. They must also consider that the design lessons developed for private sector e-commerce sites might not necessarily work for public sector sites.

User help, service navigation, and organizational structure are critical features of any public sector main portal that is dedicated to having users find its services and information. The presence or absence of these features on public sector sites can greatly affect the ability of a user to find information and services that might be available on the site and to effectively use those services.

The usability of the e-government portal interface is an important feature of human-computer interaction; to many users, the interface of the main portal is, in fact, the only important part (Singh & Kotze, 2002). Usability is typically defined as "the measure of the quality of a user's experience when interacting with a product or system—whether a Web site, a software application, mobile technology, or any user-operated device. Usability is a combination of factors that affects the user's experience with the product or system, including: ease of learning, efficiency of use, memorability, error frequency and severity, and subjective satisfaction" (U.S. Department of Health and Human Services, 2005).

Other factors that can be incorporated into usability include effectiveness, a match between the system and the real world, user control, safety, utility, flexibility, robustness, and consistency and usefulness of navigation (Nielsen, 2000; Singh & Kotze, 2002). We can also argue that usability includes adequate help features (including embedded help, interactive help, or manuals) and an information architecture that is descriptive, broad, and shallow for users to "click through" rather than relying upon a deep structure (Kitajima, Blackmon, & Polson, 2000, 2005; Nielsen, 2000).

Since the beginning of the World Wide Web, empirical studies have reported low rates of successful information and retrieval (Nielsen, 2000) and wide variation in the lengths of time taken for success (Hargittai, 2003). When Hargittai (2003) tested user ability to find the IRS 1040 tax form (given an unlimited amount of time), 93% could find the form, but the time required varied from 30 seconds to almost nine minutes. Of those participating, 60% used a search engine and 40% tried a specific URL. Among the problems encountered, particularly by those who were significantly older and by more recent users, were confusion about URLs and about page design layout.

Jenkins, Corritore, and Wiedenbeck (2003) identified four groups of users who utilized different search strategies based upon their level of expertise in subject matter and with the World Wide Web. Those who were domain or content and Web novices searched broadly first but did little evaluations of their findings. Domain experts but Web novices searched broadly first but were able to evaluate their results more thoroughly for accuracy. Domain and Web experts first looked deeply, utilizing their expertise, and were able to follow those deep trails and evaluate their findings. Those who were experts on both domain and the Web were able to quickly find and identify the information which was needed.

As Kitajima, Blackmon, and Polson (2000) describe it, if a user has a 90% chance of finding and selecting the correct link at each level, and there are five levels to go before they can access their desired services or content, the chance of successfully finding that information falls to .53 ($.9^6$) or 53% rather than the 81% chance of success if there are only two levels to move through.

Users typically seek to improve these odds by being goal-driven and focused upon descriptions of content and links that match with their understanding of reality rather than necessarily utilizing search facilities or navigation aids (Kitajima, Blackmon, & Polson, 2000, 2005). They seek out "information scent", defined as "the imperfect, subjective, perception of the value, cost or access path of information sources obtained from proximal cues, such as Web links, or icons representing the content sources" (Chi, Pirolli, & Pitkow, 2000, p. 2).

Typically, users perform this through a two-stage process. The first is an "attention" process where the user seeks to separate a Web page into sections based on labels, layout, and information on the page. To be effective in laying out information scent to guide user behavior, the layout and labels have to be able to direct the user to the appropriate section with labels that make sense for them. The second step is the "action selection" stage, where the user decides upon which link to choose. Clearly, here the appropriate labels are crucial to user success. Successful navigation thus requires gaining the user's attention and leading them to the correct selection of the appropriate link at each hierarchical level of the Web site (Blackmon, Kitajima, & Polson, 2005).

For many users seeking online government information, conducting a successful search for information means solving an unfamiliar problem (Blackmon, Kitajima, & Polson, 2005). In essence, they know too little about government and how it is structured to be able to successfully navigate and make link choices on many government Web sites.

There are numerous difficulties with this task, some of them based upon the knowledge of and familiarity with the labels themselves. Takeuchi and Kitajima (2002) effectively illustrate that, at the very least, there are gender differences in the understanding of many technical words, and these differences are further accentuated when viewed across cultural divisions. Given that there are many other differences in levels of understanding of information and a wide variety of quality in labeling and the laying of information scents, it is clear that government Web designers have a daunting task.

To overcome these many differences in abilities and understanding of how to use the technology and content, Web developers must develop effective site structures that reflect the users' views of the content at that site, not just the organization's own view of itself (based upon its organizational chart) (Nielsen, 2000). Plus, many gaps in user knowledge can also be filled with effective help systems like live chat, online learning and tutorials, online manuals, and well-structured designs which seek to define choices in terms that inexperienced users might know (Shneiderman & Hochheiser, 2001).

Usability features include those which assist the user in finding information, finding services, and in finding their way around the Web site. They include the following:

- navigation (features that assist the user in moving around the site);
- labeling (how the content is labeled, again so that the user knows how to find information);
- searching systems (the usefulness of the search features) (Rosenfeld & Morville, 1998); and
- visible help features, including a help page, frequently asked questions (FAQs) about the site, site maps (pages that literally provide a map of the entire site), and tutorials on using the site.

This previous research is important to understanding the project reported upon here, but is still not sufficient to allow us to generate meaningful hypotheses of the more specific topic explored here, user help features. Therefore, the research reported here will be structured around research questions.

STRUCTURING RESEARCH QUESTIONS ABOUT USER HELP FEATURES

Before we can identify research questions about user help features, we must identify these features. Initially, standard content analysis techniques were used to identify existing user help, navigation, and information architecture features on the Web portals. Agency and government portals were visited, features were identified and categorized, and a comprehensive list was developed. Once the list was developed, each portal to be studied was visited and coded as to the presence or absence of each feature.

Table 1 presents the types of user help features identified on government portal sites as well as a brief explanation of each. These include information about the site, an explicit Help section, FAQs (Frequently Asked Questions), information in other languages, and site maps. These features are organized in two sections according to whether or not they would be relatively easy to implement or require few resources. Thus, simple e-mail linkages for contacting the agency, to additional help, to information about the site, to user tips, and to an e-mail or comment section to provide feedback about the site would be easy to implement. Indices, site maps, FAQs, and search engines also would require minimally more work but little technical expertise to implement.

The most reasonable explanation for widespread user help features is that the features which are easiest and cheapest to produce will be utilized most frequently. There is no reason to believe that this pattern would differ across levels of government. Therefore, the first research question is:

- **R1:** The user help features which require the least technical abilities and fewest resources to implement will be found more frequently across all levels of government. The features which require the most technical abilities and greatest levels of resources to implement will be found least often.

Table 2 provides a listing of the various portal features used to provide users with assistance in finding agency online services. These features are not as common as the user help features listed above. They include agency or government calendars leading to information, as well as various ways to link to services (for example, Answers

Table 1. User help features

Feature	Explanation
Easiest and Requires Fewest Resources To Implement	
About the Site	Link to information about the site
Contact Us	Information and links to allow the user to contact the agency for more information or for help with the site
FAQs	Includes answers to Frequently Asked Questions
Feedback	Invites users to give them feedback about the site
Help	Explicit agency-provided help with the site
Index	An index of information, data, and agencies available
Search	Search engine to allow users to search the site
Site Map	Visual representation of the entire Web site
User Tips	Helpful hints on how users can use the site
More Technically Difficult or Resource-Heavy To Implement	
Live Help	Links to live chat with agency representative to provide assistance
Other Languages	Site provides information in other languages
Text Version	An alternate site is provided in text

Table 2. Service navigation aid features

Feature	Explanation
Agency Information	Listings of all agencies in directory form
Answers A to Z	Alphabetized listings of answers to questions
Calendars	Calendars of government activities and events
Contact Information	Linkages to direct contact information for agencies
Do you know how I do ___ ...?	List of questions organized according to major service areas from the citizen's point of view, stating "how do I do x or y?"
E-Government Services	Direct link from home page to all e-government services
Events	Link to information on major events
Facilities Locator	Direct linkage to way to locate government offices
Featured Link / Spotlight	Many sites have featured programs or linkages
Hot Topics	Link to information on what are considered currently important issues
Most Visited / Frequently Requested Site	Links to or listings of the most frequently visited sites, indicating the importance of that information
Popular Services / Major Programs	Highlighting of popular services or major programs
Quick Links	Listing of the commonly-asked questions in prominent format
Special Initiatives	Current, new, or special initiatives from the agency
What's New	Listing of new items posted on the site

A to Z, Do You Know?, Facilities Locators, Frequently Requested Site, Featured Links, Quick Links, and What's New).

We already know that well-planned formatting leads to success in finding sought-after information or services (Blackmon, Kitajima, & Polson, 2005) since users seek "information scent", or clues to the information they want (Chi, Pirolli, & Pitkow, 2000). Further, Web site developers can structure a site's portal entryway to separate users into knowledgeable consumers or users who might not know much about government. Thus, they are able to take advantage of the fact that users with experience and expertise typically utilize different strategies to find information (Jenkins, Corritore, & Wiedenbeck, 2003). Different agencies have used these principles to structure entry into their Web sites in different ways. This information can be used to structure service navigation schemes or the overall information organization of the entire Web portal.

However, this research is clearly exploratory, and there are few theoretical or practical reasons to expect one type or distinguish one type of service navigation scheme from another. There is no clear difference in the amount or level of technical expertise or resources needed to develop each scheme; they are just different ways of conceptualizing services and setting up the information scent discussed above. However, the most basic of the service navigation schemes are the ones which provide only basic description and require no re-conceptualization, such as E-Government Services linkages and Links to Agencies; therefore, we would suggest that these would be most popular. There would be no expectation that the usage of these labeling systems would differ from one level to another level of government.

- **R2:** The E-Government Services/Links to Agencies service navigation labeling systems would be found most commonly among government agency Web portals, no matter the level of government.

Table 3 identifies the information architecture, or structure, of systems of various Web site portals, in other words, how access to the information is organized. The various possible ways in which the Web portal can be organized include an audience/market orientation (the now familiar Citizen/Visitor/Business/Government), according to the types of services or tasks available, the kinds of topics or issues, or a hybrid of several types.

The audience/market orientation is one in which the Web portal's navigation scheme is segmented into a separate set of linkages for each potential audience. For example, the audience-oriented FirstGov.gov site has four tabs leading to four different sets of site features: For Citizens, For Businesses and Non-Profits, For Federal Employees, and Government-to-Government. States with audience/market orientations

Table 3. Types of information and service organization on government Web portals

Type of Information Architecture	Description.. Site is Organized Around:
Audience / Market	The needs of particular audiences or markets; for example, Firstgov.gov has information organized around Online Services for Citizens, for Businesses, and for Governments.
E-Government Services / Links to Agencies	The services, tasks, or functions offered by the agency
Topics / Issues	Various topics, often just miscellaneous listings of topics
Hybrid Site	Combinations of all of the above

will often have their sites segmented according to the purpose of a visitor (Access Washington's Living in Washington, Working/Employment, Doing Business, Education/Learning, and Visiting/Recreation).

A portal guiding their visitors according to the types of services or tasks available will have navigation features listing the types of services provided by the agency and providing links to information or services on those areas. Portals guiding users according to topics or issues set up navigation according to subject matter dealt with within the agency or government.

One of the few theoretical suggestions as to how these features would be clustered is by Ho (2002), who suggests that the system of information architecture used is a function of whether an agency is traditionally organized with a bureaucratic paradigm (in which case the information architecture would be structured according to a traditional listing of agencies) or whether it has moved to the more efficient e-government paradigm emphasizing a customer service orientation (with a structure according to the Web site audience or market).

However, Ho's hypothesis also suggests that there is necessarily a direct and strong linkage between design ideas within an agency's technology branch and the organizational sophistication of the overall agency, which is unlikely. Instead, staffs from these two areas are unlikely to communicate often (this is, in fact, one of the most commonly-cited breakdowns of technological systems, that there is little communication between technology developers and end users). Therefore, no research question is posited for these site features.

As discussed in the research methodology section, the components of these features on each government's main Web portal were identified for this project, their presence or absence on the portal was coded, and basic analysis was conducted.

PROJECT METHODOLOGY

The research project discussed here utilized a cross-sectional comparison that focused upon a review of federal, state, and local e-government portals, and comparisons between them. All federal agency portals from executive agencies, cabinet agencies (including sub-agencies with their own domain name), and independent agencies were included in the study. Federal boards and commissions were not included. All 50 states plus Washington, D.C. were included in the analysis, along with all cities over 100,000 in population. This resulted in 43 federal sites, 51 state sites, and 47 urban sites. The data was collected during summer of 2005.

The first stage of this analysis was to identify the user help features, service navigation features, and types of information architecture, or organization and presentation of information, that are currently being used on public sector Web sites, focusing upon the home portal of each portal. (While accessibility is also a crucial aspect of usability, it was not part of the overall project and is not reported here.)

Portals were the initial points of entry for users, as they define the usability and information architecture features for the entire site. Therefore, they are the most crucial part of an agency or government's entire Web site. The identification of help or navigation features was accomplished by content analysis of federal, state, and local home pages and the construction of coding sheets including the identified features. The presence of various features was determined through the examination of the site's portal, as this is the main entryway and where users would need these features.

All coding was conducted by one individual, the author, which is a shortcoming of this research. To attempt to overcome this issue, the author double-checked the results; of course, a simple "yes" or "no" check-off for each feature is a much less complex coding task than having to code an arbitrary scale of the effectiveness of a feature. All features were working at the time of the coding. Sixty-four variables were coded, along with three additive indices.

The author recognizes that a simple count does not address the issue of whether or not a feature is well-designed or not; however, this research is the first step in investigating this phenomena, and the first step should be whether a feature exists or not. Later, additional research should be conducted on the effectiveness of these features across jurisdictions.

USABILITY AND HELP FEATURES

The research reported here explores the simple research questions discussed above and is descriptive and exploratory in nature.

Descriptive Results

Table 4 presents basic descriptive data on user help features. As can be seen, most governments utilize more than one help feature, up to a maximum of six different features on the same portal, with state governments utilizing the most user help features. One federal and one local agency utilized none.

Table 5 reports descriptive data on service navigation features. An average of 5.1 features per government Web portal is used, with federal agencies utilizing an average of 4.3 and state agencies utilizing the highest average number, 5.6 service navigation features per site. The minimum number on a site was one for federal and local, two for state. The maximum number utilized was quite high—seven features for federal agencies, eleven for state, and ten for local agencies.

Exploration of Research Questions

The next part of the analysis is the exploration of the research questions and then, more exploratory analysis. Clearly, the first research question can be supported, as the easiest and least resource-intensive types of user help features were found much more frequently (Table 6). Among all levels of government, the most commonly-seen help feature was a search engine (found in 97.9% of all sites investigated, with no significant differences among levels of government). This was followed by invitations to Contact Us, found in 70.2% of sites, also with no significant differences across types of government. Site maps and Help areas were also found very commonly but exhibited different patterns across governments. Site maps were used most frequently by federal agencies and only by less than one-quarter of local agencies. Help areas were created most frequently by state agencies (58.8%), followed by one-quarter of federal agencies and only 12.8% of local agencies. User tips were very seldom utilized as user help features by any level of government.

Table 4. Distribution of user help features across level of government

	Total	Federal	State	Local
N	141	43	51	47
Mean Number of Features	3.7 features	3.7 features	4.3 features	3.1 features
Standard Deviation	1.36	1.35	1.30	1.17
Minimum Number of Features	0	0	2	0
Maximum Number of Features	6	6	6	6

Table 5. Distribution of service navigation features across level of government

	Total	Federal	State	Local
N	141	43	51	47
Mean Number of Features	5.1 features	4.3 features	5.6 features	5.3 features
Standard Deviation	1.78	1.59	1.62	1.85
Minimum Number of Features	1	1	2	1
Maximum Number of Features	11	7	11	10

Table 6. Distribution of help features by level of government (Ranked by most frequently used by all jurisdictions)

User Help Feature	Total	Federal (% Sites With Feature)	State (% Sites with Feature)	Local (% Sites with Feature)	Chi-Square	Probability
Easiest and Requires Fewest Resources To Implement						
Search	97.9%	97.7%	100%	95.7%	2.139	0.343
Contact Us	70.2	65.1	72.5	72.3	0.769	0.681
Site Map	***48.2***	***69.8***	***52.9***	***23.4***	***20.043 ******	***0.000***
Help	***33.3***	***25.6***	***58.8***	***12.8***	***25.021 ******	***0.000***
FAQs	19.9	27.9	21.6	10.6	4.355	0.113
About the Site	***18.4***	***11.6***	***31.4***	***10.6***	***8.901 *****	***0.012***
Feedback on Site	15.6	4.7	21.6	19.1	5.744	0.057
Index	12.8	20.9	5.9	12.8	4.744	0.093
User Tips	2.8	2.3	2	4.3	0.526	0.769
More Technically Difficult or Resource-Heavy To Implement						
Other Languages	***25.5%***	***41.9***	***11.8***	***25.5***	***11.11 *****	***0.004***
Text Version	***18.4%***	***4.7***	***31.4***	***17***	***11.17 *****	***0.004***
Live Help	***9.2%***	***0***	***19.6***	***6.4***	***11.39 *****	***0.003***

Help features which are present at significantly different levels across government levels are in bold italics.

* *Statistically different and significant at the .05 level*

** *Statistically different and significant at the .01 level*

*** *Statistically different and significant at the .000 level*

Table 7. Distribution of service navigation features by level of government (Ranked by most frequently used by all jurisdictions)

Service Navigation Feature	Total	Federal (% Sites With Feature)	State (% Sites with Feature)	Local (% Sites with Feature)	Chi-Square Statistic	Probability Level
E-Government Services	*60.3%*	*16.3%*	*72.5%*	*87.2%*	*52.2 ****	***0.000***
Featured Links	*60.3*	*44.2*	*66.7*	***68.1***	*6.7 **	***0.035***
Link to Agencies	***51.8***	***25.6***	***52.9***	***74.5***	***21.5 ******	***0.000***
Popular Services	***35.5***	***32.6***	***54.9***	***17.0***	***15.6 ******	***0.000***
Do You Know / How I Do ___?	31.9	18.6	37.3	38.3	5.1	0.080
Calendars	***27.0***	*7*	***33.3***	***38.3***	***12.8 *****	***0.002***
Link to Contacts	27.0	20.9	27.5	31.9	1.4	0.500
Events	***23.4***	***18.6***	***15.7***	***36.2***	***6.5 ****	***0.038***
What's New	22.7	27.9	17.6	23.4	1.4	0.492
Quick Links	19.1	16.3	27.5	12.8	3.7	0.154
Special Initiatives	14.9	16.3	15.7	12.8	0.3	0.879
Most Visited	***12.8***	***2.3***	***15.7***	***19.1***	***6.3 ****	***0.042***
Facilities Locator	***10.6***	***30.2***	***3.9***	***0.0***	***25.4 ******	***0.000***
Hot Topics	9.2	4.7	11.8	10.6	1.6	0.454
Answers A to Z	3.5	4.7	3.9	2.1	0.5	0.798

Service navigation features which are present at significantly different levels across government levels are in bold italics.

* *Statistically different and significant at the .05 level*

** *Statistically different and significant at the .01 level*

*** *Statistically different and significant at the .000 level*

Also as suggested in Research Question 1, those user help features that would require more resources or more technical sophistication were found less frequently on government Web portals. However, two of them (the site presented in Other Languages and an alternate Text Version, both very resource-intensive features) were available in 25.5% and 18.4% of all sites, respectively, and there were significant differences across types of governments. Federal agencies were much more likely to have sites available in other languages, and text versions were more frequently found at state sites.

Table 7 presents the distribution of service navigation features by level of government. As suggested, the very basic E-Government Services was present in 60.3% of all government sites, but more surprisingly, was seldom found on federal sites (16.3% only). It was very common on state and local sites (72.5% and 87.2%), however, and the differences between all three levels of government was statistically significant.

Table 8. Distribution of information or service organization available by level of government (Ranked by most frequently used by all jurisdictions)

Type of Organization Available	Total	Federal (% Sites With Feature)	State (% Sites with Feature)	Local (% Sites with Feature)	Chi-Square Statistic	Probability Level
Audience	35.5	14.0	49.0	40.4		
Services, Processes	34.8	44.2	43.1	17.0		
Hybrid	17.7	7.0	5.9	40.4		
Topics or Issues	11.3	34.9	2.0	2.1		
					67.7	.0000

Featured Links, Links to Agencies, and Popular Services were the next most commonly found across all levels of government, but again there were significant differences across those levels in where it was used. Featured Links were found on two-thirds of state and local sites; Agency Links were found in three-quarters of local sites, approximately one-half of the state sites, but on only one-third of the federal sites.

Features like Calendars and Events were most commonly found on state and local sites while Facilities Locators, not surprisingly, were most often found on federal sites but very seldom on state or local sites (governments evidently presume that their residents know where these government facilities are located).

Finally, Table 8 presents the distribution of information organization types across levels of government. The most commonly-utilized organizational scheme is the Audience/Market scheme, but that is because it is used by practically one-half of all states and 40% of all large cities in their Web portals. Federal agencies utilize this type only 14% of the time. A structure breaking down information by the types of services or processes offered is utilized far more often by federal agencies (44.2%) and by most of the rest of the states not using the Audience scheme (43.1%). Only 17% of the large cities used this type. Cities most frequently used a hybrid type of portal (in 40.4% of the cases), while states and federal agencies seldom used this. Finally, another third (34.9%) of federal agencies organized their information around topics or issues, a scheme avoided by states and local governments.

Clearly, the differences here are significant statistically and substantively. The types of information organization schemes utilized are a function of the types of services provided and the site managers' perceptions of their audiences. Federal agencies seem to focus on what they can offer users rather than be organized according to any anecdotal perception of their audience's identity (FirstGov.gov is a significant exception). State agencies focus on the services they offer or provide a user perspective. Cities, on the other hand, have fewer resources with which to work, which might explain the high number of hybrid sites, which are less organized. Still, 40% of local portals have taken the audience approach.

These initial results focus upon identifying user help, service navigation, and information architecture features used by the public sector. This is the first step in identifying which of these features ultimately are effective and really are helpful in assisting the general public in understanding these public sector portals and their services, and how to navigate and use them.

CONCLUSION

From the results, it appears that similar patterns do exist across levels of government in the types of user help and information organizational structure utilized. More technically-difficult features appear to be utilized by larger levels of government, so financial and staff resources are clearly determining patterns. However, there are many user help features that require little technical expertise so it is hard to explain their usage by the simple existence of resources in larger governments or agencies. In addition, it appears that states are leading the way in offering multiple types of features (see tables 4 and 5) and in offering the arguably more user-friendly audience-based type of information and service organizational structure.

Given the patterns found for some features, it appears that diffusion of these innovations and features is occurring across jurisdictions and within levels of government. Local government IT professionals meet and know one another through conferences, professional associations, and other informal networks, as do those at the federal and state levels. Certain features are discussed and popularized among IT professionals as important and useful for assisting users. Then, other governments in a network follow up and develop that feature for their own Web site. Or, Web managers visit the Web portals of their sister governments, see a feature they like that works well for their own level of government, and move to adopt it. However, there is no sense, from these results, that there is any systematic usability testing being utilized in the Web development process.

The development of user help and service navigation features, as well as systematic usability testing on Web portals, is crucial if governments really intend to effectively utilize e-government and provide electronic services. Deservedly, much focus is put upon the differences still existing between classes of users due to their access to computers and the Internet. Obviously, the inability of some groups of users to access e-government services reduces the equity of these services.

However, it should be recognized that another digital divide exists. Even if users have access to computers and the Internet, in order to fully utilize e-government services, they need government agency Web sites that can be understood and navigated successfully by everyone, not just by those who have knowledge and understanding about how government agencies and services work and are organized.

Effective user help and service navigation features can remove this second divide by allowing novice users or users unused to contacting government to understand and fully utilize e-government services and information. We should not create the "other digital divide"; we should work to ensure that all can access government services in an online context.

REFERENCES

Blackmon, M. H., Kitajima, M., & Polson, P. G. (2005). Tool for accurately predicting Web site navigation problems, non-problems, problem severity, and effectiveness of repairs. In *Proceedings of the Conference on Human Factors in Computing Systems (pp.31-40)*. Retrieved July 29, 2005, from http://staff.aist.go.jp/kitajima.muneo/English/PAPERS(E)/CHI2005.pdf

Blackmon, M. H., Polson, P. G., Kitajima, M., & Lewis, C. (2002). *Cognitive walkthrough for the Web*. Retrieved July 29, 2005, from http://staff.aist.go.jp/kitajima.muneo/English/PAPERS(E)/CHI2002.pdf

Chi, E. H., Pirolli, P., & Pitkow, J. (2000). The scent of a site: A system for analyzing and predicting information scent, usage, and usability of a Web site. In *Proceedings of CHI 2000*. ACM Press. Retrieved July 29, 2005, from http://www-users.cs.umn.edu/~echi/papers/chi2000/scent.pdf

Cohen, S. A., & Eimecke, W. B. (2001). *The use of the Internet in government service delivery.* PricewaterhouseCoopers Foundation for the Business of Government. Retrieved August 22, 2002, from http://endowment.pwcglobal.com/pdfs/CohenReport.pdf

Daabaj, Y. (2002). An evaluation of the usability of human-computer interaction methods in support of the development of interactive systems. In *Proceedings of the 35th Hawaii International Conference on System Sciences.*

Dillon, A. (2001). *Beyond usability: Process, outcome, and affect in human-computer interactions.* Canadian Journal of Information and Library Science, 26(4), 57–69.

Hargittai, E. (2003). *Serving citizens' needs: Minimizing online hurdles to accessing government information. IT and Society,* 1(3, Winter, 2003), 27–41. Retrieved July 29, 2005, from http://www.ITandSociety.org

Ho, A. T.-K. (2002). Reinventing local governments and the e-government initiative. *Public Administration Review, 62(4),* 434-444.

Huang, C. J. (2003). Usability of e-government Web sites for people with disabilities. In *Proceedings of the 36th Hawaii International Conference on System Sciences.*

Jansen, B.J., & Pooch, U. (2000). Web user studies: A review and framework for future work. *Journal of the American Society of Information Science and Technology, 52(3),* 235–246. Retrieved August 1, 2005, from http://jimjansen.tripod.com/academic/pubs/wus.pdf

Jenkins, C., Corritore, C. L., & Wiedenbeck, S. (2003). Patterns of information seeking on the Web: A qualitative study of domain expertise and Web expertise. *IT and Society, 1(3, Winter, 2003),* 64–89. Retrieved July 29, 2005, from http://www.ITandSociety.org

Jones, C. P. (2003). Usability and information design. In *Proceedings of the Annual Conference for the Society for Technical Community: Vol. 50 (pp. 333-338).*

Kitajima, M., Blackmon, M. H., & Polson, P. G. (2000). A comprehension-based model of Web navigation and its application to Web usability analysis. In S. McDonald, Y. Waern, & G. Cockton (Eds.), People and computers XIV - Usability or else! In *Proceedings of HCI 2000 (pp. 357-373).* Springer. Retrieved July 29, 2005, from http://staff.aist.go.jp/kitajima.muneo/English/PAPERS(E)/HCI2000.pdf

Kitajima, M., Blackmon, M. H., & Polson, P. G. (2005). Cognitive architecture for Web site design and usability evaluation: *Comprehension and information scent in performing by exploration. HCI International, 2005.* Retrieved July 30, 2005, from http://staff.aist.go.jp/kitajima.muneo/English/PAPERS(E)/HCII2005-CoLiDeS.html

Lazar, J., Bessiere, K., Ceaparu, I., Robinson, J., & Shneiderman, B. (2003). Help! I'm lost: User frustration in Web navigation. *IT & Society, 1(3, Winter, 2003*), 18–26. Retrieved July 29, 2005, from http://www.ITandSociety.org

Nielsen, J. (2000). Designing Web usability: *The practice of simplicity.* Indianapolis, IN: New Riders Publishing.

Norris, P. (2001). *Digital divide: Civic engagement, information poverty, and the Internet worldwide.* New York: Cambridge Press.

Paciello, M. G. (2000). *Web accessibility for people with disabilities.* Lawrence, KS: CMP Books.

Pearrow, M. (2000). Web site usability handbook. Rockland, MA: Charles River Media, Inc.

Pew Research Center (2002). Getting serious online. *Pew Internet and American Life Project.* Retrieved August 30, 2005, from http://www.pewinternet.org/reports/pdfs/PIP_Getting_Serious_Online3ng.pdf

Pew Research Center (2002). Daily Internet Activities. Retrieved August 30, 2005, from http://www.pewinternet.org/reports/chart.asp?img=Daily_Internet_Activities.jpg

Pew Research Center. (2002). Internet Activities. Retrieved August 30, 2005, from http://www.pewinternet.org/reports/chart.asp?img=Internet_Activities.jpg

Reiss, E. L. (2000). *Practical information architecture*. New York: Addison Wesley.

Rosenfeld, L. (2000). Special report: Design usability—Seven pitfalls to avoid in information architecture. *Internet World Magazine*. Retrieved July 29, 2005, from http://www.internetworld.com/magazine.php?inc=121500/12.15.00feature3long.html

Rosenfeld, L., & Morville, P. (1998). *Information architecture for the World Wide Web Sebastopol*, CA: O'Reilly and Associates.

Shneiderman, B., & Hochheiser. (2001). *Universal usability as a stimulus to advanced interface design. Human-Computer Interaction Lab*, University of Maryland. Retrieved August 1, 2005, from http://www.cs.umd.edu/hcil/pubs/tech-reports.shtml

Singh, S., & Kotze, P. (2002). Towards a framework for e-commerce usability. In *Proceedings of the 2002 Annual Research Conference of the South African Institute of Computer Scientists and Information Technologist on Enablement through Technology*. Retrieved July 29, 2005, from http://portal.acm.org/citation.cfm?id=581508&CFID=51211042&CFTOKEN=76008125

Takeuchi, H., & Kitajima, M. (2002). Web contents evaluation based on human knowledge of words. *International Conference on Soft Computing and Intelligent Systems*. Retrieved July 29, 2005, from http://staff.aist.go.jp/kitajima.muneo/English/PAPERS(E)/SCIS2002Takeuchi.pdf

U.S. Department of Commerce (2002). *A nation online: How Americans are expanding their use of the Internet*. Retrieved February 15, 2002, from http://www.ntia.doc.gov/ntiahome/dn/index.html

U.S. Department of Commerce (2000). *Falling through the net: Toward digital inclusion*. Retrieved February 21, 2001, from http://www.esa.doc.gov/fttn00.pdf

U.S. Department of Health and Human Services (2005). *Usability basics at usability.gov*. Retrieved August 4, 2005, from http://www.usability.gov/basics/index.html

U.S. Office of Management and Budget E-Government Task Force. (2002).

E-government strategy: *Simplified delivery of service to citizens*. Retrieved from http://www.whitehouse.gov/omb/inforeg/egovstrategy.pdf

West, D. M. (2005). *Global e-government, 2005*. Retrieved October 28, 2005, from http://www.insidepolitics.org/egovt05int.pdf

West, D. M. (2005). *State and federal e-government*, 2005. Retrieved October 15, 2005, from http://www.insidepolitics.org/egovt05us.pdf

This work was previously published in E-Government Research: Policy and Management, edited by D. Norris, pp. 140-157, copyright 2008 by IGI Publishing, formerly known as Idea Group Publishing (an imprint of IGI Global).

Chapter 5.11
Users' Acceptance of E-Government: A Study of Indian Central Excise

Ganesh P. Sahu
Indian Institute of Technology Delhi, India

M. P. Gupta
Indian Institute of Technology Delhi, India

ABSTRACT

The study seeks to highlight the key variables affecting usage of e-government by internal users of Indian Central Excise. An e-government acceptance model is developed and empirically tested using the 163 usable questionnaire responses from internal users of the Indian Central Excise. A priority of the variables is set by calculating the "total effect" of each variable on "intention to use e-government." Further, the "total effect" is compared with "ratio of acceptance" and clear recommendations for the Central Excise are generated for increasing the usage of e-government among it users. The model developed here can be applied in other similar e-government projects to test the users' intention to accept the system.

INTRODUCTION

Information technologies (IT), comprising of the Internet, e-mail, database, word processing applications, and so forth, have changed the way people work and live, the governments being no exceptions. IT initiatives in government services known as electronic government, or e-government, are changing the way the government works and interacts with citizens, businessmen, its employees, and other governments. E-government is supposed to provide information, services, or products through electronic means, by and from government agencies, at any given moment and place, offering an extra value for all participating players (Gupta, Kumar, & Bhattacharya, 2004). IT has the potential to transform government structures and to improve the quality of government services. Technology provides two main opportunities for government: increased operational efficiency by reducing costs and increasing productivity, and the better quality of services provided by government agencies (Garcia & Pardo, 2005).

Being the largest democracy and having one of the largest government set-ups in the world, India offers a vast potential for effective implementation of e-government (Gupta et al., 2004). The number of Internet users in India is constantly on the rise, with the focus shifting on providing more and more government services electronically. The Indian central government and state governments have problems such as delay in processes, uncertainty, lack of transparency, corruption, and so on, in their various processes. In many successful implementations of e-government, the respective governments or government departments are able to get rid of such problems to a great extent (www.mit.gov.in). The e-government market grew by 18% in 2003-2004 and is the highest growing vertical in the domestic IT market (NASSCOM, 2005). In the tenth five-year plan (2002-2007) of India, government has allocated US$4.92 billion to spend on the e-government implementation (www.mit.gov.in).

However, the failure rate of e-government project implementation is up to 85% in developing countries, which is quite high (Heeks, 2003). E-government acceptance by the end users depends on various factors, which are needed to be studied at the pilot stage of implementation and addressed while the project in on rollout. Therefore, acceptance or intention to use e-government of end users should be studied carefully to identify the various factors affecting the acceptance decision of an individual. This will help in reviewing and fine tuning the projects to achieve higher acceptability.

To identify the factors affecting e-government acceptance and also to develop a model for acceptance, literature was surveyed in the area of e-government acceptance and technology acceptance. The literature survey offered the technology acceptance model (TAM) as a proven tool. Researchers within the information systems (IS) community in the past have sought to conceptualize, empirically validate, and also extend TAM to explain IS adoption in a variety of contexts. The important constructs of TAM are "perceived ease of use," "perceived usefulness," and "attitude towards using technology" (Davis, Bagozzi, & Warshaw, 1989). Another model on the same line of TAM is "Unified Theory of Acceptance and Usage of Technology (UTAUT)" (Venkatesh, Morris, Davis, & Davis, 2003); this model is considered to be a robust model in literature. However, this model does not deal with issues related to system security and strength of control, which are critical in e-government domain. This study includes these as added variables in its research model. The motivation for this study stemmed from a desire to lay down such a model, which highlights the factors that lead to acceptance or rejection of information technology by government employees.

Low system acceptance by the end users is one of the major hurdles to the proliferation of e-government projects. Few studies in the e-government acceptance highlights that usage level of an e-government would depend on a number of criteria viz. intention to use, attitude toward using, effort expectancy, performance expectancy, and so forth. In India there is probably no evidence of such research, however there are some studies carried out in other countries. In a study, Chang, Li, Hung, and Hwang (2005) used TAM in the Taiwan government's Internet tax-filers' system to explain the taxpayers' acceptance of the system. Other studies available on the tax system of Taiwan are by Wang (2003) and Fu, Chao, and Farn (2004). Tahinakis, Mylonakis, and Protogeros (2006) studied the Hellenic Taxation System in Greece applying TAM and concluded that increased participation of taxpayers through an electronic system would create a socioeconomic

Table 1. Literature on e-government acceptance using TAM

Study	Objective	Use Context	Conclusion
Wang, 2003	To identify the factors affecting the adoption of electronic tax-filing systems using the technology acceptance model (TAM) as a theoretical framework	The Taiwanese Government Tax Agency	The findings of this study provide important implications for developing effective electronic government services in general and effective electronic tax-filing systems in particular.
Tahinakis et al., 2006	The influence of the e-government to the application of modern information systems that support direct and indirect taxation is examined	Hellenic taxation system, Greece	The function of electronic tax processes (TAXISnet) and the increased participation of taxpayers will create a socioeconomic environment, which was predicted to satisfy both the tax administration and the taxpayers.
Fu et al., 2004	To develop an understanding of the factors that influence citizens' adoption of electronic tax-filing services	Taiwan's electronic tax payment system.	Taxpayers who adopted the manual tax-filing method perceived lowest overall satisfaction level. Internet filing seemed to perform best in most of the sub dimensions of satisfaction and was perceived as the most efficient.
Chang et al., 2005	To examine taxpayers' acceptance of the Internet tax-filing system using TAM	Users Internet tax filing system	TAM proved to be a valid model to explain the taxpayers' acceptance of the Internet tax-filers' system. Meanwhile, perceived usefulness has created more impact than perceived ease of use on taxpayers' intention to use the system.
Hung, Chang, & Yu, 2006	To identify the factors that determine the publics' acceptance of e-government services	Online tax filing and payment system in Taiwan	Theory of planed behaviour with some modifications is proved to be a valid model explaining 72% variations in behaviour intention to use the system.

environment. A brief of these studies is presented in Table 1.

It was chosen to study e-governance applications in the Central Excise of India which is a part of Department of Revenue under the Ministry of Finance and responsible for collection of indirect taxes like excise levies and service tax. The government of India has identified it as one of the mission-mode e-government projects. Since a large section of the government's revenue collections comes through excise, reforms in this department could heavily benefit the Indian government and its citizens. It also has a large base of citizens which includes manufacturing organizations, importers, exporters, service organizations, and so on; thus, increased usage of e-government options in this department could have wide ranging implications for a large base of business organizations.

Considering technology acceptance factors in e-government, a research model is proposed to explain 'intention to use e-government' by the internal users of the Indian Central Excise. The model is empirically validated using 163 questionnaire responses from internal users of the Central Excise. The validated model can be used for other similar e-government projects in India to test and enhance the level of e-government acceptance.

CENTRAL EXCISE AND E-GOVERNMENT THEREIN

Central Excise is a commissionerate under the Central Board of Excise and Customs (CBEC), under the Ministry of Finance, government of India. It deals with the tasks of formulation of policy concerning levy and collection of Central Excise duties. Central Excise duty is an indirect tax levied on goods manufactured in India. Major processes in Excise include: registration of new assesses, processing of returns and refunds, reconciliation of revenue receipts, audit, and so forth.

Computerization in central excise started way back in 1985, on a limited scale, with a centralized feeding of invoices. However, the entire process took a big jump in 1991, when a application named SERMON (System for Excise Revenue Monitoring) was introduced. Brief information about all important information system application in the Central Excise and Service tax is depicted in Figure 1. The applications are classified into three categories with respect to their usage viz. internal users, external users and common for both internal and external users.

The e-government initiatives in Central Excise are guided by two principles: delivering services in ways that reflect what people need or want from the department, and making the department and its services more accessible on an anywhere, anytime basis through its Web site (http://exciseandservicetax.nic.in). This provides a platform for users to transact their work with the department from the comfort of their home or office using the Internet.

Figure 1. Central Excise e-government

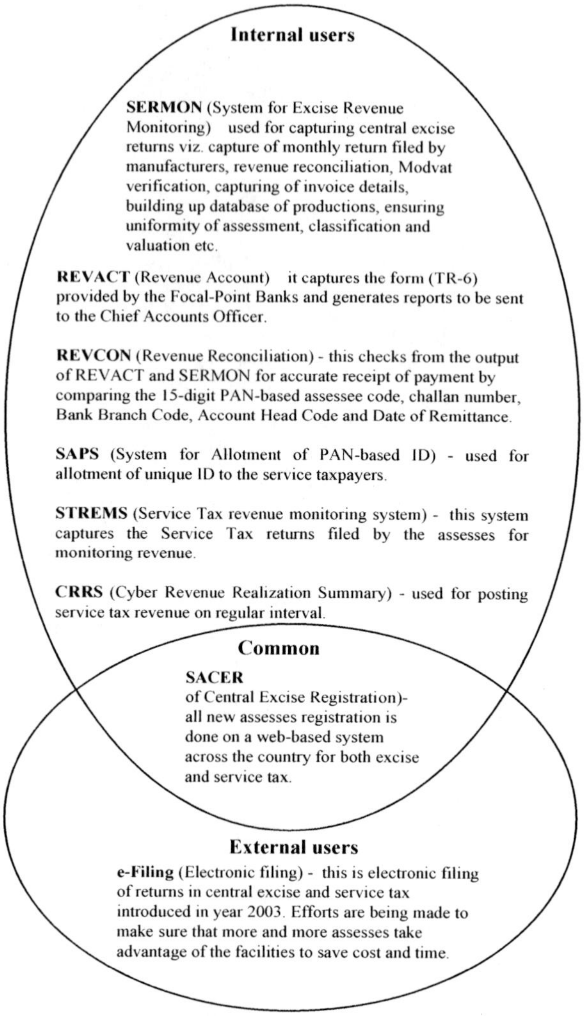

STUDY DESIGN

The study is designed with an objective to identify factors that determine acceptance or lead to rejection of e-government by its end users in the Indian Central Excise and to arrive at a model of e-government acceptance for this department. The initial study of the department by interacting with the users identified few issues related to acceptance of e-government. These issues are ease of use, control and security, skill and training, awareness about system usefulness, attitude of government employees towards using e-government, facilitating conditions, top management support, societal concerns, and so on. Many of these issues are similar to the issues of technology acceptance and therefore technology acceptance model and unified theory of acceptance and use of technology (UTAUT) are considered as base models for this study. A research model was designed that incorporates the essential variables of

TAM and UTAUT as well as a few other important variables considered relevant for the study. The additional variables are perceived strength of control, self efficacy, attitude towards using e-government, and anxiety. A brief description for all the variables is given. The research model for this study is illustrated in Figure 2.

- **Attitude toward using e-government:** This factor measures the individual's positive or negative feelings (evaluative effect) about using the e-government. This factor has been added to the model on the premise that people will use the system they enjoy working on. Originally this factor was used in the "Theory of Reason Action," which is one of the most fundamental and influential theories of human behavior (Hung, et al., 2006; Chang et al., 2005; Sheppard, Hartwick, & Warshaw, 1988; Ajzen, 1991; Chau & Hu, 2001; Taylor & Todd, 1995; Davis, 1989; Mathieson, 1991).
- **Self-efficacy:** Self-efficacy deals with an individual's perception of his or her ability to use the system on his or her own. This factor is considered important as it deals with the level of comfort a person has in working on the e-government. This factor is adapted from the social cognitive theory (SCT), which is one of the important theories of human behavior (Wang, 2003; Hung, 2006; Bandura, 1986; Compeau & Higgins, 1995).
- **Anxiety:** This factor measures anxious and emotional reactions when it comes to performing a behavior. This factor has been added to the model because it was felt that a lot of non-usage issues in government

Figure 2. Research model

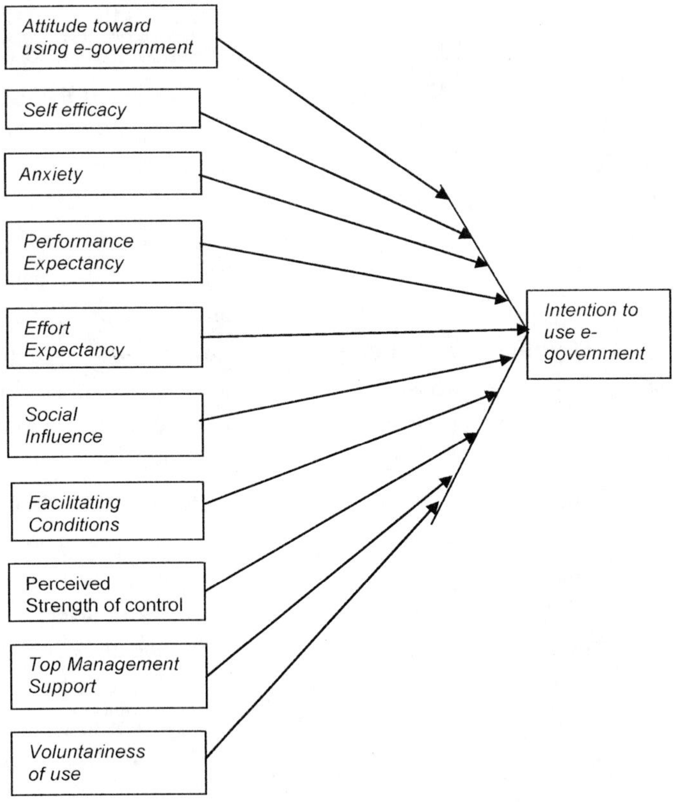

departments could be associated with fear factors relating to various technology options and fear of making mistakes while operating the system. Anxiety is adapted from the social cognitive theory (SCT) (Bandura, 1986) and is subsequently being used by other researchers in the technology acceptance research (Compeau & Higgins 1995).

- **Performance expectancy:** Performance expectancy is defined as the degree to which an individual believes that the e-government will help him or her to gain in job performance. Many users of the government department think that the new system is troublesome and is not helping individuals to improve the performance. Performance expectancy is adapted from the UTAUT model (Venkatesh et al., 2003; Davis, 1989; Compeau & Higgins, 1995; Wang, 2003; Chang et al., 2005; Hung et al., 2006).
- **Effort expectancy:** Effort expectancy is defined as the degree of ease associated with the use of e-government. This factor refers to the perceived amount of effort that the user needs to put to learn and operate the system. Effort expectancy has been adopted from the UTAUT model (Venkatesh et al., 2003; Davis, 1989; Compeau & Higgins, 1995; Wang, 2003; Chang et al., 2005; Hung et al., 2006; Fu et al., 2004).
- **Social influence:** This factor is defined as the degree to which an individual perceives that important others (such as bosses, peers, subordinate, etc.) believe that he or she should use the e-government. In the Indian government departments there is high resistance to change, therefore some initiation is needed by the some employees of the department to form the nucleus and then it percolates to other employees. Social influence construct has been used in UTAUT model (Venkatesh et al., 2003) and model of PC utilization (Thompson, Higgins, & Howell, 1991; Ajzen, 1991; Heintze & Bretschneider, 2000; Ho & Pardo, 2004; LaPorte, Demchak, & de Jong, 2002; Brown & Brudney, 2003; Edmiston, 2003; Holden, Norris, & Fletcher, 2003; Hung et al., 2006).
- **Facilitating conditions:** This is a provision of support for users in terms of computer hardware and software necessary to work on the e-government, the system compatibility with the other systems and the users who are using is also covered. The "facilitating condition" variable has been used in UTAUT model (Venkatesh et al., 2003) and model of PC utilization (Thompson et al., 1991; Hung et al., 2006).
- **Perceived strength of control:** This is about the system security, which is one of the most challenging problems faced by e-government users who wish to transact with a government online. The problem arises from the vulnerabilities of the Internet, upon which e-government is based. When a user transacts through the Internet, anyone from anywhere around the world will be able to access the information being sent or received if the system is not secured (Suh & Han, 2003; Irvine, 2000; Andersen & Dawes, 1991; Joshi, Ghafor, Aref, & Spafford, 2002; Caffrey, 1998; Milner, 2000; Moon, 2002; Duncan & Roehrig, 2003; Edmiston, 2003; Holden et al., 2003; Hung et al., 2006). The vulnerabilities of the Internet may inhibit users from participating in e-government if they feel that the level of risk is unacceptable (Newell, Goldsmith, & Banzhaf, 1998). Suh and Han (2003) have discussed the basic security control requirements of Internet transaction, which are:
  - *Authentication* ensures that the transaction parties in an electronic transaction or communication are genuine.
  - *Non-repudiation* means that neither of the participating parties should be

able to deny having participated in a transaction.

- *Confidentiality* warrants that all communications between the parties are restricted to the parties involved in the transaction.
- *Privacy protection* ensures that personal information about the user collected from their electronic transactions is protected from disclosure without permission.
- *Data integrity* means that data in transmissions are not created, intercepted, modified, or deleted illicitly. These requirements are accomplished by various technologies, such as encryption, third-party certificates, digital signatures, and compliance with privacy policy (Ahuja, 2000; Ratnasigham, 1998).

- **Top management support:** This refers to the extent to which the top management is involved into the planning and implementation of the e-government project. The top management commitment will drive involvement of the top leaders. Gibson (1998) asserted that top management involvement is critical for successful planning of information technology. Most of the government projects in India are bureaucracy driven. Hence "top management" plays an important role in implementations and making the users aware about the benefits of the e-government (Gupta et al., 2004).
- **Voluntariness of use:** This factor deals with the degree to which use of the system is perceived as being voluntary and the users are encouraged to use the system in a non-mandatory environment. Originally this construct was used in innovation diffusion theory (Moore & Benbasat, 1996). Subsequently, Venkatesh et al. (2003) used this construct as a moderating factor for the social influence and behavior intention. In this study, voluntariness of use is considered as a predictor of intention to use e-government; as the e-government are not mandatory for many groups of users. Moreover, the e-government is a new innovation and it is in the process of diffusion among the members of the society.
- **Intention to use e-government:** Intention to use e-government is a measure of the strength of one's intention to perform a specified behaviour. Actual use refers to an individual's actual direct usage of the given system. In this research, "intention to use e-government" is considered as the surrogate measure of the e-government's actual usages. Actual usage refers to hard facts that have to be ascertained. Since measuring "actual usage" is not the objective of this study, it is therefore prudent to proceed with its surrogate measure.

As shown in the research model (Figure 2), it was hypothesized that all the external variables are predictor of intention to use of e-government. Table 2 depicts the research hypotheses and their supporting studies.

A questionnaire-based approach is used in obtaining data from the e-government users in the Indian Central Excise. The development of a questionnaire involved various phases starting from clear definition of the research topic, issue identification, relationship of variables, and so forth. A precise, structured multiple-choice questionnaire was designed keeping in mind the need for eliciting the requisite information. Likert's scale was used in formulating the questionnaire, in which the respondents were asked to mark their position on the continuum having two extreme ends. The continua were divided into seven intervals of measurement. The intervals were "extremely disagree," "disagree," "partially disagree," "neutral," "partially agree," "agree," and "strongly agree." Questions were also adapted

Table 2. Summary of research hypotheses

Hypothesis		Supporting Studies
H1	Attitude towards using e-government → Intention to use e-government	Sheppard, et al., 1988; Ajzen, 1991; Chau & Hu, 2001; Taylor & Todd, 1995; Mathieson, 1991; Chang, et al., 2005; Hung, et al., 2006; Davis, 1989.
H2	Self-efficacy → Intention to use e-government	Bandura, 1986; Compeau & Higginsm, 1995; Wang, 2003; Hung, et al., 2006.
H3	Anxiety → Intention to use e-government	Bandura, 1986; Compeau & Higgins, 1995.
H4	Performance expectancy → Intention to use e-government	Venkatesh, et al., 2003; Davis, 1989; Compeau & Higgins, 1995; Wang, 2003; Chang, et al., 2005.
H5	Effort expectancy → Intention to use e-government	Venkatesh, et al., 2003; Davis, 1989; Moore & Benbasat, 1996; Fu, et al., 2004; Wang, 2003; Chang, et al., 2005.
H6	Social influence→ Intention to use e-government	Venkatesh, et al., 2003; Ajzen, 1991; Thompson, et al., 1991; Ajzen, 1991; Heintze and Bretschneider, 2000; Ho and Pardo, 2004; LaPorte, et al., 2002; Brown and Brudney, 2003; Edmiston, 2003; Holden, et al., 2003.
H7	Facilitating condition → Intention to use e-government	Venkatesh, et al., 2003; Thompson, et al., 1991; Hung, et al., 2006.
H8	Perception of authentication → Intention to use e-government	Suh & Han, 2003; Irvine, 2000; Andersen & Dawes, 1991; Joshi, et al., 2002; Caffrey, 1998; Milner, 2000; Moon, 2002; Duncan & Roehrig, 2003; Edmiston, 2003; Holden, et al., 2003; Hung, et al., 2006; Newell, et al., 1998, Ahuja, 2000; Ratnasigham, 1998.
H9	Perception of non repudiation → Intention to use e-government	Suh & Han, 2003; Irvine, 2000; Andersen & Dawes, 1991; Joshi, et al., 2002; Caffrey, 1998; Milner, 2000; Moon, 2002; Duncan & Roehrig, 2003; Edmiston, 2003; Holden, et al., 2003; Hung, et al., 2006; Newell, et al., 1998, Ahuja, 2000; Ratnasigham, 1998.
H10	Perception of confidentiality → Intention to use e-government	Suh & Han, 2003; Irvine, 2000; Andersen & Dawes, 1991; Joshi, et al., 2002; Caffrey, 1998; Milner, 2000; Moon, 2002; Duncan & Roehrig, 2003; Edmiston, 2003; Holden, et al., 2003; Hung, et al., 2006; Newell, et al., 1998, Ahuja, 2000; Ratnasigham, 1998.
H11	Perception of privacy protection → Intention to use e-government	Suh & Han, 2003; Irvine, 2000; Andersen & Dawes, 1991; Joshi, et al., 2002; Caffrey, 1998; Milner, 2000; Moon, 2002; Duncan & Roehrig, 2003; Edmiston, 2003; Holden, et al., 2003; Hung, et al., 2006; Newell, et al., 1998, Ahuja, 2000; Ratnasigham, 1998.
H12	Perception of data integration → Intention to use e-government	Suh & Han, 2003; Irvine, 2000; Andersen & Dawes, 1991; Joshi, et al., 2002; Caffrey, 1998; Milner, 2000; Moon, 2002; Duncan & Roehrig, 2003; Edmiston, 2003; Holden, et al., 2003; Hung, et al., 2006; Newell, et al., 1998, Ahuja, 2000; Ratnasigham, 1998.
H13	Top management support → Intention to use e-government	Gupta, et al., 2004; Gibson, 1998.
H14	Voluntariness of use → Intention to use e-government	Moore & Benbasat, 1996; Venkatesh, et al., 2003.

from the previous researches where the same variables were used (Ajzen, 1991; Andersen & Dawes 1991; Brown & Brudney, 2003; Caffrey, 1998; Chau & Hu, 2001; Compeau & Higgins, 1995; Davis, 1989; Duncan & Roehrig, 2003; Edmiston, 2003; Fu et al., 2004; Gibson et. al., 1998; Mathieson, 1991; Moore & Benbasat, 1996; Newell et al., 1998; Sheppard et al. 1988; Suh & Han, 2003; Taylor & Todd, 1995; Venkatesh et al., 2003; Wang, 2003). A rigorous questionnaire validation exercise was undertaken which includes face validity, criterion validity, content validity, and construct validity. Further, the questionnaire was subjected to pretesting through a pilot survey administered to a small sample of respondents and corrective modifications were made.

The final questionnaire contained 87 questions, including sub questions. The questionnaire, along with a covering letter mentioning the objective of the study, was administered across the various offices of Indian Central Excise. Mostly the questionnaires were administered personally and very few through postal services with prior telephonic talk. Many personal visits were made to the offices situated in National Capital Region (NCR) Delhi. Collection of completed questionnaires was very tedious and time consuming. The respondents were very busy in almost all the offices and few of them were ignorant about sharing information besides having prior permission of the senior authority of the office. Total 163 valid questionnaires were collected.

Structural equation modeling (SEM) is used for the multivariate analysis in this study. This allows researchers to perform path analytic modeling with latent variables. Specifically, SEM provides the researcher with the flexibility to: (a) model relationships among multiple predictor and criterion variables, (b) construct unobservable latent variables, (c) model errors in measurements for observed variables, and (d) statistically test a priori substantive/theoretical and measurement of assumptions against empirical data (i.e., confirmatory analysis). The application software used for the SEM was AMOS 5. SPSS (Version 11) was used in this study for data tabulation, descriptive analysis, reliability analysis, and it was used as back-end data support for the AMOS.

The universe of the study is the Indian Central Excise employees using e-government. This selection was made after a primary study of all major Indian e-government projects listed with Department of Information Technology, Government of India. In total a detail of 258 e-government projects were found (www.mit.gov.in). Screening of the projects was done on the basis of its size, life, and government initiatives. Indian Central Excise remained a high priority area. This was further endorsed on June 18, 2006, when the government of India announced eight mission mode projects under National E-governance Plan that includes Indian Customs and Central Excise into the list.

DATA ANALYSIS

The final questionnaire was administered through personal visits among 600 employees working at different capacity ranging from superintendent, inspector, tax assistant, operator, and so on. The number of valid responses received is 163, with a 27.17% of response rate. Reliability measurement has been carried out for the internal consistency of data.

Reliability and Validity of the Instrument

The reliability is assessed using Cronbach's alpha and confirmatory factor analysis (CFA) is used for the convergent validity. High values of Cronbach's alpha indicate high internal consistency of the multiple items measuring each construct, hence indicating high reliability of the individual construct. The reliability coefficients are more than the cut-off value of 0.6 (that is recommended as acceptable for empirical research of similar nature) except "voluntariness of use," which is 0.5732. This is accepted as it is for the further analysis since the cumulative percentage in the CFA is 55.761 (acceptable range). The reliability coefficients of the variables are tabulated in Table 3. Most of the alpha values are highly significant (above 0.75) and others are at a satisfactory level. In this view, it is concluded that the data are found significantly reliable.

CFA was carried out for validation of constructs used in this study. This was performed on all 15 variables to examine the convergent validity of each construct. Table 3 summarizes the results of the CFA. This study validates that the various items used for the variables are converging. The cumulative percentage of variance varies from 55.761 (voluntariness of use) and 93.213 (perception of data integrity). All the individual items have surpassed the recommended value of cumulative percentage of variance 50 (Hair, Tatham, Anderson, & Black, 1998), which demonstrated

Table 3. Reliability validity analysis and confirmatory factor analysis for variables (N = 163)

Sl No	Variable Name	No of Items	Alpha Value	Cumulative (Percentage of the Variance)
1	Attitude toward using e-government	4	.6664	63.858
2	Self efficacy	5	.6471	77.060
3	Anxiety	4	.7934	63.488
4	Performance expectancy	5	.6206	64.742
5	Effort expectancy	4	.6380	67.346
6	Social influence	6	.8273	58.068
7	Facilitating conditions	12	.9074	64.017
8	Intention to use e-government	4	.8647	72.208
9	Perception of authentication	3	.8660	79.940
10	Perception of non repudiation	6	.9196	76.683
11	Perception of confidentiality	4	.8548	65.726
12	Perception of privacy protection	4	.9001	77.347
13	Perception of data integrity	4	.9738	93.213
14	Voluntariness of use	3	.5732	55.761
15	Top management support	4	.8828	74.181

the convergent validity of the items used for the measurement.

Sample Profile

Questionnaire was distributed among eight different Central Excise Commissionerates in the National Capital Region Delhi and nearby cities. The final acceptable responses collected were 163 in total with a response rate of 27.17%. The majority of the respondents were at the level of superintendent (42.94%) and inspector (24.54%). Majority of the respondents were in age group of 36 to 45 (37.4%) and 46 to 55 (36.2%). Of the respondents, 31.9% had postgraduate and 55.2% had graduate degrees. There were 21 (12.88%) respondents who had some diploma courses. All the users had formal qualifications, but most of them were not provided with specific system training.

In the subsequent section structural equation modeling results are discussed.

Structural Model Result

The hypothesized research model (Figure 2) is examined for the model fit index using structural equation modeling (AMOS 5). Table 4 presents the results of the model goodness of fit along with the common recommended criteria for the structural equation modeling. Multiple iterations of path analysis were carried out using AMOS 5. A final model for e-government acceptance for Central Excise—internal user is arrived which is shown in Figure 3 along with the path coefficient. In terms of goodness of fit indicators, chi-square value is 22.22 (degree of freedom = 15) at a probability level of 0.102. This indicates that the probability of getting a chi-square statistics as large as 22.2 is 0.102. In other words, departure of data from the model is significant at the 0.1 level.

The ratio of minimum discrepancy to degree of freedom (CMIN/DF) has been suggested as measure of fit. This ratio should be close to one (Arbuckle, 1996) for correct model. In this model

Table 4. Evaluation of fitness of revised model

Measure of Fitness of Model	Recommended criteria	Results in the study
Chi Square/ Degree of Freedom (CMIN/DF)	<3	1.481
P Value	>0.05	0.102
Goodness of Fit Index (GFI)	>0.9	0.953
Adjusted Goodness of Fit Index (AGFI)	>0.9	0.899
Comparative Fit Index (CFI)	>0.9	0.982
Root Mean square Residual (RMR)	<0.05	0.057
Root mean square error of approximation RMSEA	<0.05	0.049
Boolen's Relative Fit Index (RFI)	Near to 1	0.897
Boolen's Incremental Fit Index (IFI)	Near to 1	0.983
Tucker-Lewis Index (TLI)	Near to 1	0.945

the CMIN/DF ratio is 1.481, indicating a good fit index. It is suggested in the literature that if the ratio of CMIN/DF is more than two, it indicates an inadequate fit of the model (Gillespie & Glisson, 1992). Other fitness indices such as Boolen's relative fit index (RFI), Boolen's incremental fit index (IFI) and the Tucker-Lewis index (TLI) should be close to one for good fit (Arbuckle, 1996). The values of RFI, IFI, and TLI are 0.897, 0.983, and 0.945 respectively. Table 4 shows that the modified model is having good fit index.

The root mean-square residual (RMR) is the square root of the squared amount by which the sample variance and covariance differ from their estimates obtained under the assumption that the model is correct. It is recommended in the literature that the value should be less than 0.05; the smaller the RMR the better it is. In this case the value of RMR is 0.057, which is a slightly higher value.

Further, the significance of each hypothesized path in the research model as well as the variance explained (R^2 value) by each path was examined. The result of the path analysis reports, "raw" and "standardized estimates" for all specified paths along with standard errors and test statistics for each path. Table 5 presents the squared multiple correlations of the various variables in the model.

For the "intention to use e-government," the value of R^2 is 0.65, which means the model can explain 65% variations of the "intention to use e-government."

Variance in individual "intention to use e-government" is totally explained 65% by the external variables considered in the model. The external variables includes "attitude toward using e-government," "selfefficacy," "anxiety," "performance expectancy," "effort expectancy," "social influence," "perceived strength of control," and "top management support." In this case the "top management support" is having a negative affect on "intention to use e-government," which rejects the hypothesis H13. Regarding total variance of "intention to use e-government"; "social influence" explains 29% variance along with "effort expectancy" (21%), "attitude toward using e-government" (19%), "perceived strength of control" (21%), and "effort expectancy" (8%). There are

Table 5. Squared multiple correlations

Variables	Estimate
Self-efficacy	0.24
Attitude toward using e-government	0.54
Intention to use of e-government	0.65

three variables, which are having negative affect on the variance of "intention to use e-government." They are "anxiety" (-27%), "top management support" (-27%) and "self efficacy" (-17%). Therefore "social influence" "effort expectancy," "perceived strength of control," "attitude toward using e-government," and "top management support" are more important than other determinants of the "intention to use e-government."

Further, the resulting model (Figure 3) of path analysis considers "attitude towards using e-government" and "self efficacy" as intermediary variables. Main determinants of "attitude towards using e-government" are "performance expectancy" (5%), "effort expectancy" (24%), "perceived strength of control" (25%) and "facilitating condition" (3%). Similarly, the "self efficacy" is determined by "effort expectancy" (12%). The next section presents a discussion on hypothesis testing.

Hypothesis Testing

Table 6 illustrates the relationships among the various factors studied; "Critical ratio" is presented for each relation along with the findings. Most of the relations are supported by the statistical analysis except one relation that is between "voluntariness of use" and "intention to use e-government". The hypothesis H14 ("voluntariness of use" is a predictor of "intention to use e-government") could not get support.

Critical ratio (CR) was calculated in the SEM using AMOS 5 software. CR is defined as critical ratio = estimate / standard errors. The CR values greater than 1.96 and 2.32 are statistically significant at 0.05 and 0.01 levels, respectively. The results of SEM are standardized maximum likelihood path coefficients for the hypothesized model.

Using the results of SEM, the hypotheses testing was carried out. Most of the hypotheses set in

Figure 3. Model along with path co-efficient

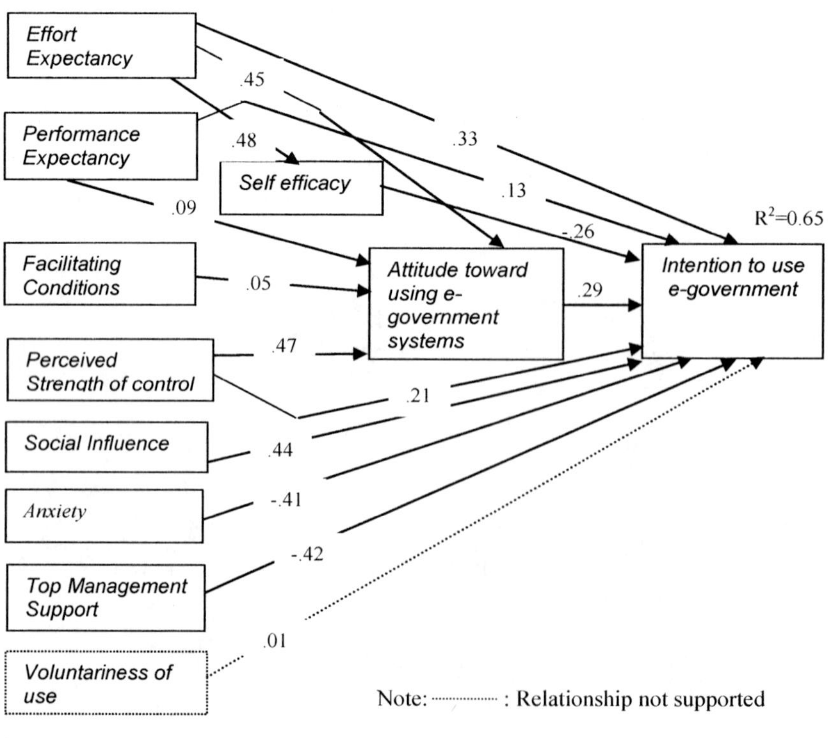

this study are accepted. Hypotheses H2, H13, and H14 (Table 7) could not get support in this study. The variables self-efficacy and top management support are proven to be the predictors of the intention to use e-government but they are having negative effect. Therefore, the hypothesis H2 and H13 are not supported. voluntariness of use did not prove to be a predictor of intention to use e-government, as this relationship is statistically insignificant, the confidence level is very low (p = 0.909). Hypothesis H7 is indirectly supported through an intermediary variable attitude towards using e-government. Table 7 presents the summary of the hypotheses testing.

Self-efficacy was found to be negatively related to intention to use e-government. A possible reason for this is that the system users are not satisfied with the initiatives being taken by the top management, most of the users are concerned about the poor computing infrastructure. There are many places where the systems were either not working or they were outdated, moreover the top management has not taken concrete initiative in improving the situation. The responses were random as respondents were reluctant about saying anything negative about the top management support. In the case of self-efficacy due to the low usage of the system the users are not proficient in using the system. Also there were some problems with the network connectivity of the system. Though 70% of the respondents rated themselves comfortable in using the computer system, the

Table 6. Summary of research findings

Sl No	Relationship	Critical Ratio	Finding
1	Intention to use of e-government ← Attitude toward using e-government	2.959*	Supported
2	Intention to use of e-government ← Effort expectancy	2.361*	Supported
3	Intention to use of e-government ← Performance expectancy	2.007	Supported
4	Intention to use of e-government ← Perceived strength of control	2.051	Supported
5	Intention to use of e-government ← Anxiety	-5.767*	Supported
6	Intention to use of e-government ← Social influence	4.298*	Supported
7	Intention to use of e-government ← Self-efficacy	-3.353*	Supported
8	Intention to use of e-government ← Top Management support	-3.815*	Supported
9	Intention to use of e-government ← Voluntariness of use	0.114	Not Supported
10	Attitude towards using e-government ← Performance expectancy	2.391*	Supported
11	Attitude towards using e-government ← Effort expectancy	8.604*	Supported
12	Attitude towards using e-government ← Facilitating condition	2.067	Supported
13	Attitude towards using e-government ← Social influence	4.756*	Supported
14	Self-efficacy ← Effort expectancy	3.531*	Supported

Table 7. Hypotheses testing

Hypothesis		Result
H1	Attitude toward using e-government → Intention to use e-government	Supported
H2	Self-efficacy → Intention to use e-government	Not Supported
H3	Anxiety → Intention to use e-government	Supported
H4	Performance expectancy → Intention to use e-government	Supported
H5	Effort expectancy → Intention to use e-government	Supported
H6	Social influence→ Intention to use e-government	Supported
H7	Facilitating condition → Intention to use e-government	Supported *
H8	Perception of authentication → Intention to use e-government	Supported
H9	Perception of non repudiation → Intention to use e-government	Supported
H10	Perception of confidentiality → Intention to use e-government	Supported
H11	Perception of privacy protection → Intention to use e-government	Supported
H12	Perception of data integration → Intention to use e-government	Supported
H13	Top management support → Intention to use e-government	Not Supported
H14	Voluntariness of use → Intention to use e-government	Not Supported

actual usage of the system in the department was poor. These are the possible reason of being the self—efficacy not a significant predictor of intention to use e-government.

This study has given a new empirically validated e-government acceptance model for the Indian Central Excise—internal users. Intention to use e-government is totally explained 65% by the external variables, which includes attitude towards using e-government, anxiety, performance expectancy, effort expectancy, social influence, perceived strength of control, and top management support.

Total Effect of Predictor Variables on Intention to Use E-Government

The total effect of a predictor variable for "intention to use e-government" is calculated using the path coefficient values and R^2 from the SEM results (Figure 3). In the case of direct relation with "intention to use e-government," multiplication of path coefficient and R^2 ($R^2 = 0.65$) is taken as the total effect. In case of indirect relation, the path coefficients are multiplied together and finally multiplied with R^2 value to get the "total effect." The value of "total effect" gives the relative importance of the variable; the higher the value, the higher the importance. The result is presented in Table 8.

The value of total effect equal to or greater than 0.065, is treated as high. This value 0.065 is arrived at by considering an ideal situation where all the ten factors considered have an equal path coefficient of 0.10 (1/10). In this case, the value of R^2 is 0.65, therefore the average value is 0.1*0.65 (i.e., 0.065).

The highest value of total effect on intention to use e-government is of social influence. Other variables having high value of total effect are

Table 8. Total effect of predictor variable on intention to use e-government

Sl No	Variable	Total effect on "Intention to use e-government"
1	Attitude toward using e-government	0.1885
2	Self-efficacy	-0.169*
3	Anxiety	-0.2665
4	Performance expectancy	0.0845
5	Effort expectancy	0.2145
6	Social influence	0.286
7	Facilitating conditions	0.009425
8	Perception of authentication	
9	Perception of non repudiation	
10	Perception of confidentiality	0.1365**
11	Perception of privacy protection	
12	Perception of data integrity	
13	Voluntariness of use	0.0065*
14	Top management support	-0.2665*

Note: * *Variables statistically not significant*

***Five sub variables of perceived strength of control are calculated together*

anxiety, effort expectancy, attitude toward using e-government, perceived strength of control, and performance expectancy.

Analysis of Ratio of Acceptance

Ratio of acceptance is calculated for each variable used in this study. Ratio of acceptance is a ratio of the value assigned to the variable by the respondent and the maximum value possible for the factor. For example, the rating scale chosen has values between 1 and 7 therefore the maximum value for any question over the 163 surveys could be 7*163 (i.e., 1141). Further, the highest value for any variable is 1141*n (where "n" is the number of questions relating to that factor in the questionnaire). Thus, for a factor having four questions the maximum value will be 1141*4 i.e. 4564. The actual value for the factor would be the sum of the values given to all the four questions across 163 surveys. A mathematical formula for the calculating the "Ratio of Acceptance" is developed (equation 1). The Table 9 gives the values of the "ratio of acceptance" for all the variables. Lower the value of the ratio of acceptance, higher is the scope for improvement.

$$Ratio\,of\;Acceptance(V) = \frac{\sum_{i=1}^{N}\left(\sum_{j=1}^{S_V} R_j^i\right)}{N * M * S_V} \qquad (1)$$

V = Variable

S_V = Number of Subvariables of Variable V

M = Maximum Rating

= Actual Rating for the jth Subvariable of the ith Response

N = Maximum Number of Responses

Variables with highest ratio of acceptance are intention to use e-government (0.843) and performance expectancy (0.840). This highlights

Table 9. Ratio of acceptance

Factor name	Ratio of acceptance
Attitude toward using e-government	0.794
Self-efficacy	0.679
Anxiety (negative predictor)	0.461
Performance expectancy	0.840
Effort expectancy	0.741
Social influence	0.696
Facilitating conditions	0.694
Perception of authentication	0.724
Perception of non-repudiation	0.658
Perception of confidentiality	0.677
Perception of privacy protection	0.713
Perception of data integrity	0.706
Voluntariness of use	0.792
Top management support	0.654
Intention to use e-government	0.843

that most of the users of the system have average intention to use e-government. The score is average as per the scale chosen for analysis. Value of ratio of acceptance less than 0.571 is the negative acceptance (rejection) and average value for acceptance is 0.786. In this study, most of the scores are below average value. The variables, which have ratio of acceptance value above average, are intention to use e-government, performance expectancy, and attitude towards using e-government. Therefore, there is a high scope for improvement in almost all the factors to attain a higher acceptance of the e-government. Variables with low ratio of acceptance are top management support (0.654), Perception of non repudiation (0.658), and other security-related factors. Anxiety is a negative predictor of intention to use e-government; therefore its value of ratio of acceptance should be as low as possible. Anxiety is having 0.461 value of ratio of acceptance, which is considered poor. This indicates considerable amount of training and counseling needed for the users to keep their anxiety level low for the use of e-government.

SYNTHESIS AND RECOMMENDATIONS

A comparative study of the ratio of acceptance and total effect gives strategic insight to increase the usage of e-government. A categorization of the factors is done on the basis of high and low value of ratio of acceptance and total effect.

A comparison of ratio of acceptance and total effect is carried out. For total effect, values greater than or equal to 0.065 are treated as high and less than 0.065 are low. In case of ratio of acceptance the value greater than or equal to 0.785 are high and less are treated as low. This value is decided after calculating the average acceptance value. This analysis seeks to prioritize investment of resources and efforts into increasing usage by highlighting whose change will bring about largest positive increase in intention to use e-government and which are right now having a low value leaving a lot of room for leverage and improvement. The comparison of values of ratio of acceptance and total effect is done using Table 8 and Table 9.

Effort expectancy, social influence, and perceived strength of control have low ratio of acceptance and high value of total effect. Therefore these factors are key inhibitors of intention to use e-government. Thus these factors are of high importance and effort should be taken to raise the ratio of acceptance value. Efforts by top management are required in the form of training employees in IT skills as well as motivational training to increase comfort with the systems, which will result in increasing the ratio of acceptance of effort expectancy. Similarly to improve the social influence, it is required to have frequent trainings and improve overall work environment by providing learning ambience. The senior executives should help their subordinates in learning to operate the new system. To improve perceived strength of control it is required to improve the system security features by providing state-of-art security technology, good network connectivity and providing training to the end users to deal with security related issues.

Anxiety is a negative predictor of intention to use e-government; therefore the value of ratio of acceptance should be maintained as low as possible. This can be achieved by keeping low anxiety level of the users.

Attitude towards using e-government and performance expectancy have high ratio of acceptance and high value of total effect. This implies that these two factors are major predictors of the intention to use e-government and simultaneously their values of ratio of acceptance are also high. Further intention to use e-government can be improved by motivating the users to use the e-government and improving the system interface, providing integrated service by clubbing all the modules of Central Excise into one single system, maintaining a central database and online updating and so on. These two factors are of high importance and need to maintain a high ratio of acceptance value.

Facilitating condition has low value of total effect on intention to use e-government and at the same time the value of ratio of acceptance is also low. Still facilitating condition is a predictor of intention to use e-government. Therefore, effort should be put to improve the facilitating condition, which includes computing facility, maintenance, peripheral devices, backup power supply, and so forth in the Central Excise offices.

In brief, the recommendations to increase intention to use e-government by the internal users of Indian Central Excise are summarized here:

- User needs to be trained in IT skills on a regular interval to increase comfort level in operating the systems.
- Improve overall work environment by providing learning ambience. The senior executives should help their subordinates in learning to operate the new system.
- It is required to improve the system security features by providing state-of-the-art security technology, good network connectivity, and providing training to the end users to deal with security related issues.
- Motivate the users to use the e-government.
- Improve the system interface to provide integrated service by clubbing all the modules of Central Excise into one single system; maintain a central database and online updating facility.
- Effort should be put forth to improve the facilitating condition in the Central Excise offices for the e-government users.
- Computing facility, maintenance, peripheral devices, backup power supply, and so forth should be improved.

CONCLUDING REMARKS

The study has identified 15 variables having predictive ability with regard to "intention to use e-government" in Indian Central Excise among their internal users. The study brought out an empirically validated model of e-government acceptance for Indian Central Excise which has helped in developing a strategic insight into various factors for improving e-government acceptance. Relative significance of the variables is also examined. The recommendations of this study would be helpful in developing and implementing new e-government plans. To achieve higher acceptance, apart from the several factors identified, user awareness of e-government services is essential. Also, users' trust depends heavily on increased transparency and therefore organizational reform must follow to ensure users' trust and in turn success. One of the major limitations of this research was that the study has been mostly done in the northern region of India. The other limitation of the research is common to most surveys related to behavioral issues and subjectivity of the questionnaire responses. Suitability of new variables should be tested to increase the overall explanatory power of the model. The e-government acceptance model developed here can be used in other similar studies of e-government acceptance.

REFERENCES

Ahuja, V. (2000). Building trust in electronic commerce. *IT Professional, 2*(3), 61-63.

Ajzen, I. (1991). Theory of planned behavior. *Organizational Behavior and Human Decision Processes, 50*(2), 179-211.

Andersen, D. F., & Dawes, S. S. (1991). *Government information management: A primer and casebook.* Englewood Cliffs, NJ: Prentice Hall.

Arbuckle, J. L. (1996). Structural equation modeling: Amos program. In *Proceedings of Eighth invitational research seminar on advanced issues in research analysis.* Case Western Reserve University.

Bandura, A. (1986). *Social foundations of thought and action: A social cognitive theory.* Englewood Cliffs, NJ: Prentice Hall.

Brown, M. M., & Brudney, J. L. (2003). Learning organizations in the public sector? A study of police agencies employing information and technology to advance knowledge. *Public Administration Review, 63*(1), 30-43.

Brown, S. A., Massey, A. P., Weiss, M. M., & Burkman, J. R. (2002). Do I really have to? User acceptance of mandated technology. *European Journal of Information Systems, 11*(3), 283-295.

Caffrey, L. (1998). Information sharing between and within governments: A study group report. *London7 Commonwealth Secretariat*

Chang, I. C., Li, Y. C., Hung, W. F., & Hwang, H. G. (2005). An empirical study on the impact of quality antecedents on tax payers' acceptance of Internet tax-filing systems. *Government Information Quarterly, 22*(3), 389-410.

Chau, P. Y. K., & Hu, P. J. (2001). Information technology acceptance by individual professionals: A model comparison approach. *Decision Sciences, 32*(4), 699-719.

*Compeau, D., Higgins, C. A., & Huff, S. (*1999). Social cognitive theory and individual reactions to computing technology: A longitudinal study. *MIS Quarterly, 23*(2), 145-158.

Davis, F. D. (1989). Perceived usefulness, perceived ease of use, and user acceptance of information technology. *MIS Quarterly, 13*(3), 318-340.

Davis, F. D., Bagozzi, P. R., & Warshaw, P. R. (1989). User acceptance of computer technology: A comparison of two theoretical models. *Management Science, 35*(8), 892-1003.

Duncan, G. T., & Roehrig, S. T. (2003). Mediating the tension between information privacy and information access: The role of digital government. In G. D. Garson (Ed.), *Public information technology: Policy and management issues.* Hershey, PA: Idea Group Publishing.

Edmiston, K. D. (2003). State and local e-government: Prospects and challenges. *American Review of Public Administration, 33*(1), 20-45.

Fu, J. R., Chao, W. P., & Farn, C. K. (2004). Determinants of taxpayers' adoption of electronic filing methods in Taiwan: An exploratory study. *Journal of Government Information, 30*(5-6), 658-683.

García, J. R. G., & Pardo, T. A. (2005). E-government success factors: Mapping practical tools to theoretical foundations. *Government Information Quarterly, 22*(2), 187-216.

Gibson, D., Kleinberg, J. M., & Raghavan, P. (1998). Inferring Web communities from link topology. In *Proceedings of ACM Hypertext '98* (pp. 225-234). Pittsburgh.

Gillespie, D. F., & Glisson, C. (1992). *Quantitative methods in social work: State of the art. Binghamton, NY: Haworth Press.*

Gupta, M. P., Kumar, P., & Bhattacharya, J. (2004). *Government online: Opportunities and challenges,* TMH, New Delhi.

Hair, J. F., Tatham, R. L., Anderson, R. E., & Black, W. (1998). *Multivariate data analysis* (5th ed.). Englewood Cliffs, NJ: Prentice Hall.

Heeks, R. (2003). Success and failure rates of e-government in developing/transitional countries: Overview. *E-government for Development,* Institute for Development Policy and Management, University of Manchester, UK.

Heintze, T., & Bretschneider, S. (2000). Information technology and restructuring in public organizations: Does adoption of information technology affect organizational structures, communications, and decision-making? *Journal of Public Administration Research and Theory, 10*(4), 801-830.

Ho, J., & Pardo, T. A. (2004). *Toward the success of e-government initiatives: Mapping known success factors to the design of practical tools.* Paper presented at the 37th Hawaii International Conference on System Sciences (HICSS), organized by the College of Business, University of Hawaii at Manoa.

Holden, S. H., Norris, D. F., & Fletcher, P. D. (2003). Electronic government at the local level: Progress to date and future issues. *Public Performance and Management Review, 26*(4), 325-344.

http://exciseandservicetax.nic.in retrieved during December 2005- July 2006.

Hung, S. Y., Chang, C. M., & Yu, T. J. (2006). Determinants of user acceptance of the e-government services: The case of online tax filing and payment system. *Government Information Quarterly, 23*(1), 97-122.

Irvine, C. E. (2000). Security issues for automated information systems. In G. D. Garson (Ed.), *Handbook of pPublic information systems.* New York: Marcel Dekker, Inc.

Joshi, J. B. D., Ghafor, A., Aref, W. G., & Spafford, E. H. (2002). Security and privacy challenges of a digital government. In W. J. McIver & A. K. Elmagarmid (Eds.), *Advances in digital government, technology, human factors, and policy.* Norwell, MA: Kluwer Academic Publishers.

LaPorte, T. M., Demchak, C. C., & de Jong, M. (2002). Democracy and bureaucracy in the age of the Web: Empirical findings and theoretical speculations. *Administration and Society, 34*(4), 411-446.

Mathieson, K. (1991). Predicting user intentions: Comparing the technology acceptance model with the theory of planned behavior. *Information Systems Research, 2*(3), 173-191.

Milner, E. M. (2000). *Managing information and knowledge in the public sector.* New York: Routledge.

MIT (Department of Information Technology, Government of India), (2005), http://www.mit.gov.in, accessed during May-June 2005

Moon, M. J. (2002). The evolution of e-government among municipalities: Rhetoric or reality? *Public Administration Review, 62*(4), 424-433.

Moore, G. C., & Benbasat, I. (1996). Integrating diffusion of innovations and theory of reasoned action models to predict utilization of information technology by end-users. In K. Kautz & J. Pries-Hege (Eds.), *Diffusion and adoption of information technology* (pp. 132-146). London: Chapman and Hall.

NASSCOM (2005). Retrieved December 3, 2005, from http://www.nasscom.org

Newell, S. J., Goldsmith, R. E., & Banzhaf, E. J. (1998). The effect of misleading environmental claims on consumer perceptions of advertisements. *Journal of Marketing: Theory and Practice, 6*(2), 48-60.

Ratnasingham, P. (1998). The importance of trust in electronic commerce. *Internet Research: Electronic Networking Applications and Policy, 8*(4), 313-321.

Sheppard, B. H., Hartwick, J., & Warshaw, P. R. (1988). The theory of reasoned action: A meta-analysis of past research with recommendations for modifications and future research. *Journal of Consumer Research, 15*(3), 325-343.

Suh, B., & Han, I. (2003). The impact of customer trust and perception of security control on the acceptance of electronic commerce. *International Journal of Electronic Commerce, 7*(3), 135-161.

Tahinakis, P., Mylonakis, J., & Protogeros, N. (2006). The contribution of e-government to the modernisation of the Hellenic taxation system. *Electronic Government, an International Journal (EG), 3*(2), 139-157.

Taylor, S., & Todd, P. A. (1995). Understanding information technology usage: A test of competing models. *Information Systems Research, 6*(2), 144-176.

Thompson, C. S. (2002). Enlisting on-line residents: Expanding the boundaries of e-government in a Japanese rural township. *Government Information Quarterly, 19*(2), 173-188.

Thompson, R. L., Higgins, C. A., & Howell, J. M. (1991). Personal computing: Toward a conceptual model of utilization. *MIS Quarterly, 15*(1), 124-143.

Venkatesh, V. (2000). Determinants of perceived ease of use: Integrating control, intrinsic motivation, and emotion into the technology acceptance model. *Information Systems Research, 11*(4), 342-365.

Venkatesh, V, & Davis, F. D. (1996). A model of the antecedents of perceived ease of use: Development and test. *Decision Science, 27*(3), 451-481.

Venkatesh, V., Morris, M. G., Davis, G. B., & Davis, F. D. (2003). User acceptance of information technology: Toward a unified view. *MIS Quarterly*, 27(3), 425-478.

Wang, Y. S. (2003). The adoption of electronic tax filing systems: An empirical study. *Government Information Quarterly, 20*(4), 333-352.

This work was previously published in International Journal of Electronic Government Research, Vol. 3, Issue 3, edited by M. Khosrow-Pour, pp. 1-21, copyright 2007 by IGI Publishing, formerly known as Idea Group Publishing (an imprint of IGI Global).

Chapter 5.12
Innovative Local E-Government:
The PEOPLE Project

Roberto De Vivo
PEOPLE project, Italy

Marco Magnani
PEOPLE project, Italy

INTRODUCTION

PEOPLE, one of the most important e-government projects in Italy, was created in 2002, when it was ranked first among almost 400 projects submitted to the Italian government according to its Piano di Azione per l'E-Government, literally, E-Government Action Plan, that is, the program to which the Italian government allocated around €120 million to finance various projects on e-government development. The financial contribution for each project did not exceed 50% of its total expected budget.

The name of the project is the acronym for Progetto Enti Online Portali Locali E-Government, literally, Project Public Bodies Online Portals E-Government.

The purpose of PEOPLE is "to innovate and to simplify the relationships between Local Public Administrations and citizens" through the online delivery of almost all the services provided by local bodies, leading to the fulfilment of 95% of individual and company requests. The project seeks to create a multichannel network system with a Web portal as the main method of access and interaction.

BACKGROUND

PEOPLE is supported by 55 Italian local authorities from 12 different regions. This group includes both metropolitan areas, like Rome and Florence, as well as small municipalities. The developers of the project therefore had to create a model that was sufficiently abstract to fit all the different contexts, irrespective of local legislation or regulation.

The total population administrated by PEOPLE amounts to 7.5 million, almost 13% of the entire Italian population.

The main reason these administrations were involved in the realization of PEOPLE is the high level of organizational and technological capabilities required. These bodies are the most

Figure 1. The areas involved in PEOPLE (Progetto PEOPLE)

dynamic in the country and represent best practices as concerns service innovation. This makes PEOPLE a sort of laboratory in which the most innovative Italian local authorities are sharing their experiences and their know-how. To this end, the PEOPLE administrations are organized in a federal model, in which every single municipality has the opportunity to participate in the creation of each single service. The choice is to preserve and enhance cultural diversity by creating a set of solutions based on a common structure and on a shared standardized platform.

The model is equally participated in by every single local authority and is built on the exchange and integration of information; the goal is to promote the sharing of services and solutions that may have been produced locally before the project started or created ad hoc. However, those solutions must be the same for each single participant and for each citizen who wants to use the solution proposed by the project. Consequently, an extremely high level of coordination is needed to make this model work, and this is one of the most critical points that PEOPLE had to face. In order to overcome this problem, the PEOPLE staff created an original management organization based on an efficient, high-tech communication system.

THE SERVICES PROVIDED

PEOPLE will provide a wide range of services concerning every single life event, as defined by the Italian government. Once the project is completed, there will be around 180 services divided in five groups:

- local tax services,
- grant and authorization services,
- geographic information-system services,
- social and welfare services, and
- register-office services.

Besides these, an efficient online payment service and a reliable registration and authorization system have been created.

Some general services are also planned, such as online ticket reservation and sale for events like exhibitions or concerts, virtual community services, and online document access.

All these services have been developed in the project itself by a well-organized division of labour between the local administrations involved. Each area has been managed by a single administration, which, without regard for the indications from the other authorities, was responsible for the development of all the services in the area.

So far, the project has developed some demonstration services, such as the change-of-address (within the same local area) or the Building Start-Up Certification (Decuncia Inizio Attività, DIA) initiatives to illustrate the technical functionalities of its software.

Table 1. The local government authorities involved in PEOPLE (Source: Progetto PEOPLE)

Local Government Administration	Citizens	Region
Comune di Ancona	100,409	Marche
Comune di Bari	347,106	Puglia
Comune di Bologna	378,356	Emilia Romagna
Comune di Bolzano - Stadtgemeinde Bozen	97,317	Trentino Alto Adige
Comune di Brescia	195,442	Lombardia
Comune di Carpi	62,104	Emilia Romagna
Comune di Cesena	90,851	Emilia Romagna
Comune di Cremona	71,321	Lombardia
Comune di Falconara Marittima	28,307	Marche
Comune di Firenze	374,000	Toscana
Comune di Genova	627,599	Liguria
Comune di Jesi	39,238	Marche
Comune di Mantova	48,341	Lombardia
Comune di Modena	176,965	Emilia Romagna
Comune di Paterno Dugnano	45,661	Lombardia
Comune di Parma	170,541	Emilia Romagna
Comune di Pesaro	90,000	Marche
Comune di Piacenza	95,594	Emilia Romagna
Comune di Ravenna	140,933	Emilia Romagna
Comune di Reggio Calabria	179,412	Reggio Calabria
Comune di Reggio Emilia	148,517	Emilia Romagna
Comune di Roma	2,665,000	Lazio
Comune di San Benedetto del Tronto	45,368	Marche
Comune di Sesto San Giovanni	81,482	Lombardia
Comune di Siena	54,344	Toscana
Comune di Trapani	69,700	Sicilia
Comune di Venezia	274,168	Veneto
Comune di Verona	258,372	Veneto
Comune di Vigevano	59,302	Lombardia
Comune di Malo	12,366	Veneto
Comune di Schio	37,662	Veneto
Comune di Tiene	21,107	Veneto
Comune di Santorso	5,305	Veneto
Comune di Torrebelvicino	5,516	Veneto
comune di Valdagno	27,136	Veneto
Comune di Arzignano	23,454	Veneto
Comune di Chiampo	12,251	Veneto
Comune di Marostica	12,823	Veneto
Comune di Pianezze	1,839	Veneto
Comune di Nove	4,901	Veneto
Comune di Schiavon	2,339	Veneto
Comune di Marano Vicentino	8,902	Veneto
Comune di Villaverla	5,384	Veneto
Provincia di Bologna	926,744	Emilia Romagna
Unione di Comuni "Caserta Sud-Ovest"	139,534	Campania

THE SOFTWARE

As stated above, PEOPLE is both the project and the aggregation. However, there is yet another interpretation; PEOPLE is the software through which each municipality will provide services to the citizens. The major benefits expected from the use of this software are the following:

- decrease in the development costs for online services;
- means to manage the complexity of e-government-related issues through coordinated and integrated investments; and
- the possibility for small-size local administrations to benefit from low-cost products and solutions provided by other PEOPLE administrations.

Each service comprises several data forms structured in different fields to complete. In order to validate the data provided, the system acts as follows:

- verifies each single word syntactically;
- marks submitted forms, ensuring that all the compulsory fields have been correctly completed; and

- validates and cross-verifies all the data after completion.

Citizens will be free to fill in the forms in any order before signing and sending the request. However, the order of the pages will be defined by the system, which will also take control if a page may not be needed (e.g., as the data has already been provided) or will block the access (e.g., depending on a user's access level as a requester, delegated, or technician). The user will be able at any moment to interrupt the procedure, save the inserted data, and return later to complete the request.

PEOPLE will also allow citizens to sign both the request and any attachment (any kind of document) digitally. In some cases, for example, the DIA, more than one person must sign the documentation, and the process above can be quite complex. PEOPLE will also guide users in this process, identifying the documents that will be needed to be signed and who is supposed to sign them. Citizens will be able to notify the local administration of people authorized to act as their proxies. Each proxy created by a citizen will be valid only within a specific local government area for a specific service and for a specific period of time.

After all documents are completed and signed, the requests will be sent to the local government through a certified e-mail system. The local government officials will receive in a special inbox an e-mail of notification with a link to the citizen's request from the certified e-mail system. This message will contain the text of the main form and all the attachments. Once the message has been read, the e-mail system will request the official to sign a receipt that will be sent to the requesting citizen.

Citizens will also be able to consult their current personal proceedings management page at any point in the application. This page will contain all the forms that have been completed, those that have been temporarily saved, and all the forms awaiting completion from the competent local authority. In the last case, the progress status will also be shown.

PEOPLE has been planned to send the requests to the local administration's back-office system directly. This operation will be started when the legislative and organizational conditions for the automatic reception of requests has been introduced.

PEOPLE 1.0 FRAMEWORK: THE REFERENCE IMPLEMENTATION

The PEOPLE 1.0 framework is the first version of the project released to allow municipalities to test the results obtained so far and to develop services and systems to link between the online front office and the back office. For this, the virtual service layer of the PEOPLE 1.0 reference implementation is required. This framework has been realized on a vendor-neutral basis in order to guarantee full accessibility and compatibility with the services developed by different ISVs (independent software vendors) in a service-oriented environment.

The framework uses J2EE (Java 2 Platform Enterprise Edition) technologies and components extensively, looking for the latest specifications and standards in Web-service technology provided by the Ministero per l'Innovazione e le Tecnologie, literally, the Ministry of Innovation and Technology, the body responsible for information and communication technology and high-tech development in Italian public administration.

Through this, PEOPLE can achieve the following:

- Allow software vendors to realize online services quickly, using the same patterns and development techniques
- Achieve the same look-and-feel experience for all online services, so standardizing the user experience

- Support the integration and certification of the online services provided by the project and guarantee compliance with architectural standards

The People framework is structured in three layers:

- The front-end layer includes the services based on a multichannel access system, a light work-flow engine used to manage user interactions, and a Web service ensuring interoperability with the other layers of the Web-service-layer and with external calls (i.e., interoperability with other domains).
- The people layer comprises the management components (the so-called PEOPLE console) and the service components (PEOPLE services).
- The back-end layer consists of Web services that answer the front-end requests and interact with the back-end systems.

As a reference implementation, the PEOPLE framework was developed and tested in the Centro di Itegrazione e Collaudo, literally, the Integration and Testing Center, which was created by the project in close collaboration with Enterprise Digital Architect, the private company that works as a technical partner of PEOPLE, in order to certify the correspondence to all PEOPLE requirements and its full usability.

The reference implementation uses vendor-neutral components in a vendor-neutral environment and cannot therefore satisfy all requirements of a given production scenario. These requirements could be trustworthiness, performance, scalability (clustered environments), fault tolerance, or recoverability (what happens to the submitted requests if the system breaks down).

Such requirements are best satisfied by commercial platforms. The project has thus collaborated with the top-five platform vendors: IBM, Microsoft, Oracle, Bea, and Sun. The problem was to implement the PEOPLE framework on those platforms, using their components and features, but without losing any characteristics or benefits in the overall product.

Four of these partners are Java based. The first technical activities concerned the translation of the reference implementation to the specific DBMS (database management system) and application-server environments. Subsequently, various devices were developed to allow the PEOPLE framework to interface with these platform components.

A different approach has been taken for the Microsoft platform because of the difficulties related to the ownership property of programming languages.

The vendor implementations kept the layered structure of the reference implementation. A test and certification process guaranteed full architectural compliance.

This result was achieved by developing a dummy service to verify the following:

- The integration with the reference-implementation PEOPLE node using the service running on the vendor's front-end node
- The integration with the vendor PEOPLE node using the service running on the reference-implementation front-end node

Another cornerstone of the PEOPLE project was the modeling approach. This was tailored to UML (Unified Modeling Language) modeling constructs used in business management.

The modeling group represented online services as business objects and designed the model. A very important distinction was made between shared objects and domain-specific objects.

The main modeling artifacts were the following:

- Business use case diagrams representing and describing online services for each category

- Activity diagrams representing the typical work flow of online services from the first step to data submission (front-end requests)
- Class diagrams referring to online services representing business objects, their associations, and hierarchies in order to distinguish between objects, documents, receipts, requests, responses, forms, and so on

UML diagrams and objects defined the data needed to support the interactions between the front-end applications (online services) and the back-end systems. Data had to implement Web-services standards fully and be generated as XML (Extensible Markup Language) schema definitions (XSDs). XML files exchanged between the front end and the back end had to be compatible with this structure.

The architecture of PEOPLE allows different ISVs with different knowledge of several application domains to be chosen without losing the coherence and the common design of the services.

After a few months, all ISVs could release online services running on a solid architecture compliant with the modeling standards already described.

A crucial part of the service implementation was the testing and certification process to guarantee that the same service would work properly on the information systems of several different municipalities, fulfilling all functional and technical requirements.

The online services certification process was divided into two main activities:

- Functional certification to guarantee the satisfaction of all functional requirements gathered by many users and domain experts belonging to different municipalities, both in the mail-sending scenario and in the Web-services scenario
- Architectural certification to certify correct interaction with the framework, the implementation of a common user experience, and compliance with XSDs generated by UML object models representing data exchanged between the front end and the back end

The functional certification activity was divided into three steps:

- Verification and certification of technical specifications sent by ISVs in order to guarantee coherence between the detailed design and the test plan
- Execution of test cases by user representatives and feedback to ISVs to fix bugs and errors
- Verification and certification of test results

The architectural certification activity involved five steps:

- Test of the services in the reference implementation in order to guarantee correct interfacing with the front-end node and with the PEOPLE node; the services that did not pass this step were returned to the suppliers
- Verification of compliance with look-and-feel standards
- Verification of compliance with accessibility guidelines
- Verification of correct interfacing of infrastructural services
- Test of the vendor implementations' front-end nodes in order to verify interoperability

Once all these activities and steps had been performed, each individual service was declared a certified PEOPLE online service, ready to work in a PEOPLE-compliant environment. In response to the municipalities' priorities, it was decided that two categories of services would be implemented: demographics and tax services. In this way, all municipalities could start the deployment process on the preferred platform, taking account of their back-end systems and integration needs. At the same time, other categories of services were developed by many ISVs for the Java and the .Net environments. To this end, a stabilized framework, a standard model for future development processes, and a tested certification process were used.

Once this first phase of deployment has been completed, all municipalities will be able to easily deploy other family services without difficulty.

FUTURE TRENDS

As mentioned above, the deployment process has already started, and before the deadline of March 2006, all the services will be available to the PEOPLE administrations' citizens. The PEOPLE network is also expected to be enlarged to at least 300 municipalities. This enlargement will be on a voluntary basis and will depend on a contribution proportional to the administrated population.

CONCLUSION

PEOPLE offers one of the most important opportunities for the local government in Italy to develop its structure in line with the European e-government legislature and to bridge the digital divide created by the massive introduction of ICTs.

The main benefits expected for all local authorities, irrespective of their size, are the following:

- A strong impulse to develop new integrated systems for companies and citizens
- Scaled costs equally distributed among each local administration taking part in the project
- The creation of online services and high—quality, innovative solutions
- The spread of technical and organizational know-how that is essential for the innovation of local administrations
- The management of the major e-government issues, using integrated, coordinated, and modular investments and architectures
- The optimization of procedural management timetables
- The rationalization of communication systems between different local administrations and within the local administration itself
- The creation of a shared and constantly updated professional level of excellence

REFERENCES

Bray, T., Paoli, J., Sperberg-McQueen, C. M., & Maler, E. (Eds.). (2000). *Extensible Markup Language (XML)* (Version 1.0).

Comitato Tecnico della Commissione Permanente per l'Innovazione e le Tecnologie. (2003). *L'e-government per un federalismo efficiente, una visione condivisa una realizzazione cooperativa.* Rome.

Cracchi Bianchi, N. (Ed.). (2004). *Sigmater, people, docarea: Un percorso di collaborazione.* Rome: Carocci Editore.

Europe Union, Communication from the Commission to the Council, the European Parliament, the European Economics and Social Committee, & the Committee for the Regions. (2003). *The role of e-government for Europe's future.* Brussels, Belgium: Europe Union.

Favaretti, G., Mantero, G., & Pigni, F. (Eds.). (2003). *PEOPLE: Analisi degli interscambi. Elementi condivisi* (Version 1.0).

Mascheroni, M., & Cozza, M. T. (Eds.). (2003). *PEOPLE: Programme management. Gruppi di lavoro* (Version 1.3).

Ministero dell'Innovazione. (2002). *Linee guida del governo per lo sviluppo della società dell'informazione nella legislatura.* Rome: Ministero per l'Innovazioni e le Tecnologie.

Ministero per l'Innovazione e le Tecnologie. (2000). *Piano d'azione per l'e-government.* Rome: Author.

OASIS. (2003). *Assertions and protocol for the OASIS security assertion markup language (SAML) V1.1* (OASIS standard).

OASIS. (2004). *Technical overview of the OASIS security assertion markup language (SAML)* (Committee draft).

Piastra, M., & Osnaghi, A. (Ed.). (2003). *PEOPLE: Linee guida per l'architettura generale* (Version 1.2).

RUR. (2004a). *Le città digitali in Italia, rapporto 2003-2004.* Milan: Franco Angeli.

RUR. (2004b). *Seconda convenzione RUR delle città italiane: Municipium le città in movimento.* Milan: Franco Angeli.

Tivelli, L. (Ed.). (2004). *Verso una nuova amministrazione, un passaggio complesso.* Naples, Italy: Fazi Editore.

Tivelli, L., & Masini, S. (2004). *Un nuovo modo di governare: L'e-government e il cambiamento della pubblica amministrazione.* Naples, Italy: Fazi Editore.

United Nations. (2004). *UN global e-government readiness report 2004: Towards access for opportunity.* New York: Author.

United Nations Division for Public Economics and Public Administration. (2002). *Benchmarking e-government: A global perspective.* New York: United Nations.

KEY TERMS

Front End and Back End: Interface of the PEOPLE program respectively for the front office and the back office.

J2EE Technologies and .Net Technologies: The project based on the Java 2 Platform Enterprise Edition (J2EE) language and the Microsoft .Net one, respectively. This choice allows each local authority to choose the preferred language, avoiding further investments to link the new interface to the internal back-office system.

Multichannel Network System: The project planned a very complex access system to the PEOPLE network that will allow the connection and the supply of the provided services through different media, such as PCs (personal computers), mobile phones, digital television, and so on.

Online Front Office: The main goal of the project is to substitute the physical front office used by public authorities to supply services with a Web portal system, giving citizens the opportunity to access those services from a simple PC.

PEOPLE Project: The most important e-government project in Italy, it aims "to innovate and to simplify the relationships between Local Public Administrations and citizens" through the online delivery of almost all the services provided by local bodies.

Virtual Service Layer: Layer of the program that acts as a connection between the front end and back end and that contains the structure of each service provided.

This work was previously published in Encyclopedia of Digital Government, edited by A. Anttiroiko and M. Malkia, pp. 1089-1094, copyright 2007 by Information Science Reference, formerly known as Idea Group Reference (an imprint of IGI Global).

Chapter 5.13
Citizen-Initiated Contacts with Ontario Local E-Government:
Administrators' Responses to Contacts

Christopher G. Reddick
University of Texas at San Antonio, USA

ABSTRACT

This study examines Ontario, Canada's municipal e-government adoption. This paper specifically focuses on how e-government has increased citizen-initiated contacts with these local governments. This study uses survey data of these local governments to determine the key factors that predict increased citizen contact with e-government. What these municipal governments most commonly are doing is informational e-government, such as providing downloadable forms for manual completion. Transactional e-government is done less often, with very few local governments offering online payment of taxes, for example. The regression results indicated that offering more online services or e-services and having a separate information technology (IT) department developing the e-government budget increased citizen contact with e-government. The traditional factors that are used to explain citizen-initiated contact, such as socioeconomic status of the community, were not found to have any impact on increasing citizen contact with e-government.

INTRODUCTION AND BACKGROUND

E-government has been defined as the use of the Internet to deliver services and information to citizens and businesses (Ho & Ni, 2004; Holden, Norris & Fletcher, 2003; Reddick, 2004a). There are several studies that examine the adoption of e-government at the local level in the U.S. (Edmiston, 2002; Fletcher, 2003; Ho, 2002; Holden, Norris & Reddick, 2004a; Moon, 2002; Reddick, 2004b). However, there are few studies that have empirically examined e-government at the local level outside the U.S. (Criado & Ramilo, 2003).

Therefore, most of the empirical evidence on local e-government adoption is provided from the analysis of a single country. In addition, most of the work on e-government literature focuses on the features of local governments that have adopted the Internet for information and e-service delivery (Edmiston, 2002; Ho, 2002; Moon, 2002; Reddick, 2004a). A smaller number of studies actually has tested the impact of key features that explain e-government adoption rates (Ho & Ni, 2004; Holden, Norris & Fletcher, 2003; Reddick, 2004b).

Citizen-initiated contacts with government occur when individual citizens contact government personnel with requests for services or complaints (Thomas & Melkers, 1999). Increased citizen initiated contact with e-government is important, since it enhances political participation and validates government institutions (Thomas & Streib, 2003). E-government is a way to enhance efficiency, effectiveness, and equity of citizen and business access to local governments. Few studies have examined how e-government has changed citizens' interaction with their local governments (Thomas & Streib, 2003). The studies that have examined citizen-initiated contact with public administrators focus on the perceptions and characteristics of citizens and their contacts (Serra, 1995; Thomas, 1982; Thomas & Melkers, 2000). Few studies examine administrators' responses to citizen-initiated contacts (Green, 1982). Therefore, the existing literature presents only one side of the relationship between citizen-initiated contacts and government, because it has not extensively considered bureaucrats and their responses to contacts.

Increased citizen interaction with government is a tool for enhancing democracy, since it represents an avenue for increasing service delivery and confidence in government (Green, 1982). With such an emphasis on enhancing performance at all levels of government, e-government is an excellent mechanism with which to achieve this goal (Ho, 2002). Therefore, this study examines through survey research, municipal e-government adoption in Ontario, Canada, to see how developed these local governments are and to discern whether e-government has increased citizen-initiated contacts with government.

Ontario, Canada, was chosen for two reasons: (1) for four years in a row, this country was rated as the most e-government-enabled national government according to Accenture, an information systems consultancy firm (Accenture, 2004); and (2) it is the most populous province in Canada with the largest city in the country; namely, Toronto.

In order to examine the impact of e-government and its relationship on citizen-initiated contacts, this paper first outlines the existing literature in both areas and demonstrates how this study fits into the literature. Second, the evidence of e-government adoption at the local level in Ontario is presented. Third, six key hypotheses are outlined, and a model of citizen-initiated contacts is tested empirically. The conclusion summarizes and suggests avenues for future research on e-government adoption at the local level.

LOCAL E-GOVERNMENT ADOPTION SURVEY LITERATURE

As previously mentioned, there are few studies that examine factors that precipitate e-government adoption at the local level, with most of this work being focused on the U.S. (Ho & Ni, 2004; Reddick, 2004b). The majority of the existing research examines the International City/County Management Association (ICMA) surveys of e-government adoption (Holden, Norris & Fletcher, 2003; Moon, 2002; Reddick, 2004a). The general consensus from their findings is that local e-government adoption is past stage one of the Layne and Lee (2001) model of cataloging information online (Holden, Norris & Fletcher, 2003; Moon, 2002; Reddick, 2004a). Stage two of transaction-based e-government is not as common, partly because of issues of privacy and security of personally identifiable information (PII) (Edmiston, 2002; Holden, Norris & Fletcher, 2003). Limited evidence exists for vertical and horizontal integration of e-government across organizational boundaries and functional areas of government (Ho, 2002). This study is different from the existing work on e-government adoption in that it focuses on whether e-government has increased citizen-initiated contact with government officials; most of the existing work has focused on explaining e-government features, as mentioned, and has concentrated mainly on the U.S.

CITIZEN-INITIATED CONTACT LITERATURE

The citizen-initiated contacts literature can be divided into two research areas, with the first examining perceived needs and awareness as the most important factors that increases contacts (Hirlinger, 1992; Jones, Greenberg, Kaufman, & Drew, 1977; Sharp, 1984; Thomas, 1982; Thomas & Melkers, 1999; Vedlitz, Durand, & Dyer 1980) and the second examining the satisfaction with bureaucracy and its impact on citizen-initiated contacts. In the second research area, some scholars have argued that citizen-initiated contact will decrease, because the bureaucracy is overwhelmed with service requests (Serra, 1995; Vedlitz & Dyer, 1984). There are also studies that show the opposite effect of increased contact because of frustration with the bureaucracy (Moon, Serra, & West, 1993; Thomas & Melkers, 2000).

A significant question in public administration is how responsive municipal bureaucracies are to citizens' needs and demands and how these can be increased (Greene, 1982). Most studies (of contacting) have examined the contactors; few studies focus directly on administrators' attitudes toward contacts (Greene, 1982). The question of responsiveness is important not only for individuals who depend on municipal services but also for democracy and political participation, since administrators are supposed to be responsible directly to mayors and council members and ultimately to citizens (Greene, 1982).

As mentioned, one reason for citizen-initiated contact with municipal government is a perceived *need* for the services that a government offers, which is usually a specific government service or modification of service (Thomas & Melkers, 2000; Thomas & Streib, 2003). Contacting behavior is also related to the *awareness* of government as the appropriate provider of these services (Vedlitz, Durand & Dyer 1980). Finally, needs and awareness are related to the relative social well being of the individual, or socioeconomic status (Jones, Greenberg, Kaufman, & Drew, 1977). Empirical evidence indicates that contacting is related to a perceived need for information or services, and socioeconomic status is of secondary importance (Hirlinger, 1992; Sharp, 1984; Thomas, 1982; Thomas & Melkers, 1999).

Other factors that influence citizen-initiated contacts are related to bureaucratic response to citizen demands. Research shows that the greater the number of demands, the more difficult it is for local governments to respond (Vedlitz & Dyer, 1984). In addition, empirical evidence indicates that citizens who are unhappy with the bureaucracy are more likely to contact members of Congress (Moon, Serra, & West, 1993). Research also shows that citizen-initiated contact increases with greater satisfaction of the bureaucracy (Serra, 1995).

There are at least two important differences between these Web contacts and traditional citizen-initiated contacts (Thomas & Streib, 2003). First, contacting via the Web may be easier and quicker than contacting by phone or in person, meaning that many contacts that have been traditionally made by the phone or in person will be made over the Web (Horrigan, 2004). Second, the Web may not have a meaningful two-way communication, because the phone has greater personal contact than a Web contact. Despite these differences, the similarities between the two types of contacts are still enough to explore citizen-initiated contacts (Thomas & Streib, 2003). This study does so by focusing on survey evidence collected from municipal administrators in Ontario, Canada.

DATA COLLECTION METHODS

The data collected for this local e-government study were from a survey conducted in the months of August and September 2004. There were 161 municipal governments surveyed in Ontario, Canada, that served populations of 10,000 or more. Chief administrative officers (CAO) of these local governments were surveyed to obtain their perceptions on e-government development. A total of 119 surveys were completed. The overall response rate was 74%. This response rate was very high, given the general hesitancy of professionals to answer surveys. This was accomplished first by sending a letter introducing the research project and then following up in a couple of weeks with the formal survey. To maximize the response rate, there was a reminder letter sent two weeks before the survey due date. In addition, only 10 key questions were asked in order to maximize the return rate. The questions were taken from the 2004 International City/County Management Association (ICMA) e-government survey and adapted to the Canadian context (ICMA, 2004). The 10 questions were used to show the major aspects of e-government relationships, specifically government-to-citizen, government-to-business, and government-to-employees. The value of a survey is to provide information on Web site content and to identify opinions of key decision makers on e-government adoption. If this study only conducted a Web site content analysis, it would be limited, since the opinions of key e-government decision makers would not be accounted for (West, 2004).

Data on the unemployment rate, median personal income, and population of the communities were taken from the most recent Statistic Canada's 2001 Community Profiles database of local governments. These socioeconomic data were used in the test of the model of citizen-initiated contact with government discussed toward the end of this paper. The responses to the survey questions are discussed in the following section in order to get a better understanding of the e-government climate that local governments face in Canada.

ONTARIO LOCAL E-GOVERNMENT SURVEY DATA

The most common services that local governments in Ontario offer to their citizens and businesses are presented in Table 1. The majority of the list of services in Table 1 was taken from ICMA e-government survey questions of e-services offered by local governments in the U.S. (ICMA, 2004). Most of the municipal governments offer informational services. For example, 103 of them post council meeting minutes online. Other common information provided online was budget documents, with three-fourths of these local governments providing this type of financial information to its citizens.

E-government in Ontario has not progressed to higher stages of development (see Table 1). For example, only around 12% of the governments surveyed provided the option of online tax payment, and 20% offered online registration for recreational facilities. In fact, the third most common response, at 68%, was providing online forms that could be downloaded for manual completion. This demonstrates the limited development of providing electronic service delivery.

Table 1 also compares Ontario local e-government adoption to municipal governments in the U.S. with ICMA (2004) data. Comparing Ontario municipalities with local governments in the U.S. indicates some interesting observations. Providing council meeting minutes online is very common in Ontario municipalities with more than 90% of these governments doing this, compared to three-

Table 1. Please provide the following information about e-government on your local government Web site (check all applicable)

	Ontario Local Governments Total Responses	Ontario Local Governments Percent of Respondents	ICMA E-Government Survey 2004 Percent of Responses
Council meeting minutes	103	91.2%	75.6%
Budget documents	83	73.5%	NA
Forms that can be downloaded for manual completion (e.g., voter registration, building permits, etc.)	77	68.1%	58.3%
Online communication with elected and appointed officials	63	55.8%	65.6%
Online complaints (e.g., reporting graffiti, missing trash pickup, etc.)	47	41.6%	NA
Online requests for local government records	36	31.9%	27.1%
Online requests for services (e.g., pothole repair)	33	29.2%	29.5%
Newsletters e-mailed to residents	26	23.0%	27.7%
Other (please specify)	25	22.1%	19.7%
Online registration for use of recreational facilities (e.g., reserving picnic areas, racquetball courts, and registering for classes)	23	20.4%	16.4%
Online delivery of local governments records to the requestor	20	17.7%	18.1%
Online payment of fines/fees	17	15.0%	7.3%
Online completion and submission of permit applications	17	15.0%	10.2%
Online payment of taxes	14	12.4%	8.6%
Online payment of utility bills	9	8.0%	9.2%
Police reports	5	4.4%	NA
Online completion and submission of business license applications/renewals	4	3.5%	6.3%
Online property registration (e.g., animal, bicycle registration)	3	2.7%	2.8%
Online voter registration	1	0.9%	2.4%
Note: NA = Not Available			

quarters in the U.S. Forms that can be downloaded for manual completion also are found more often in Ontario than the U.S. However, communication with individual elected and appointed officials is less common in Ontario than the U.S., possibly explained by more officials in the latter county running for elections. Ontario local governments also seem to be more advanced in online payment systems, with 15% doing this in Ontario and only 7.3% in the U.S. having online payments systems for fines or fees. Similarly, online payment of taxes is done by 12.4% in Ontario and 8.6% in the U.S. The overall results reveal that Ontario municipalities are not much further ahead than U.S. local governments. However, Ontario e-governments conduct more transactions than the U.S.

There is greater adoption of e-government when it comes to electronic purchasing compared to the services results in Table 1. Table 2 shows electronic purchasing with transactional-based e-government taking place when local governments purchase goods online from businesses. For example, local governments purchasing office supplies from businesses often is done, but

Table 2. Please indicate by checking the boxes below which procurement activities you complete online (check all applicable)

	Review Product Offerings Online (Percent of Responses in Brackets)	Make Purchases Online (Percent of Responses in Brackets)	Respondents Total
Property and/or liability insurance	13(100%)	0(0%)	13
Equipment	66(93%)	25(35%)	71
Office supplies	62(81%)	53(69%)	77
		Total Respondents	80

equipment purchases are done less frequently, and government purchasing insurance online is not done at all. Therefore, the development of e-purchasing seems to be more developed than e-services provided to citizens and businesses (see Table 1). The nonexistence of local governments purchasing insurance online could be the result of the lack of acceptance and technology enabling digital signatures in municipal governments. Therefore, these transactions would have to be completed on paper.

Table 3 demonstrates how e-government is used internally by these municipal governments, if they use an intranet (a Web server accessible only to local government employees). Around half of these governments have an intranet. Some of the more common intranet uses involve providing news and information, documents, and job searches. The intranet is used less often for more advanced tasks, such as online training and procurement.

When comparing what e-governments offer to its citizens, there seems to be little development in transactional-based e-government (see Table 1). This is attributed to the general hesitancy of the public conducting online transactions because of privacy and security concerns. E-purchasing is more advanced (see Table 2), and the intranet seems to be the most promising venture (see Table 3).

Table 4 demonstrates the amount that these governments are planning to budget for e-government for fiscal year 2005. In the sample, around 55% of municipalities budgeted less than $10,000 Canadian for e-government, and 21% budgeted more than $100,000 Canadian a year. Since the sample is composed of many smaller-sized local governments, this is not surprising. It demonstrated that small amounts of money are allocated to e-government, most likely attributed to the meltdown of the dot-com industry in early 2001 (Roy, 2003). This has caused many municipal governments to be hesitant to spend expansively on e-government projects, unless a sound business model can be identified.

Table 5 asks CAOs if they have a separate budget for e-government and whether the IT department develops this budget. This will give this research a sense of whether organizational structure influences e-government adoption. Around two-thirds of the local governments surveyed did not have a separate budget for e-government. Around 30% did have a separate budget for e-government, and the IT department submitted it to the budget office. Having a separate department looking after the needs of e-government is important because of the intense competition for fiscal resources. A separate department can fight for e-government more effectively, rather than being lumped together with other departments.

Table 3. Does your local government have an intranet (a Web server accessible only to local governments employees)?

	Total Responses	Percent of Responses
Yes	53	47.7%
No	58	52.3%
If "Yes," how do you use the intranet? (Check all applicable)		
Provide news and information	52	96%
Publish documents and manuals online to reduce printing costs	48	96%
Post job openings for internal recruitments	43	90%
Expand telecommuting staff access to information and data	29	71%
Provide employees with benefit forms	28	67%
Enable project teams to collaborate	26	74%
Provide online report generation	25	60%
Provide online training	21	57%
Provide online procurement tools	18	51%

Table 4. How much (Canadian dollars) do you plan to budget for e-government for the next coming fiscal year?

	Total Responses	Percent of Responses
Under $5,000	30	30.6%
$5,000-$10,000	25	25.5%
$10,000-$25,000	6	6.1%
$25,000-$50,000	8	8.2%
$50,000-$100,000	8	8.2%
Over $100,000	21	21.4%

Table 6 demonstrates that most of the sources of funds for e-government initiatives are found in the general fund. There was not a lot of non-traditional funding being used, such as grants and transaction fees. In addition, entrepreneurial efforts, such as risk sharing with private sector entities, hardly ever was done by these local governments.

Table 1 provides the evidence that there is not much transaction-based e-government taking place. Table 7 gives some indication as to why this has happened. Some e-government barriers can partially explain the situation that local governments are facing. For instance, the top responses for the barriers to e-government initiatives were lack of resources (both financial and personnel)

Table 5. Please check the box beside the option below that best describes the e-government budget process in your local government

	Total Responses	Percent of Responses
There is no separate budget item for e-government	75	67.6%
There is a separate budget item for e-government, and the information technology (or equivalent) department develops and submits the e-government budget for the local government.	34	30.6%
There is a separate budget item for e-government, and each department develops and submits its own e-government budget.	2	1.8%

Table 6. How are your current e-government efforts funded? (check all applicable)

	Total Responses	Percent of Responses
General tax revenue	75	79.8%
Federal or provincial grants	22	23.4%
Transaction fees from services provided	13	13.8%
Municipal bond financing	9	9.6%
Risk-sharing (a private sector firm provides the application and receives a percent of the revenue)	4	4.3%

Table 7. Which, if any, of the following barriers to e-government initiatives has your local government encountered? (check all applicable)

	Total Responses	Percent of Responses
Lack of financial resources	84	75.7%
Lack of technology/Web staff	64	57.7%
Lack of technology/Web expertise	50	45.0%
Issues regarding security	41	36.9%
Issues regarding privacy	37	33.3%
Need to upgrade technology (PCs, networks, etc.)	34	30.6%
Issues relating to convenience fees for online transactions	26	23.4%
Staff resistance to change	21	18.9%
Lack of collaboration among departments	20	18.0%
Lack of support from elected officials	17	15.3%
Other (please specify)	17	15.3%
Lack of information about e-government applications	13	11.7%

and issues regarding privacy and security that have not been adequately addressed. This is consistent with the lack of transaction-based e-government, as shown in Table 1. In order for citizens to feel comfortable about paying taxes online or having online voter registration, governments must address the critical issues of privacy and security. For instance, what is going to happen to citizens' PII, such as credit card information? As well, are there controls in place to prevent misuse of this PII? In addition, since transaction-based e-government is more expensive than simply providing online information, funding and staffing become critical issues that should be addressed.

Table 8 shows the most important response to what is being tested in this paper. Has e-government increased citizen-initiated contact? This was the number-one change as a result of e-government. The results in this table demonstrate that almost half of those surveyed believed that e-government had increased citizen-initiated contact. Only two municipal governments believed that e-government had reduced the number of staff. This is somewhat surprising, since this has been one of the primary reasons for many fiscally stressed local governments initiating e-government projects. E-government actually has increased the demands on staff, which is the opposite of those who argue that it will reduce transaction costs.

The results in Table 8 highlight that e-government is moving closer to achieving outcomes. Therefore, the argument presented in some of the e-government literature on reinventing government has some validity (Ho, 2002). The impact of increasing citizen contact with government officials and business processes being re-engineered, the top two changes are consistent with the reinventing government movement. Reinventing municipal government through e-government was evident for almost half of the municipal governments surveyed.

This data can now be compiled to test specific hypotheses that explain whether e-government has increased citizen-initiated contacts with elected and appointed officials.

HYPOTHESES

There are six hypotheses tested in this study that are relevant to the citizen-initiated contact and e-government literatures, namely:

1. Increases in population and median personal income will increase citizen-initiated con-

Table 8. How has e-government changed your local government? (check all applicable)

	Total Responses	Percent of Responses
Increased citizen contact with elected and appointed officials	46	48.4%
Business processes are being re-engineered	45	47.4%
Increased demands on staff	43	45.3%
Business processes are more efficient	42	44.2%
Changed the role of staff	37	38.9%
Reduced time demands on staff	29	30.5%
Reduced administrative costs	19	20.0%
Other (please specify)	10	10.5%
Reduced the number of staff	2	2.1%
Increased non-tax-based revenues from fees advertising	1	1.1%

tact with e-government because of greater socioeconomic status of the community.

2. Increases in the unemployment rate will decrease contact with e-government because of greater fiscal stress placed on local governments.
3. The greater the number of barriers to e-government adoption, such as lack of financial resources, lack of technology, issues regarding security and privacy, and so forth, that a municipal government faces inhibits e-government adoption. Therefore, less citizen-initiated contact with government will occur.
4. Having a greater Internet presence will be signaled by providing more e-services, having more e-purchasing, and having an intranet; these factors will increase citizen-initiated contact with government by providing greater opportunity for contacting.
5. If a municipal government plans to use non-traditional financing sources and has a large budget for e-government, this will increase citizen contact because of having more resources and diversity of sources of revenue.
6. If a municipal government has a separate e-government budget developed by the IT department, this will increase citizen-initiated contact with government because of increased budgetary clout.

Each of these six hypotheses will be briefly elaborated on. The first hypothesis addresses the socioeconomic status of the community. Greater socioeconomic status leads to more citizen-initiated contact with e-government because of greater resources and economies of scale in service provision (Jones, Greenberg, Kaufman, & Drew, 1977; Thomas, 1982; Thomas & Streib, 2003). Larger and wealthier cities are able to supply more e-government services and, thus, enhance contact. Personal income is one measure of wealth of a community. Higher income would signify a greater ability to tax citizens, and therefore, more money could be devoted to e-government. Local governments that serve larger population centers would have the ability to reap economies of scale in service provision, which would mean greater e-government adoption (Holden, Norris, & Fletcher, 2003).

The second hypothesis argues that the higher levels of unemployment will decrease citizen contact because of greater fiscal stress (Ho & Ni, 2004). Communities that have a higher unemployment rate will not be able to afford as much e-government, thereby reducing citizen-initiated contact. When more workers are unemployed, less tax revenue is being collected, which creates fiscal stress. Some workers would leave the community, especially in northern Ontario, where there is less work. They would search for jobs in larger cities in the southern part of the province. This further shrinks the tax base and prospects for e-government adoption.

If a municipal government identifies many barriers to e-government adoption, this would signal less citizen-initiated contact with government (Reddick, 2004b). Issues such as lack of resources (financial and personnel), privacy, and security should inhibit contact. Cities that have fewer barriers to e-government should be able to secure higher levels of adoption. Leadership is important, since champions of e-government can push projects from start to finish, creating greater e-government adoption (Ho & Ni, 2004).

The more e-services, e-purchasing, and intranet signals that the government is well developed technologically when it comes to e-government and, therefore, increases the possibility of citizen contact. Offering more opportunities for contact reflects the citizen-initiated contact research that greater demands by citizens will increase contact. Therefore, providing more services and opportunities to engage in e-government increases contact (Thomas & Melkers, 2000; Thomas & Streib, 2003). For example, if citizens are able to file their taxes online or register for recreational facilities, this will enhance citizen contact with government. In addition, if the local government has the ability to purchase office equipment or supplies online, this will signal greater acceptance of e-government as a tool for contact. Having an intranet provides more services and resources to local employees. This will enable employees to become more proficient and comfortable working online and enhance e-government acceptance and development by staff.

Larger e-government budgets and use of non-traditional sources of finance should indicate higher levels of e-government adoption (Ho & Ni, 2004). For example, using transaction fees or convenience charges to fund an e-government project indicates a more entrepreneurial spirit in financing and an increased willingness to implement e-government. In addition, merely spending more on e-government should imply greater development, leading to increased citizen-initiated contact.

A separate e-government budget developed by the IT department indicates the capability of the local governments to secure expenditures, since it has a representative that actively will pursue its interests (Reddick, 2004b). If e-government spending is lumped together with other departments, there may be no high-level official who has enough clout to find and secure appropriate funding (Wildavsky, 1974).

The following section presents the summary statistics of the dependent variable and independent variables used to test citizen-initiated contact with e-government.

SUMMARY STATISTICS OF DEPENDENT AND PREDICTOR VARIABLES

Table 9 demonstrates the descriptive statistics of data tested in this study. Since this study is interested in whether there has been increased citizen-initiated contact with elected and appointed officials, this is used as the dependent variable. The summary statistics demonstrated that, on average, 39% of CAOs believed that e-government had increased citizen contact with

Table 9. Descriptive statistics

	N	Minimum	Maximum	Mean
Increased citizen contact with elected and appointed officials	119	0	1	0.39
Barriers index	119	0	9	3.42
E-purchases index	119	0	2	0.66
E-services index	119	0	9	2.41
Intranet	119	0	1	0.45
Log of median personal income (Canadian dollars)	108	$17,382	$33,828	$24,591
Non traditional e-gov finance	119	0	1	0.31
Plan to budget > $50,000 (Canadian dollars)	119	0	1	0.18
Log of population	108	10,059	988,948	89,635
Separate e-government budget developed IT department	119	0	1	0.29
Unemployment rate	108	1.4	11.9	5.44
Note: Dependent Variable Shaded				

elected and appointed officials (This figure is less than that presented in Table 1, since there are 108 usable observations rather than 119).

In order to measure how many obstacles these governments faced in terms of implementing e-government, a barriers' index was composed (Table 9). The more barriers they faced, such as lack of financial resources and lack of technology (as reported in Table 2), the higher the index score these governments received. It is anticipated that more barriers to e-government adoption would decrease citizen-initiated contact with e-government. Out of nine possible barriers, these governments indicated that, on average, they experienced three of them.

On average, there was less than one e-purchase completed by these municipal governments (Table 9). In addition, out of the nine possible services that were available online, only two municipal governments offered eight of these e-services. (There was one city that offered nine services but wished to remain anonymous.) Two cities have the highest score for the e-services index—the City of Ottawa (http://www.ottawa.ca) with a population of three quarters of a million, and the City of Windsor (http://www.citywindsor.ca) with a population of just over 200,000. They both had an e-services index score of eight, meaning that they offered eight of the services listed in Table 1. The services considered were only those that are transaction-based, such as online payment of taxes and online payment of utility bills. There were five services that were not part of this index. They are forms that can be downloaded for manual completion, council meeting minutes, budget documents, police reports, and newsletters, since they do not involve a transaction. An intranet was found in less than half of these local governments. The average median personal income for residents was around $24,000 Canadian a year. In terms of non-traditional financing of e-government, this research found that less than one- third used this method. Most of the financing was taken from the general fund. Almost one-fifth planned to budget more than $50,000 for fiscal year 2005. The average population that these governments served was almost 90,000, a typical medium-sized municipal government. Twenty-nine percent had a separate e-government budget developed by the IT department. On average, the unemployment rate was almost 6%, which was below the national average of 7%. The following section uses the data on e-government adoption and tests a model of citizen-initiated contact.

RESULTS OF LOGISTIC REGRESSION

In order to examine the impact that these predictor variables have on citizen-initiated contact with government, logistic regression was conducted. The dependent variable is increased citizen contact with elected and appointed officials. This is a binary variable, with a *1* if this statement is true and *0* if it is not true.

As shown in Table 10, of all of the social, economic, and organizational independent variables, the most important reasons for increased citizen-initiated contact were increased e-services and a separate e-government budget developed by an IT department. None of the socioeconomic status variables, such as median personal income and the unemployment rate, had an influence on increasing citizen contact with e-government. Therefore, size or wealth of a municipal government was not a good predictor of increased contact with citizens. Having more e-government barriers was not an impediment to increased citizen contact with e-government.

Odds ratios can be used in logistic regression to find out the likelihood of observing a *1* in the dependent variable, or increased citizen-initiated contact with e-government. For the statistically significant e-services index, the odds ratio was 1.45, indicating that as a municipal government offers more online services, it was almost one and a half times more likely to have increased

Table 10. Logistic regression results

	Dependent Variable: Increased citizen contact with elected and appointed officials			
Independent or Predictor Variables	Odds Ratio	Standard Error	Wald Statistic	Prob. Significant
Barriers index	1.16	0.11	(1.86)	0.17
E-purchases index	1.35	0.29	(1.07)	0.30
E-services index	1.45	0.12	(9.72)***	0.00
Intranet	0.59	0.54	(0.99)	0.32
Log of median personal income (Canadian Dollars)	1.04	0.45	(0.01)	0.93
Non traditional e-gov finance	1.52	0.53	(0.63)	0.43
Plan to budget > $50,000 (Canadian Dollars)	0.83	0.71	(0.07)	0.79
Log of population	0.64	0.45	(0.96)	0.33
Separate e-gov budget developed IT department	3.37	0.63	(3.73)**	0.05
Unemployment rate	0.91	0.13	(0.59)	0.44
Nagelkerke-R^2	0.30			
Log-Likelihood $\chi^2(10)$	(23.08)***			
N	108			

Note: *** Significant at the 0.01 level; ** Significant at the 0.05 level.

citizen-initiated contact. In addition, if there was a separate budget developed by the IT department for e-government, this indicated that local governments would be three times more likely to increase citizen-initiated contact with e-government (i.e., the odds ratio of 3.37).

The following section analyzes the key findings of this study and presents avenues for future research.

DISCUSSION AND CONCLUSION

What do these statistical results mean for public administrators and the study of e-government? First, having more e-government services is a good predictor of increased citizen-initiated contact with government. This confirms the key hypothesis in the citizen-initiated contact literature that increased *needs* drive contacts. By increasing online services, municipal governments must answer more e-service related questions with citizens. This is somewhat surprising, since one would think that more online services would indicate less contact, because the municipal governments would conduct transactional services online.

In addition, a separate e-government budget adopted by an IT department signals a stronger command of fiscal resources, because it can fight as an autonomous unit to secure more e-government funding. This is the classic validation of the budget game applied to e-government finance (Wildavsky, 1974). This should indicate that larger and more developed e-governments that have separate IT departments interact more with the public.

What was found not to be a significant predictor of citizen-initiated contact with e-government was equally interesting. Socioeconomic status of the community that the municipal government serves did not have an impact on contact. This is consistent with the citizen-initiated contact literature showing that socioeconomic status is not an important predictor of increased contact. Common factors cited in the literature, such as the unemployment rate, personal income, and population, did not have an influence on increasing citizen contact. Therefore, being a large city serving a wealthy population did not assure greater citizen-initiated contact with e-government. This is consistent and inconsistent with the e-government adoption literature. Some studies argue that larger population centers have a positive influence on e-government adoption (Holden, Norris & Fletcher, 2003), while other studies claim that non-socioeconomic status variables have the most important influence, such as leadership (Ho & Ni, 2004).

One of the limitations of this study is that it relies on the self reporting of CAOs, who may be prone to exaggeration (Ho & Ni, 2004). For example, an examination of ICMA surveys of e-government longitudinally has shown an overestimation of plans for e-government adoption by local governments in the U.S. (Norris & Moon, 2005). A future study should combine the survey analysis of Ontario municipal governments and content analysis of their Web sites in order to verify accuracy of responses. This combined methodological approach most recently has been done in the U.S. (West, 2004). In addition, future work should examine issues such as e-government demand by the public in Canada. For instance, many studies focus on what governments supply, but what the public demands is equally important, and it is a relatively unexplored area of e-government research.

REFERENCES

Accenture. (2004). *eGovernment leadership: High performance, maximum value*. New York: Accenture.

Criado, J.I. & Ramilo, M.C. (2003). E-government in practice: An analysis of Website orientation to the citizens in Spanish municipalities. *International Journal of Public Sector Management, 16*(3), 191-218.

Edmiston, K.D. (2002). State and local e-government: Prospects and challenges. *American Review of Public Administration, 33*(1), 20-45.

Green, K.R. (1982). Municipal administrators' receptivity to citizens' and elected officials' contacts. *Public Administration Review, 42*(4), 346-353.

Hirlinger, M.W. (1992). Citizen-initiated contacting of local government officials: A multivariate explanation. *Journal of Politics, 54*(2), 553-564.

Ho, A.T.K. (2002). Reinventing local governments and the e-government initiative. *Public Administration Review, 62*(4), 434-444.

Ho, A.T.K. & Ni, A.Y. (2004). Explaining the adoption of e-government features: A case study of Iowa County treasurers' offices. *American Review of Public Administration, 34*(2), 164-180.

Holden, S.H., Norris, D.F., & Fletcher, P.D. (2003). Electronic government at the local level: Progress to date and future issues. *Public Performance & Management Review, 26*(4), 325-344.

Horrigan, J.B. (2004). *How Americans get in touch with government*. Washington, D.C.: Pew Internet & American Life Project.

ICMA. (2004). *Electronic government 2004*. Washington, D.C.: International City/County Management Association.

Jones, B.D., Greenberg, S.R., Kaufman, C., & Drew, J. (1977). Bureaucratic response to citizen-initiated contacts: Environmental enforcement in Detroit. *American Political Science Review, 71*(1), 148-165.

Layne, K. & Lee, J. (2001). Developing fully function e-government: A four stage model. *Government Information Quarterly, 18*(1), 122-136.

Moon, D., Serra, G., & West, J.P. (1993). Citizens' contacts with bureaucratic and legislative officials. *Political Research Quarterly, 46*(4), 931-941.

Moon, M.J. (2002). The evolution of e-government among municipalities: Rhetoric or reality? *Public Administration Review, 62*(4), 424-433.

Norris, D.F. & Moon, M.J. (2005). Advancing e-government at the grassroots: Tortoise or hare? *Public Administration Review, 65*(1), 64-76.

Reddick, C.G. (2004a). A two-stage model of e-government growth: Theories and empirical evidence for U.S. cities. *Government Information Quarterly, 21*(1), 51-64.

Reddick, C.G. (2004b). Empirical models of e-government growth in local governments. *e-Service Journal, 3*(2), 59-84.

Roy, J. (2003). The relational dynamics of e-governance: A case study of the city of Ottawa. *Public Performance & Management Review, 26*(4), 391-403.

Serra, G. (1995). Citizen-initiated contact and satisfaction with bureaucracy: A multivariate analysis. *Journal of Public Administration Research and Theory, 5*(2), 175-188.

Sharp, E.B. (1984). Citizen-demand making in the urban context. *American Journal of Political Science, 28*(4), 654-670.

Thomas, J.C. (1982). Citizen-initiated contacts with government agencies: A test of three theories. *American Journal of Political Science, 26*(3), 504-522.

Thomas, J.C. & Melkers, J. (1999). Explaining citizen-initiated contacts with municipal bureaucrats: Lessons from the Atlanta experience. *Urban Affairs Review, 34*(5), 667-690.

Thomas, J.C. & Melkers, J. (2000). Citizen contacting of municipal officials: Choosing between appointed administrators and elected leaders. *Journal of Public Administration Research and Theory, 11*(1), 51-71.

Thomas, J.C. & Streib, G. (2003). The new face of government: Citizen-initiated contacts in the era of e-government. *Journal of Public Administration Research and Theory, 13*(1), 83-102.

Vedlitz, A. & Dyer, J.A. (1984). Bureaucratic response to citizen contacts: Neighborhood demands and administrative reaction in Dallas. *The Journal of Politics, 46*(4), 1207-1216.

Vedlitz, A., Dyer, J.A., & Durand, R. (1980). Citizen contacts with local governments: A comparative view. *American Journal of Political Science, 24*(1), 50-67.

West, D.M. (2004). E-government and the transformation of service delivery and citizen attributes. *Public Administration Review, 61*(1), 15-27.

Wildavsky, A.B. (1974). *The politics of the budgetary process* (2nd ed.). Boston: Little Brown.

This work was previously published in International Journal of Electronic Government Research, Vol. 1, Issue 4, edited by D. Norris, pp. 45-62, copyright 2005 by IGI Publishing, formerly known as Idea Group Publishing (an imprint of IGI Global).

Chapter 5.14
Healthcare Network Centric Operations:
The Confluence of E-Health and E-Government

Dag von Lubitz
MedSMART, Inc., USA
Central Michigan University, USA

Nilmini Wickramasinghe
Illinois Institute of Technology, USA

ABSTRACT

Healthcare has yet to realize the true potential afforded by e-health. To date, technology-based healthcare operations are conducted chaotically, at a wide variety of nonintegrated fronts, with little or no long-term strategy, and at a tremendous and ever increasing cost. This chapter proposes that in order for healthcare to ever reap the full benefits from e-health, it is imperative for the development of a doctrine of healthcare network centric operations. Otherwise, millions if not billions of dollars will be spent on a futile chase of the definitions of how and when the computer, healthcare provider, and healthcare administrator interact most efficiently and at least expense. The concept of a doctrine, "conceptual platform," that outlines the consequent, goal-oriented way forward, and integrates all constituent elements into a smoothly operating whole, is utilized to great effect in the military. Drawing upon the strategies and techniques employed by the military to develop a network centric doctrine, the chapter outlines the essential components necessary for the establishment of the doctrine for healthcare network centric operations (HNCO), and in so doing not only highlights the integral role played by information computer and communication technologies (IC^2T) but also the pivotal role of policy makers and governments. In fact, HNCO underscores the important yet rarely acknowledged confluence of e-health and e-government.

INTRODUCTION

The rules of competition are changing as a result of the growth of global markets, the increased speed of business transactions, the technological revolution, and continued change in customer expectations. The growth, integration, and sophistication of information computer and communication technologies (IC^2T) are changing our society and economy. Consumers and businesses have been particularly quick to recognize the potential and realize the benefits of the Internet and Internet-facilitated computer networks. The resultant "e-revolution" changed many aspects of the traditional "way of doing business," facilitated substantial changes in internal and external management styles, enabled increased efficacy of virtually all production stages and operations, and helped to extend the customer reach. As e-commerce or the application of IC^2T to business matures, more attention is being placed on maximising its potential benefits to all areas of society. Two areas where much focus is now being placed regarding the use of IC^2T to improve access to information and provide better access to services include public institutions and governments and healthcare.

E-government is defined as the use of IC^2T to provide citizens and organizations with more convenient access to government services and embrace interactions within governments (government-to-government), between governments and citizens (government-to-citizen), and between governments and businesses (government-to-business) (Turban, King, Lee, & Viehland, 2004). An analogous definition holds for e-health, which involves the use of IC^2T to provide all participants within the healthcare domain with better access to information and services (Wickramasinghe, Geisler, & Schaffer, 2005).

IC^2T are without doubt the source and the platform of one of the greatest transformations of society since the invention of print and permit-free flow, access, and exchange of information, and the development of universal means of contact among humans. In practical terms, these technologies offer the possibilities for vast improvement of efficiency and cost reduction in business, provide a platform for dissemination of high quality education, facilitate healthcare delivery, and limit the potential for conflict. Already today, the impact of the increasingly more intensive IC^2T use can be measured in the way local, national, and global political, economical, or social transactions are conducted. Yet, with the growing employment of IC^2T in daily operations, it is also apparent that neither the optimal pattern of use has been developed (we need look no further, for example, than the productivity paradox (Haag, Cummings, & McCubbrey, 2004; Jessup & Valacich, 2005; Laudon & Laudon, 2004; O'Brien, 2005), nor a philosophy guiding such use has been contemplated despite the emerging chaos that threatens the future growth of the field. The impeding state of chaos is exemplified by the collapse of e-businesses in the 1990s (Affuah & Tucci, 2001; Kalakota & Robinson, 1999; Stiglitz, 2003; Wickramasinghe & Sharma, 2004). The need for optimization and doctrine development is most evident in the arena of healthcare that, at the moment, is the most costly budgetary item in the world's economy (McGown, Overhag, Barnes, & McDonald, 2004; Reinhardt, Hussey, & Anderson, 2002; Stats & Facts, 2002; von Lubitz & Wickramasinghe, 2005a; Wickramasinghe & Ginzberg, 2001; Wickramasinghe & Mills, 2002).

Irrespective of the particular healthcare system adopted by a country, governments will always be one of the major influencing forces and key actors of the healthcare stage. It should therefore be a logical extrapolation that e-government and e-health should share a significant overlap. One might even go to the extreme and suggest that e-health, especially for countries which only have a public healthcare system, is in fact a subset of e-government. And yet, the two are rarely if ever discussed together. This confluence between e-health and e-government is best highlighted in the doctrine of healthcare network centric operations (HNCO). We believe that by acknowledging this confluence, more effective policies and protocols can be developed which will facilitate the adoption and diffusion of HNCO and in turn will lead to more effective and efficient healthcare delivery.

In healthcare, despite their relatively late arrival, computer-based technologies will play the major role in management of services at all levels. Yet, while the concept of "e-health" brings the promise of improved economy, increased efficiency, greater equality, and wider range and availability of services, the increasingly diverging goals and philosophies, disparity in the emerging approaches, and frequent incompatibility or limited nature of the available or developed electronic platforms mitigate against such optimistic future. Moreover, the tendency to convert precise terms describing individual components of "e-operations" (operations or activities where IC^2T have been applied to make them electronic) into often meaningless "household" terminology adds superficial linguistic grandeur to quite non-glamorous and very common-sense notions, and transforms the latter into profoundly sounding expressions of a trivialized credo. The misconceptions serve to produce chaos that, in turn, diffuses the true value of the "electronic" in the context of healthcare, reduces its impact, and, consequently, delays its most significant contribution toward elimination of spatial and temporal barriers, and energized operational facilitation.

Presently, existing networks and e-health initiatives in healthcare represent distinctive and disconnected entities whose operation is, essentially, platform-centric, that is, concentrates on the operations of a single system (platform) without any regard for the operational interaction among different systems (a "system of systems" or systems network, see von Lubitz & Wickramasinghe, 2005a, b, c, 2006). The consequent fragmentation and broad incompatibility of individual efforts has, in turn, a major influence on the access range to and sharing of high quality information existing among (or even within) the existing individual systems (ibid). For these reasons, despite providing very significant advantages to the local users (Wickramasinghe & Ginzberg, 2001; Wickramasinghe & Mills; 2002), the overall impact of the electronic information systems on either national or international healthcare operations continues to be relatively limited (von Lubitz & Wickramasinghe, 2005a) and nor does it provide the promised superior quality of care (Institute of Medicine, 2001).

Healthcare operations are conducted in a complex operational space. The limitations of a platform-centric approach in such environments are compounded by the fact that the limited (or inadequate) information extraction, gathering, and manipulation capabilities of individual systems are amplified by their frequent lack of interoperability (von Lubitz & Wickramasinghe, 2005a, b, c, 2006). Such limitations severely degrade the possibility of integrating inputs of complex, highly relevant data both from a wide variety of relevant (clinical data banks, for example) as well as seemingly nonessential sources (e.g., political, economical, geographical, ethnographic data pools) and has been the justification for taking a systems approach (Checkland & Scholes, 1990; Churchman, 1968). Environmental complexity of healthcare operations is often magnified by the presence of multiple actors (agencies, governmental bodies, global organizations, etc.) performing within the same space but using a wide variety of independent and non-intercommunicating platform-centric tools. As a consequence of the resulting chaos, the attainment (mission) of healthcare goals (objectives) is uncertainty, rather than information-driven (von Lubitz & Wickramasinghe, 2005c).

HEALTHCARE NETWORK CENTRIC OPERATIONS (HNCO)

The *network-centric approach* stands in direct apposition to platform centricity (Alberts, Garstka, & Stein, 2000; Cebrowski & Garstka, 1998; von Lubitz & Wickramasinghe, 2005a, b, c, 2006). Its underlying conceptual framework is drawn from the pioneering work of Boyd (1987), who synthesized decision making, interaction with and control of a fast paced and unpredictably changing environment into a loop-like process (OODA Loop) (Figure 1) (Boyd, 1987; von Lubitz & Wickramasinghe, 2005b, c, d, 2006). Decision making in complex macroenvironments, particularly those characterized by a very rapid revolution cycle and a vast array of multispectral information inputs, is the primary beneficiary of the practical applications of Boyd's Loop. Application of Loop methodology allows for the interpretation of the environment of multidimensional action space (in this case, healthcare) as a set of simultaneous and intertwined events that characterize the space, and are both influencing and are influenced by the actor (e.g., a healthcare organization, clinician, or disease). Boyd's Loop-based thinking forces the actor into continuous extraction and synthesis of pertinent information and germane knowledge. Without such extraction / synthesis, information chaos and overload will rapidly ensue and force the operator into subjective selection of *seemingly* relevant inputs and disregard of other inputs *that appear, at the time of the analysis, to be inconsequential* (von Lubitz & Wickramasinghe, 2005c, 2006; von Lubitz et al., 2004). The ensuing responses to the objective pressures will thus derive from increasingly subjective data interpretation, leading to suboptimal decision making and the ultimate danger of catastrophic errors.

Figure 1. Boyd's (OODA) Loop depicting how the processes for making critical decisions can be framed in terms of the four key stages of orientation, observation, determination, and action.

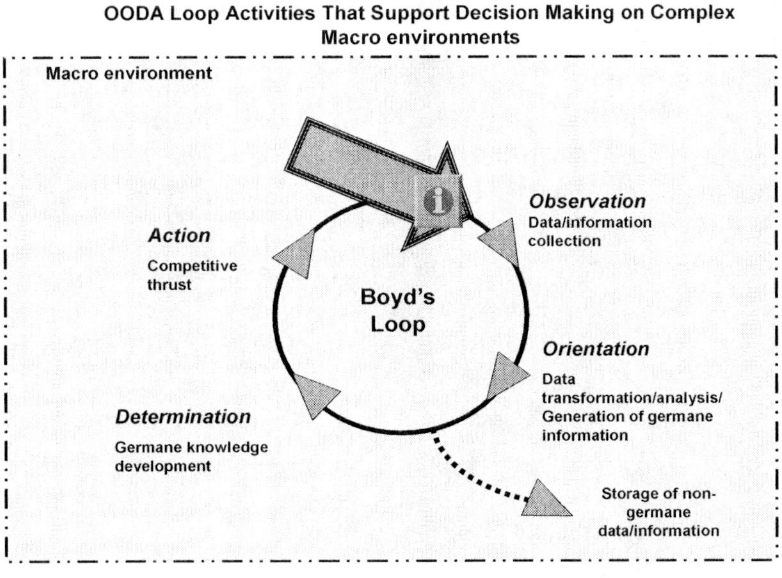

Note: The loop revolves both in time and space, and that termination of each revolution (Action stage) modifies the environment with which the Observer interacts, and imposes a new set of "unfolding circumstances" that generate "outside information" and shape the subsequent "Orient" and "Decide" stages. (Adapted from von Lubitz & Wickramasinghe, 2005a, 2005b, 2005c)

Application of Boyd's Loop and the associated continuous extraction and analysis of high quality information from the environment of the "operational space" provides yet another major advantage: the development of "information superiority" and the reduction of "information asymmetry" relative to the environment.

Each environment contains a complete set of data (information) that describe it. By extracting this information, the actor shifts the knowledge of the given environment from fully unknown (i.e., the environment containing all information that is hidden from the observer) to fully known (the observer uncovers the entire information content of the environment). In the process of uncovering the informational content of the environment, the actor shifts information asymmetry (from environment contained to actor extracted) in his favour and, at the same time, attains the state of "information superiority" (the actor knows progressively more about the faced environment, while the density of the unknown information contained within the environment diminishes during the extraction process). Hence, the highest possible rate of the shift of information asymmetry in favour of the actor and the maximum reduction of time needed for the attainment of valid information superiority are the principal goals of the actor acting in a complex, dynamically evolving environment. Both actor-biased information asymmetry and information superiority are also the principal countermeasure to the "information chaos" or information overload (Lehto, 1991; Prietula, Feltovich, & Marchak, 2000; Tole, Stephens, Harris, & Eprath, 1982)—elements that also characterize many aspects of today's healthcare (Arellano & Weber, 1998; d'Alessandro & Kreiter, 1999; Geiger, Merriles, Walo, Gordon, & Kunov, 1995).

In summary, information superiority provides asymmetric operational advantage not only assures complete control of the direction and tempo of all activities in a collaborative yet highly coordinated manner, but also facilitates attainment of the objective in the most effective and economical way possible.

The state of information superiority can be attained only through the effective use of IC²T—a critical architectural element of doctrine of "network-centric warfare" created and currently implemented by the U.S. Department of Defense (Stein, 1998). The approach calls for the development of interconnected information grids creating a multilayered, robust network that facilitates information sharing among all participants within the operational space (Arellano & Weber, 1998; d'Alessandro et al., 1999). Drawing upon these ideas and the underlying logic of Boyd's OODA, a doctrine for healthcare network-centric operations has been proposed recently (von Lubitz & Wickramasinghe, 2005a), of which the principal element is the creation and employment of an effective integrated worldwide collection/dissemination/exchange IC²T grid that will allow free flow of standardized/structured data/information among worldwide actors within the healthcare space necessary to allow the development of global information superiority state.

The doctrine of HNCO is thus defined as:

unhindered networking operations within and among all three domains that govern all activities conducted in healthcare space and are based on free, multidirectional flow and exchange of information without regard to the involved platforms or platform-systems and utilizing all available means of ICTs to facilitate such operations. (von Lubitz & Wickramasinghe, 2005a)

The three distinct domains of networkcentric operations are very closely interrelated, and the space within which the domains overlap provides physical and conceptual infrastructure within which all activities are conducted (Figure 2a):

- **Physical domain:** The target that the healthcare intends to influence directly or indirectly. In addition to the most obvious goal of eliminating disease, other aspects of healthcare, for example, research and its policies, fiscal issues, political environment of healthcare, provider personnel, and patient education, belong to this domain. The data/information/knowledge within physical domain relate to its *present rather than future state* and are the easiest to collect. Cumulatively, the physical domain represents *the current state of healthcare reality*.

- **Information domain:** Consists of all elements needed to generate, store, manipulate, disseminate/share/transform information, and disseminate/share the product of such transformation as knowledge in all its forms. All sensory inputs gathered are gathered within the information domain with the sensors representing a wide variety of entities (people and devices.) The output of the sensors may have a wide variety of forms/sensitivity (e.g., basic research data, diagnostic data from individual/multiple patient encounters, electronic health records, etc.) The information existing in this domain may not fully represent the current state of reality. However, all knowledge about that state emerges from and through the interaction with the information domain, and all communications about that occur through interactions within this domain. The information domain is particularly sensitive to incursions that may affect the quality of information contained within the domain. Hence, it must have appropriate security measures that prevent hostile intrusions in any form.
- **Cognitive domain:** Constitutes all human factors that affect healthcare operations, such as education, training, experience, personal engagement (motivation), "open-mindedness," or even intuition of individuals involved in relevant activities. All these represent highly intangible quantities that are difficult to measure but form the basis for the selection of right timing, right place, and right effect of all actions undertaken within the healthcare. Even in the presence of well developed decision support systems provided by the information domain, deep situational awareness is created and decisions are made within the cognitive domain.

The technological backbone of network-centric healthcare is the World Healthcare Information Grid (WHIG) (von Lubitz & Wickramasinghe, 2005a, b, c, 2006) which utilizes Web and related Internet technologies, for example, HTML, TCP/IP, Web, JAVA, XTML, and so forth (Eysenbach, 2001; Eysenbach & Diepgen, 1998; Glaser, 2002; McGown et al., 2004; PricewaterhouseCoopers, 2003; Sharma & Wickramasinghe, 2004a; Sieving, 1999; Umhoff & Winn, 1999; Wickramasinghe & Ginzberg, 2001; Wickramasinghe & Mills, 2002). Figure 2a depicts the WHIG with its three distinct yet interconnected domains, each made up of interconnecting grids while Figure 2b identifies the key elements of the grid with its smart access portals, analytic nodes, and intelligent sensors (von Lubitz & Wickramasinghe, 2005b). Implementation of principles based on ASP (application software provider) philosophy and fusing them together with the concept of smart portals allows direct worldwide access to the WHIG that is essentially independent of the technology existing at the user site and that opens network-centric healthcare operations to practically all involved entities — whether individual healthcare providers or national/international bodies providing healthcare governance, monitoring, and policy development.

FUTURE TRENDS: IMPLICATIONS FOR POLICY MAKERS AND GOVERNMENTS

WHIG provides the technology backbone of HNCO; however, for WHIG to function as

Figure 2. (a) The relationship among the operational domains in health care. Network-centric health care operations (NHCO) exist only in the territory where all three domains overlap; (b) The critical components of WHIG, including the smart portal, analytic nodes, and sensors (Adapted from von Lubitz & Wickramasinghe, 2005a, 2005b, 2005c, 2005d)

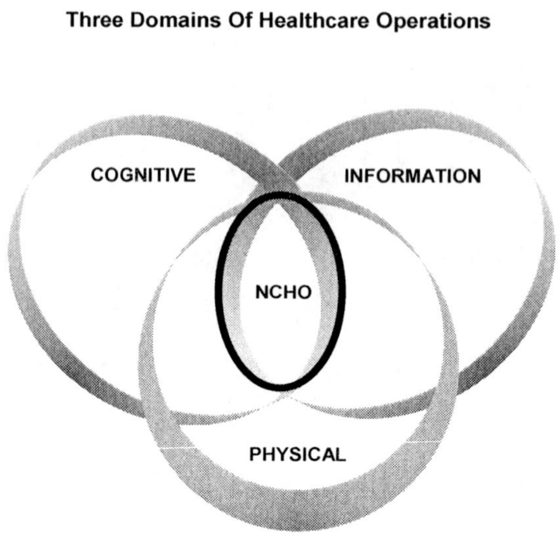

(a)

(b)

intended, providing pertinent information and germane knowledge in a seamless, effective, and efficient fashion to a decision maker anywhere anytime, various protocols and procedures must be developed at a global level. Without such standardization even the simplest of functions, such as the exchange of documents and other procurement information, connectivity, and e-commerce enabled benefits, become problematic while the critical goal of decreasing information asymmetry becomes unattainable. Unfortunately, standardization is woefully lacking in too many areas of healthcare let alone e-health. Given the global nature of WHIG, it is here that global bodies, such as the World Healthcare Organization (WHO) in conjunction with governments and policy makers, must develop policies, procedures, and standards that will enable the seamless functioning of WHIG. We identify four key areas that must be addressed:

1. **Information computer communication technology (IC^2T) architecture/infrastructure:** The generic architecture for most e-health initiatives is similar to that required by WHIG. However this infrastructure that consists of phone lines, fiber trunks and submarine cables, T1, T3 and OC-xx, ISDN, DSL and other high-speed services used by businesses as well as satellites, earth stations and teleports must be available globally.
   A sound technical infrastructure is an essential ingredient to the undertaking of e-health initiatives by any nation. Such infrastructures should also include telecommunications, electricity, access to computers, number of Internet hosts, number of ISPs (Internet service providers) and available bandwidth and broadband access. To offer a good multimedia content and thus provide a rich e-health experience, one would require a high bandwidth. ICT considerations are undoubtedly one of the most fundamental infrastructure requirements.
   Networks are now a critical component of the business strategies for organizations to compete globally. Having a fast microprocessor-based computer at home has no meaning unless you have high bandwidth based communication infrastructure available to connect computers with the ISP. With the explosion of the Internet and the advent of e-commerce, global networks need to be accessible, reliable, and fast to participate effectively in the global business environment. Telecommunications is a vital infrastructure for Internet access, hence also for e-commerce. One of the pioneering countries in establishing a complete and robust e-health infrastructure is Singapore which is in the process of wiring every home, office, and factory up to a broadband cable network which will cover 98% of Singaporean homes and offices (APEC, 2001; A report prepared for Asia Pacific Foundation, 2002a).
   It is estimated that over 70% of world telephone lines are in countries with 15% of the world's population (Parker, 1998). The average number of telephone lines in industrialized countries is one for every two persons as compared to 13 lines per thousand people in emerging economies such as India and China (ibid). A sound technical infrastructure is a key ingredient to the future economic health of any given nation and should be a priority for all governments.
   For example, in the Asia-Pacific region (APEC, 2001; Beal, 2000; Oxley & Yeung, 2001; A report prepared for Asia Pacific Foundation, 2002a; A study report on Thailand, 2001; Turpin, 2000), there are a number of "digital divides," not only between the richer and poorer countries, but divides between urban and rural populations and between more and less educated or affluent groups. Although the number of female Internet users in a number of countries in the region is catching up quickly with those of male users, women are less present when it comes to the actual use of the new technologies. Furthermore, in many of these countries, women make up the majority of the rural population, which is often marginalized in areas of telecommunication infrastructure, education, and training. Therefore, governments should formulate national IC^2T and e-commerce strategies that help to ensure universal access for all socioeconomic groups. A number of prerequisites for access to IC^2T include education and training, local content, sociocultural awareness, and a stable social, economic, and political environment. Appropriate technologies need to be developed to address the needs of disadvantaged communities.

2. **Building human capital/resources:** The disparity between educational standards of developed and developing nations in the world is significant (Roquilly, 2002; Sharma & Wickramasinghe, 2004a, b; UNCTAD, 2002). In order for healthcare network-centric operations to fully maximize the potential afforded by WHIG significant enhancement of human capital through education and training is required. Many of the developing nations through investment and foreign aid need to concentrate on developing human capacity, and increasing basic access to IC^2T, as well as rapidly increasing the presence and access to the Internet. Moreover, the governments of disadvantaged countries must also exercise significant international pressure to lower costs of hardware and software while, at the same time, contemplating to form larger multinational user blocks capable of effective implementation of ASP principles. E-commerce adoption in general requires improved e-commerce knowledge and skills, and improved language proficiency (especially in English as it is as the recognized principal technology / commerce language). For example, governments in many countries have started to introduce basic education in digital literacy in primary and secondary schools. Such training courses should be constantly updated as new innovations and practices emerge very rapidly in this field. Institutions responsible for human resource development of e-commerce personnel should provide appropriate incentives for e-commerce courses to be kept up-to-date. Increasing the number of programs or activities for human resource development for IC^2T and especially Internet use will only be effective if the education and training matches the changing needs of the industries concerned. It is important to note that only medical specialists require medical training but all people globally who need to interact with WHIG must have basic familiarity, training, and proficiency with use of IC^2T. Once again much of the onus falls on governments to set the agenda and priority for such an emphasis.
3. **Fostering consumer trust:** Consumers are also concerned about a number of dimensions of trust; trust in the security of value passed during electronic transactions with organizations that are "virtual" in a disconcertingly ineffable way and trust in the privacy of personal data arising from electronic transactions (Fjetland, 2002; Ghosh & Swaminath, 2001; Panagariya, 2000; Roquilly, 2002). Other than in North America, Japan, and integrated Europe, the infrastructure for e-commerce is not in place for effective e-commerce transactions. The key reason for slow penetration has been the scale of investment in infrastructure, and the small volume of transactions over which to amortize (Dutta, 1999; A report prepared for the Asia Pacific Foundation, 2002b).
   The security issue in particular is perceived as very important across the Asia-Pacific region, and the majority of SMEs, for instance, have a fear of electronics. This is primarily due to the low level of technology diffusion and awareness making it a psychological barrier for SMEs as confirmed in various reports (APEC, 2001; Beal, 2000; A report prepared for the Asia Pacific Foundation, 2002b). Many of these SMEs do not have technical expertise, and are not convinced that the technology standards, such as encryption, will protect them. Thus, SMEs are not willing to use electronic payment systems.
   Given such a general lack of trust in developing nations with using e-commerce, it is likely that the trust issue will be a significant factor in e-health initiatives given the general sensitivity of healthcare information. Once

again government and national bodies must make every attempt to foster trust. This will not be an easy task since in many developing countries people have a low level of trust for governments, corruption tends to be significant, and especially in rural areas, people tend to be very superstitious and leery of "modern methods." However, in many instances WHIG and healthcare network centric operations will offer these groups of people the best healthcare alternatives and thus significant effort must be made to build and foster trust.

Ethical concerns are inevitably related to healthcare operations based on network centricity. The notion of the governmental bodies having ready access to healthcare information of the citizens is among the major concerns in the U.S., and similar reservations are also voiced in Europe. The possibility of security breaches, similar to those that recently affected millions of credit card customers in the United States, demands a very stringent layer of protective layers that will assure prevention of commercial misuse of healthcare data. The seriousness of such intrusions is emphasized by the dynamic development of molecular biology and genetics that allow early determination of the likelihood to develop long-term debilitating diseases at the later stages of life. Misappropriation of such information may then affect the subsequent chances of employment, nature and availability of health insurance, and even acquisition of credit. While laws preventing such discrimination already exist in several Western countries, their enforcement is not simple and the fear of clandestine stratification into "health risk" classes whose quality and freedom of life is directly related to the long-term risk is a threat that needs to be addressed with utmost vigor now. At a less threatening, albeit far more practical level, the problems of the responsibility for the delivery of healthcare also need clarification.

Among the major obstacles to the development of an efficient national telemedicine network in the U.S. is the difficulty of assigning responsibility for treatment conducted across state borders. The dilemma becomes even more pertinent when healthcare expertise is projected across national borders. While there is no doubt that the rule of the "best medical practice" ought to be the prevailing one, the best practice has different definitions in different countries and what is considered the standard of care in one country may not be so in another. There is thus a clear need to develop generally accepted standards of delivery and the current acceptance of the concept of "evidence-based medicine" may offer the most useful foundation for further deliberations of such standards. These are but two of several problems that already either influence or are about to influence e-health in all its forms. The magnitude of network centricity and its global nature will add even greater urgency to the need for their effective operational rather than merely political or legislative solution. At a purely technical level, while network centricity strengthens the efficacy and economy of global healthcare, it may also have an impact on access to it. Ideally, network-centric operations will support a continuously broadening access to high quality healthcare across the entire globe. In practice, however, there is a chance it may support improvements there where the level of the preexisting technology and sophistication in its use are already high while leaving those who lag behind, yet needing rapid improvement of even basic healthcare in the same position they are now—desperately struggling to satisfy the most elementary healthcare needs of the local population. It is thus evident that introduction of network centricity and the creation of WHIG require a fundamentally different approach to the one currently practiced: they can be made functional only when a state of intense, multilateral, and determinedly synergistic collaboration exists between corporate and governmental entities not only at the national but, even more importantly, at the international level. Ultimately, transparency, international synergism, and adherence to the highest ethical standards of operations will be among the most instrumental factors to convince the users (i.e., both deliverers and recipients of healthcare) that network centricity in healthcare offers tangible benefits that have been unattainable prior to the implementation of the concept.

4. **Creating synergies between national and regional economic blocks:** For WHIG and HNCO to be fully functional, it is vital that synergies are created between national and economic blocks. For example, in similarity to the EU, all countries in the Asia-Pacific region should improve access to IC^{2}Ts, design the necessary legal and institutional frameworks to educate the governments, businesses, and civil society to more efficiently use IC^{2}Ts in their daily practices, and create an environment for further development of IC^{2}T use in general and in particular with a focus on healthcare. There is a tremendous need to support the integration and interoperability of regional e-commerce initiatives through various international and regional economic blocks such as the Asia-Pacific Economic Cooperation (APEC), North American Free Trade Agreement (NAFTA), and the European Union.

   Another critical aspect that requires significant consideration to enable and facilitate the required synergies is that pertaining to legal and ethical issues. In general the Internet community has developed its own distinctive culture and a great part many of these behavioural norms function outside the realm of International Law given the current maturity of International Internet Law (Commission of the European Communities, 2003; De Ly, 1992, 2000; Nielson, 2000; Polanski, 2005; Polanski & Johnston, 2002). Given the sensitive nature of much of the information contained with healthcare interactions, this poses a significant problem and major stumbling block for the adoption of HNCO. This is clearly an area that requires significant discussion and will form the center of future research; we mention it here only in passing to note that it remains as yet a key area that needs to be addressed

CONCLUSION

It is beyond the scope of this chapter to discuss the details of the technology configuration of WHIG or provide guidelines for practioners. Interested readers can refer to other research (von Lubitz & Wickramasinghe, 2005a, 2005b, 2005c, 2005d; von Lubitz, Wickramasinghe, & Yanovsky, 2005) for details. The primary focus here is to highlight the key role for governments if we are to ever realize the full benefits of e-health.

The idea of WHIG and HNCO is to span many parties and geographic dimensions. To enable such a far reaching coverage, significant amounts of document exchange and information flows must be accommodated. Standardization is the key for this. Once a country decides to undertake e-health initiatives and become a "WHIG member," standardization policies, protocols, and procedures must be developed at the outset to ensure the full realization of the goals of e-health. The transformation to e-health by any country cannot be successfully attained without the deliberate establishment of standardization policies, protocols, and procedures which play a significant role in the adoption of e-health and the reduction of many structural impediments (Panagariya, 2000; Samiee, 1998). Fortunately, the main infrastructure of WHIG is the Internet which imposes the most widely and universally accepted standard protocols such as TCP/IP and http. It is the existence of these standard protocols that has led to the widespread adoption of the Internet for e-commerce applications.

Access to the technologies of e-commerce is defined by the WTO (World Trade Organization) as consisting of two critical components: (1) access to Internet services and (2) access to e-services (Health Insurance Portability and Accountability Act, 2001); the former deals with the user infrastructure, while the latter pertains to specific commitments to electronically accessible services. The user infrastructure includes number of Internet hosts and number of Web sites, Web users as a percent of the population as well as ISP availability and costs for consumers, PC penetration level, and so forth. Integral to user infrastructure is the diffusion rate of PCs and Internet usage. The United States and the United Kingdom have experienced the greatest penetration of home computers (Samiee, 1998). For developing countries, such as India and China, there is, however, a very low PC penetration and teledensity. In such a setting it is a considerable challenge then to offer e-health, since a large part of the population is not able to afford to join the e-commerce bandwagon. Countries, thus have to balance local call charges, rentals, subscription charges, and so forth, otherwise the majority of citizens will find these costs a disincentive. This is particularly significant for developing and emerging nations where access prices tend to be out of reach for most of the population. Upcoming new technologies hold the promise to increase the connectivity as well as affordability level and developing countries will need to seriously consider these technologies. In addition to access to PCs and the Internet, computer literacy is important and users must be familiar not only with the use of computers and pertinent software products but also the benefits and potential uses of the Internet and World Wide Web (ibid).

The key challenges regarding e-health use include (1) cost effectiveness that is less costly than traditional healthcare delivery; (2) functionality and ease of use: that is, they should enable and facilitate many uses for physicians and other healthcare users by combining various types and forms of data as well as be easy to use; and (3) they must be secure. One of the most significant legislative regulations in the U.S. is the Health Insurance Portability and Accountability Act (HIPAA) (2001).

Given the nature of healthcare and the sensitivity of healthcare data and information, it is incumbent on governments not only to mandate regulations that will facilitate the exchange of healthcare documents between the various healthcare stakeholders but also to provide protection of privacy and the rights of patients (Dyer, 2001). Some countries, such as China and Singapore, even control access to certain sites for moral, social, and political reasons while elsewhere transnational data flows are hindered by a plethora of regulations aimed at protecting domestic technology and related human resource markets (Ghosh & Swaminatha, 2001; Gupta, 1992; Samiee, 1998). Irrespective of the type of healthcare system; that is, whether 100% government driven, 100% private or a combination thereof, it is clear that some governmental role is required to facilitate successful e-health initiatives.

HNCO also serves to underscore the inextricable connection and intertwining of e-health and e-government which to date has rarely been researched let alone acknowledged. Moreover, for HCNO to become adopted successfully, it requires governments to develop policies and protocols which will in turn facilitate its usability. We identify four key areas that will have an important impact on the development of the necessary policies and protocols as IT education, morbidity, cultural/social dimensions, and world economic standing as elaborated upon below. It is interesting to note that these areas also impact the development of numerous e-government initiatives (Turban et al., 2004), once again highlighting the inextricable link between e-health and e-government.

- **IT education:** A sophisticated, well educated population boosts competition and hastens innovation. According to Michael Porter, one of the key factors to a country's strength in an industry is strong customer support (Porter, 1990). Thus, a strong domestic market leads to the growth of competition which leads to innovation and the adoption of technology enabled solutions to provide more effective and efficient services such as e-health and telemedicine. As identified earlier, the health consumer is the key driving force in pushing e-health initiatives. We conjecture that a more IT educated healthcare consumer would then provide stronger impetus for e-health adoption.
- **Morbidity rate:** There is a direct relationship between health education and awareness and the overall health standing of a country. Therefore, a more health conscious society, which tends to coincide with a society that has a lower morbidity rate, is more likely to embrace e-health initiatives. Furthermore, higher morbidity rates tend to indicate the existence of more basic health needs (World Health Organization, 2003) and hence treatment is more urgent than the practice of preventative medicine and thus e-health could be considered an unrealistic luxury and, in some instances, such as when a significant percentage of a population is suffering from malnutrition related diseases, is even likely to be irrelevant, at least in the short term. Thus, we conjecture that the modifying impact of morbidity rate is to prioritize the level of spending on e-health vs. other basic healthcare needs.
- **Cultural/social dimensions:** Healthcare has been shaped by each nation's own set of cultures, traditions, payment mechanisms, and patient expectations. While the adoption of e-health, to a great extent, dilutes this cultural impact, social and cultural dimensions will still be a moderating influence on any countries e-health initiatives. Another aspect of the cultural/social dimension relates to the presentation language of the content of the e-health repositories. The entire world does not speak English, so the e-health solutions have to be offered in many other languages. The e-health supporting content in Web servers/sites must be offered in local languages, supported by pictures and universal icons. This becomes a particularly important consideration when we look at the adoption and diffusion of evidence-based medicine as it will mean that much of the available evidence and case study data will not be easily accessible globally due to language barriers.

Therefore, for successful e-health initiatives it is important to consider cultural dimensions. For instance, an international e-commerce study by International Data Corp. indicates that Web surfing and buying habits differ substantially from country to country (Wilson, 1999) and this would then have a direct impact on their comfort to use e-commerce generally and e-health in particular, especially as e-health addresses a more fundamental need. Hence, the adoption of e-health is directly related to ones comfort with using the technology and this in turn is influenced in a major way by cultural dimensions. Also connected with cultural aspects is the relative entrepreneurial spirit of a country. For example, a study (Hofstede, 1984) indicates that in a cultural context, Indians score high on "uncertainty avoidance" criteria when compared to their Western counterparts. As a result, for example, Indians do not accept change very easily and are hostile towards innovation. This then would potentially pose a challenge to the starting up of e-health initiatives whose success depends on widespread adoption for their technological innovations. Thus, we conjecture that fear of risk and absence of an entrepreneurial mindset as well as other cultural/social dimensions can also impact the success of e-health initiatives in a given country.

- **World economic standing:** Economies of the future will be built around the Internet. All governments are very aware of the importance and critical role that the Internet will play on a country's economy. This makes it critical that appropriate funding levels and budgetary allocations become a key component of governmental fiscal policies so that such initiatives will form the bridge between a traditional healthcare present and a promising e-health future. Thus, the result of which would determine success of effective e-health implementations and consequently have the potential to enhance a country's economy and future growth.

A healthy society is in the interests of all governments. As labor costs increase and productivity is critical to economic development, a healthy population is naturally able to contribute more significantly to increasing GDP. Coupled with the fact that healthcare remains the most expensive item for any government, it behooves governments to make healthcare a top priority on their agenda. The doctrine of HNCO serves to outline a coherent and systematic approach for harnessing the full potential of IC^2T for healthcare and the ability to realize the promises of e-health. However, if this is to occur, e-health must become a top priority on all government agendas. Moreover, governments must go further than just acknowledge the importance of e-health to focusing their energies and efforts to address the key impediments we have identified and that currently preclude the ubiquitous adoption of HNCO.

The World Economic Forum's Global competitiveness ranking measures the relative global competitiveness of a country. This ranking takes into account factors such as physical infrastructure, bureaucracy, and corruption. It is a simple extrapolation of the combination of these factors to postulate that the combination of a weak physical infrastructure with high levels of bureaucracy and corruption will constitute a significant impediment to the establishment of successful e-health initiatives. Surely, network-centric healthcare operations will not change these realities. On the other hand, the possibility for a rural healthcare provider working in an even most oppressive political and economical environment to enter WHIG and benefit from the combined global healthcare expertise will be without doubt a step in the right direction. And many steps in the right direction will ultimately help to redress the level of current inequalities in access to the most fundamental right of all humans across the globe — health.

REFERENCES

Affuah, A., & Tucci, C. (2001). *Internet business models and strategies*. Boston: McGraw-Hill Irwin.

Alberts, D. S., Garstka, J. J., & Stein, F. P. (2000). *Network centric warfare: Developing and leveraging information superiority* (CCRP Publication Series, pp. 1-284). Washington, DC: Department of Defense. Retrieved May 5, 2006, from http://www.dodccrp.org/publications/pdf/Alberts_NCW.pdf

APEC. (2001). *The new economy and APEC*. Report to the Economic Committee of APEC.

Retrieved May 5, 2006, from http://www.diw.de/deutsch/produkte/veranstaltungen/docs/apec-report.html

Arellano, M. G., & Weber, G. I. (1998). Issues in identification and linkage of patient records across an integrated delivery system. *Journal of Healthcare Information Management, 12*, 43-52

Beal, T. (2000). *SMEs and the World Wide Web: Opportunities and prospects.* In A. M. Asri (Ed.), *Small and medium enterprises in Asia Pacific* (Vol. III Development Prospects, pp. 102-134). Commack, NY: Nova Science Publishers.

Boyd, J. R. (1987). *COL USAF, in "Patterns of Conflict", unpublished briefing.* Retrieved from "Essence of Winning and Losing", http://www.d-n-i.net

Cebrowski, A. K, & Garstka, J. J. (1998). Network-centric warfare: Its origin and future. *US Nav. Inst. Proc., 1*, 28-35

Checkland, P., & Scholes, J. (1990). *Soft systems methodology in action.* New York: Wiley.

Churchman, C. (1968). *The systems approach.* New York: Del Publishing.

Commission of the European Communities (2003). *First report on the application of Directive 2003/31/EC of the European Parliament and of the Council of 8 June 2000 on certain legal aspects of information society services, in particular, electronic commerce, in the Internal Market (Directive on electronic commerce)* (pp. 1-25). Brussels.

d'Alessandro, D. M., & Kreiter, C. D. (1999). Improving usage of pediatric information on the Internet: The Virtual Children's Hospital. *Pediatrics, 104*, e55.

De Ly, F. (1992). *International business law and Lex Mercatoria.* Amsterdam, London, New York, Tokyo: T. M. C. Asser Instituut — The Hague.

De Ly, F. (2000). Emerging new perspectives regarding Lex Mercatoria in an era of increasing globalization. In *Festschrift für Otto Sandrock* (pp. 179-204). Heidelberg: Verlag Recht und Wirtschaft.

Dutta, A. (1999). The physical infrastructure for electronic commerce in developing nations: Historic trends and the impacts of privatization. *International Journal of Electronic Commerce, 2*(1), 63-82.

Dyer, K. A. (2001). Ethical challenges of medicine and health on the internet: A review. *JMIR, 3*(2). Retrieved from http://www.jmir.org/2001/2/e23

E-Health and the Practicing Physician. (n.d.). Retrieved May 5, 2006, from http://www.medscape.com

E-Health in the Medical Field. (n.d.). Retrieved May 5, 2006, from http://www.americantelemed.org/ehealth/ehealthH.htm

Eysenbach, G. (2001). Journal of Medical Internet Research is now indexed in Medline. *Journal of Medical Internet Research, 3*(3), e25.

Eysenbach, G., & Diepgen, T. L. (1998). Towards quality management of medical information on the Internet: Evaluation, labeling, and filtering of information. *BMJ, 317*, 1496-1500.

Fjetland, M. (2002). Global commerce and the privacy clash. *Information Management Journal, 36*(1), 54-58.

Geiger, G., Merriles, K., Walo, R., Gordon, D., & Kunov, H. (1995). An analysis of the paper-based health record: Information content and its implications for electronic patient records. *Medinfo, 8*(1), 295.

Ghosh, A. K., & Swaminatha, T. M. (2001, February). Software security and privacy risks in mobile e-commerce. *Communications of the ACM, 44*(2), 51-58.

Glaser, J. (2002). *The strategic application of information technology in health care organizations* (2nd ed.). San Francisco: Jossey Bass.

Gupta, U. (1992). Global networks: Promises and challenges. *Information Systems Management, 9*, 28-32.

Haag, S., Cummings, M., & McCubbrey, D. (2004). *Management information systems for the Information Age* (4th ed.). Boston: McGraw-Hill Irwin.

Health Insurance Portability and Accountability Act (HIPPA). (2001). *Privacy compliance executive summary.* Washington, DC: Protegrity Inc.

Health Technology Center. (2000). *A survey conducted for the Health Technology Center (HealthTech) by Harris Interactive in cooperation with Pricewaterhouse Coopers and the Institute for the Future (IFTF).* Retrieved May 5, 2006, from http://www.ncddr.org/cgi-bin/good-bye.cgi?url=http://www.healthtechcenter.org

Hofstede, G. (1984). *Culture's consequences, international work related values.* Beverly Hills: Sage.

Institute of Medicine. (2001). *Crossing the quality chasm: A new health system for the 21st Century Committee on Quality of Health Care in America Institute of Medicine.* Washington, DC: National Academy Press.

Jessup, L., & Valacich, J. (2005). *Information systems today* (2nd ed.). Upper Saddle River, NJ: Prentice Hall.

Kalakota, R., & Robinson, M. (1999). *E-business roadmap for success.* Reading, MA: Addison-Wesley.

Laudon, K., & Laudon, J. (2004). *Management information systems* (7th ed.). Upper Saddle River, NJ: Prentice Hall.

Lehto, M. R. (1991). A proposed conceptual model of human behaviour and its implications for design of warning. *Percept. Mot. Skills, 73*, 595-611.

McGowan, J. J., Overhag, J. M., Barnes, M., & McDonald, C. J. (2004). Indianapolis I3: The third generation integrated advanced information management systems. *J Med Libr Assoc, 92*, 179-187.

Nielsen, J. (2000). *Designing Web usability: The practice of simplicity.* Indianapolis, IN: New Riders Publishing.

O'Brien, J. (2005). *Management information system* (6th ed.). Boston: Irwin McGraw-Hill.

Odyssey Research. (n.d.). Retrieved May 5, 2006, from http://www.odysseyresearch.org

Oxley, J. E., & Yeung, B. (2001). E-commerce readiness: Institutional environment and international competitiveness. *Journal of International Business Studies, 32*(4), 705-723.

Panagariya, A. (2000). E-commerce, WTO and developing countries. *The World Economy, 23*(8), 959-978.

Parker, B. (1998). *Globalization and business practices.* Beverley Hills: Sage.

Polanski, P. (2005, June 17-19). Common practices in the electronic commerce and their legal significance. In *Proceedings of the 18th Bled E-Commerce Conference*, Bled, Slovenia (pp. 170-189).

Polanski, P. P., & Johnston, R. B. (2002, January 5-8). International custom as a source of law in global electronic commerce. In *Proceedings of the 35th Hawaii International Conference on System Sciences* (CD-ROM), Big Island, HI.

Porter, M. (1990). *The competitive advantage of nations.* New York: Free Press.

PricewaterhouseCoopers Healthcare Practice. (2003). Retrieved May 5, 2006, from http://www.pwchealth.com

Prietula, M. J., Feltovich, P. J., & Marchak, F. (2000). Factors influencing analysis of complex cognitive tasks: A framework and example from industrial process control. *Human Factors, 42*, 56-74.

Reinhardt, U. E., Hussey, P. S., & Anderson, G. F. (2002). Cross-national comparisons of health systems using OECD data. *Health Affairs, 3*, 169-181.

Report prepared for Asia Pacific Foundation. (2002a). *Asia-Pacific E-Commerce: B2B & B2C*. Retrieved May 5, 2006, from http://www.gii.co.jp/english/em11033_asia_ec_toc.html

Report prepared for Asia Pacific Foundation. (2002b). *E-commerce and Asia Pacific, Castle Asia Pacific*. Retrieved May 5, 2006, from http://www.gii.co.jp/english/em11033_asia_ec_toc.html

Roquilly, C. (2002). Closed distribution networks and e-commerce: Antitrust issues. *International Review of Law, Computers & Technology, 16*(1), 81-93.

Samiee, S. (1998). The Internet and international marketing: Is there a fit? *Journal of Interactive Marketing, 12*(4), 5-20.

Sharma, S., & Wickramasinghe, N. (2004a). E-health with knowledge management: Areas for tomorrow. In N. Wickramasinghe, J. Gupta, & S. Sharma (Eds.), *Creating knowledge-based healthcare organizations* (pp. 110-124). Hershey, PA: Idea Group Publishers.

Sharma, S., & Wickramasinghe, N. (2004b). Obstacles to SMEs for e-adoption in the Asia Pacific region in ebusiness, egovernment & small and medium enterprises: Opportunities and challenges. In Al-Qirim et al. (Eds.), *E-business, E-government & Small and Medium Enterprises: Opportunities and Challenges* (pp. 112-133). Hershey, PA: Idea Group Publishing.

Sieving, P. C. (1999). Factors driving the increase in medical information on the Web: One American perspective. *Journal of Medical Internet Research*, 1. Retrieved May 5, 2006, from http://www.jmir.org/1999/1/e3

Stats and facts. (2002). Global health cost and care comparisons. *Manage Care Interface, 15*, 66-77.

Stein, P. (1998). *Observations on the emergence of network centric warfare*. Retrieved May 5, 2006, from http://www.dodccrp.org/research/ncw/stein/_observations/steincw.htm

Stiglitz, J. E. (2003). *The roaring nineties.* New York: Norton & Co.

Study report on Thailand. (2001). *SMEs and e-commerce*, Asia Pacific Foundation.

The higher the connection speed, the higher the value: Broadband use as an indication of value amongst e-health users. (2001). *Cyber Dialogue Cybercitizen Health Trend Report 2001*, No. 49.

Tole, J. R., Stephens, A. T., Harris, R. L., Sr., & Eprath, A. R. (1982). Visual scanning behavior and mental worlkload of aircraft pilots. *Aviat. Space Environ. Med., 53*, 54-61.

Turban, E., King, D., Lee, J., & Viehland, D. (2004). *Electronic commerce.* Upper Saddle River, NJ: Prentice Hall.

Turpin, T. (2000). SMEs and technology diffusion in Asia Pacific-Pacific economies: Indonesia a case-study. In *Proceedings of the Annual Conference of the Academy of International Business Southeast Asia Pacific Region, International Business Research Institute,* University of Wollongong, Australia (CD-ROM).

Umhoff, B., & Winn, J. (1999, May 1). The healthcare profit pool: Who stands to gain and lose in the digital economy. *Health Forum Journal.*

von Lubitz, D., & Wickramasinghe, N. (2005a). Healthcare and technology: The doctrine of networkcentric healthcare. *International Journal Healthcare Technology Management, 4*, 322-343.

von Lubitz, D., & Wickramasinghe, N. (2005b). Networkcentric healthcare: Outline of the entry portal concept. *International Journal of Electronic Business, 1*, 16-28.

von Lubitz, D., & Wickramasinghe, N. (2005c). Networkcentric healthcare and bioinformatics. *International Journal on Expert Systems.*

von Lubitz, D., & Wickramasinghe, N. (2005d). Creating germane knowledge in dynamic environments. *International Journal of Innovation Learning.*

von Lubitz, D., & Wickramasinghe, N. (2006, January). Networkcentric healthcare: Strategies, structures and technologies for managing knowledge. In *Proceedings of the IRMA Conference*, Washington, DC.

von Lubitz, D., Wickramasinghe, N., & Yanovsky, G. (2005). Networkcentric healthcare operations: The telecommunications structure. *International Journal on Global Technology.*

von Lubitz, D., et al. (2004). Medical readiness in the context of operations other than war: Development of first responder readiness using OODA. In *Proceedings of the Loop Thinking and Advanced Distributed Interactive Simulation Technology Symposium*, Istanbul, Turkey. Retrieved May 5, 2006, from the Defence and National Intelligence Network, http://www.d-n-i.net/fcs/pdf/von_lubitz_1rp_ooda.pdf

Web Based Second Opinion. (n.d.). Retrieved May 5, 2006, from http://www.eclevelandclinic.org

Wickramasinghe, N., Fadlalla, A., Geisler, E., & Schaffer, J. (2004). A framework for assessing e-health preparedness. *International Journal on Electronic Healthcare (IJEH)1*(3), 316-334.

Wickramasinghe, N., Geisler, E., & Schaffer, J. (2005). Assessing e-health. In Spiel & Schuring (Eds.), *E-health systems diffusion and use: The innovation, the user and the use it model* (pp. 294-323). Hershey, PA: Idea Group.

Wickramasinghe, N., & Ginzberg, M. (2001). Integrating knowledge workers and the organization: The role of IT. *International Journal Healthcare Quality Assurance, 14*(6-7), 245-253.

Wickramasinghe, N., & Mills, G. (2002). Integrating e-commerce and knowledge management: What does the Kaiser experience really tell us? *International Journal of Accounting Information Systems, 3*(2), 83-98.

Wickramasinghe, N., & Sharma, S. (2004). Key factors that hinder SMEs in succeeding in today's knowledge based economy. *International Journal of Management and Enterprise Development, 2*(2), 141-158.

Wilson, T. (1999). Not a global village after all? Consumer behavior varies widely by country. *Internetweek, 792*(13), 792.

World Health Organization (WHO). (2003). Retrieved May 5, 2006, from http://www.emro.who.int/ehealth/

Chapter 5.15
The Core Governmental Perspectives of E-Health

Antti Syväjärvi
University of Lapland, Finland

Jari Stenvall
University of Lapland, Finland

INTRODUCTION

Public healthcare is facing huge future challenges in order to deal with rising costs, growing demands of customers, information flow, demographic changes, and aging population. The healthcare service sector can be seen as an information intensive area during an era of innovation and information technology (cf. Bellamy & Taylor, 1998). According to McLaughlin, Rosen, Skinner, and Webster (1999), it is common to assume that technological interventions are almost inevitable and it is humans' duty, at least to some extent, to follow the suggested development. In the organizational level of public healthcare, high expectations about the technology and its new possibilities are introduced. Additionally, the customers can seek support and advice for their healthcare needs from thousands online connections at any time of a day (e.g., Silber, 2003). The European Commission (2004) states how "eHealth offers European citizens important opportunities for improved access to better health systems" (p. 22). This trend has implications to human beings and governments.

The electronic health services produced by the information and communication technology (ICT) belong to the era of e-government. The e-government can be seen as an electronic exchange of information and services between different actors (cf. Mälkiä, Anttiroiko, & Savolainen, 2004; Oliver & Sanders, 2004). The development of information society throughout the last decades has brought up possibilities to adapt, modify, and reorganize healthcare practices and services (e.g., Gallivan, 2001; Turner, Fraser, Muir Grau, & Toth, 2002). The ICT has been used as a tool to reorganize best organizational practices, information management, and government. The ICT has also given a possibility to produce tailored healthcare services and to gain improvements in cost-effectiveness, access, safety, and quality of public healthcare services (Bates et al., 2001; Whitten et al., 2002).

In the future, the healthcare organizations in public sectors will confront many challenges by means of the ICT implementation. This situation is considered here both as the function of healthcare organizations and as the supply of knowledge intensive public health services. The current viewpoint presumes a paradigm that is structured on the basis of specific conceptualization. The purpose of this article is to conceptualize the complex topic of e-health from the governmental viewpoint and to clarify the best organizational practices. Special notation is also given for human resources, information management and the ICT implementation. Finally, some future trends are shortly discussed.

BACKGROUND

Experts define e-health differently and the term has some overlapping conceptual views. The term "e-health" is derived from the term "electronic commerce" (i.e., e-commerce), which was introduced in the mid-1990s to reflect the growing commercial use of the Internet. The e-health (cf. Eysenbach, 2001; European Commission, 2004; Silber, 2003), when recognized as a governmental issue, refers to the use of ICT applications or information systems to improve or enable health and healthcare services. Now it also refers to the main organizational and resource based factors before, during, and after an introduction of ICT. Finally, the term refers to best practices and implementations produced or needed to confront and manage with the ICT-based healthcare. The e-health concerns customers, patients, professionals, but additionally the whole primary healthcare, home care, and organizations like hospitals. It engages the terms like telemedicine, telematics, telehealth, medical and health informatics, interactive health communication, and so forth. To conclude, the e-health as a governmental concept give good reason for to describe the abovementioned combination by the means of three conceptual dimensions.

CONCEPTUAL DIMENSIONS OF THE E-HEALTH PARADIGM: THE GOVERNMENTAL PERSPECTIVE

In the first dimension, the e-health connection can be found by referring to ICT applications and information systems in healthcare and in supporting functions (cf. McGinnis, 1997; Turban, McLean, & Wetherbe, 1999). In many cases, this has included telemedicine and health informatics as patients have been informed, examined and treated over distance by using appropriate applications (e.g., Hailey, Roine, & Ohinmaa, 2002). The e-health is seen now through issues like information system, standardization, and system quality (e.g., digital referrals, data security, access, and privacy, etc.). Also, the usability or user-friendly orientation should be placed under a close scrutiny. Hence, the applications and systems require understanding about technology and its effect on organizational structures, processes, and actors.

Figure 1. E-health concept according to the core governmental dimensions

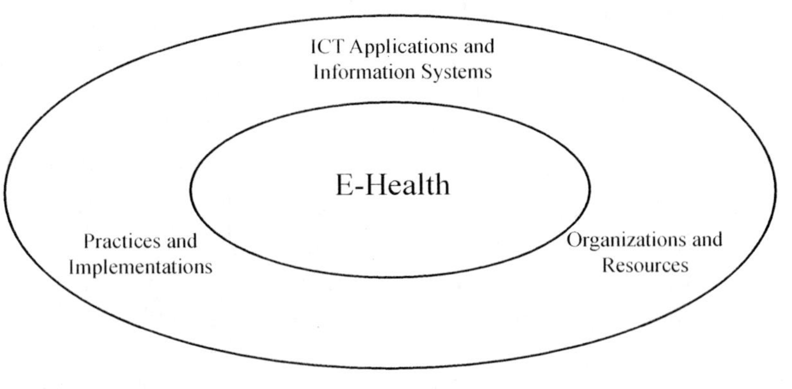

Secondly, it is considered that by e-health it is possible to renew and to produce more effective healthcare practices and implementations. Now the e-health is studied typically in conjunction with key processes like the management of ICT applications and information (Plsek & Wilson, 2001; Tachakra, El Habashy, & Dawood, 2001; Walker & Whetton, 2002) and by the means of best practices or ICT implementations in healthcare (e.g., Paré & Elam, 1999). The introduction of technology may support or change operational practices in organizations. The operational aspect engages also electronic healthcare services as the e-health services are multileveled. Services represent, for example, the possibility of consumers to interact online, the possibilities for institution-to-institution data transmissions, and the possibilities for peer-to-peer communication of consumers. However, the overall question is about the best practices and implementations in order to successfully complete the e-health in service sector.

As third dimension, the organization and its various resources (e.g., economical and humanistic) have been under intensive study. For example, Parente and Dunbar (2001) found that hospitals with integrated information systems have higher total and operating financial margins than those without these systems. Whitten et al. (2002) did a systematic review and found no good evidence that telemedicine is cost-effective. Additionally, the e-health can be seen in terms of human resources. This is the case, for example, with the acceptance of ICT-based organizational solutions (Mathieson, Peacock, & Chin, 2001) and with the professional human resources (e.g., Syväjärvi, Stenvall, Harisalo, & Jurvansuu, 2005). The interest has also been in health services and in policy to provide a diverse range of services (e.g., Silber, 2003; Turner et al., 2002). Both customers and professionals can be seen as key actors, because they use applications and participate in electronic service interaction (e.g., Hailey et al., 2002).

Hence, the e-health from governmental perspective can be defined as health service and information delivered through different technologies. Applications of the ICT and information systems support health, healthcare, and health services. In case of current governmental perspective, the dimension of ICT applications and information systems concentrates mainly on technological system, standardization, and usability issues. The ICT applications can be seen as architectures to understand and plan information system components in the form of an organizational infrastructure. The most crucial questions are the standardization of information systems and their usability in organizational environment.

It seems worldwide that open technical standards to provide e-health are lacking. McGinnis (1997) studied health informatics and stated the critical importance of data exchange standards for communication between healthcare providers. The usability instead is traditionally defined (cf. Isomäki, 2002) by attributes like learnability, efficiency, memorability, errors and satisfaction. However, without neglecting the human factors like learning, sensation, and perception, memory, problem solving, and so forth. An optimal system should be easy to learn, it should be efficient to use, the system should be easy to remember, the error rate with the system should be low, and the system should be pleasant to use. Corresponding arguments of usability and human-centered design are also offered by ISO quality standards.

Second governmental dimension of e-health was about practices and implementations. E-health as practices and implementations emphasizes the need to combine knowledge and the use of ICT in various ways. In this article, the management as an organizational process has the viewpoint of ICT-based e-health. McLaughlin et al. (1999) claimed that in hospitals it is needed a wider perspective than social, since managers and users need to have a commitment to longtime innovative process. Clark (1995) suggested that leaders have the main responsibility for development work, because the problem with technological changes was frequently that people and technology didn't meet or people didn't participate.

The management has also direct link to best practices in organization and its health service production. Martin (2000) claimed that the quality of public services and cost-effectiveness depend on management. Smith (2004) studied how to inspire and motive professional service teams and indicated the importance of discussion and collective responsibility. The e-health can be seen as a part of knowledge intensive public services in a knowledge intensive society. The previous conceptualization invoked to describe the current e-health practices and implementations more generally as seminal goals for public healthcare organizations. However, it should be reminded that information technology does not necessarily lead so radical organizational changes as expected (Bellamy & Taylor, 1998; Nicholson, 2003).

The third governmental dimension of e-health involved organizations and resources. The governments try to manage with the increasing costs of public administration. Simultaneously the need to improve the cost-effectiveness of public healthcare has become apparent. One way to resolve the dilemma has been the use of electronic health services. However, the results have been controversial. Whitten et al. (2002) made a massive evaluation and they included 24 of 612 identified articles presenting cost-benefit information. About 30% of those 24 tried to solve the economic function of telemedicine without a clear outcome.

However, in public organizations the ICT has had often a transformative role. The e-health is understood and projected as being able to reshape the way healthcare services are delivered. The demands set by stakeholders are obvious. Governments want accountability to ensure that the funds are used effectively. Healthcare providers want a better quality of work life through the ICT tools. Patients and customers want access to the high quality healthcare service. One response has been the virtual life of organizations (cf. Nicholson, 2003). The virtual life in current context can be defined as a group of people or organizations that interact through interdependent task guided by common good purpose. In addition, the actors have learned to interact across space, time and inter-professional or organizational boundaries by using the ICT-based e-health solutions (Syväjärvi et al., 2005).

ORGANIZATIONS AND E-HEALTH: IMPLEMENTATION AND HUMAN RESOURCES AS CRUCIAL FACTORS

Numerous organizational e-health projects with various goals are ongoing worldwide under public administration. For example, the European Commission launched an Action Plan for a European eHealth area in 2004. The aim is to support EU member states to materialize the benefits available from e-health, and to respond to the growing need for coordinated activities of e-health (European Commission, 2004). These kinds of activities denote a coherent agenda for the implementation of e-health. Hence, the e-health implementation may cause changes in organizational design and such changes typically require new organizational structures, processes, and personnel arrangements. From governmental perspective, the e-health either allows or forces an organization to rearrange especially its human resources. The focus is thus to analyze the relationship between e-health implementation and HR-centered organizational practice. Human resources are considered as a key area of e-health implementation.

Human resources have indeed an essential function both in knowledge intensive healthcare practices and in knowledge innovative services. The implementation of e-health has indeed organizational effects as it should concurrently support the patient mobility, facilitate the citizen-centered healthcare, but particularly to provide healthcare professionals new tools to sustain or improve the quality of public healthcare service. The implementation should allow greater flexibility, for example in case of inter-professional and organizational practices, to enhance information and knowledge exchange between humans. It is given here a synopsis of e-health implementation that contains previous governmental dimensions.

Many nations worldwide are known as countries with high technology. The extensive use of ICT and the adoption of various technological solutions represent everyday practice. In these knowledge intensive nations, the public policy has been largely based on the assumption that society will develop and succeed by focusing on ICT. For example in many European countries the information technology has been harnessed to promote social welfare. The ICT has been used for strengthening and developing the welfare society. The public service organizations and citizens thus have confronted the wave of e-government (e.g., Mälkiä et al., 2004; Oliver & Sanders, 2004). At the same time research has concentrated on the possibilities, quality, and costs of technology. However, what the implemented information technology means to public health service sector, public organizations, and especially to organizational human resources has usually received less attention. Under the issues of e-government and public services, there are several approaches to the human-centered e-health implementation.

Firstly, from the point of how the employees' attitudes and approval affect the success of implementation (Mathieson et al., 2001). This kind of approach has produced theoretical models to explain how implementation depends on reasoned action of humans and the technology acceptance. Considering a more professional view, for example, the doctors who have received training in technology and understand technological concepts are more likely to grasp the positive impact of technology in healthcare (Paré & Elam, 1999). Burge, Creps, and Wright (2001) assumed that doctors are key persons to adopt technology in healthcare organizations, however, the doctors are not enthusiastically accepting the technology if it does not help everyday work. Tachakra et al. (2001) suggest that telemedicine includes the ability to rearrange the distribution of work; especially concerning the tasks of doctors and nurses. The ICT-based e-health seems not to be a question of single profession as it reflects over entire professional work society.

Secondly, the ICT has been studied by the innovative theories. Again models have been presented how a technological innovation is adopted in an organization through various phases. Gallivan (2001) developed a frame of references how to merge a technical innovation into the organizational operation. Thus, there are themes like management support, high resources, organization culture, own responsibility of learning, broad work roles, work security, and individual characteristics, which either increase or decrease the innovative implementation. These studies argue that the success of information technology in organizations more generally reflects the systems of innovations' advance in organizations. Finally, as technology is implemented to organization more clear and exact strategies accompanied with leading spokesmen are required (Walker & Whetton, 2002).

Thirdly, the setup "e-health vs. implementation" stimulates the leadership and management dimensions. Clark (1995) suggests that the use of ICT is an organizational issue that needs efforts in the direction of change. The leaders have thus a responsibility to create and sustain participation, but also trust (cf. Harisalo & Stenvall, 2004). In good accordance, Plsek and Wilson (2001) found complexity in leadership and management of healthcare organizations. They assumed that leaders should found ways to make the change more attractive and meaningful for workers. This is done by securing the open information flow of good practices. The earlier observation about the complexity of knowledge intensive health services denotes the importance of information management. The information management refers to interdisciplinary procedures designed to provide and improve the appropriate information systems and resources by planning, organizing, executing, and evaluating necessary management operations. Thus, the human resource perspective both involves multi-professional diversity practices and presupposes the proper activities of human resource management (Syväjärvi et al., 2005).

Fourthly, the human resource centered ICT implementation considers the development of information systems according to usability factors, organizational practice, and the humanization of computerized information systems (Cummings & Worley, 2001; Isomäki, 2002). The usability of information systems is included in this framework. The information system development (ISD) can be introduced by different phases. It is stressed that the ISD tasks must be completed with knowledge concerning users and contextual analyses. Isomäki (2002) found that only a few information system designers have potential to contribute to the humanization of information systems. Cummings and Worley (2001) considered organizational change as a function of implementation process. They indicated how implementation causes organizational change and this can be controlled throughout singular phases like by information or system contracting and gathering, familiarizing, planning and accomplishing, evaluating and stabilizing. The humanization and e-health-based information system development can be seen as a part of organizational development (OD). Organization development in public health service sector applies this kind of knowledge and practice in order to help organizations to achieve effectiveness and social quality of work life.

The fifth and final aspect to comprise human resource and e-health implementation consists of the cognitive human capacity and service administration. The human capacity indicates the multilevel competencies of professionals. The service administration indicates both the service knowledge and management, which are approached in a customer-centered way. The e-health services are a challenge for both individuals and collective work society. Hence, individual, collective, and organizational competencies (e.g., Hamel & Prahalad, 1994; McLagan, 1997) are clearly required in different phases of the implementation. These competencies represent the foundation of service knowledge, which denotes the ability to arrange and manage both professionally and organizationally with the electronic public services. In present context this entirety (i.e., professional and organizational practices), the e-health implementation and customer relationships can be supported by appropriate and flexible service management. The public service management can comprise, for example, the dimensions of project management, human resource management, network management and customer relationship management. The concept of service management can be also seen as one value creator for service innovations or improvements, and with modifications, as a suitable management approach for organizations from various sectors (cf. Boyne, Martin, & Walker, 2004; Fitzsimmons & Fitzsimmons, 2004; Martin, 2000).

FUTURE TRENDS

In the near future organizations will once again face a dynamic and turbulent environment. That requires flexible and fast response ability from the healthcare organizations and public services. The ongoing era of e-government has enabled organizations to acquire such structures and processes that support new or additional ways of interaction between electronic service providers and customers. Hence, the future trends of e-health indicate implications for health service users, service suppliers and entire society. The purpose of this section is to discuss shortly some essential future trends of e-health. The future possibilities and needs of e-health are introduced according to present literature and reflected alongside the three main dimensions described in current conceptualization. Thus, the final section is based on future prospects and e-health's relationship to e-government.

The present view indicated that the public healt care services will be going through major electronic turnarounds. The e-health revolution accompanied with the future possibilities are far away from straightforward. Many different issues have to be considered in order to make successful ICT-based transitions in public services. In case of organizations and resources there is going to be a further increase in information intensity of the e-health. Public institutions and human actors are stressed and challenged over again with more sophisticated, and hopefully with more user-friendly and appropriate information technology. There will be a need for competent health professional as continuous cognitive pressure is evident. A clear e-health challenge for public healthcare organizations seems to be how to manage with differences in processes, with strong professional culture of healthcare personnel, with cognitive pressure set by ICT, and with hierarchical or traditional structures.

These prospects as seen as future trends of e-health indicate cooperation, but also knowledge and information integration both in organizational and professional level. For example, healthcare professional will probably have fast and unhindered access to the latest knowledge and to the other relevant information needed in clinical practice. It is also assumed that the number of virtual organizations and new innovative services will be increased. The organizational and resource-based future of e-health has to be affected more by customers and patients. The e-health services are targeted as support for the customers (i.e., for those who daily cope with individual health). Thus, as the impact of ICT on healthcare professionals is extensive, similarly the e-health should be harmonized to the specific needs of the users. For example, citizens will increasingly have an opportunity to access their own health data and to contact directly to health professional (e.g., online booking, e-prescribing, home-care monitoring, health information bank, etc.). It is expected that the customer-centered approach will be even more vital as a resource for the future development of e-health. In knowledge intensive society, more demanding customers can be recognized.

In the future, the applications appear to be even more plentiful for consultations with other organizations, professionals, and patients. Portable and mobile tools will be increasingly adopted in healthcare settings together with many web-based gateways or portals. For example, the question can be about the new innovative e-health systems for retrieval, feedback, participation, clinical data management, and in general about the electronic health recording systems (EHR). There will be quite many views about the needs of e-health-based information systems and probably only a few will get it right. The challenge will be the standardization of ICT applications and information systems. Also the users themselves should be equal partners in development teams. As indicated before, people will probably found themselves in the era of virtual life. This indicates the increasing use of collaboration-support information systems.

Finally, the e-health future has implication in the dimension of practices and implementations. The ICT can be seen as a powerful change agent for the whole healthcare sector and it is important to recognize the importance of non-ICT factors in e-health. In this sense, alongside the system implementation it seems to be significant to concentrate on workplace practices and implementations. The best practices and implementations will be valued even more in the complex future of e-health. The e-health interventions based on ICT re-engineering, human-centered information systems, human resource and change management, and practical work innovations will play crucial roles for wellness in workplaces.

It seems that practical work tools or models that support decision making, management, preparation and processes will have an enormous importance. Public healthcare organizations will continue to invest huge amounts of resources into the latest ICT. It seems that new investments on organizational practices and implementations should support both professionals and customers. For example, one challenge is to combine multi-professional practices and service security for the customers benefit. During the continuing era of e-government, the e-health concept will be even more inevitable and natural part of the public healthcare service.

CONCLUSION

The current governmental perspective of e-health has focused into three core dimensions. Current conceptualization has indeed some overlapping areas, but it is important that the approach to e-health is not done only by means of ICT factors or some single science. Hence, the e-health should follow the multi-scientific paradigm as the concept itself has been adopted by the experts of medicine, health science, applied information technology, social science, information and communication science, and by governmental and management science.

It was found how rich the topic of e-health is. The e-health was studied through the ICT implementation and human resources in the knowledge intensive healthcare service organizations. Hence, the implementation of e-health was recognized as a function of various practices and human resources together with future organizational possibilities in public service sector. Alongside the implementation procedures, the human resource was found to be fundamental. Thus, professional, inter-professional and customer perspectives were critical factors. Current perspectives go under the e-government. It combines the perspectives of governmental and management science, social science, health science, and applied information technology. The future trends of e-health thus involve various combined implications to customers and professionals, to service and system suppliers, and to organizations.

REFERENCES

Bates, D. W., Cohen, M., Leape, L. L., Overhage, J. M., Shabot, M. M., & Sheridan, T. (2001). Reducing the frequency of errors in medicine using information technology. *Journal of the American Medical Informatics Association, 8*(4), 299-308.

Bellamy, C., & Taylor, J. A. (1998). *Governing in the information age*. Buckingham, UK: Open University Press.

Boyne, G., Martin, S., & Walker, R. (2004). Explicit reforms, implicit theories, and public service improvement. *Public Management Review, 6*(2), 189-210.

Burge, L., Creps, L., & Wright, B. (2001). If you build it, will they come? *Health Management Technology, 22*(9), 14-20.

Clark, J. (1995). *Managing innovation and change. People, technology, and strategy*. London. Thousand Oaks, CA; New Delhi: SAGE Publications.

Cummings, T. S., & Worley, C. G. (2001). *Organization development and change* (7th ed.). Cincinnati: South-Western College Publishing.

European Commission. (2004). *eHealth—Making healthcare better for European citizens: An action plan for European eHealth area*. COM (2004) 356 final, Brussels.

Eysenbach, G. (2001). What is eHealth? *Journal of Medical Internet Research, 3*(2), e20. Retrieved from http://www.jmir.org/2001/2/e20

Fitzsimmons, J. A., & Fitzsimmons, M. J. (2004).

Service management: Operations, strategy, and information technology (4th ed.). New York: McGraw-Hill.

Gallivan, M. (2001). Organizational adoption and assimilation of complex technological innovations: Development and application of new framework. *Database of Advances in Information systems, 3*, 51-85.

Hailey, D., Roine, R., & Ohinmaa, A. (2002). Systematic review of evidence for the benefits of telemedicine. *Journal of Telemedicine & Telecare, 8*(1), 1-30.

Hamel, G., & Prahalad, C. K. (1994). *Competing for the future*. Boston: Harvard Business School Press.

Harisalo, R., & Stenvall, J. (2004). *Trust as capital: The foundation of management*. In M. L. Huotari & M. Iivonen (Eds.) Trust as knowledge management and systems in organizations. Hershey, PA: Idea Group Publishing.

Isomäki, H. (2002). *The prevailing conceptions of the human being in information systems development: Systems designers' reflections*. Doctoral dissertation, University of Tampere, Finland.

Martin, S. J. (2000). Implementing best value: Local public services in transition. *Public Administration, 78*(1), 209-227.

Mathieson, K., Peacock, E., & Chin, W. W. (2001). Extending the technology acceptance model: The influence of perceived user resources. *Database for Advances in Information Systems, 32*(3), 86-112.

McGinnis, P. J. (1997). The scope and direction of health informatics. *Aviation, Space, and Environmental Medicine, 73*(5), 503-507.

McLagan, P. (1997). Competencies: The next generation. *Training & Development, 51*, 40-47.

McLaughlin, J., Rosen, P., Skinner, D., & Webster, A. (1999). *Valuing technology: Organisations, culture, and change*. London: Routledge.

Mälkiä, M., Anttiroiko, A. V., & Savolainen, R. (2004). *eTransformation in governance: New directions in government and politics*. Hershey, PA: Idea Group Publishing.

Nicholson, N. (2003). *What stays the same?* In S. Chowdhury (Ed.), *Organization 21C—Someday all organizations will lead this way* (pp. 241-255). Upper Saddle River, NJ: Prentice Hall.

Oliver, E. L., & Sanders, L. (2004). *E-government reconsidered: Renewal of governance for the knowledge age*. Canada: Canadian Plains Research Center, University of Regina.

Paré, G., & Elam, J. J. (1999). Physicians' acceptance of clinical information systems: An empirical look at attitudes, expectations, and skills. *International Journal of Healthcare Technology and Management, 1*, 46-61.

Parente, S. T., & Dunbar, J. L. (2001). Is the health information technology investment related to the financial performance of US hospitals? An exploratory analysis. *International Journal of Healthcare Technology and Management, 3*(1), 48-58.

Plsek, P. E., & Wilson, T. (2001). Complexity, leadership, and management in healthcare organisations. *British Medical Journal, 323*(7215), 746-750.

Silber, D. (2003). *The case for eHealth*. The Netherlands: The European Commission. European Institute of Public Administration.

Smith, G. (2004). *Leading the professionals. How to inspire & motivate professional service teams*. London and Sterling, VA: Kogan Page Limited.

Syväjärvi, A., Stenvall, J., Harisalo, R., & Jurvansuu, H. (2005). The impact of information technology on human capacity, interprofessional practice, and management. *Problems and Perspectives in Management, 1*(4), 82-95.

Tachakra, S., El Habashy, A., & Dawood, M. (2001). Changes in the workplace with telemedicine. *Journal of Telemedicine and Telecare, 7*, 277-280.

Turban, E., McLean, E., & Wetherbe, J. (1999). *Information technology for management*. New York: John Wiley & Sons, Inc.

Turner, A., Fraser, V., Muir Grau, J. A., & Toth, B. (2002). A first class knowledge service: Developing the national electronic library for health. *Health Information and Libraries Journal, 19*(3), 133-145.

Walker, J., & Whetton, S. (2002). The diffusion of innovation: Factors influencing the uptake of telehealth. *Journal of Telemedicine and Telecare, 8*(3), 73-75.

Whitten, P. S., Mair, F. S., Haycox, A., May, C. R., Williams, T. L., & Hellmich, S. (2002). Systematic review of cost effectiveness studies telemedicine interventions. *British Medical Journal, 14*, 1434-1437.

KEY TERMS

E-Government: An electronic exchange of information and services between different actors. Usually refers to local or state government activities that take place by digital processes and various networks.

E-Health: Health services and information delivered through different technologies in order to improve or enable health, healthcare and services with variable contents and transactions (cf. Eysenbach, 2001).

E-Health Usability: The design and technical features that allow electronic healthcare applications and information systems to be suitable for intentional use in a user friendly way.

Health Informatics: Knowledge, skills, and tools to support the delivery of healthcare information and services (cf. Silber, 2003).

Health Information System: An ICT-based routine constructed for the purposes of delivering health and medical care. Information system can be seen as physical process that supports an organization by providing information to achieve goals.

Information Management: Interdisciplinary procedures designed to provide and improve appropriate information systems and resources. Refer to planning, organizing, executing, and evaluating the necessary management operations.

Standardization of E-Health: The method to reduce or eliminate inconsistency, potential added costs and quality problems in applications and information systems of the electronic healthcare.

This work was previously published in Encyclopedia of Digital Government, edited by A. Anttiroiko and M. Malkia, pp. 244-250, copyright 2007 by Information Science Reference, formerly known as Idea Group Reference (an imprint of IGI Global).

Chapter 5.16 Exploiting Public Sector Information through Innovative E-Government Policies

Ioannis P. Chochliouros
Hellenic Telecommunications Organization S.A. (OTE), Greece

Anastasia S. Spiliopoulou-Chochliourou
Hellenic Telecommunications Organization S.A. (OTE), Greece

INTRODUCTION

The digital, knowledge-based economy (European Commission, 2003a) has a strong impact on the life of all citizens at the global level. Under suitable terms and/or appropriate conditions, it can be a powerful "engine" for growth, competitiveness, and jobs, while at the same time it improves living standards.

The multiplicity of innovative Information Society (Dutta, Paua, & Lanvin, 2004) tools has led to unprecedented possibilities to combine data taken from different and various sources into added-value products and services. To this perspective, public sector information can be an important "prime" material for relevant applications.

For the specific framework of the European Union (EU), the public sector information (European Commission, 1998) plays a very important role in its social and economic models by supporting high levels of welfare for citizens, ensuring socioeconomic cohesion, and sustaining the functioning of a competitive and fully liberalized market environment. In particular, the public sector engages in a wide range of activities, varying from education, healthcare, and social security, to protecting consumers and strengthening the environment. Consequently, financial and business information is collected by a number of ministries and other appropriate organizations.

Company registers, usually required by law in many Member States, are also maintained by the public sector. Legal information (in particular concerning legislation and jurisprudence) and administrative information constitute another example, while patent offices are usually public sector bodies. Scientific, technical, cultural, and medical information is extensively collected by public research institutions and public archives.

Geographical information relevant to transport and tourism (e.g., maps, road traffic situation) is also available in corresponding public agencies. Furthermore, tourist information is gathered and published by public sector bodies at different levels of government.

Learning how to manage and to exploit all relevant information produced and stored could create a very high level of public value (and this is probably an unavoidable step towards a future user-centered government). Even greater potential benefits can result if governments, authorities, and/or organizations actively participate in the development of the knowledge-based society, in the true sense to create public-shared spaces for the creation and the delivery of various forms of "knowledge."

However, today there are still some "barriers" preventing the full "exploitation" of public sector information at the European level. These may originate from diversities either in language or in pricing issues, or in (administrative) rules and/or practices, such as differences in replying time, the refusal to transmit the information in digital format, the need to prove that the information is not limited by data-protection rules, and exclusive deals that already exist between public and private firms.

In fact, Europe's public sector (Cap Gemini Ernst & Young, 2004) is today at a crossroads, in front of numerous global challenging conditions, institutional change, and the profound impact of new technologies in a background which evolves very rapidly. Expectation is growing that, as it is a major economic performer for boosting growth and innovation, the public sector can (and will) play a strong role in realizing the Lisbon strategy (European Commission, 2000; European Council, 2003) for economic, social, and environmental renewal. It should be expected that the public sector would become more productive, cut the "red tape," eliminate queues, and offer services of improved quality.

Simultaneously, the European public sector will, over the next decade, undergo a number of transitions (such as increasing cultural and religious diversity, aging of the population, and changing living, working, and consumption patterns) that will require new services as well as innovative ways of delivering the existing ones. In particular, the public sector should "close" the demographic deficit, restore democratic ownership, and cope with demographic change (e.g., aging, immigration, etc.). Other perspectives may be relevant to safeguard liberty, justice, and security. The public administrations are now facing (with a medium- to long-term time horizon) very powerfully the challenge (DG Information Society of the European Commission, 2001) of improving the efficiency, productivity, and quality of their offerings, to respond to all the forthcoming needs and demands. This may result in new ways of delivering services to citizens and businesses while coping with various domains, especially if considering initiatives to extend the internal market and to deepen convergence in enlargement (OECD, 2003; IDA eGovernment Observatory, 2002; Chochliouros & Spiliopoulou-Chochliourou, 2003a). This option also implicates special perspectives such as identity management, advanced public electronic services, deployment of dynamic and personalized services, and exploitation of innovation in technology.

BACKGROUND

The initial concept of electronic government (e-government) took off a few years ago, mostly as the "*mirror image*" of electronic commerce (e-commerce) in the public sector. However, the e-government has now become an explicit component of public sector reform as a fundamental instrument to increase efficiency, strengthen competitiveness, and enhance modernization.

In particular, e-government can be now estimated (European Commission, 2003c) as:

"...the use of information and communication technologies (ICTs) in public administrations combined with organizational change and new skills in order to improve public services and democratic processes and strengthen support to public policies."

Experiences and up-to-date practices have very clearly demonstrated that relevant activities can refer to a great diversity of functions (European Institute of Public Administration, 2003), including, *inter-alia*:

- Electronic public services (e-services) to end-users, either citizens or corporate businesses; these could include applications, facilities, and/or additional electronic features related to government *online* presence/access and the provision of *online* services, customs' services, value-added taxes, *online* job search, *online* requests for personal documents, *online* book search in public libraries, and so forth.
- Electronic procurement (e-procurement)—that is, the means for the realization of *online purchases*. The adoption of electronic public procurement systems is driven by the need to reduce costs and favor purchases in large volumes, thus limiting the number of contracts. Although such an option can be occasionally included in e-services (as a specific modular component), it may follow completely different implementation dynamics. In fact, it is currently promoted by higher-level administrations and typically requires considerable internal government reorganization. Early experiences seem to suggest extra benefits in terms of cost savings and improvement of transparency, however there are still strong "resistances" by local stakeholders, threatened by the concentration of purchase activities and other constituencies.
- Electronic democracy (e-democracy), in a way to support the genuine participation of citizens in politics. Although still in its "infancy" and at elementary levels (with some pioneer experiences especially in northern Europe), e-democracy formulates a very promising expectation for the future.

E-GOVERNMENT AS THE "VEHICLE" FOR EXPLOITING "PUBLIC VALUE"

In fact, e-government implicates the use of emerging technologies to transform public administrations and to improve radically the way they work with their customers, be they citizens, enterprises, or other administrations. The e-government is now a key vehicle for the implementation and achievement of "higher policy" objectives. It is unlikely that relevant objectives on the single market freedoms, industrial policy, liberalization and competition, sustainable development, and security across the EU can be achieved (Chochliouros & Spiliopoulou-Chochliourou, 2003a) unless such interoperable services are swiftly implemented.

This places e-government at the "core" of public management renovation and reform, where technology is used as a strategic tool to modernize structures, processes, the regulatory framework (Chochliouros & Spiliopoulou-Chochliourou, 2003b), human resources, and the culture of public administrations to provide better government and, ultimately, increased "public value."

The creation of public value is a broad term that includes a multiplicity of democratic, social, economic, environmental, and governance roles. Some quite indicative but concrete examples may refer to: (a) the provision of public administration and public services (such as health, education, and social care); (b) the development and the implementation of policies, accompanied by an appropriate regulatory framework to reflect real market needs; (c) the supervision and the management of public finances; (d) the guarantee of democratic political processes, gender equality, social inclusion, and personal security; and (e) the management of environmental sustainability and development.

The target for the provision of better government depends on a variety of factors including, but not limited to, existing and developing governmental structures and processes, cost benefits and reductions, effectiveness, improved quality of services, accountability, transparency and openness, and greater participative governance and adequate accessibility, especially to avoid "digital divide" events (Department of Economic and Social Affairs of the UN, 2003).

In particular, present challenges are focused on opportunities to design, apply, and exploit methods, means, and/or other "tools" essential for new public management activities, especially focusing on the centrality of users' needs. Core drivers of such a revolutionary process could be: (a) the need to improve efficiency, productivity, and quality of public services without increasing budgets; and (b) the need to satisfy citizens' expectations of new standards of service provision allowing flexibility, personalization, and full availability, as in the private sector.

It becomes evident that e-government can be a "catalyst" to realize a more efficient administration, transforming the "balance of power" between government levels (supranational, national, regional, local) and functions. So it improves the development and implementation of public policies and helps the public sector to cope with the conflicting demands of delivering more and better services with fewer resources. While technology cannot transform "bad" procedures into good "ones," e-government creates the *choice* for the public sector to do its tasks differently. Therefore, electronic government marks "the most dramatic shift in governance in generations and offers a fundamental restructuring of the way government operates and interacts with citizens" (Holmes, 2001).

OPTIONS FOR STRUCTURING THE NECESSARY UNDERLYING PREREQUISITES

All fundamental related activities are currently built on two main but interrelated developments. The first can be estimated as the business models adopted in the recent past by the (private) enterprise sector. These were largely concerned with obtaining competitive advantage by diverse activities such as continuous process improvement, a focus on core competencies, and the reorganization of internal processes. The public and their political representatives now expect public administration to be as efficient, fast, and effective in achieving its goal, as is the private enterprise sector.

The second domain of activities is related to the effective use (Wauters, 2003) of a wide range of information and communications technologies, of which the Internet is the most "visible." The combination of advanced ICTs in the support of new ways of working in public administration, together with the "enhanced" provision of information and interactive services, accessible over different "channels" and infrastructures, is the foundation of e-government. This vision is very exciting as it progresses beyond the "simplistic" image of communication technologies, considered as "tools" for an additional delivery channel of public services. On the contrary, it constitutes a new vision of the role of government, which exploits the potential of technical innovation, without falling in the trap of any particular technological determinism. Modernizing government through ICTs is not the only driver of change in the public administration. The whole socio-political system is shifting, to incorporate new and innovative options of the evolution performed. This "variable geometry of power" scenario lends credibility to the perspective of an increasingly networked government.

In essence, interoperability between infrastructures, facilities, applications, and equipment is a fundamental requirement (European Commission, 2003b), from both the economic and technical perspectives, for the development of efficient and effective services at both the pan-European and national levels (also including the regional and local ones). Interoperability is not simply a technical issue concerned with linking up various systems; it goes beyond, to include the sharing of information between networks and the reorganization of administrative processes to support the seamless delivery of e-government services. Such a framework, which can be defined as the "wider" set of policies, standards, and guidelines describing the way in which organizations have agreed, or should agree, to do business with each other, is to provide the specifications and the guiding principles for joining together the information systems of public administrations across the EU.

FUTURE TRENDS

Apart from intergovernmental relationships (also including the local, regional, national, and EU dimensions), all principal applications currently refer to government-to-citizens (G2C) and government-to-businesses (G2B) relationships. Citizens and enterprises can greatly benefit from a sophisticated provision of various forms of public sector information on Internet-based platforms and infrastructures.

Making public sector information online available for reuse (where allowed and always under the specific requirements imposed by a proper legal framework) enables businesses (also including small and medium-sized enterprises (SMEs)) to develop attractive and competitive offers. Meanwhile, a minimum "set" of common rules could take away investment failures and most part of any probable uncertainty, to enhance the offering of suitable products.

Current trends (IDA eGovernment Observatory, 2002) promote the need to incorporate, in the delivery chain, a growing number of "intermediaries," which will play an increasing role in the delivery of public services and will ensure openness and competitiveness. Services, however, should be addressed to the citizen-centric, especially in terms of availability, usability, flexibility, and pricing.

Citizens are becoming accustomed to ever-faster response times and ever-higher quality of products-services from the private sector (OECD, 2003). Consequently, they expect to have the same (or similar) levels of performance from the public administrations. Obscure procedures, long queues, having to re-enter information that is already held by the administration, and "one-size-fits-all" approaches are all practices that are increasingly criticized. In order to face the appearing challenges (Millard, Iversen, Kubicek, Westholm, & Cimander, 2004), public service provision should be expected to become more user friendly and personalized, adapted to the specific needs of the individuals. Moreover, it needs to be "inclusive," and all citizens have to be adequately served, independently of their skills and capabilities, income, or geographical location. The public sector cannot "choose" its clients, contrary to the private sector (nor can the public usually choose whether or not to be clients of the public sector).

The e-government evolution should also address the needs of enterprises for reducing cost transactions, supporting competition in a global economic environment, and increasing speed, simplicity, and scalability. Meanwhile, the promotion of fair-trading and appropriate pricing schemes in the market(s), in order to guarantee a minimum of certainty and transparency, will be a principal factor to forward an efficient penetration of e-government. In order to respond, *properly,* to the forthcoming challenges, the enterprise sector should, with appropriate support from the EU authorities, develop fully interoperable e-business solutions.

Interoperability, therefore, for both public and enterprise sectors, will be at the heart of all the suggested policies. This implicates combined considerations at various levels, such as: (a) the technical level, which is concerned with technical issues of linking "Internet-type" technologies and systems, the definition of "open" interfaces (with appropriate standards and specifications), and realizing communications; (b) the organizational level, which deals with modeling business processes, aligning information architectures to organizational goals, and helping business processes to cooperate, to extend their activities, and to include suppliers, (business) partners, and customers; and (c) the semantics level, which is concerned with ensuring that the precise meaning of exchanged information is understandable by any other relevant application; this also entails agreement on, for example, ways to discover, represent, and give context to information, and it will allow automated tools to share and process data, even when they have been designed independently.

Citizens and businesses expect authorities to become more accountable for the management of their financial contributions and taxes to the state. They also demand more transparency of decision making (especially in the fight against corruption and fraud) and democratic involvement in all phases of policy development. More specifically, through online forums, virtual discussion rooms, and electronic voting, citizens can be able to express their views, directly question the decision makers, and so contribute with an informed opinion to the democratic process.

This constitutes an improvement towards more transparent, accountable, and open public institutions.

To ensure creation, development, and implementation of appropriate e-government- based services (Millard, 2003), the latter should be accompanied by joint actions to build up experience and validate advanced solutions for profitable collaborations. This concerns common approaches to key aspects of seamless pan-European service provision such as accessibility, user identification, security, interoperability, also including data definitions and procedures. As far as appropriate, pan-European e-government services should be integrated and interactive.

CONCLUSION

Public sector information covers a great variety of activities, while its improved use could turn all relevant resources into a valuable asset for European citizens, businesses, and administrations alike. In particular, with the advent of the Internet, governments have started exploring how they can maximize the value of their information resources.

Consequently, numerous recent European initiatives have been focused on stimulating services, applications, and content that can create new markets, reduce costs, and eventually increase productivity throughout the economy. In such a complex environment, electronic government can be a significant factor, mainly to promote solutions for an effective exploitation of the disposed information. The expected development encompasses the provision of better public administration; more efficient, transparent, open, and participative governance; and the implementation of more democratic political processes.

E-government has emerged as a means for improving government, and ultimately, for increasing public value (Centeno, van Bavel, & Burgelman, 2004). However, clearer understanding on how, and in what areas, can efficiently contribute to maintain and strengthen good governance in the knowledge society. In particular, recent development is now entering a new phase, fully characterized by the "re-engineering" of governmental processes, at all possible levels of administration, for better treatment of information.

E-government should have a strategic focus: the complete achievement of the "Lisbon goals" for realizing an appropriate "electronic Europe" capable of sustainable economic growth, and ensuring that businesses and citizens derive the maximum benefit from any progress in ICTs (European Commission, 2000; European Council, 2003). This will also contribute to the reduction of barriers to the internal market for services and mobility, effective implementation of national policies, and broader regional or local development.

Moreover, e-government should be oriented to satisfy user needs in two parallel options: (a) for living, working, and doing business; and (b) as "users" of administrative services, as taxpayers, and as interactive participants in democracy.

Public administrations can provide major key contributions to improve Europe's competitiveness, growth, innovation, and employment rates, as well as social cohesion (European Commission, 2001b).

REFERENCES

Cap Gemini Ernst & Young. (2004). *Report on online availability of public services. How is Europe processing?* Brussels, Belgium: DG Information Society of the European Commission.

Centeno, C., van Bavel, R., & Burgelman, J.-C. (Institute for Prospective Technological Studies [ITPS]). (2004). *eGovernment in the EU in the next decade: The vision and key challenges* (Technical Report EUR 21376 EN). Brussels, Belgium: Directorate General Joint Research Center (JRC) of the European Commission. Retrieved May 11, 2005, from http://www.jrc.es/home/publications/publications.html

Chochliouros, I., & Spiliopoulou-Chochliourou, A. (2003a). Perspectives for achieving competition and development in the European information and communication technology (ICT) market. *Journal of the Communications Network: TCN, 2*(3), 42-50.

Chochliouros, I., & Spiliopoulou-Chochliourou, A. (2003b). Innovative horizons for Europe: The new European telecom framework for the development of modern electronic networks and services. *Journal of the Communications Network: TCN, 2*(4), 53-62.

Department of Economic and Social Affairs of the UN. (2003). *E-government at the crossroads, world public sector report.* New York: United Nations.

DG Information Society of the European Commission. (2001). *Summary report—Web-based survey on electronic public services, results of the first measurement.* Brussels, Belgium: European Commission.

Dutta, S., Paua, F., & Lanvin, B. (Eds.). (2004). *The global information technology report 2003-2004: Readiness for the networked world.* New York: Oxford University Press.

European Commission. (1998). *Green paper on public sector information: A key resource for Europe [(COM(1998) 585), 20.01.1999].* Brussels, Belgium: European Commission.

European Commission. (2000, June 19-20). *Communication on eEurope 2002—An information society for all. Draft action plan, prepared by the European Commission for the European Council in Feira [COM(2000) 330 final, 24.05.2000].* Brussels, Belgium: European Commission.

European Commission. (2001a). *Communication on European governance—A white paper [COM(2001) 428, 25.07.2001].* Brussels, Belgium: European Commission.

European Commission. (2001b). *Communication on eEurope 2002: Creating an EU framework for the exploitation of public sector information (COM[2001]607 final, 23.10.2001).* Brussels, Belgium: European Commission.

European Commission. (2003a). *Communication on electronic communication: Road to the knowledge economy [COM(2003) 65, 11.02.2003].* Brussels, Belgium: European Commission.

European Commission. (2003b). *Communication on interoperable delivery of pan-European eGovernment services to public administrations, businesses and citizens [COM(2003) 406, 08.07.2003].* Brussels, Belgium: European Commission.

European Commission. (2003c). *Communication on the role of eGovernment for Europe's future [COM(2003)567 final, 26.09.2003].* Brussels, Belgium: European Commission.

European Council. (2003). *Resolution of 18 February 2003 on the implementation of the eEurope 2005 action plan [Official Journal (OJ) C48, 28.02.2003, pp. 02-09].* Brussels, Belgium: European Council.

European Institute of Public Administration (EIPA). (2003). *eGovernment in Europe: The state of affairs.* Maastricht, The Netherlands: EIPA.

Holmes, D. (2001). *eGov: E-business strategies for government.* London: Nicholas Brealey.

IDA eGovernment Observatory. (2002). *Survey on eGovernment services to enterprises.* Brussels, Belgium: European Commission, Enterprise Directorate General. Retrieved July 11, 2005, from http://europa.eu.int/idabc/en/document/679/5589

Millard, J. (2003). *E-public services in Europe: Past, present and future. Research findings and new challenges. Final paper.* Retrieved May 10, 2005, from ftp://ftp.cordis.lu/pub/ist/docs/epublic-services.pdf

Millard, J., Iversen, J. S., Kubicek, H., Westholm, H., & Cimander, R. (2004, January). *Reorganisation of government back offices for better electronic public services—European good practices (back-office reorganisation), final report to the European Commission, January 2004.* Brussels, Belgium: Danish Technological Institute, Institut für Informationsmanagement GmbH, University of Bremen.

OECD. (2003, March). *Engaging citizens online for better policy-making* (policy brief). Paris: Organization for Economic Co-operation and Development. Retrieved June 6, 2005, from http://www.oecd.org/dataoecd/62/23/2501856.pdf

Wauters, P. (2003). *Online availability of public services: How is Europe progressing? Web based survey on electronic public services. Results of the fourth measurement.* Brussels, Belgium: DG Information Society of the European Commission. Retrieved May 17, 2005, from http://europa.eu.int/information_society/eeurope/2005/doc/highlights/whats_new/capgemini4.pdf

KEY TERMS

E-Democracy: The utilization of electronic communications technologies, such as the Internet, in enhancing democratic processes within a democratic republic or a representative democracy. It is a political development still in its infancy, as well as the subject of much debate and activity within government, civic-oriented groups, and societies around the world. E-democracy also includes within its scope electronic voting.

E-Government: The use of information and communication technologies in public administrations, combined with organizational change and new skills in order to improve public services and democratic processes, and strengthen support to public policies.

E-Procurement: The means for the realization of *online purchases*, by using appropriate electronic communications services and infrastructures.

Information and Communication Technology (ICT): A sector including a great variety of technologies such as desktop and laptop computers, software, peripherals, and connections to the Internet that are intended to fulfill information processing and communications functions.

Interoperability Framework: Not simply a purely technical issue concerned with linking up various systems, but the "wider" set of policies, measures, standards, practices, and guidelines describing the way in which various organizations have agreed, or should agree, to do business with each other.

Knowledge-Based Economy: A form of modern economy referring to a specific structural transformation, where the fast creation of new knowledge and the improvement of access to various knowledge bases increasingly constitute the main resource for greater efficiency, novelty, and competitiveness.

Public Value: Any form of value created by governments though the provision of services, the passing of laws and regulations, and other actions. It also involves all the short-term and long-term contributions made by public administrations to society and the economy. Furthermore, it includes efficiency gains by better internal performance and, most importantly, the multiplier social and economic effects such as: (1) social development and inclusion, (2) enabling companies to lower their administrative costs and become more competitive, and (3) strengthening innovation across the economy.

This work was previously published in Encyclopedia of E-Commerce, E-Government, and Mobile Commerce, edited by M. Khosrow-Pour, pp. 508-513, copyright 2006 by Information Science Reference, formerly known as Idea Group Reference (an imprint of IGI Global).

Chapter 5.17
A Comparative Account of Joined-Up Government Initiatives in Dutch and Belgian Social Security

Vincent M.F. Homburg
Erasmus University Rotterdam, The Netherlands

EXECUTIVE SUMMARY

In this article, organizational and policy aspects of two national clearing house concepts are compared and discussed. In social security, Belgium has witnessed the emergence of the so-called Cross Point Bank and the Netherlands have produced the RINIS initiative. Although both countries are rather comparable, they differ in terms of their politico-administrative structures. From the comparison of the antecedents of both initiatives and their form and shape, it is concluded that e-government is not a universal, necessarily converged concept and that institutions and institutional matter, not so much as to how e-government is talked about (rhetorical convergence), but especially for the ways in which e-government technologies are implemented in the real world of public administration. From the case study, there is little support for decisional and operational convergence of the e-government phenomenon.

ORGANIZATIONAL BACKGROUND

One of the goals for many governments throughout the world is the realization of an administrative apparatus that not only is digitally accessible, but also works seamlessly: it should not suffer from fragmentation and lack of responsiveness. In order to achieve this goal, insights from various disciplines are used and actually implemented.

In the public administration literature, it has been said repeatedly that improving coordination inside public administration is an eternal quest (Peters, 1996, 1998; Pressman & Wildavsky, 1973). In the Anglo-Saxon world (notably the United Kingdom), in the slipstream of *new public management* reforms, emphasis has been put on the phenomenon of joined-up government (Bogdanor, 2005; Ling, 2002). Joined-up government, in general, refers to consistency between organizational arrangements of policy programmes, policies, or agency strategies, which enables them to collaborate. Joined-up government is implemented by means of (among other measures) new (merged) organizations, new ways of working across traditional organizational boundaries (for example, joined teams, pooled budgets), new ways of service delivery (joint front offices), or new accountabilities and incentives (shared performance targets, regulation) (Ling, 2002).

In the e-government literature, in many cases, there is a focus on the design and implementation of technology that fosters integration of (primarily) service delivery. Through all kinds of measures, government-to-government (G2G) exchange of information is nurtured in order to coordinate activities and processes between formerly disparate governmental bodies.

Probably inspired by technological and managerial developments; politicians, commentators, and consultants have argued for a digitally accessible, seamlessly integrated administrative apparatus that is customer-oriented, and, moreover, is able to deliver public services efficiently, comprehensively, and fast. To some degree, this ideal is a digital sublime (Mosco, 2004); however, to a certain degree, a successful marriage seems to emerge from the combined trajectories of managerial (JUG) and technological (e-government) reform (Homburg & Bekkers, 2005). One can indeed witness actual e-government initiatives being rolled out in the United States (Fountain, 2001; Moon, 2002; Tat-Kei Ho, 2002), the United Kingdom (Chadwick & May, 2003), Continental-European countries (Kubicek & Hagen, 2000), Australia (Teichert & Dow, 2002) and the developing world (Heeks, 2003; Ndou, 2004). Apparently, the "wired" government does not only exist in the minds and rhetorics of politicians and consultants, but also at the shop floor of public sector organizations throughout the world.

When it comes to reforms, there is a compelling rhetoric of convergence (Pollitt, 2002). From case studies, best practices, talk, and so on, a picture emerges of how managerial and technological reforms spread over countries, produce similar results, and result in comparable practices. One common approach is to design Web-based packages of services around life events. The general aspiration is that front-office integration around life-events obviates coordination and integration through similar, comparable management practices.

In the practice of public management and public policy, however, styles of coordination (for example French centralism, the German decentralized approach, or the Dutch consensus style of coordination) appear to be rather resistant to the pressures of technological innovation as such (6, Leat, Seltzer, & Stoker, 2002). From the relatively few documented cases and surveys of international e-government practices (Accenture, 2004; Cap Gemini, 2006), it is often concluded that institutional factors constrain (in the sense that they limit courses of action and change) e-government practices. If one takes the point of view of the "social shaping of technology"— stream in the literature (MacKenzie & Wajcman, 1985; Williams & Edge, 1996), one might hypothesize that inversely, the eventual form and shape technology takes, including the level of integration and interoperability, is largely, although not exclusively, shaped by social and institutional factors. And indeed, in a large European study of back-office integration strategies, the authors conclude that "state structures, and institutional, legal, regulatory and cultural factors can be extremely important in determining the nature, cost and success of eGovernment (…). Progress often depends on whether or not there is a history of back office integration and cooperation, but not necessarily through centralized structures" (Millard, Iversen, Kubicek, Westholm, & Cimander, 2004, p. 61). Apparently, integration and interoperability, as well as means to achieve them, are far more contextually bound than is apparent at first sight, and appears from many e-government writings.

The empirical question, therefore, is whether there actually exists a globally converged ideal of integration and joined-up government beyond the level of fallible rhetoric, and if and how integration is actually achieved on decisional and operational levels of e-government (cf. Pollitt, 2002). From a comparative point of view, it is interesting to analyze if and how interoperability and integration are interpreted in disparate institutional contexts (Esping-Andersen, 1996; Pollitt & Bouckaert, 2004), for example, in a unitary-decentralized country like Norway and in a federal—coordinated country like Belgium. Furthermore, one can ask the question how similarities and differences in ways in which integration and interoperability are achieved, can be explained.

SETTING THE STAGE

The analysis of the interpretation and implementation of joined-up government and e-government integration attempts in this paper takes place in the field of social security. Social security in OECD countries has a relatively long history, and due to the information-intensive character of claim processing and payment services, social insurance agencies (together with tax agencies, and, more recently, homeland security and intelligence services) have been leaders in the use of ICTs (Henman & Adler, 2001, p. 23). Therefore, social security is an interesting field of study if one attempts to study e-government initiatives beyond mere description and taking into account that technological and institutional reforms generally span several years if not decades.

Although the term social security is in many cases associated with the value of solidarity, the provision of services to compensate for temporary loss of income due to unemployment or illness, it must be stressed that initially, at the end of the 19th century, the provision of social services had less to do with welfare than with the maintenance of order in society: the delivery of services and beneficiaries was primarily aimed at the prevention of begging and regulation of almsgiving (Henman & Adler, 2003).

The systems of social security in most of the OECD countries have developed along various lines. In general, until the advent of the 20th century, social security was primarily aimed at the provision of social assistance to the poor. Social assistance was primarily administered locally, by officers representing voluntary sector organizations, with considerable discretion. In many western countries, the activities of the voluntary sector have been taken over by municipal government agencies. Officers generally have some discretion to determine the appropriate level of support on a case-by-case basis.

Another component of the system of social security is social insurance. Social insurance is to be distinguished from social assistance in the sense that people are entitled to receive benefits in cases of illness, involuntary unemployment, disabilities, and so forth, in recognition of contributions (premiums) to an insurance scheme. Social insurance schemes developed in Europe at the beginning of the 20th century through joined action by governments, trade unions, and employers' associations. After the Second World War, in the United States, the Anglo-Saxon countries and Continental European Countries, the Welfare State emerged and systems of social assistance and social insurances expanded. In general, national pension schemes, unemployment benefit schemes and schemes to compensate for loss of income due to illness and disability adopted bureaucratic models of organization, whereas social assistance was still predominantly administered locally. The general picture of these developments in OECD countries shows that private initiative was taken over by bureaucratic models of organization, and social services were increasingly delivered by civil servants. It must be noted that in Continental Europe, notably in corporatist countries, social partners (trade unions, employer associations) have been commissioned by central governments to deliver welfare services. This situation remained relatively undisturbed until about the 1980s, when fiscal crises and economic depressions fundamentally challenged the founding principles of social security. By then, the ever-expanding system of social security was curtailed throughout the OECD world, and fighting fraud was put on the political agenda. In order to do that, administrators had to be able to bring together all the relevant social security information on level of individual claimants (or households) that was held within specific institutions, as well as in related but disparate social security institutions.

It is in this period that information and communication technologies were first tried out to administer the complex interconnections in social security domains, and between social security and other policy domains (taxation, health care, study grants, to name a few examples) (Smith, 1985). It must be noted, though, that the application of ICTs has been notably different in emphasis in various national contexts. The history of the application of ICTs in the social security sector (Henman & Adler, 2001; Smith, 1985) shows that in Scandinavian countries, the emphasis was on empowerment of front-line social security officers (Andersen & Kraemer, 1995). In Anglo-American countries, however, the automation of decision-making from application to benefit was given priority in order to improve the efficiency of the system (Henman & Adler, 2001).

From these observations, we can infer that ICT application takes various forms and shapes in various institutional contexts, be it the liberal politico-administrative regimes in the Anglo-Saxon countries, and the corporatist welfare regimes in Continental Europe (including Scandinavian countries). The empirical question, though, is whether this is also true for attempts to foster intergovernmental cooperation through electronic means (G2G interaction), and whether there are general models to implement joined-up government in social security. After all, governments worldwide are enthusiastically using "joined-up government" and "customer orientation" as famous administrative slogans (6 et al., 2002; Ling, 2002). In order to do that, in the remainder of this paper, we focus on strategies to foster integration in social security in two comparable countries, namely the Netherlands and Belgium, that nonetheless have two distinct politico-administrative regimes.

In general, the Netherlands can be classified as being a unitary, communitarian decentralized state (Adler & Henman, 2005). Its legal model resembles the Napoleonic model, with some influences from the Constitutional State model (Steen, van den Berg, van der Meer, Overeem, & Toonen, 2005). The political system is rather consensual: almost every sector of policy consists of a myriad of consultative and advisory councils, which are deeply intertwined with government and form an "iron ring" around ministerial departments (Pollitt & Bouckaert, 2004)

Belgium, on the other hand, can be typified as a federal, corporatist state. Its legal model is a combined Napoleonic/Latin model (encompassing a relatively strong central state, hierarchical structures and a civil service system that enjoys a high level of prestige) (Steen et al., 2005). In Belgium, in contrast to the Netherlands (see above), policy preparation is predominantly the domain of the ministerial cabinets (and not the civil service, in consultation with the "iron rings" of consultative councils). Belgium has a tradition of political appointments of senior civil servants (Steen et al., 2005).

In the case description below, we will analyze (1) general social security developments and antecedents of joined-up government, (2) political and technological agreements as the backbones of joined-up government, (3) architectural foundations and organizational models used. The research approach in general is a comparative study, employing research results from a case study of ICT use in the social security sector of the Netherlands (Homburg, 1999) and additionally, a study of written sources and a literature review of the Belgian situation.

CASE DESCRIPTIONS

Social Security Developments in the Netherlands

The Netherlands can be characterized as a unitary and decentralized welfare state (Steen et al., 2005). In general, the field of social security in the Netherlands can be characterized as a divergent system of execution (Homburg, 1999).

Child Allowances and State Pensions are administered by an independent administrative body Social Insurances Bank (Dutch: Sociale Verzekeringsbank). Social Assistance, on the other hand, has been carried out by public, municipal social assistance agencies on behalf of the Ministry of Social Affairs. Until about 1995, semi-autonomous Industrial Insurance Boards had executed insurance schemes on behalf of trade unions and associations of employers. The state only had a supervisory role (Fenger, 2006). The functioning of the rather heterogeneous system of social security severely criticized in the 1990s by the Netherlands Court of Audit, a subsequent Parliamentary Research Commission (that focused on the execution of Social Insurance Acts) and a Research Committee that scrutinized implementation practices of the Social Assistance Act (the Van der Zwan Committee).

As a result of these (and other) investigations, the execution of Acts in the fields of Social Security was reorganized. Discussions about privatization emerged (especially in the field of Social Insurances), but eventually, in 2002, the Industrial Insurance Boards merged into a independent administrative body known as the *Uitvoeringsinstituut Werknemersverzekeringen* (Executive Organization of Social Insurances). This marked a more prominent role of the state as principal in the field of social security; execution of schemes and Acts, however, still takes place in a rather divergent field of hundreds of municipal social assistance agencies, the Social Insurances bank, and the Executive Organization for Social Insurances.

RINIS: A Dutch Initiative from the Field

In 1996, representatives from various quasi-autonomous executive agencies teamed up and developed ideas and concepts to fight fraud and to foster interorganizational cooperation. Partly, these initiatives can be understood as a genuine concern to prevent and/or fight fraud. Partly, the initiatives can be understood as pre-emptive action that allowed executive organizations to preserve and defend their autonomy against initiatives that were at that time prepared by central levels of government (more precisely: the Ministry of Social Affairs and Employment). With these initiatives, the Ministry attempted to impose standards and practices for information exchange in the sector of social security, and this was seen by executive organizations as an unwanted breach of their (informational) autonomy (Homburg, 1999).

In various talks and meetings, the RINIS concept was developed. RINIS is an abbreviation of the *Routeringsinstituut voor (Inter)nationale Informatie Stromen* (Router Institution for International Information Flows). The term RINIS both refers to:

- a relatively small (seven members of staff) bureau, which is controlled by a Board. The Board consists of representatives of organizations that participate in (and finance) the RINIS bureau; and
- an infrastructure that enables information exchange across participating organizations.

The RINIS concept started from the core of the Social Security Sector, but throughout time it has expanded, and currently the following organizations are involved:

- the Executive Organization of Social Insurances (*UWV*);

- the Social Insurances Bank (*SVB*);
- the Organization for Collecting Alimonies (*LBIO*);
- the Office for Enquiries in the Social Assistance domain (*IB*; an umbrella organization of municipal social assistance agencies);
- The Office for Granting Student Loans (*IB-Group*);
- The Association of (Private) Care Insurance Companies (*ZN*);
- The Office for Judicial Institutions (*DJI*);
- The National Dutch Tax Agency (*Belastingdienst*) and
- The Association of Bailiffs (*SGN*).

Characteristic for the RINIS concept of cooperation is that each of the participating organizations is a so-called authentic source of data. An authentic source of data is an organization that is responsible for the operational maintenance, content, quality and verification of a data element. For example, an executive organization is always the authentic source for a data element that results from its executive process (for example, the Social Insurances Bank is the authentic source for decisions on the basis of the National Old Age Pensions Act). But organizations may also be regarded as authentic source for other data elements; for example, the citizens' registration office is an authentic source for a client's name, date of birth, and domicile. A study in 1995 revealed that most of the data elements (about sixty) are "claimed" by one organization. About thirteen are not claimed by any organization and one data element is claimed by more than one organization (see Homburg, 1999).

The RINIS infrastructure allows for mainly back-office communication and exchange of information between participating organizations. RINIS can be seen as a so-called reference index: it routes information requests and notification of changes in status of specific citizens (in XML, EDIFACT, or the IVP format that is being used by the Dutch Tax Agency) by participating organizations to the authentic source of data. Requesting organizations therefore are not required to have knowledge in advance which organization has specific information on particular clients or households, or in which specific information system information is stored. The RINIS organization itself does not store information in any way; it merely oversees compliance with agreements that have been made (see below), facilitates routing of messages, use of software (an InfoNet X400 mailserver application, a MaxWare Remote User Agent, a StaffWare Workflow Management package and UTIMACO encryption / decryption utilities), and hosts a helpdesk for the participating organizations.

At present (2006), about 55 million information requests are annually processed through the RINIS infrastructure.

Agreements

From the beginning, it was explicitly recognized that RINIS is about making a minimum level of agreements between participating organizations, and protecting the informational autonomy of participating organizations to a maximum degree. In order to make the RINIS concept work, the following agreements are being used:

- technological agreements that refer to the data interchange standards that are being used, the requirements of the RINIS server and the encryption/decryption methods used;
- information management agreements that refer to the establishment and recognition of authentic sources of data, and the responsibility each authentic source takes for the quality of information of that specific authentic source;
- interchange agreements, in which each and every type of exchange in the RINIS concept is formalized. The purpose of each exchange is explicitly stated, and procedures to resolve

possible future disputes are explicitly stated. Interchange agreements require approval of each and every member of the RINIS Board.

The RINIS agreements focus on the exchange of information between organizations, and can be interpreted as expressions of voluntariness and self-regulation in the social security sector as a whole. Moreover, with the RINIS concept, the autonomy of the participating organization is firmly anchored.

Architectural Foundation and Organizational Model

The organizational model of RINIS and its architectural foundation strongly resembles an archetypical decentralized clearing house. Information is gathered and administered by participating organization, and ownership of information is explicitly attributed to the participating organizations. By means of interchange agreements, other organizations are in practice allowed to verify clients' characteristics (job seeking history, fiscal details, and so forth) through the RINIS infrastructure, but responsibility for information and handling is not handed over to the RINIS bureau. In fact, RINIS itself does not have any administrative tasks other than facilitating information exchange, it does not have any databases with information on citizens, and any attenuation of informational property rights requires the explicit approval of all organizations involved (through an explicit decision in the RINIS Board). Cooptation therefore plays an important role in the governance of RINIS. Moreover, RINIS is not a public body in the sense that it lacks a legal basis in Dutch administrative law.

Social Security Developments in Belgium

Until the second half of the 1980s, the Belgian National System for Social Security was heavily fragmented and supply-oriented. It has involved a mixture of public and private sector organizations, and, as had been the case in the Netherlands, both administratively as well as in terms of execution involved "tripartite" parties (state, labor unions, employers' associations). The Belgian Social Security System covers seven social risks (incapacity for work, industrial accident, occupational disease, unemployment, retirement, child care, and holiday pay—the so-called social security branches), and four social support systems (allowances for the disabled, guaranteed family allowance, minimum income and income guarantee for the elderly), which grant people specific minimum services after verifying their subsistence resources. The system covers 10,000,000 citizens and 200,000 employers (Deprest & Robben, 2003).

The following organizations can be discerned:

- National Illness and Disability Insurance Office (*Rijksinstituut voor ziekte- en invaliditeitsverzekering*);
- National Office of Social Security (*Rijksdienst voor Sociale Zekerheid*)
- National Old Age Pensions Office (*Rijksdienst voor pensioenen*);
- National Child Allowances Office (*Rijksdienst voor kinderbijslag voor werknemers*);
- National Fund for Work-related Disabilities (*Fonds voor de beroepsziektes*);
- National Fund for Work-related Accidents *(Fonds voor arbeidsongevallen);*
- National Employment Office (*Rijksdienst voor arbeidsvoorziening*) and
- National Holiday Premium Office (*Rijksdienst voor jaarlijke vakantie*).

A study conducted in 1986 (Viaene, Robben, Lahaye, & Van Steenberge, 1986) reported the following problems and shortcomings in the cooperation in the field of executive organizations:

- the existence of paper-based information flows;
- poor information requirements analyses by Offices (in the presence of changing legislation);
- repeated information request by various agencies regarding comparable or even similar topics; and
- in general, lack of focus on ways in which companies register data, and lack of citizen orientation.

Following the above analysis, and the recommendations of a National Committee on the Codification, Harmonization and Simplification of Legislation in the field of social security, an Act was drafted (15 January 1990) in which the so-called Cross Point Bank for Social Security (*Kruispuntbank* or *Banque Carrefour de la Securité Sociale)* was announced.

Cross Point Bank for Social Security: A National Initiative to Reduce Administrative Burden

In 1990, the Cross Point Bank for Social Security was established. Although the term "bank" might indicate that the organization has databases by itself, it primarily (but not exclusively) functions as a referral index that allows for information exchange between various organizations, based on the principle of authentic sources of information. There is one important difference with the Dutch connotation of authentic sources, though: if the participating organizations fail to reach agreement on the articulation of authenticity of specific sources or data, or if participating organizations are not able to meet information requirements by the sector as a whole, it is the responsibility of the Cross Point Bank to provide for that information by means of setting up dedicated databases.

The infrastructure of the Cross Point Bank connects public authorities that act as core participants (like the National Illness and Disability Insurance Office and the National Office of Social Security), and auxiliary members (like labor union's insurance companies) that connect through core participants.

Goals of the Cross Point Bank for Social Security can be stated as follows: reduction of administrative burden, increased focus on needs of citizens and corporations and stronger support for the social security policy in general (Snijkers, 2005). In order to do achieve this, harmonization of legislation and implementation practice is explicitly addressed. For instance, legislation allows for assistance from Cross Point Bank to executive organizations in the development and implementation of e-government strategies (art. 3bis Act on Establishment of the Cross Point Bank, 15 January 1990). Furthermore, although it is recognized that the Cross Point Bank should not interfere with existing tasks and responsibilities in the field of executive organizations, it is explicitly acknowledged that tasks that are not carried out by existing executive organizations can or should be performed by the Cross Point Bank.

Overall, the Cross Point Bank focuses heavily on the reduction of administrative burden of citizens and corporations through improvement of intergovernmental exchange of information. At present, the Cross Point Bank for Social Security processes hundred millions of exchanges every year (2004: 339,1 million messages). The communication takes place using the XML standard.

Agreements

Particular exchanges that use the infrastructure of the Cross Point Bank are referred to in specific Acts and Official Announcements (*Koninklijk Besluit* or *Arrêté Royal*). Therefore, exchanges are firmly anchored in legislation and are multilateral (instead of bilateral) in nature. Exchanges require approval of a dedicated Sectoral Committee of the Social Security that is installed in order to protect privacy of citizens. The Committee consists of independent members, among them experts in the fields of law, informatics and health.

Architectural Foundation and Organizational Model

In general, the architecture of the Cross Point Bank is based on the archetypical decentralized clearing house. By using a referral index and XML-based messages, the Cross Point Bank allows for the exchange of information in order to check citizens' income figures, job history, entitled benefits and so forth. It must be stated that the governance structure of the infrastructure is firmly anchored in Acts and legislation in general. The legal basis leaves room for so-called residual tasks: should central government decide that there is a need for specific information that can not be provided by individual executive organizations (or by cooperating executive organizations), the Cross Point Bank can be assigned to carry out additional tasks in order to comply with specific requests. Specific exchanges require legal status and approval by an independent committee of experts. Overall, the Cross Point Bank is the institution that governs the infrastructure in Belgian social security, but it must be stressed that it also has characteristics of a so-called missionary organization: it is explicitly stated that the Bank should assist executive organization in the development and implementation of e-government strategies. This is probably best understood in the context of the frail condition of ICT use in Belgian Social Security at the end of the previous century (Henman & Adler, 2001).

CONCLUSIONS AND LESSONS LEARNED

In the international practice of e-government, concepts like integration and joined-up government almost have mythical proportions. In policy programs, but also in the actual implementation practice at the shop floor of public administration, various initiatives are announced and implemented in order to foster inter-governmental cooperation, reduce administrative burden for citizens and corporations, and so forth.

At a global level, there seems to be a rhetorical closure: governments throughout the world seem to be busy developing and implementing same sets of concepts, be it joined-up government or interoperability, or pan-governmental integration. To the observer, intuitively appealing concepts are swept over the OECD world, or even beyond that part of the globe.

In this comparative case study, it has been our intention to scrutinize to what degree the assumed convergence actually takes place beyond levels of fallible rhetoric. We have scrutinized organizational and political practices in a specific sector of governmental activity, namely social security policy. Social security policy is an interesting field of study as it has a long-standing tradition of ICT implementation and use (so it allows for intensive study). We have compared two rather comparable countries that nonetheless have rather different politico-administrative structures: Belgium and the Netherlands. Although the countries resemble one another in terms of size and geographical proximity, there are notable institutional changes. Belgium can be portrayed as a federal, corporatist state, the Netherlands is an example of a decentralized unitary state. These countries allow for a comparison of ways in which technologies are actually implemented, and if and how technologies are shaped and crafted in various institutional contexts.

From the case study it can be concluded that at a rhetorical level, there is considerable support for assuming convergence. In both contexts, there has been a clamor for joined-up-ness (6 et al., 2002), as an answer to felt needs to fight fraud and compartmentalization. At decisional and operational levels, there is less evidence for assuming convergence. It seems that in disparate institutional contexts, especially governance structures of ICTs are notably different.

In terms of organization and organizational architecture, a notable difference is the origination of the initiative. In the decentralized unitary state of the Netherlands, the RINIS initiative emerged out of the field of executive organizations. These organizations have traditionally nourished ICT competences and could use this knowledge and their relatively strong position to promote, gain support and actually implement the RINIS initiative. By demonstrating the usefulness and effectiveness of the RINIS architecture, executive organizations could defend their traditionally strong informational autonomy and keep central levels of government out. The governance structure of RINIS is characterized by co-opting by participating organizations. The RINIS organization itself is small and does not have any other tasks than merely supporting the information exchanges. Therefore, the Dutch approach is characterized by voluntariness, mutualism and self-regulation. Harmonizing, interorganizational standardization and legal bases for exchanges are kept to the minimum level, and responsibility for fighting fraud and promoting cooperation are mainly carried by executive organizations themselves. In corporatist Belgium, the executive organizations lagged behind in terms of ICT competences and as a reaction to the same alarming signals that had hit the Netherlands, central levels of government (Ministry of Social Affairs) took the initiative to promote intra- and intersectoral information exchange initiatives like the Cross Point Bank. The Cross Point Bank therefore is different in character (missionary activities, governance structure, harmonization and standardization as explicit targets).

It must be stressed that both countries do not differ that much in terms of performance or ranking on general e-government lists. The 2006 CapGemini study positions Belgium on position 18 and the Netherlands on position 16 of European states (Cap Gemini, 2006). Accenture, on the other hand, positions Belgium and the Netherlands on positions 11 and 9 of all countries in the worlds in terms of general e-government performance, respectively.

Overall, this case analysis supports the "social shaping of technology" stream in the literature. Institutions and institutional context matter for ways in which technologies are shaped, not only rhetorically but also in (policy) practice. Therefore, any claim of convergence with respect to e-government should be approached with great caution. Obviously, institutions and institutional context matter for e-government, not only in order to explain pace of implementation or difficulty in implementation, but, more importantly, in terms of organization, management and governance structures of the technologies-in-use.

REFERENCES

6, P., Leat, D., Seltzer, K., & Stoker, G. (2002). *Toward holistic governance: the new reform agenda*. Basingstoke: Palgrave.

Accenture. (2004). *eGovernment leadership: High performance, maximum value*. Retrieved 25 August, 2006, from http://www.accenture.com/NR/rdonlyres/D7206199-C3D4-4CB4-A7D8-846C94287890/0/gove_egov_value.pdf

Adler, M., & Henman, P. (2005). Computerizing the welfare state: An international comparison of computerization in social security. *Information, Communication and Society, 8*(3), 315-342.

Andersen, K. V., & Kraemer, K. L. (1995). Information technology and transitions in the public-service - A comparison of Scandinavia and the United-States. *European Journal of Information Systems, 4*(1), pp. 51-63.

Bogdanor, V. (2005). *Joined-up government* Oxford: Oxford University Press.

Cap Gemini. (2006). *Online availability of public services: How is Europe progressing?* . Retrieved 25 August, 2006.

Chadwick, A., & May, C. (2003). Interaction between states and citizens in the age of the internet: "e-government" in the United States, Britain, and the European Union. *Governance, 16*(2), pp. 271-300.

Deprest, J., & Robben, F. (2003). *E-government: the approach of the Belgian federal administration*. Brussels: FEDICT.

Esping-Andersen, G. (1996). *Welfare states in transition. National adaptations in global economies.* London: Sage Publications.

Fenger, H. J. M. (2006). Shifts in welfare governance: the state, private and non-profit sectors in four European countries. In P. Henman & H. J. M. Fenger (Eds.), *Administering welfare reform* (73-92). Bristol: The Policy Press.

Fountain, J. (2001). *Building the virtual state*. Washington DC: The Brookings Institute.

Heeks, R. (2003). E-Government in Africa: Promise and practice. *Information Polity, 7*(2-3), pp. 97-114.

Henman, P., & Adler, M. (2001). Information technology and transformations in social security policy and administration: a review. *International Social Security Review, 54*(4), 23-47.

Henman, P., & Adler, M. (2003). Information technology and the governance of social security. *Critical Social Policy, 23*(2), 139-164.

Homburg, V. M. F. (1999). *The Political economy of information management:A theoretical and empirical analysis of decision making regarding interorganizational information systems.* Capelle aan de IJssel: Labyrinth.

Homburg, V. M. F., & Bekkers, V. J. J. M. (2005). E-government and NPM: A perfect marriage? In V. J. J. M. Bekkers & V. M. F. Homburg (Eds.), *The Information Ecology of E-Government: E-Government as Institutional and Technological Innovation in Public Administration*. Amsterdam / Berlin / Oxford / Tokyo / Washington D.C.: IOS Press.

Kubicek, H., & Hagen, M. (Eds.). (2000). *One-Stop-Government in Europe: Results from 11 national surveys.* Bremen: University of Bremen.

Ling, T. (2002). Delivering joined-up government in the UK: Dimensions, Issues and Problems. *Public Administration, 80*(4), 615-642.

MacKenzie, D., & Wajcman, J. (Eds.). (1985). *The social shaping of technology: How the refrigerator got its hum.* Milton Keynes: Open University Press.

Millard, J., Iversen, J. S., Kubicek, H., Westholm, H., & Cimander, R. (2004). *Reorganisation of government back-offices for better electronic public services – European good practices (back-office reorganisation).* Brussels: EU DG Information Society.

Moon, M. J. (2002). The evolution of e-government among municipalities: Rhetoric or reality? *Public Administration Review, 62*(4), 424-433.

Mosco, V. (2004). *The digital sublime: Myth, power and cyberspace*. Cambridge: The MIT Press.

Ndou, V. (2004). E-Government for developing countries: Opportunities and challenges. *The Electronic Journal for Information Systems in Developing Countries, 18*(1), 1-24.

Peters, B. G. (1996). *The Future of Governing: Four Emerging Models*. Kansas: Kansas University Press.

Peters, B. G. (1998). Managing horizontal government: the politics of coordination. *Public Administration, 76*(2), 295-311.

Pollitt, C. P. (2002). Clarifying convergence: Striking similarities and durable differences in public management reform. *Public Management Review, 4*(1), 471-492.

Pollitt, C. P., & Bouckaert, G. (2004). *Public management reform: A comparative analysis*. Oxford: Oxford University Press.

Pressman, J., & Wildavsky, A. (1973). *Implementation*. Berkeley, CA: University of California Press.

Smith, N. J. (1985). *Social welfare and computers: A general outline*. Melbourne: Longman Cheshire.

Snijkers, K. (2005). *eGovernment in een interbestuurlijke context. Casestudie: OCMW's en de Kruispuntbank van de Sociale Zekerheid*. Leuven: Steunpunt Beleirdsrelevant Onderzoek Bestuurlijke Organisatie Vlaanderen.

Steen, T., van den Berg, C., van der Meer, F., Overeem, P., & Toonen, T. (2005). *Modernising Governments in other countries*. The Hague: Modernising Government Project (Ministry of the Interior and Kingdom Relations).

Tat-Kei Ho, A. (2002). Reinventing local governments and the e-government initiative. *Public Administration Review, 62*(4), 434-444.

Teichert, J., & Dow, N. (2002). E-government in Australia, promise and progress. *The Information Polity, 7*(4), 231-246.

Viaene, J., Robben, F., Lahaye, D., & Van Steenberge, J. (1986). Algemene schets van een rationele informatieverwerking in de sociale zekerheid. *Belgisch Tijdschrift voor de Sociale Zekerheid, 4*(5), 399-473.

Williams, R., & Edge, D. (1996). The social shaping of technology. *Research Policy, 25*, 865-899.

This work was previously published in International Journal of Cases on Electronic Commerce, Vol. 3, Issue 2, edited by M. Khosrow-Pour, pp. 1-12, copyright 2007 by IGI Publishing, formerly known as Idea Group Publishing (an imprint of IGI Global).

Chapter 5.18
Electronic Voting in Belgium

Pascal Delwit
Université Libre de Bruxelles, Belgium

Jean-Benoit Pilet
Université Libre de Bruxelles, Belgium

Erol Kulahci
Université Libre de Bruxelles, Belgium

INTRODUCTION

Does representative democracy imply that there is … representation? What does one mean by *representation*? Looked at very generally, it means that the legislative (parliament and government) and executive (government) bodies represent the opinions of those who are represented.

The primary method for expressing opinions in democracies is by voting: the parliaments are made up of representatives that reflect the different trends of the opinion expressed by the vote (Avril, 1990). Universal suffrage is neither a historical fact nor a clear-cut contemporary feature. There have been, and there still are, individuals who are excluded from voting and universal suffrage (Rémond, 1999). For a long time, several European countries had representational parliamentary systems that were not democracies. We then experienced a *notabilization* of political relations (Deloye, 1997, p. 96). As Max Weber put it, one is not then living from politics but for politics (Weber, 1963). Several restrictions existed and still exist with universal suffrage. For many years, governments either slowed down or restrained access to voting.

Nowadays, the problems arise in new and really reverse terms. The question is more about knowing how to bring citizens back to the ballot boxes and in this manner to perpetuate the legitimacy of the democratic system. Indeed, voter turnout rates have been falling for the past 20 years (Blais & Dobrzynska, 1998; Delwit, 2002). In many European countries, abstention has risen in a straight line since the end of the 1970s right up to the present day. In view of this trend and considering the growing number of election choices for a priori nongovernment parties (Ignazi, 2003), several analysts and political leaders have been wondering about ways to curb this development.

In part, thoughts relating to *electronic voting* (e-voting) lie within this context (Birch & Watt, 2004). A certain number of academics and political leaders have been examining institutionalised restraints likely to improve the current state of affairs (Bowler, Brockington, & Donovan, 2001). Naturally in this framework, electronic vote is only one element amongst others. In this regard, Arend Lijphart has undoubtedly pursued this the furthest, since in 1997 he suggested (re)introducing compulsory voting in democratic states in order to respond to the sagging voter turnout (Lijphart, 1997, p. 11).

The will to reduce voter abstention was not the only issue at the origin of studies on the possibility of introducing or extending e-voting. The mobilization of new communication methods and technology for voting was also at issue. Particularly as the unfortunate vote counting experience in the state of Florida during the 2000 presidential election highlighted concerns about traditional methods of voting and vote counting (Jarvis, 2001).

This article will briefly discuss the issue of e-voting by looking at the response to the introduction of e-voting by Belgian citizens who used it. We will show the results of a major exit poll survey conducted on the occasion of the May 18, 2003, federal elections on Belgian's opinions with regard to e-voting. Two major issues were examined. To what extent was e-voting as it was used in Belgium considered as easy or difficult to use? Was e-voting commonly accepted or rejected by the voters who used it?

BACKGROUND: THE BELGIANS AND ELECTRONIC VOTING

In 1994, the following provision was inserted in the Belgian Electoral Law, "The King can, by decree deliberated by the Cabinet, decide that, for electoral constituencies, electoral cantons or communes that he designates, an automated voting system should be used."[1] From that moment on, computer voting was introduced in more and more Belgian municipalities. In 2003, 44% of all Belgian voters cast their vote on a computer.

To a certain extent, the use of e-voting in Belgium may look surprising. In Belgium, voting is compulsory. Voters not attending at the polls may be sued. The first time, they risk to pay from 25€ to 50€, the second from 50€ to 125€. Even if sanctions are scarcely applied (0.0015% in 1985), most Belgians respect the rule and vote. In the last federal elections (2003), the turnout was 91.9% (decreasing of 3.25 percentage points in the last 15 years). In that context, one can hardly conclude that Belgian legislators introduce e-voting to curb a growing abstention. Actually, two reasons justified this choice. First, e-voting was going to avoid a large number of invalid votes. Second, legislators wanted to reduce the length of counting procedures.

Ten years after its introduction, time had come for a first evaluation of e-voting in Belgium. On May 18, 2003, a team of 27 pollsters supervised by seven researchers and professors from the Université libre de Bruxelles (ULB) went to 13 polling stations in the country[2]. In addition, two teams of pollsters went to two municipalities where the so-called "ticketing" method was being tried out, in order to improve confidence and, eventually, recount in case of contest (Kohno, Tubblefield, Rubin, & Wallach, 2003; Maynihan, 2004, pp. 523-524).

The questionnaire submitted at the polling station exit on May 18, 2003, was in three parts[3]. The first had a series of questions that enabled defining the socio-demographic profile of the individuals interviewed. This information has a twofold use. On the one hand, it enabled assessment of the value of the sampling in terms of representativeness. On the other hand, this data also permitted us to determine whether certain socioeconomic groups or certain age categories showed any specific association with e-voting problems.

The second part of the questionnaire contributed a second round of objective data on the profile of the persons polled. Its purpose was to provide the resources needed to assess whether familiarity with computers and the information received beforehand about this new voting system tended to influence the way voters felt about e-voting.

Finally, the last part of the exit-poll questionnaire contained questions asking Belgian voters if they were satisfied with e-voting. Four questions served as indicators of this global satisfaction. First, those polled were asked to evaluate how easy they found e-voting. Second, they were asked to express the social acceptance of the new voting procedure. The third item concerned trust in e-voting. Finally, their overall feeling regarding e-voting was asked.

MAIN THRUST OF ARTICLE: ACCEPTANCE OF E-VOTING IN BELGIUM

The User Friendliness of Electronic Voting

First of all, those polled were asked the user friendliness of e-voting. Before going into the answers, one should briefly state how Belgian voters have to proceed to cast their vote electronically.[4] In the poll station, each voter receives a magnetic card. The voter enters the polling booth, inserts his or her magnetic card, and starts the process. Using an electronic pencil, the voter chooses a party first, and then a candidate. Afterward, the voter has to confirm his or her vote. At the end, the voter gives back his or her magnetic card and his or her vote is recorded.

Knowing the details of e-voting in Belgium, we can move on to the analysis of the user friendliness of e-voting. Those polled were asked to evaluate the ease/difficulty of use of e-voting by stating that e-voting as "very easy," "easy," "difficult," or "very difficult" to use. Looking at the figures, it seemed clear that if there was any criticism voiced by the interviewees about e-voting, the reproaches had nothing to do with the user friendliness of this method of voting.

Indeed, just under three fourths of respondents stated "very easy" for computerized voting. The positive comments relating to the actual operation of the e-voting mechanism even reached 95.11% if one adds the 24.92% of persons who noted "easy" to vote with computer. Except for a very small minority of 3.28%, a favorable opinion was given about the user friendliness of e-voting.

If one cross-checks ease of use with the educational background, one can analyse to what extent e-voting would be more accessible to the better educated. The data obtained in our research were able to confirm this hypothesis to a certain degree. Indeed, it was with respondents having greater educational capital (university and college qualifications) that the percentages of people who stated "very easy" for e-voting were the highest. In the two cases, it was close to 80% (78.16% for university graduates and 79.95% for those who graduated from colleges). Conversely, individuals with less educational capital gave fewer favorable answers. For example, it was only 41.67% with people whose final diploma was the one they obtained at the end of their primary school education (age 12).

Societal Acceptance of Electronic Voting

The second variable tested was societal acceptance of e-voting. Here, it dealt with assessing within our sampling if e-voting posed any philosophical problems.

In order to assess if people interviewed had any complaints to make in this realm, an ad hoc question was put to them. It asked them to state if for them, e-voting was "a major problem of principle," "a slight problem of principle," or "not a problem of principle."

The figures are clear for the matter of societal acceptance of e-voting. By a very substantial majority (84.97%), the respondents stated that for them, the new voting method was not a problem of principle. The two other replies were only given by 12.34% of those questioned.

Therefore it clearly emerged that societal acceptance of e-voting was not a disputed issue within our sampling taken on May 18, 2003, at polling station exits.

Figure 1. Ease/difficulty in using electronic voting

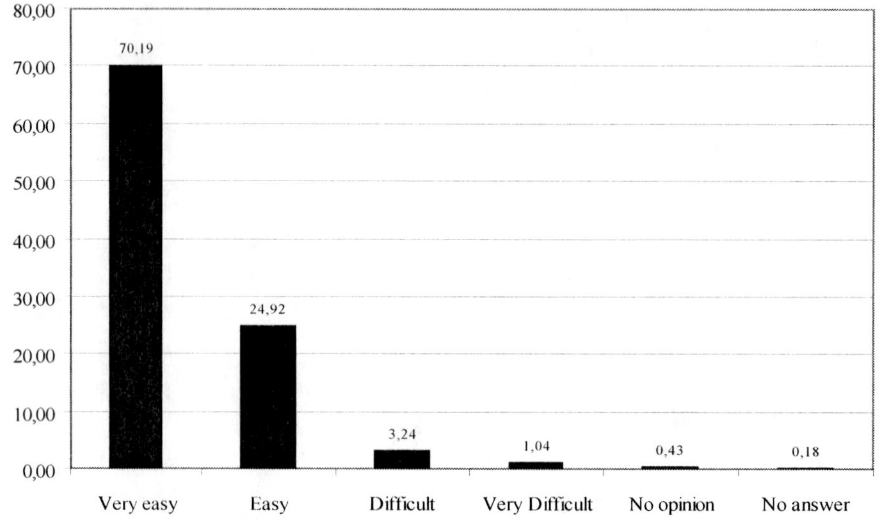

Figure 2. Degree of ease depends on educational capital

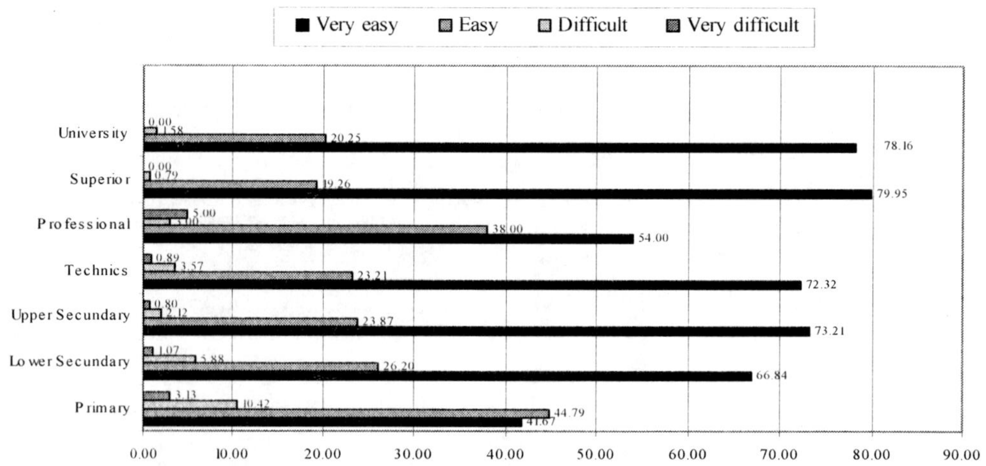

Figure 3. The matter of principle

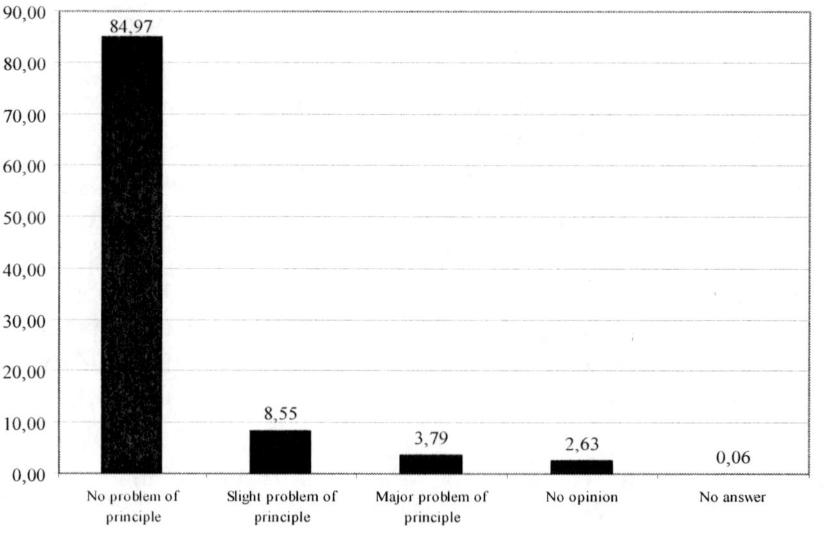

The Issue of Trust/Mistrust in E-Voting

The third and final question was about citizens' confidence in e-voting. The last variable is vital for establishing the legitimacy of computerised voting. As several authors have repeated, without this legitimacy, any wide-scale application of this method could be problematic.

Over the sampling as a whole, there was a majority feeling of trust toward e-voting. The favorable responses ("full confidence" and "rather confident") were mentioned in 88.88% of cases. Only 8.5% of those surveyed expressed mistrust ("rather not very confident" and "not at all confident") toward computerized voting.

The feeling of trust appeared to dominate to a large extent, although it was not without reservations. Indeed, a majority of respondents (54%) expressed complete confidence, but nearly a quarter of the sampling expressed qualified trust (34.88%). Thus there was now a different configuration than the one for the question on ease of use. For the latter variable, the proportion of qualified responses was much lower.

Just as with ease of use, it was interesting to cross-check this data on trust with several independent variables. The first run dealt again with educational capital. The first lesson learned was that no matter what the final diploma was, trust was expressed by the wide majority. In all cases, over 80% of respondents expressed complete or reasonable confidence in computerized voting.

Even so, some differences were noticed between the different levels of educational capital. Full confidence was highest in respondents with the lowest level of academic assets ("no diploma" [61.22%] and "primary school diploma" [60.22%]), as well as by individuals who took technical education (62.73%). Yet, the total for positive responses ("fully confident" and "rather confident") remained at around 80 to 90%, regardless of the educational capital.

The age category that least expressed "full confidence" (46.73%), the 30–39 year olds, was also the one in which the total number of confident respondents ("full confidence" or "rather confident") was the highest (91.9%). This clearly strange revelation reflected a broader trend in which it turned out that as the age of respondents increased, there was more "full confidence" but also more mistrust. The skeptical responses ("rather no confidence" and "no confidence at all") were largely in the minority no matter what the age of the respondents. On average, we had rates of mistrust between 5 and 13%.

The age category expressing the least mistrust was the 30–39 year olds with 5.3%. At the other end, we found the 60-69 year olds for whom computerized voting raised a feeling of mistrust in 13.24% of cases. For the latter, as well as with the 70+ category, the answers "not at all confident" even reached 6.85%.

It seemed, therefore, that the oldest individuals, who were also those who had the least contact with computers and information technology, expressed comparatively more caution with regard to the new way of voting. The relationship between age and mistrust was not in a straight line, however. Indeed, the 30-39 year olds and those aged 50-59 were the categories in which mistrust was the lowest. In both cases, the mistrust rates remained below 8%.

Finally, what about the experimental tests with ticketing? The experiment conducted at the Waarschot and Verlaine polling stations increased confidence a bit but it especially altered its fundamental nature. Seventy percent of voters in these polling stations actually confirmed they had complete confidence in computerzed voting compared to 52% of voters in other stations. On the contrary, the number of citizens expressing some kind of mistrust was reduced to its most simple expression, 3%, compared to 9% amongst citizens voting in a different station. It did indeed seem that ticketing had a valued-added effect.

The preceding data showed that computerized voting gave rise to relatively few negative

Figure 4. Trust/mistrust in electronic voting

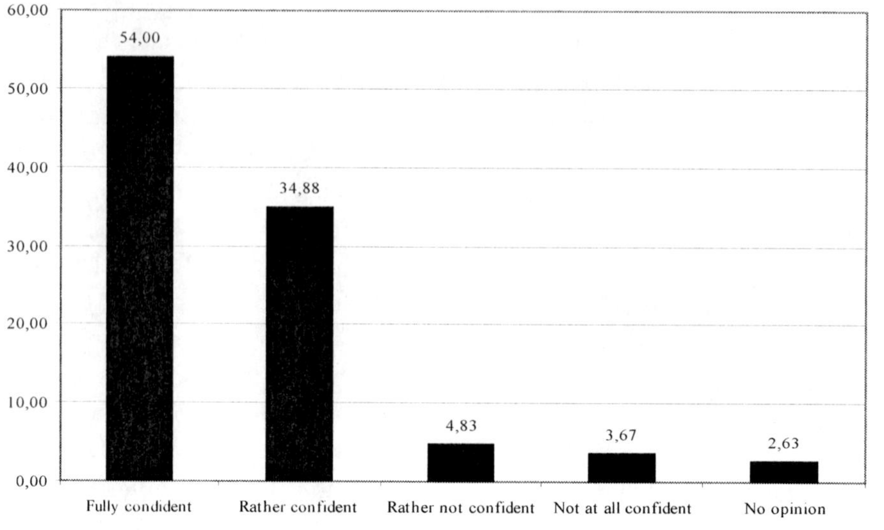

Figure 5. Trust or mistrust in the paper ballot

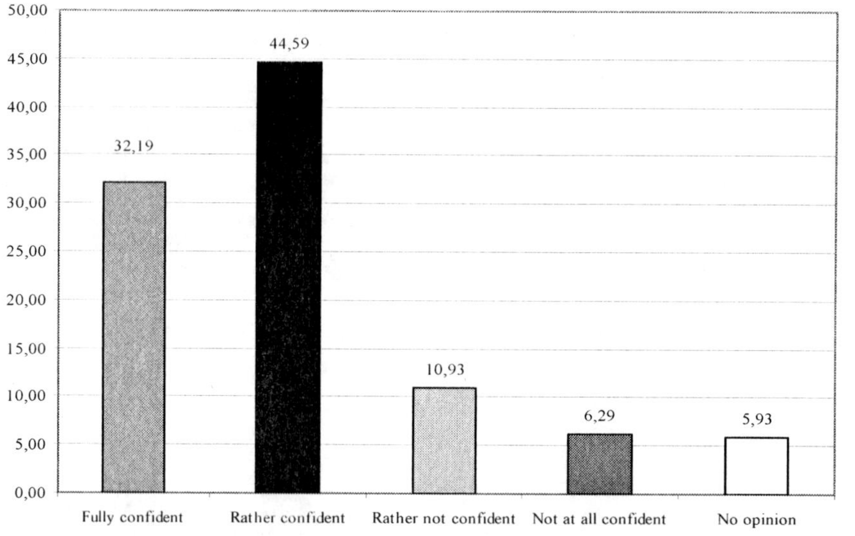

reactions on the subject of user friendliness, societal acceptance, and trust. Nonetheless, it was certainly advisable to wonder if the relationship to the new voting method was better or not as good as Belgian ties to the paper ballot. For this purpose, the questionnaire submitted at the poll exits included a question about confidence in voting with paper ballots.

A majority of respondents expressed their confidence in the paper ballot. Almost one third of them (32.19%) declared to have "full confidence" and 44.59% said they were "rather confident," which meant 76.78% positive responses. Negative responses were made by 17.26% of those polled (10.93% "relatively little confidence" and 6.29% "no confidence at all"). Finally, there were 5.93% with no opinion. Amongst the latter, one undoubtedly will find voters who have never voted with paper ballot.

Just as for e-voting, the confidence of those questioned was largely positive. Even so, it was expressed in a more nuanced manner than it was for the new voting method. The paper ballot received more "reasonably confident" than "fully confident." Conversely, 54% marked "full confidence" for e-voting compared to 34.88% "reasonably confident." Nonetheless, this comparison must be made with caution because it compared real circumstances—the e-voting done on May 18, 2003—with a past situation—voting with paper ballot—or virtual, notably in the case of the under 30s who may have never voted with paper ballot.

In short, the two voting methods inspired respondents' trust. Nevertheless, the confidence grades were more moderate for voting with paper ballot.

The positions with regard to paper balloting and e-voting could be cross-checked. The goal was to see if the positions vis-à-vis the former method were the same as for computerized voting. The figure below can be read in the following manner. The people who were completely confident about computerized voting are represented on the black columns. These respondents were subdivided between the four answers on paper ballots and according to the percentages that are above the lines. The same logic applies for the other three colours (three shades of grey).

The people who placed full confidence in e-voting most often gave the response "fully confident" for the other voting method (43.14%). The response that was in second place was "rather confident" (37.71%). Mistrust was expressed moderately in 12.71% of cases and decidedly in 6.97%. Overall, the respondents who had complete confidence in e-voting also placed much confidence in paper ballots. Even so, less than half declared full confidence in both cases.

Amongst those surveyed who said they had "reasonable confidence" in e-voting, 63.5% were also "reasonably confident" in voting with paper ballots. The second case was "full confidence" with 21.04%. Then came "relatively little confidence" with 10.24% and "no confidence at all" for 5.21% of cases.

Three quarters (73.08%) of those interviewed who noted relative mistrust in e-voting were more disposed toward the former method. With the latter, the paper ballot obtained 50% of "reasonably confident" and 23.08% of "full confidence." Finally, 5.13% had less confidence in the paper ballot.

With the voters approached at the polling station exits who declared they had "no confidence at all" in computerized voting, they also found a certain preference for the old system. Thirty-seven-and-a-half percent had complete confidence in the paper ballot and 42.86% were "reasonably confident." Next, 16.07% had "no confidence at all" in either of the two methods of voting. Finally 3.75% of respondents in this category had "relatively little confidence" in the paper ballot.

In brief, two trends appeared. A majority of those who had confidence in e-voting also had confidence in the paper ballot, but in a more moderate fashion. On the other hand, with those who mistrusted the new method, it was generally through preference to the former technique.

The respondents' positioning toward e-voting was analyzed in detail according to three variables: societal acceptance, user friendliness, and trust. A fourth and more encompassing question was added to the questionnaire. It asked the respondents to state if in the end, they were or were not favorable to computerized voting.

A vast majority (87.84%) answered yes to this question. Less than 10% gave an unfavorable answer (8.43%). The percentage of nonanswers was 3.67%. As with the totality of questions, the opinions were positive with regard to e-voting. But one should keep in mind the nuances that surfaced with socio-demographics and voter familiarity with computers.

If we differentiate between voters from polling stations with ticketing system and the others, we once again observe a high level of acceptance.

Figure 6. Cross-checking of confidence in electronic voting and paper (colors for confidence in e-voting and columns for confidence in paper ballot)

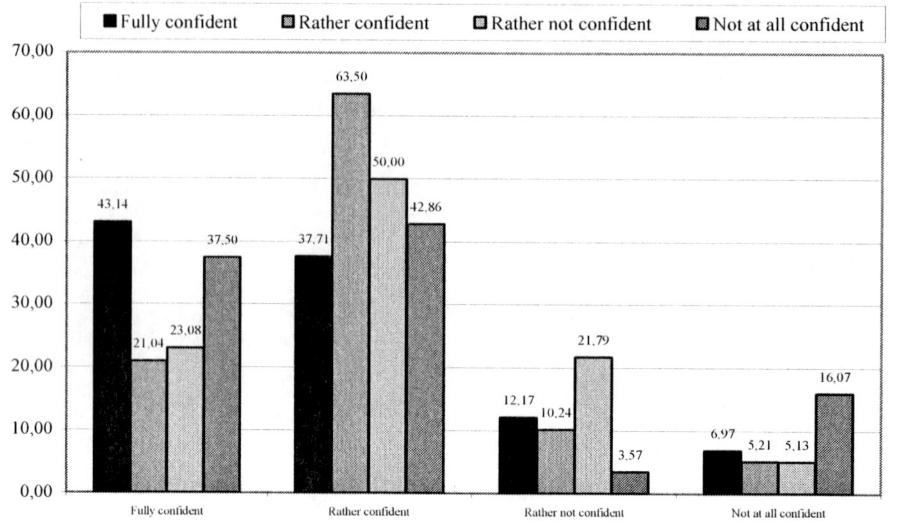

Figure 7. Overall feeling regarding electronic voting

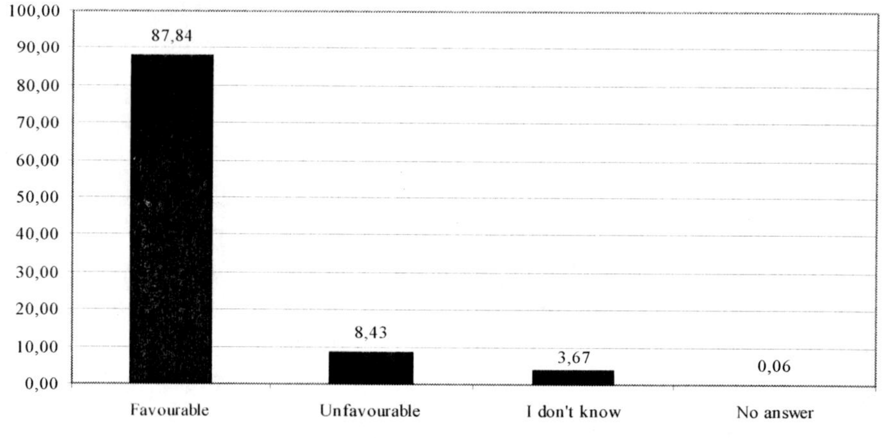

Nearly 92% of voters in Verlaine and Waarschot declared themselves in favor of computerized voting compared to 87% of surveyed voters from other polling stations. And only 6.6% had a differing opinion compared to 8.7% in the second category.

FUTURE TRENDS

Considering the low level of mistrust in e-voting among Belgian voters in 2003, one can assume that the legislator would not restrain his or her desire to go farther in the application of this new voting procedure.

In previous years, politicians from several parties declared that they want to generalize computer voting in all Belgian municipalities. Only the *Parti socialiste* does not want implement e-voting in more areas. The first goal of the promoters was to have computer voting in all municipalities for the 2006 general elections. As it was not practically possible, they will try to do it for the 2007 federal elections or for the 2009 regional and European elections.

Actually, some even want to go one step farther by introducing Internet voting in Belgium. The current Flemish State Secretary Peter Vanvelthoven (SP.A) announced his project in October 2005. No decision has been made, but no one can say that it is never going to happen.

CONCLUSION

In every representative democracy, the act of voting is without a doubt a stumbling block. Through it, citizens exercise their sovereignty; through it, they choose representatives, they exercise control over those in power, decide on societal projects. This multitude of functions fully demonstrates the importance of voting. Under these conditions, when the ballot box verdict loses representativeness, legitimacy, or credibility, it is the entire democratic system that grinds to a halt.

In the fight against abstentionism, institutional imposition is at the top of the list. This approach can lead to rather radical suggestions: the world-renown political science expert Arend Lijphart (1997) suggested (re)turning to compulsory voting. However, "more moderate" proposals are being examined. One of the key approaches aims at making voting easier.

This approach would involve making voting easier through a variety of improvements. In this way, voting would become simpler, which would have the knock-on effect of bring voters (back) to the polling stations, even if in reality abstentionists can be considered as being "in remission" from the voting system.

A few nuances should be added to this diagnosis. Some studies have well and truly shown that an evolution in voting methods can increase voter participation. Thus, Jean Blondel, Richard Sinnott, and Palle Svensson (1997) in particular plotted a higher rate of abstention in the countries where voting took place on a weekday than in countries where it took place on Sunday the 8th. Gimpel and Schuknecht (2003) have pointed out the importance of the ballot boxes' accessibility. But the main cause of the drop in voter participation did not stem from these secondary elements and basically reflected the significance of the election (see, for example, Reif, 1980).

Be that as it may, technical solutions to abstention were certainly the ones that gave rise to most of the legislative initiatives. At various levels, numerous countries experimented with technical innovations aiming at making voting *easier*. Among them, one, the electronic or computer voting is at the moment experienced at a large-scale level in Belgium, as it is in the Netherlands, Great Britain, the United States, and Brazil (Bourgaux, 2001). In Belgium, the first use of e-voting was made in 1991 in the villages of Waarschot and Verlaine. The trial was considered conclusive enough for the procedure to be expanded. At the last elections on May 18, 2003, around 44% of voters used the new method.

Nevertheless, such evolution in the process of voting is certainly not only technical. It can have several impacts on the reliability of the counting, on the secrecy of the vote, and also in terms of societal cohesion. Knowing that, the *Centre d'étude de la vie politique* of the ULB became involved in very extensive field research in 2003 (Delwit, Kulahci, & Pilet). Studies have included an "exit poll" conducted on May 18, 2003 (N = 1637).

The goal of this research was to analyze the social legitimacy of computer voting in Belgium by questioning Belgian voters. The hypotheses were that this new voting technology could affect the equal access to the right to vote. Four categories of polarization were presumed:

1. Between rich and poor
2. Between those who pursed higher academic studies and those who have minimum qualifications in academic terms
3. Between young and old
4. Between Flanders, Wallonia, and Brussels

In this concise contribution, we have given a brief presentation of the results of this survey. Looking at the figures, it seemed clear that if any criticism was made with regard to e-voting, the main concern of these reproofs had no connection with the user friendliness of this voting method. Indeed, a bit less than three quarters of respondents felt that they had used computerized voting "with the greatest of ease."

Generally speaking, the fact to have already voted by computer, but also the respondent's familiarity with IT, tended to promote to a great extent the convenience of e-voting. Apropos, modest elements of a *digital divide* were noted: there was an underlying trend for people with the lowest level of academic assets to encounter the most difficulties. These reservations only involved a minority of respondents, but the observation was verified by our exit poll and likewise for three target publics that we analyzed in a postelection survey.

At societal acceptance level, the exit poll results showed the absence of any major problems. By a very large majority (84.97%), respondents confirmed that the new method of voting did not pose any problems in principle. Societal acceptance of e-voting appeared to be contested just a little and not very strongly within the scope of our sampling taken on May 18, 2003, at the polling station exits.

The third dependent variable assessed was confidence in the new method of voting amongst Belgian voters. The favorable responses ("full confidence" and "reasonably confident") were expressed in 88.88% of the cases.

Looking at the cross-checking of certain socio-demographic data with levels of confidence in e-voting, some nuances can be established. Thus we could detect differences in terms of levels of educational capital. Full confidence was highest in respondents with the lowest one. Thus it was the opposite of the observation established for ease of use.

The second cross-checking carried out on the matter of trust/mistrust was the influence of age on the responses. Here, too, the great majority expressed confidence. In all age categories, more than 80% of respondents reported "full confidence" or "reasonably confident." However, it was noted that when the age of respondents increased, the attitudes with the most opposition increased as well: *those with complete self-confidence* and those *with deep-seated mistrust*.

The aforementioned figures show that computerized voting gave little rise to negative reactions in the realms of user friendliness, societal acceptance, and confidence. Moreover, we observed that in the Verlaine and Waarschot polling stations, where the ticketing experiment was introduced, societal acceptance and confidence in computer voting were higher than the average.

Without a doubt, and based on the data from this research using questionnaires, it is shown that the relationship of Belgian voters with e-voting is largely positive. Both in terms of ease of use as well as of societal acceptance, the surveys conducted recorded large rates of support in the new method of voting. The sole nuances to be added are expressed by senior citizens and youngest ones who expressed a more moderate level of confidence. Nonetheless, in no example did the negative opinions have the most replies. Societal legitimacy of the new voting method within the sampling of Belgian voters that this analysis is based on did not seem to pose any insurmountable problems for the interpretation of these results.

Naturally, these findings are at a *representation* level. They express the feeling of voters toward a (relatively) new method of voting. As such, they do not prove the absence or the presence of potential problems. But in the eyes of a clear majority of voters, e-voting on site at the polling station did not cause any particular difficulty with use and no specific concerns as to the tallying and announcement of the results.

REFERENCES

Avril, P. (1990). *Essais sur les partis politiques*. Paris: Payot.

Birch, S., & Watt, B. (2004). Remote electronic voting: Free, fair and secret. *The Political Quarterly, 75*(1), 60-72.

Blais, A., & Dobrzynska, A. (1998). Turnout in electoral democracies. *European Journal of Political Research, 33*(2), 239-261.

Blondel J., Sinnott R., & Svensson P. (1997). Representation and voter participation. *European Journal of Political Research, 32*(2), 243-272.

Bourgaux, A.-E. (2001). *Le vote automatisé : du mythe de Prométhée à celui de Frankenstein. Les élections dans tous leurs états. Bilan, enjeux et perspectives du droit électoral.* Centre de droit public de l'ULB. Bruxelles: Bruylant, 157-245.

Bowler, S., Brockington, D., & Donovan T. (2001). Election systems and voter turnout: Experiments in the United States. *The Journal of Politics, 63*(3), 902-915.

Deloye, Y. (1997). *Sociologie historique du politique*. Paris: La découverte.

Delwit, P. (2002). Electoral participation and European polls: A limited legitimacy. In G. Grunberg, P. Perrineau, & C. Ysmal (Eds.), *Europe at the polls. The European Elections of 1999* (pp. 207-222). New York: Palgrave-MacMillan.

Delwit, P., Kulahci, E., & Pilet, J.-B. (2004). *Le vote électronique en Belgique: un choix légitime?* Ghent, Belgium: Academia Press.

Gimpel, J. G., & Schuknecht, J. E. (2003). Political participation and the accessibility of the ballot box. *Political Geography, 22*(5), 471-488.

Ignazi, P. (2003). *Extreme Right parties in Western Europe*. Oxford, UK: Oxford University Press.

Jarvis, R. (2001), *Bush vs. Gore. The fight for Florida's vote*. New York: Kluwer.

Kohno, T., Tubblefield, A., Rubin, A., & Wallach, D. (2003). *Analysis of an electronic voting system*. Johns Hopkins University Information Security Institute Technical Report. 19. Baltimore: Johns Hopkins University.

Lijphart, A. (1997). Unequal participation: Democracy's unresolved dilemma. *American Political Science Review, 91*(1), 1-14.

Maynihan, D. (2004). Building secure elections: E-voting, security and systems theory. *Public Administration Review, 64*(5), 515-528.

Reif, K. (1980). Ten second-order national election. In *Ten European Elections* (pp. 1-36). London: Gower.

Rémond, R. (1999). Pour une histoire idéologique du suffrage universel: d'une utopie contestée au consensus relativisé. In *La politique est-elle intelligible?* (pp. 209-224). Brussels: Complexe. Weber, M. (1963). *Le savant et le politique*. Paris: Plon.

KEY TERMS

Abstention: Number of registered electors who do not go to vote on the election day. In all Western European countries (except Denmark), abstention has increased for 20 years.

Digital Divide: Hypothesis whereby the use of IT in the electoral process would put certain categories of voters at a disadvantage. Certain social classes who are less familiar with electronic voting would be deprived de facto of their right to vote.

Electronic Voting: Technique by which electors vote by following the instructions on the screen of a computer installed in a pooling booth, instead of by using a ballot paper. (In this article, used as a synonym of computer voting, automatized voting, e-voting, or computerized voting.)

Internet Voting: Technique by which electors vote by using a computer connected to the Internet. This operation can be take place in a polling booth, via interactive kiosks installed in public places, or from any computer connected to the Web.

Societal Acceptance of Electronic Voting: In order to assess if the persons interviewed had any complaints to make in this realm, an ad hoc question was put to them. It asked them to state if for them, electronic voting was "a major problem of principle," "a slight problem of principle," or "not a problem of principle."

Ticketing: Word commonly used in Belgium for *voter verifiable paper audit trail (VVAT).*

Trust in Electronic Voting: Voters were asked to declare if they were "fully confident," "rather confident," "rather not confident," or "not at all confident" in electronic voting.

User Friendliness of Electronic Voting: In the survey conducted on the occasion of the 2003 federal elections, Belgian voters were asked to evaluate the ease/difficulty of use of electronic voting by stating that electronic voting as "very easy," "easy," "difficult," or "very difficult" to use.

Voter Verifiable Paper Audit Trail: Experiences where a voting ticket is printed by the computer and collected in a sealed ballot box, in order to improve confidence in electronic voting and, eventually, recount in case of contest.

ENDNOTES

1. Loi du 11 avril 1994 organisant le vote automatisé, article 1er.
2. Four in rural areas (Lens, Asse, Waarschoot, and Verlaine), two in suburban areas (Seraing and Sart-Tilman) and seven in urban areas (Bruxelles-Ville, Saint Gilles, Jette, Anvers, Borgerhout, Anderlecht, Liège centre). All are municipalities where e-voting is used. In Waarschoot and Verlaine, a system of voter verifiable paper audit trail (VVAT) was tested.
3. Finally, the sample is composed of 1.637 voters, 51.93% are men, and 55.07% are professionally active. The age scale is as follows: 18-29 years (21.69%), 30-39 (19.24%), 40-49 (17.03%), 50-59 (14.83%), 60-69 (13.85%), 70+ (13.36%).
4. http://elections2004.belgium.be/fr/automated_voting.html# In the bilingual regions, the voter must choose a language (Dutch, French, or German) before voting.

This work was previously published in Encyclopedia of Digital Government, edited by A. Anttiroiko and M. Malkia, pp. 670-679, copyright 2007 by Information Science Reference, formerly known as Idea Group Reference (an imprint of IGI Global).

Chapter 5.19
Enabling Federated Identity for E-Government

Tanya Candia
Enosis Group, USA

Paul Madsen
NTT, USA

INTRODUCTION

Today's administrative and business environment calls for information sharing on an unprecedented scale, from government to business to citizen. Sharing and interoperating among agencies, businesses, and governments around the world create opportunities to simplify processes and unify work, as well as improve the overall performance of government. Secure interoperability, based on identity management solutions, enables substantial cost savings, streamlined processes and faster communication of vital information to the benefit of governments and citizens of all nations.

At the core of this revolution is the concept of federated identity management and the need for standards that are open, interoperable and decentralized. In addition, such standards must allow for privacy safeguard across all sectors. The Liberty Alliance Project (Liberty Alliance, n.d.) was established to address this need and tackle the twin issues of standards and trust.

BACKGROUND

Today's administrative and business environment has created an unprecedented need to securely share sensitive information among national, regional and local governments, agencies and organizations, as well as with citizens and business entities. The true distributed computing platform created by the Internet brings into sharp relief the importance of adhering to emerging privacy standards and data security regulations.

Identity is at the core of any information-sharing transaction: government to citizen, government to business or government to government. Individuals' identities not only prove that they are who they say they are, it also indicates what they can do and what resources they can access. Governments are often the source of core documents that relate to one's identity: birth certificates, drivers' licenses, employment and tax records, marriage and death certificates, and the like. Identity credentials are perhaps more relevant in today's digital society in their electronic form than on paper.

Identity Management Issues

Effectively managing one's identity means retaining control over the information relative to who one is, who has access to it and how it is used. While simple in the abstract, the task is enormously complex in reality. Even within a single organization, an individual may rely on multiple identities: an employee may need to authenticate to a database, an application or a service using completely different mechanisms. Once outside the organization, the problem is compounded. Multiple organizations will hold multiple instances of identity and attribute information. The problem of effectively managing all these instances is enormously complex, resulting in ineffective identity management and complexity.

Furthermore, as governments, citizens and businesses extend their services, they are challenged to grant access to resources and applications to the right people at the right time without sacrificing privacy, security or scalability. Since today's communities of interest are built and modified on a dynamically changing basis, trust must be able to be created or eliminated quickly. The old ways of managing identity dramatically reduce the organization's ability to move quickly enough to respond to changing relationships.

The Ideal Solution

Ideally, government would like to have the ability (whether through technology, business practices, policies, education or a combination thereof) to meet the following seemingly conflicting requirements:

- Simplify access to services and applications both inside and outside the organization
- Reduce the need to maintain and manage multiple sets of identity credentials
- Reduce the cost and complexity of managing identities
- Enable dynamic creation and management of trusted relationships
- Preserve privacy and ensure data security.

FEDERATED IDENTITY MANAGEMENT

Fortunately, there is a solution that approaches the above ideal: *federated identity management*. Federated identity management makes it possible for an authenticated identity to be recognized and take part in personalized services across multiple domains. Federated identity avoids the pitfalls of centralized storage of personal information while allowing users to link identity information among accounts. Since users can control when and how their accounts and attributes are linked and shared, they retain greater control over their personal information. In practice, this means that users can be authenticated by one organization or Web site and be recognized and receive delivered personalized content and services in other domains without having to re-authenticate.

Increasingly, governments are looking at federated identity as the preferred underlying identity architecture for interacting with their various constituencies and partners. Federated identity provides governments with an open and standards-based approach for enabling access to sensitive internal resources to external parties.

The advantages of federated identity include:

- A standards-based mechanism of both sharing and managing identity information as it moves between discrete legal, policy and organizational domains
- A cost-efficient means of establishing single sign-on to cross-domain resources
- A simpler way to grant and revoke user access to information
- A reduction in the number of sign-ons and passwords an individual must work with to access multiple systems and databases

- Greater security when it comes to user access to information.

PUBLIC SECTOR BENEFITS

Within a single government organization, a federated identity management infrastructure can bring substantial cost savings, operational efficiencies and increased security. These benefits come in the form of more effective employee provisioning and password management, focused development efforts on a single standard that will be supported by a variety of technology providers, and the ability to more easily outsource certain employee applications in a secure and flexible manner. Also, since employee identities can be managed internally and brought online and offline quickly, deployment of a federated identity infrastructure limits an organization's vulnerability to security attacks by current or former employees and contractors.

The real benefits of federated identity management can be seen when communication takes place between and among various organizations. Below, we briefly discuss several situations that call for federated identity.

Government to Government

Many types of vital information must be shared across government and organizational boundaries. Interoperability is a requirement within agencies, among organizations and even between nations. Indeed, the dynamically changing nature of national coalitions calls for dynamic circles of trust (a group of organizations that have established trusted relationships with one another and have pertinent agreements in place regarding federations). A federated architecture now allows systems to interoperate while maintaining their autonomy. The circle of trust provides participating organizations the framework to ensure that this interoperability is trusted and secure.

The compelling need for sharing sensitive information, and thus for federated identity management, can be clearly seen in times of disaster. A regional incident, such as an earthquake or avalanche, brings together myriad organizations that must freely share disasterresponse information among all relevant agencies and governments, often spanning multiple countries. When information about victims, rescue and response actions, and law enforcement activities are at stake, it is vitally important to ensure that individuals are properly authenticated prior to exchanging such sensitive information.

Government information sharing is a requirement not only in times of crisis; in fact, it permeates all aspects of government. For example, the European Commission's eEurope (eEurope, n.d.) activity covers a number of initiatives, including e-government, e-health, e-learning, and e-business, all designed to foster the development of new and better services. Examples include initiatives related to the health sector in Spain and Finland, the management of relations between administrations and companies in Belgium, the indexing of public files in Italy, e-voting in some local consultations in France, and much more. In each, the need for interchange of information requires a federated identity management framework to enable free flow of information while preserving security and privacy.

Government to Citizen

Perhaps in no other area of communication is the need for secure yet open access as important as in government-to-citizen interaction. Governments around the world are embarking on e-government and e-authentication initiatives, widespread broadband access and electronic communication programs to bring the benefits of technology to their citizens. In the public sector, various government departments and agencies give citizens and businesses access to online services through their e-authentication initiatives. The federated approach is ideal to avoid any generalized interconnection of public files containing personal information, because it ensures that data is not duplicated in a single central database.

Individual government authorities can act as identity providers for citizens by establishing circles of trust and offering a complete range of personalized applications across different government agencies and domains, such as online tax declaration, reimbursement for medical expenses, car registration, and electronic passport and driver's license renewals. In addition, with strong yet manageable authentication, governments can ensure that benefits are going to the authorized recipients. Such a scheme can quickly lead to single-sign-on, with the resultant benefits of cost reduction and increased security.

The eEurope 2005 Action Plan (eEurope, n.d.) embodies these initiatives, aimed at modernizing public services and giving everyone the opportunity to participate in the global information society. One area of particular focus is health care. Over the past few years, much progress has been made in building integrated regional health information networks, standardized electronic health records and the like. New initiatives will enable rapid reaction to health threats while protecting individuals' health information from unauthorized access.

Government to Business

Whether for government sales of assets, expanded tax products for business, one-stop business compliance, streamlining of international trade or other activities, businesses have come to expect more electronic interaction with government. This is especially true for small- and medium-size enterprises: With limited resources for interacting with government agencies, they are eager to find convenient procedures for such activities as VAT declarations or company registrations. A federated architecture is essential, as it enables a single-sign-on capability and seamless and secure interaction with distinct functions or agencies, while leaving each user in control of his or her data.

When business interacts with the government, the conflicting requirements of privacy and interoperability must both be addressed in a delicate balance. An interesting example can be seen today in Japan's EduMart, part of the e-Japan Policy Priority Program (e-Japan, n.d.) and spearheaded by the Strategic Headquarters for the Promotion of an Advanced Information and Telecommunications Network Society (IT Strategic Headquarters, n.d.). In an effort to bring rich educational content to students at more than 40,000 schools, the IT Strategic Headquarters established an open interface and built an educational content distribution network that will lead to a system in which both public institutions and private businesses can connect to interfaces and freely participate.

Additional examples can be seen across the value chain, from government-controlled health care programs that must communicate with providers and patients, to government contracts with foreign suppliers, to basic business licensing and taxation. Speed, timeliness, accuracy and user friendliness are the obvious outcomes of such initiatives.

To generalize across these public sector scenarios, the benefits of implementing a federated identity strategy and infrastructure fall into five main categories:

- Improved alliances, both within governments and between governments, through interoperability with autonomy
- Faster response time for critical communications
- Cost avoidance, cost reduction and increased operational efficiencies
- Stronger security and risk management
- Interoperability and decreased deployment time.

FEDERATED IDENTITY IN ACTION

GSA E-Authentication

The United States (U.S.) General Services Administration E-Authentication Initiative (e-Authentication, n.d.) is aimed at providing the necessary federated identity infrastructure to support a common, unified authentication process and streamline access to government online resources. Based on federated identity, E-Authentication will help government departments and agencies accelerate delivery of online services by allowing them to leverage a variety of electronic credential providers.

County Land Document Recordation Exchange

An example of cooperation between government and citizen can be seen in the U.S. initiative called the Internet-Based County Land Document Recording Exchange (Electronic Recordation Exchange, n.d.). Intended to dramatically streamline the land recordation process for participants, notably mortgage and title companies, it will save time and money while increasing the integrity of the participating local government land records systems. Users swipe smart cards through readers to access the system. The cards contain digital certificates that identify the users and can be passed along within the CoT. As other lending companies and counties join the County Land Document Recordation Exchange, they become part of the identity network and validate their own users as partners within the circle of trust. This minimizes the spiraling number of log-on credentials needed by users as they exchange documents with an ever-growing number of partners. It is only recently that such a fully electronic process became legally possible. The U.S. E-Sign (Electronic Signatures in Global and National Commerce Act, n.d.) went into effect October, 2000. The act allows suitable electronic signatures to have the same legal effect as written signatures.

Guide Project

GUIDE (Guide, n.d.) is a European Union (EU)-funded research project conducting research and technological development, with the aim of creating a technological, institutional, policy and socio-economic architecture for secure and interoperable e-government electronic identity services and transactions for Europe. Increasingly, citizens of the EU work, travel and access social security or health care services in other Member States. The primary practical objective of GUIDE is to create an architecture to solve the current cross-border compatibility issues.

Joint Warrior Interoperability Demonstration

The Joint Warrior Interoperability Demonstration 2003 (JWID) (Joint Warrior Interoperability Demonstration, 2003) demonstrated government-to-government interoperability. Spearheaded by the US joint chiefs of staff, JWID tackles identity issues across national and international boundaries. One key objective is to enable a standard solution for information sharing among coalition partners. Important issues are authentication and identity management, since each nation retains control of its own information, and desires to maintain its autonomy without impeding the free exchange of information.

In JWID 2003, military forces from six nations (Canada, Australia, New Zealand, U.S., United Kingdom, and Norway as the NATO representative) used federated identity solutions to clearly demonstrate how federated identity management could save lives, increase communication and build stronger alliances. Using its federated authentication architecture, the solution tied together message traffic from land-based and maritime units from all six countries, showing the true potential and value of this approach in scenarios that required the ability to revoke credentials from field forces that may have been compromised.

STANDARDS

Federated identity will not become ubiquitous without broadly supported standards to act as the necessary building blocks. Some key standards and proposals are discussed in the following sections.

SAML

The most successful federated identity building block to date is the Security Assertions Markup Language (SAML) (SAML, n.d.), an Extensible Markup Language (XML) framework for exchanging security information between servers.

SAML 1.0 became an OASIS standard in November 2002; SAML 1.1 followed in September 2003. SAML has seen significant success within industry—seeing successful deployments in financial services, higher education, government and other verticals. SAML has been broadly implemented by all major Web-access management vendors. SAML is also supported in major application server products, and SAML support is common among Web services management and security vendors.

SAML 2.0 reflects a three-fold convergence between SAML 1.1, Liberty ID-FF 1.2 (ID-FF 1.2, 2003) and Shibboleth (Shibboleth, n.d.) and, as such, is a critical development for federated standards.

Identity-Federation Framework

In 2003 the Liberty Alliance took SAML 1.0 and added mechanisms for account linking and session management to define its Identity Federation Framework. The extensions that Liberty defined to SAML 1.0 (and later SAML 1.1) were contributed back into SAML 2.0.

Although ID-FF is deprecated in favor of SAML 2.0 going forward, the Liberty Alliance continues to build on SAML—its Identity Web Services Framework (ID-WSF 1.1, 2005) has been adapted to include support for using SAML 2.0 assertions to communicate identity among Web services actors.

WS-Federation

A separate effort for federated identity protocols is WS-Federation (WS-Federation, 2003)—part of IBM and Microsoft's WS-* initiative for a broad set of composable standards for Web service security. Although WS-Federation has not itself been submitted to an open standards body, WS-Trust, on which WS-Federation builds, is now being developed within OASIS' WS-Secure Exchange Technical Committee. Microsoft's Infocard is a client component of the next release of Windows that may give end-users greater control over their identity by integrating through WS-Trust with identity requestors and providers.

FUTURE TRENDS

Multiple drivers and trends are pushing governments towards federated identity: greater degrees of collaboration with internal and external partners, heterogeneous security infrastrctures, regulations governing the acquisition and treatment of privacy and sensitive information all enourage government departments to implement a federated model of identity management for their constituent employees, citizens and partners. We expect that this push will continue—the future will show an increased number of deployments of federated systems, with more prototypes emerging and early prototypes evolving into full-scale deployments.

Deployments of strong authentication and federated identity are expected to go hand in hand, federated single sign-on allowing the cost of strong authentication to be borne by dedicated providers, but the value of increased security it enables shared elsewhere thereby makes strong authentication affordable and scaleable.

We also expect to see continued convergence between the various proposals and standards for the identity protocols and identifiers. The so-called identity metasystem is an encouraging development towards this end.

CONCLUSION

Sharing and interoperating among agencies, businesses and governments around the world create challenges for authentication and authorization to control aceess to distributed resources. Federated identity management, by allowing home organizations to authenticate their end users for their transactions across security domains, likely represents the best approach to addressing these challenges in a scaleable and flexible manner. To be practical, federated identity requires two key components: trust and standards. The Liberty Alliance, a global consortium of more than 150 leading global organizations, including numerous government and non-profit agencies, is leading the way in both developing the standards to enable the flow of identity information in a privacy-respecting manner, as well as defining best practices and guidelines to faciliate the establishment of trust between organizations.

REFERENCES

ACS Electronic Recordation Exchange. (n.d.). Retrieved from https://www.erxchange.com

eAuthentication. (n.d.). E-Authentication homepage. Retrieved from www.gsa.gov/e-authentication

eEurope Homepage. (n.d.). Retrieved from www.e-europestandards.org/

e-Japan. (n.d.). Retrieved from www.kantei.go.jp/foreign/it/network/0122full_e.html

Electronic Signatures in Global and National Commerce Act. (n.d.). Retrieved from www.ftc.gov/os/2001/06/esign7.htm

European Identity Management Project for eGovernment. (n.d.). Retrieved from http://guide-project.org

ID-FF 1.2. (2003). Retreived from https://www.projectliberty.org/resources/specifications.php#box1

ID-WSF 1.1. (2005). Retrieved from https://www.project liberty.org/resources/specifications.php#box2a

IT Strategic Headquarters. (n.d.). Retrieved from www.kantei.go.jp/foreign/policy/it/index_e.html

Joint Warrior Interoperability Demonstration. (2003). Retrieved from www.globalsecurity.org/military/ops/jwid.htm

Liberty Alliance Project. (n.d.). Retrieved from www. projectliberty.org

Security Assertions Markup Language. (n.d.). Retrieved from www.oasis-open.org/committees/tc_home.php? wg_abbrev=security

Shibboleth. (n.d.). Retrieved from http://shibboleth. internet2.edu/

WS-Federation. (2003). Retrieved from www-128.ibm.com/developerworks/library/specification/ws-fed/

WS-Secure Exchange Technical Committee. (n.d.). Retrieved from www.oasis-open.org/committees/tc_home.php?wg_abbrev=ws-sx

KEY TERMS

Circle of Trust: A group of organizations that have established trusted relationships with one another and have pertinent agreements in place regarding how to do business and interact with each other and manage user identities across their boundaries.

Identity: The set of behavioral or personal characteristics by which an individual is recognizable.

Identity Management: The set of processes by which individuals can be granted access to appropriate network resources, but no others.

Federated Identity: The agreements, standards and technologies that make identity and entitlements portable across autonomous policy domains.

Privacy: The right of individuals to control the collection and subsequent use of their identity information.

Single Sign-On: The sequence by which an individual can authenticate to one Web site and then be able to access protected resources at another site without additional authentication.

Web Services: A set of standards for distributed computing on the Internet.

This work was previously published in Encyclopedia of Digital Government, edited by A. Anttiroiko and M. Malkia, pp. 691-696, copyright 2007 by Information Science Reference, formerly known as Idea Group Reference (an imprint of IGI Global).

Chapter 5.20
E-Rulemaking

Cary Coglianese
Harvard University, USA

INTRODUCTION

Throughout the world, governments use regulation to combat monopoly power, protect consumers, and reduce health, safety, and environmental risks. Regulation promotes the safety of transportation, the cleanliness of the air, and the quality of their food and drugs. Today, nearly every major aspect of contemporary public life is significantly affected by rules made by regulatory agencies, ministries, or bureaus (Kerwin, 2003).

Given the consequential and complex nature of regulatory decision-making, crafting rules presents government agencies with significant informational challenges. Government regulators must collect information to understand the causes of regulatory problems, identify available regulatory options, and predict the effects of each alternative (Coglianese, Zeckhauser, & Parson, 2004). To develop a new rule, regulators must often undertake extensive studies and analyses and respond to comments from industry groups and other interested organizations.

E-rulemaking—or the use of information technology in government rulemaking—promises to help regulatory agencies make rules more efficiently and with better quality (Brandon & Carlitz, 2002; Johnson, 1998). E-rulemaking may also help expand public access to and participation in government decision making. Despite the significance of regulatory decisions, they have often been made in relative obscurity, with organized business lobbies sometimes having disproportionate influence over policymaking. Information technology may facilitate greater transparency and democratic accountability in the rulemaking process.

Already, regulatory agencies are making use of information technology to create Websites containing notices of new regulatory proposals and various background documents. They have also begun to allow citizens to use the Internet to share comments on new regulatory policies or engage in online dialogues (Beierle, 2003; Brandon & Carlitz, 2002). In early 2003, for example, the United States government launched a new Web portal called Regulations.Gov that allows the public to locate and comment on all new regulatory proposals announced by hundreds of federal regulatory agencies (Skrzycki, 2003). In addition, American officials are currently at work developing a government-wide, online docket system that will make available all the extensive information contained in each agency's rulemaking files (Skrzycki, 2004). Efforts such as these are likely to continue and can be expected in other regulatory jurisdictions around the world.

BACKGROUND

In order to understand how information technology can be used in the rulemaking process, it helps to understand the basic contours of that process. By way of illustration, consider how rulemaking operates in the United States for agencies like the Environmental Protection Agency, Department of Agriculture, and Federal Aviation Administration. These agencies typically first develop plans or "regulatory agendas" that are published twice each year in the *Federal Register*, a daily publication that includes regulatory notices and other material submitted by federal departments and agencies.

As agencies work on the items included in their agendas, they gather information, conduct analysis of the underlying problem, and identify possible regulatory solutions. They also frequently engage in discussions with industry representatives, other organized interests, and staff members from Congress or other agencies (Strauss, Rakoff, & Farina, 2003). When an agency has reached a tentative decision, it proceeds to publish a notice of proposed rulemaking (NPRM) in the *Federal Register*. In addition to describing the proposed rule, the NPRM will usually enunciate reasons for the proposed new rule and discuss the agency's underlying regulatory analysis (Administrative Procedure Act, 1946). The NPRM also informs interested parties how they can submit comments to the agency over its proposed course of action.

After reviewing the comments submitted on the NPRM and conducting any further analysis, the agency staff will make revisions to the proposed rule and then publish the final rule in the *Federal Register*. In addition to publishing the operative rule itself, the agency will also explain its decision in a preamble, a section of the *Federal Register* that accompanies the final rule. These preambles will often be longer than the final rules themselves, sometimes spanning more than a hundred pages for a single new rule.

Even after the final rule is published in the *Federal Register*, the rulemaking process continues (Coglianese, 2001). The operative rule itself, without the preamble, is later moved to and published in the relevant section of the *Code of Federal Regulations*. Furthermore, businesses or nongovernmental organizations can take the agency to court over new rules. Depending on what happens in litigation, the regulatory agency may need to revise its rules, which would start the entire process over again.

E-RULEMAKING'S PROMISE

Interest in applying information technology to the rulemaking process is growing (Shulman, Thrane, & Shelley, 2005). Already, regulatory agencies in the United States and other countries have begun to apply information technology to the rulemaking process. Agencies now permit members of the public to submit their comments by e-mail; they make the contents of their regulatory dockets available on the Internet; and they use information technology to help agency managers track the progress of rulemaking staff (Brandon & Carlitz, 2002). These existing applications only scratch the surface of information technology's potential for government rulemaking.

Researchers and public officials are contemplating a variety of new applications of digital technology in an effort to help government agencies improve the process of rulemaking—and thereby also to improve the quality of the rules themselves. Since making rules requires the acquisition, processing, and analysis of large quantities of technical and time-sensitive information, systems for information retrieval and extraction can aid the work of the regulatory analysts. Analysts could also use text categorization technology to sort public comments based on the issues they address or the departments within their agency to which they refer (Shulman, Hovy, Callan, & Zavestoski, 2004; Lau, Law, & Wiederhold, 2005). Summarization systems could automatically condense large studies or comments into more useable size for government officials to digest.

In addition, information technology can help regulators draft the text of new rules or supporting documents. Systems could be designed to flag potential inconsistencies within a proposed rule or between the proposed rule and existing rules. In order to maximize the regulated community's understanding of its obligations under a new rule, drafting software could suggest alternative sentence construction to make rules simpler and more accessible to a broad audience. Rule compliance wizards available on an agency's Web site could also help ensure that regulated entities understand and meet their regulatory obligations, even in areas with complex systems of rules (Kerrigan & Law, 2005).

Information technology can be used in a variety of ways to inform citizens about government rulemaking. Agencies can easily create automatic alerts to inform interested citizens about proposed rules under development. To help citizens offer more informed comments, information technology could provide clearer or easier access to information about a rule's development. Agencies could develop simulation software that would show how the costs and benefits of a proposed rule would vary under different parameters or assumptions, and then make that software available for the public to use to develop a better understanding of the tradeoffs implicit in a rulemaking (Belton, 2000).

Information technology could also create new opportunities for public deliberation over rulemaking. Information technology could allow members of the public to submit questions to the agency or engage in ongoing dialogue with agency staff or others interested in a proposed rule. In addition to online chat rooms, agencies could conduct digital public hearings or even convene cyber-juries that would link citizens from across the jurisdiction to deliberate over core policy issues raised by a rulemaking (Coglianese, 2005).

GOALS FOR E-RULEMAKING

As these examples show, e-rulemaking encompasses a range of new digital government applications. Some of these applications use existing technologies simply to digitize the existing rulemaking process, such as by providing documents online or allowing the submission of electronic comments. However, new applications also have the potential to transform the existing rulemaking process in significant ways (Lubbers, 2002). Whether applying existing technologies or designing new ones, decisions about whether and how to apply e-rulemaking call for attention to e-rulemaking's goals. E-rulemaking is generally thought to have the capacity to advance one or more of the following goals (Coglianese, 2004a).

1. **Enhance Democratic Legitimacy:** Increasing democratic legitimacy could be accomplished by using information technology to increase public understanding of rulemaking, make the process more interactive and deliberative, and make it easier for more democratically accountable institutions, such as the legislature, to oversee the rulemaking process
2. **Ensure Better Decisions:** E-rulemaking could improve policy decisions by making it easier for regulatory officials to analyze large volumes of data drawn from multiple sources. Simulation software could help

analysts make better predictions, and other technologies could make it easier for agencies to rely on routine use of high quality economic analysis

3. **Reduce Administrative Burdens:** Information technology can enable agency managers to coordinate rulemaking staff and other resources more efficiently. To date, a few agencies have reported some cost savings from initial applications of e-rulemaking for storage of documents
4. **Expand Regulatory Compliance:** Agencies can use information technology to increase compliance both by increasing public understanding of what regulations require and also, possibly, by reducing the cost of compliance through compliance assistance software.

FUTURE TRENDS

To achieve measurable improvements in meeting these goals, research will be needed from across both the information sciences and the social sciences (Coglianese, 2004b). Information science research will be crucial for technological design, such as developing text categorization and summarization tools for the rulemaking environment. Social science research will be needed to understand better the professional tasks of regulatory decision makers as well as the organizational environment within which technologies will be deployed. With coordinated input from across multiple disciplines, digital government researchers will be able to develop still more effective uses of information technology and better design rulemaking institutions to make better use of such technology. Future research directions will span four main areas (Coglianese, 2004a, 2004b).

1. **Information Technology:** E-rulemaking raises a series of challenges for research in the information sciences, such as designing general simulation and modeling packages or software to conduct automated consistency checking or cross-indexing and linking to related documents (Hovy & Noveck, 2004). In addition, human-computer interface research will help ensure that systems will be easy for the broad public to use and will therefore facilitate greater public participation. Any increase in citizen involvement will generate the need for information technology to help process and categorize public comments
2. **Agency Management:** E-rulemaking will give rise to a number of research questions in the field of public management or related areas of institutional or legal analysis. It will be important to study the effect on regulatory officials and their institutions from the introduction of new information technologies (Fountain, 2001). Do these technologies actually achieve their goals of improving regulatory decisions? Do agency staff members use these systems in the ways they were designed? How does the institutional environment affect the efficacy of e-rulemaking
3. **Public Participation:** Since e-rulemaking can affect how members of the public interact with government, political science research can help understand how information technology affects the involvement of businesses, interest groups, and citizens in the rulemaking process (Shulman, 2004). Such research can help assess whether information technology actually improves public understanding of rulemaking or increases the number and quality of comments filed. Of equal value will be to understand whether the types of participants in the rulemaking process change, or whether the proportion of comments from industry continues to dwarf the proportion from ordinary citizens (Coglianese, 2005). Social scientists will also be able to help determine whether e-rulemaking affects the public's overall perception of legitimacy to government regulation

4. **Regulatory Compliance:** A final avenue for future research would focus on how e-rulemaking can address regulatory compliance. Basic research on the factors that affect compliance with regulations will be helpful in identifying ways to use information technology to improve compliance. In addition, research could investigate how different kinds of compliance assistance software affect regulated actors' knowledge of rules and the obligations they impose (Kerrigan & Law, 2005). In addition, research could identify ways to use technologies such as remote sensing to supplement traditional enforcement tools

CONCLUSION

Government rulemaking affects the most significant aspects of today's economy and society. Given the importance of rulemaking, it is not surprising that government officials are beginning to investigate information technologies that can promise to improve regulatory decision-making. Regulatory agencies may be able to deploy e-rulemaking technologies to improve their information collection and regulatory analysis, enhance their interaction with the public, and ultimately implement their rules in a more effective manner.

E-rulemaking may be able to advance important goals of democratic legitimacy, improved decisions, lowered administrative costs, and increased compliance. Research will be needed to determine whether specific applications of e-rulemaking actually serve these goals. Researchers working across both the information and social sciences can help design information systems that fulfill institutional requirements and improve the rulemaking process. Building and sustaining research on e-rulemaking should be part of any strategy to improve the way government makes rules that will in turn affect every major aspect of society.

REFERENCES

Administrative Procedure Act. (1946). 5 United States Code, Section 553(b)(3).

Beierle, T. C. (2003). *Discussing the rules: Electronic rulemaking and democratic deliberation.* Resources for the Future Discussion Paper 03-22. Retrieved from http://www.rff.org/rff/Documents/RFF-DP-03-2.pdf

Belton, K. (2000). What if everyone were a policy analyst. *Regulation, 23*(3), 8-9.

Brandon, B. H., & Carlitz, R. D. (2002). Online rulemaking and other tools for strengthening our civic infrastructure. *Administrative Law Review, 54*(4), 1421-1478.

Coglianese, C. (2001). Assessing the advocacy of negotiated rulemaking. *New York University Environmental Law Journal, 9*(2), 386-447.

Coglianese, C. (2004a). E-rulemaking: information technology and the regulatory process. *Administrative Law Review, 56*(2), 353-402.

Coglianese, C. (2004b). Information technology and regulatory policy: New directions for digital government research. *Social Science Computer Review, 22*(1), 85-91.

Coglianese, C. (2005). The Internet and citizen participation in rulemaking. *I/S: Journal of Law and Policy for the Information Society, 1*(1), 33-57.

Coglianese, C., Zeckhauser, R., & Parson, E. (2004). Seeking truth for power: informational strategy and regulatory policymaking. *Minnesota Law Review, 89*(2), 277-336.

Fountain, J. E. (2001). *Building the virtual state: Information technology and institutional change.* Washington, DC: Brookings.

Hovy, E., & Noveck, B. S. (2004). E-rulemaking: Research problems for IT. In C. Coglianese

(Ed.), *E-rulemaking: Information technology and regulatory policy* (pp. 51-56). Regulatory Policy Program Report No. RPP-05, Harvard University.

Johnson, S. (1998). The Internet changes everything: Revolutionizing public participation and access to government information through the Internet. *Administrative Law Review, 50*(2), 277-337.

Kerrigan, S. L., & Law, K. H. (2005). A regulation-centric, logic-based compliance assistance framework. *Journal of Computing in Civil Engineering, 19*(1), 1-15.

Kerwin, C. M. (2003). *Rulemaking: How government agencies write law and make policy.* Washington, DC: CQ Press.

Lau, G. T., Law, K. H., & Wiederhold, G. (2005). A relatedness analysis tool for comparing drafted regulations and the associated public comments. *I/S: Journal of Law and Policy for the Information Society, 1*(1), 95-110.

Lubbers, J. S. (2002). *The future of electronic rulemaking: A research agenda.* Regulatory Policy Program Working Paper RPP-2002-04, Harvard University.

Shulman, S. W., Thrane, L., & Shelley, M. C. (2005). eRulemaking. In G. D. Garson (Ed.), *Handbook of public information systems* (2nd ed., pp. 237-254). New York: Marcel Dekker/CRC.

Shulman, S. W., Hovy, E., Callan, J., & Zavestoski, S. (2004). SGER collaborative: A testbed for eRulemaking data. *Journal of E-Government, 1*(1), 123-127.

Shulman, S. W. (2004). *The Internet still might (but probably won't) change everything: Stakeholder views on the future of electronic rulemaking.* Pittsburgh: University of Pittsburgh Report.

Skrzycki, C. (2004). *Project aims for one-stop online shopping for federal rules.* Washington Post (March 30), E1.

Skrzycki, C. (2003). *U.S. opens online portal to rulemaking; Web site invites wider participation in the regulatory process.* Washington Post (Jan. 23), E1.

Strauss, P. L., Rakoff, T. D., & Farina, C. R. (2003). *Administrative law* (10th ed.). New York: Foundation Press.

KEY TERMS

Code of Federal Regulations (CFR): The CFR is the annual publication of all federal agency regulations currently in force, with rules organized by subject matter.

Federal Register: The Federal Register is a daily publication in which federal agencies publish proposed and final rules as well as other announcements. Rules published in the Federal Register are organized in chronological order.

Final Rule: After receiving public comments, agencies publish their final rules in the Federal Register. In addition to the text of the rule, the agency must publish a statement justifying the rule. Such a statement will usually include a discussion of the major policy issues involved, the evidence relied on for the decision, and a reply to any counterarguments presented in the public comments.

Notice-and-Comment Rulemaking: Notice-and-comment, or informal, rulemaking is a process in which the agency publishes a proposed rule, receives public comments, and then publishes a final rule without holding a formal hearing on the record. Notice-and-comment rulemaking is the most common way for agencies to issue regulations.

Notice of Proposed Rulemaking (NPRM): Agencies must publish a notice of proposed rulemaking in the Federal Register to inform the public of the underlying legal authority of the proposed rule and its specific terms. The NPRM also contains information about when and where to submit public comments.

Preamble: When an agency publishes a notice of proposed rulemaking or a final rule in the Federal Register, it also publishes a statement explaining the purpose and background of the rule. This statement is the preamble. For final rules, the agency also responds to public comments in the preamble.

Regulatory Agenda: The Regulatory Flexibility Act requires that agencies publish a regulatory agenda twice each year containing a description of the subject area of rules that the agencies intends to propose, an approximate schedule for completing action on rules that the agency has already proposed, and a listing of recently completed rules.

Regulatory Docket: All materials and information related to a rulemaking are compiled in a regulatory docket. The docket includes studies, comments, and any other information on which the agency relies in developing a rule.

This work was previously published in Encyclopedia of Digital Government, edited by A. Anttiroiko and M. Malkia, pp. 713-717, copyright 2007 by Information Science Reference, formerly known as Idea Group Reference (an imprint of IGI Global).

Chapter 5.21 A Prototype Study on Electronic Rulemaking

Gloria T. Lau
Stanford University, USA

Kincho H. Law
Stanford University, USA

INTRODUCTION

The making of government regulations represents an important communication between the government and citizens. During the process of rulemaking, government agencies are required to inform and to invite the public to review the proposed rules. Interested and affected citizens participate by submitting comments accordingly. Electronic rulemaking, or e-rulemaking in short, redefines this process of rule drafting and commenting to effectively involve the public in the making of regulations. The goal of the e-rulemaking initiative is to integrate agency operations and technology investments; for instance, the electronic media, such as the Internet, is used as the means to provide a better environment for the public to comment on proposed rules and regulations. Based on the review of the received public comments, government agencies revise the proposed rules.

With the proliferation of the Internet, it becomes a growing problem for government agencies to handle the comments submitted by the public. Large amounts of electronic data (i.e., the public comments) are easily generated, and they need to be reviewed and analyzed along with the drafted rules. As such, part of e-rulemaking involves a non-trivial task of sorting through a massive volume of electronically submitted textual comments. For example, the Federal Register (2003) documented a recent case where the U.S. Alcohol and Tobacco Tax and Trade Bureau (TTB) received over 14,000 comments in seven months, majority of which are e-mails, on a flavored malt beverages proposal. The call for public comments by the TTB included the following statement:

All comments posted on our Web site will show the name of the commenter but will not show street addresses, telephone numbers, or e-mail addresses. (2003, p. 67388)

However, due to the "unusually large number of comments received," the Bureau announced later that it is difficult to remove all street addresses, telephone numbers, and e-mail addresses "in a timely manner" (2003, p. 67388). Instead, concerned individuals are asked to submit a request for removal of address information as opposed to the original statement posted in the call for comments. The example shows that an effortless electronic comment submission process has turned into a huge data processing problem for government agencies. Fortunately, the advance in information and communication technology (ICT) can help alleviate some of the barriers in e-rulemaking. This article will discuss a prototype of a comment analysis system, which classifies public comments according to related provisions in the drafted regulations. The automated relatedness analysis system can potentially save rule makers significant amount of time in reviewing public comments in regard to different provisions in the drafted regulations.

BACKGROUND

In the field of legal informatics, most research efforts focus on enhancing the search and browse aspect of legal corpus, whose targeted users are legal practitioners. Merkl and Schweighofer (1997) suggested that "[the] exploration of document archives may be supported by organizing the various documents into taxonomies or hierarchies that have been used by lawyers for centuries" (p. 465). Indeed, a hierarchical organization of relevant public comments and drafted provisions can extend the benefit to industry designers, planners, policy-makers and interested individuals as well.

Berman and Hafner (1989, p. 928) observed that legal rights of individuals are "severely compromised by the cost of legal services," and as a result suggested the potential of artificial intelligence (AI) to improve legal services. Rissland, Ashley, and Loui (2003) also noted that "the law offers structure and constraints that may enable AI techniques to handle law's complexity and diversity" (p. 6). Researchers have studied extensively the application of AI, in particular, knowledge-based systems, to the *understanding* of the law (Bench-Capon, 1991; Brüninghaus & Ashley, 2001; Schweighofer, Rauber, & Dittenbach, 2001; Thomson, Huntley, Belton, Li, & Friel, 2000; Valente & Breuker, 1995; Wahlgren, 1992). In comparison, the application of ICT or AI to help the *making* of the law is rather new.

Nonetheless, ICT *can* help streamline the development of regulatory policy in several new directions (Coglianese, 2003). One suggestion is to integrate rules with other laws, such as using ICT to "link all the traces of a rule's history, both back to the underlying statute and back to past or related rules, facilitating improved understanding of legal requirements" (Coglianese, 2004, p. 88). Previous work has shown that such an application of ICT is indeed possible. A framework for comparisons among regulations from multiple sources has been developed, with successful examples of related provisions automatically linked (Lau, Law, & Wiederhold, 2003a, 2003b). This article will exploit the use of the developed comparison framework to implement a prototype to aid the e-rulemaking process.

AUTOMATED ANALYSIS OF COMMENTS FROM E-RULEMAKING

In order to help screening and filtering of public comments, a prototype regulatory analysis system has been developed to automate the comparison between the drafted rules and their associated comments (Lau, Law, & Wiederhold, 2005). The prototyped e-rulemaking scenario incorporates public comments submitted to the U.S. Access Board, who released a drafted chapter for the Americans with Disabilities Act Accessibility Guidelines (Access Board, 1999), titled "Guidelines for Accessible Public Rights-of-way (Access Board, 2002)." The drafted chapter was less than 15 pages long. However, over a period of four months, the Board received over 1,400 public comments which totaled around 10 megabytes in size, with some comments longer than the draft itself. To facilitate understanding of the comments with reference to the draft, we have developed an automated system to perform a relatedness analysis.

Each piece of comment is compared with individual provisions from the draft. Characteristic features, such as conceptual phrases (Dörre, Gerstl, & Seiffert, 1999), are automatically extracted for the computation of the degree of similarity between provisions and comments (Bishop, 1995). The organizational structure of regulation is also exploited to review hidden relevance between neighboring provisions and references, similar to citation analysis and link analysis in the Web (Brin & Page, 1998; Garfield, 1995; Kleinberg, 1998; Page, Brin, Motwani, & Winograd, 1998). The results of this analysis are related pairs of provision from the draft and individual comment. Figure 1 shows the developed framework where users are given an overview of the draft along with related comments.

As shown in Figure 1, the drafted regulation appears in its natural tree structure with each node representing sections in the draft. Next to the section number on the node, for example, Section 1105.4, is a bracketed number that shows the number of related public comments identified. Users can follow the link to view the content of the selected section in addition to its retrieved relevant public comments. This prototype demonstrates the use of a regulatory comparison system on an e-rulemaking scenario to help review drafted rules based on a large pool of public comments.

To conceptualize the use of a comparison framework on e-rulemaking, we present some interesting results here. Figure 2 shows a typical pair of drafted section and excerpts of an identified related public comment. Section 1105.4.1 in the draft established the requirements for pedestrian refuge islands in situations where there lacks adequate signal timing for full crossing of traffic lanes. Using the prototyped system, we found that one of the reviewers complained about

Figure 1. Comparisons of drafted rules and public comments in e-rulemaking

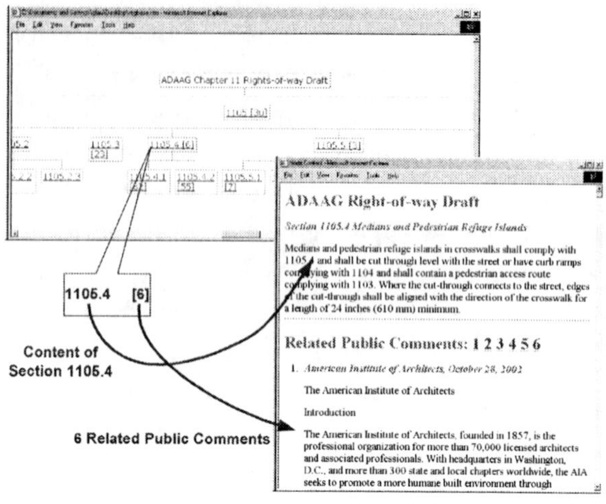

Figure 2. Related drafted rule and public comment

ADAAG Chapter 11: Rights-of-way Draft

Section 1105.4.1: Length

Where **signal timing is inadequate for full crossing of all traffic lanes** or where the crossing is not signalized, cut-through medians and pedestrian refuge islands shall be 72 inches (1830 mm) minimum in length in the direction of pedestrian travel.

Public Comment, October 29, 2002

I am a member of The American Council of the Blind. I am writing to express my desire for the use of audible pedestrian traffic signals to become common practice. Traffic is becoming more and more complex, and many traffic signals are set up for the benefit of drivers rather than of pedestrians. This often means **walk lights that are so short in duration** that by the time a person who is blind realizes they have the light, the light has changed or is about to change, and they must wait …

Figure 3. Comment intended for a single provision only

> **ADAAG Chapter 11: Rights-of-way Draft**
>
> **1109.2 Parallel Parking Spaces**
>
> An access aisle at least 60 inches (1525 mm) wide shall be provided at street level the full length of the parking space. The access aisle shall connect to a pedestrian access route serving the space. The access aisle shall not encroach on the vehicular travel lane.
> EXCEPTION: An access aisle is not required where the width of the sidewalk between the extension of the normal curb and boundary of the public right-of-way is less than 14 feet (4270 mm). When an access aisle is not provided, the parking space shall be located at the end of the block face.
>
> **Public Comment, August 26, 2002**
>
> 1109.2 Parallel Parking Spaces. An access aisle at least 60 inches (1525 mm) …
> 1. **This section** needs to be clarified, i.e., where is the access isle located? that is, "will it be on the driver side or passenger side?"
> 2. The following is more of a question/concern about this requirement: …
> I would really appreciate, if you could **forward this comments to the right individual** and hopefully get a response back …

the same situation, where in the reviewer's own words, "walk lights that are so short in duration" should be investigated. This example illustrates that our system correctly retrieves related pairs of drafted section and public comment. We also observed from this example that a full content comparison between provisions and comments is necessary, since title phrases, such as "length" in this case, are not always illustrative of the content. Automation is clearly desirable, as it would otherwise require much human effort to conduct a full content comparison to sort through piles of comments.

The pair of highly related provision and comment shown in Figure 3 suggests that a comparison between drafted provisions and comments is indeed the right approach. This commenter started by citing Section 1109.2 in the draft, followed by a list of suggestions and questions on Section 1109.2. Our system gathered the relatedness between Section 1109.2 and this comment through different features, such as the shared phrases. This piece of comment is a representative example of a lot of comments that are written similarly: comments that are concerned about a single provision in the draft. Thus, a comparison between drafted provisions and comments is important to help rule makers focus on the most related comments per provision.

FUTURE TRENDS

Based on the observations of results shown in the previous section, there seem to be room for improvement for an e-rulemaking portal. The example in Figure 3 shows that the public might find it helpful to submit comments on a per provision basis, in addition to a per draft basis. With enabling technology, it should be possible to develop an online submission system that allows for both types of comment submission. It saves participants time to paraphrase or cite their concerned provision. It also saves rule makers time to locate related comments either through human effort or an automated system. Comments submitted on a per draft basis can still be analyzed and compared with the entire draft to identify any additional relevant provisions. In the example of Figure 3, the commenter also suggested that it is important to forward the comments to the right person. An extension of this relatedness analysis framework could be developed to automatically inform any assigned personnel in charge of reviewing the provision within government agencies.

Regulations are frequently updated by agencies to reflect environmental changes and new policies. However, the desynchronized updating of regulations seems to be problematic, especially when different regulations reference one another. We observe that there is a need for consistency check among multiple sources of regulations citing each other as references. For instance, in the domain of accessibility, Balmer (2003) pointed out that the "ADAAG references the A17.1 elevator code for conformance. Since 2000 there has been no section of the A17 that references lifts for the disabled. Therefore ADAAG references a non-existent standard … if ADAAG is to reference the A18 then the A18 should contain the requirements for this application" (p. 10). In previous work, we have developed a semi-automated reference extraction parser, which can potentially be extended to locate cross citations and check for consistency of rulemaking (Kerrigan, 2003; Lau, 2004).

A public comment submission portal, an automated comment routing system and a reference tracking tool are just a few examples of the potential technology impact on the making of the law. E-rulemaking provides a rich research platform for a multi-disciplinary study involving social scientists, policy makers, computer scientists, and interested and affected citizens. Improvements and innovations of an integrated e-rulemaking system are much needed to help various parties to locate, retrieve, review, and validate regulations.

CONCLUSION

This article has demonstrated a potential use of ICT on policy making, in particular, the communication between government agencies and the public via comments on proposed rules. A short discussion is given on the observed impact of e-rulemaking on the efficiency of government agencies. This translates into a significant increase of workload for rule makers, as the drafted rules need to be analyzed, compared, and revised based on the generated public comments. One of the main barriers to e-rulemaking, namely the vast amount of public comments received through the Internet, is concretized using a recent drafted regulation as an example. We proposed to perform a relatedness analysis on the drafted regulation and its associated public comments to streamline the process.

A prototype relatedness analysis system is demonstrated to compare a drafted regulation and its associated public comments. Documented and reported here are selected examples of results, which also inspired some potential future research directions. By screening through the public comments and sorting them according to their relatedness to provisions in the draft, it helps rule makers to review and revise the draft based on the comments. It helps interested and affected individuals to focus their concerns and suggestions to drafted rules. The use of ICT on the making of regulations can undoubtedly facilitate the editorial job of policy-makers and enhance public understanding of rulemaking.

ACKNOWLEDGMENT

This research project is sponsored by the Digital Government Program and the Information Technology Research of the National Science Foundation, Grant Numbers EIA-9983368 and EIA-0085998.

REFERENCES

Access Board (U.S. Architectural and Transportation Barriers Compliance Board). (1999). *Americans with Disabilities Act Accessibility Guidelines (ADAAG) for Buildings and Facilities*. 36 Code of Federal Regulations Part 1191.

Access Board (U.S. Architectural and Transportation Barriers Compliance Board). (2002). *Draft Guidelines for Accessible Public Rights-of-Way*. Retrieved from http://access-board.gov/rowdraft.htm/.

Balmer, D. C. (2003, October 9-11). *Trends and issues in platform lift*. Presented at Space Requirements for Wheeled Mobility Workshop, Buffalo, NY.

Bench-Capon, T. J. M. (1991). *Knowledge based systems and legal applications*. San Diego: Academic Press Professional, Inc.

Berman, D. H., & Hafner, C. D. (1989). The potential of artificial intelligence to help solve the crisis in our legal system. *Communications of the ACM, 32*(8), 928-938.

Bishop, C. M. (1995). *Neural networks for pattern recognition*. New York: Oxford University Press, Clarendon Press.

Bollacker, K. D., Lawrence, S., & Giles, C. L. (1998). CiteSeer: An autonomous Web agent for automatic retrieval and identification of interesting publications. *Proceedings of the 2nd International Conference on Autonomous Agents*, Minneapolis, MN (pp. 116-123).

Brin, S., & Page, L. (1998). The anatomy of a large-scale hypertextual Web search engine. *Proceedings of the 7th International World Wide Web Conference, Brisbane, Australia* (pp. 107-117).

Brüninghaus, S., & Ashley, K. D. (2001). Improving the representation of legal case texts with information extraction methods. *Proceedings of the 8th International Conference on Artificial Intelligence and Law (ICAIL 2001), St. Louis, Missouri* (pp. 42-51).

Calado, P., Ribeiro-Neto, B., Ziviani, N., Moura, E., & Silva, I. (2003). Local versus global link information in the Web. *ACM Transactions on Information Systems (TOIS), 21*(1), 42-63.

Coglianese, C. (2003). *E-rulemaking: Information technology and regulatory policy*. Technical Report, Regulatory Policy Program, Kennedy School of Government, Harvard University, Cambridge, MA.

Coglianese, C. (2004). Information technology and regulatory policy. *Social Science Computer Review, 22*(1), 85-91.

Dörre, J., Gerstl, P., & Seiffert, R. (1999). Text mining: Finding nuggets in mountains of textual data. *Proceedings of ACM SIGKDD International Conference on Knowledge Discovery and Data Mining, San Diego, CA* (pp. 398-401).

Garfield, E. (1995). New international professional society signals the maturing of scientometrics and informetrics. *The Scientist, 9*(16), 11.

Gentner, D., & Markman, A.B. (1997). Structure mapping in analogy and similarity. *American Psychologist, 52(1)*, 45-56.

Gurrin, C., & Smeaton, A. F. (1999). A connectivity analysis approach to increasing precision in retrieval from hyperlinked documents. *Proceedings of Text Retrieval Conference (TREC)*, Gaithersburg, MD (pp. 357-366).

Kepler, J. (1992, original work published 1609). *New astronomy* (W.H. Donahue translation). Cambridge, UK: Cambridge University Press.

Kerrigan, S. (2003). *A software infrastructure for regulatory information management and compliance assistance*. Ph.D. Thesis, Department of Civil and Environmental Engineering, Stanford University, Stanford, CA.

Kleinberg, J. (1998). Authoritative sources in a hyperlinked environment. *Proceedings of the 9th ACM-SIAM Symposium on Discrete Algorithms*, San Francisco, CA (pp. 668-677).

Lau, G. (2004). *A comparative analysis framework for semi-structured documents, with applications to government regulations*. Ph.D. Thesis, Civil and Environmental Engineering, Stanford University, Stanford, CA.

Lau, G., Law, K., & Wiederhold, G. (2003a). A framework for regulation comparison with application to accessibility codes. *Proceedings of the National Conference on Digital Government Research*, Boston (pp. 251-254).

Lau, G., Law, K., & Wiederhold, G. (2003b). Similarity analysis on government regulations. *Proceedings of the 9th ACM SIGKDD International Conference on Knowledge Discovery and Data Mining,* Washington, DC (pp. 111-117).

Lau, G., Law, K., & Wiederhold, G. (2005). Legal information retrieval and application to e-rulemaking. *Proceedings of the 10th International Conference on Artificial Intelligence and Law (ICAIL 2005), Bologna, Italy* (pp. 146-154).

Merkl, D., & Schweighofer, E. (1997). En route to data mining in legal text corpora: Clustering, neural computation, and international treaties. *Proceedings of the 8th International Workshop on Database and Expert Systems Applications, Toulouse, France* (pp. 465-470).

Page, L., Brin, S., Motwani, R., & Winograd, T. (1998). *The PageRank citation ranking: Bringing order to the Web.* Technical Report, Stanford University, Stanford, CA.

Rissland, E. L., Ashley, K. D., & Loui, R. P. (2003). AI and law: A fruitful synergy. *Artificial Intelligence, 150*(1-2), 1-15.

Schweighofer, E., Rauber, A., & Dittenbach, M. (2001). Automatic text representation, classification, and labeling in European law. *Proceedings of the 8th International Conference on Artificial Intelligence and Law (ICAIL 2001), St. Louis, Missouri* (pp. 787).

Silva, I., Ribeiro-Neto, B., Calado, P., Moura, E., & Ziviani, N. (2000). Link-based and content-based evidential information in a belief network model. *Proceedings of the 23rd Annual International ACM SIGIR Conference on Research and Development in Information Retrieval, Athens, Greece* (pp. 96-103).

Thomson, R., Huntley, J., Belton, V., Li, F., & Friel, J. (2000). The legal data refinery. *International Journal of Law and Information Technology, 8*(1), 87-97.

U.S. Alcohol and Tobacco Tax and Trade Bureau (TTB). (2003). Flavored malt beverages and related proposals. Posting of comments received on the TTB Internet Web site. *Federal Register, 68*(231), 67388-67389.

Valente, A., & Breuker, J. (1995). ON-LINE: An architecture for modelling legal information. *Proceedings of the 5th International Conference on Artificial Intelligence and Law, College Park, MD* (pp. 307-315).

Wahlgren, P. (1992). *Automation of legal reasoning.* Deventer, The Netherlands: Kluwer Law and Taxation Publishers.

KEY TERMS

Academic Citation Analysis: It is the analysis of the citation pattern among scholar publications and literatures. For instance, CiteSeer is a scientific literature digital library that provides academic publications indexed with their citations (Bollacker, Lawrence, & Giles, 1998).

Characteristic Feature: Features are the evidences that identify relatedness. Examples include conceptual phrases such as "access aisle," and domain-specific terminologies such as chemical names and symbols. Often, features are constructed by hand based on some understanding of the particular problem being tackled (Bishop, 1995).

E-Rulemaking: During the process of rulemaking, government agencies are required to inform and to invite the public to review a proposed rule. E-rulemaking redefines this process in which the electronic media, such as the Internet, is used to provide a better environment for the public to locate, retrieve and comment on proposed rules.

Feature Extraction: Feature extraction is an important step in repository development when the data is voluminous. In particular, in the field of information retrieval (IR), software tools exist to fulfill the task of feature extraction to recognize and classify significant vocabulary items (Bishop, 1995).

Link Analysis: The popularity of the Internet has led to extensive examinations of different types of hyperlink topology and fitting models (Calado, Ribeiro-Neto, Ziviani, Moura, & Silva, 2003; Gurrin & Smeaton, 1999; Silva, Ribeiro-Neto, Calado, Moura, & Ziviani, 2000). Google's PageRank algorithm (Brin & Page, 1998; Page, Brin, Motwani, & Winograd, 1998) and the HITS (Hypertext Induced Topic Search) algorithm (Kleinberg, 1998) both exploit the hyperlink structures of the Web, similar to the heavy cross-references in the legal domain.

Relatedness Analysis: A comparative analysis among regulations and supplementary documents that identifies similar or related materials by computing a similarity score. Although the term relatedness appears more appropriate, the phrase "similarity score" has been used in the field of Information Retrieval (IR) traditionally.

Similarity/Relatedness: Psychologists Gentner and Markman (1997) suggested that "similarity is like analogy (p. 45)," based on the concept of analogy defined by Johannes Kepler (1609/1992). In the comparative analysis of regulatory documents, we define similarity/relatedness to describe elements of texts that are alike in substance and/or connected by reason of a discoverable relation.

This work was previously published in Encyclopedia of Digital Government, edited by A. Anttiroiko and M. Malkia, pp. 1364-1369, copyright 2007 by Information Science Reference, formerly known as Idea Group Reference (an imprint of IGI Global).

Chapter 5.22
Privacy Protection Overseas as Perceived by USA-Based IT Professionals

Jaymeen R. Shah
Texas State University—San Marcos, USA

Garry L. White
Texas State University—San Marcos, USA

James R. Cook
Texas State University—San Marcos, USA

ABSTRACT

Privacy laws for the Internet are difficult to develop and implement domestically and internationally. A clear problem is how such laws are limited to national jurisdictions. What is legal in one country may be illegal in another. Due to differences in cultures and values, and government types, it may not be possible to establish global standards and legislations to ensure privacy. Due to the nonexistence of global privacy standards, multinational (international) companies usually select one of the following two possible solutions: (1) implement a most restrictive "one size fits all" privacy policy that is used across various countries, or (2) implement different privacy policies that meet the privacy regulations of different countries and expectations of those citizens. In order to investigate a solution that may be used by multinational companies, and how companies view domestic privacy laws, the authors conducted a survey of U.S.-based employees of domestic and multinational companies. The results of the survey suggest that the majority of the multinational companies prefer the first solution—most restrictive "one size fits all" approach. They develop and implement a single set of privacy policies that is used across their operations in different countries. The majority of the companies surveyed consider domestic privacy laws in the United States to be practical, but ineffective.

INTRODUCTION

Computer technologies, especially the Internet, have created an electronically connected global community. The Internet and World Wide Web allow easy collection and distribution of information across the globe. Use of the World Wide Web has exponentially increased over the past few years. It is used by businesses as an important sales and communications channel, and by consumers for information research and e-shopping. The free flow of information is one of the most essential requirements for the economic growth of any organization (Oz, 1994).

Information on a Web page can be viewed and accessed from across national and judicial boundaries. Such universal access to Web pages allows businesses to market their products across the globe using the Web. When consumers shop on the Web, they are required to enter personally identifiable information such as their name, address, and credit card number. This personally identifiable information may be transmitted across the boundaries of states and countries depending upon the locations of the customer and the Web server hosting the Web site. Transmitting data around the world has become necessary for international business (Oz, 1994). A major issue for global e-traders is privacy (Chandran, Phatak, & Sambharya, 1987; Zuckerman, 2001). Such an issue can threaten the growth of e-commerce. Surveys have indicated that consumers have become concerned about privacy on the Internet, to such an extent, that 61% of the users refuse to shop online (Ryker, Lafleur, Mcmanis, & Cox, 2002).

The Internet has promoted direct interactions between businesses and their customers, irrespective of their locations around the world. There are no immigration or customs checks. Data flows across the globe just as it flows across a local area network. However, this has created a new problem with consumer and employee privacies as existing privacy laws do not seem to adequately address the privacy issues across geographical boundaries. Further, privacy laws across different countries differ (Zuckerman, 2001). For example, in many countries the data is owned by the data collector (e.g., United States), while in other countries, the data is owned by the person concerned (e.g., European Union). Another difference is how the laws govern the operations of law enforcement agencies and telecommunication services. This brings up the question as to how multinational companies deal with and perceive the patchwork of privacy laws that exist across the various countries of their operations. The primary purpose of this research is to answer this question.

We will first discuss the threats to privacy from the increased use of the Internet and e-commerce. Next, we will provide an overview of privacy laws of some countries. This will provide a perspective about the extent to which privacy laws differ across countries around the globe. We then discuss the survey methodology, followed by a discussion of the results of the survey.

THREATS TO PRIVACY

Privacy is defined as the right of an individual or business to determine when, how, and how much information about them should be disclosed to others (Grandinetti, 1996; Martin, 1973; Udo, 2001). The Internet and e-commerce have created potential threats to privacy, which are invisible to most users (Camp, 1999; Pedley, 2002). Although many believe that the Internet is anonymous, the reality is to the contrary. The Internet is shifting away from the assumptions of anonymity upon which it was originally designed (Bennett, 2001). For example, a client computer can be traced via the Internet Protocol (IP) address. The Web server also can place a "cookie" on a client PC, which can be subsequently used to exchange information between the client PC and the Web server. A "cookie" can keep track of user's online activities, such as Web pages visited, date and time of access, and duration of access. This information about a user's online activities can be sent back to the Web server. In certain situations, such stealthy monitoring of a user's online activities can constitute violation of a user's privacy (Rezgui, Bouguettaya, & Eltoweissy, 2003). When a user enters personal information on a Web page, more privacy issues come into play, especially when accessing a Web server located in another country. Several U.S. federal agency Web sites track users' online activities despite rules banning the practice (Mearian, 2001). Privacy advocates argue that organizations should ask permission before tracking users' online activities (Roha, 2000). Users should have the right to prevent some transfers of personally identifiable information (Graham, 1987). This may require that a user be more involved in protecting his/her privacy. For example, a user could block cookies from being placed on their computer. The most recent version of the Internet Explorer browser, allows users to select between receiving cookies from Web sites or blocking them completely. However, blocking cookies is not the default setting. Blocking cookies and the use of privacy-protecting technology/software requires time and computer skills/knowledge that many consumers may lack (Camp, 1999). It seems that only well educated users may be aware of such privacy issues and are able to deal with them.

Few Web sites have explicit privacy policies that are conspicuously posted on the Web site to protect users' privacy (Electronic privacy information center, 1997; Yang & Chiu, 2002). Many Web sites fail to provide the type of privacy protection that would be provided by the most rudimentary privacy laws in the United States (Rotenberg, 1999). Decisions about consumers' privacy are being driven by market forces and technologies rather than by ethical or legal reasoning (Camp, 1999). Laws, especially international laws, were not written to deal with privacy issues created by the use of such new technologies.

The privacy problem revolves around what data or information can be collected, and how it can be used. Since data flows across international boundaries, the use and collection of personal data may have different restrictions in different countries along the path of the data flow. What an international company can collect and do in one country, may be illegal in another country. International companies that collect customers' and employees' personally identifiable data, and transmit it across geographical boundaries, have to carefully tackle such legislative differences in privacy laws across countries of operation. There are two possible alternatives available for developing and implementing a corporate privacy policy: (1) Develop and implement different privacy policies based on the privacy laws in the various countries of operations, or (2) Develop and implement a single privacy policy by adopting the strictest elements of privacy laws across the countries of operations as the company's corporate privacy policy.

GLOBAL PRIVACY LEGISLATIONS

Cultural and political differences among different countries significantly contribute to the differences in the data protection/privacy regulations. The extent of protection to personal data varies from nation to nation, as does the regulatory agencies governing them (Chandran et al., 1987; Connolly, 2000; Oz, 1994; Rudraswamy & Vance, 2001). Perception or the definition of privacy differs across cultures (Milberg, Smith, & Burke, 2000). Some countries are democratic; the privacy of citizens is valued. Other authoritarian countries are less concerned about the privacy of their citizens.

Some governments are willing to forego some privacy to allow the free flow of information and provide better marketing. Others restrict collection of private data based on the consent of the individual (Oz, 1994). Many countries have passed privacy legislation to protect their citizens from the growing ability of computerized systems to access personal data. Some countries may refuse to allow personal data to be transmitted to other countries if the other country's privacy laws are less restrictive (Waples & Norris, 1992). Countries that favor protection of data on individuals argue that it is difficult to separate data on individuals from data regarding the business activities that are performed by the individuals (Oz, 1994).

This lack of harmonization poses a fundamental challenge to international data flows and the Internet (Reidenberg, 2000). For example, the regulatory approach to privacy protection by many foreign jurisdictions is different from the United States (Cain, 2002; Oz, 1994; Waples et al., 1992). The United States and the European Union use very different approaches to information privacy. These differences have led to regulatory and managerial conflicts between the United States and the European Union (Cambanis, 2000; Smith, 2001). European Union countries and Canada have developed comprehensive privacy protection regulations that protect personal information more stringently than in the United States. To highlight the differences in data protection and privacy laws that exist across different countries, a summary table consisting of laws from a few countries is provided in Appendix A. Thus, "one size does not fit all," with respect to regulatory implementations of privacy laws (Milberg et al., 2000).

Privacy has been on the agenda of the United Nations since the late 1970s (Bennett, 2001). Yet, today there is no global standard to ensure information privacy. With the move towards globalization of business and the use of the Internet for both business and personal use, there has been a significant increase in transmission of personal and business information across state and country borders. The Internet and e-commerce has forced states and countries to modify existing privacy legislation, and/or enact new privacy legislations in order to enhance protection of the information privacy of their citizens and corporations (Rudraswamy et al., 2001). Each country's privacy laws only apply to that legislation's jurisdiction. Due to the political and cultural differences between various countries, there are differences among these privacy laws. Unfortunately, this lack of uniformity among various countries' privacy and data protection laws has created a legal and regulatory challenge for companies operating across multiple countries (Bentivoglio, Cortez, & Kirk, 2003). When companies or customers deal with international entities using the Internet, these differences in the privacy laws produce implementation conflicts. With the worldwide trend towards enhancing the protection of personal information, businesses should be careful in developing and implementing company privacy policies. Privacy policies should comply with the privacy laws of the countries in which they operate, as any violation of a country's privacy laws could result in financial and/or criminal penalties.

SURVEY METHOD

Governments impose privacy laws in accordance with the local culture and political beliefs. Governments are oriented locally, and, thus, able to ignore what is done outside the governments' judicial boundaries. However, global businesses are unable to ignore privacy laws in other countries. The purpose of this survey was to address these issues. The following are the 11 survey questions developed:

1. Does your company do businesses in other countries?
2. Are Internet legislations by the USA government affecting your company's privacy policies?
3. Are information privacy laws in the USA practical?
4. Considering the global nature of the Internet, are current information privacy laws effective?
5. Are technologies available to effectively and economically implement information privacy laws?
6. Are information privacy lawsuits involving the Internet impeding Internet operations?
7. Do the laws of other countries impact your overall corporate information privacy policies?
8. Does your company implement different information privacy policies across different countries?

9. Does your company implement across countries the most restrictive policies as defined by the most restrictive laws of one country?
10. Where do you find the most restrictive privacy laws?
11. Were privacy laws in a foreign country so complex and restrictive, that it deterred your company from doing business there? If YES, which country?

Information systems (IS) professionals and managers of United States-based companies were surveyed. The survey was designed to see how USA-based companies deal with privacy, especially with the laws. Questions #2, #3, #4, and #7 were specific for this purpose. General conclusions for foreign-based companies were not made. USA-based companies were the focus since international legislations may never establish a common, global standard. Also, differences in cultural values and political beliefs were kept constant. Survey participants were selected from the membership list of the Association of Information Technology Professionals (AITP), a USA-based information technology (IT) professional organization. This organization provided a reasonable cross section of IT professionals in the USA. All professional members of the AITP were selected for the survey resulting in a total of 3,772 subjects.

The survey instrument consisted of eleven survey questions and two demographic questions. All respondents answered the first six survey questions. Respondents who worked for a company that did foreign business answered the last five survey questions. The two demographic questions requested information about the type of business and the position of the respondent. To maintain anonymity of the respondents, they were not required to provide their name or their company's name.

The survey instrument was distributed via e-mail to AITP members. Each e-mail contained a brief message explaining the purpose of the study and a hyperlink to access the Web-based electronic survey instrument. The electronic survey instrument was designed with the intention of ensuring that it was easy to access, contained clearly stated questions, and required a minimal amount of time to complete. The Web site survey was made available to the respondents for ten days. The bolt of responses from the e-mail Web link came within 3 days after e-mails were sent. Beginning on the 4th day, very few responses were being submitted. By the 7th day there were no responses being submitted. At the end of the survey period, there were a total of 356 valid responses. The response rate was approximately 9.4%. The demographics showed we did get a cross section of position and business types as shown in Box 1 and Table 1. Almost half of respondents were non-decision makers (technical position) and 42% did business in other countries.

Data collected from this survey were analyzed for frequencies using SPSS statistical software. Data is reported as frequency/percent in Tables 1 through 4. National and international modes are represented in bold.

Box 1. Respondents' position and company scope

	U.S. only	Foreign	**Totals**
Technical	102	72	**174**
Management	80	60	**140**
CEOs	26	16	**42**
Totals	**208**	**148**	**356**

DISCUSSION OF RESULTS

The results of the survey illustrate the attitude of the USA IT professionals toward privacy laws, national and international. These attitudes appear to be similar when the "don't know" responses are taken into consideration. A large proportion of the USA IT professionals, from both national

Table 1. Demographic data of respondents

Business Type of Respondents					
Manufacturing	50 / 14%	Financial	32 / 9%	Health Care	15 / 4%
Distribution	8 / 2%	Consulting	67 / 19%	Government	56 / 16%
Transportation	2 / 1%	Construction	6 / 2%	other	97 / 27%
Communication	11 / 3%	Retail	8 / 2%		

Position Type of Respondents	
Technical	174 / 49%
Management	140 / 39%
CEO	42 / 12%

Table 2. Company type frequencies

1. Does your company do business in other countries?	Yes No	148 / 42% (International company) 208 / 58% (National company)

companies and international companies, did not know about privacy policies and laws. Those responses were generally 20% to 30%.

Table 1 shows the percent distribution of the position type of each respondent. About 49% of the respondents were in technical positions, and the remaining 51% were in decision-making positions (managerial and corporate executive officers). The authors believe this provides a good representation of both groups. While managers and corporate executive officers make privacy policy decisions, technical personnel are more likely to be involved in the implementation of the privacy policies. Hence, these two groups of individuals may have different perspectives on these same issues. Analyses between these two groups are planned for future research.

Forty-two percent of the respondents worked for international (multinational companies operating across different countries) companies, while the other 58% worked for national (companies operating only within the United States) companies. This provided a large sample of respondents from both groups. See Table 2, company-type frequencies.

From Question #2 of the survey (Table 3), it appears that Internet legislation by the United States government affects privacy policies of international companies, while national companies tend to not be affected. It should be noted that over 25% of the respondents of both groups did not know if the Internet legislations by the United States government affected their company's privacy policies. Results seem to imply that a majority of the national companies may have imposed upon themselves voluntary self-regulation with regards to the privacy of personally identifiable information (PII). They may have proactively developed and implemented privacy policies that adequately satisfy United States privacy legislations. International companies' privacy policies may be affected, due to the differences in the privacy policies across the countries in which they operate.

The majority of each group indicated that information privacy laws in the United States were practical. This suggests that a majority of the respondents believe United States information privacy laws to be appropriate and cost-effective to implement. Less then 25% of the respondents did not know if this was true. However, the majority of each group indicated that the current information privacy laws, when considering the global nature of the Internet, are NOT effective (See Question #4 in Table 3). This could be attributed to the difficulty and ineffectiveness in

Table 3. National and international companies responses

	Overall	National	International
2. Are Internet legislations by the United States government affecting your company's privacy policies?			
Yes	**134 / 38%**	69 / 33%	**65 / 44%**
No	126 / 35%	**85 / 41%**	41 / 28%
Don't know	96 / 27%	54 / 26%	42 / 28%
3. Are information privacy laws in the United States practical?			
Yes	**191 / 54%**	**107 / 51%**	**84 / 57%**
No	96 / 27%	56 / 27%	40 / 27%
Don't know	69 / 19%	45 / 22%	24 / 16%
4. Considering the global nature of the Internet, are current information privacy laws effective?			
Yes	52 / 15%	26 / 13%	26 / 18%
No	**214 / 60%**	**123 / 59%**	**91 / 62%**
Don't know	90 / 25%	59 / 28%	31 / 21%
5. Are technologies available to effectively and economically implement information privacy laws?			
Yes	**147 / 41%**	**85 / 41%**	**62 / 42%**
No	113 / 32%	69 / 33%	44 / 30%
Don't know	96 / 27%	54 / 26%	42 / 28%
6) Are information privacy lawsuits involving the Internet impeding Internet operations?			
Yes	103 / 29%	55 / 26%	48 / 32%
No	**133 / 37%**	**83 / 40%**	**50 / 34%**
Don't know	120 / 34%	70 / 34%	**50 / 34%**

imposing national privacy laws, especially when the data transmitted across the Internet flows across national borders. Further, developing and implementing privacy policies that satisfy different and sometimes conflicting privacy laws of all countries, in which a company operates, is complex and inefficient.

Although the response trend was that technologies are available to effectively and economically implement information privacy laws, there was no clear majority of respondents indicating either "yes," "no," or "don't know."

An interesting finding is the comparison of survey questions #3 and #4. The majority of both national and international groups indicated that information privacy laws in the United Sates were practical. Yet, both groups indicated information privacy laws, when considering the global nature of the Internet, are NOT effective. These results clearly bring forth the issue of how the Internet does not recognize judicial boundaries. When laws are designed for national use, they can be enforced and implemented within the judicial boundary of a country. However, it may not be possible to enforce such national laws across judicial boundaries. Internet, e-business, and globalization may have made such national laws ineffective due to the transborder nature of the data flow enabled by the Internet. The results of this study indicate that the U.S. privacy laws are practical from the perspective of their implementation by companies. However, due to the global nature of the Internet and e-business, these privacy laws are not effective in dealing with the transborder nature of the data flow, as it may not be possible to enforce these national laws across its judicial boundary.

Table 4. International company responses

The following questions were for International companies only.

	Yes	No	Don't know
7. Do the laws of other countries impact your overall corporate information privacy policies?	**65 / 44%**	53 / 36%	30 / 20%
8. Does your company implement different information privacy policies across different countries?	28 / 19%	**75 / 51%**	45 / 30%
9. Does your company implement across countries the most restrictive policies as defined by the most restrictive laws of one country?	**81 / 55%**	40 / 27%	27 / 18%

10. Where do you find the most restrictive privacy laws?

Canada	**36 / 24%**	Japan	2 / 1%	Singapore	1 / 1%
China (Mainland)	10 / 7%	Korea	0 / 0%	United Kingdom	3 / 2%
European Union	26 / 18%	Mexico	0 / 0%	**United States**	**41 /28%**
India	0 / 0%	Russia	0 / 0%	other country	29 / 20%

11. Were privacy laws in a foreign country so complex and restrictive, that it deterred your company from doing business there? If Yes, which country?

NO	**139 / 94%**				
Canada	0 / 0%	Japan	0 / 0%	Singapore	1 / 1%
China (Mainland)	1 / 1%	Korea	0 / 0%	United Kingdom	0 / 0%
European Union	1 / 1%	Mexico	0 / 0%	other country	5 / 4%
India	1/ 1%	Russia	0 / 0%		

The response distributions for Question #6 were very close to a uniform distribution. Whether information privacy lawsuits involving the Internet are impeding Internet operations or not is inconclusive from this survey.

International companies tended to find the laws of other countries to impact their corporate information privacy policies. However, ninety-four percent did not find these laws to deter their company from doing business in other countries (See Questions #7 and #11 in Table 4).

The majority of respondents indicated that different policies are NOT implemented across different countries (Question #8). Instead, the most restrictive policies, as defined by the most restrictive laws of one country, are used (Question #9). This seems logical since it is more efficient and cost-effective to develop and implement uniform corporate information privacy policies across the corporation, compared with dealing with a different set of privacy policies in different countries of operation. Strict adoption of the latter approach may require a multinational company to develop and implement many different sets of privacy policies to comply with the privacy laws of different countries, which would be difficult to implement. It should be noted that sometimes it may not be feasible for international companies to develop corporate privacy policies based on the most restrictive laws of one country because of the differences in the privacy laws of different countries. For example, inconsistent privacy laws in Europe prompted Prudential Insurance Company to try to develop a single corporate privacy policy based on the most restrictive privacy law across all countries. According to John Smith, head of security at Prudential, "usually when differences in laws exist, Prudential implements the most restrictive law as the policy to be used across all countries." A detailed review of various countries' privacy laws revealed that such an approach was unworkable. It was found that although there were differences in privacy laws across countries, the privacy law of one country was not necessarily lower in standard than those of other countries (Cohen, 2003). In such situations, companies may still be able to develop and implement a uniform set of corporate privacy policies that complies with the privacy laws of various countries. However, these privacy policies will be based on privacy policies of multiple countries rather than the most restrictive privacy policy of a country.

The literature review indicated that privacy laws of European countries are more stringent than the privacy laws of the United States. Survey respondents most frequently selected the United States, Canada, and the European Union to have the most restrictive privacy laws. It should be noted that the respondents only compared the countries they do business with and the United States. It is very possible that the results would be different if they all did business with other countries that had stricter laws than the United States (See Questions #8, #9, and #10 in Table 4).

Chi-Square analyses were performed between decision-makers (Managers and CEOs) and non-decision makers (Technical). Three questions indicated a difference of responses. Question #2 asked if Internet legislations by the United States government affected the company's privacy policies (Chi-Square = 6.36, df = 2, $p < .05$). Managers' and CEOs' responses differed from the technical professional responses. Since this question deals with domestic laws from outside the company and the impact on the company, it stands to reason that the technical staff would be less involved. The technical respondents did have a higher percentage of "Do not know."

For companies that did foreign business, Questions #8 and #9 dealt with how companies resolved the differences in privacy laws across judicial boundaries. Question #8 asked if the respondent's company implements different information privacy policies across different countries (Chi-Square = 14.28, df = 2, $p < .001$). Question #9 asked if the respondent's company implements across countries the most restrictive policies as defined by the most restrictive laws of one country (Chi-Square = 12.72, df = 2, $p < .005$). Responses from the Managers/CEOs and technical professionals for these two questions were different. The technical professionals tended to have a higher percentage of "Do not know" for both questions.

CONCLUSION

The very nature of the Internet has created threats to privacy. Although countries have enacted privacy laws, the jurisdictions of such national privacy laws are limited within the boundaries of the country. Differences among the privacy laws of various countries have led to conflicts in data protection/privacy regulations. International companies have to tread carefully through these differences in the privacy laws of the different countries in which they do business, in order to avoid legal troubles due to noncompliance. Dealing with such a patchwork of national privacy laws is expensive for businesses. An alternative to this is to develop a set of international privacy laws. Although information privacy has emerged as an international issue, no information privacy law exists that can be uniformly applied across the reach of the Internet. International privacy laws may not be feasible, due to the cultural and political differences among countries. For example, privacy is a basic right in a democratic society. However, countries with other forms of government may view this differently. Hence, their privacy laws may be different. Different democratic countries within the European Union have differences in privacy laws due to cultural differences. Even if international privacy regulations are enacted, effectively implementing these regulations across the globe will be extremely difficult.

International legislations may never establish a common, global standard to ensure privacy. Differences in cultural values and political beliefs among countries create a significant barrier. International companies must carry the burden of safeguarding consumer, employee, and business privacies across the various countries of operation, in accordance with each country's privacy laws. Results of this study indicate that a majority of the international companies develop and implement uniform corporate privacy policies across all countries in which they operate. These privacy policies are usually based on the most restrictive privacy laws of the countries in which they operate. This is a better alternative than implementing different privacy policies in different countries, as it is more efficient and cost-effective. International companies tend to adopt the most restrictive policy, a "one size fits all" approach. Companies that were surveyed found USA privacy laws practical, less restrictive than other countries, but ineffective. The primary reason for the ineffectiveness of the USA privacy laws is the global nature of the Internet, which renders the law to be ineffective beyond the jurisdiction of the law. This suggests that there may be a need for developing uniform global privacy legislation, as it will provide stronger protection to Internet users' personal identifiable information.

FUTURE RESEARCH

An argument has been established, to ensure effective, efficient, and feasible privacy policies across judicial boundaries, the most restrictive policy that satisfies all jurisdictions is implemented. This research lays the foundation for future research on this argument with a more specific population, companies that deal with world trade. Issues and questions for future consideration are:

1. Do decision-makers (managers and CEOs) have the same opinions and attitudes as non-decision-makers (technical professionals)? Do they agree with the argument for most restrictive policies across judicial boundaries?
2. Since e-commerce is creating a global economy, is there a need for a global standard on privacy issues? Is such a standard practical? Would differences in cultures and political beliefs be a hindrance to a global standard on privacy?
3. When it comes to international privacy issues, is there a trend/attitude to share information with other parties? Do culture and political beliefs impact such a trend/attitude?

REFERENCES

Anonymous. (2003). Mrs. Field's cookies and Hershey's foods assessed largest penalties to date for COPPA violations. *Computer and Internet Lawyer, 20*(5), 30-31.

Auerbach, I. (1985). Professional responsibility for information privacy. *Computers & Security, 4*(2), 103-107.

Bennett, C. (2001). Cookies, Web bugs, Webcams, and cue cats: Patterns of surveillance on the world wide Web. *Ethics and Information Technology, 3*, 197-210.

Bentivoglio, J., Cortez, N., & Kirk, S. (2003). Global privacy law update. *The Computer & Internet Lawyer, 20*(6), 1-6.

Cain, R. (2002). Global privacy concerns and regulation—Is the United States a world apart? *International Review of Law, Computers, & Technology, 16*(1), 23.

Cambanis, T. (2000). Data-privacy accord with United States faces renegotiation in Europe. *Wall Street Journal*, July 6, A.23.

Camp, L. (1999). Web security and privacy: An American perspective. *Information Society, 15*(4), 249-256.

Cantos, L., Porcelli, N., & Selby, S. (2001). House introduces legislation requiring consumer "opt-in" for Internet cookies. *Intellectual Property & Technology Law Journal, 13*(4), 22-23.

Chandran, R., Phatak, A., & Sambharya, R. (1987). Transborder data flows: Implications for multinational corporations. *Business Horizons, 30*(6), 74-83.

Cohen, L. (2003). If it's personal, it's protected. *Security Management*, 93-98, April 2003.

Connolly, P. (2000). Privacy as global policy. *InfoWorld, 22*(37), 49-50.

Dreazen, Y. (2002). The best way to... ...guard your privacy. *Wall Street Journal*, Nov 18, R.4.

Electronic privacy information center. (1997). *Surfer beware: Personal privacy and the Internet.* Retrieved July 16, 2003, from www.epic.org/reports/surfer-beware.html

Graham, J. (1987). Privacy, computers, and the commercial dissemination of personal information. *Texas Law Review, 65*(7), 1395-1439.

Grandinetti, M. (1996). Establishing and maintaining security on the Internet. *Sacramento Business Journal, 13*(25), 22.

Martin, J. (1973). *Security, accuracy, and privacy in computer systems*. Englewood Cliffs, NJ: Prentice-Hall,

Mearian, L. (2001). Report: Many federal Web sites use cookies. *Computerworld, 35*(17), 21.

Milberg, S., Smith, J., & Burke, S. (2000). Information privacy: Corporate management and national regulation. *Organization Science, 11*(1), 35-57.

Oz, E. (1994). Barriers to international data transfer. *Journal of Global Information Management, 2*(2), 22-29.

Pedley, P. (2002). Data protection for intranets and Web sites. *Business Information Review, 19*(3), 41.

Petersen, S. (1995). Your life as open book: Has technology rendered personal privacy virtually obsolete? *Federal Communications Law Journal, 48*(1), 163-186.

Reidenberg. (2000). Resolving conflicting international data privacy rules in cyberspace. *Stanford Law Review, 52*(5), 1315-1367.

Rezgui, A., Bouguettaya, A., & Eltoweissy, M. (2003). Privacy on the Web: Facts, challenges, and solutions. *IEEE Security & Privacy*, 40-49, November/December 2003.

Robertson, C. J., & Sarathy, R. (2002, 2–5, January-February). Digital privacy: A pragmatic guide for senior managers charged with developing a strategic policy for handling privacy issues. *Business Horizons, 45*(1).

Roha, R. (2000). Prying eyes. *Kiplinger's Personal Finance, 54*(8), 118-124.

Rotenberg, M. (1999). *Oversight hearing on electronic communications privacy policy disclosures.* Subcommittee on Courts and Intellectual Property Committee on the Judiciary, United States House of Representatives, Rayburn House Office Building, May 27, 1999. Retrieved July 16, 2003, from www.epic.org/privacy/internet EPIC_testimony_599.html

Rudraswamy, V., & Vance, D. (2001). Transborder data flows: Adoption and diffusion of protective legislation in the global electronic commerce environment. *Logistics Information Management, 14*(1/2), 127.

Ryker, R., Lafleur, E., Mcmanis, B., & Cox, K. C. (2002). Online privacy policies: An assessment of The Fortune E-50. *Journal of Computer Information Systems, 42*(4), 15-20.

Smith, H. (2001). Information privacy and marketing: What the United States should (and shouldn't) learn from Europe. *California Management Review, 43*(2), 8-33.

Swartz, N. (2004). Canada's privacy law faces legal challenge. *The Information Management Journal*, 20-24, March/April 2004.

Udo, G. (2001). Privacy and security concerns as major barriers for e-commerce: A survey study. *Information Management & Computer Security, 9*(4), 165-174.

Waples, E., & Norris, D. (1992). Information systems and transborder data flow. *Journal of Systems Management, 43*(1), 28-30.

Wolf, C. (2004). California's new online privacy policy law has nationwide implications. *Journal of Internet Law*, 3-8, January 2004.

Yang, H., & Chiu, H. (2002). Privacy disclosures of Web sites in Taiwan. *Journal of Information Technology Theory and Application, 4*(3), 15.

Zuckerman, A. (2001). Order in the courts? *World Trade, 14*(9), 26-29.

This work was previously published in Journal of Global Information Management, Vol. 15, Issue 1, edited by F. B. Tan, pp. 68-81, copyright 2007 by IGI Publishing, formerly known as Idea Group Publishing (an imprint of IGI Global).

APPENDIX A. SUMMARY COMPARISON OF PRIVACY LAWS ACROSS COUNTRIES.

United States

Legislation by Congress may be the most effective way of providing information privacy in the United States (Auerbach, 1985; Dreazen, 2002; Petersen, 1995; Rotenberg, 1999). The major legislations in the United States pertaining to regulating information privacy are as follows:

Federal Laws:

- Children's Online Privacy Protection Act (COPPA) regulates Web sites targeted at children, and general audience Web sites that may collect personally identifiable information (PII) from children under the age of 13 (Wolf, 2004). COPPA requires such Web sites to prominently display a link to its privacy policy in each area of the Web site where children's PII is collected. In addition to this, COPPA requires notification of parents in order to obtain "verifiable parental consent" before collecting, using, or disclosing personal information from a child (Robertson & Sarathy, 2002).
- Graham-Leach-Bliley Act (GLB Act) requires financial institutions to provide consumers information about their current privacy policies and notify them via a notice regarding any changes to it. It mandates that consumers must be given the choice of not disclosing any non-public personal information to non-affiliated third parties (Wolf, 2004).
- Health Insurance Portability and Accountability Act (HIPAA) provides protection from the disclosure of an individual's patient records and personally identifiable health information. It requires that health care providers and other entities covered by the HIPAA provide information about their privacy practices to individuals through the publication and distribution of their privacy policies (Wolf, 2004).
- Consumer Online Privacy and Disclosure Act (H.R. 347) require Web sites to obtain consumer consent prior to tracking them (Cantos,Porcelli & Selby, 2001).
- Internet Privacy Protection Act prohibits federal agencies from disclosing confidential records about an individual on the Internet (Robertson et al., 2002).

State Laws:

- California's Online Privacy Protection Act of 2003 require operators of commercial Web sites that collect PII about California's residents to adopt privacy policies and prominently display them on their Web sites (Wolf, 2004). The Web site www.ftc.gov/bcp/conline/pubs/buspubs/coppa.htm provides further information on this subject.

The GLB Act and HIPAA are not restricted to online privacy. The Federal Trade Commission (FTC) currently has the responsibility of enforcing federal privacy legislations (Anonymous, 2003). However, companies that are not affected by these federal regulations are not required to develop and adopt privacy policies to protect consumers' PII (Wolf, 2004). Except for a few sensitive areas, the United States has adopted a hands-off approach towards the online privacy regulation, with more reliance on self-governance by businesses.

Australia

Federal privacy regulations in Australia are implemented in the form of National Privacy Principles (NPP). They govern the collection, maintenance, use, disclosure, and security of PII. Efforts are underway by various industries to develop self-regulatory codes tailored to their specific industry, which if approved by Australia's Privacy Commissioner, will replace the NPPs. Many critics have criticized NPPs for not providing adequate privacy protection compared with International Standards (Bentivoglio et al., 2003)

Canada

The Personal Information Protection and Electronic Documents Act (PIPEDA) was developed to provide a uniform and effective statutory framework for protecting consumers' PII. The Canadian business community has supported development of PIPEDA. One of the main reasons for their support is that dealing with a single federal privacy law is more efficient than complying with several different provincial laws (Swartz, 2004). PIPEDA imposes several restrictions on organizations' practice of collecting, using, and disclosing personal information (Bentivoglio et al., 2003). Businesses cannot collect, use, or disclose consumers' personal data without their consent. Collected PII cannot be used beyond the stated purpose, and information that is no longer required for the stated purpose must be destroyed or made anonymous. PIPEDA requires businesses to appoint a Privacy Officer, a person responsible for compliance with PIPEDA. Any violation of PIPEDA can result in bad publicity for the organization, and a monetary penalty in federal court (Swartz, 2004).

Japan

In 2003, Japan enacted personal data protection laws that govern both public and private sectors' use of personal data. The basic idea on which this law is based is that a consumers' PII "must be properly handled" (Bentivoglio et al., 2003). It prohibits businesses from using an individuals' PII beyond the stated purpose, and from transferring it to third parties without their prior consent. This law also precludes government agencies from releasing PII to other organizations without a justifiable reason. It is implemented via industry-specific guidelines developed and released by each national ministry, which is also responsible for the investigation and resolution of violation complaints.

European Union

The European Union (EU) has developed the Data Protection Directive for protecting personal information. Most of the member countries have developed laws implementing provisions contained within the Data Protection Directive that apply to both public- and private-sector organizations. However, it must be noted that there is lack of uniformity among member countries' implementation of the Data Protection Directive (Bentivoglio et al., 2003). For example, the amended Federal Data Protection Act of Germany is more stringent than EU's Data Protection Directive (Bentivoglio et al., 2003).

In the Data Protection Directive, there is a strict requirement for transferring personal data to non-EU countries that lack adequate privacy laws. Companies can only transfer personal data without any additional safeguard to non-EU countries that are "white-listed" (Bentivoglio et al., 2003). One of the major concerns of the European Commission is the inadequacy of data protection privacy laws in the United States and Australia. In general, EU laws have restrictions on collection, use, and sharing of personal data. Companies cannot collect data without an individuals' consent, and should erase it after a reasonable time period. Further, it provides to individuals the right to review and rectify their personal data.

Chapter 5.23
The European Commission's E-Government Initiatives and Public Participation

Christian Hunold
Drexel University, USA

INTRODUCTION

According to the European Commission (2003), increased networking of local, regional, and national administrations across the European Union (EU) is creating "a more integrated 'European public space' for EU citizens and businesses" (p. 6). This emerging public space owes its existence chiefly to improvements in information and communication technology (ICT). The Commission (2002) believes that e-government initiatives will help to build a more robust European public space capable of engendering in the public's mind a sense of democratic ownership of European institutions and policies: "E-government is helping to establish a more open, inclusive and productive public sector, in line with good governance" (p. 7). E-government as defined by the Commission (2005) as "the use of information and communication technologies, combined with organisational change and new skills, to improve public services, increase democratic participation and enhance public policy making."

Echoing the literature on e-democracy (Gibson, Rommele, & Ward, 2004), the Commission (2002) contends that e-government can improve EU democratic processes and public support for EU policies in two ways: by giving citizens greater access to information from authorities, which empowers citizens by improving the transparency and accountability of European institutions; and by fostering direct communication between citizens and policy makers, which enables improved mutual accommodation of needs and interests. This article analyzes Commission e-government initiatives, with special emphasis on the Consultation, the European Commission and Civil Society (CONECCS) directory, the interactive policy making (IPM) initiative, and the i2010: European Information Society 2010 initiative. IPM seeks to enable the Commission to collect feedback directly from citizens, consumers, and businesses via a single Internet access point for consultations (Your Voice in Europe). i2010 is a five-year strategy launched in 2005 to boost Europe's digital economy and includes proposals to enhance e-participation in Europe's emerging public space. Such proposals, I argue, will be more likely to succeed if the Commission were to move from managerial and consultative to participatory models of public involvement (Chadwick & May, 2003).

BACKGROUND

Interest group involvement in shaping Commission decisions is common and largely routine. Interest group participation can make the difference between the Commission's success and failure in the policy process (Greenwood, 1997); public consultations build cooperation around and support for its proposals and policies (Bellier, 1997). Cultivating close relationships with interest groups helps the Commission gather valuable expertise, though involving a wide range of nongovernmental groups and interests in deliberations about new policy initiatives may also help the Commission avoid obstruction by national governments (Christiansen, 1996). As Schmitter (2000) notes, however, opportunities for access to European interest representation are far from equal: "While all this pluralism (to use the American expression) is entirely appropriate in a modem democracy, its highly skewed nature does raise some questions about whether these channels for the expression of particular intensities are freely and fairly available to all citizens of Europe. So far, the evidence suggests a mobilization of bias in favor of business interests" (p. 81). Also concerned about too much backroom dealing with privileged interest groups, Watson and Shackleton (2003) call for "a more open policy debate in which more voices are heard by EU policy-makers" (p. 106).

The Commission is increasingly sensitive to these concerns. The Prodi Commission's 2001 *White Paper on European Governance* acknowledged the Commission's duty to broaden public involvement in its policy deliberations. From the Commission's perspective the problem was not that European citizens did not speak up, but that they often did so in ways the Commission could not easily understand or integrate into policy decisions. Europe's unruly public sphere often failed to produce the sort of policy-relevant communication the Commission saw as essential to make Brussels less remote to European citizens. ICTs took center stage in subsequent proposals to create a "reinforced culture of consultation and dialogue" with civil society organizations (European Commission, 2002). Moving consultations online, the Commission hoped, would improve their transparency and lower barriers to access for groups new to the European policy arena. Since taking office in late 2004, the Barroso Commission has expanded on these efforts by unleashing a slew of new e-government initiatives seen as critical to reviving Europe's economy and furthering European citizenship. According to Commissioner for Information Society and Media Viviane Reding (2004), "Information technologies encourage participation, facilitate access to information and offer new ways of learning and communicating." As well as meeting public demand for participation in European policy making, the Commission views enhancing e-government and, more broadly, nurturing a European information society, as important factors in their own right in promoting economic growth across the European Union.

THE EUROPEAN COMMISSION'S E-GOVERNMENT INITIATIVES

Consultation, the European Commission, and Civil Society

CONECCS (Consultation, the European Commission and Civil Society) is an online directory of the Commission's formal civil society consultative bodies and of civil society organizations representing a wide range of groups and interests. CONECCS can be accessed via the Commission's civil society Web site, which provides information on the Commission's dialogue and consultations with civil society. On December 2, 2005, the directory listed 738 organizations, including "third-sector" nongovernmental organizations (NGOs) as well as business federations, labor unions, and associations of governmental authorities. Registration in CONECCS is voluntary and does not confer accreditation on groups (http://europa.eu.int/comm/civil_society/coneccs/index_en.htm). The Commission hopes CONECCS will improve the openness and accountability of its policy deliberations and decisions. The directory is part of the Commission's efforts to convey to the public what issues are being developed, what mechanisms are being used to consult, who is being consulted and why, and what has influenced decisions in the formulation of policy.

Organizations wishing to participate in Commission consultations must provide the Commission and the public at large with basic information about themselves, preferably via CONECCS. As participation in CONECCS is voluntary, however, groups may provide this information in other ways, such as "special information sheets" (European Commission, 2002). As a practical matter, though, CONECCS is fairly inclusive; organizations may be searched for alphabetically or by policy area, which provides interested citizens with a convenient means of identifying and contacting civil society organizations that participate in a wide range of EU policy consultations. Technological convenience alone, however, will not solve the underlying problem for enhancing public participation and inclusion, namely that European-level associations do not play a significant role in the lives of most Europeans. Initiatives such as CONECCS are a start, but they cannot conjure by themselves a European public space where there may not be enough European-level public engagement to begin with.

Interactive Policy Making

The interactive policy making (IPM) initiative consists of two online instruments that enable the Commission to gather feedback directly from citizens, consumers, and businesses in order to better understand how they perceive Commission policies and to learn from their experience, with a view to shaping new policies and improving existing ones (European Commission, 2005a). Both instruments are available via the Your Voice in Europe Web portal, which was developed in the context of IPM and is the Commission's single access point for consultations.

A *feedback mechanism* helps the Commission collect information from citizens and businesses about their daily problems relating to different EU policies. About 300 intermediaries, such as Euro Info Centers and European Consumers Centers located across the EU, candidate countries, and European Free Trade Area countries, collect everyday problems and record them in the Commission's feedback database. This listening device allows for a constant monitoring of the application of existing legislation and provides concrete input for new policy initiatives. The Commission claims that thousands of cases are collected annually, providing several Directorate Generals with input for policy making (European Commission, 2005a).

An *online consultation mechanism* involves structured questionnaires, which citizens may answer on the Internet in order to provide the Commission with feedback on particular policy issues. As this mechanism can handle structured questions in several languages and deliver the output in the desired language, the Commission should be able to act on citizens' opinions and views more quickly and effectively than in the days of paper-based consultations. For example, a consultation in preparation for the Community Action Plan on Animal Welfare and Protection (closing date December 11, 2005) involved an 18-point questionnaire soliciting responses to various animal welfare topics. The survey covered key issues of animal welfare in food production, distribution, and consumption; however, there was no provision for submitting open-ended answers or for raising issues omitted from the questionnaire. By contrast, the Your Voice on eGovernment consultation (closing date December 4, 2005) did include a field for open-ended comments up to 450 characters. This implies that online tools like IPM have the technical capability to accommodate forms of public involvement that are more deliberative than filling out a questionnaire. Whether or not a given consultation solicits such contributions from the public therefore depends less on technological constraints than on practical judgments by Commission officials seeking to balance demands for participation and efficiency. Reading, sorting, and absorbing into policy initiatives contributions from the public requires time and money—resources often in short supply in busy public bureaucracies.

i2010

i2005 is a 5-year initiative to boost the digital economy, identified by the Commission as Europe's most promising sector, accounting for 40% of EU productivity growth and 25% of EU GDP growth. The Commission (2005b) has outlined three policy priorities for i2010:

- Creating an open and competitive single market for information society and media services within the EU;
- Increasing investment in research on ICTs by 80%; and
- Promoting an inclusive European information society.

Concerning the last point—e-inclusion—the Commission is working on several proposals aimed at closing the digital divide: an Action Plan on eGovernment for citizen-centered services (2006); three "quality of life" ICT flagship initiatives (technologies for an aging society; intelligent vehicles that are smarter, safer, and cleaner, and digital libraries making multimedia and multilingual European culture available to all (2007); and actions to overcome the geographic and social "digital divide," culminating in a European initiative on e-inclusion (2008). It is noteworthy that these policy initiatives operate with a sophisticated understanding of what is causing the digital divide. The concept of a geographic digital divide refers to disadvantaged rural areas with little access to ICT. The concept of a social digital divide recognizes that access to ICT declines with socioeconomic status, but that providing for access alone does not create the means for all citizens to use ICTs competently. The Commission's e-inclusion initiatives, therefore, aim to spread the benefits of the information society to all segments of the population, including people who are disadvantaged due to limited resources or education, age, gender, or ethnicity; people with disabilities; and those living in poor areas. The Commission (2005c) has issued a Communication on eAccessibility aimed at promoting a consistent approach to e-accessibility initiatives in the member states on a voluntary basis to foster industry self-regulation. Further, EU-level information on e-inclusion and e-accessibility can be accessed via a single Web site on the Europe's Information Society Thematic Portal (http://europa.eu.int/information_society/policy/accessibility/index_en.htm). In November 2005, Commissioner Reding described the Commission's aspirations for e-government in Europe: "Full e-government means measurably more efficient, effective, inclusive and open government for all citizens and in all areas of administration and democracy. Today's online availability is just the first step."

FROM MANAGERIAL AND CONSULTATIVE TO PARTICIPATORY MODELS OF PUBLIC INVOLVEMENT?

This section considers whether the initiatives discussed above are likely to lead to participatory forms of e-government becoming the norm. Chadwick and May (2003) differentiate between managerial, consultative, and participatory models of government-citizen interaction in e-government. At the least participatory end of their conceptual spectrum, the managerial model emphasizes using ICT to improve service delivery to citizens and businesses conceived of as "users" and "customers." The consultative model shares this basic outlook, but seeks feedback from (mainly business) interest groups to improve the technical accuracy of policies. Only the participatory model promotes democratic deliberation within civil society alongside government-citizen interactions. Each model favors its own style of information flow. Managerialism visualizes information as traveling along a one-way street from government to citizens; information under consultative auspices flows up and down a limited-access highway; the participatory model, in contrast, encourages a freewheeling, discursive flow of information: citizens to citizens, citizens to government, government to citizens (Chadwick & May, 2003). Although these models may overlap in practice, only the participatory model explicitly grants citizens a significant deliberative role in policy making; its defining logic is to politicize policy disputes through deliberation and participation. The Commission's various e-government initiatives hailing e-participation, e-inclusion, and e-accessibility may signal some willingness to move in this direction.

Early analyses of the Prodi Commission's participatory intentions as outlined in the *White Paper on European Governance* (European Commission, 2001) were skeptical. President Prodi (2001) emphasized the need to impose order on Europe's "cacophonous" public sphere before the Commission could interact more productively with citizens. Armstrong (2002) reckoned the Commission would seek out those European civil society organizations that, in return for participation in policy making, would moderate their demands to fit the Commission's policy agenda. Warleigh (2001) was concerned that the Commission's stated preference for interacting with civil society associations organized at European level would undermine its commitment to an ostensibly broad conception of civil society because Euro-associations play such a miniscule role in Europeans' associational lives. And Magnette (2001) concluded that narrowly structured forms of engagement would dominate policy making, with policies initiated and controlled by the Commission. These assessments foresaw no radical departure from the Commission's adherence to managerial and consultative practices of public involvement wherein efficient service delivery to customers trumped efforts to facilitate meaningful participation in policymaking by citizens. During the 1990s neoliberal policy discourses in Western Europe had emphasized the role of citizens as taxpayers and customers rather than participants in politics, and e-government initiatives largely reproduced this emphasis (Chadwick & May, 2003.) Why should the European Commission prove exceptional in this regard?

Any public bureaucracy, moreover, faces trade-offs between demands for greater participation and demands for greater efficiency. The Commission is aware of this dilemma. Commissioner Reding (2005) has characterized it this way: "European citizens demand better services, better democracy. Europe's businesses demand less bureaucracy, more efficiency." The Commission's proposed solution is to frame e-government as the answer to overcoming this sort of trade-off—citizens and businesses both get what they want. This solution may fall short, however, as perfecting the technological interfaces between political institutions and the public alone cannot prevent that, when push comes to shove in pluralist systems of interest representation like the EU's, public bureaucracies often side with businesses not citizens. The defeat in 2005 of the European Constitution, however, has reminded European-level policy makers that ignoring the voices of Europe's citizens for too long does not promote European integration in the long run. The European Commission has dramatically improved both the quantity and the quality of its e-government services in the past five years. It remains to be seen whether

Europe's citizens and civil society organizations seize on these opportunities with a view to steering the Commission away from old-style managerial and consultative toward new-style participatory practices and approaches.

CONCLUSION

Present-day EU-level e-government initiatives show an awareness of social and economic barriers to e-participation, e-inclusion, and e-accessibility that is far more sophisticated than earlier e-government initiatives narrowly focused on providing information and delivering services to citizens as customers. In one sense this evolution simply reflects a growing body of experience with e-government across the European Union; there has been a steep learning curve associated with e-government everywhere. But the e-government tools being deployed by the Commission today really *are* more interactive and thus perhaps more promising than their predecessors. Deploying online technologies, however, is the easy part. A more difficult challenge for policy makers wishing to make e-government more useful to Europe's citizens will be to identify ways of creating a more meaningful European public space in which Europe's citizens feel politically and emotionally invested.

REFERENCES

Armstrong, K. A. 2002. Rediscovering civil society: The European Union and the White Paper on Governance. *European Law Journal, 8*(1), 102-132.

Bellier, I. (1997). The Commission as an actor: An anthropologist's view. In H. Wallace & A. R. Young (Eds.), *Participation and policy-making in the EU* (pp. 91-115). New York: Oxford University Press.

Chadwick, A., & May, C. (2003). Interaction between states and citizens in the age of the Internet: "E-government" in the United States, Britain, and the European Union. *Governance, 16*(2), 271-300.

Christiansen, T. (1996). A maturing bureaucracy? The role of the commission in the policy process. In J. J. Richardson (Ed.), *EU: Power and policy-making* (pp. 77-95). New York: Routledge.

European Commission. (2001). *White Paper on European Governance*. Brussels, July 25. COM (2001) 428 final.

European Commission. (2002). *Towards a reinforced culture of consultation and dialogue—General principles and minimum standards for consultation of interested parties by the Commission*. COM (2002) 704.

European Commission. (2005a). *What is interactive policy making (IPM)?* Retrieved December 6, 2005, from http://europa.eu.int/yourvoice/ipm/index_en.htm

European Commission. (2005b). *Commission launches five-year strategy to boost the digital economy*. Retrieved December 6, 2005, from http://europa.eu.int/information_society/eeurope/i20lO/docs/press_ release_en.pdf

European Commission. (2005c). *Communication on eAccessibility*. Retrieved December 6, 2005, from http://europa.eu.int/information_society/policy/accessibility/com_ea_2005/index_en.htm

Gibson, R. K., Rommele, A., & Ward, S. (Eds.). (2004). *Electronic democracy: Mobilisation, organisation, and participation via new ICTs*. New York: Routledge.

Magnette, P. (2001). *European governance and civic participation: Can the EU be politicised?* Jean Monnet Working Paper. New York: New York University School of Law.

Prodi, R. (2001). *The EU and its citizens: A matter of democracy*. Speech to the European Parliament. Strasbourg, France, September 4 (Speech/01/365).

Reding, V. (2004). *Hearing of Mrs. Viviane Reding, Commissioner Designate for Information Society and Media.* Brussels, September 29. Retrieved December 2, 2005, from http://europa.eu.int/information_society/newsroom/cf/itemlongdetail.cfm?item_id=1354

Reding, V. (2005). *Speech to the Transforming Public Services Conference,* Manchester, UK, November 28. Retrieved December 6, 2005, from http://www.egovmonitor.com/node/3742

Schmitter, P.C. (2000). *How to democratize the EU ... And why bother?* Lanham, MD: Rowman & Littlefield.

Warleigh, A. (2001). "Europeanizing" civil society: NGOs as agents of political socialization. *Journal of Common Market Studies, 39*(4), 619-639.

Watson, R., & Shackleton, M. (2003). Organized interests and lobbying in the EU. In E. Bomberg & A. Stubb (Eds.), *The European Union: How does it work?* (pp. 88-110). Oxford: Oxford University Press.

KEY TERMS

CONECCS: Consultation, the European Commission and Civil Society is the European Commission's online directory of the Commission's formal civil society consultative bodies and of civil society organizations representing a wide range of groups and interests. (http://europa.eu.int/comm/civil_society/coneccs/index_ en.htm)

E-Accessibility: Policies to ensure that disadvantaged groups, for example, older people, people with disabilities, and people living in remote rural areas, can access the same e-government services as anyone else.

Europe's Information Society Thematic Portal: The EU's Web portal providing information on the EU's information society policies and activities. (http://europa.eu.int/information_society/index_en.htm)

Interactive Policy Making: Online forum used by the European Commission to gather feedback directly from citizens, consumers, and businesses in order to better understand how they perceive Commission policies and to learn from their experience, with a view to shaping new policies and improving existing ones. (http://europa.eu.int/yourvoice/ipm/index_en.htm)

i2010: European Information Society 2010: A five-year European Commission initiative to foster growth and jobs in the information society and media industries launched in 2005; includes a comprehensive strategy for modernizing and deploying all EU policy instruments to encourage the development of the digital economy: regulatory instruments, research, and partnerships with industry. (http://www.eu.int/information_society/eeurope/i2010/index_en.htm)

White Paper on European Governance: 2001 European Commission White Paper containing a set of recommendations on how to enhance democracy in Europe and increase the legitimacy of the institutions. (http://europa.eu.int/eur-lex/en/com/cnc/2001/com2001_0428en01.pdf)

Your Voice in Europe: The European Commission's "single access point" to a wide variety of consultations, discussions, and other tools that enable citizens to play an active role in the European policy-making process. (http://www.eu.int/yourvoice/index_en.htm)

This work was previously published in Encyclopedia of Digital Government, edited by A. Anttiroiko and M. Malkia, pp.763-767, copyright 2007 by Information Science Reference, formerly known as Idea Group Reference (an imprint of IGI Global).

Index

A

B

C

D

E

F

H

I

J

K

L

M

O

Q

R

S

T

U

V

W